EXCELLENCE IN

BUSINESS COMMUNICATION

Ninth Edition

EXCELLENCE IN BUSINESS COMMUNICATION

Ninth Edition

John V. Thill
Chairman and Chief Executive Officer
Global Communication Strategies

Courtland L. Bovée
Professor of Business Communication
C. Allen Paul Distinguished Chair
Grossmont College

Prentice Hall
Boston Columbus Indianapolis New York San Francisco Upper Saddle River
Amsterdam Cape Town Dubai London Madrid Milan Munich Paris Montreal Toronto
Delhi Mexico City Sao Paulo Sydney Hong Kong Seoul Singapore Taipei Tokyo

Editorial Director: Sally Yagan
Editor in Chief: Eric Svendsen
Acquisitions Editor: James Heine
Editorial Project Manager: Kierra Kashickey
Editorial Assistant: Karin Williams
Director of Marketing: Patrice Jones
Marketing Manager: Nikki A. Jones
Marketing Assistant: Ian Gold
Senior Managing Editor: Judy Leale
Senior Production Project Manager: Karalyn Holland
Senior Operations Supervisor: Arnold Vila
Senior Art Director: Janet Slowik
Interior and Cover Designer: Kristine Carney
Cover Photo: Lise Gagne/iStockphoto
Manager, Visual Research: Beth Brenzel
Photo Researcher: Kathy Ringrose
Manager, Rights and Permissions: Shannon Barbe
Image Permission Coordinator: Joanne Dippel
Media Editor: Ashley Lulling
Media Project Manager: Lisa Rinaldi
Full-Service Project Management: GGS Higher Education Resources, a Division of PreMedia Global, Inc.
Composition: GGS Higher Education Resources, a Division of PreMedia Global, Inc.
Printer/Binder: Courier/Kendallville
Cover Printer: Lehigh-Phoenix Color/Hagarstown
Text Font: 10.5/12 Minion

Credits and acknowledgments borrowed from other sources and reproduced, with permission, in this textbook appear on page AC-1.

Library of Congress Cataloging-in-Publication Data

Thill, John V.
Excellence in business communication / John V. Thill, Courtland L.Bovée. — 9th ed.
p. cm.
Includes bibliographical references and index.
ISBN-13: 978-0-13-610376-9 (alk. paper)
ISBN-10: 0-13-610376-6 (alk. paper)
1. Business communication—United States—Case studies. I. Bovée, Courtland L. II. Title.
HF5718.2.U6T45 2011
658.4′5—dc22

2009040353

Prentice Hall
is an imprint of

PEARSON

www.pearsonhighered.com

10 9 8 7 6 5 4 3 2 1
ISBN 10: 0-13-610376-6
ISBN 13: 978-0-13-610376-9

PEARSON

mybcommlab™

In mybcommlab there are activities for every facet of the course to help you achieve the key learning objectives in writing, grammar, and presentation skills.

Customized Study Plans

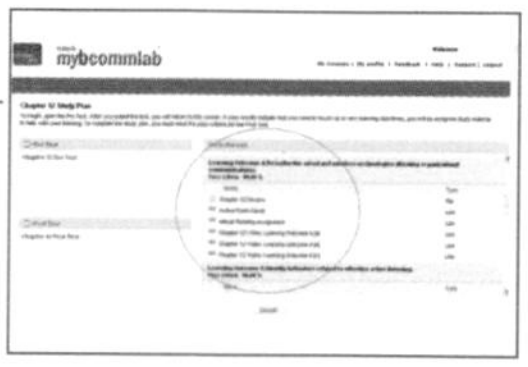

Customized Study Plans keep you on track throughout the semester.

You complete a pre-test, and the results generate a customized study plan, complete with remediation activities. Study plans tag incorrect questions from the pre-test to the appropriate textbook learning objective, enabling you to concentrate on only the topics that you need help with. Tools to help you study include flash cards, eBook reading assignments, document makeovers, and grammar and writing tutorials.

After you complete the remediation activities, you may take a post-test to validate that you have mastered the learning objectives.

Robust Self-Study and Practice Tools

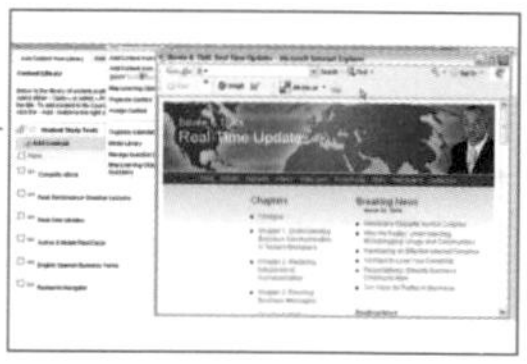

Peer Review capabilities so that you can focus on the writing process as they critique each other's work.

Model Documents help you understand the "why" and the "how" of polished communication.

Sample Presentations reinforce the presentations heard in class.

Video Applications reinforce the concepts covered in lecture.

Get the latest information and advice with Real-Time Updates

A unique integration of print and electronic media, the Real-Time Updates service provides fresh content throughout the course to reinforce learning and to keep the class relevant.

Benefits: You can stay up to date with the trends and techniques of professional business communication and be ready to hit the ground running the day you graduate.

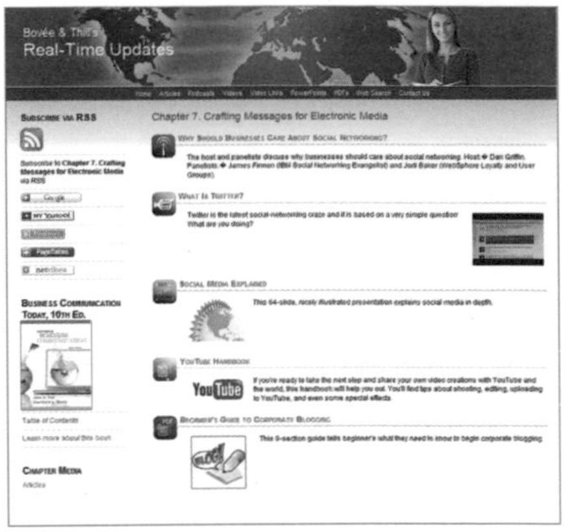

Discover a proven process for writing better messages in less time

The time-tested three-step writing process helps you craft a variety of messages for print and electronic media quickly and easily.

Benefits: Reduce the time and energy it takes to create effective business messages, both during college and throughout your entire career.

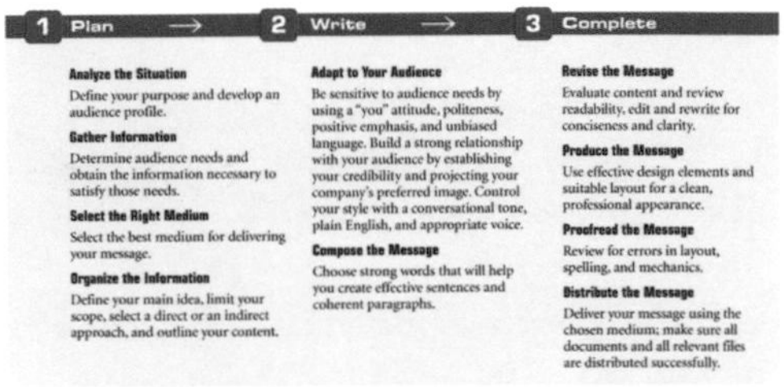

Find answers quickly with the Handbook of Grammar, Mechanics, and Usage

The integrated Handbook of Grammar, Mechanics, and Usage offers summaries of essential points of grammar, mechanics, and usage plus helpful lists of frequently confused, misused, and misspelled words.

Benefits: The handbook helps take the work and worry out of grammar, mechanics, and usage.

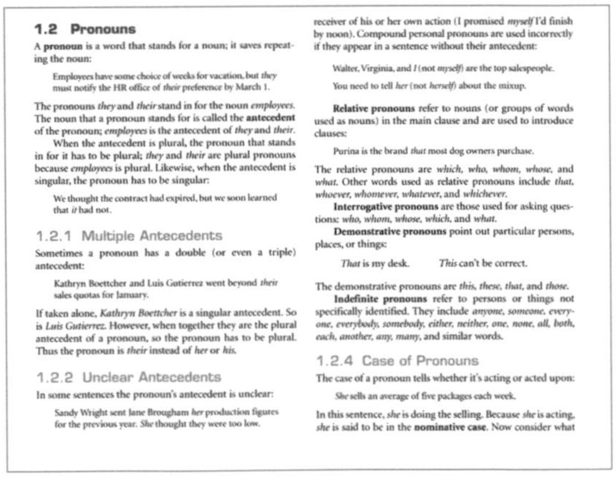

1.2 Pronouns

A **pronoun** is a word that stands for a noun; it saves repeating the noun:

Employees have some choice of weeks for vacation, but *they* must notify the HR office of *their* preference by March 1.

The pronouns *they* and *their* stand in for the noun *employees*. The noun that a pronoun stands for is called the **antecedent** of the pronoun; *employees* is the antecedent of *they* and *their*.

When the antecedent is plural, the pronoun that stands in for it has to be plural; *they* and *their* are plural pronouns because *employees* is plural. Likewise, when the antecedent is singular, the pronoun has to be singular:

We thought the contract had expired, but we soon learned that *it* had not.

1.2.1 Multiple Antecedents

Sometimes a pronoun has a double (or even a triple) antecedent:

Kathryn Boettcher and Luis Gutierrez went beyond *their* sales quotas for January.

If taken alone, *Kathryn Boettcher* is a singular antecedent. So is *Luis Gutierrez*. However, when together they are the plural antecedent of a pronoun, so the pronoun has to be plural. Thus the pronoun is *their* instead of *her* or *his*.

1.2.2 Unclear Antecedents

In some sentences the pronoun's antecedent is unclear:

Sandy Wright sent Jane Brougham *her* production figures for the previous year. *She* thought they were too low.

receiver of his or her own action (I promised *myself* I'd finish by noon). Compound personal pronouns are used incorrectly if they appear in a sentence without their antecedent:

Walter, Virginia, and *I* (not *myself*) are the top salespeople.

You need to tell *her* (not *herself*) about the mixup.

Relative pronouns refer to nouns (or groups of words used as nouns) in the main clause and are used to introduce clauses:

Purina is the brand *that* most dog owners purchase.

The relative pronouns are *which, who, whom, whose*, and *what*. Other words used as relative pronouns include *that, whoever, whomever, whatever*, and *whichever*.

Interrogative pronouns are those used for asking questions: *who, whom, whose, which*, and *what*.

Demonstrative pronouns point out particular persons, places, or things:

That is my desk. *This* can't be correct.

The demonstrative pronouns are *this, these, that*, and *those*.

Indefinite pronouns refer to persons or things not specifically identified. They include *anyone, someone, everyone, everybody, somebody, either, neither, one, none, all, both, each, another, any, many*, and similar words.

1.2.4 Case of Pronouns

The case of a pronoun tells whether it's acting or acted upon:

She sells an average of five packages each week.

In this sentence, *she* is doing the selling. Because *she* is acting, *she* is said to be in the **nominative case**. Now consider what

Simplify and accelerate learning with mybcommlab

This unique online study tool helps you identify and improve weak areas through focused practice. Test your understanding of the concepts presented in the text and explore additional materials that will bring the ideas to life in video, activities, and an online multimedia ebook.

Benefits: Make the best use of your time by identifying the areas where you need to improve, reviewing the appropriate concepts and skills, and practicing the specific techniques that will help you communicate more effectively.

PEARSON mybcommlab™

Contents in Brief

Contents

Real-Time Updates—Learn More

"Learn More" is a unique feature you will see strategically located throughout the text, connecting you with dozens of carefully screened online media. These elements, categorized by the icons shown below representing podcasts, PDFs, articles, videos, and Powerpoints, complement the text's coverage by providing contemporary examples and valuable insights from successful professionals.

REAL-TIME UPDATES Learn More

REAL-TIME UPDATES Learn More

REAL-TIME UPDATES Learn More

REAL-TIME UPDATES Learn More

REAL-TIME UPDATES Learn More

Preface

Major Changes and Improvements in This Edition

The social media revolution	New coverage of the social communication model that is redefining business communication and reshaping the relationships between companies and their stakeholders
Significant content additions	In addition to numerous updates throughout, the following sections are new: • *Getting Ready for Business Communication 2.0 (in Chapter 1)* • *Guarding Against Information Overload and Information Addiction (in Chapter 1)* • *Social Networks and Virtual Communities (in Chapter 2)* • *Business Etiquette Online (in Chapter 2)* • *Adapting to Other Business Cultures (in Chapter 3)* • *Finding Your Focus (in Chapter 4)* • *Evaluating, Editing, and Revising the Work of Others (in Chapter 6)* • *Designing Multimedia Documents (in Chapter 6)* • *Writing Persuasive Messages for Social Media (in Chapter 10)* • *Collaborating on Wikis (in Chapter 12)* • *Data Visualization (in Chapter 12)* • *Choosing Structured or Free-Form Slides (in Chapter 14)* • *Ending with Clarity and Confidence (in Chapter 14)* • *Introductory Statement (in Chapter 15)* • *Presenting a Professional Image (in Chapter 16)*
Integration with mybcommlab	Use this optional online resource to test your understanding of the concepts presented in every chapter and explore additional materials that will bring the ideas to life in video, activities, and an online multimedia e-book.
Multimedia resources	Extend the learning experience with unique Learn More media elements that connect students with dozens of handpicked videos, podcasts, and other items that complement chapter content.
New vignettes and simulations	Four new chapter-opening vignettes and accompanying end-of-chapter simulations: • *Rosen Law Firm's use of wikis to promote collaboration (Chapter 2)* • *H&R Block's extensive use of social media to communicate with customers (Chapter 4)* • *Get Satisfaction's application of new media to create a new approach to customer service (Chapter 8)* • *Leviton's tactful approach to delivering negative news to its employees during the current recession (Chapter 9)*
New communication cases	Thirty-one new communication cases, giving students the opportunity to solve real-world communication challenges using the media skills they'll be expected to have in tomorrow's workplace
New figures and tables	Thirty-six new figures and tables, including new model documents in the latest electronic business media
New highlight boxes	Seven new Business Communication 2.0 highlight boxes, exploring how companies are using—and sometimes misusing—new social media in business
Efficient presentation	Even though it covers an even wider range of topics, the new ninth edition is more than 80 pages shorter than the eighth edition.

Extend the Value of Your Textbook with Free Multimedia Content

Excellence in Business Communication's unique **Real-Time Updates** system automatically provides weekly content updates, including podcasts, PowerPoint presentations, online videos, PDFs, and articles. You can subscribe for updates chapter by chapter, so you get only the material that applies to the chapter you are studying. Access Real-Time Updates through **mybizlab** (**www.mybizlab.com**) or by visiting **http://real-timeupdates.com/ebc**.

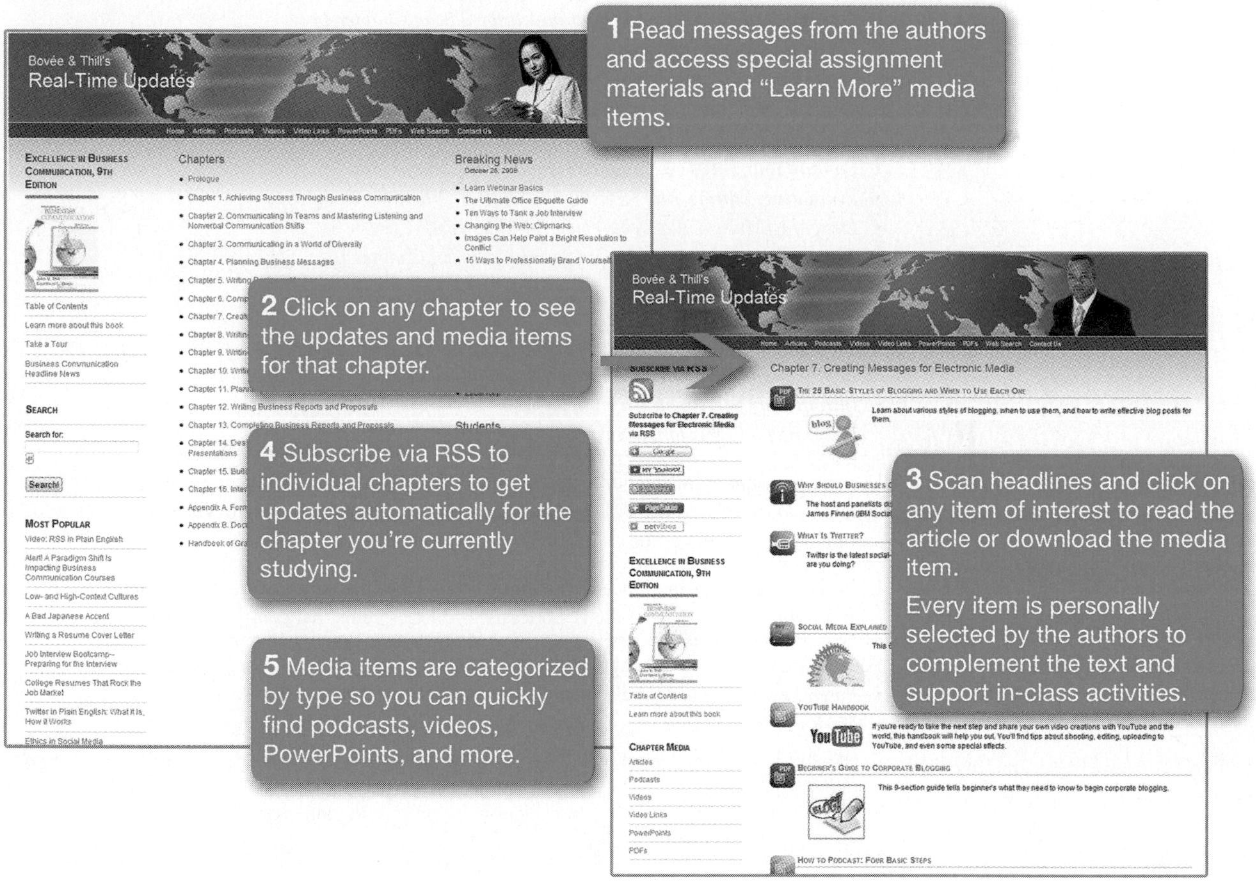

1 Read messages from the authors and access special assignment materials and "Learn More" media items.
2 Click on any chapter to see the updates and media items for that chapter.
3 Scan headlines and click on any item of interest to read the article or download the media item.
Every item is personally selected by the authors to complement the text and support in-class activities.
4 Subscribe via RSS to individual chapters to get updates automatically for the chapter you're currently studying.
5 Media items are categorized by type so you can quickly find podcasts, videos, PowerPoints, and more.
Bovée & Thill's Real-Time Updates
Chapters
Breaking News
Chapter 7. Creating Messages for Electronic Media

Career Success 101: Improving Your Communication Skills

No matter what profession you want to pursue, the ability to communicate will be an essential skill—and a skill that employers expect you to have when you enter the workforce. This course introduces you to the fundamental principles of business communication and gives you the opportunity to develop your communication skills. You'll discover how business communication differs from personal and social communication, and you'll see how today's companies are using blogging, podcasting, video, wikis, and other innovative technologies. You'll learn a simple three-step writing process that works for all types of writing and speaking projects, both in college and on the job. Along the way, you'll gain valuable insights into ethics, etiquette, listening, teamwork, and nonverbal communication. Plus, you'll learn effective strategies for the many different types of communication challenges you'll face on the job, from routine messages about transactions to complex reports and websites.

Colleges and universities vary in the prerequisites established for the business communication course, but we advise taking at least one course in English composition before taking this class. Some coursework in business studies will also give you a better perspective on communication challenges in the workplace. However, we have taken special care not to assume any in-depth business experience, so you can use *Excellence in Business Communication*, Ninth Edition, successfully even if you have limited on-the-job experience or business coursework.

HOW THIS COURSE WILL HELP YOU

Few courses can offer the three-for-the-price-of-one value you get from a business communication class. Check out these benefits:

- **In your other classes.** The communication skills you learn in this class can help you in virtually every other course you will take in college. From simple homework assignments to complicated team projects to oral presentations, you'll be able to communicate more effectively with less time and effort.
- **During your job search.** You can reduce the stress of searching for a job and stand out from the competition. As you'll see in Chapters 15 and 16, every activity in the job search process relies on communication. The better you can communicate, the more successful you'll be in landing interesting and rewarding work.
- **On the job.** After you get that great job, the time and energy you have invested in this course will continue to yield benefits year after year. As you tackle each project and every new challenge, influential company leaders—the people who largely determine how quickly you'll get promoted and how much you'll earn—will be paying close attention to how well you communicate. They will observe your interactions with colleagues, customers, and business partners. They'll take note of how well you can collect data, find the essential ideas buried under mountains of information, and convey those points to other people. They'll observe your ability to adapt to different audiences and circumstances. They'll be watching when you encounter tough situations that require careful attention to ethics and etiquette. All this may sound daunting, but every insight you gain and every skill you develop in this course will help you shine in your future career.

HOW TO SUCCEED IN THIS COURSE

Although this course explores a wide range of message types and appears to cover quite a lot of territory, the underlying structure of the course is actually rather simple. You'll learn a few basic concepts, identify some key skills to use and procedures to follow—and then practice, practice, practice. Whether you're writing a blog posting in response to one of the real-company cases or drafting a copy of your own résumé, you'll be practicing the same skills again and again. With feedback and reinforcement from your instructor and your classmates, your confidence will grow and the work will become easier and more enjoyable.

The following sections offer advice on approaching each assignment, using your book and taking advantage of some other helpful resources.

Approaching Each Assignment

In the spirit of practice and improvement, you will have a number of writing (and possibly speaking) assignments throughout this course. These suggestions will help you produce better results with less effort:

- **First, don't panic!** If the thought of writing a report or giving a speech sends a chill up your spine, you're not alone. Everybody feels that way when they are first learning business communication skills, and even experienced professionals can feel nervous about major projects. Keeping three points in mind will help. First, every project can be broken down into a series of small, manageable tasks. Don't let a big project overwhelm you; it's nothing more than a bunch of smaller tasks. Second, remind yourself that you have the skills you need to accomplish each task. As you move through the course, the assignments are carefully designed to match the skills you've developed up to that point. Third, if you feel panic creeping up on you, take a break and regain your perspective.
- **Focus on one task at a time.** A common mistake is trying to organize and express your ideas while simultaneously worrying about audience reactions, grammar, spelling, formatting, page design, print quality, and a dozen other factors. You must fight the temptation to do everything at once; otherwise, your frustration will soar and your productivity will plummet. In particular, don't worry about grammar, spelling, and word choices during your first draft. Concentrate on the organization of your ideas first, then the way you express those ideas, and then the presentation and production of your messages. Following the three-step writing process is an ideal way to focus on one task at a time in a logical sequence.
- **Give yourself plenty of time.** As with every other school project, putting things off to the last minute creates unnecessary stress. Writing and speaking projects in particular are much easier if you tackle them in small stages with breaks in between, rather than trying to get everything done in one frantic blast. Moreover, there will be instances when you simply get stuck on a project, and the best thing to do is walk away and give your mind a break. If you allow room for this in your schedule, you'll minimize the frustration and spend less time overall on your homework, too.
- **Step back and assess each project before you start.** The writing and speaking projects you'll have in this course cover a wide range of communication scenarios, and it's essential that you adapt your approach to each new challenge. Resist the urge to dive in and start writing without a plan. Ponder the assignment for a while, consider the various approaches you might take, and think carefully about your objectives before you start writing. Nothing is more frustrating than getting stuck halfway through because you're not sure what you're trying to say or you've wandered off track. Spend a little time planning, and you'll spend a lot less time writing.
- **Use the three-step writing process.** Those essential planning tasks are the first step in the three-step writing process, which you'll learn about in Chapter 4 and use throughout the course. This process has been developed and refined by professional writers with decades of experience and thousands of projects ranging from simple e-mail messages to 500-page textbooks. It works, so take advantage of it.
- **Learn from the examples and model documents.** This textbook offers dozens of realistic examples of business messages, many with notes along the sides that explain strong and weak points. Study these and any other examples that your instructor provides. Learn what works and what doesn't work, then apply these lessons to your own writing.
- **Learn from experience.** Finally, learn from the feedback you get from your instructor and from other students. Don't take the criticism personally; your instructor and your classmates are commenting about the work, not about you. View every piece of feedback as an opportunity to improve.

Using This Textbook Package

This book and its accompanying online resources introduce you to the key concepts in business communication while helping you develop essential skills. As you read each chapter, start by studying the learning objectives. These help you identify the most important concepts in the chapter and give you a feel for what you'll be learning. Following the learning objectives, the "On the Job" vignette tells a brief story of how a particular business professional met a real-life communication challenge using the same concepts and skills you'll be learning in the chapter.

As you work your way through the chapter, compare the advice given with the various examples, both the brief in-text examples and the standalone model documents. Also, keep an eye out for the *Real-Time Updates* "Learn More" elements in each chapter. The authors have selected these videos, podcasts, presentations, and other online media to provide informative and entertaining enhancements to the text material.

At the end of each chapter, the "Learning Objectives Checkup" gives you the chance to quickly verify your grasp of important concepts. Each chapter includes a variety of questions and activities that help you gauge how well you've learned the material and are able to apply it to realistic business scenarios. Several chapters have activities with downloadable media such as podcasts; if your instructor assigns these, follow the instructions in the text to locate the correct files. You can also download the two-page Quick Learning Guide to review the essential points from the chapter.

In addition to the 16 chapters of the text itself, here are some special features that will help you succeed in the course and on the job:

- **Prologue: Building a Career with Your Communication Skills.** This brief section (immediately following this Preface) helps you understand today's dynamic workplace, the steps you can take to adapt to the job market, and the importance of creating an employment portfolio.
- **Handbook.** The "Handbook of Grammar, Mechanics, and Usage" (see page H-1) serves as a convenient reference guide to essential Business English.
- **mybcommlab.** If mybcommlab (www.mybcommlab.com) is used with your course, take advantage of this unique resource to test your understanding of the concepts presented in every chapter and explore additional materials that will bring the ideas to life in video, activities, and an online multimedia e-book.
- **Real-Time Updates.** You can use this unique newsfeed service to make sure you're always kept up to date on important topics. Plus, at strategic points in every chapter, you will be directed to the Real-Time Updates website to get the latest information about specific subjects. To sign up via RSS, visit http://real-timeupdates.com/ebc. You can also access Real-Time Updates through mybcommlab.
- **Quick Learning Guides.** These downloadable, two-page study guides were specially prepared by the authors to help you study for exams or review important concepts whenever you need a quick refresher.
- **Business Communication Web Search.** With this revolutionary approach to searching developed by the authors, you quickly access more than 325 search engines. The tool uses a simple and intuitive interface engineered to help you find precisely what you want, whether it's PowerPoint files, Adobe Acrobat PDFs, Microsoft Word documents, Excel files, videos, or podcasts. Check it out at http://businesscommunicationblog.com/websearch.
- **Companion Website.** This text's Companion Website at www.pearsonhighered.com/thill offers free access to self-assessment quizzes, a student version of the PowerPoint package, an updated list of featured websites, the "English-Spanish Audio Glossary of Business Terms," an online version of the "Handbook of Grammar, Mechanics, and Usage," and the "Business Communication Study Hall," which helps you brush up on several aspects of business communication—grammar, writing skills, critical thinking, report writing, résumés, and PowerPoint development.
- **Study Guide.** The study guide includes a variety of review questions and study quizzes. Page references to the review questions and quizzes are included. If your professor

hasn't packaged your text with the study guide, you can purchase it by visiting www.mypearsonstore.com and searching for ISBN 0-13-610377-4.

- **CourseSmart eTextbooks Online.** CourseSmart is an exciting new choice for students looking to save money. As an alternative to purchasing the print textbook, you can purchase an electronic version of the same content and save up to 50% off the suggested list price of the print text. With a CourseSmart eTextbook, you can search the text, make notes online, print out reading assignments that incorporate lecture notes, and bookmark important passages for later review. For more information or to purchase access to the CourseSmart eTextbook, visit www.coursesmart.com.

FEEDBACK

The authors and the product team would appreciate hearing from you! Let us know what you think about this textbook by writing to college_marketing@prenhall.com. Please include "Feedback about Thill/Bovee EBC 9e" in the subject line.

ACKNOWLEDGMENTS

The ninth edition of *Excellence in Business Communication* reflects the professional experience of a large team of contributors and advisors.

Reviewers of Previous Editions

We express our thanks to the many individuals whose valuable suggestions and constructive comments influenced the success of this book. The authors are deeply grateful to Janet Adams, Minnesota State University–Mankato; Gus Amaya, Florida International University; Anita S. Bednar, Central State University; Donna Cox, Monroe Community College; Sauny Dills, California Polytechnic State University–San Luis Obispo; Ruthann Dirks, Emporia State University; Cynthia Drexel, Western State College; Mary DuBoise, DeVry University–Dallas; J. Thomas Dukes, University of Akron; Karen Eickhoff, University of Tennessee; Lindsay S. English, Ursuline College; Mike Flores, Wichita State University; Charlene A. Gierkey, Northwestern Michigan College; Sue Granger, Jacksonville State University; Bradley S. Hayden, Western Michigan University; Joyce Hicks, Valparaiso University; Michael Hignite, Southwest Missouri State; Mark Hilton, Lyndon State College; Cynthia Hofacker, University of Wisconsin–Eau Claire; Louise C. Holcomb, Gainesville College; Larry Honl, University of Wisconsin–Eau Claire; Kenneth Hunsaker, Utah State University; Sandie Idziak, University of Texas; Robert O. Joy, Central Michigan University; Paula R. Kaiser, University of North Carolina–Greensboro; Paul Killorin, Portland Community College; Linda M. LaDuc, University of Massachusetts–Amherst; Jennifer Loney, Portland State University; Al Lucero, East Tennessee State University; Rachel Mather, Adelphi University; Linda McAdams, Westark Community College; Melinda McCannon, Gordon College; Bronna McNeely, Midwestern State University; William McPherson, Indiana University of Pennsylvania; Russ Meade, Tidewater Community College; Betty Mealor, Abraham Baldwin College; Mary Miller, Ashland University; Joe Newman, Faulkner University; Barbara Oates, Texas A&M University; Richard Profozich, Prince George's Community College; Brian Railsback, Western Carolina University; John Rehfuss, California State University–Sacramento; Joan C. Roderick, Southwest Texas State University; Salvatore Safina, University of Wisconsin; Jean Anna Sellers, Fort Hays State University; Andrea Smith–Hunter, Siena College; Carol Smith White, Georgia State University; Karen Sneary, Northwestern Oklahoma State University; Jeanne Stannard, Johnson County Community College; Terisa Tennison, Florida International University; Michael Thompson, Brigham Young University; Betsy Vardaman, Baylor University; Robert von der Osten, Ferris State University; Karl V. Winton, Marshall University; Billy Walters, Troy State University; George Walters, Emporia State University; John L. Waltman, Eastern Michigan University; F. Stanford Wayne, Southwest Missouri State; Robert Wheatley, Troy State University; Rosemary B. Wilson, Washtenaw Community College; Beverly C. Wise, SUNY–Morrisville; Aline Wolff, New York University; and Bonnie Yarbrough, University of North Carolina–Greensboro. We also appreciate the notable talents and distinguished contributions of Deborah Valentine, Emory University; Anne Bliss, University of Colorado–Boulder; Carolyn A. Embree, University of Akron; Carla L. Sloan, Liberty University; Doris A. Van Horn Christopher, California State University–Los Angeles; and Susan S. Rehwaldt, Southern Illinois University.

Reviewers of "Document Makeover" Feature

We sincerely thank the following reviewers for their assistance with the Document Makeover feature: Lisa Barley, Eastern Michigan University; Marcia Bordman, Gallaudet University; Jean Bush-Bacelis, Eastern Michigan University; Bobbye Davis, Southern Louisiana University; Cynthia Drexel, Western State College; Kenneth Gibbs, Worcester State College; Ellen Leathers, Bradley University; Diana McKowen, Indiana University; Bobbie Nicholson, Mars Hill College; Andrew Smith, Holyoke Community College; Jay Stubblefield, North Carolina Wesleyan College; Dawn Wallace, South Eastern Louisiana University.

Reviewers of Model Documents

The many model documents in the text and their accompanying annotations received invaluable review from Dacia Charlesworth, Indiana University–Purdue University Fort Wayne; Diane Todd Bucci, Robert Morris University; Estelle Kochis, Suffolk County Community College; Sherry Robertson, Arizona State University; Nancy Goehring, Monterey Peninsula College; James Hatfield, Florida Community College at Jacksonville; Avon Crismore, Indiana University.

Personal Acknowledgments

We wish to extend a heartfelt thanks to our many friends, acquaintances, and business associates who provided materials or agreed to be interviewed so that we could bring the real world into the classroom.

A very special acknowledgment goes to George Dovel, whose superb writing and editing skills, distinguished background, and wealth of business experience assured clarity and completeness on this project. Also, recognition and thanks to Jackie Estrada for her outstanding skills and excellent attention to details. Her creation of the "Peak Performance Grammar and Mechanics" material is especially noteworthy. Jim Forgione's attention to detail improved the quality of the text throughout.

We also feel it is important to acknowledge and thank the Association for Business Communication, an organization whose meetings and publications provide a valuable forum for the exchange of ideas and for professional growth.

Additionally, we would like to thank the supplement authors who prepared material for this new edition. They include: Dacia Charlesworth, Indiana University–Purdue University Fort Wayne; Myles Hassell, University of New Orleans; William Peirce, Prince George's Community College; and Jay Stubblefield, North Carolina Wesleyan College.

We want to extend our warmest appreciation to the devoted professionals at Prentice Hall. They include Jerome Grant, president; Sally Yagan, editorial director; Eric Svendsen, editor in chief; James Heine, acquisitions editor; Kierra Kashickey, editorial project manager; Nikki Jones, marketing manager; Judy Leale, senior managing editor; Ashley Santora, product development manager; Karin Williams, editorial assistant; all of Prentice Hall Business Publishing; and the outstanding Prentice Hall sales representatives. Finally, we thank Suzanne DeWorken, permissions researcher, and Karalyn Holland, senior production project manager, for their dedication; and we are grateful to Andrea Stefanowicz, production editor at GGS Higher Education Resources, A Division of Premedia Global, Inc.; Janet Slowik, senior art director; and Kristine Carney, interior and cover designer, for their superb work.

John V. Thill
Courtland L. Bovée

About the Authors

John V. Thill and Courtland L. Bovée have been leading textbook authors for more than two decades, introducing millions of students to the fields of business and business communication. Their award-winning texts are distinguished by proven pedagogical features, extensive selections of contemporary case studies, hundreds of real-life examples, engaging writing, thorough research, and the unique integration of print and electronic resources. Each new edition reflects the authors' commitment to continuous refinement and improvement, particularly in terms of modeling the latest practices in business and the use of technology.

Mr. Thill is a prominent communications consultant who has worked with organizations ranging from Fortune 500 multinationals to entrepreneurial start-ups. He formerly held positions with Pacific Bell and Texaco. Professor Bovée has 22 years of teaching experience at Grossmont College in San Diego, where he has received teaching honors and was accorded that institution's C. Allen Paul Distinguished Chair.

John V. Thill
Courtland L. Bovée

Dedication

This book is dedicated to you and the many thousands of other students who have used this book in years past. We appreciate the opportunity to play a role in your education, and we wish you success and satisfaction in your studies and in your career.

John V. Thill

Courtland L. Bovée

Prologue

Building a Career with Your Communication Skills

USING THIS COURSE TO HELP LAUNCH YOUR CAREER

This course will help you develop vital communication skills that you'll use throughout your career—and those skills can help you launch an interesting and rewarding career, too. This brief prologue sets the stage by helping you understand today's dynamic workplace, the steps you can take to adapt to the job market, and the importance of creating an employment portfolio. Take a few minutes to read these sections while you think about the career you hope to create for yourself.

UNDERSTANDING TODAY'S DYNAMIC WORKPLACE

Social, political, and financial events continue to change workplace conditions from year to year, so the job market you read about this year might not be the same market you try to enter a year or two from now. However, you can count on a few forces that are likely to affect your entry into the job market and your career success in years to come:[1]

- **Instability and opportunity.** In addition to broad economic cycles, your career will likely be affected by globalization, mergers and acquisitions, short-term mentality driven by the demands of stockholders, ethical upheavals, and the relentless quest for lower costs. On the plus side, new opportunities, new companies, and even entire industries can appear almost overnight. In fact, trying to make a long-term career plan might not be a wise use of your time anyway. As retired Lockheed Martin CEO Norman Augustine puts it, "There are just too many changes ahead, too many things that are going to happen that you can't anticipate."[2]
- **Responsibility for your own career.** The idea of lifetime employment, in which employees spend their entire working lives with a single firm that takes care of them throughout their careers, is all but gone in many industries. Boeing, the Chicago-based aerospace giant, speaks of lifetime *employability*, rather than lifetime employment, putting the responsibility on employees to track market needs and keep their skills up to date—even changing careers if necessary. In fact, most U.S. employees will not only change employers multiple times but will even change careers anywhere from three to five times over their working lives.
- **Growth of small business.** Small businesses employ about half of the private-sector workforce in this country and from year to year create 60 to 80 percent of all new jobs, so chances are good that you'll work for a small firm at some point.
- **Increase in independent contractors.** The nature of employment itself is changing for many people. As companies try to become more flexible, more employees are going solo and setting up shop as independent contractors, sometimes selling their services back to the very companies they just left.

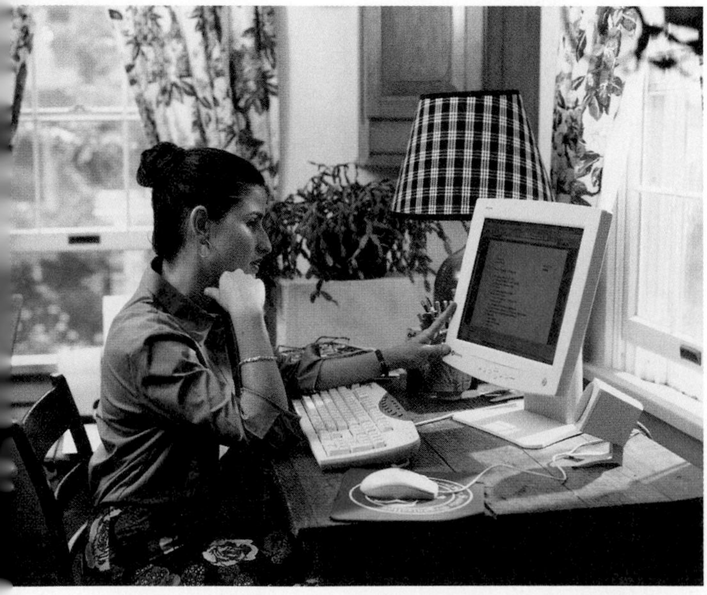

Would you like to pursue a career in business but have the flexibility to work from home? Many professionals now do so, as either independent contractors or corporate employees who telecommute.

- **Changing view of job-hopping.** Given all these changes, job-hopping doesn't have quite the negative connotation it once had. Even so, you still need to be careful about "jumping ship" at every new opportunity. Recruiting and integrating new employees takes time and costs money, and most employers are reluctant to invest in someone who has a history of switching jobs numerous times without good reason.
- **Personal branding.** With the increase in independent contracting and short-term job assignments, the need to establish yourself in the marketplace continues to increase. The idea behind *personal branding* is to create an image for yourself as a valued contributor in much the same way that marketing departments brand products, and then using online and offline networking to build awareness for your capabilities.[3]

What do all these forces mean to you? First, take charge of your career—and stay in charge of it. Understand your options, have a plan, and don't count on others to watch out for your future. Second, as you will learn throughout this course, understanding your audience is key to successful communication, starting with understanding how employers view today's job market.

How Employers View Today's Job Market

From the employer's perspective, the employment process is always a question of balance. Maintaining a stable workforce can improve practically every aspect of business performance, yet many employers want the flexibility to shrink and expand payrolls as business conditions change. Employers obviously want to attract the best talent, but the best talent is more expensive and more vulnerable to offers from competitors, so there are always financial trade-offs to consider.

Employers also struggle with the ups and downs of the economy. When unemployment is low, the balance of power shifts to employees, and employers have to compete in order to attract and keep top talent. When unemployment is high, the power shifts back to employers, who can afford to be more selective and less accommodating. In other words, pay attention to the economy; at times, you can be more aggressive in your demands, but at other times, you should be more accommodating.

Many employers now fill some labor needs by hiring temporary workers or engaging contractors on a project-by-project basis. Many U.S. employers are now also more willing to move jobs to cheaper labor markets outside the country and to recruit globally to fill positions in the United States. Both trends have stirred controversy, especially in the technology sector, as U.S. firms recruit top engineers and scientists from other countries while shifting mid- and low-range jobs to India, China, Russia, the Philippines, and other countries with lower wage structures.[4]

What Employers Look for in Job Applicants

Given the forces in the contemporary workplace, employers are looking for people who can adapt to the new dynamics of the business world, can survive and thrive in fluid and uncertain situations, and continue to learn throughout their careers. Companies want team players with strong work records, leaders who are versatile, and employees with diversified skills and varied job experience.[5] In addition, most employers expect college graduates to be sensitive to cultural differences and to have a sound understanding of international affairs.[6] In some cases, your chances of being hired are better if you've studied abroad, learned another language, or can otherwise demonstrate an appreciation of other cultures.

ADAPTING TO TODAY'S JOB MARKET

Adapting to the workplace is a lifelong process of seeking the best fit between what you want to do and what employers are willing to pay you to do. For instance, if money is more important to you than anything else, you can certainly pursue jobs that promise high pay; just be aware that most of these jobs require years of experience, and many produce a lot of stress, require frequent travel, or have other potential drawbacks you'll want to consider. In contrast, if location, lifestyle, intriguing work, or other factors are more important to you, you may well have to sacrifice some level of pay to achieve them. The important question is to know what you want to do, what you have to offer, and how to make yourself more attractive to employers.

What Do You Want to Do?

Economic necessities and the vagaries of the marketplace will influence much of what happens in your career, of course; nevertheless, it's wise to start your employment search by examining your own values and interests. Identify what you want to do first, then see whether you can find a position that satisfies you at a personal level while also meeting your financial needs.

- **What would you like to do every day?** Research occupations that interest you. Find out what people really do every day. Ask friends, relatives, or alumni from your school. Read interviews with people in various professions to get a sense of what their careers are like.
- **How would you like to work?** Consider how much independence you want on the job, how much variety you like, and whether you prefer to work with products, machines, people, ideas, figures, or some combination thereof. Do you prefer constant change or a predictable role?
- **What specific compensation do you expect?** What do you hope to earn in your first year? What's your ultimate earnings goal? Are you willing to settle for less money in order to do something you really love?
- **Can you establish some general career goals?** Consider where you'd like to start, where you'd like to go from there, and the ultimate position you'd like to attain.
- **What size company would you prefer?** Do you like the idea of working for a small, entrepreneurial operation or a large corporation?
- **What sort of corporate culture are you most comfortable with?** Would you be happy in a formal hierarchy with clear reporting relationships? Or do you prefer less structure? Do you prefer teamwork or individualism? Do you like a competitive environment?
- **What location would you like?** Would you like to work in a city, a suburb, a small town, an industrial area, or an uptown setting? Do you favor a particular part of the country? Another country?

Filling out the assessment in Table 1 on the next page might help you get a clearer picture of the nature of work you would like to pursue in your career.

What Do You Have to Offer?

Knowing what you *want* to do is one thing. Knowing what you *can* do is another. You may already have a good idea of what you can offer employers. If not, some brainstorming can help you identify your skills, interests, and characteristics. Start by jotting down 10 achievements you're proud of, such as learning to ski, taking a prize-winning photo, tutoring a child, or editing your school paper. Think carefully about what specific skills these achievements demanded of you. For example, leadership skills, speaking ability, and artistic talent may have helped you coordinate a winning presentation to your school's administration. As you analyze your achievements, you'll begin to recognize a pattern of skills. Which of them might be valuable to potential employers?

Next, look at your educational preparation, work experience, and extracurricular activities. What do your knowledge and experience qualify you to do? What have you learned from volunteer work or class projects that could benefit you on the job? Have you held any offices, won any awards or scholarships, or mastered a second language?

Take stock of your personal characteristics. Are you aggressive, a born leader? Or would you rather follow? Are you outgoing, articulate, great with people? Or do you prefer working alone? Make a list of what you believe are your four or five most important qualities. Ask a relative or friend to rate your traits as well.

If you're having difficulty figuring out your interests, characteristics, or capabilities, consult your college placement office. Many campuses administer a variety of tests to help

TABLE 1 Career Self-Assessment

What work-related activities and situations do you prefer? Evaluate your preferences in each of these following areas and use the results to help guide your job search.

ACTIVITY OR SITUATION	STRONGLY AGREE	AGREE	DISAGREE	NO PREFERENCE
1. I want to work independently.				
2. I want variety in my work.				
3. I want to work with people.				
4. I want to work with technology.				
5. I want physical work.				
6. I want mental work.				
7. I want to work for a large organization.				
8. I want to work for a nonprofit organization.				
9. I want to work for a small family business.				
10. I want to work for a service business.				
11. I want to start or buy a business someday.				
12. I want regular, predictable work hours.				
13. I want to work in a city location.				
14. I want to work in a small town or suburb.				
15. I want to work in another country.				
16. I want to work outdoors.				
17. I want to work in a structured environment.				
18. I want to avoid risk as much as possible.				
19. I want to enjoy my work, even if that means making less money.				
20. I want to become a high-level corporate manager.				

you identify interests, aptitudes, and personality traits. These tests won't reveal your "perfect" job, but they'll help you focus on the types of work best suited to your personality.

How Can You Make Yourself More Valuable?

While you're figuring out what you want from a job and what you can offer an employer, you can take positive steps now toward building your career. First, look for volunteer projects, temporary jobs, freelance work, or internships that will help expand your experience base and skill set. These temporary assignments not only help you gain valuable experience and relevant contacts but also provide you with important references and with items for your employment portfolio (see the following section).[7]

Second, consider applying your talents to *crowdsourcing* projects, in which companies and nonprofit organizations invite the public to contribute solutions to various challenges. For example, Fellowforce (www.fellowforce.com) posts projects involving advertising, business writing, photography, graphic design, programming, strategy development, and other skills.[8] Even if your contributions aren't chosen, you still have solutions to real business problems that you can show to potential employers as examples of your work. You can also find freelance projects on Craigslist (www.craigslist.org) and numerous other websites; some of these pay only nominal fees but do provide the opportunity to display your skills.

Third, learn more about the industry or industries in which you want to work, and stay on top of new developments. Join networks of professional colleagues and friends who can help you keep up with trends and events. Many professional societies have student chapters or offer students discounted memberships. Take courses and pursue other educational or life experiences that would be hard to get while working full-time. Identify insightful and influential bloggers who cover industries and professions that interest you.

Even after an employer hires you, it's a good idea to continue improving your skills, in order to distinguish yourself from your peers and to make yourself more valuable to current and potential employers. Acquire as much technical knowledge as you can, build broad-based life experience, and develop your social skills. Learn to respond to change in positive, constructive ways; doing so will help you adapt if your "perfect" career path eludes your grasp. Learn to see each job, even so-called entry-level jobs, as an opportunity to learn more and to expand your knowledge, experience, and social skills. Share what you know with others instead of hoarding knowledge in the hope of becoming indispensable; helping others excel is a skill, too.[9]

BUILDING AN EMPLOYMENT PORTFOLIO

Employers want proof that you have the skills to succeed on the job, but even if you don't have much relevant work experience, you can use your college classes to assemble that proof. Simply create and maintain an **employment portfolio**, which is a collection of projects that demonstrate your skills and knowledge. You can create both a *print portfolio* and an *e-portfolio*; both can help with your career effort. A print portfolio gives you something tangible to bring to interviews, and it lets you collect project results that might not be easy to show online, such as a handsomely bound report.

An e-portfolio is a multimedia presentation of your skills and experiences.[10] Think of it as a website that contains your résumé, work samples, letters of recommendation, articles you may have written, and other information about you and your skills. Be creative. For example, a student who was pursuing a degree in meteorology added a video clip of himself delivering a weather forecast.[11] The portfolio can be burned on a CD-ROM for physical distribution or, more commonly, posted online—whether it's a personal website, your college's site (if student pages are available), or a networking site such as www.collegegrad.com or www.creativeshake.com. To see a selection of student e-portfolios from colleges around the United States, go to http://real-timeupdates.com/ebc, click on "Student Assignments," and then click on "Prologue" to locate the link to student e-portfolios.

Throughout the course, pay close attention to the activities and cases marked "Portfolio Builder" (they start in Chapter 7). These items will make particularly good samples of not only your communication skills but also your ability to understand and solve business-related challenges. By combining these projects with samples from your other courses, you can create a compelling portfolio by the time you're ready to start interviewing. Your portfolio is also a great resource for writing your résumé because it reminds you of all the great work you've done over the years. Moreover, you can continue to refine and expand your portfolio throughout your career; many professionals use e-portfolios to advertise their services, for instance (see Figure 1 on the next page).

As you assemble your portfolio, collect anything that shows your ability to perform, whether it's in school, on the job, or in other venues. However, you *must* check with an employer before including any items that you created while you were an employee. Many business documents contain confidential information that companies don't want distributed to outside audiences.

For each item you add to your portfolio, write a brief description that helps other people understand the meaning and significance of the project. Include such items as these:

- **Background.** Why did you undertake this project? Was it a school project, or maybe an article you wrote on your own initiative.
- **Project objectives.** Explain the project's goals, if relevant.

FIGURE 1 **Professional Portfolio**
Erik Jonsson, a digital media designer, uses e-portfolio services such as Behance.net (**www.behance.net/erikj**) to display samples of his work. Potential clients or business partners can click on the images shown here to learn more about each project. No matter what your intended profession or level of experience, you can use an e-portfolio to help potential employers learn more about your skills and qualifications.

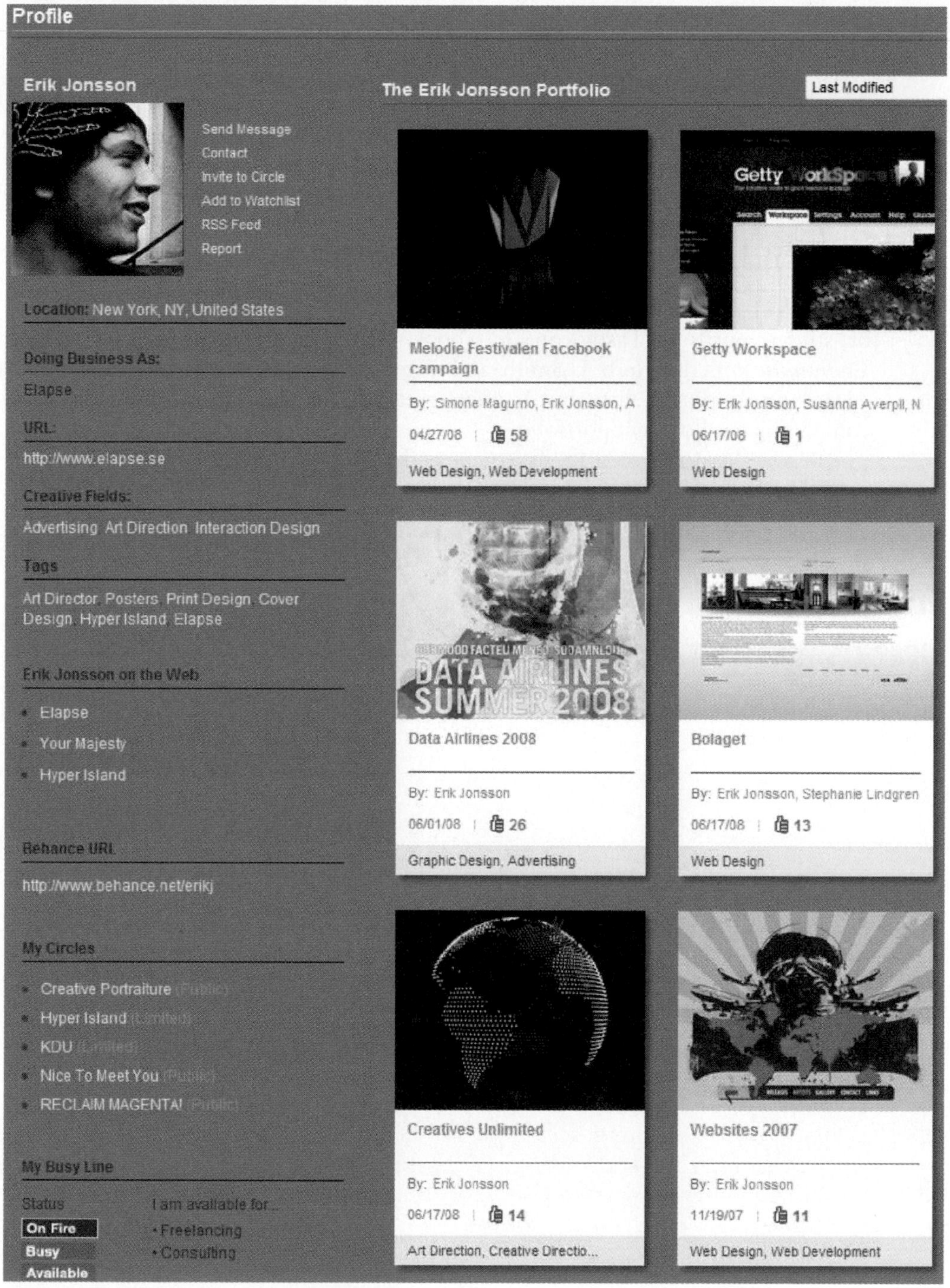

- **Collaborators.** If you worked with others, be sure to mention that and discuss team dynamics if appropriate. For instance, if you led the team or worked with others long-distance as a *virtual team*, point that out.
- **Constraints.** Sometimes the most impressive thing about a project is the time or budget constraints under which it was created. If these apply to a project, consider mentioning

them in a way that doesn't sound like an excuse for poor quality. If you had only one week to create a website, for example, you might say that "One of the intriguing challenges of this project was the deadline; I had only one week to design, compose, test, and publish this material."

- **Outcomes.** If the project's goals were measurable, what was the result? For example, if you wrote a letter soliciting donations for a charitable cause, how much money did you raise?
- **Learning experience.** If appropriate, describe what you learned during the course of the project.

Keep in mind that the portfolio itself is a communication project too, so be sure to apply everything you'll learn in this course about effective communication and good design. Assume that every potential employer will find your e-portfolio site (even if you don't tell them about it), so don't include anything that could come back to haunt you. Also, if you have anything embarrassing on Facebook, MySpace, or any other social networking site, remove it immediately.

To get started, first check with the career center at your college; many schools now offer e-portfolio systems for their students. (Some schools now require e-portfolios, so you may already be building one.) You can also find plenty of advice online; search for "e-portfolio" or "student portfolio." Lastly, consider a book such as *Portfolios for Technical and Professional Communicators*, by Herb J. Smith and Kim Haimes-Korn. This book is intended for communication specialists, but it offers great advice for anyone who wants to create a compelling employment portfolio.

Best wishes for success in this course and in your career!

Part 1

Understanding the Foundations of Business Communication

No other skill will help your career in as many different ways as communication. Discover what business communication is all about and learn how to adapt your communication experiences in life and college to the business world. Improve your skills in such vital areas as team interaction, etiquette, listening, and nonverbal communication. Explore the advantages and the challenges of a diverse workforce and develop the skills that every communicator needs to succeed in today's multicultural business environment.

1 Achieving Success Through Effective Business Communication

Learning Objectives

After studying this chapter, you will be able to

1. Explain how the Business Communication 2.0 concept is transforming the practice of business communication
2. Describe the five characteristics of effective business communication
3. Describe six strategies for communicating more effectively on the job
4. Explain what must occur for an audience to successfully receive, decode, and respond to messages
5. Explain four strategies for successfully using communication technology
6. Discuss the importance of ethics in business communication and differentiate between ethical dilemmas and ethical lapses

On the Job: Communicating at Six Apart

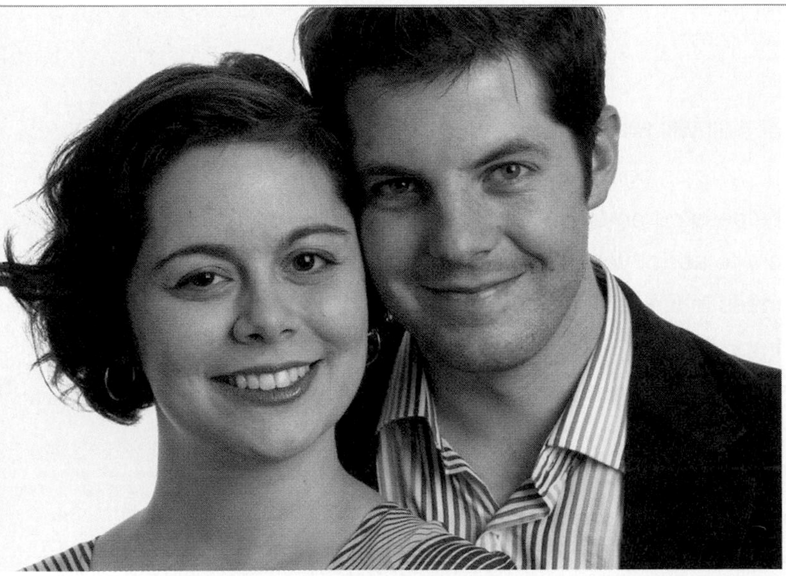

Through the company she co-founded with her husband, Ben, Six Apart's Mena Trott is an influential figure in the world of blogging.

Mena Trott Helps Redefine the Nature of Communication

Many people transform personal interests into successful business enterprises. Mena Trott used her hobby to help start a revolution. She was among the first wave of web users to keep a *web log*, or *blog*, an online journal that can cover any topic from politics to pets. As the popularity of Trott's blog grew, the rudimentary blogging tools available at the time couldn't keep up. Trott and her husband, Ben, decided to create their own software that would handle high-volume blogging—and make it easy for anyone to blog.

The Trotts' first product, Movable Type, caught on quickly as web users around the world welcomed the opportunity to become instant online publishers. Before long, Ben and Mena become first-name celebrities in the "blogosphere," and an effort that had started as an extension of a hobby soon grew into a multinational firm that now lays claim to being the world's leading provider of blogging tools and services. (The Trotts named their new company Six Apart in honor of the fact that the two of them were born just six days apart.)

With help from companies such as Six Apart, bloggers began to influence virtually every aspect of contemporary life, from politics to journalism to business. The best of these business blogs tear down the barriers that can make companies seem impersonal or unresponsive. Companies ranging from Boeing to General Motors to Microsoft now use blogs to put a human face on commercial organizations, and millions of people read these blogs to keep up on the latest news about the products and companies that interest them.

Six Apart continues to offer consumers and businesspeople new ways to communicate, such as making its TypePad blogging system available on Apple's popular iPhone and helping bloggers connect with companies that want to advertise on popular blogs. Blogging is changing so rapidly that it's hard to predict what the future holds for Six Apart, but Trott summed up the impact of blogging when she said, "I can't imagine where we'll be in a year, let alone five years, but I'm certain web logging is here to stay."[1]

www.sixapart.com

GETTING READY FOR BUSINESS COMMUNICATION 2.0

1 LEARNING OBJECTIVE

Explain how the Business Communication 2.0 concept is transforming the practice of business communication.

Back in the old days—you know, two or three years ago—business communication was largely defined by a *publishing* or *broadcasting* mindset. Externally, a company released carefully scripted messages to a mass audience that often had few, if any, ways to respond. Likewise, customers and other interested parties had few ways to connect with one another to ask questions, share information, or offer support. Internally, communication tended to follow the same "we talk, you listen" model, with upper managers issuing directives to lower-level supervisors and employees.

The conversational and interactive social communication model *is revolutionizing business communication.*

However, thanks to the efforts of innovators such as Mena Trott (profiled in the chapter-opening "On the Job" vignette), a variety of technologies have enabled and inspired a new approach to business communication. In contrast to the publishing mindset, this new **social communication model** is *interactive* and *conversational.* As corporate communication specialist Caroline Kealey puts it, traditional practices of "issuing messages through static, hierarchical and largely one-way channels are fading into obsolescence."[2] The audience is no longer a passive recipient of messages but an active participant in the conversation. Just as **Web 2.0** signifies the second generation of World Wide Web technologies (blogs, wikis, podcasts, and other *social media* tools that you'll read about in Chapter 7), **Business Communication 2.0** is a convenient label for this new approach to business communication.

Practically every assumption about business communication needs to be reconsidered under the Business Communication 2.0 approach.

On the surface, this approach might look as if it has just added a few new media tools, such as blogs, podcasts, and wikis. However, as Figure 1.1 shows, the changes are much deeper and more profound. In a typical "1.0" approach, messages are scripted by

FIGURE 1.1 Business Communication: 1.0 Versus 2.0
Business Communication 2.0 differs from conventional communication strategies and practices in a number of significant ways.

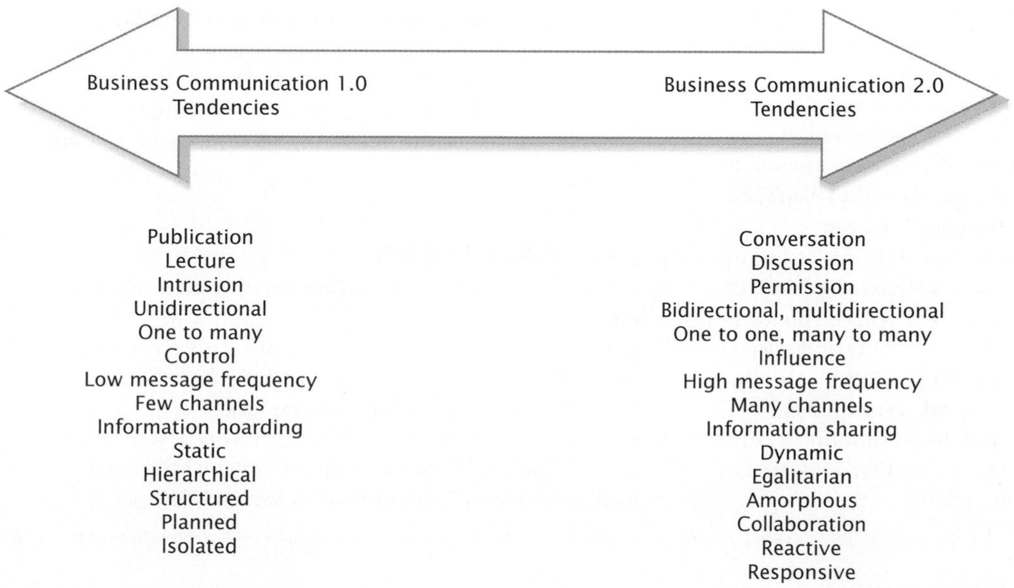

—REAL-TIME UPDATES
Learn More

See how businesses are using Facebook, YouTube, and other social media

This interview with social media expert Ben Wills discusses the growing role of social media in business. Go to **http://real-timeupdates.com/ebc** and click on "Learn More." If you are using mybcommlab, you can access Real-Time Updates within each chapter or under Student Study Tools.

designated communicators, approved by someone in authority, distributed through selected channels, and delivered without modification to a passive audience that is not invited or even expected to respond. In the 2.0 approach, the rules change dramatically; none of these assumptions can be taken for granted.

Of course, no company, no matter how enthusiastically it embraces the 2.0 mindset, is going to be run as a social club in which everyone has a say and a vote. Instead, a hybrid approach is emerging in which some communications (such as strategic plans and policy documents) follow the traditional approach and others (such as project management updates and customer support messages) follow the 2.0 approach.

Throughout this book, you'll find many discussions of how the nature of business communication is changing. Here are some of the major Business Communication 2.0 topics you'll read about:

- Social networking technologies (Chapter 2)
- Social media (including blogs and podcasts) for short messages (Chapter 7)
- The challenge of negative information spread through social media (Chapter 9)
- Social commerce and new approaches to persuasive messages (Chapter 10)

Business Communication 2.0

Putting Their Communication Skills to Work

The authors have recently met a number of young professionals who use the latest media tools to improve communication in their work. Here are a few of their stories:

- Meg Stivison (University of Massachusetts–Amherst) writes a blog and maintains a Flickr photo-sharing collection for the Stickley Museum at Craftsman Farms in Cary, North Carolina.
- Aga Westfall (Northern Arizona University) of The Santy Agency, an advertising firm in Phoenix, Arizona, uses the Twitter microblogging tool for research and networking.
- Melissa Popp (Millersville University), who is employed by Best Buy in Dover, Delaware, uses YouTube to educate her customers about electronic products.
- Matthew Nederlanden (Palm Beach Atlantic University) of Pompano Beach, Florida, just launched a new *crowdsourcing* advertising agency that allows anyone to create a concept for a commercial, post it on YouTube, and get paid based on how many people view it.
- Jerrold Thompson (Evergreen State College) of Clinton, Washington, just launched In My Life Video, a service that produces personal autobiographies. The skills he honed in class helped him write content for his website and a script for a promotional video he posted on YouTube.
- Philip Beech (Brooks Institute of Photography) of Portland, Oregon, uses Facebook to communicate with other Home Video Studio franchise owners and to promote his business to prospective clients.
- Chris Millichap (University of Wisconsin–Madison) of Chicago, Illinois, uses Facebook to promote Boosh Magazine, an online college entertainment publication.
- Matthew Meyer (Indiana University) of Oakland, California, is an e-learning developer for Adecco who has written and produced a series of training podcasts for a major pharmaceutical client.
- Liz Wise (Art Institute of Colorado) and her colleagues at Drillspot.com, a tools and hardware website based in Boulder, Colorado, use a wiki to minimize the number of meetings held and to store and share instructions for tasks and procedures.
- Ted Rubin (State University of New York–Purchase) of Atlanta, Georgia, is a remote server support analyst for Career Connection who uses Really Simple Syndication (RSS) newsfeeds to receive updates from vendors and to track the continuous results from his searches on Google News.

CAREER APPLICATIONS

1. If you are currently working, how could you use electronic media to improve the way you communicate with customers or colleagues? (If you're not currently working, think about a job you had in the past or think about a friend's or classmate's job for this exercise.)
2. In what ways have you used electronic media in your college classes? Can you identify any disadvantages of using these media to communicate with instructors and classmates?

- Social bookmarking and tagging as research tools (Chapter 11)
- Social media (wikis) for longer messages (Chapter 12)
- Social media tools used in recruiting and job searches (Chapter 15)

If you're an active user of Web 2.0 technologies, you'll fit right in with this new communication environment—and possibly even have a head start on more experienced professionals who are still adapting to the new tools and techniques (see "Business Communication 2.0: Putting Their Communication Skills to Work"). For the latest information on communicating in a Web 2.0 environment, visit **http://real-timeupdates.com/ebc** and select Chapter 1.

ACHIEVING SUCCESS IN TODAY'S COMPETITIVE ENVIRONMENT

Communication skills are essential to your career success.

No matter what career path you pursue, communication skills will be essential to your success. In fact, if you're looking for a surefire way to stand out from your competition, improving your communication skills may be the single most important step you can take. Employers often express frustration at the poor communication skills of many employees—particularly recent college graduates who haven't yet learned how to adapt their communication styles to a professional business environment. If you learn to write well, speak well, listen well, and recognize the appropriate way to communicate in various business situations, you'll gain a major advantage that will serve you throughout your career.[3]

Communication is the process of transferring information and meaning between *senders* and *receivers*, using one or more written, oral, visual, or electronic channels. The essence of communication is sharing—providing data, information, and insights in an exchange that benefits both you and the people with whom you are communicating.[4] Effective communication helps businesses in numerous ways. These benefits include:[5]

Effective communication yields numerous business benefits.

- Stronger decision making based on timely, reliable information
- Faster problem solving, in which less time is spent on understanding problems and more time is spent on creating solutions
- Earlier warning of potential problems, from rising business costs to critical safety issues
- Increased productivity and lower costs (In the words of business writing expert Jack Appleman, "Bad writing wastes time, and time is money."[6])
- Stronger business relationships
- Clearer and more persuasive marketing messages
- Enhanced professional images for both employers and companies
- Greater employee engagement with their work, leading to higher employee satisfaction and lower employee turnover
- Better financial results and higher return for investors

Effective communication strengthens the connection between a company and all of its **stakeholders**, those groups affected in some way by the company's actions: customers, employees, shareholders, suppliers, neighbors, the community, and the nation.[7] Conversely, when communication breaks down, the results can range from time wasting to tragic. At every stage of your career, communication will help you succeed, and the higher you rise in your organization, the more important communication becomes. Top managers spend as much as 85 percent of their time communicating with others.[8]

Communicating in Organizational Settings

Messages flow into, through, and out of business organizations in a variety of ways. **Internal communication** takes place between people inside a company, whereas **external communication** takes place between a company and outside parties.

FIGURE 1.2 **Formal Communication Network**
A formal communication network, defined by the relationships between the various job positions in an organization, generally follows Business Communication 1.0 conventions. Messages can flow *upward* (from a lower-level employee to a higher-level employee), *downward* (from a higher-level employee to a lower-level employee), and *horizontally* (across the organization, between employees at the same or similar levels).

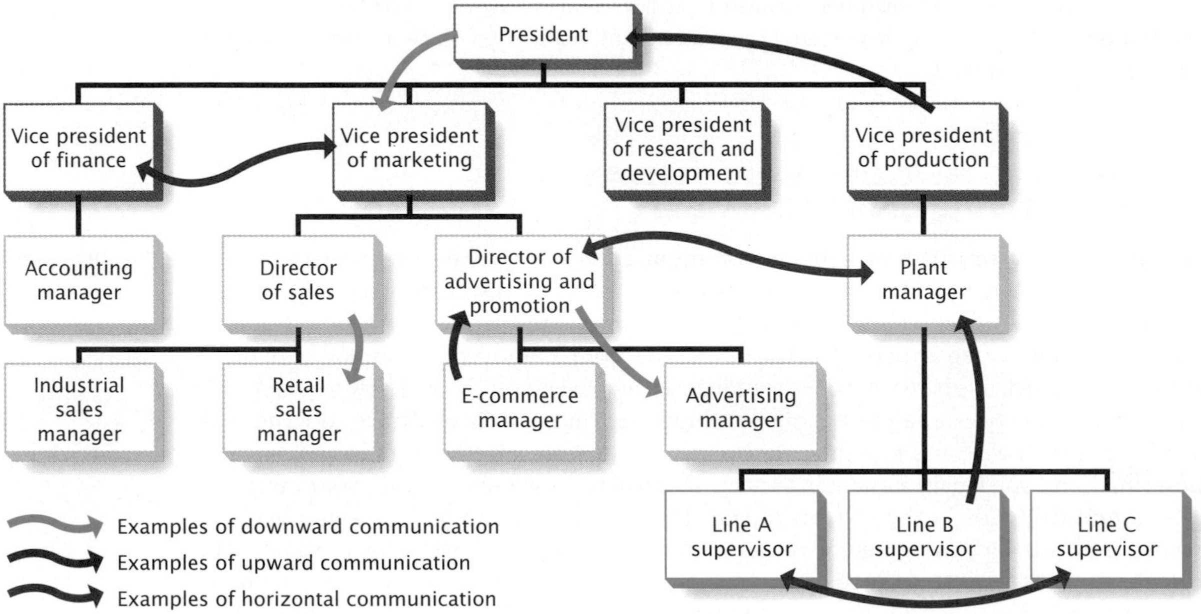

A formal communication network mirrors the company's organizational structure.

Every organization has a **formal communication network**, in which ideas and information flow along the lines of command (the hierarchical levels) in the company's organization structure (see Figure 1.2). Although these communication efforts might use social media, they tend to follow the conventional Business Communication 1.0 mindset.

Throughout the internal formal network, information flows in three directions. *Downward communication* flows from executives to employees, conveying executive decisions and providing information that helps employees do their jobs. *Upward communication* flows from employees to executives, providing insight into problems, trends, opportunities, grievances, and performance—thus allowing executives to solve problems and make intelligent decisions. *Horizontal communication* flows between departments to help employees share information, coordinate tasks, and solve complex problems.[9]

Social media play an increasingly important role in the informal communication network.

Every organization also has an **informal communication network**, often referred to as the *grapevine* or the *rumor mill*, that encompasses all communication that takes place outside the formal network. Some of this informal communication takes place naturally as a result of employee interaction both on the job and in social settings, and some of it takes place when the formal network doesn't provide information that employees want. In fact, the inherent limitations of formal communication networks helped spur the growth of social media and the Business Communication 2.0 concept.

Recognizing Effective Communication

2 LEARNING OBJECTIVE

Describe the five characteristics of effective business communication.

To make your messages effective, you need to make them practical, factual, concise, clear, and persuasive:[10]

- **Provide practical information.** Give recipients useful information, whether it's to help them perform a desired action or understand a new company policy.
- **Give facts rather than vague impressions.** Use concrete language, specific detail, and information that is clear, convincing, accurate, and ethical. When an opinion is called for, present compelling evidence to support your conclusion—and make sure readers know you're offering an opinion.

FIGURE 1.3 Ineffective Business Communication
At first glance, this e-mail message looks like a reasonable attempt at communicating with the members of a project team. However, review the blue annotations to see just how many problems the message really has.

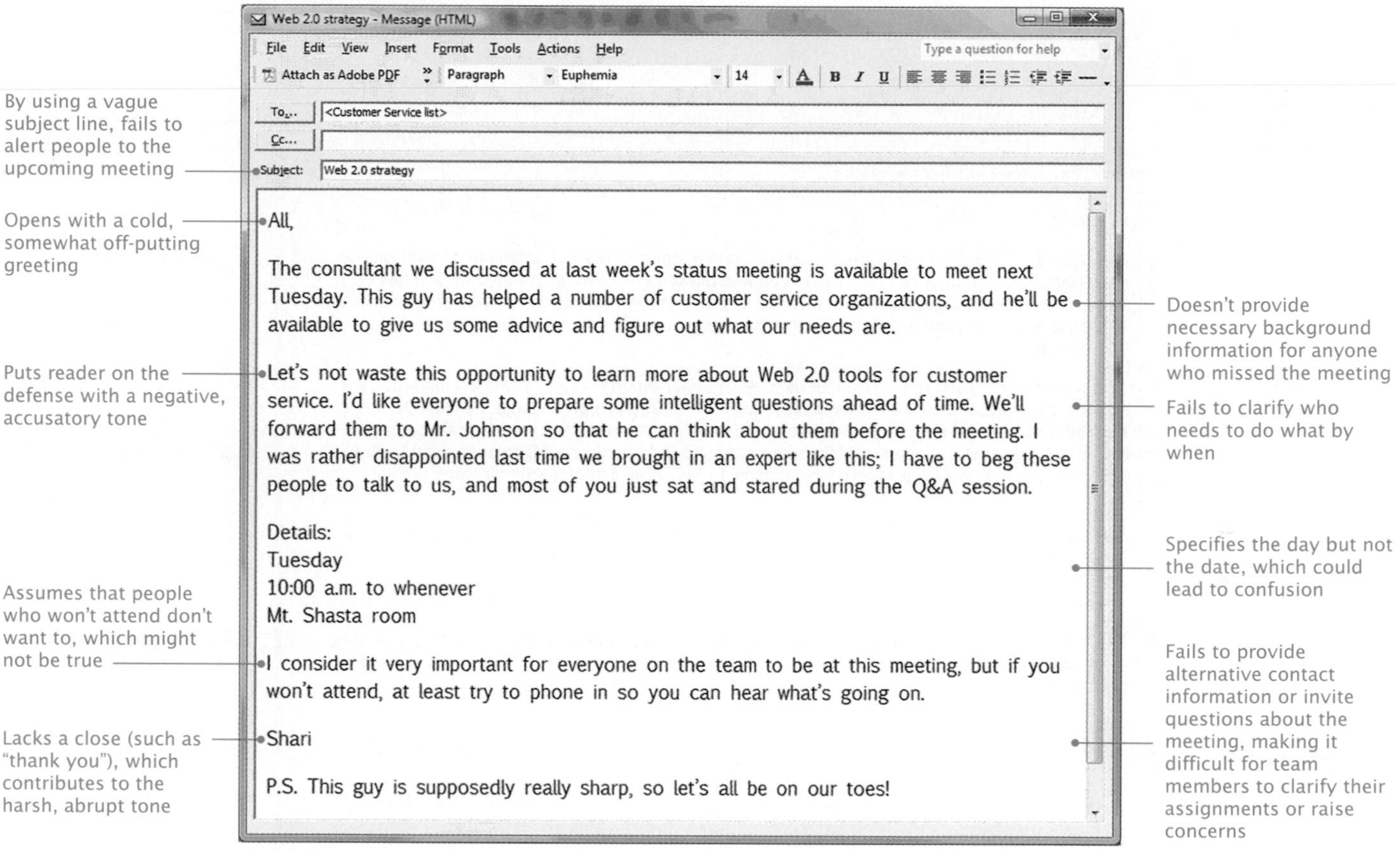
Web 2.0 strategy - Message (HTML)

To... <Customer Service list>
Cc...
Subject: Web 2.0 strategy

All,

The consultant we discussed at last week's status meeting is available to meet next Tuesday. This guy has helped a number of customer service organizations, and he'll be available to give us some advice and figure out what our needs are.

Let's not waste this opportunity to learn more about Web 2.0 tools for customer service. I'd like everyone to prepare some intelligent questions ahead of time. We'll forward them to Mr. Johnson so that he can think about them before the meeting. I was rather disappointed last time we brought in an expert like this; I have to beg these people to talk to us, and most of you just sat and stared during the Q&A session.

Details:
Tuesday
10:00 a.m. to whenever
Mt. Shasta room

I consider it very important for everyone on the team to be at this meeting, but if you won't attend, at least try to phone in so you can hear what's going on.

Shari

P.S. This guy is supposedly really sharp, so let's all be on our toes!

By using a vague subject line, fails to alert people to the upcoming meeting
Opens with a cold, somewhat off-putting greeting
Puts reader on the defense with a negative, accusatory tone
Assumes that people who won't attend don't want to, which might not be true
Lacks a close (such as "thank you"), which contributes to the harsh, abrupt tone
Doesn't provide necessary background information for anyone who missed the meeting
Fails to clarify who needs to do what by when
Specifies the day but not the date, which could lead to confusion
Fails to provide alternative contact information or invite questions about the meeting, making it difficult for team members to clarify their assignments or raise concerns

- **Present information in a concise, efficient manner.** Audiences respond more positively to messages that highlight and summarize essential points, rather than burying them under mountains of disorganized facts and figures.
- **Clarify expectations and responsibilities.** Write messages to generate a specific response from a specific audience. Clearly state what you expect from audience members or what you can do for them.
- **Offer compelling, persuasive arguments and recommendations.** Show your readers precisely how they will benefit from responding to your message the way you want them to.

Keep these five important characteristics in mind as you review Figures 1.3 and 1.4. At first glance, both e-mails appear to be well constructed, but Figure 1.4 is far more effective, as the comments in blue explain.

Understanding What Employers Expect from You

Employers expect you to possess a wide range of communication skills.

In any business-related career, employers expect you to be competent at a wide range of communication tasks. Fortunately, the skills that employers expect from you are the same skills that will help you advance in your career:[11]

- Organizing ideas and information logically and completely
- Expressing ideas and information coherently and persuasively—in oral, written, visual, and electronic media
- Actively listening to others

FIGURE 1.4 Effective Business Communication
This improved version of the e-mail message from Figure 1.3 does a much better job of communicating the essential information the team members need in order to effectively prepare for the meeting.

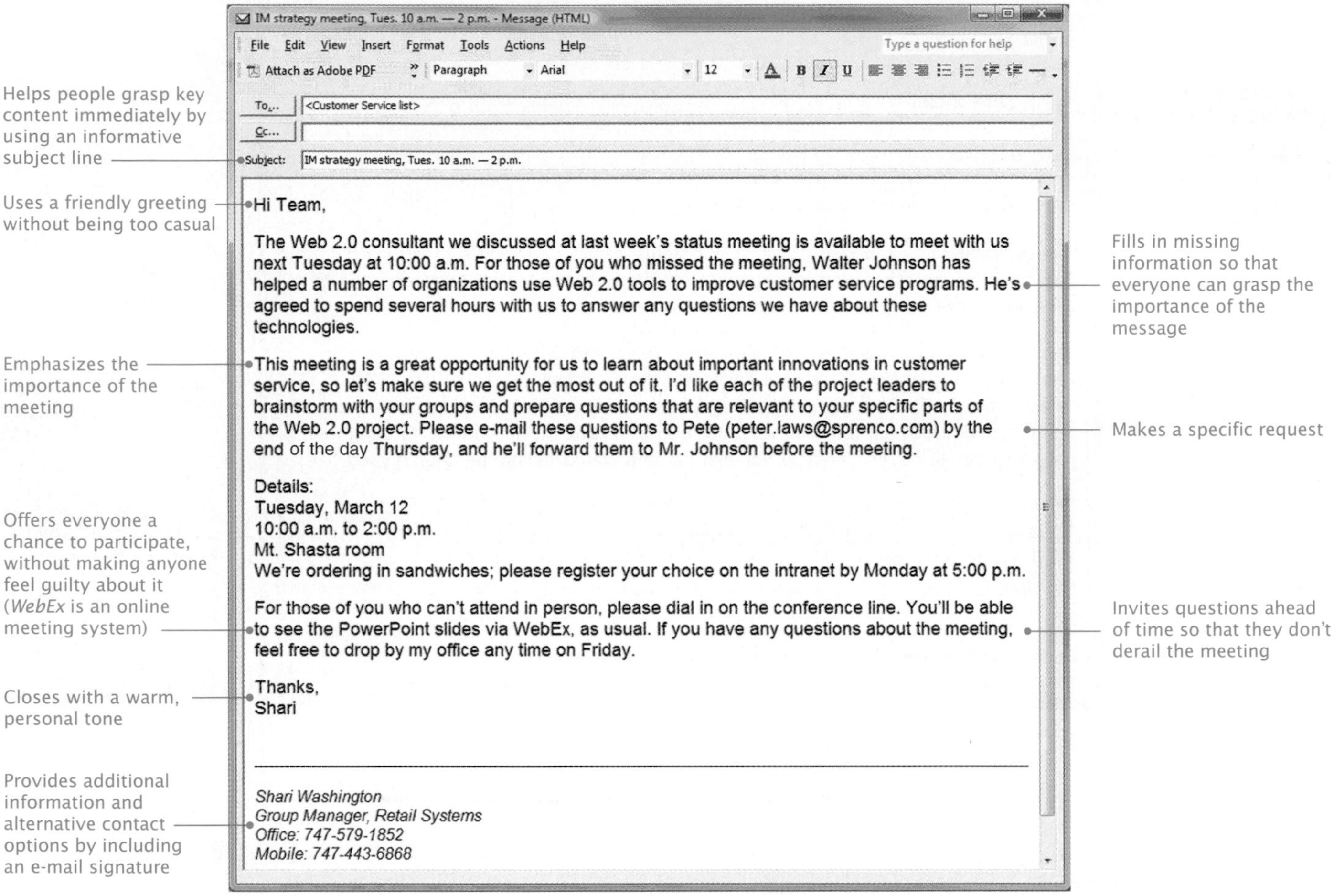

- Communicating effectively with people from diverse backgrounds and experiences
- Using communication technologies effectively and efficiently
- Following accepted standards of grammar, spelling, and other aspects of high-quality writing and speaking
- Adapting your messages and communication styles to specific audiences and situations
- Communicating in a civilized manner that reflects contemporary expectations of business etiquette, even when dealing with indifferent or hostile audiences
- Communicating ethically, even when choices aren't crystal clear
- Managing your time wisely and using resources efficiently

You'll have the opportunity to practice these skills throughout this course—but don't stop there. Successful professionals continue to hone communication skills throughout their careers.

Understanding the Unique Challenges of Business Communication

Although you have been communicating with some success your entire life, business communication is often more complicated and demanding than the social communication you typically engage in with family, friends, and school associates. Five issues help illustrate why business communication requires a high level of skill and attention: the globalization of business and the increase in workforce diversity, the increasing value of business information, the pervasiveness of technology, the evolution of organizational structures, and the growing reliance on teamwork.

Successful companies know that diverse workforces can create powerful competitive advantages, but managers must pay close attention to communication in order to eliminate barriers between groups with different communication styles.

The Globalization of Business and the Increase in Workforce Diversity

Today's businesses increasingly reach across international borders to market their products, partner with other businesses, and employ workers and executives—an effort known as **globalization.** Many U.S. companies rely on exports for a significant portion of their sales, sometimes up to 50 percent or more, and managers and employees in these firms need to communicate with many other cultures. Moreover, thousands of companies from all around the world vie for a share of the massive U.S. market, so chances are you'll do business with or even work for a company based in another country at some point in your career.

Businesses are paying more attention to **workforce diversity**—all of the differences among the people who work together, including differences in age, gender, sexual orientation, education, cultural background, religion, ability, and life experience. As Chapter 3 discusses, successful companies realize that a diverse workforce can yield a significant competitive advantage, but it also requires a more conscientious approach to communication.

The Increasing Value of Business Information

As global competition for talent, customers, and resources continues to grow, the importance of information continues to escalate as well. Even companies not usually associated with the so-called Information Age often rely on **knowledge workers,** employees at all levels of an organization who specialize in acquiring, processing, and communicating information. Three examples help to illustrate the value of information in today's economy:

Information has become one of the most important resources in business today.

- **Competitive insights.** The more a company knows about its competitors and their plans, the better able it will be to adjust its own business plans.
- **Customer needs.** Information about customer needs is analyzed and summarized in order to develop goods and services that better satisfy customer demands.
- **Regulations and guidelines.** Today's businesses must understand and follow a wide range of government regulations and guidelines covering such areas as employment, environment, taxes, and accounting.

No matter what the specific type of information, the better you are able to understand it, use it, and communicate it to others, the more competitive you and your company will be.

The Pervasiveness of Technology

The innovations that enable the Business Communication 2.0 approach highlight an important fact of business communication today: Technology influences virtually every aspect of the field. To benefit from this technology, however, you need to have at least a basic level of skills. If your level of technical expertise doesn't keep up with that of your colleagues and co-workers, the imbalance can put you at a disadvantage and complicate the communication process. Throughout this course, you'll learn how to use numerous technological tools and systems more effectively.

Business communication today depends heavily on a growing array of technologies.

The Evolution of Organizational Structures

Every firm has a particular structure that defines the relationships between various units in the company, and these relationships influence the nature and quality of communication throughout the organization. *Tall structures* have many layers of management between the lowest and highest positions, so they can suffer communication breakdowns and delays as messages are passed up and down through multiple layers.[12]

Organizations with tall structures may unintentionally restrict the flow of information; flatter structures can make it easier to communicate effectively.

To overcome such problems, many businesses are adopting *flat structures* that reduce the number of layers. With fewer layers, communication generally flows faster and with fewer disruptions and distortions. On the other hand, with fewer formal lines of control and communication in these organizations, individual employees are expected to assume more responsibility for communication—particularly in the horizontal direction, from department to department across the company.

Newer types of organization structures such as matrixes and networks present new communication challenges.

Specific types of organization structures present unique communication challenges. In a *matrix structure*, for example, employees report to two managers at the same time, such as a project manager and a department manager. The need to coordinate workloads, schedules, and other matters increases the communication burden on everyone involved. In a *network structure*, sometimes known as a *virtual organization*, a company supplements the talents of its employees with services from one or more external partners, such as a design lab, a manufacturing firm, or a sales and distribution company.

Open corporate cultures benefit from free-flowing information and employee input.

Regardless of the particular structure a company uses, your communication efforts will also be influenced by the organization's **corporate culture**, the mixture of values, traditions, and habits that gives a company its atmosphere and personality. Many successful companies encourage employee contributions by fostering *open climates* that encourage candor and honesty, helping employees feel free enough to admit their mistakes, disagree with the boss, and share negative or unwelcome information.

The Growing Reliance on Teamwork

Working in a team makes you especially responsible for communicating effectively.

Both traditional and innovative company structures can rely heavily on teamwork, and you will probably find yourself on dozens of teams throughout your career. Teams are commonly used in business today, but they're not always successful—and a key reason that teams fail to meet their objectives is poor communication. Chapter 2 offers insights into the complex dynamics of team communication and identifies skills you need in order to be an effective communicator in group settings.

3 LEARNING OBJECTIVE

Describe six strategies for communicating more effectively on the job.

COMMUNICATING MORE EFFECTIVELY ON THE JOB

Communication in today's business environment is clearly a challenge, but you can meet that challenge by learning to connect with your audiences, minimizing distractions, adopting an audience-centered approach, improving your basic communication skills, using constructive feedback, and being sensitive to business etiquette.

Connecting with Your Audience

Human communication is a complex process with many opportunities for messages to get lost, ignored, or misinterpreted. Fortunately, by understanding this process, you can improve the odds that your messages will reach their intended audiences and produce the intended effects.

The Communication Process

Viewing communication as a process helps you identify steps you can take to make yourself a more successful communicator.

By viewing communication as a process (see Figure 1.5), you can identify and improve the skills you need to be more successful. Many variations on this process model exist, but these eight steps provide a practical overview:

1. **The sender has an idea.** Whether a communication effort will ultimately be effective starts right here. For example, if you have a clear idea about a procedure change that will save your company time and money, the communication process is off to a strong start. On the other hand, if all you want to do is complain about how the company is wasting time and money, but you don't know how to fix the situation, you might be able to get your point across, but you probably won't communicate anything of value to your audience.

FIGURE 1.5 The Communication Process
These eight steps illustrate how ideas travel from sender to receiver. After you explore the process in more detail in the following pages, Figure 1.8 on page 22 offers advice on improving your skills at each step.

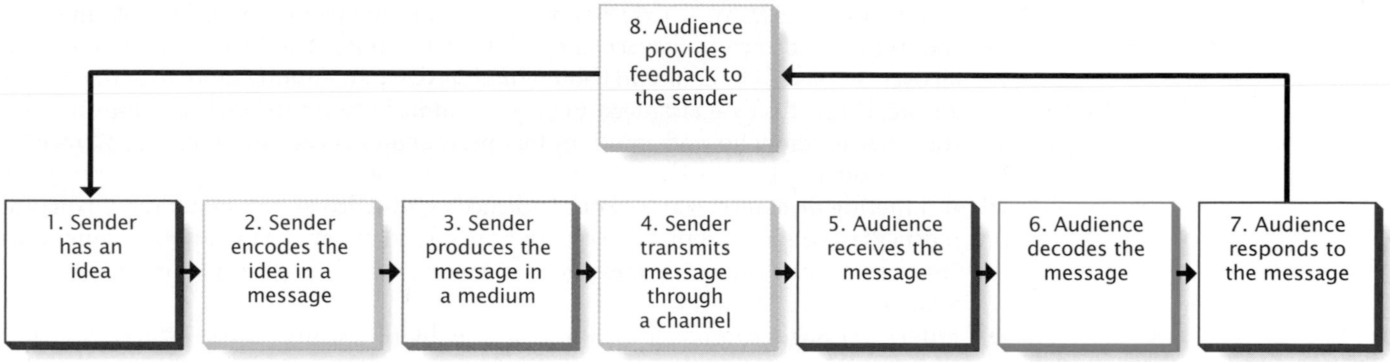

2. **The sender encodes the idea as a message.** When you put your idea into a message (words, images, or a combination of both), you are **encoding** it. Much of the focus of this course is on developing the skills needed to successfully encode your ideas into effective messages.
3. **The sender produces the message in a transmittable medium.** With the appropriate message to express your idea, you now need some way to present that message to your intended audience. As you'll read in Chapter 4, media for transmitting messages can be divided into *oral, written, visual,* and *electronic* forms. Selecting the best medium for each message is an important communication skill, particularly as electronic media options continue to multiply.
4. **The sender transmits the message through a channel.** Just as technology continues to increase the number of media options at your disposal, it continues to provide new **communication channels** you can use to transmit your messages. The distinction between medium and channel can get a bit murky, but think of the medium as the *form* a message takes and the channel as the system used to *deliver* the message. The channel can be a face-to-face conversation, the Internet, or another company—any method or system capable of delivering messages.
5. **The audience receives the message.** If all goes well, your message survives the trip through the channel and arrives at your intended audience. However, mere arrival at the destination is not a guarantee that the message will be noticed or understood correctly. As "How Audiences Receive Messages" explains, many messages are either ignored or misinterpreted as noise.
6. **The audience decodes the message.** If the message is actually received, the audience then needs to extract your idea from the message, a step known as **decoding**. "How Audiences Decode Messages" takes a closer look at this complex and subtle step in the process.
7. **The audience responds to the message.** By crafting your messages in ways that show the benefits of responding, you can increase the chances that your audiences will respond as you'd like them to. See "How Audiences Respond to Messages" for more information.
8. **The audience provides feedback.** In addition to responding (or not responding) to the message, audience members may give **feedback** that helps you evaluate the effectiveness of your communication effort.

The following sections take a closer look at two important aspects of the process: environmental barriers that can block or distort messages and the steps audiences take to receive, decode, and respond to messages.

Barriers in the Communication Environment

Within any communication environment, messages can be disrupted by a variety of **communication barriers.** These include noise and distractions, competing messages, filters, and channel breakdowns:

A number of barriers can block or distort messages before they reach the intended audience.

- **Noise and distractions.** External distractions range from uncomfortable meeting rooms to crowded computer screens with instant messages and reminders popping up all over the place. The common habit of *multitasking*, attempting more than one task at a time, is practically guaranteed to create communication distractions. Internal distractions are thoughts and emotions that prevent audiences from focusing on incoming messages.
- **Competing messages.** Having your audience's undivided attention is a rare luxury. In most cases, you must compete with other messages that are trying to reach your audience at the same time. Any message that is more compelling than yours can pull the audience's attention away.
- **Filters.** Messages can be blocked or distorted by *filters*, any human or technological interventions between the sender and the receiver. Filtering can be both intentional (such as automatically filing e-mail messages based on sender or content) or unintentional (such as an overly aggressive *spam* filter that deletes legitimate e-mail). As you read earlier, the structure and culture of an organization can also inhibit the flow of vital messages.
- **Channel breakdowns.** Sometimes the channel simply breaks down and fails to deliver your message at all. A colleague you were counting on to deliver a message to your boss might have forgotten to do so, or a computer server might have crashed and prevented your blog from updating.

As a communicator, try to be aware of any barriers that could prevent your messages from reaching their intended audiences. As a manager, keep an eye out for any organizational barriers that could be inhibiting the flow of information.

4 LEARNING OBJECTIVE

Explain what must occur for an audience to successfully receive, decode, and respond to messages.

Inside the Mind of Your Audience

After a message works its way through the communication channel and reaches the intended audience, it encounters a whole new set of challenges. Understanding how audiences receive, decode, and respond to messages will help you create more effective messages.

How Audiences Receive Messages

For an audience member to receive a message, three events need to occur: The receiver has to *sense* the presence of a message, *select* it from all the other messages clamoring for attention, and *perceive* it as an actual message (as opposed to random, pointless noise).[13]

To actually receive a message, audience members need to sense it, select it, and perceive it as a message.

Today's business audiences are much like drivers on busy streets. They are inundated with so many messages and so much noise that they can miss or ignore many of the messages intended for them. Through this course, you will learn a variety of techniques to craft messages that get noticed. In general, follow these five principles to increase your chances of success:

- **Consider audience expectations.** Deliver messages using the media and channels that the audience expects. If colleagues expect meeting notices to be delivered by e-mail, don't suddenly switch gears and start delivering the notices via blog postings without telling anyone.
- **Ensure ease of use.** Even if audiences are actively looking for your messages, they probably won't see the messages if you make them hard to find, hard to access, or hard to read. Poorly designed websites with confusing navigation are common culprits in this respect.
- **Emphasize familiarity.** Use words, images, and designs that are familiar to your audience. For example, most visitors to company websites now expect to see information about the company on a page called "About Us."

- **Practice empathy.** Make sure your messages speak to the audience by clearly addressing *their* wants and needs—not yours. People are inclined to notice messages that relate to their individual concerns.[14]
- **Design for compatibility.** For the many messages delivered electronically these days, be sure to verify technological compatibility with your audience. For instance, if your website requires visitors to have the Adobe Flash capability on their computers, you won't reach those audience members who don't have that software installed.

Message overload is a constant challenge in contemporary life; your messages must compete with many others clamoring for the audience's attention.

How Audiences Decode Messages

A received message doesn't "mean" anything until the recipient decodes it and assigns meaning to it, and there is no guarantee that your audience will assign the same meaning that you intended. Even well-crafted, well-intentioned communication efforts can fail at this stage because assigning meaning through decoding is a highly personal process that is influenced by culture, individual experience, learning and thinking styles, hopes, fears, and even temporary moods. Moreover, audiences tend to extract the meaning they expect to get from a message, even if it's the opposite of what the sender intended.[15] In fact, rather than extract your meaning, it's more accurate to say that audience members recreate their own meaning—or meanings—from the message.

As you'll discover in Chapter 3, culture shapes people's views of the world in profound ways, from determinations of right and wrong to details such as the symbolic meanings attached to specific colors. For instance, because U.S. culture celebrates youth and individual accomplishment, it is "natural" for people raised in this country to admire young, independent-minded leaders who rebel against older, established ways of doing business. A culture such as Japan's, however, generally places a higher value on respect for older colleagues, consensus decision making, and group accomplishment. Given these differences, a younger colleague's bold proposal to radically reshape business strategy could be interpreted more positively in one culture than in the other—quite independent of the proposal's merits alone.

Decoding a message to assign meaning to it is a complicated and often highly personal process.

At an individual level, beliefs and biases influence the meaning that audiences extract from messages. For instance, the human brain organizes incoming sensations into a mental "map" that represents each person's individual **perception** of reality. If a detail doesn't quite fit for any reason, people are inclined to distort the information rather than rearrange their mental map—a process known as **selective perception.**[16] For example, an executive who has staked her reputation on a particular business strategy might distort or ignore evidence that suggests the strategy is failing.

Selective perception occurs when people ignore or distort incoming information to fit their preconceived notions of reality.

Differences in language and usage also influence received meaning. If you ask an employee to send you a report on sales figures "as soon as possible," does that mean within 10 seconds, 10 minutes, or 10 days? By clarifying expectations and resolving potential ambiguities in your messages, you can minimize such uncertainties. In general, the more experiences you share with another person, the more likely you are to share perception and thus share meaning (see Figure 1.6 on page 14).

Individual thinking styles are another important factor in message decoding. For example, someone who places a high value on objective analysis and clear logic might interpret a message differently from someone who values emotion or intuition (reaching conclusions without using rational processes).

How Audiences Respond to Messages

Audiences will likely respond to a message if they remember it, if they're able to respond, and if they're properly motivated to respond.

Your message has been delivered, received, and correctly decoded. Will audience members respond in the way you'd like them to? Only if three events occur.

First, the recipient has to *remember* the message long enough to act on it. Simplifying greatly, memory works in several stages: *Sensory memory* momentarily captures incoming data from the senses; then, whatever the recipient pays attention to is transferred to *short-term memory.* Information in short-term memory will quickly disappear if it isn't transferred to *long-term memory,* which can be done either actively (such as when a person memorizes a list of items) or passively (such as when a new piece of information connects

FIGURE 1.6 How Shared Experience Affects Understanding
The more that two people or two groups of people share experiences—personal, professional, and cultural—the more likely it is that receivers will extract the intended meanings that senders encode into the messages.

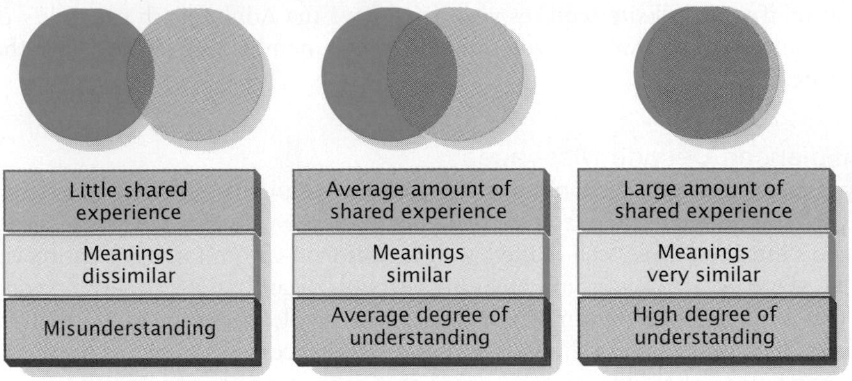

with something else the recipient already has stored in long-term memory). Finally, the information needs to be *retrieved* when the recipient wants to act on it.[17] In general, people find it easier to remember and retrieve information that is important to them personally or professionally. Consequently, by communicating in ways that are sensitive to your audience's wants and needs, you greatly increase the chance that your messages will be remembered and retrieved.

Second, the recipient has to be *able* to respond as you wish. Obviously, if recipients simply cannot do what you want them to do, they will not respond according to your plan. By understanding your audience (you'll learn more about audience analysis in Chapter 4), you can work to minimize these scenarios.

By explaining how audiences will benefit by responding to your messages, you'll increase their motivation to respond.

Third, the recipient has to be *motivated* to respond. You'll encounter many situations in which your audience has the option of responding but isn't required to. For instance, a record company may or may not offer your band a contract, or your boss may or may not respond to your request for a raise. Throughout this course, you'll learn techniques for crafting messages that can help motivate readers to respond.

Minimizing Distractions

Overcome distractions by
- *Using common sense and courtesy*
- *Not sending unnecessary messages*
- *Not isolating yourself*
- *Informing receivers of message priority*

Communicating in emotionally charged situations requires extra care.

Distractions are a major problem in business communication, but everyone in an organization can help minimize them. A small dose of common sense and courtesy goes a long way. Turn off that mobile phone before you step into a meeting. Don't talk across the tops of other people's cubicles. Be sensitive to personal differences, too; for instance, some people enjoy working with music on, but music is an enormous distraction for others.[18]

Take steps to insulate yourself from distractions, too. Don't let e-mail, instant messaging (IM), telephone calls, or Twitter updates interrupt you every minute of the day. Set aside time to attend to messages all at once so that you can focus the rest of the time.

Finally, recognize that emotions—yours and your audience's—can create distractions. Try to overcome these distractions by being aware of your own feelings and by anticipating emotional reactions from others.[19] For example, when communicating about an emotionally charged situation, choose your words carefully to minimize overreactions that could keep your message from getting through.

Adopting an Audience-Centered Approach

Keeping your audience's needs in mind helps you ensure successful messages.

An **audience-centered approach** involves understanding and respecting the members of your audience and making every effort to get your message across in a way that is meaningful to them (see Figure 1.7). This approach is also known as adopting the **"you" attitude**, in contrast to messages that are about "me." Learn as much as possible about the biases, education, age, status, style, and personal and professional concerns of your receivers. If you're

FIGURE 1.7 Audience-Centered Communication
This blog post from the developers of the popular TypePad blogging system demonstrates concern for the audience in several ways, including content that addresses audience interests, multiple options for consuming the information, a design that makes the content easy to absorb, and the opportunity for readers to participate in the conversation.

February 11, 2009

Add Your Latest Twitter Tweets to Your TypePad Blog

Twitter is a microblogging service that lets you share ideas and news with your friends in 140 character updates. Here's how to add your latest Twitter updates - called *tweets* - to your TypePad blog: (instructions below)

Explains the context of the message for those readers who might not be familiar with twitter

blogging tips
hosted by Professor Andy Wibbels
Tip:
Add Your Latest Twitter Updates to Your TypePad Blog
00:00
00:00

Offers the information in video format for those who prefer this medium

1. Go to http://www.twitter.com/widgets/ and select TypePad and click on Continue. Select the number of tweets you want to display and give your list of updates a name. Click Install Widget on TypePad.
2. You'll be sent into TypePad to then choose the blog you want to add the Twitter widget to.
3. Check the checkbox of the blog and click Add Widget. The Widget has been added to your sidebars.
4. Go out to your blog and reload it and you should see your latest Twitter updates your sidebar.

Complements the video message with textual material in an easy-to-follow list of steps for those who prefer reading to viewing

To change the position of the Twitter widget, go to Weblogs > (your blog) > Design > Content and then drag-and-drop the widgets in the order your like and then Save Changes.

☆☆☆☆☆ rated **4.67** by 3 people [?]

Offers an article rating system that lets readers judge the value of the material

Posted by Andy Wibbels on February 11, 2009 at 03:02 PM in Business, Tips and Tricks | Permalink
ShareThis

Tags the post with keywords that readers can use to find similar posts

TrackBack

TrackBack URL for this entry:
http://www.typepad.com/services/trackback/6a00d83451c82369e20111685be18d970c
Listed below are links to weblogs that reference Add Your Latest Twitter Tweets to Your TypePad Blog:

Comments

Offers a commenting feature (comments not shown here) to let readers participate in the conversation

addressing people you don't know and you're unable to find out more about them, try to project yourself into their position by using common sense and imagination. This ability to relate to the needs of others is a key part of *emotional intelligence*, which is widely considered to be a vital characteristic of successful managers and leaders.[20] The more you know about the people you're communicating with, the easier it will be to concentrate on their needs—which, in turn, will make it easier for them to hear your message, understand it, and respond positively.

Recognizing and adapting to the diverse styles of all the audiences you'll encounter on the job will improve not only the effectiveness of your communication but also the quality of your working relationships.[21] The audience-centered approach is emphasized throughout this book, so you'll have plenty of opportunity to practice this approach.

Fine-Tuning Your Business Communication Skills

Work on your communication skills now, before you start (or restart) your business career.

Many employers provide ongoing communication training in both general skills and specific communication challenges, but don't wait to master these skills. Begin mastering them now, using this course and the opportunity to practice in an environment that provides honest and constructive feedback. You'll have ample opportunity to plan and produce documents, collaborate in teams, listen effectively, improve nonverbal communication, use a variety of technologies, and communicate across cultures—all skills that will serve your career well.

Giving—and Responding to—Constructive Feedback

Constructive feedback focuses on improvement, not personal criticism.

You'll encounter numerous situations in which you are expected to give and receive feedback regarding communication efforts. Whether giving or receiving criticism, be sure to do so in a constructive way. **Constructive feedback**, sometimes called *constructive criticism*, focuses on improvement (see Table 1.1). In contrast, **destructive feedback** simply criticizes with no effort to stimulate improvement.[22] For example, "This proposal is a confusing mess, and you failed to convince me of anything" is destructive feedback. Your goal is to be more constructive: "Your proposal could be more effective, with a clearer description of the manufacturing process you advocate and a well-organized explanation of why the positives outweigh the negatives." When giving feedback, avoid personal attacks and give the person clear guidelines for improvement.

Try to react unemotionally when you receive constructive feedback.

When you receive constructive feedback, resist the urge to defend your work or deny the validity of the feedback. Remaining open to criticism isn't easy when you've poured

TABLE 1.1 Giving Constructive Feedback

HOW TO BE CONSTRUCTIVE	EXPLANATION
Think through your suggested changes carefully.	Because many business documents must illustrate complex relationships between ideas and other information, isolated and superficial edits can do more harm than good.
Discuss improvements rather than flaws.	Instead of saying "this is confusing," explain how the writing can be improved to make it clearer.
Focus on controllable behavior.	Because the writer may not have control over every variable that affected the quality of the message, focus on the aspects the writer can control.
Be specific.	Comments such as "I don't get this" or "Make this clearer" don't identify what the writer needs to fix.
Keep feedback impersonal.	Focus comments on the message, not the person who created it.
Verify understanding.	Ask for confirmation from the recipient to make sure that the person understands your feedback.
Provide your feedback in a timely fashion.	Make sure the writer will have sufficient time to implement the changes you suggest.
Highlight any limitations your feedback may have.	If you didn't have time to give the document a thorough edit, or if you're not an expert in some aspect of the content, let the writer know so that he or she can handle your comments appropriately.

your heart and soul into a project, but feedback is a valuable opportunity to learn and improve. Try to disconnect your emotions from the work and view it simply as something—a thing apart from yourself—that you can make better. Many writers find it helpful to step back, think about the feedback for a while, and let their emotions settle down before diving in to make corrections. Of course, don't automatically assume that even well-intentioned feedback is necessarily correct. You have the responsibility for the final content and quality of every message you produce, so make sure that any suggested changes are valid.

Being Sensitive to Business Etiquette

Understanding communication etiquette can help you avoid needless blunders.

A vital element of audience-centered communication is **etiquette**, the expected norms of behavior in any particular situation. In today's hectic, competitive world, etiquette might seem a quaint and outdated notion. However, the way you conduct yourself and interact with others can have a profound influence on your company's success and your career. When executives hire and promote you, they expect your behavior to protect the company's reputation. The more you understand such expectations, the better chance you have of avoiding career-damaging mistakes.

Throughout this book, you'll encounter etiquette advice for a variety of business situations, but even if you don't know the specific expectations in a given situation, some general guidelines will get you through any rough spots. Start by being sensitive to the fact that etiquette is culturally based, and people from different cultures can have different expectations about the same situation. Something you find appalling or embarrassing might be business as usual for a colleague and vice versa.

Respect, courtesy, and common sense will get you through most etiquette challenges on the job.

Long lists of etiquette "rules" can be overwhelming, and you'll never be able to memorize all of them. Fortunately, you can count on three principles to get you through any situation: respect, courtesy, and common sense. Moreover, following these principles will encourage forgiveness if you do happen to make a mistake. As you prepare to encounter new situations, take some time to learn the expectations of the other people involved. Travel guidebooks are a great source of information about norms and customs in other countries. Check to see if your library has online access to the CultureGrams database, or review the country profiles at www.kwintessential.co.uk. Don't be afraid to ask questions, either. People will respect your concern and curiosity. You'll gradually accumulate considerable knowledge, which will help you feel comfortable and be effective in a wide range of business situations.

Applying What You've Learned to the Communication Process

Now that you have some additional insights into what makes communication succeed, take another look at the communication process model. Figure 1.8 on page 22 identifies the key challenges in the process and summarizes the steps you can take along the way to become a more effective communicator.

USING TECHNOLOGY TO IMPROVE BUSINESS COMMUNICATION

5 LEARNING OBJECTIVE

Explain four strategies for successfully using communication technology.

Today's businesses rely heavily on technology to facilitate the communication process. In fact, many of the technologies you might use in your personal life, from microblogs to video games to virtual worlds, are also used in business. You will find technology discussed extensively throughout this book, with specific advice on using both common and emerging tools. The four-page photo essay "Powerful Tools for Communicating Efficiently" (see pages 18–21) provides an overview of the technologies that connect people in offices, factories, and other business settings.

Communicating in today's business environment requires at least a basic level of technological competence.

Anyone who has used a computer, a smartphone, or other advanced gadget knows that the benefits of technology are not automatic. Poorly designed or inappropriately used technology can hinder communication more than it helps. To communicate effectively, learn to

(*Text continues on page 22*)

Powerful Tools for Communicating Effectively

The tools of business communication evolve with every new generation of digital technology. Selecting the right tool for each situation can enhance your business communication in many ways. In today's flexible office settings, communication technology helps people keep in touch and stay productive. When co-workers in different cities need to collaborate, they can meet and share ideas without costly travel. Manufacturers use communication technology to keep track of parts, orders, and shipments—and to keep customers well-Informed. Those same customers can also communicate with companies in many ways at any time of day or night.

REDEFINING THE OFFICE

Technology makes it easier for people to stay connected with co-workers and retrieve needed information. Some maintain that connection without having a permanent office, a desktop PC, or even a big filing cabinet. For example, Sun Microsystems lets staff members choose to work either at the main office or at remote offices called "drop-in centers." Many Sun facilities have specially equipped "iWork" areas where phone and computer connections can be quickly reconfigured to meet individual requirements.

Electronic Presentations

Combining a color projector with a laptop or personal digital assistant (PDA) running the right software lets people give business presentations that are enhanced with sound, animation, and website hyperlinks.

Wireless Networks

Wireless access lets workers with laptop PCs and other devices stay connected from just about anywhere—around the corporate campus and from coffee shops, airports, hotels, and other remote locations.

Virtual Meeting Spaces

A number of companies (such as Cranial Tap, whose virtual headquarters is shown here) are experimenting with meeting spaces in virtual worlds such as Second Life. Advantages include being able to explore three-dimensional product models and data visualization displays.

Electronic Whiteboards

Electronic whiteboards can capture, store, and e-mail the results of brainstorming sessions and other meetings. The newest versions work with electronic presentations, too, letting users write and draw directly on displayed slides.

Unified Communications

Many workers can now access all their voice and e-mail communication through a single portal. *Follow-me phone service* automatically forwards incoming calls to remote sites, home offices, or mobile phones. Integrated systems can retrieve voice-mail messages via computer or read e-mail messages over the phone.

Wikis

Wikis promote collaboration by simplifying the process of creating and editing online content. Anyone with access (some wikis are private, while some are public) can add and modify pages as new information becomes available.

Web-Based Meetings

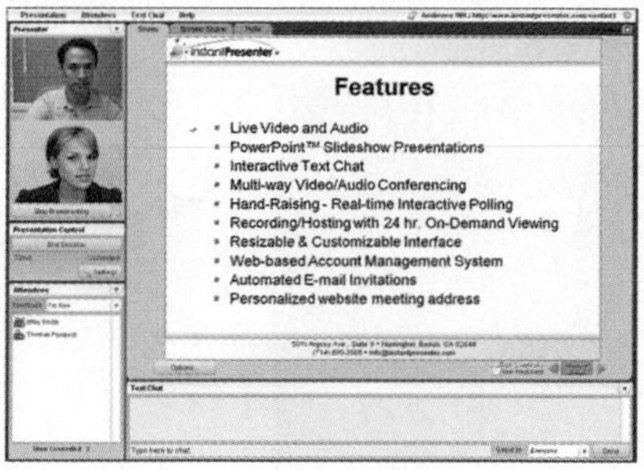

Web-based meetings allow team members from all over the world to collaborate online. Various systems support instant messaging, live video, real-time editing tools, and more.

COLLABORATING

Working in teams is essential in almost every business. Teamwork can become complicated, however, when team members work in different parts of the company, in different time zones, or even for different companies. Technology helps bridge the distance by making it possible to brainstorm, attend virtual meetings, and share files from widely separated locations. Communication technology also helps companies save money on costly business travel without losing most of the benefits of face-to-face collaboration.

Shared Workspaces

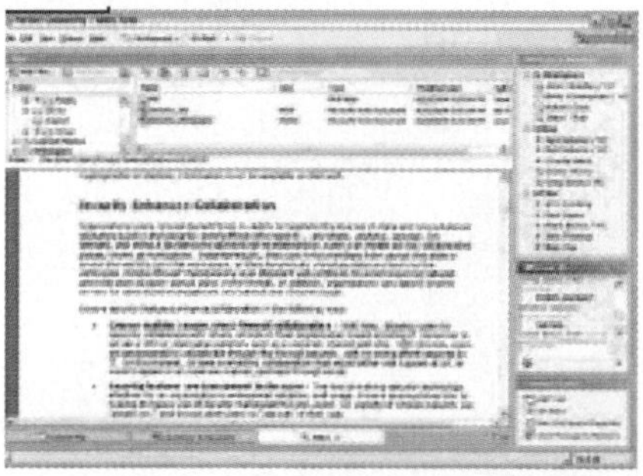

Online workspaces such as eRoom and Groove make it easy for far-flung team members to access shared files anywhere, anytime. Accessible through a browser, the workspace contains a collection of folders and has built-in intelligence to control which team members can read, edit, and save specific files.

Videoconferencing and Telepresence

Videoconferencing provides many of the same benefits as in-person meetings at a fraction of the cost. Advanced systems feature *telepresence*, in which the video images are life sized and extremely realistic.

Voice Technologies

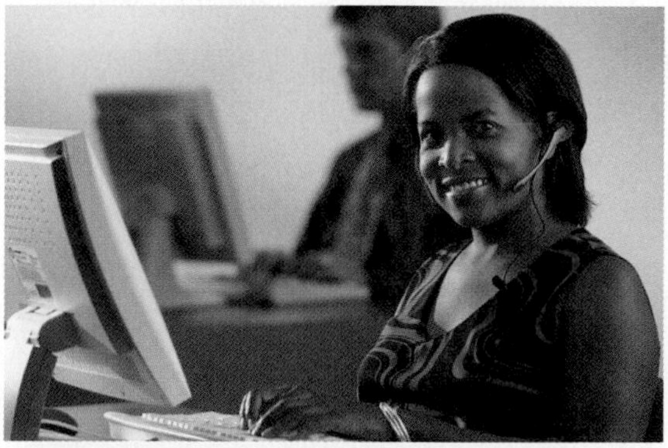

The human voice is being supplemented by a variety of technologies. *Voice synthesis* generates a human speaking voice from computer files. *Voice recognition* converts human speech to computer-compatible data.

SHARING THE LATEST INFORMATION

Companies use a variety of communication technologies to create products and services and deliver them to customers. The ability to easily access and share the latest information improves the flow and timing of supplies, lowers operating costs, and boosts financial performance. Easy information access also helps companies respond to customer needs by providing them timely, accurate information and service and by delivering the right products to them at the right time.

RSS Newsfeeds and Aggregators

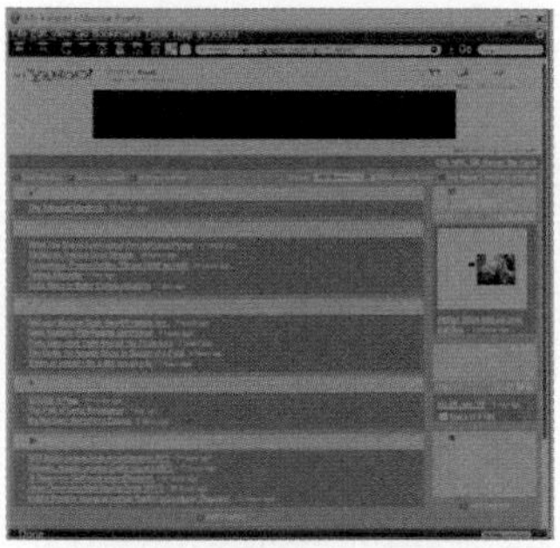

Aggregators, sometimes called *newsreaders*, automatically collect information about new blog postings and podcasts via Really Simple Syndication (RSS) newsfeeds. They give audiences more control over the content they receive from businesses. Businesses are now sending some messages to internal and external audiences via RSS newsfeeds instead of e-mail.

Social Tagging and Bookmarking

Audiences get involved in the communication process when they find and recommend online content through tagging and bookmarking sites such as Delicious.com.

Location and Tracking Technologies

Location and tracking technologies can replace manual reporting. Radio-frequency identification (RFID) tags enable automated tracking of goods and containers. Geographic data from the Global Positioning System (GPS) enables new forms of communication, such as location-based advertising (getting an ad on your mobile phone from a store you're walking past, for instance) and remote monitoring of medical patients and trucking fleets.

Extranets

Extranets are secure, private websites and networks that share information with suppliers, business partners, and customers. Think of an extranet as an extension of a company intranet that is available to people outside the organization by invitation only.

Supply Chain Management Software

Manufacturers, distributors, and retailers now automatically share information that used to require labor-intensive manual reporting. Improved information flow increases report accuracy and helps each company in the *supply chain* manage stock levels.

INTERACTING WITH CUSTOMERS

Maintaining an open dialog with customers is a great way to gain a better understanding of their likes and dislikes. Today's communication technologies make it easier for customers to interact with a company whenever, wherever, and however they wish. A well-coordinated approach to phone, web, and in-store communication helps a company build stronger relationships with its existing customers, which increases the chances of doing more business with each one.

Online Customer Support

For online shoppers who need instant help, many retail websites make it easy to connect with a live sales rep via phone or instant messaging. In addition, software tools known as *virtual agents* or *bots* can perform a variety of communication tasks, such as answering simple questions and responding to requests for electronic documents.

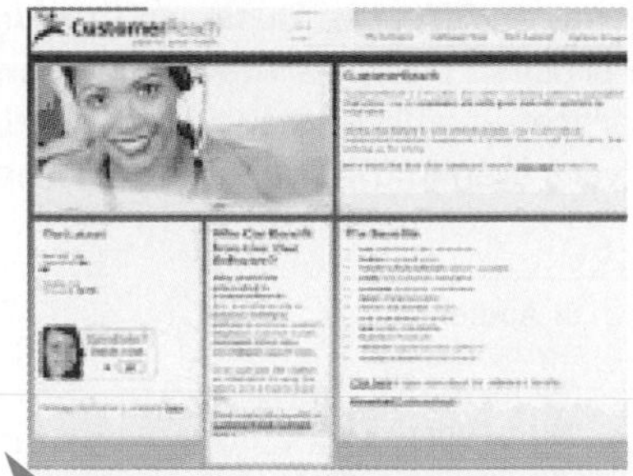

Help Lines

Some people prefer the personal touch of contact by phone. Moreover, some companies assign preferred customers special ID numbers that let them jump to the front of the calling queue. Many companies offer multilingual support as well.

Podcasts

With the portability and convenience of downloadable audio and video recordings, podcasts have quickly become a popular means of delivering everything from college lectures to marketing messages. Podcasts are also used for internal communication, replacing conference calls, newsletters, and other media.

In-Store Kiosks

Staples is among the retailers that let shoppers buy from the web while they're still in the store. Web-connected kiosks give customers quick access to thousands of in-store items and many more that are available online.

Blogs

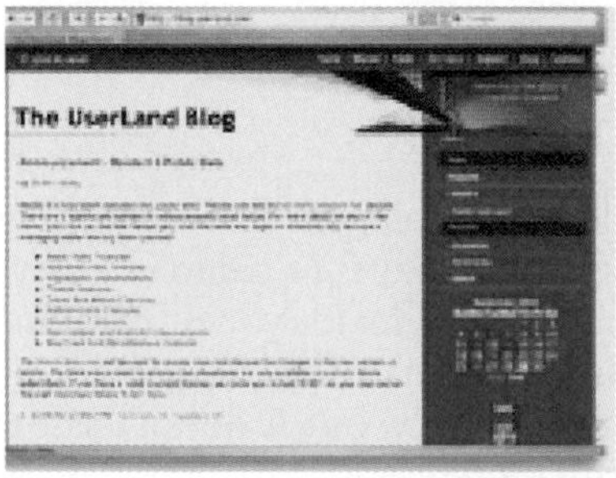

Blogs let companies connect with customers and other audiences in a fast and informal way. Commenting features let audiences participate in the conversation, too.

FIGURE 1.8 Becoming an Effective Business Communicator
The communication process presents many opportunities for messages to get lost, distorted, or misinterpreted as they travel from sender to receiver. Fortunately, you can take action at every step in the process to increase your chances of success.

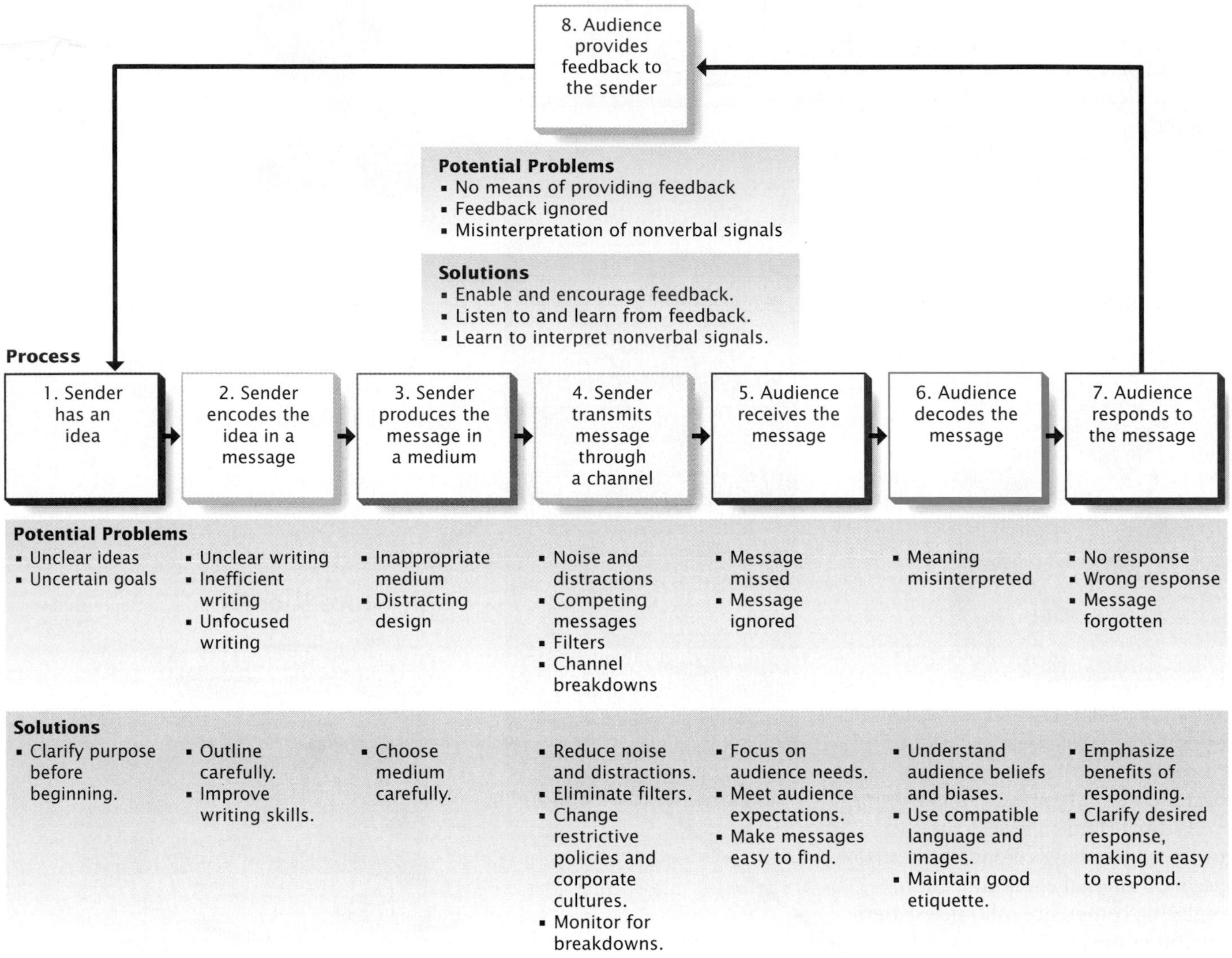

keep technology in perspective, guard against information overload and information addiction, use technological tools productively, and disengage from the computer frequently to communicate in person.

Keeping Technology in Perspective

Don't rely too much on technology or let it overwhelm the communication process.

Perhaps the single most important point to remember about technology is that it is simply a tool, a means by which you can accomplish certain tasks. Technology is an aid to interpersonal communication, not a replacement for it. Technology can't think for you or communicate for you, and if you lack some essential skills, technology can't fill in the gaps. Your spell checker is happy to run all your words through a dictionary, but it doesn't know whether you're using the correct words or crafting powerful sentences.

While this advice might sound obvious, it is easy to get caught up in the "gee whiz" factor, particularly when new and different technologies first appear. No matter how exotic or cutting edge it may be, technology has value only if it helps deliver the right information to the right people at the right time.

Guarding Against Information Overload

Information overload results when people receive more information than they can effectively process.

The overuse or misuse of communication technology can lead to **information overload**, in which people receive more information than they can effectively process. Information overload makes it difficult to discriminate between useful and useless information, lowers productivity, and amplifies employee stress both on the job and at home—even to the point of causing health and relationship problems.[23] Information overload has become such a serious productivity concern that research organizations such as the Information Overload Research Group have been founded to search for solutions.[24]

As a recipient, you often have some level of control over the number and types of messages you choose to receive. For example, corporate e-mail systems usually have powerful filtering and tagging capabilities that can automatically sort incoming messages based on criteria you set. Use this feature to isolate high-priority messages that deserve your attention. Also, be wary of subscribing to too many blog feeds, Twitter follows, and other sources of recurring messages. Separate your *need-to-know* information from *nice-to-know* information and make sure the latter doesn't drown out the former.

An important step in reducing information overload is to avoid sending unnecessary messages.

As a sender, you can help reduce information overload by making sure you don't send unnecessary messages. You don't want to undercommunicate, but sending unnecessary messages or sending the right message to the wrong people is almost as bad. In addition, if you must send a message that isn't urgent or crucial, let people know so they can prioritize. If a report requires no action from recipients, tell them up front so they don't have to search through it, looking for action items that apply to them. Also, most communication systems let you mark messages as urgent; however, use this feature only when it is truly needed. Sending too many so-called urgent messages that aren't really urgent will lead to annoyance and anxiety, not action.

Using Technological Tools Productively

Facebook, Twitter, YouTube, IM, and other technologies are key parts of what has been called the "information technology paradox," in which information tools can waste as much time as they save. Moreover, many employers are so concerned about productivity losses and legal issues from inappropriate use of the Internet and e-mail at work that they are placing restrictions on how employees can use them, such as installing software that limits Internet access to business-related sites during working hours.[25]

For instance, inappropriate web surfing not only distracts employees from work responsibilities but can also leave employers open to lawsuits for sexual harassment if inappropriate images are displayed in or transmitted around the company.[26] Blogging has created another set of managerial challenges, given the risk that employee blogs can expose confidential information or damage a firm's reputation in the marketplace. With all these technologies, the best solution lies in developing clear policies that are enforced evenly for all employees.[27]

Managers need to help ensure that employees can productively use the communication tools at their disposal.

Managers need to guide their employees in productive use of information tools because the speed and simplicity of these tools are also some of their greatest weaknesses: It's too easy to send too many messages and to subscribe to too many blog feeds, Twitter feeds, and other information sources. The flood of messages from an expanding array of electronic sources can significantly affect employees' ability to focus on their work. In one study, workers exposed to a constant barrage of e-mail, IM, and phone calls experienced an average 10-point drop in their functioning intelligence quotient (IQ).[28]

Simply knowing how to use your tools can make a big difference in your productivity. You don't have to become an expert in most cases, but you need to be familiar with the basic features and functions of the tools you are expected to use on the job. As a manager, you also need to ensure that your employees have sufficient training to productively use the tools you expect them to use. To access a variety of online tutorials on various communication tools, visit http://real-timeupdates.com/ebc and click on Chapter 1.

REAL-TIME UPDATES
Learn More

Steps you can take to help reduce information overload

Everyone needs to a play a part in reducing the burden of too much data and information in the work environment; this document has plenty of helpful tips. Go to **http://real-timeupdates.com/ebc** and click on "Learn More." If you are using mybcommlab, you can access Real-Time Updates within each chapter or under Student Study Tools.

Reconnecting with People

No matter how much technology is involved, communication is about people connecting with people.

Let's say you IM a colleague asking how she did with her sales presentation to an important client, and her answer comes back simply as "Fine." What does *fine* mean? Is an order expected soon? Or did she lose the sale and doesn't want to talk about it? If you visit with her in person, or at least talk over the phone, she might provide additional information, or you might be able to offer advice or support during a difficult time.

Moreover, even the best technologies cannot truly match the rich experience of person-to-person contact. For example, *telepresence* videoconferencing systems (discussed in Chapter 2) can create a convincing illusion of everyone being in the same room, even if they are thousands of miles apart. However, even enthusiastic users know that this technology has limits. Jill Smart, an executive with the consulting firm Accenture, often takes advantage of the company's advanced telepresence facilities but still travels frequently to meet with clients—particularly clients in other countries and cultures: "You get things from being there, over breakfast and dinner, building relationships face to face."[29]

6 LEARNING OBJECTIVE

Discuss the importance of ethics in business communication and differentiate between ethical dilemmas and ethical lapses.

MAKING ETHICAL COMMUNICATION CHOICES

Ethics are the accepted principles of conduct that govern behavior within a society. Put another way, ethical principles define the boundary between right and wrong. Former Supreme Court Justice Potter Stewart defined ethics as "knowing the difference between what you have a right to do and what is the right thing to do."[30] To make the right choices as a business communicator, you have a responsibility to think through not only what you say but also the consequences of saying it.

Ethical behavior is a companywide concern, but because communication efforts are the public face of a company, they are subjected to particularly rigorous scrutiny from regulators, legislators, investors, consumer groups, environmental groups, labor organizations, and anyone else affected by business activities. **Ethical communication** includes all relevant information, is true in every sense, and is not deceptive in any way. In contrast, unethical communication can distort the truth or manipulate audiences in a variety of ways:[31]

Any time you try to mislead an audience, the result is unethical communication.

- **Plagiarism.** Plagiarism is presenting someone else's words or other creative product as your own. Note that plagiarism can be illegal if it violates a **copyright**, which is a form of legal protection for the expression of creative ideas.[32]
- **Omitting essential information.** Information is essential if your audience needs it to make an intelligent, objective decision. For example, homebuyers in an Orlando, Florida, housing development were sold houses without being told that the area was once a U.S. Army firing range and that live bombs and ammunition are still buried in multiple locations around the neighborhood.[33]
- **Selective misquoting.** Distorting or hiding the true intent of someone else's words is unethical.
- **Misrepresenting numbers.** Statistics and other data can be unethically manipulated by increasing or decreasing numbers, exaggerating, altering statistics, or omitting numeric data.
- **Distorting visuals.** Images can be manipulated in unethical ways, such as making a product seem bigger than it really is or changing the scale of graphs and charts to exaggerate or conceal differences.
- **Failing to respect privacy or information security needs.** Ethical concerns involve more than just the content of messages. Failing to respect the privacy of others or failing to adequately protect information entrusted to your care can also be considered unethical (and is sometimes illegal).

REAL-TIME UPDATES
Learn More

Take the quiz: Are you an ethical decision maker?

Take this online quiz to see if you can identify and deal with the rights, the wrongs, and the gray areas of the business world. Go to **http://real-timeupdates.com/ebc** and click on "Learn More." If you are using mybcommlab, you can access Real-Time Updates within each chapter or under Student Study Tools.

In some situations, ethical choices are clear, but in others, the right path is not always easy to identify. Deciding what is ethical can be a considerable challenge in complex business situations.

Distinguishing Ethical Dilemmas from Ethical Lapses

An ethical dilemma is a choice between alternatives that may all be ethical and valid.

Every company has responsibilities to its multiple stakeholders, and those various groups often have competing interests. An **ethical dilemma** involves making a choice when the alternatives aren't completely wrong or completely right. Perhaps two conflicting alternatives are both ethical and valid, or perhaps the alternatives lie somewhere in the gray area between clearly right and clearly wrong. Suppose you are the chief executive of a company whose sales are declining, and you might be forced to reduce costs by laying off 100 employees. You've decided to monitor sales for two more months before making this tough decision. Here's your dilemma: Do you tell the workforce now that 100 jobs could disappear in the near future? Telling them now would give people more time to look for new jobs and adjust their finances—clearly a good thing. However, if you tell them now, essential employees might leave immediately to find new jobs, which could drive down sales even more and possibly force you to eventually lay off even more than 100 employees. And what if you tell them now, and many people leave but then sales improve enough in the next two months that you can avoid the layoffs? You will have unnecessarily disrupted many careers and families. Situations such as these often have no clear answer.

An ethical lapse is making a choice that you know to be unethical.

In contrast, an **ethical lapse** is a clearly unethical choice. If you tell employees their jobs are "absolutely safe" even though you know there is a strong likelihood that some of them will be laid off, you have committed an ethical lapse. With both internal and external communication efforts, the pressure to produce results or justify decisions can make unethical communication a tempting choice. (Compare the messages in Figures 1.9 and 1.10.)

FIGURE 1.9 Unethical Communication
The writers of this memo clearly want the company to continue funding their pet project, even though the marketing research doesn't support such a decision. By comparing this memo with the version shown in Figure 1.10, you can see how the writers twisted the truth and omitted evidence in order to put a positive "spin" on the research.

SunStar Sports

Confidential Memorandum

TO: Executive Committee
FROM: Darcy O'Leary & Bob Caruthers, Product Management
DATE: October 23, 2010
SUBJECT: Pegasus market confirmation

We're pleased to announce that the numbers are in, and as we predicted before the research began, consumers show strong support for the Pegasus product concept. The results validate the several months we've invested in product design and should give a green light to fund the completion of the project.

We're particularly pleased with the results in this case, since the research was directed by Sadie McMahon at Bowerman Research. She has conducted hundreds of research projects and is known for her keen insights into the consumer market. Only a third of the consumers surveyed expressed little or no interest in Pegasus, and Ms. McMahon said that doesn't worry her at all since few products ever appeal to the entire market. With a two-thirds majority in our favor, this looks to be a winner before we even bring it to market.

Given the momentum we've already built up, coupled with this powerful endorsement of the concept, we're confident the executive committee will reach the same strategic conclusion that we have and continue funding the project.

Thank you for your support.

Uses a biased subject line to slant readers' perceptions before they have a chance to read the research results

Suggests O'Leary and Caruthers had their minds made up before the research even started, which means that their analysis may be biased

Mixes McMahon's opinions and conclusions with O'Leary and Caruthers' own opinions

Pulls selectively from McMahon's summary, leaving out information that doesn't support the writers' own conclusion

Misrepresents the research results; two-thirds of the market did *not* express interest in the product concept

Biases the conversation again by implying that the executive committee would be making a mistake if it disagreed with them

Assumes the writers have the committee's support, which may not be true

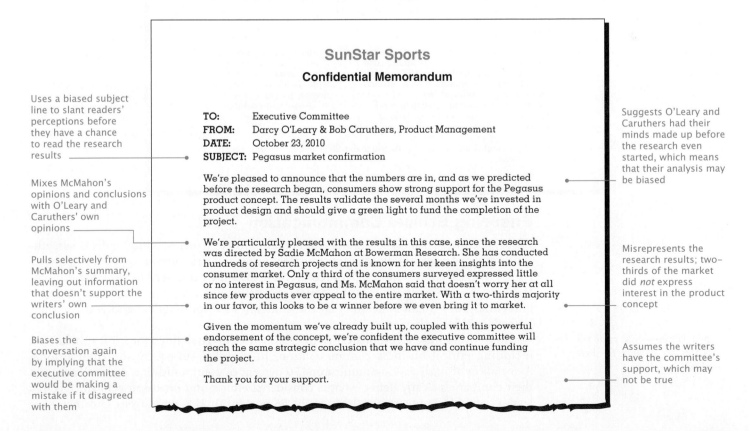

FIGURE 1.10 Ethical Communication
This version of the memo shown in Figure 1.9 presents the evidence in a more honest and ethical manner.

SunStar Sports

Confidential Memorandum

TO: Executive Committee
FROM: Darcy O'Leary & Bob Caruthers, Product Management
DATE: October 23, 2010
SUBJECT: Market research summary for Pegasus project

Tries not to "sell" the conclusion ahead of time, using an even-handed subject line

The market research for the Pegasus Project concluded last week with phone interviews of 236 sporting goods buyers in 18 states. As in the past, we used Bowerman Research to conduct the interviews, under the guidance of Bowerman's survey supervisor, Sadie McMahon. Ms. McMahon has directed surveys on more than 200 consumer products, and we've learned to place a great deal of confidence in her market insights.

Emphasizes the skills of the researcher without biasing the readers regarding her conclusions

A complete report, including all raw data and verbatim quotes, will be available for downloading on the Engineering Department intranet by the end of next week. However, in light of the project-funding discussions going on this week, we believe the conclusions from the research warrant your immediate attention.

Offers full disclosure of all the background information

Explains that more in-depth information will be available soon but emphasizes the importance of reviewing this summary right now

Sadie McMahon's research summary

Consumer interest in the new product code-named Pegasus is decidedly mixed, with 34% expressing little or no interest in the product but 37% expressing moderate to strong interest. The remaining 29% expressed confusion about the basic product concept and were therefore unable to specify their level of interest. The segment expressing little or no interest is not a cause for concern in most cases; few products appeal to the entire consumer market.

Provides the complete text of the researcher's summary

However, the portion of the market expressing confusion about the fundamental design of the product is definitely cause for concern. We rarely see more than 10 or 15% confusion at this stage of the design process. A 29% confusion figure suggests that the product design does not fit many consumers' expectations and that it might be difficult to sell if SunStar goes ahead with production.

Illustrates clearly that the market expert is concerned about the project

Our recommendations

At $7.6 million, the development costs for Pegasus are too high to proceed with this much uncertainty. The business case we prepared at the beginning of the project indicated that at least 50% consumer acceptance would be needed in order to generate enough sales to produce an acceptable return on the engineering investment. We would need to convince nearly half of the "confused" segment in order to reach that threshold. We recommend that further development be put on hold until the design can be clarified and validated with another round of consumer testing.

Separates the researcher's observations and opinions from the writers' own

States clearly and honestly that the project will not live up to original hopes

Please contact Darcy at ext. 2354 or Bob at ext. 2360 if you have any questions or concerns.

Invites further discussion of the situation

Ensuring Ethical Communication

Ensuring ethical business communication requires three elements: ethical individuals, ethical company leadership, and the appropriate policies and structures to support employees' efforts to make ethical choices.[34] Moreover, these three elements need to work in harmony. If employees see company executives making unethical decisions and flouting company guidelines, they might conclude that the guidelines are meaningless and emulate their bosses' unethical behavior.

Responsible employers establish clear ethical guidelines for their employees to follow.

Employers have a responsibility to establish clear guidelines for ethical behavior, including ethical business communication. In a global survey by the International Association of Business Communicators, 70 percent of communication professionals said their companies clearly define what is considered ethical and unethical behavior.[35] On a less encouraging note, in another survey, 56 percent of U.S. employees said they have observed unethical behavior by people in their organizations—and more than 40 percent of those who witnessed unethical behavior did not report it.[36]

Many companies establish an explicit ethics policy by using a written **code of ethics** to help employees determine what is acceptable. For example, Gap Inc. (the owner of the Gap, Banana Republic, and Old Navy retail chains) publishes a detailed Code of Business Conduct for its employees, addressing such areas as conflicts of interest, product integrity, health and safety, protection of company assets and information, and political activities by employees.[37] A code is often part of a larger program of employee training and communication channels that allow employees to ask questions and report instances of questionable ethics. To ensure ongoing compliance with their codes of ethics, many companies also conduct **ethics audits** to monitor ethical progress and to point out any weaknesses that need to be addressed.

However, whether or not formal guidelines are in place, every employee has a responsibility to communicate in an ethical manner. In the absence of clear guidelines, ask yourself the following questions about your business communications:[38]

- Have you defined the situation fairly and accurately?
- What is your intention in communicating this message?
- What impact will this message have on the people who receive it, or who might be affected by it?
- Will the message achieve the greatest possible good while doing the least possible harm?
- Will the assumptions you've made change over time? That is, will a decision that seems ethical now seem unethical in the future?
- Are you comfortable with your decision? Would you be embarrassed if it were printed in tomorrow's newspaper or spread across the Internet? Think about a person whom you admire and ask yourself what he or she would think of your decision.

If you can't decide whether a choice is ethical, picture yourself explaining it to someone whose opinion you value.

Ensuring Legal Communication

In addition to ethical guidelines, business communication is also bound by a wide variety of laws and regulations, including the following areas:

Business communication is governed by a wide variety of laws designed to ensure accurate, complete messages.

- **Promotional communication.** Marketing specialists need to be aware of the many laws that govern truth and accuracy in advertising. These laws address such issues as false and deceptive advertising, misleading or inaccurate labels on product packages, and "bait and switch" tactics in which a store advertises a lower-priced product to lure consumers into a store but then tries to sell them a more expensive item.[39] Chapter 10 explores this area in more detail.
- **Contracts.** A **contract** is a legally binding promise between two parties, in which one party makes a specified offer and the other party accepts. Contracts are fundamental to virtually every aspect of business, from product sales to property rental to credit cards and loans to professional service agreements.[40]
- **Employment communication.** A variety of local, state, and federal laws govern communication between employers and both potential and current employees. For example, job descriptions must be written in a way that doesn't intentionally or unintentionally discriminate against women, minorities, or people with disabilities.[41]
- **Intellectual property.** In an age when instant global connectivity makes copying and retransmitting electronic files effortless, the protection of intellectual property (IP) has become a widespread concern. **Intellectual property** includes patents, copyrighted materials, trade secrets, and even Internet domain names.[42] Bloggers need to be particularly careful about IP protection, given the carefree way that some post the work of others without offering proper credit. For guidelines on this hot topic, get the free *Legal Guide for Bloggers* at **www.eff.org/issues/bloggers/legal**.
- **Financial reporting.** Finance and accounting professionals who work for publicly traded companies (those that sell stock to the public) must adhere to stringent reporting laws. For instance, a number of corporations have recently been targets of both

government investigations and shareholder lawsuits for offering misleading descriptions of financial results and revenue forecasts.

- **Defamation.** Negative comments about another party raise the possibility of **defamation**, the intentional communication of false statements that damage character or reputation.[43] (Written defamation is called *libel*; spoken defamation is called *slander*.) Someone suing for defamation must prove (1) that the statement is false, (2) that the language is injurious to the person's reputation, and (3) that the statement has been published.

If you have any doubts about the legality of a message you intend to distribute, ask for advice from your company's legal department. A small dose of caution can prevent huge legal headaches and protect your company's reputation in the marketplace.

For the latest information on ethical and legal issues in business communication, visit **http://real-timeupdates.com/ebc** and click on Chapter 1.

APPLYING WHAT YOU'VE LEARNED

At the beginning of this chapter, you met Six Apart's Mena Trott in "On the Job: Communicating at Six Apart." Trott is just one of the many real business professionals you'll meet throughout this book—people who successfully handle the same communication challenges you'll face on the job. Each chapter opens with one of these slice-of-life vignettes, and as you read through each chapter, think about the person and the company highlighted in the vignette. Become familiar with the various concepts presented in the chapter, and imagine how they might apply to the featured scenario.

At the end of each chapter, you'll take part in an innovative simulation called "On the Job: Solving Communication Dilemmas." You'll play the role of a person working in the highlighted organization, and you'll face situations you'd encounter on the job. You will be presented with several communication scenarios, each with several possible courses of action. It's up to you to recommend one course of action from each scenario as homework, as teamwork, as material for in-class discussion, or in a host of other ways. These scenarios let you explore various communication ideas and apply the concepts and techniques from the chapter.

Now you're ready for the first simulation. As you tackle each problem, think about the material you covered in this chapter and consider your own experience as a communicator. You'll probably be surprised to discover how much you already know about business communication.

Document Makeover

Improve This Memo

To practice correcting drafts of actual documents, visit the "Document Makeovers" section in mybcommlab. Refer to the User Guide for specific instructions on how to access the content for this chapter. You will find a memo that contains problems and errors related to what you've learned in this chapter about improving business communication. Use the Final Draft decision tool to create an improved version of this memo. Check the message for ethical communication and an audience-centered approach.

On the Job: Solving Communication Dilemmas at Six Apart

In 2007, Ben and Mena Trott promoted Chris Alden to president and chief executive officer (CEO) of Six Apart. Alden plays a vital role in keeping communication flowing within the company and between the company and external audiences. To help him with a growing workload of communication tasks, he has recently hired you as an assistant with special responsibilities for communication. Use your knowledge of communication to choose the best response for each of the following situations. Be prepared to explain why your choice is best.

1. One of the reasons for Six Apart's success is its friendly, open style of communication with its customers, even those occasional customers who make unrealistic demands or expect special treatment. Unfortunately, you've learned that some of the customer service representatives have been letting their emotions get in the way when dealing with these difficult customers. Several customers have complained about rude treatment. You're sensitive to the situation because you know that customer service can be a difficult job. However, having a reputation for hostile customer service could spell doom for the company, so you need to

communicate your concerns immediately. Which of the following sentences would be the best way to begin an e-mail message to the customer service staff?

a. "We must all work harder at serving customers in an efficient, timely manner."
b. "The growing problem of abusive customers communications must stop immediately—after all, without customers, we have no revenue; without revenue, you have no jobs."
c. "Positive customer support is one of our most important competitive advantages, but it has come to management's attention that some of you are ruining the company's reputation by mistreating customers."
d. "Thank you for your continued efforts at supporting our customers; I know this can be a challenging task at times."

2. Six Apart has developed a corporate culture that reflects both the engaging personalities of Ben and Mena Trott and the generally informal "vibe" of the blogosphere. However, as the company continues to grow, new employees bring a variety of communication styles and expectations. In particular, the new accounting manager tends to communicate in a formal, distant style that some company old-timers find off-putting and impersonal. Several of these people have expressed concerns that the new manager "doesn't fit in," even though she's doing a great job otherwise. How should you respond?

a. Tell these people to stop complaining; the accounting manager is doing her job well, and that's what counts.
b. In a private conversation with the accounting manager, explain the importance of fitting into the corporate culture and give her a four-week deadline to change her style.
c. In a private conversation with the accounting manager, explain the reasoning behind the company's informal culture and its contribution to the company's success; suggest that she might find her work here more enjoyable if she modifies her approach somewhat.
d. Allow the accounting manager to continue communicating in the same style; after all, that's her personal style, and it's not up to the company to change it.

3. A false rumor has begun circulating online that Six Apart plans to sell one of its product lines to a competitor and lay off most of the employees who currently work on those products. Alden asks your advice in handling the situation. Which of the following would you recommend?

a. Try to plant a counter-rumor on the online grapevine so that the employees who are worried about their jobs will get the right message the same way they got the wrong one.
b. Immediately schedule a companywide, in-person meeting to set the record straight, emphasizing to everyone in the firm that Six Apart has no plans to shed that product line.
c. Post a message on an internal blog, setting the record straight and assuring the workforce that all jobs are safe; employees and customers alike are accustomed to getting information from this blog, so it's the right way to communicate this message.
d. Ignore the rumor. Like all other false rumors, it will eventually die out.

4. As Microsoft, Google, and other major companies join the market for blogging software and services, Six Apart is forced to lower its prices to remain competitive. Unfortunately, lower prices mean the company will have to lower its operating costs if it is to remain profitable, and employee salaries are the single biggest cost. The management team has decided to enact a 10 percent salary reduction for the next six months and then reevaluate the company's financial health at that point. However, some of the executives are convinced that the salary reductions will have to continue for a year at least—and perhaps even be permanent. In light of this knowledge, which of the following communication strategies would best balance the needs of the company and the needs of the employees?

a. Tell employees that the 10 percent pay cut will last six months, without implying that it could last longer or even be permanent. If employees worry that their income could be reduced permanently, they'll start looking for other jobs now, which will be a big drain on worker productivity and make the financial situation even worse.
b. Tell employees that the 10 percent pay cut *is scheduled* to last six months, leaving open the possibility that it could last longer without stating so.
c. Explain that the pay reduction is likely to be permanent, even if you're not sure that will be the case; it's better to give employees the worst possible news and then offer a pleasant surprise if the situation works out more favorably than expected.
d. Tell employees that the pay cut will last for six months, at which point the management team will evaluate the situation and decide if the cut needs to be extended beyond that. Explain that you'd like to be able to provide more solid information, but the uncertainties in the market make that unrealistic. The best that you can do is tell employees everything you know—and don't know.

LEARNING OBJECTIVES CHECKUP

Assess your understanding of the principles in this chapter by reading each learning objective and studying the accompanying exercises. For fill-in-the-blank items, write the missing text in the blank provided; for multiple-choice items, circle the letter of the correct answer. You can check your responses against the answer key on page AK-1.

Objective 1.1: Explain how the Business Communication 2.0 concept is transforming the practice of business communication.

1. Communication style using the Business Communication 2.0 concept is best described as
   a. Conversational
   b. Multilingual
   c. Technical
   d. Playful
2. What role do social media play in the Business Communication 2.0 concept?
   a. They facilitate internal communication but have no role in external communication.
   b. They facilitate external communication but have no role in internal communication.
   c. They enable an interactive, conversational approach to business communication.
   d. They are social tools only and have no role in business communication.

Objective 1.2: Describe the five characteristics of effective business communication.

3. Effective business messages are
   a. Entertaining, blunt, direct, opinionated, and persuasive
   b. Practical, objective, concise, clear, and persuasive
   c. Personal, clear, short, catchy, and challenging
4. Why is it important for a business message to clearly state expectations regarding who is responsible for doing what in response to the message?
   a. To make sure other employees don't avoid their responsibilities
   b. To make sure that the person who sent the message isn't criticized if important tasks don't get completed
   c. To eliminate confusion by letting each affected person know what his or her specific responsibilities are

Objective 1.3: Describe six strategies for communicating more effectively on the job.

5. An audience-centered approach to communication
   a. Starts with the assumption that the audience is always right
   b. Improves the effectiveness of communication by focusing on the information needs of the audience
   c. Is generally a waste of time because it doesn't accommodate the needs of the sender
   d. Always simplifies the tasks involved in planning and creating messages
6. Constructive feedback focuses on _____ rather than criticism.
7. Sensitivity to business etiquette
   a. Reduces the chance of interpersonal blunders that might negatively affect communication
   b. Is considered by most companies to be a waste of time in today's fast-paced markets
   c. Is now legally required in all 50 states
   d. Always increases the cost of business communication

Objective 1.4: Explain what must occur for an audience to successfully receive, decode, and respond to messages.

8. In order for audience members to successfully receive messages, they must first _____ the presence of the message, then _____ it from other sensory input, and then _____ it as a message.
9. In order for the receiver of a message to respond in the manner desired by the sender, the receiver needs to
   a. Remember the message
   b. Be able to respond to the message
   c. Have the motivation to respond to the message
   d. Do all of the above

Objective 1.5: Explain four strategies for successfully using communication technology.

10. Communication technology has value only if it helps deliver the right _____ to the right _____ at the right time.
11. The information technology paradox means that
    a. Communication tools can sometimes waste more time than they save
    b. Computers lose as much information as they save
    c. People are no longer needed to create messages
    d. Technology isn't as expensive as it used to be
12. Reconnecting frequently with colleagues and customers in person
    a. Is widely considered an inappropriate use of time, given all the electronic options now available
    b. Is frowned on by successful managers
    c. Is critical because it helps ensure that technology doesn't hinder human interaction

Objective 1.6: Discuss the importance of ethics in business communication and differentiate between ethical dilemmas and ethical lapses.

13. Ethical communication
    a. Is the same thing as legal communication
    b. Costs more because there are so many rules to consider

c. Is important only for companies that sell to consumers rather than to other businesses
d. Is important because communication is the public face of a company

14. An ethical _____ exists when a person is faced with two conflicting but ethical choices; an ethical _____ occurs when a person makes an unethical choice.

PEARSON mybcommlab™

Log on to www.mybcommlab.com to access the following study and assessment aids associated with this chapter:

- Video applications
- Real-Time Updates
- Peer review activity
- Quick Learning Guides
- Pre/post test
- Personalized study plan
- Model documents
- Sample presentations

If you are not using mybcommlab, you can access Real-Time Updates and Quick Learning Guides through http://real-timeupdates.com/ebc. The Quick Learning Guide (located under "Learn More" on the website) hits all the high points of this chapter in just two pages. This guide, especially prepared by the authors, will help you study for exams or review important concepts whenever you need a quick refresher.

Apply Your Knowledge

1. How are blogs, wikis, and other Web 2.0 technologies changing the practice of business communication?
2. Is it possible for companies to be too dependent on communication technology? Explain briefly.
3. How can a lack of shared experience between sender and receiver result in communication failures?
4. How does the presence of a reader comments feature on a corporate blog reflect audience-centered communication?
5. **Ethical Choices** Because of your excellent communication skills, your boss always asks you to write his reports for him. When you overhear the CEO complimenting him on his logical organization and clear writing style, your boss responds as if he'd written all those reports himself. What kind of ethical choice does your boss's response represent? What can you do in this situation? Briefly explain your solution and your reasoning.

Practice Your Knowledge

Message for Analysis

Read the following blog posting and then (1) analyze whether the message is effective or ineffective communication (be sure to explain why) and (2) revise the message so that it follows this chapter's guidelines.

> It has come to my attention that many of you are lying on your time cards. If you come in late, you should not put 8:00 on your card. If you take a long lunch, you should not put 1:00 on your time card. I will not stand for this type of cheating. I simply have no choice but to institute an employee monitoring system. Beginning next Monday, video cameras will be installed at all entrances to the building, and your entry and exit times will be logged each time you use electronic key cards to enter or leave.
>
> Anyone who is late for work or late coming back from lunch more than three times will have to answer to me. I don't care if you had to take a nap or if you girls had to shop. This is a place of business, and we do not want to be taken advantage of by slackers who are cheaters to boot.
>
> It is too bad that a few bad apples always have to spoil things for everyone.

Exercises

Active links for all websites in this chapter can be found on mybcommlab; see your User Guide for instructions on accessing the content for this chapter.

1.1 **Business Communication 2.0: Convincing Your Colleagues to Open the Door** You are the customer service manager for a company that sells a software package used by not-for-profit organizations to plan and manage fundraising campaigns. The powerful software is complicated enough to require a fairly extensive user's manual, and the company has always provided a printed manual to customers. Customers frequently e-mail your department with questions about using the software and suggestions for using the software to maximize fundraising efforts. You know that many customers could benefit from the answers to those questions and the suggestions from fellow customers, but with a printed manual issued once every couple years, you don't have any way to collect and distribute this information in a timely fashion.

You've been researching wikis and believe this would be a great way to let customers participate in an ongoing conversation about using the software. In fact, you'd like to convert the printed manual to a wiki on which any registered customer could add or edit pages. Rather than spend thousands of dollars printing a manual that is difficult to expand or update, the wiki would be a "living" document that continually evolves as people ask and answer questions and offer suggestions. The rest of the management team is extremely nervous, however. "We're the experts—not the customer," one says. Another asks, "How can we ensure the quality of the information if any customer can change it?" They don't deny that customers have valuable information to add; they just don't want customers to have control of an important company document. Making up any information you need, write a brief e-mail to your colleagues, explaining the benefits of letting customers contribute to a wiki-based user manual. (You can refer to pages 37–38 to learn more about wikis.)

1.2 **Effective Business Communication: Understanding the Difference** Bring to class a sales message that you received in the mail or via e-mail. Comment on how well the communication

- **a.** Provides practical information
- **b.** Gives facts rather than impressions
- **c.** Clarifies and condenses information
- **d.** States precise responsibilities
- **e.** Persuades others and offers recommendations

1.3 **Internal Communication: Planning the Flow** For the following tasks, identify the necessary direction of communication (downward, upward, horizontal), suggest an appropriate type (or types) of communication (casual conversation, formal interview, meeting, workshop, web conference, instant message, memo, blog, bulletin board notice, and so on), and briefly explain your suggestions.

- **a.** As human resources manager, you want to announce details about this year's company picnic.
- **b.** As director of internal communication, you want to convince top management of the need for an internal executive blog.
- **c.** As production manager, you want to make sure that both the sales manager and the finance manager receive your scheduling estimates.
- **d.** As marketing manager, you want to help employees throughout the company understand the marketplace and customer needs.

1.4 **Ethical Choices** In less than a page, explain why you think each of the following is or is not ethical.

- **a.** Keeping quiet about a possible environmental hazard you've just discovered in your company's processing plant
- **b.** Overselling the benefits of instant messaging to your company's managers; they never seem to understand the benefits of technology, so you believe it's the only way to convince them to make the right choice
- **c.** Telling an associate and close friend that she needs to pay more attention to her work responsibilities or management will fire her
- **d.** Recommending the purchase of excess equipment to use up your allocated funds before the end of the fiscal year so that your budget won't be cut next year

1.5 **The Changing Workplace: Personal Expression at Work** Blogging has become a popular way for employees to communicate with customers and other parties outside the company. In some cases, employee blogs have been quite beneficial for both companies and their customers by providing helpful information and "putting a human face" on otherwise formal and imposing corporations. However, in some other cases, employees have been fired for posting information that their employers said was inappropriate. One particular area of concern is criticism of the company or individual managers. Should employees be allowed to criticize their employers in a public forum such as a blog? In a brief e-mail message, argue for or against company policies that prohibit critical information in employee blogs.

1.6 **Internet** Cisco, a leading manufacturer of equipment for the Internet and corporate networks, has developed a code of ethics that it expects employees to abide by. Visit the company's website, at www.cisco.com, and find the *Code of Conduct*. In a brief paragraph, describe three specific examples of things you could do that would violate these provisions; then list at least three opportunities that Cisco provides its employees to report ethics violations or ask questions regarding ethical dilemmas.

1.7 **Communication Etiquette** Potential customers frequently visit your production facility before making purchase decisions. You and the people who report to you in the sales department have received extensive training in etiquette issues because you deal with high-profile clients so often. However, the rest of the workforce has not received such training, and you worry that someone might inadvertently say or do something that would offend one of these potential customers. In a two-paragraph e-mail, explain to the general manager why you think anyone who might come in contact with customers should receive basic etiquette training.

1.8 **Ethical Choices** Knowing that you have numerous friends throughout the company, your boss relies on you for feedback concerning employee morale and other issues affecting the staff. She recently asked you to start reporting any behavior that might violate company polices, from taking office supplies home to making personal long-distance calls. List the issues you'd like to discuss with her before you respond to her request.

1.9 **Formal Communication: Self-Introduction** Write an e-mail message or prepare an oral presentation introducing yourself to your instructor and your class. Include such things as your background, interests, achievements, and goals. If you write an e-mail message, keep it under one normal screen in length, and use Figure 1.4 as a model for the format. If you prepare an oral presentation, plan to speak for no more than two minutes.

1.10 **Teamwork** Your boss has asked your work group to research and report on corporate child-care facilities. Of course, you'll want to know who (besides your boss) will be reading your report. Working with two team members, list four or five other things you'll want to know about the situation and about your audience before starting your research. Briefly explain why each of the items on your list is important.

1.11 Communication Process: Analyzing Miscommunication Use the eight phases of the communication process to analyze a miscommunication you've recently had with a co-worker, supervisor, classmate, teacher, friend, or family member. What idea were you trying to share? How did you encode and transmit it? Did the receiver get the message? Did the receiver correctly decode the message? How do you know? Based on your analysis, identify and explain the barriers that prevented your successful communication in this instance.

1.12 Ethical Choices You've been given the critical assignment of selecting the site for your company's new plant. After months of negotiations with landowners, numerous cost calculations, and investments in ecological, social, and community impact studies, you are about to recommend building the new plant on the Lansing River site. Now, just 15 minutes before your big presentation to top management, you discover a possible mistake in your calculations: Site-purchase costs appear to be $500,000 more than you calculated, nearly 10 percent over budget. You don't have time to recheck all your figures, so you're tempted to just go ahead with your recommendation and ignore any discrepancies. You're worried that management won't approve this purchase if you can't present a clean, unqualified solution. You also know that many projects run over their original estimates, so you can probably work the extra cost into the budget later. On your way to the meeting room, you make your final decision. In a few paragraphs, explain the decision you make.

1.13 Communication Etiquette In group meetings, some of your colleagues have a habit of interrupting and arguing with the speaker, taking credit for ideas that aren't theirs, and shooting down ideas they don't agree with. You're the newest person in the group and not sure if this is accepted behavior in this company, but it concerns you both personally and professionally. Should you go with the flow and adopt their behavior or stick with your own communication style, even though you might get lost in the noise? In two paragraphs, explain the pros and cons of both approaches.

Expand Your Knowledge

Learning More on the Web

Check Out These Resources at the Business Writer's Free Library

www.managementhelp.org/commskls/cmm_writ.htm
The Business Writer's Free Library is an excellent resource for business communication material. Categories of information include basic composition skills, basic writing skills, correspondence, reference material, and general resources and advice. Log on and read about the most common errors in English, become a word detective, ask Miss Grammar, review samples of common forms of correspondence, fine-tune your interpersonal skills, join a newsgroup, and more. Follow the links and improve your effectiveness as a business communicator.

1. What are some common causes of problems in internal communication?
2. What is the value of diversity in the workplace?
3. Why is bad etiquette bad for business?

Sharpening Your Career Skills Online

Bovée and Thill's Business Communication Web Search, at **http://businesscommunicationblog.com/websearch**, is a unique research tool designed specifically for business communication research. Use the Web Search function to find an online video, a podcast, or a PowerPoint presentation that explains at least one essential business communication skill. Write a brief e-mail message to your instructor, describing the item that you found and summarizing the career skills information you learned from it.

Improve Your Grammar, Mechanics, and Usage

The following exercises help you improve your knowledge of and power over English grammar, mechanics, and usage. Turn to the Handbook of Grammar, Mechanics, and Usage at the end of this book and review all of Section 1.1 (Nouns). Then look at the following 10 items. Underline the preferred choice within each set of parentheses. (Answers to these exercises appear on page AK-3.)

1. She remembered placing that report on her (*bosses, boss's*) desk.
2. We mustn't follow their investment advice like a lot of (*sheep, sheeps*).
3. Jones founded the company back in the early (*1990's, 1990s*).
4. Please send the (*Joneses, Jones'*) a dozen of the following: (*stopwatchs, stopwatches*), canteens, and headbands.
5. Our (*attorneys, attornies*) will talk to the group about incorporation.
6. Make sure that all (*copys, copies*) include the new addresses.
7. Ask Jennings to collect all (*employee's, employees'*) donations for the Red Cross drive.
8. Charlie now has two (*sons-in-law, son-in-laws*) to help him with his two online (*business's, businesses*).
9. Avoid using too many (*parentheses, parenthesis*) when writing your reports.
10. Follow President (*Nesses, Ness's*) rules about what constitutes a (*weeks, week's*) work.

For additional exercises focusing on nouns, visit mybcommlab. Click on Chapter 1, click on "Additional Exercises to Improve Your Grammar, Mechanics, and Usage," and then click on "1. Possessive nouns" or "2. Antecedents."

2 Mastering Team Skills and Interpersonal Communication

Learning Objectives

After studying this chapter, you will be able to

1. Highlight the advantages and disadvantages of working in teams
2. Identify eight guidelines for successful collaborative writing
3. Explain how to make meetings more productive, and describe the emerging role of social networking technologies in business communication
4. Describe the listening process, and explain how good listeners overcome barriers at each stage of the process
5. Clarify the importance of nonverbal communication, and briefly describe six categories of nonverbal expression
6. Discuss the importance of business etiquette

On the Job: Communicating at Rosen Law Firm

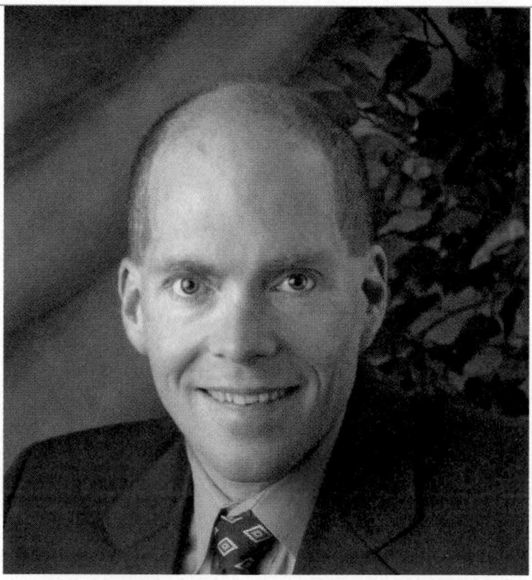

Lee Rosen's law firm uses a wiki to manage thousands of documents while boosting teamwork and collaboration.

The Wiki Way to Cut Costs and Build Team Spirit

When communication tools function at their best, they can go beyond mere facilitation to transformation. Such was the case at Rosen Law Firm, based in Raleigh, North Carolina. Lee Rosen, the firm's owner and chief executive, wanted to replace an expensive, complicated, and inflexible computer system that employees relied on for everything from contact lists to appointment calendars to document storage. The solution he chose for his small law firm was a wiki, the same technology that enables nearly 100,000 people around the world to contribute to Wikipedia.

The wiki certainly helped cut costs, and it also did much more. In addition to handling much of the firm's document storage and formal communication, the wiki introduced an informal social element that is helping employees bond as a community. Many employees have added personal pages with information about themselves, helping employees get to know their colleagues on a more intimate level.

In implementing the wiki, Rosen faced a common challenge with new communication tools: getting people to give up familiar ways of doing things and embrace change. Knowing that the value of a company wiki depends on the level of employee contribution and that having some of the staff switch while others cling to old ways would seriously disrupt communication, he encouraged use of the new wiki with a friendly competition. For each page an employee created during the three-month competition, he or she was given one possible combination to the company safe, which contained a $1,000 cash prize. From time to time, Rosen also forced use of the wiki by publishing important information only on the wiki.

As often happens when companies face significant changes, the move to the wiki did cause some turmoil. Two camps of employees argued over the best way to organize information and got caught up in an "edit war" on the wiki, repeatedly undoing each other's decisions. They eventually reached a compromise that resolved the disagreement and had lasting benefits for teamwork and interpersonal communication across the firm. According to Rosen, "It forced everybody to learn about each other's job."[1]

www.rosen.com

COMMUNICATING EFFECTIVELY IN TEAMS

Team members have a shared mission and are collectively responsible for their work.

The teamwork interactions among the employees at Rosen Law Firm (profiled in the chapter-opening "On the Job" vignette) represent one of the essential elements of interpersonal communication. A **team** is a unit of two or more people who share a mission and the responsibility for working to achieve a common goal.[2] **Problem-solving teams** and **task forces** assemble to resolve specific issues and then disband when their goals have been accomplished. Such teams are often *cross-functional*, pulling together people from a variety of departments who have different areas of expertise and responsibility. The diversity of opinions and experiences can lead to better decisions, but competing interests can lead to tensions that highlight the need for effective communication.

Committees are formal teams that usually have a long life span and can become a permanent part of the organizational structure. Committees typically deal with regularly recurring tasks, such as an executive committee that meets monthly to plan strategies and review results.

Effective communication is essential to every aspect of team performance.

Whatever the purpose and function of a team, you and your fellow team members must be able to communicate effectively with each other and with people outside your team. As Chapter 1 points out, this ability often requires taking on additional responsibility for communication: sharing information with team members, listening carefully to their inputs, and crafting messages that reflect the team's collective ideas and opinions.

Advantages and Disadvantages of Teams

1 LEARNING OBJECTIVE

Highlight the advantages and disadvantages of working in teams.

When teams are successful, they can improve productivity, creativity, employee involvement, and even job security.[3] Teams are often at the core of **participative management**, the effort to involve employees in the company's decision making. Teams can play a vital role in helping an organization reach its goals, but they are not appropriate for every situation, and even when they are appropriate, companies need to weigh both the advantages and disadvantages of a team-based approach. A successful team can provide a number of advantages:[4]

Effective teams can pool knowledge, take advantage of diverse viewpoints, and increase acceptance of solutions the team proposes.

- **Increased information and knowledge.** By pooling the experience of several individuals, a team has access to more information in the decision-making process.
- **Increased diversity of views.** Team members can bring a variety of perspectives to the decision-making process. Keep in mind, however, that unless these diverse viewpoints are guided by a shared goal, the multiple perspectives can hamper a team's efforts.[5]
- **Increased acceptance of a solution.** Those who participate in making a decision are more likely to support it and encourage others to accept it.
- **Higher performance levels.** Working in teams can unleash new levels of creativity and energy in workers who share a sense of purpose and mutual accountability. Effective teams can be better than top-performing individuals at solving complex problems.[6] Furthermore, teams fill an individual worker's need to belong to a group, reduce employee boredom, increase feelings of dignity and self-worth, and reduce stress and tension between workers.

Teams need to avoid the negative impact of groupthink, hidden agendas, and excessive costs.

Although teamwork has many advantages, it also has a number of potential disadvantages. At the worst, working in teams can be a frustrating waste of time. Teams need to be aware of and work to counter the following potential disadvantages:

- **Groupthink.** Like other social structures, business teams can generate tremendous pressures to conform with accepted norms of behavior. **Groupthink** occurs when peer pressures cause individual team members to withhold contrary or unpopular opinions. The result can be decisions that are worse than the choices the team members might have made individually.
- **Hidden agendas.** Some team members may have a **hidden agenda**—private, counterproductive motives, such as a desire to take control of the group, to undermine someone else on the team, or to pursue a business goal that runs counter to the team's mission.
- **Cost.** Aligning schedules, arranging meetings, and coordinating individual parts of a project can eat up a lot of time and money.

Characteristics of Effective Teams

To be effective collaborators in a team setting, you and your colleagues must recognize that each individual brings valuable assets, knowledge, and skills to the team. Strong collaborators are willing to exchange information, examine issues, and work through conflicts that arise. They trust each other and work toward the greater good of the team and organization rather than focus on personal agendas.[7]

Effective teams have a clear sense of purpose, open and honest communication, consensus-based decision making, creativity, and effective conflict resolution.

The most effective teams have a clear objective and a shared sense of purpose, communicate openly and honestly, reach decisions by consensus, think creatively, and know how to resolve conflict.[8] Learning these team skills takes time and practice, so U.S. companies now teach teamwork more frequently than any other aspect of business.[9]

In contrast, unsuccessful teamwork can waste time and money, generate lower-quality work, and frustrate both managers and employees. A lack of trust is cited as the most common reason for the failure of teams. A lack of trust can result from team members being suspicious of one another's motives or ability to contribute.[10] Another common reason for failure is poor communication, particularly when teams operate across cultures, countries, and time zones.[11] Poor communication can also result from basic differences in conversational styles. Some people expect conversation to follow an orderly pattern in which team members wait their turn to speak. Others view conversation as more spontaneous and are comfortable with an overlapping, interactive style.[12]

Collaborative Communication

When a team collaborates on reports, websites, presentations, and other communication projects, the collective energy and expertise of the various members can lead to results that transcend what each individual could do otherwise.[13] However, collaborating on team messages requires special effort; the following section offers a number of helpful guidelines.

2 LEARNING OBJECTIVE

Identify eight guidelines for successful collaborative writing.

Guidelines for Collaborative Writing

In any collaborative effort, it's important to recognize that team members coming from different backgrounds may have different work habits or priorities: A technical expert may focus on accuracy and scientific standards; an editor may be more concerned about organization and coherence; a manager may focus on schedules, cost, and corporate goals. In addition, team members differ in writing styles and personality traits—two factors that can complicate the creative nature of communication.

To collaborate effectively, everyone involved must be flexible and open to other opinions, focusing on team objectives rather than on individual priorities.[14] Successful writers know that most ideas can be expressed in many ways, so they avoid the "my way is best" attitude. The following guidelines will help you collaborate more successfully:[15]

Successful collaboration requires a number of steps, from selecting the right partners and agreeing on project goals to establishing clear processes and avoiding writing as a group.

- **Select collaborators carefully.** Choose a combination of people who have the experience, information, and talent needed for each project.
- **Agree on project goals before you start.** Starting without a clear idea of what the team hopes to accomplish inevitably leads to frustration and wasted time.

- **Give your team time to bond before diving in.** If people haven't had the opportunity to work together before, make sure they can get to know each other before being asked to collaborate.
- **Clarify individual responsibilities.** Because members will be depending on each other, make sure individual responsibilities are clear, including who is supposed to do what and by when.
- **Establish clear processes.** Make sure everyone knows how the work will be done, including checkpoints and decisions to be made along the way.
- **Avoid writing as a group.** The actual composition is the only part of developing team messages that does not usually benefit from group participation. In most cases, the best approach is to plan, research, and outline together but assign the task of writing to one person or divide larger projects among multiple writers. If you divide the writing, try to have one person do a final revision pass to ensure a consistent style.
- **Make sure tools and techniques are ready and compatible across the team.** Even minor details such as different versions of software can delay projects. If you plan to use technology for sharing or presenting materials, test the system before work begins.
- **Check to see how things are going along the way.** Don't assume that everything is working just because you don't hear anything negative.

Technologies for Collaborative Writing

Collaboration tools include multiauthor blogs, content management systems, and wikis.

A variety of collaboration tools exist to help teams write together, including group review and editing features in both word processors and the Adobe Acrobat electronic document system (PDF files), multiauthor blogs, and **content management systems** that organize and control the content for websites. A **wiki**, from the Hawaiian word for *quick*, is a website that allows anyone with access to add new material and edit existing material (see Figure 2.1).

FIGURE 2.1 Using a Wiki for Collaborative Communication

This page from the Public Relations Wiki (**http://pr.wikia.com**) shows the features typically used to create and edit wiki pages.

Public wikis allow any registered user to edit pages; private wikis such as the one in use at Rosen Law Firm (featured at the beginning of the chapter) are accessible only with permission. Yahoo! uses private wikis to facilitate communication among hundreds of team members around the world involved in creating and documenting new services.[16] Chapter 12 offers guidelines for effective wiki collaboration.

Benefits of wikis include simple operation and the ability to post new or revised material instantly, without a formal review process.

Key benefits of wikis include simple operation—writers don't need to know any of the techniques normally required to create web content—and the freedom to post new or revised material without prior approval. This approach is quite different from a content management system, in which both the organization of the website and the *workflow* (the rules for creating, editing, reviewing, and approving content) are tightly controlled.[17] With a wiki, if you see a way to improve a particular page or want to add a new page, you simply edit or write, using your web browser, and it's done. A content management system is a great tool for maintaining consistent presentation on a company's primary public website, whereas a wiki allows a team to collaborate with speed and flexibility.

Enterprise wiki systems extend the wiki concept with additional features for business use that ensure information quality and confidentiality and also provide the speed and flexibility of a wiki. For instance, *access control* lets a team leader identify who is allowed to read and modify a wiki. *Change monitoring* alerts team members when significant changes or additions are made. And *rollback* allows a team to "travel back in time" to see all previous versions of pages.[18]

To facilitate collaboration on a broad scale, using a variety of resources, many teams now take advantage of **groupware**, computer-based systems that let people communicate, share files, present materials, and work on documents simultaneously. **Shared workspaces** are online "virtual offices" that give everyone on a team access to the same set of resources and information: databases, calendars, project plans, pertinent instant messaging (IM) and e-mail exchanges, shared reference materials, and team-created documents (see Figure 2.2). To maintain security, shared workspaces and other team

FIGURE 2.2 Shared Workspaces

Shared workspaces, such as this example from Microsoft's Office Live Workspace system, give virtual teams instant access to the documents, calendars, and other files and information needed for successful collaboration. Carefully designed intranet tools such as this can boost team productivity and help prevent communication breakdowns.

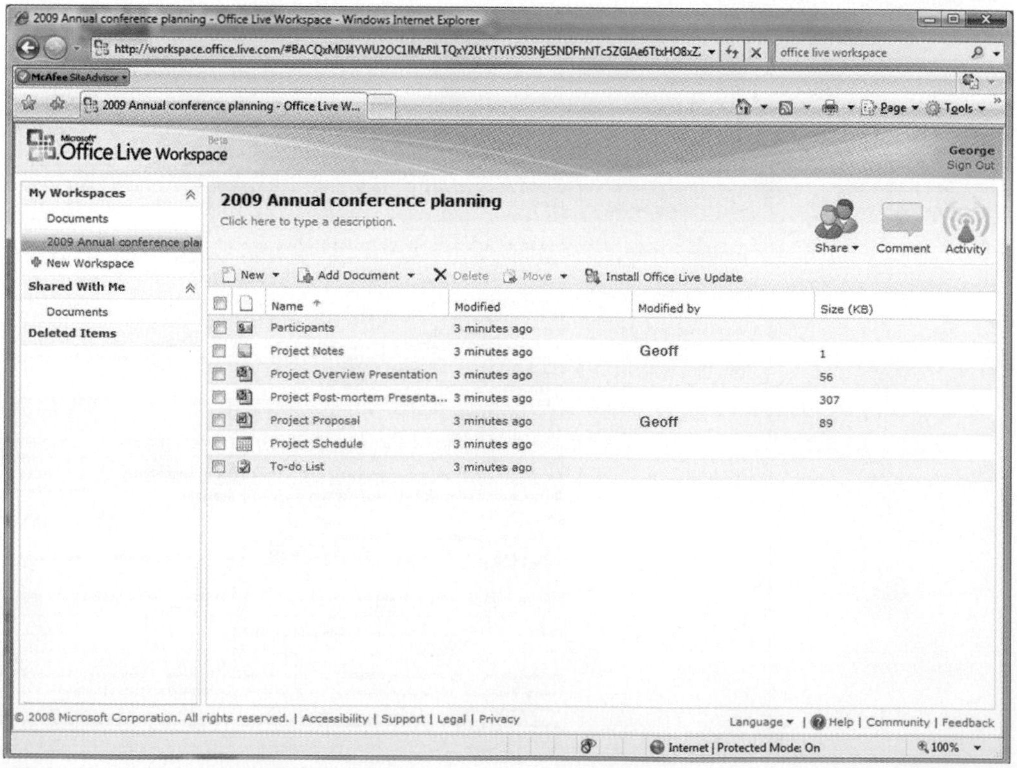

resources are hosted on *intranets* (restricted-access websites that are open to employees only) or *extranets* (restricted sites that are available to employees and to outside parties by invitation only).

Most groupware systems have built-in intelligence to control which team members can read, edit, and save specific files. *Revision control* goes one step further: It allows only one person at a time to check out a given file or document and records all the changes that person makes.[19]

In the coming years, keep an eye out for emerging technologies that can help teams collaborate. For example, Google's new Wave technology combines writing and communication tools in a way that could enable new forms of online collaboration.

Group Dynamics

Group dynamics are the interactions and processes that take place in a team.

The interactions and processes that take place among the members of a team are called **group dynamics**. Productive teams tend to develop rules of interaction that are conducive to business. Often unstated, these rules become group **norms**—informal standards of conduct that members share and that guide member behavior. For example, some teams develop a casual approach to schedules, with members routinely showing up 10 or 15 minutes late for meetings, while other teams expect strict adherence to time commitments. Group dynamics are influenced by several factors: the roles that team members assume, the current phase of team development, the team's success in resolving conflict, and the team's success in overcoming resistance.

Assuming Team Roles

Each member of a group plays a role that affects the outcome of the group's activities.

Members of a team can play various roles, which fall into three categories (see Table 2.1). Members who assume **self-oriented roles** are motivated mainly to fulfill personal needs, so they tend to be less productive than other members. "Dream teams" composed of multiple superstars often don't perform as well as one might expect because high-performing individuals can have trouble putting the team's needs ahead of their own.[20] In addition, highly skilled and experienced people with difficult personalities might not contribute for the simple reason that other team members may avoid interacting with them.[21] Far more likely to contribute to team goals are members who assume **team-maintenance roles** to help everyone work well together and those who assume **task-oriented roles** to help the team reach its goals.[22]

Roles can change over time. For instance, in a self-directed team with no formal leader, someone may assume a task-oriented leadership role early in the team's evolution. If this person doesn't prove to be a capable leader, someone else may emerge as a leader as the group searches for more effective direction.[23]

TABLE 2.1 Team Roles—Functional and Dysfunctional

DYSFUNCTIONAL: SELF-ORIENTED ROLES	FUNCTIONAL: TEAM-MAINTENANCE ROLES	FUNCTIONAL: TASK-FACILITATING ROLES
Controlling: Dominating others by exhibiting superiority or authority	**Encouraging:** Drawing out other members by showing verbal and nonverbal support, praise, or agreement	**Initiating:** Getting the team started on a line of inquiry
Withdrawing: Retiring from the team either by becoming silent or by refusing to deal with a particular aspect of the team's work	**Harmonizing:** Reconciling differences among team members through mediation or by using humor to relieve tension	**Information giving or seeking:** Offering (or seeking) information relevant to questions facing the team
Attention seeking: Calling attention to oneself and demanding recognition from others	**Compromising:** Offering to yield on a point in the interest of reaching a mutually acceptable decision	**Coordinating:** Showing relationships among ideas, clarifying issues, summarizing what the team has done
Diverting: Focusing the team's discussion on topics of interest to the individual rather than on those relevant to the task		**Procedure setting:** Suggesting decision-making procedures that will move the team toward a goal

FIGURE 2.3 Phases of Group Development
Groups generally progress through several stages on their way to becoming productive and reaching their objectives.

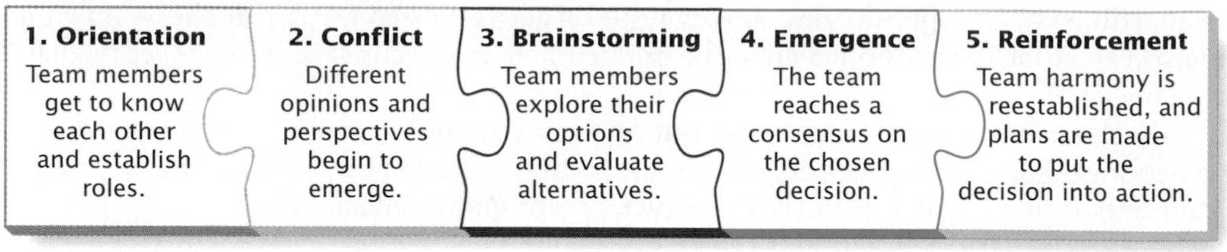

1. Orientation
Team members get to know each other and establish roles.
2. Conflict
Different opinions and perspectives begin to emerge.
3. Brainstorming
Team members explore their options and evaluate alternatives.
4. Emergence
The team reaches a consensus on the chosen decision.
5. Reinforcement
Team harmony is reestablished, and plans are made to put the decision into action.

Allowing for Team Evolution

Teams typically evolve through a variety of phases, such as orientation, conflict, brainstorming, emergence, and reinforcement.

Teams typically evolve through a number of phases on their way to becoming productive (see Figure 2.3). A variety of models have been proposed to describe the evolution toward becoming a productive team. Here is how one commonly used model identifies the phases a problem-solving team goes through as it evolves:[24]

1. **Orientation.** Team members socialize, establish their roles, and begin to define their task or purpose. Many companies use a variety of team-building exercises and activities to help teams break down barriers and develop a sense of shared purpose.[25] Note that team building can be a particular challenge with geographically dispersed virtual teams (see page 45) because the members may never meet in person. Sharing a "team operating agreement" that sets expectations for online meetings, communication processes, and decision making can help teams overcome the disadvantages of distance.[26]
2. **Conflict.** Team members begin to discuss their positions and become more assertive in establishing their roles. Disagreements and uncertainties are natural in this phase.
3. **Brainstorming.** Team members air all the options and fully discuss the pros and cons. At the end of this phase, members begin to settle on a single solution to the problem. Note that while group brainstorming remains a highly popular activity in today's companies, it may not always be the most productive way to generate new ideas. Some research indicates that having people brainstorm individually and then bring their ideas to a group meeting is more successful.[27]
4. **Emergence.** Consensus is reached when the team finds a solution that all members are willing to support (even if they have reservations).
5. **Reinforcement.** The team clarifies and summarizes the agreed-upon solution. Members receive their assignments for carrying out the group's decision, and they make arrangements for following up on those assignments.

You may also hear the process defined as *forming, storming, norming, performing,* and *adjourning,* the phases identified by researcher Bruce Tuckman when he proposed one of the earliest models of group development.[28] Regardless of the model you consider, recognize that these stages are a general framework for team development. Some teams may move forward and backward through several stages before they become productive, and other teams may be productive right away, even while some or all members are in a state of conflict.[29]

Resolving Conflict

Conflict in teams can be either constructive or destructive.

Conflict in team activities can arise for a number of reasons: competition for resources; disagreement over goals or responsibilities; poor communication; power struggles; or fundamental differences in values, attitudes, and personalities.[30] Although the term *conflict* sounds negative, conflict isn't necessarily bad. Conflict can be *constructive* if it forces important issues into the open, increases the involvement of team members, and generates creative ideas for solving a problem. Teamwork isn't necessarily about happiness and harmony; even teams that have some interpersonal friction can excel with effective leadership and team players committed to strong results. As teamwork experts Andy Boynton and Bill Fischer put it, "Virtuoso teams are not about getting polite results."[31]

In contrast, conflict is *destructive* if it diverts energy from more important issues, destroys the morale of teams or individual team members, or polarizes or divides the team.[32] Destructive conflict can lead to *win–lose* or *lose–lose* outcomes, in which one or both sides lose, to the detriment of the entire team. If you approach conflict with the idea that both sides can satisfy their goals to at least some extent (a *win–win strategy*), you can minimize losses for everyone. For a win–win strategy to work, everybody must believe that (1) it's possible to find a solution that both parties can accept, (2) cooperation is better for the organization than competition, (3) the other party can be trusted, and (4) greater power or status doesn't entitle one party to impose a solution.

—REAL-TIME UPDATES
Learn More

Use negotiation skills to resolve conflicts

This two-part video series teaches managers and entrepreneurs to resolve conflicts through the win–win strategies of empathetic negotiation. Go to **http://real-timeupdates.com/ebc** and click on "Learn More." If you are using mybcommlab, you can access Real-Time Updates within each chapter or under Student Study Tools.

The following seven measures can help team members successfully resolve conflict:

- **Proaction.** Deal with minor conflict before it becomes major conflict.
- **Communication.** Get those directly involved in a conflict to participate in resolving it.
- **Openness.** Get feelings out in the open before dealing with the main issues.
- **Research.** Seek factual reasons for a problem before seeking solutions.
- **Flexibility.** Don't let anyone lock into a position before considering other solutions.
- **Fair play.** Insist on fair outcomes and don't let anyone avoid a fair solution by hiding behind the rules.
- **Alliance.** Get opponents to fight together against an "outside force" instead of against each other.

Overcoming Resistance

One particular type of conflict that can affect team progress is resistance to change. Sometimes this resistance is clearly irrational, such as when people resist any kind of change, whether it makes sense or not. Sometimes, however, resistance is perfectly logical. A change may require someone to relinquish authority or give up comfortable ways of doing things. If someone is resisting change, you can be persuasive with calm, reasonable communication:

When you encounter resistance or hostility, try to maintain your composure and address the other person's emotional needs.

- **Express understanding.** You might say, "I understand that this change might be difficult, and if I were in your position, I might be reluctant myself." Help the other person relax and talk about his or her anxiety so that you have a chance to offer reassurance.[33]
- **Bring resistance out into the open.** When people are noncommittal and silent, they may be tuning you out without even knowing why. Continuing with your argument is futile. Deal directly with the resistance, without accusing. You might say, "You seem cool to this idea. Have I made some faulty assumptions?" Such questions force people to face and define their resistance.[34]
- **Evaluate others' objections fairly.** Use active listening to focus on what the other person is expressing, both the words and the feelings. Get the person to open up so that you can understand the basis for the resistance. Others' objections may raise legitimate points that you'll need to discuss, or they may reveal problems that you'll need to minimize.[35]
- **Hold your arguments until the other person is ready for them.** Getting your point across depends as much on the other person's frame of mind as it does on your arguments. You can't assume that a strong argument will speak for itself. By becoming more audience centered, you will learn to address the other person's emotional needs first.

Sometimes you need to address the other party's emotional needs before attempting to resolve underlying conflict.

Social Networks and Virtual Communities

Chapter 1 explains how social media and the Web 2.0 approach are redefining business communication. Within that context, **social networking technologies** are redefining teamwork and team communication by helping erase the constraints of

Social networking technologies are becoming vital communication linkages in many companies.

geographic and organization boundaries. In addition to enabling and enhancing teamwork, social networks have numerous other business applications and benefits (see Table 2.2).

The two fundamental elements of social networking technology are *profiles* (the information stored about each member of the network) and *connections* (mechanisms for finding and communicating with other members).[36] If you're familiar with MySpace or Facebook, you have a basic idea of how social networks function. Business-oriented networks such as LinkedIn (www.linkedin.com), Ryze (www.ryze.com), and Xing (www.xing.com) function in much the same way, and they also have the potential to become vital elements of an organization's structure and communication channels. For example, some companies use social networking technologies to form *virtual communities* or *communities of practice* that link employees with similar professional interests throughout the company and sometimes with customers and suppliers as well. Given its ability to connect people across organizational boundaries, networking technology is an essential element of the network organizational structure discussed on page 10 in Chapter 1.

The heavy-equipment manufacturer Caterpillar has more than 2,700 virtual teams or communities that discuss problems and share insights into improving quality and productivity. In some companies, these teams or communities

REAL-TIME UPDATES
Learn More

Social media for professionals

See several intriguing new examples of social networks designed exclusively for members of certain professions or industries. Go to **http://real-timeupdates.com/ebc** and click on "Learn More." If you are using mybcommlab, you can access Real-Time Updates within each chapter or under Student Study Tools.

TABLE 2.2 Business Uses of Social Networking Technology

BUSINESS CHALLENGE	EXAMPLE OF SOCIAL NETWORKING IN ACTION
Supporting customers	Allowing customers to develop close relationships with product experts within the company
Integrating new employees	Helping new employees navigate their way through the organization, finding experts, mentors, and other important contacts
Easing the transition after reorganizations and mergers	Helping employees connect and bond after internal staff reorganizations or mergers with other organizations
Overcoming structural barriers in communication channels	Bypassing the formal communication system in order to deliver information where it is needed in a timely fashion
Assembling teams	Identifying the best people, both inside the company and in other companies, to collaborate on projects
Fostering the growth of communities	Helping people with similar—or complementary—interests and skills find each other in order to provide mutual assistance and development
Solving problems	Finding "pockets of knowledge" within the organization—the expertise and experience of individual employees
Preparing for major meetings and events	Giving participants a way to meet before an event takes place, helping to ensure that the meeting or event becomes more productive more quickly
Accelerating the evolution of teams	Accelerating the sometimes slow process of getting to know one another and identifying individual areas of expertise
Maintaining business relationships	Giving people an easy way to stay in contact after meetings and conferences
Sharing and distributing information	Making it easy for employees to share information with people who may need it and for people who need information to find employees who might have it
Finding potential customers, business partners, and employees	Identifying strong candidates by matching user profiles with current business needs and linking from existing member profiles

are informal and "organic," springing up and growing as employees connect with one another. In other companies, including Caterpillar, they are planned and managed in a more formal fashion.[37] The huge advantage that social networking brings to these team efforts is in identifying the best people to collaborate on each problem or project, no matter where they are located around the world or what their official roles are in the organization.

MAKING YOUR MEETINGS MORE PRODUCTIVE

3 LEARNING OBJECTIVE

Explain how to make meetings more productive, and describe the emerging role of social networking technologies in business communication.

Well-run meetings can help you solve problems, develop ideas, and identify opportunities. Much of your workplace communication is likely to occur in small-group meetings; therefore, your ability to contribute to the company and to be recognized for those contributions will depend on your meeting skills.

Unfortunately, many meetings are unproductive. In one study, senior and middle managers reported that only 56 percent of their meetings were actually productive and that 25 percent of them could have been replaced by a phone call or a memo.[38] The three most frequently reported problems with meetings are getting off the subject, not having an agenda, and running too long.[39] You can help ensure productive meetings by preparing carefully, conducting meetings efficiently, and using meeting technologies wisely.

Preparing for Meetings

Careful preparation helps you avoid the two biggest meeting mistakes: (1) holding a meeting when a blog posting or some other message would do the job and (2) holding a meeting without a specific goal in mind. Before you even begin preparing for a meeting, make sure holding a meeting is truly necessary. Once you're sure, proceed with four preparation tasks:

To ensure a successful meeting, decide on your purpose ahead of time, select the right participants, choose the time and facility carefully, and set a clear agenda.

- **Identify your purpose.** *Informational meetings* involve sharing information and answering audience questions. *Decision-making meetings* involve persuasion, analysis, problem solving, and planning. Whatever your purpose, identify what the best possible result of the meeting would be (such as "we carefully evaluated all three product ideas and decided which one to invest in"). Use this hoped-for result to shape the direction and content of the meeting.[40]
- **Select participants for the meeting.** Be sure to invite everyone who needs to participate—but don't invite anyone who doesn't need to be there. The more people you have, the longer it will take to reach consensus. Meetings with more than 10 or 12 people can become unmanageable if everyone is expected to participate in the discussion and decision making.
- **Choose the time and prepare the facility.** Morning meetings can be more productive than afternoon sessions because people are fresher and not yet involved in the various problems and concerns of their working days. After selecting the time, plan the facility and layout carefully. For instance, if you want to encourage interaction, arranging chairs in a circle or U shape is more effective than seating in rows. Plus, give some attention to details such as room temperature, lighting, ventilation, acoustics, and refreshments; any of these details can make or break a meeting. If the meeting will take place online, you need to consider a variety of other factors (see page 459).
- **Set the agenda.** The success of a meeting depends on the preparation of the participants. Distribute a carefully written agenda to participants, giving them enough time to prepare as needed (see Figure 2.4 on the next page). A productive agenda answers three key questions: (1) What do we need to do in this meeting to accomplish our goals? (2) What issues will be of greatest importance to all participants? (3) What information must be available in order to discuss these issues?[41]

FIGURE 2.4 Typical Meeting Agenda
Agenda formats vary widely, depending on the complexity of the meeting and the presentation technologies that will be used. For an online meeting, for instance, a good approach is to first send a detailed planning agenda in advance of the meeting so that presenters know what they need to prepare. You can then create a simpler display agenda, similar to this one, to guide the progress of the meeting.

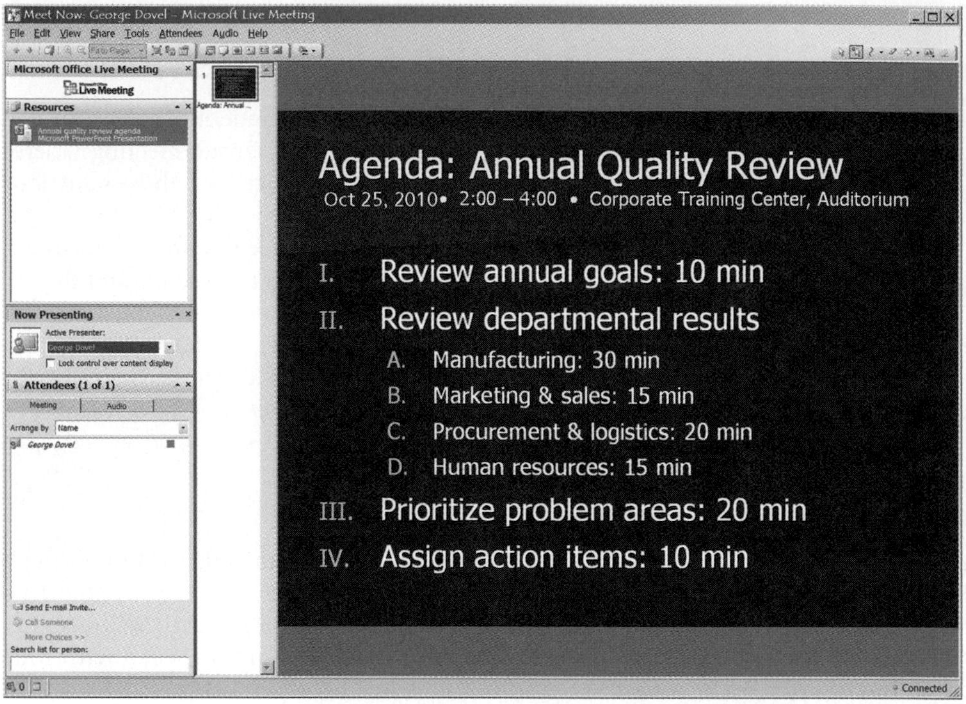

Conducting and Contributing to Efficient Meetings

Everyone shares the responsibility for successful meetings.

Everyone in a meeting shares the responsibility for making the meeting productive. If you're the designated leader of a meeting, however, you have an extra degree of responsibility and accountability. To ensure productive meetings, be sure to do the following:

- **Keep the discussion on track.** A good meeting leader draws out the best ideas the group has to offer and resolves differences of opinion while maintaining progress toward achieving the meeting's purpose and staying on schedule.
- **Follow agreed-upon rules.** The larger the meeting, the more formal you need to be to maintain order. Formal meetings use **parliamentary procedure**, a time-tested method for planning and running effective meetings. The best-known guide to this procedure is *Robert's Rules of Order*.
- **Encourage participation.** On occasion, some participants will be too quiet and others too talkative. The quiet participants may be shy, they may be expressing disagreement or resistance, or they may be working on unrelated tasks. Draw them out by asking for their input on issues that pertain to them.
- **Participate actively.** If you're a meeting participant, try to contribute to both the subject of the meeting and the smooth interaction of the group. Speak up if you have something useful to say, but don't monopolize the discussion or talk simply to bring attention to yourself.

PDF — **REAL-TIME UPDATES**
Learn More

Keep those meetings on track with simple parliamentary procedures

These condensed guidelines to parliamentary procedures can help a group transform meetings from chaos to controlled efficiency. Go to **http://real-timeupdates.com/ebc** and click on "Learn More." If you are using mybcommlab, you can access Real-Time Updates within each chapter or under Student Study Tools.

CHECKLIST: Improving Meeting Productivity

A. Prepare carefully.

- Make sure the meeting is necessary.
- Decide on your purpose.
- Select participants carefully.
- Choose the time and prepare the facility.
- Establish and distribute a clear agenda.

B. Lead effectively and participate fully.

- Keep the meeting on track.
- Follow agreed-upon rules.
- Encourage participation.
- Participate actively.
- Close effectively.

- **Close effectively.** At the conclusion of the meeting, verify that the objectives have been met or arrange for follow-up work, if needed. Summarize either the general conclusion of the discussion or the actions to be taken. Make sure all participants have a chance to clear up any misunderstandings.

To review the tasks that contribute to productive meetings, refer to "Checklist: Improving Meeting Productivity."

For formal meetings, it's good practice to appoint one person to record the **minutes**, a summary of the important information presented and the decisions made during a meeting. In smaller or informal meetings, attendees often make their own notes on their copies of the agenda. In either case, a clear record of the decisions made and the people responsible for follow-up action is essential. If your company doesn't have a specific format for minutes, follow the generic format shown in Figure 2.5 on the next page.

Using Meeting Technologies

You can expect to use a variety of meeting-related technologies throughout your career. In some instances, technology is used to promote interaction among participants in the same location, such as *electronic whiteboards* that can print or e-mail information recorded on them during a meeting and a variety of *electronic presentation tools* (see Chapter 14).

The focus of most meeting technologies is to enable participation among people in two or more locations. These technologies have spurred the emergence of **virtual teams,** whose members work in different locations and interact electronically in **virtual meetings**.

The simplest of the long-distance meeting tools provide communication through a single medium, such as audio **teleconferencing**, in which three or more people are connected by phone simultaneously. IM chat sessions can also serve as virtual meetings, with people participating by typing instead of talking.

Videoconferencing combines audio communication with live video, letting team members see each other, demonstrate products, and transmit other visual information. Videoconferencing can take place using PC-based systems over the web or through dedicated networks with specially built rooms. The most advanced systems feature *telepresence*, in which the interaction feels so lifelike that participants can forget that the person "sitting" on the other side of the table is actually in another city.[42]

Web-based meeting systems combine the best of IM, shared workspaces, and videoconferencing with other tools such as *virtual*

How many people are in this conference room in Chicago? Only the two people in the foreground are in the conference room; the other six are in Atlanta and London. Virtual meeting technologies such as this *telepresence* system connect people spread across the country or around the world.

FIGURE 2.5 Typical Minutes of a Meeting
Intranets and blogs are commonly used to distribute meeting minutes. The specific format of minutes is less important than making sure you record all the key information, particularly regarding responsibilities assigned during the meeting. No matter what medium is used, key elements of meeting minutes include a list of those present and a list of those who were invited but didn't attend, followed by the times the meeting started and ended, all major decisions reached at the meeting, all assignments of tasks to meeting participants, and all subjects that were deferred to a later meeting. Minutes objectively summarize important discussions, noting the names of those who contributed major points. Outlines, subheadings, and lists help organize the minutes; additional documentation is noted in the minutes and attached.

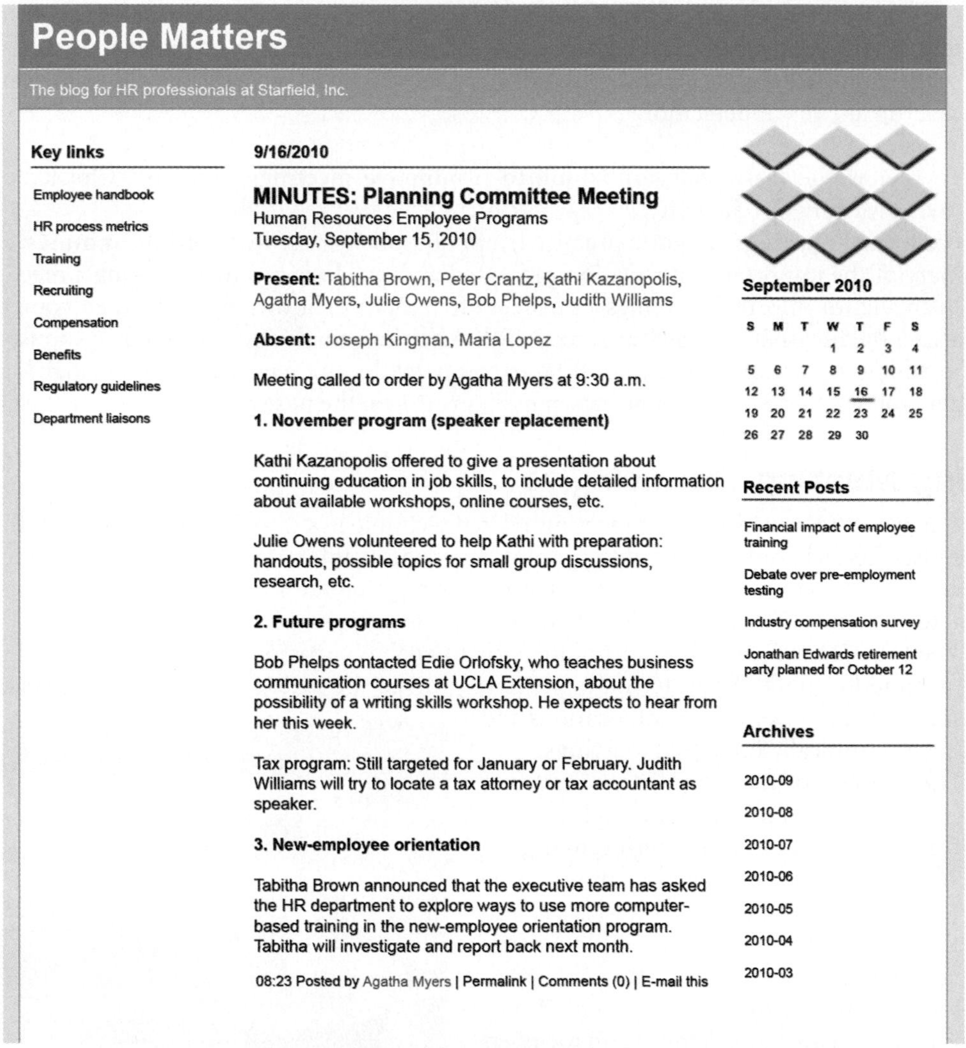

People Matters

The blog for HR professionals at Starfield, Inc.

Key links

- Employee handbook
- HR process metrics
- Training
- Recruiting
- Compensation
- Benefits
- Regulatory guidelines
- Department liaisons

9/16/2010

MINUTES: Planning Committee Meeting
Human Resources Employee Programs
Tuesday, September 15, 2010

Present: Tabitha Brown, Peter Crantz, Kathi Kazanopolis, Agatha Myers, Julie Owens, Bob Phelps, Judith Williams

Absent: Joseph Kingman, Maria Lopez

Meeting called to order by Agatha Myers at 9:30 a.m.

1. November program (speaker replacement)

Kathi Kazanopolis offered to give a presentation about continuing education in job skills, to include detailed information about available workshops, online courses, etc.

Julie Owens volunteered to help Kathi with preparation: handouts, possible topics for small group discussions, research, etc.

2. Future programs

Bob Phelps contacted Edie Orlofsky, who teaches business communication courses at UCLA Extension, about the possibility of a writing skills workshop. He expects to hear from her this week.

Tax program: Still targeted for January or February. Judith Williams will try to locate a tax attorney or tax accountant as speaker.

3. New-employee orientation

Tabitha Brown announced that the executive team has asked the HR department to explore ways to use more computer-based training in the new-employee orientation program. Tabitha will investigate and report back next month.

08:23 Posted by Agatha Myers | Permalink | Comments (0) | E-mail this

September 2010

S	M	T	W	T	F	S
			1	2	3	4
5	6	7	8	9	10	11
12	13	14	15	16	17	18
19	20	21	22	23	24	25
26	27	28	29	30		

Recent Posts

- Financial impact of employee training
- Debate over pre-employment testing
- Industry compensation survey
- Jonathan Edwards retirement party planned for October 12

Archives

- 2010-09
- 2010-08
- 2010-07
- 2010-06
- 2010-05
- 2010-04
- 2010-03

whiteboards that let teams collaborate in real time (see Figure 2.6). Using such systems, attendees can log on from almost anywhere in the world.

Technology continues to create intriguing opportunities for online interaction. For instance, one of the newest virtual tools is *online brainstorming*, in which companies conduct "idea campaigns" to generate new ideas from people across the organization. These range from small team meetings to huge events such as IBM's giant InnovationJam, in which 100,000 IBM employees, family members, and customers from 160 countries were invited to brainstorm online for three days.[43]

Companies are also beginning to experiment with virtual meetings and other communication activities in *virtual worlds*, most notably Second Life (www.secondlife.com). In much

FIGURE 2.6 Web-Based Meetings
You can expect to participate in many online meetings during your career. Web-based meeting systems offer powerful tools for communication, and you need to be proficient at using these tools to be effective during online meetings.

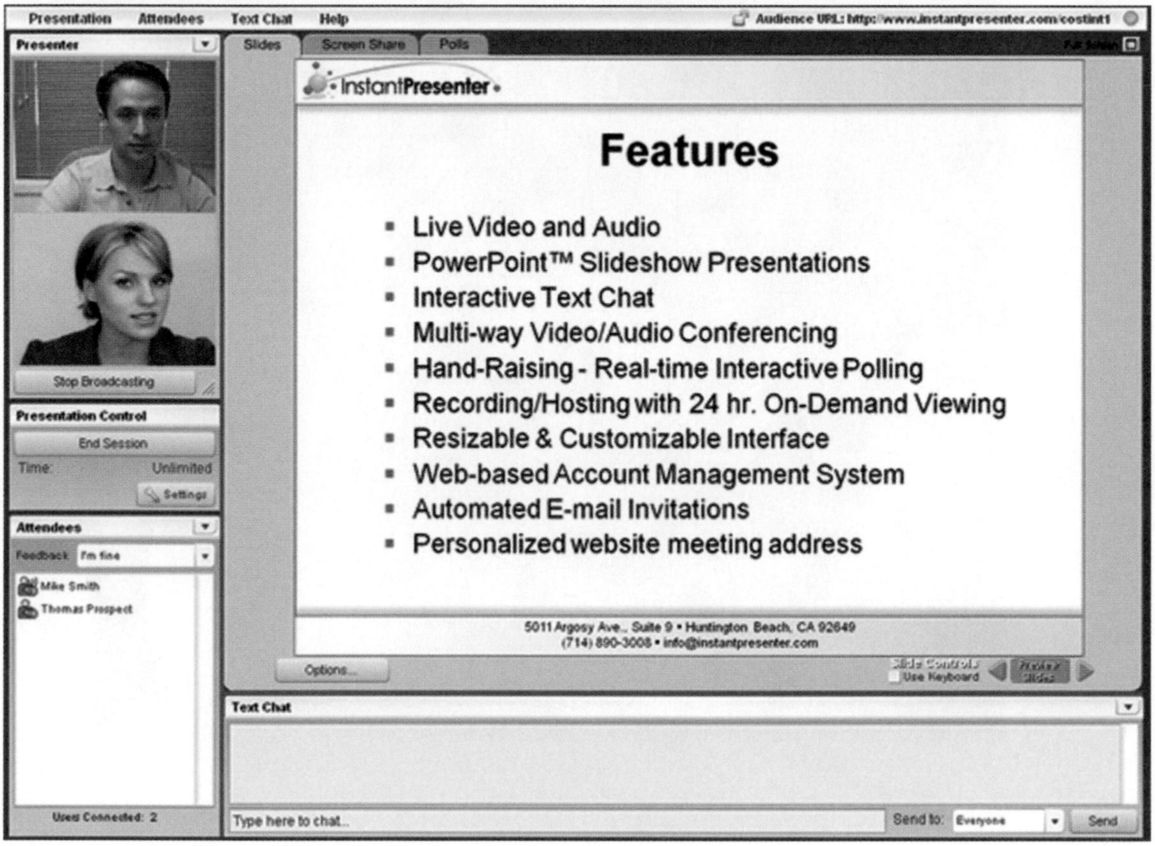

the same way that gamers can create and control characters (often known as *avatars*) in a multiplayer video game, professionals can create online versions of themselves to participate in meetings, training sessions, sales presentations, and other activities (see Figure 2.7). To learn more about business communication in Second Life, you can read the Business Communicators of Second Life blog at **http://freshtakes.typepad.com/sl_communicators**.

For the latest information on meeting technologies, visit **http://real-timeupdates.com/ebc** and click on Chapter 2.

IMPROVING YOUR LISTENING SKILLS

4 LEARNING OBJECTIVE

Describe the listening process, and explain how good listeners overcome barriers at each stage of the process.

Effective listening strengthens organizational relationships, enhances product delivery, alerts an organization to opportunities for innovation, and allows an organization to manage diversity both in the workforce and in the customers it serves.[44] Companies whose employees and managers listen effectively stay in touch, up to date, and out of trouble. Some 80 percent of top executives say that listening is the most important skill needed to get things done in the workplace.[45] In fact, many of the leading business schools in the United States have begun retooling their curricula in recent years to put more emphasis on "soft skills" such as listening.[46]

Listening is one of the most important skills in the workplace.

Poor listening skills can cost companies millions of dollars a year as a result of lost opportunities, legal mistakes, and other errors. Effective listening is vital to the process of building trust not only between organizations but also between individuals.[47] Throughout your career, effective listening will give you a competitive edge, enhancing your performance and thus the influence you have within your company and your industry.

FIGURE 2.7 **Virtual Meetings in a Virtual World**
Cranial Tap, whose online headquarters is shown here, is one of a growing number of firms that use Second Life as a virtual meeting place.

Recognizing Various Types of Listening

To be a good listener, adapt the way you listen to suit the situation.

Effective listeners recognize several types of listening and choose the best approach for each situation. The primary goal of **content listening** is to understand and retain the speaker's message. Because you're not evaluating the information at this point, it doesn't matter whether you agree or disagree, approve or disapprove—only that you understand. Try to overlook the speaker's style and any limitations in the presentation; just focus on the information.[48]

The goal of **critical listening** is to understand and evaluate the meaning of the speaker's message on several levels: the logic of the argument, the strength of the evidence, the validity of the conclusions, the implications of the message, the speaker's intentions and motives, and the omission of any important or relevant points. If you're skeptical, ask questions to explore the speaker's point of view and credibility. Be on the lookout for bias that could color the way the information is presented and be careful to separate opinions from facts.[49]

The goal of **empathic listening** is to understand the speaker's feelings, needs, and wants so that you can appreciate his or her point of view, regardless of whether you share that perspective. By listening with empathy, you help the individual vent the emotions that prevent a calm, clear-headed approach to the subject. Avoid the temptation to jump in with advice unless the person specifically asks for it. Also, don't judge the speaker's feelings and don't try to tell people they shouldn't feel this or that emotion. Instead, let the speaker know that you appreciate his or her feelings and understand the situation. After you establish that connection, you can help the speaker move on to search for a solution.[50]

No matter what mode they are using at any given time, effective listeners try to engage in **active listening**, making a conscious effort to turn off their own filters and biases to truly hear and understand what the other party is saying. They ask questions to verify key points and encourage the speaker through positive body language.[51]

Understanding the Listening Process

Listening is a far more complex process than most people think—and most of us aren't very good at it. People typically listen at no better than a 25 percent efficiency rate, remember only about half of what's said during a 10-minute conversation, and forget half of that within 48 hours.[52] Furthermore, when questioned about material they've just heard, they are likely to get the facts mixed up.[53]

Listening involves five steps: receiving, decoding, remembering, evaluating, and responding.

Listening follows the same sequence as the general communication process model described in Chapter 1 (page 11), with the added challenge that it happens in real time. To listen effectively, you need to successfully complete five separate steps:[54]

1. **Receiving.** You start by physically hearing the message and acknowledging it. Physical reception can be blocked by noise, impaired hearing, or inattention. Some experts also include nonverbal messages as part of this stage because these factors influence the listening process as well.
2. **Decoding.** Your next step is to assign meaning to sounds, which you do according to your own values, beliefs, ideas, expectations, roles, needs, and personal history.
3. **Remembering.** Before you can act on the information, you need to store it for future processing. As you learned in Chapter 1, incoming messages must first be captured in short-term memory before being transferred to long-term memory for more permanent storage.
4. **Evaluating.** Your next step is to evaluate the message by applying critical thinking skills to separate fact from opinion and evaluate the quality of the evidence.
5. **Responding.** After you've evaluated the speaker's message, you react. If you're communicating one-on-one or in a small group, the initial response generally takes the form of verbal feedback. If you're one of many in an audience, your initial response may take the form of applause, laughter, or silence. Later on, you may act on what you have heard.

If any one of these steps breaks down, the listening process becomes less effective or even fails entirely. As both a sender and a receiver, you can reduce the failure rate by recognizing and overcoming a variety of physical and mental barriers to effective listening.

Overcoming Barriers to Effective Listening

Good listeners actively try to overcome the barriers to effective listening.

Good listeners look for ways to overcome potential barriers throughout the listening process (see Table 2.3). **Selective listening** is one of the most common barriers to effective listening. If your mind wanders, you may stay tuned out until you hear a word or phrase that gets your attention again. But by that time, you're unable to recall what the speaker *actually* said; instead, you remember what you *think* the speaker probably said.[55]

Your mind can process information much faster than most speakers talk, so you need to focus to listen effectively.

One reason listeners' minds tend to wander is that people think faster than they speak. Most people speak at about 120 to 150 words per minute, but listeners can process audio information at up to 500 words per minute.[56] In other words, your brain has a lot of free time whenever you're listening, and if you don't focus, it will find a thousand other things to think about.

When information is crucial, don't count on your memory.

Overcoming interpretation barriers can be difficult because you may not even be aware of them. As Chapter 1 notes, selective perception leads listeners to mold messages to fit their own conceptual frameworks. Listeners sometimes make up their minds before fully hearing the speaker's message, or they engage in defensive listening—protecting their self-esteem by tuning out anything that doesn't confirm their view of themselves.

Overcoming memory barriers is a comparatively easy problem to solve, but it takes some work. One simple rule is: Don't count on your memory. If the information is crucial,

TABLE 2.3 What Makes an Effective Listener?

EFFECTIVE LISTENERS	INEFFECTIVE LISTENERS
• Listen actively.	• Listen passively.
• Take careful and complete notes.	• Take no notes or ineffective notes.
• Make frequent eye contact with the speaker (depending on the culture).	• Make little or no eye contact.
• Stay focused on the speaker and the content.	• Allow their minds to wander; are easily distracted.
• Mentally paraphrase key points to maintain attention level and ensure comprehension.	• Fail to paraphrase.
• Adjust listening style to the situation.	• Listen with the same style, regardless of the situation.
• Give the speaker nonverbal cues (such as nodding to show agreement or raising eyebrows to show surprise or skepticism).	• Fail to give the speaker nonverbal feedback.
• Save questions or points of disagreement until an appropriate time.	• Interrupt whenever they disagree or don't understand.
• Overlook stylistic differences and focus on the speaker's message.	• Are distracted by or unduly influenced by stylistic differences; are judgmental.
• Make distinctions between main points and supporting details.	• Are unable to distinguish main points from details.
• Look for opportunities to learn.	• Assume that they already know everything that's important to know.

record it. You can hold information in short-term memory by repeating it silently or organizing a long list of items into several shorter lists. To store information in long-term memory—particularly information that you might not be immediately interested in—four techniques can help: (1) Associate new information with something closely related (such as the restaurant in which you met a new client), (2) categorize the new information into logical groups (such as alphabetizing the names of products you're trying to remember), (3) visualize words and ideas as pictures, and (4) create mnemonics such as acronyms or rhymes. Note that all four techniques have an important factor in common: You have to *do* something to make the information stick.

For a reminder of the steps you can take to overcome listening barriers, see "Checklist: Overcoming Barriers to Effective Listening."

REAL-TIME UPDATES
Learn More

Are you a good listener?

Most of us believe we are good listeners, but frequent communication breakdowns in business and personal settings are evidence that we could all improve. This video can help. Go to **http://real-timeupdates.com/ebc** and click on "Learn More." If you are using mybcommlab, you can access Real-Time Updates within each chapter or under Student Study Tools.

CHECKLIST: Overcoming Barriers to Effective Listening

- Control whatever barriers to physical reception you can (such as avoiding interrupting speakers by asking questions or by exhibiting disruptive nonverbal behaviors).
- Avoid selective listening by focusing on the speaker and carefully analyzing what you hear.
- Keep an open mind by avoiding any prejudgment and by not listening defensively.
- Try to paraphrase the speaker's ideas, giving that person a chance to confirm or correct your interpretation.
- Don't count on your memory; write down or record important information.
- Improve your short-term memory by repeating information or breaking it into shorter lists.
- Improve your long-term memory by using association, categorization, visualization, and mnemonics.

IMPROVING YOUR NONVERBAL COMMUNICATION SKILLS

5 LEARNING OBJECTIVE

Clarify the importance of nonverbal communication, and briefly describe six categories of nonverbal expression.

Nonverbal communication is the interpersonal process of sending and receiving information, both intentionally and unintentionally, without using written or spoken language. Nonverbal signals play a vital role in communication because they can strengthen a verbal message (when the nonverbal signals match the spoken words), weaken a verbal message (when nonverbal signals don't match the words), or replace words entirely. For example, you might tell a client that a project is coming along nicely, but your forced smile and nervous glances send an entirely different message. In fact, nonverbal communication often conveys more to listeners than the words you speak—particularly when they're trying to decide how you really feel about a situation or when they're trying to judge your credibility and aptitude for leadership.[57]

Nonverbal communication supplements spoken language.

Recognizing Nonverbal Communication

Paying special attention to nonverbal signals in the workplace will enhance your ability to communicate successfully. Moreover, as you interact with business associates from other backgrounds, you'll discover that some nonverbal signals don't necessarily translate across cultures. You'll learn more about cultural influences on nonverbal communication in Chapter 3. The range and variety of nonverbal signals are almost endless, but you can grasp the basics by studying six general categories:

Nonverbal signals include facial expression, gestures and posture, vocal characteristics, personal appearance, touch, and use of time and space.

- **Facial expression.** Your face is the primary vehicle for expressing your emotions; it reveals both the type and the intensity of your feelings.[58] Your eyes are especially effective for indicating attention and interest, influencing others, regulating interaction, and establishing dominance.[59]
- **Gesture and posture.** The way you position and move your body expresses both specific and general messages, some voluntary and some involuntary. Many gestures—a wave of the hand, for example—have specific and intentional meanings. Other types of body movement are unintentional and express more general messages. Slouching, leaning forward, fidgeting, and walking briskly are all unconscious signals that reveal whether you feel confident or nervous, friendly or hostile, assertive or passive, or powerful or powerless.
- **Vocal characteristics.** Voice carries both intentional and unintentional messages. A speaker can intentionally control pitch, pace, and stress to convey a specific message. For instance, consider the question, "What are you doing?" with the emphasis on *what* versus the emphasis on *you*. Unintentional vocal characteristics can convey happiness, surprise, fear, and other emotions (for example, fear often increases the pitch and the pace of your speaking voice).
- **Personal appearance.** People respond to others on the basis of their physical appearance, sometimes fairly and other times unfairly. Although an individual's body type and facial features impose limitations, people can control grooming, clothing, accessories, and overall personal style. If your goal is to make a good impression, adopt the style of the people you want to impress.
- **Touch.** Touch is an important way to convey warmth, comfort, and reassurance—as well as control. Touch is so powerful, in fact, that it is governed by cultural customs that establish who can touch whom and how in various circumstances. In the United States and Great Britain, for instance, people usually touch less frequently than people in France or Costa Rica. Even within each culture's norms, however, individual attitudes toward touch vary widely. A manager might be comfortable using hugs to express support or congratulations, but his or her subordinates could interpret those hugs as either a show of dominance or sexual interest.[60] Touch is a complex subject. The best advice is: When in doubt, don't touch.
- **Time and space.** Like touch, time and space can be used to assert authority, imply intimacy, and send other nonverbal messages. For instance, some people try to demonstrate their own importance or disregard for others by making other people wait; others show respect by being on time. The manipulation of space works in a similar way. For example, the decision to respect or violate someone's "private space" sends a powerful nonverbal signal.

Sharpening Your Career Skills

Sending the Right Signals

The nonverbal signals you send can enhance—or undermine—your verbal message, so make sure to use nonverbal cues to your advantage. In U.S. business culture, the following signals are key to building and maintaining professional credibility:

- **Eye behavior.** Maintain direct, but not continuous, eye contact. Don't look down before responding to a question, and be careful not to shift your eyes around. Don't look away from the other person for extended periods, and try not to blink excessively.
- **Gestures.** When using gestures to emphasize points or convey the intensity of your feelings, keep them spontaneous, unrehearsed, and relaxed. Keep your hands and elbows away from your body, and avoid hand-to-face gestures, throat clearing, fidgeting, and tugging at clothing. Don't lick your lips, wring your hands, tap your fingers, or smile out of context.
- **Posture.** Assume an open and relaxed posture. Walk confidently, with grace and ease. Stand straight, with both feet on the floor, and sit straight in your chair without slouching. Hold your head level, and keep your chin up. Shift your posture while communicating, leaning forward and smiling as you begin to answer a question. Avoid keeping your body rigid or otherwise conveying a sense of tension.
- **Voice.** Strive for a conversational style, while speaking at a moderately fast rate. Use appropriate variation in pitch, rate, and volume. Avoid speaking in a monotone. Avoid sounding flat, tense, or nasal. Do your best to avoid ahs or ums, repeating words, interrupting or pausing midsentence, omitting parts of words, and stuttering.

CAREER APPLICATIONS

1. What message might you get if your boss smiles but looks away when you ask if you'll be getting a raise this year? Explain your interpretation of these nonverbal signals.
2. Would you be reluctant to hire a job candidate who stares intently at you through an entire job interview? Why or why not?

Using Nonverbal Communication Effectively

Work to make sure your nonverbal signals match the tone and content of your spoken communication.

Paying attention to nonverbal cues will make you both a better speaker and a better listener. When you're talking, be more conscious of the nonverbal cues you could be sending. Are they effective without being manipulative? Consider a situation in which an employee has come to you to talk about a raise. This situation is a stressful one for the employee, so don't say you're interested in what she has to tell you and then spend your time glancing at your computer or checking your watch. Conversely, if you already know you won't be able to give her the raise, be honest in your expression of emotions. Don't overcompensate for your own stress by smiling too broadly or shaking her hand too vigorously. Both nonverbal signals would raise her hopes without justification. In either case, match your nonverbal cues to the tone of the situation.

What signals does your personal appearance send?

Also consider the nonverbal signals you send when you're not talking, such as the clothes you wear, the way you sit, or the way you walk. Are you talking like a serious business professional but dressing like you belong in a dance club or a frat house? (Appropriate clothing for work situations is discussed in the next section, on business etiquette.)

CHECKLIST: Improving Nonverbal Communication Skills

- Understand the roles that nonverbal signals play in communication, complementing verbal language by strengthening, weakening, or replacing words.
- Nonverbal signals often reveal the truth, sometimes conveying more to listeners than spoken words.
- Note that facial expressions (especially eye contact) reveal the type and intensity of a speaker's feelings.
- Watch for cues from gestures and posture.
- Listen for vocal characteristics that signal who the speaker is, the speaker's relationship with the audience, and the emotions underlying the speaker's words.
- Recognize that listeners are influenced by physical appearance.
- Be careful with physical contact; touch can convey positive attributes but can also be interpreted as dominance or sexual interest.
- Pay attention to the use of time and space.

When you listen, be sure to pay attention to the speaker's nonverbal cues. Do they amplify the spoken words or contradict them? Is the speaker intentionally using nonverbal signals to send you a message that he or she can't put into words? Be observant but don't assume that you can "read someone like a book." Nonverbal signals are powerful, but they aren't infallible. Contrary to popular belief, for instance, just because someone doesn't look you squarely in the eye doesn't mean he or she is lying.[61] If something doesn't feel right, ask the speaker an honest and respectful question; doing so may clear everything up, or it may uncover issues you need to explore further. See "Checklist: Improving Nonverbal Communication Skills" for a summary of key ideas regarding nonverbal skills.

DEVELOPING YOUR BUSINESS ETIQUETTE

6 LEARNING OBJECTIVE

Discuss the importance of business etiquette.

You may have noticed a common thread running through the topics of successful teamwork, productive meetings, effective listening, and nonverbal communication: All these activities depend on mutual respect and consideration among all participants. As Chapter 1 notes, etiquette is now considered an essential business skill. Nobody wants to work with someone who is rude to colleagues or an embarrassment to the company. Moreover, shabby treatment of others in the workplace can be a huge drain on morale and productivity.[62] Poor etiquette can drive away customers, investors, and other critical audiences—and it can limit your career potential. This section addresses some key etiquette points to remember when you're in the workplace, out in public, and online.

Business Etiquette in the Workplace

Personal appearance can have considerable impact on your success in business.

Workplace etiquette includes a variety of behaviors, habits, and aspects of nonverbal communication. Although it isn't always thought of an as element of etiquette, your personal appearance in the workplace sends a strong signal to managers, colleagues, and customers. Pay attention to the style of dress where you work and adjust your style to match. Observe others and don't be afraid to ask for advice. If you're not sure, dress modestly and simply—earn a reputation for what you can *do*, not for what you can wear. Table 2.4 offers

TABLE 2.4 Assembling a Business Wardrobe

1 SMOOTH AND FINISHED (START WITH THIS)	2 ELEGANT AND REFINED (TO COLUMN 1, ADD THIS)	3 CRISP AND STARCHY (TO COLUMN 2, ADD THIS)	4 UP-TO-THE-MINUTE TRENDY (TO COLUMN 3, ADD THIS)
1. Choose well-tailored clothing that fits well; it doesn't have to be expensive, but it does have to fit and be appropriate for business. 2. Keep buttons, zippers, and hemlines in good repair. 3. Select shoes that are comfortable enough for long days but neither too casual nor too dressy for the office; keep shoes clean and in good condition. 4. Make sure the fabrics you wear are clean, are carefully pressed, and do not wrinkle easily. 5. Choose colors that flatter your height, weight, skin tone, and style; sales advisors in good clothing stores can help you choose.	1. Choose form-fitting (but not skin-tight) clothing—not swinging or flowing fabrics, frills, or fussy trimmings. 2. Choose muted tones and soft colors or classics, such as a dark blue suit or a basic black dress. 3. If possible, select a few classic pieces of jewelry (such as a string of pearls or diamond cuff links) for formal occasions. 4. Wear jackets that complement an outfit and lend an air of formality to your appearance. Avoid jackets with more than two tones; one color should dominate.	1. Wear blouses or shirts that are or appear starched. 2. Choose closed top-button shirts or button-down shirt collars, higher-neckline blouses, or long sleeves with French cuffs and cuff links. 3. Wear creased trousers or a longer skirt hemline.	1. Supplement your foundation with pieces that reflect the latest styles. 2. Add a few pieces in bold colors but wear them sparingly to avoid a garish appearance. 3. Embellish your look with the latest jewelry and hairstyles but keep the overall effect looking professional.

some general guidelines on assembling a business wardrobe that's cost-effective and flexible.

Grooming is as important as attire. Pay close attention to cleanliness and avoid using products with powerful scents, such as perfumed soaps, colognes, shampoos, and after-shave lotions (many people are bothered by these products, and some are allergic to them). Shampoo frequently, keep hands and nails neatly manicured, use mouthwash and deodorant, and make regular trips to a barber or hairstylist.[63] Some companies have specific policies regarding hairstyles, which you may be expected to follow.[64]

If you work in a conventional office setting, you'll spend as much time with your officemates as you spend with family and friends. Personal demeanor is therefore a vital element of workplace harmony. No one expects (or wants) you to be artificially upbeat and bubbly every second of the day, but a single negative personality can make an entire office miserable and unproductive. Every person in the company has a responsibility to contribute to a positive, energetic work environment.

Plan important phone calls as carefully as you plan meetings.

Given the telephone's central role in business communication, phone skills are essential in most professions. Because phone calls lack the visual richness of face-to-face conversations, you have to rely on your attitude and tone of voice to convey confidence and professionalism. Table 2.5 summarizes helpful tips for placing and receiving phone calls in a confident, professional manner.

TABLE 2.5 Quick Tips for Improving Your Phone Skills

GENERAL TIPS	PLACING CALLS	RECEIVING CALLS	USING VOICE MAIL
Use frequent verbal responses that show you're listening ("Oh yes," "I see," "That's right").	Be ready before you call so that you don't waste the other person's time.	Answer promptly and with a smile so that you sound friendly and positive.	When recording your outgoing message, make it brief and professional.
Increase your volume just slightly to convey your confidence.	Minimize distractions and avoid making noise that could annoy the other party.	Identify yourself and your company. (Some companies have specific guidelines on what to say when you answer.)	If you can, record temporary greetings on days when you are unavailable all day so that callers will know you're gone for the day.
Don't speak in a monotone; vary your pitch and inflections so people know you're interested.	Identify yourself and your organization, briefly describe why you're calling, and verify that you've called at a good time.	Establish the needs of your caller by asking, "How may I help you?" If you know the caller's name, use it.	Check your voice-mail messages regularly and return all necessary calls within 24 hours.
Slow down when conversing with people whose native language isn't the same as yours.	Don't take up too much time. Speak quickly and clearly and get right to the point of the call.	If you can, answer questions promptly and efficiently; if you can't help, tell the caller what you can do for him or her.	Leave simple, clear messages, with your name, number, purpose for calling, and times when you can be reached.
Stay focused on the call throughout; others can easily tell when you're not paying attention.	Close in a friendly, positive manner and double-check all vital information, such as meeting times and dates.	If you must forward a call or put someone on hold, explain what you are doing before you do it.	State your name and telephone number slowly so that the other person can easily write them down; repeat both if the other person doesn't know you.
		If you forward a call to someone else, try to speak with that person first to verify that he or she is available and to introduce the caller.	Be careful what you say; most voice-mail systems allow users to forward messages to anyone else in the system.
		If you take a message for someone else, be complete and accurate, including the caller's name, number, and organization.	Replay your message before leaving the system to make sure it is clear and complete.

If you're accustomed to using your mobile phone anywhere and everywhere, get ready to change your habits. Mobile phones are causing so much disruption in the workplace that some senior executives now ban their use in meetings.[65] Other companies prohibit their use throughout the entire workday. Even if mobile phones aren't banned in your office, don't let yours become a source of annoyance to your colleagues.

Business Etiquette in Social Settings

You represent your company when you're in public, so etiquette continues to be important outside the organization's walls.

From business lunches to industry conferences, you may represent your company when you're out in public. Make sure your appearance and actions are appropriate to the situation. Get to know the customs of the culture when you meet new people. For example, in North America, a firm handshake is expected when two people meet, whereas a respectful bow of the head is more appropriate in Japan. If you are expected to shake hands, be aware that the passive "dead fish" handshake creates an extremely negative impression. If you are physically able, always stand when shaking someone's hand.

When introducing yourself, include a brief description of your role in the company. When introducing two other people, speak their first and last names clearly and then try to offer some information (perhaps a shared professional interest) to help the two people ease into a conversation.[66] Generally speaking, the lower-ranking person is introduced to the senior-ranking person, without regard to gender.[67]

Business is often conducted over meals, and knowing the basics of dining etiquette will make you more effective in these situations.[68] Start by choosing foods that are easy to eat. Avoid alcoholic beverages in most instances, but if one is appropriate, save it for the end of the meal. Leave business documents under your chair until entrée plates have been removed; the business aspect of the meal doesn't usually begin until then.

Just as in the office, when you use your mobile phone in public, you send the message that people around you aren't as important as your call and that you don't respect your caller's privacy.[69] If it's not a matter of life and death, or at least an urgent request from your boss or a customer, wait until you're back in the office.

Finally, always remember that business meals are a forum for business, period. Don't get on your soapbox about politics, religion, or any other topic that's likely to stir up emotions. Don't complain about work, don't ask deeply personal questions, avoid profanity, and be careful with humor—a joke that entertains some people could easily offend others.

Business Etiquette Online

When you represent your company online, you must adhere to a high standard of etiquette and respect for others.

Electronic media seem to be a breeding ground for poor etiquette. Learn the basics of professional online behavior to avoid mistakes that could hurt your company or your career. Here are some guidelines to follow whenever you are representing your company while using electronic media:[70]

- **Avoid personal attacks.** The anonymous and instantaneous nature of online communication can cause even level-headed people to strike out in blog postings and on message threads.
- **Stay focused on the original topic.** If you want to change the subject of an e-mail exchange, a forum discussion, or a blog comment thread, start a new message.
- **Don't present opinions as facts; support facts with evidence.** This guideline applies to all communication, of course, but online venues in particular seem to tempt people into presenting their beliefs and opinions as unassailable truths.
- **Follow basic expectations of spelling, punctuation, and capitalization.** Sending acronym-filled messages that look like you're texting your high school buddies makes you look like an amateur.
- **Use virus protection and keep it up to date.** Sending or posting a file that contains a computer virus is rude.

REAL-TIME UPDATES
Learn More

Don't let etiquette blunders derail your career

Get great advice on developing professional telephone skills, making a positive impression while dining, and dressing for success in any career environment (including great tips on buying business suits). Go to **http://real-timeupdates.com/ebc** and click on "Learn More." If you are using mybcommlab, you can access Real-Time Updates within each chapter or under Student Study Tools.

Document Makeover

Improve This E-Mail Message

To practice correcting drafts of actual documents, visit the "Document Makeovers" section in mybcommlab. Refer to the User Guide for specific instructions on how to access the content for this chapter. You will find an e-mail message that contains problems and errors related to what you've learned in this chapter about communicating in teams. Use the Final Draft decision tool to create an improved version of the e-mail. Check the message for clarity, relevance of topics to meeting participants, proper approach to group collaboration, and attention to etiquette.

- **Ask if this is a good time for an IM chat.** Don't assume that just because a person is showing as "available" on your IM system that he or she wants to chat with you right this instant.
- **Watch your language and keep your emotions under control.** A moment of indiscretion could haunt you forever.
- **Avoid multitasking while using IM.** You might think you're saving time by doing a dozen things at once, but you're probably making the other person wait while you bounce back and forth between IM and your other tasks.
- **Never assume privacy.** Assume that anything you type will be stored forever, could be forwarded to other people, and might be read by your boss or the company's security staff.
- **Don't use "reply all" in e-mail unless everyone can benefit from your reply.** If one or more recipients of an e-mail message don't need the information in your reply, remove their addresses before you send.
- **Don't waste others' time with sloppy, confusing, or incomplete messages.** Doing so is disrespectful.

On the Job: Solving Communication Dilemmas at Rosen Law Firm

You recently joined Rosen Law Firm and love the spirit of camaraderie and mutual support that most employees exhibit. Of course, even in the best work environments, conflicts and misunderstandings can arise. Study these scenarios and decide how to respond.

1. You're an enthusiastic contributor to the Rosen wiki, but one particular employee keeps editing your pages on the wiki, often making changes that appear to add no value, as far as you can see. She doesn't seem to be editing other employees' pages nearly so often, so you are beginning to wonder if she has a personal grudge against you. You want to address this uncomfortable situation without dragging your boss into it. How should you handle it?
   a. Edit some of her pages needlessly to help her understand how annoying this behavior is.
   b. Approach her in person and ask her if there is something about your writing style that she finds unclear. That will open a conversation in a nonthreatening way.
   c. Post a notice on the wiki, emphasizing that all edits should be useful and unnecessary edits waste everybody's time.
   d. Ignore her behavior; confronting her will get you nowhere.

2. You've been asked to take over leadership of a group of paralegals that once had a reputation for being a tight-knit, supportive team, but you quickly figure out that this team is in danger of becoming dysfunctional. For example, minor issues that functional teams in a law office routinely handle, from helping each other with computer questions to covering the phones when someone has an outside appointment, frequently generate conflict within this group. What steps should you take to help your crew return to positive behavior?
   a. Give the team the task of healing itself, without getting directly involved. Explain the steps necessary in forming an effective team and then let them figure out how to make it happen.
   b. Lead the "team restoration" project yourself so that you can mediate whatever conflicts arise, at least until the team is able to function on its own in a more positive manner.
   c. Don't try to interfere; the negative behaviors were probably caused by an ineffective manager in the past, but now that you're in charge, the team will return to positive behavior under your enlightened guidance.
   d. Your professional reputation is on the line, so you don't have time for the niceties of team building. Sit down with the group and demand that the negative, unprofessional behavior stop immediately.

3. After a few weeks with the paralegal team, you notice that team meetings often degenerate into little more than complaint sessions. Workers seem to gripe about everything from difficult clients to the temperature in the office. Some of these complaints sound like valid business issues that might require additional training or other employee support efforts; others are superficial issues that you suspect are simply by-products of the negative atmosphere. How should you handle complaints during the meetings?

a. Try to defuse each complaint with humor; after awhile, employees will begin to lighten up and stop complaining so much.
b. Ask employees to refrain from complaining during meetings; after all, these are important business meetings, not random social gatherings.
c. Set up a whiteboard and write down each issue that is raised. After you've compiled a list over the course of a week or so, add a problem-solving segment to each meeting, in which you and the team tackle one issue per meeting to determine the scope of each problem and identify possible solutions.
d. Whenever a complaint is raised, stop the meeting and confront the person who raised the issue. Challenge him or her to prove that the problem is a real business issue and not just a personal complaint. By doing this, you will not only identify the real problems that need to be fixed but also discourage people from raising petty complaints that shouldn't be aired in the workplace.

4. You're in charge of hiring a replacement for a paralegal who recently retired. Four job candidates are waiting outside your office, and you have a few moments to observe them before inviting them in for an initial interview (you can see them through the glass wall but can't hear them). Based on the following descriptions, which of these people seems like the best fit for the firm? Why?
a. **Candidate A:** A woman who is dressed perfectly for an interview at Rosen. Her appearance is contemporary but business appropriate, which suggests that she appreciates and shows respect for the situation she finds herself in. However, you are slightly troubled by the fact that she's listening to her iPod and has kicked off her shoes and tucked her feet under her while she waits in the chair.
b. **Candidate B:** A man who has also dressed the part, although this candidate's behavior is nothing like the relaxed, carefree attitude that Candidate A is showing. He seems to be juggling multiple tasks at once: checking notes on some sort of digital device, organizing a collection of papers he pulled from his briefcase, reattaching several sticky notes that keep falling loose, and fiddling with a mobile phone that he has answered at least twice in the few minutes you've been watching.
c. **Candidate C:** A woman who closed the notebook she was scanning in order to help Candidate B with some problem he was having with his mobile phone. (If you had to guess, he was having trouble figuring out how to silence the ringer.) After their interaction, they shake hands and appear to be introducing themselves with cordial smiles. Unfortunately, although the city is suffering through record high temperatures, her casual dress and sandals strike you as too informal for a job interview at a law firm.
d. **Candidate D:** A man wearing what appears to be a finely tailored, conservative suit. His appearance is more dignified and businesslike than the other three, and he knows how to dress for success—carefully knotted tie, starched shirt, perfect posture, the works. He keeps to himself and avoids bothering the other candidates, although his facial expressions make it clear that he disapproves of the noise Candidate B is making with his mobile phone.

LEARNING OBJECTIVES CHECKUP

Assess your understanding of the principles in this chapter by reading each learning objective and studying the accompanying exercises. For fill-in-the-blank items, write the missing text in the blank provided; for multiple-choice items, circle the letter of the correct answer. You can check your responses against the answer key on page AK-1.

Objective 2.1: Highlight the advantages and disadvantages of working in teams.

1. Teams can achieve a higher level of performance than individuals alone because
a. They combine the intelligence and energy of multiple individuals
b. Motivation and creativity flourish in team settings
c. They involve more input and a greater diversity of views, which tends to result in better decisions
d. They do all of the above

2. Which of the following is a potential disadvantage of working in teams?
a. Teams always stamp out creativity by forcing people to conform to existing ideas and practices.
b. Teams increase a company's clerical workload because of the additional government paperwork required for administering workplace insurance.
c. Team members are never held accountable for their individual performance.

d. Social pressure within the group can lead to groupthink, in which people go along with a bad idea or poor decision even though they may not really believe in it.

Objective 2.2: Identify eight guidelines for successful collaborative writing.

3. Which of the following is the best way for a team of people to write a report?
   a. Each member should plan, research, and write his or her individual version and then the group can select the strongest report.
   b. The team should divide and conquer, with one person doing the planning, one doing the research, one doing the writing, and so on.
   c. To ensure a true group effort, every task from planning through final production should be done as a team, preferably with everyone in the same room at the same time.
   d. Research and plan as a group but assign the actual writing to one person, or at least assign separate sections to individual writers and have one person edit them all to achieve a consistent style.

4. Which of the following steps should be completed before anyone from the team does any planning, researching, or writing?
   a. The team should agree on the project's goals.
   b. The team should agree on the report's title.
   c. To avoid compatibility problems, the team should agree on which word processor or other software will be used.
   d. The team should always step away from the work environment and enjoy some social time in order to bond effectively before starting work.

Objective 2.3: Explain how to make meetings more productive, and describe the emerging role of social networking technologies in business communication.

5. What are the three key steps to making sure meetings are productive?
   a. Planning, planning, and more planning
   b. Preparing carefully, conducting meetings efficiently, and using meeting technologies wisely
   c. Preparing carefully, conducting meetings using true democratic participation, and using meeting technologies wisely
   d. Preparing carefully, using meeting technologies wisely, and distributing in-depth minutes to everyone in the company

6. Which of the following is not a benefit of using social media for business communication?
   a. Social media are "out in the open," so messages are easier for managers to monitor and control.
   b. Social media help erase geographic and organization boundaries.
   c. Social media give customers an easy way to voice their opinions and concerns.
   d. Social media can help "faceless" companies adopt a more human, conversational tone.

Objective 2.4: Describe the listening process, and explain how good listeners overcome barriers at each stage of the process.

7. After receiving messages, listeners _______ what they've heard by assigning meaning to the sounds.

8. If you're giving an important presentation and notice that many of the audience members look away when you try to make momentary eye contact, which of the following is most likely going on?
   a. These audience members don't want to challenge your authority by making direct eye contact.
   b. You work with a lot of shy people.
   c. The information you're presenting is making your audience uncomfortable in some way.
   d. The audience is taking time to carefully think about the information you're presenting.

9. If you don't agree with something the speaker says in a large, formal meeting, the best response is to
   a. Signal your disagreement by folding your arms across your chest and staring defiantly back at the speaker
   b. Use your mobile phone to begin sending text messages to other people in the room, explaining why the speaker is wrong
   c. Immediately challenge the speaker so that the misinformation is caught and corrected
   d. Quietly make a note of your objections and wait until a question-and-answer period to raise your hand

Objective 2.5: Clarify the importance of nonverbal communication, and briefly describe six categories of nonverbal expression.

10. Nonverbal signals can be more influential than spoken language because
   a. Body language is difficult to control and therefore difficult to fake, so listeners often put more trust in nonverbal cues than in the words a speaker uses
   b. Nonverbal signals communicate faster than spoken language, and most people are impatient
   c. Body language saves listeners from the trouble of paying attention to what a speaker is saying

11. Which of the following is true about nonverbal signals?
   a. They can strengthen a spoken message.
   b. They can weaken a spoken message.
   c. They can replace spoken messages.
   d. All of the above are true.

Objective 2.6: Discuss the importance of business etiquette.

12. Which of the following is the best characterization of etiquette in today's business environment?
   a. Business etiquette is impossible to generalize because every company has its own culture; you have to make it up as you go along.
   b. With ferocious international competition and constant financial pressure, etiquette is an old-fashioned luxury that businesses simply can't afford today.
   c. Ethical businesspeople don't need to worry directly about etiquette because ethical behavior automatically leads to good etiquette.

d. Etiquette plays an important part in the process of forming and maintaining successful business relationships.

13. If you forgot to shut off your mobile phone before stepping into a business meeting and you receive a call during the meeting, the most appropriate thing to do is to
    a. Lower your voice to protect the privacy of your phone conversation
    b. Answer the phone and then quickly hang it up to minimize the disruption to the meeting
    c. Excuse yourself from the meeting and find a quiet place to talk
    d. Continue to participate in the meeting while taking the call; this shows everyone that you're an effective multitasker

14. Your company has established a designated "quiet time" from 1:00 to 3:00 every afternoon, during which office phones, IM, and e-mail are disabled so that people can concentrate on planning, researching, writing, and other intensive tasks without being interrupted. However, a number of people continue to flout the guidelines by leaving their mobile phones on, saying their families and friends need to able to reach them. With all the various ringtones going off at random, the office is just as noisy as it was before. What is the best response?
    a. Agree to reactivate the office phone system if everyone will shut off their mobile phones, but have all incoming calls routed through a receptionist who will take messages for all routine calls and deliver a note if an employee truly is needed in an emergency.
    b. Give up on quiet time; with so many electronic gadgets in the workplace today, you'll never achieve peace and quiet.
    c. Get tough on the offenders by confiscating mobile phones whenever they ring during quiet time.
    d. Without telling anyone, simply install one of the available mobile phone jamming products that block incoming and outgoing mobile phone calls.

15. Constantly testing the limits of your company's dress and grooming standards sends a strong signal that you
    a. Don't understand or don't respect your company's culture
    b. Are a strong advocate for worker's rights
    c. Are a creative and independent thinker who is likely to generate lots of successful business ideas
    d. Represent the leading edge of a new generation of enlightened workers who will redefine the workplace according to contemporary standards

PEARSON mybcommlab™

Log on to www.mybcommlab.com to access the following study and assessment aids associated with this chapter:

- Video applications
- Real-Time Updates
- Peer review activity
- Quick Learning Guides
- Pre/post test
- Personalized study plan
- Model documents
- Sample presentations

If you are not using mybcommlab, you can access Real-Time Updates and Quick Learning Guides through http://real-timeupdates.com/ebc. The Quick Learning Guide (located under "Learn More" on the website) hits all the high points of this chapter in just two pages. This guide, especially prepared by the authors, will help you study for exams or review important concepts whenever you need a quick refresher.

Apply Your Knowledge

1. How can nonverbal communication help you run a meeting? How can it help you call a meeting to order, emphasize important topics, show approval, express reservations, regulate the flow of conversation, and invite a colleague to continue with a comment?
2. Whenever your boss asks for feedback during department meetings, she blasts anyone who offers criticism, which causes people to agree with everything she says. You want to talk to her about it, but what should you say? List some of the points you want to make when you discuss this issue with your boss.
3. Is conflict in a team good or bad? Explain your answer.
4. You and another manager in your company disagree about whether employees should be encouraged to create online profiles on LinkedIn and other business-oriented social networking websites. You say these connections can be valuable to employees by helping them meet their peers throughout the industry and valuable to the company by identifying potential sales leads and business partners. The other manager says that encouraging employees to become better known in the industry will only make it easier for competitors to lure them away with enticing job offers. Write a brief e-mail message that outlines your argument. (Make up any information you need about the company and its industry.)

5. **Ethical Choices** Strange instant messages occasionally pop up on your computer screen during your team's virtual meetings, followed quickly by embarrassed apologies from one of your colleagues in another city. You eventually figure out that this person is working from home, even though he says he's in the office; moreover, the messages suggest that he's running a sideline business from his home. You're concerned about the frequent disruptions, not to mention your colleague's potential ethical violations. What should you do? Explain your choice.

Practice Your Knowledge

Message for Analysis

A project leader has made notes about covering the following items at the quarterly budget meeting. Prepare a formal agenda by putting these items into a logical order and rewriting, where necessary, to give phrases a more consistent sound.

- Budget Committee Meeting to be held on December 12, 2010, at 9:30 a.m.
- I will call the meeting to order.
- Real estate director's report: A closer look at cost overruns on Greentree site.
- The group will review and approve the minutes from last quarter's meeting.
- I will ask the finance director to report on actual versus projected quarterly revenues and expenses.
- I will distribute copies of the overall divisional budget and announce the date of the next budget meeting.
- Discussion: How can we do a better job of anticipating and preventing cost overruns?
- Meeting will take place in Conference Room 3, with WebEx active for remote employees.
- What additional budget issues must be considered during this quarter?

Exercises

Active links for all websites in this chapter can be found on mybcommlab; see your User Guide for instructions on accessing the content for this chapter.

2.1 **Teamwork** With a classmate, attend a local community or campus meeting where you can observe a group discussion, vote, or take other group action. During the meeting, take notes individually and, afterward, work together to answer the following questions.

   a. What is your evaluation of this meeting? In your answer, consider (1) the leader's ability to articulate the meeting's goals clearly, (2) the leader's ability to engage members in a meaningful discussion, (3) the group's dynamics, and (4) the group's listening skills.
   b. How did group members make decisions? Did they vote? Did they reach decisions by consensus? Did those with dissenting opinions get an opportunity to voice their objections?
   c. How well did the individual participants listen? How could you tell?
   d. Did any participants change their expressed views or their votes during the meeting? Why might that have happened?
   e. Did you observe any of the communication barriers discussed in Chapter 1? Identify them.
   f. Compare the notes you took during the meeting with those of your classmate. What differences do you notice? How do you account for these differences?

2.2 **Team Communication: Overcoming Barriers** Every month, each employee in your department is expected to give a brief oral presentation on the status of his or her project. However, your department has recently hired an employee who has a severe speech impediment that prevents people from understanding most of what he has to say. As department manager, how will you resolve this dilemma? Please explain.

2.3 **Team Development: Resolving Conflict** Describe a recent conflict you had with a team member at work or at school and explain how you resolved it. Did you find a solution that was acceptable to both of you and to the team?

2.4 **Ethical Choices** During team meetings, one member constantly calls for votes or decisions before all the members have voiced their views. As the leader, you asked this member privately about his behavior. He replied that he was trying to move the team toward its goals, but you are concerned that he is really trying to take control. How can you deal with this situation without removing the member from the group?

2.5 **Online Communication: Staying on Track with Blog Replies** As the leader of a product development team, you write a daily blog to inform team members of questions, concerns, and other developments related to your project. Team members are always encouraged to reply to your online posts, but lately a number of people have been wandering off track with their replies, raising new issues in the middle of a discussion thread, or posting on matters unrelated to the item to which they're replying. The blog is becoming less useful for everyone because individual message threads no longer stick to a single topic. Write a brief blog posting, three or four sentences at most, courteously reminding readers why it's important to stick to the subject at hand when replying to blog items.

2.6 **Internet** Visit the PolyVision website, at www.websterboards.com, and read about electronic whiteboards. What advantages do you see in using this kind of whiteboard during a meeting? Draft a short e-mail message to your boss, outlining the product's advantages.

2.7 **Telephones and Voice Mail** Late on a Friday afternoon, you learn that the facilities department is going to move you—and your computer, your desk, and all your files—to another office first thing Monday morning. However, you have an important client meeting scheduled in your office for Monday afternoon, and you need to finalize some contract details on Monday morning. You simply can't lose access to your office at this point, and you're more than a little annoyed that your boss didn't ask you before approving the move. He has already left for the day, but you know he usually checks his voice mail over the weekend, so you decide to leave a message, asking him to cancel the move or at least call you at home as soon as possible. Using the voice-mail guidelines listed in Table 2.5, plan your message (use an imaginary phone number as your contact number and make up any other details you need for the call). As directed by your instructor, submit either a written script of the message or a podcast recording of the actual message.

2.8 **Nonverbal Communication: Analyzing Written Messages** Select a business letter and envelope that you have received at work or home. Analyze their appearance. What nonverbal messages do they send? Are these messages consistent with the content of the letter? If not, what could the sender have done to make the nonverbal communication consistent with the verbal communication?

2.9 **Nonverbal Communication: Analyzing Body Language** Describe what the following body movements suggest when someone exhibits them during a conversation. How do such movements influence your interpretation of spoken words?
   a. Shifting one's body continuously while seated
   b. Twirling and playing with one's hair
   c. Sitting in a sprawled position
   d. Rolling one's eyes
   e. Extending a weak handshake

2.10 **Etiquette: Coaching New Hires** As the local manager of an international accounting firm, you place high priority on professional etiquette. Not only does it communicate respect to your clients, but it also instills confidence in your firm by showing that you and your staff are aware of and able to meet the expectations of almost any audience. Earlier today, you took four recently hired college graduates to lunch with an important client. You've done this for years, and it's usually an upbeat experience for everyone, but today's lunch was a disaster. One of the new employees made not one, not two, but *three* calls on his mobile phone during lunch. Another interrupted the client several times and even got into a mild argument. The third employee kept making sarcastic jokes about politics, making everyone at the table uncomfortable. And the fourth showed up dressed like she was expecting to bale hay or work in coal mine, not have a business lunch in a posh restaurant. You've already called the client to apologize, but now you need to coach these employees on proper business etiquette. Draft a brief memo to these employees, explaining why etiquette is so important to the company's success—and to their individual careers.

2.11 **Listening Skills: Self-Assessment** How good are your listening skills? Use the following chart to rate yourself on each element of listening. Then examine your ratings to identify where you are strongest and where you can improve, using the tips in this chapter.

ELEMENT OF LISTENING	ALWAYS	FREQUENTLY	OCCASIONALLY	NEVER
1. I look for areas of interest when people speak.	____	____	____	____
2. I focus on content rather than delivery.	____	____	____	____
3. I wait to respond until I understand the content.	____	____	____	____
4. I listen for ideas and themes, not isolated facts.	____	____	____	____
5. I take careful notes to make sure I understand and analyze the message correctly.	____	____	____	____
6. I really concentrate on what speakers are saying.	____	____	____	____
7. I stay focused even when the ideas are complex.	____	____	____	____
8. I keep an open mind despite emotionally charged language.	____	____	____	____

Expand Your Knowledge

Learning More on the Web

Make Your Meetings More Productive

www.effectivemeetings.com

From preparing effective agendas to dealing with "meeting addicts," the Effective Meetings website offers advice to make business meetings more productive. Peruse the list of articles and answer the following questions.

1. What are four questions to ask to determine whether a meeting is necessary? (Look under Meeting Basics.)
2. What steps can you take to make sure meetings start and end on schedule? (Look under Meeting Planning.)
3. How can a "scrum meeting" help a team stay on target toward meeting its goals? (Look under Teams.)

Sharpening Your Career Skills Online

Bovée and Thill's Business Communication Web Search, at **http://businesscommunicationblog.com/websearch**, is a unique research tool designed specifically for business communication research. Use the Web Search function to find an online video, a podcast, or a PowerPoint presentation that offers advice on improving your active listening skills in business situations. Write a brief e-mail message to your instructor, describing the item that you found and summarizing the career skills information you learned from it.

Improve Your Grammar, Mechanics, and Usage

The following exercises help you improve your knowledge of and power over English grammar, mechanics, and usage. Turn to the Handbook of Grammar, Mechanics, and Usage at the end of this book and review all of Section 1.2 (Pronouns). Then look at the following 10 items. Underline the preferred choice within each set of parentheses. (Answers to these exercises appear on page AK-3.)

1. The sales staff is preparing guidelines for (*their, its*) clients.
2. Few of the sales representatives turn in (*their, its*) reports on time.
3. The board of directors has chosen (*their, its*) officers.
4. Gomez and Archer have told (*his, their*) clients about the new program.
5. Each manager plans to expand (*his, their, his or her*) sphere of control next year.
6. Has everyone supplied (*his, their, his or her*) Social Security number?
7. After giving every employee (*his, their, a*) raise, George told (*them, they, all*) about the increased work load.
8. Bob and Tim have opposite ideas about how to achieve company goals. (*Who, Whom*) do you think will win the debate?
9. City Securities has just announced (*who, whom*) it will hire as CEO.
10. Either of the new products would readily find (*their, its*) niche in the marketplace.

For additional exercises focusing on pronouns, visit mybcommlab. Click on Chapter 2, click on "Additional Exercises to Improve Your Grammar, Mechanics, and Usage," and then click on "3. Case of pronouns" or "4. Possessive pronouns."

Communicating in a World of Diversity

3

Learning Objectives

After studying this chapter, you will be able to

1 Discuss the opportunities and challenges of intercultural communication

2 Define *culture*, and explain how culture is learned

3 Define *ethnocentrism* and *stereotyping*, and give three suggestions for overcoming these limiting mindsets

4 Explain the importance of recognizing cultural variations, and list eight categories of cultural differences

5 Identify steps you can take to improve your intercultural communication skills

6 List seven recommendations for writing clearly in multilanguage business environments

On the Job: Solving Communication Dilemmas at IBM

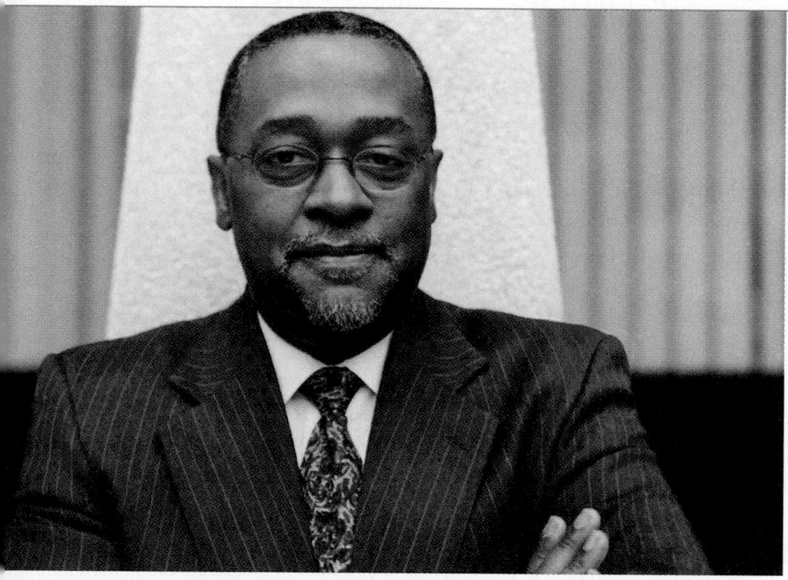

Ron Glover oversees IBM's efforts to build competitive advantage by capitalizing on the benefits of a diverse workforce.

Building Competitive Advantage by Embracing Diversity

The *I* in IBM stands for *International*, but it could just as easily stand for *Intercultural*, as a testament to the computer giant's long-standing commitment to embracing diversity. Ron Glover, IBM's vice president of global workforce diversity, knows from years of experience that communicating successfully across cultures is no simple task, however—particularly in a company that employs more than 350,000 people and sells to customers in roughly 175 countries around the world.

Language presents a formidable barrier to communication when you consider that IBM's employees speak more than 165 languages. But language is just one of many elements that play a role in communication between cultures. Differences in age, ethnic background, gender, sexual orientation, physical ability, and economic status can all affect the communication process. Glover emphasizes that "to operate successfully, we must be especially mindful of how we respect and value differences among people in countries and regions." He recognizes that these differences represent both a challenge and an opportunity, and a key part of his job is helping IBM executives and employees work together in a way that transforms their cultural differences into a critical business strength. Diversity, he explains, is "an essential aspect of IBM's broader business strategy."

Throughout its long history of employing and working with people from a variety of cultures, IBM has learned some powerful lessons. Perhaps the most significant is its conclusion that successfully managing a diverse workforce and competing in a diverse marketplace start with embracing those differences, not trying to ignore them or pretending they don't affect interpersonal communication. Take Ron Glover's advice when he says that even if your company never does business outside the United States, "you will need to effectively engage differences to remain viable in the economy of the future."[1]

www.ibm.com

UNDERSTANDING THE OPPORTUNITIES AND CHALLENGES OF COMMUNICATION IN A DIVERSE WORLD

IBM's experience (profiled in the chapter-opening "On the Job" vignette) illustrates both the challenges and the opportunities for business professionals who know how to communicate with diverse audiences. Although the concept is often framed in terms of ethnic background, a broader and more useful definition of **diversity** "includes all the characteristics and experiences that define each of us as individuals."[2] As you'll learn in this chapter, these characteristics and experiences can have a profound effect on the way businesspeople communicate.

Diversity includes all the characteristics that define people as individuals.

Intercultural communication is the process of sending and receiving messages between people whose cultural backgrounds could lead them to interpret verbal and nonverbal signs differently. Every attempt to send and receive messages is influenced by culture, so to communicate successfully, you need a basic grasp of the cultural differences you may encounter and how you should handle them. Your efforts to recognize and bridge cultural differences will open up business opportunities throughout the world and maximize the contributions of all the employees in a diverse workforce.

1 LEARNING OBJECTIVE

Discuss the opportunities and challenges of intercultural communication.

The Opportunities in a Global Marketplace

Chances are good that you'll be looking across international borders sometime in your career. Thanks to communication and transportation technologies, natural boundaries and national borders are no longer the impassable barriers they once were. Local markets are opening to worldwide competition as businesses of all sizes look for new growth opportunities outside their own countries. Thousands of U.S. businesses depend on exports for significant portions of their revenues. Every year, these companies export hundreds of billions of dollars worth of materials and merchandise, along with billions more in personal and professional services. If you work in one of these companies, you may well be called on to visit or at least communicate with a wide variety of people who speak languages other than English and who live in cultures quite different from what you're used to (see Figure 3.1). Of the top ten export markets for U.S. products, only two, Canada and Great Britain, speak English as an official language—and Canada also has French as an official language.[3]

You will communicate with people from other cultures throughout your career.

The Advantages of a Diverse Workforce

Even if you never visit another country or transact business on a global scale, you will interact with colleagues from a variety of cultures, with a wide range of characteristics and life experiences. Over the past few decades, many innovative companies have changed the way they approach diversity, from seeing it as a legal requirement (providing equal opportunities for all) to seeing it as a strategic opportunity to connect with customers and take advantage of the broadest possible pool of talent.[4] Smart business leaders such as IBM's Ron Glover recognize the competitive advantages of a diverse workforce that offers a broader spectrum of viewpoints and ideas, helps companies understand and identify with diverse markets, and enables companies to benefit from a wider range of employee talents. According to Glover, more diverse teams tend to be more innovative over the long term than more homogeneous teams.[5]

The diversity of today's workforce brings distinct advantages to businesses:

- *A broader range of views and ideas*
- *A better understanding of diverse, fragmented markets*
- *A broader pool of talent from which to recruit*

FIGURE 3.1 Languages of the World
This map illustrates the incredible array of languages used around the world. Each dot represents the geographic center of one of the more than 6,900 languages tracked by the linguistic research firm SIL International. Even if all your business communication takes place in English, you will interact with audience members who speak a variety of other native languages.

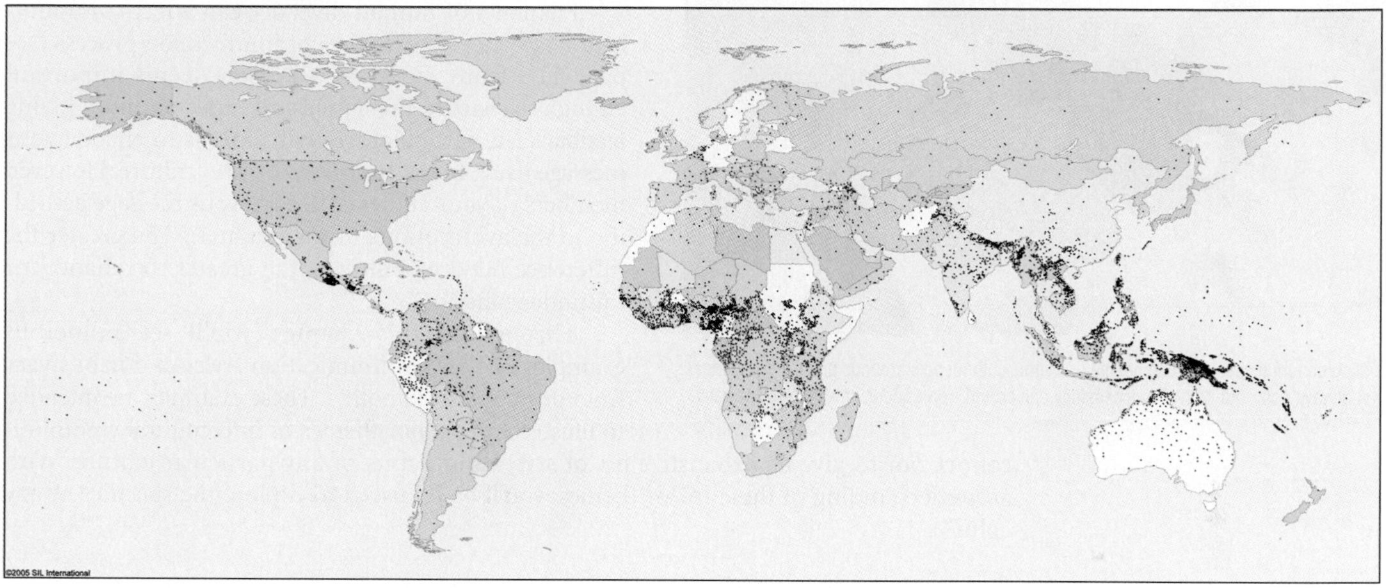

Diversity is simply a fact of life for all companies. The United States has been a nation of immigrants from the beginning, and that trend continues today. The western and northern Europeans who made up the bulk of immigrants during the nation's early years now share space with people from across Asia, Africa, eastern Europe, and Central and South America. Even the term *minority*, as it applies to nonwhite residents, makes less and less sense every year: In two states (California and New Mexico), in several dozen large cities, and in several hundred counties across the United States, Caucasian Americans make up less than half the population.[6] This pattern of immigration isn't unique to the United States. For example, workers from Africa, Asia, and the Middle East are moving to Europe in search of new opportunities, while workers from India, the Philippines, and Southeast Asia contribute to the employment base of the Middle East.[7]

However, you and your colleagues don't need to be recent immigrants to constitute a diverse workforce. Differences in everything from age and gender to religion and ethnic heritage to geography and military experience enrich the workplace. Both immigration and workforce diversity create advantages—and challenges—for business communicators throughout the world.

The Challenges of Intercultural Communication

A company's cultural diversity affects how its business messages are conceived, composed, delivered, received, and interpreted.

Culture influences everything about communication, including:
- *Language*
- *Nonverbal signals*
- *Word meaning*
- *Time and space issues*
- *Rules of human relationships*

Today's increasingly diverse workforce encompasses a wide range of skills, traditions, backgrounds, experiences, outlooks, and attitudes toward work—all of which can affect communication in the workplace. Supervisors face the challenges of connecting with these diverse employees, motivating them, and fostering cooperation and harmony among them. Teams face the challenge of working together closely, and companies are challenged to coexist peacefully with business partners and with the community as a whole.

The interaction of culture and communication is so pervasive that separating the two is virtually impossible. The way you communicate is deeply influenced by the culture in which you were raised. The meaning of words, the significance of gestures, the importance of time and space, the rules of human relationships, and many other aspects of

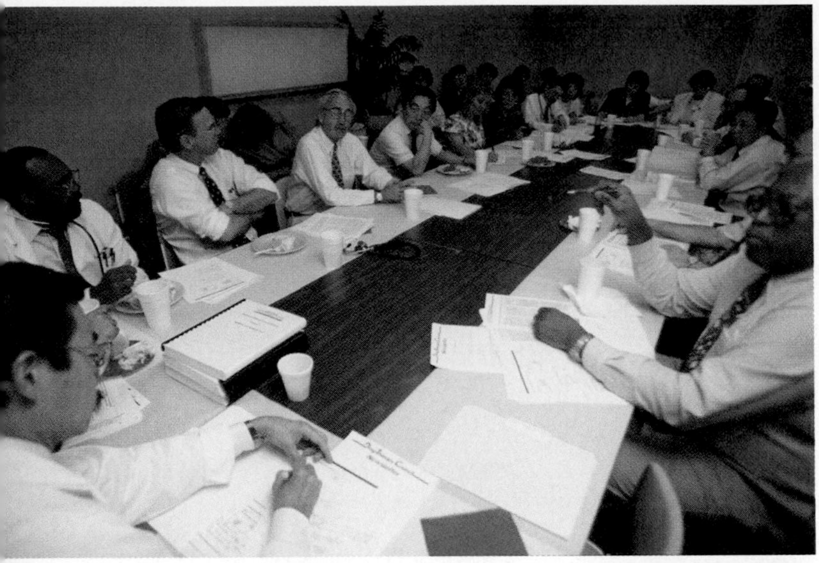

Handling communication among people of diverse cultural backgrounds and life experiences is not always easy, but doing it successfully can create tremendous strategic advantages.

communication are defined by culture. To a large degree, your culture influences the way you think, which naturally affects the way you communicate as both a sender and a receiver.[8] Intercultural communication is much more complicated than simply matching language between sender and receiver—it goes beyond mere words to beliefs, values, and emotions.

Elements of human diversity can affect communication at every stage of the communication process (see page 11), from the ideas a person deems important enough to share to the habits and expectations of giving feedback. In particular, your instinct is to encode your message using the assumptions of *your* culture. However, members of your audience decode your message according to the assumptions of *their* culture. The greater the difference between cultures, the greater the chance for misunderstanding.[9]

Throughout this chapter, you'll see numerous examples of how communication styles and habits vary from one culture to another. These examples are intended to illustrate the major themes of intercultural communication, not to give an exhaustive list of styles and habits of any particular culture. With an understanding of these major themes, you'll be prepared to explore the specifics of any culture.

ENHANCING YOUR SENSITIVITY TO CULTURE AND DIVERSITY

The good news is that you're already an expert in culture, at least in the culture in which you grew up. You understand how your society works, how people are expected to communicate, what common gestures and facial expressions mean, and so on. The bad news is that because you're such an expert in your own culture, your communication is largely automatic; that is, you rarely stop to think about the communication rules you're following. An important step toward successful intercultural communication is becoming more aware of these rules and of the way they influence your communication.

Understanding the Concept of Culture

2 LEARNING OBJECTIVE

Define *culture*, and explain how culture is learned.

Culture is a shared system of symbols, beliefs, attitudes, values, expectations, and behavior norms.

Culture is a shared system of symbols, beliefs, attitudes, values, expectations, and norms for behavior. Your cultural background influences the way you prioritize what is important in life, helps define your attitude toward what is appropriate in a situation, and establishes rules of behavior.[10]

You belong to several cultures, each of which affects the way you communicate.

Actually, you belong to several cultures. In addition to the culture you share with all the people who live in your own country, you belong to other cultural groups, including an ethnic group, possibly a religious group, and perhaps a profession that has its own special language and customs. With its large population and long history of immigration, the United States is home to a vast array of cultures. As one indication of this diversity, the inhabitants of this country now speak more than 160 languages.[11] In contrast, Japan is much more homogeneous, having only a few distinct cultural groups.[12]

Members of a given culture tend to have similar assumptions about how people should think, behave, and communicate, and they all tend to act on those assumptions in much the same way. Cultures can differ widely and vary in their rate of change, their degree of complexity, and their tolerance toward outsiders. These differences affect the level of trust and openness that you can achieve when communicating with people of other cultures.

You learn culture both directly (by being instructed) and indirectly (by observing others).

People learn culture directly and indirectly from other members of their group. As you grow up in a culture, you are taught by the group's members who you are and how best to function in that culture. Sometimes you are explicitly told which behaviors are acceptable; at other times, you learn by observing which values work best in a particular group. In these ways, culture is passed on from person to person and from generation to generation.[13]

In addition to being automatic, culture tends to be *coherent*; that is, a culture appears to be fairly logical and consistent when viewed from the inside. Certain norms within a culture may not make sense to someone outside the culture, but they probably make sense to those inside. Such coherence generally helps a culture function more smoothly internally, but it can create disharmony between cultures that don't view the world in the same way.

Cultures tend to offer views of life that are both coherent (internally logical) and complete (answering all of life's big questions).

Finally, cultures tend to be *complete*; that is, they provide most of their members with most of the answers to life's big questions. This idea of completeness dulls or even suppresses curiosity about life in other cultures. Not surprisingly, such completeness can complicate communication with other cultures.[14]

Overcoming Ethnocentrism and Stereotyping

3 LEARNING OBJECTIVE

Define *ethnocentrism* and *stereotyping*, and give three suggestions for overcoming these limiting mindsets.

Ethnocentrism is the tendency to judge other groups according to the standards, behaviors, and customs of one's own group. Given the automatic influence of one's own culture, when people compare their culture to others, they often conclude that their own group is superior.[15] An even more extreme reaction is **xenophobia**, a fear of strangers and foreigners. Clearly, businesspeople who take these views are not likely to communicate successfully across cultures.

Distorted views of other cultures or groups also result from **stereotyping**, assigning a wide range of generalized attributes to an individual on the basis of membership in a particular culture or social group. For instance, assuming that an older colleague will be out of touch with the youth market or that a younger colleague can't be an inspiring leader are examples of stereotyping age groups.

Ethnocentrism is the tendency to judge other groups according to the standards, behaviors, and customs of one's own group.

Stereotyping is assigning generalized attributes to an individual on the basis of membership in a particular group.

Cultural pluralism is the acceptance of multiple cultures on their own terms.

You can avoid ethnocentrism and stereotyping by avoiding assumptions and judgments and by acknowledging differences.

Those who want to show respect for other people and to communicate effectively in business need to adopt a more positive viewpoint, in the form of **cultural pluralism**—the practice of accepting multiple cultures on their own terms. When crossing cultural boundaries, you'll be even more effective if you move beyond simple acceptance and adapt your communication style to that of the new cultures you encounter—even integrating aspects of those cultures into your own.[16] A few simple habits can help:

- **Avoiding assumptions.** Don't assume that others will act the same way you do, use language and symbols the same way you do, or even operate from the same values and beliefs. For instance, in a comparison of the 10 most important values in three cultures, people from the United States had *no* values in common with people from Japanese or Arab cultures.[17]
- **Avoiding judgments.** When people act differently, don't conclude that they are in error or that their way is invalid or inferior.
- **Acknowledging distinctions.** Don't ignore the differences between another person's culture and your own.

Unfortunately, overcoming ethnocentrism and stereotyping is not a simple task, even for people who are highly motivated to do so. Moreover, research suggests that people often have beliefs and biases that they're not even aware of—and that may even conflict with the beliefs they *think* they have. (To see if you have some of these *implicit beliefs*, visit the Project Implicit website, at **https://implicit.harvard.edu/implicit**, and take some of the simple online tests.)[18]

Recognizing Variations in a Diverse World

4 LEARNING OBJECTIVE

Explain the importance of recognizing cultural variations, and list eight categories of cultural differences.

You can begin to learn how people in other cultures want to be treated by recognizing and accommodating eight main types of cultural differences: contextual, legal and ethical, social, nonverbal, age, gender, religious, and ability.

Communicating Across Cultures

Test Your Intercultural Knowledge

Even well-intentioned businesspeople can make mistakes if they aren't aware of simple but important cultural differences. Can you spot the erroneous assumptions in these scenarios?

1. You're tired of the discussion, and you want to move on to a new topic. You ask your Australian business associate, "Can we table this for a while?" To your dismay, your colleague ignores the request and keeps right on discussing the topic.
2. You finally made the long trip overseas to meet the new director of your German division. Despite slow traffic, you arrive only four minutes late. His door is shut, so you knock on it and walk in. The chair is too far away from the desk, so you pick it up and move it closer. Then you lean over the desk, stick out your hand, and say, "Good morning, Hans. It's nice to meet you." Why is his reaction so chilly?
3. Your meeting went better than you'd ever expected. In fact, you found the Japanese representative for your new advertising agency to be very agreeable; she said yes to just about everything. When you share your enthusiasm with your boss, he doesn't appear very excited. Why?

Here's what went wrong in each situation:

1. To "table" something in Australia means to bring it forward for discussion, the opposite of the usual U.S. meaning.
2. You've just broken four rules of German polite behavior: punctuality, privacy, personal space, and proper greetings. In time-conscious Germany, guests should never arrive even a few minutes late. Also, Germans like their privacy and space, and many adhere to formal greetings of "Frau" and "Herr," even if the business association has lasted for years.
3. The word *yes* may not always mean "yes" in the Western sense. Japanese people may say *yes* to confirm that they have heard or understood something but not necessarily to indicate that they agree with it. You'll seldom get a direct *no*. Some of the ways that Japanese people say no indirectly include "It will be difficult," "I will ask my supervisor," "I'm not sure," "We will think about it," and "I see."

CAREER APPLICATIONS

1. Have you ever been on the receiving end of an intercultural communication error, such as when someone inadvertently used an inappropriate gesture or figure of speech? How did you respond?
2. After arriving late at the office of the German colleague, what would have been a better way to handle the situation?

Contextual Differences

Cultural context is a pattern of physical cues, environmental stimuli, and implicit understanding that conveys meaning between members of the same culture.

High-context cultures rely heavily on nonverbal actions and environmental setting to convey meaning; low-context cultures rely more on explicit verbal communication.

Low-context cultures tend to value written agreements and interpret laws strictly, whereas high-context cultures view adherence to laws as being more flexible.

Every attempt at communication occurs within a **cultural context**, the pattern of physical cues, environmental stimuli, and implicit understanding that convey meaning between two members of the same culture. However, cultures around the world vary widely in the role that context plays in communication (see Figure 3.2).

In a **high-context culture**, people rely less on verbal communication and more on the context of nonverbal actions and environmental setting to convey meaning. For instance, a Chinese speaker expects the receiver to discover the essence of a message and uses indirectness and metaphor to provide a web of meaning.[19] In high-context cultures, the rules of everyday life are rarely explicit; instead, as individuals grow up, they learn how to recognize situational cues (such as gestures and tone of voice) and how to respond as expected.[20] The primary role of communication is building relationships, not exchanging information.[21]

In a **low-context culture**, people rely more on verbal communication and less on circumstances and cues to convey meaning. In such cultures, rules and expectations are usually spelled out through explicit statements such as, "Please wait until I'm finished" or "You're welcome to browse."[22] The primary task of communication in low-context cultures is exchanging information.[23]

Contextual differences are apparent in the way people approach situations such as decision making, problem solving, and negotiating. For instance, in low-context cultures, businesspeople tend to focus on the results of the decisions they face, a reflection of the cultural emphasis on logic and progress (for example, "Will this be good for our company? For my career?"). In comparison, higher-context cultures emphasize the means or the method by which a decision will be made. Building or protecting relationships can be as important as the facts and information used in making the decisions.[24] Consequently, negotiators working on business deals in such cultures may spend most of their time together building relationships rather than hammering out contractual details.

FIGURE 3.2 How Cultural Context Affects Business
Cultural context influences the nature of business communication in many ways. Note that these are generalized assessments of each culture; contextual variations can be found within each culture and from one individual to another.

IN LOW-CONTEXT CULTURES	IN HIGH-CONTEXT CULTURES
Executive offices are separate with controlled access.	Executive offices are shared and open to all.
Workers rely on detailed background information.	Workers do not expect or want detailed information.
Information is highly centralized and controlled.	Information is shared with everyone.
Objective data are valued over subjective relationships.	Subjective relationships are valued over objective data.
Business and social relationships are discrete.	Business and social relationships overlap.
Competence is valued as much as position and status.	Position and status are valued much more than competence.
Meetings have fixed agendas and plenty of advance notice.	Meetings are often called on short notice, and key people always accept.

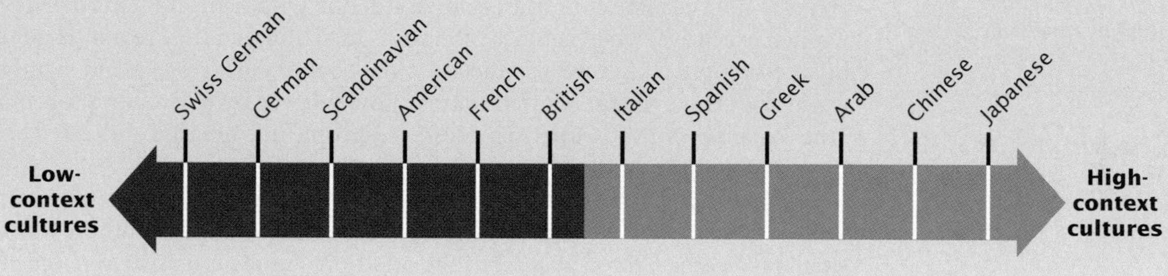

The distinctions between high and low context are generalizations, of course, but they are important to keep in mind as guidelines. Communication tactics that work well in a high-context culture may backfire in a low-context culture and vice versa.

Legal and Ethical Differences

Cultural context influences legal and ethical behavior, which in turn can affect communication. For example, because low-context cultures value the written word, they consider written agreements binding. But high-context cultures put less emphasis on the written word and consider personal pledges more important than contracts. They also tend to take a more flexible approach regarding adherence to the law, whereas low-context cultures adhere to the law strictly.[25]

As you conduct business around the world, you'll find that both legal systems and ethical standards differ from culture to culture. Making ethical choices across cultures can seem complicated, but you can keep your messages ethical by applying four basic principles:[26]

Honesty and respect are cornerstones of ethical communication, regardless of culture.

- **Seek mutual ground.** To allow the clearest possible exchange of information, both parties must be flexible and avoid insisting that an interaction take place strictly in terms of one culture or another.
- **Send and receive messages without judgment.** To allow information to flow freely, both parties must recognize that values vary from culture to culture, and they must trust each other.
- **Send messages that are honest.** To ensure that information is true, both parties must see things as they are—not as they would like them to be. Both parties must be fully aware of their personal and cultural biases.
- **Show respect for cultural differences.** To protect the basic human rights of both parties, each must understand and acknowledge the other's needs and preserve each other's dignity by communicating without deception.

REAL-TIME UPDATES
Learn More

Video guide puts culture in context

Enjoy a pictorial tour of cultures around the world as you learn more about communication across the spectrum of cultural context. Go to **http://real-timeupdates.com/ebc** and click on "Learn More." If you are using mybcommlab, you can access Real-Time Updates within each chapter or under Student Study Tools.

Social Differences

The nature of social behavior varies among cultures, sometimes dramatically. Walmart learned this lesson the hard way when the giant retailer tried to expand into Germany. Store clerks resisted the company requirement of always smiling at customers—a cornerstone of customer relationship strategies in the United States—because customers sometimes misinterpreted smiling as flirting. Walmart dropped the requirement but, after a number of other cultural and strategic missteps, eventually left the German market.[27]

Formal rules of etiquette are explicit and well defined, but informal rules are learned through observation and imitation.

Some behavioral rules are formal and specifically articulated (table manners are a good example), and others are informal and learned over time (such as the comfortable distance to stand from a colleague during a discussion). In addition to the factors already discussed, social norms can vary from culture to culture in the following areas:

- **Attitudes toward work and success.** Many U.S. citizens hold the view that material comfort earned by individual effort is a sign of superiority and that people who work hard are better than those who don't.

Respect and rank are reflected differently from culture to culture in the way people are addressed and in their working environment.

- **Roles and status.** Culture dictates, or at least tries to dictate, the roles that people play, including who communicates with whom, what they communicate, and in what way. For example, in some countries, women still don't play a prominent role in business, so women executives who visit these countries may find that they're not taken seriously as businesspeople.[28] Culture also dictates how people show respect and signify rank. For example, people in the United States show respect by addressing top managers as "Mr. Roberts" or "Ms. Gutierrez." However, people in China are addressed according to their official titles, such as "President" or "Manager."[29]

The rules of polite behavior vary from country to country.

- **Use of manners.** What is polite in one culture may be considered rude in another. For instance, asking a colleague "How was your weekend?" is a common way of making small talk in the United States, but the question sounds intrusive to people in cultures in which business and private lives are seen as totally separate.

Attitudes toward time, such as strict adherence to meeting schedules, vary throughout the world.

- **Concepts of time.** People in low-context cultures see time as a way to plan the business day efficiently, viewing time as a limited resource. However, executives from high-context cultures often see time as more flexible. Meeting a deadline is less important than building a business relationship.[30]
- **Future orientation.** Successful companies tend to have a strong *future orientation*, planning for and investing in the future, but national cultures around the world vary widely in this viewpoint (see Figure 3.3). Some societies encourage a long-term outlook that emphasizes planning, investing, and making short-term sacrifices for long-term outcomes. Others are oriented more toward the present, even to the point of viewing the future as hopelessly remote and not worth planning for.[31]

Cultures around the world exhibit varying degrees of openness toward outsiders and people whose personal identities don't align with prevailing social norms.

- **Openness and inclusiveness.** At both the national level and within smaller groups, cultures vary on how open they are to accepting people from other cultures and people who don't necessarily fit the prevailing norms within the culture. An unwillingness to accommodate others can range from outright exclusion to subtle pressures to conform to majority expectations. IBM has long been a leader in the effort to create an inclusive environment that ensures fair opportunities for both employees and external business partners. For example, executive-led task forces at the company represent women; Asian American, African American, Hispanic American, and Native American people; people with disabilities; and gay, lesbian, bisexual, and transgender employees.[32]

Nonverbal Differences

The meanings of nonverbal signals vary widely from culture to culture, so you can't rely on assumptions.

Nonverbal communication habits can vary widely across cultures. For instance, a gesture that communicates good luck in Brazil is the equivalent of giving someone "the finger" in Colombia.[33] Don't assume that the gestures you grew up with will translate to another culture; doing so could lead to embarrassing mistakes (see Figure 3.4).

When you have the opportunity to interact with people in another culture, the best advice is to study the culture in advance and then observe the way people behave in the following areas:

- **Greetings.** Do people shake hands, bow, or kiss lightly (on one side of the face or both)? Do people shake hands only when first introduced or every time they say hello or good-bye?

FIGURE 3.3 Future Orientation and National Competitiveness
Countries vary widely in the degree to which they are willing to embrace and invest in the future. As this graph shows, there appears to be a strong correlation between a country's future orientation and its ability to compete in global markets. A culture's attitude about the future is one of several social elements that influence the communication process.

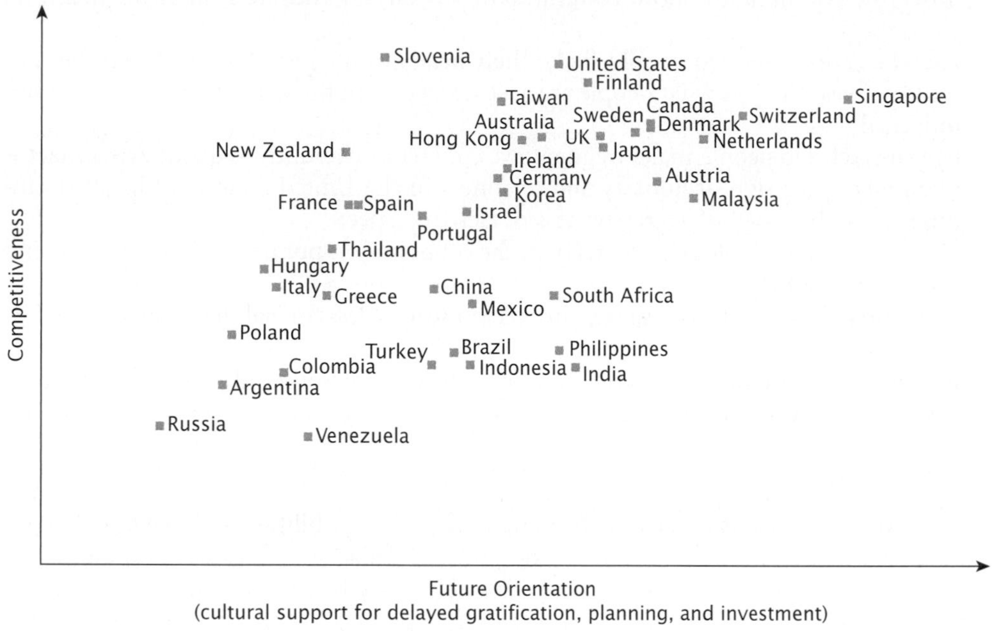

FIGURE 3.4 Avoiding Nonverbal Mishaps
The smile is about the only nonverbal gesture that has the same meaning in all cultures. But even a simple smile isn't all that simple. People in many cultures do not smile at strangers as much as people in the United States do, so travelers from the United States are sometimes put off by what they consider unfriendly responses from strangers. Conversely, people from other cultures can be put off by the U.S. habit of frequent smiling, which some view as insincere.

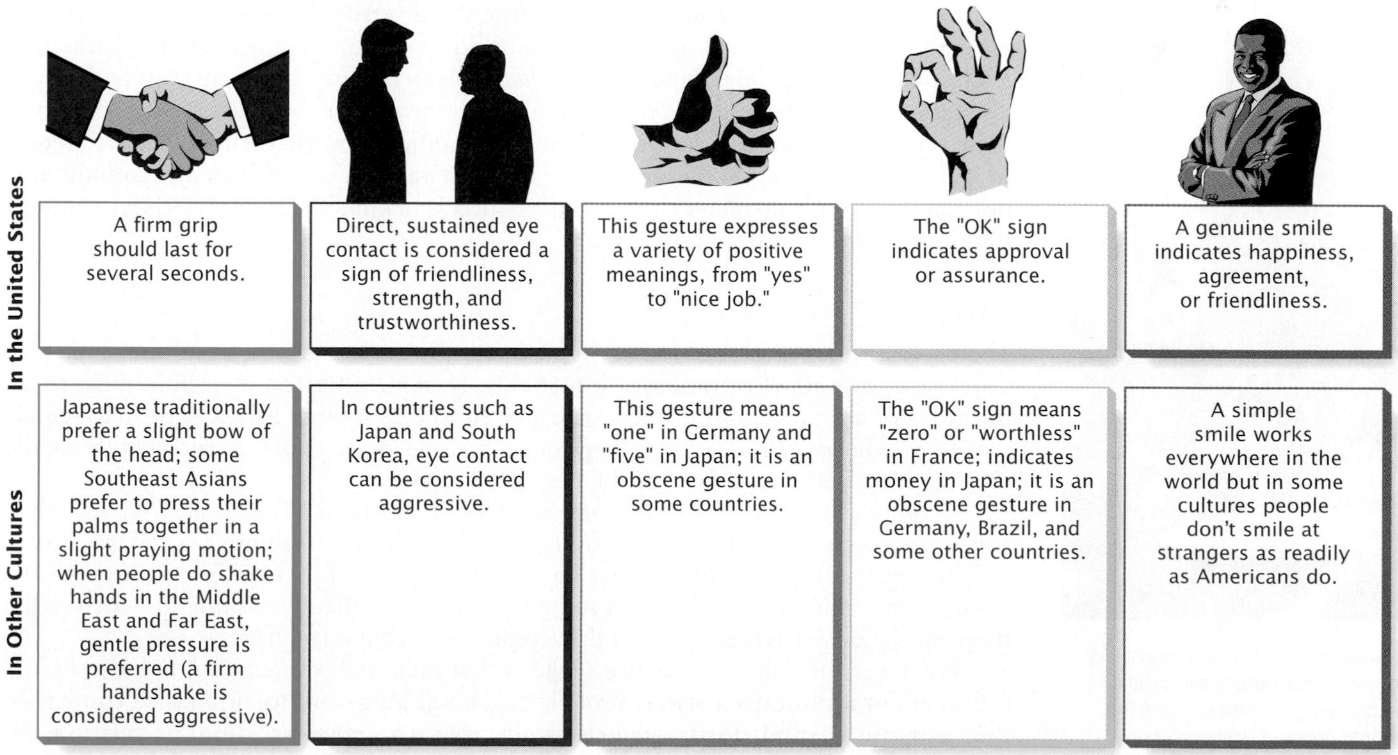

In the United States
A firm grip should last for several seconds.
Direct, sustained eye contact is considered a sign of friendliness, strength, and trustworthiness.
This gesture expresses a variety of positive meanings, from "yes" to "nice job."
The "OK" sign indicates approval or assurance.
A genuine smile indicates happiness, agreement, or friendliness.
In Other Cultures
Japanese traditionally prefer a slight bow of the head; some Southeast Asians prefer to press their palms together in a slight praying motion; when people do shake hands in the Middle East and Far East, gentle pressure is preferred (a firm handshake is considered aggressive).
In countries such as Japan and South Korea, eye contact can be considered aggressive.
This gesture means "one" in Germany and "five" in Japan; it is an obscene gesture in some countries.
The "OK" sign means "zero" or "worthless" in France; indicates money in Japan; it is an obscene gesture in Germany, Brazil, and some other countries.
A simple smile works everywhere in the world but in some cultures people don't smile at strangers as readily as Americans do.

- **Personal space.** When people are conversing, do they stand closer together or farther away than you are accustomed to?
- **Touching.** Do people touch each other on the arm to emphasize a point or slap each other on the back to show congratulations? Or do they refrain from touching altogether?
- **Facial expressions.** Do people shake their heads to indicate "no" and nod them to indicate "yes"? This is what people are accustomed to in the United States, but it is not universal.
- **Eye contact.** Do people make frequent eye contact or avoid it? Frequent eye contact is often taken as a sign of honesty and openness in the United States, but in other cultures, it can be a sign of aggressiveness or lack of respect.
- **Posture.** Do people slouch and relax in the office and in public, or do they sit up and stand up straight?
- **Formality.** In general, does the culture seem more or less formal than yours?

Following the lead of people who grew up in the culture is not only a great way to learn but also a good way to show respect.

Age Differences

A culture's views on youth and aging affect how its people communicate with one another.

In U.S. culture, youth is associated with strength, energy, possibilities, and freedom. In contrast, age is often associated with declining powers and a loss of respect and authority. However, older workers can offer broader experience, the benefits of important business relationships nurtured over many years, and high degrees of "practical intelligence"—the ability to solve complex, poorly defined problems.[34]

In contrast, in cultures that value age and seniority, longevity earns respect and increasing power and freedom. For instance, in many Asian societies, the oldest employees hold the most powerful jobs, the most impressive titles, and the greatest degrees of freedom and decision-making authority. If a younger employee disagrees with one of these senior executives, the discussion is never conducted in public. The notion of "saving face," of avoiding public embarrassment, is too strong. Instead, if a senior person seems to be in error about something, other employees will find a quiet, private way to communicate whatever information they feel is necessary.[35]

In addition to cultural values associated with various life stages, the multiple generations within a culture present another dimension of diversity. Today's workplaces can have as many as four distinct generations working side by side, generally defined as *traditionalists* (those born before 1946), *baby boomers* (born between 1946 and 1964), *generation X* (born between 1965 and 1980), and *generation Y* (born after 1980).[36] Each of these generations has been shaped by dramatically different world events and social trends, so it is not surprising that they often have different values, expectations, and communication habits. As with all other cultural matters, success in building bridges starts with understanding the gaps between the two sides.

Communication styles and expectations can vary widely among age groups, putting extra demands on teams that include workers of varying ages.

Gender Differences

The perception of men and women in business varies from culture to culture, and these differences can affect communication efforts. In some cultures, men hold most or all positions of authority, and women are expected to play a more subservient role. Female executives who visit these cultures may not be taken seriously until they successfully handle challenges to their knowledge, capabilities, and patience.[37]

As more women enter the workforce and take on positions of increasing responsibility, enlightened company leaders are making a point to examine past assumptions and practices.[38] For instance, company cultures that have been dominated by men for years may have adopted communication habits that some women have difficulty relating to—such as the frequent use of sports metaphors or the acceptance of coarse language.

Whatever the culture, evidence suggests that men and women tend to have slightly different communication styles. Broadly speaking, men tend to emphasize content in their communication efforts, whereas women place a higher premium on relationship maintenance.[39] This difference can create friction when two parties in a conversation have different needs and expectations from the interchange. Again, these are broad generalizations that do not apply to every person in every situation, but keeping them in mind can help men and women overcome communication hurdles in the workplace.

Generally speaking, men tend to emphasize content in their messages, and woman tend to emphasize relationship maintenance.

Religious Differences

Religion is a dominant force in many cultures and the source of many differences between cultures.[40] The effort to accommodate employees' life interests on a broader scale has led a number of companies to address the issue of religion in the workplace. As one of the most personal and influential aspects of life, religion brings potential for controversy in a work setting. On the one hand, some employees feel they should be able to express their beliefs in the workplace and not be forced to "check their faith at the door" when they come to work. On the other hand, companies want to avoid situations in which openly expressed religious differences cause friction between employees or distract employees from their responsibilities. To help address such concerns, firms such as Ford, Intel, Texas Instruments, and American Airlines allow employees to form faith-based employee support groups as part of their diversity strategies. In contrast, Procter & Gamble is among the companies that don't allow organized religious activities at their facilities.[41]

Religion in the workplace is a complex and contentious issue—and it's getting more so every year, at least as measured by a significant rise in the number of religious discrimination lawsuits.[42] Beyond accommodating individual beliefs to a reasonable degree, as required by U.S. law, companies occasionally need to resolve situations that pit one group of employees against another or against the company's policies.[43] As more companies work to establish inclusive workplaces and as more employees seek to integrate religious convictions into their daily work, you can expect to see this issue being discussed at many companies in the coming years.

U.S. law requires employers to accommodate employees' religious beliefs to a reasonable degree.

Ability Differences

Colleagues and customers with disabilities that affect communication represent an important aspect of the diversity picture. People whose hearing, vision, cognitive ability, or physical ability to operate computers is impaired can be at a significant disadvantage in today's workplace. As with other elements of diversity, success starts with respect for individuals and sensitivity to differences. Employers can also invest in a variety of *assistive technologies* that help people with disabilities perform activities that might otherwise be difficult or impossible. These technologies include devices and systems that help people communicate orally and visually, interact with computers and other equipment, and enjoy greater mobility in the workplace. For example, designers can emphasize *web accessibility*, taking steps to make websites more accessible to people whose vision is limited. Assistive technologies create a vital link for thousands of employees with disabilities, giving them opportunities to pursue a greater range of career paths and giving employers access to a broader base of talent. With the United States heading for a potentially serious shortage of workers in a few years, the economy will need all the workers who can make a contribution, and assistive technologies will be an important part of the solution.[44]

Assistive technologies help employers create more inclusive workplaces and benefit from the contributions of people with physical or cognitive impairments.

Adapting to Other Business Cultures

Culture is obviously a complex topic that requires a lifetime commitment to learning and growth. You'll find a variety of specific tips in "Improving Intercultural Communication Skills," starting on page 74, but here are four general guidelines that can help all business communicators improve their cultural competency:

- **Become aware of your own biases.** Successful intercultural communication requires more than just an understanding of the other party's culture; you need to understand your own culture and the way it shapes your communication habits.[45] For instance, knowing that you value independence and individual accomplishment will help you communicate more successfully in a culture that values consensus and group harmony.

An important step in understanding and adapting to other cultures is to recognize the influences that your own culture has on your communication habits.

REAL-TIME UPDATES
Learn More

Overcoming culture shock

This entertaining five-part video series shares the experience of an Israeli journalist undergoing culture shock when coming to graduate school in New York City. Go to **http://real-timeupdates.com/ebc** and click on "Learn More." If you are using mybcommlab, you can access Real-Time Updates within each chapter or under Student Study Tools.

- **Ignore the "Golden Rule."** You probably heard this growing up: "Treat people the way you want to be treated." The problem with the Golden Rule is that people *don't* always want to be treated the same way you want to be treated, particularly across cultural boundaries. The best approach is to treat people the way *they* want to be treated.
- **Exercise tolerance, flexibility, and respect.** As IBM's Ron Glover puts it, "To the greatest extent possible, we try to manage our people and our practices in ways that are respectful of the core principles of any given country or organization or culture."[46]
- **Practice patience and maintain a sense of humor.** Even the most committed and attuned business professionals can make mistakes in intercultural communication, so it is vital for all parties to be patient with one another. As business becomes ever more global, even the most tradition-bound cultures are learning to deal with outsiders more patiently and overlook occasional cultural blunders.[47] A sense of humor is a helpful asset as well, allowing people to move past awkward and embarrassing moments. When you make a mistake, simply apologize, if appropriate, ask the other person to explain the accepted way, and then move on.

Adapting to U.S. Business Culture

If you are a recent immigrant to the United States or grew up in a culture outside the U.S. mainstream, you can apply all the concepts and skills in this chapter to help adapt to U.S. business culture. Here are some key points to remember as you become accustomed to business communication in this country:[48]

The values espoused by U.S. culture include individualism, equality, and privacy.

- **Individualism.** In contrast to cultures that value group harmony and group success, U.S. culture generally expects individuals to succeed by their own efforts, and it rewards individual success. Even though teamwork is emphasized in many companies, competition between individuals is expected and even encouraged in many cases.
- **Equality.** Although the country's historical record on equality has not always been positive, and inequalities still exist, equality is considered a core American value. This applies to race, gender, social background, and even age.
- **Privacy and personal space.** People in the United States are accustomed to a fair amount of privacy, and this includes their "personal space" at work. For example, they expect you to knock before entering a closed office and to avoid asking questions about personal beliefs or activities until they get to know you well.
- **Time and schedules.** U.S. businesses value punctuality and the efficient use of time. For instance, meetings are expected to start and end at designated times.
- **Religion.** The United States does not have an official state religion. Many religions are practiced throughout the country, and people are expected to respect each other's beliefs.
- **Communication style.** Communication tends to be direct and focused on content and transactions, not relationships or group harmony.

These are generalizations, of course. However, following these guidelines will help you succeed in most business communication situations.

IMPROVING INTERCULTURAL COMMUNICATION SKILLS

5 LEARNING OBJECTIVE

Identify steps you can take to improve your intercultural communication skills.

Communicating successfully between cultures requires a variety of skills (see Figure 3.5). You can improve your intercultural skills throughout your career by studying other cultures and languages, respecting preferences for communication styles, learning to write and speak clearly, listening carefully, knowing when to use interpreters and translators, and helping others adapt to your culture.

FIGURE 3.5 **Components of Successful Intercultural Communication**
Communicating in a diverse business environment is not always an easy task, but you can continue to improve your sensitivity and build your skills as you progress in your career.

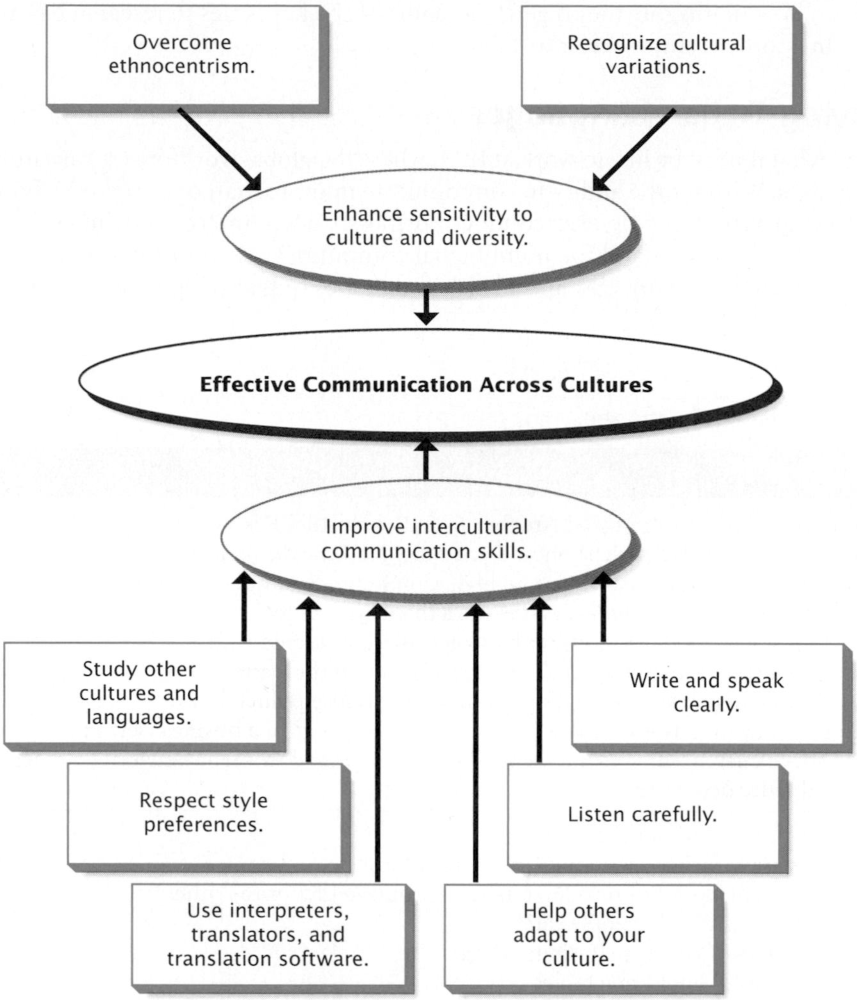

Studying Other Cultures

Effectively adapting your communication efforts to another culture requires not only knowledge about the culture but also both the ability and the motivation to change your personal habits as needed.[49] Fortunately, you don't need to learn about the whole world all at once. Many companies appoint specialists for specific countries or regions, giving employees a chance to focus on just one culture at a time. Some firms also provide resources to help employees prepare for interaction with other cultures. On IBM's Global Workforce Diversity intranet site, for instance, employees can click on the "GoingGlobal" link to learn about customs in specific cultures.[50]

Successful intercultural communication can require the modification of personal communication habits.

Even a small amount of research and practice will help you get through many business situations. In addition, most people respond positively to honest effort and good intentions, and many business associates will help you along if you show an interest in learning more about their cultures.

Numerous websites and books offer advice on traveling to and working in specific cultures. Also try to sample newspapers, magazines, and even the music and movies of

REAL-TIME UPDATES
Learn More

Essential guidelines for adapting to other business cultures

This brief PowerPoint presentation offers great etiquette tips for doing business in France, Germany, Japan, Mexico, and Russia. Go to **http://real-timeupdates.com/ebc** and click on "Learn More." If you are using mybcommlab, you can access Real-Time Updates within each chapter or under Student Study Tools.

Making an effort to learn about another person's culture is a sign of respect.

another country. For instance, a movie can demonstrate nonverbal customs even if you don't grasp the language. (However, be careful not to rely solely on entertainment products. If people in other countries based their opinions of U.S. culture only on the silly teen flicks and violent action movies that the United States exports around the globe, what sort of impression do you imagine they'd get?) For some of the key issues to research before doing business in another country, refer to Table 3.1.

Studying Other Languages

Consider what it must be like to work at IBM, where the global workforce speaks more than 165 languages. Without the ability to communicate in more than one language, how could this diverse group of people ever conduct business? As commerce continues to become more globalized, the demand for multilingual communicators continues to grow as well. For instance, with so many U.S. and British companies outsourcing business functions to

TABLE 3.1 Doing Business in Other Cultures

ACTION	DETAILS TO CONSIDER
Understand social customs	• How do people react to strangers? Are they friendly? Hostile? Reserved? • How do people greet each other? Should you bow? Nod? Shake hands? • How do you express appreciation for an invitation to lunch, dinner, or someone's home? Should you bring a gift? Send flowers? Write a thank-you note? • Are any phrases, facial expressions, or hand gestures considered rude? • How do you attract the attention of a waiter? Do you tip the waiter? • When is it rude to refuse an invitation? How do you refuse politely? • What topics may or may not be discussed in a social setting? In a business setting? • How do social customs dictate interaction between men and women? Between younger people and older people?
Learn about clothing and food preferences	• What occasions require special clothing? • What colors are associated with mourning? Love? Joy? • Are some types of clothing considered taboo for one gender or the other? • How many times a day do people eat? • How are hands or utensils used when eating? • Where is the seat of honor at a table?
Assess political patterns	• How stable is the political situation? • Does the political situation affect businesses in and out of the country? • Is it appropriate to talk politics in social or business situations?
Understand religious and social beliefs	• To which religious groups do people belong? • Which places, objects, actions, and events are sacred? • Do religious beliefs affect communication between men and women or between any other groups? • Is there a tolerance for minority religions? • How do religious holidays affect business and government activities? • Does religion require or prohibit eating specific foods? At specific times?
Learn about economic and business institutions	• Is the society homogeneous or heterogeneous? • What languages are spoken? • What are the primary resources and principal products? • Are businesses generally large? Family controlled? Government controlled? • What are the generally accepted working hours? • How do people view scheduled appointments? • Are people expected to socialize before conducting business?
Appraise the nature of ethics, values, and laws	• Is money or a gift expected in exchange for arranging business transactions? • Do people value competitiveness or cooperation? • What are the attitudes toward work? Toward money? • Is politeness more important than factual honesty?

facilities in India, many Indians now view English skills as an important career asset. Conversely, China's continued growth as a manufacturing powerhouse is prompting many professionals in the United Sates and other countries to learn Mandarin, the official language in China.[51]

A number of U.S. companies are teaching their English-speaking employees a second language to facilitate communication with customers and co-workers. The Target retail chain is among those sponsoring basic Spanish classes for English-speaking supervisors of immigrant employees. Elsewhere around the country, enrollment is growing in specialized classes such as health-care Spanish and Spanish for professionals.[52] Informal coaching is helpful, too, such as having English- and Spanish-speaking employees teach each other a few business or technical terms every day.[53]

Even if your colleagues or customers in another country speak your language, it's worth the time and energy to learn common phrases in theirs. Learning the basics not only helps you get through everyday business and social situations but also demonstrates your commitment to the business relationship. After all, the other person probably spent years learning your language.

Finally, don't assume that people from two countries who speak the same language speak it the same way. The French spoken in Quebec and other parts of Canada is often noticeably different from the French spoken in France. Similarly, it's often said that the United States and the United Kingdom are two countries divided by a common language. For instance, *period* (punctuation), *elevator*, and *gasoline* in the United States are *full stop*, *lift*, and *petrol* in the United Kingdom.

English is the most prevalent language in international business, but don't assume that everyone understands it or speaks it the same way.

Respecting Preferences for Communication Style

Communication style varies widely from culture to culture. For instance, U.S. workers typically prefer an open and direct communication style; they find other styles frustrating or suspect. Directness is also valued in Sweden as a sign of efficiency; but, unlike with discussions in the United States, heated debates and confrontations are unusual. Italian, German, and French executives don't soften up colleagues with praise before they criticize—doing so seems manipulative to them. However, professionals from high-context cultures, such as Japan or China, tend to be less direct.[54] Finally, in general, business correspondence in other countries is often more formal than the style used by U.S. businesspeople (see Figure 3.6).

Writing Clearly

6 LEARNING OBJECTIVE

List seven recommendations for writing clearly in multilanguage business environments.

When sending written communication to businesspeople from another culture, familiarize yourself with their written communication preferences and adapt your approach, style, and tone to meet their expectations. Follow these recommendations:[55]

- **Use simple, clear language.** Use precise words that don't have the potential to confuse with multiple meanings. For instance, the word *right* has several dozen different meanings and usages, so look for a synonym that conveys the precise meaning you intend, such as *correct*, *appropriate*, *desirable*, *moral*, *authentic*, or *privilege*.[56]
- **Be brief.** Use simple sentences and short paragraphs, breaking information into smaller chunks that are easier for your reader to capture and translate. Remember that your messages need to be translated one word at a time.[57]
- **Use transitional elements.** Help readers follow your train of thought by using plenty of transitional words and phrases. Precede related points with expressions such as *in addition* and *first*, *second*, and *third*.
- **Address international correspondence properly.** Table A.5 in Appendix A shows address elements and salutations commonly used in various countries.
- **Cite numbers and dates carefully.** In the United States, 12-05-10 means December 5, 2010, but in many other countries, it means May 12, 2010. Dates in Japan and China are usually expressed with the year first, followed by the month and then the day; therefore, to write December 5, 2010, in Japan, write it as 2010-12-05. Similarly, 1.000 means one with three decimal places in the United States and Great Britain, but it means one thousand in many European countries.

Clarity and simplicity are essential when writing to or speaking with people who don't share your native language.

FIGURE 3.6 Effective German Business Letter (Translated)
In Germany, business letters usually open with a reference to the business relationship and close with a compliment to the recipient. In this letter written by a supplier to a nearby retailer, you can see that the tone is more formal than would typically be used in the United States.

Furtwangen Handcrafts
Kussenhofstrasse 150
Furtwangen, Germany

Mister
Karl Wieland
Business Leader
Black Forest Gifts
Friedrichstrasse 98
70174 Stuttgart
GERMANY

15.5.2010

Very honorable Mister Wieland,

Because the tourist season will begin soon, we would like to take the opportunity to introduce our new line of hand-carved cuckoo clocks to you. Last year you were so friendly as to buy two dozen of our clocks. In recognition of our good business relationship, we now offer you the opportunity to select the new models before we offer this line to other businesses for purchase.

As you know, our artisans use only the best wood. According to time-honored patterns that are passed on from generation to generation, they carefully carve every detail by hand. Our clockworks are of superior quality, and we test every clock before it is painted and shipped. We give you a guarantee of five years on all Furtwangen Handcrafts clocks.

Enclosed you will find a copy of our newest brochure and an order form. To express our appreciation, we will take over the shipping costs if you order before 15 June 2010.

We continue to wish you a lot of success in your new Stuttgart location. We are convinced that you will continue to satisfy your regular clientele with your larger exhibition area and expanded stock and that you will also gain many new visitors.

With friendly greetings

Frederick Semper

Frederick Semper

Literal translation of *Geschäftsführer* (Common English translation would be "managing director")

Refers to the ongoing business relationship

Uses language a bit more formally than U.S. letters do, such as "We give you a guarantee . . ."

Uses a complimentary close typical of German business letters (note the lack of punctuation)

Places the date to the right and below the address block (some German writers use the format 15 May 2010)

Shows concern for the audience

Ends with a compliment to the receiver

Does not include a title with the typed name

- **Avoid slang, idiomatic phrases, and business jargon.** Everyday speech and writing are full of slang and **idiomatic phrases**, phrases that mean more than the sum of their literal parts. Examples from U.S. English include phrases such as, "Off the top of my head" and "More bang for the buck." Your audience may have no idea what you're talking about when you use such phrases.

Humor does not "travel well" because it usually relies on intimate knowledge of a particular culture.

- **Avoid humor and other references to popular culture.** Jokes and references to popular entertainment usually rely on subtle cultural issues that might be completely unknown to your audience.

Although some of these differences may seem trivial, meeting the expectations of an international audience illustrates both knowledge of and respect for the other cultures (see Figures 3.7 and 3.8 on pages 79 and 80).

FIGURE 3.7 Ineffective Intercultural Letter
This letter from a U.S. sales representative to a manager in France exhibits several intercultural mistakes, including the informal tone and use of U.S. slang. Compare this with the improved version in Figure 3.8.

La Cristallerie

Troy Halford, U.S. Sales Representative
163 Pico Boulevard
Los Angeles, CA 90032
Voice: (213) 975-8924
Fax: (213) 860-3489
halford@home.com

April 7, 2010

Mr. Pierre Coll
Director of Accounting
La Cristallerie
22 Marne Blvd.
Beaune, France 21200

Dear Pierre:

I know you've had gorgeous spring weather, with sunny skies and balmy days. But here in the States, it's been a spring of another color. We've been hammered with storms, flooding, and even late snow. Travel over here has been a nightmare, which is why you'll find my expenses a bit elevated this month.

I realize that you've asked all the reps to reduce rather than increase our expenses, but there were extenuating circumstances this last month. All the bad weather we've been having has caused major bottlenecks, with flights canceled and people forced to sleep in the terminals wherever they could find a spot.

After being stuck in the Chicago airport for 18 hours straight, I was desperate for a hot shower and some shut-eye, so I decided to wait out the crunch in a hotel. I know that hotels near airports are expensive, but I struck out trying to book a cheaper room in town. The bottom line is I had to spend extra funds for a hotel at $877; meals, which came to some $175; $72 just in transportation from the terminal to the hotel, and extra phone calls totaling $38.

I appreciate your understanding these unique circumstances. I was really in a jam.

Sincerely,

Troy Halford

Troy Halford
U.S. Sales Rep

Annotations:

- Uses the U.S. format for the date, rather than the international format typically used by French writers
- Fails to follow French preferences for title and address format
- Uses reader's first name, which is much too informal for most French business correspondence
- Wastes reader's time with unnecessarily dramatic and long description of weather problems
- Uses slang and idioms throughout the message, creating the potential for confusion (e.g., hammered, bottlenecks, shut-eye, crunch, struck out, jam)
- Buries specific information in awkward phrasing
- Fails to provide a total of the extra expenses
- Closes with a self-centered tone rather than trying to help the reader
- Fails to alert the reader that other documents are enclosed

Speaking and Listening Carefully

Languages vary considerably in the significance of tone, pitch, speed, and volume. The English word *progress* can be a noun or a verb, depending on which syllable you accent. In Chinese, the meaning of the word *mà* changes, depending on the speaker's tone; it can mean *mother*, *pileup*, *horse*, or *scold*. Routine Arabic speech can sound excited or angry to an English-speaking U.S. listener.[58]

When talking with people whose native language is different from yours, remember that the processing of even everyday conversations can be difficult. For instance, speakers from the United States are notorious for stringing together multiple words into a single, mystifying pseudoword, such as turning "Did you eat yet?" into "Jeetyet?" The French language uses a concept known as *liaison*, in which one word is intentionally joined with the next. New French speakers have a hard time telling when one word ends and the next one begins.

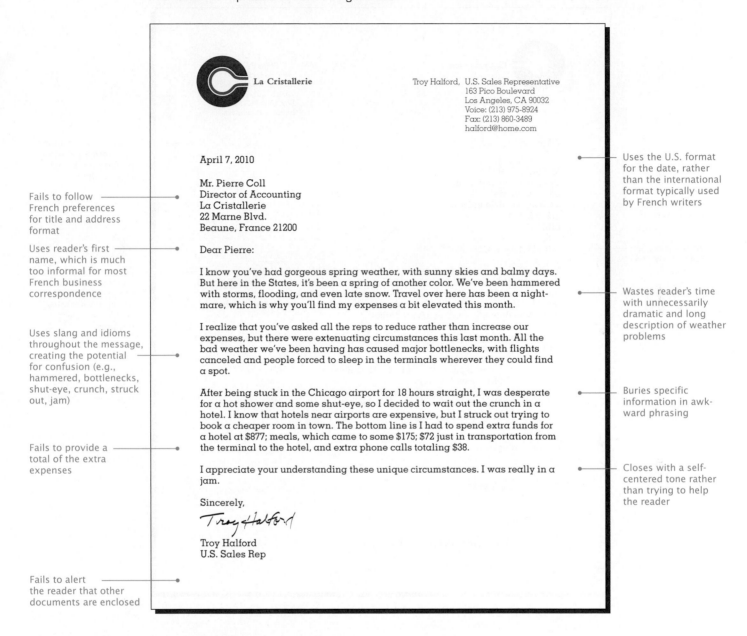

FIGURE 3.8 Effective Intercultural Letter
This version of the letter in Figure 3.7 follows French standards for correspondence and is also easier to read and to scan.

La Cristallerie

Troy Halford, U.S. Sales Representative
163 Pico Boulevard
Los Angeles, CA 90032
Voice: (213) 975-8924
Fax: (213) 860-3489
halford@home.com

7 April 2010

Uses the international date format, which is preferred in French correspondence

M. Pierre Coll
Commissaire aux Comptes
La Cristallerie
22, Boulevard de la Marne
21200 Beaune
FRANCE

Follows French preferences for title and address format

Dear Monsieur Coll:

Addresses the reader more formally in the salutation, as is expected in most French correspondence

Enclosed are my expense statement and receipts for March 2010. My expenses are higher than usual this month because an unexpected snowstorm that closed the airport in Chicago left me stranded for nearly five days. I was able to get a hotel for the duration of the storm, although the only room available was far more expensive than my usual accommodations.

States the main idea directly and clearly in the opening, leaving no room for confusion about the letter's purpose

Uses clear and conventional language that is easier for non-native English speakers

In addition to the regular expenses identified in the enclosed report, here are the additional expenditures caused by the weather delay:

Three nights at the Carlton-O'Hare Hotel	$ 877
Meals over four days	175
Transportation between hotel and terminal	72
Phone calls to reschedule meetings	38
Total extra expenses	**$1,162**

Clearly identifies the extra expenses in a list that is easy to read

Provides a total of the extra expenses

If you have any questions or need any more information about these expenses, please contact me.

Closes with an offer to help the reader with any further needs

Sincerely,

Troy Halford

Troy Halford
U.S. Sales Rep

Enclosures: Expense statement and receipts

Indicates that additional materials are enclosed with the letter

Speaking clearly and getting plenty of feedback are two of the keys to successful intercultural conversations.

To be more effective in intercultural conversations, remember these tips: (1) Speak slowly and clearly; (2) don't rephrase until it's obviously necessary (immediately rephrasing something you've just said doubles the translation workload for the listener); (3) look for and ask for feedback to make sure your message is getting through; (4) don't talk down to the other person by overenunciating words or oversimplifying sentences; and (5) at the end of the conversation, double-check to make sure you and the listener agree on what has been said and decided.

To listen more effectively in intercultural situations, accept what you hear without judgment and let people finish what they have to say.

As a listener, you'll need some practice to get a sense of vocal patterns. The key is simply to accept what you hear first, without jumping to conclusions about meaning or motivation. Let other people finish what they have to say. If you interrupt, you may miss something important. You'll also show a lack of respect. If you do not understand a comment, ask the person to repeat it. Any momentary awkwardness you might feel in asking for extra help is less important than the risk of unsuccessful communication.

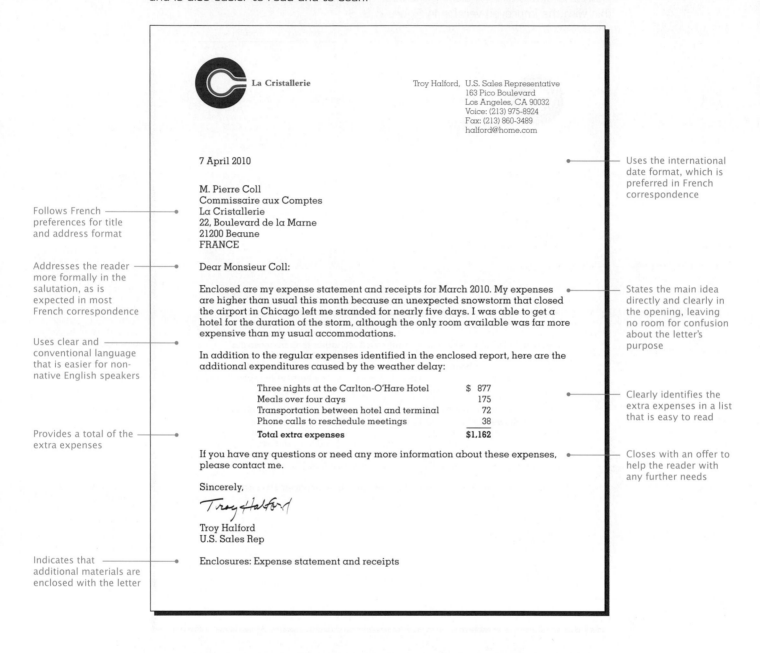

Using Interpreters, Translators, and Translation Software

You may encounter business situations that require using an *interpreter* (for spoken communication) or a *translator* (for written communication). Interpreters and translators can be expensive, but skilled professionals provide invaluable assistance for communicating in other cultural contexts.[59] Keeping up with current language usage in a given country or culture is also critical in order to avoid embarrassing blunders. Landor Associates, a leading marketing agency, usually engages three native-language speakers to review translated materials to make sure the sense of the message is compatible with current usage and slang in a given country.[60] Some companies use *back-translation* to ensure accuracy. After a translator encodes a message into another language, a different translator retranslates the same message into the original language. This back-translation is then compared with the original message to discover any errors or discrepancies.

Experienced international speakers, such as Dr. Eric Schmidt, Google's chairman and CEO, are careful to incorporate culture and language variations into their communication efforts.

The time and cost required for professional translation has encouraged the development of translation software. Online services such as WorldLingo (www.worldlingo.com) offer various forms of automated translation. Major search engines let you request translated versions of the websites you find. Although none of these tools can translate as well as human translators, they can help with individual words and phrases, and they can often give you the overall gist of a message.[61]

For important business communication, use a professional interpreter (for oral communication) or translator (for written communication).

Helping Others Adapt to Your Culture

Whether a younger person is unaccustomed to the formalities of a large corporation or a colleague from another country is working on a team with you, look for opportunities to help people fit in and adapt their communication style. For example, if a nonnative English speaker is making mistakes that could hurt his or her credibility, you can offer advice on the appropriate words and phrases to use. Most language learners truly appreciate this sort of assistance, as long as it is offered in a respectful manner.

You can also take steps to simplify the communication process. For example, oral communication in a second language is usually more difficult than written forms of communication, so instead of asking a foreign colleague to provide information in a conference call, you could use written electronic media instead.

Help others adapt to your culture; doing so will create a more productive workplace and teach you about their cultures as well.

CHECKLIST: Improving Intercultural Communication Skills

- Understand your own culture so that you can recognize its influences on your communication habits.
- Study other cultures so that you can appreciate cultural variations.
- Study the languages of people with whom you communicate, even if you can learn only a few basic words and phrases.
- Help nonnative speakers learn your language.
- Respect cultural preferences for communication style.
- Write clearly, using brief messages, simple language, generous transitions, and appropriate international conventions.
- Avoid slang, humor, and references to popular culture.
- Speak clearly and slowly, giving listeners time to translate your words.
- Ask for feedback to ensure successful communication.
- Listen carefully and ask speakers to repeat anything you don't understand.
- Use interpreters and translators for important messages.

Document Makeover

Improve This Letter

To practice correcting drafts of actual documents, visit the "Document Makeovers" section in mybcommlab. Refer to the User Guide for specific instructions on how to access the content for this chapter. You will find a letter that contains problems and errors related to what you've learned in this chapter about developing effective intercultural communication skills. Use the Final Draft decision tool to create an improved version of this letter. Check the message for a communication style that keeps the message brief; does not become too familiar or informal; uses transitional elements appropriately; and avoids slang, idioms, jargon, and technical language.

Whatever assistance you can provide will be greatly appreciated because smart businesspeople recognize the value of intercultural communication skills. Moreover, chances are that while you're helping others, you'll learn something about other cultures, too.

For a brief summary of ideas to improve intercultural communication in the workplace, see "Checklist: Improving Intercultural Communication Skills." For additional information on communicating in a world of diversity, visit **http://real-timeupdates.com/ebc** and click on Chapter 3.

On the Job: Solving Communication Dilemmas at IBM

Ron Glover is responsible for overall diversity planning and strategy at IBM, but every manager throughout the company is expected to foster a climate of inclusion and support for employees of every cultural background. As a team leader in one of IBM's software development labs, you're learning to exercise sound business judgment and use good listening skills to help resolve situations that arise within your diverse group of employees. How would you address each of these challenges?

1. Joo Mi Kang, a recent immigrant from South Korea, is a brilliant programmer who continues to impress everyone with her technical innovations. Unfortunately, she usually doesn't do a good job of documenting her code, an admittedly tedious process in which programmers are supposed to write descriptions of what they've created and explain how it works so that other people can come in later and fix it if needed. You suspect from seeing some of her e-mails that she has trouble writing in English. What should your first step be?

a. Send her an e-mail reminding her of the need to document her code; attach a copy of her job description.
b. Suggest that she find a tutor to help her develop her English skills.
c. Visit her in her office and discuss the situation; ask if she understands the importance of documenting her code and whether she has encountered any difficulty in doing so.
d. Assign several other programmers the task of pitching in to take care of her documentation chores.

2. Your employees are breaking into ethnically based cliques. Members of ethnic groups eat together, socialize together, and often chat in their native languages while they work. You appreciate how these groups give their members a sense of community, but you worry that these informal communication channels are alienating nonmembers and fragmenting the flow of information. How do you encourage a stronger sense of community and teamwork across your department?

a. Ban the use of languages other than English at work.
b. Do nothing. This is normal behavior, and any attempt to disrupt it will only generate resentment.
c. Structure work assignments and other activities (such as volunteer projects) in ways that bring people from the various cultural groups into regular contact with one another and make them more dependent on one another as well.
d. Send all your employees to diversity training classes.

3. Vasily Pevsner, a Russian immigrant, has worked in the department for five years. He works well alone, but he resists working with other employees, even in team settings where collaboration is expected. How do you handle the situation?

a. Stay out of the way and let the situation resolve itself. Pevsner has to learn how to get along with the other team members.
b. Tell the rest of the team to work harder at getting along with Pevsner.
c. Tell Pevsner he must work with others or he will not progress in the company.
d. Talk privately with Pevsner and help him understand the importance of working together as a team. During the conversation, try to uncover why he doesn't participate more in team efforts.

4. IBM boasts one of the most highly educated workforces in the world, and your department is no exception. However, you've been surprised at the confusion that some of your memos and other written messages have generated lately. You suspect your casual and often humorous writing style might be the culprit and decide to "test drive" a different writing style. You've drafted four versions of a blog posting that explains a new policy aimed at keeping software projects on schedule as they near completion. Which of these do you choose and why?
   a. "As each new project nears completion, I recognize how hard you all try to keep projects on schedule, even with the last-minute problems that are always part of software projects. To lighten your workload during the hectic final phase, you'll no longer be expected to attend routine department meetings or tend to other nonessential tasks during the final four weeks of each project."
   b. "As each new project races toward the finish line, I appreciate that all of you work like dogs to keep projects on schedule, even with the inevitable glitches and gremlins that always seem to attack software projects at the last minute. Good news: During the last four weeks of every project, you'll be excused from nonessential tasks such as routine department meetings so that you can focus on your programming work (admit it—I know you hate coming to these meetings anyway!)."
   c. "As usual, the solution to all of life's problems can be found on television! While watching the Raiders–Chiefs game yesterday, I realized that we need to have our own version of the two-minute drill. To help avoid schedule slippage during the crazy final few weeks of each project, team members will be excused from routine meetings and other nonessential tasks not directly related to their project responsibilities."
   d. "As you should all be aware, numerous entities both internal and external to the corporation rely on us for timely project completion. While the inherent nature of software development presents unexpected difficulties during the final stages of a project, it is incumbent upon us to employ every tactic possible to avoid significant completion delays. Henceforth, team members will be excused from nonessential tasks during the final four weeks of every development project."

LEARNING OBJECTIVES CHECKUP

Assess your understanding of the principles in this chapter by reading each learning objective and studying the accompanying exercises. For fill-in-the-blank items, write the missing text in the blank provided; for multiple-choice items, circle the letter of the correct answer. You can check your responses against the answer key on page AK-1.

Objective 3.1: Discuss the opportunities and challenges of intercultural communication.

1. Which of the following factors is a significant reason U.S. business professionals often need to understand the cultures of other countries?
   a. Recent changes to government regulations require cultural education before companies are granted export licenses.
   b. The U.S. economy has been shrinking for the past 20 years, forcing companies to look overseas.
   c. Many countries require business executives to be fluent in at least two languages.
   d. Thousands of U.S. companies, including many of the largest corporations in the country, rely on markets in other countries for a significant portion of their sales.

2. Which of the following is a benefit of a multicultural workforce?
   a. Providing a broader range of viewpoints and ideas
   b. Giving companies a better understanding of diverse markets
   c. Enabling companies to recruit workers from the broadest possible pool of talent
   d. All of the above

3. A culturally rich workforce, composed of employees representing a wide range of ethnicities, religions, ages, physical abilities, languages, and other factors
   a. Always slows down the decision-making process
   b. Can be more challenging to manage but can pay off in a variety of important ways
   c. Is easier to manage because so many new ideas are present
   d. Is a concern only for companies that do business outside the United States

Objective 3.2: Define *culture*, and explain how culture is learned.

4. Culture is defined as
   a. A distinct group that exists within a country
   b. A shared system of symbols, beliefs, attitudes, values, expectations, and norms for behavior
   c. The pattern of cues and stimuli that convey meaning between two or more people
   d. Serious art forms such as classical music, painting, sculpture, drama, and poetry

5. Which of the following is *not* an example of a cultural group?
   a. Hindus
   b. Wrestling fans
   c. Television viewers
   d. Members of a fraternity

6. Culture is learned from
   a. Family members
   b. Explicit teaching by others in the culture
   c. Observations of the behavior of others in the culture
   d. All of the above

Objective 3.3: Define *ethnocentrism* and *stereotyping*, and give three suggestions for overcoming these limiting mindsets.

7. _____ is the tendency to judge all other groups according to the standards, behaviors, and customs of one's own group.

8. _____ is the mistake of assigning a wide range of generalized attributes to individuals on the basis of their membership in a particular culture or social group, without considering an individual's unique characteristics.

9. Which of the following is one of several techniques you can use to make sure you don't fall into the traps of ethnocentrism and stereotyping?
   a. Minimize interactions with people whose cultures you don't understand.
   b. Make sure that the people you work with clearly understand your culture.
   c. Insist that every employee who works for you strictly follows the company's guidelines for intercultural communication.
   d. Avoid making assumptions about people in other cultures.

Objective 3.4: Explain the importance of recognizing cultural variations, and list eight categories of cultural differences.

10. In business, recognizing cultural differences is important because
    a. Doing so helps reduce the chances for misunderstanding
    b. Someone from another culture may try to take advantage of your ignorance
    c. If you don't, you'll be accused of being politically incorrect
    d. Doing so helps you become more ethnocentric

11. An example of low-context cultural communication would be
    a. Someone from China using metaphors to convey meaning
    b. Someone from Greece insisting that the details of an agreement can be worked out later
    c. Someone from Germany vigorously arguing his point of view in a problem-solving situation
    d. Someone from Japan encouraging socializing before entering into official negotiations

12. Which of the following is generally true about high-context cultures?
    a. Employees work shorter hours in such cultures because context allows them to communicate less often.
    b. People rely less on verbal communication and more on the context of nonverbal actions and environmental setting to convey meaning.
    c. People rely more on verbal communication and less on the context of nonverbal actions and environmental setting to convey meaning.
    d. The rules of everyday life are explicitly taught to all people within the culture.

13. Contextual differences between cultures refer to
    a. The degree to which various cultures rely on verbal or nonverbal actions to convey meaning
    b. Whether cultures emphasize written or spoken communication
    c. The role of the Internet (including e-mail and instant messaging) in international communication
    d. Attitudes toward work and success

14. Differing attitudes toward greetings, personal space, touching, facial expression, eye contact, posture, and formality are common examples of _____ differences between cultures.

Objective 3.5: Identify steps you can take to improve your intercultural communication skills.

15. When communicating orally to those who speak English as a second language, you should make a habit to always
    a. Immediately rephrase every important point you make in order to give your listeners two options to choose from
    b. Speak louder if listeners don't seem to understand you
    c. Ignore the other person's body language
    d. Rephrase your key points if you observe body language that suggests a lack of understanding

16. Understanding the nuances of a culture can take years to learn, so the best approach when preparing to communicate with people in a culture that you don't know well is to
    a. Learn as much as you can from websites, travel guides, and other resources and not be afraid to ask for help while you are communicating in that new culture
    b. Learn as much as you can from websites, travel guides, and other resources but never ask for help because doing so will only show everyone how ignorant you are
    c. Learn as much as you can from television shows and movies that feature the other culture; the combination of spoken words, visuals, and music is the best way to learn a culture
    d. Not worry about cultural variations; you'll never have time to understand them all, so your energy is better spent on other business issues

Objective 3.6: List seven recommendations for writing clearly in multilanguage business environments.

17. When writing for audiences who don't speak the same native language as you speak, you can improve communication by
    a. Spelling out numbers rather than writing them as figures
    b. Using simple sentences and careful word choices
    c. Using long paragraphs to reduce the number of visual breaks on the page
    d. Doing all of the above

18. When you are writing for multilanguage audiences, humor
    a. Should be used often because it makes your audience feel welcome on a personal level
    b. Should rarely, if ever, be used because humor is one of the most difficult elements of communication to encode or decode in a second language
    c. Should never be used because movies and other entertainment products rarely cross over national boundaries
    d. Should be used at least once per letter to show that you appreciate your audience as human beings

PEARSON **mybcommlab**

Log on to **www.mybcommlab.com** to access the following study and assessment aids associated with this chapter:

- Video applications
- Pre/post test
- Real-Time Updates
- Personalized study plan
- Peer review activity
- Model documents
- Quick Learning Guides
- Sample presentations

If you are not using mybcommlab, you can access Real-Time Updates and Quick Learning Guides through **http://real-timeupdates.com/ebc.** The Quick Learning Guide (located under "Learn More" on the website) hits all the high points of this chapter in just two pages. This guide, especially prepared by the authors, will help you study for exams or review important concepts whenever you need a quick refresher.

Apply Your Knowledge

1. What are some of the intercultural differences that managers of a U.S.-based firm might encounter during a series of business meetings with a China-based company whose managers speak English fairly well?
2. What are some of the intercultural communication issues to consider when deciding whether to accept a job in an overseas branch of a U.S. company? How about a job in the United States with a local branch of a foreign-owned firm? Explain.
3. How do you think company managers from a country that has a relatively homogeneous culture might react when they do business with the culturally diverse staff of a company based in a less homogeneous country? Explain your answer.
4. Make a list of the top five priorities in your life (for example, fame, wealth, family, spirituality, peace of mind, individuality, artistic expression). Compare your list with the priorities that appear to be valued in the culture in which you are currently living. (You can be as broad or as narrow as you like in defining *culture* for this exercise, such as overall U.S. culture or culture in your college or university.) Do your personal priorities align with the culture's priorities? If not, how might this disparity affect your communication with other members of the culture?
5. **Ethical Choices** Your office in Turkey desperately needs the supplies that have been sitting in Turkish customs for a month. Should you bribe a customs official to speed up delivery? Explain your decision.

Practice Your Knowledge

Message for Analysis

Your boss wants to send a brief e-mail message, welcoming employees recently transferred to your department from the company's Hong Kong branch. They all speak English, but your boss asks you to review his message for clarity. What would you suggest your boss change in the following e-mail message, and why? Would you consider this message to be audience centered? Why or why not?

> I wanted to welcome you ASAP to our little family here in the States. It's high time we shook hands in person and not just across the sea. I'm pleased as punch about getting to know you all, and I for one will do my level best to sell you on America.

Exercises

Active links for all websites in this chapter can be found on mybcommlab; see your User Guide for instructions on accessing the content for this chapter.

3.1 **Intercultural Sensitivity: Recognizing Variations** You represent a Canadian toy company that's negotiating to buy miniature truck wheels from a manufacturer in Osaka, Japan. In your first meeting, you explain that your company expects to control the design of the wheels as well as the materials that are used to make them. The manufacturer's representative looks down and says softly, "Perhaps that will be difficult." You press for agreement, and to emphasize your willingness to buy, you show the prepared contract you've brought with you. However, the manufacturer seems increasingly vague and uninterested. What cultural differences may be interfering with effective communication in this situation? Explain.

3.2 **Ethical Choices** A U.S. manager wants to ship machine parts to a West African country, but a government official there expects a special payment before allowing the shipment into the country. How can the two sides resolve their different approaches without violating U.S. rules against bribing foreign officials? On the basis of the information presented in Chapter 1, would you consider this situation an ethical dilemma or an ethical lapse? Please explain.

3.3 **Teamwork** Working with two other students, prepare a list of 10 examples of slang (in your own language) that might be misinterpreted or misunderstood during a business conversation with someone from another culture. Next to each example, suggest other words you might use to convey the same message. Do the alternatives mean *exactly* the same as the original slang or idiom?

3.4 **Intercultural Communication: Studying Cultures** Choose a specific country, such as India, Portugal, Bolivia, Thailand, or Nigeria, with which you are not familiar. Research the culture and write a brief summary of what a U.S. manager would need to know about concepts of personal space and rules of social behavior in order to conduct business successfully in that country.

3.5 **Multicultural Workforce: Bridging Differences** Differences in gender, age, and physical abilities contribute to the diversity of today's workforce. Working with a classmate, role-play a conversation in which

a. A woman is being interviewed for a job by a male personnel manager.
b. An older person is being interviewed for a job by a younger personnel manager.
c. An employee who is a native speaker of English is being interviewed for a job by a hiring manager who is a recent immigrant with relatively poor English skills.

How did differences between the applicant and the interviewer shape the communication? What can you do to improve communication in such situations?

3.6 **Intercultural Sensitivity: Understanding Attitudes** As the director of marketing for a telecommunications firm based in Germany, you're negotiating with an official in Guangzhou, China, who's in charge of selecting a new telephone system for the city. You insist that the specifications be spelled out in the contract. However, your Chinese counterpart seems to have little interest in technical and financial details. What can you do or say to break this intercultural deadlock and obtain the contract so that both parties are comfortable?

3.7 **Cultural Variations: Ability Differences** You are a new manager at K & J Brick, a masonry products company that is now run by the two sons of the man who founded it 50 years ago. For years, the co-owners have invited the management team to a wilderness lodge for a combination of outdoor sports and annual business planning meetings. You don't want to miss the event, but you know that the outdoor activities weren't designed for someone with your physical impairments. Draft a short memo to the rest of the management team, suggesting changes to the annual event that will allow all managers to participate.

3.8 **Culture and Time: Dealing with Variations** When a company knows that a scheduled delivery time given by an overseas firm is likely to be flexible, managers may buy in larger quantities or may order more often to avoid running out of product before the next delivery. Identify three other management decisions that may be influenced by differing cultural concepts of time and make notes for a short (two-minute) presentation to your class.

3.9 **Intercultural Communication: Using Interpreters** Imagine that you're the lead negotiator for a company that's trying to buy a factory in Prague, the capital of the Czech Republic. Although you haven't spent much time in the country in the past decade, your parents grew up near Prague, so you understand and speak the language fairly well. However, you wonder about the advantages and disadvantages of using an interpreter anyway. For example, you may have more time to think if you wait for an intermediary to translate the other side's position. Decide whether to hire an interpreter and write a brief e-mail message (two or three paragraphs) explaining your decision.

3.10 **Internet: Translation Software** Explore the powers and limitations of computer translation at Babel Fish, **http://babelfish.yahoo.com**. Click on "Translate" and enter a sentence such as, "We are enclosing a purchase order for four dozen computer monitors." Select "English to Spanish" and click to complete the translation. Once you've read the Spanish version, cut and paste it into the "text for translation" box, select "Spanish to English," and click to translate. Try translating the same English sentence into German, French, or Italian and then back into English. How do the results of each translation differ? What are the implications for the use of automated translation services and back-translation? How could you use this website to sharpen your intercultural communication skills? Summarize your findings in a brief report.

3.11 **Intercultural Communication: Improving Skills** You've been assigned to host a group of Swedish college students who are visiting your college for the next two weeks. They've all studied English, but this is their first trip to your area. Make a list of at least eight slang terms and idioms they are likely to hear on campus. How will you explain each phrase? When speaking with the Swedish students, what word or words might you substitute for each slang term or idiom?

3.12 **Intercultural Communication: Podcasting** Your company was one of the first to use podcasting (see page 190 for more information) as a business communication tool. Executives frequently record messages (such as monthly sales summaries) and post them on the company's intranet site; employees from the 14 offices in Europe, Asia, and North America then download the files to their music players and listen to the messages while riding the train to work, eating lunch at their desks, and so on. Your boss asks you to draft the opening statement for a podcast that will announce a revenue drop caused by intensive competitive pressure. She reviews your script and hands it back with a gentle explanation that it needs to be revised for international listeners. Improve the following statement in as many ways as you can:

> Howdy, comrades. Shouldn't surprise anyone that we took a beating this year, given the insane pricing moves our knucklehead competitors have been making. I mean, how those clowns can keep turning a profit is beyond me, what with steel costs still going through the roof and labor costs heating up—even in countries where everybody goes to find cheap labor—and hazardous waste disposal regs adding to operating costs, too.

Expand Your Knowledge

Learning More on the Web

Cultural Savvy for Competitive Advantage

www.executiveplanet.com

Want to be more competitive when doing business across borders? Executive Planet offers quick introductions to expected business practices in a number of countries, from setting up appointments to giving gifts to negotiating deals. Visit www.executiveplanet.com and browse the business culture guides to answer the following questions.

1. What sort of clothes should you pack for a business trip to Mexico that will include both meetings and social events?
2. You've been trying to sell your products to a Saudi Arabian company whose executives treat you to an extravagant evening of dining and entertainment. Can you take this as a positive sign that they're likely to buy from you?
3. You collect antique clocks as a hobby, and you plan to give one of your favorites to the president of a Chinese company you plan to visit. Would such a gift likely help or hurt your relationship with this person?

Sharpening Your Career Skills Online

Bovée and Thill's Business Communication Web Search, at http://businesscommunicationblog.com/websearch, is a unique research tool designed specifically for business communication research. Use the Web Search function to find a website, video, podcast, or PowerPoint presentation that offers advice on communicating with business contacts in another country or culture. Write a brief e-mail message to your instructor, describing the item that you found and summarizing the career skills information you learned from it.

Improve Your Grammar, Mechanics, and Usage

The following exercises help you improve your knowledge of and power over English grammar, mechanics, and usage. Turn to the Handbook of Grammar, Mechanics, and Usage at the end of this book and review all of Section 1.3 (Verbs). Then look at the following 10 items. Circle the letter of the preferred choice in the following groups of sentences. (Answers to these exercises appear on page AK-3.)

1. Which sentence contains a verb in the present perfect form?
   - **a.** I became the resident expert on repairing the copy machine.
   - **b.** I have become the resident expert on repairing the copy machine.
2. Which sentence contains a verb in the simple past form?
   - **a.** She knows how to conduct an audit when she came to work for us.
   - **b.** She knew how to conduct an audit when she came to work for us.
3. Which sentence contains a verb in the simple future form?
   - **a.** Next week, call John to tell him what you will do to help him set up the seminar.
   - **b.** Next week, call John to tell him what you will be doing to help him set up the seminar.
4. Which sentence is in the active voice?
   - **a.** The report will be written by Leslie Cartwright.
   - **b.** Leslie Cartwright will write the report.
5. Which sentence is in the passive voice?
   - **a.** The failure to record the transaction was mine.
   - **b.** I failed to record the transaction.
6. Which sentence contains the correct verb form?
   - **a.** Everyone upstairs receives mail before we do.
   - **b.** Everyone upstairs receive mail before we do.
7. Which sentence contains the correct verb form?
   - **a.** Neither the main office nor the branches is blameless.
   - **b.** Neither the main office nor the branches are blameless.
8. Which sentence contains the correct verb form?
   - **a.** C&B Sales are listed in the directory.
   - **b.** C&B Sales is listed in the directory.
9. Which sentence contains the correct verb form?
   - **a.** When measuring shelves, 7 inches is significant.
   - **b.** When measuring shelves, 7 inches are significant.
10. Which sentence contains the correct verb form?
    - **a.** About 90 percent of the employees plans to come to the company picnic.
    - **b.** About 90 percent of the employees plan to come to the company picnic.

For additional exercises focusing on verbs, visit mybcommlab. Click on Chapter 3, click on "Additional Exercises to Improve Grammar, Mechanics, and Usage," and then click on "5. Verb tenses," "6. Transitive and intransitive verbs," or "7. Voice of verbs."

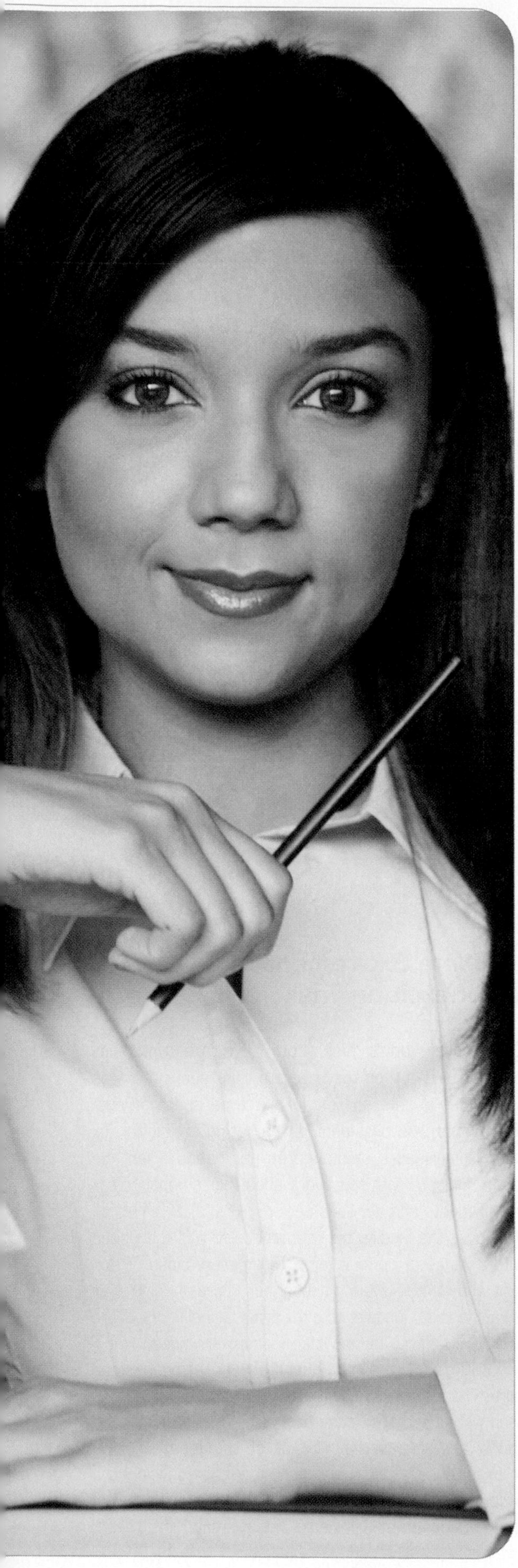

Part 2

Applying the Three-Step Writing Process

Every professional can learn to write more effectively while spending less time and energy creating effective messages. Discover a proven writing process that divides the challenge of communicating into three simple steps: planning, writing, and completing messages. The process works for everything from blog posts to formal reports to your résumé. With a bit of practice, you'll be using the process without even thinking about it.

4 Planning Business Messages

Learning Objectives

After studying this chapter, you will be able to

1. Describe the three-step writing process
2. Explain why it's important to analyze the situation, and define your purpose carefully before writing a message
3. Discuss information-gathering options for simple messages, and identify three attributes of quality information
4. List the factors to consider when choosing the most appropriate medium for a message
5. Explain why good organization is important to both you and your audience
6. Explain the differences between the direct and indirect approaches to organizing a message

On the Job: Communicating at H&R Block

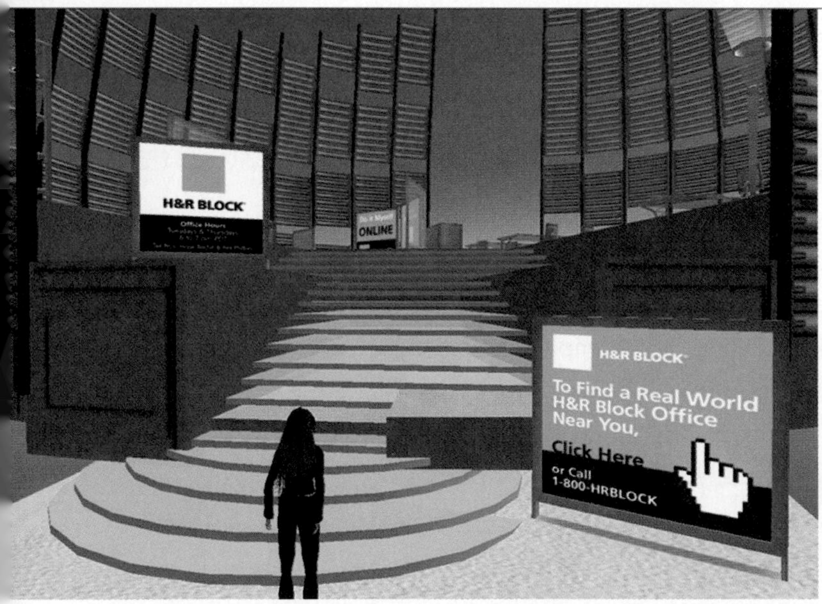

H&R Block Island in the virtual world Second Life is just one of many social media efforts that Paula Drum and her team at H&R Block use to communicate with customers about tax preparation products and services.

Adding Some Excitement to a Most Unexciting Task

Many U.S. taxpayers don't think about their taxes until they absolutely have to, and then they want to think about taxes as little as possible. In this context of extreme apathy, Paula Drum, H&R Block's vice president of marketing for digital tax solutions, certainly has a challenge on her hands when she wants to communicate with taxpayers about her company's tax preparation products and services.

H&R Block is the leading tax-preparation firm in the United States, with a range of options for virtually every class of taxpayer. Those who want to avoid the laborious chore of doing their own taxes can hand the job over to a tax professional in one of the company's 13,000 offices nationwide. In contrast, those taxpayers who are willing to do most or all of the work themselves can choose from a variety of digital alternatives, including both PC software and web-based solutions.

Although tax preparation is one of the least exciting consumer experiences, Drum and her staff have developed a reputation for creative communication efforts that make use of the latest innovations in social media. For example, in a recent product launch that noted media expert Shel Israel characterized as "among the most extensive business-to-consumer social media campaigns in history," Drum and her crew used a variety of techniques to connect with potential customers: video on YouTube (including a contest for user-created videos), profiles on MySpace and Facebook, Twitter microblogging, and "H&R Block Island" in the virtual world Second Life.

Drum's innovations aren't simply about technology, however. In the spirit of Business Communication 2.0 (see Chapter 1), she emphasizes a conversational, two-way approach in which the company listens as carefully as it speaks. For example, her staffers follow a large number of Twitter users who have asked tax questions in the past, with the goal of maintaining an open channel of communication. Sometimes H&R Block personnel answer specific tax questions, and sometimes they just "offer moral support," according to Drum.

Particularly coming from a company that has a stodgy, old-school image in the minds of many people, this cutting-edge communication has surprised more than a few social media observers. Perhaps even more amazing is that Drum has actually generated some interest in the field of tax preparation.[1]

www.hrblock.com

UNDERSTANDING THE THREE-STEP WRITING PROCESS

1 LEARNING OBJECTIVE

Describe the three-step writing process.

The emphasis that H&R Block's Paula Drum (profiled in the chapter-opening "On the Job" vignette) puts on connecting with audiences is a lesson that applies to every business message. By following a proven process, you can learn to create successful messages that meet audience needs and highlight your skills as a perceptive business professional.

The three-step writing process consists of planning, writing, and completing your message.

The three-step writing process (see Figure 4.1) helps ensure that your messages are both *effective* (meeting your audience's needs and getting your points across) and *efficient* (making the best use of your time and your audience's time):

- **Step 1: Planning business messages.** To plan any message, first *analyze the situation* by defining your purpose and developing a profile of your audience. When you're sure about what you need to accomplish with your message, *gather information* that will meet your audience's needs. Next, *select the right medium* (oral, written, visual, or electronic) to deliver your message. Then *organize the information* by defining your main idea, limiting your scope, selecting the direct or indirect approach, and outlining your content. Planning messages is the focus of this chapter.

FIGURE 4.1 The Three-Step Writing Process
This three-step process will help you create more effective messages in any medium. As you get more practice with the process, it will become easier and more automatic.

1 Plan →

Analyze the Situation
Define your purpose and develop an audience profile.

Gather Information
Determine audience needs and obtain the information necessary to satisfy those needs.

Select the Right Medium
Select the best medium for delivering your message.

Organize the Information
Define your main idea, limit your scope, select a direct or an indirect approach, and outline your content.

2 Write →

Adapt to Your Audience
Be sensitive to audience needs by using a "you" attitude, politeness, positive emphasis, and unbiased language. Build a strong relationship with your audience by establishing your credibility and projecting your company's preferred image. Control your style with a conversational tone, plain English, and appropriate voice.

Compose the Message
Choose strong words that will help you create effective sentences and coherent paragraphs.

3 Complete

Revise the Message
Evaluate content and review readability, edit and rewrite for conciseness and clarity.

Produce the Message
Use effective design elements and suitable layout for a clean, professional appearance.

Proofread the Message
Review for errors in layout, spelling, and mechanics.

Distribute the Message
Deliver your message using the chosen medium; make sure all documents and all relevant files are distributed successfully.

- **Step 2: Writing business messages.** After you've planned your message, *adapt to your audience* with sensitivity, relationship skills, and an appropriate writing style. Then you're ready to *compose your message* by choosing strong words, creating effective sentences, and developing coherent paragraphs. Writing business messages is discussed in Chapter 5.
- **Step 3: Completing business messages.** After writing your first draft, *revise your message* by evaluating the content, reviewing readability, and editing and rewriting until your message comes across concisely and clearly, with correct grammar, proper punctuation, and effective format. Next, *produce your message.* Put it into the form that your audience will receive, and review all design and layout decisions for an attractive, professional appearance. *Proofread* the final product to ensure high quality and then *distribute your message.* Completing business messages is discussed in Chapter 6.

As a starting point, allot half your available time for planning, one-quarter for writing, and one-quarter for completing your messages—but adjust these percentages for each project.

The more you use the three-step writing process, the more intuitive and automatic it will become. You'll also get better at allotting your time for each task during a writing project. As a general rule, set aside roughly 50 percent of that time for planning, 25 percent for writing, and 25 percent for completing. The optimum percentages will vary widely from project to project, naturally.

Trying to save time by skimping on planning usually costs you more time in the long run.

As soon as the need to create a message appears, inexperienced communicators are often tempted to dive directly into writing. However, even a few minutes of planning can save hours of rework and frustration later on. Analyzing your audience helps you find and assemble the facts they're looking for and to deliver that information in a concise and compelling way. Planning your message reduces indecision as you write, it reduces rework during the completing step, and it can save you from embarrassing blunders that could hurt your company or your career.

2 LEARNING OBJECTIVE

Explain why it's important to analyze the situation, and define your purpose carefully before writing a message.

ANALYZING YOUR SITUATION

A successful message starts with a clear purpose that connects the sender's needs with the audience's needs. Identifying your purpose and your audience is usually a straightforward task for simple, routine messages. However, this task can be more demanding in more intricate situations. For instance, if you need to communicate about a shipping problem between your Beijing and Los Angeles factories, your purpose might simply be to alert upper management to the situation, or it might involve asking the two factory managers to explore and solve the problem. These two scenarios have different purposes and different audiences, so they require distinctly different messages. If you launch directly into writing without clarifying both your purpose and your audience, you'll waste time and energy, and you'll probably generate a less effective message.

Defining Your Purpose

Your general purpose may be to inform, to persuade, or to collaborate.

All business messages have a **general purpose**: to inform, to persuade, or to collaborate with the audience. In addition to defining the overall direction of your message, the general purpose also determines both the appropriate degree of audience participation and the amount of control you have over your message (see Figure 4.2).

To determine the specific purpose, think of how the audience's ideas or behavior should be affected by the message.

Within the scope of its general purpose, each message also has a **specific purpose**, which identifies what you hope to accomplish with your message and what your audience should do or think after receiving your message. For instance, is your goal simply to update your audience about some upcoming event, or do you want people to take immediate action? State your specific purpose as precisely as possible, even to the point of identifying which audience members should respond, how they should respond, and when.

After you have defined your specific purpose, take a moment for a reality check. Decide whether that purpose merits the time and effort required for you to prepare and send the

FIGURE 4.2 The Relationship Between General Purpose and Communicator Control
Your control over a message is inversely related to the degree of audience participation. The more participation from the audience, the less control you'll have, and vice versa.

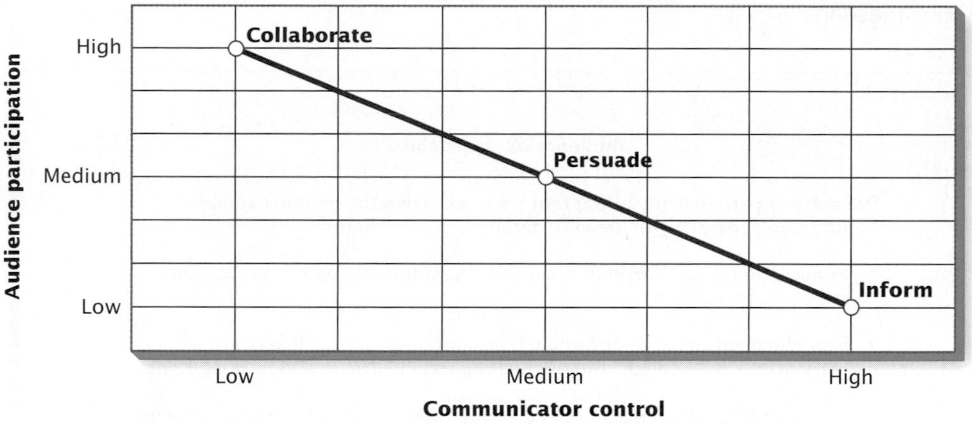

message—and for your audience to read it, view it, or listen to it. Test your purpose by asking these four questions:

- **Will anything change as a result of your message?** Make sure you don't contribute to information overload by sending messages that won't change anything. Complaining about things that you have no influence over is a good example of a message that probably shouldn't be sent.
- **Is your purpose realistic?** Recognizing whether a goal is realistic is an important part of having good business sense. For example, if you request a raise while the company is struggling, you might send the message that you're not tuned into the situation around you.
- **Is the time right?** People who are busy or distracted when they receive your message are less likely to pay attention to it.
- **Is your purpose acceptable to your organization?** Your company's business objectives and policies, and even laws that apply to your particular industry, may dictate whether a particular purpose is acceptable.

Defer sending a message, or do not send it at all, if
- *Nothing will change as a result of sending it*
- *The purpose is not realistic*
- *The timing is not right*
- *The purpose is not acceptable to your organization*

When you are satisfied that you have a clear and meaningful purpose and that this is a smart time to proceed, your next step is to understand the members of your audience and their needs.

Developing an Audience Profile

Before audience members will take the time to read or listen to your messages, they need to be interested in what you're saying. They need to see what's in it for them: How will listening to your advice or doing what you ask help them, personally or professionally? The more you know about your audience members, their needs, and their expectations, the more effectively you'll be able to communicate with them. For an example of the kind of information that is helpful to compile in an audience analysis, see Figure 4.3 on the next page. Follow these steps to conduct a thorough audience analysis:

Ask yourself some key questions about your audience:
- *Who are the most important people in the audience?*
- *How many people do you need to reach?*
- *How much do they already know about the subject?*
- *What is their probable reaction to your message?*

- **Identify your primary audience.** For some messages, certain audience members may be more important than others. Don't ignore the needs of less influential members, but make sure you address the concerns of the key decision makers.
- **Determine audience size and geographic distribution.** A message aimed at 10,000 people spread around the globe will probably require a different approach than one aimed at a dozen people down the hall.

FIGURE 4.3 Audience Analysis Helps You Plan Your Message
For simple, routine messages, you usually don't need to analyze your audience in depth. However, for complex messages or messages for indifferent or hostile audiences, take the time to study their information needs and potential reactions to your message.

Audience analysis notes

Project: A report recommending that we close down the on-site exercise facility and subsidize private memberships at local health clubs.

- **Primary audience:** Nicole Perazzo, vice president of operations, and her supervisory team.
- **Size and geographic distribution:** Nine managers total; Nicole and five of her staff are here on site; three other supervisors are based in Hong Kong.
- **Composition:** All have experience in operations management, but several are new to the company.
- **Level of understanding:** All will no doubt understand the financial considerations, but the newer managers may not understand the importance of the on-site exercise facility to many of our employees.
- **Expectations and preferences.** They're expecting a firm recommendation, backed up with well-thought-out financial rationale and suggestions for communicating the bad news to employees. For a decision of this magnitude, a formal report is appropriate; e-mail distribution is expected.
- **Probable reaction.** From one-on-one discussions, I know that several of the managers receiving this report are active users of the on-site facility and won't welcome the suggestion that we shut it down. However, some nonexercisers generally think it's a luxury the company can't afford. Audience reactions will range from highly positive to highly negative; the report should focus on overcoming the highly negative reactions since they're the ones I need to address.

- **Determine audience composition.** Look for both similarities and differences in culture, language, age, education, organizational rank and status, attitudes, experience, motivations, and any other factors that could affect the successful reception and decoding of your message.
- **Gauge audience members' level of understanding.** If audience members share your general background, they'll probably understand your material without difficulty. If not, your message will need an element of education.
- **Understand audience expectations and preferences.** Will members of your audience expect complete details or just a summary of the main points? In general, for internal communication, the higher up the organization your message goes, the fewer details people want to see.
- **Forecast probable audience reaction.** As you'll read later in the chapter, potential audience reaction affects message organization. If you expect a favorable response, you can state conclusions and recommendations up front and offer minimal supporting evidence. If you expect skepticism, you can introduce conclusions gradually and with more proof.

If audience members have different levels of understanding of the topic, aim your message at the most influential decision makers.

To win over a skeptical audience, use a gradual approach and plenty of evidence.

3 LEARNING OBJECTIVE

Discuss information-gathering options for simple messages, and identify three attributes of quality information.

GATHERING INFORMATION

When you have a clear picture of your audience, your next step is to assemble the information that you will include in your message. For simple messages, you may already have all the information at hand, but for more complex messages, you may need to do considerable research and analysis before you're ready to begin writing. Chapter 11 explores formal techniques for finding, evaluating, and processing information, but you can often use a variety of informal techniques to gather insights and guide your research efforts:

- **Consider the audience's perspective.** Put yourself in the audience's position; what are these people thinking, feeling, or planning? What information do they need to move forward?
- **Read reports and other company documents.** Annual reports, financial statements, news releases, blogs by industry experts, marketing reports, and customer surveys are just a few of the many potential sources. Find out whether your company has a *knowledge-management system*, a centralized database that collects the experiences and insights of employees throughout the organization.
- **Talk with supervisors, colleagues, or customers.** Fellow workers and customers may have information you need, or they may know what your audience will be interested in.
- **Ask your audience for input.** If you're unsure what audience members need from your message, ask them. Admitting you don't know but want to meet their needs will impress an audience more than guessing and getting it wrong.

Uncovering Audience Needs

If you're given a vague request, ask questions to clarify it before you plan a response.

In many situations, your audience's information needs are readily apparent; in others, your audience may be unable to articulate exactly what is needed. If someone makes a vague or broad request, ask questions to narrow the focus. If your boss says, "Find out everything you can about Interscope Records," narrow the investigation by asking which aspect of the company and its business is most important. Asking a question or two often forces the person to think through the request and define more precisely what is required.

If appropriate, include additional information that might be helpful, even though the requester didn't specifically ask for it.

In addition, try to think of information needs that your audience may not have expressed. Suppose you've been asked to compare two health insurance plans for your firm's employees, but your research has uncovered a third alternative that might be even better. You could then expand your report to include a brief explanation of why the third plan should be considered and compare it to the two original plans. Use judgment, however; in some situations you need to provide only what the audience expects and nothing more.

Finding Your Focus

You may encounter situations in which the assignment or objective is so vague that you have no idea how to get started in determining what the audience needs to know. In such cases, you can use some *discovery techniques* to help generate ideas and uncover possible avenues to research. One popular technique is **free writing**, in which you write whatever comes to mind, without stopping to make any corrections, for a set period of time. The big advantage of free writing is that you silence your "inner critic" and just express ideas as they come to you. You might end up with a rambling mess by any conventional measure, but that's not important. Within that tangle of expressions, you might also find some useful ideas and angles that hadn't occurred to you yet—perhaps the crucial idea that will jump-start the entire project.

The best discovery option in some cases might not be writing at all, but rather *sketching*. If you're unable to come up with any words, grab a sketchpad and starting drawing. While you're thinking visually, your brain might release some great ideas that were trapped behind words.

The techniques listed under "Defining Your Main Idea" on page 104 can also be helpful if you don't know where to start.

Providing Required Information

Test the completeness of your document by making sure it answers all six journalistic questions: who, what, when, where, why, *and* how.

After you've defined your audience's information needs, be sure you satisfy those needs completely. One good way to test the thoroughness of your message is to use the **journalistic approach**: Check to see whether your message answers *who, what, when, where, why*, and *how* so readers or listeners get all the information they need.

To gauge the quality of the information you provide in your messages, check to ensure that the information is accurate, ethical, and pertinent:

- **Is the information accurate?** Inaccuracies can cause a host of problems, from embarrassment and lost productivity to serious safety and legal issues. Be sure to review any mathematical or financial calculations. Check all dates and schedules. Examine your own assumptions and conclusions to be certain they are valid.
- **Is the information ethical?** By working hard to ensure the accuracy of the information you gather, you'll also avoid many ethical problems in your messages. However, messages can also be unethical if important information is omitted or obscured.
- **Is the information pertinent?** Remember that some points will be more important to your audience than others. Moreover, by focusing on the information that concerns your audience the most, you increase your chances of sending an effective message.

Some messages necessarily reach audiences with a diverse mix of educational levels, subject awareness, and other variables. In these cases, your only choice is to try to accommodate the likely range of audience members (see Figure 4.4).

4 LEARNING OBJECTIVE

List the factors to consider when choosing the most appropriate medium for a message.

SELECTING THE RIGHT MEDIUM

Selecting the best medium for your message can make the difference between effective and ineffective communication.[2] A **medium** is the form through which you choose to communicate a message. You may choose to talk with someone face to face, post to a blog, send an e-mail message, or create a webcast; the range of media possibilities is wide and growing wider all the time. Although media categories have become increasingly blurred in recent years, for the sake of discussion, you can think of media as being *oral*, *written*, *visual*, or *electronic* (which often combines several media types).

Oral Media

Oral communication is best when you need to encourage interaction, express emotions, or monitor emotional responses.

Oral media include face-to-face conversations, interviews, speeches, and in-person presentations and meetings. By giving communicators the ability to see, hear, and react to each other, oral media are useful for encouraging people to ask questions, make comments, and work together to reach a consensus or decision. For example, experts recommend that managers engage in frequent "walk-arounds," chatting with employees to get input, answer their questions, and interpret important business events and trends.[3]

Of course, if you don't want a lot of questions or interaction, using oral media can be an unwise choice. However, consider your audience carefully before deciding to limit interaction by choosing a different medium. As a manager, you will encounter unpleasant situations (declining an employee's request for a raise, for example) in which sending an e-mail message or otherwise avoiding personal contact will seem appealing to you. In many such cases, though, you owe the other party the opportunity to ask questions or express concerns. Moreover, facing the tough situations in person will earn you a reputation as an honest, caring manager.

Written Media

Printed messages have been replaced in many instances by electronic media, although the print medium still has a place in business today.

Written messages take many forms, from traditional memos to glossy reports that rival magazines in production quality. **Memos** are brief printed documents traditionally used for the routine, day-to-day exchange of information within an organization. In many organizations, instant messaging (IM), e-mail, blogs, and other electronic media have largely replaced paper memos.

Letters are brief written messages generally sent to recipients outside the organization. In addition to conveying a particular message, they perform an important public relations function in fostering good working relationships with customers, suppliers, and others. Many organizations rely on *form letters* to save time and money on routine communication.

FIGURE 4.4 An Audience-Focused Report (Selected Pages)
These two pages from a local water district's annual water quality report do a good job of presenting a technical subject to the general public (all the households in this particular city). Notice how the report presents scientific information accurately and supplements it with clear explanations of what the information means and how it pertains to water users.

ANNUAL WATER QUALITY REPORT

Important Terms Used In This Report

Helps readers understand the scientific terms used to describe water quality

Maximum Contaminant Level Goal (MCLG) - The maximum goal level of a contaminant in drinking water below which there is no known or expected risk to health MCLG's allow for a margin of safety.

Maximum Contaminant Level (MCL) - The level of a contaminant allowed in drinking water.

Treatment Technique (TT) - A required process intended to reduce the level of contaminant in drinking water.

Action Level (AL) - The concentration of a contaminant which, if exceeded, triggers treatment or other requirements that a water system must follow.

Parts per Million (ppm) Parts per Billion (ppb) - A part per million means that one part of a particular contaminant is present for every million parts of water. Similarly, parts per billion indicate the amount of contaminant per billion parts of water.

Not Applicable (NA) – Means that EPA has not established MCLG's for these substances.

Disinfection By-Products (DBP's) - Organic compounds resulting from the interaction of chlorine with natural organic matter in water supplies.

Who Can I Contact For More Information?

Provides helpful contact information

To obtain more information on water quality issues contact any of the following agencies:

Alderwood Water & Wastewater District
Water Quality Division
Telephone: 425-787-0250
www.alderwoodwater.com

U.S. Environmental Protection Agency
Safe Drinking Water Hotline
Telephone: 800-426-4791

Washington State Department of Health
Regional DOH Office
Telephone: 253-395-6750
www.doh.wa.gov/ehp/dw

How can I get involved in water quality decisions?

Answers a question that many concerned customers are likely to have

The Alderwood Water & Wastewater District regular Board of Commissioners meetings are scheduled at the District Administration Building at 3626 156th Street SW, Lynnwood WA. each first and third Monday of the month.

Terms Simply Stated

Helps readers grasp significance of very small numbers by providing a selection of analogous measurements

Parts per million (ppm)	Parts per billion (ppb)
3 drops in 42 gallons	1 drop in 14,000 gallons
1 second in 12 days	1 second in 32 years
1 penny in $10,000	1 penny in $10,000,000
1 inch in 16 miles	1 inch in 16,000 miles

ANNUAL WATER QUALITY REPORT

Water Quality Results

Last year, your drinking water was tested for hundreds of possible contaminants. The contaminants that were detected are listed in the following tables. In reading this data, it is important to note that all of these contaminants were present in amounts below the United States Environmental Protection Agency's (USEPA) allowable levels. To ensure tap water is safe to drink USEPA prescribes regulations that limit the amount of certain contaminants in the water provided by public water systems.

Shows test results in appropriate scientific format but helps nontechnical readers by explaining what the various substances are and whether the water complies with government standards

Regulated Contaminants		EPA Regulations		Your Water Results		
SUBSTANCE	UNITS	IDEAL LEVEL/ GOAL (MCLG)	MAXIMUM ALLOWABLE (MCL)	Range or Other	Average Value or Highest Result	Comply?
Nitrate	ppm	10	10	0.05 - 0.12	0.09	YES
The small amount of Nitrate comes from natural sources in the water source						
Total Coliform Bacteria	% Positive	0	Not More Than 5% Positive Per Month	0%	0%	YES
Total coliform bacteria testing is used to monitor microbial quality in the water distribution system. In Alderwood, a minimum of 100 samples must be collected each month. Not more than 5% of the monthly total can be positive for total coliforms.						
Fluoride	ppm	2	4	0.7 - 1.1	1.0	YES
Fluoride is added to your water in carefully controlled levels for dental health.						
Haloacetic Acids (5)	ppb	NA	60	16.6 - 45.1	35.5	YES
Total Triholomethanes	ppb	NA	80	30.2 - 58.7	47.3	YES
Haloacetic acids and trihalomethanes form as by-products of the chlorination process that is used to kill or inactivate disease-causing microbes.						
Turbidity	NTU	NA	TT	100%	0.08	YES
Turbidity is a measurement of the amount of particulates in water measured in Nephelometric Turbidity Units (NTU). Particulates in water can include bacteria, viruses and protozoans that can cause disease. Turbidity measurements are used to determine the effectiveness of the treatment processes used to remove these particulates. Values reported are the lowest monthly percentage of samples that met the turbidity limit (0.3 NTU for EPA and 0.1 NTU for theState) and the highest filtered water turbidity measurement obtained in 2004.						

Cryptosporidium Reporting

Cryptosporidium is a microscopic organism that, when ingested, may cause diarrhea, fever, and other gastrointestinal distress. It can be found in all of Washington's rivers and streams and comes from animal wastes in the watershed. Cryptosporidium is eliminated by effective treatment including filtration, sedimentation and disinfection. Your water is tested regularly for the presence of Cryptosporidium. In 2004, one of the 12 monthly samples of the raw, source water showed the presence of Cryptosporidium. However, no Cryptosporidium was detected in the finished/treated water you receive.

Cryptosporidium	Units	Ideal Level/ Goal (MCLG)	Your Water Results	
			Range	Average
Cryptosporidium parvum oocysts	oocysts/L	N/A	0 - 1	0
One monthly sample of the raw, source water showed the presence of Cryptosporidium.				

Reports and proposals are usually longer than memos and letters, although both can be created in memo or letter format. These documents come in a variety of lengths, ranging from a few pages to several hundred, and are usually fairly formal in tone. Chapters 11 through 13 discuss reports and proposals in detail.

Visual Media

In some situations, a message that is predominantly visual, with text used to support the illustration, can be more effective that a message that relies primarily on text.

Traditional business messages rely primarily on text, with occasional support from graphic elements such as charts, graphs, or diagrams to help illustrate points discussed in the text. However, many business communicators are discovering the power of messages in which the visual element is dominant and supported by small amounts of text. For the purposes of this discussion, you can think of *visual media* as any formats in which one or more visual elements play a central role in conveying the message content (see Figure 4.5).

Messages that combine powerful visuals with supporting text can be effective for a number of reasons. Today's audiences are pressed for time and bombarded with messages, so anything that communicates quickly is welcome. Visuals are also effective at describing complex ideas and processes because they can reduce the work required for an audience to identify the parts and relationships that make up the whole. Also, in a multilingual business world, diagrams, symbols, and other images can lower communication barriers by requiring less language processing. Finally, visual depictions can be easier to remember than purely textual descriptions or explanations.

Electronic Media

In general, use electronic media to deliver messages quickly, to reach widely dispersed audiences, and to take advantage of rich multimedia formats.

The range of electronic media is broad and continues to grow even broader, from phone calls and podcasts to blogs and wikis to e-mail and text messaging. When you want to make a powerful impression, using electronic media can increase the excitement and visual appeal with interactivity, animation, audio, and video.

The growth of electronic communication options is both a blessing and a curse for business communicators. On the one hand, you have more tools than ever before to choose

FIGURE 4.5 Visual Media
In traditional business messages, visual elements usually support the text. However, in some instances, the message can be presented more effectively by reversing that relationship—basing the message on a dominant visual and using text to support that image.

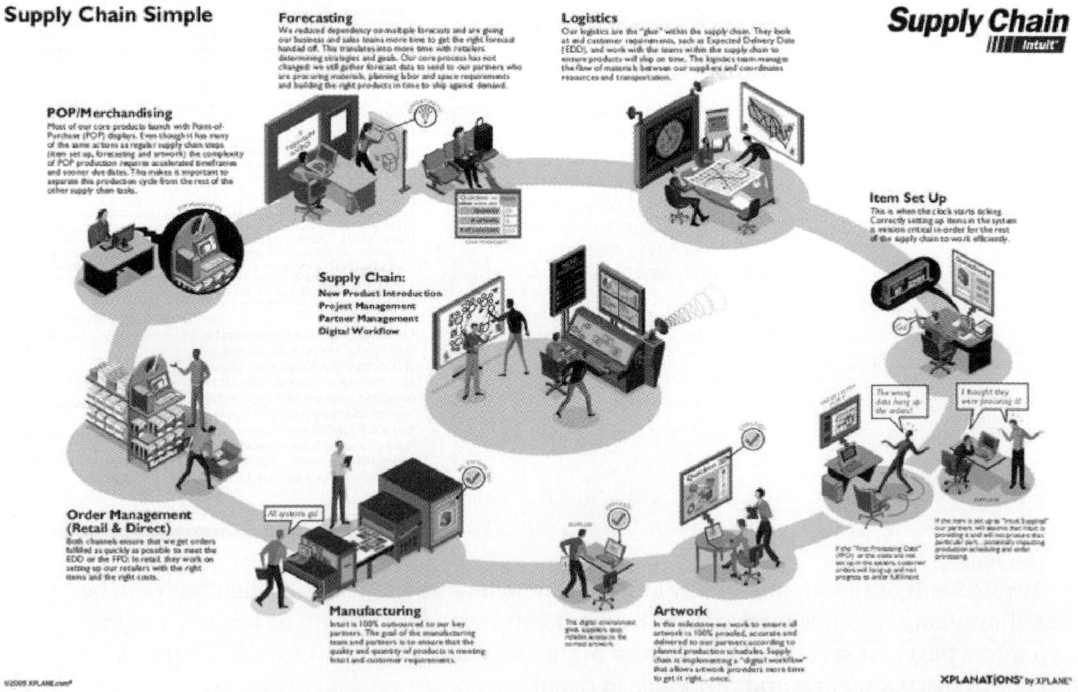

FIGURE 4.6 **Electronic Oral Media**
Many websites now feature talking animated figures, sometimes called *avatars*, offering website visitors a more engaging experience.

from, with more ways to deliver rational and emotional content. On the other hand, the sheer range of choices can complicate your job because you often need to choose among multiple media, and you need to know how to use each medium successfully.

You'll learn more about using electronic media throughout this book (in Chapter 7, in particular), but for now, here is a quick overview of the major electronic media being used in business:

- **Electronic versions of oral media.** These media include telephone calls, teleconferencing, voice-mail messages, audio recordings such as compact discs and podcasts, voice synthesis (creating audio signals from computer data), voice recognition (converting audio signals to computer data), and even animated online characters (see Figure 4.6). The simple telephone call is still a vital communication link for many organizations, but even it has joined the Internet age, thanks to *Internet telephony*, also known by the technical term VoIP (which stands for *Voice over IP*, the Internet Protocol). Although telephone calls can't convey all the nonverbal signals of an in-person conversation, they can convey quite a few, including tone of voice, pace, laughter, pauses, and so on. Using voice mail is a handy way to send brief messages when an immediate response isn't crucial, but it's a poor choice for lengthy messages because the information is difficult to retrieve. You'll learn about podcasts in particular in Chapter 7.
- **Electronic versions of written media.** These options range from e-mail and IM to blogs, websites, social networks, and wikis. These media are in a state of constant change, in terms of both what is available and who tends to use which media. For example, e-mail has been a primary business medium for the past decade or two, but it is being replaced in many cases by IM, blogs, text messaging, and communication via social networks.[4] Chapter 7 takes a closer look at e-mail, IM, blogs, and social networks; Chapter 13 discusses wikis in more detail.
- **Electronic versions of visual media.** These choices can include electronic presentations (using Microsoft PowerPoint and other software), computer animation (using software such as Adobe Flash to create many of the animated sequences you see on websites, for example), and video. Businesses have made extensive use of video (particularly for training, new product promotions, and executive announcements) for years—first on tape, then on DVD, and now online. Video is also incorporated in podcasting, creating *vidcasts*, and in blogging, creating *video blogs* (*vlogs*) and *mobile blogs* (*moblogs*).[5] **Multimedia** refers to use of two or more media to craft a single message, typically some combination of audio, video, text, and visual graphics.

For more on the latest innovations in electronic media, visit **http://real-timeupdates.com/ebc** and click on Chapter 4.

Factors to Consider When Choosing Media

Table 4.1 lists the general advantages and disadvantages of each medium. In addition, be sure to consider how your message is affected by these important factors:

Complicated messages often benefit from richer media.

- **Media richness.** Richness is a medium's ability to (1) convey a message through more than one *informational cue* (visual, verbal, and vocal), (2) facilitate feedback, and (3) establish personal focus. The richest medium is face-to-face communication; it's personal, it provides immediate feedback (verbal and nonverbal), and it conveys the emotion behind a message.[6] Multimedia presentations and webpages are also quite rich, with the ability to present images, animation, text, music, sound effects, and other elements. Many electronic media are also *interactive*, in that they enable audiences to participate in the communication process. At the other end of the continuum are the leanest media—those that communicate in the simplest ways, provide no opportunity for audience feedback, and aren't personalized (see Figure 4.7). In general, use richer media to send nonroutine or complex messages, to humanize your presence throughout the organization, to communicate caring to employees, and to gain employee commitment to company goals. Use leaner media to send routine messages or to transfer information that doesn't require significant explanation.[7]

TABLE 4.1 Media Advantages and Disadvantages

MEDIA TYPE	ADVANTAGES	DISADVANTAGES
Oral	• Provide opportunity for immediate feedback • Promote interaction • Involve rich nonverbal cues (both physical gesture and vocal inflection) • Allow the expression of the emotions behind the message	• Restrict participation to those physically present • Unless recorded, provide no permanent, verifiable record of the communication • In most cases, reduce communicator's control over the message • Other than for messages that are prewritten and rehearsed, offer no opportunity to revise or edit spoken words
Written	• Allow planning and control of message • Reach geographically dispersed audiences • Offer a permanent, verifiable record • Minimize the distortion that can result with oral and some forms of electronic messages • Can be used to avoid immediate interactions • Can help control the emotional aspects of an interchange by eliminating interpersonal communication	• Usually not conducive to speedy feedback • Lack the rich nonverbal cues provided by oral media • Often take more time and more resources to create and distribute • For elaborate documents, can require special skills in preparation and production
Visual	• Can convey complex ideas and relationships quickly • Often less intimidating than long blocks of text, particularly for nonnative readers • Can reduce the burden on the audience to figure out how the pieces fit	• Can require artistic skills to design • Require some technical skills to create • Can require more time to create than an equivalent amount of text • More difficult to transmit and store than simple textual messages
Electronic	• Deliver messages quickly • Reach geographically dispersed audiences • Offer the persuasive power of multimedia formats • Can increase accessibility and openness in an organization	• Easy to overuse (sending too many messages to too many recipients) • Present privacy risks and concerns (exposing confidential data; employer monitoring of e-mail, IM, and blogs; accidental forwarding) • Present security risks (viruses and spyware) • Create productivity concerns (frequent interruptions, lack of integration among multiple electronic media in use at the same time, and time wasted on nonbusiness uses)

FIGURE 4.7 Media Richness
Business media vary widely in terms of *richness*, which is the number of informational cues available, the medium's ability to incorporate feedback, and the degree to which the medium can be personalized.

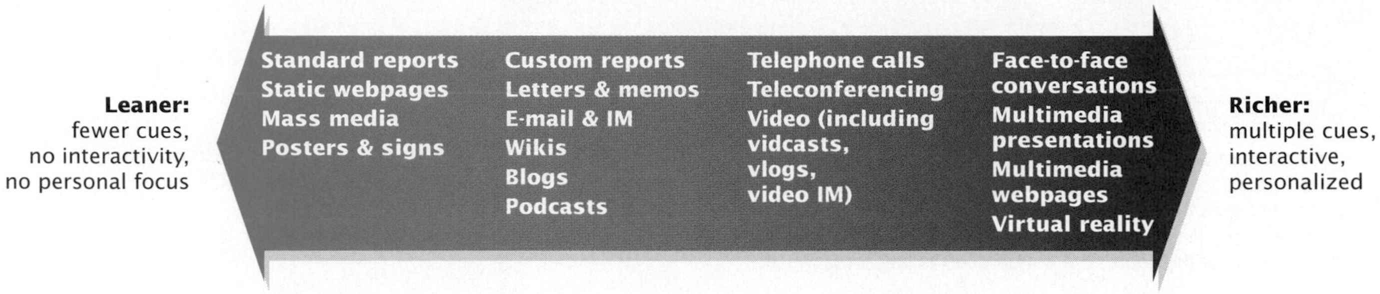

- **Message formality.** Your media choice is a nonverbal signal that affects the style and tone of your message. For example, a printed memo letter is likely to be perceived as a more formal gesture than an e-mail message.
- **Media limitations.** Every medium has limitations. For example, IM and text are great for simple, straightforward messages, but they are ineffective for sending complex messages.
- **Urgency.** Some media establish a connection with the audience faster than others, so choose wisely if your message is urgent. However, be sure to respect audience members' time and workloads. If a message isn't urgent and doesn't require immediate feedback, choose a medium such as e-mail that allows people to respond at their convenience.

Some media deliver messages faster than others; avoid using instantaneous delivery to create a false sense of urgency.

- **Cost.** Cost is both a real financial factor and a perceived nonverbal signal. For example, depending on the context, extravagant (and expensive) video or multimedia presentations can send a nonverbal signal of sophistication and professionalism—or careless disregard for company budgets.
- **Audience preferences.** Be sure to consider which medium or media your audience expects or prefers.[8] For instance, some cultures tend to favor one channel over another. The United States, Canada, and Germany emphasize written messages, for example, whereas Japan emphasizes oral messages—perhaps because its high-context culture carries so much of the message in nonverbal cues and "between-the-lines" interpretation.[9]

When choosing the appropriate medium, don't forget to consider your audience's preferences and expectations.

After you select the best medium for your purpose, situation, and audience, you are ready to start thinking about the organization of your message.

ORGANIZING YOUR INFORMATION

5 LEARNING OBJECTIVE

Explain why good organization is important to both you and your audience.

Organization can make the difference between success and failure. Compare the two versions of the message in Figure 4.8 on the next page. The ineffective version exhibits several common organization mistakes: taking too long to get to the point, including irrelevant material, getting ideas mixed up, and leaving out necessary information.

Recognizing the Importance of Good Organization

The ability to present information in an organized fashion is an essential business skill.

Good organization helps audience members understand your message, accept your message, and save time.

Good organization helps your readers or listeners in three key ways. First, it helps them understand your message. In a well-organized message, you make the main point clear at the outset, present additional points to support that main idea, and satisfy all the information needs of the audience. But if your message is poorly organized, your meaning can be obscured, and your audiences may form inaccurate conclusions about what you've written or said.

Second, good organization helps receivers accept your message. If your writing appears confused and disorganized, people will likely conclude that the *thinking* behind the writing

FIGURE 4.8 Improving the Organization of a Message
The improved version of this e-mail message is clear and efficient, presenting only the necessary information in a logical sequence.

Ineffective

Defective D... r (HTML)

File ... sert Format Tools Actions Help — Type a question for help

To: customer_service@computertime.com

Cc...:

Subject: Defective DVD recorder

General Nutrition Corporation has been doing business with ComputerTime since I was hired six years ago. Your building was smaller then, and it was located on the corner of Federal Avenue and 2nd N.W. Jared Mallory, our controller, was one of your first customers. I still remember the day. It was the biggest check I'd ever written. Of course, over the years, I've gotten used to larger purchases.

Fails to explain the purpose of the letter and immediately gets bogged down in irrelevant details

Our department now has 15 employees. As accountants, we need to have our computers working so that we can do our jobs. The DVD recorder we bought for my assistant, Suzanne, has been a problem. We've taken it in for repairs three times in three months to the authorized service center, and Suzanne is very careful with the machine and hasn't abused it. After all those repairs, it still doesn't work right, and she's tired of hauling it back and forth. We're all putting in longer hours because it is our busy season, and none of us have a lot of spare time.

Waits until the second paragraph to even introduce the main idea

Fails to provide specific information about the problem

This is the first time we've returned anything to your store, and I hope you'll agree that we deserve a better deal.

Fails to specify what she wants the reader to do

Effective

Defective DVD recorder (HTML)

File Edit ... ert Format Tools Actions Help — Type a question for help

To: customer_service@computertime.com

Cc...:

Subject: Defective DVD recorder: request for replacement

Dear Customer Service Representative:

Can you please exchange the faulty DVD record/play drive (Olympic Systems, Model PRS-2) that GNC purchased on November 15, 2010? The drive began malfunctioning soon after my assistant installed it on her computer (an HP Compaq dc5100), and we've had trouble with it ever since.

Opens with her request and immediately follows that with relevant details

We took the drive to the authorized service center and were assured that the problem was merely a loose connection. The service representative fixed the drive, but in April we had to have it fixed again—another loose connection. For the next three months, the drive worked reasonably well, although the recording time was occasionally slow. Two months ago, the drive stopped working again. Once more, the service representative blamed a loose connection and made the repair. The drive is again operational, but it occasionally makes odd noises and takes an inordinate amount of time to record a disc.

Provides details in the body so that the reader can understand why Saunders thinks a problem exists

Provides a detailed history of the problem so that the reader clearly understands her frustration

Although all the repairs have been relatively minor and have been covered by the one-year warranty, we are not satisfied with the drive. We would like to exchange it for a similar model from another manufacturer.

GNC has done business with your store for six years, and we look forward to purchasing from you in the future after this matter is resolved successfully. Please let us know your answer by September 20.

Requests a specific action from the reader

Emphasizes (in a calm, respectful way) that GNC won't be buying anything else until this problem is resolved

Sincerely,
Jill Saunders
Accounting Supervisor

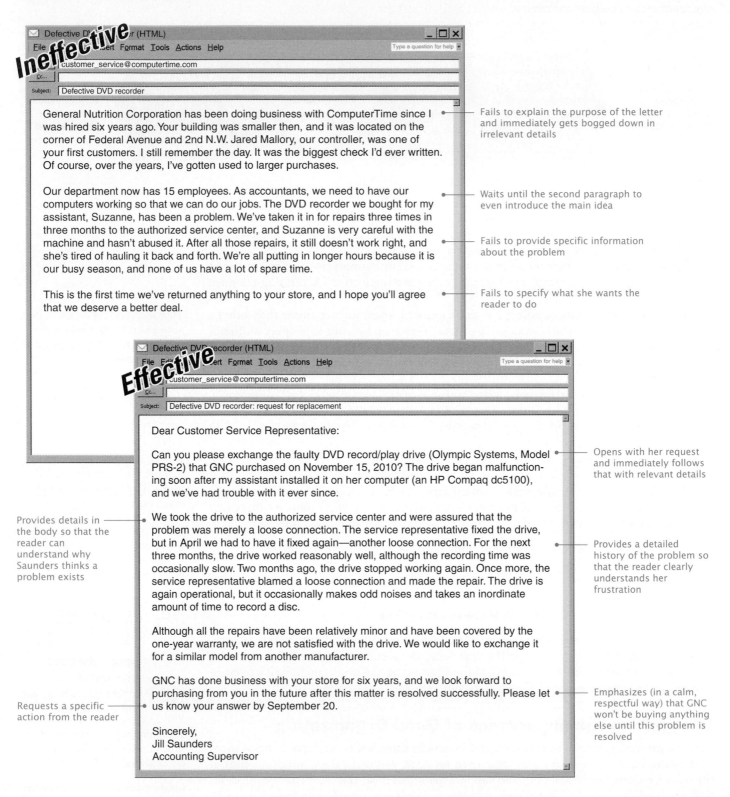

FIGURE 4.9 Message Demonstrating a Diplomatic Organization Plan
In the case of ComputerTime's response to Jill Saunders's request for a replacement product from a different manufacturer, ComputerTime isn't able to do exactly what Saunders requested. (It has arranged a replacement from the same manufacturer instead.) Consequently, the response letter from Linda Davis has a negative aspect to it, but the style of the letter is tactful and positive.

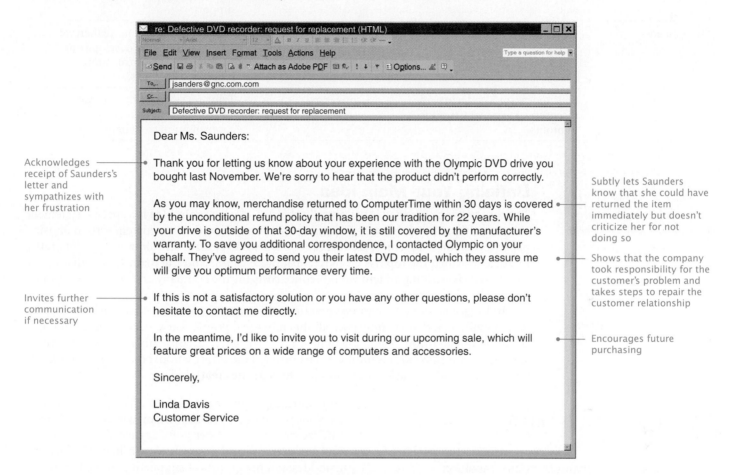

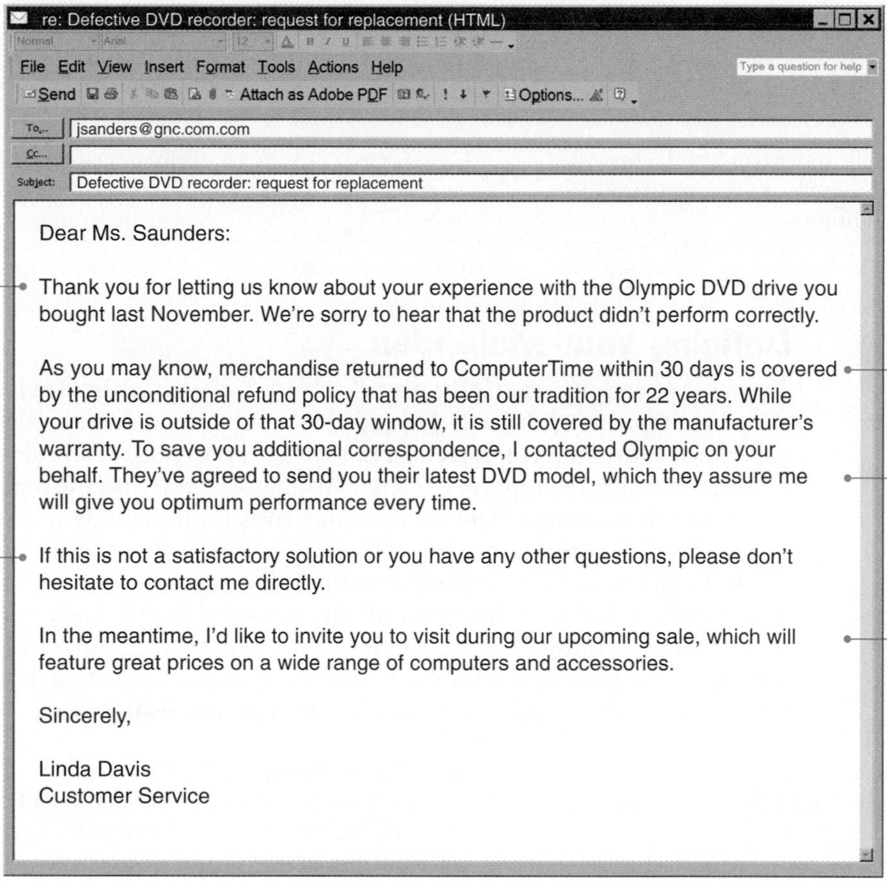
re: Defective DVD recorder: request for replacement (HTML)

File Edit View Insert Format Tools Actions Help

Send Attach as Adobe PDF Options...

To... jsanders@gnc.com.com

Cc...

Subject: Defective DVD recorder: request for replacement

Dear Ms. Saunders:

Thank you for letting us know about your experience with the Olympic DVD drive you bought last November. We're sorry to hear that the product didn't perform correctly.

As you may know, merchandise returned to ComputerTime within 30 days is covered by the unconditional refund policy that has been our tradition for 22 years. While your drive is outside of that 30-day window, it is still covered by the manufacturer's warranty. To save you additional correspondence, I contacted Olympic on your behalf. They've agreed to send you their latest DVD model, which they assure me will give you optimum performance every time.

If this is not a satisfactory solution or you have any other questions, please don't hesitate to contact me directly.

In the meantime, I'd like to invite you to visit during our upcoming sale, which will feature great prices on a wide range of computers and accessories.

Sincerely,

Linda Davis
Customer Service

is also confused and disorganized. Moreover, effective messages often require a bit more than simple, clear logic. A diplomatic approach helps receivers accept your message, even if it's not exactly what they want to hear (see Figure 4.9). In contrast, a poorly organized message on an emotionally charged topic can alienate the audience before you have the chance to get your point across.

Third, good organization saves your audience time. Well-organized messages are efficient. They contain only relevant ideas, and they are brief. Moreover, each piece of information is located in a logical place in the overall flow; each section builds on the one before to create a coherent whole, without forcing people to look for missing pieces.

In addition to saving time and energy for your readers, good organization saves you time and consumes less of your creative energy. Writing proceeds more quickly because you don't waste time putting ideas in the wrong places or composing material that you don't need. You spend far less time rewriting, trying to extract sensible meaning from disorganized rambling.

Good organization saves you time and energy in the writing and completing phases.

Good organizational skills are also good for your career because they help you develop a reputation as a clear thinker who cares about your readers. If you get a reputation as a disorganized communicator, people will begin to ignore your messages and question your thinking skills. In other words, poorly organized messages are bad for business and bad for your career.

TABLE 4.2 Defining Topic and Main Idea

GENERAL PURPOSE	SPECIFIC PURPOSE	TOPIC	MAIN IDEA
To inform	Teach customer service representatives how to edit and expand the technical support wiki	Technical support wiki	Careful, thorough edits and additions to the wiki help the entire department provide better customer support.
To persuade	Convince top managers to increase spending on research and development	Funding for research spending on research and development	Competitors spend more than we do on research and development, enabling them to create more innovative products.
To collaborate	Solicit ideas for a companywide incentive system that ties wages to profits	Incentive pay	Tying wages to profits motivates employees and reduces compensation costs in tough years.

Defining Your Main Idea

The topic is the overall subject; the main idea is a specific statement about the topic.

The **topic** of your message is the overall subject, and your **main idea** is a specific statement about that topic (see Table 4.2). For example, if you believe that the current system of using paper forms for filing employee insurance claims is expensive and slow, you might craft a message in which the topic is employee insurance claims and the main idea is that a new web-based claim-filing system would reduce costs for the company and reduce reimbursement delays for employees.

In longer documents and presentations, you often need to unify a mass of material with a main idea that encompasses all the individual points you want to make. Finding a common thread through all these points can be a challenge. Sometimes you won't even be sure what your main idea is until you sort through the information. For tough assignments like these, consider a variety of techniques to generate creative ideas:

- **Brainstorming.** Working alone or with others, generate as many ideas and questions as you can, without stopping to criticize or organize. After you capture all these pieces, look for patterns and connections to help identify the main idea and the groups of supporting ideas. For example, if your main idea concerns whether to open a new restaurant in Denver, you'll probably find a group of ideas related to financial return, another related to competition, and so on. Identifying such groups helps you see the major issues that will lead you to a conclusion you can feel confident about.
- **Journalistic approach.** Introduced earlier in the chapter, the journalistic approach asks *who*, *what*, *when*, *where*, *why*, and *how* questions to distill major ideas from unorganized information.
- **Question-and-answer chain.** Start with a key question, from the audience's perspective, and work back toward your message. In most cases, you'll find that each answer generates new questions until you identify the information that needs to be in your message.
- **Storyteller's tour.** Some writers find it best to talk through a communication challenge before they try to write. Record yourself as you describe what you intend to write. Then listen to the playback, identify ways to tighten and clarify the message, and repeat the process until you distill the main idea down to a single concise message.

REAL-TIME UPDATES
Learn More

Smart advice for brainstorming sessions

Generate better ideas in less time with these helpful tips. Go to **http://real-timeupdates.com/ebc** and click on "Learn More." If you are using mybcommlab, you can access Real-Time Updates within each chapter or under Student Study Tools.

REAL-TIME UPDATES
Learn More

Wrap your mind around mind mapping

See mind mapping in action in this colorfully illustrated presentation. Go to **http://real-timeupdates.com/ebc** and click on "Learn More." If you are using mybcommlab, you can access Real-Time Updates within each chapter or under Student Study Tools.

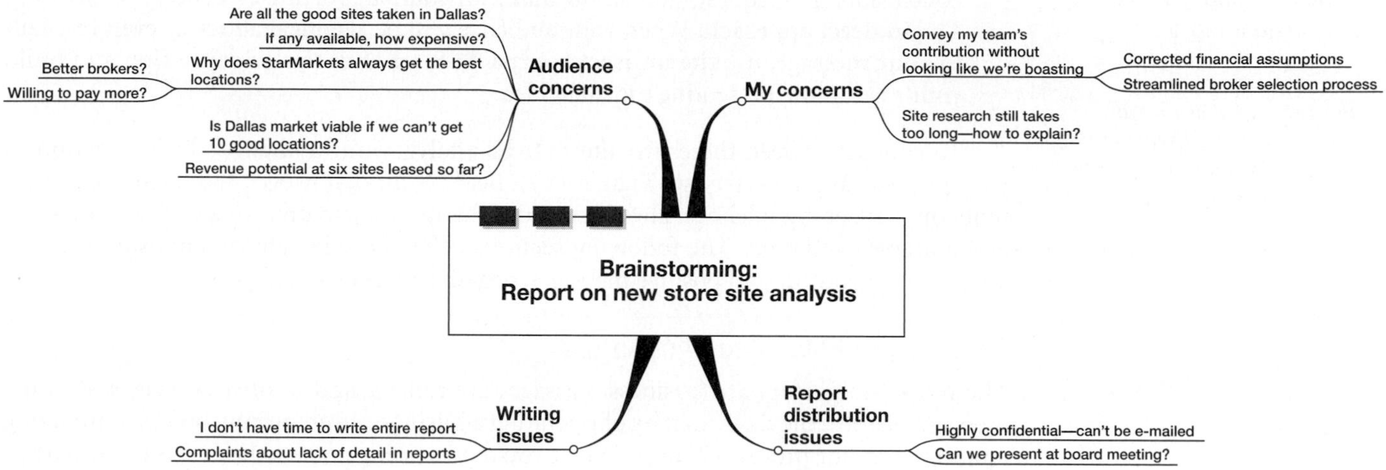

FIGURE 4.10 Using the Mind-Mapping Technique to Plan a Writing Project
Mind mapping is a helpful technique for identifying and organizing the many ideas and pieces of information that a complex writing task usually entails. Software (MindJet's MindManager in this case) makes it easy to create graphical output—such as this diagram, which shows the writer's own concerns about a report, her insights into the audience's concerns, and several issues related to writing and distributing the report.

- **Mind mapping.** You can generate and organize ideas using a graphic method called *mind mapping.* Start with a main idea and then branch out to connect every other related idea that comes to mind (see Figure 4.10). You can learn more about mind mapping from the Mind Mapping Software Weblog, at **http://mindmapping.typepad.com**, and try a free online tool at **http://bubbl.us**.[10]

Limiting Your Scope

The **scope** of a message is the range of information presented, the overall length of the message, and the level of detail—all of which need to correspond to the main idea. Some business messages have a preset length limit, whether from a boss's instructions, the technology you're using, or a time frame, such as individual speaker slots during a seminar. Even if you don't have a preset length, it's vital to limit yourself to the scope needed to convey your message—and no more.

Limit the number of support points; having fewer, stronger points is a better approach than using many, weaker points.

Whatever the length of your message, keep the number of major supporting points to half a dozen or so. If you can get your idea across with fewer than that, all the better. Listing 20 or 30 supporting points might feel as though you're being thorough, but your audience is likely to view such detail as rambling and mind numbing. Instead, look for ways to group supporting points under major headings, such as finance, customers, competitors, employees, or whatever is appropriate for your subject. You may need to refine your major supporting points so that you have a smaller number with greater impact.

If your message needs to be brief, your main idea will have to be easy to understand and easy to accept. However, if your message can be somewhat longer, you can develop the major points in more detail. How much space you need to communicate and support your main idea depends on your subject, your audience members' familiarity with the material and their receptivity to your conclusions, and your credibility with them. You'll need fewer words to present routine information to a knowledgeable audience that already knows and respects you. You'll need more words to build a consensus about a complex and controversial subject, especially if the members of your audience are skeptical or hostile strangers.

6 LEARNING OBJECTIVE

Explain the differences between the direct and indirect approaches to organizing a message.

Use the direct approach if the audience's reaction is likely to be positive and the indirect approach if it is likely to be negative.

Choosing Between Direct and Indirect Approaches

After you've defined your main idea and supporting points, you're ready to decide on the sequence you will use to present your information. You have two basic options:

- **The direct approach.** When you know your audience will be receptive to your message, use the **direct approach**: Start with the main idea (such as a recommendation, a conclusion, or a request) and follow that with your supporting evidence.
- **The indirect approach.** When your audience will be skeptical about or even resistant to your message, use the **indirect approach**: Start with the evidence first and build your case before presenting the main idea.

To choose between these two alternatives, analyze your audience's likely reaction to your purpose and message (see Figure 4.11). Bear in mind, however, that Figure 4.11 presents only general guidelines; always consider the unique circumstances of each message and audience situation. The following sections offer more insight on choosing the best approach for routine and positive messages, negative messages, and persuasive messages.

Routine and Positive Messages

The most straightforward business messages are *routine* and *positive* messages. Routine messages involve the daily matters of operating a business, from placing orders to updating employees about process changes. When you're providing routine information as part of your regular business, your audience will probably be neutral—neither pleased nor displeased. Positive messages convey some sort of good news, whether you're announcing a price cut, accepting an invitation, or congratulating a colleague. In most instances, your audience will be pleased to hear from you.

Routine and positive messages nearly always use the direct approach.

Aside from being easy to understand, such messages are easy to prepare. In most cases, you can use the direct approach. In the opening, state your main idea directly. If you have good news to share, conveying that right away puts your audience members in a positive

FIGURE 4.11 Choosing Between the Direct and Indirect Approaches
Think about the way your audience is likely to respond before choosing your approach.

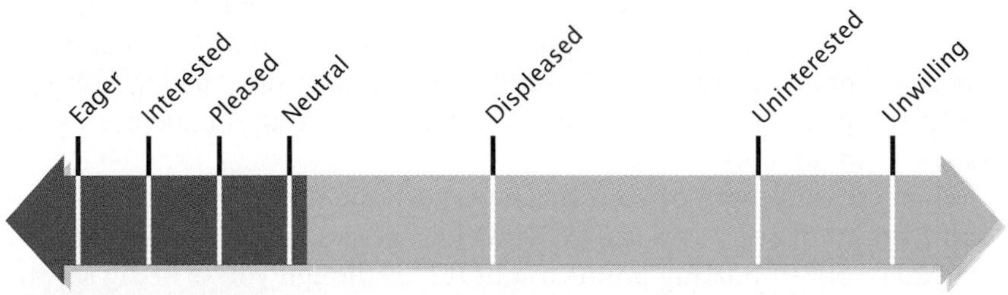

	Direct Approach	Indirect Approach	
Audience Reaction	Eager/interested/ pleased/neutral	Displeased	Uninterested/unwilling
Message Opening	Start with the main idea, the request, or the good news.	Start with a neutral statement that acts as a transition to the reasons for the bad news.	Start with a statement or question that captures attention.
Message Body	Provide necessary details.	Give reasons to justify a negative answer. State or imply the bad news, and make a positive suggestion.	Arouse the audience's interest in the subject. Build the audience's desire to comply.
Message Close	Close with a cordial comment, a reference to the good news, or a statement about the specific action desired.	Close cordially.	Request action.

frame of mind and encourages them to be receptive to whatever else you have to say. The body of your message can then provide all necessary details. The close is cordial and emphasizes your good news or makes a statement about the specific action desired. Routine and positive messages are discussed in greater detail in Chapter 8.

Negative Messages

In any profession, you will face situations in which you need to deliver bad news. Because your audience will be disappointed, these messages usually benefit from the indirect approach—putting the evidence first and building up to the main idea. This approach strengthens your case as you go along, making the receiver more receptive to the eventual conclusion.

Successful communicators take extra care with negative messages. They often open with a neutral statement that acts as a transition to the reasons for the bad news. In the body, they give the reasons that justify the negative answer, announcement, or information before they state or imply the bad news. And they are always careful to close cordially. Negative messages are discussed further in Chapter 9.

In many situations, you can cushion the blow of negative news by introducing it with other, more positive information.

Persuasive Messages

Persuasive messages present a special communication challenge because you're asking your audience to give, do, or change something, whether it's buying a product or agreeing to fund a new project. Before you try to persuade people to do something, you need to capture their attention and get them to consider your message with an open mind. In other words, the indirect approach is usually ideal for persuasive messages. Open with an interesting point and provide supporting facts that encourage your audience to continue paying attention. Then use the body of the message to build interest in the subject and arouse audience members' desire to respond. Once you have them thinking, you can introduce your main idea and request the desired action. Persuasive messages are discussed at greater length in Chapter 10.

Persuasive messages can be a challenge because you're asking your audience to give up something, such as time, money, beliefs, or habits.

Outlining Your Content

After you have chosen the right approach, it's time to figure out the most logical and effective way to present your major points and supporting details. Even if you've resisted creating outlines in your school assignments over the years, try to get into the habit of creating outlines when you're preparing business messages. You'll save time, get better results, and do a better job of navigating through complicated business situations. Even if you're just jotting down three or four points on a notepad, making a plan and sticking to it will help you cover the important details.

Particularly with longer messages, using an outline is an indispensable way to visualize how all the points will fit together.

When you're preparing a longer, more complex message, an outline is indispensable because it helps you visualize the relationships among the various parts. Without an outline, you may be inclined to ramble. As you're describing one point, another point may occur to you, so you describe it as well. One detour leads to another, and before you know it, you've forgotten the original point and wasted precious time and energy.

You may want to experiment with other organizational schemes in addition to traditional outlines.

You're no doubt familiar with the basic outline formats that identify each point with a number or letter and that indent certain points to show which ones are of equal status. A good outline divides a topic into at least two parts, restricts each subdivision to one category, and ensures that each subdivision is separate and distinct (see Figure 4.12).

Another way to visualize the outline of your message is to create an organization chart similar to the charts used to show a company's management structure (see Figure 4.13). Show the main idea, like the top executive in a company, in the highest-level box to establish the big picture. The lower-level ideas, like lower-level employees, provide the details. All the ideas are logically organized into divisions of thought,

REAL-TIME UPDATES
Learn More

Get helpful tips on creating an outline for any project

Learn these proven steps for creating robust, practical outlines. Go to **http://real-timeupdates.com/ebc** and click on "Learn More." If you are using mybcommlab, you can access Real-Time Updates within each chapter or under Student Study Tools.

FIGURE 4.12 Two Common Outline Forms
Your company may have a tradition of using a particular outline form for formal reports and other documents. If not, either of these two approaches will work for almost any writing project.

Alphanumeric Outline

- I. First major point
  - A. First subpoint
  - B. Second subpoint
    - 1. Evidence
    - 2. Evidence
      - a. Detail
      - b. Detail
    - 3. Evidence
  - C. Third subpoint
- II. Second major point
  - A. First subpoint
    - 1. Evidence
    - 2. Evidence
  - B. Second subpoint

Decimal Outline

- 1.0 First major point
  - 1.1 First subpoint
  - 1.2 Second subpoint
    - 1.2.1 Evidence
    - 1.2.2 Evidence
      - 1.2.2.1 Detail
      - 1.2.2.2 Detail
    - 1.2.3 Evidence
  - 1.3 Third subpoint
- 2.0 Second major point
  - 2.1 First subpoint
    - 2.1.1 Evidence
    - 2.1.2 Evidence
  - 2.2 Second subpoint

just as a company is organized into divisions and departments.[11] Using a visual chart instead of a traditional outline has many benefits. Charts help you (1) see the various levels of ideas and how the parts fit together, (2) develop new ideas, and (3) restructure your information flow. The mind-mapping technique used to generate ideas works in a similar way.

Whichever outlining or organizing scheme you use, start your message with the main idea, follow that with major supporting points, and then illustrate these points with evidence.

Start with the Main Idea

The main idea helps you establish the goals and general strategy of the message, and it summarizes two vital considerations: (1) *what* you want your audience members to do or think and (2) *why* they should do so. Everything in your message should either support the main idea or explain its implications. As discussed earlier, the direct approach states the main idea quickly and directly, whereas the indirect approach delays the main idea until after the evidence is presented.

FIGURE 4.13 Organization Chart Method for Outlining
The organization chart approach is helpful when you're faced with a large variety of facts, figures, and other bits of information and aren't quite sure how they all might relate to one another. When you gather pieces of evidence under major points, a clearer picture of the main idea will emerge.

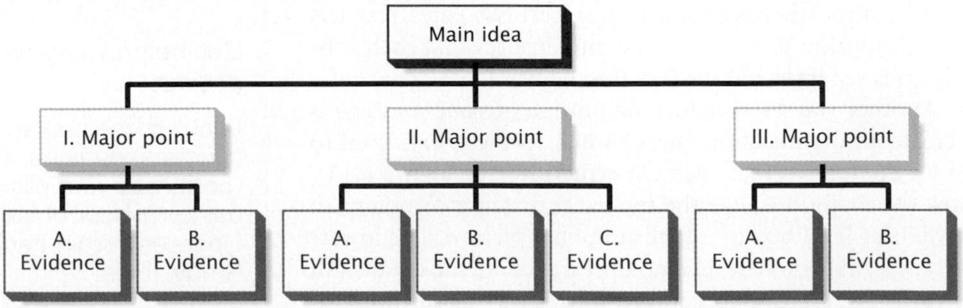

State the Major Points

You need to support your main idea with major points that clarify and explain your ideas in more concrete terms. If your purpose is to inform and the material is factual, your major points may be based on something physical or financial—something you can visualize or measure, such as activities to be performed, functional units, spatial or chronological relationships, or parts of a whole. When you're describing a process, the major points are almost inevitably steps in the process. When you're describing an object, the major points often correspond to the parts of the object. When you're giving a historical account, major points represent events in the chronological chain of events. If your purpose is to persuade or to collaborate, select major points that develop a line of reasoning or a logical argument that proves your central message and motivates your audience to act.

Major supporting points clarify and explain your main idea.

Illustrate with Evidence

After you've defined the main idea and identified major supporting points, you're ready to illustrate each of those points with specific evidence that helps audience members understand, accept, and remember your message. To a certain extent, the more evidence you provide, the more conclusive your case will be. If your subject is complex and unfamiliar or if your audience is skeptical, you may need a lot of facts and figures to demonstrate your points. On the other hand, if your subject is routine and your audience is positively inclined, you can be more sparing with the evidence. You want to provide enough support to be convincing but not so much that your message becomes boring or inefficient.

Each major point must be supported with enough specific evidence to be convincing, but don't pile on so much evidence that your message becomes overly long or boring.

As you draft your message, try to incorporate the methods described in Table 4.3. Switch from facts and figures to narration, add a dash of description, and throw in some

Business Communication 2.0

Who's Responsible Here?

When companies engage in *comparative advertising,* making explicit comparisons between their products and those of their competitors, complaints of false statements and defamation are fairly common. In that sense, a lawsuit that Subway recently filed against Quiznos is not in itself unusual. Subway claims that Quiznos made unfair and untrue comparisons about the size and meat content of one of its sandwiches and failed to disclose the fact that the larger Quiznos sandwich cost nearly twice as much as the Subway sandwich.

What makes this case unusual—and gives it potentially far-reaching impact for business communication—is the Web 2.0 angle of *user-generated content* (UGC). As part of its efforts to promote this particular sandwich, Quiznos sponsored a contest in which members of the public were invited to create their own commercials. The contest encouraged people to highlight the "meat, no meat" theme, suggesting that the Quiznos sandwich had copious amounts of beef, while the Subway sandwich had far less. More than 100 people submitted videos, which were posted to a Quiznos website and to iFilm, a now-defunct video clip website owned by the media giant Viacom.

Subway's lawsuit claims that some of the videos contain false and disparaging content for which Quiznos and iFilm should be held liable. Subway asserts that Quiznos specifically encouraged contestants to promote one product at the expense of the other, so it should not be immune from responsibility. Quiznos's lawyers responded by claiming that the company did not create these videos and is therefore not liable. "We're just facilitating consumers who go out and create their own expression in the form of a commercial." The company tried to have the UGC part of the lawsuit dismissed by claiming the same immunity that YouTube and other services have regarding the content on their websites, but a judge refused, saying the law that protects YouTube (the Communications Decency Act) doesn't necessarily protect Quiznos in this case.

Contests involving consumer-generated ads and other forms of UGC have become popular in recent years, but if Quiznos is found liable (legal action is ongoing), the trend of inviting UGC could shrink dramatically because other companies won't want to expose themselves to similar lawsuits.

CAREER APPLICATIONS

1. Legal issues aside, in your opinion, is Quiznos ethically responsible for any false or misleading information that may be found in the user-generated videos? Why or why not?
2. Most consumers lack the skills and equipment needed to produce professional-quality video commercials. Why would companies such as Quiznos invite them to create commercials?

TABLE 4.3 Six Types of Detail

TYPE OF DETAIL	EXAMPLE	COMMENT
Facts and figures	Sales are strong this month. We have two new contracts worth $5 million and a good chance of winning another worth $2.5 million.	Adds more credibility than any other type. Can become boring if used excessively. Most common type used in business.
Example or illustration	We've spent four months trying to hire recent accounting graduates, but so far, only one person has joined our firm. One candidate told me that she would love to work for us, but she can get $10,000 more a year elsewhere.	Adds life to a message, but one example does not prove a point. Idea must be supported by other evidence as well.
Description	Upscale hamburger restaurants target burger lovers who want more than the convenience and low prices of a McDonald's. These places feature wine and beer, half-pound burgers, and generous side dishes (nachos, potato skins). Atmosphere is key.	Helps audience visualize the subject by creating a sensory impression. Does not prove a point but clarifies it and makes it memorable. Begins with an overview of the function; defines its purpose, lists major parts, and explains how it operates.
Narration	Under former management, executives worked in blue jeans, meetings rarely started on time, and lunches ran long. When Jim Wilson became CEO, he completely overhauled the operation. A Harvard MBA who favors Brooks Brothers suits, Wilson has cut the product line in half and chopped $12 million off expenses.	Works well for attracting attention and explaining ideas but lacks statistical validity.
Reference to authority	I discussed this idea with Jackie Loman in the Chicago plant, and she was very supportive. As you know, Jackie has been in charge of that plant for the past six years. She is confident that we can speed up the number 2 line by 150 units an hour if we add another worker.	Bolsters a case while adding variety and credibility. Works only if authority is recognized and respected by audience.
Visual aids	Graphs, charts, and tables.	Helps audience grasp specific data. Used more in memos and reports than in letters.

CHECKLIST: Planning Business Messages

A. Analyze the situation.

- Determine whether the purpose of your message is to inform, persuade, or collaborate.
- Identify what you want your audience to think or do after receiving the message.
- Make sure your purpose is worthwhile and realistic.
- Make sure the time is right for your message.
- Make sure your purpose is acceptable to your organization.
- Identify the primary audience.
- Determine the size and composition of your audience.
- Estimate your audience's level of understanding and probable reaction to your message.

B. Gather information.

- Decide whether to use formal or informal techniques for gathering information.
- Find out what your audience needs to know.
- Provide all required information and make sure it's accurate, ethical, and pertinent.

C. Select the best medium for your message.

- Understand the advantages and disadvantages of oral, written, visual, and electronic media.
- Consider media richness, formality, media limitations, urgency, cost, and audience preference.

D. Organize your information.

- Define your main idea.
- Limit your scope.
- Choose the direct or indirect approach.
- Outline content by starting with the main idea, adding major points, and illustrating with evidence.

Document Makeover

Improve This Letter

To practice correcting drafts of actual documents, visit the "Document Makeovers" section in mybcommlab. Refer to the User Guide for specific instructions on how to access the content for this chapter. You will find a letter that contains problems and errors related to what you've learned in this chapter about planning and organizing business messages. Use the Final Draft decision tool to create an improved version of this letter. Check the document for audience focus, the right choice of medium, and the proper choice of direct or indirect approach.

examples or a reference to authority. If doing so makes sense, you can reinforce all these details with visual aids.

If your schedule permits, put your outline aside for a day or two before you begin composing your first draft. Then review it with a fresh eye, looking for opportunities to improve the flow of ideas. For a reminder of the planning tasks involved in preparing your messages, see "Checklist: Planning Business Messages."

On the Job: Solving Communication Dilemmas at H&R Block

Paula Drum was impressed enough with your communication skills to add you to the team that markets H&R Block's digital tax-preparation solutions. Using the insights you gained in this chapter, address these internal and external communication challenges.

1. A carefully defined purpose is essential for every message, but particularly so with marketing messages. These persuasive messages can accomplish any number of different tasks, from changing perceptions about an overall category of products to encouraging shoppers to visit a retail store to enticing people to place an order for a specific product right away. Any confusion about purpose will result in a message that either doesn't know what it's trying to accomplish or tries to accomplish too much. Drum has asked you to plan a promotional campaign that encourages people who do their own taxes but have never used tax preparation software to at least consider these products. Which of the following statements does the best job of defining the specific purpose of this message?

a. To persuade everyone who visits the H&R Block website to order a copy of TaxCut software within two hours of landing on the website.
b. To persuade people who do their own taxes but have never used tax software to visit the H&R Block website and order a copy of TaxCut software.
c. To persuade at least 75 percent of all visitors to the H&R Block website to learn more about the advantages of using software to prepare their taxes.
d. To persuade people who do their own taxes but have never used tax software to visit the H&R Block website to learn more about the advantages of using software to prepare their taxes.

2. You've just learned that the company's software developers are going to redesign TaxCut to make it easier to use, and they have asked for feedback from Drum's department to help prioritize their work. Unfortunately, they actually made the request about a month ago, but the message fell through the cracks somehow and no one in marketing has prepared any information. The design team needs the information first thing tomorrow morning, and it's already 3:00 P.M. You have a couple of hours to gather as much information as possible, then you can write a brief report this evening and e-mail it to the development manager. Which of these is the best way to gather useful information?

a. Interview the customer service manager to find out which features and functions have generated the most calls from frustrated customers.
b. Use the software yourself for two hours, analyzing its usability and taking note of functions that are difficult to use.
c. Do an extensive Internet search using several search engines. Look for negative reviews in software and financial magazines, negative comments from bloggers, and other feedback.
d. Recruit a dozen people in your office for a panel discussion, asking them to share their own experiences with learning the software and to pass along any feedback they've heard from family, friends, and customers.

3. After submitting the emergency report on usability frustrations, you realize the company could benefit from a more systematic way of collecting feedback from customers. Which of the following media choices would you recommend and why?

a. Publish the software development manager's e-mail address and invite customers to write to that address whenever they get frustrated with any aspect of the software.

b. Publish a toll-free telephone number that users can call whenever they are frustrated with the software. Operators can record the information and then e-mail the results of each call to the software development manager.
c. Build an Internet link into the software that gives users access to a feedback form whenever they get frustrated or confused. They can instantly record their grievances, and the information will then be transmitted to H&R Block and automatically fed into a searchable database.
d. Create the same form and database described in choice (c) but put the form on the H&R Block website, rather than embedding it in the TaxCut software.

4. You think you've spotted a potential business opportunity for H&R Block. After scanning some of the many "apps" (software applications) for the Apple iPhone (**www.apple.com/iphone/apps-for-iphone**), you think H&R Block should explore the possibility of creating an app for the iPhone as well. Most consumers don't use tax software more than once a year and don't need to do their taxes on the run, so an iPhone version of TaxCut might not make sense. However, a general-purpose financial app that would let them track expenses, balance their checkbook, and perform other routine tasks could be used quite often and therefore be a good candidate for the iPhone. You know that such a product would be a strategic departure for H&R Block, which has always been all about taxes, so your proposal will surely encounter some resistance and skepticism. Which of the following approaches should you take in organizing a proposal that recommends the company explore the possibility of creating this new iPhone app?

a. Launching a new product is a serious business decision, so be direct. Come right out and say what you propose in the opening paragraph of your proposal and then back that up with details in the body of the message. Your readers will study the supporting details and then evaluate your idea on its merits alone.
b. They don't want to create an iPhone app? Everybody wants to create iPhone apps—and virtually everybody is doing so. Your proposal needs to be not only direct but also blunt: If H&R Block doesn't create such an app, somebody else surely will. Without exactly saying so, you need to convey the message that only a fool would ignore an opportunity like this.
c. Your proposal should take an indirect approach because your readers will initially be resistant to the idea. Moreover, it would be bad form to dictate precisely what the solution should be, so write only in general terms (such as "the opportunity for smartphone software apps is significant") and let the readers reach a conclusion on their own (as in, deciding specifically to create a personal finance manager for the iPhone).
d. If the proposal doesn't quickly address the audience's reservations regarding moving beyond tax preparation tools into general-purpose financial tools, audience members won't bother to read the details or consider the proposal. Consequently, an indirect approach is best. Start by announcing that you've identified a business opportunity that is ideal for H&R Block but needs to be acted upon soon or a competitor will get there first. After you've captured the audience's attention with that intriguing opening, continue with your persuasive argument in favor of the iPhone app.

LEARNING OBJECTIVES CHECKUP

Assess your understanding of the principles in this chapter by reading each learning objective and studying the accompanying exercises. For fill-in-the-blank items, write the missing text in the blank provided; for multiple-choice items, circle the letter of the correct answer. You can check your responses against the answer key on page AK-1.

Objective 4.1: Describe the three-step writing process.

1. The three major steps in the three-step writing process are
   a. Writing, editing, and producing
   b. Planning, writing, and completing
   c. Writing, editing, and distributing
   d. Organizing, defining your purpose, and writing

2. The first step of the three-step writing process is
   a. Writing the first draft
   b. Organizing your information
   c. Planning your message
   d. Preparing an outline

3. The purpose of limiting your scope when planning a writing project is to
   a. Make your job easier
   b. Reduce the number of things you need to think about
   c. Make sure your memos are never longer than one page
   d. Make sure that your message stays focused on the main idea and any necessary supporting details

4. Which of the following tasks should you do when you're planning a writing project?
   a. Define your purpose
   b. Revise carefully to make sure you haven't made any embarrassing mistakes
   c. Choose words and sentences carefully to make sure the audience understands your main idea
   d. Do all of the above

5. The _____ of a message indicates whether you intend to use the message to inform, to persuade, or to collaborate.

Objective 4.2: Explain why it's important to analyze the situation, and define your purpose carefully before writing a message.

6. If you were to write a letter to a manufacturer complaining about a defective product and asking for a refund, your general purpose would be
   a. To inform
   b. To persuade
   c. To collaborate
   d. To entertain

7. No matter what the message is or the audience you want to reach, you should always
   a. Determine the information your audience needs in order to grasp your main idea
   b. Learn the names of everyone in the target audience
   c. Estimate the percentage of audience members who are likely to agree with your message
   d. Determine a complete demographic profile of your audience

8. If audience members will vary in terms of the amount of information they already know about your topic, your best approach is to
   a. Provide as much extra information as possible to make sure everyone gets every detail
   b. Provide just the basic information; if your audience needs to know more, they can find out for themselves
   c. Gear your coverage to your primary audience and provide the information most relevant to them
   d. Include lots of graphics

Objective 4.3: Discuss information-gathering options for simple messages, and identify three attributes of quality information.

9. To make sure you have provided all the necessary information, use the journalistic approach, which is to
   a. Interview your audience about its needs
   b. Check the accuracy of your information
   c. Verify whether your message answers the questions of *who, what, when, where, why,* and *how*
   d. Make sure your information is ethical

10. To determine whether the information you've gathered is good enough, verify that it is
   a. Accurate
   b. Ethical
   c. Pertinent to the audience's needs
   d. All of the above

11. If you realize you have given your audience incorrect information, the most ethical action would be to
   a. Say nothing and hope no one notices
   b. Wait until someone points out the error and then acknowledge the mistake
   c. Post a correction on your website
   d. Contact the audience immediately and correct the error

Objective 4.4: List the factors to consider when choosing the most appropriate medium for a message.

12. A medium's ability to convey a message using more than one informational cue, to facilitate feedback, and to establish personal focus is a measure of its _____.

13. Which of the following choices would be best for communicating a complex policy change to employees in a company with offices all over the world?
   a. A teleconference followed by an e-mail message
   b. Instant messaging (IM)
   c. A traditional typed memo sent via regular postal mail
   d. A website posting with an e-mail message alerting employees to the change and directing them to the website for more information

14. Media richness is a measure of
   a. A medium's ability to use more than one informational cue, facilitate feedback, and establish personal focus
   b. A medium's ability to use more than one informational cue, limit destructive feedback, and establish personal focus
   c. How expensive the delivery options are likely to be, particularly for large or geographically dispersed audiences
   d. How much total employee cost is involved in creating messages using a particular medium

Objective 4.5: Explain why good organization is important to both you and your audience.

15. Which of the following is an important benefit of taking time to organize your business messages?
   a. You can delay the actual writing.
   b. You save time and conserve creative energy because the writing process is quicker.
   c. Organizing your thoughts and information saves you the trouble of asking colleagues for input.
   d. In many cases, you can simply send a detailed outline and save the trouble of writing the document.

Objective 4.6: Explain the differences between the direct and indirect approaches to organizing a message.

16. Starting with the main idea and then offering supporting evidence is known as the _____ approach.

17. Starting with evidence first and building toward your main idea is known as the _____ approach.

18. When your audience is likely to have a skeptical or even hostile reaction to your main idea, you should generally use
   a. An indirect approach
   b. A direct approach
   c. An open-ended approach
   d. A closed approach

PEARSON mybcommlab™

Log on to www.mybcommlab.com to access the following study and assessment aids associated with this chapter:

- Video applications
- Pre/post test
- Real-Time Updates
- Personalized study plan
- Peer review activity
- Model documents
- Quick Learning Guides
- Sample presentations

If you are not using mybcommlab, you can access Real-Time Updates and Quick Learning Guides through http://real-timeupdates.com/ebc. The Quick Learning Guide (located under "Learn More" on the website) hits all the high points of this chapter in just two pages. This guide, especially prepared by the authors, will help you study for exams or review important concepts whenever you need a quick refresher.

Apply Your Knowledge

1. Some writers argue that planning messages wastes time because they inevitably change their plans as they go along. How would you respond to this argument? Briefly explain.
2. As a member of the public relations department, which medium (or media) would you recommend using to inform the local community that your toxic waste cleanup program has been successful? Why?
3. Would you use the direct or indirect approach to ask employees to work overtime to meet an important deadline? Please explain.
4. You have been invited to speak at an annual industry conference. After preparing the outline for your presentation, you see that you've identified 14 different points to support your main idea. Should you move ahead with creating the slides for your presentation or move back and rethink your outline? Why?
5. **Ethical Choices** A day after sending an e-mail to all 1,800 employees in your company regarding income tax implications of the company's retirement plan, you discover that one of the sources you relied on for your information plagiarized from other sources. You quickly double-check all the information in your message and confirm that it is accurate. However, you are concerned about using plagiarized information, even though you did nothing wrong. Write a brief e-mail message to your instructor, explaining how you would handle the situation.

Practice Your Knowledge

Message for Analysis

A writer is working on an insurance information brochure and is having trouble grouping the ideas logically into an outline. Using the following information, prepare the outline, paying attention to the appropriate hierarchy of ideas. If necessary, rewrite phrases to make them all consistent.

Accident Protection Insurance Plan

- Coverage is only pennies a day
- Benefit is $100,000 for accidental death on common carrier
- Benefit is $100 a day for hospitalization as result of motor vehicle or common carrier accident
- Benefit is $20,000 for accidental death in motor vehicle accident
- Individual coverage is only $17.85 per quarter; family coverage is just $26.85 per quarter
- No physical exam or health questions
- Convenient payment—billed quarterly
- Guaranteed acceptance for all applicants
- No individual rate increases
- Free, no-obligation examination period
- Cash paid in addition to any other insurance carried
- Covers accidental death when riding as fare-paying passenger on public transportation, including buses, trains, jets, ships, trolleys, subways, or any other common carrier
- Covers accidental death in motor vehicle accidents occurring while driving or riding in or on automobile, truck, camper, motor home, or nonmotorized bicycle

Exercises

Active links for all websites in this chapter can be found on mybcommlab; see your User Guide for instructions on accessing the content for this chapter.

4.1 **Message Planning Skills: Self-Assessment** How good are you at planning business messages? Use the chart below to rate yourself on each element of planning an audience-centered business message. Then examine your ratings to identify where you are strongest and where you can improve, using the tips in this chapter.

ELEMENT OF PLANNING	ALWAYS	FREQUENTLY	OCCASIONALLY	NEVER
1. I start by defining my purpose.	___	___	___	___
2. I analyze my audience before writing a message.	___	___	___	___
3. I investigate what my audience wants to know.	___	___	___	___
4. I check that my information is accurate, ethical, and pertinent.	___	___	___	___
5. I consider my audience and purpose when selecting media.	___	___	___	___

4.2 Planning Messages: General and Specific Purposes Make a list of communication tasks you'll need to accomplish in the next week or so (for example, a homework assignment, an e-mail message to an instructor, a job application, or a speech to a class). For each, determine a general and a specific purpose.

4.3 Planning Messages: Specific Purpose For each of the following communication tasks, state a specific purpose (if you have trouble, try beginning with "I want to . . .").

a. A report to your boss, the store manager, about the outdated items in the warehouse
b. A memo to clients about your booth at the upcoming trade show
c. A letter to a customer who hasn't made a payment for three months
d. A memo to employees about the department's high phone bills
e. A phone call to a supplier, checking on an overdue parts shipment
f. A report to future users of the computer program you have chosen to handle the company's mailing list

4.4 Planning Messages: Audience Profile For each communication task that follows, write brief answers to three questions: Who is the audience? What is the audience's general attitude toward my subject? What does the audience need to know?

a. A final-notice collection letter from an appliance manufacturer to an appliance dealer that is 3 months behind on payments, sent 10 days before initiating legal collection procedures
b. An advertisement for digital cameras
c. A proposal to top management, suggesting that the four sales regions in the United States be combined into just two regions
d. Fliers to be attached to doorknobs in the neighborhood, announcing reduced rates for chimney cleaning or repairs
e. A cover letter sent along with your résumé to a potential employer
f. A website that describes the services offered by a consulting firm that helps accounting managers comply with government regulations

4.5 Meeting Audience Needs: Necessary Information Choose a fairly simple electronic device (such as a digital music player or digital camera) that you know how to operate well. Write two sets of instructions for operating the device: one set for a reader who has never used that type of device and one set for someone who is generally familiar with that type of machine but has never operated the specific model. Briefly explain how your two audiences affect your instructions.

4.6 Selecting Media: Defining the Purpose List five messages you have received lately, such as direct-mail promotions, letters, e-mail messages, phone solicitations, and lectures. For each, determine the general purpose and the specific purpose; then answer the following questions: (1) Was the message well-timed? (2) Did the sender choose an appropriate medium for the message? (3) Was the sender's purpose realistic?

4.7 Selecting Media: Identifying an Audience Barbara Marquardt is in charge of public relations for a cruise line that operates out of Miami. She is shocked to read a letter in a local newspaper from a disgruntled passenger, complaining about the service and entertainment on a recent cruise. Marquardt will have to respond to these publicized criticisms in some way. What audiences will she need to consider in her response? What medium should she choose? If the letter had been published in a travel publication widely read by travel agents and cruise travelers, how might her course of action have differed? Summarize your recommendations in an e-mail message.

4.8 Teamwork: Audience Analysis Your team has been studying a new method for testing the durability of your company's power tools. Now the team needs to prepare three separate reports on the findings: first, a report for the administrator who will decide whether to purchase the equipment needed for this new testing method; second, a report for the company's engineers who design and develop the hand tools; and third, a report for the trainers who will be showing workers how to use the new equipment. To determine the audience's needs for each of these reports, the team has listed the following questions: (1) Who are the readers? (2) Why will they read my report? (3) Do they need introductory or background material? (4) Do they need definitions of terms? (5) What level or type of language is needed? (6) What level of detail is needed? (7) What result does my report aim for? Working with two other students, answer the questions for each of these audiences and summarize your analysis in a brief report:

a. The administrator
b. The engineers
c. The trainers

4.9 **Internet: Planning Your Message** Go to the PepsiCo website, at www.pepsico.com, and locate the latest annual report under the Investors tab. Read the annual report's letter to shareholders. Who is the audience for this message? What is the general purpose of the message? What do you think this audience wants to know from the chairman of PepsiCo? Summarize your answers in a brief (one-page) memo or oral presentation.

4.10 **Message Organization: Outlining Your Content** Using the improved version of the GNC e-mail message in Figure 4.8, draw an organizational chart similar to the one shown in Figure 4.13. Fill in the main idea, the major points, and the evidence provided in this letter. (*Note:* Your diagram may be smaller than the one shown in Figure 4.13.)

4.11 **Message Organization: Limiting Scope** Suppose you are preparing to recommend that top management install a new heating system that uses the cogeneration process. The following information is in your files. Eliminate topics that aren't essential and then arrange the other topics so that your report will give top managers a clear understanding of the heating system and a balanced, concise justification for installing it.

- History of the development of the cogeneration heating process
- Scientific credentials of the developers of the process
- Risks assumed in using this process
- Your plan for installing the equipment in the headquarters building
- Stories about the successful use of cogeneration technology in comparable facilities
- Specifications of the equipment that would be installed
- Plans for disposing of the old heating equipment
- Costs of installing and running the new equipment
- Advantages and disadvantages of using the new process
- Detailed 10-year cost projections
- Estimates of the time needed to phase in the new system
- Alternative systems that management might want to consider

4.12 **Message Organization: Choosing an Approach** Indicate whether the direct or indirect approach would be best in each of the following situations and briefly explain why. Would any of these messages be inappropriate for e-mail? Explain.

a. A message to the owner of an automobile dealership, complaining about poor service work
b. A message from a recent college graduate, requesting a letter of recommendation from a former instructor
c. A message turning down a job applicant
d. A message announcing that because of high air-conditioning costs, the plant temperature will be held at 78°F during the summer
e. A message from an advertising agency to a troublesome long-term client, explaining that the agency will no longer be able to work on the client's account

4.13 **Message Organization: Audience Focus** If you were trying to persuade people to take the following actions, how would you organize your argument?

a. You want your boss to approve your plan for hiring two new people.
b. You want to be hired for a job.
c. You want to be granted a business loan.
d. You want to collect a small amount of money from a regular customer whose account is slightly past due.
e. You want to collect a large amount of money from a customer whose account is seriously past due.

4.14 **Ethical Choices: Providing Information** Your supervisor, whom you respect, has asked you to withhold important information that you think should be included in a report you are preparing. Disobeying him could be disastrous for your relationship and your career. Obeying him could violate your personal code of ethics. What should you do? On the basis of the discussion in Chapter 1, would you consider this situation to be an ethical dilemma or an ethical lapse? Please explain.

4.15 **Three-Step Process: Other Applications** How can the material discussed in this chapter also apply to meetings, as discussed in Chapter 2? (*Hint:* Review the section headings in this chapter and think about making your meetings more productive.)

Expand Your Knowledge

Learning More on the Web

Ready to Make a Buck on Blogging?

Millions of people now blog for fun or free, but a few are figuring out how to earn part or all of their income from their blogging efforts. ProBlogger (www.problogger.net) can help you get started with advice on setting up a blog, using Google's popular AdSense program, and identifying multiple ways to generate income with a blog. Explore ProBlogger's advice and answer these questions:

1. What are the various ways bloggers can make money from their work?
2. How can you go about choosing a topic for a blog?
3. How can the Google AdSense program help bloggers cover their costs and perhaps even turn a profit?

Sharpening Your Career Skills Online

Bovée and Thill's Business Communication Web Search, at **http://businesscommunicationblog.com/websearch**, is a unique research tool designed specifically for business communication research. Use the Web Search function to find a website, video, podcast, or PowerPoint presentation that offers advice on planning a report, speech, or other business message. Write a brief e-mail message to your instructor, describing the item that you found and summarizing the career skills information you learned from it.

Improve Your Grammar, Mechanics, And Usage

The following exercises help you improve your knowledge of and power over English grammar, mechanics, and usage. Turn to the Handbook of Grammar, Mechanics, and Usage at the end of this book and review all of Section 1.4 (Adjectives). Then look at the following 10 items. Underline the preferred choice within each set of parentheses. (Answers to these exercises appear on page AK-3.)

1. Of the two products, this one has the (*greater, greatest*) potential.
2. The (*most perfect, perfect*) solution is *d.*
3. Here is the (*interesting, most interesting*) of all the ideas I have heard so far.
4. The (*hardest, harder*) part of my job is firing people.
5. A (*highly placed, highly-placed*) source revealed Dotson's (*last ditch, last-ditch*) efforts to cover up the mistake.
6. A (*top secret, top-secret*) document was taken from the president's office last night.
7. A (*30 year old, 30-year-old*) person should know better.
8. The two companies are engaged in an (*all-out no-holds-barred; all-out, no-holds-barred*) struggle for dominance.
9. A (*tiny metal; tiny, metal*) shaving is responsible for the problem.
10. You'll receive our (*usual cheerful prompt; usual, cheerful, prompt; usual cheerful, prompt*) service.

For additional exercises focusing on adjectives, visit mybcommlab. Click on Chapter 4, click on "Additional Exercises to Improve Your Grammar, Mechanics, and Usage," and then click on "8. Adjectives."

5 Writing Business Messages

Learning Objectives

After studying this chapter, you will be able to

1. Explain the importance of adapting to your audiences, and list three techniques for doing so
2. Explain why establishing credibility is vital to the success of your communication efforts
3. Discuss four ways of achieving a businesslike tone with a style that is clear and concise
4. Briefly describe how to select words that are not only correct but also effective
5. Explain how sentence style affects emphasis in a message
6. List five ways to develop unified, coherent paragraphs

On the Job: Communicating at Creative Commons

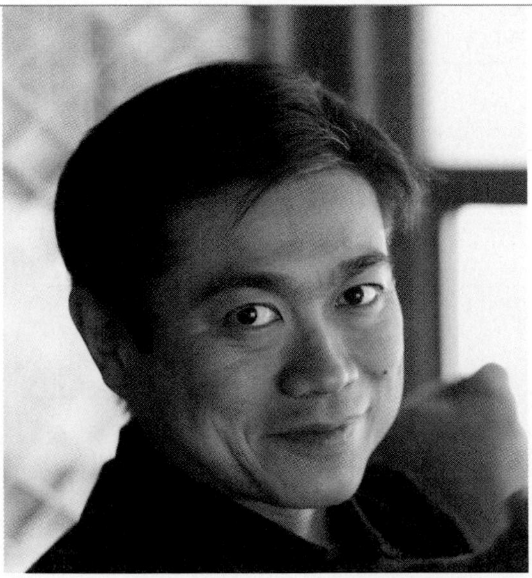

Joi Ito, CEO of Creative Commons, uses a variety of communication vehicles to convince copyright owners to explore new ways of sharing and protecting their creative works.

Redefining Two Centuries of Copyright Law for the Digital Age

Have you ever noticed that tiny © symbol on books, DVDs, music CDs, and other media products? It means that the person or organization that created the item is granted *copyright* protection, the exclusive legal right to produce, distribute, and sell that creation. Anyone who wants to resell, redistribute, or adapt such works usually needs to secure permission from the current copyright holder.

However, what if you *want* people to remix the song you just recorded or use your graphic designs in whatever artistic compositions they might want to create? Or what if you want to give away some of your creative works to get your name out there, without giving up all your legal rights to them? Alternatively, suppose you need a few photos or a video clip for a website? Other than for limited personal and educational use, a conventional copyright requires every person to negotiate a contract for every application or adaptation of every piece of work he or she wants to use.

The search for some middle ground between "all rights reserved" and simply giving your work away led Stanford University law professor Lawrence Lessig to co-found Creative Commons. This nonprofit organization's goal is to provide a simple, free, and legal way for musicians, artists, writers, teachers, scientists, and others to collaborate and benefit through the sharing of art and ideas. Instead of the everything-or-nothing approach of traditional copyright, Creative Commons offers a more flexible range of "some rights reserved" options.

In 2008, Japanese venture capitalist Joichi ("Joi") Ito took over as CEO, bringing an entrepreneur's perspective to the Creative Commons business model. Through a variety of media, Ito continues to promote the benefits of simplifying the legal constraints on sharing and reusing intellectual property, whether for creative expression or scientific research. Millions of Creative Commons licenses have been initiated for musical works, images, short films, educational materials, novels, and more. This approach can't solve the entire dilemma of copyrights in the digital age, and not everyone agrees with the Creative Commons model, but it has created an easier way for creative people to communicate and collaborate.[1]

http://creativecommons.org

BRINGING YOUR IDEAS TO LIFE

As they work to persuade their audiences to consider new forms of copyright protection, Joi Ito and his colleagues at Creative Commons (profiled in the chapter-opening "On the Job" vignette) realize it takes more than just a great idea to change the way people think. Expressing ideas clearly and persuasively starts with adapting to one's audience.

ADAPTING TO YOUR AUDIENCE

1 LEARNING OBJECTIVE

Explain the importance of adapting to your audiences, and list three techniques for doing so.

Whether consciously or not, audiences greet most incoming messages with a selfish question: "What's in this for me?" If your intended audience members think a message does not apply to them or doesn't meet their needs, they won't be inclined to pay attention to it. Follow the example set by the Creative Commons website, which addresses a diverse audience of artists, lawyers, and business professionals but fine-tunes specific messages for each group of people.

Readers and listeners want to know how your messages will benefit them.

To adapt to your audiences in a way that provides a compelling answer to the "What's in this for me?" question, be sensitive to your audience members' needs, build strong relationships, and control your style to maintain a professional tone.

Being Sensitive to Your Audience's Needs

If your readers or listeners don't think you understand or care about their needs, they won't pay attention, plain and simple. You can improve your audience sensitivity by adopting the "you" attitude, maintaining good standards of etiquette, emphasizing the positive, and using bias-free language.

Using the "You" Attitude

Chapter 1 introduced the notion of audience-centered communication and the "you" attitude—speaking and writing in terms of your audience's wishes, interests, hopes, and preferences. On the simplest level, you can adopt the "you" attitude by replacing terms such as *I*, *me*, *mine*, *we*, *us*, and *ours* with *you* and *yours*:

The "you" attitude is best implemented by expressing your message in terms of the audience's interests and needs.

INSTEAD OF THIS	WRITE THIS
Tuesday is the only day that we can promise a quick response to purchase order requests; we are swamped the rest of the week.	If you need a quick response, please submit your purchase order requests on Tuesday.
We offer MP3 players with 50, 75, or 100 gigabytes of storage capacity.	You can choose an MP3 player with 50, 75, or 100 gigabytes of storage.

Messages that emphasize "I" and "we" risk sounding selfish and uninterested in the audience. Such messages feel like they are all about the sender, not the receiver.

However, the "you" attitude is more than simply using particular pronouns; it's a matter of genuine interest and concern. You can use *you* 25 times in a single page and still ignore your audience's true concerns. If you're talking to a retailer, try to think like a retailer; if you're dealing with a production supervisor, put yourself in that position; if you're writing to a dissatisfied customer, imagine how you would feel at the other end of the transaction.

Avoid using you *and* yours *when doing so*
- *Makes you sound dictatorial*
- *Could make someone else feel unnecessarily guilty*
- *Is inappropriate for the culture*
- *Goes against your organization's style*

Be aware that on some occasions, it's better to avoid using *you*, particularly if doing so will sound overly authoritative or accusing:

INSTEAD OF THIS	WRITE THIS
You failed to deliver the customer's order on time.	The customer didn't receive the order on time. *or* Let's figure out a system that will ensure on-time deliveries.
You must correct all five copies by noon.	All five copies must be corrected by noon.

As you practice using the "you" attitude, be sure to consider the attitudes of other cultures and the policies of your organization. In some cultures, it is improper to single out one person's achievements because the whole team is responsible for the outcome; in that case, using the pronoun *we* or *our* (when you and your audience are part of the same team) would be more appropriate. Similarly, some companies have a tradition of avoiding references to *you* and *I* in most messages and reports.

Maintaining Standards of Etiquette

You know how it feels to be treated inconsiderately; when that happens, you probably react emotionally and then pay less attention to the offending message. By being courteous to members of your audience, you show consideration for them and foster a more successful environment for communication.

Although you may be tempted now and then to be brutally frank, try to express the facts in a kind and thoughtful manner.

On occasions when you experience frustration with co-workers, customers, or others, you may be tempted to say what you think in blunt terms. But venting your emotions rarely improves the situation and can jeopardize your audience's goodwill. Demonstrate your diplomatic skills by controlling your emotions and communicating calmly and politely:

INSTEAD OF THIS	WRITE THIS
Once again, you've managed to bring down the entire website through your incompetent programming.	Let's review the last website update to explore ways to improve the process.
You've been sitting on our order for two weeks, and we need it now!	Our production schedules depend on timely delivery of parts and supplies, but we have not yet received the order you promised to deliver two weeks ago. Please respond today with a firm delivery commitment.

Written communication and most forms of electronic media generally require more tact than oral communication (see Figure 5.1). When you're speaking, your words are softened by your tone of voice and facial expression. Plus, you can adjust your approach according to the feedback you get. If you inadvertently offend someone in writing or in a podcast, for example, you usually don't get the immediate feedback you would need to resolve the situation. In fact, you may never know that you offended your audience.

FIGURE 5.1 Fostering a Positive Relationship with an Audience
In the "ineffective" example, notice how the customer service agent's unfortunate word choices immediately derail this *instant messaging* (IM) exchange. In the "effective" example, a more sensitive approach allows both people to focus on solving the problem.

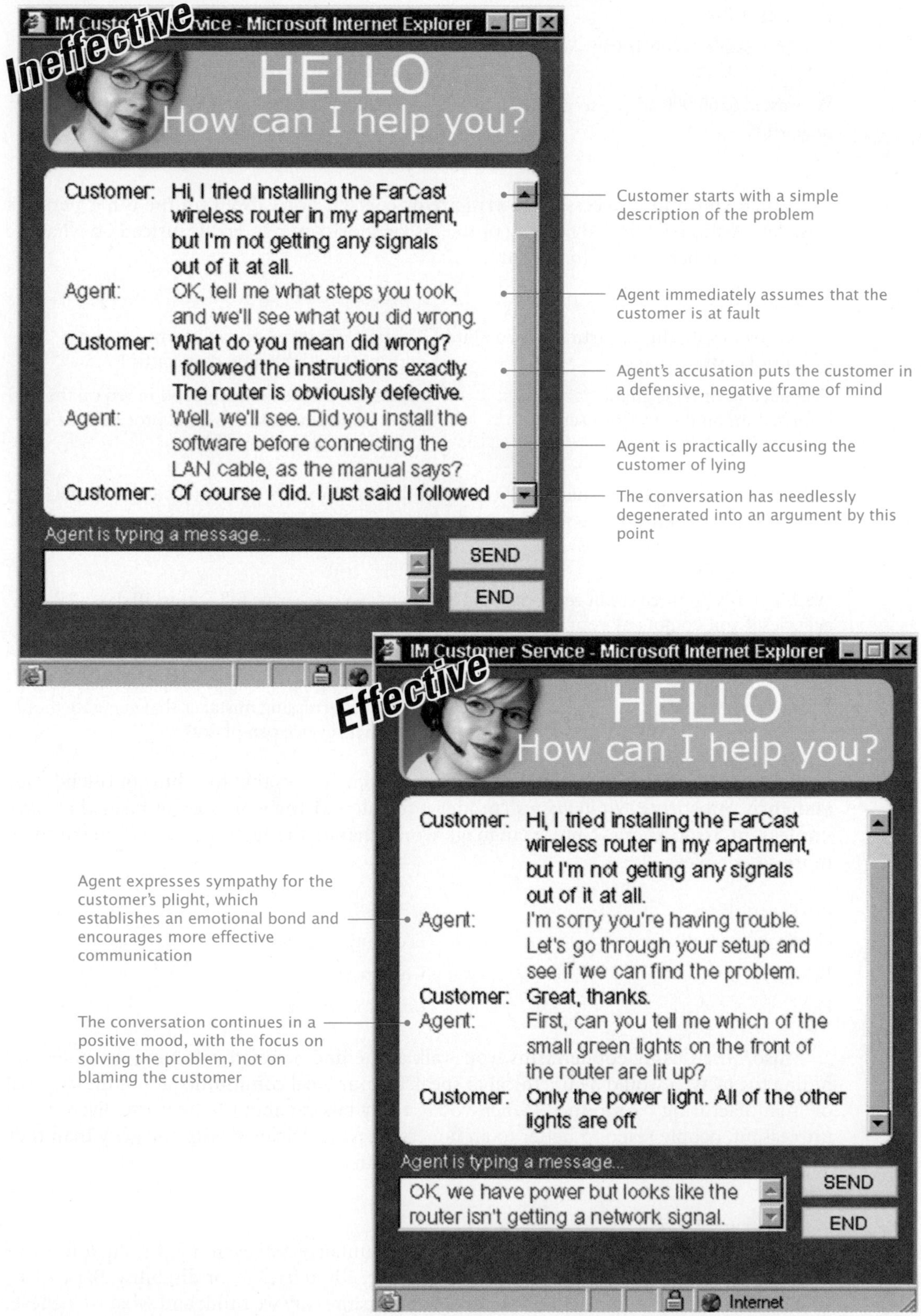

Emphasizing the Positive

You can communicate negative news without being negative.

Sensitive communicators understand the difference between delivering negative news and being negative. Never try to hide negative news, but always be on the lookout for positive points that will foster a good relationship with your audience:[2]

INSTEAD OF THIS	WRITE THIS
It is impossible to repair your laptop today.	Your computer can be ready by Tuesday. Would you like a loaner until then?
We wasted $300,000 advertising in that magazine.	Our $300,000 advertising investment did not pay off; let's analyze the experience and apply the insights to future campaigns.

When you are offering criticism or advice, focus on what the person can do to improve.

When you find it necessary to criticize or correct, don't dwell on the other person's mistakes. Avoid referring to failures, problems, or shortcomings. Focus instead on what the audience members can do to improve:

INSTEAD OF THIS	WRITE THIS
The problem with this department is a failure to control costs.	The performance of this department can be improved by tightening cost controls.
You failed to provide all the necessary information on the previous screen.	Please review the items marked in red on the previous screen so that we can process your order as quickly as possible.

Show your audience members how they will benefit from complying with your message.

If you're trying to persuade audience members to buy a product, pay a bill, or perform a service for you, emphasize what's in it for them:

INSTEAD OF THIS	WRITE THIS
We will notify all three credit reporting agencies if you do not pay your overdue bill within 10 days.	Paying your overdue bill within 10 days will prevent a negative entry on your credit record.
I am tired of seeing so many errors in the customer service blog.	Proofreading your blog postings will help you avoid embarrassing mistakes that generate more customer service complaints.

Try to avoid words with unnecessarily negative connotations; use meaningful euphemisms instead.

In general, try to state your message without using words that may hurt or offend your audience. Substitute *euphemisms* (milder equivalents) for words or phrases that have unpleasant associations. Gentle language won't change the facts, but it will make them more acceptable:

INSTEAD OF THIS	WRITE THIS
Cheap merchandise	Economy merchandise
Failing	Underperforming
Fake	Imitation or faux

Also, when using euphemisms, you walk a fine line between softening the blow and hiding the facts. It would be unethical to speak to your local community about the disposal of "manufacturing by-products" when you're really talking about toxic waste. Even if it is unpleasant, people respond better to an honest message delivered with integrity than they do to a sugar-coated message that obscures the truth.

Using Bias-Free Language

Biased language can perpetuate stereotypes and prejudices.

Bias-free language avoids words and phrases that unfairly and even unethically categorize or stigmatize people in ways related to gender, race, ethnicity, age, or disability. Biased language is not simply about "labels." Language reflects the way we think and what we believe, and biased language may well perpetuate the underlying stereotypes and prejudices that it represents[3]. Moreover, because communication is all about perception, simply *being* fair and objective isn't enough. To establish a good relationship with your audience, you must also *appear* to be fair[4]. Good communicators make every effort to change biased language (see Table 5.1). Bias can come in a variety of forms:

- **Gender bias.** Avoid sexist language by using the same label for everyone (don't call a woman *chairperson* and then call a man *chairman*; use *chair, chairperson,* or *chairman* consistently). Rather than refer to all individuals as *he*, reword sentences to use the plural *they* or avoid using a pronoun altogether.

TABLE 5.1 Overcoming Bias in Language

EXAMPLES	UNACCEPTABLE	PREFERABLE
Gender Bias		
Using words containing *man*	Man-made	Artificial, synthetic, manufactured, constructed, human-made
	Mankind	Humanity, human beings, human race, people
	Manpower	Workers, workforce
	Businessman	Executive, manager, businessperson, professional
	Salesman	Sales representative, salesperson
	Foreman	Supervisor
Using female-gender words	Actress, stewardess	Actor, flight attendant
Using special designations	Woman doctor, male nurse	Doctor, nurse
Using *he* to refer to "everyone"	The average worker . . . he	The average worker . . . he or she *OR* Average workers . . . they
Identifying roles with gender	The typical executive spends four hours of his day in meetings.	Most executives spend four hours a day in meetings.
	The consumer . . . she	Consumers . . . they
	The nurse/teacher . . . she	Nurses/teachers . . . they
Identifying women by marital status	Mrs. Norm Lindstrom	Maria Lindstrom *OR* Ms. Maria Lindstrom
	Norm Lindstrom and Ms. Drake	Norm Lindstrom and Maria Drake *OR* Mr. Lindstrom and Ms. Drake
Racial and Ethnic Bias		
Assigning stereotypes	Not surprisingly, Shing-Tung Yau excels in mathematics.	Shing-Tung Yau excels in mathematics.
Identifying people by race or ethnicity	Mario M. Cuomo, Italian-American politician and ex-governor of New York	Mario M. Cuomo, politician and ex-governor of New York
Age Bias		
Including age when irrelevant	Mary Kirazy, 58, has just joined our trust department.	Mary Kirazy has just joined our trust department.
Disability Bias		
Putting the disability before the person	Disabled workers face many barriers on the job.	Workers with physical disabilities face many barriers on the job.
	An epileptic, Tracy has no trouble doing her job.	Tracy's epilepsy has no effect on her job performance.

> **REAL-TIME UPDATES**
> **Learn More**
>
> **Get detailed advice on using bias-free language**
>
> This in-depth guide offers practical tips for avoiding many types of cultural bias in your writing and speaking. Go to **http://real-timeupdates.com/ebc** and click on "Learn More." If you are using mybcommlab, you can access Real-Time Updates within each chapter or under Student Study Tools.

- **Racial and ethnic bias.** Avoid identifying people by race or ethnic origin unless such a label is relevant to the matter at hand—and it rarely is.
- **Age bias.** Mention the age of a person only when it is relevant. Moreover, be careful of the context in which you use words that refer to age. For example, *young* can imply youthfulness, inexperience, or even immaturity, depending on how it's used.
- **Disability bias.** If you must refer to someone's disability, put the person first and the disability second.[5] For example, by saying "employees with physical disabilities," not "handicapped employees," you focus on the whole person, not the disability. Finally, never use outdated terminology such as *crippled* or *retarded.*

Building Strong Relationships with Your Audience

Whether a one-time interaction or a series of exchanges over the course of many months or years, successful communication relies on a positive relationship existing between sender and receiver. Establishing your credibility and projecting your company's image are two vital steps in building and fostering positive business relationships.

Establishing Your Credibility

> **2 LEARNING OBJECTIVE**
> Explain why establishing credibility is vital to the success of your communication efforts.

Audience responses to your messages depend heavily on your **credibility**, a measure of your believability, based on how reliable you are and how much trust you evoke in others. With audiences that don't know you and trust you already, you need to establish credibility before they'll accept your messages (see Figure 5.2). To build, maintain, or repair your credibility, emphasize the following characteristics:

- **Honesty.** Demonstrating honesty and integrity will earn you the respect of your audiences, even if they don't always agree with or welcome your messages.

FIGURE 5.2 Building Credibility
Lisa Ford is a highly regarded expert in the field of customer service, but she still takes care to communicate her qualifications as a presenter so that potential audience members who aren't familiar with her work can appreciate the expertise she has to offer.

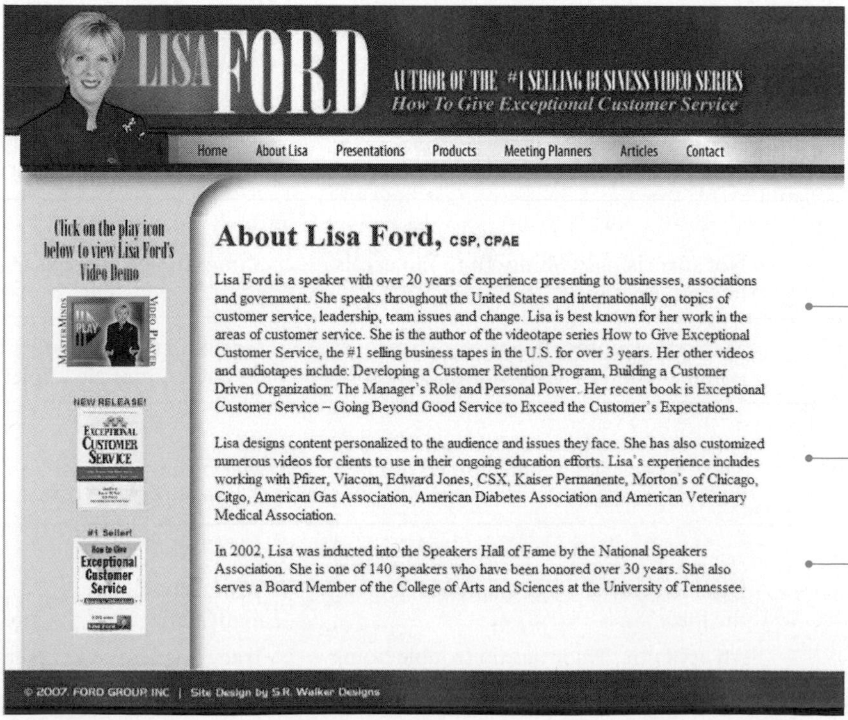

Summarizes Ford's background and describes the services she offers

Builds her credibility as a customer service expert by listing major clients

Builds her credibility as a presenter by mentioning a prestigious honor related to public speaking

- **Objectivity.** Show that you can distance yourself from emotional situations and look at all sides of an issue.
- **Awareness of audience needs.** Let your audiences know that you understand what's important to them.
- **Credentials, knowledge, and expertise.** Audiences need to know that you have whatever it takes to back up your message, whether it's education, professional certification, special training, past successes, or simply the fact that you've done your research.
- **Endorsements.** An *endorsement* is a statement on your behalf by someone who is accepted by your audience as an expert.
- **Performance.** Demonstrating impressive communication skills is not enough; people need to know they can count on you to get the job done.
- **Confidence.** Audiences need to know that you believe in yourself and your message. If you are convinced that your message is sound, you can state your case confidently, without sounding boastful or arrogant.
- **Communication style.** Support your points with evidence, not empty terms such as *amazing, incredible,* or *extraordinary.*
- **Sincerity.** When you offer praise, don't use *hyperbole,* such as "You are the most fantastic employee I could ever imagine." Instead, point out specific qualities that warrant praise.

People are more likely to react positively to your message when they have confidence in you.

To enhance your credibility, emphasize such factors as honesty, objectivity, and awareness of audience needs.

In addition, audiences need to know that you believe in yourself and your message. If you lack faith in yourself, you're likely to communicate an uncertain attitude that undermines your credibility. Try to avoid phrases that contain words such as *if, hope,* and *trust,* which can drain the audience's confidence in your message:

INSTEAD OF THIS	WRITE THIS
We hope this recommendation will be helpful.	We're glad to make this recommendation.
If you'd like to order, please visit our website.	To order, please visit our website.
We trust that you'll want to extend your service contract.	By extending your service contract, you can continue to enjoy top-notch performance from your equipment.

Projecting Your Company's Image

When you communicate with anyone outside your organization, it is more than a conversation between two individuals. You represent your company and therefore play a vital role in helping the company build and maintain positive relationships with all of its stakeholders. Most successful companies work hard to foster a specific public image, and your external communication efforts need to project that image. As part of this responsibility, the interests and preferred communication style of your company must take precedence over your own views and personal communication style.

Your company's interests and reputation take precedence over your personal communication style.

Many organizations have specific communication guidelines that show everything from the correct use of the company name to preferred abbreviations and other grammatical details. Specifying a desired style of communication is more difficult, however. Observe more experienced colleagues to see how they communicate and never hesitate to ask for editorial help to make sure you're conveying the appropriate tone. For instance, with clients entrusting thousands or millions of dollars to it, an investment firm communicates in a style quite different from that of a clothing retailer. And a clothing retailer specializing in high-quality business attire communicates in a different style than a store catering to the latest trends in casual wear.

3 LEARNING OBJECTIVE

Discuss four ways of achieving a businesslike tone with a style that is clear and concise.

—REAL-TIME UPDATES
Learn More

Building credibility online

Follow these steps to build your credibility as an online voice. Go to **http://real-timeupdates.com/bia** and click on "Learn More." If you are using mybizlab, you can access Real-Time Updates within each chapter or under Student Study Tools.

Controlling Your Style and Tone

Your communication **style** involves the choices you make to express yourself: the words you select, the manner in which you use those words in sentences, and the way you build paragraphs from individual sentences. Your style creates a certain **tone**, or overall impression, in your messages. You can vary your style to sound forceful or objective, personal or formal, colorful or dry. The right choice depends on the nature of your message and your relationship with the reader. Although style can be refined during the revision phase (see Chapter 6), you'll save time and a lot of rewriting if you use a style that allows you to achieve the desired tone from the start.

Using a Conversational Tone

The tone of your business messages can range from informal to conversational to formal. If you're in a large organization and you're communicating with your superiors or with customers, your tone may tend to be more formal and respectful.[6] However, that formal tone might sound distant and cold if used with close colleagues.

Most business messages aim for a conversational style that is warm but businesslike.

Compare the three versions of the message in Table 5.2. The first is too formal and stuffy for today's audiences, whereas the third is inappropriately casual for business. The second message demonstrates the conversational tone used in most business communication—plain language that sounds businesslike without being stuffy, full of jargon, or sounding like texting between two friends who are out clubbing. You can achieve a tone that is conversational but still businesslike by following these guidelines:

- **Understand the difference between texting and writing.** The casual language used in text messaging and instant messaging (IM) between friends is not considered

TABLE 5.2 Finding the Right Tone

TONE	EXAMPLE
Stuffy: too formal for today's audiences	Dear Ms. Navarro: Enclosed please find the information that was requested during our telephone communication of May 14. As was mentioned at that time, Midville Hospital has significantly more doctors of exceptional quality than any other health facility in the state. As you were also informed, our organization has quite an impressive network of doctors and other health-care professionals with offices located throughout the state. In the event that you should need a specialist, our professionals will be able to make an appropriate recommendation. In the event that you have questions or would like additional information, you may certainly contact me during regular business hours. Most sincerely yours, Samuel G. Berenz
Conversational: just right for most business communication	Dear Ms. Navarro: Here's the information you requested during our phone conversation on Friday. As I mentioned, Midville Hospital has the highest-rated doctors and more of them than any other hospital in the state. In addition, we have a vast network of doctors and other health professionals with offices throughout the state. If you need a specialist, they can refer you to the right one. If you would like more information, please call any time between 9:00 and 5:00, Monday through Friday. Sincerely, Samuel G. Berenz
Unprofessional: too casual for business communication	Here's the 411 you requested. IMHO, we have more and better doctors than any other hospital in the state. FYI, we also have a large group of doctors and other health professionals w/offices close to U at work/home. If U need a specialist, they'll refer U to the right one. Any ? just ring or msg. L8R, S

TABLE 5.3 Weeding Out Obsolete Phrases

OBSOLETE PHRASE	UP TO DATE REPLACEMENT
we are in receipt of	we received
kindly advise	please let me/us know
attached please find	enclosed is *or* I/we have enclosed
it has come to my attention	I have just learned *or* [someone] has just informed me
the undersigned	I/we
in due course	(specify a time or date)
permit me to say that	(omit; just say whatever you need to say)
pursuant to	(omit; just say whatever you need to say)
in closing, I'd like to say	(omit; just say whatever you need to say)
we wish to inform you that	(omit; just say whatever you need to say)
please be advised that	(omit; just say whatever you need to say)

professional business writing. Yes, texting style is an efficient way for friends to communicate—particularly taking into account the limitations of a phone keypad—but if you want to be taken seriously in business, you simply cannot write like this on the job.

- **Avoid stale and pompous language.** Many phrases that were once common in business now sound stale and pompous to contemporary audiences (see Table 5.3).
- **Avoid preaching and bragging.** Few things are more irritating than know-it-alls who like to preach or brag. However, if you need to remind your audience of something that should be obvious, try to work in the information casually, perhaps in the middle of a paragraph, where it will sound like a secondary comment rather than a major revelation.
- **Be careful with intimacy.** Business messages should generally avoid intimacy, such as sharing personal details or adopting a casual, unprofessional tone. However, when you have a close relationship with audience members, such as among the members of a close-knit team, a more intimate tone is sometimes appropriate and even expected.
- **Be careful with humor.** Humor can easily backfire and divert attention from your message. If you don't know your audience well or you're not skilled at using humor in a business setting, don't use it at all. Never use humor in formal messages or when you're communicating across cultural boundaries.

Using Plain Language

What do you think this sentence is trying to say?

> We continually exist to synergistically supply value-added deliverables such that we may continue to proactively maintain enterprise-wide data to stay competitive in tomorrow's world.[7]

Audiences can understand and act on plain English without having to reread material to comprehend it.

If you don't have any idea what it means, you're not alone. However, this is a real sentence from a real company, written in an attempt to explain what the company does and why. This sort of incomprehensible, buzzword-filled writing is driving a widespread call to use *plain language* (or *plain English* specifically when English is involved).

Using plain language is a way of presenting information in a simple, unadorned style so that your audience can easily grasp your meaning, without struggling through specialized, technical, or convoluted language. The Plain English Campaign (a nonprofit group in England that's campaigning for clear language) defines *plain English* as language "that the intended audience can read, understand and act upon the first time they read it."[8] You can see how this definition supports using the "you" attitude and shows respect for your

Communicating Across Cultures

Communicating with a Global Audience on the Web

Reaching an international audience on the web involves more than simply offering translations of the English language. Successful global sites address the needs of international customers in five ways:

1. **Consider the reader's perspective.** Many communication elements that you may take for granted may be interpreted differently by audiences in different countries. Should you use the metric system, different notations for times or dates, or even different names for countries? For example, German citizens don't refer to their country by the English word *Germany*; it's *Deutschland* to them. Review the entire online experience and look for ways to improve communication, including such helpful tools as interactive currency converters and translation dictionaries.
2. **Take cultural differences into account.** For instance, because humor is rooted in cultural norms, U.S. humor may not be so funny to readers from other countries. Avoid idioms and references that aren't universally recognized, such as "putting all your eggs in one basket" or "jumping out of the frying pan into the fire."
3. **Keep the message clear.** Choose simple, unambiguous words; construct short, clear, sentences; and write in the active voice whenever possible. Define abbreviations, acronyms, and words an international audience may not be familiar with.
4. **Complement language with visuals.** Use drawings, photos, videos, and other visual elements to support written messages.
5. **Consult local experts.** Seek the advice of local experts about phrases and references that may be expected. Even terms as simple as *homepage* differ from country to country. Spanish readers refer to the "first page," or *pagina inicial*, whereas the French term is "welcome page," or *page d'accueil*.

CAREER APPLICATIONS

1. Visit Sony's Global Headquarters website, at www.sony.net, and find Sony's music websites for Australia (www.sonymusic.com.au), France (www.sonymusic.fr), and Germany (www.sonybmg.de). How does Sony localize each country's site?
2. Compare Sony's international sites to IBM's global webpages, at www.ibm.com/us/, www.ibm.com/au/, www.ibm.com/fr/, and www.ibm.com/de. How does Sony's approach differ from IBM's? Do both corporations successfully address the needs of a global audience? Write a two-paragraph summary that compares the international sites of the two companies.

audience. In addition, plain language can make companies more productive and more profitable simply because people spend less time trying to figure out messages that are confusing or aren't written to meet their needs.[9]

On the Creative Commons website, for instance, licensing terms are available in two versions: a complete "legal code" document that spells out contractual details in specific legal terms that meet the needs of legal professionals and a second version labeled "license deed," which explains the licensing terms in nontechnical language that anyone can understand.[10]

Selecting Active or Passive Voice

Your choice of active or passive voice affects the tone of your message. You are using **active voice** when the subject performs the action and the object receives the action: "Jodi sent the e-mail message." You're using **passive voice** when the subject receives the action: "The e-mail message was sent by Jodi." As you can see, the passive voice combines the helping verb *to be* with a form of the verb that is usually the past tense.

Use passive sentences to soften bad news, to put yourself in the background, or to create an impersonal tone.

Using the active voice helps make your writing more direct, livelier, and easier to read (see Table 5.4). Passive voice is not wrong grammatically, but it can be cumbersome, lengthy, and vague. In most cases, the active voice is the best choice.[11] Nevertheless, using the passive voice can help you demonstrate the "you" attitude in some situations:

- When you want to be diplomatic about pointing out a problem or an error of some kind
- When you want to point out what's being done without taking or attributing either the credit or the blame
- When you want to avoid personal pronouns (*I* and *we*) in order to create an objective tone

TABLE 5.4 Choosing Active or Passive Voice

In general, avoid passive voice in order to make your writing lively and direct.

DULL AND INDIRECT IN PASSIVE VOICE	LIVELY AND DIRECT IN ACTIVE VOICE
The new procedure was developed by the operations team.	The operations team developed the new procedure.
Legal problems are created by this contract.	This contract creates legal problems.
Reception preparations have been undertaken by our PR people for the new CEO's arrival.	Our PR people have begun planning a reception for the new CEO.

However, passive voice is helpful when you need to be diplomatic or want to focus attention on problems or solutions rather than on people.

ACCUSATORY OR SELF-CONGRATULATORY IN ACTIVE VOICE	MORE DIPLOMATIC IN PASSIVE VOICE
You lost the shipment.	The shipment was lost.
I recruited seven engineers last month.	Seven engineers were recruited last month.
We are investigating the high rate of failures on the final assembly line.	The high rate of failures on the final assembly line is being investigated.

The second half of Table 5.4 illustrates several other situations in which the passive voice helps you focus your message on your audience.

COMPOSING YOUR MESSAGE

After you have decided how to adapt to your audience, you're ready to begin composing your message. As you write your first draft, let your creativity flow. Don't try to draft and edit at the same time or worry about getting everything perfect. Make up words if you can't think of the right word, draw pictures, or talk out loud—do whatever it takes to get the ideas out of your head and onto your computer screen or a piece of paper. If you've planned well, you'll have time to revise and refine the material later, before showing it to anyone. In fact, many writers find it helpful to establish a personal rule of *never* showing a first draft to anyone. By working in this "safe zone," away from the critical eyes of others, your mind will stay free to think clearly and creatively.

As you create and refine your messages, learn to view your writing on three levels: strong words, effective sentences, and coherent paragraphs.

Choosing Strong Words

4 LEARNING OBJECTIVE

Briefly describe how to select words that are not only correct but also effective.

Successful writers pay close attention to the correct use of words[12]. If you make grammatical or usage errors, you lose credibility with your audience—even if your message is otherwise correct. Poor grammar implies that you're uninformed, and audiences may choose not to trust an uninformed source. Moreover, poor grammar can imply that you don't respect your audience enough to get things right.

The "rules" of grammar and usage can be a source of worry for writers because some of these rules are complex and some evolve over time. Even professional editors and grammarians occasionally have questions about correct usage, and they sometimes disagree about the answers. For example, the word *data* is the plural form of *datum*, yet some experts now prefer to treat *data* as a singular noun when it's used in nonscientific material to refer to a body of information.

With practice, you'll become more skilled in making correct choices over time. If you have doubts about what is correct, you have many ways to find the answer. Check the

REAL-TIME UPDATES
Learn More

Grammar questions? Click here for help

This comprehensive online guide can help you out of just about any grammar dilemma. Go to **http://real-timeupdates.com/ebc** and click on "Learn More." If you are using mybcommlab, you can access Real-Time Updates within each chapter or under Student Study Tools.

FIGURE 5.3 Choosing Strong Words
Through the use of such words and phrases as *premiere showcase*, *latest news*, *innovators*, and *industry leaders*, this e-mail message promotes the many benefits of the annual VTCE trade show.

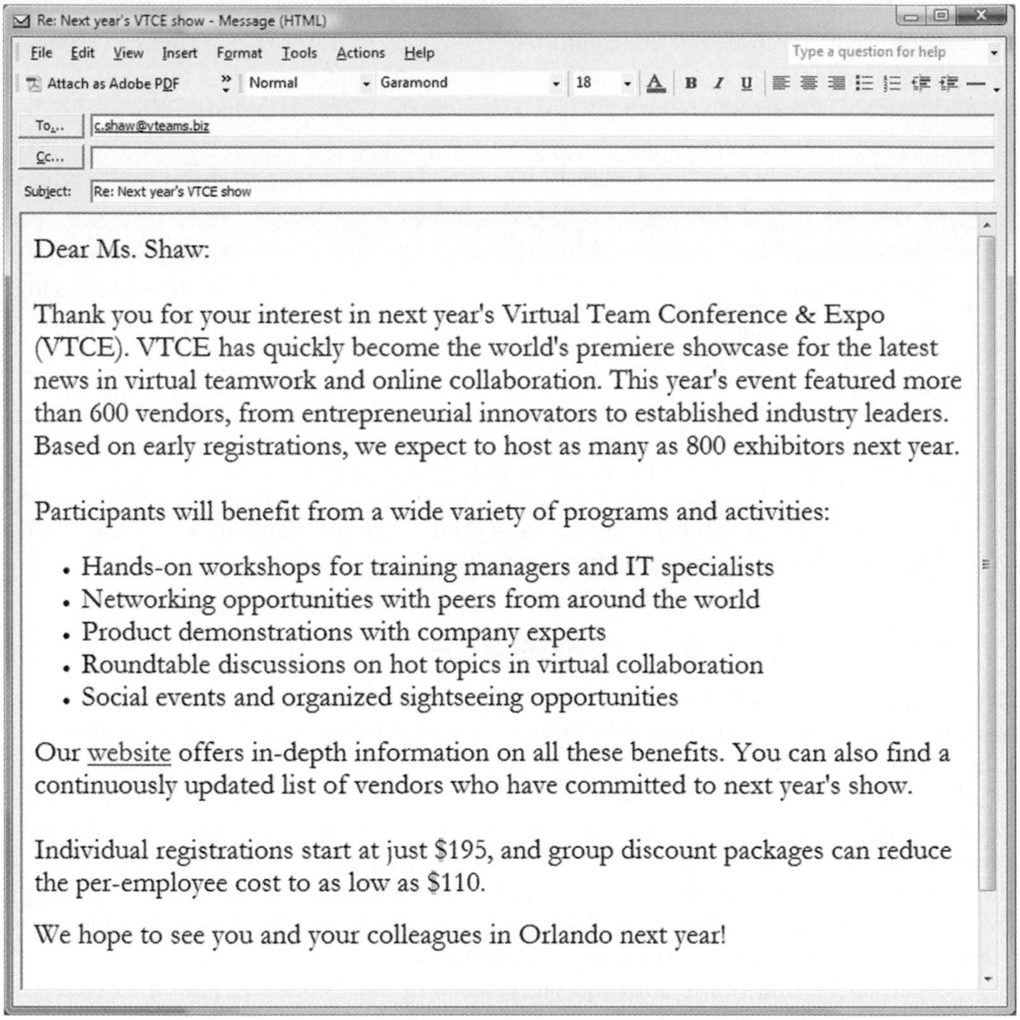

Correctness is the first consideration when choosing words.

If you're not sure of correct grammar or usage, look it up; you'll avoid embarrassing mistakes and learn at the same time.

"Handbook of Grammar, Mechanics, and Usage" at the end of this book or consult the many special reference books and resources available in libraries, in bookstores, and on the Internet.

Effectiveness is the second consideration when choosing words.

In addition to using words correctly, successful writers and speakers take care to find the most effective words and phrases to use. Selecting and using words effectively is often more challenging than using words correctly because it's a matter of judgment and experience. Careful writers continue to work at their craft to find words that communicate with power (see Figure 5.3).

Understanding Denotation and Connotation

Many words have both a denotative (explicit, specific) meaning and a connotative (implicit, associative) meaning.

A word may have both a denotative and a connotative meaning. The **denotative meaning** is the literal, or dictionary, meaning. The **connotative meaning** includes all the associations and feelings evoked by the word.

The denotative meaning of *desk* is "a piece of furniture with a flat work surface and various drawers for storage." The connotative meaning of *desk* may include thoughts associated with work or study, but the word *desk* has fairly neutral connotations—neither strong nor emotional. However, some words have much stronger connotations than others and should be used with care. For example, the connotations of the word *fail* are negative and can carry strong emotional meaning. If you say that the sales department *failed* to meet its annual quota, the connotative meaning suggests that the group is inferior, incompetent, or below some standard of performance. However, the reason for not achieving 100 percent might be an inferior product, incorrect pricing, or some other factor outside the control of the sales department. In contrast, by saying that the sales department achieved 85 percent of its quota, you clearly communicate that the results were less than expected—without triggering all the negative emotions associated with *failure.*

Balancing Abstraction and Concreteness

The more abstract a word is, the more it is removed from the tangible, objective world that can be perceived with the senses.

Words vary dramatically in their degree of abstraction or concreteness. An **abstract word** expresses a concept, quality, or characteristic. Abstractions are usually broad, encompassing a category of ideas, and are often intellectual, academic, or philosophical. *Love, honor, progress, tradition,* and *beauty* are abstractions, as are such important business concepts as *satisfaction, inspiration,* and *motivation.* In contrast, a **concrete word** stands for something you can touch, see, or visualize. Most concrete terms are anchored in the tangible, material world. *Chair, table, horse, rose, kick, kiss, red, green,* and *two* are concrete words; they are direct, clear, and exact. Incidentally, technology continues to generate new words and new meanings that describe things that don't have a physical presence but are nonetheless concrete; for example, *software, database, signal,* and *code* are all concrete terms as well.

As you can imagine, abstractions tend to cause more trouble for writers and readers than concrete words. Abstractions tend to be "fuzzy" and can be interpreted differently, depending on the audience and the circumstances. The best way to minimize such problems is to blend abstract terms with concrete ones, the general with the specific. State the concept and then pin it down with details expressed in more concrete terms. Save the abstractions for ideas that cannot be expressed any other way. In addition, abstract words such as *small, numerous, sizable, near, soon, good,* and *fine* are imprecise, so try to replace them with terms that are more accurate. Instead of referring to a *sizable loss,* talk about a *loss of $32 million.*

Finding Words That Communicate Well

Try to use words that are powerful and familiar.

When you compose business messages, look for the most powerful words for each situation (see Table 5.5 on the next page):

- **Choose powerful words.** Choose words that express your thoughts clearly, specifically, and dynamically. If you find yourself using a lot of adjectives and adverbs, you're probably trying to compensate for weak nouns and verbs. Saying that *sales plummeted* is stronger and more efficient than saying *sales dropped dramatically* or *sales experienced a dramatic drop.*
- **Choose familiar words.** You'll communicate best with words that are familiar to both you and your readers. Moreover, trying to use an unfamiliar word for the first time in an important document can lead to embarrassing mistakes.
- **Avoid clichés and be careful with buzzwords.** Although familiar words are generally the best choice, avoid *clichés*—terms and phrases so common that they have lost some of their power to communicate. *Buzzwords,* newly coined terms often associated with technology, business, or cultural changes, are slightly more difficult to handle than clichés because in small doses and in the right situation, they can be useful. The careful use of a buzzword can signal that you're an insider, someone in the know.[13] However, buzzwords quickly become clichés, and using them too late in their "life cycle" can mark you as an outsider desperately trying to look like an insider.
- **Use jargon carefully.** *Jargon,* the specialized language of a particular profession or industry, has a bad reputation, but it's not always bad. Using jargon is usually an efficient way to communicate within the specific groups that understand these terms. After all, that's how jargon develops in the first place, as people with similar interests develop ways to communicate complex ideas quickly.

Avoid clichés, be extremely careful with trendy buzzwords, and use jargon only when your audience is completely familiar with it.

If you need help finding the right words, try some of the visual dictionaries and thesauruses available online. For example, Visuwords (**www.visuwords.com**) shows words

TABLE 5.5 Selected Examples of Finding Powerful Words

WEAK WORDS AND PHRASES	STRONGER ALTERNATIVES (EFFECTIVE USAGE DEPENDS ON THE SITUATION)
Increase (as a verb)	Accelerate, amplify, augment, enlarge, escalate, expand, extend, magnify, multiply, soar, swell
Decrease (as a verb)	Curb, cut back, depreciate, dwindle, shrink, slacken
Large, small	(Use a specific number, such as $100 million)
Good	Admirable, beneficial, desirable, flawless, pleasant, sound, superior, worthy
Bad	Abysmal, corrupt, deficient, flawed, inadequate, inferior, poor, substandard, worthless
We are committed to providing . . .	We provide . . .
It is in our best interest to . . .	We should . . .
UNFAMILIAR WORDS	**FAMILIAR WORDS**
Ascertain	Find out, learn
Consummate	Close, bring about
Peruse	Read, study
Circumvent	Avoid
Unequivocal	Certain
CLICHÉS AND BUZZWORDS	**PLAIN LANGUAGE**
An uphill battle	A challenge
Writing on the wall	Prediction
Call the shots	Lead
Take by storm	Attack
Costs an arm and a leg	Expensive
A new ballgame	Fresh start
Fall through the cracks	Be overlooked
Think outside the box	Be creative
Run it up the flagpole	Find out what people think about it
Eat our own dog food	Use our own products
Mission-critical	Vital
Disintermediate	Get rid of
Green light (as a verb)	Approve
Architect (as a verb)	Design
Space (as in, "we compete in the XYZ space")	Market or industry
Blocking and tackling	Basic skills
Trying to boil the ocean	Working frantically but without focus
Human capital	People, employees, workforce
Low-hanging fruit	Tasks that are easy to complete or sales that are easy to close
Pushback	Resistance

that are similar to or different from a given word and helps you see subtle differences to find the perfect word.[14]

Creating Effective Sentences

Arranging your carefully chosen words in effective sentences is the next step in creating powerful messages. Start by selecting the optimum type of sentence to communicate each point you want to make.

Choosing from the Four Types of Sentences

Sentences come in four basic varieties: simple, compound, complex, and compound–complex. A **simple sentence** has one main *clause* (a single subject and a single predicate), although it may be expanded by nouns and pronouns that serve as objects of the action and by modifying phrases. Here's an example with the subject noun underlined once and the predicate verb underlined twice:

A simple sentence has one main clause.

> Profits increased in the past year.

A **compound sentence** has two main clauses that express two or more independent but related thoughts of equal importance, usually joined by *and, but,* or *or.* In effect, a compound sentence is a merger of two or more simple sentences (independent clauses) that are related. For example:

A compound sentence has two main clauses.

> Wages have declined by 5 percent, and employee turnover has been high.

The independent clauses in a compound sentence are always separated by a comma or by a semicolon (in which case the conjunction—*and, but, or*—is dropped).

A **complex sentence** expresses one main thought (the independent clause) and one or more subordinate, related thoughts (dependent clauses that cannot stand alone as valid sentences). Independent and dependent clauses are usually separated by a comma. In this example, "Although you may question Gerald's conclusions" is a subordinate thought expressed in a dependent clause:

A complex sentence has one main clause and one subordinate clause.

> Although you may question Gerald's conclusions, you must admit that his research is thorough.

A **compound–complex sentence** has two main clauses, at least one of which contains a subordinate clause:

A compound–complex sentence has two main clauses and at least one dependent clause.

> Profits have increased in the past year, and although you may question Gerald's conclusions, you must admit that his research is thorough.

To make your writing as effective as possible, strive for variety and balance, using all four sentence types. If you use too many simple sentences, you won't be able to properly express the relationships among your ideas, and your writing will sound choppy and abrupt. At the other extreme, a long series of compound, complex, or compound–complex sentences can be tiring to read.

Writing is usually more effective if it balances all four sentence types.

Using Sentence Style to Emphasize Key Thoughts

5 LEARNING OBJECTIVE

Explain how sentence style affects emphasis in a message.

In every message, some ideas are more important than others. You can emphasize these key ideas through your sentence style. One obvious technique is to give important points the most space. When you want to call attention to a thought, use extra words to describe it. Consider this sentence:

> The chairperson called for a vote of the shareholders.

To emphasize the importance of the chairperson, you might describe her more fully:

> Having considerable experience in corporate takeover battles, the chairperson called for a vote of the shareholders.

You can emphasize ideas in a sentence by

- *Devoting more words to them*
- *Putting them at the beginning or at the end of the sentence*
- *Making them the subject of the sentence*

You can increase the emphasis even more by adding a separate, short sentence to augment the first:

> The chairperson called for a vote of the shareholders. She has considerable experience in corporate takeover battles.

You can also call attention to a thought by making it the subject of the sentence. In the following example, the emphasis is on the person:

> I can write letters much more quickly by using a computer.

However, by changing the subject, the computer takes center stage:

> The computer enables me to write letters much more quickly.

Another way to emphasize an idea is to place it either at the beginning or at the end of a sentence:

> **Less emphatic:** We are cutting the price to stimulate demand.
> **More emphatic:** To stimulate demand, we are cutting the price.

Dependent clauses can determine emphasis.

In complex sentences, the placement of the dependent clause hinges on the relationship between the ideas expressed. If you want to emphasize the subordinate idea, put the dependent clause at the end of the sentence (the most emphatic position) or at the beginning (the second most emphatic position). If you want to downplay the idea, put the dependent clause within the sentence:

> **Most emphatic:** The electronic parts are manufactured in Mexico, *which has lower wage rates than the United States.*
> **Emphatic:** *Because wage rates are lower in Mexico than in the United States,* the electronic parts are manufactured there.
> **Least emphatic:** Mexico, *which has lower wage rates than the United States,* was selected as the production site for the electronic parts.

Techniques such as these give you a great deal of control over the way your audience interprets what you have to say.

6 LEARNING OBJECTIVE

List five ways to develop unified, coherent paragraphs.

Crafting Unified, Coherent Paragraphs

Paragraphs organize sentences related to the same general topic. Readers expect every paragraph to be *unified*—focusing on a single topic—and *coherent*—presenting ideas in a logically connected way. By carefully arranging the elements of each paragraph, you help your readers grasp the main idea of your document and understand how the specific pieces of support material back up that idea (see Figure 5.4).

Elements of a Paragraph

Paragraphs vary widely in length and form, but a typical paragraph contains three basic elements: a topic sentence, support sentences that develop the topic, and transitional words and phrases.

FIGURE 5.4 Unified Paragraphs
In two brief paragraphs, Whirlpool assured its trade partners (retailers and commercial laundries) that business would continue as usual after its acquisition of Maytag.

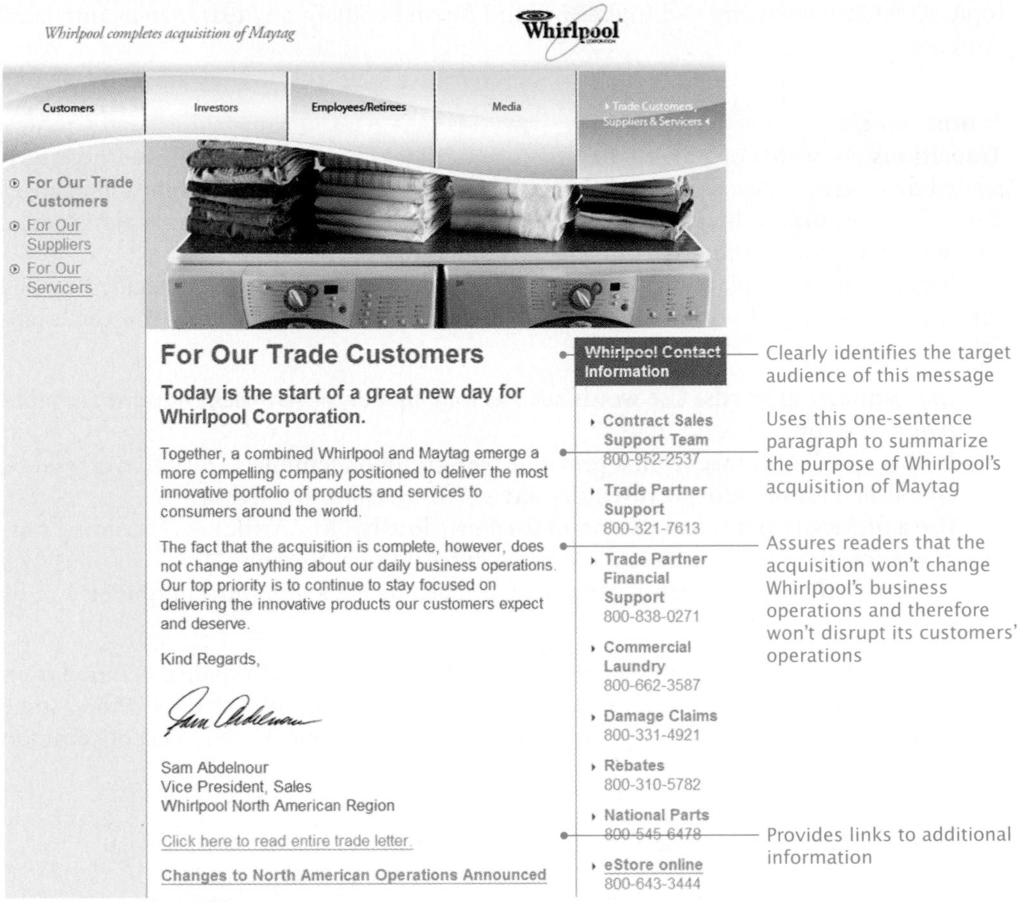

Topic Sentence

An effective paragraph deals with a single topic, and the sentence that introduces that topic is called the **topic sentence**. The topic sentence, usually the first sentence in the paragraph, gives readers a summary of the general idea that will be covered in the rest of the paragraph. The following examples show how a topic sentence can introduce the subject and suggest the way the subject will be developed:

Most paragraphs consist of
- *A topic sentence that reveals the subject of the paragraph*
- *Related sentences that support and expand the topic*
- *Transitions that help readers move between sentences and between paragraphs*

> The medical products division has been troubled for many years by public relations problems. [In the rest of the paragraph, readers will learn the details of the problems.]
>
> To get a refund, please supply us with the following information. [The details of the necessary information will be described in the rest of the paragraph.]

Support Sentences

In most paragraphs, the topic sentence needs to be explained, justified, or extended with one or more support sentences. These related sentences must all have a bearing on the general subject and must provide enough specific details to make the topic clear:

> The medical products division has been troubled for many years by public relations problems. Since 2002 the local newspaper has published 15 articles that portray the division in a negative light. We have been accused of everything from mistreating laboratory animals to polluting the local groundwater. Our facility has been described as a health hazard. Our scientists are referred to as "Frankensteins," and our profits are considered "obscene."

The support sentences are all more specific than the topic sentence. Each one provides another piece of evidence to demonstrate the general truth of the main thought. Also, each sentence is clearly related to the general idea being developed, which gives the paragraph unity. A paragraph is well developed when it contains enough information to make the topic sentence convincing and interesting and doesn't contain any extraneous, unrelated sentences.

Transitions

Transitions are words or phrases that tie together ideas by showing how one thought is related to another. They also alert the reader to what lies ahead so that shifts and changes don't cause confusion. In addition to helping readers understand the connections you're trying to make, transitions give your writing a smooth, even flow.

Transitional elements include
- *Connecting words (conjunctions)*
- *Repeated words or phrases*
- *Pronouns*
- *Words that are frequently paired*

Ideally, you begin planning transitions while you're outlining, as you decide how the various ideas and blocks of information will be arranged and connected.[15] You can establish transitions in a variety of ways:

- **Use connecting words.** Use words such as *and, but, or, nevertheless, however, in addition*, and so on.
- **Echo a word or phrase from a previous paragraph or sentence.** "A system should be established for monitoring inventory levels. *This system* will provide . . ."
- **Use a pronoun that refers to a noun used previously.** "Ms. Arthur is the leading candidate for the president's position. *She* has excellent qualifications."
- **Use words that are frequently paired.** "The machine has a *minimum* output of. . . . Its *maximum* output is . . ."

Some transitions serve as mood changers, alerting the reader to a change in mood from the previous material. Some announce a total contrast with what's gone on before, some announce a causal relationship, and some signal a change in time. Here is a list of common transitions:

Additional detail: moreover, furthermore, in addition, besides, first, second, third, finally
Causal relationship: therefore, because, accordingly, thus, consequently, hence, as a result, so
Comparison: similarly, here again, likewise, in comparison, still
Contrast: yet, conversely, whereas, nevertheless, on the other hand, however, but, nonetheless
Condition: although, if
Illustration: for example, in particular, in this case, for instance
Time sequence: formerly, after, when, meanwhile, sometimes
Intensification: indeed, in fact, in any event
Summary: in brief, in short, to sum up
Repetition: that is, in other words, as mentioned earlier

Consider using a transition whenever it could help the reader understand your ideas and follow you from point to point. You can use transitions inside paragraphs to link related points and between paragraphs to ease the shift from one distinct thought to another. In longer reports, a transition that links major sections or chapters may be a complete paragraph that serves as a mini-introduction to the next section or as a summary of the ideas presented in the section just ending

Five Ways to Develop a Paragraph

Five ways to develop paragraphs:
- *Illustration*
- *Comparison or contrast*
- *Cause and effect*
- *Classification*
- *Problem and solution*

You have a variety of options for developing paragraphs. Five of the most common approaches are illustration, comparison or contrast, cause and effect, classification, and problem and solution (see Table 5.6).

In practice, you'll occasionally combine two or more methods of development in a single paragraph. For instance, you could begin by using illustration, shift to comparison or

TABLE 5.6 Five Techniques for Developing Paragraphs

TECHNIQUE	DESCRIPTION	EXAMPLE
Illustration	Giving examples that demonstrate the general idea	Some of our most popular products are available through local distributors. For example, Everett & Lemmings carries our frozen soups and entrees. The J. B. Green Company carries our complete line of seasonings, as well as the frozen soups. Wilmont Foods, also a major distributor, now carries our new line of frozen desserts.
Comparison or contrast	Using similarities or differences to develop the topic	When the company was small, the recruiting function could be handled informally. The need for new employees was limited, and each manager could comfortably screen and hire her or his own staff. However, our successful bid on the Owens contract means that we will be doubling our labor force over the next six months. To hire that many people without disrupting our ongoing activities, we will create a separate recruiting group within the human resources department.
Cause and effect	Focusing on the reasons for something	The heavy-duty fabric of your Wanderer tent probably broke down for one of two reasons: (1) a sharp object punctured the fabric, and without reinforcement, the hole was enlarged by the stress of pitching the tent daily for a week or (2) the fibers gradually rotted because the tent was folded and stored while still wet.
Classification	Showing how a general idea is broken into specific categories	Successful candidates for our supervisor trainee program generally come from one of several groups. The largest group by far consists of recent graduates of accredited business management programs. The next largest group comes from within our own company, as we try to promote promising staff workers to positions of greater responsibility. Finally, we occasionally accept candidates with outstanding supervisory experience in related industries.
Problem and solution	Presenting a problem and then discussing the solution	Selling handmade toys online is a challenge because consumers are accustomed to buying heavily advertised toys from major chain stores or well-known websites such as Amazon.com. However, if we develop an appealing website, we can compete on the basis of product novelty and quality. In addition, we can provide unusual crafts at a competitive price: a rocking horse of birch, with a hand-knit tail and mane; a music box with the child's name painted on the top; and a real teepee, made by Native American artisans.

contrast, and then shift to problem and solution. However, when combining approaches, do so carefully so that you don't lose readers partway through the paragraph. In addition, before settling for the first approach that comes to mind, consider the alternatives. Think through various methods before committing yourself, or even write several test paragraphs to see which method works best. By avoiding the easy habit of repeating the same old paragraph pattern time after time, you can keep your writing fresh and interesting.

USING TECHNOLOGY TO COMPOSE AND SHAPE YOUR MESSAGES

Take advantage of the tools in your word processor or online publishing systems to write more efficiently and effectively. The names and details vary from system to system, but you'll probably find most of these capabilities:

Take full advantage of your software's formatting capabilities to help produce effective, professional messages in less time.

- **Style sheets, style sets, templates, and themes.** *Style sheets*, *style sets*, *templates*, and *themes* are various ways of ensuring consistency throughout a document and from document to document. Capabilities vary, but in general these tools establish the design choices for everything from page layout to fonts. Rather than manually formatting every element in a document, you simply select one of the available styles. This approach also makes it easy to redesign an entire document simply by redefining the various styles or selecting a different design theme.
- **Smart documents.** *Smart documents* are word processor files based on special templates that can retrieve information from databases and other information sources. For

CHECKLIST: Writing Business Messages

A. Adapt to your audience.
- Use the "you" attitude.
- Maintain good etiquette through polite communication.
- Emphasize the positive whenever possible.
- Use bias-free language.
- Establish credibility in the eyes of your audience.
- Project your company's preferred image.
- Use a conversational but still professional and respectful tone.
- Use plain language for clarity.

B. Compose your message.
- Choose strong words that communicate efficiently.
- Pay attention to the connotative meaning of your words.
- Balance abstract and concrete terms to convey your meaning accurately.
- Avoid clichés and be careful with trendy buzzwords.
- Use jargon only when your audience understands it and prefers it.
- Vary your sentence structure for impact and interest.
- Develop coherent, unified paragraphs.
- Use transitions generously to help your audience follow your message.

example, a smart document can pull data directly from the sales department's reporting system and insert these figures into ready-made tables in a monthly sales report.
- **Master documents.** Long reports with multiple sections are sometimes easier to handle as multiple *subdocuments*, particularly if different authors are in charge of the different sections. Using a *master document*, you can then organize and integrate all the subdocuments when you're ready to print and distribute the report.
- **Autocompletion.** *Autocompletion* inserts a ready-made block of text when you type the first few characters, which saves time and reduces errors.
- **Autocorrection.** An automatic feature in some programs instantly corrects spelling and typing errors and converts text to symbols, such as converting (c) to the © copyright symbol. If autocorrection is active, be sure to verify the changes your software makes; they're not always desirable.
- **Endnotes, footnotes, indexes, and tables of contents.** Your computer can also help you track footnotes and endnotes, renumbering them every time you add or delete references.
- **Wizards.** Some programs offer *wizards* that guide you through the process of creating letters, résumés, webpages, and other common documents.
- **Mail merge.** *Mail merge* lets you personalize form letters by inserting names and addresses from a database.

For the latest information on using technology to compose messages, visit **http://real-timeupdates.com/ebc** and click on Chapter 5. For a reminder of the tasks involved in writing messages, see "Checklist: Writing Business Messages."

Document Makeover

Improve This Letter

To practice correcting drafts of actual documents, visit the "Document Makeovers" section in mybcommlab. Refer to the User Guide for specific instructions on how to access the content for this chapter. You will find a letter that contains problems and errors related to what you've learned in this chapter about establishing a good relationship with your audience. Use the Final Draft decision tool to create an improved version of this letter. Check the document for "you" attitude, positive language, communication etiquette, bias-free language, and phrases that establish credibility.

On the Job: Solving Communication Dilemmas at Creative Commons

To achieve their mission of popularizing a new approach to copyrighting songs, artwork, literature, and other creative works, Joi Ito and his staff at Creative Commons need to convince people that the traditional approach to copyright doesn't meet the needs of today's digital society. This is no small challenge: Not only do they need to convince people to reconsider more than 200 years of legal precedent and habit, they also need to communicate with an extremely diverse audience—everyone from lawyers and business managers to artists, writers, musicians, and scientists. After graduating with a business degree, you've joined Creative Commons as a communication intern for a year before entering law school. Apply your knowledge of effective writing to the following scenarios.

1. Creative Commons offers six levels of licensing agreements with varying degrees of restrictions on what others can

do with the licensed content. The least restrictive, known as "Attribution," gives others the right to do whatever they want with a piece of work—remix it, expand it, or even sell it for profit, as long as they give the originator credit. At the other extreme, the "Attribution Non-Commercial No Derivatives" license lets others redistribute an original work, but that is all; they can't modify it or use it in any commercial way, including advertising. Which of these statements does the most effective job of explaining to content creators (those who wish to use a license to protect their works) that Creative Commons offers a range of licensing options?

a. Creative Commons licenses combine four features—(1) attribution (giving credit to the creator), (2) the freedom to make derivatives based on original creations, (3) restrictions on whether someone can make commercial products or use a derivative commercially, and (4) requirements to share a derivative with exactly the same licensing terms—to create six different levels of licensing options.
b. Creative Commons offers six levels of licensing agreements with varying degrees of restrictions on what others can do with the licensed content.
c. Creative Commons offers a range of licensing options.
d. No matter what level of licensing you need, Creative Commons has it.

2. A key part of the communication challenge for Creative Commons is translating legal documents into language that musicians, artists, and others with no legal training can easily understand. Which of the following does the best job of adapting the following legal phrase (which is part of the licensing contracts) into language for a general audience?

The above rights may be exercised in all media and formats whether now known or hereafter devised. The above rights include the right to make such modifications as are technically necessary to exercise the rights in other media and formats, but otherwise you have no rights to make adaptations.

a. The rights granted by this licensing contract extend to any current or future media, and you also have the right to modify the material as needed to meet the technical needs of any media.
b. You may use this material in any present or future media and modify it as needed to work with any media.
c. Be advised that your rights within the scope of this contract include the right to use this material in any media that either exists now or might be devised in the future. Moreover, you are also granted the right to modify the material as any current or future media might technically demand.
d. You are hereby granted the right to use this material in any media, including modifications required by that media.

3. The single most important concept in the Creative Commons approach is the idea of a spectrum of possibilities between *all rights reserved* (a conventional copyright) and *no rights reserved* (being in the *public domain*, where anybody is free to use material in any way the person pleases). Review the structure of the following four sentences and choose the one that does the best job of emphasizing the importance of the "spectrum of possibilities."

a. Conventional copyrights, in which the creator reserves all rights to a work, and the public domain, in which the creator gives up all rights, represent two black-and-white extremes.
b. Between the all-or-nothing extremes of a conventional copyright and being in the public domain, Creative Commons sees a need for other possibilities.
c. The primary contribution of Creative Commons is enabling a range of possibilities between the extremes of *all rights reserved* (conventional copyright) and *no rights reserved* (public domain).
d. The black-and-white choice of *all rights reserved* (conventional copyright) and *no rights reserved* (public domain) does not meet everyone's needs, so Creative Commons is developing a range of possibilities between these two extremes.

4. Like many other organizations these days, Creative Commons must occasionally deal with online rumors spread by bloggers who aren't always sure of their facts. You've been asked to reply to an e-mail query from a *Wall Street Journal* reporter who read a blog rumor that the real objective of Creative Commons is to destroy ownership of all copyrights. Which of the following has the right style and tone for your response?

a. That blog posting is an absolute crock. The person who wrote it is either a liar or a fool.
b. As our website and other materials strive to make clear, the objective of Creative Commons is to work within the framework of existing copyright law but to establish a range of possibilities for people whose needs aren't met by conventional copyright choices.
c. You wouldn't believe how much time and energy we have to spend defending ourselves against idiotic rumors like this.
d. Creative Commons has never expressed, in print or in online materials, nor in any speeches or presentations given by any of our current or former staff or board members, any plans or strategies that would allow anyone to reach a valid conclusion that our intent is to weaken existing copyright protections.

Individual Challenge: Visit the licensing section of the Creative Commons website, at **http://creativecommons.org/about/licenses**, and read the information on Attribution Non-Commercial Share Alike, Attribution Non-Commercial, and Attribution No Derivatives licenses. Write a brief description that explains how these three licenses differ. Imagine that your audience is a group of music and art majors.

LEARNING OBJECTIVES CHECKUP

Assess your understanding of the principles in this chapter by reading each learning objective and studying the accompanying exercises. For fill-in-the-blank items, write the missing text in the blank provided; for multiple-choice items, circle the letter of the correct answer. You can check your responses against the answer key on page AK-1.

Objective 5.1: Explain the importance of adapting to your audiences, and list three techniques for doing so.

1. Why should you take the time to adapt your messages to your audience?
   a. People are more inclined to read and respond to messages that they believe apply to them and their concerns.
   b. Adapting messages to audiences is corporate policy in nearly all large companies.
   c. Adapting your message saves time during planning and writing.
   d. You can manipulate audience responses more easily by adapting your messages.
2. How is your audience likely to respond to a message that doesn't seem to be about their concerns or that is written in language they don't understand?
   a. They will ignore the message.
   b. If they read the message, they will be less inclined to respond in a positive way.
   c. They will assume that the writer doesn't respect them enough to adapt the message.
   d. All of the above could occur.

Objective 5.2: Explain why establishing credibility is vital to the success of your communication efforts.

3. Credibility is a measure of
   a. Your power within the organization
   b. The length of time the audience has known you
   c. Your confidence
   d. The audience's perception of your believability
4. If you have developed a reputation for missing deadlines on projects you manage, which of the following statements would do the best job of helping to rebuild your credibility? [You have previously committed to a project completion date of April 1.]
   a. No April foolin' this time; we'll be finished by April 1.
   b. After analyzing past projects, I now realize that a failure to clarify project objectives up front created significant delays down the line. In order to meet the April 1 deadline, I will make sure to clarify the objective as soon as the team assembles.
   c. I plan to work extra hard this time to make sure we will be finished by April 1.
   d. I hope that we will be finished by April 1.

Objective 5.3: Discuss four ways of achieving a businesslike tone with a style that is clear and concise.

5. A good way to achieve a businesslike tone in your messages is to
   a. Use formal business terminology, such as "In re your letter of the 18th"
   b. Brag about your company
   c. Use a conversational style that is not intimate or chatty
   d. Use plenty of humor
6. Plain English is
   a. Never recommended when speaking with people for whom English is a second language
   b. A movement toward using "English only" in American businesses
   c. A way of writing and arranging content to make it more readily understandable
   d. An attempt to keep writing at a fourth- or fifth-grade level
7. If you want to avoid attributing blame or otherwise calling attention to a specific person, the _____ voice is a more diplomatic approach.
8. The _____ voice usually makes sentences shorter, more direct, and livelier.

Objective 5.4: Briefly describe how to select words that are not only correct but also effective.

9. Which of the following defines the connotative meaning of the word *flag*?
   a. A flag is a piece of material with a symbol of some kind sewn on it.
   b. A flag is a symbol of everything that a nation stands for.
   c. A flag is fabric on a pole used to mark a geographic spot.
   d. A flag is an object used to draw attention.
10. Which of the following is a concrete word?
   a. Little
   b. Mouse
   c. Species
   d. Kingdom

11. If you're not sure about the meaning of a word you'd like to use, which of the following is the most appropriate way to handle the situation?
    a. Your readers probably have instant access to online dictionaries these days, so go ahead and use the word.
    b. Use the word but include a humorous comment in parentheses saying that you're not really sure what this big, important word means.
    c. Either verify the meaning of the word or rewrite the sentence so that you don't need to use it.
    d. Find a synonym in a thesaurus and use that word instead.

12. Using jargon is
    a. Often a good idea when discussing complex subjects with people who are intimately familiar with the subject and common jargon relating to it
    b. Never a good idea
    c. A good way to build credibility, no matter what the purpose of the message
    d. A sign of being an "insider"

Objective 5.5: Explain how sentence style affects emphasis in a message.

13. Where is the most emphatic place to put a dependent clause?
    a. At the end of the sentence
    b. At the beginning of the sentence
    c. In the middle of the sentence
    d. Anywhere in the sentence

14. Devoting a lot of words to a particular idea shows your audience that
    a. The idea is complicated
    b. The idea is the topic sentence
    c. The idea is important
    d. The idea is new and therefore requires more explanation

Objective 5.6: List five ways to develop unified, coherent paragraphs.

15. When developing a paragraph, keep in mind
    a. That you should stick to one method of development within a single paragraph
    b. That once you use one method of development, you should use that same method for all the paragraphs in a section
    c. That your choice of technique should take into account your subject, your intended audience, and your purpose
    d. All of the above

16. To develop a paragraph by illustration, give your audience enough _____ to help them grasp the main idea.

17. Paragraphs organized by comparison and contrast point out the _____ or _____ between two or more items.

18. To explain the reasons something happened, which of these paragraph designs should you use?
    a. Cause–effect
    b. Opposition and argument
    c. Classification
    d. Prioritization

PEARSON **mybcommlab**

Log on to www.mybcommlab.com to access the following study and assessment aids associated with this chapter:

- Video applications
- Pre/post test
- Real-Time Updates
- Personalized study plan
- Peer review activity
- Model documents
- Quick Learning Guides
- Sample presentations

If you are not using mybcommlab, you can access Real-Time Updates and Quick Learning Guides through http://real-timeupdates.com/ebc. The Quick Learning Guide (located under "Learn More" on the website) hits all the high points of this chapter in just two pages. This guide, especially prepared by the authors, will help you study for exams or review important concepts whenever you need a quick refresher.

Apply Your Knowledge

1. How can you apply the "you" attitude when you don't know your audience personally?
2. How does plain language demonstrate the "you" attitude?
3. What steps can you take to make abstract concepts such as *opportunity* feel more concrete in your messages?
4. Should you bother using transitional elements if the logical sequence of your message is obvious? Why or why not?
5. **Ethical Choices** Eleven million people in the United States are allergic to one or more food ingredients. Each year, 30,000 of these people end up in the emergency room after suffering allergic reactions, and hundreds of them die. Many of these tragic events are tied to poorly written food labels that either fail to identify dangerous allergens or use scientific terms that most consumers don't recognize.[16] Do food manufacturers have a responsibility to ensure that consumers read, understand, and follow warnings on food products? Explain your answer.

Practice Your Knowledge

Message for Analysis

Read the following e-mail draft and then (1) analyze the strengths and weaknesses of each sentence and (2) revise the document so that it follows this chapter's guidelines. The message was written by the marketing manager of an online retailer of baby-related products in the hope of becoming a retail outlet for Inglesina strollers and high chairs. As a manufacturer of stylish, top-quality products, Inglesina (based in Italy) is extremely selective about the retail outlets through which it allows its products to be sold.

> Our e-tailing site, **www.BestBabyGear.com**, specializes in only the very best products for parents of newborns, infants, and toddlers. We constantly scour the world looking for products that are good enough and well-built enough and classy enough—good enough that is to take their place alongside the hundreds of other carefully selected products that adorn the pages of our award-winning website, **www.bestbabygear.com**. We aim for the fences every time we select a product to join this portfolio; we don't want to waste our time with onesey-twosey products that might sell a half dozen units per annum—no, we want every product to be a top-drawer success, selling at least one hundred units per specific model per year in order to justify our expense and hassle factor in adding it to the abovementioned portfolio. After careful consideration, we thusly concluded that your Inglesina lines meet our needs and would therefore like to add it.

Exercises

Active links for all websites in this chapter can be found on mybcommlab; see your User Guide for instructions on accessing the content for this chapter.

5.1 **Audience Relationship: Courteous Communication** Substitute a better phrase for each of the following:

- **a.** You claim that
- **b.** It is not our policy to
- **c.** You neglected to
- **d.** In which you assert
- **e.** We are sorry you are dissatisfied
- **f.** You failed to enclose
- **g.** We request that you send us
- **h.** Apparently you overlooked our terms
- **i.** We have been very patient
- **j.** We are at a loss to understand

5.2 **Audience Relationship: The "You" Attitude** Rewrite these sentences to reflect your audience's viewpoint.

- **a.** Your e-mail order cannot be processed; we request that you use the order form on our website instead.
- **b.** We insist that you always bring your credit card to the store.
- **c.** We want to get rid of all our 15-inch LCD screens to make room in our warehouse for the new 19-, 23-, and 35-inch monitors. Thus, we are offering a 25 percent discount on all sales of 15-inch models this week.
- **d.** I am applying for the position of bookkeeper in your office. I feel my grades prove that I am bright and capable, and I think I can do a good job for you.
- **e.** As requested, we are sending the refund for $25.
- **f.** If you cared about doing a good job, you would've made the extra effort required to learn how to use the machinery properly.
- **g.** Your strategy presentation this morning absolutely blew me away; there's no way we can fail with all the brilliant ideas you've pulled together—I'm so glad you're running the company now!
- **h.** Regarding your e-mail message from September 28 regarding the slow payment of your invoice, it's important for you to realize that we've just undergone a massive upgrade of our accounts payable system and payments have been delayed for everybody, not just you.
- **i.** I know I'm late with the asset valuation report, but I haven't been feeling well and I just haven't had the energy needed to work through the numbers yet.
- **j.** With all the online news sources available today, I can't believe you didn't know that MyTravel and Thomas Cook were in merger talks—I mean, you don't even have to get up from your computer to learn this!

5.3 **Audience Relationship: Emphasize the Positive** Revise these sentences to be positive rather than negative.

- **a.** To avoid damage to your credit rating, please remit payment within 10 days.
- **b.** We don't offer refunds on returned merchandise that is soiled.
- **c.** Because we are temporarily out of Baby Cry dolls, we won't be able to ship your order for 10 days.
- **d.** You failed to specify the color of the blouse that you ordered.
- **e.** You should have realized that waterbeds will freeze in unheated houses during winter. Therefore, our guarantee does not cover the valve damage, and you must pay the $9.50 valve-replacement fee (plus postage).

5.4 **Audience Relationship: Euphemisms** Provide euphemisms for the following words and phrases:

- **a.** Stubborn
- **b.** Wrong
- **c.** Stupid
- **d.** Incompetent
- **e.** Loudmouth

5.5 **Audience Relationship: Bias-Free Language** Rewrite each of the following to eliminate bias:

- **a.** For an Indian, Maggie certainly is outgoing.
- **b.** He needs a wheelchair, but he doesn't let his handicap affect his job performance.
- **c.** A pilot must have the ability to stay calm under pressure, and then he must be trained to cope with any problem that arises.
- **d.** Candidate Renata Parsons, married and the mother of a teenager, will attend the debate.
- **e.** Senior citizen Sam Nugent is still an active salesman.

5.6 **Ethical Choices** Your company has been a major employer in the local community for years, but shifts in the global marketplace have forced some changes in the company's long-term direction. In fact, the company plans to reduce local staffing by as much as 50 percent over the next 5 to 10 years, starting with a small layoff next month. The size and timing of future layoffs have not been decided, although there is little doubt that more layoffs will happen at some point. In the first draft of a letter aimed at community leaders, you write, "This first layoff is part of a continuing series of staff reductions anticipated over the next several years." However, your boss is concerned about the vagueness and negative tone of the language and asks you to rewrite that sentence to read "This layoff is part of the company's ongoing efforts to continually align its resources with global market conditions." Do you think this suggested wording is ethical, given the company's economic influence in the community? Explain your answer in an e-mail message to your instructor.

5.7 **Message Composition: Controlling Style** Rewrite the following e-mail to customer Betty Crandall so that it conveys a helpful, personal, and interested tone:

We received your order complaint via our website response system. Owing to the fact that you neglected to include the size of the dress you ordered, please be advised that no shipment of your order was made, but the aforementioned shipment will occur at such time as we are in receipt of the aforementioned information.

5.8 **Message Composition: Selecting Words** Write a concrete phrase for each of these vague phrases:

a. Sometime this spring
b. A substantial savings
c. A large number attended
d. Increased efficiency
e. Expanded the work area
f. Flatten the website structure

5.9 **Message Composition: Selecting Words** List terms that are stronger than the following:

a. Ran after
b. Seasonal ups and downs
c. Bright
d. Suddenly rises
e. Moves forward

5.10 **Message Composition: Selecting Words** As you rewrite these sentences, replace the clichés and buzzwords with plain language (if you don't recognize any of these terms, you can find definitions online):

a. Being a jack-of-all-trades, Dave worked well in his new general manager job.
b. Moving Leslie into the accounting department, where she was literally a fish out of water, was like putting a square peg into a round hole, if you get my drift.
c. My only takeaway from the offsite was that Laird threw his entire department under the bus for missing the deadline.
d. I'd love to help with that project, but I'm bandwidth-constrained.
e. The board green-lighted our initiative to repurpose our consumer products for the commercial space.

5.11 **Message Composition: Selecting Words** Suggest short, simple words to replace each of the following:

a. Inaugurate
b. Terminate
c. Utilize
d. Anticipate
e. Assistance
f. Endeavor
g. Ascertain
h. Procure
i. Consummate
j. Advise
k. Alteration
l. Forwarded
m. Fabricate
n. Nevertheless
o. Substantial

5.12 **Message Composition: Selecting Words** Write up-to-date, less stuffy versions of these phrases; write *none* if you think there is no appropriate substitute or "delete" if the phrase should simply be deleted:

a. As per your instructions
b. Attached herewith
c. In lieu of
d. In reply I wish to state
e. Please be advised that

5.13 **Message Composition: Creating Sentences** Suppose that end-of-term frustrations have produced the following e-mail message to Professor Anne Brewer from a student who believes he should have received a B in his accounting class. If this message were recast into three or four clear sentences, the teacher might be more receptive to the student's argument. Rewrite the message to show how you would improve it:

I think that I was unfairly awarded a C in your accounting class this term, and I am asking you to change the grade to a B. It was a difficult term. I don't get any money from home, and I have to work mornings at the Pancake House (as a cook), so I had to rush to make your class, and those two times that I missed class were because they wouldn't let me off work because of special events at the Pancake House (unlike some other students who just take off when they choose). On the midterm examination, I originally got a 75 percent, but you said in class that there were two different ways to answer the third question and that you would change the grades of students who used the "optimal cost" method and had been counted off 6 points for doing this. I don't think that you took this into account, because I got 80 percent on the final, which is clearly a B. Anyway, whatever you decide, I just want to tell you that I really enjoyed this class, and I thank you for making accounting so interesting.

5.14 **Message Composition: Creating Sentences** Rewrite each sentence so that it is active rather than passive:

a. The raw data are entered into the customer relationship management system by the sales representative each Friday.
b. High profits are publicized by management.
c. The policies announced in the directive were implemented by the staff.

d. Our computers are serviced by the Santee Company.
e. The employees were represented by Janet Hogan.

5.15 Message Composition: Writing Paragraphs In the following paragraph, identify the topic sentence and the related sentences (those that support the idea of the topic sentence):

> Sync is a snap with Auto-Sync. By default, iTunes automatically copies your entire music library to iPod and deletes songs on iPod that are not listed in iTunes. Or you can use Playlist Sync and select the playlists you want to sync with your iPod. If you have more songs in your iTunes library than you can fit on your iPod, let iTunes create a playlist to fill your iPod, or just update your iPod by dragging over individual songs.[17]

Now add a topic sentence to this paragraph:

> Our analysis of the customer experience should start before golfers even drive through the front gate here at Glencoe Meadows; it should start when they phone in or log onto our website to reserve tee times. When they do arrive, the first few stages in the process are also vital: the condition of the grounds leading up to the club house, the reception they receive when they drop off their clubs, and the ease of parking. From that point, how well are we doing with check-in at the pro shop, openings at the driving range, and timely scheduling at the first tee? Then there's everything associated with playing the course itself and returning to the club house at the end of the round.

5.16 Teamwork Working with four other students, divide the following five topics among yourselves and each write one paragraph on your selected topic. Be sure each student uses a different technique when writing his or her paragraph: One student should use the illustration technique, one the comparison or contrast technique, one a discussion of cause and effect, one the classification technique, and one a discussion of problem and solution. Then exchange paragraphs within the team and pick out the main idea and general purpose of the paragraph one of your teammates wrote. Was everyone able to correctly identify the main idea and purpose? If not, suggest how the paragraph could be rewritten for clarity.

a. Types of digital cameras (or dogs or automobiles) available for sale
b. Advantages and disadvantages of eating at fast-food restaurants
c. Finding that first full-time job
d. Good qualities of my car (or house, or apartment, or neighborhood)
e. How to make a dessert (or barbecue a steak or make coffee)

5.17 Internet Download the Security and Exchange Commission's (SEC's) *A Plain English Handbook,* from www.sec.gov/pdf/handbook.pdf. In one or two sentences, summarize what the SEC means by the phrase *plain English.* Now scan the SEC's introduction to mutual funds at www.sec.gov/investor/pubs/inwsmf.htm. Does this information follow the SEC's plain English guidelines? Cite several examples that support your assessment.

5.18 Message Organization: Transitional Elements Add transitional elements to the following sentences to improve the flow of ideas. (*Note:* You may need to eliminate or add some words to smooth out your sentences.)

a. Steve Case saw infinite possibilities in online business. Steve Case was determined to turn his vision into reality. The techies scoffed at his strategy of building a simple Internet service for ordinary people. Case doggedly pursued his dream. He analyzed other online services. He assessed the needs of his customers. He responded to their desires for an easier way to access information over the Internet. In 1992, Steve Case named his company America Online (AOL). Critics predicted the company's demise. By the end of the century, AOL was a profitable powerhouse. An ill-fated merger with Time Warner was a financial disaster and led to Case's ouster from the company.

b. Facing some of the toughest competitors in the world, Harley-Davidson had to make some changes. The company introduced new products. Harley's management team set out to rebuild the company's production process. New products were coming to market and the company was turning a profit. Harley's quality standards were not on par with those of its foreign competitors. Harley's costs were still among the highest in the industry. Harley made a U-turn and restructured the company's organizational structure. Harley's efforts have paid off.

c. Whether you're indulging in a doughnut in New York or California, Krispy Kreme wants you to enjoy the same delicious taste with every bite. The company maintains consistent product quality by carefully controlling every step of the production process. Krispy Kreme tests all raw ingredients against established quality standards. Every delivery of wheat flour is sampled and measured for its moisture content and protein levels. Krispy Kreme blends the ingredients. Krispy Kreme tests the doughnut mix for quality. Krispy Kreme delivers the mix to its stores. Financial critics are not as kind to the company as food critics have been. Allegations of improper financial reporting have left the company's future in doubt.

5.19 Ethical Choices Under what circumstances would you consider the use of terms that are high in connotative meaning to be ethical? When would you consider it to be unethical? Explain your reasoning.

Expand Your Knowledge

Learning More on the Web

Compose a Better Business Message

http://owl.english.purdue.edu

At Purdue University's Online Writing Lab (OWL), http://owl.english.purdue.edu, you'll find tools to help you improve your business messages. For advice on composing written messages, for help with grammar, and for referrals to other information sources, you'd be wise to visit this site. Purdue's OWL offers online services and an introduction to Internet search tools. You can also download a variety of handouts on writing skills. Check out the resources at the OWL homepage and then answer the following questions. (Note that some of the advice you read on OWL may differ from the advice in your textbook in some respects.)

1. Explain why positive wording in a message is more effective than negative wording. Why should you be concerned about the position of good news or bad news in your written message?
2. What six factors of tone should you consider when conveying your message to your audience?
3. What points should you include in the close of your business message? Why?

Sharpening Your Career Skills Online

Bovée and Thill's Business Communication Web Search, at **http://businesscommunicationblog.com/websearch**, is a unique research tool designed specifically for business communication research. Use the Web Search function to find a website, video, PDF document, or PowerPoint presentation that offers advice on writing effective sentences. Write a brief e-mail message to your instructor, describing the item that you found and summarizing the career skills information you learned from it.

Improve Your Grammar, Mechanics, And Usage

The following exercises help you improve your knowledge of and power over English grammar, mechanics, and usage. Turn to the Handbook of Grammar, Mechanics, and Usage at the end of this book and review all of Section 1.5 (Adverbs). Then look at the following 10 items. Underline the preferred choice within each set of parentheses. (Answers to these exercises appear on page AK-3.)

1. Their performance has been (*good, well*).
2. I (*sure, surely*) do not know how to help you.
3. He feels (*sick, sickly*) again today.
4. Customs dogs are chosen because they smell (*good, well*).
5. The redecorated offices look (*good, well*).
6. Which of the two programs computes (*more fast, faster*)?
7. Of the two we have in stock, this model is the (*best, better*) designed.
8. He doesn't seem to have (*any, none*).
9. That machine is scarcely (*never, ever*) used.
10. They (*can, can't*) hardly get replacement parts for this equipment (*any, no*) more.

For additional exercises focusing on adverbs, visit mybcommlab. Click on Chapter 5; click on "Additional Exercises to Improve Your Grammar, Mechanics, and Usage;" and then click on "9. Adverbs."

6 Completing Business Messages

Learning Objectives

After studying this chapter, you will be able to

1. Discuss the value of careful revision, and list the main tasks involved in completing a business message
2. List four writing techniques you can use to improve the readability of your messages
3. Describe the steps you can take to improve the clarity of your writing and to make your writing more concise
4. Explain how design elements help determine the effectiveness of your documents
5. List eight tips for improving message quality through careful proofreading
6. Discuss the most important issues to consider when distributing your messages

On the Job: Communicating at Mercedes-AMG

Elegant design and attention to every detail are hallmarks of Mercedes-AMG automobiles, and that same concern for quality design is reflected in the company's communication efforts.

Promoting "Powerful Luxury" Through Careful Communication Design

Every business message tries to create a particular impression in the minds of the audience. What if the impression you want to create is how it feels to drive one of the world's most luxurious cars that has been customized with one of the world's most powerful engines? Merely saying the words *power* and *luxury* isn't likely to be too convincing in today's advertising-saturated world.

The German firm AMG is revered among automotive connoisseurs for its high-performance engines, which are available in special Mercedes-Benz models. To promote the newest models, the marketing communication specialists at the Mercedes-AMG partnership knew they needed to go beyond mere words and photos and use every media option and design technique possible to reach their target audience. "Our goal was to create immersive experiences that build an emotional connection between the Mercedes-AMG brand and automotive enthusiasts," said Scott Preacher, vice president of Mercedes-AMG's interactive advertising agency, Avenue A | Razorfish. The result was an innovative multimedia website that won the Webby award from the International Academy of Digital Arts and Sciences, considered by many to be the online media equivalent of an Oscar or Emmy.

When visitors "start" the virtual engine to begin a virtual tour of the AMG factory in Affalterbach, Germany, their web browsers even shake slightly to suggest the physical sensation of firing up the mighty AMG engine they can hear growling through their computer speakers. Visitors "drive" to the factory via online video and then enter various buildings to learn more about Mercedes-AMG products.

The message of powerful luxury is delivered in ways that business communicators could only dream about even a few years ago, and it does so with ageless attention to quality. In every respect—word choices, color palette, photography, audio, video, and interactive features—the website reflects the renowned "fit and finish" of the cars it represents.[1] www.mercedes-amg.com

MOVING BEYOND YOUR FIRST DRAFT

First drafts are rarely as effective as they could be, so take the time to improve them through revision.

Your business messages may not require the sophisticated design or technology of the Mercedes-AMG website (profiled in the chapter-opening "On the Job" vignette), but they can benefit from the same rigorous attention to detail in the third step of the three-step writing process: completing your messages.

After you've completed a first draft, you may be tempted to breathe a sigh of relief, send the message on its way, and move on to the next project. Resist the temptation. Successful communicators recognize that the first draft is rarely as tight, clear, and compelling as it needs to be. Careful revision can mean the difference between a rambling, unfocused message and a lively, direct message that gets results. The third step of the three-step writing process involves four key tasks: revising your message to achieve optimum quality and then producing, proofreading, and distributing it.

REVISING YOUR MESSAGE

1 LEARNING OBJECTIVE

Discuss the value of careful revision, and list the main tasks involved in completing a business message.

The revision task can vary somewhat, depending on the medium and the nature of your message. For informal messages to internal audiences, particularly when using instant messaging, text messaging, e-mail, or blogging, the revision process is often as simple as quickly looking over your message to correct any mistakes before sending or posting it. However, don't fall into the common trap of thinking that you don't need to worry about grammar, spelling, clarity, and other fundamentals of good writing when you use these media. These qualities can be *especially* important in electronic media, particularly if these messages are the only contact your audience has with you. Audiences are likely to equate the quality of your writing with the quality of your thinking. Poor-quality messages create an impression of poor-quality thinking. Moreover, even minor errors can cause confusion, frustration, and costly delays.

In any medium, readers tend to equate the quality of your writing with the quality of your thinking.

If you have time, put aside your draft for a day or two before you begin the revision process.

With more complex messages, try to put your draft aside for a day or two before you begin the revision process so that you can approach the material with a fresh eye. Then start with the "big picture," making sure that the document accomplishes your overall goals before moving to finer points, such as readability, clarity, and conciseness. Compare Figures 6.1 and 6.2 on the following pages to see how careful revision improves a customer letter.

Evaluating Your Content, Organization, Style, and Tone

When you begin the revision process, focus your attention on content, organization, style, and tone. To evaluate the content of your message, answer these questions:

- Is the information accurate?
- Is the information relevant to the audience?
- Is there enough information to satisfy the readers' needs?
- Is there a good balance between general information (giving readers enough background information to appreciate the message) and specific information (giving readers the details they need to understand the message)?

FIGURE 6.1 Improving a Message Through Careful Revision
Careful revision makes this draft shorter, clearer, and more focused. These *proofreading symbols* (see Appendix C) are still widely used when printed documents are edited and revised. However, in many instances, you'll use the electronic markup features in your word processor or other software, as shown on pages 156 and 157.

YAMAHA

YAMAHA CORPORATION OF AMERICA

6600 Orangethorpe Avenue, P.O. Box 6600, Buena Park, CA 90622-6600 (714) 522-9011

June 21, 2010

Ms. Claudia Banks
122 River Heights Drive
Bettendorf, IA 52722

Dear Ms. Banks:

On behalf of everyone at Yamaha Corporation of America, it is my pleasure to thank you for your recent purchase of a Yamaha CG1 grand piano. The Cg1 carries more than a century of Yamaha's heritage in design and production of world-class musical instruments and ~~you can bet it~~ will give you many years of playing and listening pleasure. Our commitment to your satisfaction doesn't stop with your purchase, however. ~~Much to the contrary, it continues for as long as you own your piano, which we hope, of course, is for as long as you live.~~ As a vital first step, please remember to call your Yamaha dealer sometime within three to eight months after your piano was delivered to take advantage of the ~~free~~ Yamaha Servicebond[SM] Assurance Program. This free service ~~program~~ includes a thorough evaluation and ~~adjusting~~ adjustment of the instrument after you've had some time to play your piano and your piano has had time to adapt to its environment. In addition to this ~~vital~~ important service ~~appointment~~, a regular program of tuning is ~~absolutely~~ essential to ensure ~~its~~ your piano's impeccable performance. Our piano specialists recommend four tunings during the first year and two tunings every year thereafter ~~that~~. Your Yamaha dealer is ideally positioned to provide you with optimum service for both regular tuning and any maintenance or repair needs you may have ~~over the years.~~

~~All of us at Yamaha~~ thank you for your recent purchase. We wish you many, many years of satisfaction with your new CG1 grand piano.

Respectfully, ~~yours in beautiful music,~~

Dirk Allen
Yamaha Corporation of America

Replaces the first sentence with the sentence from below (the two sentences said essentially the same thing)

Changes *adjusting* to *adjustment* to make it parallel with *evaluation*

Replaces *its* with *your piano's* to avoid confusion

Simplifies an over-the-top complimentary close

Removes a phrase (*you can bet*) that is too informal for this fairly formal message

Removes an awkward and unnecessary sentence

Inserts a missing word (*dealer*)

Removes unnecessary words in several places

Common Proofreading Symbols (see page A-29 for more)

~~strikethrough~~	Delete text
ℓ	Delete individual character or a circled block of text
∧	Insert text (text to insert is written above)
⊙	Insert period
∧ with comma	Insert comma
⌐	Start new line
¶	Start new paragraph
≡	Capitalize

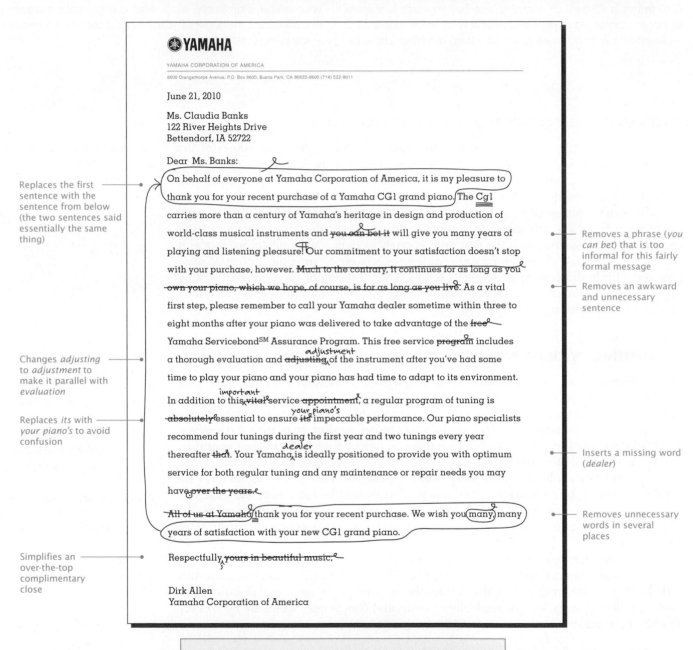

FIGURE 6.2 Revised Customer Letter
This revised letter provides the requested information more clearly, in a more organized fashion, with a friendlier style, and with precise mechanics.

YAMAHA

YAMAHA CORPORATION OF AMERICA

6600 Orangethorpe Avenue, P.O. Box 6600, Buena Park, CA 90622-6600 (714) 522-9011

June 21, 2010

Ms. Claudia Banks
122 River Heights Drive
Bettendorf, IA 52722

Dear Ms. Banks:

Thank you for your recent purchase. We wish you many years of satisfaction with your new CG1 grand piano. The CG1 carries more than a century of Yamaha's heritage in design and production of world-class musical instruments and will give you many years of playing and listening pleasure.

Our commitment to your satisfaction doesn't stop with your purchase, however. As a vital first step, please remember to call your Yamaha dealer sometime within three to eight months after your piano was delivered to take advantage of the Yamaha Servicebond^{SM} Assurance Program. This free service includes a thorough evaluation and adjustment of the instrument after you've had some time to play your piano and your piano has had time to adapt to its environment.

In addition to this important service, a regular program of tuning is essential to ensure your piano's impeccable performance. Our piano specialists recommend four tunings during the first year and two tunings every year thereafter. Your Yamaha dealer is ideally positioned to provide you with optimum service for both regular tuning and any maintenance or repair needs you may have.

Respectfully,

Dirk Allen
Yamaha Corporation of America

When you are satisfied with the content of your message, you can review its organization:

- Are all the points covered in the most logical order?
- Do the most important ideas receive the most space, and are they placed in the most prominent positions?
- Would the message be more convincing if it were arranged in another sequence?
- Are any points repeated unnecessarily?
- Are details grouped logically, or are some still scattered throughout the document?

Next, consider whether you have achieved the right style and tone for your audience. Is your writing formal enough to meet the audience's expectations, without being too formal or academic? Is it too casual for a serious subject? Does your message emphasize the audience's needs over your own?

The beginning and end of a message usually have the greatest impact on your readers, so make sure they are clear, concise, and compelling.

Finally, spend a few extra moments on the beginning and end of your message; these sections usually have the greatest impact on the audience. Be sure that the opening is relevant, interesting, and geared to the reader's probable reaction. In longer messages, ensure that the first few paragraphs establish the subject, purpose, and organization of the material. Review the conclusion to be sure that it summarizes the main idea and leaves the audience with a positive impression.

Reviewing for Readability

After confirming the content, organization, style, and tone of your message, make a second pass to improve *readability*. Most professionals are inundated with more reading material than they can ever hope to consume, and they'll appreciate your efforts to make your documents easier to read. You'll benefit from this effort, too: If you earn a reputation for creating well-crafted documents that respect the audience's time, people will pay more attention to your work.

Readability formulas can give you a helpful indication, but they can't measure everything that affects readability.

You may be familiar with one of the many indexes that have been developed over the years in an attempt to measure readability. If these measurements aren't built into your word processing software, you can find a number of calculators for various indexes at websites such as www.editcentral.com. These indexes offer a useful reference point, but they are limited by what they are able to measure: word length, number of syllables, sentence length, and paragraph length. They can't measure any of the other factors that affect readability, such as document design, the "you" attitude, clear sentence structure, smooth transitions, and proper word usage.

2 LEARNING OBJECTIVE

List four writing techniques you can use to improve the readability of your messages.

Beyond using shorter words and simpler sentences, you can improve the readability of a message by making the document interesting and easy to skim. Most business audiences—particularly influential senior managers—tend to skim documents, looking for key ideas, conclusions, and recommendations. If they determine that a document contains valuable information or requires a response, they will read it more carefully when time permits. Four techniques will make your message easier to read and easier to skim: varying sentence length, using shorter paragraphs, using lists and bullets instead of narrative, and adding effective headings and subheadings.

Varying Your Sentence Length

To keep readers' interest, use a variety of long, medium, and short sentences.

Effective documents usually combine a mixture of sentences that are short (up to 15 words or so), medium (15–25 words), and long (more than 25 words). Each sentence length has advantages. Short sentences can be processed quickly and are easier for nonnative speakers and translators to interpret. Medium-length sentences are useful for showing the relationships among ideas. Long sentences are often the best way to convey complex ideas, list multiple related points, or summarize or preview information.

Of course, each sentence length also has disadvantages. Too many short sentences in a row can make your writing choppy and disconnected. Medium sentences lack the punch of short sentences and the informative power of longer sentences. Long sentences can be difficult to understand because they are packed with information. They are also harder to skim because readers can absorb only a few words per glance.

Keeping Your Paragraphs Short

Long paragraphs are visually intimidating and can be difficult to read.

Large blocks of text can be visually daunting, so the optimum paragraph length is short to medium in most cases. Short paragraphs, generally 100 words or fewer (this paragraph has 58 words), are easier to read than long ones, and they make your writing look inviting. You can also emphasize ideas by isolating them in short, forceful paragraphs.

However, don't go overboard with short paragraphs. In particular, be careful to use one-sentence paragraphs only occasionally and only for emphasis. Also, if you need to divide a subject into several pieces in order to keep paragraphs short, be sure to help your readers keep the ideas connected by guiding them with plenty of transitional elements.

Using Lists and Bullets to Clarify and Emphasize

An effective alternative to using conventional sentences is to set off important ideas in a list. Lists can show the sequence of your ideas, heighten their impact visually, and increase the likelihood that a reader will find key points. In addition, lists help simplify complex subjects, highlight main points, break up a page or screen visually, ease the skimming process for busy readers, and give readers a breather. Consider the difference between the following two presentations of the same information:

Lists are effective tools for highlighting and simplifying material.

NARRATIVE

Owning your own business has many potential advantages. One is the opportunity to pursue your own personal passion. Another advantage is the satisfaction of working for yourself. As a sole proprietor, you also have the advantage of privacy because you do not have to reveal your financial information or plans to anyone.

LIST

Owning your own business has three advantages:

- Opportunity to pursue personal passion
- Satisfaction of working for yourself
- Financial privacy

Note how the sentence that introduces this bullet list ends in a colon. If this introduction is not a complete sentence, however, don't use any punctuation.

You can separate list items with numbers, letters, or bullets (a general term for any kind of graphical element that precedes each item). Bullets are generally preferred over numbers, unless the list is in some logical sequence or ranking or you need to refer to specific list items elsewhere in the document.

Regardless of the format you choose, the items in a list should be parallel; that is, they should all use the same grammatical pattern. Parallel forms are easier to read and skim. You can create parallelism by repeating the pattern in words, phrases, clauses, or entire sentences (see Table 6.1).

Adding Headings and Subheadings

A **heading** is a brief title that tells readers about the content of the section that follows. **Subheadings** are subordinate to headings, indicating subsections with a major section. Headings and subheadings serve these important functions:

Use headings and subheadings to show the organization of your material, draw the reader's attention to key points, and show connections between ideas.

- **Organization.** Headings show your reader at a glance how the document is organized.
- **Attention.** Informative, inviting, and in some cases intriguing headings grab the reader's attention, make the text easier to read, and help the reader find the parts he or she needs to read—or skip.
- **Connection.** Using headings and subheadings together helps readers see the relationship between your main ideas and between each main idea and its supporting minor ideas.

Descriptive headings, such as "Cost Considerations," identify a topic but do little more. **Informative headings**, such as "A New Way to Cut Costs," guide readers to think in a certain way about the topic. Well-written informative headings are self-contained, which means readers can read just the headings and subheadings and understand them without reading the rest of the document. Whatever types of headings you choose, keep them brief and use parallel construction throughout the entire document.

Informative headings are generally more helpful than descriptive ones.

TABLE 6.1 Achieving Parallelism

METHOD	EXAMPLE
Parallel words	The letter was approved by Clausen, Whittaker, Merlin, and Carlucci.
Parallel phrases	We are gaining market share in supermarkets, in department stores, and in specialty stores.
Parallel clauses	I'd like to discuss the issue after Vicki gives her presentation but before Marvin shows his slides.
Parallel sentences	In 2007, we exported 30 percent of our production. In 2008, we exported 50 percent.

3 LEARNING OBJECTIVE

Describe the steps you can take to improve the clarity of your writing and to make your writing more concise.

Editing for Clarity and Conciseness

After you've reviewed and revised your message for readability, your next step is to make sure your message is as clear and as concise as possible. See Table 6.2 for examples of the following tips:

- **Break up overly long sentences.** If you find yourself stuck in a long sentence, you're probably trying to make the sentence do more than it can reasonably do, such as expressing two dissimilar thoughts or peppering the reader with too many pieces of supporting evidence at once. (Did you notice how difficult this long sentence was to read?)

TABLE 6.2 Revising for Clarity

ISSUES TO REVIEW	INEFFECTIVE	EFFECTIVE
Overly Long Sentences		
Taking compound sentences too far	The magazine will be published January 1, and I'd better meet the deadline if I want my article included because we want the article to appear before the trade show.	The magazine will be published January 1. I'd better meet the deadline because we want the article to appear before the trade show.
Hedging Sentences		
Overqualifying sentences	I believe that Mr. Johnson's employment record seems to show that he may be capable of handling the position.	Mr. Johnson's employment record shows that he is capable of handling the position.
Unparallel Sentences		
Using dissimilar construction for similar ideas	Mr. Simms had been drenched with rain, bombarded with telephone calls, and his boss shouted at him.	Mr. Sims had been drenched with rain, bombarded with telephone calls, and shouted at by his boss.
	To waste time and missing deadlines are bad habits.	Wasting time and missing deadlines are bad habits.
Dangling Modifiers		
Placing modifiers close to the wrong nouns and verbs	Walking to the office, a red sports car passed her.	A red sports car passed her while she was walking to the office.
	Reduced by 25 percent, Europe had its lowest semiconductor output in a decade.	Europe reduced semiconductor output by 25 percent, its lowest level in a decade.
Long Noun Sequences		
Stringing too many nouns together	The window sash installation company will give us an estimate on Friday.	The company that installs window sashes will give us an estimate on Friday.
Camouflaged Verbs		
Changing verbs and nouns into adjectives	The manager undertook implementation of the rules.	The manager implemented the rules.
	Verification of the shipments occurs weekly.	We verify shipment weekly
Changing verbs into nouns	reach a conclusion about	conclude
	give consideration to	consider
Sentence Structure		
Separating subject and predicate	A 10% decline in market share, which resulted from quality problems and an aggressive sales campaign by Armitage, the market leader in the Northeast, was the major problem in 2008.	The major problem in 2008 was a 10% loss of market share, which resulted from quality problems and an aggressive sales campaign by Armitage, the market leader in the Northeast.
Separating adjectives, adverbs, or prepositional phrases from the words they modify	Our antique desk lends an air of strength and substance with thick legs and large drawers.	With its thick legs and large drawers, our antique desk lends an air of strength and substance.
Awkward References	The Law Office and the Accounting Office distribute computer supplies for legal secretaries and beginning accountants, respectively.	The Law Office distributes computer supplies for legal secretaries; the Accounting Office distributes those for beginning accountants.

- **Rewrite hedging sentences.** *Hedging* means pulling back from making an absolutely certain, definitive statement about a topic. Granted, sometimes you have to write *may* or *seems* to avoid stating a judgment as a fact. However, when you hedge too often or without good reason, you come across as being unsure of what you're saying.
- **Impose parallelism.** When you have two or more similar ideas to express, make them parallel by using the same grammatical construction. Parallelism shows that the ideas are related, of similar importance, and on the same level of generality.
- **Correct dangling modifiers.** Sometimes a modifier is not just an adjective or an adverb but an entire phrase modifying a noun or a verb. Be careful not to leave this type of modifier *dangling*, with no connection to the subject of the sentence.
- **Reword long noun sequences.** When multiple nouns are strung together as modifiers, the resulting sentence can be hard to read. See if a single well-chosen word will do the job. If the nouns are all necessary, consider moving one or more to a modifying phrase, as shown in Table 6.2.
- **Replace camouflaged verbs.** Watch for words that end in *-ion*, *-tion*, *-ing*, *-ment*, *-ant*, *-ent*, *-ence*, *-ance*, and *-ency*. These endings often change verbs into nouns and adjectives, requiring you to add a verb in order to get your point across.
- **Clarify sentence structure.** Keep the subject and predicate of a sentence as close together as possible. Similarly, adjectives, adverbs, and prepositional phrases usually make the most sense when they're placed as close as possible to the words they modify.
- **Clarify awkward references.** Try to avoid vague references such as *the above-mentioned*, *as mentioned above*, *the aforementioned*, *the former*, *the latter*, and *respectively*. Use a specific pointer such as "as described in the second paragraph on page 22."

Clarity is essential to getting your message across accurately and efficiently.

If you qualify or hedge too often, you undermine your credibility.

Camouflaged verbs are verbs that have been changed into nouns; they often increase the length of a sentence without adding any value.

Subject and predicate should be placed as close together as possible, as should modifiers and the words they modify.

The next step is to examine the text with the goal of reducing the number of words you use. See Table 6.3 for examples of the following tips:

Improving clarity often makes messages shorter, but you can make them shorter still by using some specific revision techniques.

Early drafts often have words and phrases that don't add anything and can easily be cut out.

- **Delete unnecessary words and phrases.** To test whether a word or phrase is essential, try the sentence without it. If the meaning doesn't change, leave it out.
- **Shorten long words and phrases.** Short words and phrases are generally more vivid and easier to read than long ones. Also, by using infinitives (the "to" form of a verb) in place of some phrases, you can often shorten sentences while making them clearer.
- **Eliminate redundancies.** In some word combinations, the words say the same thing. For instance, "visible to the eye" is redundant because *visible* is enough without further clarification; "to the eye" adds nothing.
- **Recast "It is/There are" starters.** If you start a sentence with an indefinite pronoun such as *it* or *there*, odds are the sentence could be shorter and more active. For instance, "We believe . . ." is a stronger opening than "It is believed that . . ."

As you rewrite, concentrate on how each word contributes to an effective sentence and on how each sentence helps build a coherent paragraph. For a reminder of the tasks involved in revision, see "Checklist: Revising Business Messages."

Evaluating, Editing, and Revising the Work of Others

At many points in your career, you will be asked to evaluate, edit, or revise the work of others. Whether you're suggesting improvements or actually making the improvements yourself (as you might on a wiki site, for example), you can make a contribution by using all the skills you've learned in this chapter as well as in Chapters 4 and 5.

Before you dive into someone else's work, recognize the dual responsibility that doing so entails. First, unless you've been specifically asked to rewrite something in your own style

Evaluating and revising the work of others is an important responsibility.

TABLE 6.3 Revising for Conciseness

ISSUES TO REVIEW	INEFFECTIVE	EFFECTIVE
Unnecessary Words and Phrases		
Using wordy phrases	for the sum of	for
	in the event that	if
	prior to the start of	before
	in the near future	soon
	at this point in time	now
	due to the fact that	because
	in view of the fact that	because
	until such time as	when
	with reference to	about
Using too many relative pronouns	Cars that are sold after January will not have a six-month warranty.	Cars sold after January will not have a six-month warranty.
	Employees who are driving to work should park in the underground garage.	Employees driving to work should park in the underground garage. OR Employees should park in the underground garage.
Using too few relative pronouns	The project manager told the engineers last week the specifications were changed.	The project manager told the engineers last week that the specifications were changed. The project manager told the engineers that last week the specifications were changed.
Long Words and Phrases		
Using overly long words	During the preceding year, the company accelerated productive operations.	Last year the company sped up operations.
	The action was predicated on the assumption that the company was operating at a financial deficit.	The action was based on the belief that the company was losing money.
Using wordy phrases rather than infinitives	If you want success as a writer, you must work hard.	To succeed as a writer, you must work hard.
	He went to the library for the purpose of studying.	He went to the library to study.
	The employer increased salaries so that she could improve morale.	The employer increased salaries to improve morale.
Redundancies		
Repeating meanings	absolutely complete	complete
	basic fundamentals	fundamentals
	follows after	follows
	free and clear	free
	refer back	refer
	repeat again	repeat
	collect together	collect
	future plans	plans
	return back	return
	important essentials	essentials
	end result	result
	actual truth	truth

(continued)

TABLE 6.3 Revising for Conciseness *(continued)*

ISSUES TO REVIEW	INEFFECTIVE	EFFECTIVE
Redundancies		
	final outcome	outcome
	uniquely unusual	unique
	surrounded on all sides	surrounded
Using double modifiers	modern, up-to-date equipment	modern equipment
It Is/There Are Starters	It would be appreciated if you would sign the lease today.	Please sign the lease today.
Starting sentences with *It* or *There*	There are five employees in this division who were late to work today.	Five employees in this division were late to work today.

or change the emphasis of the message, remember that your job is to help the other writer succeed at his or her task, not to impose your writing style or pursue your own agenda. In other words, make sure your input focuses on making the piece more effective, not on making it more like something you would've written. Second, make sure you understand the writer's intent before you begin suggesting or making changes. If you try to edit or revise without knowing what the writer hoped to accomplish, you run the risk of making the piece less effective, not more. With those thoughts in mind, answer the following questions as you evaluate someone else's writing:

- What is the purpose of this document or message?
- Who is the target audience?
- What information does the audience need?
- Does the document provide this information in a well-organized way?
- Does the writing demonstrate the "you" attitude toward the audience?
- Is the tone of the writing appropriate for the audience?
- Can the readability be improved?
- Is the writing clear? If not, how can it be improved?
- Is the writing as concise as it could be?
- Does the design support the intended message?

You can read more about using these skills in the context of wiki writing in Chapter 12.

CHECKLIST: Revising Business Messages

A. Evaluate content, organization, style, and tone.
- Make sure the information is accurate, relevant, and sufficient.
- Check that all necessary points appear in logical order.
- Verify that you present enough support to make the main idea convincing and interesting.
- Be sure the beginning and end are effective.
- Make sure you've achieved the right tone.

B. Review for readability.
- Consider using a readability index but be sure to interpret the answer carefully.
- Use a mix of short and long sentences.
- Keep paragraphs short.
- Use bulleted and numbered lists to emphasize key points.
- Make the document easy to scan with headings and subheadings.

C. Edit for clarity.
- Break up overly long sentences and rewrite hedging sentences.
- Impose parallelism to simplify reading.
- Correct dangling modifiers.
- Reword long noun sequences and replace camouflaged verbs.
- Clarify sentence structure and awkward references.

D. Edit for conciseness.
- Delete unnecessary words and phrases.
- Shorten long words and phrases.
- Eliminate redundancies.
- Rewrite sentences that start with "It is" or "There are."

Using Technology to Revise Your Message

Revision marks and commenting features are great ways to track the revision process when multiple reviewers are involved.

When it's time to revise and polish your message, be sure to use the revision features in your software to full advantage. For instance, *revision tracking* (look for a feature called "track changes" or something similar) and *commenting* keep track of proposed editing changes and provide a history of a document's revisions. In Microsoft Word, for example, revisions appear in a different color (see Figure 6.3), giving you a chance to review changes before accepting or rejecting them. Adobe Acrobat lets you attach comments to PDF files (see Figure 6.4). Using revision marks and commenting features is also a great way to keep track of editing changes made by team members. Both Word and Acrobat let you use different colors for each reviewer, so you can keep everyone's comments separate.

Spell checkers, grammar checkers, and computerized thesauruses can all help with the revision process, but they can't take the place of good writing and editing skills.

Four other software tools can help you find the best words and use them correctly. First, a *spell checker* compares your document with an electronic dictionary, highlights unrecognized words, and suggests correct spellings. Spell checkers are wonderful for finding typos, but they are no substitute for careful reviewing. For example, if you use *their* when you mean to use *there*, your spell checker won't notice because *their* is spelled correctly.

Second, a computer *thesaurus* gives you alternative words, just as a printed thesaurus does. The best uses of any thesaurus, printed or computerized, are to find fresh, interesting

FIGURE 6.3 Revision Marks in Microsoft Word
Microsoft Word, the most commonly used word processor in business offices, offers handy tools for reviewing draft documents. In this example, text to be added is underlined, and text to be deleted is struck through. The writer can then choose to accept or reject each suggested change.

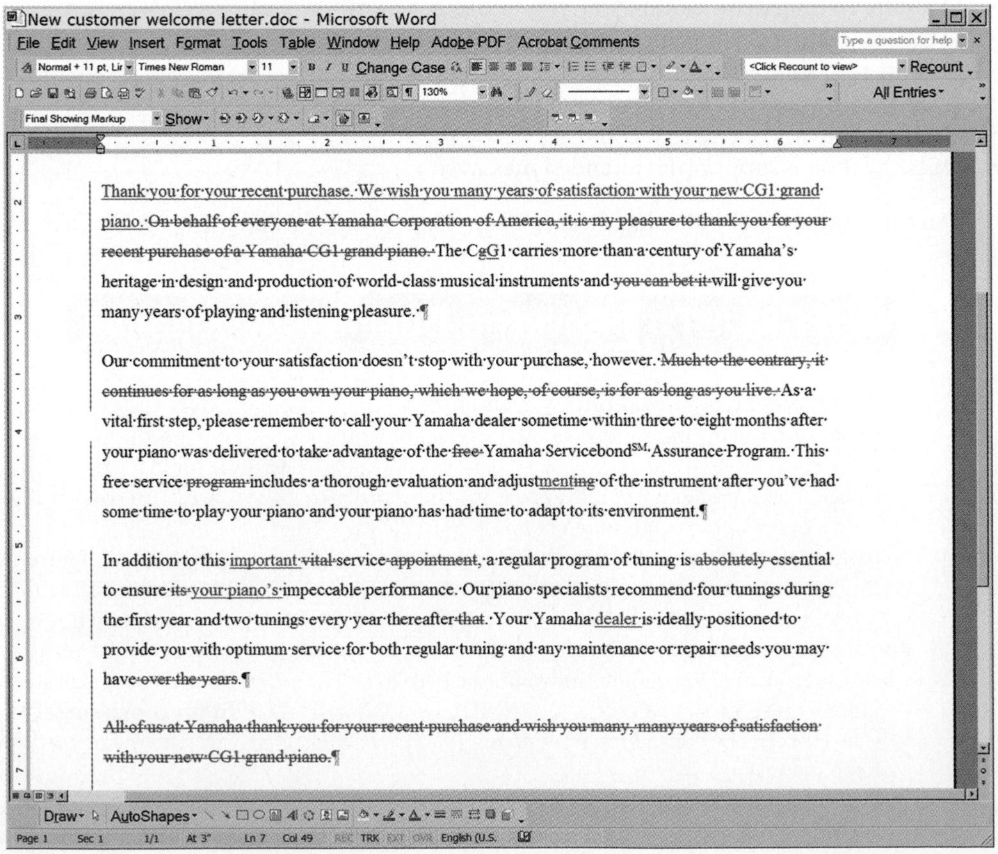
New customer welcome letter.doc - Microsoft Word

Thank you for your recent purchase. We wish you many years of satisfaction with your new CG1 grand piano. ~~On behalf of everyone at Yamaha Corporation of America, it is my pleasure to thank you for your recent purchase of a Yamaha CG1 grand piano.~~ The CgG1 carries more than a century of Yamaha's heritage in design and production of world-class musical instruments and ~~you can bet it~~ will give you many years of playing and listening pleasure. ¶

Our commitment to your satisfaction doesn't stop with your purchase, however. ~~Much to the contrary, it continues for as long as you own your piano, which we hope, of course, is for as long as you live.~~ As a vital first step, please remember to call your Yamaha dealer sometime within three to eight months after your piano was delivered to take advantage of the ~~free~~ Yamaha Servicebond℠ Assurance Program. This free service ~~program~~ includes a thorough evaluation and adjustment~~ing~~ of the instrument after you've had some time to play your piano and your piano has had time to adapt to its environment.¶

In addition to this important ~~vital~~ service ~~appointment~~, a regular program of tuning is ~~absolutely~~ essential to ensure ~~its~~ your piano's impeccable performance. Our piano specialists recommend four tunings during the first year and two tunings every year thereafter ~~that~~. Your Yamaha dealer is ideally positioned to provide you with optimum service for both regular tuning and any maintenance or repair needs you may have ~~over the years.~~¶

~~All of us at Yamaha thank you for your recent purchase and wish you many, many years of satisfaction with your new CG1 grand piano.~~¶

FIGURE 6.4 Comments Attached to a PDF File
Adobe Acrobat lets reviewers attach comments to any document in PDF format, even if it was originally created using software that the reviewers don't have. (Note that this commenting capability is not available in the free Adobe Reader product.)

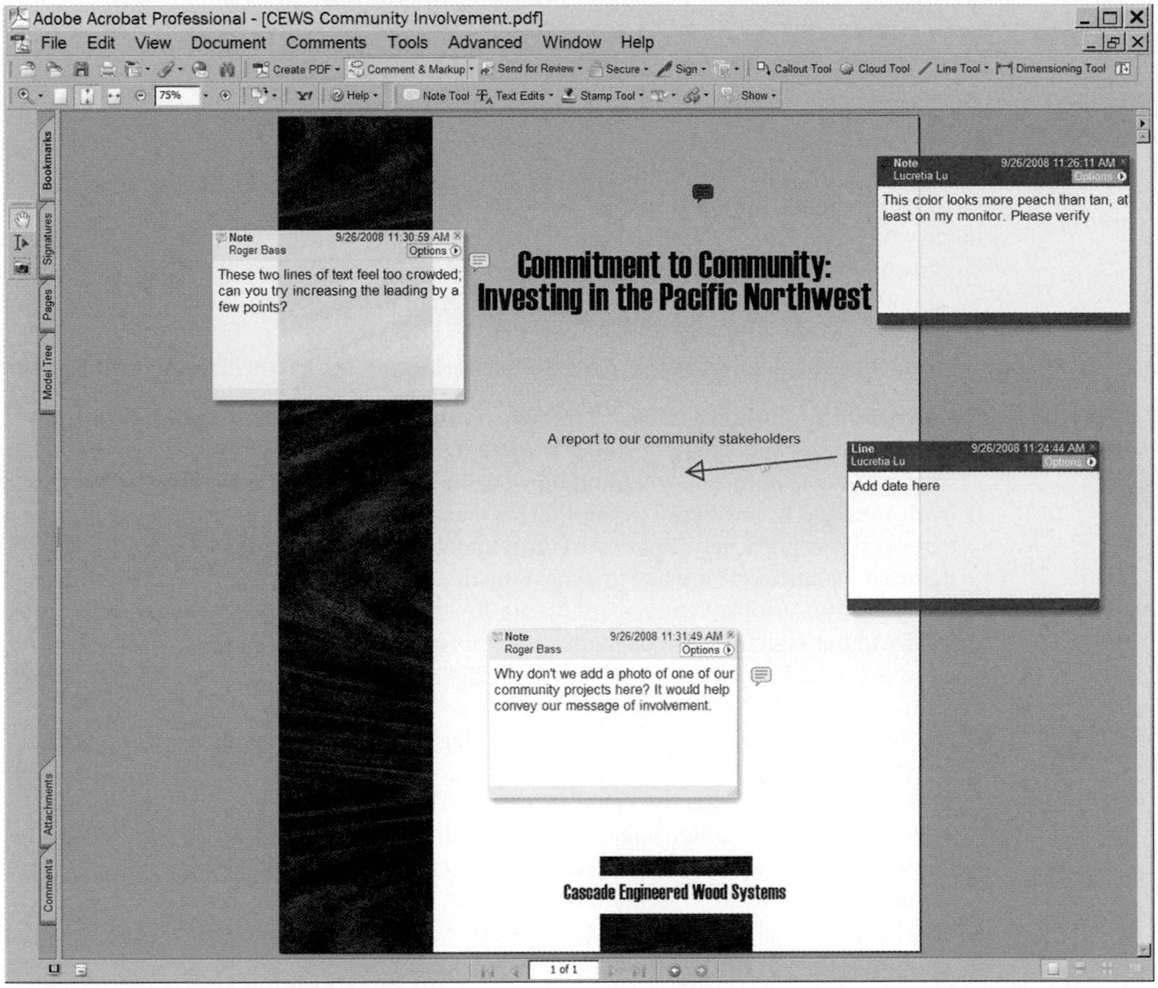

words when you've been using the same word too many times and to find words that most accurately convey your intended meaning. Don't use a thesaurus simply to find impressive words, however.

Third, a *grammar checker* tries to do for your grammar what a spell checker does for your spelling. Because the program doesn't have a clue about what you're trying to say, it can't tell whether you've said it clearly or completely. However, grammar checkers can highlight items you should consider changing, such as passive voice, long sentences, and words that tend to be misused.

Fourth, a *style checker* can monitor your word and sentence choices and suggest alternatives that might produce more effective writing. For instance, the style-checking options in Microsoft Word range from basic issues, such as spelling out numbers and using contractions, to more subjective matters, such as sentence structure and the use of technical terminology.

By all means, use any software tools that you find helpful when revising your documents. Just remember that it's unwise to rely on them to do all your revision work and that you're responsible for the final product.

PRODUCING YOUR MESSAGE

Production quality affects readability and audience perceptions of you and your message.

Now it's time to put your hard work on display. The *production quality* of your message—the total effect of page or screen design, graphical elements, typography, and so on—plays an important role in the effectiveness of your message. A polished, inviting design not only makes your material easier to read but also conveys a sense of professionalism and importance.[2]

Designing for Readability

Document design sends strong nonverbal signals. Make sure they are positive and appropriate signals.

Design affects readability in two important ways. First, if used carefully, design elements can improve the effectiveness of your message. If used poorly, design elements can act as barriers, blocking your communication. Second, the visual design sends a nonverbal message to your readers, influencing their perceptions of the communication before they read a single word (see Figure 6.5). For example, the elegant style of the Mercedes-AMG website conveys a message that matches the nature of the products themselves. The black, silver, gray, and white color palette sends a distinctly different message than a website with vibrant or clashing colors would send.

To achieve an effective design, pay careful attention to the following design elements:

Aim for consistent design within each message and from message to message.

- **Consistency.** Throughout each message, be consistent in your use of margins, typeface, type size, and space. Also be consistent when using recurring design elements, such as vertical lines, columns, and borders. In many cases, you'll want to be consistent from message to message as well; that way, audiences who receive multiple messages from you recognize your documents and know what to expect.
- **Balance.** Balance is a subjective issue. One document may have a formal, rigid design in which the various elements are placed in a grid pattern, while another may have a less formal design in which elements flow more freely across the page—and both could be in balance. Like the tone of your language, visual balance can be too formal, just right, or too informal for a given message.
- **Restraint.** Strive for simplicity in design. Elegant simplicity, using only enough text, graphics, audio, and video to get each point across, is one of the reasons the Mercedes-AMG website is so effective. Don't clutter your message with too many design elements, too much highlighting, too many colors, or too many decorative touches. Let "simpler" and "fewer" be your guiding concepts.
- **Detail.** Pay attention to details that affect your design and thus your message. For instance, extremely wide columns of text can be difficult to read; in many cases a better solution is to split the text into two narrower columns.

Simple designs are usually more effective than more complex ones.

4 LEARNING OBJECTIVE

Explain how design elements help determine the effectiveness of your documents.

You can make both printed and electronic messages more effective by understanding the use of white space, margins and line justification, typefaces, and type styles.

White Space

White space separates elements in a document and helps guide the reader's eye.

Any space that doesn't contain any text or artwork, both in print and online, is considered **white space**. (Note that "white space" isn't necessarily white; it is simply blank.) These unused areas provide visual contrast and important resting points for your readers. White space includes the open area surrounding headings, margins, paragraph indents, space around images, vertical space between columns, and horizontal space between paragraphs or lines of text. To increase the chance that readers will read your messages, be generous with white space; it makes pages and screens feel less intimidating and easier to read.[3]

Margins and Justification

Margins define the space around text and between text columns. In addition to their width, the look and feel of margins is influenced by the way you arrange lines of text, which can be set (1) *justified* (which means they are *flush*, or aligned vertically, on the left and also flush on the right), (2) flush left with a *ragged-right* margin, (3) flush right with a *ragged-left* margin, or (4) centered. This paragraph is justified, whereas the paragraphs in Figure 6.2 on page 149 are flush left with a ragged-right margin.

FIGURE 6.5 Ineffective and Effective Design
Compare these two e-mail screens. They contain virtually the same information but send dramatically different messages to the reader. The unprofessional appearance of the "ineffective" version makes it uninviting and difficult to read. The amateurish use of color is distracting. In contrast, the "effective" version is clear, inviting, and easy to either read entirely or scan quickly.

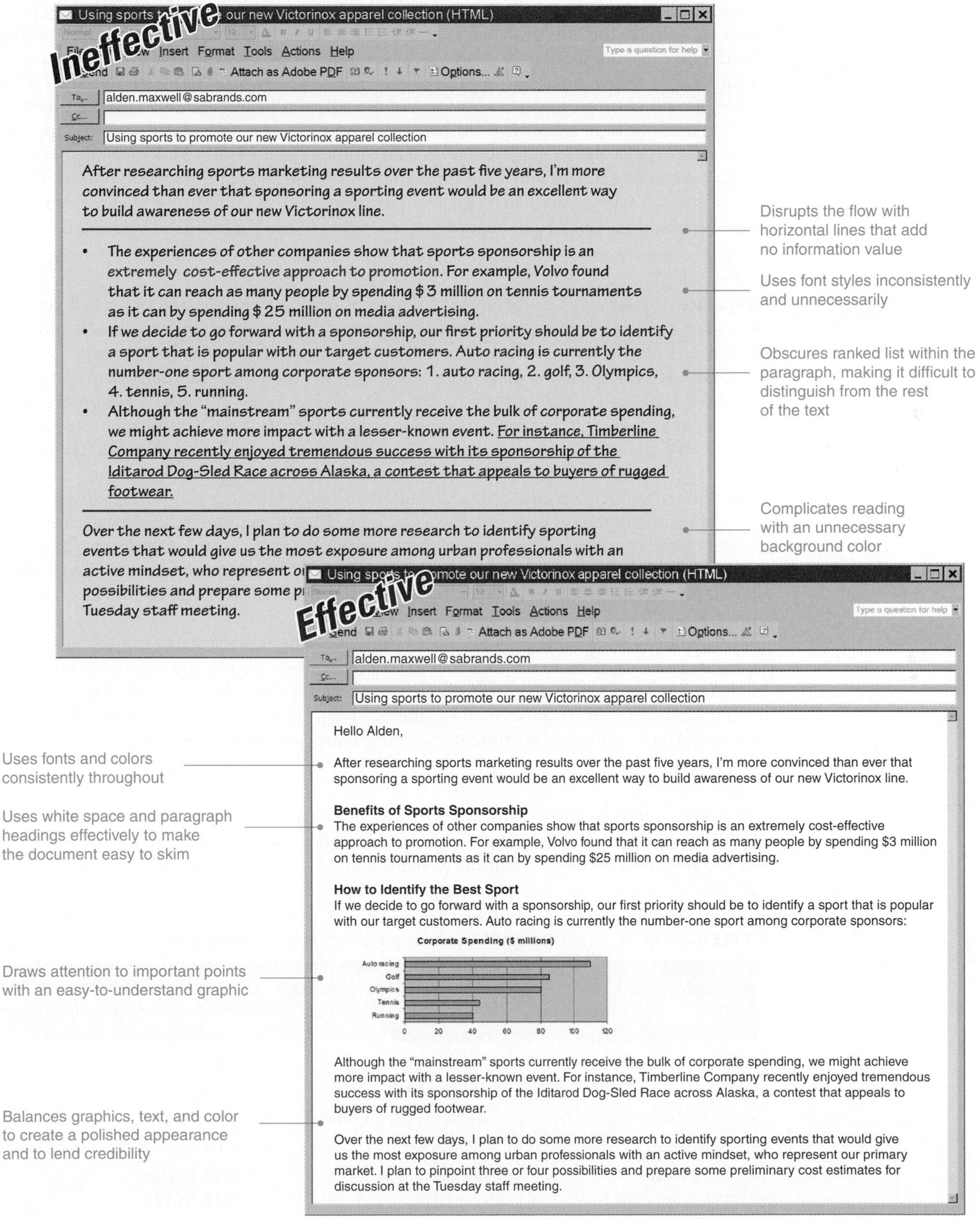

Ineffective
Using sports to promote our new Victorinox apparel collection (HTML)
File Edit View Insert Format Tools Actions Help
Send Attach as Adobe PDF Options...
To... alden.maxwell@sabrands.com
Cc...
Subject: Using sports to promote our new Victorinox apparel collection
After researching sports marketing results over the past five years, I'm more convinced than ever that sponsoring a sporting event would be an excellent way to build awareness of our new Victorinox line.
• The experiences of other companies show that sports sponsorship is an extremely cost-effective approach to promotion. For example, Volvo found that it can reach as many people by spending $ 3 million on tennis tournaments as it can by spending $ 25 million on media advertising.
• If we decide to go forward with a sponsorship, our first priority should be to identify a sport that is popular with our target customers. Auto racing is currently the number-one sport among corporate sponsors: 1. auto racing, 2. golf, 3. Olympics, 4. tennis, 5. running.
• Although the "mainstream" sports currently receive the bulk of corporate spending, we might achieve more impact with a lesser-known event. For instance, Timberline Company recently enjoyed tremendous success with its sponsorship of the Iditarod Dog-Sled Race across Alaska, a contest that appeals to buyers of rugged footwear.
Over the next few days, I plan to do some more research to identify sporting events that would give us the most exposure among urban professionals with an active mindset, who represent o possibilities and prepare some p Tuesday staff meeting.
Disrupts the flow with horizontal lines that add no information value
Uses font styles inconsistently and unnecessarily
Obscures ranked list within the paragraph, making it difficult to distinguish from the rest of the text
Complicates reading with an unnecessary background color
Effective
Using sports to promote our new Victorinox apparel collection (HTML)
Send Attach as Adobe PDF Options...
To... alden.maxwell@sabrands.com
Cc...
Subject: Using sports to promote our new Victorinox apparel collection
Hello Alden,
After researching sports marketing results over the past five years, I'm more convinced than ever that sponsoring a sporting event would be an excellent way to build awareness of our new Victorinox line.
Benefits of Sports Sponsorship
The experiences of other companies show that sports sponsorship is an extremely cost-effective approach to promotion. For example, Volvo found that it can reach as many people by spending $3 million on tennis tournaments as it can by spending $25 million on media advertising.
How to Identify the Best Sport
If we decide to go forward with a sponsorship, our first priority should be to identify a sport that is popular with our target customers. Auto racing is currently the number-one sport among corporate sponsors:
Corporate Spending ($ millions)
Auto racing
Golf
Olympics
Tennis
Running
0 20 40 60 80 100 120
Although the "mainstream" sports currently receive the bulk of corporate spending, we might achieve more impact with a lesser-known event. For instance, Timberline Company recently enjoyed tremendous success with its sponsorship of the Iditarod Dog-Sled Race across Alaska, a contest that appeals to buyers of rugged footwear.
Over the next few days, I plan to do some more research to identify sporting events that would give us the most exposure among urban professionals with an active mindset, who represent our primary market. I plan to pinpoint three or four possibilities and prepare some preliminary cost estimates for discussion at the Tuesday staff meeting.
Uses fonts and colors consistently throughout
Uses white space and paragraph headings effectively to make the document easy to skim
Draws attention to important points with an easy-to-understand graphic
Balances graphics, text, and color to create a polished appearance and to lend credibility

Most business documents use a flush-left margin and a ragged-right margin.

Magazines, newspapers, and books often use justified type because it can accommodate more text in a given space. However, justified type needs to be used with care. First, it creates a denser look because the uniform line lengths decrease the amount of the white space along the right margin. Second, it produces a more formal and less personalized look. Third, unless it is used with some skill and attention, justified type can be more difficult to read because it can produce large gaps between words and excessive hyphenation at the ends of lines. The publishing specialists who create magazines, newspapers, and books have the time and skill needed to carefully adjust character and word spacing to eliminate these problems. (In some cases, sentences are even rewritten in order to improve the appearance of the printed page.) Because most business communicators don't have that time or skill, it's best to avoid justified type in most business documents.

In contrast to justified type, flush-left, ragged-right type creates a more open appearance on the page, producing a less formal and more contemporary look. Spacing between words is consistent, and only long words that fall at the ends of lines are hyphenated.

Centered type is rarely used for text paragraphs but is commonly used for headings and subheadings. Flush-right, ragged-left type is rarely used in business documents.

Typefaces

Typeface or **font** refers to the physical design of letters, numbers, and other text characters. The choice of typefaces influences the tone of your message, making it look authoritative or friendly, businesslike or casual, classic or modern, and so on. In other words, typefaces send nonverbal signals independent of what the words themselves say, so be sure to choose fonts that are appropriate for your message (see Table 6.4). Computers offer dozens of font choices, but most of these are inappropriate for general business usage.

Serif typefaces are commonly used for regular paragraph text; sans serif typefaces are commonly used for headings and subheadings.

Serif typefaces have small crosslines (called serifs) at the ends of each letter stroke. Serif typefaces such as Times Roman are commonly used for regular paragraph text (as in this book), but they can look busy and cluttered when set in large sizes for headings.

Sans serif typefaces have no serifs (*sans* is French for "without"). The visual simplicity of sans serif typefaces such as Helvetica and Arial makes them ideal for the larger sizes used in headlines. However, these typefaces can be difficult to read in long blocks of text. They look best when surrounded by plenty of white space—as in headings or in widely spaced lines of text.

For most documents, generally avoid using more than two typefaces, although if you want to make captions or another special text element stand out, you can use a third font for that.[4] You can't go too far wrong with a sans serif typeface (such as Arial) for heads and subheads and a serif typeface (such as Times New Roman) for text and captions. Using too many typefaces clutters a document and can produce an amateurish look.

Type Styles

Type style refers to any modification that lends contrast or emphasis to type, including boldface, italic, underlining, and color. For example, you can boldface individual words or phrases to draw more attention to them. Italic type has specific uses as well, such as

TABLE 6.4 Typeface Purposes and Personalities

SERIF TYPEFACES [BEST FOR TEXT]	SANS SERIF TYPEFACES [BEST FOR HEADLINES; SOME WORK WELL FOR TEXT]	SPECIALTY TYPEFACES [FOR DECORATIVE PURPOSES ONLY]
Bookman Old Style	Arial	ANNA
Century Schoolbook	**Eras Bold**	Bauhaus
Courier	Franklin Gothic Book	Edwardian
Garamond	Frutiger	*Lucida Handwriting*
Rockwell	Gill Sans	Old English
Times Roman	Verdana	**STENCIL**

highlighting quotations and indicating foreign words, irony, humor, book and movie titles, and unconventional usage.

As a general rule, avoid using any style in a way that slows your audience's progress through the message. For instance, underlining or using all-uppercase letters can interfere with a reader's ability to recognize the shapes of words, and shadowed or outlined type can seriously hinder legibility.

Avoid using any type style in ways that might interfere with reading.

For most printed business messages, use a type size of 10 to 12 points for regular text and 12 to 18 points for headings and subheadings (1 point is approximately 1/72 inch). Type that is too small is hard to read, whereas extra-large type looks unprofessional.

Designing Multimedia Documents

A **multimedia document** contains a combination of text, graphics, photographs, audio, animation, video, and interactivity (such as hyperlinks that access webpages or software programs). Most electronic media now support multiple media formats, so you have a variety of options for creating multimedia documents. For example, you can add photos to a word processor file, audio commentary to a PDF, video clips to a blog posting, and animation to webpages.

As rich media, multimedia documents can convey large amounts of information quickly, engage people in multiple ways, express emotions, and allow recipients to personalize the communication process to their own needs. However, these documents are more difficult to create than documents that contain only text and static images. To design and create multimedia documents, you need to consider the following factors:

Multimedia documents can be powerful communication vehicles, but they require more time, tools, and skills to create.

- **Creative and technical skills.** Depending on what you need to accomplish, creating and integrating multimedia elements can require some creative and technical skills. Fortunately, many basic tasks, such as adding photographs or video clips to a webpage, have gotten much easier in recent years. And even if you don't have the advantage of formal training in design, by studying successful examples such as the Mercedes-AMG website, you can start to get a feel for what works and what doesn't.
- **Tools.** The hardware and software tools needed to create and integrate media elements are now widely available and generally affordable. For example, with simpler and less expensive consumer versions of professional photo and video editing software, you can often perform all the tasks you need for business multimedia (see Figure 6.6).
- **Time and cost.** The time and cost of creating multimedia documents has dropped dramatically in recent years. However, you still need to consider time and cost—and exercise good judgment when deciding whether to include multimedia and how much to include. Make sure the time and money you plan to spend will be paid back in communication effectiveness.
- **Content.** To include various media elements in a document, you obviously need to create or acquire them. If you have the skills, time, and tools, you might be able to create graphics or other media elements. If not, you'll need to find these items and secure the right to use them. Millions of graphics, photos, video clips, and other elements are available online, but you need to make sure you can legally use each item. One good option is to search Creative Commons (**www.creativecommons.org**) for multimedia elements available for use at no charge but with various restrictions (such as giving the creator credit).
- **Message structure.** Multimedia documents often lack a rigid linear structure from beginning to end, which means you need to plan for readers to take multiple, individualized paths through the material. In other words, a conventional outline is often inadequate. Chapter 11 discusses the challenge of *information architecture*, the structure and navigational flow of websites and other multimedia documents.
- **Compatibility.** Some multimedia elements require specific software to be installed on the recipient's viewing device. Another challenge is the variety of screen sizes and resolutions, from large, high-resolution computer monitors to tiny, low-resolution mobile phone displays. Make sure you understand the demands your message will place on the audience.

Make sure you have the legal right to use any media elements that you include in your documents.

FIGURE 6.6 Multimedia Tools
Software such as Adobe Photoshop Elements makes it easy for anyone with basic computer skills to create and modify content for multimedia documents. A simple *cropping* operation on a photo is shown here.

Using Technology to Produce Your Message

Production tools vary widely, depending on the software and systems you're using. Some instant messaging (IM) and e-mail systems offer limited formatting and production capabilities, whereas most word processors now offer some capabilities that rival those of professional publishing software for many day-to-day business needs. *Desktop publishing* software, such as QuarkXPress and Adobe InDesign, goes beyond word processing, offering more advanced and precise layout capabilities that meet the technical demands of publication-quality printing. (These programs are used mainly by design professionals.)

For online content, web publishing systems make it easy to produce great-looking webpages quickly. Similarly, most blogging systems now simplify the production of blog content, letting you rapidly post new material without worrying too much about design or production. Multimedia production tools such as Microsoft Producer let you combine slides, audio commentary, video clips, and other features into computer-based presentations that once cost thousands of dollars to create.

Learning to use the basic features of your communication tools will help you produce better messages in less time.

No matter what system you're using, become familiar with the basic formatting capabilities. A few hours of exploration on your own or an introductory training course can help you dramatically improve the production quality of your documents. Depending on the types of messages you're creating, you'll benefit from being proficient with the following features:

- **Templates and style sheets.** As Chapter 5 notes, you can save a tremendous amount of time by using templates and style sheets.
- **Page setup.** Use page setup to control margins, orientation (*portrait* is vertical; *landscape* is horizontal), and the location of *headers* (text and graphics that repeat at the top of every page) and *footers* (similar to headers but at the bottom of the page).
- **Column formatting.** Most business documents use a single column of text per page, but multiple columns can be an attractive format for documents such as newsletters. Columns are also handy for formatting long lists.

- **Paragraph formatting.** Take advantage of paragraph formatting controls to enhance the look of your documents. For instance, you can offset quotations by increasing margin width around a single paragraph, subtly compress line spacing to fit a document on a single page, or use hanging indents to offset the first line of a paragraph.
- **Numbered and bulleted lists.** Let your word processor or online publishing system do the busywork of formatting numbered and bulleted lists. It can also automatically renumber lists when you add or remove items, saving you the embarrassment of misnumbered lists.
- **Tables.** Tables are great for displaying any information that lends itself to rows and columns, including calendars, numeric data, comparisons, and multicolumn bullet lists. Use paragraph and font formatting thoughtfully within tables for the best look.
- **Images, text boxes, and objects.** Word processing and desktop publishing software lets you insert a wide variety of images (using industry-standard formats such as JPEG and GIF). *Text boxes* are small blocks of text that stand apart from the main text and can be placed anywhere on the page; they are great for captions, callouts, margin notes, and so on. *Objects* can be anything from a spreadsheet to a sound clip to an engineering drawing. Similarly, blogging systems, wikis, and other web development tools let you insert a variety of pictures, audio and video clips, and other multimedia elements.

By improving the appearance of your documents with these tools, you'll improve your readers' impressions of you and your messages, too.

Formatting Formal Letters and Memos

Formal business letters usually follow certain design conventions, as the letter in Figure 6.2 (see page 149) illustrates. Most business letters are printed on *letterhead stationery*, which includes the company's name, address, and other contact information. The first element to appear after the letterhead is the date, followed by the inside address, which identifies the person receiving the letter. Next is the salutation, usually in the form of *Dear Mr.* or *Ms. Last Name*. The message comes next, followed by the complimentary close, usually *Sincerely* or *Cordially*. And last comes the signature block: space for the signature, followed by the sender's printed name and title. Your company will probably have a standard format to follow for letters, possibly along with a template in Microsoft Word or whatever word processor is standard in the organization. For in-depth information on letter formats, see Appendix A, "Format and Layout of Business Documents."

Letters typically have the following elements:
- *Preprinted letterhead stationery*
- *Date*
- *Inside address*
- *Salutation*
- *Complimentary close*
- *Signature block*

Like letters, business memos usually follow a preset design (see Figure 6.7 on the next page). Memos have largely been replaced by e-mail, IM, and other electronic media in many companies, but if they are still in use at the firm you join, the company may have a standard format or template for you to use. Most memos begin with a title such as *Memo*, *Memorandum*, or *Interoffice Correspondence*. Following that are usually four headings: *Date*, *To*, *From*, and *Subject*. (*Re:*, short for *Regarding*, is sometimes used instead of *Subject*.) Memos usually don't use a salutation, complimentary close, or signature, although signing your initials next to your name on the *From* line is standard practice in most companies. Bear in mind that memos are often distributed without sealed envelopes, so they are less private than most other message formats.

Memos are usually identified by a title such as Memo *or* Memorandum.

PROOFREADING YOUR MESSAGE

Proofreading is the quality inspection stage for your documents, your last chance to make sure that your document is ready to carry your message—and your reputation—to the intended audience. Even a small mistake can doom your efforts, so take proofreading seriously.

Look for two types of problems: (1) undetected mistakes from the writing, design, and layout stages and (2) mistakes

REAL-TIME UPDATES
Learn More

Practical advice for thorough proofreading

Identify and correct common problems in business writing with this handy guide. Go to **http://real-timeupdates.com/ebc** and click on "Learn More." If you are using mybcommlab, you can access Real-Time Updates within each chapter or under Student Study Tools.

FIGURE 6.7 A Typical Business Memo
This document shows the elements usually included in a formal business memo. Note that in many instances today, this information would be transmitted via e-mail, IM, or other electronic media instead.

Uses standard company memo stationery with title indicating that this is a memo

Uses four standard headings for memos

Does not begin with a salutation

Does not include a complimentary close or a signature block

Carnival

INTERNAL MEMORANDUM

TO: Lauren Eastman
FROM: Brad Lymans
DATE: June 11, 2009
SUBJECT: Capacity for Carnival Corporation Cruise Ships

Here is the capacity data you requested along with a brief explanation of the figures:

Cruise Brand	Number of Ships	Passenger Capacity	Primary Market
Carnival	15	30,020	North America
Holland America	10	13,348	North America
Costa	7	9,200	Europe
Cunard	2	2,458	Worldwide
Seabourn	6	1,614	North America
Windstar	4	756	North America
Airtours-Sun	4	4,352	Europe
Total	48	61,748	

All passenger capacities are calculated based on two passengers per cabin, even though some cabins can accommodate three or four passengers.

Cruising capacity has grown in recent years, and management expects it to continue because all the major cruise companies are planning to introduce new ships into service. Carnival Corporation will build 16 additional cruise ships over the next five years, increasing the company's passenger capacity by 36,830, which will bring the total to 98,578.

To utilize this new capacity, we must increase our share of the overall vacation market. Keep in mind that demand for cruises may be affected by (1) the strength of the countries where the ships operate; (2) political instability in areas where the ships travel; and (3) adverse incidents involving cruise ships in general.

Please let me know if you have any further questions or need any additional data.

5 LEARNING OBJECTIVE

List eight tips for improving message quality through careful proofreading.

A methodical approach to proofreading will help you find the problems that need to be fixed.

that crept in during production. For the first category, you can review format and layout guidelines in Appendix A on page A-1 and brush up on writing basics with Handbook of Grammar, Mechanics, and Usage on page H-1. The second category can include anything from computer glitches such as missing fonts and broken web links to problems with the ink used in printing. Be particularly vigilant with complex documents and production processes that involve teams of people and multiple computers. Strange things can happen as files move from computer to computer, especially when lots of fonts and multimedia elements are involved.

Far from being a casual scan up and down the page (or screen, for online material), proofreading should be a methodical procedure in which you look for specific problems that might occur. Start by reviewing the advice in "Sharpening Your Career Skills: Proofread Like a Pro to Create Perfect Documents." You might also find it helpful to create a checklist of items to review; this can be handy when you need to review one of your own documents or you're asked to review someone else's work.

Sharpening Your Career Skills

Proofread Like a Pro to Create Perfect Documents

Before you click on "Send" or tote that stack of reports off to the shipping department, make sure your document represents the best possible work you can do. Your colleagues will usually overlook errors in everyday e-mails, but higher-profile mistakes in messages to outside audiences can damage your company and hinder your career.

Use these techniques from professional proofreaders to help ensure high-quality output:

- **Make multiple passes.** Go through the document several times, focusing on a different aspect each time. The first pass may be to look for omissions and errors in content; the second pass may be to check for typographical, grammatical, and spelling errors; and a final pass could be for layout, spacing, alignment, colors, page numbers, margins, and other design features.
- **Use perceptual tricks.** You've probably experienced the frustration of reading over something a dozen times and still missing an obvious error that was staring you right in the face. This happens because your brain has developed a wonderful skill of subconsciously supplying missing pieces and correcting mistakes when it "knows" what is supposed to be on the page. To keep your brain from tricking you, you need to trick it by changing the way you process the visual information. Try (1) reading each page backward, from the bottom to the top; (2) placing your finger under each word and reading it silently; (3) making a slit in a sheet of paper that reveals only one line of type at a time; (4) reading the document aloud and pronouncing each word carefully; and (5) temporarily reformatting the document so that it looks fresh to your eyes.
- **Double-check high-priority items.** Double-check the spelling of names and the accuracy of dates, addresses, and any number that could cause grief if incorrect (such as telling a potential employer that you'd be happy to work for $5,000 a year when you meant to say $50,000).
- **Give yourself some distance.** If possible, don't proofread immediately after finishing a document; let your brain wander off to new topics and then come back fresh later on.
- **Be vigilant.** Avoid reading large amounts of material in one sitting and try not to proofread when you're tired.
- **Stay focused.** Concentrate on what you're doing. Try to block out distractions and focus as completely as possible on your proofreading task.
- **Review complex electronic documents on paper.** Some people have trouble proofreading webpages, online reports, and other electronic documents on-screen. If you have trouble, try to print the materials so you can review them on paper.
- **Take your time.** Quick proofreading is not careful proofreading.

CAREER APPLICATIONS

1. Why is it so valuable to have other people proofread your documents?
2. Proofread and correct the following sentence:
   aplication of thse methods in stores in San Deigo nd Cinncinati have resultted in a 30 drop in roberies an a 50 precent decling in violnce there, acording ot thedevelpers if the securty sytem, Hanover brothrs, Inc.

The amount of time you need to spend on proofing depends on the length and complexity of the document and the situation. A typo in an e-mail message to your team may not be a big deal; but a typo in a financial report, a contract, or a medical file certainly could be serious. As with every other task in the writing process, with proofreading, practice helps—you become not only more familiar with what errors to look for but also more skilled in identifying those errors. See "Checklist: Proofing Business Messages" for a handy list of items to review during proofing.

REAL-TIME UPDATES
Learn More

Proofread with advice from Stanford Business School

Prepare world-class business documents with help from this 32-page writing and editing style guide. Go to **http://real-timeupdates.com/ebc** and click on "Learn More." If you are using mybcommlab, you can access Real-Time Updates within each chapter or under Student Study Tools.

DISTRIBUTING YOUR MESSAGE

6 LEARNING OBJECTIVE

Discuss the most important issues to consider when distributing your messages.

With the production finished, you're ready to distribute your message. You often have several options for distribution; consider the following factors when making your choice:

- **Cost.** Cost isn't a concern for most messages, but for lengthy reports or multimedia productions, it may well be. Printing, binding, and delivering reports can be expensive, so weigh the cost versus the benefits before you decide. If you're trying to land a

CHECKLIST: Proofing Business Messages

A. Look for writing errors.
- Typographical mistakes
- Misspelled words
- Grammatical errors
- Punctuation mistakes

B. Look for missing elements.
- Missing text sections
- Missing exhibits (drawings, tables, photographs, charts, graphs, online images, and so on)
- Missing source notes, copyright notices, or other reference items

C. Look for design, formatting, and programming mistakes.
- Incorrect or inconsistent font selections
- Problems with column sizing, spacing, and alignment
- Incorrect margins
- Incorrect special characters
- Clumsy line and page breaks
- Problems with page numbers
- Problems with page headers and footers
- Lack of adherence to company standards
- Inactive or incorrect links
- Missing files

million-dollar client, spending $1,000 on presentation materials could be a wise investment.

Make sure your delivery method is convenient for your audience members.

- **Convenience.** How much work is involved for you and your audience? Although it's easy to attach a document to an IM or e-mail message, things might not be so simple for the people on the other end. They may not have access to a printer, might be accessing your message from slow wireless connections or on handheld devices with tiny screens, or might not have the software needed to open your file. If you're sending large files as IM or e-mail attachments, consider using a file-compression utility to shrink the file first (but make sure your recipients have the means to expand the files upon arrival). For extremely large files, see whether your audience would prefer a DVD or flash drive instead.
- **Time.** How soon does the message need to reach the audience? Don't waste money on overnight delivery if the recipient won't read the report for a week.
- **Security and privacy.** The convenience offered by IM, e-mail, blogs, and other technologies needs to be weighed against security and privacy concerns. For the most sensitive documents, your company will probably restrict both the people who can receive the documents and the means you can use to distribute them. In addition, most computer users are wary of opening attachments these days. Instead of sending word processor files (which are vulnerable to macro viruses and other risks), you can convert your documents to PDF files using Adobe Acrobat or an equivalent product.

Chapter 7 offers more advice on distributing podcasts, blogs, and other messages in electronic formats. For news on the latest advances in message distribution technologies, visit http://real-timeupdates.com/ebc and click on Chapter 6.

Document Makeover

Improve This Letter

To practice correcting drafts of actual documents, visit the "Document Makeovers" section in mybcommlab. Refer to the User Guide for specific instructions on how to access the content for this chapter. You will find a letter that contains problems and errors related to what you've learned in this chapter about revising messages. Use the Final Draft decision tool to create an improved version of this letter. Check the message for organization, readability, clarity, and conciseness.

On the Job: Solving Communication Dilemmas at Mercedes-AMG

You've just joined the Mercedes-AMG marketing team as a communication specialist. Your duties include creating new material for the Mercedes-AMG website and, occasionally, reviewing materials created by your colleagues. Using what you've learned in this chapter about revising for readability, clarity, and conciseness, address these challenges.[5]

1. You've been asked to review the following statement that concerns the protection of personal data collected from website visitors (Daimler is the parent company of Mercedes-Benz, so its name appears in all legal documentation):

> Daimler appreciates your interest in its products and your visit to this website. Your privacy is important to us and we want you to feel comfortable visiting our site. The protection of your privacy in the processing of your personal data is an important concern to which we pay special attention during our business processes. Personal data collected during visits to our website are processed by us according to the legal provisions valid for the countries in which the websites are maintained. In addition, our data protection policy complies with the Data Protection Code of Conduct applicable company-wide for Daimler. The Daimler website may include, however, links to other websites which are not covered by this privacy statement.

Which of the following revisions is the best way to shorten this statement to 50 words or fewer (it is currently 123 words) without losing any essential information?

a. Daimler promises to protect your privacy whenever you enter personal data on our website.

b. Daimler uses a wide variety of technical and organizational security measures in order to protect the data we have under our control against accidental or intentional manipulation, loss, destruction, or unauthorized access. Our security procedures are continually enhanced as new technology becomes available.

c. As a worldwide leader in the automotive industry, Daimler protects the data we have under our control against accidental or intentional manipulation, loss, or destruction. We also use these measures in order to protect said collected data against access by persons unauthorized to access such information.

d. Daimler uses a wide variety of technical and organizational security measures in order to protect the data we have under our control against accidental or intentional manipulation, loss, or destruction. We also use these measures in order to protect said collected data against access by persons unauthorized to access such information. Of course, we constantly strive to maintain the latest and most sophisticated data protection possible, so our security procedures are continually enhanced as new technology becomes available.

2. In a section that discusses the history of AMG from its founding as a manufacturer of race car engines, the Mercedes-AMG website includes the following sentence: "The technology transfer from the race circuit to the road is still an integral part of the company's philosophy, which is to the benefit of every Mercedes-AMG customer." Which of these revised statements does the best job of communicating this message without using the term *technology transfer*?

a. Every Mercedes-AMG customer benefits from the technologies we develop for race cars.

b. It has always been the philosophy of Mercedes-AMG to transfer technologies we develop for the race track to the road, which benefits every Mercedes-AMG customer.

c. Making sure customers benefit from our racing experience has always been an important part of Mercedes-AMG's philosophy.

d. Transferring technologies developed for racing to our regular passenger cars remains an integral part of the company's philosophy.

3. Although your manager speaks English as a second language, he is an accomplished communicator and adamant about clear writing. He circled the following sentence in your draft of a report but left you to figure out what is wrong: "We have implemented improvements in quality control at every stage of the manufacturing process." How should you revise the sentence?

a. We have implemented improvements in quality control at every phase of the manufacturing process.

b. At every stage of the manufacturing process, we have implemented improvements in quality control.

c. We have improved quality control at every stage of the manufacturing process.

d. At every stage, we have implemented improvements in quality control of the manufacturing process.

4. While reviewing a draft of a new promotional brochure, you find a paragraph that you believe would be more effective as a bulleted list:

The exclusive character of the new Mercedes-Benz CL 63 AMG two-door coupé is immediately reflected in the high-tech equipment package: AMG body styling, AMG 19-inch light-alloy wheels, AMG sports suspension with Active Body Control, AMG high-performance braking system, the distinctive AMG interior as well as the Mercedes-Benz PRE SAFE® anticipatory occupant protection system, which uses radar to recognize potentially dangerous situations and automatically adjust the vehicle's speed to avoid collisions.

Which of these following does the most effective job of communicating this information in list form? (Remember that Mercedes-AMG models are special adaptations of standard Mercedes-Benz models.)

a. The exclusive character of the new Mercedes-Benz CL 63 AMG two-door coupé is immediately reflected in the high-tech equipment package:
   - AMG body styling
   - AMG 19-inch light-alloy wheels
   - AMG sports suspension with Active Body Control
   - AMG high-performance braking system
   - Distinctive AMG interior
   - Mercedes-Benz PRE SAFE® anticipatory occupant protection system, which uses radar to recognize potentially dangerous situations and automatically adjust the vehicle's speed to avoid collisions

b. The exclusive character of the new Mercedes-Benz CL 63 AMG two-door coupé is immediately reflected in the high-tech equipment package, which features a number of unique AMG features:
   - Body styling
   - 19-inch light-alloy wheels
   - Sports suspension with Active Body Control
   - High-performance braking system
   - Distinctive interior

   In addition, every Mercedes-AMG model features such Mercedes-Benz innovations as the PRE SAFE® anticipatory occupant protection system, which uses radar to recognize potentially dangerous situations and automatically adjust the vehicle's speed to avoid collisions.

c. The exclusive character of the new Mercedes-Benz CL 63 AMG two-door coupé is immediately reflected in the high-tech equipment package:
   - AMG features:
     - Body styling
     - 19-inch light-alloy wheels
     - Sports suspension with Active Body Control
     - High-performance braking system
     - Distinctive interior
   - Mercedes-Benz features:
     - Innovations such as the PRE SAFE® anticipatory occupant protection system, which uses radar to recognize potentially dangerous situations and automatically adjust the vehicle's speed to avoid collisions

LEARNING OBJECTIVES CHECKUP

Assess your understanding of the principles in this chapter by reading each learning objective and study the accompanying exercises. For fill-in-the-blank items, write the missing text in the blank provided; for multiple-choice items, circle the letter of the correct answer. You can check your responses against the answer key on page AK-1.

Objective 6.1: Discuss the value of careful revision, and list the main tasks involved in completing a business message.

1. Which of these is the most important reason you should take care to revise messages before sending them?
   a. Revising shows your audience how hard you work.
   b. Revising lowers the word count.
   c. Revising makes it cheaper to e-mail messages.
   d. Revising can usually make your messages more successful.

2. Which of the following is not one of the main tasks involved in completing a business message?
   a. Drafting the message
   b. Revising the message
   c. Producing the message
   d. Proofreading the message

Objective 6.2: List four writing techniques you can use to improve the readability of your messages.

3. Regarding sentence length, the best approach for business messages is to
   a. Keep all sentences as short as possible
   b. Make most of your sentences long since you will usually have complex information to impart
   c. Vary the length of your sentences
   d. Aim for an average sentence length of 35 words

4. Regarding paragraph length, the best approach for business messages is to
   a. Keep paragraphs short
   b. Make most of your paragraphs long since that is standard practice in business writing
   c. Make most of your paragraphs one sentence in length
   d. Aim for an average paragraph length of 200 words
5. Regarding the use of lists, the best approach for business messages is to
   a. Avoid using lists except where absolutely necessary
   b. Make sure listed items are in parallel form
   c. Use numbered lists rather than bulleted ones
   d. Do all of the above
6. Which of the following is not an informative heading?
   a. Why We Need a New Distributor
   b. Five Challenges Facing Today's Distributors
   c. Distributors Are a Better Choice for Us Than Wholesalers
   d. Distributor Choices

Objective 6.3: Describe the steps you can take to improve the clarity of your writing and to make your writing more concise.

7. Which of the following sentences contains hedging words?
   a. It appears that we may have a problem completing the project by May 20.
   b. There is a possibility that the project might be done by May 20.
   c. It seems that the project could possibly miss its completion date of May 20.
   d. All of the above contain hedging words.
8. Which of the following sentences lacks parallelism?
   a. Consumers can download stock research, electronically file their tax returns, create a portfolio, or choose from an array of recommended mutual funds.
   b. Consumers can download stock research, can electronically file their tax returns, create a portfolio, or they can choose from an array of recommended mutual funds.
   c. Consumers can download stock research, can electronically file their tax returns, can create a portfolio, or can choose from an array of recommended mutual funds.
   d. Consumers can download stock research, they can electronically file their tax returns, they can create a portfolio, or they can choose from an array of recommended mutual funds.
9. Which of the following sentences does not have a dangling modifier?
   a. Lacking brand recognition, some consumers are wary of using Internet-only banks.
   b. Because Internet-only banks lack brand recognition, some consumers are wary of using them.
   c. Because of a lack of brand recognition, some consumers are wary of using Internet-only banks.
   d. All have dangling modifiers.
10. When editing for conciseness, you should look for
   a. Unnecessary words and phrases
   b. Dangling modifiers
   c. Lack of parallelism
   d. Awkward references
11. Which of the following is not an example of a redundancy?
   a. Visible to the eye
   b. Free gift
   c. Very useful
   d. Repeat again

Objective 6.4: Explain how design elements help determine the effectiveness of your documents.

12. A well-designed document
   a. Includes a wide variety of typefaces
   b. Balances the space devoted to text, artwork, and white space
   c. Fills as much of the available space as possible with text and art
   d. Does all of the above
13. Any blank areas in a document are referred to as ______.
14. Type that is "justified" is
   a. Flush on the left and ragged on the right
   b. Flush on the right and ragged on the left
   c. Flush on both the left and the right
   d. Centered
15. A sans serif typeface would be best for
   a. The headings in a report
   b. The text of a report
   c. Both the headings and the text of a report
   d. Elements such as footnotes and endnotes

Objective 6.5: List eight tips for improving message quality through careful proofreading.

16. The best time to proofread is
   a. As you are writing
   b. Immediately after you finish the first draft, while the information is still fresh in your mind
   c. A day or so after you finish the first draft
   d. After you distribute the document
17. When proofreading, you should look for errors in
   a. Spelling and punctuation
   b. Grammar and usage
   c. Typography and format
   d. All of the above

Objective 6.6: Discuss the most important issues to consider when distributing your messages.

18. As a general rule, the cost of distributing a business message should be balanced against
   a. The importance and urgency of the message
   b. The length of the message
   c. Your career goals as they relate to the message
   d. The number of recipients
19. Which of the following concerns is the most important to consider when distributing messages through electronic media such as e-mail?
   a. The difficulty of reading on-screen
   b. Privacy and security
   c. Differences between flat-panel and CRT monitors
   d. The difficulty of keeping e-mail addresses current

PEARSON mybcommlab

Log on to www.mybcommlab.com to access the following study and assessment aids associated with this chapter:

- Video applications
- Real-Time Updates
- Peer review activity
- Quick Learning Guides
- Pre/post test
- Personalized study plan
- Model documents
- Sample presentations

If you are not using mybcommlab, you can access Real-Time Updates and Quick Learning Guides through http://real-timeupdates.com/ebc. The Quick Learning Guide (located under "Learn More" on the website) hits all the high points of this chapter in just two pages. This guide, especially prepared by the authors, will help you study for exams or review important concepts whenever you need a quick refresher.

Apply Your Knowledge

1. Why is it helpful to put your first draft aside for a while before you begin the editing process?
2. How do careful revision and quality document production reflect the "you"attitude?
3. Why is it important to spend extra time reviewing and polishing the beginning and end of a message?
4. How can you demonstrate good business judgment when it comes to multimedia documents?
5. **Ethical Choices** What are the ethical implications of murky, complex writing in a document that is supposed to explain how customers can appeal the result of a decision made in the company's favor during a dispute?

Practice Your Knowledge

Messages for Analysis

Message 6.A: Improving Readability

Analyze the strengths and weaknesses of this message and then revise it so that it follows the guidelines in Chapters 4 through 6:

> As an organization, the North American Personal Motorsports Marketing Association has committed ourselves to helping our members—a diverse group comprising of dealers of motorcycles, all-terrain vehicles, Snowmobiles, and personal watercraft—achieve their business objectives. Consequently, our organization, which usually goes under the initials NAPMMA, has the following aims, goals, and objectives. Firstly, we endeavor to aid or assist our members in reaching their business objectives. Second, NAPMMA communicates ("lobbying" in slang terms) with local, state, and national governmental agencies and leaders on issues of importance to our members. And lastly, we educate the motorsports public, that being current motorsports vehicle owners, and prospective owners of said vehicles, on the safe and enjoyable operation of they're vehicles.

Message 6.B: Improving the Layout of a Word Document

To access this message, visit http://real-timeupdates.com/ebc, click on "Student Assignments,"select Chapter 6, and then select Page 170, Message 6.B. Download and open the Microsoft Word document. Using the various page, paragraph, and font formatting options available in your word processor, modify the formatting of the document so that its visual tone matches the tone of the message.

Message 6.C: Helping Another Writer Improve Readability

To access this message, visit http://real-timeupdates.com/ebc, click on "Student Assignments,"select Chapter 6, and then select Page 170, Message 6.C. Download and open the Microsoft Word document. Using your knowledge of effective writing and the tips on pages 153–155 for evaluating the work of other writers, evaluate this message. After you set Microsoft Word to track changes, make any necessary corrections. Insert comments, as needed, to explain your changes to the author.

Exercises

Active links for all websites in this chapter can be found on mybcommlab; see your User Guide for instructions on accessing the content for this chapter.

6.1 **Message Readability: Writing Paragraphs** Rewrite the following paragraph to vary the length of the sentences and to shorten the paragraph so it looks more inviting to readers:

> Although major league baseball remains popular, more people are attending minor league baseball games because they can spend less on admission, snacks, and parking and still enjoy the excitement of America's pastime. Connecticut, for example, has three AA minor league teams, including the New Haven Ravens, who are affiliated with the St. Louis Cardinals; the Norwich Navigators, who are affiliated with the New York Yankees; and the New Britain Rock Cats, who are affiliated with the Minnesota Twins. These teams play in relatively small stadiums, so fans are close enough to see and hear everything, from the swing of the bat connecting with the ball to the thud of the ball landing in the outfielder's glove. Best of all, the cost of a family outing to see rising stars play in a local minor league game is just a fraction of what the family would spend to attend a major league game in a much larger, more crowded stadium.

6.2 Message Readability: Using Bullets Rewrite the following paragraph using a parallel bulleted list and one introductory sentence:

Our forensic accounting services provide the insights needed to resolve disputes, recover losses, and manage risk intelligently. One of our areas of practice is insurance claims accounting and preparation services, designed to help you maximize recovery of insured value. Another practice area is dispute advisory, in which we can assist with discovery, expert witness testimony, and economic analysis. A third practice: construction consulting. This service helps our clients understand why large-scale construction projects fail to meet schedule or budget requirements. Fourth, we offer general investigative and forensic accounting services, including fraud detection and proof of loss analysis.[6]

6.3 Revising Messages: Clarity Break the following sentences into shorter ones by adding more periods and revise as needed for smooth flow:

a. The next time you write something, check your average sentence length in a 100-word passage, and if your sentences average more than 16 to 20 words, see whether you can break up some of the sentences.

b. Don't do what the village blacksmith did when he instructed his apprentice as follows: "When I take the shoe out of the fire, I'll lay it on the anvil, and when I nod my head, you hit it with the hammer."The apprentice did just as he was told, and now he's the village blacksmith.

c. Unfortunately, no gadget will produce excellent writing, but using a yardstick like the Fog Index gives us some guideposts to follow for making writing easier to read because its two factors remind us to use short sentences and simple words.

d. Know the flexibility of the written word and its power to convey an idea, and know how to make your words behave so that your readers will understand.

e. Words mean different things to different people, and a word such as *block* may mean city block, butcher block, engine block, auction block, or several other things.

6.4 Revising Messages: Conciseness Cross out unnecessary words in the following phrases:

a. Consensus of opinion
b. New innovations
c. Long period of time
d. At a price of $50
e. Still remains

6.5 Revising Messages: Conciseness Revise the following sentences, using shorter, simpler words:

a. The antiquated calculator is ineffectual for solving sophisticated problems.

b. It is imperative that the pay increments be terminated before an inordinate deficit is accumulated.

c. There was unanimity among the executives that Ms. Jackson's idiosyncrasies were cause for a mandatory meeting with the company's personnel director.

d. The impending liquidation of the company's assets was cause for jubilation among the company's competitors.

e. The expectations of the president for a stock dividend were accentuated by the preponderance of evidence that the company was in good financial condition.

6.6 Revising Messages: Conciseness Use infinitives as substitutes for the overly long phrases in these sentences:

a. For living, I require money.

b. They did not find sufficient evidence for believing in the future.

c. Bringing about the destruction of a dream is tragic.

6.7 Revising Messages: Conciseness Rephrase the following in fewer words:

a. In the near future
b. In the event that
c. In order that
d. For the purpose of
e. With regard to
f. It may be that
g. In very few cases
h. With reference to
i. At the present time
j. There is no doubt that

6.8 Revising Messages: Conciseness Revise to condense these sentences to as few words as possible:

a. We are of the conviction that writing is important.

b. In all probability, we're likely to have a price increase.

c. Our goals include making a determination about that in the near future.

d. When all is said and done at the conclusion of this experiment, I'd like to summarize the final windup.

e. After a trial period of three weeks, during which time she worked for a total of 15 full working days, we found her work was sufficiently satisfactory so that we offered her full-time work.

6.9 Revising Messages: Modifiers Remove all the unnecessary modifiers from these sentences:

a. Tremendously high pay increases were given to the extraordinarily skilled and extremely conscientious employees.

b. The union's proposals were highly inflationary, extremely demanding, and exceptionally bold.

6.10 Revising Messages: Hedging Rewrite these sentences so that they no longer contain any hedging:

a. It would appear that someone apparently entered illegally.

b. It may be possible that sometime in the near future the situation is likely to improve.

c. Your report seems to suggest that we might be losing money.

d. I believe Nancy apparently has somewhat greater influence over employees in the e-marketing department.

e. It seems as if this letter of resignation means you might be leaving us.

6.11 Revising Messages: Indefinite Starters Rewrite these sentences to eliminate the indefinite starters:

a. There are several examples here to show that Elaine can't hold a position very long.

b. It would be greatly appreciated if every employee would make a generous contribution to Mildred Cook's retirement party.
c. It has been learned in Washington today from generally reliable sources that an important announcement will be made shortly by the White House.
d. There is a rule that states that we cannot work overtime without permission.
e. It would be great if you could work late for the next three Saturdays.

6.12 Revising Messages: Parallelism Revise these sentences in order to present the ideas in parallel form:
a. Mr. Hill is expected to lecture three days a week, to counsel two days a week, and must write for publication in his spare time.
b. She knows not only accounting, but she also reads Latin.
c. Both applicants had families, college degrees, and were in their thirties, with considerable accounting experience but few social connections.
d. This book was exciting, well written, and held my interest.
e. Don is both a hard worker and he knows bookkeeping.

6.13 Revising Messages: Awkward References Revise the following sentences to delete the awkward references:
a. The vice president in charge of sales and the production manager are responsible for the keys to 34A and 35A, respectively.
b. The keys to 34A and 35A are in executive hands, with the former belonging to the vice president in charge of sales and the latter belonging to the production manager.
c. The keys to 34A and 35A have been given to the production manager, with the aforementioned keys being gold embossed.
d. A laser printer and an inkjet printer were delivered to John and Megan, respectively.
e. The walnut desk is more expensive than the oak desk, the former costing $300 more than the latter.

6.14 Revising Messages: Dangling Modifiers Rewrite these sentences to clarify the dangling modifiers:
a. Full of trash and ripped-up newspapers, we left Dallas on a plane that apparently hadn't been cleaned in days.
b. Lying on the shelf, Ruby found the operations manual.
c. With leaking plumbing and outdated wiring, I don't think we should buy that property.
d. Being cluttered and filthy, Sandy took the whole afternoon to clean up her desk.
e. After proofreading every word, the letter was ready to be signed.

6.15 Revising Messages: Noun Sequences Rewrite the following sentences to eliminate the long strings of nouns:
a. The focus of the meeting was a discussion of the bank interest rate deregulation issue.
b. Following the government task force report recommendations, we are revising our job applicant evaluation procedures.
c. The production department quality assurance program components include employee training, supplier cooperation, and computerized detection equipment.
d. The supermarket warehouse inventory reduction plan will be implemented next month.
e. The State University business school graduate placement program is one of the best in the country.

6.16 Revising Messages: Sentence Structure Rearrange the following sentences to bring the subjects closer to their verbs:
a. Trudy, when she first saw the bull pawing the ground, ran.
b. It was Terri who, according to Ted, who is probably the worst gossip in the office (Tom excepted), mailed the wrong order.
c. William Oberstreet, in his book *Investment Capital Reconsidered*, writes of the mistakes that bankers through the decades have made.
d. Judy Schimmel, after passing up several sensible investment opportunities, despite the warnings of her friends and family, invested her inheritance in a jojoba plantation.
e. The president of U-Stor-It, which was on the brink of bankruptcy after the warehouse fire, the worst tragedy in the history of the company, prepared a press announcement.

6.17 Revising Messages: Camouflaged Verbs Rewrite each sentence so that the verbs are no longer camouflaged:
a. Adaptation to the new rules was performed easily by the employees.
b. The assessor will make a determination of the tax due.
c. Verification of the identity of the employees must be made daily.
d. The board of directors made a recommendation that Mr. Ronson be assigned to a new division.
e. The auditing procedure on the books was performed by the vice president.

6.18 Producing Messages: Design Elements Review a copy of the syllabus your instructor provided for this course. Which design elements were used to improve readability? Can you identify ways to make the document easier to read or more user friendly in general? Create your own version, experimenting with different design elements and design choices. How do your changes affect readability? Exchange documents with another student and critique each other's work.

6.19 Web Design Visit the stock market page of Bloomberg's website at www.bloomberg.com and evaluate the use of design in presenting the latest news. What design improvements can you suggest to enhance readability of the information posted on this page? Summarize your recommendations in an e-mail message to your instructor.

6.20 Teamwork Team up with another student and exchange your revised versions of Message 6.A (in the exercises under "Messages for Analysis"). Evaluate each other's work to see if it could be improved. After you have critiqued each other's work, take a moment to examine the way you expressed your comments and the way you felt listening to the other student's comments. Can you identify ways to improve the critiquing process in situations such as this? For example, did your comments focus on the writing and not the writer?

6.21 Proofreading Messages: E-Mail Proofread the following e-mail message and revise it to correct any problems you find:

Our final company orrientation of the year will be held on Dec. 20. In preparation for this sesssion, please order 20 copies of the Policy handbook, the confindentiality agreenemt, the employee benefits Manual, please let me know if you anticipate any delays in obtaining these materials.

6.22 Ethical Choices The time and energy required for careful revision can often benefit you or your company directly, such as by increasing the probability that website visitors will buy your products. But what about situations in which the quality of your writing and revision work really doesn't stand to benefit you directly? For instance, assume that you are putting a notice on your website, informing the local community about some upcoming construction to your manufacturing plant. The work will disrupt traffic for nearly a year and generate a significant amount of noise and air pollution, but knowing the specific dates and times of various construction activities will allow people to adjust their commutes and other activities to minimize the negative impact on their daily lives. However, your company does not sell products in the local area, so the people affected by all this are not potential customers. Moreover, providing accurate information to the surrounding community and updating it as the project progresses will take time away from your other job responsibilities. Do you have an ethical obligation to keep the local community informed with accurate, up-to-date information? Why or why not?

Expand Your Knowledge

Learning More on the Web

Write It Right: Tips to Help You Rethink and Revise

www.powa.org

Are you sure that readers perceive your written message as you intended? If you want help revising a message that you're completing, use the Paradigm Online Writing Assistant (POWA; www.powa.org). With this interactive writer's guide, you can select topics to get tips on how to edit your work, reshape your thoughts, and rewrite for clarity. Read discussions about perfecting your writing skills, complete one of the many online activities provided to reinforce what you've learned, or join a special-interest group to talk about writing. At POWA's website, you'll learn how to improve the final draft of your message. (Note that you may find advice that differs in some respects from the information in this textbook.) Explore POWA's advice and then answer the following questions:

1. Why is it better to write out ideas in a rough format and later reread your message to revise its content? When revising your message, what questions can you ask about your writing?
2. Name the four elements of the "writing context." Imagine that you're the reader of your message. What questions might you ask?
3. When you revise a written message, what is the purpose of "tightening"? What is one way to tighten your writing as you complete a message?

Sharpening Your Career Skills Online

Bovée and Thill's Business Communication Web Search, at **http://businesscommunicationblog.com/websearch**, is a unique research tool designed specifically for business communication research. Use the Web Search function to find a website, video, PDF document, or PowerPoint presentation that offers advice on effective proofreading. Write a brief e-mail message to your instructor, describing the item that you found and summarizing the career skills information you learned from it.

Improve Your Grammar, Mechanics, and Usage

The following exercises help you improve your knowledge of and power over English grammar, mechanics, and usage. Turn to the Handbook of Grammar, Mechanics, and Usage at the end of this book and review Section 1.6.1 (Prepositions). Then look at the following 10 items. Underline the preferred choice within each set of parentheses. (Answers to these exercises appear on page AK-3.)

1. Where was your argument (*leading to, leading*)?
2. I wish he would get (*off, off of*) the phone.
3. U.S. Mercantile must become (*aware, aware of*) and sensitive to its customers' concerns.
4. Dr. Namaguchi will be talking (*with, to*) the marketing class, but she has no time for questions.
5. Matters like this are decided after thorough discussion (*among, between*) all seven department managers.
6. We can't wait (*on, for*) their decision much longer.
7. Their computer is similar (*to, with*) ours.
8. This model is different (*than, from*) the one we ordered.
9. She is active (*in not only, not only in*) a civic group but also in an athletic organization.
10. Carolyn told Jorge not to put the used inkjet cartridges (*in, into*) the trash can.

For additional exercises focusing on prepositions, visit mybcommlab. Click on Chapter 6; click on Additional Exercises to Improve Your Grammar, Mechanics, and Usage; and then click on "10. Prepositions."

Part **3**

Crafting Brief Messages

Most of your communication on the job will be through brief messages, from Twitter updates and text messages to formal letters that might run to several pages. Learning how to write these messages effectively is key to maintaining productive working relationships with colleagues and customers. Start by adapting what you probably already know about electronic media to the professional challenges of business communication. Then learn specific techniques for crafting routine, positive, negative, and persuasive messages—techniques that will help you in everything from getting a raise to calming an angry customer to promoting your next great idea.

7 Crafting Messages for Electronic Media

Learning Objectives

After studying this chapter, you will be able to

1. Compare the strengths and weaknesses of the electronic media available for short messages
2. Outline six guidelines for creating successful social media content
3. Explain the need to treat e-mail as a professional medium, and identify the qualities of an effective e-mail subject line
4. Identify guidelines for successful instant messaging in the workplace
5. Describe the role of blogging in business communication today, and explain how to adapt the three-step writing process to blogging
6. Explain how to adapt the three-step writing process to podcasting, and describe the syndication process for blogs and podcasts

On the Job: Communicating at Southwest Airlines

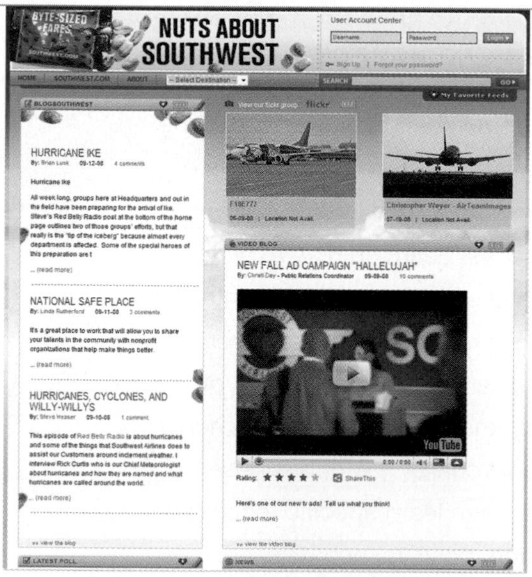

Southwest Airlines's multiauthor blog, Nuts About Southwest, features a variety of entertaining writers from around the company.

Online Uproar Triggers Change in Company Policy

Southwest Airlines's blog is usually a love fest—or a "luv" fest, to use one of the company's favorite words. In fact, the blog's official name is Nuts About Southwest. A typical post might highlight the community service efforts of a group of employees or congratulate a team of Southwest mechanics for winning gold at the Aviation Maintenance Olympics. Devoted customers post enthusiastic comments on nearly every article, and many seem to have bonded in virtual friendship with dozens of employees on the Emerging Media Team who take turns writing the blog.

Bill Owens probably didn't expect a bubbly reception to a rather workaday post titled "Why can't I make reservations further in advance?" in which he calmly explained why the company usually didn't let customers make reservations as far into the future as other airlines do.

But he probably wasn't expecting the response he *did* get, either. In his words, "Talk about sticking your head in a hornet's nest!" Instead of the usual dozen or so happy responses to a typical post, he received several hundred responses—many of which expressed disappointment, unhappiness, and downright anger.

Customers described one scenario after another in which they had a real need to book travel farther in advance than Southwest allowed, and many complained that the policy was forcing them to fly other airlines. Some Southwest employees chimed in too, expressing their frustration with not being able to meet customer needs at times.

After bravely and patiently addressing specific customer responses over a period of several months, Owens responded with a new post titled "I blogged. You flamed. We changed." In this message, he explained that the company had listened and was changing its scheduling policies to better accommodate customer needs.

In fact, feedback from blog readers is so important that Southwest CEO Colleen Barrett considers the blog a "customer service laboratory" that helps the company learn how to better serve its customers.[1]

www.blogsouthwest.com

CHOOSING ELECTRONIC MEDIA FOR BRIEF MESSAGES

1 LEARNING OBJECTIVE

Compare the strengths and weaknesses of the electronic media available for short messages.

Southwest's experience with customer feedback (profiled in the chapter-opening "On the Job" vignette) is just one of many cases in which electronic media and Web 2.0 media in particular are changing business communication. In fact, with so many media options for brief messages, a key challenge these days is often figuring out which is the best medium for each message:

- **Social networks and user-generated content sites.** Social networking sites such as Facebook and user-generated content sites such as Flickr and YouTube provide a variety of communication tools, including user comments and personal profiles, that support brief messages. In addition, a number of companies now host their own social networking sites, where product enthusiasts interact by sharing personal stories, offering advice, and commenting on products and company news—all brief-message functions that replace more traditional media options. For example, Specialized, a major bicycle manufacturer based in Morgan Hill, California, hosts the Specialized Riders Club (www.specializedriders.com), where customers can interact with each other and the professional riders the company sponsors.[2]
- **E-mail.** Thanks to its high speed and low cost, e-mail is a primary medium for most companies. However, as technologies continue to evolve and users tire of fighting the flood of spam, viruses, and other problems related to e-mail, this medium is being replaced in many instances by instant messaging, blogging, wikis, and other tools that provide better support for instant communication and real-time collaboration.
- **Instant messaging (IM).** After consumers around the world began to adopt IM as a faster and simpler alternative to e-mail, businesses weren't far behind; computer-based IM usage now rivals e-mail in many companies. IM offers even greater speed than e-mail, as well as simple operation and—so far at least—fewer problems with unwanted messages or security and privacy problems.
- **Text messaging.** Small screen sizes and the lack of a regular keyboard on many phone devices make text messaging somewhat less convenient than computer-based IM. However, text messaging is beginning to make inroads into business communication in such areas as marketing, customer service (airline flight updates and credit reporting alerts, for example), and online banking.[3]
- **Blogs.** The ability to update content quickly and easily makes blogs a natural medium when communicators need to get messages out in a hurry; bloggers can also publish information to vast audiences with relatively little effort.
- **Podcasts.** You may be familiar with podcasts as the online equivalent of recorded radio or video broadcasts (video podcasts are often called

REAL-TIME UPDATES
Learn More

Explore the business value of social networking

See how businesses can improve internal and external communication with social networking tools. Go to **http://real-timeupdates.com/ebc** and click on "Learn More." If you are using mybcommlab, you can access Real-Time Updates within each chapter or under Student Study Tools.

Carleton University in Ottawa, Ontario, Canada, reaches students all over the world with its lecture vodcasts.

vidcasts or *vodcasts*). Businesses are now using podcasts to replace or supplement conference calls, training courses, and other communication activities.
- **Online video.** Creating high-quality videos (such as for formal training and marketing activities) requires some time and expertise, but even the simple video functions now widely available in cameras and mobile phones can be useful for research interviews, location surveys, product demonstrations, and other communication tasks.

While e-mail and other electronic media have largely replaced traditional printed memos for internal communication, don't dismiss the benefits of printed messages. (For more on formatting printed letters and memos, see Chapter 6 and Appendix A.) Here are several situations in which you should consider using a printed message rather than electronic alternatives:

Consider using printed messages
- *To create a more formal impression*
- *When you are legally or contractually required to do so*
- *To stand out from electronic messages*
- *When you need a permanent or secure record*

- When you want to make a formal impression
- When you are legally required to provide information in printed form
- When you want to stand out from the flood of electronic messages
- When you need a permanent, unchangeable, or secure record

Again, most of your on-the-job communication is going to be through electronic media, which is the focus of this chapter. The following sections offer advice on creating content for social media and using e-mail, IM, blogging, and podcasting for business communication. Another vital Web 2.0 medium, wikis, is covered in Chapter 12.

CREATING CONTENT FOR SOCIAL MEDIA

Writing for social media requires a different approach than that used for traditional business media.

2 LEARNING OBJECTIVE

Outline six guidelines for creating successful social media content.

As Chapter 1 points out in the discussion of Business Communication 2.0, social media change the relationship between sender and receiver. Because the relationship has changed, the nature of the messages between them needs to change as well. Whether you're writing a blog or posting a product demonstration video to YouTube, consider these tips for creating successful content for social media:[4]

- **Remember that it's a conversation, not a lecture or a sales pitch.** One of the great appeals of social media is the feeling of conversation, of people talking *with* one another instead of one person talking *at* everyone else.
- **Write informally but not carelessly.** Write as a human being, not as a cog in a faceless corporate machine. At the same time, don't get sloppy; no one wants to slog through misspelled words and half-baked sentences, looking for a message.
- **Create concise, specific, and informative headlines.** Avoid the temptation to engage in clever wordplay with headlines. Readers don't want to spend the time and energy required to figure out what your witty headlines mean. Search engines won't know what they mean, either, so fewer people will find your content.
- **Get involved and stay involved.** Companies and individual executives can and do get criticized all the time in social media. However, don't hide from criticism. Take the opportunity to correct misinformation or explain how mistakes will be fixed.
- **If you need to promote something, do so indirectly.** Just as you wouldn't hit people with a company sales pitch during an informal social gathering, refrain from blatant promotional efforts in social media. For example, instead of listing selling features of a product, tell a story about how the product changed someone's life.
- **Be transparent and honest.** Honesty is always essential, of course, but a particular issue that has tripped up a few companies in recent years is hiding behind an online blogging persona—either a fictitious character whose writing is actually done by a corporate marketing specialist or a real person who fails to disclose an affiliation with a corporate sponsor.

CREATING EFFECTIVE E-MAIL MESSAGES

E-mail in the workplace is a more formal medium than you are probably accustomed to for personal communication (see Figure 7.1). It's important to approach e-mail as a professional communication medium and an important company resource, as explained in the following section.

FIGURE 7.1 E-Mail for Business Communication

In this response to an e-mail query from a colleague, Elaine Burgman takes advantage of her e-mail system's features to create an efficient and effective message.

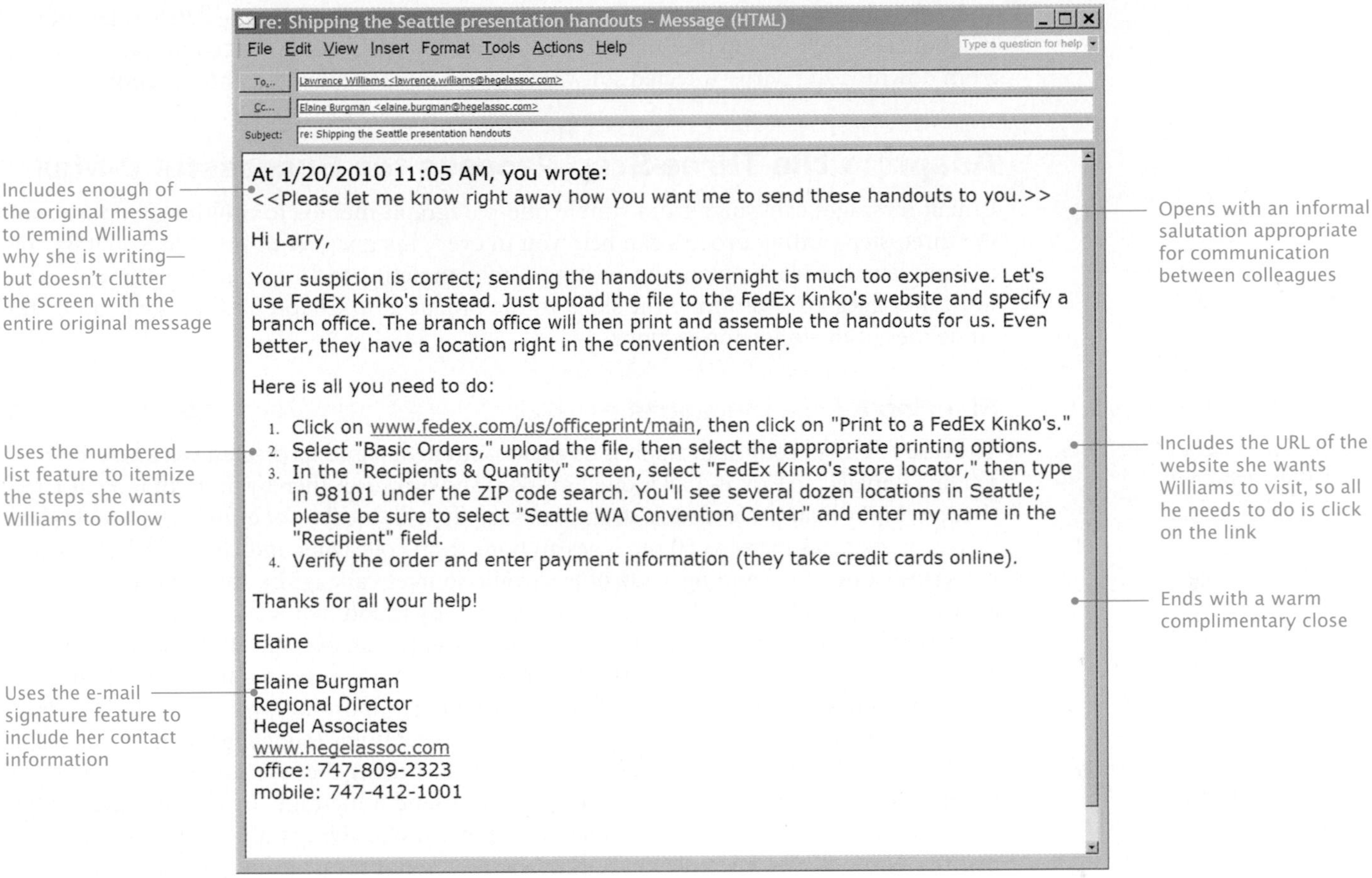
re: Shipping the Seattle presentation handouts - Message (HTML)
File Edit View Insert Format Tools Actions Help
Type a question for help
To... Lawrence Williams <lawrence.williams@hegelassoc.com>
Cc... Elaine Burgman <elaine.burgman@hegelassoc.com>
Subject: re: Shipping the Seattle presentation handouts
At 1/20/2010 11:05 AM, you wrote:
<<Please let me know right away how you want me to send these handouts to you.>>
Hi Larry,
Your suspicion is correct; sending the handouts overnight is much too expensive. Let's use FedEx Kinko's instead. Just upload the file to the FedEx Kinko's website and specify a branch office. The branch office will then print and assemble the handouts for us. Even better, they have a location right in the convention center.
Here is all you need to do:
1. Click on www.fedex.com/us/officeprint/main, then click on "Print to a FedEx Kinko's."
2. Select "Basic Orders," upload the file, then select the appropriate printing options.
3. In the "Recipients & Quantity" screen, select "FedEx Kinko's store locator," then type in 98101 under the ZIP code search. You'll see several dozen locations in Seattle; please be sure to select "Seattle WA Convention Center" and enter my name in the "Recipient" field.
4. Verify the order and enter payment information (they take credit cards online).
Thanks for all your help!
Elaine
Elaine Burgman
Regional Director
Hegel Associates
www.hegelassoc.com
office: 747-809-2323
mobile: 747-412-1001
Includes enough of the original message to remind Williams why she is writing—but doesn't clutter the screen with the entire original message
Uses the numbered list feature to itemize the steps she wants Williams to follow
Uses the e-mail signature feature to include her contact information
Opens with an informal salutation appropriate for communication between colleagues
Includes the URL of the website she wants Williams to visit, so all he needs to do is click on the link
Ends with a warm complimentary close

Treating E-Mail as a Professional Communication Medium

3 LEARNING OBJECTIVE

Explain the need to treat e-mail as a professional medium, and identify the qualities of an effective e-mail subject line.

The most important single point to recognize about e-mail in the workplace is that business e-mail is dramatically different from personal e-mail. The expectations of writing quality are higher, and the consequences of bad writing or poor judgment can be much more serious. For example, e-mail and other electronic message forms have been used as evidence in numerous lawsuits and criminal investigations involving everything from sexual harassment to financial fraud.[5] Other e-mail concerns include the possibility of disclosing confidential information and exposing company networks to security problems. In fact, the problem of internal information being leaked through e-mail and winding up on public blogs—sometimes within a matter of minutes—is growing so acute that some companies are becoming wary of disclosing sensitive information to employees, and some are hiring investigating firms to track down the sources of leaks.[6]

To minimize the potential for trouble, many companies now have formal e-mail policies that specify how employees can use e-mail, including restrictions against using company e-mail service for personal messages and sending material that might be deemed objectionable. More than one-quarter of U.S. employers have terminated employees for misuse of company e-mail systems, according to one survey.[7] In addition, roughly the same percentage of employers now monitor

REAL-TIME UPDATES
Learn More

Take a crash course in e-mail etiquette

Learn career-enhancing tips on using e-mail in professional settings. Go to **http://real-timeupdates.com/ebc** and click on "Learn More." If you are using mybcommlab, you can access Real-Time Updates within each chapter or under Student Study Tools.

Because e-mail presents considerable technical and legal hazards, many companies have formal e-mail policies.

internal e-mail, and half of them monitor external e-mail. This monitoring can involve both automated scans using software programmed to look for sensitive content and manual scans in which security staff actually read selected e-mail messages.[8]

E-mail hygiene refers to all the efforts that companies are making to keep e-mail clean and safe—from spam blocking and virus protection to content filtering.[9] Regardless of formal policies, every e-mail user has a responsibility to avoid actions that could cause trouble, from downloading virus-infected software to sending objectionable photographs.

Adapting the Three-Step Process for Successful E-Mail

E-mail messages can range from simple one-paragraph memos to multipage reports, and the three-step writing process can help you in every instance. With practice, you'll be able to complete the various planning, writing, and completing tasks in a matter of minutes for most messages. In addition to the skills you've practiced in Chapter 4 through 6, apply the guidelines in the following sections.

Planning E-Mail Messages

Attention to etiquette is vital with e-mail communication.

The ease of e-mail communication is its greatest strength—and its greatest weakness. Because sending e-mail is so easy, e-mail is often misused and overused, thereby undermining its effectiveness. Many busy professionals struggle to keep up with the flow of e-mail messages—some report receiving as many as 50 messages an hour from colleagues and clients.[10] The flood of messages from an expanding array of electronic sources can significantly affect employees' ability to focus on their work. In fact, one recent study found that workers exposed to a constant barrage of e-mail, IM, and phone calls experienced an average 10-point drop in their functioning IQ.[11] In addition to making sure every e-mail you send is necessary so that you don't contribute to the deluge of messages of dubious importance, you can help keep electronic messages from causing problems in your organization by following the tips in Table 7.1.

Do your part to stem the flood of e-mail by making sure you don't send unnecessary messages or cc people who don't really need to see particular messages.

When analyzing your audience, think twice before using the *cc* (courtesy copy) function to send copies to multiple recipients. Let's say you send a message to your boss and cc five colleagues simply because you want them to see that you're giving the boss some good information. Those five people now not only have to read your message but might also feel compelled to reply so that the boss doesn't think they're being negligent. Then everyone will start replying to *those* replies, and on and on. What should have been a single message exchange between you and your boss quickly turns into a flurry of messages that wastes a lot of time.

Writing E-Mail Messages

You don't need to compose perfect works of literature to inform people that lunch will be served in the conference room, but even in routine matters, well-crafted messages demonstrate professionalism and respect for your audience. The time you might save with careless e-mail writing isn't worth the damage it can do to your career.[12]

Careless writing might save you time, but it costs your readers time.

First, haphazard planning and sloppy writing may require less time for writers, but they usually demand *more* time from readers forced to dig the meaning out of misspelled words, confusing sentences, and disjointed paragraphs. Making readers do work you should have done is the very antithesis of the "you" attitude. Second, people who care about effective communication—a group that includes most senior executives, the people who often decide whether you'll get promoted and how much you'll get paid—often judge the quality of your *work* by the quality of your *writing.* Third, at the click of somebody else's mouse, e-mail messages can travel to places you never imagined, including the CEO's computer screen, a lawyer's office, or off into the blogosphere. Always assume that whatever you write in an e-mail message will be stored forever and could become public knowledge inside or outside the firm.

Writing Effective Subject Lines

A poorly written subject line could lead to a message being deleted or ignored.

The subject line might seem like a minor detail, but it's actually one of the most important parts of every e-mail message because it helps recipients decide which messages to read and when to read them. Missing or poorly written subject lines often result in messages

TABLE 7.1 Tips for Effective E-Mail Messages

TIP	WHY IT'S IMPORTANT
When you request information or action, make it clear what you're asking for, why it's important, and how soon you need it; don't make your reader write back for details.	People will be tempted to ignore your messages if it's not clear what you want or how soon you want it.
When responding to a request, either paraphrase the request or include enough of the original message to remind the reader what you're replying to.	Some businesspeople get several hundred or more e-mail messages every day and may need to be reminded what your specific response is about.
If possible, avoid sending long, complex messages via e-mail.	Long messages are easier to read as printed reports or web content.
Adjust the level of formality to the message and the audience.	Overly formal messages to colleagues are perceived as stuffy and distant; overly informal messages to customers or top executives are perceived as disrespectful.
Activate a signature file, which automatically pastes your contact information into every message you create.	You save the trouble of retyping vital information and ensure that recipients know how to reach you through other means.
Don't let unread messages pile up in your in-box.	You'll miss important information and create the impression that you're ignoring other people.
Never type in all caps.	ALL CAPS ARE INTERPRETED AS SCREAMING.
Don't over-format your messages with background colors, colored type, complicated fonts, and so on.	Such messages can be difficult and annoying to read on-screen.
Remember that messages can be forwarded anywhere and saved forever.	A moment of anger or poor judgment could haunt you for the rest of your career.
Use the "return receipt requested" feature only for the most critical messages.	This feature triggers a message back to you whenever someone receives or opens your message; many consider this an invasion of privacy.
Make sure your computer has up-to-date virus protection.	One of the worst breaches of "netiquette" is unknowingly infecting other computers because you haven't protected your own system.
Pay attention to grammar, spelling, and capitalization.	Some people don't think e-mail needs formal rules, but careless messages make you look unprofessional and can annoy readers.
Use acronyms sparingly.	Acronyms such as *IMHO* ("in my humble opinion") and *LOL* ("laughing out loud") can be useful in informal correspondence between close colleagues, but don't use them in important messages.

being deleted without even being opened. To capture your audience's attention, make sure your subject line is informative and compelling. Go beyond simply describing or classifying your message; use the opportunity to build interest with keywords, quotations, directions, or questions:[13]

INEFFECTIVE SUBJECT LINE	EFFECTIVE SUBJECT LINE
July sales results	July sales results: good news and bad news
Friday meeting	Be ready for some tough questions at Friday's meeting
Marketing reports	Marketing reports are due Monday morning
Employee parking	Revised resurfacing schedule for parking lot
Status report	Website redesign is falling behind schedule

Consider the first of these examples. "July sales results" accurately describes the content of the message, but "July sales results: good news and bad news" is more intriguing. Readers will want to know why some news is good and some is bad. "Status report" doesn't even specify which project the report is about, but "Website redesign is falling behind schedule" identifies the project and alerts people to a problem.

Also, if you and someone else are replying back and forth based on the same original message, periodically modify the subject line of your message to reflect the revised message content. When numerous messages have identical subject lines, trying to find a particular one can be confusing and frustrating.

Keeping Your Emotions Under Control

Keep your emotions in check when you compose e-mail messages; flaming can damage relationships and reputations.

Given the spontaneous nature of e-mail and other electronic media, you may sometimes need to work hard to keep your emotions under control. A message that contains insensitive, insulting, or critical comments is called a *flame*. If you're angry, calm down before composing an e-mail message. If you do write an emotionally charged message, let it sit for at least a day and then revise it—if it even needs to be sent. Ask yourself two questions: First, "Would I say this to my audience face to face?" And second, "Am I comfortable with this message becoming a permanent part of the company's communication history?" Remember that a living, breathing human being is on the receiving end of your communication—and that your message can be forwarded easily and stored forever.

Completing E-Mail Messages

Don't let the speed and simplicity of e-mail lull you into thinking that careless presentation is acceptable. Particularly for important messages, a few moments of revising and proofing might save you hours of headaches and damage control. Also, lean in favor of simplicity when it comes to producing your e-mail messages. A clean, easily readable font, in black on a white background, is sufficient for nearly all e-mail messages.

Take advantage of your e-mail system's ability to include a *signature* (most corporate systems support this). This is a small text file that is automatically appended to your outgoing messages. Use it to include your full name, job title, company, and contact information. A signature gives your messages a more professional appearance and makes it easy for others to communicate with you through multiple channels.

When you're ready to distribute your message, pause to verify what you're doing before you click Send. Double-check your addressees to make sure you've included everyone necessary—and no one else. Don't click Reply All when you mean to click Reply. The difference could be embarrassing or even career threatening. Don't include people in the cc (courtesy copy) or bcc (blind courtesy copy) fields unless you know how these features work. (Everyone

CHECKLIST: Creating Effective E-Mail Messages

A. Treat e-mail as a professional communication medium.
- Remember that business e-mail is more formal than personal e-mail.
- Recognize that e-mail messages carry the same legal weight as other business documents.
- Follow company e-mail policy; understand the restrictions your company places on e-mail usage.
- Practice good e-mail hygiene by not opening suspicious messages, keeping virus protection up to date, and following other company guidelines.

B. Adapt the three-step process for effective e-mail.
- Make sure every e-mail message you send is necessary.
- Don't cc or bcc anyone who doesn't really need to see the message.
- Follow the chain of command.
- Pay attention to the quality of your writing and use correct grammar, spelling, and punctuation.
- Make your subject lines informative by clearly identifying the purpose of your message.
- Make your subject lines compelling by wording them in a way that intrigues your audiences.
- Update the subject line if you reply to the same message back and forth multiple times.
- Keep your emotions under control.
- Don't mark messages as "urgent" unless they truly are urgent.

who receives the message can see who is on the cc line but not who is on the bcc line.) Also, don't set the message priority to "high" or "urgent" unless your message is truly urgent.

To review the tips and techniques for successful e-mail, see "Checklist: Creating Effective E-Mail Messages" or click on Chapter 7 at http://real-timeupdates.com/ebc.

CREATING EFFECTIVE INSTANT MESSAGES AND TEXT MESSAGES

While e-mail isn't going away anytime soon, its disadvantages—including viruses, spam, and rampant overuse—are driving many people to explore alternatives. No single replacement has emerged, but social networks such as Facebook, microblogging services such as Twitter, and instant messaging (IM) are all being used as alternatives to e-mail.[14]

IM is taking the place of e-mail for much of the routine communication in many companies.

IM capabilities are also being embedded into other communication media, including social networks and online meeting systems, further extending the reach of this convenient technology.[15] Business-grade IM systems offer a range of capabilities, including basic chat, *presence awareness* (the ability to quickly see which people are at their desks and available to IM), remote display of documents, video capabilities, remote control of other computers, automated newsfeeds from blogs and websites, and automated *bot* (derived from the word *robot*) capabilities in which a computer can carry on simple conversations.[16]

Phone-based **text messaging** has long been popular in other parts of the world, where it is often referred to as *short messaging service* (*SMS*) and was widely available for years before it caught on in North America. Text messaging applications in business include marketing (alerting customers about new sale prices, for example), customer service (such as airline flight status, package tracking, and appointment reminders), security (for example, authenticating mobile banking transactions), crisis management (such as updating all employees working at a disaster scene), and process monitoring (alerting computer technicians to system failures, for example).[17]

Phone-based text messaging is fast and portable but not yet as versatile as computer-based IM.

Because IM is currently more versatile and more widely used in business than text messaging, the following sections focus on IM. However, as text messaging evolves along with wireless devices and networking, you can expect that many of the benefits, risks, and guidelines that pertain to IM will eventually pertain to text messaging as well.

Understanding the Benefits and Risks of IM

The benefits of IM include the possibility of rapid response to urgent messages, lower cost than phone calls, ability to mimic conversation more closely than e-mail, and availability on a wide range of devices.[18] In addition, because it more closely resembles one-on-one conversation, IM doesn't get misused as a one-to-many broadcast method as often as e-mail does.[19]

IM offers many benefits:

- *Rapid response*
- *Low cost*
- *Ability to mimic conversation*
- *Wide availability*

Of course, wherever technology goes, trouble seems to follow. The potential drawbacks of IM include security problems (computer viruses, network infiltration, and the possibility that sensitive messages might be intercepted by outsiders), the need for *user authentication* (making sure that online correspondents are really who they appear to be), the challenge of logging messages for later review and archiving, incompatibility between competing IM systems, and *spim* (unsolicited commercial messages, similar to e-mail spam). Fortunately, with the growth of *enterprise instant messaging* (*EIM*), or IM systems designed for large-scale corporate use, many of these problems are being overcome. However, security remains a significant concern for corporate IM systems.[20]

Adapting the Three-Step Process for Successful IM

Although instant messages are often conceived, written, and sent within a matter of seconds, the principles of the three-step process still apply, particularly when communicating with customers and other important audiences:

- **Planning instant messages.** View every IM exchange as a conversation; while you may not deliberately plan every individual statement you make or question you pose, take a moment to plan the overall exchange. If you're requesting something, think through exactly what you need and the most effective way to ask for it. If someone is asking you for something, consider his or her needs and your ability to meet them before you respond. And although you rarely organize instant messages in the sense of creating an outline, try to deliver information in a coherent, complete way that minimizes the number of individual messages required.

- **Writing instant messages.** As with e-mail, the appropriate writing style for business IM is more formal than the style you may be accustomed to with personal IM or text messaging. You should generally avoid IM acronyms (such as *FWIW* for "for what it's worth" or *HTH* for "hope that helps") except when communicating with close colleagues. In the IM exchange in Figure 7.2, notice how the participants communicate quickly and rather informally but still maintain good etiquette and a professional tone. This style is even more important if you or your staff use IM to communicate with customers and other outside audiences.
- **Completing instant messages.** One of the biggest attractions of IM is that the completing step is so easy. You don't have to produce the message in the usual sense, and distribution is as simple as clicking the Send button. However, don't skip over the revising and proofreading tasks. Quickly scan each message before you send to make sure you don't have any missing or misspelled words and that your message is clear and complete.

When using IM, be aware of the potential for constant interruptions and wasted time.

To use IM effectively, keep in mind some important behavioral issues: the potential for constant interruptions, the ease of accidentally mixing personal and business messages, the risk of being out of the loop (if a hot discussion or an impromptu meeting flares up when you're away from your PC or other IM device), and the "vast potential for wasted time" (in the words of MIT labor economist David Autor). On top of all that, users are at the mercy of other people's typing abilities, which can make IM agonizingly slow.[21]

FIGURE 7.2 Instant Messaging for Business Communication
Instant messaging is widely used in business, but you should not use the same informal style of communication you probably use for IM with your friends and family.

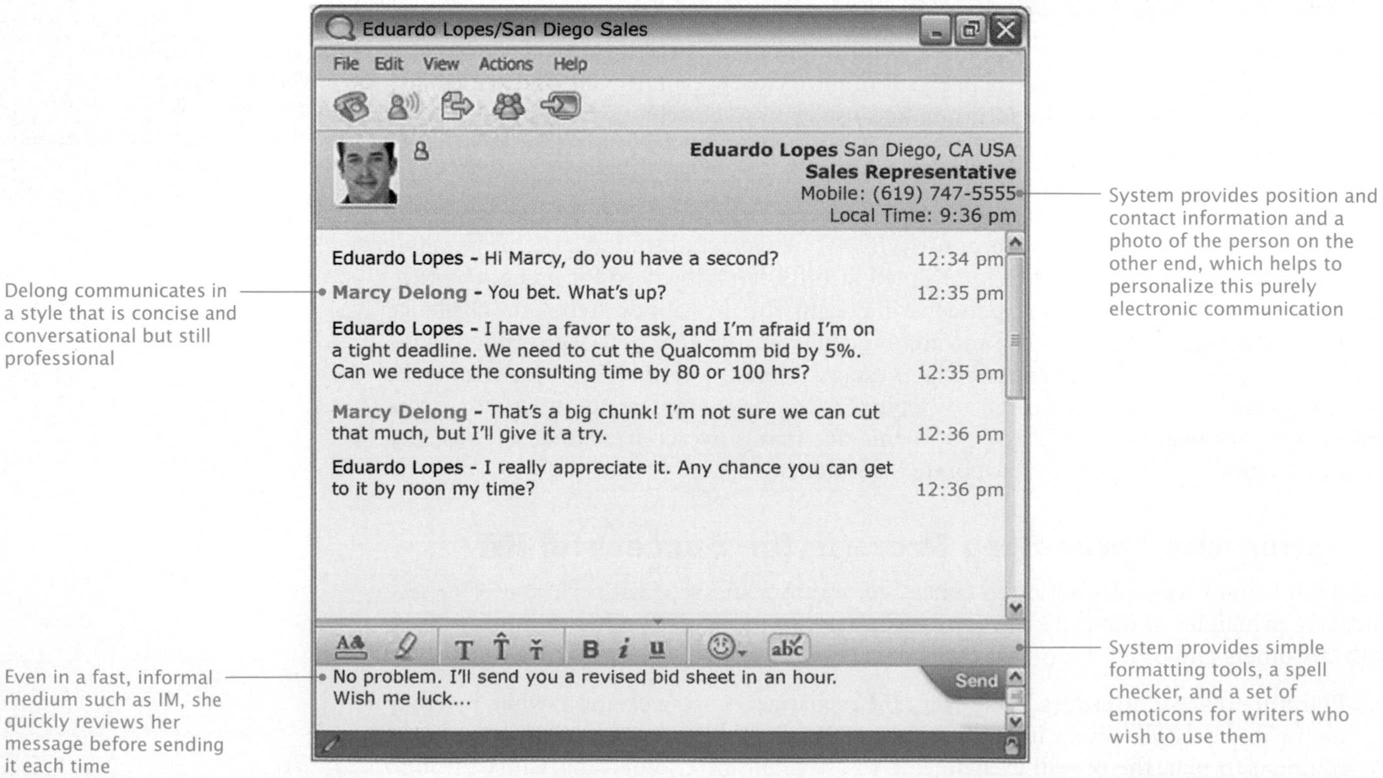

CHECKLIST: Using IM Productively

- Pay attention to security and privacy issues and be sure to follow all company guidelines.
- Treat IM as a professional communication medium, not an informal, personal tool; avoid using IM slang with all but close colleagues.
- Maintain good etiquette, even during simple exchanges.
- Protect your own productivity by making yourself unavailable when you need to focus.
- In most instances, don't use IM for confidential messages, complex messages, or personal messages.

Regardless of the system you're using, you can make IM more efficient and effective by following these tips:[22]

Understand the guidelines for successful business IM before you begin to use it.

4 LEARNING OBJECTIVE

Identify guidelines for successful instant messaging in the workplace.

- Unless a meeting is scheduled or you're expected to be available for other reasons, make yourself unavailable when you need to focus on other work.
- If you're not on a secure system, don't send confidential information using IM.
- Be extremely careful about sending personal messages—they have a tendency to pop up on other people's computers at embarrassing moments.
- Don't use IM for important but impromptu meetings if you can't verify that everyone concerned will be available.
- Don't use IM for lengthy, complex messages; e-mail is better for those.
- Try to avoid carrying on multiple IM conversations at once, to minimize the chance of sending messages to the wrong people or making one person wait while you tend to another conversation.
- Follow all security guidelines designed to keep your company's information and systems safe from attack.

To review the advice for effective IM in the workplace, see "Checklist: Using IM Productively" or click on Chapter 7 at **http://real-timeupdates.com/ebc**.

CREATING EFFECTIVE BUSINESS BLOGS

Blogging combines the global reach and reference value of a conventional website with the conversational exchanges of e-mail or IM. Good business blogs pay close attention to several important elements:

Blogs encourage interaction with a large, geographically dispersed audience.

- **Communicating with personal style and an authentic voice.** Most business messages designed for large audiences are carefully scripted and written in a "corporate voice" that is impersonal and objective. In contrast, successful business blogs such as Southwest Airlines's are written by individuals and exhibit their personal style. Audiences relate to this fresh approach and often build closer emotional bonds with the blogger's organization as a result.
- **Delivering new information quickly.** Today's blogging tools let you post new material as soon as you write or film it (see Figure 7.3). Not only does this feature allow you to respond quickly when needed—such as during a corporate crisis—it also lets your audiences know that an active conversation is taking place. Blogs that don't offer a continuous stream of new and interesting content are quickly ignored in today's online environment. Topics don't need to be earth shaking or cutting edge, either. They just need to be things that people care about and are willing to spend time reading. For instance, Harold Baker, a researcher at Clorox, blogs for the company under the name "Dr. Laundry," dispensing helpful advice on removing stains and tackling other household chores.[23]
- **Choosing topics of peak interest to audiences.** Successful blogs cover topics that readers care about. General Motors's (GM) popular FastLane blog (**http://fastlane.gmblogs.com**) features top executives writing about GM automobiles and responding to questions and criticisms from car enthusiasts. The people who read the blog and write comments obviously care about cars and want the latest information from GM.[24]

FIGURE 7.3 Video Blogging
With the addition of video, blogging becomes a true multimedia experience that gives bloggers an easy way to share sights and sounds with their audiences.

Most business blogs invite readers to leave comments, although many review comments before displaying them.

- **Encouraging audiences to join the conversation.** Not all blogs invite comments, although most do. These comments can be a valuable source of news, information, and insights. In addition, the relatively informal nature of blogging seems to make it easier for company representatives to let their guards down and converse with their audiences. Of course, not all comments are helpful or appropriate, which is why many bloggers review all comments and select the most helpful or interesting ones to post. In addition to enabling comments, blogs such as GM's FastLane offer online chat sessions, giving readers an even more direct link to executives.

Given the unique ability of blogs to convey topical information quickly and in a conversational format, their rapid adoption by businesses in virtually every industry should come as no surprise. The following sections offer an overview of the business applications of blogging, and Table 7.2 offers a number of suggestions for successful blogging.

Understanding the Business Applications of Blogging

The business applications of blogs include a wide range of internal and external communication tasks.

Blogs are a potential solution whenever you have a continuing stream of information to share with an online audience—and particularly when you want the audience to have the opportunity to respond. Here are some of the many ways businesses are using blogs:[25]

TABLE 7.2 Tips for Effective Business Blogging

TIP	WHY IT'S IMPORTANT
Don't blog without a clear plan.	Without a clear plan, your blog is likely to wander from topic to topic and fail to build a sense of community with your audience.
Post frequently; the whole point of a blog is fresh material.	If you won't have a constant supply of new information or new links, create a traditional website instead.
Make it about your audience and the issues that are important to them.	Readers want to know how your blog will help them, entertain them, or give them a chance to communicate with others who have similar interests.
Write in an authentic voice; never create an artificial character who supposedly writes a blog.	*Flogs*, or fake blogs, violate the spirit of blogging, show disrespect for your audience, and may turn audiences against you as soon as they uncover the truth.
Link generously—but carefully.	Providing interesting links to other blogs and websites is a fundamental aspect of blogging, but make sure the links will be of value to your readers and don't point to inappropriate material.
Keep it brief.	Most online readers don't have the patience to read lengthy reports.
Don't post anything you wouldn't want the entire world to see.	Future employers, government regulators, competitors, journalists, and community critics are just a few of the people who might eventually see what you've written.
Don't engage in blatant product promotion.	Readers who think they're being advertised to will stop reading.
Take time to write compelling, specific headlines for your posts.	Readers usually decide within a few seconds whether to read your posts; boring or vague headlines will turn them away instantly.
Pay attention to spelling, grammar, and mechanics.	No matter how smart or experienced you are, poor-quality writing undermines your credibility with intelligent audiences.
Respond to criticism openly and honestly.	Hiding sends the message that you don't have a valid response to the criticism. If your critics are wrong, patiently explain why you think they're wrong. If they are right, explain how you'll fix the situation.
Listen and learn.	If you don't take the time to analyze the comments people leave on your blog or the comments other bloggers make about you, you're missing out on one of the most valuable aspects of blogging.
Respect intellectual property.	You not only have an ethical obligation to not use material you don't own, but doing so can also violate copyright laws.
Be scrupulously honest and careful with facts.	Honesty is an absolute requirement for every ethical business communicator, of course, but you need to be extra careful online because inaccuracies (both intentional and unintentional) are likely to be discovered quickly and shared widely.

- **Project management and team communication.** Using blogs is a good way to keep project teams up to date, particularly when team members are geographically dispersed. For instance, the trip reports that employees file after visiting customers or other external parties can be enhanced vividly with *mobile blogs*, or *moblogs*. Thanks to the convenience of camera phones and other multimedia wireless devices, employees on the go can send text, audio, images, and video to their colleagues. Conversely, mobile employees can also stay in touch with their team blogs by using handheld devices.
- **Company news.** Companies can use blogs to keep employees informed about general business matters, from facility news to benefit updates. Blogs also serve as online community forums, giving everyone in the company a chance to raise questions and voice concerns by using the commenting feature.
- **Customer support.** Building on the tradition of online customer support forums that have been around since the earliest days of the Internet, customer support blogs answer questions, offers tips and advice, and inform customers about new products.

5 LEARNING OBJECTIVE

Describe the role of blogging in business communication today, and explain how to adapt the three-step writing process to blogging.

Moblogs are blogs adapted for display on mobile devices such as phones.

- **Public relations and media relations.** Many company employees and even high-ranking executives now share company news with both the general public and journalists via their blogs. The Nuts About Southwest blog featured at the beginning of the chapter is a great example.
- **Recruiting.** Using a blog is a great way to let potential employees know more about your company, the people who work there, and the nature of the company culture.
- **Policy and issue discussions.** Executive blogs in particular provide a public forum for discussing legislation, regulations, and other broad issues of interest to an organization.
- **Crisis communication.** Using blogs is an efficient way to provide up-to-the-minute information during emergencies, correct misinformation, or respond to rumors.
- **Market research.** Blogs can be a clever mechanism for soliciting feedback from customers and experts in the marketplace. In addition to using their own blogs for research, today's companies need to monitor blogs that are likely to discuss them, their executives, and their products. *Reputation analysts* such as Evolve24 (www.evolve24.com) have developed ways to automatically monitor blogs and other online sources to see what people are saying about their corporate clients and evaluate risks and opportunities in the global online conversation.[26]
- **Brainstorming.** Online brainstorming via blogs offers a way for people to toss around ideas and build on each others' contributions.

Blogs are an ideal medium for viral marketing, the organic spread of messages from one audience member to another.

- **Viral marketing.** The interconnected nature of the blogosphere makes it a natural vehicle for spreading the word about your company and your products. *Viral marketing* refers to the transmission of messages in much the same way that biological viruses are transmitted from person to person.
- **E-mail replacement.** As spam filters and message overload make it increasingly difficult to reach people via e-mail, many companies have turned to using blogs as a way to distribute information to customers and other audiences.
- **News syndication.** Blogging allows both individuals and companies to become publishers of news and other information. Syndication is explained on page 193.
- **Community building.** Blogging is a great way to connect people with similar interests. **Microblogging**, of which Twitter (http://twitter.com) is the best-known example, is essentially blogging via short messages. Starbucks, Whole Foods Market, The Home Depot, and Comcast are among the growing number of firms using Twitter to build communities of enthusiasts who participate in research studies or other conversations or who simply want to follow along with news and events that involve their favorite products or companies.[27]

> **REAL-TIME UPDATES**
> **Learn More**
>
> **Convincing corporate holdouts of the value of business blogs**
>
> If you need to convince anyone that a blog can be good for business—including why blogs outperform static webpages in search engine results—check out this compelling presentation. Go to **http://real-timeupdates.com/ebc** and click on "Learn More." If you are using mybcommlab, you can access Real-Time Updates within each chapter or under Student Study Tools.

The possibilities of blogs are almost unlimited, so be on the lookout for new ways to use them to foster positive relationships with colleagues, customers, and other important audiences (see Figure 7.4).

Adapting the Three-Step Process for Successful Blogging

The three-step writing process is easy to adapt to blogging. The planning step is particularly important if you're considering starting a blog because you're planning an entire communication channel, not just a single message. Pay close attention to your audience, your purpose, and your scope:

Before you launch a blog, make sure you have a clear understanding of your target audience, the purpose of your blog, and the scope of subjects you plan to cover.

- **Audience.** Except for team project blogs and other efforts with an obvious and well-defined audience, defining your target audience can be challenging. You want an

FIGURE 7.4 Elements of an Effective Business Blog
Blogs exist in many forms and formats, but visitors expect a few basic elements, such as access to archives, links to related information, and a convenient way to subscribe to an automatic newsfeed. Note the style and tone of the writing in this blog; it is far more engaging and conversational than the traditional "corporate voice." Moreover, it is about the *customers*, not the *company*.

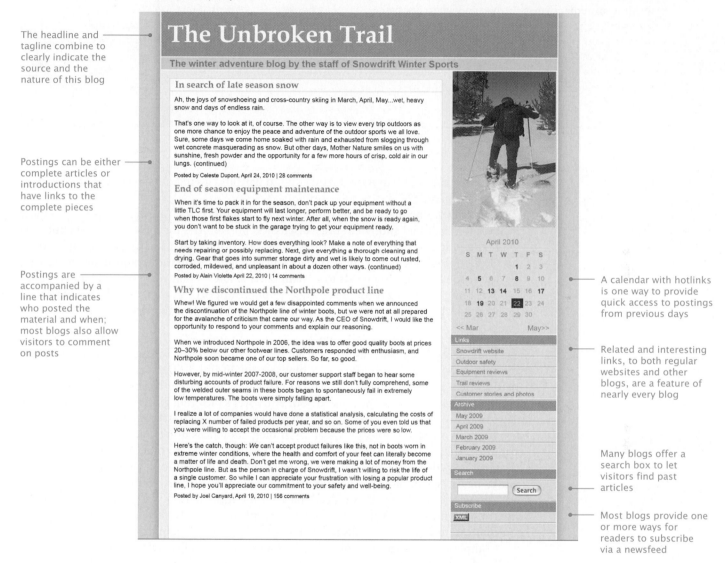

The headline and tagline combine to clearly indicate the source and the nature of this blog

Postings can be either complete articles or introductions that have links to the complete pieces

Postings are accompanied by a line that indicates who posted the material and when; most blogs also allow visitors to comment on posts

A calendar with hotlinks is one way to provide quick access to postings from previous days

Related and interesting links, to both regular websites and other blogs, are a feature of nearly every blog

Many blogs offer a search box to let visitors find past articles

Most blogs provide one or more ways for readers to subscribe via a newsfeed

audience large enough to justify the time you'll be investing but narrow enough that you can provide a clear focus for the blog. For instance, if you work for a firm that develops computer games, would you focus your blog on "hardcore" players, the type who spend thousands of dollars on super-fast PCs optimized for video games, or would you broaden the reach to include all video gamers? The decision often comes down to business strategy.

- **Purpose.** Unlike a personal blog, in which you typically write about whatever interests you, a business blog needs to have a business-related purpose that is important to your company and to your chosen audience. Moreover, the *general purpose* of your blog must "have legs"—that is, it needs to be something that can drive the blog's content for months or years and provide a cohesive framework for the *specific purpose* of each blog post. And like many websites, business blogs often need to address more than one purpose. For instance, Adam C. Haver writes the blog for SendOutCards, a Salt Lake City, Utah, greeting card company. Haver explains that the blog has two purposes: keeping

CHECKLIST: Blogging for Business

- Consider creating a blog whenever you have a continuing stream of information to share with an online audience.
- Identify an audience that is broad enough to justify the effort but narrow enough to have common interests.
- Identify a purpose that is comprehensive enough to provide ideas for a continuing stream of posts.
- Consider the scope of your blog carefully; make it broad enough to attract an audience but narrow enough to keep you focused.
- Communicate with a personal style and an authentic voice but don't write carelessly.
- Deliver new information quickly.
- Choose topics of peak interest to your audience.
- Encourage audiences to join the conversation.
- Offer a newsfeed option so that subscribers can get automatic updates.

the company's distribution partners up to date and giving outsiders "an inside look at our company."[28]

- **Scope.** Defining the scope of your blog can be a bit tricky. You want to cover a subject area that is broad enough to offer discussion possibilities for months or years but narrow enough to have an identifiable focus. For instance, GM's FastLane blog is about GM automobiles only—not GM's stock price, labor negotiations, and so on. Moreover, the scope of your blog needs to remain fairly stable so that you can build an audience over time. If you start out discussing product support but then shift to talking about your company's advertising programs, you'll probably lose readers along the way.

Careful planning needs to continue with each message. Unless you're posting to a restricted-access blog, such as an internal blog on a company intranet, you can never be sure who might see your posts. Other bloggers might link to them months or years later. Also, if you are not writing an official company blog but rather blogging as an individual employee, make sure you understand your employer's blogging guidelines. More and more companies are putting policies in place to prevent employee missteps with blogging.[29]

Write blog posts in a comfortable—but not careless—style.

Write in a comfortable, personal style. Blog audiences don't want to hear from your company; they want to hear from *you.* Bear in mind, though, that *comfortable* does not mean *careless.* Sloppy writing damages your credibility. In addition, while audiences expect you to be knowledgeable in the subject area your blog covers, you don't need to know everything about a topic. If you don't have all the information yourself, provide links to other blogs and websites that supply relevant information. In fact, many blog audiences consider carefully screened links to be an essential part of blogging.

Completing messages for your blog is usually quite easy. Evaluate the content and readability of your message, proofread to correct any errors, and post using your blogging system's tools for doing so. If your blog doesn't already have one, be sure to include one or more *newsfeed* options so that your audience can automatically receive updates of new blog posts (see "Distributing Blog and Podcast Content" on page 193).

"Checklist: Blogging for Business" summarizes some of the key points to remember when creating and writing a business blog. You can also visit http://real-timeupdates.com/ebc and click on Chapter 7 for the latest advice on blogging.

CREATING EFFECTIVE PODCASTS

Podcasting can be used to deliver a wide range of audio and video messages.

Podcasting offers a number of interesting possibilities for business communication. Its most obvious use is to replace existing audio and video messages, such as one-way teleconferences in which a speaker provides information without expecting to engage in conversation with the listeners. Training is another good use of podcasting. One of the first podcasts recorded by technical experts at IBM gave other employees advice on setting up blogs, for example.[30] Sales representatives who travel to meet with potential customers can listen to

Business Communication 2.0

Help! I'm Drowning in Social Media!

Anyone who has sampled today's social media offerings has probably experienced this situation: You find a few fascinating blogs, a few interesting people to follow on Twitter, a couple of podcast channels with helpful business tips, and then wham—within a few hours of signing up, your computer is overflowing with updates. Even if every new item is useful (which is rather unlikely), you receive so many that you can't stay ahead of the incoming flood. Between Twitter updates, newsfeeds, e-mail, instant messaging, and social networks—not to mention a desk phone and a mobile phone—today's business professionals could easily spend their entire day just trying to keep up with incoming messages and never get any work done.

To keep social media from turning into a source of stress and information anxiety, consider these tips:

- **Understand what information you really need in order to excel in your current projects and along your intended career path.** Unfortunately, taking this advice is even trickier than it sounds because you can't always know what you need to know, so you can't always predict which sources will be helpful. However, don't gather information simply because it is interesting or entertaining; collect information that is useful or at least potentially useful.
- **Face the fact that you cannot possibly handle every update from every potentially interesting and helpful source.** You have to set priorities and make tough choices to protect yourself from information overload.
- **Add new information sources slowly.** Give yourself a chance to adjust to the flow and judge the usefulness of each new source.
- **Prune your sources vigorously and frequently.** Bloggers can run out of things to say; your needs and interests may change; higher-priority sources might appear.
- **Remember that information is an enabler, a means to an end.** Collecting vast amounts of information won't get you a sweet promotion with a big, juicy raise. *Using* information creatively and intelligently will.

CAREER APPLICATIONS

1. How can you determine whether a social media source is worth paying attention to?
2. Should you allow any information source to interrupt your work flow during the day (even just to signal that a new message is available)? Why or why not?

audio podcasts or view video podcasts to get the latest information on their companies' products. Podcasts are also an increasingly common feature on blogs, letting audiences listen to or watch recordings of their favorite bloggers. New services can even transcribe blogs into podcasts and vice versa.[31]

As more businesspeople become comfortable with podcasting, it should find applications in a variety of new areas, wherever audio or video content can convey business messages effectively. For instance, real estate agents can record audio podcasts that potential homebuyers can listen to while walking through houses. Marketing departments can replace expensive printed brochures with video podcasts that demonstrate new products in action. Human resources departments can offer video tours of their companies to entice new recruits.

Adapting the Three-Step Process for Successful Podcasting

6 LEARNING OBJECTIVE

Explain how to adapt the three-step writing process to podcasting, and describe the syndication process for blogs and podcasts.

Although it might not seem obvious at first, the three-step writing process adapts quite nicely to podcasting. You've already chosen the medium, so focus the planning step on analyzing the situation, gathering the information you'll need, and organizing your material. One vital planning step depends on whether you intend to create podcasts for limited use and distribution (such as a weekly audio update to your virtual team) or to create a **podcasting channel** with regular recordings on a consistent theme, designed for a wider public audience.

If you plan to create a podcast channel, make sure your subject has "legs"—enough interesting topics to sustain an ongoing effort.

As with planning a blog, if you intend to create a podcasting channel, be sure to think through the range of topics you want to address over time to verify that you have a sustainable purpose. If you plan to comment on the stock market or breaking news in your industry, for instance, you'll have a recurring source of topics to discuss. In contrast, if you plan to share marketing ideas for small business owners, make sure you have or can find plenty of ideas over time so that your podcasting efforts don't run out of steam. If you bounce from one theme to another over time, you risk losing your audience.[32]

Generous use of previews, transitions, and reviews helps podcast audiences follow the thread of your recording.

As you organize and begin to think about the words or images you'll use as content, pay close attention to previews, transitions, and reviews. These steering devices are especially vital in audio and video recordings because these formats lack the "street signs" (such as headings) that audiences rely on in print media. Moreover, scanning back and forth to find specific parts of an audio or video message is much more difficult than with textual messages, so you need to do everything possible to make sure your audience successfully receives and interprets your message on the first try. Another way to help listeners and viewers is to provide detailed written descriptions of your podcasts (on your blog, for example) so that they understand what each recording offers.

One of the attractions of podcasting is the conversational, person-to-person feel of the recordings, so unless you need to capture exact wording, speaking from an outline and notes rather than a prepared script is often the best choice. However, no one wants to listen to rambling podcasts that struggle to make a point, so don't try to make up your content on the fly. An effective podcast, like an effective story, has a clear beginning, middle, and end.

Plan your podcast content carefully; edits are much more difficult to make than in textual messages.

In the completing step, keep in mind that making edits is much more difficult with audio or video than with textual media. Take extra care to revise your script or think through your speaking notes before you begin to record. You don't want to get halfway through the recording process and realize that you should have said something else in the introduction.

Finally, consider integrating your podcasting efforts with a related blog. Not only can you provide additional information, but you can also use the commenting feature of the blog to encourage feedback from your audience.[33]

—REAL-TIME UPDATES
Learn More

Step-by-step advice for recording your first podcast

You'll be podcasting in no time with this hands-on advice, which includes step-by-step instructions for using the free Audacity audio recording software. Go to **http://real-timeupdates.com/ebc** and click on "Learn More." If you are using mybcommlab, you can access Real-Time Updates within each chapter or under Student Study Tools.

With a few upgrades beyond a basic computer, you can assemble a studio capable of producing professional-quality podcasts.

Assembling a Podcasting System

The equipment needed to record podcasts depends on the degree of production quality you want to achieve. For the most basic podcasts, such as those you might record for internal audiences, most contemporary personal computers probably have the equipment you need: a low-cost microphone (most laptop computers now have built-in microphones), a sound card to convert the microphone signal to digital format (most computers have them now), and some recording software (free versions are available online). Many handheld digital recorders can also record audio files that you can upload to a PC for editing and distribution.

However, a basic system might not deliver the audio quality or production flexibility you need for a public podcast. For instance, the microphone built into your laptop can't reproduce sound nearly as well as a professional-quality microphone can, and because it's physically located on the computer, the built-in microphone will pick up the noise from the computer's fan. Similarly, the low-cost sound cards built into many computers can add a significant amount of noise to your signal.[34]

If you require higher production quality or greater flexibility, you'll need additional pieces of hardware and software, such as an audio processor (to filter out extraneous noise and otherwise improve the audio signal), a mixer (to combine multiple audio or video signals), a better microphone, and more sophisticated recording and editing software (see Figure 7.5). You may also need to improve the acoustics of the room in which you are recording in order to minimize echoes, noise, and other problems. To learn more about the technical requirements of podcasting, pick up one of the many books on the subject. Some of them even come with free recording software.[35]

FIGURE 7.5 The Podcasting Process
Creating a podcast requires just a few easy steps, and basic podcasts can be created using free or low-cost hardware and software.

1. Install recording software
2. Connect and verify microphone
3. Click the record button and start talking
4. Review your file and edit if needed
5. Convert file to MP3 format and save
6. Create and validate your feed
7. Upload your file and let RSS alert your subscribers
Program_01.mp3
http://www.myshow.com/podcasts/program_01.xml
Validate
The Marketing Show

For a quick review of the key points of business podcasting, see "Checklist: Planning and Producing Business Podcasts." For news on the latest developments in podcasting, visit **http://real-timeupdates.com/ebc** and click on Chapter 7.

DISTRIBUTING BLOG AND PODCAST CONTENT

With today's blog and podcast technologies, you can easily reach a vast audience—an audience that can continue to grow as your readers or listeners help spread the word for you.

Syndicating Your Content

The distribution process for blogs and podcasts is called **syndication** (see Figure 7.6).[36] As a content creator, you initiate syndication by creating a **feed**, or *newsfeed*, a file that contains information about the items you have written or recorded. In the case of podcasts, the audio or video file is enclosed within the feed file as well. Several formats now exist for these feeds; the most common is known as **RSS**, which is short for *really simple syndication*. (Although this process sounds fairly technical, popular blogging and podcasting systems take care of most of the details for you.) The benefit of syndication via an RSS feed is that you have the potential to build up a vast audience over time, provided that you offer compelling content and make that content easy to find.

Syndication is the process of distributing blog and podcast content via feeds.

On the receiving end, audiences subscribe to your content either through their web browser or using a piece of software called an **aggregator** or a *newsreader*. (*Aggregating* is simply another word for *collecting*.) Basic aggregators can collect messages with both text and static images, and some aggregators specialize in certain types of media. Aggregators specifically for podcasts are usually called **podcatchers**. Whenever you create a feed for a new blog post or podcast, your subscribers are automatically alerted via the feed. In the case

Aggregators automatically collect information about new blog posts and podcasts.

FIGURE 7.6 The Syndication Process for Blogs
The publish/subscribe model lets bloggers reach a potentially vast audience and lets audiences automatically acquire fresh content from an unlimited number of sources.

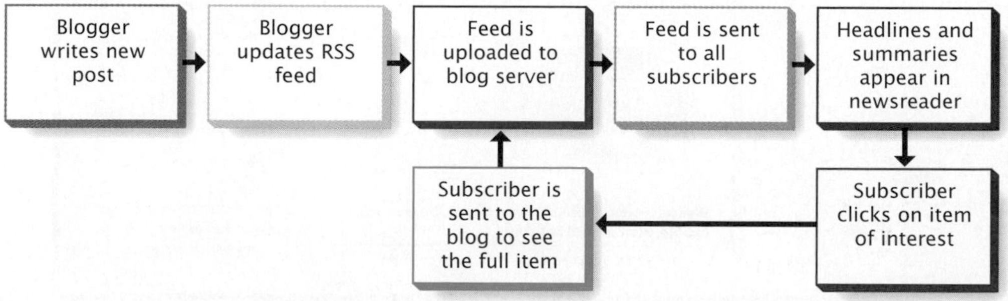
Blogger writes new post
Blogger updates RSS feed
Feed is uploaded to blog server
Feed is sent to all subscribers
Headlines and summaries appear in newsreader
Subscriber clicks on item of interest
Subscriber is sent to the blog to see the full item

CHECKLIST: Planning and Producing Business Podcasts

- Consider podcasting whenever you have the opportunity to replace existing audio or video messages.
- If you plan a podcast channel with a regular stream of new content, make sure you've identified a theme or purpose that is rich enough to sustain your effort.
- Pay close attention to previews, transitions, and reviews to help prevent your audience from getting lost.
- Decide whether you want to improvise your podcast or speak or film from a written script.
- If you improvise, do enough planning and organization to avoid floundering and rambling in search of a point.
- Remember that editing is much more difficult to do with audio or video than with textual media and plan your content and recording carefully.
- Consider linking your podcast to a blog in order to provide additional information and a forum for audience feedback.
- Syndicate your podcast, if appropriate, via RSS enclosures.

of blogs, aggregators usually display a headline and brief summary of your post. Anyone who wants to read the full item can click on the headline to be directed back to your blog to see the entire post (see Figure 7.7). In the case of podcasts, subscribers can choose to have new podcasts downloaded to their computer or other device automatically, or they can

FIGURE 7.7 Viewing Blog Updates in Web Browsers
With newsfeed capability now built into web browsers, collecting updates from your favorite bloggers and news sources is effortless.

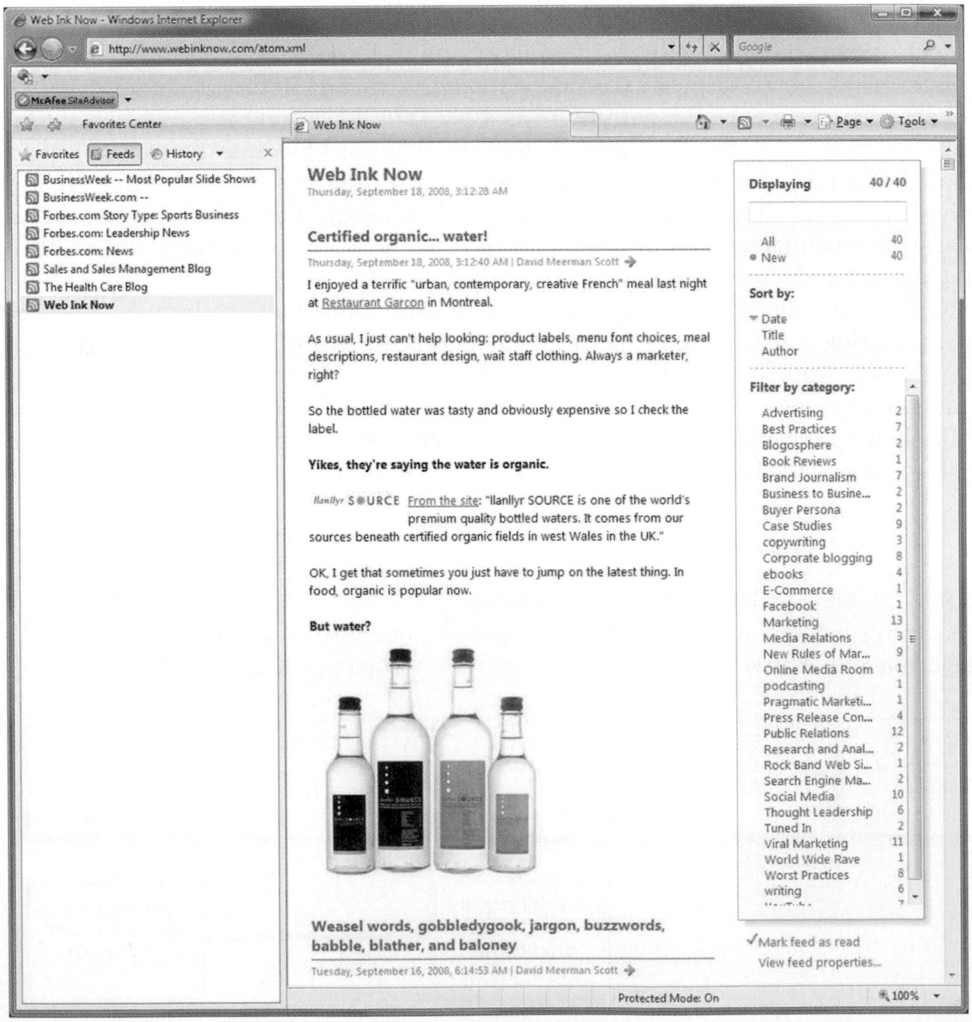

download them manually. For audiences, the key benefit of syndication is automatically collecting interesting content from many sources in a variety of formats. In a sense, it's like creating personal versions of the Internet.

Connecting with Audiences

Adding feed capability is the most important step in staying connected with your blog or podcast audiences.

Of course, content creators and audiences need ways to find each other for blogging and podcasting to have any value. This connection can happen in a variety of ways. The most fundamental step for bloggers is to add the feed capability to their blogs so that interested audiences can easily subscribe through their aggregators. Bloggers and podcasters can also take advantage of services such as Google's FeedBurner (**http://feedburner.google.com**), which make sure files are properly formatted and help publicize content.[37]

Beyond that, bloggers and podcasters can get themselves listed in a variety of directories, some of which specialize in blogs (such as Technorati, **http://technorati.com**), others in podcasts (such as Juice, **http://juicereceiver.sourceforge.net**), and others in two or more media types (such as Mefeedia, **www.mefeedia.com**, which covers podcasts and vodcasts).

Content creators can also make their material easier to find through **tagging**, which involves assigning descriptive words to each post or podcast. For instance, for a blog post on clever techniques for attracting new employees, you might tag the post with the word *recruiting*. Visitors to your blog who want to read everything you've written about recruiting just click on that word to see all your posts on that subject. Tagging can also help audiences locate your posts on blog trackers such as Technorati or on *social bookmarking* or *social news* sites such as Delicious (**http://delicious.com**) and Digg (**http://digg.com**). You can read more about social bookmarking as a research tool in Chapter 11.

Bloggers can help each other find audiences by listing favorite blogs in their blogrolls.

Bloggers can help each other by identifying blogs they themselves read. This list, called a *blogroll*, can be found on many blogs. In addition, when bloggers comment on individual posts on other blogs, they can use a feature called *trackback* to let readers of the original post know that other bloggers have commented on it. Both blogrolls and trackbacks help "spread the word" for bloggers by showing audiences other blogs they might like.

Document Makeover

Improve This Blog

To practice correcting drafts of actual documents, visit the "Document Makeovers" section in mybcommlab. Refer to the User Guide for specific instructions on how to access the content for this chapter. You will find a blog post that contains problems and errors related to what you've learned in this chapter about writing for electronic media. Use the Final Draft decision tool to create an improved version of this post.

On the Job: Solving Communication Dilemmas at Southwest Airlines

You recently joined the corporate communications group at Southwest Airlines, and one of your responsibilities is overseeing the Nuts About Southwest blog. Study the scenarios that follow and apply what you learned about blogging in this chapter to choose the best course of action.

1. Pressure is building to stop the practice of moderating the blog by reviewing reader comments and selecting which ones will appear on the blog. You've received a number of adamant messages saying that Nuts About Southwest won't be a "real" blog until anyone is allowed to write any sort of comment without being "censored" by the company. However, you know that every blog is vulnerable to rude, inappropriate, and irrelevant comments, and you don't want Nuts About Southwest to turn into a free-for-all shouting match. Which of the following messages should you post on the blog to explain that the current policy of reviewing and filtering comments will continue?

a. There are plenty of free-for-all blogs and websites on the Internet; if you want to rant and rave, I suggest you try one of those.

b. Please bear in mind that this blog is a Southwest company commercial communication endeavor and, as such, it must adhere to company standards for communication style. I therefore regret to inform you that we cannot allow a free-form, unmonitored exchange as part of this blog.

c. Our blog; our rules. Seriously, though, this is a professional communication channel designed primarily to give Southwest employees the opportunity to share their thoughts with customers and vice versa. As such, we need to make sure that primary messaging effort doesn't get lost in the noise that can flare up in unregulated online forums.

d. Every web surfer knows that online discussions can get a little out of hand at times, degenerating into shouting matches, name calling, and off-topic rants. In order to continue providing the congenial, information-driven blog that readers have come to expect, we believe it is necessary to exercise a minimal amount of control over the content.

2. Southwest's change in scheduling policy (allowing customers to reserve seats slightly further into the future) placated many customers but not everyone. Some still want to book travel up to a year or more in advance. You don't want to ignore these complaints, but the company has decided that scheduling that far out just isn't feasible. You therefore decide to post a few representative complaints and respond to them as best you can. In addition to letting customers know that the schedule window won't be extended that far, you'd like to curtail any further discussion on this topic. Which of the following would be the best way to respond to these complaints?

a. Folks, you don't really understand how complicated running an airline truly is. You can't just slap a time schedule together and have it magically happen. Every single flight involves a flight crew, a ground crew, catering, gates at both ends, fees, clearances—you name it. Zillions of details have to be coordinated for every flight we put on the schedule, and it's a major job. We manage to handle 3,000 flights a day, so trust us; we know what we're doing.

b. Thanks for your input. We realize air travel isn't as smooth or as simple as we'd all like, so it's helpful to hear from all of our valued customers. I'll make sure the rest of the scheduling team reads your comments, and if anything changes in the scheduling policy, I'll post the new information here immediately.

c. Thanks for taking the time to post your comments. You're certainly welcome to book your travel on other airlines if you need to nail down a reservation 6 to 12 months into the future. However, I should warn you that the further into the future you make a reservation, the greater the chances that the airline will change the schedule on you. Let's say it's January 10, and you want to book a flight from Denver to San Jose on December 20. Fine, you're all set. Then along comes October or November, and the airline realizes it needs that plane for the Denver to Chicago leg on December 20 instead. What happens then? You get a phone call or e-mail saying "Sorry, we've had to book you on a different flight at a different time." What's the point of nailing down your plans 11 or 12 months in advance if they're just going to change on you?

d. Thanks for taking the time to post your comments. When we're considering the scheduling question, let's remember why all of us—employees included—are nuts about flying Southwest: low fares, predictable schedules, and on-time performance. In order to maintain those benefits, we've learned over the years that we need to make certain choices about how we run the airline. One of those choices is to operate a shorter reservation window than many other airlines. I realize this doesn't meet the needs of every passenger in every situation, but experience shows that it's the best way to make most passengers happy most of the time. In that light, I hope the decision not to extend scheduling beyond six months makes sense to everyone.

3. The multiauthor concept generally works well for Nuts About Southwest. It divides the writing workload, and it gives readers the opportunity to hear from a variety of voices across the company. One member of the team is retiring, so you need to recruit a new blogger to replace her. Your plan is to send an e-mail message to everyone in the company, providing a brief reminder of the blog's purpose, describing the writing style you're looking for, and inviting interested writers to submit sample blog entries for evaluation. Which of the following paragraphs is the best way to describe the preferred writing style for the blog? (This message is for employees only; it won't be seen by the public.)

a. Nuts About Southwest has connected with thousands of readers because the writing is *engaging* (people want to read and respond), *personal* (readers want to get to know real, live human beings, not a faceless corporation), *honest* (we don't sugar-coat anything or hide from criticism), and *friendly* (our readers want to enjoy the experience).

b. What kind of writing are we looking for? Well, let me tell you exactly what we need. We need writing that is above all (a) engaging—it makes people *want* to read and become involved in the conversation. Plus, (b), the writing must be *personal*; we don't need anybody to repeat "the company line" here; we want *your unique* thoughts and opinions. However, (c), we, of course (!), need writing that is consistent with Southwest's culture that combines honesty with friendliness.

c. You should be able to produce copy that meets the following criteria: Your writing must be engaging, personal, honest, and friendly. Writing that does not meet these criteria, no matter how well written in other respects, will not be accepted for online publication.

d. I'll be short and to the point: the writing we want for this blog must be engaging, personal, honest, and friendly.

4. For the sample blog entries you solicited in your e-mail message, you asked candidates to start their entries with a brief paragraph introducing themselves. Which of the following seems like the most compatible style for Nuts About Southwest?

a. Hi everyone! I'm Janice McNathan, and I couldn't be more excited to be joining the Nuts About Southwest blog cuz—hey, I'm nuts! I've worked at some goofball companies before, but nobody has as much fun as the loonies here at Southwest, so I know I'm going to have a great time writing for this blog!

b. Howdy folks, Charlie Parker here. No, not the famous jazz musician! I'm just a lowly fuel inventory auditor here in Dallas. Pretty much, I keep tabs on the fuel that goes into our planes and I make sure we get the best deals possible and all the paperwork stays in order. I can't promise any exciting stories of adventure like the pilots and other people write here, but I'll keep my eyes peeled around the airport here, and maybe something interesting will come up.

c. I'm Rick Munoz, and I've always wanted to be a professional writer. My career sort of took a detour, though, and I wound up as a programmer who works behind the scenes at the Southwest website. I really appreciate this opportunity to hone my craft, and who knows—maybe this will be the break I need to make it as a "real" writer. You'll be able to say "I knew that guy before he became famous!"

d. Excuse me while I wipe the grease off my hands; I don't want to mess up this shiny new keyboard! Hi, I'm Kristal Yan, an airframe and powerplant mechanic at Southwest's facility in Oakland, California. I've been an avid reader of Nuts About Southwest since it started, and I really look forward to participating in this wonderful worldwide conversation. I hope to provide some interesting observations from a mechanic's perspective, and I hope you'll feel free to ask any questions you may have about how we keep Southwest's planes running smoothly and safely.

LEARNING OBJECTIVES CHECKUP

Assess your understanding of the principles in this chapter by reading each learning objective and studying the accompanying exercises. For fill-in-the-blank items, write the missing text in the blank provided; for multiple-choice items, circle the letter of the correct answer. You can check your responses against the answer key on page AK-1.

Objective 7.1: Compare the strengths and weaknesses of the electronic media available for short messages.

1. To express sympathy to the family of one of your employees who recently died in a traffic accident, which of these media would you choose and why?

a. Printed memo
b. Printed letter
c. E-mail
d. Instant message

2. Which of the following best describes an advantage of computer-based instant messaging over phone-based text messaging?

a. A computer keyboard and full-size display make IM more convenient to use than text messaging.
b. IM is cheaper because everybody has computers these days.
c. IM is faster than text messaging.
d. Computer-based IM is currently available in more languages than phone-based text messaging.

Objective 7.2: Outline six guidelines for creating successful social media content.

3. Which of these descriptions best captures the preferred style of writing for social media in business?

a. Businesslike and message-driven
b. Unplanned, unrehearsed, and super casual
c. Conversational, supportive, and engaged
d. Funny, quirky, and intriguing

4. The best way to promote companies and products through social media is to

a. Mention at least one product benefit every time you mention your product
b. Promote indirectly, such as mentioning how a product helped change someone's life for the better
c. Give everyone in the firm the responsibility to promote the company through social media
d. Never, ever mention your company or its products in any social medium

Objective 7.3: Explain the need to treat e-mail as a professional medium, and identify the qualities of an effective e-mail subject line.

5. E-mail hygiene refers to

a. Keeping e-mail safe and productive through such steps as keeping virus protection up to date and not downloading questionable software onto company systems

b. Making multiple backup copies of every message sent and received
c. Always washing your hands before and after you use the keyboard
d. Refraining from using any hard or unkind language in e-mail messages

6. Which of the following is true of e-mail subject lines?
a. Only "newbies" bother to use them anymore.
b. Subject lines should never give away the content of the message because no one will bother to read it if they already know what the message is about.
c. They can make the difference between a message being read right away, skipped over for later attention, or ignored entirely.
d. They should always be in all caps to get the audience's attention.

7. Which of the following is the most effective e-mail subject line?
a. Production line: wiring issues
b. Wiring errors in production: let's analyze the problem and explore solutions
c. Wiring errors on the production line MUST STOP NOW!
d. Careless employees ⇒ unhappy customers ⇒ fewer customers ⇒ fewer employees

8. You work in a customer service department, answering e-mails from customers. This morning you received an angry message from a customer who has a legitimate complaint about your company's warranty policies. After responding to the message as best you can, which of the following steps should you take?
a. Forward the message to your immediate supervisor and suggest that the company might want to reconsider its warranty policies.
b. Forward the message to the CEO and suggest that the company might want to reconsider its warranty policies.
c. Forward the message to everyone in the department so they are aware of the problem with the warranty policy.
d. Delete the customer's message; you can't fix the warranty policy.

Objective 7.4: Identify guidelines for successful instant messaging in the workplace.

9. Which of the following reasons helps explain why IM usage is overtaking e-mail in some companies?
a. People don't have to be so formal when they use IM; it saves time to use acronyms and emoticons and to avoid using capitalization, punctuation, and other time wasters.
b. IM works better as a broadcast mechanism than e-mail.
c. IM is faster than e-mail and mimics human conversation better than e-mail, so many people find it a more natural way to communicate.
d. IM systems let you communicate using different colors of text, which is vital for highlighting key points and conveying nonverbal aspects that are impossible to communicate in e-mail.

10. Which of these statements best describes how the three-step writing process applies to IM?
a. Because there is no planning step and no completing step in IM, the three-step process does not apply.
b. The real beauty of IM in the business world is that people don't have to spend so much time composing; they just zap out whatever is on their minds and get back to work.
c. The three-step process for IM works exactly the same way as it does with letters, memos, and reports. Every message requires audience analysis, information gathering, and outlining.
d. IM exchanges should be planned the same way conversations are planned to minimize confusion and the number of messages required. And instant messages don't have to be great works of literature, but they do need to be efficient and effective, so some degree of care in writing and revising is important.

11. Which of the following types of messages are most appropriate for IM?
a. Long, complex messages
b. Brief conversational messages
c. Confidential or highly personal messages
d. All of the above

Objective 7.5: Describe the role of blogging in business communication today, and explain how to adapt the three-step writing process to blogging.

12. Which of the following is a good strategy for using blogs to promote products and services?
a. Write in a style that is personal and conversational; minimize direct promotion of your products and services. Focus instead on topics that your customers and potential customers find helpful and interesting.
b. In order to cut through the noise in the blogosphere, promote your products and services constantly. If you don't, your competitors will drown you out.
c. Make sure the blog matches all other corporate communications in both style and content; customers get confused when a company communicates in more than one style.
d. Blogs should never be used for marketing and selling.

13. Which of the following best describes the idea of an "authentic voice" in blogging?
a. A writing style that is scrupulously precise and free from technical and grammatical errors
b. The voice of a real, living, breathing human being, communicating to other human beings on a personal level
c. Writing that is always highly emotional so as to counteract the dehumanizing logic and linear thinking that dominates business today
d. A detached, professional voice that is careful not to take sides, voice opinions, or otherwise inject elements into the conversation that could disturb or disappoint audiences

14. Blogs are a natural tool for _____, the transmission of product messages in a voluntary, organic way from one interested party to another.

15. Which of the following best describes the optimum audience of a blog?
    a. Always the largest audience possible
    b. Only people who are experts in the subject matter so that comments and discussions aren't pulled off track by "newbies" who don't know what they are talking about
    c. An audience large enough to justify the time required to maintain the blog but narrow enough to ensure a clear focus
    d. Whatever audience happens to find the blog on the web

16. Which of the following is *not* a good general purpose for a blog?
    a. Sharing news from the racing circuit, describing how the racers we sponsor are faring and how they use our products
    b. Commenting on economic and social policy decisions that affect the national and international business environment
    c. Explaining to the local community why we've decided not to expand employment at the Nampa facility
    d. Describing the work going on in our research and development labs

Objective 7.6: Explain how to adapt the three-step writing process to podcasting, and describe the syndication process for blogs and podcasts.

17. If one of the attractions of podcasting is its spontaneous, conversational feel, why should podcasters take the time to plan their recordings?
    a. Individual podcasts that aren't well thought out can end up being rambling, confusing, and repetitive.
    b. Podcasts are more difficult to edit than textual messages, so it's important to do enough planning to help avoid major mistakes.
    c. If you don't plan ahead, you could run out of ideas and therefore have no reason to continue podcasting.
    d. All of the above are reasons to plan podcasts.

18. A/an _____ is an ongoing series of podcasts on the same general topic.

19. _____ is the process of publishing blog and podcast content to the web so that audiences can find your content and be automatically updated when new content is available.

20. Which of the following tools is used to collect new blog postings, podcasts, and other fresh content automatically?
    a. A newsreader or aggregator
    b. A feeder
    c. A news scooper
    d. An RSS publisher

PEARSON **mybcommlab**™

Log on to www.mybcommlab.com to access the following study and assessment aids associated with this chapter:

- Video applications
- Real-Time Updates
- Peer review activity
- Quick Learning Guides
- Pre/post test
- Personalized study plan
- Model documents
- Sample presentations

If you are not using mybcommlab, you can access Real-Time Updates and Quick Learning Guides through http://real-timeupdates.com/ebc. The Quick Learning Guide (located under "Learn More" on the website) hits all the high points of this chapter in just two pages. This guide, especially prepared by the authors, will help you study for exams or review important concepts whenever you need a quick refresher.

Apply Your Knowledge

1. Is instant messaging replacing many instances of e-mail for the same reasons that e-mail replaced many instances of printed memos and letters? Explain your answer.
2. If one of the benefits of blogging is the personal, intimate style of writing, is it a good idea to limit your creativity by adhering to conventional rules of grammar, spelling, and mechanics? Why or why not?
3. In your work as a video game designer, you know that eager players search the web for any scrap of information they can find about upcoming releases. In fact, to build interest, your company's public relations department carefully doles out small bits of information in the months before a new title hits the market. However, you and others in the company are also concerned about competitors getting their hands on all this "prerelease" information. If they learn too much too soon, they can use the information to improve their own products more quickly. You and several other designers and programmers maintain blogs that give players insights into game design techniques and that occasionally share tips and tricks. You have thousands of readers, and you know your blog helps build customer loyalty. The company president wants to ban blogging entirely so that bloggers don't accidentally share too much prerelease information about upcoming games. Would this be a wise move? Why or why not?

4. In what ways does carefully planning a podcast reflect the "you" attitude?
5. **Ethical Choices** You work for a midsize freight delivery company that has been using text messaging as the primary communication channel between drivers and the central dispatch office. Drivers send a text message to confirm the time and location whenever they've made a delivery or a pickup, and whenever dispatchers get an urgent request from a customer, they send messages to the trucks to find out who is nearby and available. This manual system is clumsy and prone to errors, and the company's owners want to replace it with a fully computerized mapping system that uses the global positioning system (GPS) to automatically monitor the location of every truck in the fleet. Some drivers are in an uproar over the plan, saying it invades their privacy by tracking their every move all day long. Should the company proceed with the plan even though some drivers object? Summarize your opinion in a brief e-mail message to your instructor (or blog post, if your course uses a blog).

Practice Your Knowledge

Messages for Analysis

Message 7.A: Improving IM Skills

Review this IM exchange and explain how the customer service agent could have handled the situation more effectively.

Agent:	Thanks for contacting Home Exercise Equipment. What's up?
Customer:	I'm having trouble assembling my home gym.
Agent:	I hear that a lot! LOL
Customer:	So is it me or the gym?
Agent:	Well, let's see. Where are you stuck?
Customer:	The crossbar that connects the vertical pillars doesn't fit.
Agent:	What do you mean doesn't fit?
Customer:	It doesn't fit. It's not long enough to reach across the pillars.
Agent:	Maybe you assembled the pillars in the wrong place. Or maybe we sent the wrong crossbar.
Customer:	How do I tell?
Agent:	The parts aren't labeled so could be tough. Do you have a measuring tape? Tell me how long your crossbar is.

Message 7.B: Drafting Effective Blog Posts

Revise this blog post based on what you've learned in this chapter.

[headline]

We're DOOMED!!!!!

[post]

I was at the Sikorsky plant in Stratford yesterday, just checking to see how things were going with the assembly line retrofit we did for them last year. I think I saw the future, and it ain't pretty. They were demo'ing a prototype robot from Motoman that absolutely blows our stuff out of the water. They wouldn't let me really see it, but based on the 10-second glimpse I got, it's smaller, faster, and more maneuverable than any of our units. And when I asked about the price, the guy just grinned. And it wasn't the sort of grin designed to make me feel good.

I've been saying for years that we need to pay more attention to size, speed, and maneuverability instead of just relying on our historical strengths of accuracy and payload capacity, and you'd have to be blind not to agree that this experience proves me right. If we can't at least show a design for a better unit within two or three months, Motoman is going to lock up the market and leave us utterly in the dust.

Believe me, being able to say "I told you so" right now is not nearly as satisfying as you might think!!

Message 7.C: Plan a Better Podcast

To access this message, visit **http://real-timeupdates.com/ebc**, click on "Student Assignments," select Chapter 7, and then select page 200, Message 7.C. Download and listen to this podcast. Identify at least three ways in which the podcast could be improved and draft a brief e-mail message that you could send to the podcaster, giving your suggestions for improvement.

Exercises

Active links for all websites in this chapter can be found on mybcommlab; see your User Guide for instructions on accessing the content for this chapter.

7.1 **Choose Your Medium: Selecting the Best Technology for a Message** For each of these message needs, choose a medium that you think would work effectively and explain your choice. (More than one medium could work in some cases; just be able to support your particular choice.)
   a. A technical support service for people trying to use their digital music players
   b. A message of condolence to the family of an employee who passed away recently
   c. A message from the CEO of a small company, explaining that she is leaving the company to join a competitor
   d. A series of observations on the state of the industry
   e. A series of messages, questions, and answers surrounding the work of a project team

7.2 **E-Mail: Making Subject Lines Informative** Using your imagination to make up whatever details you need, revise the following e-mail subject lines to make them more informative:
   a. New budget figures
   b. Marketing brochure—your opinion
   c. Production schedule

7.3 **E-Mail: Message Outlining a New Employee Procedure** The following e-mail message contains numerous errors related to what you've learned about planning and writing business messages. Using the information it contains, write a more effective version.

TO: Felicia August <fb_august@evertrust.com>

SUBJECT: Those are the breaks, folks

Some of you may not like the rules about break times; however, we determined that keeping track of employees while they took breaks at times they determined rather than regular breaks at prescribed times was not working as well as we would have liked it to work. The new rules are not going to be an option. If you do not follow the new rules, you could be docked from your pay for hours when you turned up missing, since your direct supervisor will not be able to tell whether you were on a "break" or not and will assume that you have walked away from your job. We cannot be responsible for any errors that result from your inattentiveness to the new rules. I have already heard complaints from some of you and I hope this memo will end this issue once and for all. The decision has already been made.

Starting Monday, January 1, you will all be required to take a regular 15-minute break in the morning and again in the afternoon, and a regular thirty-minute lunch at the times specified by your supervisor, NOT when you think you need a break or when you "get around to it."

There will be no exceptions to this new rule!

Felicia August

Manager

Billing and accounting

7.4 Instant Messaging: Let's Get Professional Your firm, which makes professional paint sprayers, uses IM extensively for internal communication and frequently for external communication with customers and suppliers. Several customers have recently forwarded copies of messages they've received from your staff, asking if you know how casually some employees are treating this important medium. You decide to revise parts of several messages to show your staff a more appropriate writing style. Rewrite these sentences, making up any information you need, to convey a more businesslike style and tone. (Look up the acronyms online if you need to.)

a. IMHO, our quad turbo sprayer is best model 4U.
b. No prob; happy2help!
c. FWIW, I use the L400 myself & it rocks
d. Most cust see 20-30% reduct in fumes w/this sprayer —— of course, YMMV.

7.5 Blogging: Keeping Emotions Under Control The members of the project team of which you are the leader have enthusiastically embraced blogging as a communication medium. Unfortunately, as emotions heat up during the project, some of the blog posts are getting too casual, too personal, and even sloppy. Because your boss and other managers around the company also read this project blog, you don't want the team to look unprofessional in anyone's eyes. Revise the following blog post so that it communicates in a more businesslike manner while retaining the informal, conversational tone of a blog. (Be sure to correct any spelling and punctuation mistakes you find as well.)

Well, to the profound surprise of absolutely nobody, we are not going to be able meet the June 1 commitment to ship 100 operating tables to Southeast Surgical Supply. (For those of you who have been living in a cave the past six month, we have been fighting to get our hands on enough high-grade chromium steel to meet our production schedule.) Sure enough, we got news, this morning that we will only get enough for 30 tables. Yes, we look lik fools for not being able to follow through on promises we made to the customer, but no, this didn't have to happpen. Six month's ago, purchasing warned us about shrinking supplies and suggested we advance-buy as much as we would need for the next 12 months, or so. We naturally tried to followed their advice, but just as naturally were shot down by the bean counters at corporate who trotted out the policy about never buying more than three months worth of materials in advance. Of course, it'll be us—not the bean counters who'll take the flak when everybody starts asking why revenues are down next quarter and why Southeast is talking to our friends at Crighton Manuf!!! Maybe, some day this company will get its head out of the sand and realize that we need to have some financial flexibility in order to compete.

7.6 Blogging: Blog Post Informing Employees About an Office Relocation From what you've learned about effective blogging as well as planning and writing business messages in general, you should be able to identify numerous errors made by the writer of the following blog post. After identifying the flaws, draft a version that fixes them.

Get Ready!

We are hoping to be back at work soon, with everything running smoothly, same production schedule and no late projects or missed deadlines. So you need to clean out your desk, put your stuff in boxes, and clean off the walls. You can put the items you had up on your walls in boxes, also.

We have provided boxes. The move will happen this weekend. We'll be in our new offices when you arrive on Monday.

We will not be responsible for personal belongings during the move.

Posted by David Burke at 10:42 AM 09-27-09

7.7 Podcasting: Where Are We Going with This, Boss? You recently began recording a weekly podcast to share information with your large and far-flung staff. Now after a month, you've asked for feedback from several of your subordinates, and you're disappointed to learn that some people stopped listening to the podcast after the first couple weeks. Someone eventually admits that many staffers feel the recordings are too long and rambling, and the information they contain isn't valuable enough to justify the time it takes to listen. You aren't pleased, but you want to improve. An assistant transcribes the introduction to last week's podcast so you can review it. You immediately see two problems. Revise the introduction based on what you've learned in this chapter.

So there I am, having lunch with Selma Gill, who just joined and took over the Northeast sales region from

Jackson Stroud. In walks our beloved CEO with Selma's old boss at Uni-Plex; turns out they were finalizing a deal to co-brand our products and theirs and to set up a joint distribution program in all four domestic regions. Pretty funny, huh? Selma left Uni-Plex because she wanted to sell our products instead, and now she's back selling her old stuff, too. Anyway, try to chat with her when you can; she knows the biz inside and out and probably can offer insight into just about any sales challenge you might be running up against. We'll post more info on the co-brand deal next week; should be a boost for all of us. Other than those two news items, the other big news this week is the change in commission reporting. I'll go into the details in minute, but when you log onto the intranet, you'll now see your sales results split out by product line and industry sector. Hope this helps you see where you're doing well and where you might beef things up a bit. Oh yeah, I almost forgot the most important bit. Speaking of our beloved CEO, Thomas is going to be our guest of honor, so to speak, at quarterly sales meeting next week and wants an update on how petroleum prices are affecting customer behavior. Each district manager should be ready with a brief report. After I go through the commission reporting scheme, I'll outline what you need to prepare.

Expand Your Knowledge

Learning More on the Web

Ready to Start Blogging?

www.website101.com/RSS-Blogs-Blogging

Blogging is easy to do if you have the right information. These helpful tutorials cover everything from creating a blog to attracting more readers to setting up RSS newsfeeds. Learn techniques for adding audio and photo files to your blog. Review how search engines treat blogs and how you can use search engines to help more people find your blog. Then answer the following questions:

1. What are five ways to attract more readers to your blog?
2. Why are blogs good for marketing?
3. What is a newsfeed, and why is it a vital part of blogging?

Sharpening Your Career Skills Online

Bovée and Thill's Business Communication Web Search, at http://businesscommunicationblog.com/websearch, is a unique research tool designed specifically for business communication research. Use the Web Search function to find a website, video, PDF document, podcast, or PowerPoint presentation that offers advice on using social media in business. Write a brief e-mail message to your instructor, describing the item that you found and summarizing the career skills information you learned from it.

Improve Your Grammar, Mechanics, and Usage

The following exercises help you improve your knowledge of and power over English grammar, mechanics, and usage. Turn to the Handbook of Grammar, Mechanics, and Usage at the end of this book and review Section 1.6.1 (Prepositions), Section 1.6.2 (Conjunctions), and Section 1.6.3 (Articles and Interjections). Then look at the following 10 items. Circle the letter of the preferred choice in the following groups of sentences. (Answers to these exercises appear on page AK-3.)

1. **a.** The response was not only inappropriate but it was also rude.
   b. The response was not only inappropriate but also rude.
2. **a.** Be sure to look the spelling up in the dictionary.
   b. Be sure to look up the spelling in the dictionary.
3. **a.** We didn't get the contract because our proposal didn't comply with the request for proposal (RFP).
   b. We didn't get the contract because our proposal didn't comply to the RFP.
4. **a.** Marissa should of known not to send that e-mail to the CEO.
   b. Marissa should have known not to send that e-mail to the CEO.
5. **a.** The Phalanx 1000 has been favorably compared to the Mac iBook.
   b. The Phalanx 1000 has been favorably compared with the Mac iBook.
6. **a.** What are you looking for?
   b. For what are you looking?
7. **a.** Have you filed an SEC application?
   b. Have you filed a SEC application?
8. **a.** The project turned out neither to be easy nor simple.
   b. The project turned out to be neither easy nor simple.
9. **a.** If you hire me, you will not regret your decision!
   b. If you hire me, you will not regret your decision.
10. **a.** This is truly an historic event.
    b. This is truly a historic event.

For additional exercises focusing on conjunctions, articles, and prepositions, visit mybcommlab. Click on Chapter 7, click on "Additional Exercises to Improve Your Grammar, Mechanics, and Usage," and click on "11. Conjunctions, articles, and interjections."

CASES

Applying the Three-Step Writing Process to Cases

Apply each step to the following cases, as assigned by your instructor.

1 Plan →	2 Write →	3 Complete
Analyze the Situation Identify both your general purpose and your specific purpose. Clarify exactly what you want your audience to think, feel, or believe after receiving your message. Profile your primary audience, including their backgrounds, differences, similarities, and likely reactions to your message. **Gather Information** Identify the information your audience will need to receive, as well as other information you may need in order to craft an effective message. Select the right medium. The medium is identified for each case here, but when on the job, make sure your medium is both acceptable to the audience and appropriate for the message. **Organize the Information** Define your main idea, limit your scope, choose a direct or indirect approach, and outline necessary support points and other evidence.	**Adapt to Your Audience** Show sensitivity to audience needs with a "you"attitude, politeness, positive emphasis, and bias-free language. Understand how much credibility you already have—and how much you may need to establish. Project your company's image by maintaining an appropriate style and tone. Consider cultural variations and the differing needs of internal and external audiences. **Compose the Message** For written messages, draft your message using clear but sensitive words, effective sentences, and coherent paragraphs. For podcasts, outline your message and draft speaking notes to ensure smooth recording; use plenty of previews, transitions, and review to help audiences follow along.	**Revise the Message** Evaluate content and review readability, then edit and rewrite for conciseness and clarity. **Produce the Message** For written messages, use effective design elements and suitable layout for a clean, professional appearance. For podcasts, record your messages using whatever equipment you have available (professional podcasts may require upgraded equipment). **Proofread the Message** Review for errors in layout, spelling, and mechanics. Listen to podcasts to check for recording problems. **Distribute the Message** Deliver your message using the chosen medium; make sure all documents and all relevant files are distributed successfully.

BLOGGING SKILLS

1. Come on to Comic-Con: Explaining the benefits of attending. Comic-Con International is an annual convention that highlights a wide variety of pop culture and entertainment media, from comic books and collectibles to video games and movies. From its early start as a comic book convention that attracted several hundred fans and publishing industry insiders, Comic-Con has become a major international event with more than 100,000 attendees.

Your task: Several readers of your pop culture blog have been asking for your recommendation about visiting Comic-Con in San Diego next summer. Write a two- or three-paragraph post for your blog that explains what Comic-Con is and what visitors can expect to experience at the convention. Be sure to address your post to fans, not industry insiders. You can learn more at www.comic-con.org.[38]

E-MAIL SKILLS

2. Keeping the fans happy: Analyzing advertising on ESPN.com. ESPN leads the pack both online and off. Its well-known cable television sports channels are staple fare for sports enthusiasts, and ESPN.com (**http://espn.go.com**) is the leader in sports websites, too. Advertisers flock to ESPN.com because it delivers millions of visitors in the prime 18- to 34-year-old demographic group. With a continually refreshed offering of sporting news, columnists, video replays, and fantasy leagues (online competitions in which participants choose players for their teams, and the outcome is based on how well the real players do in actual live competition), ESPN.com has become one of the major advertising venues on the web.

As an up-and-coming web producer for ESPN.com, you're concerned about the rumblings of discontent you've heard from friends and read in various blogs and other sources. ESPN.com remains popular with millions of sports fans, but some say they are getting tired of all the ads—both ads on the site itself and pop-up ads. A few say they are switching to other websites that have fewer advertising intrusions. Your site traffic numbers are holding fairly steady for now, but you're worried that the few visitors leaving ESPN.com might be the start of a significant exodus in the future.

Your task: Write an e-mail message to your manager, expressing your concern about the amount of advertising content on ESPN.com. Acknowledge that advertising is a vital source of revenue, but share what you've learned about site visitors who claim to be migrating to other sites. Offer to lead a comprehensive review effort to compare the advertising presence on ESPN.com with that of other sports websites and explore ways to maintain strong advertising sales without alienating readers.[39]

E-MAIL SKILLS

3. Clothes for real women: Changing the look at La Maison Simons. The physical difference between the women who model clothes and women who buy them has long been a point of contention for shoppers—and a point of concern for health advocates who say that top fashion models have become too thin in recent years. Not only is the super-thin look unhealthy for the models, but critics say it encourages eating disorders among girls and women who aspire to look like them.

Some industry insiders admit that the images portrayed in fashion advertising are often unrealistic. Designer and television host Tim Gunn says the problem starts with an unrealistic assumption in the illustration stage, when designers are sketching new clothes. "The way in which we illustrate [a model's body] is seven heads high, which isn't normal. We're always striving to have the same look of the illustration on the runway, and it's impossible. You have a few—forgive me—freaky people who can approximate that size and shape, but this look is not part of the real world."

Models weren't always much thinner than the general population, and the pendulum seems to be swinging back toward more normal body types—at least slightly. In the summer of 2008, La Maison Simons, a Canadian retailer, pulled its back-to-school catalog following complaints that its models were too thin; the company replaced the catalog and issued an apology. Ken Downing, fashion director at the upscale American retailer Neiman-Marcus, explains, "Any retailer has to consider [its] customer and who [it's] trying to appeal to. There are models of all shapes and sizes, and the people who do the advertising and marketing really have to be conscious that they're portraying healthy, beautiful women of many ages and many colors from many backgrounds."[40]

Your task: Imagine that you're the director of catalog operations at La Maison Simons, and you want to make sure that the embarrassing episode with the summer 2008 catalog isn't repeated. Write a brief e-mail to the catalog staff, outlining the company's new policy of using only models with healthy body mass indexes. (Make up any information you need to draft the message.) You can visit the company's website, at www.simons.ca, to learn more about its products, and you can research body mass index at a variety of health-related websites.

E-MAIL SKILLS

4. There must be an opportunity in here somewhere: The growing market of women living without husbands. For the first time in history (aside from special situations such as major wars), more than half—51 percent—of all U.S. adult women now live without a spouse. (In other words, they live alone, with roommates, or as part of an unmarried couple.) Twenty-five percent have never married, and 26 percent are divorced, widowed, or married but living apart from their spouses. In the 1950s and into the 1960s, only 40 percent of women lived without a spouse, but every decade since, the percentage has increased. In your work as a consumer trend specialist for Seymour Powell (www.seymourpowell.com), a product design firm based in London that specializes in the home, personal, leisure, and transportation sectors, it's your business to recognize and respond to demographic shifts such as this.

Your task: With a small team of classmates, brainstorm possible product opportunities that respond to this trend. In an e-mail message to be sent to the management team at Seymour Powell, list your ideas for new or modified products that might sell well in a society in which more than half of all adult women live without a spouse. For each idea, provide a one-sentence explanation of why you think the product has potential.[41]

E-MAIL SKILLS PORTFOLIO BUILDER

5. A jolt of encouragement: The Chevy Volt is on the way. The "Big Three" U.S. automakers—GM, Chrysler, and Ford—haven't had much good news to share lately. GM, in particular, has been going through a rough time, entering bankruptcy, shedding assets, and relying on bailouts from the U.S. and Canadian governments to stay in business. The news isn't entirely bleak, however. Chevrolet, one of the brands in the GM automotive stable, is about to introduce the Volt, a gas/electric hybrid that might finally give drivers a viable alternative to the wildly popular Toyota Prius.

Your task: Write an e-mail to be sent to all Chevy dealers in North America, briefly describing the new Volt and the benefits it offers car owners. You can learn more about the Volt at Chevy's website, www.chevrolet.com.

BLOGGING SKILLS

6. Legitimate and legal: Defending technology sales to Chinese police agencies. Cisco, a leading manufacturer of computer networking equipment, is one of several technology companies that have been criticized recently for selling high-tech equipment to police agencies in China. After the Chinese government killed hundreds of protestors in Tiananmen Square in 1989, U.S. officials began restricting the export of products that could be used by Chinese security forces. The restrictions cover a range of low-tech devices, from helmets and handcuffs to fingerprint powder and teargas, but not certain high-tech products, such as the networking equipment that Cisco sells, which can conceivably be used by security forces in ways that violate human rights. Critics contend that by not restricting products such as Cisco's, the U.S. government is not enforcing the full intent of the restrictions. Moreover, they suggest that Cisco could be enabling abuse. For example, its Chinese marketing brochure promotes the equipment's ability to "strengthen police control."

Your task: Write a brief post for the Cisco executive blog that explains the following points: The company rigorously follows all U.S. export regulations; the company's marketing efforts in China are consistent with the way it markets products to other police organizations throughout the world; the products are simply tools, and like all other tools, they can be applied in good or bad ways, and responsible application is the customer's responsibility, not Cisco's; if Cisco didn't sell this equipment to the Chinese government, another company from another country would.[42]

IM SKILLS

7. The very definition of confusion: Helping consumers sort out high-definition television. High-definition television can be a joy to watch-but, oh, what a pain to buy. The field is littered with competing technologies and arcane terminology that is meaningless to most consumers. Moreover, it's nearly impossible to define one technical term without invoking two or three others, leaving consumers swimming in an alphanumeric soup of confusion. The manufacturers themselves can't even agree on which of the *18* different digital TV formats truly qualify as "high definition." As a sales support manager for Crutchfield (www.crutchfield.com), a leading online retailer of audio and video systems, you understand the frustration buyers feel; your staff is deluged daily by their questions.

Your task: To help your staff respond quickly to consumers who ask questions via Crutchfield's online IM chat service, you are developing a set of "canned" responses to common questions. When a consumer asks one of these questions, a sales advisor can simply click on the ready-made answer. Start by writing concise, consumer-friendly definitions of the following terms: *resolution*, *HDTV*, *1080p*, and *HDMI*. Explore the Crutchfield Learning Center (visit www.crutchfield.com, click on "Learn" and then "Home Theater & Audio") to learn more about these terms. Answers.com and CNET.com are two other handy sources.[43]

PODCASTING SKILLS PORTFOLIO BUILDER

8. Based on my experience: Recommending your college or university. With any purchase decision, from a restaurant meal to a college education, recommendations from satisfied customers are often the strongest promotional messages.

Your task: Write a script for a one- to two-minute podcast (roughly 150 to 250 words), explaining why your college or university is a good place to get an education. Your audience is high school juniors and seniors. You can choose to craft a general message, something that would be useful to all prospective students, or you can focus on a specific academic discipline, the athletic program, or some other important aspect of your college experience. Either way, make sure your introductory comments make it clear whether you are offering a general recommendation or a specific recommendation. If your instructor asks you to do so, record the podcast and submit the file electronically.

PODCASTING SKILLS

9. Based on my experience: Suggestions for improving your college or university. Every organization, no matter how successfully it operates, can find ways to improve its customer service.

Your task: Write a script for a one- to two-minute podcast (roughly 150 to 250 words), identifying at least one way in which your college experience could have been or still could be improved through specific changes in policies, programs, facilities, or other elements. Your audience is the school's administration. Offer constructive criticism and specific arguments about why your suggestions would help you—and possibly other students as well. Be sure to focus on meaningful and practical opportunities for improvement. If your instructor asks you to do so, record the podcast and submit the file electronically.

BLOGGING SKILLS

10. Look sharp: Travel safety tips for new employees. As the travel director for a global management consulting firm, your responsibilities range from finding the best travel deals to helping new employees learn the ins and outs of low-risk, low-stress travels. One of the ways in which you dispense helpful advice is through an internal blog.

Your task: Research advice for safe travel and identify at least six tips that every employee in your company should know. Write a brief blog post that introduces and identifies the six tips.

E-MAIL SKILLS

11. Your work does matter: Encouraging an unhappy colleague. You certainly appreciate your company's "virtual team" policy of letting employees live wherever they want and using technology to communicate and collaborate. The company is headquartered in a large urban area, but you get to live in the mountains, only a step or two away from some of the best fly fishing in the world. Most of the time, this approach to work couldn't get any better.

However, the lack of face-to-face contact with your colleagues definitely has disadvantages. For example, when a teammate seems to be upset about something, you wish you could go for a walk with the person and talk it out rather than rely on phone calls, e-mail, or IM. In the past couple of weeks, Chris Grogan, the graphic designer working with you on a new e-commerce website project, seems to be complaining about everything. His negative attitude is starting to wear down the team's enthusiasm at a critical point in the project. In particular, he has complained several times that no one on the team seems to care about his design work. It is rarely mentioned in team teleconferences, and no one asks him about it. That part is true, actually, but the reason is that there is nothing wrong with his work—some critical technical issues unrelated to the graphic design are consuming everyone's attention.

Your task: After a couple of unsuccessful attempts at encouraging Grogan over the phone, you decide to write a brief e-mail message to assure him of the importance of his work on this project and the quality of his efforts. Let him know that graphic design is a critical part of the project's success and that as soon as those technical issues are resolved and the project is completed, everyone will have a chance to appreciate his contribution to the project. Make up whatever details you need to craft your message.

E-MAIL SKILLS

12. She's one of us: Promoting a new lifestyle magazine. Consumers looking for beauty, health, and lifestyle magazines have an almost endless array of choices, but even in this crowded field, Logan Olson found her own niche. Olson, who was born with congenital heart disease, suffered a heart attack at age 16 that left her in a coma and caused serious brain damage. The active and outgoing teen had to relearn everything from sitting up to feeding herself. As she recovered, she looked for help and advice in conquering such daily challenges as finding fashionable clothes that were easier to put on and makeup that was easier to apply. Mainstream beauty magazines didn't seem to offer any information for young women with disabilities, so she started her own magazine. Oprah Winfrey has *Oprah*, and now Logan Olson has *Logan*. The magazine not only gives young women tips on buying and using a variety of products but lets women with disabilities know there are others like them, facing and meeting the same challenges.

Your task: Write a promotional e-mail message to be sent to young women with disabilities as well as families and friends who might like to give gift subscriptions, promoting the benefits of subscribing to *Logan*. You can learn more about *Logan* at **www.loganmagazine.com**.[44]

E-MAIL SKILLS PORTFOLIO BUILDER

13. We're the one: Explaining why a company should hire your firm. You work for Brainbench (**www.brainbench.com**), one of many companies that offer employee screening services. Brainbench's offerings include a variety of online products and consulting services, all designed to help employers find and develop the best possible employees. For example, Brainbench's Pre-Hire Testing products help employers test for job skills, communication skills, personality, and employment history red flags (such as chronic absenteeism or performance problems). Employers use these test results to either screen out candidates entirely or ask focused interview questions about areas of concern.

Sonja Williamson, the human resources director of a large retail company, has just e-mailed your sales team. She would like an overview of the Pre-Hire Testing products and some background on your company.

Your task: Write an e-mail response to Williamson's query. Be sure to thank her for her interest, briefly describe the Pre-Hire Testing products, and summarize Brainbench's qualifications. Include at least one hyperlink to the Brainbench website and consider attaching one or more PDF files from the website as well.

E-MAIL SKILLS

14. Firing the customer: When a particular customer is always wrong. Many companies operate on the principle that the customer is always right, even when the customer *isn't* right. They take any steps necessary to ensure happy customers, lots of repeat sales, and a positive reputation among potential buyers. Overall, this is a smart and successful approach to business. However, most companies eventually encounter a nightmare customer who drains so much time, energy, and profit that the only sensible option is to refuse the customer's business. For example, the nightmare customer might be someone who constantly berates you and your employees, repeatedly makes outlandish demands for refunds and discounts, or simply requires so much help that you not only lose money on this person but also no longer have enough time to help your other customers. "Firing" a customer is an unpleasant step that should be taken only in the most extreme cases and only after other remedies have been attempted (such as talking with the customer about the problem), but it is sometimes necessary for the well-being of your employees and your company.

Your task: If you are currently working or have held a job in the recent past, imagine that you've encountered just such a customer. If you don't have job experience to call on, imagine that you work in a retail location somewhere around campus or in your neighborhood. Identify the type of behavior this imaginary customer exhibits and the reasons the behavior can no longer be accepted. Write a brief e-mail message to the customer to explain that you will no longer be able to accommodate him or her as a customer. Calmly explain why you have had to reach this difficult decision. Maintain a professional tone and keep your emotions in check.

PODCASTING SKILLS

15. Podcasting pitch: Training people to sell your favorite product. What product do you own (or use regularly) that you can't live without? It could be something as seemingly minor as a favorite pen or something as significant as a medical device that you literally can't live without. Now imagine you're a salesperson for this product; think about how you would sell it to potential buyers. How would you describe it and how would you explain the benefits of owning it? After you've thought about how you would present the product to others, imagine that you've been promoted to sales manager, and it is your job to train other people to sell the product.

Your task: Write the script for a brief podcast (200 to 300 words) that summarizes for your sales staff the most important points to convey about the product. Imagine that they'll listen to your podcast while driving to a customer's location or preparing for the day's activity in a retail store (depending on the nature of the product). Be sure to give your staffers a concise overview message about the product and several key support points.

BLOGGING SKILLS

16. Everybody's doing it, and maybe it's not so bad: Dispelling some misconceptions about teenagers and video games. The fact that 97 percent of American youth ages 12 to 17 play video games is not much of a surprise, but more than a few nongaming adults might be surprised to learn that game playing might not be quite the social and civic catastrophe it is sometimes made out to be. A recent study by the Pew Internet & American Life Project puts a least a few cracks in the stereotyped image of gamers being loners who live out violent fantasies while learning few if any skills that could make them positive members of society.[45]

Your task: Imagine that you're on the public relations staff at the Entertainment Software Association (ESA), an industry group that represents the interests of video game companies. You'd like to share the results of the Pew survey with parents to help ease their concerns. Visit **http://real-timeupdates.com/bct**, click on "Student Assignments," Chapter 7, and then Case 18. Download this PDF file, which is a summary of the Pew results. Find at least three positive aspects of video game playing and write a brief message that could be posted on an ESA public affairs blog.

E-MAIL SKILLS PORTFOLIO BUILDER

17. Safe at any angle: Explaining the benefits of side-impact safety features. One-quarter of all motor vehicle accidents that involve children under age 12 are side-impact crashes—and these crashes result in higher rates of injuries and fatalities than those with front or rear impacts.[46]

Your task: You work in the consumer information department at Britax, a leading manufacturer of car seats. Your manager has asked you to prepare an e-mail message that can be sent out whenever parents request information about side-impact crashes and the safety features of Britax seats. Start by research side-impact crashes at www.britaxusa.com (click on "Safety Center" and then "Side Impact Protection Revealed"). Write a three-paragraph message that explains the seriousness of side-impact crashes, describes how injuries and fatalities can be minimized in these crashes, and describes how Britax's car seats are designed to help protect children in side-impact crashes.

MICROBLOGGING SKILLS

18. Airfare auction: Alerting JetBlue's Twitter fans about fare auctions on eBay. JetBlue is known for its innovations in customer service and customer communication, including its pioneering use of the Twitter microblogging system. Thousands of JetBlue fans and customers follow the company on Twitter to get updates on flight status during weather disruptions, facility upgrades, and other news.[47]

Your task: Write a Twitter update that announces the limited-time availability of flights and travel packages (flights plus hotel rooms, for example) at JetBlue's store on eBay. The key selling point is that travelers may be able to purchase flights they want at steep discounts. Include the URL http://jetblue.com/ebay. The URL takes up 24 characters, so you have a maximum of 116 characters for the rest of your message, including spaces. (The limit for Twitter updates is 140 characters.)

PODCASTING SKILLS

19. Why me? Introducing yourself to a potential employer. While writing the many letters and e-mail messages that are part of the job search process, you find yourself wishing that you could just talk to some of these companies so your personality could shine through. Well, you've just gotten that opportunity. One of the companies that you've applied to has e-mailed you back, asking you to submit a two-minute podcast, introducing yourself and explaining why you would be a good person to hire.

Your task: Identify a company that you'd like to work for after graduation and select a job that would be a good match for your skills and interests. Write a script for a two-minute podcast (roughly 250 words). Introduce yourself and the position you're applying for, describe your background, and explain why you think you're a good candidate for the job. Make up any details you need. If your instructor asks you to do so, record the podcast and submit the file.

SOCIAL NETWORKING SKILLS

20. "Hi, my name is . . .": Introducing yourself on a business network. Business networking websites such as www.linkedin.com, www.ryze.com, and www.spoke.com have become popular places for professionals to make connections that would be difficult or impossible to make without the Internet. You might be familiar with MySpace.com or Friendster.com, sites that help individuals meet through networks of people they already know and trust. These business-oriented sites follow the same principle, but instead of using them to find new friends or dates, you use them to find new customers, new suppliers, or other important business connections. For instance, you might find that the ideal contact person in a company you'd like to do business with is the aunt of your boss's tennis partner.

An important aspect of business networking is being able to provide a clear description of your professional background and interests. For example, a manufacturing consultant can list the industries in which she has experience, the types of projects she has worked on, and the nature of work she'd like to pursue in the future (such as a full-time position for a company or additional independent projects).

Your task: Write a brief statement, introducing yourself, including your educational background, your job history, and the types of connections you'd like to make. Feel free to "fast forward" to your graduation and list your degree, the business specialty you plan to pursue, and any relevant experience. If you have business experience already, feel free to use that information instead. Make sure your statement is clear, concise (no more than two sentences), and compelling so that anyone looking for someone like you would want to get in touch with you after reading your introduction.

8 Writing Routine and Positive Messages

Learning Objectives
After studying this chapter, you will be able to

1. Apply the three-step writing process to routine and positive messages
2. Outline an effective strategy for writing routine requests
3. Explain how to ask for specific action in a courteous manner
4. Describe a strategy for writing routine replies and positive messages
5. Discuss the importance of knowing who is responsible when granting claims and requests for adjustment
6. Describe the importance of goodwill messages, and explain how to make them effective

On the Job: Communicating at Get Satisfaction

Co-founder Thor Muller helped Get Satisfaction create a new way for companies and their customers to exchange routine messages.

Applying Business Communication 2.0 Concepts to Customer Support

For about as long as online communication has been possible, frustrated customers have been going online to complain about faulty products, confusing instructions, and poor service. When Web 2.0 tools hit the scene a few years ago, giving even nontechnical consumers a ready voice, the stream of "I need help!" messages turned into a full-time flood. On product review and shopping websites, enthusiast blogs, and various "complaint sites," consumers can vent their frustrations and ask for help when they feel they aren't getting satisfaction from the companies with which they do business.

These various websites can occasionally provide answers, but they suffer from four fundamental drawbacks. First, they are randomly scattered all over the web, so many consumers are never quite sure where to look for help. Second, the right experts from the right companies often aren't involved, meaning that customers often have to rely on each other—which sometimes works but sometimes doesn't. Third, even companies that make a valiant effort to keep their customers satisfied know that everyone can benefit if customers can share ideas, learn from one another, and participate in ongoing conversation. Fourth, companies often find that multiple customers have the same routine questions, but communicating with every customer individually can be time-consuming and expensive.

The San Francisco–based startup Get Satisfaction is working to address all these issues. Founder Thor Muller explains that the company is "creating a kind of social network designed for companies and customers to communicate with each other." Consumers can post questions or complaints and request e-mail notification whenever a response is posted. If someone else has already posted the same complaint, all a visitor needs to do is ask to be notified when the issue is resolved, saving time for the people asking and answering questions. Consumers can also suggest ideas for new products and services or improvements to existing offerings.

On the other side of the relationship, employees from companies that sell products and services can register as official representatives to answer questions, solve problems, and solicit feedback. As both knowledgeable consumers and company representatives provide answers and solutions, the responses voted most useful rise to the top, ensuring that visitors always get the most helpful information available. Companies can also put a *widget* on their websites to direct customer service inquiries to the Get Satisfaction site or replicate the Get Satisfaction capabilities right on their own websites. Plus, the Overheard feature lets companies monitor Twitter conversations about their products, so they can stay tuned in to complaints, questions, and compliments. As Muller explains, "When customers start to converge and talk, for many companies this is gold—real engagement with current or future customers."[1]

http://getsatisfaction.com

USING THE THREE-STEP WRITING PROCESS FOR ROUTINE AND POSITIVE MESSAGES

1 LEARNING OBJECTIVE

Apply the three-step writing process to routine and positive messages.

Get Satisfaction's Thor Muller (profiled in the chapter-opening "On the Job" vignette) knows that much of the vital communication between a company and its customers is about routine matters, from product operation hints and technical support to refunds and ordering glitches. Whether you're writing these messages in a Web 2.0 environment such as Get Satisfaction's website or using more conventional tools, the three-step writing process gives you a great way to produce these messages effectively and efficiently.

Step 1: Planning a Routine or Positive Message

Even simple, routine messages can benefit from thoughtful planning.

Even though planning routine and positive messages may take only a few minutes, the four tasks of planning still apply. First, analyze the situation, making sure that your purpose is clear and that you know enough about your audience to craft a successful message. Second, gather the information your audience needs to know. Third, select the right medium for the message, the audience, and the particular situation at hand. Fourth, organize your information effectively. Throughout this chapter, you'll learn more about performing all four of these tasks for a variety of routine and positive message types.

Step 2: Writing a Routine or Positive Message

With all messages, you need to adapt to your audience by being sensitive to their needs: Maintain the "you" attitude, be polite, emphasize the positive, and use bias-free language. To strengthen your relationship with your audience, establish your credibility and project your company's image. And keep in mind that even if you normally use a conversational tone, some messages need to be more formal than others. Finally, use plain English and try to use the active voice as much as possible.

With some practice, you'll be able to compose most routine messages quickly. Your main idea is probably well defined already; just be sure you stick to it by limiting the scope of your message (see Figure 8.1 on the next page).

For routine requests and positive messages
- *Open by stating the request or main idea*
- *Give necessary details in the body*
- *Close with a cordial request for specific action*

In most cases, your readers will be interested or at least neutral, so you can usually adopt the direct approach for routine and positive messages: Open with a clear statement of the main idea, include all necessary details in the body, and then close cordially. Keep in mind that even though these messages are the least complicated to write, communicating across cultural boundaries can be challenging, especially if you're not familiar with the cultural differences involved.

FIGURE 8.1 Routine Messages
Routine and positive messages are best conveyed using a direct approach. Google uses this blog to keep users of its AdWords search engine advertising system up to date on maintenance interruptions and other important news.

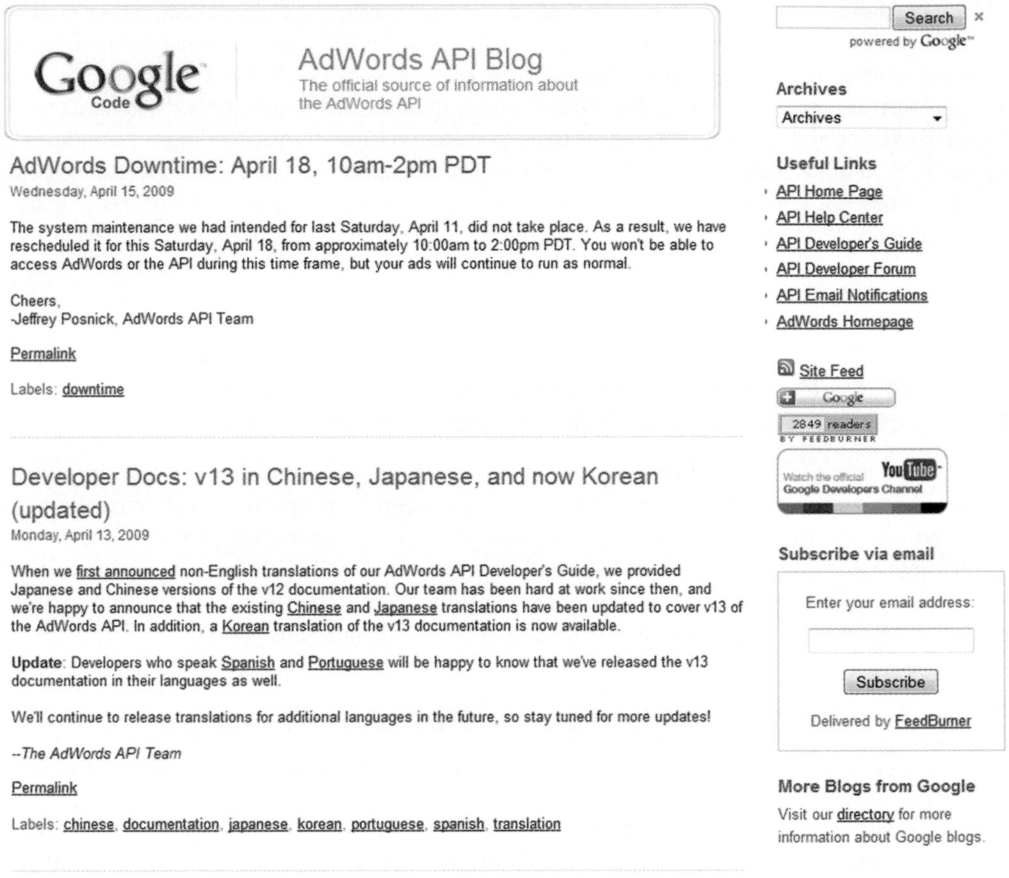
Google Code

AdWords API Blog
The official source of information about the AdWords API

AdWords Downtime: April 18, 10am-2pm PDT
Wednesday, April 15, 2009

The system maintenance we had intended for last Saturday, April 11, did not take place. As a result, we have rescheduled it for this Saturday, April 18, from approximately 10:00am to 2:00pm PDT. You won't be able to access AdWords or the API during this time frame, but your ads will continue to run as normal.

Cheers,
-Jeffrey Posnick, AdWords API Team

Permalink

Labels: downtime

Developer Docs: v13 in Chinese, Japanese, and now Korean (updated)
Monday, April 13, 2009

When we first announced non-English translations of our AdWords API Developer's Guide, we provided Japanese and Chinese versions of the v12 documentation. Our team has been hard at work since then, and we're happy to announce that the existing Chinese and Japanese translations have been updated to cover v13 of the AdWords API. In addition, a Korean translation of the v13 documentation is now available.

Update: Developers who speak Spanish and Portuguese will be happy to know that we've released the v13 documentation in their languages as well.

We'll continue to release translations for additional languages in the future, so stay tuned for more updates!

--The AdWords API Team

Permalink

Labels: chinese, documentation, japanese, korean, portuguese, spanish, translation

Search
powered by Google

Archives
Archives

Useful Links
- API Home Page
- API Help Center
- API Developer's Guide
- API Developer Forum
- API Email Notifications
- AdWords Homepage

Site Feed
Google
2849 readers BY FEEDBURNER

Watch the official Google Developers Channel YouTube

Subscribe via email
Enter your email address:
Subscribe
Delivered by FeedBurner

More Blogs from Google
Visit our directory for more information about Google blogs.

Step 3: Completing a Routine or Positive Message

No matter how brief or straightforward your message, maximize its impact by giving yourself plenty of time to revise, produce, proofread, and distribute it. First, revise your message by evaluating content and organization to make sure you've said what you want to in the order you want to say it. Review your message's readability. Edit and rewrite to make it concise and clear. Second, design your document to suit your purpose and your audience. Even simple messages can benefit from careful font selection, the wise use of white space, and other design choices. Next, proofread the final version of your message, looking for typos, errors in spelling and mechanics, alignment problems, poor print quality, and so on. Finally, choose a distribution method that balances cost, convenience, time, security, and privacy. Refer to Chapter 7 for the most common media formats for brief messages.

MAKING ROUTINE REQUESTS

Making requests—for information, action, products, adjustments, or other matters—is a routine part of business. In most cases, your audience will be prepared to comply, as long as you're not being unreasonable or asking people to do something they would expect you to do yourself. By applying a clear strategy and tailoring your approach to each situation, you'll be able to generate effective requests quickly.

Strategy for Routine Requests

2 LEARNING OBJECTIVE

Outline an effective strategy for writing routine requests.

Like all other business messages, a routine request has three parts: an opening, a body, and a close. Using the direct approach, open with your main idea, which is a clear statement of your request. Use the body to give details and justify your request. Finally, close by requesting specific action.

Stating Your Request Up Front

Take care that your direct approach doesn't come across as abrupt or tactless.

Begin routine requests by placing your initial request first; up front is where it stands out and gets the most attention. Of course, getting right to the point should not be interpreted as license to be abrupt or tactless:

- **Pay attention to tone.** Even though you expect a favorable response, the tone of your initial request is important. Instead of demanding action ("Send me the latest personnel cost data"), soften your request with words such as *please* and *I would appreciate.*
- **Assume that your audience will comply.** An impatient demand for rapid service isn't necessary. You can generally assume that your readers will comply with your request when they clearly understand the reason for it.
- **Be specific.** State precisely what you want. For example, if you request the latest market data from your research department, be sure to say whether you want a brief summary or 100 pages of raw data.

Explaining and Justifying Your Request

Use the body of your message to explain your request. Make the explanation a smooth and logical outgrowth of your opening remarks. If possible, point out how complying with the request could benefit the reader. For instance, if you would like some assistance interpreting complex quality-control data, you might point out how a better understanding of quality-control issues would improve customer satisfaction and ultimately lead to higher profits for the entire company.

Using a list format helps readers sort through multiple questions or requests.

Whether you're writing a formal letter or a simple instant message, you can use the body of your request to list a series of questions. This list of questions helps organize your message and helps your audience identify the information you need. Just keep in mind a few basics:

- **Ask the most important questions first.** If cost is your main concern, you might begin with a question such as "What is the cost for shipping the merchandise by air versus truck?" Then you might want to ask more specific but related questions about, say, discounts for paying early.
- **Ask only relevant questions.** To help expedite the response to your request, ask only questions that are central to your main request. Doing so will generate an answer sooner and make better use of the other person's time.
- **Deal with only one topic per question.** If you have an unusual or complex request, break it down into specific, individual questions so that the reader can address each one separately. Don't put the burden of untangling a complicated request on your reader. This consideration not only shows respect for your audience's time but also gets you a more accurate answer in less time.

3 LEARNING OBJECTIVE

Explain how to ask for specific action in a courteous manner.

Requesting Specific Action in a Courteous Close

Close request messages with
- *A request for some specific action*
- *Information about how you can be reached*
- *An expression of appreciation*

Close your message with three important elements: (1) a specific request, (2) information about how you can be reached (if it isn't obvious), and (3) an expression of appreciation or goodwill. When you ask readers to perform a specific action, ask that they respond by a specific time, if appropriate (for example, "Please send the figures by May 5 so that I can return first-quarter results to you before the May 20 conference"). Plus, by including your phone number, e-mail address, office hours, and other contact information, you help your readers respond easily.

CHECKLIST: Writing Routine Requests

A. State your request up front.
- Write in a polite, undemanding, personal tone.
- Use the direct approach because your audience will probably respond favorably to your request.
- Be specific and precise in your request.

B. Explain and justify your request.
- Justify the request or explain its importance.
- Explain any potential benefits of responding.
- Ask the most important questions first.
- Break complex requests into individual questions that are limited to only one topic each.

C. Request specific action in a courteous close.
- Make it easy to comply by including appropriate contact information.
- Express your gratitude.
- Clearly state any important deadlines for the request.

Conclude your message by sincerely expressing your goodwill and appreciation. However, don't thank the reader "in advance" for cooperating. If the reader's reply warrants a word of thanks, send it after you've received the reply. To review, see "Checklist: Writing Routine Requests."

Common Examples of Routine Requests

Many of the routine messages you'll be writing will likely fall into a few main categories: asking for information and action, asking for recommendations, and making claims and requesting adjustments.

Asking for Information and Action

When you need to know about something, elicit an opinion from someone, or request a simple action, you usually need only ask. In essence, simple requests say

- What you want to know or what you want readers to do
- Why you're making the request
- Why it may be in your readers' interest to help you

For simple, straightforward requests for information or action, use the direct approach.

If your reader is able to do what you want, such a straightforward request gets the job done quickly. Use the direct approach by opening with a clear statement of your reason for writing. In the body, provide whatever explanation is needed to justify your request. Then close with a specific description of what you expect and include a deadline, if appropriate (see Figure 8.2). In some situations, readers might be unwilling to respond unless they understand how the request benefits them, so be sure to include this information in your explanation. You can assume some shared background when communicating about a routine matter to someone in the same company. In contrast to requests sent internally, those sent to people outside the organization usually adopt a more formal tone.

Asking for Recommendations

Always ask for permission before using someone as a reference.

The need to inquire about people arises often in business. For example, before extending credit or awarding contracts, jobs, promotions, or scholarships, companies often ask applicants to supply references. Companies ask applicants to list references who can vouch for their ability, skills, integrity, character, and fitness for the job. Before you volunteer someone's name as a reference, ask permission to do so. Some people don't want you to use their names, perhaps because they don't know enough about you to feel comfortable writing a letter or because they or their employers have a policy of not providing recommendations.

FIGURE 8.2 Effective Message Requesting Action

In this e-mail request to district managers across the country, Helene Clausen asks them to fill out an attached information collection form. Although the request is not unusual and responding to it is part of the managers' responsibility, Clausen asks for their help in a courteous manner and points out the benefits of responding.

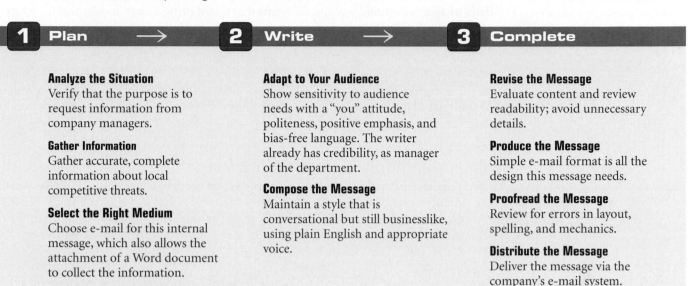

1 Plan →

Analyze the Situation
Verify that the purpose is to request information from company managers.

Gather Information
Gather accurate, complete information about local competitive threats.

Select the Right Medium
Choose e-mail for this internal message, which also allows the attachment of a Word document to collect the information.

Organize the Information
Clarify that the main idea is collecting information that will lead to a better competitive strategy, which will in turn help the various district managers.

2 Write →

Adapt to Your Audience
Show sensitivity to audience needs with a "you" attitude, politeness, positive emphasis, and bias-free language. The writer already has credibility, as manager of the department.

Compose the Message
Maintain a style that is conversational but still businesslike, using plain English and appropriate voice.

3 Complete

Revise the Message
Evaluate content and review readability; avoid unnecessary details.

Produce the Message
Simple e-mail format is all the design this message needs.

Proofread the Message
Review for errors in layout, spelling, and mechanics.

Distribute the Message
Deliver the message via the company's e-mail system.

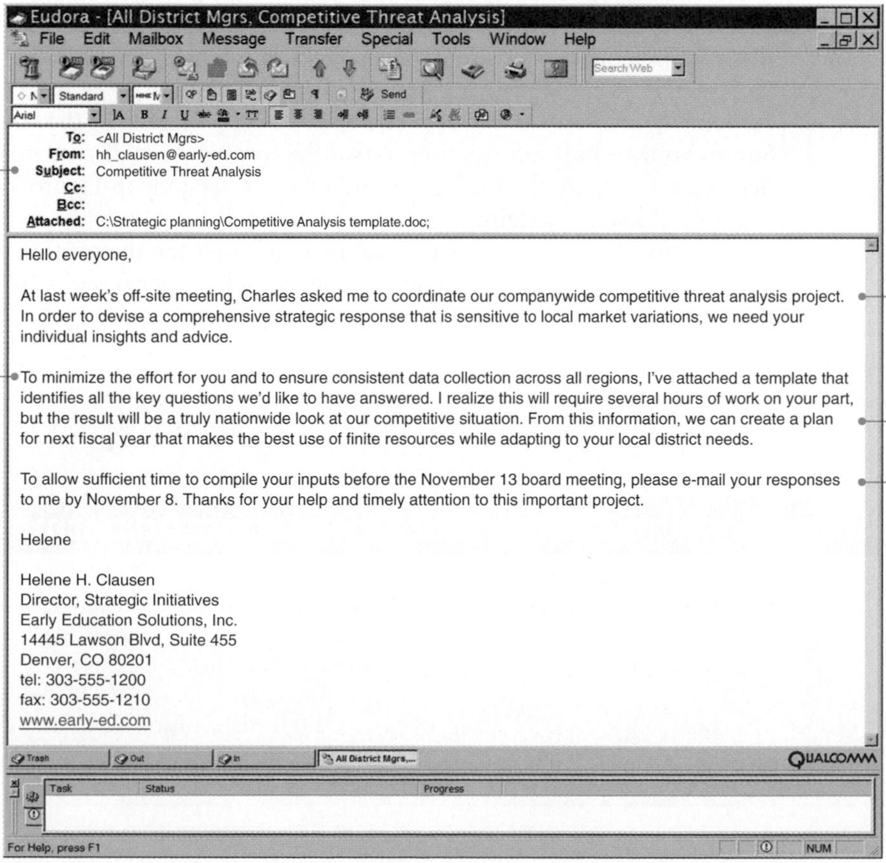

Eudora - [All District Mgrs, Competitive Threat Analysis]

To: <All District Mgrs>
From: hh_clausen@early-ed.com
Subject: Competitive Threat Analysis
Cc:
Bcc:
Attached: C:\Strategic planning\Competitive Analysis template.doc;

Hello everyone,

At last week's off-site meeting, Charles asked me to coordinate our companywide competitive threat analysis project. In order to devise a comprehensive strategic response that is sensitive to local market variations, we need your individual insights and advice.

To minimize the effort for you and to ensure consistent data collection across all regions, I've attached a template that identifies all the key questions we'd like to have answered. I realize this will require several hours of work on your part, but the result will be a truly nationwide look at our competitive situation. From this information, we can create a plan for next fiscal year that makes the best use of finite resources while adapting to your local district needs.

To allow sufficient time to compile your inputs before the November 13 board meeting, please e-mail your responses to me by November 8. Thanks for your help and timely attention to this important project.

Helene

Helene H. Clausen
Director, Strategic Initiatives
Early Education Solutions, Inc.
14445 Lawson Blvd, Suite 455
Denver, CO 80201
tel: 303-555-1200
fax: 303-555-1210
www.early-ed.com

Identifies the subject of the e-mail
Gets right to the point of the message
Acknowledges that responding to the request will require some work, but the result will benefit everyone
Explains the benefit of responding to the request
Provides a clear and meaningful deadline, then closes in a courteous manner

Refresh the memory of any potential reference you haven't been in touch with for a while.

Because requests for recommendations and references are routine, you can organize your inquiry using the direct approach. Open your message by clearly stating why the recommendation is required (if it's not for a job, be sure to explain what it is for) and that you would like your reader to write the letter. If you haven't had contact with the person for some time, use the opening to trigger the reader's memory of the relationship you had, the dates of association, and any special events that might bring a clear and favorable picture of you to mind. Consider including an updated résumé if you've had significant career advancement since your last contact.

Close your message with an expression of appreciation and the full name and address of the person to whom the letter should be sent. When asking for an immediate recommendation, you should also mention the deadline. Always be sure to enclose a stamped, preaddressed envelope as a convenience to the other party. Figure 8.3 provides an example of a request that follows these guidelines.

Making Claims and Requesting Adjustments

In claim letters

- *Explain the problem and give details*
- *Provide backup information*
- *Request specific action*

Be prepared to document your claim. Send copies and keep the original documents.

If you're dissatisfied with a company's product or service, you can opt to make a **claim** (a formal complaint) or request an **adjustment** (a settlement of a claim). In either case, it's important to maintain a professional tone in all your communication, no matter how angry or frustrated you are. Keeping your cool will help you get the situation resolved sooner.

In most cases, and especially in your first message, assume that a fair adjustment will be made and use a direct request. Open with a straightforward statement of the problem. In the body, give a complete, specific explanation of the details; provide any information an adjuster would need to verify your complaint. In your close, politely request specific action or convey a sincere desire to find a solution. And, if appropriate, suggest that the business relationship will continue if the problem is solved satisfactorily. Be prepared to back up your claim with invoices, sales receipts, canceled checks, dated correspondence, and any other relevant documents. Send copies and keep the originals for your files.

If the remedy is obvious, tell your reader exactly what you expect from the company, such as exchanging incorrectly shipped merchandise for the right item or issuing a refund if the item is out of stock. In some cases, you might ask the reader to resolve a problem. However, if you're uncertain about the precise nature of the trouble, you could ask the company to make an assessment and then advise you on how the situation could be fixed. Supply your contact information so that the company can discuss the situation with you, if necessary. Compare the ineffective and effective versions in Figure 8.4 on page 216 for an example of making a claim.

A rational, clear, and courteous approach is best for any routine request. To review the tasks involved in making claims and requesting adjustments, see "Checklist: Making Claims and Requesting Adjustments."

CHECKLIST: Making Claims and Requesting Adjustments

- Maintain a professional tone, even if you're extremely frustrated.
- Open with a straightforward statement of the problem.
- Provide specific details in the body.
- Present facts honestly and clearly.
- Politely summarize the desired action in the closing.
- Clearly state what you expect as a fair settlement or ask the reader to propose a fair adjustment.
- Explain the benefits of complying with the request, such as your continued patronage.

FIGURE 8.3 Effective Letter Requesting a Recommendation

This writer uses the direct approach when asking for a recommendation from a former professor. Note how she takes care to refresh the professor's memory because she took the class a year and a half ago. She also indicates the date by which the letter is needed and points to the enclosure of a stamped, preaddressed envelope.

1 Plan → 2 Write → 3 Complete

1 Plan

Analyze the Situation
Verify that the purpose is to request a recommendation letter from a college professor.

Gather Information
Gather information on classes and dates to help the reader recall you and to clarify the position you seek.

Select the Right Medium
The letter format gives this message an appropriate level of formality, although many professors prefer to be contacted by e-mail.

Organize the Information
Messages like this are common and expected, so a direct approach is fine.

2 Write

Adapt to Your Audience
Show sensitivity to audience needs with a "you" attitude, politeness, positive emphasis, and bias-free language.

Compose the Message
Style is respectful and businesslike, while still using plain English and appropriate voice.

3 Complete

Revise the Message
Evaluate content and review readability; avoid unnecessary details.

Produce the Message
Simple letter format is all the design this message needs.

Proofread the Message
Review for errors in layout, spelling, and mechanics.

Distribute the Message
Deliver the message via postal mail or e-mail if you have the professor's e-mail address.

1181 Ashport Drive
Tate Springs, TN 38101
March 14, 2010

Professor Lyndon Kenton
School of Business
University of Tennessee, Knoxville
Knoxville, TN 37916

Dear Professor Kenton:

I recently interviewed with Strategic Investments and have been called for a second interview for their Analyst Training Program (ATP). They have requested at least one recommendation from a professor, and I immediately thought of you. May I have a letter of recommendation from you?

[Opens by stating the purpose of the letter and making the request, assuming the reader will want to comply with the request]

As you may recall, I took BUS 485, Financial Analysis, from you in the fall of 2007. I enjoyed the class and finished the term with an "A." Professor Kenton, your comments on assertiveness and cold-calling impressed me beyond the scope of the actual course material. In fact, taking your course helped me decide on a future as a financial analyst.

[Includes information near the opening to refresh the reader's memory about this former student]

My enclosed résumé includes all my relevant work experience and volunteer activities. I would also like to add that I've handled the financial planning for our family since my father passed away several years ago. Although I initially learned by trial and error, I have increasingly applied my business training in deciding what stocks or bonds to trade. This, I believe, gives me a practical edge over others who may be applying for the same job.

[Refers to résumé in the body and mentions experience that could set applicant apart from other candidates]

If possible, Ms. Blackmon in Human Resources needs to receive your letter by March 30. For your convenience, I've enclosed a preaddressed, stamped envelope.

[Gives a deadline for response and includes information about the person expecting the recommendation]

[Mentions the pre-addressed, stamped envelope to encourage a timely response]

I appreciate your time and effort in writing this letter of recommendation for me. It will be great to put my education to work, and I'll keep you informed of my progress. Thank you for your consideration in this matter.

Sincerely,

Joanne Tucker

Joanne Tucker

Enclosure

FIGURE 8.4 Ineffective and Effective Versions of a Claim
Note the difference in tone and information content in these two versions. The ineffective version is emotional and unprofessional, whereas the effective version communicates calmly and clearly.

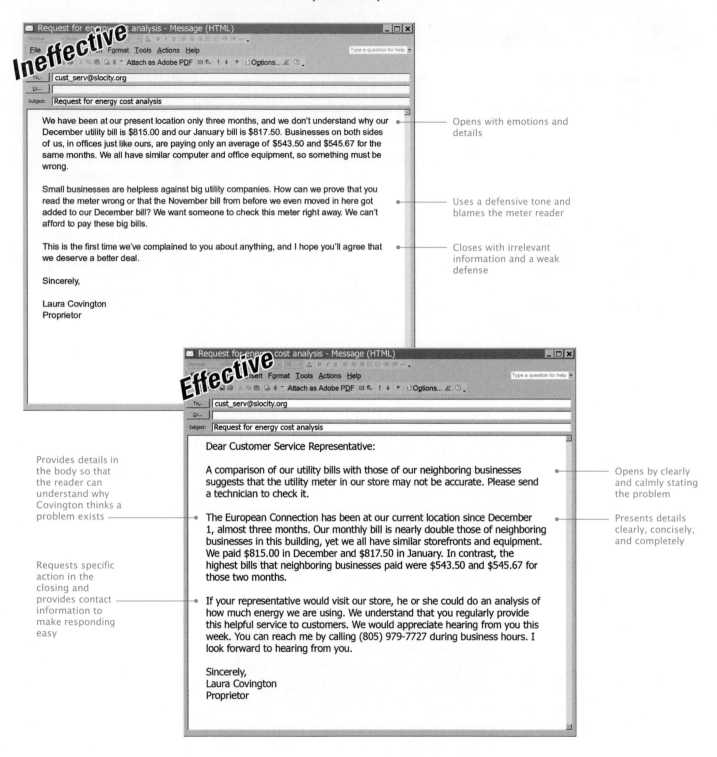

Ineffective

Request for energy cost analysis - Message (HTML)

To: cust_serv@slocity.org
Cc:
Subject: Request for energy cost analysis

We have been at our present location only three months, and we don't understand why our December utility bill is $815.00 and our January bill is $817.50. Businesses on both sides of us, in offices just like ours, are paying only an average of $543.50 and $545.67 for the same months. We all have similar computer and office equipment, so something must be wrong.

Opens with emotions and details

Small businesses are helpless against big utility companies. How can we prove that you read the meter wrong or that the November bill from before we even moved in here got added to our December bill? We want someone to check this meter right away. We can't afford to pay these big bills.

Uses a defensive tone and blames the meter reader

This is the first time we've complained to you about anything, and I hope you'll agree that we deserve a better deal.

Closes with irrelevant information and a weak defense

Sincerely,

Laura Covington
Proprietor

Effective

Request for energy cost analysis - Message (HTML)

To: cust_serv@slocity.org
Cc:
Subject: Request for energy cost analysis

Dear Customer Service Representative:

A comparison of our utility bills with those of our neighboring businesses suggests that the utility meter in our store may not be accurate. Please send a technician to check it.

Opens by clearly and calmly stating the problem

The European Connection has been at our current location since December 1, almost three months. Our monthly bill is nearly double those of neighboring businesses in this building, yet we all have similar storefronts and equipment. We paid $815.00 in December and $817.50 in January. In contrast, the highest bills that neighboring businesses paid were $543.50 and $545.67 for those two months.

Provides details in the body so that the reader can understand why Covington thinks a problem exists

Presents details clearly, concisely, and completely

If your representative would visit our store, he or she could do an analysis of how much energy we are using. We understand that you regularly provide this helpful service to customers. We would appreciate hearing from you this week. You can reach me by calling (805) 979-7727 during business hours. I look forward to hearing from you.

Requests specific action in the closing and provides contact information to make responding easy

Sincerely,
Laura Covington
Proprietor

SENDING ROUTINE REPLIES AND POSITIVE MESSAGES

Just as you'll make numerous requests for information and action throughout your career, you'll also respond to requests and send a variety of positive messages. You have several goals for such messages: to communicate the information or the good news, to answer all questions, to provide all required details, and to leave your reader with a good impression of you and your firm.

Strategy for Routine Replies and Positive Messages

4 LEARNING OBJECTIVE

Describe a strategy for writing routine replies and positive messages.

Like a request, a routine reply or positive message has an opening, a body, and a close. Because readers receiving these messages will generally be interested in what you have to say, you can usually use the direct approach. Place your main idea (the positive reply or the good news) in the opening, use the body to explain all the relevant details, and close cordially—perhaps highlighting a benefit to your reader.

Starting with the Main Idea

Use the direct approach for positive messages.

Prepare your audience for the detail that follows by beginning your positive message with the main idea or good news.

By opening a routine and positive message with the main idea or good news, you're preparing your audience for the detail that follows. Make your opening clear and concise. Although the following introductory statements make the same point, one is cluttered with unnecessary information that buries the purpose, whereas the other is brief and to the point:

INSTEAD OF THIS	WRITE THIS
I am pleased to inform you that after careful consideration of a diverse and talented pool of applicants, each of whom did a thorough job of analyzing Trask Horton Pharmaceuticals's training needs, we have selected your bid.	Trask Horton Pharmaceuticals has accepted your bid to provide public speaking and presentation training to the sales staff.

The best way to write a clear opening is to have a clear idea of what you want to say. Before you put one word on paper, ask yourself, "What is the single most important message I have for the audience?"

Providing Necessary Details and Explanation

Use the body to explain your point completely so that your audience won't be confused or doubtful about your meaning. As you provide the details, maintain the supportive tone established in the opening. This tone is easy to continue when your message is entirely positive, as in this example:

> Your educational background and internship have impressed us, and we believe you would be a valuable addition to Green Valley Properties. As discussed during your interview, your salary will be $4,300 per month, plus benefits. Please plan to meet with our benefits manager, Paula Sanchez, at 8 a.m. on Monday, March 21. She will assist you with all the paperwork necessary to tailor our benefit package to your family situation. She will also arrange various orientation activities to help you acclimate to our company.

Look for ways to present negative information in a positive context.

However, if your routine message is mixed and must convey mildly disappointing information, put the negative portion of your message into as favorable a context as possible:

INSTEAD OF THIS	WRITE THIS
No, we no longer carry the Sportsgirl line of sweaters.	The new Olympic line has replaced the Sportsgirl sweaters that you asked about. Olympic features a wider range of colors and sizes and more contemporary styling.

CHECKLIST: Writing Routine Replies and Positive Messages

A. Start with the main idea.
- Be clear and concise.
- Identify the single most important message before you start writing.

B. Provide necessary details and explanation.
- Explain your point completely to eliminate any confusion or lingering doubts.
- Maintain a supportive tone throughout.
- Embed negative statements in positive contexts or balance them with positive alternatives.
- Talk favorably about the choices the customer has made.

C. End with a courteous close.
- Let your readers know that you have their personal well-being in mind.
- If further action is required, tell readers how to proceed and encourage them to act promptly.

In this example, the more complete description is less negative and emphasizes how the recipient can benefit from the change. Be careful, though: You can use negative information in this type of message *only* if you're reasonably sure the audience will respond positively. Otherwise, use the indirect approach (discussed in Chapter 9).

If you are communicating with a customer, you might also want to use the body of your message to assure the customer of the wisdom of his or her purchase selection (without being condescending or self-congratulatory). Using such favorable comments, often known as *resale*, is a good way to build customer relationships. These comments are commonly included in acknowledgments of orders and other routine announcements to customers, and they are most effective when they are relatively short and specific:

> The zipper on the laptop carrying case you purchased is double-stitched and guaranteed for the life of the product.
>
> The KitchenAid mixer you ordered is our best-selling model. It should meet your cooking needs for many years.

Ending with a Courteous Close

Make sure audience members understand what to do next and how that action will benefit them.

Your message is most likely to succeed if your readers are left feeling that you have their best interests in mind. You can accomplish this task either by highlighting a benefit to the audience or by expressing appreciation or goodwill. If follow-up action is required, clearly state who will do what next. See "Checklist: Writing Routine Replies and Positive Messages" to review the primary tasks involved in this type of business message.

Common Examples of Routine Replies and Positive Messages

Most routine and positive messages fall into six main categories: answers to requests for information and action, grants of claims and requests for adjustment, recommendations, informative messages, good-news announcements, and goodwill messages.

Answering Requests for Information and Action

Every professional answers requests for information and action from time to time. If the response to a request is a simple "yes" or some other straightforward information, the direct approach is appropriate. A prompt, gracious, and thorough response will positively influence how people think about you and the organization you represent (see Figure 8.5).

To handle repetitive queries quickly and consistently, companies usually develop form responses that can be customized as needed (see Figure 8.6 on page 220). These ready-made message templates can be printed forms, word-processor documents, e-mail templates, or blocks of instant messaging (IM) text that can be dropped into a messaging window with the click of a mouse.

When you're answering requests and a potential sale is involved, you have three main goals: (1) to respond to the inquiry and answer all questions, (2) to leave your reader with

FIGURE 8.5 Effective IM Response to an Information Request
This quick and courteous exchange is typical of IM communication in such areas as customer service and technical support. The agent (Janice) solves the problem quickly and leaves the customer with a positive impression of the company.

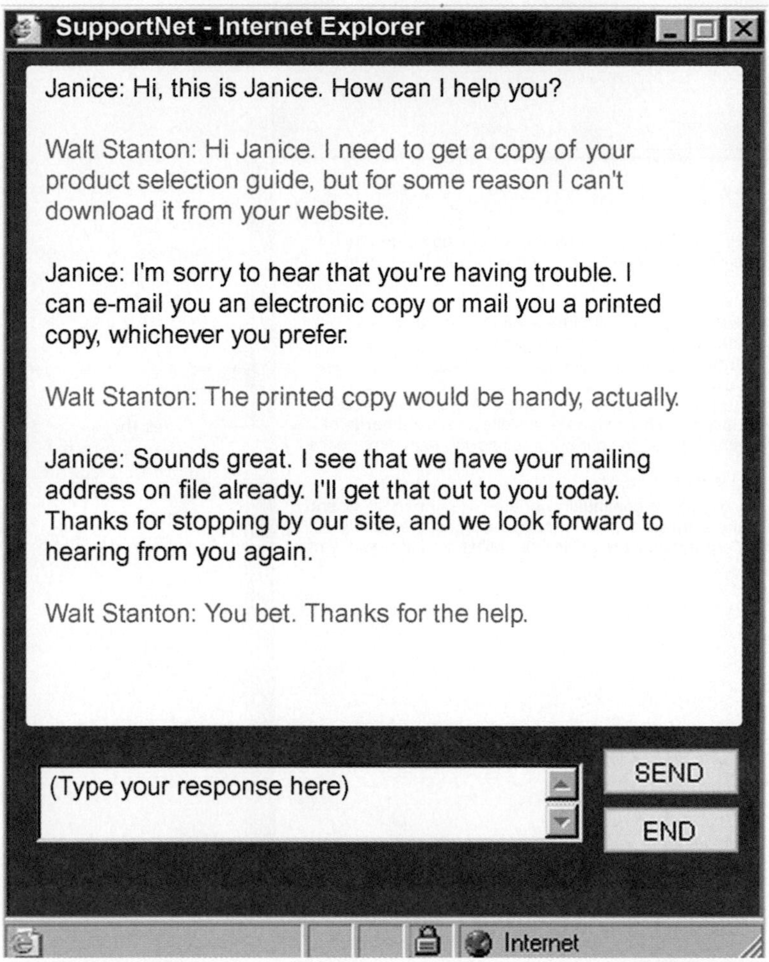
SupportNet - Internet Explorer
Janice: Hi, this is Janice. How can I help you?
Walt Stanton: Hi Janice. I need to get a copy of your product selection guide, but for some reason I can't download it from your website.
Janice: I'm sorry to hear that you're having trouble. I can e-mail you an electronic copy or mail you a printed copy, whichever you prefer.
Walt Stanton: The printed copy would be handy, actually.
Janice: Sounds great. I see that we have your mailing address on file already. I'll get that out to you today. Thanks for stopping by our site, and we look forward to hearing from you again.
Walt Stanton: You bet. Thanks for the help.
(Type your response here)
SEND
END
Internet

a good impression of you and your firm, and (3) to encourage the future sale. The following message meets all three objectives:

> Here is the brochure "Entertainment Unlimited" that you requested. This booklet describes the vast array of entertainment options available to you with an Ocean Satellite Device (OSD).
>
> On page 12 you'll find a list of the 338 channels that the OSD brings into your home. You'll have access to movie, sports, and music channels; 24-hour news channels; local channels; and all the major television networks. OSD gives you a clearer picture and more precise sound than those old-fashioned dishes that took up most of your yard—and OSD uses only a small dish that mounts easily on your roof.
>
> More music, more cartoons, more experts, more news, and more sports are available to you with OSD than with any other cable or satellite connection in this region. It's all there, right at your fingertips.
>
> Just call us at 1-800-786-4331, and an OSD representative will come to your home to answer your questions. You'll love the programming and the low monthly cost. Call us today!

Starts with a clear statement of the main point, which is responding to a consumer inquiry

Creates a positive impression of the product offered

Encourages readers to move toward a purchase by continuing to highlight product benefits

Points toward the sale confidently

FIGURE 8.6 Personalized Reply to a Request for Information
This e-mail message personalizes a standardized response by including the recipient's name in the greeting.

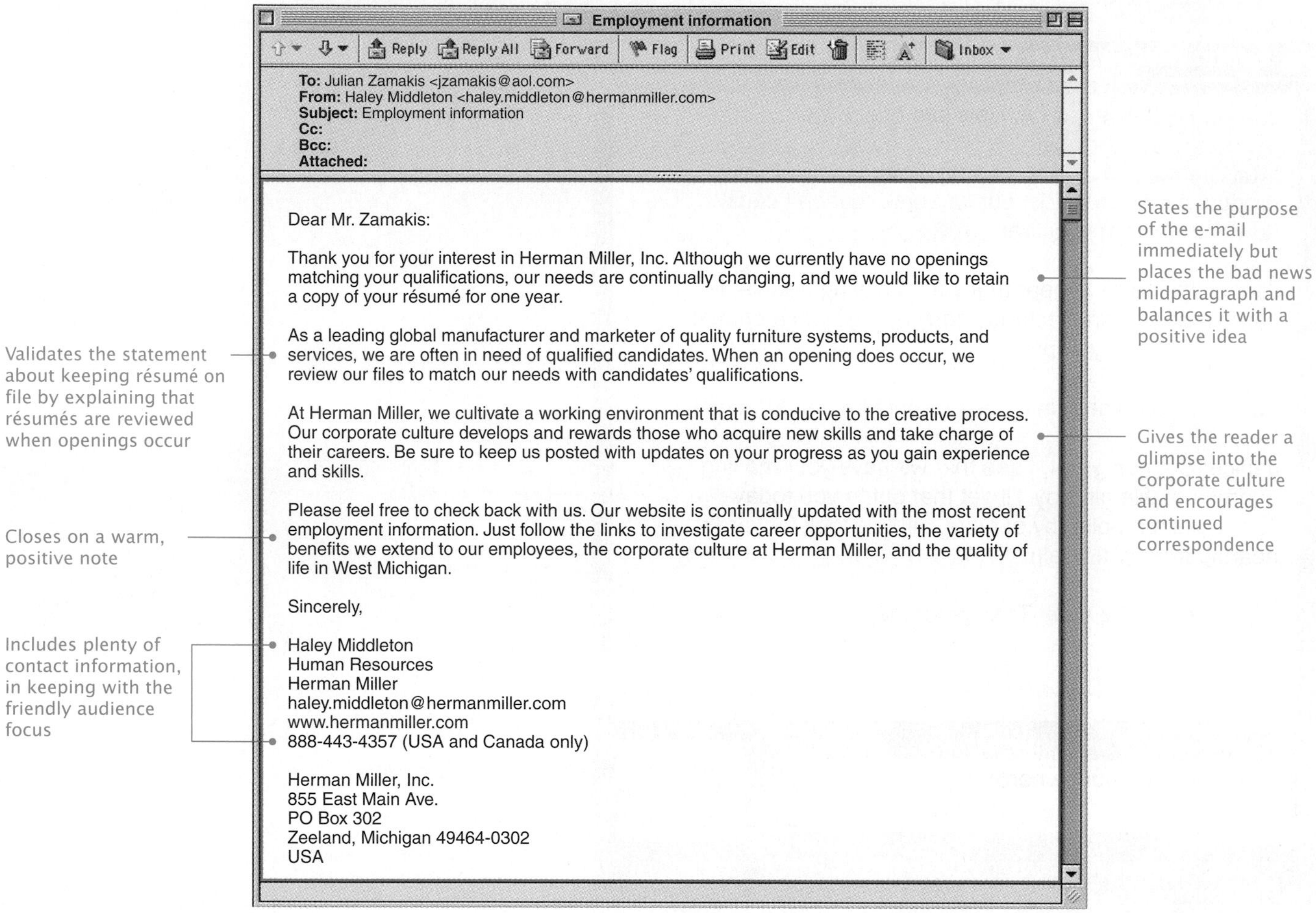
Employment information
Reply
Reply All
Forward
Flag
Print
Edit
Inbox
States the purpose of the e-mail immediately but places the bad news midparagraph and balances it with a positive idea
Validates the statement about keeping résumé on file by explaining that résumés are reviewed when openings occur
Gives the reader a glimpse into the corporate culture and encourages continued correspondence
Closes on a warm, positive note
Includes plenty of contact information, in keeping with the friendly audience focus

To: Julian Zamakis <jzamakis@aol.com>
From: Haley Middleton <haley.middleton@hermanmiller.com>
Subject: Employment information
Cc:
Bcc:
Attached:

Dear Mr. Zamakis:

Thank you for your interest in Herman Miller, Inc. Although we currently have no openings matching your qualifications, our needs are continually changing, and we would like to retain a copy of your résumé for one year.

As a leading global manufacturer and marketer of quality furniture systems, products, and services, we are often in need of qualified candidates. When an opening does occur, we review our files to match our needs with candidates' qualifications.

At Herman Miller, we cultivate a working environment that is conducive to the creative process. Our corporate culture develops and rewards those who acquire new skills and take charge of their careers. Be sure to keep us posted with updates on your progress as you gain experience and skills.

Please feel free to check back with us. Our website is continually updated with the most recent employment information. Just follow the links to investigate career opportunities, the variety of benefits we extend to our employees, the corporate culture at Herman Miller, and the quality of life in West Michigan.

Sincerely,

Haley Middleton
Human Resources
Herman Miller
haley.middleton@hermanmiller.com
www.hermanmiller.com
888-443-4357 (USA and Canada only)

Herman Miller, Inc.
855 East Main Ave.
PO Box 302
Zeeland, Michigan 49464-0302
USA

Granting Claims and Requests for Adjustment

Even the best-run companies make mistakes, from shipping the wrong order to billing a customer's credit card inaccurately. In other cases, a customer or a third party might be responsible for a mistake, such as misusing a product or damaging a product in shipment. Each of these events represents a turning point in your relationship with your customer. If you handle the situation well, your customer is likely to be even more loyal than before because you've proven that you're serious about customer satisfaction. However, if a customer believes that you mishandled a complaint, you'll make the situation even worse. Dissatisfied customers often take their business elsewhere without notice and tell numerous friends and colleagues about the negative experience. A transaction that might be worth only a few dollars by itself could cost you many times that amount in lost business. In other words, every mistake is an opportunity to improve a relationship.

5 LEARNING OBJECTIVE

Discuss the importance of knowing who is responsible when granting claims and requests for adjustment.

Your response to a customer complaint depends on your company's policies for resolving such issues and your assessment of whether the company, the customer, or some third party is at fault.

Responding to a Claim When Your Company Is at Fault

Before you respond after your company has made a mistake, make sure you know your company's policies, which might dictate specific legal and financial steps to be taken. For serious problems that go beyond routine errors, your company should have a *crisis management plan* that outlines communication steps both inside and outside the organization (see Chapter 9).

Most routine responses should take your company's specific policies into account and do the following:

- **Acknowledge receipt of the customer's claim or complaint.** Even if you can't solve the problem immediately, at least let the other party know that somebody is listening.
- **Take (or assign) personal responsibility for setting matters straight.** Customers want to know that someone is listening and responding.
- **Sympathize with the customer's inconvenience or frustration.** Letting the customer see that you're on his or her side helps defuse the emotional element of the situation.
- **Explain precisely how you have resolved or plan to resolve the situation.** If you can respond exactly as the customer requested, be sure to communicate that. If you can't, explain why.
- **Take steps to repair the relationship.** Keeping your existing customers is almost always less expensive than acquiring new customers, so look for ways to mend the relationship and encourage future business.
- **Follow up to verify that your response was correct.** Follow-up not only helps improve customer service but also gives you another opportunity to show how much you care about your customer.

In addition to taking these positive steps, maintain a professional demeanor. Don't blame anyone in your organization by name; don't make exaggerated, insincere apologies; don't imply that the customer is at fault; and don't promise more than you can deliver.

As with requests for information or action, companies often create customizable templates for granting claims and requests for adjustment. In the following example, a large online clothing company created an e-mail form to respond to customers who complain that they haven't received exactly what was ordered:

> Your e-mail message concerning your recent Klondike order has been forwarded to our director of order fulfillment. Your complete satisfaction is our goal, and a customer service representative will contact you within 48 hours to assist with the issues raised in your letter.
>
> In the meantime, please accept the enclosed $5 gift certificate as a token of our appreciation for your business. Whether you're skiing or driving a snowmobile, Klondike Gear offers you the best protection from wind, snow, and cold—and Klondike has been taking care of customers' outdoor needs for over 27 years.
>
> Thank you for taking the time to write to us. Your input helps us better serve you and all our customers.

Acknowledges receipt of the customer's message

Explains what will happen next and when, without making promises the writer can't keep

Takes steps to repair the relationship and ensure continued business

Closes with a statement of the company's concern for all its customers

Responding to a Claim When the Customer Is at Fault

Communication about a claim is a delicate matter when the customer is clearly at fault. If you refuse the claim, you may lose your customer—as well as many of the customer's friends and colleagues, who will hear only one side of the dispute. You must weigh the cost of making the adjustment against the cost of losing future business from one or more customers. Some companies have strict guidelines on responding to such claims, whereas others give individual employees and managers some leeway in making case-by-case decisions.

If you grant a claim when the customer is at fault, look for diplomatic ways to discourage the errant behavior in the future.

If you choose to grant a claim, you can simply open with the good news, being sure to specify exactly what you're agreeing to do. The body of the message is tricky because you want to discourage such claims in the future by steering the customer in the right direction. For example, customers sometimes misuse products or fail to follow the terms of service agreements, such as forgetting to cancel hotel reservations at least 24 hours in advance and thereby incurring the cost of one night's stay. Even if you do grant a particular claim, you don't want to imply that you will grant similar claims in the future. The challenge is to diplomatically remind the customer of proper usage or procedures without being condescending ("Perhaps you failed to read the instructions carefully") or preachy ("You should know that wool shrinks in hot water"). Close in a courteous manner that expresses your appreciation for the customer's business (see Figure 8.7 on the next page).

FIGURE 8.7 Responding to a Claim When The Buyer Is at Fault
In the interest of positive customer relationships, this company agreed to provide replacement parts for a customer's in-line skates, even though the product is outside its warranty period. (For the sake of clarity, the content of the customer's original e-mail message is not reproduced here.)

1 Plan →

Analyze the Situation
The purpose is to grant the customer's claim, tactfully educate him, and encourage further business.

Gather Information
Gather information on product care, warranties, and resale information.

Select the Right Medium
An e-mail message is appropriate in this case because the customer contacted the company via e-mail.

Organize the Information
You're responding with a positive answer, so the direct approach is fine.

2 Write →

Adapt to Your Audience
Show sensitivity to audience needs with a "you" attitude, politeness, positive emphasis, and bias-free language.

Compose the Message
Style is respectful while still managing to educate the customer on product usage and maintenance.

3 Complete

Revise the Message
Evaluate content and review readability; avoid unnecessary details.

Produce the Message
Emphasize a clean, professional appearance.

Proofread the Message
Review for errors in layout, spelling, and mechanics.

Distribute the Message
E-mail the reply.

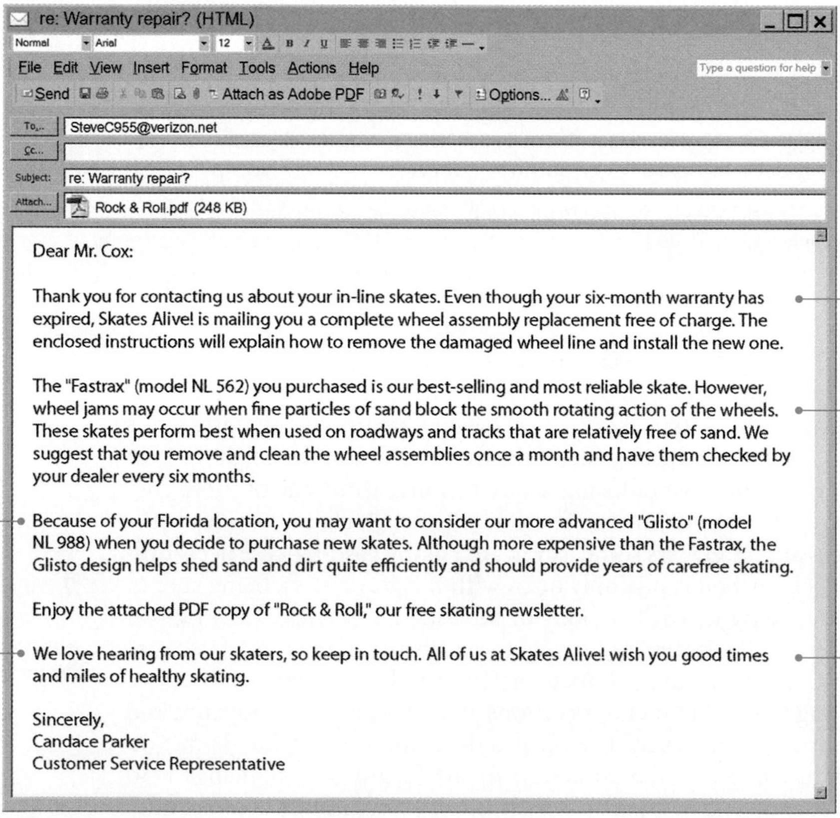
re: Warranty repair? (HTML)

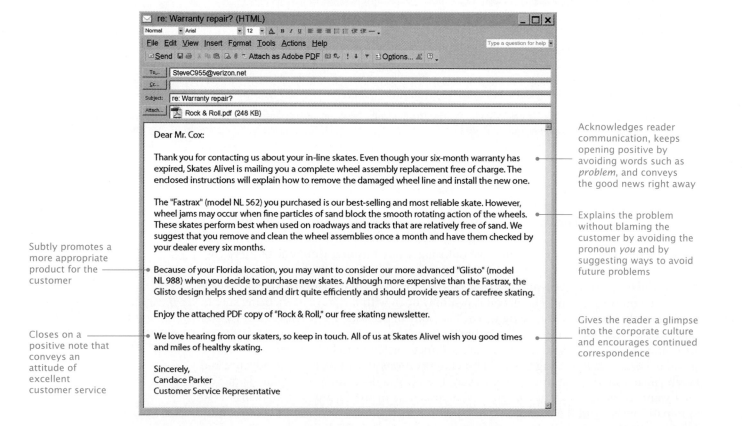

To: SteveC955@verizon.net
Cc:
Subject: re: Warranty repair?
Attach: Rock & Roll.pdf (248 KB)

Dear Mr. Cox:

Thank you for contacting us about your in-line skates. Even though your six-month warranty has expired, Skates Alive! is mailing you a complete wheel assembly replacement free of charge. The enclosed instructions will explain how to remove the damaged wheel line and install the new one.

The "Fastrax" (model NL 562) you purchased is our best-selling and most reliable skate. However, wheel jams may occur when fine particles of sand block the smooth rotating action of the wheels. These skates perform best when used on roadways and tracks that are relatively free of sand. We suggest that you remove and clean the wheel assemblies once a month and have them checked by your dealer every six months.

Because of your Florida location, you may want to consider our more advanced "Glisto" (model NL 988) when you decide to purchase new skates. Although more expensive than the Fastrax, the Glisto design helps shed sand and dirt quite efficiently and should provide years of carefree skating.

Enjoy the attached PDF copy of "Rock & Roll," our free skating newsletter.

We love hearing from our skaters, so keep in touch. All of us at Skates Alive! wish you good times and miles of healthy skating.

Sincerely,
Candace Parker
Customer Service Representative

Acknowledges reader communication, keeps opening positive by avoiding words such as *problem*, and conveys the good news right away

Explains the problem without blaming the customer by avoiding the pronoun *you* and by suggesting ways to avoid future problems

Subtly promotes a more appropriate product for the customer

Gives the reader a glimpse into the corporate culture and encourages continued correspondence

Closes on a positive note that conveys an attitude of excellent customer service

CHECKLIST: Granting Claims and Adjustment Requests

A. **Responding when your company is at fault**
- Be aware of your company's policies in such cases before you respond.
- For serious situations, refer to the company's crisis management plan.
- Start by acknowledging receipt of the claim or complaint.
- Take or assign personal responsibility for resolving the situation.
- Sympathize with the customer's frustration.
- Explain how you have resolved the situation (or plan to).
- Take steps to repair the customer relationship.
- Verify your response with the customer and keep the lines of communication open.

B. **Responding when the customer is at fault**
- Weigh the cost of complying with or refusing the request.
- If you choose to comply, open with the good news.
- Use the body of the message to respectfully educate the customer about steps needed to avoid a similar outcome in the future.
- Close with an appreciation for the customer's business.

C. **Responding when a third party is at fault**
- Evaluate the situation and review your company's policies before responding.
- Avoid placing blame; focus on the solution.
- Regardless of who is responsible for resolving the situation, let the customer know what will happen to resolve the problem.

Responding to a Claim When a Third Party Is at Fault

Sometimes neither your company nor your customer is at fault. For example, ordering a book from Amazon.com involves not only Amazon.com but also a delivery service such as FedEx or the U.S. Postal Service, the publisher and possibly a distributor of the book, a credit card issuer, and a company that processes credit card transactions. Any one of these other partners might be at fault in the event of a problem, but the customer is likely to blame Amazon.com because that is the entity primarily responsible for the transaction.

No general scheme applies to every case involving a third party, so evaluate the situation carefully and know your company's policies before responding. For instance, an online retailer and the companies that manufacture its merchandise might have an agreement that specifies that the manufacturers automatically handle all complaints about product quality. However, regardless of who eventually resolves the problem, if customers contact you, you need to respond with messages that explain how the problem will be solved. Pointing fingers is unproductive and unprofessional; resolving the situation is the only issue customers care about. See "Checklist: Granting Claims and Adjustment Requests" to review the tasks involved in these kinds of business messages.

When a third party is at fault, your response depends on your company's agreements with that organization.

Providing Recommendations

When writing a letter of recommendation, your goal is to convince readers that the person being recommended has the characteristics necessary for the job, project assignment, scholarship, or other objective the person is seeking. A successful recommendation letter contains a number of relevant details:

- The candidate's full name
- The position or other objective the candidate is seeking
- The nature of your relationship with the candidate
- An indication of whether you're answering a request from the person or taking the initiative to write
- Facts and evidence relevant to the candidate and the opportunity
- A comparison of this candidate's potential with that of his or her peers, if available (for example, "Ms. Jonasson consistently ranked in the top 10 percent of her class")
- Your overall evaluation of the candidate's suitability for the opportunity

As surprising as this might sound, the most difficult recommendation letters to write are often those for truly outstanding candidates. Your audience will have trouble believing uninterrupted praise for someone's talents and accomplishments. To enhance your credibility—and the candidate's—illustrate your general points with specific examples that highlight the candidate's abilities and fitness for the job opening.

Most candidates aren't perfect, however, and you'll need to decide how to handle each situation that comes your way. Omitting a reference to someone's shortcomings may be tempting, especially if the shortcomings are irrelevant to the demands of the job in question. Even so, you have an obligation to refer to any serious shortcoming that could be related to job performance. You owe it to your audience, to your own conscience, and even to better-qualified candidates. You don't have to present the shortcomings as simple criticisms, however. A good option is to list them as areas for improvement or as areas the person might be working on now.

REAL-TIME UPDATES
Learn More

Get expert tips on writing (or requesting) a letter of recommendation

Find helpful advice on employment recommendations, academic recommendations, and character references. Go to **http://real-timeupdates.com/ebc** and click on "Learn More." If you are using mybcommlab, you can access Real-Time Updates within each chapter or under Student Study Tools.

A serious shortcoming cannot be ignored in letters of recommendation, but beware of being libelous:
- *Include only relevant, factual information*
- *Avoid value judgments*
- *Balance criticisms with favorable points*

The danger in writing a critical letter is that you might inadvertently engage in *libel*, publishing a false and malicious written statement that injures the candidate's reputation. On the other hand, if that negative information is truthful and relevant, it may be unethical and even illegal to omit it from your recommendation.

If you must refer to a shortcoming, you can best protect yourself by sticking to the facts, avoiding value judgments, and placing your criticism in the context of a generally favorable recommendation, as in Figure 8.8. In this letter, the writer supports all statements and judgments with evidence.

Practicing Ethical Communication

What's Right to Write in a Recommendation Letter?

Recommendation letters are classified as routine messages, but with all the legal troubles they can get employers into these days, they've become anything but routine. Over the years, employees have won thousands of lawsuits that charged former employers with defamation related to job recommendations. In addition to charges of defamation—which can be successfully defended if the "defamatory" statements are proven to be true—employers have been sued for retaliation by ex-employees who believed that negative letters were written expressly for purposes of revenge. And as if that weren't enough, employers have even sued each other over recommendation letters when the recipient of a letter believed the writer failed to disclose important negative information.

No wonder many companies now refuse to divulge anything more than job titles and dates of employment. But even that doesn't always solve the problem: Ex-employees have been known to sue for retaliation when their employers refused to write on their behalf. (This refusal to write recommendations also causes problems for hiring companies. If they can't get any real background information on job candidates, they risk hiring employees who lack the necessary skills or who are disruptive or even dangerous in the workplace.)

For companies that let managers write recommendations, what sort of information should or should not be included? Even though the majority of states now have laws protecting companies against recommendation-related lawsuits when the employer acts in good faith, individual cases vary so much that no specific guidelines can ever apply to all cases. However, answering the following questions before drafting a recommendation letter will help you avoid trouble:

- Does the party receiving this personal information have a legitimate right to it?
- Does all the information I've presented relate directly to the job or benefit being sought?
- Have I put the candidate's case as strongly and as honestly as I can?
- Have I avoided overstating the candidate's abilities or otherwise misleading the reader?
- Have I based all my statements on firsthand knowledge and provable facts?

No matter what the circumstances, experts also advise that you always consult your human resources or legal department for advice.

CAREER APPLICATIONS

1. A former employee was often late for work but was an excellent and fast worker who got along well with everyone. Do you think it's important to mention the tardiness to potential employers? If so, how would you handle it?
2. Step outside yourself for a moment and write a letter of recommendation about you from a former employer's perspective. Make sure your letter embodies honesty, integrity, and prudence.

FIGURE 8.8 Effective Recommendation Letter
This letter clearly states the nature of the writer's relationship to the candidate and provides specific examples to support the writer's endorsements.

AIRBUS

November 15, 2010

Ms. Clarice Gailey
Director of Operations
McNally and Associates, Inc.
8688 Southgate Ave.
Augusta, GA 30906

Dear Ms. Gailey:

I am pleased to recommend Talvin Biswas for the marketing position at McNally and Associates. Mr. Biswas has worked with Airbus Americas as an intern for the past two summers while pursuing his degree in marketing and advertising. His duties included customer correspondence, web content updates, and direct-mail campaign planning.

As his supervisor, in addition to knowing his work here, I also know that Mr. Biswas has served as secretary for the International Business Association at the University of Michigan. He tutored other international students in the university's writing center. His fluency in three languages (English, French, and Hindi) and sensitivity to other cultures will make him an immediate contributor to your international operations.

Mr. Biswas is a thoughtful and careful professional who will not hesitate to contribute ideas when invited to do so. In addition, because Mr. Biswas learns and adapts quickly, he will learn your company's methods with ease.

Mr. Biswas will make an excellent addition to your staff at McNally and Associates. If I can provide any additional information, please call me at the number below. If you prefer to communicate by e-mail, please contact me at angela_leclerc@airbus.com.

Sincerely,

Angela LeClerc

Angela LeClerc
Vice President, Marketing

AIRBUS INDUSTRIE OF NORTH AMERICA, INC.
198 Van Buren Street • Suite 300 • Herndon, VA 20170
Telephone (703) 834-3400 • Facsimile (703) 834-3440 • Website: www.airbus.com

Before you dash off any recommendation letter, even for someone you know closely and respect without reservation, keep in mind that every time you write a recommendation, you're putting your own reputation on the line. If the person's shortcomings are so pronounced that you don't think he or she is a good fit for the job, the only choice is to not write the letter at all. Unless your relationship with the person warrants an explanation, simply suggest that someone else might be in a better position to provide a recommendation.

Creating Informative Messages

When writing informative messages
- *State the purpose in the opening and briefly mention the nature of the information you are providing*
- *Provide necessary details in the body*
- *End with a courteous close*

Companies send a variety of routine informative messages, from updated policies to reminder notices. Use the opening of informative messages to state the purpose and briefly mention the nature of the information you are providing. Unlike the replies discussed earlier, informative messages are not solicited by your reader, so make it clear up front why the reader is receiving this particular message. Provide the necessary details in the body and end your message with a courteous close.

Most informative communications are neutral. That is, they stimulate neither a positive nor a negative response from readers. For example, when you send departmental meeting announcements and reminder notices, you'll generally receive a neutral response from your readers (unless the purpose of the meeting is unwelcome). Simply present the factual information in the body of the message and don't worry too much about the reader's attitude toward the information.

Some informative messages may require additional care. For instance, policy statements or procedural changes may be good news for a company, perhaps by saving money. However, it may not be obvious to employees that such savings may make available additional employee resources or even pay raises. In instances in which the reader may not initially view the information positively, use the body of the message to highlight the potential benefits from the reader's perspective.

Announcing Good News

To develop and maintain good relationships, smart companies recognize that it's good business to spread the word about positive developments. These can include opening new facilities, hiring a new executive, introducing new products or services, or sponsoring community events. Because good news is always welcome, use the direct approach.

In a traditional news release, the primary audience is not the ultimate reader or viewer but rather editors in the news media.

Good-news announcements are usually communicated via a letter or a **news release**, also known as a *press release*, a specialized document used to share relevant information with the news media. (News releases are also used to announce negative news, such as plant closings.) In most companies, news releases are usually prepared or at least supervised by specially trained writers in the public relations department. The content follows the customary pattern for a positive message: good news followed by details and a positive close. However, traditional news releases have a critical difference: You're not writing directly to the ultimate audience (such as the readers of a newspaper); you're trying to interest an editor or a reporter in a story, and that person will then write the material that is eventually read by the larger audience. To write a successful news release, keep the following points in mind:[2]

- Above all else, make sure your information is newsworthy and relevant to the specific publications or websites to which you are sending it.
- Focus on one subject; don't try to pack a single news release with multiple, unrelated news items.
- Put your most important idea first. Don't force editors to hunt for the news.
- Be brief: Break up long sentences and keep paragraphs short.
- Eliminate clutter, such as redundancy and extraneous facts.
- Be as specific as possible.
- Minimize self-congratulatory adjectives and adverbs; if the content of your message is newsworthy, the media professionals will be interested in the news on its own merits.
- Follow established industry conventions for style, punctuation, and format.

Until recently, news releases were intended only for members of the news media and were crafted in a way to provide information to reporters who would then write their own articles if the subject matter was interesting to their readers. Thanks to the Internet, however, the nature of the news release is changing. Many companies now view it as a general-purpose tool for communicating directly with customers and other audiences, creating *direct-to-consumer news releases* (see Figure 8.9). As new-media expert David Meerman Scott puts it, "Millions of people read press releases directly, unfiltered by the media. You need to be speaking directly to them."[3]

6 LEARNING OBJECTIVE

Describe the importance of goodwill messages, and explain how to make them effective.

Fostering Goodwill

All business messages should be written with an eye toward fostering goodwill among business contacts, but some messages are written primarily and specifically to build goodwill. You can use these messages to enhance your relationships with customers, colleagues, and other businesspeople by sending friendly—even unexpected—notes with no direct business purpose.

Goodwill is the positive feeling that encourages people to maintain a business relationship.

FIGURE 8.9 Announcing Positive News
Blogs have become a popular mechanism for announcing positive company news. Some companies even forgo the traditional news release in favor of controlling and distributing such messages themselves.

Effective goodwill messages must be sincere and honest. Otherwise, you'll appear to be interested in personal gain rather than in benefiting customers, fellow workers, or your organization. To come across as sincere, avoid exaggerating and back up any compliments with specific points. In addition, readers often regard more restrained praise as being more sincere. Consider the following example:

Make sure compliments are sincere and honest.

INSTEAD OF THIS	WRITE THIS
Words cannot express my appreciation for the great job you did. Thanks. No one could have done it better. You're terrific! You've made the whole firm sit up and take notice, and we are ecstatic to have you working here.	Thanks again for taking charge of the meeting in my absence and doing such an excellent job. With just an hour's notice, you managed to pull the legal and public relations departments together so that we could present a united front in the negotiations. Your dedication and communication abilities have been noted and are truly appreciated.

Sending Congratulations

One prime opportunity for sending goodwill messages is to congratulate individuals or companies for significant business achievements—perhaps for being promoted or for attaining product sales milestones (see Figure 8.10 on the next page). Other reasons for sending congratulations include the highlights in people's personal lives, such as weddings,

Taking note of significant events in someone's personal life helps cement a business relationship.

FIGURE 8.10 Goodwill Messages
Goodwill messages serve a variety of business functions. In this news release, Nike announces new policies aimed at reducing the deforestation effects of cattle ranching in the Amazon region. Although the message does not promote Nike products, it does build goodwill for the company by signaling Nike's commitment to reducing the environmental impact of its supply chain activities.

NIKE, Inc. Commits to Helping Halt Amazon Deforestation
22 July, 2009

Identifies the environmental issue at stake and emphasizes the company's commitment

BEAVERTON, Ore. (July 22, 2009) – NIKE, Inc. today reinforced its commitment to the environment by releasing new leather sourcing guidelines aimed at helping slow the rate of Amazon deforestation due to cattle grazing within the basin.

Reminds readers of the positive work the company has done in the past in this aspect of its business

Given Nike's proven track record on environmental and sustainability issues, Nike responded quickly when Greenpeace identified that cattle grazing for meat production, and leather as a by-product of meat production, are contributors to Amazon deforestation.

Explains how the company initially responded to this issue

Nike has had extensive conversations with its leather suppliers to gain the most accurate picture possible of our leather sourcing footprint. Nike can say with a high level of certainty that leather used in Nike products is not sourced within the Amazon basin.

Explains additional steps the company will be taking

However, recognizing that there is no current leather traceability system to track the origins of leather with 100 percent confidence we have released a policy which requires our suppliers to establish a traceability system over the coming year. In addition, we have also signed Greenpeace's 'Commit or Cancel' principles which call for a moratorium on deforestation.

Beyond traceability, Nike would also call for the establishment of an enforceable certification system for all industries involved in the Brazilian meat and leather supply chain. Nike values collaboration and continued dialogue on important issues in order to implement change for a more sustainable future.

To this end Nike will continue to work with the industry's Leather Working Group, Greenpeace and other stakeholders to address this issue across the supply chain. Moving forward, we will also require all suppliers of leather for Nike product to join the Leather Working Group by December 2009.

Nike and Greenpeace share a common interest in addressing the causes of climate change. Nike has demonstrated its commitment by calling for US legislative action through its initiation of the Business for Innovative Climate and Energy Policy (BICEP) coalition, eliminating the global warming gas SF6 used in Air-Sole cushioning units, and in 2007 reducing our annual CO2 emissions to 18 percent below 1998 levels.

Provides additional information (the new policy mentioned earlier)

Read Nike's Amazon Leather Policy

births, graduations, and success in nonbusiness competitions. You may congratulate business acquaintances on their own achievements or on the accomplishments of a family member. You may also take note of personal events, even if you don't know the reader well. If you're already friendly with the reader, a more personal tone is appropriate.

Congratulations can also be incorporated into promotional campaigns, such as when companies send messages to new parents or to recent homebuyers. Some companies even develop a mailing list of potential customers by assigning an employee to clip newspaper announcements of births, engagements, weddings, and graduations or to obtain information on real estate transactions in the local community. Then they introduce themselves by sending out a form letter that might read like this:

> Congratulations on your new home! All of us at Klemper Security Solutions hope it brings you and your family many years of security and happiness.

> Please accept the enclosed *Homeowner's Guide to Home Security* with our compliments. It lists a number of simple steps you can take to keep your home, your family, and your possessions safe.

This simple message has a natural, friendly tone, even though the sender has never met the recipient.

Sending Messages of Appreciation

An important managerial quality is the ability to recognize the contributions of employees, colleagues, suppliers, and other associates. Your praise does more than just make the person feel good; it encourages further excellence. Moreover, a message of appreciation may become an important part of someone's personnel file. So when you write a message of appreciation, try to specifically mention the person or people you want to praise. The brief message that follows expresses gratitude and reveals the happy result:

An effective message of appreciation documents a person's contributions.

> Thank you and everyone on your team for the heroic efforts you took to bring our servers back up after last Friday's flood. We were able to restore business right on schedule first thing Monday morning. You went far beyond the level of contractual service in restoring our data center within 16 hours. I would especially like to highlight the contribution of networking specialist Julienne Marks, who worked for 12 straight hours to reconnect our Internet service. If I can serve as a reference in your future sales activities, please do not hesitate to ask.

Offering Condolences

In times of serious trouble and deep sadness, well-written condolences and expressions of sympathy can mean a great deal to people who've experienced loss. This type of message is difficult to write, but don't let the difficulty of the task keep you from responding promptly.

The primary purpose of condolence messages is to let the reader know that you and the organization you represent care about the person's loss.

Open a condolence message with a brief statement of sympathy, such as "I am deeply sorry to hear of your loss" in the event of a death, for example. In the body, mention the good qualities or the positive contributions made by the deceased. State what the person meant to you or your colleagues. In closing, you can offer your condolences and your best wishes. Here are a few general suggestions for writing condolence messages:

- **Keep reminiscences brief.** Recount a memory or an anecdote (even a humorous one), but don't dwell on the details of the loss, lest you add to the reader's anguish.
- **Write in your own words.** Write as if you were speaking privately to the person. Don't quote "poetic" passages or use stilted or formal phrases. If the loss is a death, refer to it as such rather than as "passing away" or "departing."
- **Be tactful.** Mention your shock and dismay but remember that bereaved and distressed loved ones take little comfort in lines such as "Richard was too young to die" or "Starting all over again will be so difficult." Try to strike a balance between superficial

CHECKLIST: Sending Goodwill Messages

- Be sincere and honest.
- Don't exaggerate or use vague, grandiose language; support positive statements with specific evidence.
- Use congratulatory messages to build goodwill with clients and colleagues.
- Send messages of appreciation to emphasize how much you value the work of others.
- When sending condolence messages, open with a brief statement of sympathy followed by an expression of how much the deceased person meant to you or your firm (as appropriate); close by offering your best wishes for the future.

REAL-TIME UPDATES
Learn More

Simple rules for writing effective thank-you notes

These tips are easy to adapt to any business or social occasions in which you need to express appreciation. Go to **http://real-timeupdates.com/ebc** and click on "Learn More." If you are using mybcommlab, you can access Real-Time Updates within each chapter or under Student Study Tools.

Document Makeover

Improve This E-Mail Message

To practice correcting drafts of actual documents, visit the "Document Makeovers" section in mybcommlab. Refer to the User Guide for specific instructions on how to access the content for this chapter. You will find an e-mail message that contains problems and errors related to what you've learned in this chapter about routine, good-news, and goodwill messages. Use the Final Draft decision tool to create an improved version of this routine e-mail. Check the message for skilled presentation of the main idea, clarity of detail, appropriate use of resale, and the inclusion of a courteous close.

expressions of sympathy and painful references to a happier past or the likelihood of a bleak future.

- **Take special care.** Be sure to spell names correctly and be accurate in your review of facts. Try to be prompt.
- **Write about special qualities of the deceased.** You may have to rely on reputation to do this, but let the grieving person know you valued his or her loved one.
- **Write about special qualities of the bereaved person.** A pat on the back helps a bereaved family member feel more confident about handling things during such a traumatic time.[4]

Supervisor George Bigalow sent the following condolence letter to his administrative assistant, Janice Case, after learning of the death of Janice's husband:

> My sympathy to you and your children. All your friends at Carter Electric were so very sorry to learn of John's death. Although I never had the opportunity to meet him, I do know how very special he was to you. Your tales of your family's camping trips and his rafting expeditions were always memorable.

To review the tasks involved in writing goodwill messages, see "Checklist: Sending Goodwill Messages." For the latest information on writing routine and positive messages, visit **http://real-timeupdates.com/ebc** and click on Chapter 8.

On the Job: Solving Communication Dilemmas at Get Satisfaction

After reading the many helpful responses you, as a representative of your company, posted on the Get Satisfaction website, new CEO Wendy Lea invited you to join the Get Satisfaction team as a customer service specialist; your job is to communicate with the companies that use Get Satisfaction's online services. Take what you've learned in this chapter and put it to good use as you address the following challenges. (View some of the postings for various companies on **http://getsatisfaction.com** to get a feel for how the system works.)[5]

1. When people are frustrated with a problem and are trying to discuss it via a lean medium such as online postings, emotions can sometimes boil over. You've been monitoring a conversation between a representative for one of the companies that uses Get Satisfaction and one of its customers. Over the past couple of days, their online conversation has turned into an ugly argument, with accusations of incompetence and even dishonesty flying back and forth. Although the situation doesn't involve Get Satisfaction directly, you think it reflects poorly on your company because the dispute is taking place in full public view on your website—and it certainly isn't doing anybody any good to let this "flame war" keep raging. What is the best way to handle this situation?
   a. E-mail the company representative privately and offer to mediate the dispute.
   b. Post a public message offering to mediate the dispute.
   c. Post a public message reminding both sides to be civil.
   d. Ignore the dispute; it's between the company and its customer.

2. Web-based businesses occasionally suffer from "page loading" problems, when a particular webpage a visitor requests will not display, even when the rest of a

website seems to be working normally. Get Satisfaction recently had a spate of these problems. Which of these is the best way to respond to queries while the company is working to fix the situation?

a. Yes, we've noticed this problem ourselves, but we hope to have everything stabilized soon.
b. We are soooooo sorry! We're working to resolve the situation as soon as possible.
c. Don't you just hate computers sometimes? We're working to resolve the situation as soon as possible.
d. We're having some problems with our host, which seems to be resulting in a lot of these errors. We're working on it now and hope to have everything stabilized soon.

3. In July 2009, Get Satisfaction released version 2.0 of its software. Which of the following is the best one-sentence summary of this major milestone?

a. Version 2.0 is a major update that unleashes the full value of customer community to answer questions, solve problems, and collect ideas for developing the next generation of your products and services.
b. Version 2.0 rocks in every way imaginable.
c. Version 2.0 is our best work yet. It clearly shows how far we've come as a company and how much we've learned in the last two years.
d. Version 2.0 is a major update, incorporating multiple new features, expanded customizability, and a vastly improved and simplified user interface.

4. Get Satisfaction has just announced an *enterprise* version of its customer support software that companies can customize as part of their own information systems. The software is available in *beta release* form, a free pre-release version that software companies often release to encourage people to use as a way to see if anything needs to be changed or fixed before the official product is released. Get Satisfaction hasn't yet announced how much the software is going to cost when it is officially released, so not surprisingly, more than a few interested customers have written questions about the anticipated price. Small business owners in particular want to know if a less-expensive version will be available to small companies. The company is working on a pricing structure that would charge by the volume of usage, meaning that small companies would probably pay less than large companies. Which of the following responses is the most effective response to this question?

a. The pricing structure will be announced when the product is ready for formal release.
b. We can't specify exact pricing yet, because we're still working on those details.
c. We can't specify exact pricing yet, because we're still working on those details. We will make sure that the pricing structure does in fact work both for small companies and large ones, and that if there is a tiered structure, that it scales according to a reliable set of figures/metrics that reflect those size differences.
d. We can't specify exact pricing yet, because we're still working on those details. However, we are trying to figure out a tiered pricing structure that would be fair to both large and small companies.

LEARNING OBJECTIVES CHECKUP

Assess your understanding of the principles in this chapter by reading each learning objective and studying the accompanying exercises. For fill-in-the-blank items, write the missing text in the blank provided; for multiple-choice items, circle the letter of the correct answer. You can check your responses against the answer key on pages AK-1 and AK-2.

Objective 8.1: Apply the three-step writing process to routine and positive messages.

1. When it comes to routine messages, you can
   a. Skip the planning stage
   b. Keep the planning stage brief
   c. Begin by gathering all the information you'll need
   d. Begin by choosing the channel and medium
2. When writing routine messages, you
   a. Can assume that your readers will be interested or neutral
   b. Should open with an "attention getter"
   c. Should use the indirect approach with most audiences
   d. Need not allow much time for revision, production, or proofreading

Objective 8.2: Outline an effective strategy for writing routine requests.

3. When writing a routine request, the best approach is to begin

a. With a personal introduction, such as "My name is Lee Marrs, and I am . . ."
b. With a vague reference to what you are writing about, such as "I have something to ask you."
c. With a strong demand for action
d. By politely stating your request

4. What should you do when asking questions in a routine request?
a. Begin with the least important question and work your way up to the most important question.
b. Include all possible questions about the topic, even if the list gets long.
c. Deal with only one topic per question.
d. Do all of the above.

5. Which of the following should you do when closing a routine request?
a. Be sure to thank the reader "in advance" for complying with the request.
b. Ask the reader to respond by a specific and appropriate time.
c. Ask any remaining questions you have.
d. Do all of the above.

Objective 8.3: Explain how to ask for specific action in a courteous manner.

6. A courteous close contains
a. A specific request
b. Information about how you can be reached (if it isn't obvious)
c. An expression of appreciation or goodwill
d. All of the above

Objective 8.4: Describe a strategy for writing routine replies and positive messages.

7. If you are making a routine reply to a customer, it's a good idea to
a. Leave out any negative information
b. Include resale information to assure the customer of the wisdom of his or her purchase
c. Leave out sales promotion material, which would be tacky to include
d. Do all of the above

8. A positive message should open with a clear and concise statement of _____.

9. If a message has both positive and negative elements, you should
a. Always start with the bad news to get it out of the way first
b. Write two separate messages; never mix good and bad news
c. Put the bad news in a postscript (p.s.) at the bottom of the letter
d. Try to put the negative news in a positive context

Objective 8.5: Discuss the importance of knowing who is responsible when granting claims and requests for adjustment.

10. Which of the following is not among the recommended elements to include in your message if you are responding to a claim or complaint when your company is at fault?
a. An acknowledgement that you received the customer's claim or complaint
b. An expression of sympathy for the inconvenience or loss the customer has experienced
c. An explanation of how you will resolve the situation
d. Complete contact information for your corporate legal staff

11. If a customer who is clearly at fault requests an adjustment, you should
a. Ignore the request; the customer is clearly wasting your time
b. Carefully weigh the cost of complying with the request against the cost of denying it and then decide how to respond based on the overall impact on your company
c. Always agree to such requests because unhappy customers spread bad publicity about a company
d. Suggest in a firm but professional tone that the customer take his or her business elsewhere in the future

12. If a third party (such as a shipping company) is at fault when one of your customers makes a claim or requests an adjustment, the best response is to
a. Follow the terms of whatever customer service agreement your company has with the third party
b. Explain to the customer that your company is not at fault
c. Always grant the request; after all, it's your customer, and the customer holds you responsible
d. Forward the message to the third party as quickly as possible

Objective 8.6: Describe the importance of goodwill messages, and explain how to make them effective.

13. The purpose of goodwill messages is to
a. Generate sales
b. Impress others
c. Make yourself feel better
d. Enhance relationships with customers, colleagues, and other businesspeople

14. The most effective goodwill messages
a. Always try to find an "angle" that benefits the sender in addition to the receiver
b. Avoid details and focus on the emotions of the situation
c. Are sincere and honest
d. Do all of the above

PEARSON mybcommlab™

Log on to www.mybcommlab.com to access the following study and assessment aids associated with this chapter:

- Video applications
- Pre/post test
- Real-Time Updates
- Personalized study plan
- Peer review activity
- Model documents
- Quick Learning Guides
- Sample presentations

If you are not using mybcommlab, you can access Real-Time Updates and Quick Learning Guides through http://real-timeupdates.com/ebc. The Quick Learning Guide (located under "Learn More" on the website) hits all the high points of this chapter in just two pages. This guide, especially prepared by the authors, will help you study for exams or review important concepts whenever you need a quick refresher.

Apply Your Knowledge

1. Why is it good practice to explain why replying to a request could benefit the reader?
2. The latest issue of a local business newspaper names 10 area executives who have exhibited excellent leadership skills in the past year. You are currently searching for a job, and a friend suggests that you write each executive a congratulatory letter and mention in passing that you are looking for new career opportunities and would appreciate the opportunity for an interview. Is this a smart strategy? Why or why not?
3. You've been asked to write a letter of recommendation for an employee who worked for you some years ago. You recall that the employee did an admirable job, but you can't remember any specific information at this point. Should you write the letter anyway? Explain.
4. Every time you send a direct-request e-mail message to Ted Jackson, who works in another department in your company, he delays or refuses to comply. You're beginning to get impatient. Should you send Jackson a memo to ask what's wrong? Complain to your supervisor about Jackson's uncooperative attitude? Arrange a face-to-face meeting with Jackson? Bring up the problem at the next staff meeting? Explain your answer.
5. **Ethical Choices** You have a complaint against one of your suppliers, but you have no documentation to back it up. Should you request an adjustment anyway? Why or why not?

Practice Your Knowledge

Messages for Analysis

Read the following messages and then (1) analyze the strengths and weaknesses of each sentence and (2) revise each document so that it follows this chapter's guidelines.

Message 8.A: Requesting Routine Information from a Business

I'm fed up with the mistakes that our current accounting firm makes. I run a small construction company, and I don't have time to double-check every bookkeeping entry and call the accountants a dozen times when they won't return my messages. Please explain how your firm would do a better job than my current accountants. You have a good reputation among homebuilders, but before I consider hiring you to take over my accounting, I need to know that you care about quality work and good customer service.

Message 8.B: Making Claims and Requests for Adjustment

At a local business-supply store, I recently purchased your *Negotiator Pro* for my computer. I bought the CD because I saw your ad for it in *Macworld* magazine, and it looked as if it might be an effective tool for use in my corporate seminar on negotiation.

Unfortunately, when I inserted it in my office computer, it wouldn't work. I returned it to the store, but because I had already opened it, they refused to exchange it for a CD that would work or give me a refund. They told me to contact you and that you might be able to send me a version that would work with my computer.

You can send the information to me at the letterhead address. If you cannot send me the correct disc, please refund my $79.95. Thanks in advance for any help you can give me in this matter.

Message 8.C: Responding to Claims and Adjustment Requests When the Customer Is at Fault

We read your letter, requesting your deposit refund. We couldn't figure out why you hadn't received it, so we talked to our maintenance engineer, as you suggested. He said you had left one of the doors off the hinges in your apartment in order to get a large sofa through the door. He also confirmed that you had paid him $5.00 to replace the door since you had to turn in the U-Haul trailer and were in a big hurry.

This entire situation really was caused by a lack of communication between our housekeeping inspector and the maintenance engineer. All we knew was that the door was off the hinges when it was inspected by Sally Tarnley. You know that our policy states that if anything is wrong with the apartment, we keep the deposit. We had no way of knowing that George just hadn't gotten around to replacing the door.

But we have good news. We approved the deposit refund, which will be mailed to you from our home office in Teaneck, New Jersey. I'm not sure how long that will take, however. If you don't receive the check by the end of next month, give me a call.

Next time, it's really a good idea to stay with your apartment until it's inspected, as stipulated in your lease agreement. That way, you'll be sure to receive your refund when you expect it. Hope you have a good summer.

Message 8.D: Letter of Recommendation

Your letter to Kunitake Ando, President of Sony, was forwarded to me because I am the human resources director. In my job as head of HR, I have access to performance reviews for all of the Sony employees in the United States. This means, of course, that I would be the person best qualified to answer your request for information on Nick Oshinski.

In your letter of the 15th, you asked about Nick Oshinski's employment record with us because he has applied to work for your company. Mr. Oshinski was employed with us from January 5, 1998, until March 1, 2008. During that time, Mr. Oshinski received ratings ranging from 2.5 up to 9.6, with 10 being the top score. As you can see, he must have done better reporting to some managers than to others. In addition, he took all vacation days, which is a bit unusual. Although I did not know Mr. Oshinski personally, I know that our best workers seldom use all the vacation time they earn. I do not know if that applies in this case.

In summary, Nick Oshinski performed his tasks well depending on who managed him.

Exercises

Active links for all websites in this chapter can be found on mybcommlab; see your User Guide for instructions on accessing the content for this chapter.

8.1 Revising Messages: Directness and Conciseness Revise the following short e-mail messages so that they are more direct and concise; develop a subject line for each revised message.

- **a.** I'm contacting you about your recent e-mail request for technical support on your cable Internet service. Part of the problem we have in tech support is trying to figure out exactly what each customer's specific problem is so that we can troubleshoot quickly and get you back in business as quickly as possible. You may have noticed that in the online support request form, there are a number of fields to enter your type of computer, operating system, memory, and so on. While you did tell us you were experiencing slow download speeds during certain times of the day, you didn't tell us which times specifically, nor did you complete all the fields telling us about your computer. Please return to our support website and resubmit your request, being sure to provide all the necessary information; then we'll be able to help you.
- **b.** Thank you for contacting us about the difficulty you had collecting your luggage at Denver International Airport. We are very sorry for the inconvenience this has caused you. As you know, traveling can create problems of this sort regardless of how careful the airline personnel might be. To receive compensation, please send us a detailed list of the items that you lost and complete the following questionnaire. You can e-mail it back to us.
- **c.** Sorry it took us so long to get back to you. We were flooded with résumés. Anyway, your résumé made the final 10, and after meeting three hours yesterday, we've decided we'd like to meet with you. What is your schedule like for next week? Can you come in for an interview on June 15 at 3:00 p.m.? Please get back to us by the end of this workweek and let us know if you will be able to attend. As you can imagine, this is our busy season.
- **d.** We're letting you know that because we use over a ton of paper a year and because so much of that paper goes into the wastebasket to become so much more environmental waste, starting Monday, we're placing white plastic bins outside the elevators on every floor to recycle that paper and in the process, minimize pollution.

8.2 Revising Messages: Directness and Conciseness Rewrite the following sentences so that they are direct and concise. If necessary, break your answer into two sentences.

- **a.** We wanted to invite you to our special 40 percent off by-invitation-only sale; the sale is taking place on November 9.
- **b.** We wanted to let you know that we are giving a tote bag and a voucher for five iTunes downloads with every $50 donation you make to our radio station.
- **c.** The director planned to go to the meeting that will be held on Monday at a little before 11 a.m.
- **d.** In today's meeting, we were happy to have the opportunity to welcome Paul Eccelson, who reviewed the shopping cart function on our website and offered some great advice; if you have any questions about these new forms, feel free to call him at his office.

8.3 Internet Visit the Workplace eCards section of the Blue Mountain site, at **www.bluemountain.com**, and analyze one of the electronic greeting cards bearing a goodwill message of appreciation for good performance. Under what circumstances would you send this electronic message? How could you personalize it for the recipient and the occasion? What would be an appropriate close for this message?

8.4 Teamwork With another student, identify the purpose and select the most appropriate medium for communicating the following written messages. Next, consider how the audience is likely to respond to each message. Based on this audience analysis, determine whether the direct or indirect approach would be effective for each message and explain your reasoning.

  a. A notice to all employees about the placement of recycling bins by the elevator doors

  b. The first late-payment notice to a good customer who usually pays his bills on time

8.5 Revising Messages: Conciseness, Courteousness, and Specificity Critique the following closing paragraphs. How would you rewrite each to be concise, courteous, and specific?

  a. I need your response sometime soon so I can order the parts in time for your service appointment. Otherwise, your air-conditioning system may not be in tip-top condition for the start of the summer season.

  b. Thank you in advance for sending me as much information as you can about your products. I look forward to receiving your package in the very near future.

  c. To schedule an appointment with one of our knowledgeable mortgage specialists in your area, you can always call our hotline at 1-800-555-8765. This is also the number to call if you have more questions about mortgage rates, closing procedures, or any other aspect of the mortgage process. Remember, we're here to make the home-buying experience as painless as possible.

8.6 Ethical Choices Your company markets a line of automotive accessories for people who like to "tune" their cars for maximum performance. A customer has just written a furious e-mail, claiming that a supercharger he purchased from your website didn't deliver the extra engine power he expected. Your company has a standard refund process to handle situations such as this, and you have the information you need to inform the customer about that. You also have information that could help the customer find a more compatible supercharger from one of your competitors, but the customer's e-mail message is so abusive that you don't feel obligated to help. Is this an appropriate response? Why or why not?

Expand Your Knowledge

Learning More on the Web

Recommended Advice for Recommendation Letters

http://businessmajors.about.com

Whether you're continuing on to graduate school or entering the workforce with your undergraduate degree, recommendation letters could play an important role in the next few steps of your career. From selecting the people to ask for recommendation letters to knowing what makes an effective letter, About.com extends the advice offered in this chapter with real-life examples and suggestions. Visit About.com's Business Majors website and click on "Recommendation Letters." Read the advice you find and answer the following questions:

1. What is a good process for identifying the best people to ask for recommendation letters?
2. What information should you provide to letter writers to help them produce credible and compelling letters on your behalf?
3. What are the most common mistakes you need to avoid with recommendation letters?

Sharpening Your Career Skills Online

Bovée and Thill's Business Communication Web Search, at **http://businesscommunicationblog.com/websearch**, is a unique research tool designed specifically for business communication research. Use the Web Search function to find a website, video, PDF document, podcast, or PowerPoint presentation that offers advice on writing goodwill messages such as thank-you notes or congratulatory letters. Write a brief e-mail message to your instructor, describing the item that you found and summarizing the career skills information you learned from it.

Improve Your Grammar, Mechanics, and Usage

The following exercises help you improve your knowledge of and power over English grammar, mechanics, and usage. Turn to the Handbook of Grammar, Mechanics, and Usage at the end of this book and review all of Section 1.7 (Sentences). Then look at the following 10 items. Circle the letter of the preferred choice within each group of sentences. (Answers to these exercises appear on page AK-3.)

1. **a.** Joan Ellingsworth attends every stockholder meeting. Because she is one of the few board members eligible to vote.
   b. Joan Ellingsworth attends every stockholder meeting. She is one of the few board members eligible to vote.
2. **a.** The executive director, along with his team members, is working quickly to determine the cause of the problem.
   b. The executive director, along with his team members, are working quickly to determine the cause of the problem.
3. **a.** Listening on the extension, details of the embezzlement plot were overheard by the security chief.
   b. Listening on the extension, the chief overheard details of the embezzlement plot.
4. **a.** First the human resources department interviewed dozens of people. Then it hired a placement service.
   b. First the human resources department interviewed dozens of people then it hired a placement service.
5. **a.** Andrews won the sales contest, however he was able to sign up only two new accounts.
   b. Andrews won the sales contest; however, he was able to sign up only two new accounts.
6. **a.** To find the missing file, the whole office was turned inside out.
   b. The whole office was turned inside out to find the missing file.

7. a. Having finally gotten his transfer, he is taking his assistant right along with him.
   b. Having finally gotten his transfer, his assistant is going right along with him.
8. a. Irene was recruiting team members for her project, she promised supporters unprecedented bonuses.
   b. Because Irene was recruiting team members for her project, she promised supporters unprecedented bonuses.
9. a. He left the office unlocked overnight. This was an unconscionable act, considering the high crime rate in this area lately.
   b. He left the office unlocked overnight. An unconscionable act, considering the high crime rate in this area lately.
10. a. When it comes to safety issues, the abandoned mine, with its collapsing tunnels, are cause for great concern.
    b. When it comes to safety issues, the abandoned mine, with its collapsing tunnels, is cause for great concern.

For additional exercises focusing on sentences, visit mybcommlab. Click on Chapter 8, click on "Additional Exercises to Improve Your Grammar, Mechanics, and Usage," and click on "12. Longer sentences," "13. Sentence fragments," "15. Misplaced modifiers," or "24. Transitional words and phrases."

CASES

Applying the Three-Step Writing Process to Cases

Apply each step to the following cases, as assigned by your instructor.

ROUTINE REQUESTS

E-MAIL SKILLS

1. Breathing life back into your biotech career: E-mail requesting a recommendation. After five years of work in the human resources department at Cell Genesys (a company that is developing cancer treatment drugs), you were laid off in a round of cost-cutting moves that rippled through the biotech industry in recent years. The good news is that you found stable employment in the grocery distribution industry. The bad news is that in the three years since you left Cell Genesys, you have truly missed working in the exciting biotechnology field and having the opportunity to be a part of something as important as helping people recover from life-threatening diseases. You know that careers in biotech are uncertain, but you have a few dollars in the bank now, and you're willing to ride that rollercoaster again.

Your task: Draft an e-mail to Calvin Morris, your old boss at Cell Genesys, reminding him of the time you worked together and asking him to write a letter of recommendation for you.[6]

IM SKILLS

2. Trans-global exchange: Instant message request for information from Chinese manufacturer. Thank goodness your company, Diagonal Imports, chose the Sametime enterprise instant messaging software produced by IBM Lotus. Other products also allow you to carry on real-time exchanges with colleagues on the other side of the planet, but Sametime supports bidirectional machine translation, and you're going to need it.

The problem is that production on a popular line of decorative lighting appliances produced at your Chinese manufacturing plant inexplicably came to a halt last month. As the product manager in the United States, you have many resources you could call on for help, such as new sources for faulty parts. But you can't do anything if you don't know the details. You've tried telephoning top managers in China, but they're evasive, telling you only what they think you want to hear.

Finally, your friend Kuei-chen Tsao has returned from a business trip. You met her during your trip to China last year. She doesn't speak English, but she's the line engineer responsible for this particular product: a fiber-optic lighting display that features a plastic base with a rotating color wheel. As the wheel turns, light emitted from the spray of fiber-optic threads changes color in soothing patterns. Product #3347XM is one of Diagonal's most popular items, and you have orders from novelty stores around the United States waiting to be filled. Kuei-chen should be able to explain the problem, determine whether you can help, and tell you how long before regular shipping resumes.

Your task: Write the first of what you hope will be a productive instant message exchange with Kuei-chen. Remember that your words will be machine translated.[7]

TEXT MESSAGING SKILLS

3. Tracking the new product buzz: Text message to colleagues at a trade show. The vast Consumer Electronics Show (CES) is the premier promotional event in the industry. More than 130,000 industry insiders from all over the world come to see the exciting new products on display from nearly 1,500 companies—everything from video game gadgets to Internet-enabled refrigerators with built-in computer screens. You've just stumbled on a video game controller that has a built-in webcam to allow networked gamers to see and hear each other while they play. Your company also makes game controllers, and you're worried that your customers will flock to this new controller-cam. You need to know how much buzz is circulating around the show: Have people seen it? What are they saying about it? Are they excited about it?

Your task: Compose a text message to your colleagues at the show, alerting them to the new controller-cam and asking them to listen for any buzz it might be generating among the attendees at the Las Vegas Convention Center and the several surrounding hotels where the show takes place. Here's the catch: Your text-messaging service limits messages to 160 characters, including spaces and punctuation, so your message can't be any longer than this.[8]

LETTER WRITING SKILLS

4. Step on it: Letter to Floorgraphics requesting information about underfoot advertising. You work for Alberta Greenwood, owner of Better Bike and Ski Shop. Yesterday, Alberta met with the Schwinn sales representative, Tom Beeker, who urged her to sign a contract with Floorgraphics. That company leases floor space from retail stores and creates and sells floor ads to manufacturers such as Schwinn. Floorgraphics will pay Alberta a fee for leasing the floor space, as well as a percentage for every ad it sells. Alberta was definitely interested and turned to you after Beeker left.

"Tom says that advertising decals on the floor in front of the product reach consumers right where they're standing when making a decision," explained Alberta. "He says the ads increase sales from 25 to 75 percent."

You both look down at the dusty floor, and Alberta laughs. "It seems funny that manufacturers will pay hard cash to put their names where customers are going to track dirt all over them! But if Tom's telling the truth, we could profit three ways: from the leasing fee, the increased sales of products being advertised, and the share in ad revenues. That's not so funny."

Your task: Alberta Greenwood asks you to write a letter for her signature to CEO Richard Rebh at Floorgraphics, Inc. (5 Vaughn Dr., Princeton, NJ 08540) asking for financial details and practical information about the ads. For example, how will you clean your floors? Who installs and removes the ads? Can you terminate the lease if you don't like the ads?[9]

E-MAIL SKILLS

5. Sour note: Requesting a refund for repeated service outages. Love at first listen is the only way to describe the way you felt when you discovered SongThrong.com. You enjoy dozens of styles of music, from Afrobeat and Tropicalia to mainstream pop and the occasional blast of industrial metal, and SongThrong.com has them all for only $9.99 a month. You can explore every genre imaginable, listening to as many tracks as you like for a fixed monthly fee. The service sounded too good to be true—and sadly, it was. The service was so unreliable that you began keeping note of when it was unavailable. Last month, it was down for all or part of 12 days—well over a third of the month. As much as you like it, you've had enough.

Your task: Write an e-mail to support@songthrong.com, requesting a full refund. To get the $9.99 monthly rate, you prepaid for an entire year ($119.88), and you've been a subscriber for two months now. You know the service has been out for at least part of the time on 12 separate days last month, and while you didn't track outages during the first month, you believe it was about the same number of days.

LETTER WRITING SKILLS

6. Unhappy customer: Claim letter requesting an adjustment. As a consumer, you've probably bought something that didn't work right or paid for a service that did not turn out the way you expected. Maybe it was a pair of jeans with a rip in a seam that you didn't find until you got home or a watch that broke a week after you bought it. Or maybe a lawn service your family hired didn't finish the agreed-upon tasks and damaged valuable plants.

Your task: Choose an incident from your own experience and write a claim letter, asking for a refund, repair, replacement, or other adjustment. You'll need to include all the details of the transaction, plus your contact address and phone number. If you can't think of such an experience, make up details for an imaginary situation. If your experience is real, you might want to mail the letter. The reply you receive will provide a good test of your claim-writing skills.

E-MAIL SKILLS

7. A juicy position: E-mail requesting information about careers at Jamba Juice. You did not expect to find a job while working out at 24-Hour Fitness, but you're willing to explore an opportunity when it appears. As you were buying a smoothie at the Jamba Juice bar inside the gym, you overheard the manager talking about the company's incentives for employees, especially those interested in becoming managers. You ask her about it, and she suggests you log on to the company's website (www.jambajuice.com) for more information.

You're still in business school, and you need a part-time job. Finding one at a company that offers a good future after graduation would be even better than simply earning some money to keep you going now. You check the Jamba Juice website. You discover that the juice-bar chain has created a good reputation in the health, fitness, and nutrition industry. Also, you can submit your résumé online for an entry-level job. That sounds promising. If you could start now while finishing your degree, you'd be in a prime spot for promotion once you graduate. You start to wonder if Jamba Juice could be a long-term career opportunity.

Your task: Write an e-mail message requesting additional information about careers and advancement at Jamba Juice. First, visit www.jambajuice.com to learn all that you can about the company; then compose your message. Specifically, ask for information about career long-term advancement beyond the store level, to corporate management. You might want to mention that you're still in school, studying business (make up any details you need).[10]

E-MAIL SKILLS

8. Looking for the best minds: Identifying local retail experts for a new business initiative. You head up the corporate marketing department for a nationwide chain of clothing stores. The company has decided to launch a new store-within-a-store concept, in which a small section of each store will showcase "business casual" clothing. To ensure a successful launch of this new strategy, you want to get input from the best retailing minds in the company. You also know it's important to get regional insights from around the country, because a merchandising strategy that works in one area might not succeed in another.

Your task: Write an e-mail message to all 87 store managers, asking them to each nominate one person to serve on an advisory team (managers can nominate themselves if they are local market experts). Explain that you want to find people with at least five years of retailing experience, a good understanding of the local business climate, and thorough knowledge of the local retail competition. In addition, the best candidates will be good team players who are comfortable collaborating long distance, using virtual meeting technologies. Also, explain that while you are asking each of the 87 stores to nominate someone, the team will be limited to no more than eight people. You've met many of the store managers, but not all of them, so be sure to introduce yourself at the beginning of the message.

ROUTINE MESSAGES

BLOGGING SKILLS

9. Here's how it will work: Explaining the brainstorming process. Austin, Texas, advertising agency GSD&M Advertising brainstorms new advertising ideas using a process it calls *dynamic collaboration*. A hand-picked team of insiders and outsiders is briefed on the project and given a key question or two to answer. The team members then sit down at computers and anonymously submit as many responses as they can within five minutes. The project moderators then pore over these responses, looking for any sparks that can ignite new ways of understanding and reaching out to consumers.

Your task: For these brainstorming sessions, GSD&M recruits an eclectic mix of participants from inside and outside the agency—figures as diverse as economists and professional video gamers. To make sure everyone understands the brainstorming guidelines, prepare a message to be posted on the project blog. In your own words, convey the following four points as clearly and succinctly as you can:

- **Be yourself.** We want input from as many perspectives as possible, which is why we recruit such a diverse array of participants. Don't try to get into what you believe is the mindset of an advertising specialist; we want you to approach the given challenge using whatever analytical and creative skills you normally employ in your daily work.
- **Create, don't edit.** Don't edit, refine, or self-censor while you're typing during the initial five-minute session. We don't care if your ideas are formatted beautifully, phrased poetically, or even spelled correctly. Just crank 'em out as quickly as you can.
- **It's about the ideas, not the participants.** Just so you know up front, all ideas are collected anonymously. We can't tell who submitted the brilliant ideas, the boring ideas, or the already-tried-that ideas. So while you won't get personal credit, you can also be crazy and fearless. Go for it!
- **The winning ideas will be subjected to the toughest of tests.** Just in case you're worried about submitting ideas that could be risky, expensive, or difficult to implement—don't fret. As we narrow down the possibilities, the few that remain will be judged, poked, prodded, and assessed from every angle. In other words, let us worry about containing the fire; you come up with the sparks.[11]

PODCASTING SKILLS PORTFOLIO BUILDER

10. Listening to business: Using the iPod to train employees. As a training specialist in Winnebago Industry's human resources department, you're always on the lookout for new ways to help employees learn vital job skills. While watching a production worker page through a training manual while learning how to assemble a new recreational vehicle, you get what seems to be a great idea: Record the assembly instructions as audio files that workers can listen to while performing the necessary steps. With audio instructions, they wouldn't need to keep shifting their eyes between the product and the manual—and constantly losing their place. They could focus on the product and listen for each instruction. Plus, the new system wouldn't cost much at all; any computer can record the audio files, and you'd simply make them available on an intranet site for download into iPods or other digital music players.

Your task: You immediately run your new idea past your boss, who has heard about podcasting but doesn't think it has any place in business. He asks you to prove the viability of the idea by recording a demonstration. Choose a process that you engage in yourself—anything from replacing the strings on a guitar to sewing a quilt to changing the oil in a car—and write a brief (one page or less) description of the process that could be recorded as an audio file. Think carefully about the limitations of the audio format as a replacement for printed text (for instance, do you need to tell people to pause the audio while they perform a time-consuming task?). If directed by your instructor, record your instructions as a podcast.

BLOGGING SKILLS PORTFOLIO BUILDER

11. Now hear this: Not-so-subtle request from the boss for better listening skills. You are normally an easygoing manager who gives your employees a lot of leeway in using their own personal communication styles. However, the weekly staff meeting this morning pushed you over the edge. People were interrupting one another, asking questions that had already been answered, sending text messages during presentations, and exhibiting just about every other poor listening habit imaginable.

Your task: Review the advice in Chapter 2 on good listening skills and then write a post for the internal company blog. Emphasize the importance of effective listening and list at least five steps your employees can take to become better listeners.

ROUTINE REPLIES

E-MAIL SKILLS PORTFOLIO BUILDER

12. Window shopping at Walmart: Offering advice to the webmaster. Walmart has grown to international success because it rarely fails to capitalize on a marketing scheme, and its website is no exception. To make sure the website remains effective and relevant, the webmaster asks various people to check out the site and give their feedback. As administrative assistant to Walmart's director of marketing, you have just received a request from the webmaster to visit Walmart's website and give your feedback.

Your task: Visit www.walmart.com and do some online "window shopping." As you browse through the site, consider the language, layout, graphics, and overall ease of use. In particular, look for aspects of the site that might be confusing or frustrating—annoyances that could prompt shoppers to abandon their quests and head to a competitor such as Target. Summarize your findings and recommendations in an e-mail message to the webmaster.

LETTER WRITING SKILLS

13. The special courier: Letter of recommendation for an old friend. In today's mail, you get a letter from Non-Stop Messenger Service, 899 Sparks St., Ottawa, Ontario K1A 0G9, Canada. It concerns a friend of yours who has applied for a job. Here is the letter:

Kathryn Norquist has applied for the position of special courier with our firm, and she has given us your name as a reference. Our special couriers convey materials of considerable value or confidentiality to their recipients. It is not an easy job. Special couriers must sometimes remain alert for periods of up to 20 hours, and they cannot expect to follow the usual "three square meals and a full night's sleep" routine because they often travel long distances on short notice. On occasion, a special courier must react quickly and decisively to threatening situations.

For this type of work, we hire only people of unquestioned integrity, as demonstrated both by their public records and by references from people, like you, who have known them personally or professionally.

We would appreciate a letter from you, supplying detailed answers to the following questions: (1) How long and in what circumstances have you known the applicant? (2) What qualities does she possess that would qualify her for the position of special courier? (3) What qualities might need to be improved before she is put on permanent assignment in this job?

As vice president of human resources at UPS, you know how much weight a strong personal reference can carry, and you don't really mind that Kathryn never contacted you for permission to list your name—that's Kathryn. You met her during your sophomore year at San Diego State University—that would have been

1994—and you two were roommates for several years after. Her undergraduate degree was in journalism, and her investigative reporting was relentless. You have never known anyone who could match Kathryn's stamina when she was on a story. Of course, when she was between stories, she could sleep longer and do less than anyone else you have ever known.

After a few years of reporting, Kathryn went back to school and earned her MBA from the University of San Diego. After that, you lost track of her for a while. Somebody said that she had joined the FBI—or was it the CIA?—you never really knew. You received a couple of postcards from Paris and one from Madrid.

Two years ago, you met Kathryn for dinner. Only in town for the evening, she was on her way to Borneo to "do the text" for a photographer friend of hers who worked for *National Geographic*. You read the article last year on the shrinking habitat for orangutans. It was powerful.

Although you're in no position to say much about Kathryn's career accomplishments, you can certainly recommend her energy and enthusiasm, her ability to focus on a task or an assignment, her devotion to ethics, and her style. She always seems unshakable—organized, thorough, and honorable—whether digging into political corruption or trudging the jungles of Borneo. You're not sure that her free spirit would flourish in a courier's position, and you wonder if she is a bit overqualified for the job. But knowing Kathryn, you're confident she wouldn't apply for a position unless she truly wanted it.

Your task: Supplying any details you can think of, write as supportive a letter as possible about your friend Kathryn to Roscoe de la Penda, Human Resources Specialist, Non-Stop Messenger.

E-MAIL SKILLS

14. Red dirt to go: Positive e-mail reply from Paradise Sportswear. As the owner of Paradise Sportswear in Hawaii, Robert Hedin was nearly done in by Hurricane Iniki in 1992, which wiped out his first silk-screened and airbrushed T-shirt business. He tried again, but then Hawaii's red dirt started seeping into his warehouse and ruining his inventory. Finally, a friend suggested that he stop trying to fight Mother Nature. Hedin took the hint: He mortgaged his condo and began producing Red Dirt Shirts, all made with dye created from the troublesome local dirt.

Bingo. Hedin's Red Dirt Sportswear designs are so popular, they're being snapped up by locals and tourists in Hedin's eight Paradise Sportswear retail outlets and in every Kmart on the islands. Hedin even added a new line, Lava Blues, made with real Hawaiian lava rock.

"You can make 500 shirts with a bucket of dirt," grins Hedin as he shows you around the operation on your first day. He's just a few years away from the usual retirement age, but he looks like a kid who's finally found the right playground.

Recently, Hedin decided to capitulate to all the requests he's received from retail outlets on the mainland. Buyers kept coming to the islands on vacation, discovering Hedin's "natural" sportswear, and begging him to set up a deal. For a long time, his answer was no; he simply couldn't handle the extra work. But now he's hired you.

As special sales representative, you'll help Hedin expand slowly into this new territory, starting with one store. Wholesaling to the local Kmarts is easy enough, but handling all the arrangements for shipping to the mainland would be too much for the current staff. So you'll start with the company Hedin has chosen to become the first mainland retailer to sell Red Dirt and Lava Blues sportswear: Surf's Up in Chicago, Illinois—of all places. The boss figures that with less competition than he'd find on either coast, his island-influenced sportswear will be a big hit in Chicago, especially in the dead of winter.

Your task: Write a positive response to the e-mail received from Surf's Up buyer Ronald Draeger, who says he fell in love with the Paradise clothing concept while on a surfing trip to Maui. Let him know he'll have a temporary exclusive and that you'll be sending a credit application and other materials by snail mail. His e-mail address is surfsup@insnet.com.[12]

E-MAIL SKILLS

15. Lighten up: E-mail reply to a website designer at Organizers Unlimited. When Kendra Williams, owner of Organizers Unlimited, wanted to create a website to sell her Superclean Organizer, she asked you, her assistant, to find a designer. After some research, you found three promising individuals. Williams chose Pete Womack, whose résumé impressed both of you. Now he's e-mailed his first design proposal, and Williams is not happy.

"I detest cluttered websites!" she explodes. "This homepage has too many graphics and animations, too much 'dancing baloney.' He must have included at least a megabyte of bouncing cotton balls and jogging soap bars! Clever, maybe, but we don't want it! If the homepage takes too long to load, our customers won't wait for it, and we'll lose sales."

Williams's dislike of clutter is what inspired her to invent the Superclean Organizer in the first place, a neat device for organizing bathroom items.

Your task: "You found him," says Williams. "Now you can answer and tell him what's wrong with this design." Before you write the e-mail reply to Womack explaining the need for a simpler homepage, read some of the articles offering tips at **www.sitepoint.com**. On the homepage, under "Before You Code," select "Site Planning." Under "Design and Layout," select "Design Principles." Use the ideas you find to support your message.[13]

LETTER WRITING SKILLS

16. Impressive trainee: Letter of recommendation for a top-notch intern. As a project manager at Orbitz, one of the largest online travel services in the world, you've seen plenty of college interns in action. However, few have impressed you as much as Maxine "Max" Chenault. For one thing, she learned how to navigate the company's content management system virtually overnight and always used it properly, whereas other interns sometimes left things in a hopeless mess. She asked lots of intelligent questions about the business. You've been teaching her blogging and website design principles, and she's picked them up rapidly. Moreover, she is always on time, professional, and eager to assist. Also, she didn't mind doing mundane tasks.

On the downside, Chenault is a popular student. Early on, you often found her busy on the phone planning her many social activities when you needed her help. However, after you had a brief talk with her, this problem vanished.

You'll be sorry to see Chenault leave when she returns to school in the fall, but you're pleased to respond when she asks you for a letter of recommendation. She's not sure where she'll apply for work after graduation or what career path she'll choose, so she asks you to keep the letter fairly general.

Your task: Working with a team of your classmates, discuss what should and should not be in the letter. Prepare an outline based on your discussion and then draft the letter.

IM SKILLS

17. Lease the light: Solar power financing options. As energy costs trend ever upward and more people become attuned to the geopolitical complexities of petroleum-based energy, interest in solar, wind, and other alternative energy sources continues to grow. In locations with high *insolation*, a measure of cumulative sunlight, solar panels can be cost-effective solutions over the long term. However, the upfront costs are still daunting for most homeowners. To help lower the entry barrier, the Foster City, California–based firm Solar City now lets homeowners lease solar panels for monthly payments that are less than their current electricity bills.[14]

Your task: Assume that Solar City is about to add an IM chat function to its website. Prepare a standard response (one or two sentences) that briefly describes the company's SolarLease option. The response will be programmed into the system, and with a few mouse clicks, operators can send it whenever website visitors ask for more information about a solar panel lease. To learn more, visit www.solarcity.com, click on "Solar 101," and then click "About SolarLease." In one or two sentences—you can't go into a lot of detail, of course—explain what the lease means and list several key benefits.

POSITIVE MESSAGES

BLOGGING SKILLS PORTFOLIO BUILDER

18. Leveraging the good news: Blog announcement of a prestigious professional award. You and your staff in the public relations (PR) department at Epson of America were delighted when the communication campaign you created for the new PictureMate Personal Photo Lab (www.epson.com/picturemate) was awarded the prestigious Silver Anvil award by the Public Relations Society of America. Now you'd like to give your team a pat on the back by sharing the news with the rest of the company.

Your task: Write a one-paragraph message for the PR department blog (which is read by people throughout the company but is not accessible outside the company) announcing the award. Take care not to "toot your own horn" as the manager of the PR department. Use the opportunity to compliment the rest of the company for designing and producing such an innovative product.[15]

LETTER WRITING SKILLS

19. Intercultural condolences: Letter conveying sympathy at IBM. You've been working for two years as administrative assistant to Ron Glover, vice president of global workforce diversity at IBM in Armonk, New York. Chana Panichpapiboon has been with Glover even longer than you have, and, sadly, her husband was killed (along with 19 others) in a bus accident yesterday. The bus skidded on icy pavement into a deep ravine, tipping over and crushing the occupants before rescue workers could get to them.

You met Surin last year at a company banquet. You can still picture his warm smile and the easy way he joked with you and others over chicken Florentine, even though you were a complete stranger to him. He was only 32 years old, and he left Chana two children, a 12-year-old boy, Arsa, and a 10-year-old girl, Veera. His death is a terrible tragedy.

Normally, you'd write a condolence letter immediately. Chana is a native of Thailand, and so was Surin. You know you better do a little research first. Is Chana Buddhist or Catholic? Is there anything about the typical Western practice of expressing sympathy that might be inappropriate? Offensive?

After making some discreet inquiries among Chana's closest friends at work, you've learned that she is Theravada Buddhist, as are most people in Thailand. From a reference work in the company library about doing business around the world, you've gleaned only that, in the beliefs of many people in Thailand, "the person takes precedence over rule or law" and "people gain their social position as a result of karma, not personal achievement," which means Chana may believe in reincarnation. But the book also says that Theravada Buddhists are free to choose which precepts of their religion, if any, they will follow. So Chana's beliefs are still a mystery.

You do know that her husband was very important to her and much loved by all their family. That, at least, is universal. And you're toying with a phrase you once read, "The hand of time lightly lays, softly soothing sorrow's wound." Is it appropriate?

Your task: You've decided to handwrite the condolence note on a blank greeting card you've found that bears a peaceful, "Eastern-flavor" image. You know you're risking a cultural gaffe, but at least you won't commit the greater offense of not writing at all. Choose the most sincere wording you can, which should resonate through any differences in custom or tradition.[16]

BLOGGING SKILLS PORTFOLIO BUILDER

20. Green is the new green: Blog update on energy savings. Adobe Systems is well known as the maker of Acrobat, Photoshop, Flash, and other programs that are fundamental tools in the Internet Age. It is also becoming well known as one of the "greenest" companies in the country, adopting a variety of techniques and technologies that have not only reduced its energy usage considerably but also cut nearly $1 million a year from its utility bills. In 2006, Adobe became the first company ever to receive the Platinum Certification from the U.S. Green Building Council.

Your task: Write a one- or two-paragraph post for an internal blog at Adobe, letting employees know how well the company is doing in its efforts to reduce energy usage and thanking employees for the energy-saving ideas they've submitted and the individual efforts they've made to reduce, reuse, and recycle. Learn more about the company's accomplishments by searching for the news release "Adobe Headquarters Awarded Highest Honors from U.S. Green Building Council," available on the Adobe website, at www.adobe.com/aboutadobe/pressroom. Select a few key details from this news release to include in your message.[17]

9 Writing Negative Messages

Learning Objectives

After studying this chapter, you will be able to

1. Apply the three-step writing process to negative messages
2. Explain the differences between the direct and the indirect approaches to negative messages, including when it's appropriate to use each one
3. Identify the risks of using the indirect approach, and explain how to avoid such problems
4. Explain the importance of maintaining high standards of ethics and etiquette when delivering negative messages
5. Explain the role of communication in crisis management
6. List three guidelines for delivering negative news to job applicants, and give a brief explanation of each one

On the Job: Communicating at Leviton

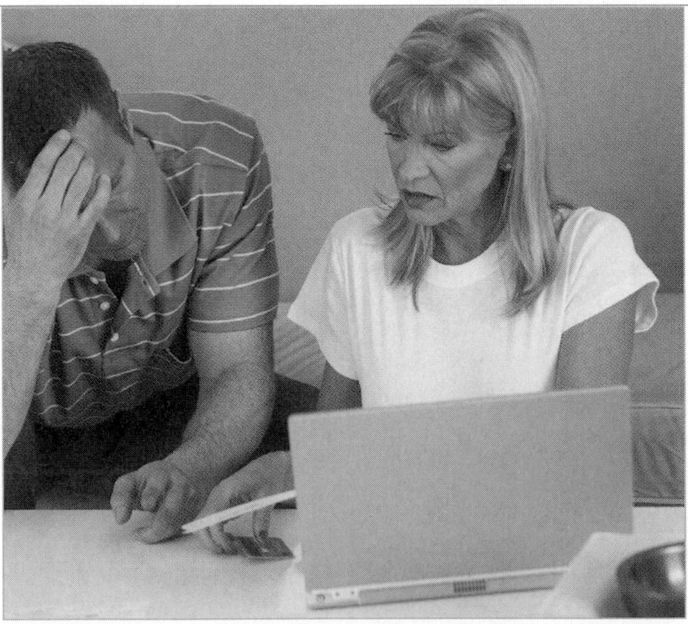

With the economy struggling in 2009, many employees were worried about losing retirement benefits. Executives at Leviton Manufacturing faced the unenviable task of telling employees the company was forced to temporarily suspend funding of their retirement accounts.

Breaking the Bad News About Retirement Accounts

Leviton Manufacturing, based in Little Neck, New York, is one of the world's leading manufacturers of electrical and electronic components used in lighting, energy management, and data communication. In fact, 90 percent of all U.S. homes have Leviton light switches, outlets, and other electrical devices. Unfortunately, with its business so heavily dependent on the construction industry, the company was particularly vulnerable to the virtual collapse of the housing market in 2008.

By January 2009, Leviton executives found it necessary to suspend the company's matching contributions to employees' 401(k) accounts. A 401(k) is a widely used type of savings and investing account that is vital to the retirement plans of millions of employees nationwide. Employees can put aside a portion of their pretax income in a 401(k), which lowers their current income tax and lets their retirement nest eggs grow tax-free as well. Employers typically match all or part of an employee's investment, making the 401(k) one of the most highly prized benefits available to employees today.

With the decision made to temporarily suspend matching contributions, Fran Ruderman, Leviton's senior director of benefits and compensation, faced a significant communication challenge—how to break the news to Leviton's 3,600 employees.

Delivering bad news is never easy, but Ruderman and Leviton CEO Don Hendler demonstrated the right way to do it. First, they shared the news via e-mail as soon as possible after the decision was made, giving employees time to adjust their financial strategies. Second, Ruderman and Hendler didn't hide behind lower-level employees or organizational boundaries. Hendler insisted on sending the message himself so that employees knew he took responsibility for the decision. Third, Ruderman sent the message to managers and human resources (HR) representatives before sending it to employees, giving these vital intermediaries time to prepare for the inevitable questions and concerns from employees. Fourth, Ruderman assured these managers and HR staffers that they had backup at the corporate level if needed. "I followed up with them to let everyone know that if they needed any assistance or help answering questions to come to me or someone else in the corporate office," she explained. Fifth, the message emphasized that the situation was not permanent, and that matching contributions would be restored when the company's finances permitted.

By communicating with honesty, attention to detail, and real concern for their employees, Ruderman and Hendler demonstrated a fundamental principle: it is possible to deliver negative news in a positive way.[1]
www.leviton.com

USING THE THREE-STEP WRITING PROCESS FOR NEGATIVES MESSAGES

1 LEARNING OBJECTIVE

Apply the three-step writing process to negative messages.

With any luck you'll never be forced to deliver bad news like Leviton's Fran Ruderman (profiled in the chapter-opening "On the Job" vignette), but communicating other kinds of negative news is a fact of life for all business professionals, from rejecting job applicants to telling customers that shipments will be late to turning down speaking invitations.

When you need to send a negative message, you have five goals: (1) to convey the bad news, (2) to gain acceptance for the bad news, (3) to maintain as much goodwill as possible with your audience, (4) to maintain a good image for your organization, and (5) if appropriate, to reduce or eliminate the need for future correspondence on the matter (however, in a few cases, you may want to encourage discussion). Five goals are clearly a lot to accomplish in one message. However, by learning some simple techniques and following the three-step process, you can develop negative messages that reduce the stress for everyone involved and improve the effectiveness of your communication efforts.

Five goals of negative messages:
- *Give the bad news*
- *Ensure acceptance of the bad news*
- *Maintain reader's goodwill*
- *Maintain organization's good image*
- *Minimize or eliminate future correspondence on the matter, as appropriate*

Step 1: Planning a Negative Message

When planning negative messages, you can't avoid the fact that your audience does not want to hear what you have to say. To minimize the damage to business relationships and to encourage the acceptance of your message, analyze the situation carefully to better understand the context in which the recipient will process your message.

Analysis, investigation, and adaptation help you avoid alienating your readers.

Be sure to consider your purpose thoroughly—whether it's straightforward (such as rejecting a job applicant) or more complicated (such as drafting a negative performance review, in which you not only give the employee feedback on past performance but also help the person develop a plan to improve future performance). Similarly, your audience profile can be simple and obvious in some situations (such as rejecting a credit request) and far more complex in others (such as telling a business partner that you've decided to terminate the partnership).

With a clear purpose and your audience's needs in mind, identify and gather the information your audience requires in order to understand and accept your message. Negative messages can be intensely personal to the recipient, and in many cases, recipients have a right to expect a thorough explanation of your answer.

Selecting the right medium is critical. Experts advise that bad news for employees be delivered in person whenever possible, both to show respect for the employees and to give them an opportunity to ask questions. Of course, delivering bad news is never easy, and an increasing number of managers appear to be using e-mail and other electronic media to convey negative messages to employees.[2]

When preparing negative messages, choose the medium with care.

Defining your main idea in a negative message is often more complicated than simply saying no. For instance, if you need to respond to a hardworking employee who requested

Appropriate organization helps readers accept your negative news.

TABLE 9.1 Choosing Positive Words

EXAMPLES OF NEGATIVE PHRASINGS	POSITIVE ALTERNATIVES
Your request *doesn't make any sense.*	Please clarify your request.
The *damage won't be fixed* for a week.	The item will be repaired next week.
Although it wasn't *our fault*, there will be an *unavoidable delay* in your order.	We will process your order as soon as we receive an aluminum shipment from our supplier, which we expect to happen within 10 days.
You are clearly *dissatisfied.*	I recognize that the product did not live up to your expectations.
I was *shocked* to learn that you're *unhappy.*	Thank you for sharing your concerns about your shopping experience.
Unfortunately, we haven't received it.	The item hasn't arrived yet.
The enclosed statement is *wrong.*	Please verify the enclosed statement and provide a correct copy.

a raise, your message might go beyond saying no to explaining how she can improve her performance by working smarter, not just harder.

Step 2: Writing a Negative Message

When you are adapting a negative message to your audience, pay close attention to effectiveness and diplomacy. After all, your audience does not want to hear bad news or might disagree strongly with you, so messages perceived as being unclear or unkind will amplify the audience's stress.

If your credibility hasn't already been established with the audience, lay out your qualifications for making the decision in question. Recipients of negative messages who don't think you are credible are more likely to challenge your decision or reject your message. And, as always, projecting and protecting your company's image are prime concerns; if you're not careful, a negative answer could spin out of control into negative feelings about your company.

When you use language that conveys respect and avoids an accusing tone, you protect your audience's pride. This kind of communication etiquette is always important, but it demands special care with negative messages. Moreover, you can ease the sense of disappointment by using positive words rather than negative, counterproductive ones (see Table 9.1).

Step 3: Completing a Negative Message

Your need for careful attention to detail continues as you complete your message. Revise your content to make sure everything is clear, complete, and concise—bearing in mind that even small flaws are magnified as readers react to your negative news. Produce clean, professional documents and proofread carefully to eliminate mistakes. Finally, be especially sure that your negative messages are delivered promptly and successfully; waiting for bad news is difficult, and wondering whether a message was lost makes it worse.

DEVELOPING NEGATIVE MESSAGES

As you apply the three-step writing process to negative messages, keep three important aspects in mind. First, before you organize the main points of a message, determine whether it will be better to use the direct or indirect approach (see Figure 9.1). Second, before composing your message, be sensitive to variations across cultures or between internal and external audiences. Third, to fulfill the spirit of audience focus, be sure you maintain high ethical standards.

FIGURE 9.1 Choosing the Indirect or Direct Approach for Negative Messages
Analyze the situation carefully before choosing your approach to organizing negative messages.

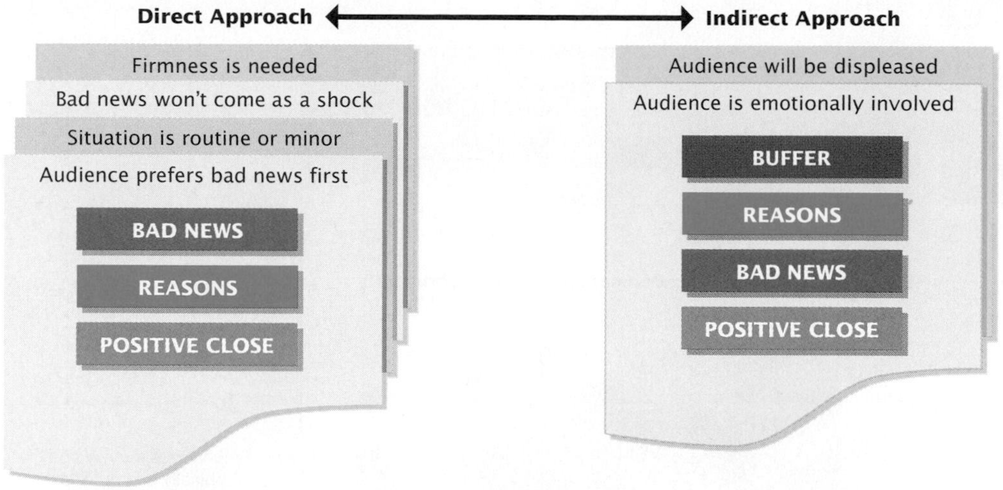

Choosing the Right Approach for the Situation

2 LEARNING OBJECTIVE

Explain the differences between the direct and the indirect approaches to negative messages, including when it's appropriate to use each one.

To choose an approach for negative business messages—direct or indirect—answer the following questions:

- **Will the bad news come as a shock?** The direct approach is fine for business situations in which people understand the possibility of receiving bad news. However, if the bad news might come as a shock to readers, use the indirect approach to help them prepare for it.
- **Does the audience prefer short messages that get right to the point?** For example, if you know that your boss always wants brief messages that get right to the point, use the direct approach.
- **How important is this news to the audience?** For minor or routine scenarios, the direct approach is nearly always better. However, if the audience has an emotional investment in the situation or the consequences are considerable, the indirect approach is less jarring.
- **Do you need to maintain a close working relationship with the audience?** The indirect approach makes it easier to soften the blow of bad news and can therefore be the better choice when you need to preserve a good relationship.
- **Do you need to get the audience's attention?** If someone hasn't responded to repeated indirect messages, the direct approach can help you get his or her attention. In some situations, you have no choice but to confront an employee or other party with a forceful message, and the direct approach is better in these uncomfortable cases. Conversely, if readers have grown accustomed to routine, nonemergency messages from you but then you have a real crisis on your hands that demands their immediate attention, the direct approach is better. For example, like most other lenders, the home mortgage giant Countrywide (now part of Bank of America) sends customers a variety of routine and promotional messages—many of which are no doubt tossed aside without being read. However, after an employee illegally sold highly sensitive personal information that exposed customers to potential identify theft, the company used the direct approach in a letter to affected customers. The letter announced the theft in the first sentence, and then it went on to outline exactly what types of information were stolen.[3] Anyone taking even a cursory glance at the letter would recognize that this was not a routine message.
- **What is your organization's preferred style?** Companies often have a distinct communication style, ranging from blunt and direct to gentle and indirect. However, going against expectations can be an effective way to get people's attention in a dramatic way.

You need to consider a variety of factors when choosing between the direct and indirect approaches for negative messages.

FIGURE 9.2 Negative Message Using the Direct Approach
Spherion Corporation, a recruiting and staffing firm based in Fort Lauderdale, Florida, conducts monthly surveys of the U.S. workforce. The company used the direct approach to announce a decline in employee confidence.

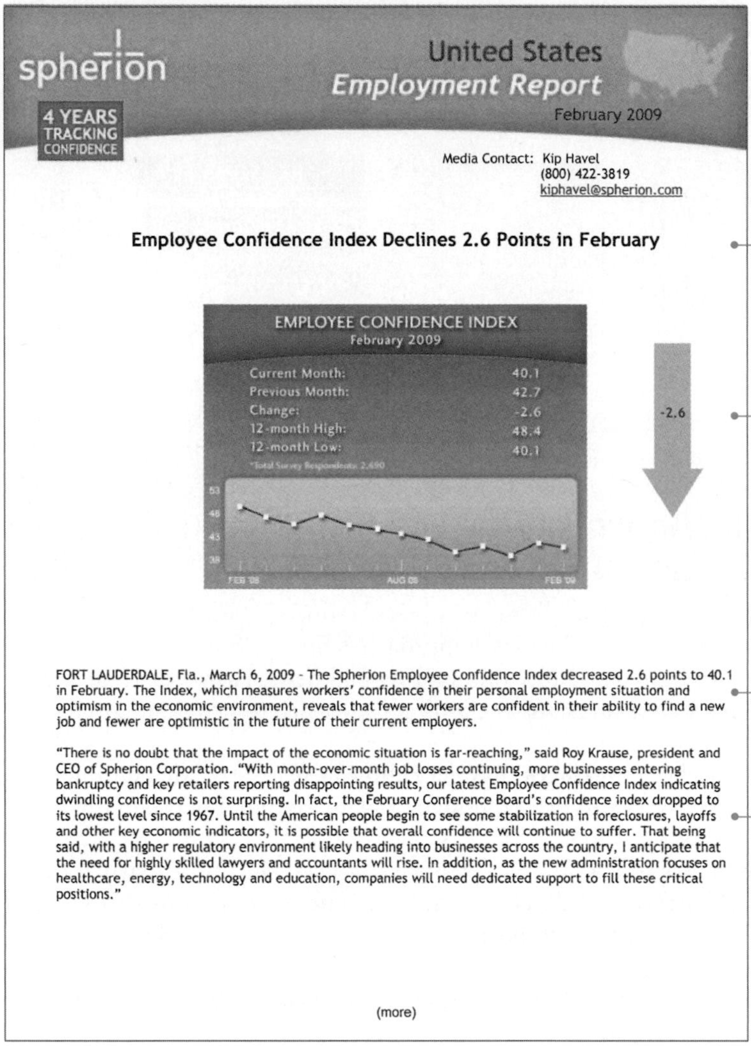
spherion

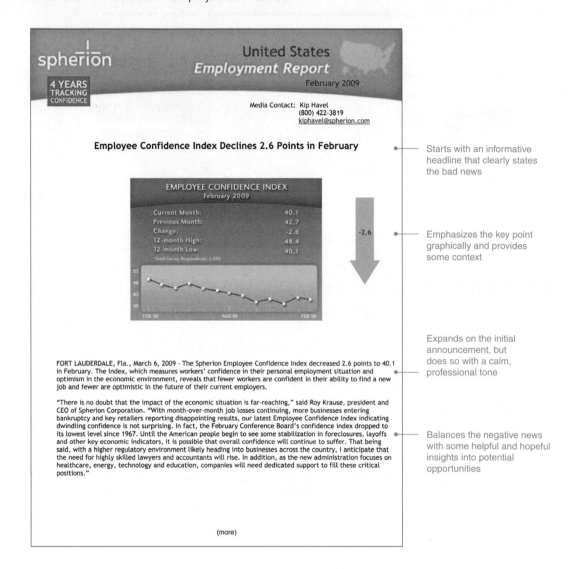

4 YEARS TRACKING CONFIDENCE

United States
Employment Report
February 2009

Media Contact: Kip Havel
(800) 422-3819
kiphavel@spherion.com

Employee Confidence Index Declines 2.6 Points in February

FORT LAUDERDALE, Fla., March 6, 2009 - The Spherion Employee Confidence Index decreased 2.6 points to 40.1 in February. The Index, which measures workers' confidence in their personal employment situation and optimism in the economic environment, reveals that fewer workers are confident in their ability to find a new job and fewer are optimistic in the future of their current employers.

"There is no doubt that the impact of the economic situation is far-reaching," said Roy Krause, president and CEO of Spherion Corporation. "With month-over-month job losses continuing, more businesses entering bankruptcy and key retailers reporting disappointing results, our latest Employee Confidence Index indicating dwindling confidence is not surprising. In fact, the February Conference Board's confidence index dropped to its lowest level since 1967. Until the American people begin to see some stabilization in foreclosures, layoffs and other key economic indicators, it is possible that overall confidence will continue to suffer. That being said, with a higher regulatory environment likely heading into businesses across the country, I anticipate that the need for highly skilled lawyers and accountants will rise. In addition, as the new administration focuses on healthcare, energy, technology and education, companies will need dedicated support to fill these critical positions."

(more)

Starts with an informative headline that clearly states the bad news

Emphasizes the key point graphically and provides some context

Expands on the initial announcement, but does so with a calm, professional tone

Balances the negative news with some helpful and hopeful insights into potential opportunities

No matter which approach you choose for a given message, don't lose sight of your purpose and your audience. A sensitive, personal tone can be more important to your readers than your choice of message organization.[4]

Using the Direct Approach Effectively

Use the direct approach when your negative answer or information will have minimal personal impact.

A negative message using the direct approach opens with the bad news, proceeds to the reasons for the situation or the decision, and ends with a positive statement aimed at maintaining a good relationship with the audience (see Figure 9.2). Depending on the circumstances, the message may also offer alternatives or a plan of action to fix the situation under discussion. Stating the bad news at the beginning can have two advantages: (1) It makes a shorter message possible, and (2) it allows the audience to reach the main idea of the message in less time.

Opening with a Clear Statement of the Bad News

No matter what the news is, come right out and say it. However, even if the news is likely to be devastating, maintain a calm, professional tone that keeps the focus on the news and not on individual failures or other personal factors. Also, if necessary, remind the reader why you're writing.

After an explosion that killed one employee and worried local residents about the potential release of toxic chemicals, Bayer CropScience plant manager Nick Crosby said, "We are truly sorry for the serious issues caused by the incident at our facility. . . . We understand the anxiety in the community resulting from the incident." He also apologized to people living near the Institute, West Virginia, plant for failing to clarify that there was no danger of toxic emissions: "We could have communicated, and we should have communicated, much better with the community that night."

Providing Reasons and Additional Information

In most cases, you follow the direct opening with an explanation of why the news is negative. The extent of your explanation depends on the nature of the news and your relationship with the reader. For example, if you want to preserve a long-standing relationship with an important customer, a detailed explanation could well be worth the extra effort such a message would require.

However, you will encounter some situations in which explaining negative news is neither appropriate nor helpful, such as when the reasons are confidential, excessively complicated, or irrelevant to the reader. To maintain a cordial working relationship with the reader, you might want to explain why you can't provide the information.

Should you apologize when delivering bad news? The answer isn't quite as simple as one might think. The notion of *apology* is hard to pin down. To some people, it simply means an expression of sympathy that something negative has happened to another person. At the other extreme, it means admitting fault and taking responsibility for specific compensations or corrections to atone for the mistake.

Some experts have advised that a company should never apologize, even when it knows it has made a mistake, as the apology might be taken as a confession of guilt that could be used against the company in a lawsuit. However, several states have laws that specifically prevent expressions of sympathy from being used as evidence of legal liability. In fact, judges, juries, and plaintiffs tend to be more forgiving of companies that express sympathy for wronged parties; moreover, an apology can help repair a company's reputation. Recently, some prosecutors have begun pressing executives to publicly admit guilt and apologize as part of the settlement of criminal cases—unlike the common tactic of paying fines but refusing to admit any wrongdoing.[5]

Although corporate apologies have been more common in recent years, the worldwide crises in the business and consumer credit markets that began in 2008 might signal a new phase in apology strategies. After the failure of risky investment strategies led to billions of dollars in corporate losses, massive layoffs, the collapse of some of the country's biggest banking companies, and widespread damage to the economy, the lack of public apologies angered both consumers and executives in other companies. As the crisis continues to unfold and inevitable lawsuits appear, it remains to be seen whether any top managers in the firms at the center of the calamity will step forward with apologies.[6]

The best general advice in the event of a serious mistake or accident is to immediately and sincerely express sympathy and offer help if appropriate, without admitting guilt; then seek the advice of your company's lawyers before elaborating. As one survey concluded, "The risks of making an apology are low, and the potential reward is high."[7]

No matter how trivial or serious the situation, if you do apologize, make it a real apology. Don't say "I'm sorry if anyone was offended" by what you did—this statement implies that you're not sorry at all and that it's the other party's fault for being offended.[8] Moreover, if appropriate, explain what steps you are taking to avoid similar mistakes in the future.

Closing on a Positive Note

After you've explained the negative news, close the message in a positive but still honest and respectful manner. Consider offering your readers an alternative solution if you can. Depending on the situation, you might also explain how you or your organization plans to respond to the negative news.

3 LEARNING OBJECTIVE

Identify the risks of using the indirect approach, and explain how to avoid such problems.

Using the Indirect Approach Effectively

The indirect approach helps readers prepare for the bad news by presenting the reasons for it first. However, the indirect approach is *not* meant to obscure bad news, delay it, or limit your responsibility. Rather, the purpose of this approach is to ease the blow and help readers accept the situation. When done poorly, the indirect approach can be disrespectful and even unethical. But when done well, it is a good example of audience-oriented communication crafted with attention to ethics and etiquette. Showing consideration for the feelings of others is never dishonest.

Use the indirect approach when some preparation will help your audience accept your bad news.

Opening with a Buffer

Messages using the indirect approach open with a **buffer**: a neutral, noncontroversial statement that establishes common ground with the reader (refer to Figure 9.1). A good buffer can express your appreciation for being considered (if you're responding to a request), assure your reader of your attention to the request, or indicate your understanding of the reader's needs. A good buffer also needs to be relevant and sincere. In contrast, a poorly written buffer might trivialize the reader's concerns, divert attention from the problem with insincere flattery or irrelevant material, or mislead the reader into thinking your message actually contains good news.

A well-written buffer establishes common ground with the reader.

Consider these possible responses to a manager of the order-fulfillment department who requested some temporary staffing help from your department (a request you won't be able to fulfill):

- Our department shares your goal of processing orders quickly and efficiently. — Establishes common ground with the reader and validates the concerns that prompted the original request—without promising a positive answer
- As a result of the last downsizing, every department in the company is running shorthanded. — Establishes common ground, but in a negative way that downplays the recipient's concerns
- You folks are doing a great job over there, and I'd love to be able to help out. — Potentially misleads the reader into concluding that you will comply with the request
- Those new state labor regulations are driving me crazy over here; how about in your department? — Trivializes the reader's concerns by opening with an irrelevant issue

Only the first of these buffers can be considered effective; the other three are likely to damage your relationship with the other manager—and lower his or her opinion of you. Table 9.2 shows several types of effective buffers you could use to tactfully open a negative message.

A poorly written buffer may mislead or insult the reader.

Given the damage that a poorly composed buffer can do, consider every buffer carefully before you send it. Is it respectful? Is it relevant? Is it neutral, implying neither yes nor no? Does it provide a smooth transition to the reasons that follow? If you can answer yes to every question, you can proceed confidently to the next section of your message. However, if a little voice inside your head tells you that your buffer sounds insincere or misleading, it probably is, in which case you'll need to rewrite it.

Providing Reasons and Additional Information

Phrase your reasons to signal the negative news ahead.

An effective buffer serves as a stepping-stone to the next part of your message, in which you build up the explanations and information that will culminate in your negative news. An ideal explanation section leads readers to your conclusion before you come right out and say it. In other words, before you actually say no, the reader has followed your line of reasoning and is ready for the answer. By giving your reasons effectively, you help maintain focus on the issues at hand and defuse the emotions that always accompany significantly bad news.

As you lay out your reasons, guide your reader's response by starting with the most positive points first and moving forward to increasingly negative ones. Be concise but provide enough detail for the audience to understand your reasons. You need to convince your audience that your decision is justified, fair, and logical. If appropriate, you can use the explanation section to suggest how the negative news might in fact benefit your reader in

TABLE 9.2 Types of Buffers

BUFFER TYPE	STRATEGY	EXAMPLE
Agreement	Find a point on which you and the reader share similar views.	We both know how hard it is to make a profit in this industry.
Appreciation	Express sincere thanks for receiving something.	Your check for $127.17 arrived yesterday. Thank you.
Cooperation	Convey your willingness to help in any way you realistically can.	Employee Services is here to assist all associates with their health insurance, retirement planning, and continuing education needs.
Fairness	Assure the reader that you've closely examined and carefully considered the problem, or mention an appropriate action that has already been taken.	For the past week, we have had our bandwidth monitoring tools running around the clock to track your actual upload and download speeds.
Good news	Start with the part of your message that is favorable.	We have credited your account in the amount of $14.95 to cover the cost of return shipping.
Praise	Find an attribute or an achievement to compliment.	The Stratford Group clearly has an impressive record of accomplishment in helping clients resolve financial reporting problems.
Resale	Favorably discuss the product or company related to the subject of the letter.	With their heavy-duty, full-suspension hardware and fine veneers, the desks and file cabinets in our Montclair line have long been popular with value-conscious professionals.
Understanding	Demonstrate that you understand the reader's goals and needs.	So that you can more easily find the printer with the features you need, we are enclosing a brochure that describes all the Epson printers currently available.

some way—but only if this is true and only if you can do so without offending your audience.

Avoid hiding behind company policy to cushion your bad news. If you say, "Company policy forbids our hiring anyone who does not have two years' supervisory experience," you imply that you won't consider anyone on his or her individual merits. Skilled and sympathetic communicators explain company policy (without referring to it as "policy") so that the audience can try to meet the requirements at a later time. Consider this response to an employee:

Don't hide behind "company policy" when you deliver bad news; present logical answers instead.

> Because these management positions are quite challenging, the human relations department has researched the qualifications needed to succeed in them. The findings show that the two most important qualifications are a bachelor's degree in business administration and two years' supervisory experience.

Shows the reader that the decision is based on a methodical analysis of the company's needs and not on some arbitrary guideline

Establishes the criteria behind the decision and lets the reader know what to expect

This paragraph does a good job of stating reasons for the refusal:

- It provides enough detail to logically support the refusal.
- It implies that the applicant is better off avoiding a program in which he or she might fail.
- It shows that the company's policy is based on experience and careful analysis.
- It doesn't offer an apology for the decision because no one is at fault.
- It avoids negative personal expressions (such as "You do not meet our requirements").

Well-written reasons are
- *Detailed*
- *Tactful*
- *Individualized*
- *Unapologetic if no one is at fault*
- *Positive*

Even valid, well-thought-out reasons won't convince every reader in every situation. However, if you've done a good job of laying out your reasoning, you've done everything you can to prepare the reader for the main idea, which is the negative news itself.

To handle bad news carefully
- *De-emphasize the bad news visually and grammatically*
- *Use a conditional statement, if appropriate*
- *Tell what you did do, not what you didn't do*

Continuing with a Clear Statement of the Bad News

After you've prepared the audience to receive the bad news, the next task is to present the news as clearly and as kindly as possible. Three techniques are especially useful for saying no. First, de-emphasize the bad news:

- Minimize the space or time devoted to the bad news—without trivializing it or withholding any important information.
- Subordinate bad news in a complex or compound sentence ("My department is already shorthanded, so I'll need all my staff for at least the next two months"). This construction presents the bad news in the middle of the sentence, the point of least emphasis.
- Embed bad news in the middle of a paragraph or use parenthetical expressions ("Our profits, which are down, are only part of the picture").

However, keep in mind that it's possible to abuse de-emphasis. For instance, if the primary point of your message is that profits are down, it would be inappropriate to marginalize that news by burying it in the middle of a sentence. State the negative news clearly and then make a smooth transition to any positive news that might balance the story.

Second, use a conditional (*if* or *when*) statement to imply that the audience could have received, or might someday receive, a favorable answer ("When you have more managerial experience, you are welcome to reapply"). Such a statement could motivate applicants to improve their qualifications.

Third, emphasize what you can do or have done rather than what you cannot do. Say "We sell exclusively through retailers, and the one nearest you that carries our merchandise is . . ." rather than "We are unable to serve you, so please call your nearest dealer." Also, by implying the bad news, you may not need to actually state it ("The five positions currently open have been filled by people whose qualifications match those uncovered in our research"). By focusing on the facts and implying the bad news, you make the impact less personal.

Don't disguise bad news when you emphasize the positive.

When implying bad news, however, be sure your audience will be able to grasp the entire message—including the bad news. Withholding negative information or overemphasizing positive information is unethical and unfair to your reader. If an implied message might lead to uncertainty, state your decision in direct terms. Just be sure to avoid overly blunt statements that are likely to cause pain and anger:

INSTEAD OF THIS	WRITE THIS
I *must refuse* your request.	I will be out of town on the day you need me.
We *must deny* your application.	The position has been filled.
I *am unable* to grant your request.	Contact us again when you have established . . .
We *cannot afford to* continue the program.	The program will conclude on May 1.
Much as I would like to attend . . .	Our budget meeting ends too late for me to attend.
We *must turn down* your extension request.	Please send in your payment by June 14.

Closing on a Positive Note

As in the direct approach, the close in the indirect approach offers an opportunity to emphasize your respect for your audience, even though you've just delivered unpleasant news. Express best wishes without ending on a falsely upbeat note. If you can find a positive angle that's meaningful to your audience, by all means consider adding it to your conclusion. However, don't try to pretend that the negative news didn't happen or that it won't affect the reader. Suggest alternative solutions if such information is available. If you've asked readers to decide between alternatives or to take some action, make sure that they know what to do, when to do it, and how to do it. Whatever type of conclusion you use, follow these guidelines:

A positive close
- *Builds goodwill*
- *Offers a suggestion for action*
- *Provides a look toward the future*

- **Avoid a negative or uncertain conclusion.** Don't refer to, repeat, or apologize for the bad news. Refrain from expressing any doubt that your reasons will be accepted. (Avoid statements such as "I trust our decision is satisfactory.")

- **Limit future correspondence.** Encourage additional communication *only* if you're willing to discuss your decision further. (If you're not, avoid wording such as "If you have further questions, please write.")
- **Be optimistic about the future.** If the situation might improve in the future, share that with your readers if it's relevant. For example, when Leviton's Fran Ruderman (page 242) crafted her message to employees about the suspension of the 401(k) matching program, she made it clear that the company intended to reinstate the matching program when economic conditions improved.
- **Be sincere.** Steer clear of clichés that are insincere in view of the bad news. (If you can't help, don't say, "If we can be of any help, please contact us.")

Keep in mind that the close is the last thing audience members have to remember you by. Even though they're disappointed, leave them with the impression that they were treated with respect.

Adapting to Your Audience

The disappointing nature of negative messages requires that you maintain your audience focus and be as sensitive as possible to audience needs. As part of this effort, you may need to adapt your message to cultural differences or to the differences between internal and external audiences.

Cultural Variations

Expectations for the handling of bad news vary from culture to culture.

Bad news is unwelcome in any language, but the conventions for conveying it can vary considerably from culture to culture. For instance, French business letters are traditionally quite formal and writer oriented, often without reference to audience needs or benefits. Moreover, when the news is bad, French writers take the direct approach. They open with a reference to the problem or previous correspondence and then state the bad news clearly. While they don't refer to the audience's needs, they often do apologize and express regret for the problem.[9]

In contrast, Japanese letters traditionally open with remarks about the season, business prosperity, or health. When the news is bad, these opening formalities serve as the buffer. Explanations and apologies follow, and then comes the bad news or refusal. Japanese writers protect their readers' feelings by wording the bad news ambiguously. Western readers may even misinterpret this vague language as a condition of acceptance rather than as the refusal it actually is.[10]

Whenever you are communicating across cultures, use the tone, organization, and other cultural conventions that your audience expects. Only then can you avoid the inappropriate or even offensive approaches that could jeopardize your business relationship.[11]

Internal Versus External Audiences

Compared to external audiences, internal audiences often expect more detail in negative messages.

Internal audiences often have expectations for negative messages that differ from those of external audiences. In some cases, the two groups can interpret the news in different or even opposite ways. For example, employees will react negatively to news of an impending layoff, but company shareholders might welcome the news as evidence that management is trying to control costs. In addition, if a negative message such as news of a layoff is being sent to internal and external audiences, employees will expect not only more detail but also to be informed before the public is told. However, given the speed at which internal announcements can be leaked to the outside world via blogs, some companies are now informing employees and the public at the same time in order to control the release of information.[12]

You may need to adjust the content of negative messages for various external audiences.

Negative messages to outside audiences require attention to the diverse nature of the audience and the concern for confidentiality of internal information. A single message might have a half-dozen audiences, all with differing opinions and agendas. You may not be able to explain things to the level of detail that some of these people want if doing so would release proprietary information such as future product plans.

4 LEARNING OBJECTIVE

Explain the importance of maintaining high standards of ethics and etiquette when delivering negative messages.

Maintaining High Standards of Ethics and Etiquette

All business messages demand attention to ethics and etiquette, of course, but these considerations take on special importance when you are delivering bad news—for several reasons. First, a variety of laws and regulations dictate the content and delivery of many business messages with potentially negative content, such as the release of financial information by a public company. Second, negative messages can have a significant negative impact on the lives of those receiving them. Even if the news is conveyed legally and conscientiously, good ethical practice demands that these situations be approached with care and sensitivity. Third, emotions often run high when negative messages are involved, for both the sender and the receiver. Senders need to not only manage their own emotions but also consider the emotional state of their audiences.

The challenge of sending—and receiving—negative messages fosters a tendency to delay, downplay, or distort the bad news.[13] However, doing so may be unethical, if not illegal. In recent years, numerous companies have been sued by shareholders, consumers, employees, and government regulators for allegedly withholding or delaying negative information in such areas as company finances, environmental hazards, and product safety. In many of these cases, the problem was slow, incomplete, or inaccurate communication between the company and external stakeholders. In others, problems stemmed from a reluctance to send or receive negative news within the organization.

Employees who observe unethical or illegal behavior may face the challenge of whistleblowing to bring appropriate attention to the situation.

Employees who observe unethical or illegal behavior within their companies and are unable to resolve the problems through normal channels may have no choice but to resort to **whistleblowing**—expressing their concerns through company ethics hot lines or even going to the news media if they perceive no other options. The decision to "blow the whistle" on one's own employer is rarely easy or without consequences; more than 80 percent of whistleblowers in a recent survey said they were punished in some way for coming forward with their concerns.[14] Although whistleblowing is sometimes characterized as "ratting on" colleagues or managers, it has an essential function. According to international business expert Alex MacBeath, "Whistleblowing can be an invaluable way to alert management to poor business practice within the workplace. Often whistleblowing can be the only way that information about issues such as rule breaking, criminal activity, cover-ups, and fraud can be brought to management's attention before serious damage is suffered."[15] Recognizing the value of this feedback, many companies have formal reporting mechanisms that give employees a way to voice ethical and legal concerns to management.

Negative situations can put your sense of self-control and business etiquette to the test.

Finally, recognize that some negative news scenarios will test your self-control and tempt you to respond with a personal attack. However, keep in mind that negative messages can have a lasting impact on the people who receive them and the people who send them. As a communicator, you have a responsibility to minimize the negative impact of your negative messages through careful planning and sensitive, objective writing. As much as possible, focus on the actions or conditions that led to the negative news, not on personal shortcomings or character issues. Develop a reputation as a professional who can handle the toughest situations with dignity.

For a reminder of successful strategies for creating negative messages, see "Checklist: Creating Negative Messages."

EXPLORING COMMON EXAMPLES OF NEGATIVE MESSAGES

The following sections offer examples of the most common negative messages, dealing with topics such as routine business matters, organizational news, and employment messages.

Sending Negative Messages on Routine Business Matters

As you progress in your career and become more visible in your industry and community, you will receive a variety of invitations to speak at private or public functions or to volunteer your time for a variety of organizations. In addition, routine business matters such as credit applications and requests for adjustment will often require you to make negative

FIGURE 9.3 Effective Letter Declining a Routine Request

May Yee Kwan's company has a long-standing relationship with the college Sandra Wofford represents and wants to maintain that positive relationship, but she can't meet this particular request. To communicate negative news, she therefore uses the indirect approach. If Kwan and Wofford shared a closer relationship (if they worked together in a volunteer organization, for instance), the direct approach might be more appropriate.

1 Plan →

Analyze the Situation

Verify that the purpose is to decline a request and offer alternatives; audience is likely to be surprised by the refusal.

Gather Information

Determine audience needs and obtain the necessary information.

Select the Right Medium

For formal messages, printed letters on company letterhead are best.

Organize the Information

The main idea is to refuse the request so limit your scope to that; select the indirect approach based on the audience and the situation.

2 Write →

Adapt to Your Audience

Adjust the level of formality based on your degree of familiarity with the audience; maintain a positive relationship by using the "you" attitude, politeness, positive emphasis, and bias-free language.

Compose the Message

Use a conversational but professional style and keep the message brief, clear, and as helpful as possible.

3 Complete

Revise the Message

Evaluate content and review readability to make sure the negative information won't be misinterpreted; make sure your tone stays positive without being artificial.

Produce the Message

Maintain a clean, professional appearance on company letterhead.

Proofread the Message

Review for errors in layout, spelling, and mechanics.

Distribute the Message

Deliver your message using the chosen medium.

InfoTech

927 Dawson Valley Road, Tulsa, Oklahoma 74151
Voice: (918) 669-4428 Fax: (918) 669-4429
www.infotech.com

March 6, 2010

Dr. Sandra Wofford, President
Whittier Community College
333 Whittier Avenue
Tulsa, OK 74150

Dear Dr. Wofford:

Infotech has been happy to support Whittier Community College in many ways over the years, and we appreciate the opportunities you and your organization provide to so many deserving students. Thank you for considering our grounds for your graduation ceremony on June 3.

Buffers negative response by demonstrating respect and recapping the request

We would certainly like to accommodate Whittier as we have in years past, but our companywide sales meetings will be held this year during the weeks of May 29 and June 5. With more than 200 sales representatives and their families from around the world joining us, activities will be taking place throughout our facility.

States a meaningful reason for the negative response, without apologizing (because the company is not at fault)

My assistant, Robert Seagers, suggests you contact the Municipal Botanical Gardens as a possible graduation site. He recommends calling Jerry Kane, director of public relations.

Suggests an alternative, showing that Kwan cares about the college and has given the matter some thought

We remain firm in our commitment to you, President Wofford, and to the fine students you represent. Through our internship program, academic research grants, and other initiatives, we will continue to be a strong corporate partner to Whittier College and will support your efforts as you move forward.

Closes by emphasizing the importance of the relationship and the company's continuing commitment

Sincerely,

May Yee Kwan

May Yee Kwan
Public Relations Director

lc

CHECKLIST: Creating Negative Messages

A. Choose the right approach for the situation.
- Consider using the direct approach when the audience is aware of the possibility of negative news, when the reader is not emotionally involved in the message, when you know that the reader would prefer the bad news first, when you know that firmness is necessary, and when you want to discourage a response.
- Consider using the indirect approach when the news is likely to come as a shock or surprise, when your audience has a high emotional investment in the outcome, and when you want to maintain a good relationship with the audience.

B. For the indirect approach, open with an effective buffer.
- Establish common ground with the audience.
- Validate the request, if you are responding to a request.
- Don't trivialize the reader's concerns.
- Don't mislead the reader into thinking the coming news might be positive.

C. Provide reasons and additional information.
- Explain why the news is negative.
- Adjust the amount of detail to fit the situation and the audience.
- Avoid explanations when the reasons are confidential, excessively complicated, or irrelevant to the reader.
- If appropriate, state how you plan to correct or respond to the negative news.
- Seek the advice of company lawyers if you're unsure what to say.

D. Clearly state the bad news.
- State the bad news as positively as possible, using tactful wording.
- To help protect readers' feelings, de-emphasize the bad news by minimizing the space devoted to it, subordinating it, or embedding it.
- If your response might change in the future if circumstances change, explain the conditions to the reader.
- Emphasize what you can do or have done rather than what you can't or won't do.

E. Close on a positive note.
- Express best wishes without being falsely positive.
- Suggest actions readers might take, if appropriate, and provide them with necessary information.
- Encourage further communication only if you're willing to discuss the situation further.
- Keep a positive outlook on the future.

responses. Neither you nor your company will be able to say yes to every request, so crafting negative responses quickly and graciously is an important skill for many professionals.

Refusing Routine Requests

When turning down an invitation or a request for a favor, consider your relationship with the reader.

When you are unable to meet a request, your primary communication challenge is to give a clear negative response without generating negative feelings or damaging either your personal reputation or the company's. As simple as these messages may appear to be, they can test your skills as a communicator because you often need to deliver negative information while maintaining a positive relationship with the other party.

The direct approach works best for most routine negative responses. It not only helps your audience get your answer quickly and move on to other possibilities but also helps you save time because the direct approach is often easier to write than the indirect approach.

The indirect approach works best when the stakes are high for you or for the receiver, when you or your company has an established relationship with the person making the request, or when you're forced to decline a request that you might have said yes to in the past (see Figure 9.3 on the next page).

Consider the following points as you develop your routine negative messages:

- Manage your time carefully; focus on the most important relationships and requests.
- If the matter is closed, don't imply that it's still open by using phrases such as "Let me think about it and get back to you" as a way to delay saying no.
- Offer alternative ideas if you can, particularly if the relationship is important.
- Don't imply that other assistance or information might be available if it isn't.

Handling Bad News About Transactions

Bad news about routine transactions is always unwelcome and usually unexpected. Such messages have three goals: (1) to modify the customer's expectations, (2) to explain how you plan to resolve the situation, and (3) to repair whatever damage might have been done to the business relationship.

The specific content and tone of each message can vary widely, depending on the nature of the transaction and your relationship with the customer. Telling an individual consumer that his new sweater will be arriving a week later than you promised is a much simpler task than telling Toyota that 30,000 transmission parts will be a week late, especially when you know the company will be forced to idle a multimillion-dollar production facility as a result.

Your approach to bad news about business transactions depends on the nature of the transaction and your relationship with the customer.

If you haven't done anything specific to set the customer's expectations—such as promising delivery within 24 hours—the message simply needs to inform the customer of the situation, with little or no emphasis on apologies (see Figure 9.4).

If you did set the customer's expectations and now find that you can't meet them, your task is more complicated. In addition to resetting those expectations and explaining how you'll resolve the problem, you may need to include an element of apology. The scope of the apology depends on the magnitude of the mistake. For the customer who ordered the sweater, a simple apology followed by a clear statement of when the sweater will arrive would probably be sufficient. For larger business-to-business transactions, the customer may want an explanation of what went wrong to determine whether you'll be able to perform as you promise in the future.

If you've failed to meet expectations that you set for the customer, you should consider including an element of apology.

To help repair the damage to the relationship and encourage repeat business, many companies offer discounts on future purchases, free merchandise, or other considerations. Even modest efforts can go a long way to rebuilding a customer's confidence in your company. To review the concepts covered in this section, see "Checklist: Handling Bad News About Transactions."

FIGURE 9.4 Effective E-Mail Message Advising of a Back Order

This message, which is a combination of good and bad news, uses the indirect approach—with the good news serving as a buffer for the bad news. In this case, the customer wasn't promised delivery by a certain date, so the writer simply informs the customer when to expect the rest of the order. The writer also takes steps to repair the relationship and encourage future business with her firm.

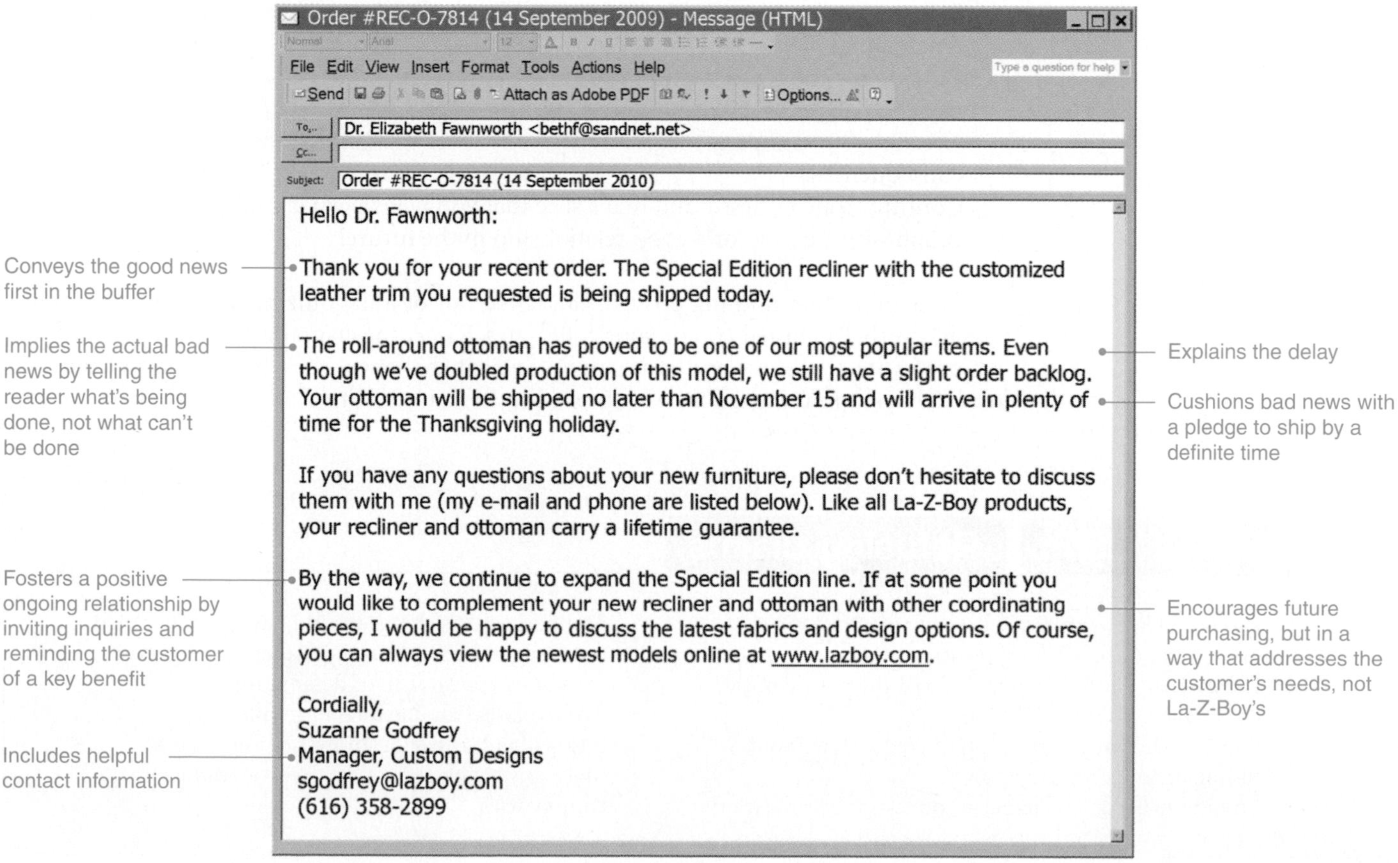

Order #REC-O-7814 (14 September 2009) - Message (HTML)

To: Dr. Elizabeth Fawnworth <bethf@sandnet.net>

Subject: Order #REC-O-7814 (14 September 2010)

Hello Dr. Fawnworth:

Thank you for your recent order. The Special Edition recliner with the customized leather trim you requested is being shipped today.

The roll-around ottoman has proved to be one of our most popular items. Even though we've doubled production of this model, we still have a slight order backlog. Your ottoman will be shipped no later than November 15 and will arrive in plenty of time for the Thanksgiving holiday.

If you have any questions about your new furniture, please don't hesitate to discuss them with me (my e-mail and phone are listed below). Like all La-Z-Boy products, your recliner and ottoman carry a lifetime guarantee.

By the way, we continue to expand the Special Edition line. If at some point you would like to complement your new recliner and ottoman with other coordinating pieces, I would be happy to discuss the latest fabrics and design options. Of course, you can always view the newest models online at www.lazboy.com.

Cordially,
Suzanne Godfrey
Manager, Custom Designs
sgodfrey@lazboy.com
(616) 358-2899

Conveys the good news first in the buffer
Implies the actual bad news by telling the reader what's being done, not what can't be done
Fosters a positive ongoing relationship by inviting inquiries and reminding the customer of a key benefit
Includes helpful contact information
Explains the delay
Cushions bad news with a pledge to ship by a definite time
Encourages future purchasing, but in a way that addresses the customer's needs, not La-Z-Boy's

CHECKLIST: Handling Bad News About Transactions

- Reset the customer's expectations regarding the transaction.
- Explain what happened and why, if appropriate.
- Explain how you'll resolve the situation.
- Repair any damage done to the business relationship, perhaps offering future discounts, free merchandise, or other considerations.
- Offer a professional, businesslike expression of apology if your organization made a mistake.

Refusing Claims and Requests for Adjustment

Use the indirect approach in most cases of refusing claims.

Almost every customer who makes a claim or requests an adjustment is emotionally involved; therefore, the indirect method is usually the best approach for a refusal. To avoid accepting responsibility for the unfortunate situation and avoid blaming or accusing the customer, pay special attention to the tone of your letter. A tactful and courteous message can build goodwill even while denying the claim (see Figure 9.5).

When refusing a claim
- *Demonstrate your understanding of the complaint*
- *Explain your refusal*
- *Suggest alternative action*

When refusing a claim, avoid language that might have a negative impact on the reader. Instead, demonstrate that you understand and have considered the complaint carefully. Then, even if the claim is unreasonable, rationally explain why you are refusing the request, without hiding behind "company policy." End the message on a respectful and action-oriented note.

If you deal with enough customers over a long enough period, chances are you'll get a request that is particularly outrageous. You might even be positive that the person is being dishonest. However, you need to control your emotions and approach the situation as calmly as possible to avoid saying or writing anything that the recipient might interpret as defamation (see page 28 in Chapter 1). To avoid being accused of defamation, follow these guidelines:

You can help avoid committing defamation by not responding emotionally or abusively.

- Refrain from using any kind of abusive language or terms that could be considered defamatory.
- Provide accurate information and stick to the facts.
- Never let anger or malice motivate your messages.
- Consult your company's legal advisers whenever you think a message might have legal consequences.
- Communicate honestly and make sure that you believe what you're saying is true.
- Emphasize a desire for a good relationship in the future.

Remember that nothing positive can come out of antagonizing a customer, even one who has verbally abused you or your colleagues. Reject the claim or request for adjustment in a professional manner and move on to the next challenge. For a brief review of the tasks involved when refusing claims, see "Checklist: Refusing Claims."

CHECKLIST: Refusing Claims

- Use the indirect approach because the reader is expecting or hoping for a positive response.
- Indicate your full understanding of the nature of the complaint.
- Explain why you are refusing the request, without hiding behind company policy.
- Provide an accurate, factual account of the transaction.
- Emphasize ways things should have been handled rather than dwelling on the reader's negligence.
- Avoid any appearance of defamation.
- Avoid expressing personal opinions.
- End with a positive, friendly, helpful close.
- Make any suggested action easy for readers to comply with.

FIGURE 9.5 Effective Letter Refusing a Claim

Daniel Lindmeier, who purchased a digital video camera from Village Electronics a year ago, wrote to say that the unit doesn't work properly and to inquire about the warranty. He incorrectly believed that the warranty covers one year, when it actually covers only three months. In this response, Walter Brodie uses the indirect approach to convey the bad news and to offer additional helpful information.

1 Plan → 2 Write → 3 Complete

1 Plan

Analyze the Situation

Verify that the purpose is to refuse a warranty claim and offer repairs; audience's likely reaction will be disappointment and surprise.

Gather Information

Gather information on warranty policies and procedures, repair services, and resale information.

Select the Right Medium

Choose the best medium for delivering your message; for formal messages, printed letters on company letterhead are best.

Organize the Information

Your main idea is to refuse the claim and promote an alternative solution; select an indirect approach based on the audience and the situation.

2 Write

Adapt to Your Audience

Adjust the level of formality based on degree of familiarity with the audience; maintain a positive relationship by using the "you" attitude, politeness, positive emphasis, and bias-free language.

Compose the Message

Use a conversational but professional style and keep the message brief, clear, and as helpful as possible.

3 Complete

Revise the Message

Evaluate content and review readability to make sure the negative information won't be misinterpreted; make sure your tone stays positive without being artificial.

Produce the Message

Emphasize a clean, professional appearance appropriate for a letter on company stationery.

Proofread the Message

Review for errors in layout, spelling, and mechanics.

Distribute the Message

Deliver your message using the chosen medium; make sure the reader receives any necessary support documents as well.

NUMBER ONE IN ENTERTAINMENT
Village Electronics
68 Lake Itasca Boulevard • Hannover, MN 55341
Voice: (612) 878-1312 • Fax: (612) 878-1316

May 2, 2010

Mr. Daniel Lindmeier
849 Cedar St.
Lake Elmo, MN 55042

Dear Mr. Lindmeier:

Thank you for your letter about the battery release switch on your JVC digital camera. Village Electronics believes, as you do, that electronic equipment should be built to last. That's why we stand behind our products with a 90-day warranty.

[Buffers the bad news by emphasizing a point the reader and writer both agree on]

Even though your JVC camera is a year old and therefore out of warranty, we can still help. Please package your camera carefully and ship it to our store in Hannover. Include your complete name, address, phone number, and a brief description of the malfunction, along with a check for $35 for an initial examination. After assessing the unit, we will give you a written estimate of the needed parts and labor. Then just let us know whether you want us to make the repairs—either by phone or by filling out the prepaid card we'll send you with the estimate.

[Puts company's policy in a favorable light]

[States bad news indirectly, tactfully leaving the repair decision to the customer]

If you choose to repair the unit, the $35 will be applied toward your bill, the balance of which is payable by check or credit card. JVC also has service centers available in your area. If you would prefer to take the unit to one of them, please see the enclosed list.

[Helps soothe the reader with a positive alternative]

Thanks again for inquiring about our service. I've also enclosed a catalog of our latest cameras and accessories, in which you'll find information about JVC's "Trade-Up Special." If you're ready to move up to one of the newest cameras, JVC will offer a generous trade-in allowance on your current model.

[Closes by blending sales promotion with an acknowledgment of the customer's interests]

Sincerely,

Walter Brodie

Walter Brodie
Customer Service Manager

Enclosures: List of service centers
Catalog

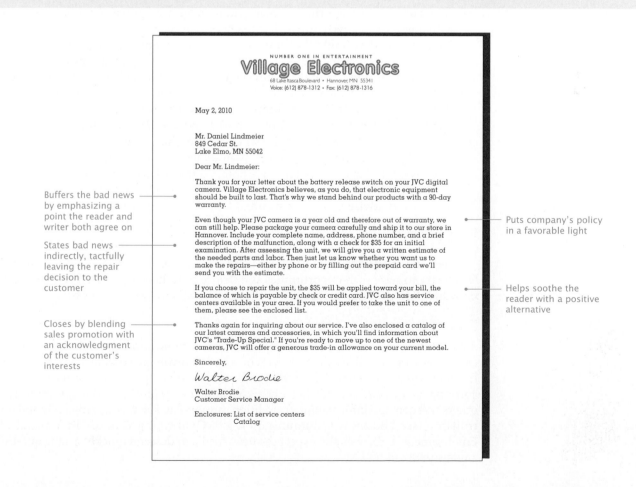

Sending Negative Organizational News

As a manager, you may need to issue negative announcements regarding some aspect of your products, services, or operations. Most of these scenarios have unique challenges that must be addressed on a case-by-case basis, but the general advice offered here applies to all of them. One key difference among all these messages is whether you have time to plan the announcement. The following section addresses negative messages that you do have time to plan for, and "Communicating in a Crisis" offers advice on communication during emergencies.

Communicating Under Normal Circumstances

Negative organizational messages to external audiences can require extensive planning.

Businesses must convey a range of negative messages regarding their ongoing operations. As you plan such messages, take extra care to consider all your audiences and their unique needs. A significant negative event such as a plant closing can affect hundreds or thousands of people in many organizations. Employees need to find new jobs, get training in new skills, or perhaps get emergency financial help. School districts may have to adjust budgets and staffing levels if many of your employees plan to move in search of new jobs. Your customers need to find new suppliers. Your suppliers may need to find other customers. Government agencies may need to react to everything from a decrease in tax revenues to an influx of people seeking unemployment benefits.

When making negative announcements, follow these guidelines:

- **Match your approach to the situation.** If the news will be shocking or highly disruptive, consider the indirect approach.
- **Consider the unique needs of each group.** As the plant closing example illustrates, various people have different information needs.
- **Give each audience enough time to react as needed.** For instance, employees, particularly high-level professionals and managers, may need up to six months or more to find new jobs.
- **Give yourself enough time to plan and manage a response.** You're going to get hit with questions, so make sure you're ready with answers.
- **Look for positive angles but don't exude false optimism.** If eliminating a seldom-used employee benefit means employees will save money, by all means promote that positive angle. On the other hand, laying off 10,000 people does not give them "an opportunity to explore new horizons." It's a traumatic event that can affect employees, their families, and their communities for years. The best you may be able to do is to thank people for their past support and wish them well in the future.
- **Minimize the element of surprise whenever possible.** This step can require considerable judgment on your part, as well as awareness of any applicable laws. In general, if you recognize that current trends are pointing toward negative results sometime in the near future, it's often best to let your audience know ahead of time.
- **Seek expert advice if you're not sure.** Many significant negative announcements have important technical, financial, or legal elements that require the expertise of lawyers, accountants, or other specialists.

Give people as much time as possible to react to negative organizational news.

Ask for legal help and other assistance if you're not sure how to handle a significant negative announcement.

Negative situations will test your skills as a communicator and leader. Inspirational leaders try to seize such opportunities as a chance to reshape or reinvigorate the organization, and they offer encouragement to those around them (see Figure 9.6).

5 LEARNING OBJECTIVE

Explain the role of communication in crisis management.

Communicating in a Crisis

Some of the most critical instances of business communication occur during crises, which can include industrial accidents, crimes or scandals involving company employees, on-site hostage situations, terrorist attacks, information theft, product tampering incidents, and financial calamities. During a crisis, customers, employees, local communities, and others will demand information. In addition, rumors can spread unpredictably and uncontrollably (see "Business Communication 2.0: Controlling Rumors in a Social Media Environment"). You can also expect the news media to descend quickly, asking questions of anyone they can find.

FIGURE 9.6 Effective E-Mail Message Providing Bad News About Company Operations
In this message to employees at Sybervantage, Frank Leslie shares the unpleasant news that a hoped-for licensing agreement with Warner Brothers has been rejected. Rather than dwell on the bad news, he focuses on options for the future. The upbeat close diminishes the effect of the bad news without hiding or downplaying the news itself.

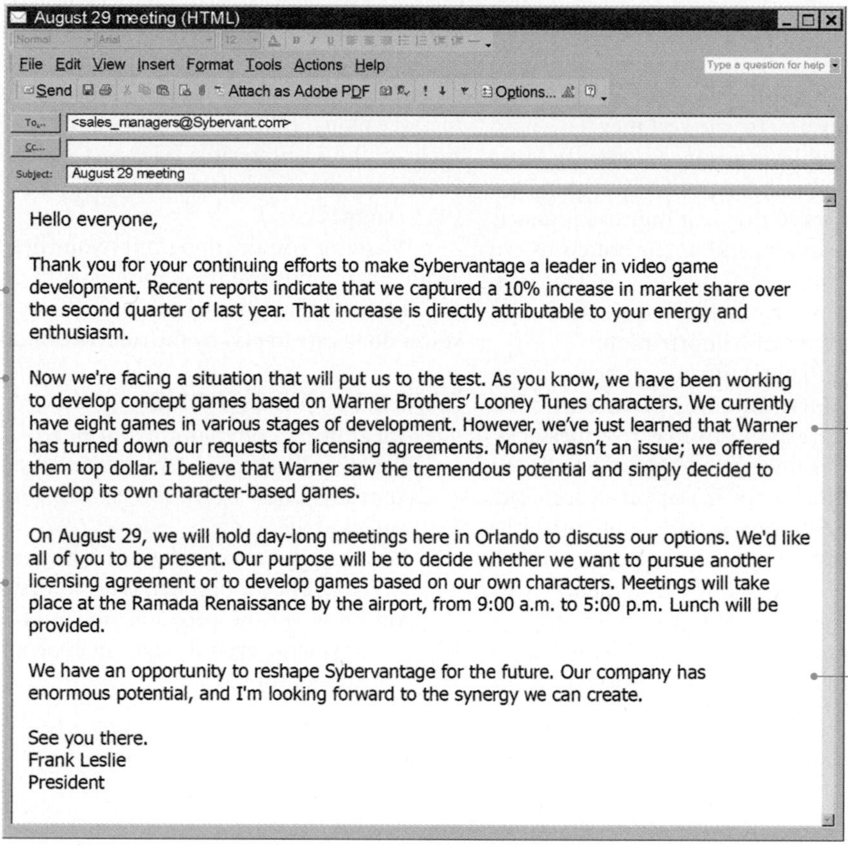
August 29 meeting (HTML)

File Edit View Insert Format Tools Actions Help

Send Attach as Adobe PDF Options...

To... <sales_managers@Sybervant.com>

Cc...

Subject: August 29 meeting

Hello everyone,

Thank you for your continuing efforts to make Sybervantage a leader in video game development. Recent reports indicate that we captured a 10% increase in market share over the second quarter of last year. That increase is directly attributable to your energy and enthusiasm.

Now we're facing a situation that will put us to the test. As you know, we have been working to develop concept games based on Warner Brothers' Looney Tunes characters. We currently have eight games in various stages of development. However, we've just learned that Warner has turned down our requests for licensing agreements. Money wasn't an issue; we offered them top dollar. I believe that Warner saw the tremendous potential and simply decided to develop its own character-based games.

On August 29, we will hold day-long meetings here in Orlando to discuss our options. We'd like all of you to be present. Our purpose will be to decide whether we want to pursue another licensing agreement or to develop games based on our own characters. Meetings will take place at the Ramada Renaissance by the airport, from 9:00 a.m. to 5:00 p.m. Lunch will be provided.

We have an opportunity to reshape Sybervantage for the future. Our company has enormous potential, and I'm looking forward to the synergy we can create.

See you there.
Frank Leslie
President

Opens on a complimentary note and buffers the bad news with some good news about sales

Moves readers from good news to bad news with an effective transition

Presents the bad news along with the possible explanations

Involves readers in the challenge of finding a solution

Closes by being positive, looking toward the future, and encouraging the audience

Although you can't predict these events, you can prepare for them. Analysis of corporate crises over the past several decades reveals that companies that respond quickly with the information people need tend to fare much better in the long run than those that go into hiding or release inconsistent or incorrect information.[16]

Anticipation and planning are key to successful communication in a crisis.

The key to successful communication efforts during a crisis is having a **crisis management plan**. In addition to defining operational procedures to deal with the crisis, this plan outlines communication tasks and responsibilities, which can include everything from media contacts to news release templates (see Table 9.3). The plan should clearly specify which people are authorized to speak for the company, contact information for all key executives, and a list of the media outlets and technologies that will be used to disseminate information. Many companies now go one step further by regularly testing crisis communications in realistic practice drills that last a full day or more.[17]

REAL-TIME UPDATES
Learn More

Take some of the sting out of delivering bad news

No one likes to deliver bad news, but these techniques can make it easier for you and the recipient. Go to **http://real-timeupdates.com/ebc** and click on "Learn More." If you are using mybcommlab, you can access Real-Time Updates within each chapter or under Student Study Tools.

Sending Negative Employment Messages

Most managers must convey bad news about individual employees from time to time. Recipients have an emotional stake in your message, so taking the indirect approach is usually advised. In addition, use great care in choosing media for

Business Communication 2.0

Controlling Rumors in a Social Media Environment

For all the benefits they bring to business, social media and other communication technologies have created a major new challenge: responding to online rumors and attacks on a company's reputation. Disappointed consumers can now communicate through blogs, social networking sites, social commerce sites, advocacy sites such as www.walmartwatch.com, general complaint websites such as www.planetfeedback.com, and company-specific sites such as www.verizonpathetic.com.

On the positive side, consumers who feel they have been treated unfairly can use the public exposure as leverage. Many companies appreciate the feedback from these sites, too, and even buy complaint summaries so they can improve products and services. However, false rumors and unfair criticisms can spread around the world in a matter of minutes. McDonald's, Coca-Cola, Pepsi, and Snapple are just a few of the brand names that have been harmed by false information.

Controlling rumors is difficult, but you can help contain them by taking five steps. First, monitor blogs and other online sources to catch and respond to negative messages. Second, decide whether each rumor or complaint justifies an official public response. If the rumor is not yet widespread, responding privately to a small number of people might be more effective than broadcasting a public response—which might just help spread the rumor to a wider audience. Also, some instances of misinformation might be so mild or vague that confronting them could cause more problems than it solves. In those cases, your best course might be to ignore the rumor but communicate positive information that indirectly counters the rumor. Third, if you determine that a rumor requires a direct strategy, respond quickly with clear information. Some companies set up special websites or sections on their sites, such as www.walmart.com/FactsNews, to answer public criticisms. Fourth, respond to rumors wherever they appear, even if this means digging back through e-mail threads to respond personally to everyone who passed the message along. Fifth, enlist the help of government agencies such as the Centers for Disease Control and Prevention (www.cdc.gov) and debunking sites such as Snopes.com (www.snopes.com).

Whatever you do, don't bury your head in the sand and assume that a positive reputation doesn't need to be guarded and defended. Everybody has a voice now, and some of those voices don't care to play by the rules of ethical communication.

CAREER APPLICATIONS

1. A legitimate complaint about one of your products on PlanetFeedback.com also contains a statement that your company "doesn't care about its customers." How should you respond?
2. A few bloggers are circulating false information about your company, but the problem is not widespread—yet. Should you jump on the problem now and tell the world the rumor is false, even though most people haven't heard it yet? Explain your answer.

TABLE 9.3 How to Communicate in a Crisis

WHEN A CRISIS HITS:	
DO	**DON'T**
Prepare for trouble ahead of time by identifying potential problems, appointing and training a response team, and preparing and testing a crisis management plan.	Don't blame anyone for anything.
Get top management involved as soon as the crisis hits.	Don't speculate in public.
Set up a news center for company representatives and the media that is equipped with phones, computers, and other electronic tools for preparing news releases and online updates. At the news center, take the following steps: • Issue frequent news updates and have trained personnel available to respond to questions around the clock. • Provide complete information packets to the media as soon as possible. • Prevent conflicting statements and provide continuity by appointing a single person trained in advance to speak for the company. • Tell receptionists and other employees to direct all media calls to the designated spokesperson in the news center. • When new information is available, provide updates via blog postings, microblog updates, text messaging, and other appropriate tools.	Don't refuse to answer questions.
Tell the whole story—openly, completely, and honestly. If you are at fault, apologize.	Don't release information that will violate anyone's right to privacy.
Demonstrate the company's concern through your statements and your actions.	Don't use the crisis to pitch products or services.
	Don't play favorites with media representatives.

these messages. For instance, e-mail and other written forms let you control the message and avoid personal confrontation, but one-on-one conversations are more sensitive and facilitate questions and answers.

Refusing Requests for Employee References and Recommendation Letters

When sending refusals to prospective employers who have requested information about past employees, your message can be brief and direct:

> Our human resources department has authorized me to confirm that Yolanda Johnson worked for Tandy, Inc., for three years, from June 2005 to July 2007. Best of luck as you interview applicants.

Implies that company policy prohibits the release of any more information but does provide what information is available

Ends on a positive note

This message doesn't need to say, "We cannot comply with your request." It simply gives the reader all the information that is allowable.

Refusing an applicant's direct request for a recommendation letter is another matter. Any refusal to cooperate may seem to be a personal slight and a threat to the applicant's future. Diplomacy and preparation help readers accept your refusal:

> Thank you for letting me know about your job opportunity with Coca-Cola. Your internship there and the MBA you've worked so hard to earn should place you in an excellent position to land the marketing job.
>
> Although we do not send out formal recommendations here at PepsiCo, I can certainly send Coca-Cola a confirmation of your employment dates. And if you haven't considered this already, be sure to ask several of your professors to write evaluations of your marketing skills. Best of luck to you in your career.

Uses the indirect approach since the other party is probably expecting a positive response

Announces that the writer cannot comply with the request, without explicitly blaming it on "policy"

Offers to fulfill as much of the request as possible and offers an alternative

Ends on a positive note

This message tactfully avoids hurting the reader's feelings because it makes positive comments about the reader's recent activities, implies the refusal, suggests an alternative, and uses a polite close.

Rejecting Job Applicants

6 LEARNING OBJECTIVE

List three guidelines for delivering negative news to job applicants, and give a brief explanation of each one.

Tactfully telling job applicants that you won't be offering them employment is a common communication challenge. Poorly written rejection letters can have negative consequences, ranging from the loss of qualified candidates for future openings to the loss of potential customers (not only the rejected applicants but also their friends and family members).[18] Badly phrased rejection letters can even invite legal troubles. When delivering bad news to job applicants, follow three guidelines:[19]

Poorly written rejection letters tarnish your company's reputation and can even invite legal troubles.

- **Choose your approach carefully.** Experts disagree on whether the direct or indirect approach is best for rejection letters. On the one hand, job applicants know they won't get every position they apply for, so negative news during a job search is not generally a shock. On the other hand, people put their hopes and dreams on the line when they apply for work, so job applicants have a deep emotional investment in the process—which is one of the factors to consider in using the indirect approach. If you opt for the direct approach, be tactful in the opening. Tell your reader that the position has been filled rather than saying, "Your application has been rejected." If you opt for the indirect approach, be careful not to mislead the reader or delay the bad news for more than a sentence or two. A simple "Thank you for considering ABC as the place to start your career" is a quick, courteous buffer that shows your company is flattered to be considered. Don't mislead the reader in your buffer by praising his or her qualifications in a way that could suggest good news is soon to follow.
- **Clearly state why the applicant was not selected.** Make your rejection less personal by stating that you hired someone with more experience or whose qualifications match the position requirements more closely.

- **Close by suggesting alternatives.** If time permits, you might suggest other positions for which the applicant is qualified or professional organizations that could help the applicant find employment.

Compare the ineffective and effective versions of the message in Figure 9.7 to see how one writer followed these guidelines.

FIGURE 9.7 Ineffective and Effective E-Mail Messages Rejecting a Job Applicant
This e-mail response was drafted by Marvin Fichter to communicate bad news to Carol DeCicco following her interview with Bradley Jackson. After reviewing the first draft, Fichter made several changes to improve the communication. The revised e-mail helps DeCicco understand that (1) she would have been hired if she'd had more tax experience and (2) she shouldn't be discouraged.

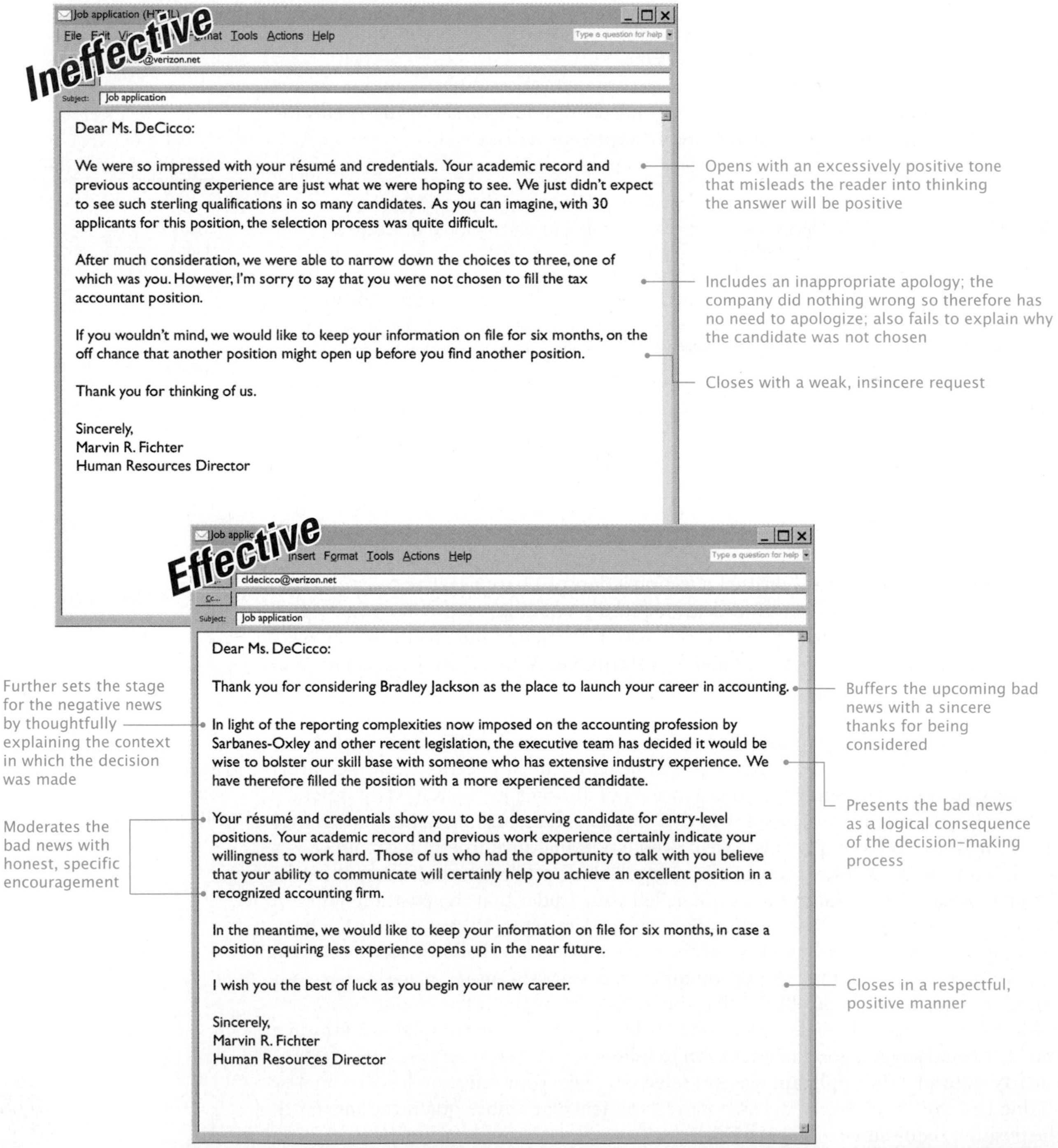

Ineffective
Job application
Tools Actions Help
@verizon.net
Subject: Job application

Dear Ms. DeCicco:

We were so impressed with your résumé and credentials. Your academic record and previous accounting experience are just what we were hoping to see. We just didn't expect to see such sterling qualifications in so many candidates. As you can imagine, with 30 applicants for this position, the selection process was quite difficult.

After much consideration, we were able to narrow down the choices to three, one of which was you. However, I'm sorry to say that you were not chosen to fill the tax accountant position.

If you wouldn't mind, we would like to keep your information on file for six months, on the off chance that another position might open up before you find another position.

Thank you for thinking of us.

Sincerely,
Marvin R. Fichter
Human Resources Director

Opens with an excessively positive tone that misleads the reader into thinking the answer will be positive
Includes an inappropriate apology; the company did nothing wrong so therefore has no need to apologize; also fails to explain why the candidate was not chosen
Closes with a weak, insincere request

Effective
Insert Format Tools Actions Help
cldecicco@verizon.net
Subject: Job application

Dear Ms. DeCicco:

Thank you for considering Bradley Jackson as the place to launch your career in accounting.

In light of the reporting complexities now imposed on the accounting profession by Sarbanes-Oxley and other recent legislation, the executive team has decided it would be wise to bolster our skill base with someone who has extensive industry experience. We have therefore filled the position with a more experienced candidate.

Your résumé and credentials show you to be a deserving candidate for entry-level positions. Your academic record and previous work experience certainly indicate your willingness to work hard. Those of us who had the opportunity to talk with you believe that your ability to communicate will certainly help you achieve an excellent position in a recognized accounting firm.

In the meantime, we would like to keep your information on file for six months, in case a position requiring less experience opens up in the near future.

I wish you the best of luck as you begin your new career.

Sincerely,
Marvin R. Fichter
Human Resources Director

Further sets the stage for the negative news by thoughtfully explaining the context in which the decision was made
Moderates the bad news with honest, specific encouragement
Buffers the upcoming bad news with a sincere thanks for being considered
Presents the bad news as a logical consequence of the decision-making process
Closes in a respectful, positive manner

Giving Negative Performance Reviews

An important goal of any performance evaluation is to give the employee a plan of action for improving his or her performance.

The main purpose of a **performance review** is to improve employee performance by (1) emphasizing and clarifying job requirements, (2) giving employees feedback on their efforts toward fulfilling those requirements, and (3) guiding continued efforts by developing a plan of action, which includes rewards and opportunities. Performance reviews help companies set organizational standards and communicate organizational values.[20] Documentation of performance problems can also protect a company from being sued for unlawful termination.[21]

Criticizing others is difficult for most people, but discussing shortcomings is a necessary first step to improvement for both an employee and an organization. When you need to give a negative performance review, follow these guidelines:[22]

- **Confront the problem right away.** Avoiding mention of performance problems usually only makes them worse—and it robs the employee of the opportunity to improve. Moreover, if you don't document problems when they occur, you may make it more difficult to terminate employment later on if the situation comes to that.[23]
- **Plan what to say.** Be clear about your concerns and include examples of the employee's specific actions. Think about any possible biases you may have and get feedback from others. Collect and verify all relevant facts (both strengths and weaknesses).
- **Deliver the message in private.** Whether in writing or in person, be sure to address the performance problem privately. Don't send performance reviews by e-mail or fax. If you're reviewing an employee's performance face to face, conduct that review in a meeting arranged expressly for that purpose and consider holding that meeting in a conference room or some other neutral area.
- **Focus on the problem.** Without attacking the employee, discuss the problems caused by his or her performance and explain how it doesn't meet expectations established for the position. In other words, "evaluate the work, not the worker."[24] Identify the consequences of continuing poor performance and show that you're committed to helping solve the problem.
- **Ask for a commitment from the employee.** Help the employee understand that planning for and making improvements are the employee's responsibility. However,

Address performance problems in private.

CHECKLIST: Writing Negative Employment Messages

A. Refusing requests for employee references and recommendation letters
- Don't feel obligated to write a recommendation letter if you don't feel comfortable doing so.
- Take a diplomatic approach to minimize hurt feelings.
- Compliment the reader's accomplishments.
- Suggest alternatives, if available.

B. Rejecting job applicants
- If possible, respond to all applications, even if you use only a form message to acknowledge receipt.
- If you use the direct approach, take care to avoid being blunt or cold.
- If you use the indirect approach, don't mislead the reader in your buffer or delay the bad news for more than a sentence or two.
- Clearly state why the applicant was rejected.
- Suggest alternatives if possible.

C. Giving negative performance reviews
- Maintain an objective and unbiased tone.
- Use nonjudgmental language.
- Focus on problem resolution.
- Make sure negative feedback is documented and shared with the employee.
- Don't avoid confrontations by withholding negative feedback.
- Ask the employee for a commitment to improve.

D. Terminating employment
- State your reasons accurately and make sure they are objectively verifiable.
- Avoid statements that might expose your company to a wrongful termination lawsuit.
- Consult company lawyers to clarify all terms of the separation.
- End the relationship on terms as positive as possible.

finalize decisions jointly so that you can be sure any action to be taken is achievable. Set a schedule for improvement and for following up with evaluations of that improvement.

If an employee's performance has been disappointing, clearly and tactfully state how the employee can better meet the responsibilities of the job. If the performance review is to be effective, be sure to suggest ways that the employee can improve.[25] Remember that the ultimate goal is not to criticize but to help the employee succeed.

Terminating Employment

Carefully word a termination message to avoid creating undue ill will and grounds for legal action.

The decision to terminate employees is rarely easy or simple, but doing it effectively is an important managerial responsibility. When writing a termination message, you have three goals: (1) to present the reasons for this difficult action, (2) to avoid statements that might expose the company to a wrongful termination lawsuit, and (3) to leave the relationship between the terminated employee and the firm as favorable as possible. For both legal and personal reasons, present specific justification for asking the employee to leave and make sure that personnel policies have been applied consistently to avoid the appearance of unfair treatment.[26] Your company's lawyers will be able to tell you whether the employee's performance is legal grounds for termination.

Make sure that all your reasons are accurate and verifiable. Avoid words that are open to interpretation, such as *untidy* and *difficult.* You can help protect personal feelings as you end the relationship by telling the truth about the termination and by helping as much as you can to make the employee's transition as smooth as possible.[27] To review the tasks involved in this type of message, see "Checklist: Writing Negative Employment Messages." For the latest information on writing negative messages, visit **http://real-timeupdates.com/ebc** and click on Chapter 9.

Document Makeover

Improve This Memo

To practice correcting drafts of actual documents, visit the "Document Makeovers" section in mybcommlab. Refer to the User Guide for specific instructions on how to access the content for this chapter. You will find a memo that contains problems and errors related to what you've learned in this chapter about handling negative messages. Use the Final Draft decision tool to create an improved version of this memo. Check the message for the use of buffers, apologies, explanations, subordination, embedding, positive action, conditional phrases, and upbeat perspectives.

On the Job: Solving Communication Dilemmas at Leviton

Thanks to your effective leadership skills, you didn't take long to move up to a management position in the corporate HR department at Leviton. You oversee a staff of HR specialists at corporate headquarters and also manage the HR representatives that support Leviton's other facilities around the country. Use what you've learned about negative messages to address these communication dilemmas.

1. Another manager in corporate headquarters stopped by this morning with a request to borrow two of your best employees for a three-week emergency. Under normal conditions, you wouldn't hesitate to help, but your team has its own scheduling challenges to deal with. Plus, this isn't the first time this manager has run into trouble, and you are confident that poor project management is the reason. Which of the following is the most diplomatic way to state your refusal while suggesting that your colleague's management skills need improvement?
   a. With the commitments we've made on our own projects, we won't be able to bail you out this time.
   b. I sympathize with the trouble you've gotten yourself into again, I really do, but the commitments we've made on our own projects prevent us from releasing any employees for temporary assignments.
   c. The commitments we've made on our own projects prevent us from releasing any workers for temporary assignments. However, I would be happy to meet with you to discuss the techniques I've been using to manage project workloads.

d. Instead of shifting resources around as usual, why don't we meet to discuss some new strategies for staffing and project management?

2. The HR department acts as an internal service provider, helping various divisions throughout the company with hiring, benefits, training, and other employment functions. An HR rep is assigned to each division, working with the managers and employees in that division, but reporting to HR executives in the corporate office. As in all other professional relationships, personal aspects can enter the relationship. Even competent professionals can start to rub each other the wrong way at a personal level, which can corrode the business relationship over time. Unfortunately, that has happened with one of your best staff members. Shirley Jackson is widely admired for her HR skills, but the general manager of the division where she is assigned has asked you to replace her with a new HR representative. Although you'd prefer to tell Jackson in person, schedule conflicts dictate that you send her an e-mail. Which of these buffers would be the best way to open the message?

a. Your work for the St. Louis Division continues to be first rate, but you never can tell how these things are going to work out, can you?
b. If it were up to me, Shirley, I would never deliver a message like this, but the St. Louis Division has asked me to re-evaluate the HR staffing assignments.
c. As I've expressed on many occasions, thank you once again for the top-quality work you've done for the St. Louis Division over the years.
d. As you know, Shirley, I continually evaluate the HR staffing assignments to make sure the various divisions are satisfied with the quality of our work and the overall nature of our relationship with them.

3. Although your project management skills are quite good, you do occasionally run into unforeseen circumstances that lead to less-than-ideal results. Halfway through the installation of a new résumé scanning system, you realized that you underestimated the complexity of linking this new technology to the company's existing applicant tracking system. You now have the unpleasant task of explaining to your boss that the project will be coming in at least 20 percent over budget and possibly as high as 30 percent over. Which of the following is the best way to begin an e-mail message to your boss?

a. I messed up, big time. The résumé scanning project is going to come in over budget.
b. The résumé scanning project is going to come in at least 20 percent over budget and possibly as much as 30 percent over.
c. I recently discovered that linking the new résumé scanner to our applicant tracking system was more complicated than anyone realized when we established the budget for this project. As a result of the extra work required to customize the software, the project is going to run 20 to 30 percent over budget.
d. I recently discovered that linking the new résumé scanner to our applicant tracking system was more complicated than anyone realized when we established the budget for this project. The fact that there is extra work is not really my fault, per se, since it would've been necessary in any case, but as a result of the extra work required to customize the software, the project is going to run 20 to 30 percent over budget.

4. You've found it easy to say "yes" to recommendation letter requests from former employees who were top performers, and you've learned to say "no" to people who didn't perform so well. The requests you struggle with are from employees in the middle, people who didn't really excel but didn't really cause any trouble, either. You've just received a request from an HR specialist who falls smack in the middle of the middle. Unfortunately, he's applying for a job at a firm that you know places high demands on its employees and generally hires the best of the best. He's a great person, and you'd love to help, but in your heart, you know that if by some chance he does get the job, he probably won't last. Plus, you don't want to get a reputation in the industry for recommending weak candidates. How do you set the stage for the negative news?

a. As your former manager, I'd like to think I can still look out for your best interests, and I'm sorry to say, but based on what I know about the position you're applying for, this might not be the best career move for you at this point.
b. In my view, the responsibility of writing a letter of recommendation goes beyond simply assessing a person's skills; it must consider whether the person is applying for the right job.
c. One of the most important factors I consider when deciding whether to endorse an applicant is whether he or she is pursuing an opportunity that offers a high probability of success.
d. Writing recommendation letters bears a heavy responsibility for the job applicant and the person writing the letter. After all, I have my own reputation to protect, too.

LEARNING OBJECTIVES CHECKUP

Assess your understanding of the principles in this chapter by reading each learning objective and studying the accompanying exercises. For fill-in-the-blank items, write the missing text in the blank provided; for multiple-choice items, circle the letter of the correct answer. You can check your responses against the answer key on page AK-2.

Objective 9.1: Apply the three-step writing process to negative messages.

1. Which of the following should be a goal of every negative message?
   a. To convey the bad news clearly
   b. To gain audience acceptance for the news
   c. To maintain as much goodwill as possible with the audience
   d. To maintain a good image for your organization
   e. To reduce or eliminate the need for future correspondence on the matter, if appropriate
   f. None of the above
   g. (a), (c), and (d)
   h. All of the above

2. Which of the following is an effective way to maintain the "you" attitude when crafting negative messages?
   a. Make sure the reader clearly understands that he or she is at fault; after all, recognizing a mistake is the first step toward improvement.
   b. Make it clear that you don't enjoy giving out bad news.
   c. Show respect for the reader by "soft peddling" the negative news, implying it without really coming out and saying it directly.
   d. Show respect for the reader by avoiding negative, accusatory language and emphasizing positives whenever possible.

Objective 9.2: Explain the differences between the direct and the indirect approaches to negative messages, including when it's appropriate to use each one.

3. When using the direct approach with negative messages, you begin with
   a. A buffer
   b. An attention-getter
   c. The bad news
   d. Any of the above

4. An advantage of using the direct approach with negative messages is that it
   a. Saves readers time by helping them reach the main idea more quickly
   b. Eases readers into the message
   c. Is diplomatic
   d. Does all of the above

5. When using the indirect approach with negative messages, you begin with
   a. A buffer
   b. An attention-getter
   c. The bad news
   d. Any of the above

6. Which of the following is an advantage of using the indirect approach with negative messages?
   a. Most readers prefer the direct approach for such messages.
   b. It makes a shorter message possible.
   c. It eases the reader into the message.
   d. It does all of the above.

Objective 9.3: Identify the risks of using the indirect approach, and explain how to avoid such problems.

7. The purpose of using the indirect approach is to
   a. Help the writer avoid the unpleasant task of delivering bad news
   b. Help the reader avoid the unpleasant task of receiving bad news
   c. Soften the blow of the bad news for the reader
   d. Reduce the word count in your messages

8. A/an _____ is a neutral, noncontroversial opening statement that establishes common ground with your reader.

9. Which of the following is a good possibility to consider for use in writing a buffer?
   a. Look for subtle opportunities to promote your company and its products.
   b. Assure the reader that your company always follows all applicable laws and regulations.
   c. Indicate your understanding of the reader's situation.
   d. All of the above are useful approaches.

Objective 9.4: Explain the importance of maintaining high standards of ethics and etiquette when delivering negative messages.

10. Which of the following is an important reason to take particular care to maintain ethics and etiquette when crafting negative messages?
   a. In many cases, the communicator needs to adhere to a variety of laws and regulations when delivering negative messages.
   b. Good ethical practice demands care and sensitivity in the content and delivery of negative messages, as these messages can have a profoundly negative effect on the people who receive them.
   c. Communicators need to manage their own emotions when crafting and distributing negative messages while at the same time considering the emotional needs of their audiences.
   d. All of the above are important reasons to maintain ethics and etiquette in negative messages.

11. Which of the following is most characteristic of organizational cultures that emphasize open communication?
    a. Managers are willing to listen to bad news from employees, but they understand if employees don't want to deliver bad news.
    b. Managers expect employees to alert them to problems so that corrective action can be taken.
    c. Managers reward employees who deliver bad news with extra vacation time, extra pay, or both.
    d. None of the above are true.

Objective 9.5: Explain the role of communication in crisis management.

12. Which of the following best characterizes the nature of crisis management planning?
    a. Good managers should be able to anticipate the specific crisis scenarios their companies might encounter and therefore should be able to plan for every crisis in a specific way.
    b. Faced with everything from terrorism to technological disasters, there's no way for managers to anticipate which crisis might hit any given business, so it's a waste of time to plan a response.
    c. Although you can't anticipate the nature and circumstance of every possible crisis, you can prepare by deciding how to handle such issues as communication with employees and the public.
    d. Only negatively focused managers worry about crisis planning; positive managers keep their organizations moving toward company goals.

13. Continuing advances in communication technology make it
    a. Easier to control rumors through Internet filters and other means
    b. More difficult to control rumors
    c. Easier to find the people who start rumors
    d. Illegal to spread false rumors about public corporations

Objective 9.6: List three guidelines for delivering negative news to job applicants, and give a brief explanation of each one.

14. Why do many experts recommend using an indirect approach when rejecting job applicants?
    a. Applicants have a deep emotional investment in the decision.
    b. Laws in most states require an indirect approach.
    c. Indirect approaches are easier to write.
    d. Indirect approaches are shorter.

15. When explaining why an applicant wasn't chosen for a position, you should
    a. Be specific without being too personal, such as explaining that the position requires specific skills that the applicant doesn't yet possess
    b. Point out the person's shortcomings as that's the honest way and the only way the person knows what he or she need to improve
    c. Be as vague as possible to avoid hurting the person's feelings
    d. Never explain why an applicant wasn't chosen

PEARSON mybcommlab™

Log on to www.mybcommlab.com to access the following study and assessment aids associated with this chapter:

- Video applications
- Pre/post test
- Real-Time Updates
- Personalized study plan
- Peer review activity
- Model documents
- Quick Learning Guides
- Sample presentations

If you are not using mybcommlab, you can access Real-Time Updates and Quick Learning Guides through http://real-timeupdates.com/ebc. The Quick Learning Guide (located under "Learn More" on the website) hits all the high points of this chapter in just two pages. This guide, especially prepared by the authors, will help you study for exams or review important concepts whenever you need a quick refresher.

Apply Your Knowledge

1. Why is it important to end a negative message on a positive note?
2. If company policy changes, should you explain those changes to employees and customers at about the same time? Why or why not?
3. Why is whistleblowing a controversial activity?
4. When a company suffers a setback, should you soften the impact by letting out the bad news a little at a time? Why or why not?
5. **Ethical Choices** Is intentionally de-emphasizing bad news the same as distorting graphs and charts to de-emphasize unfavorable data? Why or why not?

Practice Your Knowledge

Messages for Analysis

Read the following messages and then (1) analyze the strengths and weaknesses of each sentence and (2) revise each message so that it follows this chapter's guidelines.

Message 9.A: Providing Negative News About Company Operations

Date: Wed, 28 May 2010 4:20:15 -0800

From: M. Juhasz, Travel & Meeting Services <mjuhasz@blackanddecker.com>

To: [mailing list]

Subject: Travel

Dear Traveling Executives:

We need you to start using some of the budget suggestions we are going to issue as a separate memorandum. These include using videoconference equipment and web conferencing instead of traveling to meetings, staying in cheaper hotels, arranging flights for cheaper times, and flying from less-convenient but also less-expensive suburban airports.

The company needs to cut travel expenses by 50 percent, just as we've cut costs in all departments of Black & Decker. This means you'll no longer be able to stay in fancy hotels and make last-minute, costly changes to your travel plans.

You'll also be expected to avoid hotel surcharges for phone calls and Internet access. If the hotel you want to stay in doesn't offer free wireless, go somewhere else. And never, NEVER return a rental car with an empty tank! That causes the rental agency to charge us a premium price for the gas they sell when they fill it up upon your return.

You'll be expected to make these changes in your travel habits immediately.

Sincerely,

M. Juhasz

Travel & Meeting Services

Message 9.B: Refusing Requests for Claims and Adjustments

I am responding to your letter of about six weeks ago asking for an adjustment on your wireless hub, model WM39Z. We test all our products before they leave the factory; therefore, it could not have been our fault that your hub didn't work.

If you or someone in your office dropped the unit, it might have caused the damage. Or the damage could have been caused by the shipper if he dropped it. If so, you should file a claim with the shipper. At any rate, it wasn't our fault. The parts are already covered by warranty. However, we will provide labor for the repairs for $50, which is less than our cost, since you are a valued customer.

We will have a booth at the upcoming trade show there and hope to see you or someone from your office. We have many new models of hubs, routers, and other computer gear that we're sure you'll want to see. I've enclosed our latest catalog. Hope to see you there.

Message 9.C: Rejecting Job Applicants

I regret to inform you that you were not selected for our summer intern program at Equifax. We had over a thousand résumés and cover letters to go through and simply could not get to them all. We have been asked to notify everyone that we have already selected students for the 25 positions based on those who applied early and were qualified.

We're sure you will be able to find a suitable position for summer work in your field and wish you the best of luck. We deeply regret any inconvenience associated with our reply.

Exercises

Active links for all websites in this chapter can be found on mybcommlab; see your User Guide for instructions on accessing the content for this chapter.

9.1. Selecting the Approach Select which approach you would use (direct or indirect) for the following negative messages.

- **a.** An e-mail message to your boss, informing her that one of your key clients is taking its business to a different accounting firm
- **b.** An e-mail message to a customer, informing her that one of the books she ordered over the Internet is temporarily out of stock
- **c.** An instant message to a customer, explaining that the DVD recorder he ordered for his new computer is on back order and that, as a consequence, the shipping of the entire order will be delayed
- **d.** A blog post to all employees, notifying them that the company parking lot will be repaved during the first week of June and that the company will provide a shuttle service from a remote parking lot during that period
- **e.** A letter from a travel agent to a customer, stating that the airline will not refund her money for the flight she missed but that her tickets are valid for one year
- **f.** A form letter from a U.S. airline to a customer, explaining that the company cannot extend the expiration date of the customer's frequent flyer miles even though the customer was living overseas for the past three years and unable to use the miles during that time
- **g.** A letter from an insurance company to a policyholder, denying a claim for reimbursement for a special medical procedure that is not covered under the terms of the customer's policy
- **h.** A letter from an electronics store, stating that the customer will not be reimbursed for a malfunctioning mobile phone that is still under warranty (because the terms of the warranty do not cover damages to phones that were accidentally dropped from a moving car)
- **i.** An announcement to the repairs department, listing parts that are on back order and will be three weeks late

9.2. Teamwork Working alone, revise the following statements to de-emphasize the bad news. (*Hint*: Minimize the space devoted to the bad news, subordinate it, embed it, or use the passive voice.) Then team up with a classmate and read each other's revisions. Did you both use the same approach in every case? Which approach seems to be most effective for each of the revised statements?

a. The airline can't refund your money. The "Conditions" section on the back of your ticket states that there are no refunds for missed flights. Sometimes the airline makes exceptions, but only when life and death are involved. Of course, your ticket is still valid and can be used on a flight to the same destination.

b. I'm sorry to tell you, we can't supply the custom decorations you requested. We called every supplier, and none of them can do what you want on such short notice. You can, however, get a standard decorative package on the same theme in time. I found a supplier that stocks these. Of course, it won't have quite the flair you originally requested.

c. We can't refund your money for the malfunctioning MP3 player. You shouldn't have immersed the unit in water while swimming; the users' manual clearly states that the unit is not designed to be used in adverse environments.

9.3. **Using Buffers** As a customer service supervisor for a telephone company, you're in charge of responding to customers' requests for refunds. You've just received an e-mail from a customer who unwittingly ran up a $500 bill for long-distance calls after mistakenly configuring his laptop computer to dial an Internet access number that wasn't a local call. The customer says it wasn't his fault because he didn't realize he was dialing a long-distance number. However, you've dealt with this situation before; you know that the customer's Internet service provider warns its customers to choose a local access number because customers are responsible for all long-distance charges. Draft a short buffer (one or two sentences) for your e-mail reply, sympathizing with the customer's plight but preparing him for the bad news (that company policy specifically prohibits refunds in such cases).

9.4. **Internet** Public companies occasionally need to issue news releases to announce or explain downturns in sales, profits, demand, or other business factors. Search the web to locate a company that has issued a press release that recently reported lower earnings or other bad news and access the news release on that firm's website. Alternatively, find the type of press release you're seeking by reviewing press releases at www.prnewswire.com or www.businesswire.com. How does the headline relate to the main message of the release? Is the release organized according to the direct or the indirect approach? What does the company do to present the bad news in a favorable light—and does this effort seem sincere and ethical to you?

9.5. **Ethical Choices** The insurance company where you work is planning to raise all premiums for health-care coverage. Your boss has asked you to read a draft of her letter to customers announcing the new, higher rates. The first two paragraphs discuss some exciting medical advances and the expanded coverage offered by your company. Only in the final paragraph do customers learn that they will have to pay more for coverage starting next year. What are the ethical implications of this draft? What changes would you suggest?

Expand Your Knowledge

Learning More on the Web

Protect Yourself When Sending Negative Employment Messages

www.toolkit.com

A visit to Business Owner's Toolkit can help you reduce your legal liability, whether you are laying off an employee, firing an employee, or contemplating a companywide reduction in your workforce. Find out the safest way to fire someone from a legal standpoint before it's too late. Learn why it's important to document disciplinary actions. Discover why some bad news should be given face-to-face and never with a letter or over the phone. Read the site's advice under "Firing and Termination" to find answers to these questions:

1. What should a manager communicate to an employee during a termination meeting?
2. Why is it important to document employee disciplinary actions?
3. What steps should you take before firing an employee for misconduct or poor work?

Sharpening Your Career Skills Online

Bovée and Thill's Business Communication Web Search, at http://businesscommunicationblog.com/websearch, is a unique research tool designed specifically for business communication research. Use the Web Search function to find a website, video, PDF document, podcast, or PowerPoint presentation that offers advice on writing messages that convey negative information. Write a brief e-mail message to your instructor, describing the item that you found and summarizing the career skills information you learned from it.

Improve Your Grammar, Mechanics, and Usage

The following exercises help you improve your knowledge of and power over English grammar, mechanics, and usage. Turn to the Handbook of Grammar, Mechanics, and Usage at the end of this book and review all of Section 2.6 (Commas). Then look at the following 10 items. Circle the letter of the preferred choice in the following groups of sentences. (Answers to these exercises appear on page AK-3.)

1. a. Please send us four cases of filters two cases of wing nuts and a bale of rags.
   b. Please send us four cases of filters, two cases of wing nuts and a bale of rags.
   c. Please send us four cases of filters, two cases of wing nuts, and a bale of rags.
2. a. Your analysis, however, does not account for returns.
   b. Your analysis however does not account for returns.
   c. Your analysis, however does not account for returns.

3. a. As a matter of fact she has seen the figures.
   b. As a matter of fact, she has seen the figures.
4. a. Before May 7, 1999, they wouldn't have minded.
   b. Before May 7, 1999 they wouldn't have minded.
5. a. Stoneridge Inc. will go public on September 9 2003.
   b. Stoneridge, Inc., will go public on September 9, 2003.
   c. Stoneridge Inc. will go public on September 9, 2003.
6. a. "Talk to me" Sandra said "before you change a thing."
   b. "Talk to me," Sandra said "before you change a thing."
   c. "Talk to me," Sandra said, "before you change a thing."
7. a. The firm was founded during the long hard recession of the mid-1970s.
   b. The firm was founded during the long, hard recession of the mid-1970s.
   c. The firm was founded during the long hard, recession of the mid-1970s.
8. a. You can reach me at this address: 717 Darby St., Scottsdale, AZ 85251.
   b. You can reach me at this address: 717 Darby St., Scottsdale AZ 85251.
   c. You can reach me at this address: 717 Darby St., Scottsdale, AZ, 85251.
9. a. Transfer the documents from Fargo, North Dakota to Boise, Idaho.
   b. Transfer the documents from Fargo North Dakota, to Boise Idaho.
   c. Transfer the documents from Fargo, North Dakota, to Boise, Idaho.
10. a. Sam O'Neill the designated representative is gone today.
    b. Sam O'Neill, the designated representative, is gone today.
    c. Sam O'Neill, the designated representative is gone today.

For additional exercises focusing on commas, visit mybcommlab. Click on Chapter 9, click on "Additional Exercises to Improve Your Grammar, Mechanics, and Usage," and then click on "14. Fused sentences and comma splices."

CASES

Applying the Three-Step Writing Process to Cases

Apply each step to the following cases, as assigned by your instructor.

NEGATIVE MESSAGES ON ROUTINE BUSINESS MATTERS

TELEPHONE SKILLS

1. When a recall isn't really a recall: Voice recording informing customers that an unsafe product won't be replaced. Vail Products of Toledo, Ohio, manufactured a line of beds for use in hospitals and other institutions where there is a need to protect patients who might otherwise fall out of bed and injure themselves (including patients with cognitive impairments or patterns of spasms or seizures). These "enclosed bed systems" use a netted canopy to keep patients in bed rather than the traditional method of using physical restraints such as straps or tranquilizing drugs. The intent is humane, but the design is flawed: At least 30 patients have become trapped in the various parts of the mattress and canopy structure, and 8 of them have suffocated.

Working with the U.S. Food and Drug Administration (FDA), Vail issued a recall on the beds, as manufacturers often do in the case of unsafe products. However, the recall is not really a recall. Vail will not be replacing or modifying the beds, nor will it accept returns. Instead, the company is urging institutions to move patients to other beds, if possible. Vail has also sent out revised manuals and warning labels to be placed on the beds. The company also announced that it is ceasing production of enclosed beds.

Your task: A flurry of phone calls from concerned patients, family members, and institutional staff is overwhelming the support staff. As a writer in Vail's corporate communications office, you've been asked to draft a short script to be recorded on the company's phone system. When people call the main number, they'll hear "Press 1 for information regarding the recall of Model 500, Model 1000, and Model 2000 enclosed beds." After they press 1, they'll hear the message you're about to write, explaining that although the action is classified as a recall, Vail will not be accepting returned beds, nor will it replace any of the affected beds. The message should also assure customers that Vail has already sent revised operating manuals and warning labels to every registered owner of the beds in question. The phone system has limited memory, and you've been directed to keep the message to 75 words or less.[28]

E-MAIL SKILLS PORTFOLIO BUILDER

2. Message to the boss: Refusing a project on ethical grounds. A not-so-secret secret is getting more attention than you'd really like after an article in *BusinessWeek* gave the world an inside look at how much money you and other electronics retailers make from extended warranties (sometimes called service contracts). The article explained that typically half of the warranty price goes to the salesperson as a commission and that only 20 percent of the total amount customers pay for warranties eventually goes to product repair.

You also know why extended warranties are such a profitable business. Many electronics products follow a predictable pattern of failure: a high failure rate early in their lives, then a "midlife" period during which failures go way down, and concluding with an "old age" period when failure rates ramp back up again (engineers refer to the phenomenon as the *bathtub curve* because it looks like a bathtub from the side—high at both ends and low in the middle). The early failures are usually covered by manufacturers' warranties, and the extended warranties you sell are designed to cover that middle part of the life span. In other words, many extended warranties cover the period of time during which consumers are *least* likely to need them and offer no coverage when consumers need them *most.* (Consumers can actually benefit from extended warranties in a few product categories, including laptop computers and plasma televisions. Of course, the more sense the warranty makes for the consumer, the less financial sense it makes for your company.)[29]

Your task: Worried that consumers will stop buying so many extended warranties, your boss has directed you to put together a sales training program that will help cashiers sell the extended warranties even more aggressively. The more you ponder this challenge, though, the more you're convinced that your company should change its strategy so it doesn't rely on profits from these warranties so much. In addition to offering questionable value to the consumer, the warranties risk creating a consumer backlash that could lead to lower sales of all your products. You would prefer to voice your concerns to your boss in person, but both of you are traveling on hectic schedules for the next week. You'll have to write an e-mail instead. Draft a brief message, explaining why you think the sales training specifically and the warranties in general are both bad ideas.

MICROBLOGGING SKILLS

3. Hurricane heads-up: Alerting JetBlue passengers about possible flight delays and cancellations. JetBlue was one of the first companies to incorporate the Twitter microblogging service into its customer communications, and thousands of flyers and fans now follow the airline's Twittering staff members. Messages include announcements about fare sales (such as limited-time auctions on eBay or special on-site sales at shopping malls), celebrations of company milestones (such as the opening of the carrier's new terminal at New York's JFK airport in 2008), schedule updates, and even personalized responses to people who Twitter with questions or complaints about the company.[30]

Your task: Write a Tweet alerting JetBlue customers to the possibility that Hurricane Isaac might disrupt flight schedules from August 13 through August 15. Tell them that decisions about delays and cancellations will be made on a city-by-city basis and will be announced on Twitter and the company's website at www.jetblue.com. Your message must be no more than 140 characters (including spaces) and must include the 15-character URL.

WEB WRITING SKILLS PORTFOLIO BUILDER

4. Coffee offer overflow: Undoing a marketing mistake at Starbucks. Marketing specialists usually celebrate when target audiences forward their messages to friends and family—essentially acting as unpaid advertising and sales representatives. In fact, the practice of viral marketing (see page 188) is based on this hope. For one Starbucks regional office, however, viral marketing started to make the company just a bit sick. The office sent employees in the Southeast an e-mail coupon for a free iced drink and invited them to share the coupon with family and friends. To the surprise of virtually no one who understands the nature of online life, the e-mail coupon multiplied rapidly, to the point that Starbucks stores all around the country were quickly overwhelmed with requests for free drinks. The company decided to immediately terminate the free offer, a month ahead of the expiration date on the coupon.[31]

Your task: Write a one-paragraph message that can be posted on the Starbucks website and at individual stores, apologizing for the mix-up and explaining that the offer is no longer valid.

E-MAIL SKILLS

5. Retail rejection: Turning down a request to carry a product. Lee Valley Tools (www.leevalley.com) sells high-quality woodworking tools across Canada through its retail stores and around the world through its website and catalogs. While weekend hobbyists can pick up a mass-produced hand plane (a tool for smoothing wood) for $20 or $30 at the local hardware store, serious woodworkers pay up to ten times that much for one of Lee Valley's precision Veritas planes. For the price, they get top-quality materials, precision manufacturing, and innovative designs that help them do better work in less time.

Lee Valley sells both its own Veritas brand tools as well as 5,000 tools made by other manufacturers. One of those companies has just e-mailed you to ask if Lee Valley would like to carry a new line of midrange hand planes that would cost more than the mass-market, hardware-store models but less than Lee Valley's own Veritas models. Your job is to filter requests such as this, rejecting those that don't meet Lee Valley's criteria and forwarding those that do to the product selection committee for further analysis. After one quick read of this incoming e-mail message, you realize there is no need to send this idea to the committee. While these planes are certainly of decent quality, they achieve their lower cost through lower-quality steel that won't hold an edge as long and through thinner irons (the element that holds the cutting edge) that will be more prone to vibrate during use and thus produce a rougher finish. These planes have a market, to be sure, but they're not a good fit for Lee Valley's top-of-the-line product portfolio. Moreover, the planes don't offer any innovations in terms of ease of use or any other product attribute.[32]

Your task: Reply to this e-mail message, explaining that the planes appear to be decent tools, but they don't fit Lee Valley's strategy of offering only the best and most innovative tools. Support your decision with the three criteria described above. Choose the direct or indirect approach carefully, taking into consideration your company's relationship with this other company.

LETTER WRITING SKILLS

6. Enough is enough: Alerting a service provider that its services will no longer be needed. Your company, PolicyPlan Insurance Services, is a 120-employee insurance claims processor based in Milwaukee. PolicyPlan has engaged Midwest Sparkleen for interior and exterior cleaning for the past five years. Midwest Sparkleen did exemplary work for the first four years, but after a change of ownership last year, the level of service has plummeted. Offices are no longer cleaned thoroughly, you've had to call the company at least six times to remind them to take care of spills and other messes that they're supposed to address routinely, and they've left toxic cleaning chemicals in a public hallway on several occasions. You have spoken with the owner about your concerns twice in the past three months, but his assurances that service would improve have not resulted in any noticeable improvements. When the evening cleaning crew forgot to lock the lobby door last Thursday—leaving your entire facility vulnerable to theft from midnight until 8 a.m. Friday morning—you decided it was time for a change.

Your task: Write a letter to Jason Allred, owner of Midwest Sparkleen, 4000 South Howell Avenue, Milwaukee, WI, 53207, telling him that PolicyPlan will not be renewing its annual cleaning contract with Midwest Sparkleen when the current contract expires at the end of this month. Cite the examples identified above, and keep the tone of your letter professional.

E-MAIL SKILLS

7. That's why we offer free trials: Rejecting a refund request. Like many other software companies, the Swiss company Fookes Software (www.fookes.com) lets potential customers download free evaluation copies of its software before deciding to purchase. By using the free trial versions, people can verify that the software meets their needs and is compatible with their PCs. Because it allows potential buyers to try products for 30 days before purchasing, the company does not provide refunds except in the case of accidental duplicate orders. Here is the company's refund policy, as shown on its website:

All of Fookes Software's products can be evaluated, **free of charge,** through a trial mode or separate trial version that can be downloaded directly from our web site. Use the trial **before you purchase** to ensure that the full product will be compatible with your computer systems and satisfy your requirements. If you do not, you accept that the product may not meet your needs and that this will not justify a refund or chargeback. If you experience an issue with our software, then please contact our customer support service for help in solving the problem.

All sales are final and refunds are provided only for accidental duplicate orders. Refunds will only be made to the credit card or PayPal account through which the original purchase was made. An administration fee may apply in such cases to cover processing costs and third-party commissions.

Ordering a software license signifies your acceptance of this Refund Policy.

In addition, the ordering page on the website asks potential buyers to read the refund policy before ordering and provides a link to the policy page.

This morning you received an e-mail message from a customer who purchased a copy of Album Express, a software package that helps people organize photos in attractive online albums and slide shows. After purchasing the program, the customer discovered that his computer has only 16 MB of memory, which is not enough to run the software effectively. He is now requesting a refund of the purchase price of $24.95. The website clearly states that Album Express requires at least 32 MB of memory, but the customer's e-mail doesn't mention whether he read this.[33]

Your task: Write an e-mail message, denying the customer's request for a refund.

NEGATIVE ORGANIZATIONAL NEWS

BLOGGING SKILLS

8. We're going to catch some flak for this: Alerting employees to the removal of a popular product. XtremityPlus is known for its outlandish extreme-sports products, and the Looney Launch is no exception. Fulfilling the dream of every childhood daredevil, the Looney Launch is an aluminum and fiberglass contraption that quickly unfolds to create the ultimate bicycle jump. The product has been selling as fast as you can make it, even though it comes plastered with warning labels proclaiming that its use is inherently dangerous.

As XtremityPlus's CEO, you were nervous about introducing this product, and your fears were just confirmed: You've been notified of the first lawsuit by a parent whose child broke several bones after crash-landing off a Looney Launch.

Your task: Write a post for your internal blog, explaining that the Looney Launch is being removed from the market immediately. Tell your employees to expect some negative reactions from enthusiastic customers and retailers but explain that (a) the company can't afford the risk of additional lawsuits, and (b) even for XtremityPlus, the Looney Launch pushes the envelope a bit too far. The product is simply too dangerous to sell in good conscience.

E-MAIL SKILLS

9. Looney Launch coming back to Earth: Informing retailers about the demise of a popular product. Now it's time to follow up the internal employee message about the Looney Launch (see Case 8) with a message to the retailers that carry the product.

Your task: Write an e-mail message to retailers, explaining that the Looney Launch is being removed from the market and explaining why you've reached this decision. Apologize for the temporary disruption this will cause to their businesses but emphasize that it's the right decision from both legal and social perspectives. Thank them for their continuing efforts to sell XtremityPlus products and assure them that your company will continue to offer exciting and innovative products for extreme-sports enthusiasts.

BLOGGING SKILLS PORTFOLIO BUILDER

10. Communicating in a crisis: Informing the local community about a serious accident. One of your company's worst nightmares has just come true. EQ Industrial Services (EQIS), based in Wayne, Michigan, operates a number of facilities around the country that dispose of, recycle, and transport hazardous chemical wastes. Last night, explosions and fires broke out at the company's Apex, North Carolina, facility, forcing the evacuation of 17,000 local residents.

Your task: It's now Friday, the day after the fire. Write a brief post for the company's blog, covering the following points:

- A fire broke out at the Apex facility at approximately 10 P.M. Thursday.
- No one was in the facility at the time.
- Because of the diverse nature of the materials stored at the plant, the cause of the fire is not yet known.
- Rumors that the facility stores extremely dangerous chlorine gas and that the fire was spreading to other nearby businesses are not true.
- Special industrial firefighters hired by EQIS have already brought the fire under control.
- Residents in the immediate area were evacuated as a precaution, and they should be able to return to their homes tomorrow, pending permission from local authorities.
- Several dozen residents were admitted to local hospitals with complaints of breathing problems, but most have been released already; about a dozen emergency responders were treated as well.
- At this point (Friday afternoon), tests conducted by the North Carolina State Department of Environment and Natural Resources "had not detected anything out of the ordinary in the air."

Conclude by thanking the local police and fire departments for their assistance and directing readers to EQIS's toll-free hot line for more information.[34]

BLOGGING SKILLS

11. The economy claims another one: Blog post announcing the closing of a Shaw Industries yarn plant. As the U.S. economy continued to sag in 2009 after receiving multiple blows from the housing and financial sectors, plant closures were a common tragedy across many industries. Shaw Industries, the world's largest manufacturer of carpeting, was among those suppliers to the housing industry that suffered as fewer houses were built or remodeled.

Your task: Write a brief message for Shaw's corporate blog, covering the following points:

- With more than $5 billion in annual sales, Shaw Industries is the world's number one carpet manufacturer.
- Shaw's Milledgeville, Georgia, plant makes yarn used in the manufacture of carpeting.
- The continuing struggles in the new-housing market and the inability of many current homeowners to afford remodeling projects have lowered demand for carpet. With less demand for carpet, the Milledgeville plant can no longer operate at a profit.
- Shaw is forced to close the Milledgeville plant and lay off all 150 employees at the plant.

- The plant will close in three to four weeks from the current date.
- As openings become available in other Shaw facilities, the company hopes to be able to place some of the workers in those jobs.
- Georgia Labor Commissioner Michael Thurmond promised to help the affected employees. "The layoff at Shaw Industries in Milledgeville will create a difficult situation for the workers and their families, and I want them to know they're not alone in dealing with this problem. Our staff will work closely with the laid-off workers, company officials, and local elected officials in determining how to best assist the affected employees."
- Assistance to be provided by the State of Georgia includes career counseling, unemployment benefits, and job retraining.[35]

E-MAIL SKILLS

12. Pulling the plug won't pull the plug: Alerting ATV owners to a serious safety problem. People who live for an adrenaline rush can find a way to go fast from Canada's Bombardier Recreational Products. Bombardier is one of the world's top makers of snowmobiles, personal watercraft, engines for motorboats, and all-terrain vehicles (ATVs)—all designed for fast fun.

Because it sends customers hurtling across snow, water, or land at high speeds, Bombardier takes safety quite seriously. However, problems do arise from time to time, requiring a rapid response with clear communication to the company's customer base. Bombardier recently became aware of a potentially hazardous situation with the "race-ready" version of its Can-Am DS 90 X ATVs. This model is equipped with a safety device called a tether engine shutoff switch, in which a cord is connected to a special switch that turns off the engine in the event of an emergency. On the affected units, pulling the cord might not shut off the motor, which is particularly dangerous if the rider falls off—the ATV will continue on its own until the engine speed returns to idle.

Your task: Write an e-mail message that will be sent to registered owners of 2008 and 2009 DS 90 X ATVs that include the potentially faulty switch. Analyze the situation carefully as you choose the direct or indirect approach for your message. Explain that the tether engine shutoff switch may not deactivate the engine when it is pulled in an emergency situation. To prevent riders from relying on a safety feature that might not work properly, Bombardier, in cooperation with transportation safety authorities in the United States and Canada, is voluntarily recalling these models to have the tether switch removed. Emphasize the serious nature of the situation by explaining that if the rider is ejected and the engine shutoff switch does not work properly, the ATV will run away on its own, potentially resulting in significant injuries or deaths. Owners should stop riding their vehicles immediately and make an appointment with an authorized dealer to have the switch removed. The service will be performed at no charge, and customers will receive a $50 credit voucher for future purchases of Bombardier accessories. Include the following contact information: www.can-am.brp.com and 1-888-638-5397.[36]

E-MAIL SKILLS PORTFOLIO BUILDER

13. Sorry, but we don't have a choice: E-mail about monitoring employee blogs. You can certainly sympathize with employees when they complain about having their e-mail and instant messages monitored, but you're implementing a company policy that all employees agree to abide by when they join the company. Your firm, Webcor Builders of San Mateo, California, is one of the estimated 60 percent of U.S. companies with such monitoring systems in place. More and more companies use these systems (which typically operate by scanning messages for keywords that suggest confidential, illegal, or otherwise inappropriate content) in an attempt to avoid instances of sexual harassment and other problems.

As the chief information officer, the manager in charge of computer systems in the company, you're often the target when employees complain about being monitored. Consequently, you know you're really going to hear it when employees learn that the monitoring program will be expanded to personal blogs as well.

Your task: Write an e-mail message to be distributed to the entire workforce, explaining that the automated monitoring program is about to be expanded to include employees' personal blogs. Explain that, while you sympathize with employee concerns regarding privacy and freedom of speech, it is the management team's responsibility to protect the company's intellectual property and the value of the company name. Therefore, employees' personal blogs will be added to the monitoring system to ensure that employees don't intentionally or accidentally expose company secrets or criticize management in a way that could harm the company.[37]

LETTER WRITING SKILLS PORTFOLIO BUILDER

14. Listen to the music, partner: Delivering an ultimatum to a business associate. You're a marketing manager for Stanton, one of the premier suppliers of DJ equipment (turntables, amplifiers, speakers, mixers, and related accessories). Your company's latest creation, the FinalScratch system, has been flying off retailers' shelves. Both professional and amateur DJs love the way that FinalScratch gives them the feel of working with vinyl records by letting them control digital music files from any analog turntable or CD player while giving them access to the endless possibilities of digital music technology. (For more information about the product, go to www.stantondj.com.) Sales are strong everywhere except in Music99 stores, a retail chain in the Mid-Atlantic region. You suspect the cause: The owners of this chain refused to let their salespeople attend the free product training you offered when FinalScratch was introduced, claiming their people were smart enough to train themselves.

To explore the situation, you head out from Stanton headquarters in Hollywood, Florida, on an undercover shopping mission. After visiting a few Music99 locations, you're appalled by what you see. The salespeople in these stores clearly don't understand the FinalScratch concept, so they either give potential customers bad information about it or steer them to products from your competitors. No wonder sales are so bad at this chain.

Your task: You're tempted to pull your products out of this chain immediately, but you know how difficult and expensive it is to recruit new retailers in this market. However, this situation can't go on; you're losing thousands of dollars of potential business every week. Write a letter to Jackson Fletcher, the CEO of Music99 (14014 Preston Pike, Dover, DE 19901), expressing your disappointment in what you observed and explaining that the Music99 sales staff will need to agree to attend product training or else your company's management team will consider terminating the business relationship. You've met Mr. Fletcher in person once and talked to him on the phone several times, and you know him well enough to know that he will not be pleased by this ultimatum. Music99 does a good job selling other Stanton products—and he'll probably be furious to learn that you were "spying" on his sales staff.[38]

PODCASTING SKILLS

15. Say good-bye to the concierge: Podcast announcing the end of a popular employee benefit. An employee concierge seemed like a great idea when you added it as an employee benefit last year. The concierge handles a wide variety of personal chores for employees, everything from dropping off dry cleaning to ordering event tickets to sending flowers. Employees love the service, and you know that the time they save can be devoted to work or family activities. Unfortunately, profits are way down, and concierge usage is up—up so far that you'll need to add a second concierge to keep up with the demand. As painful as it will be for everyone, you decide that the company needs to stop offering the service.

Your task: Script a brief podcast, announcing the decision and explaining why it was necessary. Make up any details you need. If your instructor asks you to do so, record your podcast and submit the file.

WEB WRITING SKILLS

16. A rash of rashes: Alerting clothing customers to potential skin irritation. Sewn-in clothing tags carry essential information about size and garment care, but no matter where they are located inside a garment, they seem to have a knack for poking and scratching. Pestered consumers consequently welcomed the switch by many clothing makers to *tagless labels*, in which information is printed directly onto the fabric, and no physical tag is sewn into the garment. Carter's, one of the leading manufacturers and retailers of children's clothing, is one of those companies. Unfortunately, a small number of parents have contacted Carter's to complain that their children have developed rashes where their skin came in contact with a tagless label.

Your task: Write an announcement for Carter's website, explaining that the company has heard some reports of babies whose skin appeared to be irritated by the tagless labels. Cover the following points: (1) the situation applies only to clothes from the fall 2007 product line, in which the tagless label has a solid white printed background on which the label text is printed (as opposed to newer and older garments, in which the label text is printed directly on the fabric, without the solid background); (2) of the 100 million garments sold in the fall 2007 line, the company has received only 400 complaints of rashes; (3) based on a thorough analysis by the company, its suppliers, and several independent doctors and other specialists, Carter's has found that the labels contain no known skin irritants or abrasive chemicals, and the problem seems to affect only a very small number of children with sensitive skin; (4) because the problem is so limited in scope and the skin rashes are not serious, after discussions with the U.S. Consumer Products Safety Commission, the company has opted not to recall the clothes but is instead advising parents of affected children to switch to other garments; and (5) as is always the case with Carter's clothes, consumers can return unsatisfactory products for a full refund. You will be able to show two comparative photos on the website to help consumers identify the garments in question, one showing clothes from the fall 2007 line, with the solid-background labels, and one showing a newer line of clothes that have a different label style.[39]

NEGATIVE EMPLOYMENT MESSAGES

TELEPHONE SKILLS

17. Reacting to a lost contract: Phone call rescinding a job offer. As the human resources manager at Alion Science and Technology, a military research firm in McLean, Virginia, you were thrilled when one of the nation's top computer visualization specialists accepted your job offer. Claus Gunnstein's skills would have made a major contribution to Alion's work in designing flight simulators and other systems. Unfortunately, the day after he accepted the offer, Alion received news that a major Pentagon contract had been canceled. In addition to letting several dozen current employees know that the company will be forced to lay them off, you need to tell Gunnstein that Alion has no choice but to rescind the job offer.

Your task: Outline the points you'll need to make in a telephone call to Gunnstein. Pay special attention to your opening and closing statements. (You'll review your plans for the phone call with Alion's legal staff to make sure everything you say follows employment law guidelines; for now, just focus on the way you'll present the negative news to Gunnstein. Feel free to make up any details you need.)[40]

E-MAIL SKILLS

18. Career moves: E-mail refusing to write a recommendation. Tom Weiss worked in the office at Opal Pools and Patios for four months under your supervision (you're the office manager). On the basis of what he told you he could do, you started him off as a file clerk. However, his organizational skills proved inadequate for the job, so you transferred him to logging in accounts receivable, where he performed almost adequately. Then he assured you that his "real strength" was customer relations, so you moved him to the complaint department. After he spent three weeks making angry customers even angrier, you were convinced that no place in your office was appropriate for his talents. Five weeks ago, you encouraged him to resign before being formally fired.

Today's e-mail brings a request from Weiss, asking you to write a letter recommending him for a sales position with a florist shop. You can't assess Weiss's sales abilities, but you do know him to be an incompetent file clerk, a careless bookkeeper, and an insensitive customer service representative. Someone else is more likely to deserve the sales job, so you decide that you have done enough favors for Tom Weiss for one lifetime and plan to refuse his request.

Your task: Write an e-mail reply to Weiss (tomweiss@mailnet.com), indicating that you have chosen not to write a letter of recommendation for him.

LETTER WRITING SKILLS

19. Bad news for 80: Form letter to unsuccessful job candidates. The dean's selection committee screened 85 applications for the position of dean of arts and sciences at your campus. After two rounds of eliminations, the top five candidates were invited to "airport interviews," in which the committee managed to meet with each candidate for an hour. Then the top three candidates were invited to the campus to meet with students, faculty, and administrators.

The committee recommended to the university president that the job be given to Constance Pappas, who has a doctorate in American studies and has been chairperson of the history department at Minneapolis Metropolitan College for the past three years. The president agreed, and Dr. Pappas accepted the offer.

One final task remains before the work of the dean's selection committee is finished: Letters must be sent to the 84 unsuccessful candidates. The 4 who reached the "airport interview" stage will receive personal letters from the chairperson of the committee. Your job, as secretary of the committee, is to draft the form letter that will be sent to the other 80 applicants.

Your task: Draft a letter of 100 to 200 words. All copies will be individually addressed to the recipients but will carry identical messages.

PORTFOLIO BUILDER

20. What we have here is a failure to communicate: Writing a negative performance review. Elaine Bridgewater, the former professional golfer you hired to oversee your golf equipment company's relationship with retailers, knows the business inside and out. As a former touring pro, she has unmatched credibility. She also has seemingly boundless energy, solid technical knowledge, and an engaging personal style. Unfortunately, she hasn't been quite as attentive as she needs to be when it comes to communicating with retailers. You've been getting complaints about voice-mail messages gone unanswered for days, confusing e-mails that require two or three rounds of clarification, and reports that are haphazardly thrown together. As valuable as Bridgewater's other skills are, she's going to cost the company sales if this goes on much longer. The retail channel is vital to your company's survival, and she's the employee most involved in this channel.

Your task: Draft a brief (one page maximum) informal performance appraisal and improvement plan for Bridgewater. Be sure to compliment her on the areas in which she excels but don't shy away from highlighting the areas in which she needs to improve, too: punctual response to customer messages; clear writing; and careful revision, production, and proofreading. Use what you've learned in this course so far to supply any additional advice about the importance of these skills.

Writing Persuasive Messages

10

Learning Objectives

After studying this chapter, you will be able to

1. Apply the three-step writing process to persuasive messages
2. Identify seven ways to establish credibility in persuasive messages
3. Describe the AIDA model for persuasive messages
4. Distinguish between emotional and logical appeals, and discuss how to balance them
5. Describe seven essential steps in developing marketing and sales messages
6. Identify steps you can take to avoid ethical lapses in marketing and sales messages

On the Job: Communicating at CafeMom

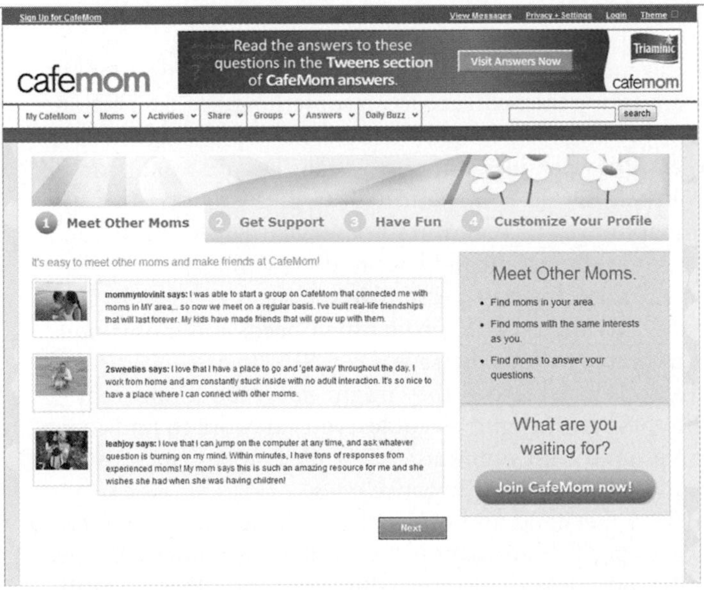

CafeMom appeals to new members with a variety of attractive images and brief, upbeat statements that emphasize the benefits of joining.

Creating a Business by Connecting Mothers Everywhere

Few roles in life require more information and insight than parenting. From prenatal care to early childhood development to education to socialization issues, parents are in continuous learning mode as their children grow. Parents also need to learn about themselves as they grow in their roles, from balancing work and home life to nurturing their own relationships. At the same time, parenting can be one of the most isolating experiences for people, often making it difficult for them to acquire the information and support they need to succeed as parents.

Two lifelong friends, actor and activist Andrew Shue and entrepreneur Michael Sanchez, pondered this age-old challenge and saw the web as a solution. The pair co-founded CafeMom, an online community and information resource that helps mothers find answers, insights, and each other.

Information resources and social networks abound on the web, and like any other web start-up, CafeMom faced the challenges of standing apart from the crowd and growing its membership large enough to create a viable business. One of the keys to its success is clear, audience-focused messages that make a compelling case for joining CafeMom. Using straightforward statements such as "CafeMom is an online community where thousands of moms come together every day to connect with each other" and "Whatever you're going through, chances are another mom has been there and can help," the company communicates the features of its various online services and the benefits of joining.

The persuasive communication effort certainly seems to have been successful: CafeMom is now one of the largest social networking communities for mothers and continues to expand as more mothers join in search of helpful insights and friendly support from their peers.[1]
www.cafemom.com

1 LEARNING OBJECTIVE

Apply the three-step writing process to persuasive messages.

USING THE THREE-STEP WRITING PROCESS FOR PERSUASIVE MESSAGES

Professionals such as Michael Sanchez, CEO of CafeMom (profiled in the chapter-opening "On the Job" vignette), realize that successful businesses rely on persuasive messages in both internal and external communication. Whether you're trying to convince your boss to open a new office in Europe or encourage potential customers to try your products, you need to call on your abilities of **persuasion**—the attempt to change an audience's attitudes, beliefs, or actions.[2] Successful professionals understand that persuasion is not about trickery or getting people to make choices that aren't in their best interests; rather, persuasion lets your audience members know they have a choice and helps them choose to agree with you.[3] As with every other type of business message, the three-step writing process improves persuasive messages.

Persuasion is the attempt to change someone's attitudes, beliefs, or actions.

Step 1: Planning a Persuasive Message

Every day, untold numbers of good ideas go unheeded and good products go unsold simply because the messages meant to promote them aren't compelling enough. Even if audiences agree that your idea or product is attractive, they usually have other options to consider as well, so you will need to convince them that your choice is the best of all the attractive alternatives. Creating successful persuasive messages in these challenging situations starts with an insightful analysis of the situation.

Analyzing the Situation

Failing to clarify your purpose is a common mistake with persuasive messages.

Demographics include characteristics such as age, gender, occupation, income, and education.

Psychographics include characteristics such as personality, attitudes, and lifestyle.

A clear purpose is important in every message, of course, but clarity is doubly important in persuasive messages because you are asking the audience to do something—to take action, make decisions, and so on. Let's say you want to persuade members of top management to support a particular research project. But what does "support" mean? Do you want them to pat you on the back and wish you well? Or do you want them to give you a staff of five researchers and a $1 million annual budget? If you don't know what you want or can't express it clearly, you'll never be able to convince an audience to do anything.

In addition to having a clear purpose, the best persuasive messages are closely connected to audience members' desires and interests.[4] Consider their needs and motivations (the reasons they might respond favorably to your message), as well as their concerns and objections (the reasons they might *not* respond favorably). With these two insights as guides, you can work to find common ground with your audience while emphasizing positive points and minimizing negative ones.

To understand and categorize audience needs, you can refer to specific information such as **demographics** (the age, gender, occupation, income, education, and other quantifiable characteristics of the people you're trying to persuade) and **psychographics** (personality, attitudes, lifestyle, and other psychological characteristics). Be sure to consider cultural expectations so that you don't undermine your persuasive message by using an inappropriate appeal or by organizing your message in a way that seems unfamiliar or uncomfortable to your audience.

REAL-TIME UPDATES
Learn More

Persuasion skills for every business professional

Persuasion is an essential business skill, no matter what career path you follow. This video offers great tips for understanding, practicing, and applying persuasive skills. Go to **http://real-timeupdates.com/ebc** and click on "Learn More." If you are using mybcommlab, you can access Real-Time Updates within each chapter or under Student Study Tools.

If you aim to change someone's attitudes, beliefs, or actions through a persuasive message, it is vital to understand his or her **motivation**—the combination of forces that drive people to satisfy their needs. Table 10.1 lists some of the needs that psychologists have identified or suggested as being important in influencing human motivation. Obviously, the more closely a persuasive message aligns with a recipient's existing motivation, the more effective the message is likely to be. For example, if you try to persuade consumers to purchase a product on the basis of its fashion appeal, that message will connect with consumers who are motivated by a desire to be in style but probably won't connect with consumers driven by practical function or financial concerns.

Effective persuasive messages are closely aligned with audience motivations, those forces that drive people to satisfy their needs.

TABLE 10.1 Human Needs That Influence Motivation

NEED	IMPLICATIONS FOR COMMUNICATION
Basic physiological requirements: The needs for food, water, sleep, oxygen, and other essentials	Everyone has these needs, but the degree of attention an individual gives to them often depends on whether the needs are being met; for instance, an advertisement for sleeping pills will have greater appeal to someone suffering from insomnia than to someone who has no problem sleeping.
Safety and security: The needs for protection from bodily harm, to know that loved ones are safe, and for financial security, protection of personal identity, career security, and other assurances	These needs influence both consumer and business decisions in a wide variety of ways; for instance, advertisements for life insurance often encourage parents to think about the financial security of their children and other loved ones.
Affiliation and belonging: The needs for companionship, acceptance, love, popularity, etc.	The need to feel loved, accepted, or popular drives a great deal of human behavior, from the desire to be attractive to potential mates to wearing the clothing style that a particular social group is likely to approve.
Power and control: The need to feel in control of situations or to exert authority over others	You can see many examples appealing to this need in advertisements: *Take control of your life, your finances, your future, your career*, and so on. Many people who lack power want to know how to get it, and people who have power often want others to know they have it.
Achievement: The need to feel a sense of accomplishment—or to be admired by others for accomplishments	This need can involve both *knowing* (when people experience a feeling of accomplishment) and *showing* (when people are able to show others that they've achieved success); advertising for luxury consumer products frequently appeals to this need.
Adventure and distraction: The need for excitement or relief from daily routine	People vary widely in their need for adventure; some crave excitement—even danger—while others value calmness and predictability. Some needs for adventure and distraction are met *virtually*, such as through horror movies, thriller novels, etc.
Knowledge, exploration, and understanding: The need to keep learning	For some people, learning is usually a means to an end, a way to fulfill some other need; for others, acquiring new knowledge is the goal.
Aesthetic appreciation: The desire to experience beauty, order, symmetry, etc.	Although this need may seem "noncommercial" at first glance, advertisers appeal to it frequently, from the pleasing shape of a package to the quality of the gemstones in a piece of jewelry.
Self-actualization: The need to "be all that one can be," to reach one's full potential as a human being	Psychologists Kurt Goldstein and Abraham Maslow popularized self-actualization as the desire to make the most of one's potential, and Maslow identified it as one of the higher-level needs in his classic hierarchy; even if people met most or all of their other needs, they would still feel the need to self-actualize. An often-quoted example of appealing to this need is the U.S. Army's one-time advertising slogan "Be all that you can be."
Helping others: The need to believe that one is making a difference in the lives of other people	This need is the central motivation in fundraising messages and other appeals to charity.

Gathering Information

Once your situation analysis is complete, you need to gather the information necessary to create a compelling persuasive message. Chapter 11 offers advice on using the latest research techniques to find the information you need.

Selecting the Right Medium

Persuasive messages can be found in virtually every communication medium, from instant messages and podcasts to radio advertisements and skywriting. In fact, advertising agencies employ media specialists whose only jobs are to analyze the media options available and select the most cost-effective combination for each client and each advertising campaign.

You may need to use multiple media to reach your entire audience.

In some situations, various members of your audience might prefer different media for the same message. Some consumers like to do all their car shopping in person, whereas

Business Communication 2.0

Building an Audience Through Search Engine Optimization

Have you ever wondered why certain websites and blogs appear at the top of the list when you use an online search engine? Or why a site you might expect to find doesn't show up at all? Such questions are at the heart of one of the most important activities in online communication: *search engine optimization* (SEO). (SEO applies to the *natural* or *organic* search results, not the sponsored, paid results you see above, beside, or below the main search results listing.)

SEO involves three major parties: web users, website owners, and search engine developers such as Google, Yahoo!, and Microsoft. Most web users rely heavily on search engines to find relevant websites for shopping, research, and other online tasks. Website owners often rely on search engines to steer potential customers and other valuable visitors their way. To bring these two parties together while building lots of web traffic and advertising opportunities for themselves, search engine developers constantly fine-tune their engines to produce relevant, helpful search results.

And that's where things get interesting. Using sophisticated—and secret—algorithms, search engines rank search results by relevance to the user's input terms, starting with the most relevant results at the top of the list. Web users typically choose sites that show up in the first few pages of search results, so site owners naturally want to be ranked as high as possible.

Given the secrecy and the high stakes, the online search business has become something of a cat-and-mouse game in which website owners try to figure out what they can do to improve their rankings, while search engine developers work to improve the quality of results—partly by blocking website owners' attempts to "game" the system. For instance, in the early days of online search, some website owners would embed dozens of popular search terms in their websites, even if those terms had nothing to do with their site content. Search engine developers responded with ways to detect such tactics and penalize sites that use them by either lowering the sites' rankings in the search results or leaving them out entirely.

SEO has become a complex topic as search engines and the web itself have continued to evolve and as motivated website owners have looked for ways to boost their rankings. For instance, Google now evaluates more than 100 factors to determine search rankings. Without becoming an expert in SEO, however, you can work toward improving rankings for your website by focusing on four important areas: (1) offer fresh, high-quality, audience-oriented content; (2) use relevant keywords judiciously, particularly in important areas such as the page title that displays at the top of the browser screen; and (3) encourage links to your site from other high-quality sites with relevant content. In addition, make sure search engines can find your valuable content, particularly if you have a lot of Web 2.0 and multimedia technologies on your site. For example, search engines tend to find blogs and wikis easily, but techniques for finding content in podcasts, online videos, and Flash animation are still developing. You can learn more from Google's Webmaster Guidelines, www.google.com/support/webmasters.

CAREER APPLICATIONS

1. Locate a website for any company that sells products to consumers and write a new title for the site's homepage (the title that appears at the top of a web browser). Make the title short enough to read quickly while still summarizing what the company offers. Be sure to use one or more keywords that online shoppers would likely use when searching for the types of products the company sells.
2. Identify three high-quality websites that would be good sites to link to the site you chose in Question 1. For instance, if you chose a website that sells automotive parts and supplies, one of the three linking sites could be a popular blog that deals with automotive repair. Or if the site you chose sells golf equipment, you might find a sports website that covers the professional golf tours or one that provides information about golf courses around the world.

others do most of their car-shopping research online. Some people don't mind promotional e-mails for products they're interested in; others resent every piece of commercial e-mail they receive. If you can't be sure you can reach most or all of your audience through a single medium, you need to use two or more, such as following up an e-mail campaign with printed letters.

Social media (see Chapter 7) provide some exciting options for persuasive messages, particularly marketing and sales messages. However, as "Writing Persuasive Messages for Social Media" on page 296 explains, messages in these media require a unique approach.

Another important area of development is combining personal attention with technological reach and efficiency. For example, a customer support agent can carry on multiple instant messaging conversations at once, responding to one customer while other customers are typing messages. Even perceptions of human interaction created by animated *avatars* such as IKEA's "Anna" (www.ikea.com) can create a more sociable experience for shoppers, which can make websites more effective as a persuasive medium.[5]

Organizing Your Information

Successful persuasion requires close attention to all four aspects of organizing your information: defining your main idea, limiting your scope, choosing the direct or indirect approach, and grouping your points in a meaningful way. The most effective main ideas for persuasive messages have one thing in common: They are about the receiver, not the sender. For instance, if you're trying to convince others to join you in a business venture, explain how it will help them, not how it will help you.

Limit your scope to include only the information needed to help your audience take the next step toward making a favorable decision.

To limit your scope effectively, include only the information needed to help your audience take the next step toward the ultimate decision or ultimate action you want. In simple scenarios such as persuading teammates to attend a special meeting, you might put everything you have to say into a single, short message. But if you want your company to invest several million dollars in your latest product idea, the scope of your first message might be limited to securing 10 minutes at the next executive committee meeting so that you can introduce your idea and get permission to explore it.

Use the direct approach if your audience is ready to hear your proposal.

Most persuasive messages use the indirect approach because it gives the writer the opportunity to explain his or her reasons and build interest before asking for a decision or action. However, consider using the direct approach whenever you know your audience is ready to hear your proposal. Similarly, if there's a good chance your audience members will agree with your message, don't force them to wade through pages of reasoning before seeing your main idea (see Figure 10.1 on the next page).

The choice of direct or indirect approach is influenced by your authority, expertise, or power within the organization.

Your choice between the direct and indirect approaches is also influenced by the extent of your authority, expertise, or power in an organization. Generally, the more of these qualities you have in a given situation, the more likely that the direct approach will work for you because audience members are more apt to accept whatever you have to say. Conversely, if you're writing on a subject outside your recognized expertise, or if you're trying to persuade higher-level managers, the indirect approach is usually better because it allows you to build credibility as you present your reasoning.

Step 2: Writing a Persuasive Message

Persuasive messages are often unexpected or even unwelcome, so the "you" attitude is crucial.

Persuasive messages are often uninvited and occasionally even unwelcome, so adopting the "you" attitude is particularly critical when you write them. Most people won't even pay attention to your message, much less respond to it, if it isn't about them. You can encourage a more welcome reception by (1) using positive and polite language, (2) understanding and respecting cultural differences, (3) being sensitive to organizational cultures, and (4) taking steps to establish your credibility.

Positive language usually happens naturally with persuasive messages because you're promoting an idea or a product that you believe has benefits for your audience. However, polite language isn't as automatic as you might think. Don't insult the readers by implying that they are incapable of making smart decisions without your wise advice.

Make sure your persuasive messages consider the culture of your audience.

Demonstrating an understanding of and respect for cultural differences is crucial to persuasion. For example, an aggressive, hard-sell technique is likely to antagonize a

FIGURE 10.1 Proposal Using the Direct Approach
Bette McGiboney, an administrative assistant to the athletic director of Auburn University, presented a solution to the problem of high phone bills during the month of August. She already has a close relationship with her boss, who is likely to welcome the money-saving idea, so the direct approach is a fast, efficient way to communicate her proposal.

Proposal to save on toll-free number - Message (HTML)

File Edit View Insert Format Tools Actions Help

Type a question for help

To... houseI@ath.auburn.edu

Cc...

Subject: Proposal to save on toll-free number

Attach... New phone message (28 KB)

Uses the subject line to announce the nature of the message (a proposal) and a compelling benefit to the reader (saving money)

David,

I've learned that we can save money, time, and frustration with a simple modification to our toll-free message system. Currently, the bill for our toll-free number at the ticket office runs at least $3,000 for August (compared with $493 on average for the other 11 months). Plus, we're so busy fielding calls during August that our other work piles up. In addition, Tiger fans who call in August are frustrated by having to wait on hold at least five minutes and often longer.

Follows the opening statement with a summary of the problem she proposes to solve

Describes the solution in enough detail to help the reader imagine how it will work

By providing callers with an additional option, we can relieve a lot of the pressure. Under the new system, callers will hear all the same messages and have all the same options as before. But if no operator is available when a caller presses "0" for ticket information, a new message will request the caller's name and phone number so that we can return the call within the next two business days.

This new message system will help us in multiple ways:

- Save money on our toll-free line
- Manage our time and stress levels
- Provide better customer service

Builds interest in the solution by highlighting key benefits in a bulleted list and then provides additional details

Reducing the on-hold time should eliminate at least $2,000 from our August bill (according to a conversation with Tandy Robertson, our AT&T representative). Adding a new message option costs nothing, and we can implement the plan immediately. We will be able to manage our work more effectively by returning phone calls during quiet times of the day. And, not least important, Tiger fans can avoid the frustration of waiting on hold.

Our staff is enthusiastic about trying this new plan. If we implement it this August, then after football season, we could call a random selection of customers to see how they liked the new system.

Motivates the reader with implied endorsement from other people and then asks for an answer by a specific time

I've attached a draft of the possible wording for the new message. Please let me know by the end of the month whether you'd like to give this a try.

Thanks,
Bette

French audience. In Germany, where people tend to focus on technical matters, make sure you provide solid supporting evidence for all messages. In Sweden, audiences tend to focus on theoretical questions and strategic implications, whereas U.S. audiences are usually concerned with more practical matters.[6]

The culture within an organization also affects persuasive efforts. For instance, some organizations handle disagreement and conflict in an indirect, behind-the-scenes way, whereas others accept and even encourage open discussion and the sharing of viewpoints. When you accept and follow these traditions, you show your audience members that you understand them and respect their values.

2 LEARNING OBJECTIVE

Identify seven ways to establish credibility in persuasive messages.

Finally, when trying to persuade a skeptical or hostile audience, you must convince people that you are credible before they will pay much attention to your message. According to recent research, most managers overestimate their own credibility.[7] Chapter 5 lists characteristics essential to building and maintaining your credibility, including honesty, objectivity, awareness of audience needs, knowledge and expertise, endorsements, performance, and communication style. In addition to those elements, you can improve your credibility in persuasive messages with these techniques:

- **Using simple language.** In most persuasive situations, your audience will be cautious, watching for fantastic claims, insupportable descriptions, and emotional manipulation.

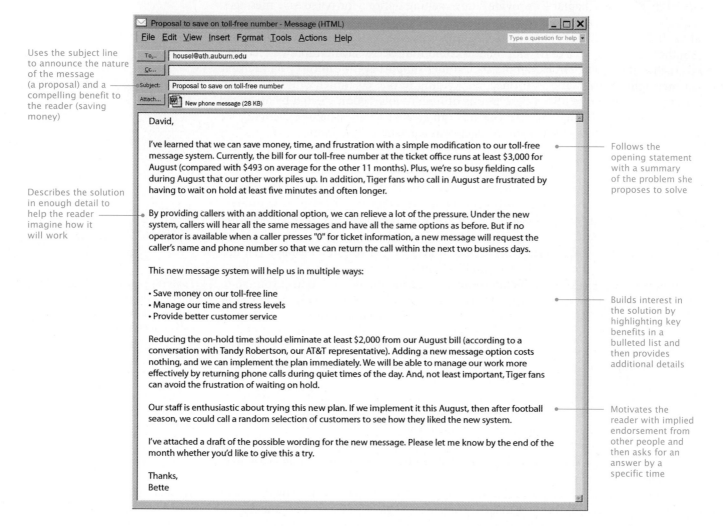

- **Supporting your message with facts.** Provide objective evidence for the claims and promises you make.
- **Identifying your sources.** Telling your audience where you got your information improves your credibility, especially if your audience already respects those sources.
- **Establishing common ground.** Beliefs, attitudes, and background experiences that you have in common with members of your audience will help them identify with you.
- **Being objective.** Your ability to understand and acknowledge all sides of an issue helps you present fair and logical arguments in your persuasive message.
- **Displaying your good intentions.** Your willingness to keep your audience's best interests in mind helps you create persuasive messages that are both effective and ethical.
- **Avoiding the "hard sell."** You've no doubt experienced a "hard sell," an aggressive approach that uses strong, emotional language and high-pressure tactics to convince people to make a firm decision in a hurry. Audiences tend to instinctively resist this approach because communicators who take this approach can come across as being more concerned with meeting their own goals than with satisfying the needs of their audiences. In contrast, a "soft sell" is more like a comfortable conversation in which the sender uses calm, rational persuasion to help the recipient make a smart choice.

Audiences resist the high-pressure tactics of the "hard sell" and tend to distrust communicators who take this approach.

Step 3: Completing a Persuasive Message

The pros know from experience that details can make or break a persuasive message, so they're careful not to skimp on this part of the writing process. For instance, advertisers may have a dozen or more people review a message before it's released to the public.

When you evaluate your content, try to judge your argument objectively and try not to overestimate your credibility. If possible, ask an experienced colleague who knows your audience well to review your draft. Make sure your design elements complement, rather than detract from, your persuasive argument. In addition, meticulous proofreading will help you identify any mechanical or spelling errors that would weaken your persuasive potential. Finally, make sure your distribution methods fit your audience's expectations and preferences.

With the three-step model in mind, you're ready to begin composing persuasive messages, starting with *persuasive business messages* (those that try to convince audiences to approve new projects, enter into business partnerships, and so on), followed by *marketing and sales messages* (those that try to convince audiences to consider and then purchase products and services).

DEVELOPING PERSUASIVE BUSINESS MESSAGES

Persuasive business messages comprise a broad and diverse category, with audiences that range from a single person in your own department to government agencies, investors, business partners, community leaders, and other external groups. Your success as a businessperson is closely tied to your ability to convince others to accept new ideas, change old habits, or act on your recommendations. As you move into positions of greater responsibility in your career, your persuasive messages could start to influence multimillion-dollar investments and the careers of hundreds or thousands of employees. Obviously, you need to match the increase in your persuasive skills with the care and thoroughness of your analysis and planning so that the ideas you convince others to adopt are sound.

No matter where your career leads, your success will depend on your ability to craft effective persuasive messages.

Strategies for Persuasive Business Messages

Even if you have the power to compel others to do what you want them to do, persuading them is more effective than forcing them. People who are forced into accepting a decision or plan are less motivated to support it and more likely to react negatively than if they're persuaded.[8] Within the context of the three-step process, effective persuasion involves four essential strategies: framing your arguments, balancing emotional and logical appeals, reinforcing your position, and anticipating objections. (Note that all these concepts in this section apply as well to marketing and sales messages, covered later in the chapter.)

3 LEARNING OBJECTIVE

Describe the AIDA model for persuasive messages.

Using the AIDA model is an effective way to organize most persuasive messages:
- *Attention*
- *Interest*
- *Desire*
- *Action*

Structuring Persuasive Business Messages

As noted earlier, most persuasive messages use the indirect approach. Experts in persuasive communication have developed a number of indirect models for such messages. One of the best known is the **AIDA model**, which organizes messages into four phases:

- **Attention.** Your first objective is to engage your readers or listeners in a way that encourages them to want to hear about your main idea. Write a brief and compelling sentence, without making extravagant claims or irrelevant points. Look for some common ground on which to build your case (see Figure 10.2). And while you want to be positive and confident, make sure you don't start out with a *hard sell*—a pushy, aggressive opening. Doing so often puts audiences on guard and on the defensive.
- **Interest.** Explain the relevance of your message to your audience. Continuing the theme you started with, paint a more detailed picture of the problem you propose to solve with the solution you're offering (whether it's a new idea, a new process, a new product, or whatever).
- **Desire.** Help audience members embrace your idea by explaining how the change will benefit them, either personally or professionally. Reduce resistance by identifying and answering in advance any questions the audience might have. If your idea is complex, you might need to explain how you would implement it. Back up your claims in order to increase audience willingness to take the action you suggest in the next section.
- **Action.** Suggest the action you want readers to take and phrase it in a way that emphasizes the benefits to them or to the organization they represent. Make the action as easy as possible to take, including offering to assist, if appropriate. Be sure to provide all the information the audience needs to take the action, including deadlines and contact details.

The AIDA model and similar plans are ideal for the indirect approach.

The AIDA model is tailor-made for using the indirect approach, allowing you to save your main idea for the action phase. However, you can also use it for the direct approach, in which case you use your main idea as an attention-getter, build interest with your argument, create desire with your evidence, and reemphasize your main idea in the action phase with the specific action you want your audience to take.

When your AIDA message uses the indirect approach and is delivered by memo or e-mail, keep in mind that your subject line usually catches your reader's eye first. Your challenge is to make it interesting and relevant enough to capture reader attention without revealing your main idea. If you put your request in the subject line, you might just get a quick no before you've had a chance to present your arguments:

INSTEAD OF THIS	WRITE THIS
Request for development budget to add automated IM response system	Reducing the cost of customer support inquiries

The AIDA model has limitations, and it needs to be modified for use with social media.

With either the direct or indirect approach, AIDA and similar models do have limitations. First, AIDA is a unidirectional method that essentially talks *at* audiences, not *with* them. Second, AIDA is built around a single event, such as asking an audience for a decision, rather than on building a mutually beneficial, long-term relationship.[9] AIDA is still a valuable tool for the right purposes, but as you'll read later in the chapter, a conversational approach is more compatible with today's social media.

4 LEARNING OBJECTIVE

Distinguish between emotional and logical appeals, and discuss how to balance them.

Balancing Emotional and Logical Appeals

Imagine you're sitting at a control panel with one knob labeled "logic" and another labeled "emotion." As you prepare your persuasive message, you carefully adjust each knob, tuning the message for maximum impact. Too little emotion, and your audience might not care enough to respond. Too much emotion, and your audience might think you are ignoring tough business questions or even being irrational.

Generally speaking, persuasive business messages rely more heavily on logical appeals than on emotional appeals because the main idea is usually to save money, increase quality,

FIGURE 10.2 Persuasive Message Using the AIDA Model

Randy Thumwolt uses the AIDA model in a message about a program that would reduce Host Marriott's annual plastics costs and address consumer complaints about the company's recycling record. Note how Thumwolt "sells the problem" before attempting to sell the solution. Few people are interested in hearing about solutions to problems they don't know about or don't believe exist.

1 Plan → 2 Write → 3 Complete

1 Plan

Analyze the Situation
Verify that the purpose is to solve an ongoing problem, so the audience will be receptive.

Gather Information
Determine audience needs and obtain the necessary information on recycling problem areas.

Select the Right Medium
Verify that an e-mail message is appropriate for this communication.

Organize the Information
Limit the scope to the main idea, which is to propose a recycling solution; use the indirect approach to lay out the extent of the problem.

2 Write

Adapt to Your Audience
Adjust the level of formality based on the degree of familiarity with the audience; maintain a positive relationship by using the "you" attitude, politeness, positive emphasis, and bias-free language.

Compose the Message
Use a conversational but professional style and keep the message brief, clear, and as helpful as possible.

3 Complete

Revise the Message
Evaluate content and review readability to make sure the information is clear and complete without being overwhelming.

Produce the Message
Emphasize a clean, professional appearance.

Proofread the Message
Review for errors in layout, spelling, and mechanics.

Distribute the Message
Verify that the right file is attached and then deliver the message.

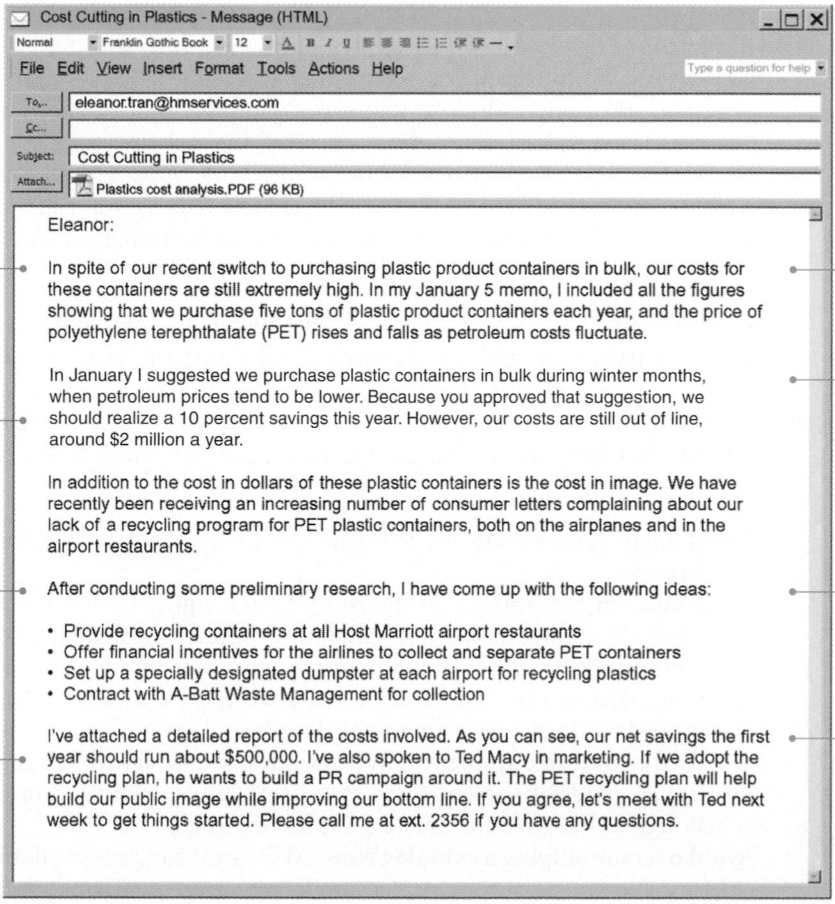

Cost Cutting in Plastics - Message (HTML)

To...: eleanor.tran@hmservices.com
Cc...:
Subject: Cost Cutting in Plastics
Attach...: Plastics cost analysis.PDF (96 KB)

Eleanor:

A — In spite of our recent switch to purchasing plastic product containers in bulk, our costs for these containers are still extremely high. In my January 5 memo, I included all the figures showing that we purchase five tons of plastic product containers each year, and the price of polyethylene terephthalate (PET) rises and falls as petroleum costs fluctuate.

Catches the reader's attention with a blunt statement of a major problem

I — In January I suggested we purchase plastic containers in bulk during winter months, when petroleum prices tend to be lower. Because you approved that suggestion, we should realize a 10 percent savings this year. However, our costs are still out of line, around $2 million a year.

In addition to the cost in dollars of these plastic containers is the cost in image. We have recently been receiving an increasing number of consumer letters complaining about our lack of a recycling program for PET plastic containers, both on the airplanes and in the airport restaurants.

Builds interest in a potential solution to the problem by emphasizing how bad it is and highlighting an associated problem

D — After conducting some preliminary research, I have come up with the following ideas:

- Provide recycling containers at all Host Marriott airport restaurants
- Offer financial incentives for the airlines to collect and separate PET containers
- Set up a specially designated dumpster at each airport for recycling plastics
- Contract with A-Batt Waste Management for collection

Increases the recipient's desire or willingness to take action by outlining a solution

A — I've attached a detailed report of the costs involved. As you can see, our net savings the first year should run about $500,000. I've also spoken to Ted Macy in marketing. If we adopt the recycling plan, he wants to build a PR campaign around it. The PET recycling plan will help build our public image while improving our bottom line. If you agree, let's meet with Ted next week to get things started. Please call me at ext. 2356 if you have any questions.

Motivates the reader one last time with a specific cost-savings figure, then requests a specific action

REAL-TIME UPDATES
Learn More

Choose the most effective emotional appeal

Understand the different types of emotional appeals and select the most effective appeal for any marketing or sales message. Go to **http://real-timeupdates.com/ebc** and click on "Learn More." If you are using mybcommlab, you can access Real-Time Updates within each chapter or under Student Study Tools.

or improve some other practical, measurable aspect of business. To find the optimum balance, consider four factors: (1) the actions you hope to motivate, (2) your readers' expectations, (3) the degree of resistance you need to overcome, and (4) how far you feel empowered to go in order to sell your point of view.[10]

Emotional Appeals

Emotional appeals attempt to connect with the reader's feelings or sympathies.

As its name implies, an **emotional appeal** calls on audience feelings and sympathies rather than facts, figures, and rational arguments. For instance, you can make use of the emotion surrounding certain words. The word *freedom* evokes strong feelings, as do words such as *success*, *prestige*, *compassion*, *security*, and *comfort*. Such words can help put your audience members in a positive frame of mind and help them accept your message. However, emotional appeals in business messages usually aren't effective by themselves because the audience wants proof that you can solve a business problem. Even if your audience members reach a conclusion based primarily on emotions, they'll look to you to provide logical support as well.

Logical Appeals

Logical appeals are based on the reader's notions of reason; these appeals can use analogy, induction, or deduction.

A **logical appeal** calls on reasoning and evidence. The basic approach with a logical appeal is to make a claim based on a rational argument, supported by solid evidence. When appealing to your audience's logic, you might use three types of reasoning:

- **Analogy.** With analogy, you reason from specific evidence to specific evidence. For instance, to convince management to buy a more robust firewall to protect your company's computer network, you might use the analogy of "circling the wagons," as when covered wagons crossing the continent gathered in a circle every night to form a safe space within.
- **Induction.** With inductive reasoning, you work from specific evidence to a general conclusion. To convince your team to change to a new manufacturing process, for example, you could point out that every company that has adopted it has increased profits, so it must be a smart idea.
- **Deduction.** With deductive reasoning, you work from a generalization to a specific conclusion. To persuade your boss to hire additional customer support staff, you might point to industry surveys that show how crucial customer satisfaction is to corporate profits.

Every method of reasoning is vulnerable to misuse, both intentional and unintentional, so verify your rational arguments carefully. For example, in the case of the manufacturing process, are there any other factors that affect the integrity of your reasoning? What if that process works well only for small companies with few products, and your firm is a multinational behemoth with 10,000 products? To avoid faulty logic, follow these guidelines:[11]

Logical flaws include hasty generalizations, circular reasoning, attacks on opponents, oversimplifications, false assumptions of cause and effect, faulty analogies, and illogical support.

- **Avoid hasty generalizations.** Make sure you have plenty of evidence before drawing conclusions.
- **Avoid circular reasoning.** *Circular reasoning* is a logical fallacy in which you try to support your claim by restating it in different words. The statement "We know temporary workers cannot handle this task because temps are unqualified for it" doesn't prove anything because the claim and the supporting evidence are essentially identical. It doesn't prove *why* the temps are unqualified.
- **Avoid attacking an opponent.** If your persuasive appeal involves countering a competitive appeal made by someone else, make sure you attack the argument your opponent is making, not his or her character or qualifications.
- **Avoid oversimplifying a complex issue.** Make sure you present all the factors and don't reduce a wide range of choices to a simple "either/or" scenario if that isn't the case.

- **Avoid mistaken assumptions of cause and effect.** If you can't isolate the impact of a specific factor, you can't assume it's the cause of whatever effect you're discussing. The weather improves in spring, and people start playing baseball in spring. Does good weather cause baseball? No. There is a *correlation* between the two—meaning the data associated with them tend to rise and fall at the same time, but there is no *causation*—no proof that one causes the other. The complexity of many business situations makes cause and effect a particular challenge. You lowered prices, and sales went up. Were lower prices the cause of the increased sales? Perhaps, but the increase in sales might have been caused by a better advertising campaign, a competitor's delivery problems, or some other factor.

REAL-TIME UPDATES
Learn More

Make sure your logic can stand on solid ground

Get sound advice on using logical appeals correctly and effectively. Go to **http://real-timeupdates.com/ebc** and click on "Learn More." If you are using mybcommlab, you can access Real-Time Updates within each chapter or under Student Study Tools.

- **Avoid faulty analogies.** Be sure that the two objects or situations being compared are similar enough for the analogy to hold. For instance, the analogy between circling the wagons and using a network firewall isn't entirely valid because circling the wagons is a temporary move and computer networks need permanent protection.
- **Avoid illogical support.** Make sure the connection between your claim and your support is truly logical and not based on a leap of faith, a missing premise, or irrelevant evidence.

Reinforcing Your Position

Choose your words carefully and use abstractions to enhance emotional content.

After you've worked out the basic elements of your argument, step back and look for ways to bolster the strength of your position. Can you find more powerful words to convey your message? For example, if your company is in serious financial trouble, talking about *fighting for survival* is a more powerful emotional appeal than talking about *ensuring continued operations.* Using vivid abstractions such as this along with basic facts and figures can bring your argument to life. As with any other powerful tool, though, vivid language and abstractions must be used carefully and honestly. If the company's survival isn't on the line, don't state or imply that it is.

In addition to individual word choices, consider using *metaphors* and other figures of speech. If you want to describe a quality-control system as being designed to catch every possible product flaw, you might call it a *spider web* to imply that it catches everything that comes its way. Similarly, anecdotes and stories can help your audience grasp the meaning and importance of your arguments. Instead of just listing the number of times the old laptop computers in your department have failed, you could describe how you lost a sale when your computer broke down during a critical sales presentation.

Highlight the direct and indirect benefits of complying with your request.

Beyond specific words and phrases, look for other factors that can reinforce your position. When you're asking for something, your audience members will find it easier to grant your request if they stand to benefit from it as well. The timing of your message can also help. Virtually all organizations operate in cycles of some sort—incoming payments from major customers, outgoing tax payments, seasonal demand for products, and so on. Study these patterns to see whether they might work for or against you. For example, the best time to ask for additional staff might be right after a cyclical period of intense activity that generated complaints about poor customer service, while the experience is still fresh in everyone's mind. If you wait too long before asking, the emotional aspect of the experience will have faded, and your request might look like just another cost increase.

Anticipating Objections

Even powerful persuasive messages can encounter resistance from the audience.

Even the most compelling ideas and proposals can be expected to encounter some initial resistance. The best way to deal with audience resistance is to anticipate as many objections as you can and address them in your message before your audience can even bring them up. For instance, if you know that your proposal to switch to lower-cost materials will raise concerns about product quality, address this issue head on in your message. If you wait until people raise the concern after reading your message, they may gravitate toward a firm *no* before you have a chance to address their concerns. By bringing up such potential problems right away, you also demonstrate a broad appreciation of the issue and imply confidence in your message.[12] This anticipation is particularly important in written messages, when you don't have the opportunity to detect and respond to objections on the spot.

To uncover potential audience objections, try to poke holes in your own theories and ideas before your audience does. Then find solutions to the problems you've uncovered. If possible, ask your audience members for their thoughts on the subject before you put together your argument; people are more likely to support solutions they help create.

Present both sides of an issue when you expect to encounter strong resistance.

Keep two things in mind when anticipating objections. First, you don't always have to explicitly discuss a potential objection. You could simply mention that the lower-cost materials have been tested and approved by the quality-control department. Second, if you expect a hostile audience, one biased against your plan from the beginning, present all sides of the story. As you cover each option, explain the pros and cons. You'll gain additional credibility if you present these options before presenting your recommendation or decision.[13]

To review the steps involved in developing persuasive messages, refer to "Checklist: Developing Persuasive Messages."

Common Examples of Persuasive Business Messages

Throughout your career, you'll have numerous opportunities to write persuasive messages within your organization, such as reports suggesting more efficient operating procedures or memos requesting money for new equipment. Similarly, you may produce a variety of persuasive messages for people outside the organization, such as websites shaping public opinions or letters requesting adjustments that go beyond a supplier's contractual obligations. In addition, many of the routine requests you studied in Chapter 8 can become persuasive messages if you want a nonroutine result or believe that you haven't received fair treatment. Most of these messages can be divided into persuasive requests for action, persuasive presentations of ideas, and persuasive claims and requests for adjustment.

Persuasive Requests for Action

When making a persuasive request for action, explain why the request is reasonable.

The bulk of your persuasive business messages will involve requests for action. In some cases, your request will be anticipated or will require minimal effort on the recipient's part, so the direct approach is fine. In others, you'll need to introduce your intention indirectly.

CHECKLIST: Developing Persuasive Messages

A. Get your reader's attention.
- Open with an audience benefit, a stimulating question, a problem, or an unexpected statement.
- Establish common ground by mentioning a point on which you and your audience agree.
- Show that you understand the audience's concerns.

B. Build your reader's interest.
- Expand and support your opening claim or promise.
- Emphasize the relevance of your message to your audience.

C. Increase your reader's desire.
- Make audience members want to change by explaining how the change will benefit them.
- Back up your claims with relevant evidence.

D. Motivate your reader to take action.
- Suggest the action you want readers to take.
- Stress the positive results of the action.
- Make the desired action clear and easy.

E. Balance emotional and logical appeals.
- Use emotional appeals to help the audience accept your message.
- Use logical appeals when presenting facts and evidence for complex ideas or recommendations.
- Avoid faulty logic.

F. Reinforce your position.
- Provide additional evidence of the benefits of your proposal and your own credibility in offering it.
- Use abstractions, metaphors, and other figures of speech to bring facts and figures to life.

G. Anticipate objections.
- Anticipate and answer potential objections.
- Present the pros and cons of all options if you anticipate a hostile reaction.

Open with an attention-getting device and show readers that you know something about their concerns. Use the interest and desire sections of your message to demonstrate that you have good reasons for making such a request and to cover what you know about the situation: the facts and figures, the benefits of helping, and any history or experience that will enhance your appeal. Your goals are (1) to gain credibility and (2) to make your readers believe that helping you will indeed help solve a significant problem. When you've demonstrated that your message is relevant to your readers, you can close with a request for some specific action or decision.

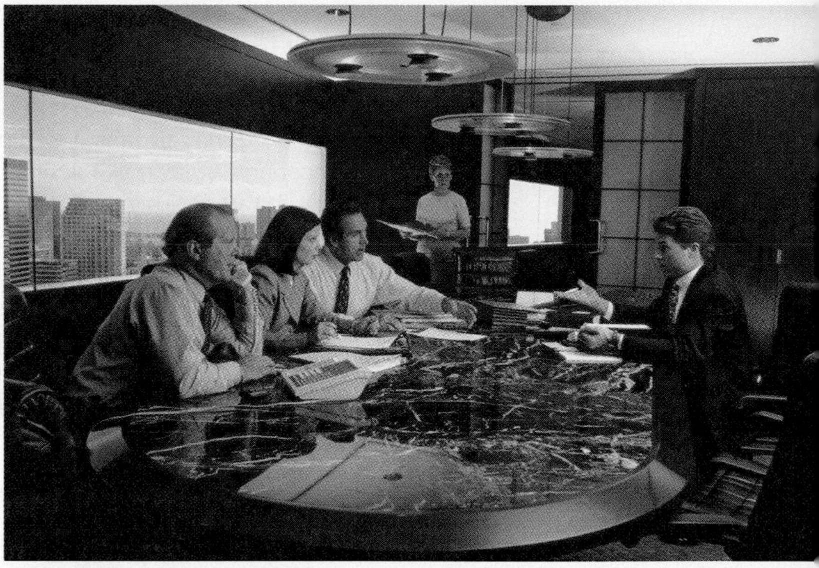

The ability to persuade others to accept and support your ideas is an essential career skill.

Persuasive Presentations of Ideas

Most internal persuasive messages focus on getting the audience to make a specific decision or take some specific action. However, you will encounter situations in which you simply want to change attitudes or beliefs about a particular topic, without asking the audience to decide or do anything—at least not yet. In complicated, multistep persuasive efforts, the goal of your first message might be nothing more than convincing your audience members to reexamine their opinions or assumption or to admit the possibility of new ways of thinking.

Sometimes the objective of persuasive messages is simply to encourage people to consider a new idea.

For instance, the World Wide Web Consortium (a global association that defines many of the guidelines and technologies behind the World Wide Web) has launched a campaign called the Web Accessibility Initiative. Although the consortium's ultimate goal is making websites more accessible to people who have disabilities or age-related limitations, a key interim goal is simply making website developers more aware of the need. As part of this effort, the consortium has developed a presentation that highlights the nature of the problems that many web visitors face.[14]

Persuasive Claims and Requests for Adjustments

Most claims and requests for adjustment are routine messages and use the direct approach discussed in Chapter 8. However, both consumers and business professionals sometimes encounter situations in which they believe they haven't received a fair deal by following normal procedures. These situations require a more persuasive message.

If a routine claim or request is unsuccessful, you may need to craft a more persuasive message to explain why you deserve a more satisfactory response.

The key ingredients of a good persuasive claim are a complete and specific review of the facts and a confident, positive tone. Assume that the other person is not trying to cheat you and that you have the right to be satisfied with the transaction. Begin persuasive claims by stating the basic problem or reviewing what has been done about the problem so far. Include a statement that you and your audience can agree with or that clarifies what you want to convince your audience about. Be as specific as possible about what you want to happen. Next, give your reader a good reason for granting your claim. Show how your audience is responsible for the problem and appeal to your reader's sense of fair play, goodwill, or moral responsibility. Explain how you feel about the problem but don't get carried away, don't complain too much, and don't make threats. People generally respond more favorably to requests that are calm and reasonable.

DEVELOPING MARKETING AND SALES MESSAGES

Marketing and sales messages use the same techniques as other persuasive messages, with the added emphasis of encouraging someone to participate in a commercial transaction. Although the terms *marketing message* and *sales message* are often used interchangeably, they represent separate but related efforts: Marketing messages usher potential buyers

Marketing and sales messages use many of the same techniques as persuasive business messages.

FIGURE 10.3 Marketing Messages
The blog written by Jim Cosgrove of Newcastle Square Realty in Damariscotta, Maine, illustrates the key difference between marketing and sales messages. Cosgrove uses the blog to build a sense of community, educate potential buyers about the local housing market, and share opinions about the real estate business. None of these postings try to make an immediate sale, but they position Cosgrove and his company as knowledgeable guides who can help consumers when they are ready to buy houses in the area.

through the purchasing process without asking them to immediately make a decision. Marketing messages focus on such tasks as introducing new brands to the public, providing competitive comparison information, encouraging customers to visit websites for more information, reminding buyers that a particular product or service is available, and building relationships for the purpose of future sales activities (see Figure 10.3). In contrast, a sales message makes a specific request for people to purchase a particular product or service.

5 LEARNING OBJECTIVE

Describe seven essential steps in developing marketing and sales messages.

Most marketing and sales messages, particularly in larger companies, are created and delivered by professionals with specific training in marketing, advertising, sales, or public relations. However, as a manager, you may be called on to review the work of these specialists or even to write such messages in smaller companies, and having a good understanding of how these messages work will help you be a more effective manager. The essential steps to address include assessing customer needs; analyzing your competition; determining key selling points and benefits; anticipating purchase objections; applying the AIDA model or a similar organizational plan; adapting your writing to social media, if appropriate; and maintaining high standards of ethics, legal compliance, and etiquette.

Assessing Audience Needs

Successful marketing and sales messages start with an understanding of audience needs. For some products and services, this assessment is a fairly simple matter. For instance, customers compare only a few basic attributes when purchasing paper, including its weight, brightness, color, and finish. In contrast, they might consider dozens of features when shopping for real estate, cars, professional services, and other complex purchases. In addition, customer needs often extend beyond the basic product or service. For example, clothes do far more than simply keep you warm. What you wear can also make a statement about who you are, which social groups you want to be associated with (or not), and how you view your relationships with the people around you.

Purchasing decisions often involve more than just the basic product or service.

Begin by assessing audience needs, interests, and emotional concerns—just as you would for any other business message. Try to form a mental image of the typical buyer for the product you want to sell. Ask yourself what your audience members might want to know about this product. How can your product help them? Are they driven by price, or is quality more important to them?

Analyzing Your Competition

Marketing and sales messages nearly always compete with messages from other companies trying to reach the same audience. When Nike plans a marketing campaign to introduce a new shoe model to current customers, the company knows that its audience has also been exposed to messages from New Balance, Reebok, and numerous other shoe companies. In crowded markets, writers sometimes have to search for words and phrases that other companies aren't already using. They might also want to avoid themes, writing styles, or creative approaches that are too similar to those of competitors' messages.

Most marketing and sales messages have to compete for the audience's attention.

Determining Key Selling Points and Benefits

With some insight into audience needs and existing messages from the competition, you're ready to decide which benefits and features of your product or service to highlight. For all but the simplest products and services, you want to prioritize the items you plan to discuss. You also want to distinguish between the features of the product or service and the benefits that those features offer the customers. As Table 10.2 shows, **selling points** are the most attractive features of a product or service, whereas **benefits** are the particular advantages that readers will realize from those features. Put another way, selling points focus on the product or service, whereas benefits focus on the user.

Selling points focus on the product; benefits focus on the user.

For example, CafeMom doesn't stress the online networking feature of its services; rather, it stresses the opportunity to connect with other moms who have similar concerns and interests—which is the benefit enabled by the networking feature. A common approach to communicating features and benefits is to show them in a list or a table, identifying each feature and describing the benefits it offers (see Figure 10.4 on the next page).

TABEL 10.2 Features Versus Benefits

PRODUCT OR SERVICE FEATURE	CUSTOMER BENEFIT
Carrier's Hybrid Heat dual-fuel system combines our Infinity 19 fuel pump with our Infinity 96 furnace.[i]	Carrier's Hybrid Heat dual-fuel system provides the optimum balance of comfort and energy efficiency.
Our marketing communication audit accurately measures the impact of your advertising and public relations efforts.	Find out whether your message is reaching the target audience and whether you're spending your marketing budget in the best possible manner.
The spools in our fly-fishing reels are machined from solid blocks of aircraft-grade aluminum.	Go fishing with confidence: These lightweight reels will stand up to the toughest conditions.

FIGURE 10.4 Explaining the Benefits of Product Features
This interactive webpage explains the user benefits made possible by key features of the BlackBerry Pearl smartphone. Website visitors simply click the "hotspot" associated with each feature to display an explanation of the benefits that feature provides.

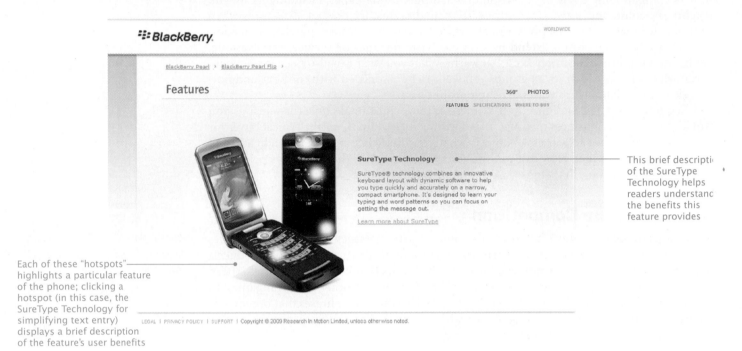

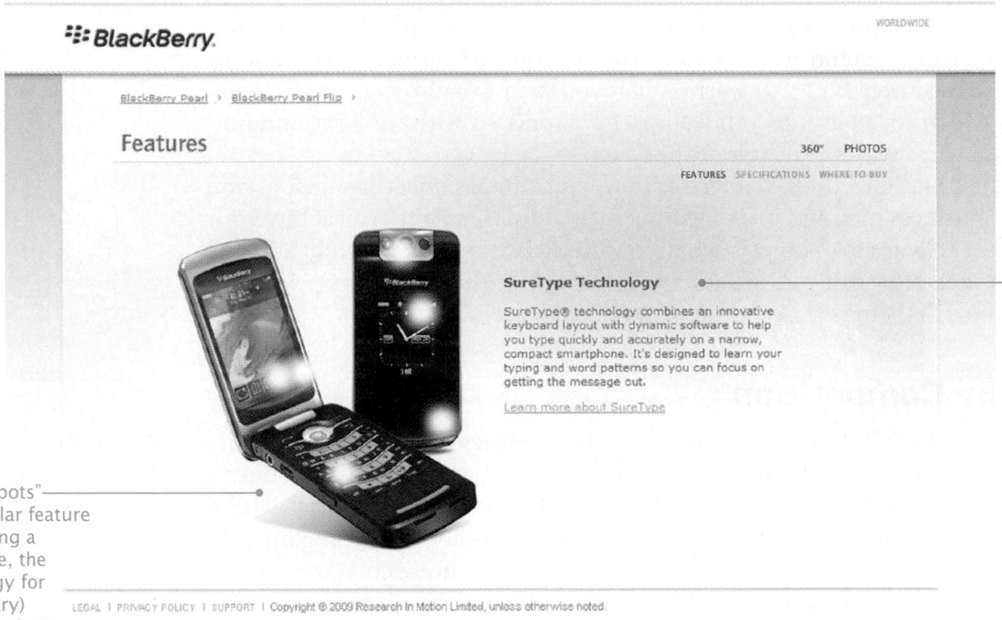

This brief descripti of the SureType Technology helps readers understanc the benefits this feature provides

Each of these "hotspots" highlights a particular feature of the phone; clicking a hotspot (in this case, the SureType Technology for simplifying text entry) displays a brief description of the feature's user benefits

Anticipating Purchase Objections

Anticipating objections is crucial to effective marketing and sales messages.

As with persuasive business messages, marketing and sales messages often encounter objections; once again, the best way to handle them is to identify them up front and try to address as many as you can. Objections can include perceptions of high price, low quality, incompatibility, or unacceptable risk. Consumers might worry that a car won't be safe enough for a family, that a jacket will make them look unattractive, or that a hair salon will botch a haircut. Business buyers might worry about disrupting operations or failing to realize the financial returns on a purchase.

Price can be a particularly tricky issue in any message. Whether you highlight or downplay the price of your product, prepare your readers for it. Words such as *luxurious* and *economical* provide clues about how your price compares with that of competitors. Such words help your readers accept your price when you finally state it.

If price is a major selling point, give it a position of prominence, such as in the headline or as the last item in a paragraph. If price is not a major selling point, you can handle it in several ways: You can leave the price out altogether or de-emphasize it by putting the figure in the middle of a paragraph that comes well after you've presented the benefits and selling points. Here's an example:

Emphasizes the rarity of the edition to signal value and thus prepares the reader for the big-ticket price that follows

Embeds the price in the middle of a sentence and ties it in with a reminder of the exclusivity of the offer

> Only 100 prints of this exclusive, limited-edition lithograph will be created. On June 15, they will be made available to the general public, but you can reserve one now for only $350, the special advance reservation price. Simply rush the enclosed reservation card back today so that your order is in before the June 15 publication date.

Whenever price is likely to cause an objection, look for ways to increase the perceived value of the purchase and decrease the perceived cost. For example, to help blunt the impact of the price of a home gym, you might say that it costs less than a year's worth of health club dues—plus, customers save on transportation costs by exercising at home. Of course, any attempts to minimize perceptions of price or other potential negatives must be ethical.

Applying AIDA or a Similar Model

Most marketing and sales messages are prepared according to the AIDA model or some variation of it. (But compare this approach with how *conversation marketing* messages are prepared in "Writing Persuasive Messages for Social Media" on page 296.) A typical AIDA-organized message begins with an attention-getting introduction, generates interest by describing some of the product's or service's unique features, increases desire by highlighting the benefits that are most appealing to the audience, and closes by suggesting the action the sender would like the audience members to take.

Getting Attention

You can use a variety of attention-getting devices in marketing and sales messages.

You can use a wide range of techniques to attract your audience's attention:

- **Your product's strongest feature or benefit.** "A little video for everyone" (promoting Apple's iPod nano with improved video-playing capabilities).[15]
- **A piece of genuine news.** "HealthGrades Reveals America's Best Hospitals."[16]
- **A point of common ground with the audience.** "An SUV adventurous enough to accommodate your spontaneity and the gear that comes with it."[17]
- **A personal appeal to the reader's emotions or values.** "Elastin Renewal: Our latest weapon in the fight against wrinkles."[18]
- **The promise of insider information.** "France may seem familiar, but nearly everything—from paying taxes to having a baby—is done quite differently. Get the practical answers to nearly 300 questions about making a life in France."[19]
- **The promise of savings.** "Through its initiative Save Energy Now, DOE's Industrial Technologies Program (ITP) helps industrial plants operate more efficiently and profitably by identifying ways to reduce energy use in key industrial process systems."[20]
- **A sample or demonstration of the product.** "In this real-time, online test drive, you'll be exploring the 2007 Microsoft Office release through your Web browser within minutes—with no product installation or download required!"[21]
- **A solution to a problem.** "This backpack's designed to endure all a kid's dropping and dragging."[22]

Of course, words aren't the only attention-getting device at your disposal. Strong, evocative images are common attention-getters. With online messages, you have even more options, including audio, animation, and video.

Even more so than in persuasive business messages, it's important to carefully balance emotion and logic in marketing and sales messages. Figure 10.5 on the next page suggests the range of logical and emotional appeals that marketing messages can achieve, based on the product and the target audience.

Building Interest

To build interest, expand on and support the promises in your attention-getting opening.

Use the interest section of your message to build on the intrigue you created with your opening. This section should also offer support for any claims or promises you made in the opening. For instance, after opening with the headline "A little video for everyone," the Apple iPod nano webpage continues with the following:[23]

> It's the small iPod with one very big idea: Video. Now the world's most popular music player lets you enjoy TV shows, movies, video podcasts, and more. The larger, brighter display means amazing picture quality. In six eye-catching colors, iPod nano is stunning all around. And with 4 GB and 8 GB models starting at just $149, little speaks volumes.

Explains the headline message of "a little video"

After establishing the key selling point (video), continues with other product features and benefits

At this point in the message, Apple has offered enough information to help people understand how they might use the product, and it has spoken to a couple potential objections as well (the quality of the video experience on such a small display and the price). Anyone interested in a digital music player with video capability is probably intrigued enough to keep reading.

FIGURE 10.5 Emotional and Logical Appeals in Marketing and Sales Messages
Both of these websites promote materials used in homes, but their respective messages use different blends of logical and emotional appeals. Premier Building Systems relies primarily on logical appeals in its messages to architects and home builders. In contrast, in its messages to homeowners, Gladiator GarageWorks balances logical and emotional appeals in describing its garage organizers.

To help convince home builders to use its innovative panel system instead of traditional frame construction, Premier Building Systems focuses on logical factors such as cost, efficiency, and quality

Gladiator GarageWorks uses a combination of logical and emotional appeals by promising to make your garage "a place to work, entertain, and show off to your friends and neighbors."

Website photograph used with permission of Whirlpool Corporation

Increasing Desire

Add details and audience benefits to increase desire for the product or service.

To build desire for a product, a service, or an idea, continue to expand on and explain how accepting it will benefit the recipient. Think carefully about the sequence of support points and use plenty of subheadings, hyperlinks, and other devices to help people quickly find the information they need. For example, after reading this much about the iPod, some

FIGURE 10.6 Flexible Communication on the Web
Want to try on a thousand pairs of eyeglasses without leaving home? You can, thanks to interactive websites such as FramesDirect.com, which lets you upload a photo of yourself and then see how you look in a variety of eyeglass styles. Flexible media technologies make it easy to adapt promotional messages to the interests of individual audience members.

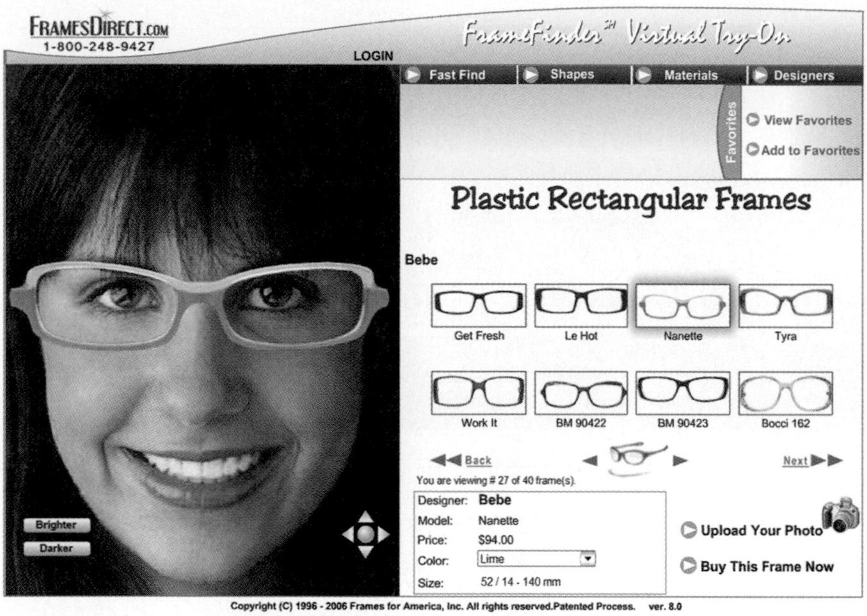

users might want to know more about the iTunes media store, whereas others will want technical specifications. The iPod product page continues with detailed discussions of various product features and benefits, and it offers numerous links to pages with other kinds of support information. The ability to provide flexible access to information is just one of the reasons the web is such a powerful medium for marketing and sales (see Figure 10.6).

Throughout the body of your message, remember to keep the focus on the audience, not on your company or your product. When you talk about product features, remember to stress the benefits and talk in terms that make sense to users. For instance, after stating that the maximum memory capacity of the iPod nano is 8 GB, Apple "translates" that technical specification into various media storage capacities that have practical meaning to users, such as 2,000 songs, 7,000 photos, or 8 hours of video.[24]

Avoid being so enthusiastic that you lose credibility.

As you work to build reader interest, be careful not to get so enthusiastic that you lose credibility. If Apple said that the video viewing experience on the iPod nano was as "satisfying as watching a full-size TV," most people would scoff at the notion of comparing a two-inch display with a full-size television.

To increase desire, as well as boost your credibility, provide support for your claims. Creative writers find many ways to provide support, including testimonials from satisfied users, articles written by industry experts, competitive comparisons, product samples and free demonstrations, independent test results, and movies or computer animations that show a product in action. You can also highlight guarantees that demonstrate your faith in your product and your willingness to back it up.

Motivating Action

After you've generated sufficient interest and desire, you're ready to persuade readers to take the preferred action.

After you have raised interest and built up the reader's desire for your product or service, you're ready to ask your audience to take action. Whether you want people to pick up the phone to place an order or visit your website to download a free demo version of your software, try to persuade them to do it right away with an effective *call to action*. You might offer a discount for the first 1,000 people to order, put a deadline on the offer, or simply

FIGURE 10.7 **The Call to Action in a Sales Message**
Notice how many calls to action are built into the homepage of the American Council on Exercise's (ACE) website. ACE is a not-for-profit organization committed to encouraging physical fitness through safe and effective exercise. In pursuit of that goal, it offers certification and training for people who want to become personal trainers, and it helps consumers find certified trainers.

remind them that the sooner they order, the sooner they'll be able to enjoy the product's benefits (see Figure 10.7). Even potential buyers who want the product can get distracted or forget to respond, so encouraging immediate action is important. Make the response action as simple and as risk-free as possible. If the process is confusing or time-consuming, you'll lose potential customers.

Take care to maintain the respectful, professional tone you've been using up to this point. Don't resort to gimmicks and desperate-sounding pleas for the customer's business. Make sure your final impression is compelling and positive. For instance, in a printed sales letter, the postscript (P.S.) below your signature is often one of the first or last parts people read. Use this valuable space to emphasize the key benefit you have to offer and to emphasize the advantages of ordering soon.

Writing Persuasive Messages for Social Media

Social commerce involves the use of social media in buying, selling, and customer support.

The AIDA model and similar approaches have been successful with marketing and sales messages for decades, but communicating with customers in the social media landscape requires a different approach. As earlier chapters emphasize, potential buyers in a social media environment are no longer willing to be passive recipients in a structured, one-way information delivery process or to rely solely on promotional messages from marketers. This notion of interactive participation is the driving force behind **conversation marketing**, in which companies initiate and facilitate conversations in a networked community of customers, journalists, bloggers, and other interested parties. The term **social commerce** encompasses any aspect of buying and selling products and services or supporting customers through the use of social media.

Given this shift from unidirectional speeches to multidirectional conversations, marketing and sales professionals must adapt their approach to planning, writing, and completing persuasive messages. Follow these guidelines:[25]

Promoting products and services through social media requires a more conversational approach.

- **Facilitate community building.** Make sure customers and other audiences can connect with your company and each other. Accomplishing this goal can be as simple as activating the commenting feature on a blog, or it may involve having a more elaborate *social commerce system.*
- **Initiate and respond to conversations within the community.** Through content on your website, blog postings, RSS newsfeeds, newsletters, and other tools, make sure you provide the information customers need in order to evaluate your products and services (see Figure 10.8 on the next page). Use an objective, conversational style; people in social networks want useful information, not "advertising speak."
- **Identify and support your champions.** In marketing, *champions* are enthusiastic fans of your company and its products. Champions are so enthusiastic that they help spread your message (through their blogs, for instance), defend you against detractors, and help other customers use your products.
- **Don't rely on the news media to distribute your message.** In traditional public relations efforts, marketers have to persuade the news media to distribute their messages to consumers and other audiences by producing news stories. These media are still important, but you can also speak directly to these audiences through blogs and other electronic tools.
- **Use the AIDA model at the right time and in the right places.** The AIDA approach is still valid for specific communication tasks, such as conventional advertising and the product promotion pages on your website.

For the latest information on using social media for persuasive communication, visit http://real-timeupdates.com/ebc and click on Chapter 10.

Maintaining High Standards of Ethics, Legal Compliance, and Etiquette

6 LEARNING OBJECTIVE

Identify steps you can take to avoid ethical lapses in marketing and sales messages.

The word *persuasion* has negative connotations for some people, especially in a marketing or sales context. They associate persuasion with dishonest and unethical practices that lead unsuspecting audiences into accepting unworthy ideas or buying unneeded products. However, effective businesspeople view persuasion as a positive force, aligning their own interests with what is best for their audiences. They influence audience members by providing information and aiding understanding, which allows audiences the freedom to choose.[26] To maintain the highest standards of business ethics, always demonstrate the "you" attitude by showing honest concern for your audience's needs and interests.

A good example of ethical complexities in persuasive messages is **stealth marketing**, in which customers don't know they're being marketed to. One common stealth-marketing technique is sending people into public places to use particular products in a conspicuous manner and then discuss them with strangers—as though they were just regular people on the street, when in fact they are employed by a marketing firm. Another is paying consumers or rewarding them with insider information and other benefits to promote products to their friends without telling the friends it's a form of advertising. Critics complain that such techniques are deceptive because they don't give

FIGURE 10.8 Conversation Marketing
Talk about putting your money where your mouth is. To promote his book *Conversation Marketing*, Ian Lurie, the marketing strategist who helped popularize the concept of conversation marketing, gave everyone free access to the entire book online (a printed copy is also available for sale). By letting his blog subscribers, journalists, and potential clients of his consulting business read the book for free, Lurie stimulated multiple online conversations—some of which he discusses in brief updates inserted into the online text.

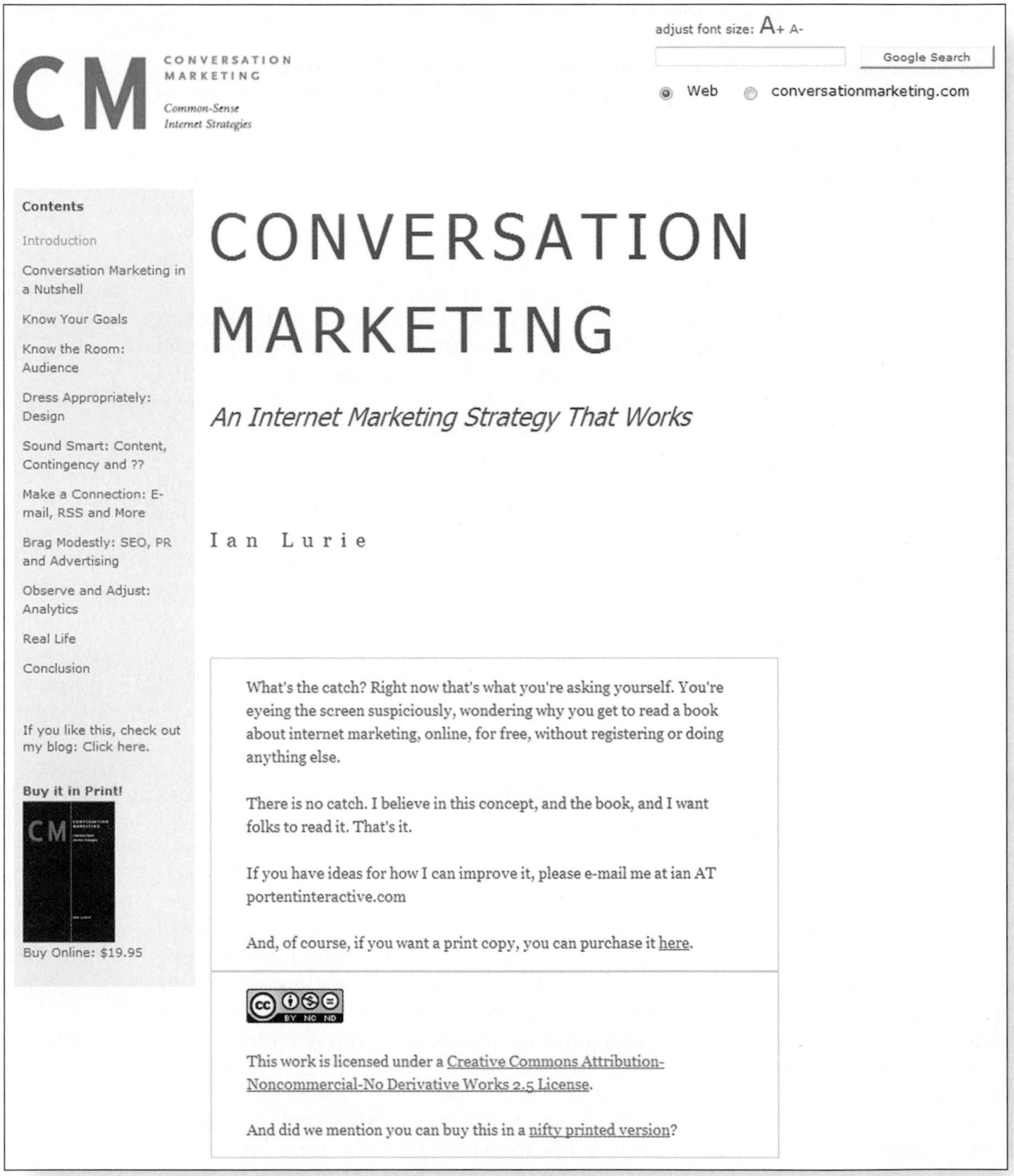

their targets the opportunity to raise their instinctive defenses against the persuasive powers of marketing messages.[27]

As marketing and selling grow increasingly complex, so do the legal ramifications of marketing and sales messages. In the United States, the Federal Trade Commission (FTC) has the authority to impose penalties (ranging from cease-and-desist orders to multimillion-dollar fines) against advertisers who violate federal standards for truthful advertising. Other federal agencies have authority over advertising in specific industries, such as transportation and financial services. Individual states have additional laws that apply. The legal aspects of promotional communication can be quite complex, from state to state and from country to country, and most companies require marketing and sales people to get clearance from company lawyers before sending messages. In any event, pay close attention to the following legal aspects of marketing and sales communication:[28]

Marketing and sales messages are covered by a wide range of laws and regulations.

- **Marketing and sales messages must be truthful and nondeceptive.** The FTC considers messages to be deceptive if they include statements that are likely to mislead reasonable customers and the statements are an important part of the purchasing decision. Failing to include important information is also considered deceptive. The FTC also looks at *implied claims*—claims you don't explicitly make but that can be inferred from what you do or don't say.
- **You must back up your claims with evidence.** According to the FTC, offering a money-back guarantee or providing letters from satisfied customers is not enough; you must still be able to support your claims with objective evidence such as a survey or scientific study. If you claim that your food product lowers cholesterol, you must have scientific evidence to support that claim.
- **Marketing and sales messages are considered binding contracts in many states.** If you imply or make an offer and then can't fulfill your end of the bargain, you can be sued for breach of contract.
- **In most cases, you can't use a person's name, photograph, or other identity without permission.** Doing so is considered an invasion of privacy. You can use images of people considered to be public figures as long as you don't unfairly imply that they endorse your message.

Before you launch a marketing or sales campaign, make sure you're up to date on the latest regulations affecting spam (or *unsolicited bulk e-mail*, as it's formally known), customer privacy, and data security. New laws are likely to appear in all three areas in the next few years.

Document Makeover

Improve This E-Mail Message

To practice correcting drafts of actual documents, visit the "Document Makeovers" section in mybcommlab. Refer to the User Guide for specific instructions on how to access the content for this chapter. You will find an e-mail message that contains problems and errors related to what you've learned in this chapter about writing persuasive messages. Use the "Final Draft" decision tool to create an improved version of this persuasive e-mail request for action. Check the message for its effectiveness at gaining attention, building interest, stimulating desire, motivating action, focusing on the primary goal, and dealing with resistance.

Meeting your ethical and legal obligations will go a long way toward maintaining good communication etiquette as well. However, you may still face etiquette decisions within ethical and legal boundaries. For instance, you can produce a marketing campaign that complies with all applicable laws and yet is offensive or insulting to your audience. Taking an audience-centered approach, involving respect for your readers and their values, should help you avoid any such etiquette missteps.

Maintaining high ethical standards is a key aspect of good communication etiquette.

Technology also gives communicators new ways to demonstrate sensitivity to user needs. One example is automated RSS newsfeeds from blogs that alert customers to information in which they've expressed an interest. *Opt-in* e-mail newsletters are another technology that shows the "you" attitude at work. Unlike the unwelcome spam messages that litter e-mail in-boxes these days, opt-in messages are sent only to people who have specifically requested information.

Communication technologies such as opt-in e-mail and blog syndication can help you be sensitive to audience needs.

On the Job: Solving Communication Dilemmas at CafeMom

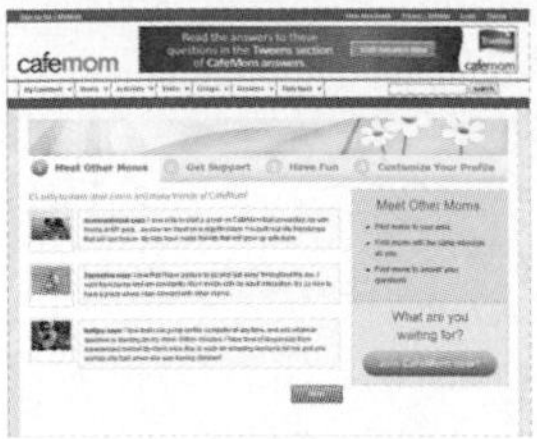

You're the vice president of member services at CafeMom, reporting to CEO Michael Sanchez. In addition to developing new online services, a key part of your job responsibility is crafting messages that describe the new services and persuade members to try them. Use what you've learned in this chapter and in your own experiences as a consumer (and as a parent, if applicable) to address these challenges.

1. You asked one of your staffers to write a benefit statement to communicate the advantages of the Groups section of the CafeMom website, which lets members find and join any of the thousands of existing groups or create new groups focused on just about any topic imaginable. She e-mails the following sentence: "We've worked hard to define and create a powerful online group capability; you can search far and wide on the Web, but you won't find anything as great as what we've created." You then write back, explaining why it's important to make marketing messages about the *customer*, not about the *company*. Which of these versions best illustrates this vital aspect of the "you" attitude? (You can learn more about the Groups feature at the CafeMom website, **www.cafemom.com/groups**.)

a. Group members at CafeMom support one another and share their knowledge, experience, and opinions on a wide variety of subjects, from pregnancy to schooling to religion.
b. Get support, information, and thought-provoking opinions from CafeMom groups.
c. Join a ClubMom group (or start your own) to get support, information, and thought-provoking opinions from other moms on a wide variety of subjects, from pregnancy to schooling to religion.
d. Social networking has rapidly become a popular way for web surfers to get insights, information, and thought-provoking opinions, and the CafeMom groups will help you, too.

2. A common challenge in marketing communication is distilling a long list of features to a single compelling message that can serve as the product's "headline." Review the following list of features and benefits (extracted from various communications presented by CafeMom and its business partners):

- The experiences of thousands of moms are now aggregated in a single place online.
- Connect with moms like you; search for moms by personal and family challenges, interests, age of kids, or location.
- Get and give support; find support and swap advice with other moms on a wide range of topics that matter most to you.
- Post questions online and get input from mothers who've been there before.
- Joining CafeMom is absolutely free.
- Setting up your own personal profile is fast and easy.
- Join groups who share your likes and concerns.
- Write as much or as little as you want to share in your personal profile.
- You have complete control over the privacy of your information.

Which of these statements is the best single-sentence encapsulation of the wide range of benefits that CafeMom offers? Obviously, a single sentence can't communicate every point listed; think more about an initial, high-level message that will entice people to keep reading.

a. Connecting and collecting; caring and sharing: The online community at CafeMom lets you network with other moms and find information you can use to help make motherhood successful and satisfying.
b. The online community at CafeMom lets you connect with other moms and find valuable information to help make motherhood successful and satisfying.
c. CafeMom offers moms everywhere a unique online experience.
d. CafeMom offers the best moms everywhere an absolutely unique online experience, with unparalleled access to valuable knowledge and rewarding camaraderie.

3. Membership in CafeMom is free, so price isn't a potential purchase objection. However, CafeMom does collect a fair amount of information from its members, including information about members themselves, their families, and their product purchase and usage habits. Which of the following statements would you put on the website to encourage anyone who is concerned about privacy and data security to read CafeMom's privacy policy? You can read the policy by clicking on "Privacy Policy" at the bottom of the CafeMom homepage. (Assume that the statement will contain the necessary hyperlink to take visitors to the privacy policy page on the website.)

a. See why you never have to worry about data security or personal privacy on CafeMom.
b. Learn more about how we protect the information we collect in order to continue making CafeMom a great web destination.
c. We implement SSL for credit card transactions and other sensitive transactions.
d. Like most websites, we collect only the information necessary to provide the valuable services we offer on this website.

4. Which of the following is the most effective call to action to encourage interested moms to sign up for free CafeMom membership?
   a. Sign up for your free Join CafeMom membership today and get knowledge and camaraderie you can't get anywhere else.
   b. Visit CafeMom.com today and learn about the many benefits of free membership.
   c. Every mom belongs in CafeMom; won't you please join today?
   d. CafeMom will change your life in ways you could never have imagined, and it's free!

LEARNING OBJECTIVES CHECKUP

Assess your understanding of the principles in this chapter by reading each learning objective and studying the accompanying exercises. For fill-in-the-blank items, write the missing text in the blank provided; for multiple-choice items, circle the letter of the correct answer. You can check your responses against the answer key on page AK-2.

Objective 10.1: Apply the three-step writing process to persuasive messages.

1. Which of the following is true about persuasive business messages?
   a. They require government approval before they can be printed or posted on websites.
   b. They are always welcomed by audiences.
   c. They often involve a combination of emotional and logical elements.
   d. They require less planning than any other type of message.

2. Why is the indirect approach often used in persuasive messages?
   a. It is more courteous and therefore gives the writer the opportunity to build up goodwill before slipping in the sales pitch.
   b. It takes less time.
   c. It is the traditional way to do persuasive messages and therefore expected.
   d. It lets the writer build audience interest and desire before asking for action or commitment.

Objective 10.2: Identify seven ways to establish credibility in persuasive messages.

3. Which of the following is not a good way to establish credibility with your audience?
   a. Support your argument with plenty of facts.
   b. Name your sources.
   c. Be enthusiastic and sincere.
   d. Present only your side of the argument to avoid reminding the audience of alternatives.

4. If you lack credibility with an audience, which of the following would be a good technique to use in a persuasive message?
   a. Make your message overly detailed so the audience will focus on the content.
   b. Include information or endorsements from recognized experts.
   c. Use plenty of humor to help bring the audience over to your side.
   d. Use multimedia to give yourself more ways to get your points across.

Objective 10.3: Describe the AIDA model for persuasive messages.

5. The first phase in the AIDA model is to
   a. Do your research
   b. Gain the audience's attention
   c. Analyze the audience
   d. Call for action

6. The body of a message that follows the AIDA model
   a. Captures the audience's attention
   b. Contains the buffer
   c. Generates interest and heightens desire
   d. Calls for action

7. Which of the following is a good way to build desire using the AIDA approach?
   a. Explain how the proposed change will help your audience.
   b. Reduce resistance by addressing objections the audience might have.
   c. Explain complex ideas or products in more detail.
   d. Do all of the above.

8. The final phase of the AIDA method
   a. Provides in-depth information to help generate interest
   b. Reduces resistance by increasing the audience's desire
   c. Calls for action
   d. Captures the audience's attention

Objective 10.4: Distinguish between emotional and logical appeals, and discuss how to balance them.

9. An argument that is based on human feelings is known as a/an ________ appeal.

10. An argument that is based on facts and reason is known as a/an ________ appeal.

11. The best approach to using emotional appeals is usually to
   a. Use them by themselves
   b. Use them in conjunction with logical appeals

c. Use them only when the audience is particularly hostile
d. Avoid them in all business messages

12. Which of the following is a type of logical appeal?
a. Deduction
b. Reduction
c. Reverse engineering
d. All of the above

Objective 10.5: Describe seven essential steps in developing marketing and sales messages.

13. Why is it important to anticipate objections when planning and writing persuasive messages?
a. You are legally required to anticipate audience objections in all marketing messages.
b. By anticipating potential objections, you have the opportunity to address them in a persuasive manner before the audience settles on a firm no answer.
c. By anticipating potential objections, you have the opportunity to explain to audience members why they are viewing the situation incorrectly.
d. By anticipating potential objections, you can explain to the audience all the negative consequences of accepting your message.

14. Why is anticipating objections particularly important in written persuasive messages?
a. Written messages are inherently less believable than oral messages.
b. Responding to questions takes longer in writing than orally.
c. Because they have more time to study them, audiences tend to have more objections to written messages than to messages in other media.
d. You often don't have the opportunity to detect and respond to objections, as you might with an oral message, for instance.

15. Prioritizing which features and benefits to write about is
a. A waste of time because people don't read in sequential order
b. Important because doing so lets you start with low-priority issues and work your way up to high-priority issues
c. Important because it helps you focus your message on items and issues that the audience cares about the most
d. Important because it helps ensure that you remember to talk about every single feature and benefit, no matter how inconsequential

16. What is the relationship between features and benefits?
a. They are different words for the same idea.
b. Features are aspects of an idea or product; benefits are the advantages that readers will realize from those features.
c. Features tell people how to use a product; benefits tell them how a product differs from the competition.
d. Features are the primary advantages of a product; benefits are the secondary advantages.

Objective 10.6: Identify steps you can take to avoid ethical lapses in marketing and sales messages.

17. Which of the following steps should you take to make sure your persuasive messages are ethical?
a. Align your interest with your audience's interests.
b. Choose words that offer multiple interpretations.
c. Limit the amount of information you provide to avoid overloading the audience and thereby confusing your readers.
d. Do all of the above.

18. If it adheres to all applicable federal laws, a marketing or sales message
a. Is certain to be both legal and ethical
b. Could still violate some state laws
c. Could still be unethical
d. Both b and c

PEARSON
mybcommlab

Log on to www.mybcommlab.com to access the following study and assessment aids associated with this chapter:

- Video applications
- Pre/post test
- Real-Time Updates
- Personalized study plan
- Peer review activity
- Model documents
- Quick Learning Guides
- Sample presentations

If you are not using mybcommlab, you can access Real-Time Updates and Quick Learning Guides through http://real-timeupdates.com/ebc. The Quick Learning Guide (located under "Learn More" on the website) hits all the high points of this chapter in just two pages. This guide, especially prepared by the authors, will help you study for exams or review important concepts whenever you need a quick refresher.

Apply Your Knowledge

1. Why is it important to present both sides of an argument when writing a persuasive message to a potentially hostile audience?
2. How are persuasive messages different from routine messages?
3. Why do the AIDA model and similar approaches need to be modified when writing persuasive messages in social media?
4. What is likely to happen if your persuasive message starts immediately with a call to action? Why?
5. **Ethical Choices** Are emotional appeals ethical? Why or why not?

Practice Your Knowledge

Messages for Analysis

For Message 10.A and Message 10.B, read the following documents and then (1) analyze the strengths and weaknesses of each sentence and (2) revise each document so that it follows this chapter's guidelines.

Message 10.A: Writing Persuasive Claims and Requests for Adjustment

Dear TechStar Computing:

I'm writing to you because of my disappointment with my new multimedia PC display. The display part works all right, but the audio volume is also set too high and the volume knob doesn't turn it down. It's driving us crazy. The volume knob doesn't seem to be connected to anything but simply spins around. I can't believe you would put out a product like this without testing it first.

I depend on my computer to run my small business and want to know what you are going to do about it. This reminds me of every time I buy electronic equipment from what seems like any company. Something is always wrong. I thought quality was supposed to be important, but I guess not.

Anyway, I need this fixed right away. Please tell me what you want me to do.

Message 10.B: Writing Sales Letters

We know how awful dining hall food can be, and that's why we've developed the "Mealaweek Club." Once a week, we'll deliver food to your dormitory or apartment. Our meals taste great. We have pizza, buffalo wings, hamburgers and curly fries, veggie roll-ups, and more!

When you sign up for just six months, we will ask what day you want your delivery. We'll ask you to fill out your selection of meals. And the rest is up to us. At "Mealaweek," we deliver! And payment is easy. We accept MasterCard and Visa or a personal check. It will save money especially when compared with eating out.

Just fill out the enclosed card and indicate your method of payment. As soon as we approve your credit or check, we'll begin delivery. Tell all your friends about Mealaweek. We're the best idea since sliced bread!

Message 10.C: Making a Podcast More Persuasive

To access this message, visit **http://real-timeupdates.com/ebc**, click on "Student Assignments," and select Chapter 10, page 303, Message 10.C. Download and listen to this podcast. Identify at least three ways in which the podcast could be more persuasive and draft a brief e-mail message that you could send to the podcaster with your suggestions for improvement.

Exercises

Active links for all websites in this chapter can be found on mybcommlab; see your User Guide for instructions on accessing the content for this chapter.

10.1 Teamwork With another student, analyze the persuasive e-mail message to Eleanor Tran at Host Marriott (see Figure 10.2) by answering the following questions:

- **a.** What techniques are used to capture the reader's attention?
- **b.** Does the writer use the direct or indirect organizational approach? Why?
- **c.** Is the subject line effective? Why or why not?
- **d.** Does the writer use an emotional or a logical appeal? Why?
- **e.** What reader benefits are included?
- **f.** How does the writer establish credibility?
- **g.** What tools does the writer use to reinforce his position?

10.2 Composing Subject Lines Compose effective subject lines for the following persuasive messages:

- **a.** A recommendation sent by e-mail to your branch manager to install wireless networking throughout the facility. Your primary reason is that management has encouraged more teamwork, but teams often congregate in meeting rooms, the cafeteria, and other places that lack network access—without which they can't do much of the work they are expected to do.
- **b.** A letter to area residents, soliciting customers for your new business, "Meals à la Car," a carryout dining service that delivers from most of the local restaurants. All local restaurant menus are on the Internet. Mom and Dad can dine on egg rolls and chow mein while the kids munch on pepperoni pizza.
- **c.** An e-mail message to the company president, asking that employees be allowed to carry over their unused vacation days to the following year. Apparently, many employees canceled their fourth-quarter vacation plans to work on the installation of a new company computer system. Under their current contract, vacation days not used by December 31 can't be carried over to the following year.

10.3 Ethical Choices Your boss has asked you to post a message on the company's internal blog, urging everyone in your department to donate money to the company's favorite charity, an organization that operates a summer camp for physically challenged children. You wind up writing a lengthy posting, packed with facts and heartwarming anecdotes about the camp and the children's experiences. When you must work that hard to persuade your audience to take an action such as donating money to a charity, aren't you being manipulative and unethical? Explain.

10.4 **Focusing on Benefits** Determine whether the following sentences focus on features or benefits; rewrite as necessary to focus all the sentences on benefits.

a. All-Cook skillets are coated with a durable, patented nonstick surface.
b. You can call anyone and talk as long as you like on Saturdays and Sundays with our new FamilyTalk wireless plan.
c. With 8-millisecond response time, the Samsung LN-S4095D 40-inch LCD TV delivers fast video action that is smooth and crisp.[29]

10.5 **Internet** Download the Federal Trade Commission document "Social Networking Sites: Safety Tips for Tweens and Teens" from www.ftc.gov/bcp/edu/pubs/consumer/ tech/tec14.pdf. Keeping in mind the target audience, analyze the effectiveness of this publication. Do you think it does a good job of persuading young people to surf the Internet safely? Write a brief summary of your analysis, along with any recommendations you might have for conveying the message more persuasively.

10.6 **Analyzing a Sales Package: Learning from the Direct-Mail Pros** The daily mail often brings a selection of sales messages. Find a direct-mail package from your mailbox that includes a sales letter. Then answer the following questions to help analyze and learn from the approach used by the communication professionals who prepare these glossy sales messages. Your instructor might also ask you to share the package and your observations in a class discussion.

a. Who is the intended audience?
b. What are some of the demographic and psychographic characteristics of the intended audience?
c. What is the purpose of the direct-mail package? Has it been designed to solicit a phone-call response, make a mail-order sale, obtain a charitable contribution, or do something else?
d. What technique was used to encourage you to open the envelope?
e. Did the letter writer follow the AIDA model or something similar? If not, explain the letter's organization.
f. What emotional appeals and logical arguments does the letter use?
g. What selling points and consumer benefits does the letter offer?
h. Did the letter and the rest of the package provide convincing support for the claims made in the letter? If not, what is lacking?

Expand Your Knowledge

Learning More on the Web

Influence an Official and Promote Your Cause

http://thomas.loc.gov

At the Thomas site compiled by the Library of Congress, you'll discover voluminous information about federal legislation, congressional members, and committee reports. You can also access committee homepages and numerous links to government agencies, current issues, and historical documents. You'll find all kinds of regulatory information, including laws and relevant issues that might affect you in the business world. Visit the site and stay informed. Maybe you'll want to convince a government official to support a business-related issue that affects you. Explore the data at the Thomas site and find an issue you can use to practice your skills at writing a persuasive message.

1. What key ideas would you include in an e-mail message to persuade your congressional representative to support an issue that is important to you?
2. In a letter to a senator or member of Congress, what information would you include to convince the reader to vote for an issue related to small business?
3. When sending a message to someone who receives hundreds of written appeals daily, what attention-getting techniques can you use? How can you get support for a cause that concerns you as a businessperson?

Sharpening Your Career Skills Online

Bovée and Thill's Business Communication Web Search, at http://businesscommunicationblog.com/websearch, is a unique research tool designed specifically for business communication research. Use the Web Search function to find a website, video, PDF document, podcast, or PowerPoint presentation that offers advice on writing persuasive messages (either persuasive business messages or marketing and sales messages). Write a brief e-mail message to your instructor, describing the item that you found and summarizing the career skills information you learned from it.

Improve Your Grammar, Mechanics, and Usage

The following exercises help you improve your knowledge of and power over English grammar, mechanics, and usage. Turn to the Handbook of Grammar, Mechanics, and Usage at the end of this book and review all of Sections 2.4 (Semicolons) and 2.5 (Colons). Then look at the following 10 items. Circle the letter of the preferred choice in the following groups of sentences. (Answers to these exercises appear on page AK-3.)

1. a. This letter looks good; that one doesn't.
   b. This letter looks good: that one doesn't.
2. a. I want to make one thing clear: None of you will be promoted without teamwork.
   b. I want to make one thing clear; none of you will be promoted without teamwork.

c. I want to make one thing clear: None of you will be promoted; without teamwork.

3. a. The Zurich airport has been snowed in, therefore I can't attend the meeting.
   b. The Zurich airport has been snowed in, therefore, I can't attend the meeting.
   c. The Zurich airport has been snowed in; therefore, I can't attend the meeting.
4. a. His motivation was obvious: to get Meg fired.
   b. His motivation was obvious; to get Meg fired.
5. a. Only two firms have responded to our survey; J. J. Perkins and Tucker & Tucker.
   b. Only two firms have responded to our survey: J. J. Perkins and Tucker & Tucker.
6. a. Send a copy to: Nan Kent, CEO, Bob Bache, president, and Dan Brown, CFO.
   b. Send a copy to Nan Kent, CEO; Bob Bache, president; and Dan Brown, CFO.
   c. Send a copy to Nan Kent CEO; Bob Bache president; and Dan Brown CFO.
7. a. You shipped three items on June 7; however, we received only one of them.
   b. You shipped three items on June 7, however; we received only one of them.
   c. You shipped three items on June 7; however we received only one of them.
8. a. Workers wanted an immediate wage increase: they hadn't had a raise in 10 years.
   b. Workers wanted an immediate wage increase; because they hadn't had a raise in 10 years.
   c. Workers wanted an immediate wage increase; they hadn't had a raise in 10 years.
9. a. His writing skills are excellent however; he needs to polish his management style.
   b. His writing skills are excellent; however, he needs to polish his management style.
   c. His writing skills are excellent: however he needs to polish his management style.
10. a. We want to address three issues; efficiency; profitability; and market penetration.
    b. We want to address three issues; efficiency, profitability, and market penetration.
    c. We want to address three issues: efficiency, profitability, and market penetration.

For additional exercises focusing on semicolons and colons, visit mybcommlab. Click on Chapter 10, click on "Additional Exercises to Improve Your Grammar, Mechanics, and Usage," and click on "16. Punctuation A."

CASES

Applying the Three-Step Writing Process to Cases

Apply each step to the following cases, as assigned by your instructor.

PERSUASIVE BUSINESS MESSAGES

E-MAIL SKILLS PORTFOLIO BUILDER

1. That's the point: E-mail encouraging your boss to blog. You've been trying for months to convince your boss, Will Florence, to start blogging. You've told him that top executives in many industries now use blogging as a way to connect with customers and other stakeholders without going through the filters and barriers of formal corporate communications. He was just about convinced—until he read the blog by Bob Lutz, the co-chair and design chief of General Motors.

"Look at this!" he calls from his office. "Bob Lutz is one of the most respected executives in the world, and all these people are criticizing him on his own blog. Sure, a lot of the responses are positive, but quite a few are openly hostile, disagreeing with GM strategy, criticizing the products, criticizing the subjects he chooses for his blog—you name it. If blogging is all about opening yourself up to criticism from every bystander with a keyboard, no way am I going to start a blog."

Your task: Write an e-mail message to Florence (w_florence@sprenco.com), persuading him that the freewheeling nature of blog communication is its key advantage, not a disadvantage at all. While they may not always agree with what he has to say, automotive enthusiasts and car buyers respect Lutz for communicating in his own words—and for giving them the opportunity to respond. For background information, read some of the postings from Lutz and other GM executives at http://fastlane.gmblogs.com.[30]

E-MAIL SKILLS

2. Give a little to get a lot: Suggesting free wireless at Starbucks. Like many other students at the University of Wisconsin—Madison, you like to escape from your cramped apartment to work on school projects at local coffee shops. With your wireless-equipped laptop, you hunt for places that offer free wireless so you can access course websites, do research, and occasionally see how Badgers athletic teams are doing. But there's a problem: At the Starbucks right around the corner, you have to pay for wireless access through the service offered by T-Mobile. Several of the locally owned coffeehouses offer free wireless, but the closest one is a mile from your apartment. That's a long walk in a Wisconsin winter.

Your task: Write a persuasive message to Starbucks, suggesting that the company drop its agreement with T-Mobile and offer free wireless instead. Try to convince the firm that free wireless will attract enough additional coffee-buying customers to offset the loss of revenue from wireless—and help Starbucks overcome the "big corporation" image that prompts some coffee drinkers to patronize locally owned establishments instead. While you don't have the data to prove that the cost of offering free wireless would be more than offset by increased coffee sales, at least make a convincing argument that Starbucks should consider making the change. You'll post your message to the Starbucks website, www.starbucks.com, which has a limit of 2,600 characters for such messages.[31]

E-MAIL SKILLS PORTFOLIO BUILDER

3. Network disconnect: Building a business case for using social media at work. As someone who came of age in the "post e-mail" world of blogs, wikis, social networks, and other Web 2.0 technologies, you were rather disappointed to find your new employer solidly stuck in the age of e-mail. You use e-mail, of course, but it is only one of the tools in your communication toolbox. From your college years, you have hands-on experience with a wide range of social media tools, having used them to collaborate on school projects, to become involved in your local community, to learn more about various industries and professions, and to research potential employers during your job search. (In fact, without social media, you might've never heard about your current employer in the first place.) Moreover, your use of social media on the job has already paid several important dividends, including finding potential sales contacts at several large companies, connecting with peers in other companies to share ideas for working more efficiently, and learning about some upcoming legislative matters in your state that could profoundly hamper your company's current way of doing business.

You hoped that by setting an example through your own use of social media at work, your new colleagues and company management would quickly adopt these tools as well. However, just the opposite has happened. Waiting in your e-mail in-box this morning was a message from the CEO, announcing that the company is now cutting off access to social networking websites and banning the use of any social media at work. The message says that using company time and company computers for socializing is highly inappropriate and might be considered grounds for dismissal in the future if the problem gets out of hand.

Your task: You are stunned by the message. You fight the urge to fire off a hotly worded reply to straighten out the CEO's misperceptions. Instead, you wisely decide to send a message to your immediate superior first, explaining why you believe the new policy should be reversed. Using your boss's favorite medium (e-mail, of course!), write a persuasive message, explaining why Facebook, Twitter, and other social networking technologies are valid—and valuable—business tools. Bolster your argument with examples from other companies and advice from communication experts. (To access a list of links to get your research started, visit http://real-timeupdates.com/ebc, click on "Student Assignments," and select Chapter 10, page 306, Case 3.)

E-MAIL SKILLS

4. Life's little hassles: E-mail requesting satisfaction. It's hard to go through life without becoming annoyed at the way some things work. You have undoubtedly been dissatisfied with a product you've bought, a service you've received, or an action of some elected official or government agency.

Your task: Write a three- to five-paragraph persuasive e-mail message request, expressing your dissatisfaction in a particular case. Specify the action you want the reader to take.

IM SKILLS

5. Helping children: Instant message holiday fund drive at IBM. At IBM, you're one of the coordinators for the annual Employee Charitable Contributions Campaign. Since 1978, the company has helped employees contribute to more than 2,000 health and human service agencies. These groups may offer child care; treat substance abuse; provide health services; or fight illiteracy, homelessness, and hunger. Some offer disaster relief or care for the elderly. All deserve support. They're carefully screened by IBM, one of the largest corporate contributors of cash, equipment, and people to nonprofit organizations and educational institutions in the United States and around the world. As your literature states, the program "has engaged our employees more fully in the important mission of corporate citizenship."

During the winter holidays, you target agencies that cater to the needs of displaced families, women, and children. It's not difficult to raise enthusiasm. The prospect of helping children enjoy the holidays—children who otherwise might have nothing—usually awakens the spirit of your most distracted workers. But some of them wait until the last minute and then forget.

They have until December 16 to come forth with cash contributions. To make it in time for holiday deliveries, they can also bring in toys, food, and blankets through Tuesday, December 20. They shouldn't have any trouble finding the collection bins; they're everywhere, marked with bright red banners. But some will want to call you with questions or (you hope) to make credit card contributions: 800-658-3899, ext. 3342.

Your task: It's December 14. Write a 75- to 100-word instant message, encouraging last-minute holiday gifts.[32]

E-MAIL SKILLS

6. Tangled web: E-mail to PurelySoftware regarding an online order duplication. Last week you ordered new design software for your boss, Martin Soderburgh, at ArtAlive, the small art consulting business where you work. As he requested, you used his Visa card to order Adobe InDesign and Adobe Photoshop from an Internet vendor, PurelySoftware.com.

When you didn't receive the usual e-mail order confirmation, you called the company's toll-free number. The operator said the company's website was having problems, and he took a second order over the phone: $649 for Adobe InDesign, $564 for Adobe Photoshop, including tax and shipping. Four days later, ArtAlive received two shipments of the software, and your boss's credit card was charged $1,213 twice, for a total of $2,426.

Your task: Strictly speaking, you did authorize both orders. But you understood during the phone call that the first order was canceled, although you have no written proof. Send a persuasive e-mail to customerservice@purelysoftware.com, requesting (1) an immediate credit to your boss's Visa account and (2) a postage-paid return label for the duplicate order.[33]

E-MAIL SKILLS

7. No more driving: Telecommuting to Bachman, Trinity, and Smith. Sitting in your Dallas office at the accounting firm Bachman, Trinity, and Smith, clacking away on your computer, it seems as though you could be doing this work from your home. You haven't spoken to any co-workers in more than two hours. As long as you complete your work on time, does your location matter?

As an entry-level accountant, you've participated in on-location audits at major companies for nearly a year now. If your bosses trust you to work while staying at a hotel, why not let you work from home, where you already have an office with a computer, phone, and fax machine? You'd love to regain those two hours you lose commuting to and from work every day.

Your task: To gather support for this idea, visit the website of the International Telework Coalition website, at www.telcoa.org. Find statistics and other support and write an e-mail message persuading your boss, senior partner Marjorie Bachman, to grant you a six-month trial as a telecommuter.[34]

MEMO WRITING SKILLS

8. Always urgent: Memo pleading case for hosting a Red Cross blood drive. This morning as you drove to your job as food services manager at the Pechanga Casino Entertainment Center in Temecula, California, you were concerned to hear on the radio that the local Red Cross chapter put out a call for blood because national supplies have fallen dangerously low. During highly publicized disasters, people are emotional and eager to help out by donating blood. But in calmer times, only 5 percent of eligible donors think of giving blood. You're one of those few.

Not many people realize that donated blood lasts for only 72 hours. Consequently, the mainstay of emergency blood supplies must be replenished in an ongoing effort. No one is more skilled, dedicated, or efficient in handling blood than the American Red Cross, which is responsible for half the nation's supply of blood and blood products.

Donated blood helps victims of accidents and disease, as well as surgery patients. Just yesterday you were reading about a girl named Melissa, who was diagnosed with multiple congenital heart defects and underwent her first open-heart surgery at one week of age. Now five years old, she's used well over 50 units of donated blood, and she wouldn't be alive without them. In a thank-you letter, her mother lauded the many strangers who had "given a piece of themselves" to save her precious daughter—and countless others. You also learned that a donor's pint of blood can benefit up to four other people.

Today, you're going to do more than just roll up your own sleeve. You know the local Red Cross chapter takes its Blood Mobile to corporations, restaurants, salons—anyplace willing to host public blood drives. What if you could convince the board of directors to support a blood drive at the casino? The slot machines and gaming tables are usually full, hundreds of employees are on hand, and people who've never visited before might come down to donate blood. The positive publicity certainly couldn't hurt Pechanga's community image. With materials from the Red Cross, you're confident you can organize Pechanga's hosting effort and handle the promotion. (Last year, you headed the casino's successful Toys for Tots drive.)

To give blood, one must be healthy, be at least 17 years old (with no upper age limit), and weigh at least 110 pounds. Donors can give every 56 days. You'll be urging Pechanga donors to eat well, drink water, and be rested before the Blood Mobile arrives.

The local Red Cross chapter's mission statement says, in part, that the Red Cross is "a humanitarian organization led by volunteers and guided by the Fundamental Principles of the International Red Cross Movement" that will "prevent and alleviate human suffering wherever it may be found." All assistance is given free of charge, made possible by "contributions of people's time, money, and skills"—and in the case of you and your coworkers, a piece of yourselves.

Your task: Write a memo persuading the Pechanga board of directors to host a public Red Cross blood drive. You can learn more about what's involved in hosting a blood drive at www.givelife.org (click on "Sponsor a Drive"). Ask the board to provide bottled water, orange juice, and snacks for donors. You'll organize food service workers to handle the distribution, but you'll need the board's approval to let your team volunteer during work hours. Use a combination of logical and emotional appeals.[35]

E-MAIL SKILL PORTFOLIO BUILDER

9. Message to an angel: Introducing your company to an investor. Your new company, WorldConnect Language Services, started well and is going strong. However, to expand beyond your Memphis, Tennessee, home market, you need a one-time infusion of cash to open branch offices in other cities around the Southeast. At the Entrepreneur's Lunch Forum you attended yesterday, you learned about several *angels*, as they are called in the investment community—private individuals who invest money in small companies in exchange for a share of ownership. One such angel, Melinda Sparks, told the audience that she is looking for investment opportunities outside of high technology, where angels often invest their money. She also indicated that she looks for entrepreneurs who know their industries and markets well, who are passionate about the value they bring to the marketplace, who are committed to growing their businesses, and who have a solid plan for how they will spend an investor's money. Fortunately, you meet all of her criteria.

Your task: Draft an e-mail message to Sparks, introducing yourself and your business and asking for a meeting at which you can present your business plan in more detail. Explain that your Memphis office was booked to capacity within two months of opening, thanks to the growing number of international business professionals looking for translators and interpreters. You've researched the entire Southeast region and identified at least 10 other cities that could support a language services office such as yours. Making up whatever other information you need, draft a four-paragraph message following the AIDA model, ending with a request for a meeting within the next four weeks.

BLOGGING SKILLS PORTFOLIO BUILDER

10. Web accessibility advocacy: It's not "World Wide" if it doesn't include everybody. Like most other companies today, your firm makes extensive use of the web for internal and external communication. However, after reading about the Web Accessibility Initiative (WAI), you've become concerned that your company's various websites haven't been designed to accommodate people with disabilities or age-related limitations. Fortunately, as one of the company's top managers, you have a perfect forum for letting everyone in the company know how important accessible web design is: Your internal blog is read by the vast majority of employees and managers throughout the company.

Your task: Visit the WAI website, at www.w3.org/WAI, and read the two articles "Introduction to Web Accessibility" (look in the "Introducing Accessibility" section) and "Developing a Web Accessibility Business Case for Your Organization" (in the "Managing Accessibility" section). Using the information you learn in these articles, write a post for your blog that emphasizes how important it is for your company's websites to be made more accessible. You don't have direct authority over the company's web developers, so it would be inappropriate for you to request them to take any specific action. Your goal is simply to raise awareness and encourage everyone to consider the needs of the company's online audiences. Don't worry about the technical aspects of web accessibility; focus instead on the benefits of improving accessibility.[36]

E-MAIL SKILLS

11. No wonder nobody ever calls me: E-mail to InstantCall, requesting adjustment. You thought it was strange that no one called you on your new mobile phone, even though you had given your family members, friends, and boss your new number. Two weeks after getting the new phone and agreeing to a $49 monthly fee, you called the service provider, InstantCall, just to see if everything was working. Sure enough, the technician discovered that your incoming calls were being routed to an inactive number. You're glad she found the problem, but then it took the company nearly two more weeks to fix it. When you called to complain about paying for service you didn't receive, the customer service agent suggested you send an e-mail to Judy Hinkley at the company's regional business office to request an adjustment.

Your task: Decide how much of an adjustment you think you deserve under the circumstances and then send an e-mail message to Hinkley, at judyh@instantcall.net, to request the adjustment to your account. Write a summary of events in chronological order, supplying exact dates for maximum effectiveness. Make up any information you need, such as problems that the malfunctioning service caused at home or at work.

LETTER MARKETING AND SALES MESSAGES

LETTER WRITING SKILLS PORTFOLIO BUILDER

12. Your new Kentucky home: Letter promoting the Bluegrass State. Like all other states, Kentucky works hard to attract businesses that are considering expanding into the state or relocating entirely from another state. The Kentucky Cabinet for Economic Development is responsible for reaching out to these companies and overseeing the many incentive programs the state offers to new and established businesses.

Your task: As the communication director of the Kentucky Cabinet for Economic Development, you play the lead role in reaching out to companies that want to expand or relocate to Kentucky. Visit www.thinkkentucky.com and download the

Kentucky Facts brochure (look under the "Why Kentucky" link). Identify the major benefits the state uses to promote Kentucky as a great place to locate a business. Summarize these reasons in a form letter that will be sent to business executives throughout the country. Be sure to introduce yourself and your purpose in the letter, and close with a compelling call to action (have them reach you by telephone at 800-626-2930 or by e-mail at econdev@ky.gov). As you plan your letter, try to imagine yourself as the CEO of a company and consider what a complex choice it would be to move to another state.

E-MAIL SKILLS

13. Slimming down: Shortening the Curves company history. Curves is a fitness center franchise that caters to women who may not feel at home in traditional gyms. With its customer-focused and research-based approach, Curves has become a significant force in the fitness industry and one of the most successful franchise operations in history.

Your task: Both potential customers and potential franchise owners can learn about the history of Curves at www.curves.com/about-curves/history.php. Using this 450-word article as a starting point, write a shorter version (no more than 150 words) that the company could use for automated e-mail and IM responses.

LETTER WRITING SKILLS

14. Selling your idea: Sales message promoting a product of your own invention. You never intended to become an inventor, but you saw a way to make something work more easily, so you set to work. You developed a prototype, found a way to mass-produce the product, and set up a small manufacturing studio in your home. You know that other people are going to benefit from your invention. Now all you need is to reach that market.

Your task: Imagine a useful product that you might have invented—perhaps something related to a hobby or sporting activity. List the benefits and features of your imaginary product. Then write a sales letter for it, using what you've learned in this chapter and making up details as you need them.

PODCASTING SKILLS

15. Listen up: Podcast promoting a podcast station. Podcasting, the technique of recording individual sound files that people download from the Internet to listen to on their computers or music players, is quickly redefining the concept of radio. A growing crowd of musicians, essayists, journalists, and others with compelling content use podcasting to reach audiences they can't get to through traditional broadcast radio. The good news is that anyone with a microphone and a computer can record podcasts. That's also the bad news, at least from your perspective as a new podcaster: With so many podcasters now on the Internet, potential listeners have thousands and thousands of audio files to select from.

Your new podcast, School2Biz, offers advice to business students making the transition from college to career. You provide information on everything from preparing résumés to interviewing to finding one's place in the business world and building a successful career. As you expand your audience, you'd eventually like to turn School2Biz into a profitable operation (perhaps by selling advertising time during your podcasts). For now, you're simply offering free advice.

Your task: You've chosen The Podcast Bunker (www.podcastbunker.com) as the first website on which to promote School2Biz. The site lets podcasters promote their feeds with brief text listings, such as this description of Pet Talk Radio: "A weekly lifestyle show for people with more than a passing interest in pets. Hosted by Brian Pickering & Kaye Browne with Australia's favourite vet Dr Harry Cooper & animal trainer Steve Austin."

Option A: Write a 50-word description of your new podcast, making up any information you need to describe School2Biz. Be sure to mention who you are and why the information you present is worth listening to. Option B: If your instructor tells you to do so, script and record a brief podcast (no more than three minutes) that describes and promotes School2Biz.[38]

WEB WRITING SKILLS PORTFOLIO BUILDER

16. Don't forget print: Using the web to promote Time Inc.'s magazine advertising. After getting a shaky start as the technology matured and advertisers tried to figure out this new medium, online advertising has finally become a significant force in consumer and business marketing. Companies in a wide variety of industries are shifting some of the advertising budgets from traditional media such as television and magazines to the increasing selection of advertising possibilities online—and more than a few companies now advertise almost exclusively online. That's fine for companies that sell advertising time and space for websites and blogs, but your job involves selling advertising in print magazines that are worried about losing market share to online publishers.

Online advertising has two major advantages that you can't really compete with: interactivity and the ability to precisely target individual audience members. On the other hand, you have several advantages going for you, including the ability to produce high-color photography, the physical presence of print (such as when a magazine sits on a table in a doctor's waiting room), portability, guaranteed circulation numbers, and close reader relationships that go back years or decades in many cases.

Your task: You work as an advertising sales specialist for the Time Inc. division of Time Warner, which publishes more than 150 magazines around the world. Write a brief persuasive message about the benefits of magazine advertising; the statement will be posted on the individual websites of Time Inc.'s numerous magazines, so you can't narrow in on any single publication. Also, Time Inc. coordinates its print publications with an extensive online presence (including thousands of paid online advertisements), so you can't bash online advertising, either.[39]

E-MAIL SKILLS PORTFOLIO BUILDER

17. Insure.com: E-mail promoting a better way to buy insurance. The great thing about Insure.com is that no one is obligated to buy a thing, which makes your job in the company's marketing department easier. Free of charge, consumers can log on to your website, ask for dozens of insurance quotes, and then go off and buy elsewhere. They can look at instant price-comparison quotes from more than 200 insurers, covering every kind of insurance from term life and medical to private passenger auto insurance. All rates are guaranteed up-to-the-day accurate against a $500 reward. And so far the online service has received positive press from *Nation's Business, Kiplinger's Personal Finance, Good Housekeeping, The Los Angeles Times, Money, U.S. News & World Report*, and *Forbes*.

Insure.com generates revenues primarily from the receipt of commissions and fees paid by insurers based on the volume of business produced. Customers can purchase insurance from the company of their choice via the Insure.com website, or they can call a toll-free number to speak to one of the company's representatives. The reps are paid salaries versus commissions and do not directly benefit by promoting one insurance company's product over another.

And all this is free. Too bad more people don't know about your services.

Your task: It's your job to lure more insurance customers to Insure.com. You've decided to use direct e-mail marketing (using a list of consumers who have inquired about rates in the past but never committed to purchase anything). Write an e-mail sales message promoting the benefits of Insure.com's services. Be sure your message is suited to e-mail format, with an appropriate subject heading.[40]

LETTER WRITING SKILLS PORTFOLIO BUILDER

18. Outsourcing: Letter from Kelly Services, offering solutions. Kelly Services is a global Fortune 500 company that offers staffing solutions that include temporary services, staff leasing, outsourcing, and vendor on-site and full-time placement. Kelly provides employees who have a wide range of skills across many disciplines, including office services, accounting, engineering, information technology, law, science, marketing, light industrial, education, health care, and home care.

Companies use Kelly Services to strategically balance workload and workforce during peaks and valleys of demand, to handle special projects, and to evaluate employees prior to making full-time hiring decisions. The dramatic changes in business have spurred the rapid growth of the contingent employment industry.

In turn, many individuals are choosing the flexibility of personal career management, increasing options of where, when, and how to work. Therefore, more and more workers are becoming receptive to being contract, temporary, or consulting employees.

The flexibility of a temporary services firm offers advantages to both the company and the employee. Both have the opportunity to evaluate one another prior to making a long-term commitment. Kelly Services earns a fee when its employees are hired permanently, but employers find that it's a small price to pay for such valuable preview time, which saves everyone the cost and pain of a bad hiring decision.

With 2,500 offices in 26 countries, Kelly provides its customers nearly 700,000 employees annually. The company provides staffing solutions to more than 90 percent of the Fortune 500 companies. Kelly has received many supplier awards for providing outstanding and cost-efficient staffing services, including Chrysler's Gold Award, Ford Motor Company's Q1 Preferred Quality Award, Intel Corporation's Supplier Continuous Quality Improvement (SCQI) Award, and DuPont Legal's Challenge Award.

As companies increasingly face new competitive pressures to provide better service and quality at lower prices, many are turning to outsourcing suppliers to deliver complete operational management of specific functions or support departments, allowing the company the necessary time to focus on its core competencies. One solution is to choose a single supplier such as the Kelly Management Services (KMS) division to deliver "full-service" outsourcing.

KMS combines management experience, people process improvements, technology enhancements, and industry expertise to optimize customer operations and reduce cost. KMS understands the unique challenges companies face in today's increasingly fast-paced business world and can provide customers with services across multiple functional offerings, including call center operations, warehousing, distribution and light assembly, back-office and administrative functions, and mail and reprographic services.

Your task: Write a sales letter to companies similar to Chrysler, Ford, Intel, and DuPont, explaining what Kelly has to offer. For current information, visit the Kelly website, at www.kellyservices.com.[41]

BLOGGING SKILLS

19. True green: Explaining why Hangers Cleaners is different. Other than possibly wrinkling their noses at that faint smell that wafts out of the plastic bags when they bring clothes home from the dry cleaner, many consumers probably don't pay much attention to the process that goes on behind the scenes at their neighborhood cleaner. However, traditional dry cleaning is a chemically intense process—so much so that these facilities require special environmental permits and monitoring by government agencies.

At Kansas City's Hangers Cleaners, the process is different—much different. The company's innovative machines use safe liquid carbon dioxide (CO_2) and specially developed detergents to clean clothes. The process requires no heat (making it easier on clothes) and has no need for the toxic, combustible perchloroethylene used in conventional dry cleaning (making it safer for employees and the environment). Customers can tell the difference, too. As one put it, "Since I started using Hangers, my clothes are softer, cleaner and they don't have that chemical smell."

Your task: Because many consumers aren't familiar with traditional dry cleaning, they don't immediately grasp why Hangers's method is better for clothes, employees, and the environment. Write a post for the company blog, explaining why Hangers is different. Limit yourself to 400 words. You can learn more about the company and its unique process at www.hangerskc.com.[42]

PORTFOLIO BUILDER

20. Try it; you just might like it: Convincing consumers to sample beefalo. You know enough about human nature to know that people tend to resist new ideas when it comes to food. In your job as public communications director for American Beefalo International, this knowledge presents a professional challenge as you try to convince people to give beefalo a try. The beefalo is a cross between bison (American buffalo) and beef cattle, and even though these animals are primarily cattle (genetically speaking), many consumers are reluctant to give up their familiar beef for something most have never tried.

But here's the good news: Many people are looking for healthier foods, and according to government tests, beefalo is lower in cholesterol, saturated fat, total fat, and calories. The table below compares the nutritional data of beefalo with other foods.

Your task: Write a small flier to be displayed in food stores that sell beefalo cuts. The page size will be 8 1/2 inches tall by 3 3/4 inches wide, so format your word processing page accordingly. Allow room for a photograph, and don't try to cram too much text on the page. Emphasize beefalo as a healthy alternative for people who want to continue enjoying meat in their diets.[37]

	PROTEIN (G)	CHOLESTEROL (MG)	SATURATED FATS (G)	TOTAL FAT (G)	CALORIES	PERCENTAGE OF CALORIES FROM FAT
Fish	22.9	47	0.104	0.81	105	6.9
Chicken	31.0	85	1.0	3.5	165	19.5
Pork	29.3	86	3.4	9.7	212	41.0
Beef	25.9	88	8.5	21.5	305	63.6
Beefalo	30.7	58	2.7	6.3	188	30.3

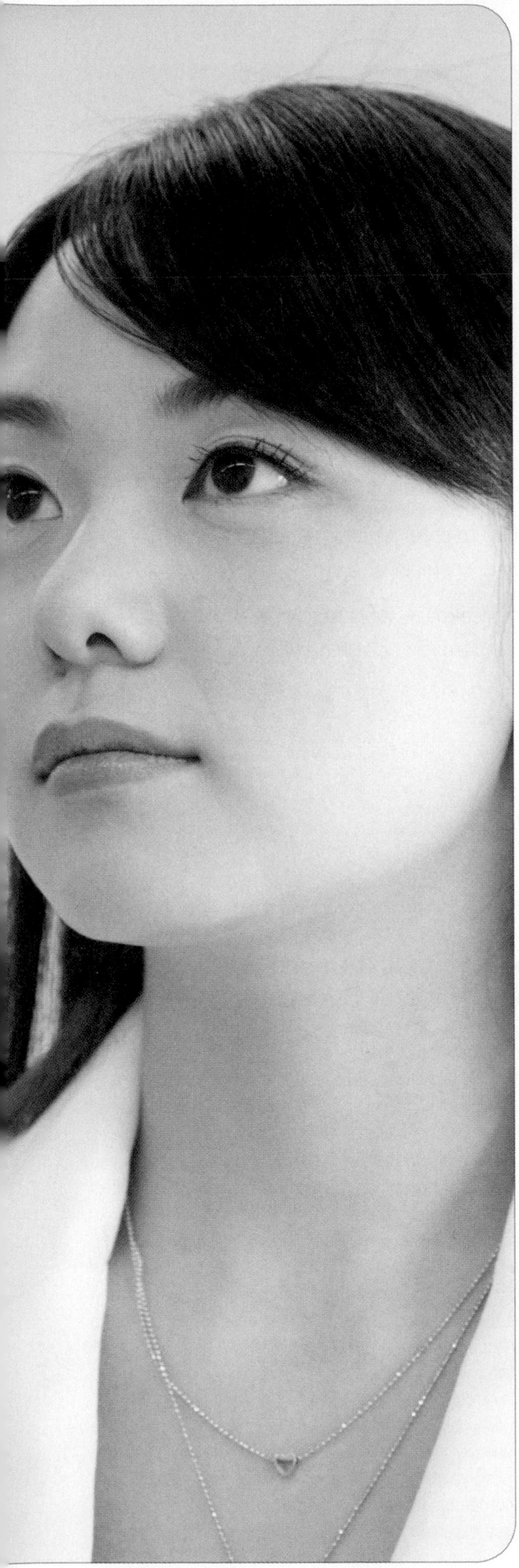

Part 4

Preparing Reports and Oral Presentations

Reports and presentations offer important opportunities to demonstrate your value to the organization. Depending on the project, you might analyze complex problems, educate audiences, address opportunities in the marketplace, win contracts, or even launch an entire company with the help of a compelling business plan. Adapt what you've learned so far to the particular challenges of long format messages, including some special touches that can make formal reports stand out from the crowd. Learn how to plan effective presentations, overcome the anxieties that every speaker feels, and respond to questions from the audience. Complement your talk with compelling visual materials and learn how to create presentation slides that engage and excite your audience. Finally, discover some tips and techniques for succeeding with online presentations.

11 Planning Reports and Proposals

Learning Objectives

After studying this chapter, you will be able to

1 Adapt the three-step writing process to reports and proposals

2 Describe an effective process for conducting business research, and explain the difference between primary and secondary research

3 Provide five guidelines for conducting an effective online search

4 Describe the major tasks involved in processing and applying your research results

5 Explain how to organize informational reports and website content

6 Discuss three major ways to organize analytical reports, and explain how to plan proposals

On the Job: Communicating at Tesco

British retail giant Tesco relies on extensive audience research to plan and craft its consumer messages.

Listening to Customers Is Part of the Recipe of Success

Most consumers enjoy the benefits of stiff price competition among their local grocery stores, but the competition is anything but enjoyable for grocery retailers. In the United States, the average grocery store's after-tax profit margin hovers around 1 percent. With so little room for error, grocers need to stay on top of consumer behavior to make sure they offer the right mix of products at the right prices.

Tesco, the leading grocery retailer in the United Kingdom, is not only surviving but thriving in this tough industry. Under the leadership of Richard Brasher, the company's top marketing executive in the United Kingdom, Tesco devotes considerable effort to acquiring and processing information about its customers, information that is used in a variety of documents to drive both strategic and tactical decisions.

For example, when demographic research indicated a growing number of immigrants from Poland, the store reached out to Polish-speaking consumers to learn more about their wants and needs. After a successful experiment on a small scale, Tesco expanded its Polish foods selection to as many as

100 other stores. In another instance, the marketing team couldn't figure out why flowers and wine had become such hot sellers during a particular week at the beginning of summer that didn't coincide with any regular holidays. Analysis of sales data revealed that families were buying these items as gifts for their children's teachers at the end of the school year, so the company responded by making sure both items were stocked in plentiful supply during that week.

Tesco is now busy applying its information-driven approach to the competitive U.S. market. After studying the market for two decades, the company made its move in 2007 and now has more than 50 Fresh & Easy Neighborhood Markets in California, Nevada, and Arizona. True to form, Tesco is emphasizing research and information every step of the way in every facet of the business. When the company approached the Phoenix-based dessert manufacturer Berto's Gelato and Sorbet about carrying its premium gelato in Fresh & Easy stores, Berto's CEO Ed DeBartolo was amazed at the amount of information the company demanded. Tesco even sent auditors and food scientists to the Berto's facility to conduct their own research. DeBartolo so admires Tesco's emphasis on information that he has applied the giant retailer's methods to all the products his company makes. And, he says, "I want to be a Tesco supplier for life."[1]

www.tesco.com

APPLYING THE THREE-STEP WRITING PROCESS TO REPORTS AND PROPOSALS

1 LEARNING OBJECTIVE

Adapt the three-step writing process to reports and proposals.

Reports play a significant role in Richard Brasher's success with Tesco (profiled in the chapter-opening "On the Job"vignette), as they do in the careers of all other business professionals. Reports fall into three basic categories:

Reports can be classified as informational reports, analytical reports, and proposals.

- **Informational reports** offer data, facts, feedback, and other types of information, without analysis or recommendations.
- **Analytical reports** offer both information and analysis, and they can also include recommendations.
- **Proposals** offer structured persuasion for internal or external audiences.

The purpose and content of business reports vary widely; in some cases, you follow a strict guideline, but in others, the organization and format are up to you.

The nature of reports varies widely, from one-page trip reports that follow a standard format to detailed business plans and proposals that can run hundreds of pages. No matter what the circumstances, try to view every business report as an opportunity to demonstrate your understanding of your audience's challenges and your ability to contribute to your organization's success.

The three-step process you studied in Chapters 4 though 6 and applied to short messages in Chapters 7 through 10 is easy to adapt to longer message formats (see Figure 11.1). This chapter addresses the planning step, focusing on two major areas that require special attention in long documents: gathering and organizing information. Chapter 12 covers the writing step and also includes advice on creating effective visuals for your reports and proposals. Chapter 13 describes the tasks involved in completing reports and proposals.

Analyzing the Situation

Define your purpose clearly so you don't waste time.

The complexity of many reports and the amount of work involved put a premium on carefully analyzing the situation before you begin to write. Pay special attention to your **statement of purpose**, which explains *why* you are preparing the report and *what* you plan to deliver in the report (see Table 11.1 on the next page).

The most useful way to phrase a purpose statement is to begin with an infinitive phrase (*to* plus a verb), which helps pin down your general goal (*to inform, to identify, to analyze*, and so on). For instance, in an informational report, your statement of purpose can be as simple as one of these:

To identify potential markets for our new phone-based video games
To update the board of directors on the progress of the research project
To submit required information to the Securities and Exchange Commission

Longer reports may have several related purposes.

Your statement of purpose for an analytical report often needs to be more comprehensive. When Linda Moreno, the cost accounting manager for Electrovision, a high-tech

FIGURE 11.1 Three-Step Writing Process for Reports and Proposals
The three-step writing process is especially valuable with reports and proposals. By guiding your work at each step, the process helps you make the most of the time and energy you invest.

1 Plan →

Analyze the Situation
Clarify the problem or opportunity at hand, define your purpose, develop an audience profile, and develop a work plan.

Gather Information
Determine audience needs and obtain the information necessary to satisfy those needs; conduct a research project, if necessary.

Select the Right Medium
Choose the best medium for delivering your message; consider delivery through multiple media.

Organize the Information
Define your main idea, limit your scope, select the direct or indirect approach, and outline your content using an appropriate structure for an informational report, an analytical report, or a proposal.

2 Write →

Adapt to Your Audience
Be sensitive to audience needs with a "you" attitude, politeness, positive emphasis, and bias-free language. Build a strong relationship with your audience by establishing your credibility and projecting your company's image. Control your style with a tone and voice appropriate to the situation.

Compose the Message
Choose strong words that will help you create effective sentences and coherent paragraphs throughout the introduction, body, and close of your report or proposal.

3 Complete

Revise the Message
Evaluate content and review readability, then edit and rewrite for conciseness and clarity.

Produce the Message
Use effective design elements and suitable layout for a clean, professional appearance; seamlessly combine text and graphical elements.

Proofread the Message
Review for errors in layout, spelling, and mechanics.

Distribute the Message
Deliver your report using the chosen medium; make sure all documents and all relevant files are distributed successfully.

TABLE 11.1 Problem or Opportunity Statements Versus Purpose Statements

PROBLEM STATEMENT	STATEMENT OF PURPOSE
Our company's market share is steadily declining.	To explore new ways of promoting and selling our products and to recommend the approaches most likely to stabilize our market share
Our current computer network lacks sufficient bandwidth and cannot be upgraded to meet our future needs.	To analyze various networking options and to recommend the system that will best meet our company's current and future needs
We need $2 million to launch our new product.	To convince investors that our new business would be a sound investment so that we can obtain desired financing
Our current operations are too decentralized and expensive.	To justify the closing of the Newark plant and the transfer of East Coast operations to a single Midwest location in order to save the company money

company based in Los Gatos, California, was asked to find ways of reducing employee travel and entertainment costs, she phrased her statement of purpose accordingly:

> . . . to analyze the T&E [travel and entertainment] budget, evaluate the impact of recent changes in airfares and hotel costs, and suggest ways to tighten management's control over T&E expenses.

Because Moreno was assigned an analytical report rather than an informational report, she had to go beyond merely collecting data; she had to draw conclusions and make recommendations. You'll see her complete report in Chapter 13.

When writing a proposal, you must also be guided by a clear statement of purpose to help focus on crafting a persuasive message. Here are several examples:

> To secure funding in next year's budget for new conveyor systems in the warehouse
>
> To get management approval to reorganize the North American salesforce
>
> To secure $2 million from outside investors to start production of the new titanium mountain bike

In addition to considering your purpose carefully, you will also want to prepare a *work plan* for most reports and proposals in order to make the best use of your time. For simpler reports, the work plan can be an informal list of tasks and a simple schedule. However, if you're preparing a lengthy report, particularly when you're collaborating with others, you'll want to develop a more detailed work plan (see Figure 11.2 on the next page).

A detailed work plan saves time and often produces more effective reports.

Gathering Information

The sheer volume of information needed for many reports and proposals requires careful planning—and may even require a separate research project to acquire the data and information you need (see "Supporting Your Messages with Reliable Information" on page 320). To stay on schedule and on budget, be sure to review your statement of purpose and your audience's needs so that you collect all the information you need—and only the information you need.

Some reports require formal research projects to gather all the necessary information.

Selecting the Right Medium

Just as you would for other business messages, select the medium for your report based on the needs of your audience and the practical advantages and disadvantages of the choices available to you. In addition to the general media selection criteria discussed in Chapter 4, consider several points for reports and proposals. First, for many reports and proposals, audiences have specific media requirements, and you might not have a choice. For instance, executives in many corporations now expect to review reports via their in-house intranets, sometimes in conjunction with an *executive dashboard*, a customized online presentation of key operating variables such as revenue, profits, quality, customer satisfaction, and project progress. Second, consider how your audience wants to provide feedback on your report or proposal. Do they prefer to write comments on a printed document or to use the commenting and markup features in a word processing program or Adobe Acrobat? Third, will multiple people need to update the document over time? A wiki could be an ideal choice. Fourth, bear in mind that your choice of media also sends a message. For instance, a routine sales report dressed up in expensive multimedia could look like a waste of time and money.

The best medium for any given report might be anything from a professionally printed and bound document to an online executive dashboard that displays nothing but report highlights.

Organizing Your Information

Both the direct and indirect approaches are used in business reports. The direct approach is popular because it is efficient and easy to follow. It can also produce a more forceful report. However, if the audience is unsure about your credibility or is not ready to accept your main idea without first seeing some reasoning or evidence, the indirect approach is a better

FIGURE 11.2 Work Plan for a Report

A formal work plan such as this is a vital tool for planning and managing complex writing projects. The preliminary outline here helps guide the research; the report writers may modify the outline when they begin writing the report.

> Clearly and succinctly defines the problem

STATEMENT OF THE PROBLEM
The rapid growth of our company over the past five years has reduced the sense of community among our staff. People no longer feel like part of an intimate organization that values teamwork.

> Identifies exactly what will be covered by the research and in the final report

PURPOSE AND SCOPE OF WORK
The purpose of this study is to determine whether social networking technology such as Facebook and Socialtext would help rebuild a sense of community within the workforce and whether encouraging the use of such tools in the workplace will have any negative consequences. The study will attempt to assess the impact of social networks in other companies in terms of community-building, morale, project communication, and overall productivity.

> Explains how the researchers will find the data and information they need

SOURCES AND METHODS OF DATA COLLECTION
Data collection will start with secondary research, including a review of recently published articles and studies on the use of social networking in business and a review of product information published by technology vendors. Primary research will focus on an employee and management survey to uncover attitudes about social networking tools. We will also collect anecdotal evidence from bloggers and others with experience using networks in the workplace.

> Offers a preliminary outline with sufficient detail to guide the research and set reader expectations

PRELIMINARY OUTLINE
The preliminary outline for this study is as follows:

I. What experiences have other companies had with social networks in the workplace?
   A. Do social networks have a demonstrable business benefit?
   B. How do employees benefit from using these tools?
   C. Has network security and information confidentiality been an issue?
II. Is social networking an appropriate solution for our community-building needs?
   A. Is social networking better than other tools and methods for community building?
   B. Are employees already using social networking tools on the job?
   C. Will a company-endorsed system distract employees from essential duties?
   D. Will a company system add to managerial workloads in any way?
III. If we move ahead, should we use a "business-class" network such as Socialtext or a consumer tool such as Facebook?
   A. How do the initial and ongoing costs compare?
   B. Do the additional capabilities of a business-class network justify the higher costs?
IV. How should we implement a social network?
   A. Should we let it grow "organically," with employees choosing their own tools and groups?
   B. Should we make a variety of tools available and let employees improvise on their own?
   C. Should we designate one system as the official company social network and make it a permanent, supported element of the information technology infrastructure?
VI. How can we evaluate the success of a new social network?
   A. What are the criteria of success or failure?
   B. What is the best way to measure these criteria?

> Clearly lists responsibilities and due dates

TASK ASSIGNMENTS AND SCHEDULE
Each phase of this study will be completed by the following dates:

Secondary research: Hank Waters	September 15, 2010
Employee and management survey: Julienne Cho	September 22, 2010
Analysis and synthesis of research: Hank Waters/Julienne Cho	October 6, 2010
Comparison of business and consumer solutions: Julienne Cho	October 13, 2010
Comparison of implementation strategies: Hank Waters	October 13, 2010
Final report: Hank Waters	October 20, 2010

choice because it gives you a chance to prove your points and gradually overcome audience reservations. The longer the message, though, the less effective the indirect approach is likely to be.

Both approaches have merit, so businesspeople often combine them, revealing their conclusions and recommendations in stages as they go along rather than putting them all first or last (see Figure 11.3).

When you outline your content, use informative ("talking") headings rather than simple descriptive ("topical") headings (see Table 11.2). When in question or summary form, informative headings force you to really think through the content rather than

FIGURE 11.3 Direct Approach Versus Indirect Approach in an Introduction
In the direct version of this introduction, the writer quickly presents the report's recommendation, followed by the conclusions that led to that recommendation. In the indirect version, the same topics are introduced in the same order, but no conclusions are drawn about them; the conclusions and the ultimate recommendation appear later, in the body of the report.

DIRECT APPROACH

Since the company's founding 25 years ago, we have provided regular repair service for all our electric appliances. This service has been an important selling point as well as a source of pride for our employees. However, rising labor costs have made it impossible to maintain profitability while offering competitive service rates. Last year, we lost $500,000 on our repair business.

Because of your concern over these losses, you asked me to study whether we should discontinue our repair service. After analyzing the situation in depth, I have concluded that the repair service is an expensive, impractical tradition, and I recommend that the service be discontinued.

By withdrawing from the electric appliance repair business, we can substantially improve our financial performance without damaging our reputation with customers. This conclusion is based on three basic points that are covered in the following pages:

- It is highly unlikely that we will ever be able to make a profit in the repair business.
- We can refer customers to a variety of qualified repair firms without significantly reducing customer satisfaction.
- Closing down the service operation will create few internal problems.

Summarizes the situation

Immediately introduces one of the report's major conclusions

Reminds the audience why the report was prepared

Presents the report's key recommendation, that the repair service should be discontinued

Emphasizes the benefits of acting on the recommendation and addresses any fears about possible negative consequences

Lists three important conclusions that led to the recommendation to end the service (notice how the indirect approach that follows presents these same three points as questions to be considered)

INDIRECT APPROACH

Since the company's founding 25 years ago, we have provided regular repair service for all our electric appliances. This service has been an important selling point as well as a source of pride for our employees. However, rising labor costs have made it impossible to maintain profitability while offering competitive service rates.

Because of your concern over these losses, you have asked me to study whether we should discontinue our repair service. I have analyzed the situation in depth, and the following pages present my findings and recommendations for your review. The analysis addressed three basic questions:

- What is the extent of our losses, and what can we do to turn the business around?
- Would withdrawal hurt our sales of electrical appliances?
- What would be the internal repercussions of closing down the repair business?

Summarizes the situation

Reminds the audience why the report was prepared

Indicates that conclusions and a recommendation will be presented later in the report

Introduces the three points that will eventually lead to the conclusions and ultimately to the recommendation

TABLE 11.2 Types of Outline Headings

DESCRIPTIVE (TOPICAL) OUTLINE	INFORMATIVE (TALKING) OUTLINE	
	QUESTION FORM	SUMMARY FORM
I. Industry characteristics	I. What is the nature of the industry?	I. Flour milling is a mature industry.
A. Annual sales	A. What are the annual sales?	A. Market is large.
B. Profitability	B. Is the industry profitable?	B. Profit margins are narrow.
C. Growth rate	C. What is the pattern of growth?	C. Growth is modest.
1. Sales	1. Sales growth?	1. Sales growth averages less than 3 percent a year.
2. Profit	2. Profit growth?	2. Profits are flat.

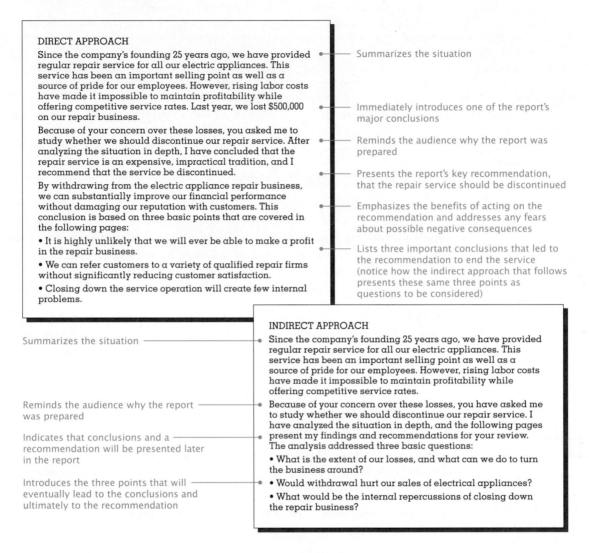

CHECKLIST: Adapting the Three-Step Writing Process to Informational and Analytical Reports

A. Analyze the situation.
- Clearly define your purpose before you start writing.
- If you need to accomplish several goals in the report, identify all of them in advance.
- Prepare a work plan to guide your efforts.

B. Gather information.
- Determine whether you need to launch a separate research project to collect the necessary information.
- Reuse or adapt existing material whenever possible.

C. Select the right medium.
- Base your decision on audience expectations (or requirements, as the case may be).
- Consider the need for commenting, revising, distributing, and storing.
- Remember that the medium you choose also sends a message.

D. Organize your information.
- Use a direct approach if your audience is receptive.
- Use an indirect approach if your audience is skeptical.
- Use an indirect approach when you don't want to risk coming across as arrogant.
- Combine approaches if doing so will help build support for your primary message.

simply identify the general topic area. Using informative headings will not only help you plan more effectively but also facilitate collaborative writing. A heading such as "Industry characteristics" could mean five different things to the five people on your writing team, so use a heading that conveys a single, unambiguous meaning, such as "Flour milling is a mature industry."

For a quick review of adapting the three-step process to long reports, refer to "Checklist: Adapting the Three-Step Writing Process to Informational and Analytical Reports." The following sections provide specific advice on how to plan informational reports, analytical reports, and proposals.

2 LEARNING OBJECTIVE

Describe an effective process for conducting business research, and explain the difference between primary and secondary research.

SUPPORTING YOUR MESSAGES WITH RELIABLE INFORMATION

Follow a clear process to ensure successful research.

Audiences expect you to support your message with solid research. As you've probably discovered while doing school projects, research involves a lot more than simply typing a few terms into a search engine. Good research requires a clear process:

1. **Plan your research.** A solid plan yields better results in less time.
2. **Locate the data and information you need.** The research plan tells you *what* to look for; your next step is to figure out *where* the data and information are and *how* to access them.
3. **Process the data and information you've located.** The data and information you find probably won't be in a form you can use immediately and will require some processing, which might involve anything from statistical analysis to resolving the differences between two or more expert opinions.
4. **Apply your findings.** You can apply your research findings in three ways: summarizing information for someone else's benefit, drawing conclusions based on what you've learned, or developing recommendations.
5. **Manage information efficiently.** Many companies today are trying to maximize the return on the time and money they invest in business research by collecting and sharing research results in a variety of computer-based systems, known generally as **knowledge management systems.** At the very least, be sure to share your results with any colleagues who may be able to benefit from them.

You can see the sequence of these steps in Figure 11.4; the following sections offer more details, starting with planning your research.

FIGURE 11.4 The Research Process
By following a methodical research process, you can save time and money while uncovering better information.

1 Plan	2 Locate data and information	3 Process data and information	4 Apply your findings	5 Manage information
▪ Maintain research ethics and etiquette ▪ Familiarize yourself with the subject; develop problem statement ▪ Identify information gaps ▪ Prioritize research needs	▪ Evaluate sources ▪ Collect secondary information at the library, online, or elsewhere ▪ Document your sources ▪ Collect primary information through surveys and interviews	▪ Quote, paraphrase, or summarize textual information ▪ Analyze numerical information	▪ Summarize findings ▪ Draw conclusions ▪ Make recommendations	▪ Make research results available to others via your company's knowledge management system

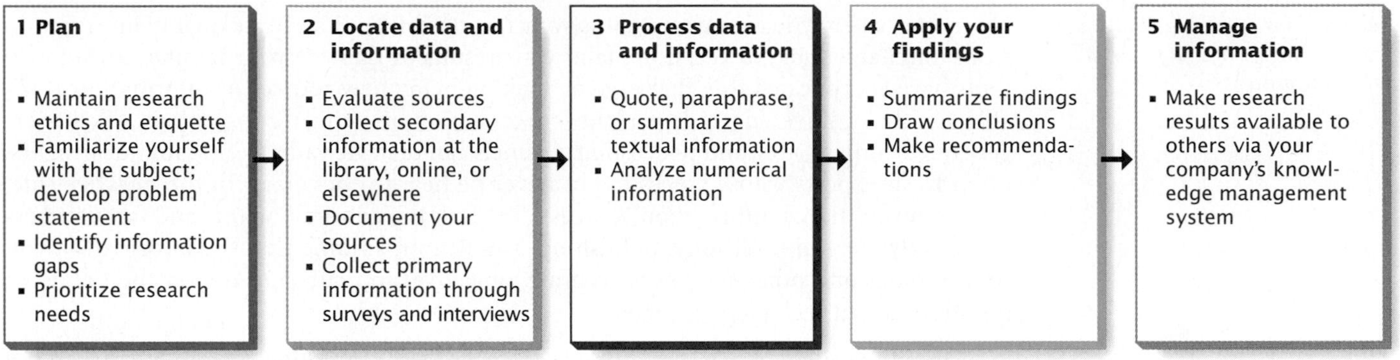

Planning Your Research

With so much information online these days, it's tempting just to punch some keywords into a search engine and then dig through the results, looking for something, anything, that looks promising. However, this haphazard approach limits your effectiveness.

To avoid expensive and embarrassing research mistakes, start by familiarizing yourself with the subject so that you can frame insightful questions. As you explore the general subject area, try to identify basic terminology, significant trends, important conflicts, influential people, and potential sources of information. Next, develop a **problem statement** that will define the purpose of your research. This statement should explicitly define the decision you need to make or the conclusion you need to reach at the end of the process. For example, Tesco's Richard Brasher might want to know whether consumers are starting to turn away from bottled water because of concerns about cost and the environmental impact of plastic packaging and transportation. His problem statement could be "We need to determine whether we should we reduce the number or variety of bottled water brands carried in our stores."

Before you begin your research project, recognize that research carries some significant ethical responsibilities. To avoid ethical lapses, keep the following points in mind:

- Don't force a specific outcome by skewing your research.
- Respect the privacy of your research participants.
- Document sources and give appropriate credit.
- Respect *intellectual property rights*, the ownership of unique ideas that have commercial value in the marketplace.[2]
- Don't distort information from your sources.
- Don't misrepresent who you are or what you intend to do with the research results.

In addition to ethics, research etiquette deserves careful attention, too. For example, respect the time of anyone who agrees to be interviewed or to be a research participant, and maintain courtesy throughout the interview or research process.

Locating Data and Information

The range of sources available to business researchers today is remarkable—almost overwhelming at times. If you have a question about an industry, a company, a market, a new technology, or a financial topic, chances are that somebody else has already researched the subject. Research conducted previously for another purpose is considered **secondary research** when the results are reused in a new project. This secondary information can be anything from magazine articles to survey results. Whenever it is available, review secondary research results that could apply to your research challenge; doing so might save you time and money. Before you use any secondary sources, however, you need to know whether you can trust them, as the following section explains. **Primary research** is

Researching without a plan wastes time and usually produces unsatisfactory results.

Guide your research with a clear problem statement that defines the purpose of your research.

Primary research contains information that you gather specifically for a new research project; secondary research contains information that others have gathered for other purposes.

new research done specifically for the current project and includes surveys, interviews, observations, and experiments.

Evaluating Sources

Evaluate your sources carefully to avoid embarrassing and potentially damaging mistakes.

No matter where you're searching, it is your responsibility to separate quality information from unreliable junk, so you don't taint your results or damage your reputation. Web 2.0 tools have complicated this challenge by making many new sources of information available. On the positive side, independent sources communicating through blogs, wikis, user-generated content sites, and podcasting channels can provide valuable and unique insights, often from experts whose voices might never be heard otherwise. On the negative side, these nontraditional information sources often lack the editorial boards and fact checkers commonly used in traditional publishing. You cannot assume that the information you find in blogs and other sources is accurate, objective, and current. Answer the following questions about each piece of material:

- **Does the source have a reputation for honesty and reliability?** Naturally, you can feel more comfortable using information from an established source that has a reputation for accuracy (see Figure 11.5). But don't let your guard down completely; even the finest reporters and editors can make mistakes. For sources that are new or relatively obscure, your safest bet is to corroborate anything you learn with information from several other sources.
- **Is the source potentially biased?** To interpret an organization's information, you need to know its point of view.
- **What is the purpose of the material?** For instance, was the material designed to inform others of new research, advance a political position, or promote a product? Was

FIGURE 11.5 Getting Information from Reliable Sources
The U.S. Census Bureau is a trusted source of information about people and businesses in the United States.

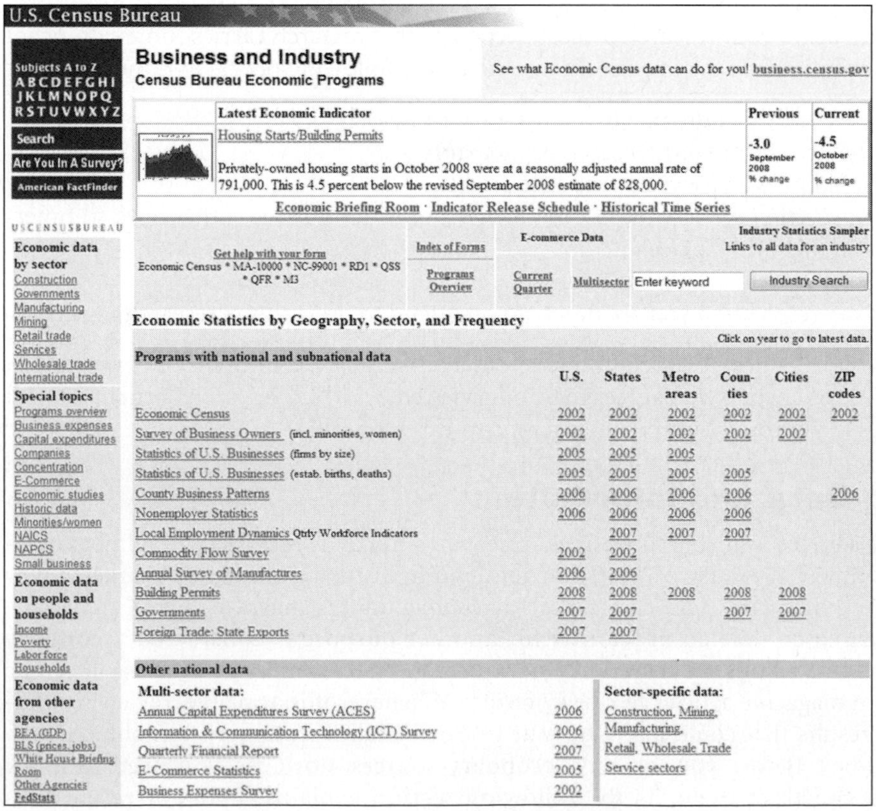

it designed to promote or sell a product? Be sure to distinguish among advertising, advocating, and informing. And don't lower your guard just because an organization has a reassuring name like the American Institute for the Advancement of All Things Good and Wonderful; many innocuously labeled groups advocate a particular line of political, social, or economic thinking.

- **Is the author credible?** Is the author a professional journalist? An informed amateur? Merely someone with an opinion?
- **Where did the source get its information?** Try to find out who collected the data, the methods they used, their qualifications, and their professional reputation.
- **Can you verify the material independently?** Verification can uncover biases or mistakes, which is particularly important when the information goes beyond simple facts to include projections, interpretations, and estimates. If you can't verify critical information, let your audience know that.
- **Is the material current?** Make sure you are using the most current information available by checking the publication date of a source.
- **Is the material complete?** Have you accessed the entire document or only a selection from it? If it's a selection, which parts were excluded? Do you need more detail?

You probably won't have time to conduct a thorough background check on all your sources, so focus your efforts on the most important or most suspicious pieces of information.

Conducting Secondary Research

Even if you intend to eventually conduct primary research, start with a review of any available secondary research. Inside the company, you might be able to find a variety of documents prepared for other projects that offer helpful information. Outside the company, business researchers can choose from a wide range of print and online resources. Table 11.3 provides a small sample of the many secondary resources available.[3]

Before you conduct primary research, see if there is any secondary research you can take advantage of first.

TABLE 11.3 Important Resources for Business Research

COMPANY, INDUSTRY, AND PRODUCT RESOURCES (URLs are provided for online resources)

AnnualReports.com (www.annualreports.com). Free access to annual reports from thousands of public companies.

Brands and Their Companies/Companies and Their Brands. Contains data on more than 430,000 consumer products and 100,000 manufacturers, importers, marketers, and distributors. Also available as an online database; ask at your library.

CNN/Money (http://money.cnn.com). News, analysis, and financial resources covering companies, industries, and world markets.

D&B Directories. A variety of directories, including *America's Corporate Families* (ownership connections among companies), *Business Rankings* (25,000 leading companies), *Directory of Service Companies* (more than 50,000 companies in the service sector), and *Industrial Guide* (more than 120,000 manufacturing companies).

Hoover's Handbook of American Business. Profiles of 750 influential public and private corporations.

Hoover's Online (www.hoovers.com). Database of 12 million companies worldwide, including in-depth coverage of 35,000 leading companies around the world. Basic information available free; in-depth information requires a subscription.

Manufacturing and Distribution USA. Data on thousands of companies in the manufacturing, wholesaling, and retailing sectors.

NAICS Codes (www.census.gov/eos/www/naics). North American Industry Classification System.

Reference USA. Concise information on millions of U.S. companies; subscription database.

SEC filing (www.sec.gov/edgar.shtml). SEC filings, including 10Ks, 10Qs, annual reports, and prospectuses for U.S. public firms.

Standard & Poor's Industry Surveys. Concise investment profiles for a broad range of industries. Coverage is extensive, with a focus on current situation and outlook. Includes some summary data on major companies in each industry. Also available in a subscription database, as part of the NetAdvantage product line.

(*continued*)

TABLE 11.3 Important Resources for Business Research *(continued)*

Standard & Poor's Register of Corporations, Directors, and Executives. Index of major U.S. and international corporations. Lists officers, products, sales volume, and number of employees. Also available in a subscription database, as part of the NetAdvantage product line.

Thomas's Register of American Manufacturers (www.thomasnet.com). Information on thousands of U.S. manufacturers, indexed by company name and product.

RESEARCH DIRECTORIES AND INDEXES

Books in Print. Database indexes nearly 20 million book, audio book, and video titles from around the world. Available in print and professional online versions.

Directories in Print. Information on more than 15,000 business and industrial directories.

Encyclopedia of Associations. Index of thousands of associations, listed by broad subject category, specific subject, association, and location. Available as an online database as well.

Reader's Guide to Periodical Literature. Classic index of general-interest magazines, categorized by subject and author; also available in electronic format, including a version with the full text of thousands of articles.

TRADEMARKS AND PATENTS

Official Gazette of the United States Patent and Trademark Office (www.uspto.gov). Weekly publication (one for trademarks and one for patents) providing official record of newly assigned trademarks and patents, product descriptions, and product names.

United States Patent and Trademark Office (www.uspto.gov). Trademark and patent information records.

STATISTICS AND OTHER BUSINESS DATA

Bureau of Economic Analysis (www.bea.gov). Large collection of economic and government data.

Europa—The European Union Online (http://europa.eu/index_en.htm). A portal that provides up-to-date coverage of current affairs, legislation, policies, and EU statistics.

FedStats (www.fedstats.gov). Access to a full range of statistics and information from more than 70 U.S. government agencies.

Industry Norms and Key Business Ratios (Dun & Bradstreet). Industry, financial, and performance ratios.

Information Please Almanac. Compilation of broad-range statistical data, with strong focus on labor force.

Annual Statement Studies. Industry, financial, and performance ratios published by the Risk Management Association.

Statistical Abstract of the United States (www.census.gov). Annual compendium of U.S. economic, social, political, and industrial statistics.

STAT-USA (www.stat-usa.gov). Large collection of economic and government data.

The World Almanac and Book of Facts. Facts on economic, social, educational, and political events for major countries.

U.S. Bureau of Labor Statistics (www.bls.gov). Extensive national and regional information on labor and business, including employment, industry growth, productivity, the Consumer Price Index (CPI), and the overall U.S. economy.

U.S. Census Bureau (www.census.gov). Demographic data and analysis on consumers and businesses based on census results.

COMMERCIAL DATABASES (Require subscriptions; check with your school library)

ABI/INFORM Trade & Industry. Access to more than 750 periodicals and newsletters that focus on specific trades or industries.

Business Source Premier (Ebsco). Access to a variety of databases on a wide range of disciplines from leading information providers.

Dialog. Hundreds of databases that include areas such as business and finance, news and media, medicine, pharmaceuticals, reference, social sciences, government and regulation, science and technology, and more.

HighBeam Research. Thousands of full-text newspaper, magazine, and newswire sources, plus maps and photographs.

Gale Business & Company Resource Center. A comprehensive research tool designed for undergraduate and graduate students, job searchers, and investors; offers a wide variety of information on companies and industries.

LexisNexis. Several thousand databases covering legal, corporate, government, and academic subjects.

ProQuest. Thousands of periodicals and newspapers; archives continue to expand through its program to digitize more than 5 billion pages of microfilm.

SRDS Media Solutions. A comprehensive database of magazine information and advertising rates, cataloging more than 100,000 U.S. and international media properties.

Finding Information at the Library

Public, corporate, and university libraries offer printed sources with information that is not available online and online sources that are available only by subscription. Libraries are also where you'll find one of your most important resources: librarians. Reference librarians are trained in research techniques and can often help you find obscure information you can't find on your own.

Libraries offer information and resources you can't find anywhere else—including experienced research librarians.

Whether you're trying to locate information in printed materials or in databases, each type of resource serves a special function:

- **Newspapers and periodicals.** Libraries offer access to a wide variety of popular magazines, general business magazines, *trade journals* (which provide information about specific professions and industries), and *academic journals* (which provide research-oriented articles from researchers and educators).
- **Business books.** Although less timely than newspapers and periodicals, business books provide in-depth coverage of a variety of business topics.
- **Directories.** Thousands of directories are published in print and electronic formats in the United States, and many include membership information for all kinds of professions, industries, and special-interest groups.
- **Almanacs and statistical resources.** Almanacs such as the *Statistical Abstract of the United States* (www.census.gov) are handy guides to factual and statistical information about countries, politics, the labor force, and other topics.
- **Government publications.** Information on laws, court decisions, tax questions, regulatory issues, and other governmental matters is often available in collections of government documents.
- **Electronic databases.** Databases offer vast collections of computer-searchable information, often in specific areas, such as business, law, science, technology, and education. Some libraries offer remote online access to some or all databases; for others, you need to visit in person.

Local, state, and federal government agencies publish a huge array of information that is helpful to business researchers.

Finding Information Online

3 LEARNING OBJECTIVE

Provide five guidelines for conducting an effective online search.

The Internet can be a tremendous source of business information, provided that you know where to look and how to use the tools available. **Search engines** identify individual webpages or files that either contain or are tagged with specific words or phrases. Search engines have the advantage of scanning millions or billions of individual webpages and using powerful ranking algorithms to present the pages that might be the most relevant to your search request. In addition, search engines such as Google Book Search now allow you to search through scanned copies of printed books (see Figure 11.6 on the next page).

For all their ease and power, though, search engines have three disadvantages you should be aware of: (1) no human editors are involved in evaluating the quality of the content on these pages; (2) various engines use different search techniques, so one engine might miss a site that another one finds; and (3) conventional search engines can't reach the content on restricted websites. These out-of-reach pages are sometimes called the *hidden Internet* or the *deep web* because regular search techniques can't access them. Fortunately, new search tools continue to reach more and more of this vast content; see the "Real-Time Updates–Learn More" link on this page.

Conduct online research with extreme care; much of the information online has not been subjected to the same quality controls common in traditional offline publishing.

The good news is that you can get around all three shortcomings of search engines, at least partly, although doing so is sometimes expensive. **Web directories** address the first major shortcoming of search engines by using human editors to categorize and evaluate websites. Directories such as those offered by Yahoo!, About, and the Open Directory Project at www.dmoz.org present lists of websites chosen by a team of editors. And as Chapter 7 points out, a number of directories (and search engines) specialize in specific media types, such as Technorati's focus on blogs.

REAL-TIME UPDATES
Learn More

See your way into the invisible Internet

These innovative search tools can access valuable information beyond the reach of conventional search engines. Go to **http://real-timeupdates.com/ebc** and click on "Learn More." If you are using mybcommlab, you can access Real-Time Updates within each chapter or under Student Study Tools.

FIGURE 11.6 Searching Printed Sources Online
The ability to search through printed texts electronically is a significant advantage for researchers in all subject areas. Google Book Search currently offers restricted previews but will soon offer full-access options.

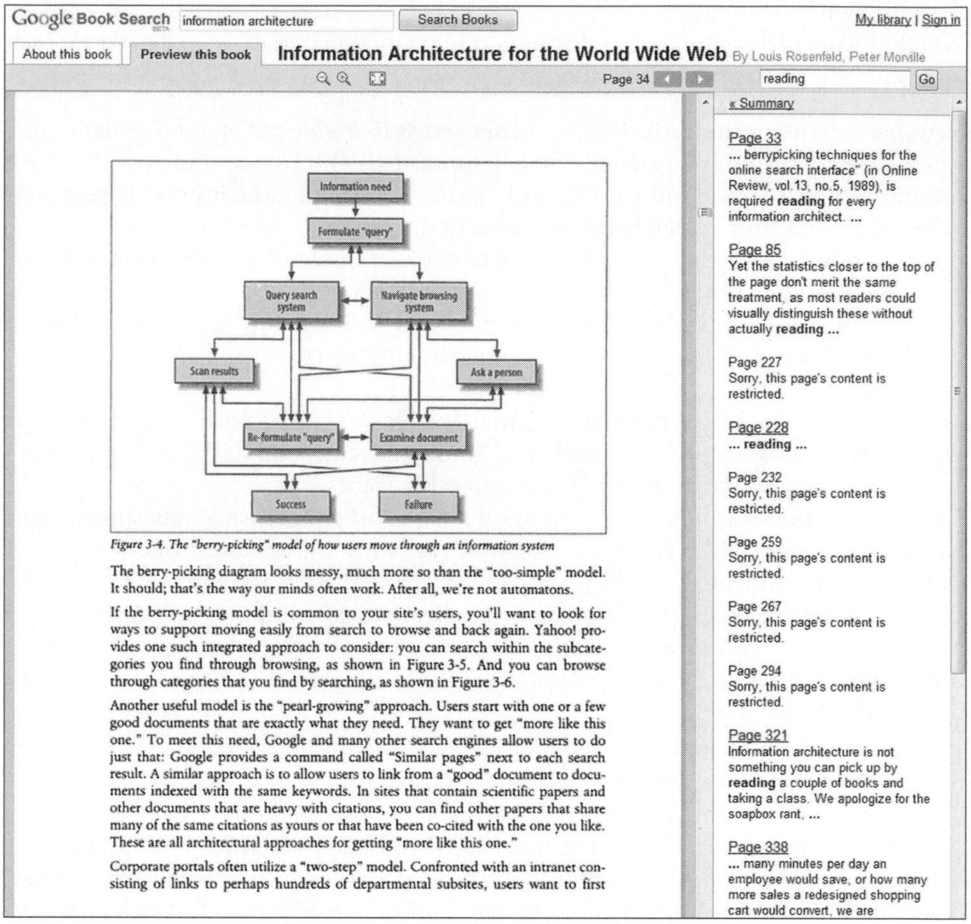

Web directories rely on human editors to evaluate and select websites.

Metacrawlers can save you time by employing multiple search engines at once.

Online databases give you access to some of the most important resource that search engines often can't reach: millions of newspaper, magazine, and journal articles.

Make sure you know how each search engine, directory, database, or metacrawler works before you use it.

Metasearch engines, or *metacrawlers* (such as Bovée and Thill's Web Search, at **http://businesscommunicationblog.com/websearch**), address the second shortcoming of search engines by formatting your search request for the specific requirements of multiple search engines and then telling you how many hits each engine was able to find for you. Table 11.4 lists some of the most popular search engines, metacrawlers, and directories.

Online databases help address the third shortcoming of search engines by offering access to newspapers, magazines, journals, and other resources. Some databases, such as High Beam (**www.highbeam.com**), are priced to attract individual users, whereas others, such as LexisNexis (**http://corporate.lexisnexis.com**) and ProQuest (**www.proquest.com**), are intended for use by companies, libraries, and other institutions. In addition to periodical databases, specialized databases such as Hoover's (**www.hoovers.com**) offer detailed information on thousands of companies. Also, you can obtain news releases at no charge from PRNewswire (**www.prnewswire.com**) and Business Wire (**www.businesswire.com**). Ask your librarian for advice on accessing all these resources.

As search engines, metacrawlers, and databases continue to multiply and offer new ways to find information, using them can become a challenge. Make sure you understand what each search tool expects from you before you enter your query. With a *keyword search*, the engine or database attempts to find items that include all the words you enter. A *Boolean search* lets you define a query with greater precision, using such operators as AND (the search must include the two terms linked by the AND), OR (the search can include either word or both words), or NOT (the search ignores items with whatever word comes after NOT). In contrast to keyword and Boolean searches, *natural language searches* let you

TABLE 11.4 The Broad Spectrum of Online Search Tools

GENERAL-PURPOSE SEARCH ENGINES			
AOL Search	http://search.aol.com	Google	www.google.com
AlltheWeb	www.alltheweb.com	Viewzi	www.viewzi.com
AltaVista	www.altavista.com	Windows Live Search	www.live.com
Ask.com	www.ask.com	Yahoo! Search	http://search.yahoo.com
METACRAWLERS, CLUSTERING ENGINES, AND HYBRID SITES			
Clusty	http://clusty.com	Search.com	www.search.com
Dogpile	www.dogpile.com	SurfWax	www.surfwax.com
ixquick	www.ixquick.com	WebBrain	www.webbrain.com
jux2	www.jux2.com	WebCrawler	www.webcrawler.com
KartOO	www.kartoo.com	Yahoo!	www.yahoo.com
Mamma	www.mamma.com	ZapMeta	www.zapmeta.com
MetaCrawler	www.metacrawler.com		
WEB DIRECTORIES AND ONLINE LIBRARIES			
About	www.about.com	Library of Congress	www.loc.gov/rr/business
Answers.com	www.answers.com	Library Spot	www.libraryspot.com
Beaucoup!	www.beaucoup.com	Open Directory Project	www.dmoz.com
CEOExpress	http://ceoexpress.com	Questia (requires subscription)	www.questia.com
Digital Librarian	www.digital-librarian.com/business.html	USA.gov (U.S. government portal)	www.usa.gov
Google Directory	www.google.com/dirhp	Virtual Learning Resources Center	www.virtuallrc.com
INFOMINE	http://infomine.ucr.edu		
Internet Public Library	www.ipl.org		
Librarians' Internet Index	http://lii.org		
NEWS SEARCH ENGINES AND SOCIAL TAGGING SITES			
10 × 10	http://tenbyten.org	Newseum	www.newseum.org
AlltheWeb News	http://www.alltheweb.com/?cat=news	NewsNow	www.newsnow.co.uk
		Topix	www.topix.net
AltaVista News	http://news.altavista.com	World News	www.wn.com
Delicious	http://delicious.com	Yahoo! News	http://news.yahoo.com
Digg	www.digg.com		
Google News	http://news.google.com		
BLOG, VIDEO, AND PODCAST SEARCH ENGINES AND DIRECTORIES			
American Rhetoric (speeches)	www.americanrhetoric.com	Podcast Bunker	www.podcastbunker.com
blinkx	www.blinkx.com	Podcast Pickle	www.podcastpickle.com
Bloglines	www.bloglines.com	Podcast Network	www.thepodcastnetwork.com
BlogPulse	www.blogpulse.com	podscope	www.podscope.com
Google Blog search	http://blogsearch.google.com	Technorati	www.technorati.com
Google Video search	http://video.google.com	Yahoo! Video search	http://video.search.yahoo.com
Podcast Alley	www.podcastalley.com	YouTube	www.youtube.com
PERIODICAL AND BOOK SEARCH ENGINES			
FindArticles.com	www.findarticles.com	Google Scholar	http://scholar.google.com
Google Book Search	http://books.google.com		

— REAL-TIME UPDATES
Learn More

A practical guide to selecting the best online search tools

Different research projects require different search tools, and this article provides great advice for selecting search tools based on the requirements of each project. Go to **http://real-timeupdates.com/ebc** and click on "Learn More." If you are using mybcommlab, you can access Real-Time Updates within each chapter or under Student Study Tools.

ask questions in everyday English. *Forms-based searches* help you create powerful queries by simply filling out an online form that lets you specify such parameters as date ranges, language, Internet domain name, and file and media types.[4]

To make the best use of any search engine or database, keep the following points in mind:

- **Read the instructions.** Unfortunately, there is no universal set of instructions that applies to every search tool, so visit the Help page for advice on how to use a particular tool most effectively.
- **Pay attention to the details.** For instance, some search engines treat *AND* (uppercase) as a Boolean search operator but ignore *and* (lowercase) and conjunctions and articles (called *stopwords*) because they are so common they show up in every webpage or database entry. Again, read the Help page to learn more.
- **Review the search and display options carefully.** For example, some article databases search only the title unless you specifically ask them to search through the article text as well—a distinction that dramatically affects your results.
- **Try variations of your terms.** If you can't find what you're looking for, try abbreviations (*CEO, CPA*), synonyms (*man, male*), related terms (*child, adolescent, youth*), different spellings (*dialog, dialogue*), singular and plural forms (*woman, women*), nouns and adjectives (*management, managerial*), and open and compound forms (*online, on line, on-line*).
- **Adjust the scope of your search, if needed.** If a search yields little or no information, broaden your search by specifying fewer terms. Conversely, if you're inundated with too many hits, use more terms to narrow your search.

Take advantage of the latest research technologies, including desktop and enterprise searches, research and content managers, social bookmarking sites, and newsfeeds.

As you conduct research throughout your career, keep an eye out for the latest technologies that can help you research more effectively and more efficiently. Current examples include desktop search engines that search all the files on your personal computer (PC) (see Figure 11.7), enterprise search engines that search all the PCs on a company's network, *research and content managers* such as the free Zotero extension for FireFox (www.zotero.com), *social tagging* or *bookmarking sites* such as Digg (http://digg.com) and Delicious (http://delicious.com), and newsfeeds from blogs and websites.

For more on the latest developments in online research tools, visit http://real-timeupdates.com/ebc and click on Chapter 11.

Documenting Your Sources

Proper documentation of the sources you use is both ethical and an important resource for your readers.

Documenting the sources you use in your writing serves three important functions: It properly and ethically credits the person who created the original material; it shows your audience that you have credible support for your message; and it helps your readers explore your topic in more detail, if desired. Be sure to take advantage of the source documentation tools in your word processing or note-management software, such as Microsoft's OneNote, or the bibliographic tools available in many online databases.

You can document your sources through footnotes, endnotes, or some similar system (see Appendix B, "Documentation of Report Sources"). Whatever method you choose, documentation is necessary for such sources as books, articles, tables, charts, diagrams, song lyrics, scripted dialogue, letters, speeches—and anything else you take from someone else, including ideas and information that you've reexpressed through paraphrasing or summarizing. However, you do not have to cite a source for general knowledge or for specialized knowledge that's generally known among your readers, such as the fact that Nike is a large sporting goods and sportswear company or that computers are pervasive in business today.

Copyright law covers the expression of creative ideas, and copyrights can cover a wide range of materials, including reports and other documents, web content, movies, musical compositions, lectures, computer programs, and even choreographed dance routines. Copyright protection is initiated the moment the expression is put into fixed form.

FIGURE 11.7 Desktop Search Engines
Desktop search engines are part of the new generation of software tools that can help businesspeople find vital information on personal computers. In this example using Copernic Desktop Search (**www.copernic.com**), a user searching for *agreements* found 127 documents in a variety of formats.

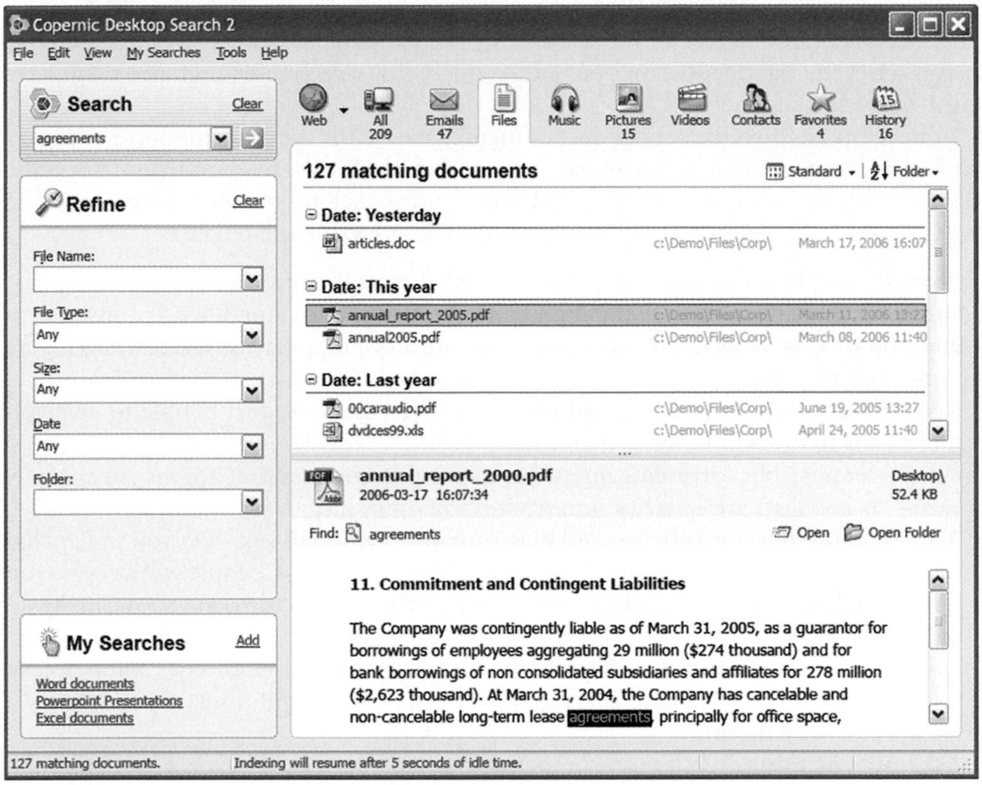

Copyright law does not protect such elements as titles, names, short phrases, slogans, familiar symbols, or lists of ingredients or contents. It also doesn't protect ideas, procedures, methods, systems, processes, concepts, principles, discoveries, or devices, although it does cover their description, explanation, or illustration.[5] However, many of the entities not covered under copyright law are covered under other legal protections, such as patents for devices and processes and trademarks for slogans.

Merely crediting the source is not always enough. According to the *fair use doctrine*, you can use other people's work only as long as you don't unfairly prevent them from benefiting as a result. For example, if you reproduce someone else's copyrighted questionnaire in a report you're writing, even if you identify the source thoroughly, you may be preventing the author from selling a copy of that questionnaire to your readers.

Conducting Primary Research

Surveys and interviews are the most common primary research techniques.

If secondary research can't provide the information and insights you need, you may need to gather the information yourself with primary research. The two most common primary research methods are surveys and interviews. (Other primary techniques are observations and experiments in special situations such as test marketing, but they're not commonly used for day-to-day business research.)

Conducting Surveys

A carefully prepared and conducted survey can provide invaluable insights, but only if it is *reliable* (would produce identical results if repeated) and *valid* (measures what it's supposed to measure). To avoid errors in design and implementation, consider hiring a research specialist for important surveys.

For a survey to produce valid results, it must be based on a representative sample of respondents.

When selecting people to participate in a survey, the most critical task is getting a representative *sample* of the entire population in question. For instance, if you want to know how U.S. consumers feel about something, you can't just survey a few hundred people in a shopping mall. Different types of consumers shop at different times of the day and different days of the week, and many consumers do not shop at malls. The online surveys you see on many websites today potentially suffer from the same *sampling bias*: They capture only the opinions of people who visit the sites and want to participate, which might not be a representative sample of the population. A good handbook on survey research will help you select the right people for your survey, including selecting enough people to have a statistically valid survey.[6]

To develop an effective survey questionnaire, start with the information needs you identified at the beginning of the research process. Then break these points into specific questions, choosing an appropriate type of question for each point (see Figure 11.8). The following guidelines will help you produce results that are valid and reliable:[7]

Provide clear instructions to prevent mistaken answers.

- **Provide clear instructions.** Entry mistakes will distort your results.
- **Don't ask for information that people can't be expected to remember.** For instance, a question such as "How many times did you go grocery shopping last year?" will generate unreliable answers.
- **Keep the questionnaire short and easy to answer.** Don't expect people to give you more than 10 or 15 minutes of their time.
- **Whenever possible, formulate questions to provide answers that are easy to analyze.** Numbers and facts are easier to summarize than opinions, for instance.
- **Avoid leading questions that could bias your survey.** If you ask, "Do you prefer that we stay open in the evenings for customer convenience?" many people will say yes even if they don't shop in the evenings. Instead, ask, "What time of day do you normally do your shopping?"
- **Avoid ambiguous questions.** If you ask, "Do you shop online often?" some people might interpret *often* to mean "every day," whereas others might think it means "once a week" or "once a month."
- **Ask only one thing at a time.** A compound question such as "Do you read books and magazines?" doesn't allow for the respondent who reads one but not the other.
- **Make the survey adaptive.** With an online survey, you can program the software to branch automatically based on audience inputs. Not only does this sort of real-time adaptation deliver better answers, but it reduces frustration for survey respondents as well.[8]

The Internet is now a preferred survey mechanism for many researchers, and dozens of companies offer online survey services (see Figure 11.9 on page 332).[9] Compared to traditional mail and in-person techniques, online surveys are usually faster to create, easier to administer, faster to analyze, and less expensive overall. The interactive capabilities of the web can enhance all kinds of surveys, from simple opinion polls to complex purchase simulations. However, don't let the speed and convenience of online surveys lower the requirements for careful planning; online surveys require the same care as any other type of survey, including being on guard against sampling bias.[10]

Conducting Interviews

Interviews are easy to conduct but require careful planning to produce useful results.

Getting in-depth information straight from an expert can be a great method for collecting primary information. Interviews can take a variety of formats, from e-mail exchanges to group discussions. For example, Tesco invites thousands of customers to visit its stores every year for meetings known as Customer Question Time, when it asks customers how the company can serve them better.[11]

Be aware that the answers you receive in an interview are influenced by the types of questions you ask, by the way you ask them, and by each subject's cultural and language background. Potentially significant factors include the person's race, gender, age, educational level, and social status.[12]

Choose question types that will generate the specific information you need.

Ask **open-ended questions** (such as "Why do you believe that South America represents a better opportunity than Europe for this product line?") to solicit opinions, insights,

FIGURE 11.8 **Types of Survey Questions**
For each question you have in your survey, choose the type of question that will elicit the most useful answers.

QUESTION TYPE	EXAMPLE
Open-ended	How would you describe the flavor of this ice cream?
Either-or	Do you think this ice cream is too rich? _____ Yes _____ No
Multiple choice	Which description best fits the taste of this ice cream? (Choose only one.) a. Delicious b. Too fruity c. Too sweet d. Too intense e. Bland f. Stale
Scale	Please mark an X on the scale to indicate how you perceive the texture of this ice cream. ◄————————————————► Too light Light Creamy Too creamy
Checklist	Which of the following ice cream brands do you recognize? (Check all that apply.) _____ Ben & Jerry's _____ Breyers _____ Carvel _____ Dreyer's _____ Häagen-Dazs
Ranking	Rank these flavors in order of your preference, from 1 (most preferred) to 5 (least preferred): _____ Vanilla _____ Cherry _____ Strawberry _____ Chocolate _____ Coconut
Short-answer	In the past 2 weeks, how many times did you buy ice cream in a grocery store? __________ In the past 2 weeks, how many times did you buy ice cream in an ice cream shop? __________

and information. Ask **closed questions** to elicit a specific answer, such as yes or no. However, don't use too many closed questions in an interview, or the experience will feel more like a simple survey and won't take full advantage of the interactive interview setting.

Think carefully about the sequence of your questions and the subject's potential answers so you can arrange questions in an order that helps uncover layers of information. Also consider providing the other person with a list of questions at least a day or two before the interview, especially if you'd like to quote your subject in writing or if your questions might require your subject to conduct research or think extensively about the answers. If you want to record the interview, ask the person ahead of time and respect his or her wishes.

FIGURE 11.9 Online Survey Tools
Online survey systems such as this one, offered by Object Planet, make it easy to create, administer, and analyze surveys.

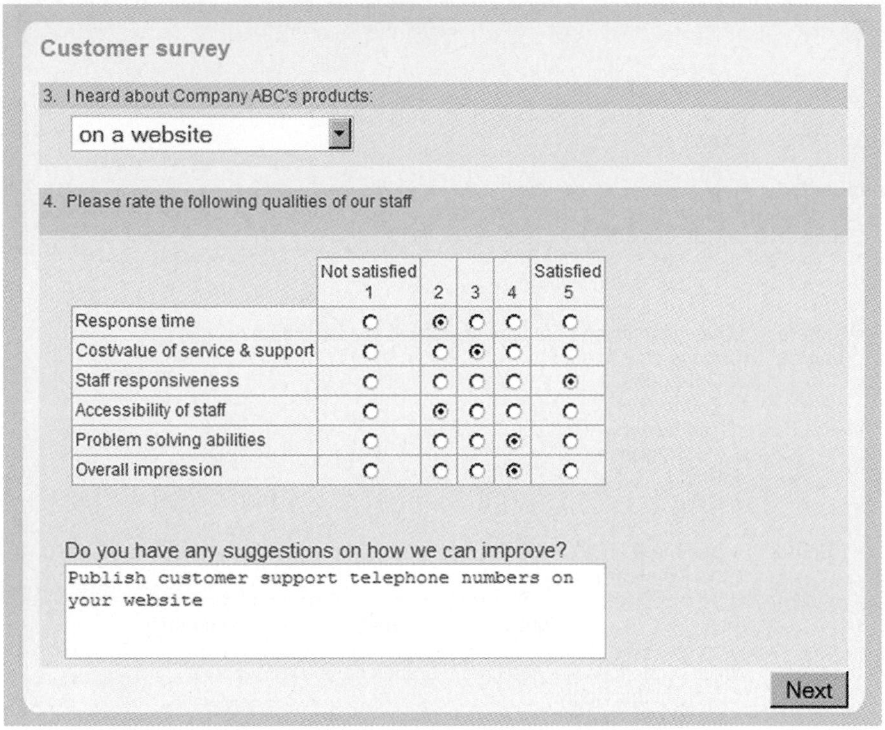

As soon as possible after the interview, take a few moments to write down your thoughts, go over your notes, and organize your material. Look for important themes, helpful facts or statistics, and direct quotes. If you made a tape recording, *transcribe* it (take down word for word what the person said) or take notes from the tape just as you would while listening to someone in person.

Face-to-face interviews give you the opportunity to gauge nonverbal responses.

Face-to-face interviews give you the opportunity to gauge the reaction to your questions and observe the nonverbal signals that accompany the answers, but interviews don't necessarily have to take place in person. E-mail interviews are becoming more common, partly because they give subjects a chance to think through their responses thoroughly rather than rushing to fit the time constraints of a face-to-face interview.[13] Also, e-mail interviews might be the only way you will be able to access some experts.

In addition to individual interviews, business researchers can also use a form of group interview known as the **focus group**. In this format, a moderator guides a group through a series of discussion questions while the rest of the research team observes through a one-way mirror. The key advantage of focus groups is the opportunity to learn from group

CHECKLIST: Conducting Effective Information Interviews

- Learn about the person you are going to interview.
- Formulate your main idea to ensure effective focus.
- Choose the length, style, and organization of the interview.
- Select question types to elicit the specific information you want.
- Design each question carefully to collect useful answers.
- Limit the number of questions you ask.
- Consider recording the interview if the subject permits.
- Review your notes as soon as the interview ends.

dynamics as the various participants bounce ideas and questions off each other. By allowing a group to discuss topics and problems in this manner, the focus group technique can uncover much richer information than a series of individual interviews.[14]

As a reminder of the tasks involved in interviews, see "Checklist: Conducting Effective Information Interviews."

Using Your Research Results

4 LEARNING OBJECTIVE

Describe the major tasks involved in processing and applying your research results.

After you've collected all the necessary secondary and primary information, the next step is to transform it into the specific content you need. For simple projects, you may be able to drop your material directly into your report, presentation, or other application. However, when you have gathered a significant amount of information or raw data from surveys, you need to process the material before you can use it. This step can involve analyzing numeric data; quoting, paraphrasing, or summarizing textual material; drawing conclusions; and making recommendations.

Analyzing Data

Mean, median, and mode provide insight into sets of data.

Business research often produces numeric data, but by themselves, these numbers might not provide the insights managers need in order to make good business decisions. Fortunately, even without advanced statistical techniques, you can use simple arithmetic to help extract meaning from sets of research data. Table 11.5 shows several answers you can gain about a collection of numbers, for instance. The **mean** (which is what most people refer to when they use the term *average*) is the sum of all the items in the group divided by the number of items in that group. The **median** is the "middle of the road," or the midpoint of a series, with an equal number of items above and below. The **mode** is the number that occurs more often than any other in the sample; it's the best answer to a question such as "What is the usual amount?" Each of the three measures can tell you different things about a set of data.

Trends suggest directions or patterns in a series of data points.

It's also helpful to look for **trends**, any repeatable patterns taking place over time, including growth, decline, and cyclical trends that vary between growth and decline. Trend analysis is common in business. By looking at data over a period of time, you can detect patterns and relationships that help you answer important questions. In addition, researchers frequently explore the relationships between subsets of data, using a technique called **cross-tabulation**. For instance, if you're trying to figure out why total sales rose or fell, you might look separately at sales data by age, gender, location, and product type.

Whenever you process numeric data, keep in mind that numbers are easy to manipulate and misinterpret, particularly with spreadsheets and other computer tools. Make sure to double-check all your calculations and document the operation of any spreadsheets you plan to share with colleagues. Also, step back and look at your entire set of data before proceeding with any analysis. Do the numbers make sense based on what you know about the subject?

TABLE 11.5 Three Types of Data Measures: Mean, Median, and Mode

Wilson	$3,000	
Green	5,000	
Carrick	6,000	
Cho	7,000	Mean
Keeble	7,500	Median
Lopes	8,500	Mode
O'Toole	8,500	Mode
Mannix	8,500	Mode
Caruso	9,000	
Total	$63,000	

Are there any individual data points that stand out as suspect? Business audiences like the clarity of numbers; it's your responsibility to deliver numbers they can count on.

Quoting, Paraphrasing, and Summarizing Information

Quoting a source means reproducing the content exactly and indicating who originally created the information.

You can use textual information from sources in three ways. *Quoting* a source means you reproduce it exactly as you found it, and you either set it off with quotation marks (for shorter passages) or extract it in an indented paragraph (for longer passages). Use direct quotations when the original language will enhance your argument or when rewording the passage would lessen its impact. However, try not to quote sources at great length. Too much quoting creates a choppy patchwork of varying styles and gives the impression that all you've done is piece together the work of other people.

Paraphrasing is expressing someone else's ideas in your own words.

You can often maximize the impact of secondary material in your own writing by *paraphrasing* it, restating it in your own words and with your own sentence structures.[15] Paraphrasing helps you maintain a consistent tone while using vocabulary familiar to your audience. Of course, you still need to credit the originator of the information, but not with quotation marks or indented paragraphs.

To paraphrase effectively, follow these tips:[16]

- Reread the original passage until you fully understand its meaning.
- Record your paraphrase on a note card or in an electronic format.
- Use language that your audience is familiar with.
- Check your version with the original source to verify that you have not altered the meaning.
- Use quotation marks to identify any unique terms or phrases you have borrowed exactly from the source.
- Record the source so that you can give proper credit if you use this material in your report.

Summarizing is similar to paraphrasing but distills the content into fewer words.

Summarizing is similar to paraphrasing but presents the gist of the material in fewer words than the original. An effective summary identifies the main ideas and major support points from your source material but leaves out most details, examples, and other information that is less critical to your audience. Summarizing is not always a simple task, and your audience will judge your ability to separate significant issues from less significant details. Identify the main idea and the key support points, and separate these from details, examples, and other supporting evidence (see Table 11.6).

TABLE 11.6 Summarizing Effectively

ORIGINAL MATERIAL (116 WORDS)	45-WORD SUMMARY	22-WORD SUMMARY
Our facilities costs spiraled out of control last year. The 23 percent jump was far **ahead of every other cost category in the company and many times higher than the 4 percent average rise for commercial real estate in the Portland metropolitan area. The rise can be attributed to many factors, but the major factors include repairs** (mostly electrical and structural problems at the downtown office), **energy** (most of our offices are heated by electricity, the price of which has been increasing much faster than for oil or gas), **and last but not least, the loss of two sublease tenants** whose rent payments made a substantial dent in our cost profile for the past five years. **Main idea** **Major support points** Details	**Our facilities costs jumped 23 percent last year,** far ahead of every other cost category in the company and many times higher than the 4 percent local average. The major factors contributing to the increase are repairs, energy, and the loss of two sublease tenants.	**Our facilities costs jumped 23 percent last year,** primarily because of rising repair and energy costs and the loss of sublease income.

Of course, all three approaches require careful attention to ethics. When quoting directly, take care not to distort the original intent of the material by quoting selectively or out of context. And never resort to plagiarism.

Drawing Conclusions

A **conclusion** is a logical interpretation of the facts and other information in a report. A sound conclusion is not only logical but flows from the information included in a report, meaning that it should be based on the information included in the report and shouldn't rely on information that isn't in the report. Moreover, if you or the organization you represent have certain biases that influence your conclusion, ethics obligate you to inform the audience accordingly.

Reaching good conclusions based on the evidence at hand is one of the most important skills you can develop in your business career. In fact, the ability to see patterns and possibilities that others can't see is one of the hallmarks of innovative business leaders. Consequently, take your time with this part of the process. Play "devil's advocate" against yourself, attacking your conclusion as an audience might to make sure it stands up to rigorous scrutiny.

Making Recommendations

Whereas a conclusion interprets information, a **recommendation** suggests action—what to do in response to the information. The following example illustrates the difference between a conclusion and a recommendation:

CONCLUSION	RECOMMENDATION
On the basis of its track record and current price, I conclude that this company is an attractive buy.	I recommend that we offer to buy the company at a 10 percent premium over the current market value of its stock.

To be credible, recommendations must be based on logical analysis and sound conclusions. They must also be practical and acceptable to the people who have to make your recommendations work. Finally, when making a recommendation, be certain that you have adequately described the steps needed to implement your recommendation.

PLANNING INFORMATIONAL REPORTS

5 LEARNING OBJECTIVE

Explain how to organize informational reports and website content.

Informational reports provide the material that employees, managers, and others need in order to make decisions, take action, and respond to dynamic conditions inside and outside the organization. Although these reports come in dozens of particular formats, they can be grouped into four general categories:

Informational reports are used to monitor and control operations, to implement policies and procedures, to demonstrate compliance, and to document progress.

- **Reports to monitor and control operations.** Managers rely on a wide range of reports to see how well their companies are functioning. *Plans* establish expectations and guidelines to direct future action. The most important of these are *business plans* (see "Sharpening Your Career Skills: Creating an Effective Business Plan"). Many business plans are actually a combination of an informational report (describing conditions in the marketplace), an analytical report (analyzing threats and opportunities and recommending specific courses of action), and a proposal (persuading investors to put money into the firm in exchange for a share of ownership). *Operating reports* provide feedback on a wide variety of an organization's functions, including sales, inventories, expenses, shipments, and so on. *Personal activity reports* provide information regarding an individual's experiences during sales calls, industry conferences, market research trips, and so on.
- **Reports to implement policies and procedures.** Reports are the most common vehicle for conveying guidelines, approved procedures, and other organizational decisions. *Policy reports* range from brief descriptions of business procedures to manuals that are

—REAL-TIME UPDATES
Learn More

Step-by-step advice for developing a successful business plan

Take advantage of the Small Business Administration's comprehensive guide to preparing a business plan. Go to **http://real-timeupdates.com/ebc** and click on "Learn More." If you are using mybcommlab, you can access Real-Time Updates within each chapter or under Student Study Tools.

dozens or hundreds of pages long. *Position papers* outline an organization's official position on issues that affect the company's success.

- **Reports to demonstrate compliance.** Businesses are required to submit a variety of *compliance reports,* from tax returns to reports that describe the proper handling of hazardous materials.
- **Reports to document progress.** Supervisors, investors, and customers frequently expect to be informed of the status of projects and other activities via *progress reports.*

Figure 11.10 shows the major subcategories within each of the three major report categories, along with examples of the more common types.

Sharpening Your Career Skills

Creating an Effective Business Plan

The most important report you may ever get the chance to write is a business plan for a new company. A comprehensive business plan forces you to think about personnel, marketing, facilities, suppliers, distribution, and a host of other issues that are vital to your success. If you are starting out on a small scale and using your own money, your business plan may be relatively informal. But at a minimum, you should describe the basic concept of the business and outline its specific goals, objectives, and resource requirements. A formal plan, suitable for use with banks or investors, should cover these points:

- **Summary.** In one or two pages, summarize your business concept. Describe your product or service and its market potential. Highlight some things about your company and its owners that will distinguish your firm from the competition. Summarize your financial projections and the amount of money investors can expect to make on their investment. Be sure to indicate how much money you will need and what it will be spent on.
- **Mission and objectives.** Explain the purpose of your business and what you hope to accomplish—and before you take another step, make sure that this is a mission you can pursue with passion, through thick and thin, with every ounce of commitment and energy you can muster.
- **Company and industry.** Give full background information on the origins and structure of your venture and the characteristics of its industry.
- **Products or services.** Give a complete but concise description of your products or services, focusing on their unique attributes. Explain how customers will benefit from using your products or services instead of those of your competitors.
- **Market and competition.** Provide data that will persuade investors that you understand your target market and can achieve your sales goals. Be sure to identify the strengths and weaknesses of your competitors.
- **Management.** Summarize the background and qualifications of the key management personnel in your company. Include résumés in an appendix.
- **Marketing strategy.** Provide projections of sales and market share and outline a strategy for identifying and contacting customers, setting prices, providing customer services, advertising, and so forth. Whenever possible, include evidence of customer acceptance, such as advance product orders.
- **Design and development plans.** If your product requires design or development, describe the nature and extent of what needs to be done, including costs and possible problems.
- **Operations plan.** Provide information on the facilities, equipment, and labor needed.
- **Overall schedule.** Forecast development of the company in terms of completion dates for major aspects of the business plan.
- **Critical risks and problems.** Identify all negative factors and discuss them honestly.
- **Financial projections and requirements.** Include a detailed budget of start-up and operating costs, as well as projections for income, expenses, and cash flow for the first three years of business. Identify the company's financing needs and potential sources.
- **Exit strategy.** Explain how investors will be able to cash out or sell their investment, such as through a public stock offering, sale of the company, or a buyback of the investors' interest.

A complete business plan obviously requires a considerable amount of work. However, by thinking your way through all these issues, you'll enjoy a smoother launch and a greater chance of success in your new adventure.

CAREER APPLICATIONS

1. Why is it important to identify critical risks and problems in a business plan?
2. Many experts suggest that you write a business plan yourself rather than hire a consultant to write it for you. Why is this a good idea?

FIGURE 11.10 **Common Types of Business Reports and Proposals**
You will have the opportunity to read and write many types of reports in your career; here are some of the most common.

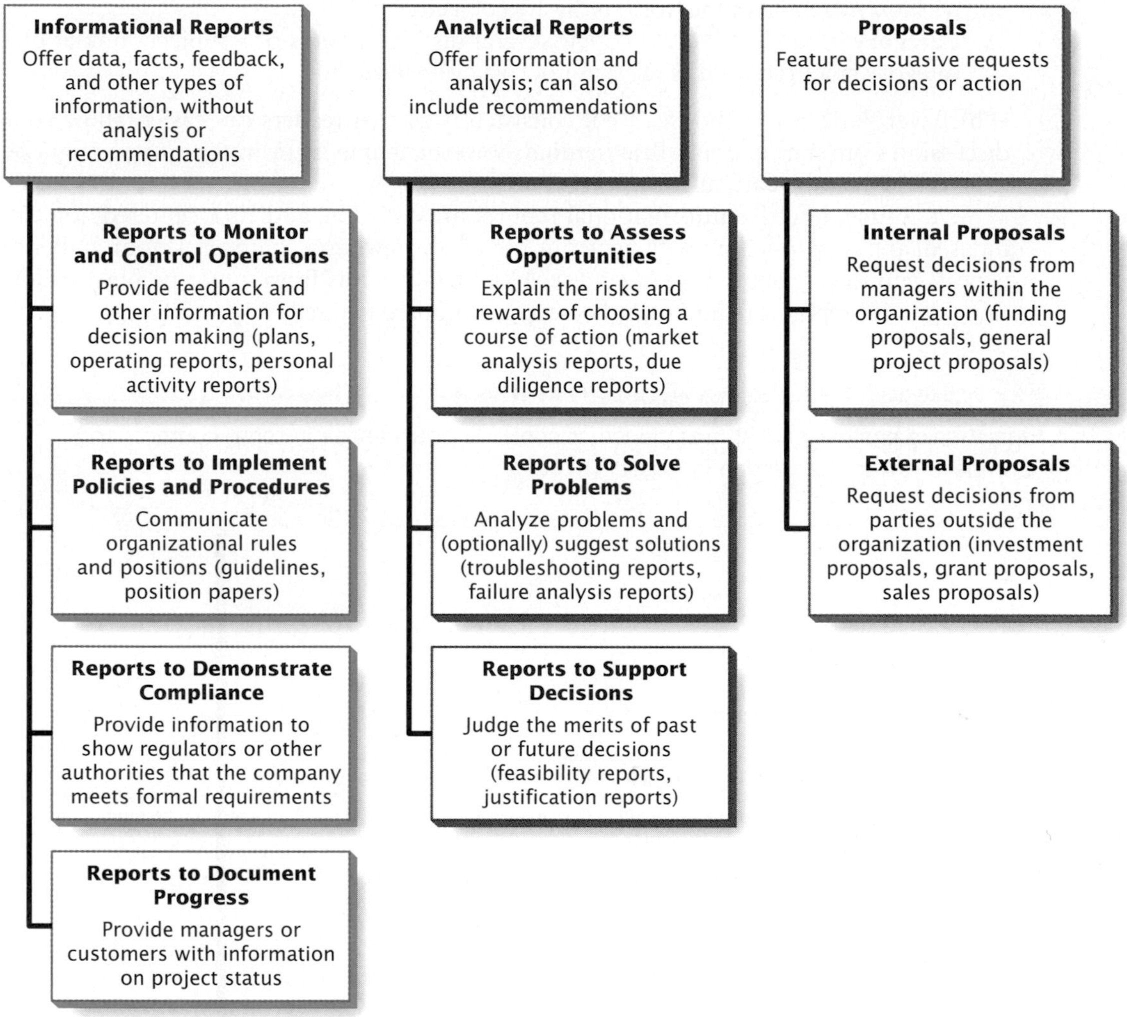

Organizing Informational Reports

Informational reports usually use a topical organization.

In most cases, the direct approach is the best choice for informational reports. However, if the information is both surprising and disappointing, such as a project that is behind schedule or over budget, you might consider using the indirect approach to build up to the bad news. Most informational reports use a **topical organization**, arranging material in one of the following ways:

- **Comparison.** If you need to show similarities and differences (or advantages and disadvantages) between two or more entities, organize your report in a way that helps your readers see those similarities and differences clearly.
- **Importance.** Build up from the least important item to most important, or start with the most important item and progress to the least important if you suspect readers are interested in only the most important items.
- **Sequence.** Describe processes or procedures by following the individual steps or stages in order.
- **Chronology.** Describe a development or an event by the order in which things occurred.

- **Spatial orientation.** Describe physical objects or spaces from left to right (or right to left, in some cultures), top to bottom, or outside to inside—in whatever order makes the most sense.
- **Geography.** If location is important, organize your study according to geography, perhaps by region of the world or by area of a city.
- **Category.** If you're asked to review several distinct aspects of a subject, look at one category at a time, such as sales, profit, cost, or investment.

Whichever pattern you choose, use it consistently so that readers can easily follow your discussion from start to finish. Bear in mind, however, that in many instances, you might be expected to follow a particular organization.

Of course, effective informational reports must also be audience centered, logical, focused, and easy to follow, with generous use of previews and summaries. Your audience expects you to sort out the details and separate major points from minor points. In addition, effective reports are honest and objective (compare Figures 11.11 and 11.12).

FIGURE 11.11 Ineffective Informational Report

While this report looks professional at first glance, it contains weaknesses in tone, content, and formatting. Compare it with the version in Figure 11.12.

MEMO

TO: Jeff Black and HR staff
FROM: Carrie Andrews *Ca*
DATE: March 14, 2010
SUBJECT: Recruiting and hiring seminar

Last week I attended an American Management Association seminar on recruiting, screening, and hiring new employees. I got enough useful information to warrant updating our online personnel handbook and perhaps developing a quick training session for all interviewing teams to avoid some of the stupid mistakes we've made in the past. Here's a quick look at the things I learned.

We should avoid legal mistakes, screen and interview applicants more effectively, and measure applicants more accurately. We need to write recruiting ads that accurately portray job openings and that don't discriminate. We need to sort through résumés more efficiently while still looking for telltale signs of false information. And we need more information on which types of preemployment tests are most effective.

I learned how best to comply with the Americans with Disabilities Act and how to use an employment agency effectively and safely (without risk of legal entanglements). The conference also covered how to screen and interview applicants more effectively, how to avoid interview questions that could get us into legal trouble, and when and how to check criminal records. In addition, I learned which drug-testing issues and recommendations affect us.

As you can see, the seminar addressed a lot of important information. I attended six sessions in all to gather exactly the information we needed. We covered the basic guidelines for much of this already, but a number of specific recommendations and legal concepts should be emphasized. Also, over the 4 day conference, I attended three workshop lunches that addressed specific applications for much of what was presented during the regular sessions. I was amazed by the valuable information I received in addition to the cruise-ship-style buffet lunches. The food was fantastic.

Updating the personnel handbook will take a couple of weeks, but we don't have any immediate hiring plans. Contact me if you need any information before then. Everyone will have a lot to review to get up to speed. Also, we have a lot of new information that may well affect our need to train the interviewing team members.

Please don't hesitate to e-mail me or drop by to discuss this matter.

Fails to state why Andrews attended the seminar

Injects inappropriate personal opinion and criticism

Does nothing to help readers focus on what is important

Uses running text instead of bullets, making it difficult for readers to identify the new knowledge

Fails to present pertinent material in a way that would be meaningful and useful to readers

Wastes time on some unimportant activities, such as how many sessions were offered during the seminar and what the lunches were like

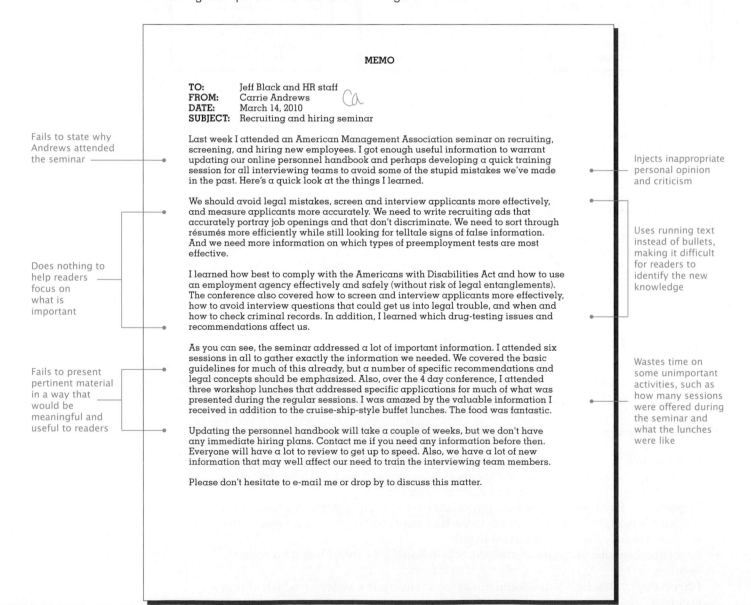

FIGURE 11.12 Effective Informational Report
This version of the report is much easier to read than the version in Figure 11.11 and presents pertinent information in a clear, concise way.

MEMO

TO: Jeff Black and HR staff
FROM: Carrie Andrews Ca
DATE: March 14, 2010
SUBJECT: Important insights from recruiting and hiring seminar

Captures reader interest with descriptive subject line

States Andrews's reason for attending the seminar

As you all know, the process of recruiting, screening, and hiring new employees presents a number of legal risks. Because we don't have an in-house lawyer to help us make every decision, it's important for all of us to be aware of what is legally acceptable and what isn't.

Last week I attended an American Management Association seminar on this subject. I received enough useful information to warrant updating our online personnel handbook and perhaps developing a quick training session for all interviewing teams. Here's a quick look at the things I learned.

Uses lists to help readers focus on key points

AVOIDING LEGAL MISTAKES
- How to write recruiting ads that accurately portray job openings and that don't discriminate
- How best to comply with the Americans with Disabilities Act
- How to use an employment agency effectively and safely (without risk of legal entanglements)

SCREENING AND INTERVIEWING MORE EFFECTIVELY
- How to sort through résumés more efficiently (including looking for telltale signs of false information)
- How to avoid interview questions that could get us into legal trouble
- When and how to check criminal records

MEASURING APPLICANTS
- Which types of pre-employment tests have been proven most effective
- Which drug-testing issues and recommendations affect us

As you can see, the seminar addressed some important topics. Our handbook addresses basic guidelines for much of this already, but it could be improved with a number of specific recommendations and legal concepts.

Respects readers' time by not including irrelevant information

Concludes with information that the recipients need, along with an estimate of when it will be available

Updating the personnel handbook will take a couple of weeks, but we don't have any immediate hiring plans. I'll keep the seminar handouts and my notes on my desk, in case you want to read them. After I've updated the handbook, we can get together and decide whether we need to train the interviewing team members. Although we have a lot of new information, we can highlight what people need to be aware of and let them read the new sections as their schedules allow.

If you have any questions in the meantime, don't hesitate to e-mail me or drop by my office.

Organizing Website Content

Many websites, particularly company websites, function as informational reports, offering sections with information about the company, its history, its products and services, its executive team, and so on. While most of what you've already learned about informational reports applies to website writing, the online experience requires some special considerations and practices.

As you begin to plan a website, start by recognizing the unique nature of online communication:

- **Web readers are demanding.** If site visitors can't find what they're looking for in a matter of minutes, they'll leave and look elsewhere.[17]
- **Reading online can be difficult.** Studies show that reading speeds are about 25 percent slower on a monitor than on paper.[18] Reading from computer screens can also be

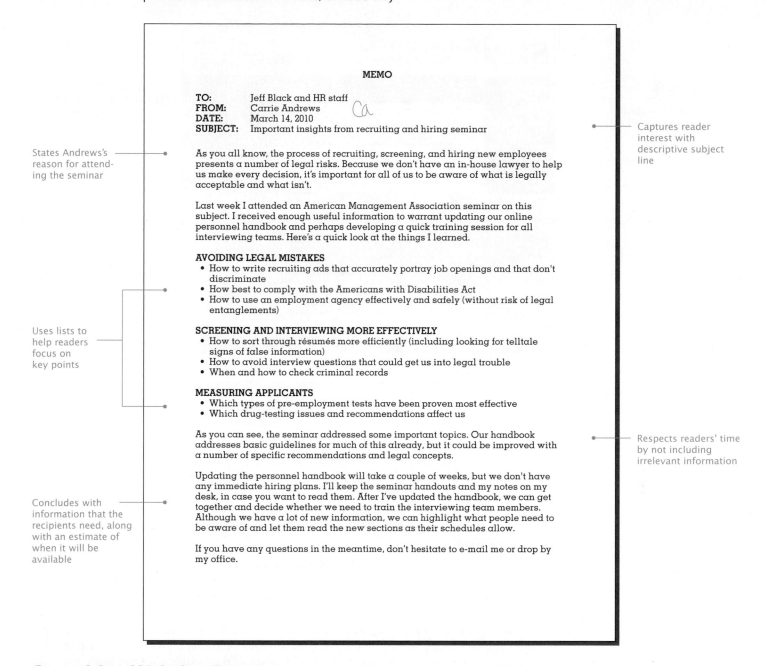

FIGURE 11.13 Information Architecture
The website of the U.S. Small Business Administration uses clearly defined and labeled navigation choices to help site visitors quickly find the information they need.

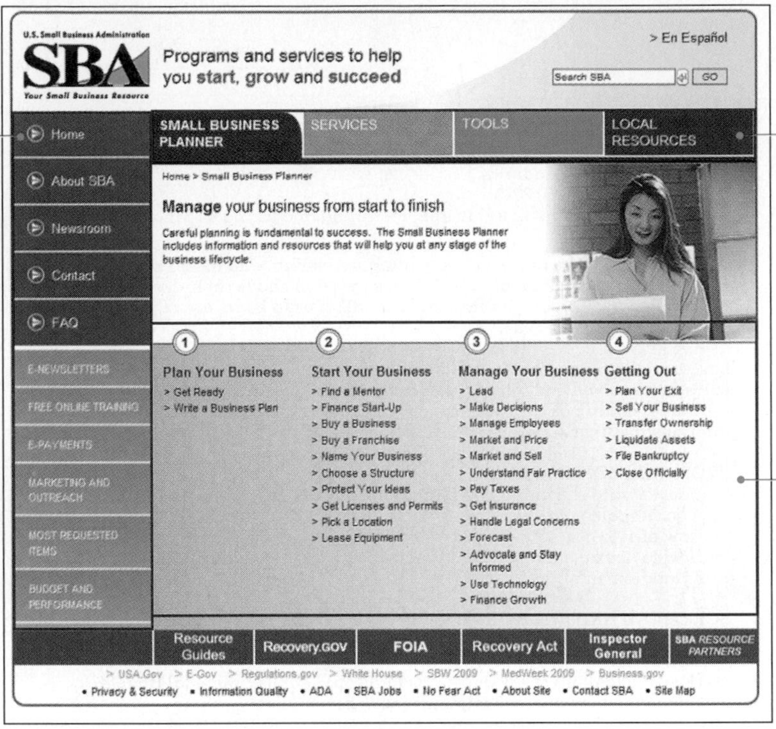

tiring on the eyes, even to the point of causing headaches, double vision, blurred vision, and other physical problems.[19]

- **The web is a nonlinear, multidimensional medium.** Readers of online material move around in any order they please; there often is no beginning, middle, or end. As a web writer, you need to anticipate the various paths your readers will want to follow and to make sure you provide the right hyperlinks in the right places to help readers explore successfully.

Many websites have multiple audiences and multiple communication functions, so planning websites is more challenging than planning printed reports. Professional website designers often use the term **information architecture** to describe the structure and navigational flow of all the parts of a website (see Figure 11.13). In a sense, the information architecture is a three-dimensional outline of the site, showing (1) the vertical hierarchy of pages from the homepage down to the lower level, (2) the horizontal division of pages across the various sections of the site, and (3) the links that tie all these pages together, both internally (between various pages on the site) and externally (between your site and other websites).

To organize your site effectively, keep the following advice in mind:

- Design the information architecture before you develop content.
- Let your readers be in control; give them clearly labeled pathways that let them explore on their own.
- Break your information into small chunks that are linked together logically.

6 LEARNING OBJECTIVE

Discuss three major ways to organize analytical reports, and explain how to plan proposals.

PLANNING ANALYTICAL REPORTS

The purpose of analytical reports is to analyze, to understand, to explain—to think through a problem or an opportunity and figure out how it affects the company and how the company should respond. In many cases, you'll also be expected to make a recommendation based on your analysis. As you saw in Figure 11.10, analytical reports fall into three basic categories:

Analytical reports are used to assess opportunities, solve problems, and support decisions.

- **Reports to assess opportunities.** Every business opportunity carries some degree of risk and also requires a variety of decisions and actions in order to capitalize on the opportunity. You can use analytical reports to assess risk and required decisions and actions. For instance, *market analysis reports* are used to judge the likelihood of success for new products or sales. *Due diligence reports* examine the financial aspects of a proposed decision, such as acquiring another company.
- **Reports to solve problems.** Managers often ask for *troubleshooting reports* when they need to understand why something isn't working properly and what needs to be done to fix it. A variation, the *failure analysis report*, studies events that happened in the past, with the hope of learning how to avoid similar failures in the future.
- **Reports to support decisions.** *Feasibility reports* are called for when managers need to explore the ramifications of a decision they're about to make, such as switching materials used in a manufacturing process. *Justification reports* explain a decision that has already been made.

Writing analytical reports presents a greater challenge than writing informational reports because you need to use your reasoning abilities and persuasive skills in addition to your writing skills. With analytical reports, you're doing more than simply delivering information: You're also thinking through a problem or an opportunity and presenting your conclusions in a compelling and persuasive manner. Finally, because analytical reports often convince other people to make significant financial and personnel decisions, your reports carry the added responsibility of the consequences of these decisions.

To help define the problem that your analytical report will address, answer these questions:

Clarify the problem in an analytical report by determining what you need to analyze, why the issue is important, who is involved, where the trouble is located, and how and when the problem started.

- What needs to be determined?
- Why is this issue important?
- Who is involved in the situation?
- Where is the trouble located?
- How did the situation originate?
- When did it start?

Not all of these questions apply in every situation, but asking them helps you define the problem being addressed and limits the scope of your discussion.

Also try **problem factoring**, dividing the problem into a series of logical, connected questions that try to identify cause and effect. When you speculate on the cause of a problem, you're forming a **hypothesis**, a potential explanation that needs to be tested. By subdividing a problem and forming hypotheses based on available evidence, you can tackle even the most complex situations.

Use problem factoring to divide a complex problem into more manageable pieces.

As with all other business messages, the best organizational structure for each analytical report depends largely on your audience's likely reaction. The three basic structures involve focusing on conclusions, focusing on recommendations, and focusing on logic (see Table 11.7 on the next page).

Before you choose an approach, determine whether your audience is receptive or skeptical.

Focusing on Conclusions

When writing for audiences that are likely to accept your conclusions—either because they've asked you to perform an analysis or they trust your judgment—consider using a direct approach that focuses immediately on your conclusions. This structure communicates the main idea quickly, but it presents some risks. Even if audiences trust your judgment, they may have questions about your data or the methods you used. Moreover, starting with a conclusion may create the impression that you have oversimplified the situation. You're generally better off taking the direct approach in a report only when your credibility is high—when your readers trust you and are willing to accept your conclusions (see Figure 11.14 on the next page).

Focusing on conclusions is often the best approach when you're addressing a receptive audience.

TABLE 11.7 Common Ways to Structure Analytical Reports

ELEMENT	FOCUS ON CONCLUSIONS OR RECOMMENDATIONS	FOCUS ON LOGICAL ARGUMENT: USE 2 + 2 = 4 MODEL	FOCUS ON LOGICAL ARGUMENT: USE YARDSTICK MODEL
Reader mindset	Are likely to accept	Hostile or skeptical	Hostile or skeptical
Approach	Direct	Indirect	Indirect
Writer credibility	High	Low	Low
Advantages	Readers quickly grasp conclusions or recommendations	Works well when you need to show readers how you built toward an answer by following clear logical steps	Works well when you have a list of criteria (standards) that must be considered in a decision; alternatives are all measured against the same criteria
Drawbacks	Structure can make topic seem too simple	Can make report longer	Readers must agree on criteria; can be lengthy because of the need to address each criterion for every alternative

FIGURE 11.14 Preliminary Outline of a Research Report Focusing on Conclusions
Cynthia Zolonka works on the human resources staff of a bank in Houston, Texas. Her company decided to have an outside firm handle its employee training, and a year after the outsourcing arrangement was established, Zolonka was asked to evaluate the results. Her analysis shows that the outsourcing experiment was a success; she opens with that conclusion and supports it with clear evidence. Readers who accept the conclusion can stop reading, and those who desire more information can continue.

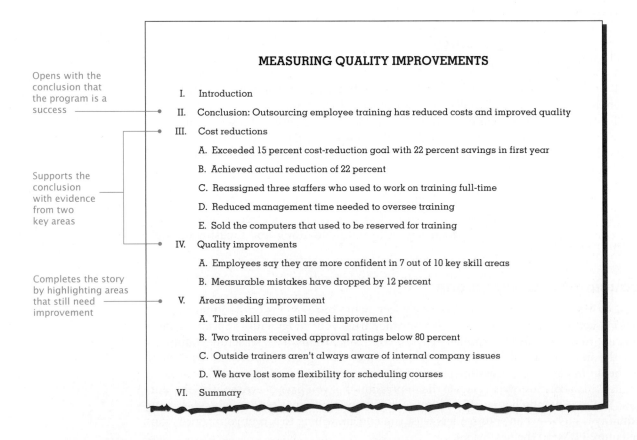

MEASURING QUALITY IMPROVEMENTS

I. Introduction

II. Conclusion: Outsourcing employee training has reduced costs and improved quality

Opens with the conclusion that the program is a success

III. Cost reductions

- A. Exceeded 15 percent cost-reduction goal with 22 percent savings in first year
- B. Achieved actual reduction of 22 percent
- C. Reassigned three staffers who used to work on training full-time
- D. Reduced management time needed to oversee training
- E. Sold the computers that used to be reserved for training

IV. Quality improvements

- A. Employees say they are more confident in 7 out of 10 key skill areas
- B. Measurable mistakes have dropped by 12 percent

Supports the conclusion with evidence from two key areas

V. Areas needing improvement

- A. Three skill areas still need improvement
- B. Two trainers received approval ratings below 80 percent
- C. Outside trainers aren't always aware of internal company issues
- D. We have lost some flexibility for scheduling courses

Completes the story by highlighting areas that still need improvement

VI. Summary

Focusing on Recommendations

A slightly different approach is useful when your readers want to know what they ought to do in a given situation (as opposed to what they ought to conclude). You'll often be asked to solve a problem or assess an opportunity rather than just study it. The actions you want your readers to take become the main subdivisions of your report.

When readers want to know what you think they should do, organize your report to focus on recommendations.

When structuring a report around recommendations, use the direct approach as you would for a report that focuses on conclusions. Then unfold your recommendations using a series of five steps:

1. Establish the need for action in the introduction by briefly describing the problem or opportunity.
2. Introduce the benefit(s) that can be achieved if the recommendation is adopted, along with any potential risks.
3. List the steps (recommendations) required to achieve the benefit, using action verbs for emphasis.
4. Explain each step more fully, giving details on procedures, costs, and benefits; if necessary, also explain how risks can be minimized.
5. Summarize your recommendations.

Focusing on Logical Arguments

When readers are skeptical or hostile to the conclusion or recommendation you plan to make, use an indirect approach that logically builds toward your conclusion or recommendation. If you guide the audience along a rational path toward the answer, they are more likely to accept it when they encounter it. The two most common logical approaches are known as the *2 + 2 = 4 approach* and the *yardstick approach.*

Logical arguments can follow two basic approaches: 2 + 2 = 4 (adding everything up) and the yardstick method (comparing ideas against a predetermined set of standards).

The 2 + 2 = 4 Approach

The 2 + 2 = 4 approach is so named because it convinces readers of your point of view by demonstrating that everything adds up. The main points in your outline are the main reasons behind your conclusions and recommendations. You support each reason with the evidence you collected during your analysis. With its natural feel and versatility, the 2 + 2 = 4 approach is generally the most persuasive and efficient way to develop an analytical report for skeptical readers, so try this structure first. You'll find that most of your arguments fall naturally into this pattern.

Try using the 2 + 2 = 4 approach; it's familiar and easy to develop.

As national sales manager of a New Hampshire sporting goods company, Binh Phan was concerned about his company's ability to sell to its largest customers. His boss, the vice president of marketing, shared these concerns and asked Phan to analyze the situation and recommend a solution. As Phan says, "We sell sporting goods to retail chains across the country. Large nationwide chains such as Sports Authority have been revolutionizing the industry, but we haven't had as much success with these big customers as we've had with smaller companies that operate strictly on a local or regional basis. With more and more of the industry in the hands of the large chains, we knew we had to fix the situation."

Phan's troubleshooting report appears in Figure 11.15 on the next page. The main idea is that the company should establish separate sales teams for these major accounts rather than continue to service them through the company's four regional divisions. However, Phan knew his plan would be controversial because it required a big change in the company's organization and in the way sales reps are paid. His thinking had to be clear and easy to follow, so he used the 2 + 2 = 4 approach to focus on his reasons.

The Yardstick Approach

The **yardstick approach** is useful when you need to use a number of criteria to decide which option to select from two or more possibilities. With this approach, you begin by discussing the problem or opportunity, and then you list the criteria that will guide the decision. The body of the report then evaluates the alternatives against those criteria.

The yardstick approach compares alternatives to a set of predetermined standards without conducting experiments or evaluating hypotheses.

FIGURE 11.15 Analytical Report Using the 2 + 2 = 4 Approach
To make his logical argument clear and compelling, Binh Phan used the 2 + 2 = 4 approach.

MEMO

TO: Robert Mendoza, Vice President of Marketing
FROM: Binh Phan, National Sales Manager BP
DATE: September 12, 2010
SUBJECT: Major accounts sales problems

As you requested on August 20, this report outlines the results of my investigation into the recent slowdown in sales to major accounts and the accompanying rise in sales- and service-related complaints from some of our largest customers.

Over the last four quarters, major account sales dropped 12%, whereas overall sales were up 7%. During the same time, we've all noticed an increase in both formal and informal complaints from larger customers, regarding how confusing and complicated it has become to do business with us.

My investigation started with in-depth discussions with the four regional sales managers, first as a group and then individually. The tension I felt in the initial meeting eventually bubbled to the surface during my meetings with each manager. Staff members in each region are convinced that other regions are booking orders they don't deserve, with one region doing all the legwork only to see another region get the sale, the commission, and the quota credit.

I followed up these formal discussions by talking informally and exchanging e-mail with several sales representatives from each region. Virtually everyone who is involved with our major national accounts has a story to share. No one is happy with the situation, and I sense that some reps are walking away from major customers because the process is so frustrating.

The decline in sales to our major national customers and the increase in their complaints stem from two problems: (1) sales force organization and (2) commission policy.

ORGANIZATIONAL PROBLEMS

When we divided the national sales force into four geographical regions last year, the idea was to focus our sales efforts and clarify responsibilities for each prospective and current customer. The regional managers have gotten to know their market territories very well, and sales have increased beyond even our most optimistic projections.

However, while solving one problem, we have created another. In the past 12 to 18 months, several regional customers have grown to national status, and a few retailers have taken on (or expressed interest in) our products. As a result, a significant portion of both current sales and future opportunities lies with these large national accounts.

I uncovered more than a dozen cases in which sales representatives from two or more regions found themselves competing with each other by pursuing the same customers from different locations. Moreover, the complaints from our major accounts about overlapping or nonexistent account coverage are a direct result of the regional organization. In some cases, customers aren't sure which of our representatives they're supposed to call with problems and orders. In other cases, no one has been in contact with them for several months.

- Clarifies who requested the report, when it was requested, and who wrote it
- Highlights the serious nature of the problem
- Explains how the information used in the analysis was collected
- Organizational problems are the first "2" in Phan's 2 + 2 = 4 approach
- Describes the first problem and explains how it occurred, without blaming anyone personally

(continued)

Figure 11.16 on page 346 is an outline of a feasibility report that uses the yardstick approach, using five criteria to evaluate two alternative courses of action.

The yardstick approach has two potential drawbacks. First, your audience needs to agree with the criteria you're using in your analysis. If they don't, they won't agree with the results of the evaluation. If you have any doubt about their agreement, build consensus before you start your report, if possible, or take extra care to explain why the criteria you're using are the best ones in this particular case. Second, the yardstick approach can get a little boring when you have many options to consider or many criteria to compare them against. One way to minimize the repetition is to compare the options in tables and then highlight the most unusual or important aspects of each alternative in the text so that you get the best of both worlds. This approach allows you to compare all the alternatives against the same yardstick while calling attention to the most significant differences among them.

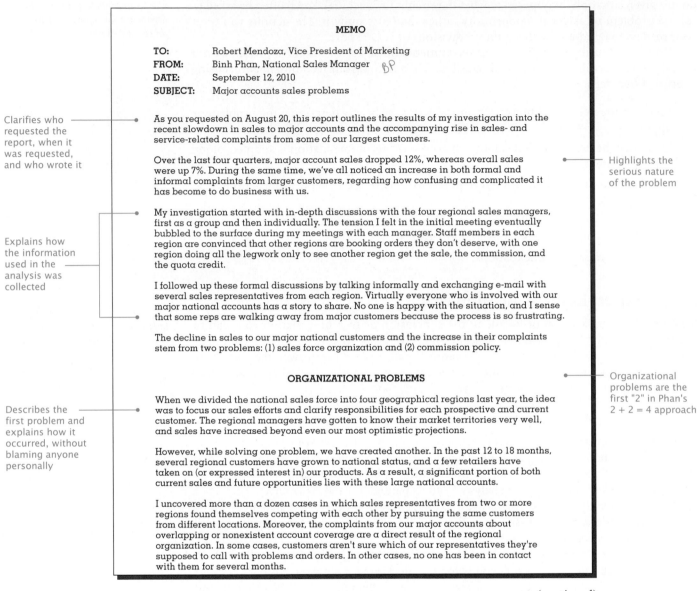

FIGURE 11.15 *(continued)*

2

For example, having retail outlets across the lower tier of the country, AmeriSport received pitches from reps out of our West, South, and East regions. Because our regional offices have a lot of negotiating freedom, the three were offering different prices. But all AmeriSport buying decisions were made at the Tampa headquarters, so all we did was confuse the customer. The irony of the current organization is that we're often giving our weakest selling and support efforts to the largest customers in the country.

Brings the first problem to life by complementing the general description with a specific example

COMMISSION PROBLEMS

Commission problems are the second "2" in Phan's 2 + 2 = 4 approach

The regional organization problems are compounded by the way we assign commissions and quota credit. Salespeople in one region can invest a lot of time in pursuing a sale, only to have the customer place the order in another region. So some sales rep in the second region ends up with the commission on a sale that was partly or even entirely earned by someone in the first region. Therefore, sales reps sometimes don't pursue leads in their regions, thinking that a rep in another region will get the commission.

Simplifies the reader's task by maintaining a parallel structure for the discussion of the second problem: a general description followed by a specific example

For example, Athletic Express, with outlets in 35 states spread across all four regions, finally got so frustrated with us that the company president called our headquarters. Athletic Express has been trying to place a large order for tennis and golf accessories, but none of our local reps seem interested in paying attention. I spoke with the rep responsible for Nashville, where the company is headquartered, and asked her why she wasn't working the account more actively. Her explanation was that last time she got involved with Athletic Express, the order was actually placed from their L.A. regional office, and she didn't get any commission after more than two weeks of selling time.

RECOMMENDATIONS

Phan concludes the 2 + 2 = 4 approach: organizational problems + commission problems = the need for a new sales structure

Our sales organization should reflect the nature of our customer base. To accomplish that goal, we need a group of reps who are free to pursue accounts across regional borders—and who are compensated fairly for their work. The most sensible answer is to establish a national account group. Any customers whose operations place them in more than one region would automatically be assigned to the national group.

Explains how the new organizational structure will solve both problems

In addition to solving the problem of competing sales efforts, the new structure will also largely eliminate the commission-splitting problem because regional reps will no longer invest time in prospects assigned to the national accounts team. However, we will need to find a fair way to compensate regional reps who are losing long-term customers to the national team. Some of these reps have invested years in developing customer relationships that will continue to yield sales well into the future, and everyone I talked to agrees that reps in these cases should receive some sort of compensation. Such a "transition commission" would also motivate the regional reps to help ensure a smooth transition from one sales group to the other. The exact nature of this compensation would need to be worked out with the various sales managers.

Acknowledges that the recommended solution does create a temporary compensation problem, but expresses confidence that a solution to that can be worked out

3

SUMMARY

The regional sales organization is effective at the regional and local levels but not at the national level. We should establish a national accounts group to handle sales that cross regional boundaries. Then we'll have one set of reps who are focused on the local and regional levels and another set who are pursuing national accounts.

Neatly summarizes both the problem and the recommended solution

To compensate regional reps who lose accounts to the national team, we will need to devise some sort of payment to reward them for the years of work invested in such accounts. This can be discussed with the sales managers once the new structure is in place.

FIGURE 11.16 Outline of an Analytical Report Using the Yardstick Approach
This report was provided by J. C. Hartley, a market analyst for a large Sacramento company that makes irrigation equipment for farms and ranches. "We've been so successful in the agricultural market that we're starting to run out of customers to sell to," says Hartley. "To keep the company growing, we needed to find another market. Two obvious choices to consider were commercial buildings and residences, but we needed to evaluate them carefully before making a decision."

Main Idea: We should move into the commercial irrigation equipment market but not into the residential market.

I. Introduction
II. Criteria for entering new markets
  A. Size and growth
  B. Profit potential
  C. Ability to compete
  D. Distribution costs and opportunities
  E. Fit with current capabilities
III. Irrigation equipment trends
  A. Water shortages leading to demand for more efficient irrigation
  B. Labor costs encouraging automation
  C. More homeowners attempting do-it-yourself projects
IV. Comparison of new market opportunities
  A. Commercial landscapers and building owners
    1. Size and growth
    2. Profit potential
    3. Ability to compete
    4. Distribution costs and opportunities
    5. Fit with current capabilities
  B. Residential landscapers and homeowners
    1. Size and growth
    2. Profit potential
    3. Ability to compete
    4. Distribution costs and opportunities
    5. Fit with current capabilities
V. Recommendations
  A. Enter the commercial segment
    1. Select a test market
    2. Learn from the test and refine our approach
    3. Roll out product marketing nationwide
  B. Do not attempt to enter the residential market at this point

Establishes the five criteria (the standards or rules) that will be used in the evaluation; these criteria are the "yardstick" in the yardstick approach

Gives readers important background information about current trends in the marketplace

Evaluates the two alternatives by judging them according to the five criteria

Recommends in favor of one alternative but against the other, based on how each alternative was judged according to the criteria

PLANNING PROPOSALS

The specific formats for proposals are innumerable, but they can be grouped into two general categories. *Internal proposals* request decisions from managers within the organization, such as proposals to buy new equipment or launch new research projects. *External proposals* request decisions from parties outside the organization. Examples of external proposals include *investment proposals*, which request funding from external investors; *grant proposals*, which request funds from government agencies and other sponsoring organizations; and *sales proposals*, which suggest individualized solutions for potential customers and request purchase decisions.

Buyers solicit proposals by publishing a request for proposals (RFP).

The most significant factor in planning a proposal is whether the recipient has asked you to submit a proposal. *Solicited proposals* are generally prepared at the request of external parties that require a product or a service, but they may also be requested by such internal sources as management or the board of directors. Some external parties prepare a formal invitation to bid on their contracts, called a **request for proposals (RFP)**, which

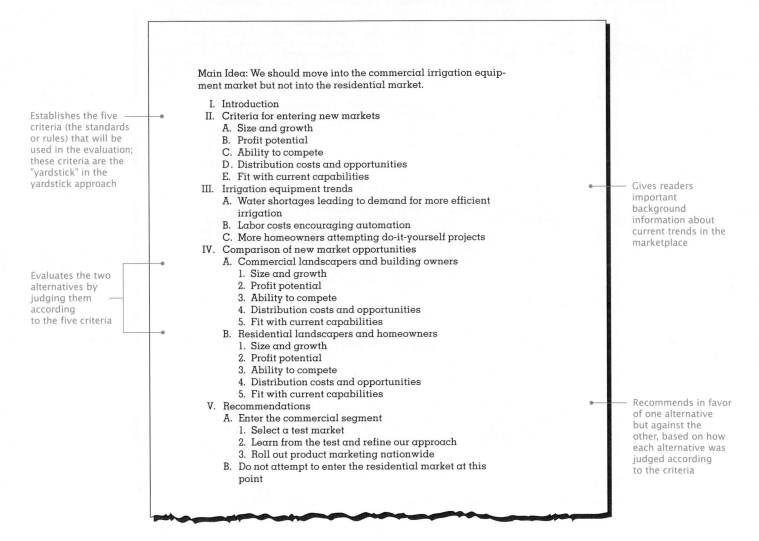

FIGURE 11.17 Internal Proposal
Shandel Cohen's internal proposal seeks management's approval to install an automatic mail-response system. Because the company manufactures computers, she knows that her boss won't object to a computer-based solution. Also, because profits are always a concern, her report emphasizes the financial benefits of her proposal.

MEMO

TO: Jamie Engle
FROM: Shandel Cohen SC
DATE: July 8, 2010
SUBJECT: Saving $145k/year with an automated e-mail response system

Catches the reader's attention with a compelling promise in subject line

THE PROBLEM:
Expensive and Slow Response to Customer Information Requests

Our new product line has been very well received, and orders have surpassed our projections. This very success, however, has created a shortage of printed brochures, as well as considerable overtime for people in the customer response center. As we introduce upgrades and new options, our printed materials quickly become outdated. If we continue to rely on printed materials for customer information, we have two choices: Distribute existing materials (even though they are incomplete or inaccurate) or discard existing materials and print new ones.

Describes the current situation and explains why it should be fixed

THE SOLUTION:
Automated E-Mail Response System

Explains the proposed solution in enough detail to make it convincing, without burdening the reader with excessive detail

With minor additions and modifications to our current e-mail system, we can set up an automated system to respond to customer requests for information. This system can save us time and money and can keep our distributed information current.

Automated e-mail response systems have been tested and proven effective. Many companies already use this method to respond to customer information requests, so we won't have to worry about relying on untested technology. Using the system is easy, too: Customers simply send a blank e-mail message to a specific address, and the system responds by sending an electronic copy of the requested brochure.

Benefit #1: Always-Current Information

Builds reader interest in the proposed solution by listing a number of compelling benefits

Rather than discard and print new materials, we would only need to keep the electronic files up to date on the server. We could be able to provide customers and our field sales organization with up-to-date, correct information as soon as the upgrades or options are available.

Benefit #2: Instantaneous Delivery

Almost immediately after requesting information, customers would have that information in hand. Electronic delivery would be especially advantageous for our international customers. Regular mail to remote locations sometimes takes weeks to arrive, by which time the information may already be out of date. Both customers and field salespeople will appreciate the automatic mail-response system.

Benefit #3: Minimized Waste

With our current method of printing every marketing piece in large quantities, we discard thousands of pages of obsolete catalogs, data sheets, and other materials every year. By maintaining and distributing the information electronically, we would eliminate this waste. We would also free up a considerable amount of expensive floor space and shelving that is required for storing printed materials.

(continued)

includes instructions that specify exactly the type of work to be performed or products to be delivered, along with budgets, deadlines, and other requirements. Suppose that the National Aeronautics and Space Administration (NASA) decides to develop a new satellite. The agency prepares an RFP that specifies exactly what the satellite should accomplish, and it sends the RFP to several aerospace companies, inviting them to bid on the job. The companies respond by preparing proposals that show how they would meet NASA's needs. In most cases, organizations that issue RFPs also provide strict guidelines on what the

FIGURE 11.17 *(continued)*

2

Of course, some of our customers may still prefer to receive printed materials, or they may not have access to electronic mail. For these customers, we could simply print copies of the files when we receive such requests. The new Xerox DocuColor printer just installed in the Central Services building would be ideal for printing high-quality materials in small quantities.

Benefit #4: Lower Overtime Costs

Acknowledges one potential shortcoming with the new approach but provides a convincing solution to that as well

In addition to saving both paper and space, we would also realize considerable savings in wages. Because of the increased interest in our new products, we must continue to work overtime or hire new people to meet the demand. An automatic mail response system would eliminate this need, allowing us to deal with fluctuating interest without a fluctuating workforce.

Cost Analysis

The necessary equipment and software cost approximately $15,000. System maintenance and upgrades are estimated at $5,000 per year. However, those costs are offset many times over by the predicted annual savings:

Itemizes the cost savings in order to support the $145k/year claim made in the subject line

Printing	$100,000
Storage	25,000
Postage	5,000
Wages	20,000
Total	**$150,000**

Based on these figures, the system would save $130,000 the first year and $145,000 every year after that.

CONCLUSION

Summarizes the benefits and invites further discussion

An automated e-mail response system would yield considerable benefits in both customer satisfaction and operating costs. If you approve, we can have it installed and running in 6 weeks. Please give me a call if you have any questions.

Document Makeover

Improve This Report

To practice correcting drafts of actual documents, visit the "Document Makeovers" section in mybcommlab. Refer to the User Guide for specific instructions on how to access the content for this chapter. You will find an informational report that contains problems and errors related to what you've learned in this chapter about planning business reports and proposals. Use the "Final Draft" decision tool to create an improved version of this personal activity report. Check the report for parallel construction, appropriate headings, suitable content, positive and bias-free language, and use of the "you" attitude.

proposals should include, and you need to follow these guidelines carefully in order to be considered. RFPs can seem surprisingly picky, even to the point of specifying the size of paper to use, but you must follow every detail.

Unsolicited proposals offer more flexibility but a completely different sort of challenge than solicited proposals because recipients aren't expecting to receive them. In fact, your audience may not be aware of the problem or opportunity you are addressing, so before you can propose a solution, you might first need to convince your readers that a problem or an opportunity exists. Consequently, using an indirect approach is often a wise choice for unsolicited proposals.

Regardless of its format and structure, a good proposal explains what a project or course of action will involve, how much it will cost, and how the recipient and his or her organization will benefit. You can see all these elements in Figure 11.17, which starts on the previous page.

On the Job: Solving Communication Dilemmas at Tesco

As a market development manager working for Richard Brasher, you are responsible for a variety of research, planning, and customer communication projects. Using what you've learned in this chapter about effective research methods and report planning, choose appropriate solutions to these challenges.

1. Tesco has created several online stores (see **www.tesco.com**) and would like to expand the number of consumers who order goods and services online. Which of the following problem statements best encapsulates the research that would be needed to devise a plan to attract more online shoppers?

a. Why aren't more consumers buying online?
b. We need to identify whether consumers are buying similar goods and services from competitive websites.
c. We need to understand the behavior of Tesco shoppers—and potential shoppers—in much more detail.
d. We need to identify potential changes to our business strategy and tactics that would prompt more consumers to purchase from Tesco online stores.

2. Which of the following research methods should Tesco use to find out what U.S. consumers think of the Tesco brand name?

a. Conduct a telephone survey of a carefully selected sample of U.S. residents.
b. Interview a dozen or so experts in consumer psychology to see what they think about Tesco; they're likely to know much more about how consumers respond to brands than consumers themselves.
c. Put a brief survey on Tesco's website. Consumers visiting the site are obviously interested in the company, so they are well positioned to comment on it.
d. Conduct a thorough review of all U.S. magazine and newspaper articles published in the past 12 months, looking specifically for mentions of Tesco.

3. Shoppers often make purchase decisions in the store rather than arriving with a preset list of specific brands to purchase. Brasher would like more information on why consumers choose one brand over another while standing in front of an array of products on the shelf. Is it the brand name? Something about the packaging? The price? Other factors? Which would be the best way to collect this information from at least 500 shoppers?

a. Install hidden cameras at strategic locations throughout a selected group of Tesco stores; be sure to record audio as well so you can hear what families discuss as they make product selections.
b. In a selection of stores covering neighborhoods that represent Tesco's overall market, attach brief survey forms to several hundred products throughout each store. Shoppers can fill out the surveys while they wait in the checkout line and hand them to the cashier.
c. Position data collection personnel throughout a representative selection of stores and interview shoppers just after they've made product selections.
d. Mail survey forms to 500 U.S. households selected at random.

4. Even though you have been with the company for only three months, you've learned quickly and believe that you have a solid understanding of Tesco's strategic challenges and opportunities. Brasher recently assigned you to write an analytical report on competition in the U.S. grocery market. His directive was to study the major players in the market and assess each one's strengths and weaknesses in preparation for Tesco's major rollout across the country. The report will be distributed to all top executives in the company. In the course of your research, however, you conclude that the entire strategy is a mistake and that the competition in the U.S. market is too strong for Tesco to make any sort of meaningful progress. You believe the company will waste millions, perhaps billions, of dollars on the venture. How should you handle this unexpected conclusion?

a. The decision to enter the U.S. market has already been made, and it's not your job to question it. Don't mention this conclusion at all in your report.
b. Discuss your concerns with Brasher before you write your first draft and don't add this conclusion to your report unless he instructs you do to so.
c. Your conclusion is more important than following Brasher's instructions to the letter. Moreover, your discovery is too important to keep from the executive team. Organize your report with the direct approach, opening immediately with your conclusion and then offering supporting evidence and reasons.
d. Add your conclusion to the report but organize the report indirectly. Insert your surprising conclusion at the very end of the report, after you've discussed the competitive situation in detail.

LEARNING OBJECTIVES CHECKUP

Assess your understanding of the principles in this chapter by reading each learning objective and studying the accompanying exercises. For fill-in-the-blank items, write the missing text in the blank provided; for multiple-choice items, circle the letter of the correct answer. You can check your responses against the answer key on page AK-2.

Objective 11.1: Adapt the three-step writing process to reports and proposals.

1. Why is it particularly important in long reports to clearly identify your purpose before you begin writing?
   a. A clear statement of purpose helps you avoid extensive revisions.
   b. A clear statement of purpose gives you the opportunity to decline projects that don't match your skill set or professional interests.
   c. A clear statement of purpose helps you avoid time-consuming research.
   d. All of the above are important factors.

2. What does it mean to define the *scope* of a project when you're preparing a work plan?
   a. The scope is the range of your investigation and subsequent reporting; you address all the important topics within the defined scope of your project and ignore issues that are outside your scope.
   b. The scope refers to the level of detail, in much the same way that microscopes and telescopes provide varying levels of detail.
   c. Scope indicates how long you'll spend on the project.
   d. None of the above are correct.

3. ______ reports focus on the delivery of facts, figures, and other types of information, without making recommendations or proposing new ideas or solutions.

4. ______ reports assess a situation or problem and recommend a course of action in response.

5. ______ present persuasive messages that encourage readers to take a specific course of action.

Objective 11.2: Describe an effective process for conducting business research, and explain the difference between primary and secondary research.

6. Which of the following is the appropriate first step in any research project?
   a. Evaluate secondary research to see if you can reuse anything from earlier research projects.
   b. Conduct a preliminary phone survey to measure the extent of the issue you're about to research.
   c. Conduct a thorough statistical analysis of any existing data.
   d. Develop a research plan by familiarizing yourself with the subject, identifying information gaps, and prioritizing research needs.

7. Consider this series of values: 14, 37, 44, 44, 44, 74, 76, 88, 93, 100, and 112.
   a. The mean is 66.
   b. The median is 74.
   c. The mode is 44.
   d. All of the above are correct.

8. Research being conducted for the first time is called ______ research.

9. Research that was conducted for other projects but is being considered for a new project is called ______ research.

10. Secondary research is
    a. Generally used before primary research
    b. Generally used after primary research
    c. Generally used at the same time as primary research
    d. Another name for unpaid research

11. Why does information found on the Internet need to be used with extreme care?
    a. Most sources on the Internet are false.
    b. You can be sued for using anything found online.
    c. Online sources often lack the fact-checking and other quality control procedures usually found in traditional offline publishing.
    d. Online information often contains computer viruses.

12. Why is it important to understand the purpose for which source material was created?
    a. Knowing the purpose helps alert you to any potential biases.
    b. You are required to indicate this purpose in your bibliography.
    c. The purpose tells you whether the material is copyrighted.
    d. The purpose tells you whether you need to pay usage rights.

13. If you uncover critically important information (the sort that could make or break your company) that is from a credible source and appears to be unbiased, well documented, current, and complete but is the only source of this information you can find, how should you handle this situation in your subsequent reporting?
    a. Use it as you would use any other information.
    b. Use it but clearly indicate the source in your report.
    c. Use it but clearly indicate in your report that this is the only source of the information and you weren't able to verify it through a second, independent source.
    d. Don't use it.

Objective 11.3: Provide five guidelines for conducting an effective online search.

14. Why is it important to fully understand the instructions for using an individual search engine, web directory, database, or other computer-based research tool?
    a. You can be fined if you use these tools improperly.
    b. Most search tools don't return any results if you don't know how to use them.
    c. Using the tool without understanding how it works can produce unpredictable and misleading results.
    d. Today's search tools are so easy to use that you don't need to worry about learning the details.

15. What should you do if your first attempt to find something with a search engine doesn't return anything useful?
    a. Try again with fewer search terms (which will broaden your search).
    b. Try again with fewer search terms (which will narrow your search).
    c. Try again with more search terms (which will broaden your search).
    d. Try again with more search terms (which will narrow your search).

Objective 11.4: Describe the major tasks involved in processing and applying your research results.

16. A ______ is a shortened version of one or more documents, research results, or other information; it filters out details and presents only the most important ideas.

17. A ______ is your analysis of what the findings mean (an interpretation of the facts).

18. A ______ is your opinion (based on reason and logic) about the course of action that should be taken.

Objective 11.5: Explain how to organize informational reports and website content.

19. Which of the following is not a common way to organize informational reports?
    a. Comparison
    b. Section size
    c. Sequence
    d. Chronology

20. The structure and navigational flow of all the parts of a website are commonly referred to as ______ ______.

Objective 11.6: Discuss three major ways to organize analytical reports, and explain how to plan proposals.

21. If you have a long history of success in business and are highly regarded by your audience, which two organizing models will probably be sufficient for most reports to this audience?
    a. Focusing on conclusions or focusing on recommendations
    b. Focusing on conclusions and focusing on troubleshooting
    c. Focusing on logic or focusing on analysis
    d. Focusing on reason and focusing on logic

22. RFP stands for
    a. Request for proposals
    b. Reason for proposing
    c. Release form project
    d. Research for proposal

PEARSON
mybcommlab™

Log on to www.mybcommlab.com to access the following study and assessment aids associated with this chapter:

- Video applications
- Pre/post test
- Real-Time Updates
- Personalized study plan
- Peer review activity
- Model documents
- Quick Learning Guides
- Sample presentations

If you are not using mybcommlab, you can access Real-Time Updates and Quick Learning Guides through http://real-timeupdates.com/ebc. The Quick Learning Guide (located under "Learn More" on the website) hits all the high points of this chapter in just two pages. This guide, especially prepared by the authors, will help you study for exams or review important concepts whenever you need a quick refresher.

Apply Your Knowledge

1. Why must you be careful when using information from a webpage in a business report?
2. Why do you need to evaluate the sources you uncover in your research?
3. If you were writing a recommendation report for an audience that doesn't know you, would you use a direct approach focusing on the recommendation or an indirect approach focusing on logic? Why?
4. Why are unsolicited proposals more challenging to write than solicited proposals?
5. **Ethical Choices** Companies occasionally make mistakes that expose confidential information, such as when employees lose laptop computers containing sensitive data files or webmasters forget to protect confidential webpages

from search engine indexes. If you conducted an online search that turned up competitive information on webpages that were clearly intended to be private, what would you do? Explain your answer.

Practice Your Knowledge

Message for Analysis: Evaluating a Report

The Securities and Exchange Commission (SEC) requires every public company to file a comprehensive annual report (form 10-K) electronically. Many companies post links to these reports on their websites, along with links to other company reports. Visit the website of Dell, at www.dell.com, and find the company's most recent annual reports: 10-K and Year in Review (click on "About Dell" on the homepage and then click on the "Investors" link). Compare the style and format of the two reports. For which audience(s) is the Year in Review targeted? Who besides the SEC might be interested in the Annual Report 10-K? Which report do you find easier to read? More interesting? More detailed?

Exercises

Active links for all websites in this chapter can be found on mybcommlab; see your User Guide for instructions on accessing the content for this chapter.

11.1 **Understanding Business Reports and Proposals: How Companies Use Reports** Interview several people working in a career you might like to enter and ask them about the reports they receive and prepare. How do these reports tie in to the decision-making process? Who reads the reports they prepare? Do they write or read electronic, online reports? Summarize your findings in writing, give them to your instructor, and be prepared to discuss them with the class.

11.2 **Understanding Business Reports and Proposals: Report Classification** Using the information presented in this chapter, identify the report type represented by each of the following examples. In addition, write a brief paragraph about each, explaining who the audience is likely to be, what type of data would be used, and whether conclusions and recommendations would be appropriate.

- **a.** A statistical study of the pattern of violent crime in a large city during the past five years
- **b.** A report prepared by a seed company demonstrating the benefits of its seed corn for farmers
- **c.** A report prepared by an independent testing agency evaluating various types of nonprescription cold remedies
- **d.** A trip report submitted at the end of a week by a traveling salesperson
- **e.** A report indicating how 45 acres of undeveloped land could be converted into an industrial park
- **f.** An annual report to be sent to the shareholders of a large corporation
- **g.** A report from a U.S. National Park wildlife officer to Washington, D.C., headquarters showing the status of the California condor (an endangered species)
- **h.** A written report by a police officer who has just completed an arrest

11.3 **Informational Reports: Personal Activity Report** Imagine you're the manager of campus recruiting for Nortel, a Canadian telecommunications firm. Each of your four recruiters interviews up to 11 college seniors every day. What kind of personal activity report can you design to track the results of these interviews? List the areas you would want each recruiter to report on and explain how each would help you manage the recruiting process (and the recruiters) more effectively.

11.4 **Understanding Your Topic: Subquestions** Your boss has asked you to do some research on franchising. Actually, he's thinking about purchasing a few Subway franchises, and he needs some information. Visit www.amazon.com and perform a keyword search on "franchises." Explore some of the books that you find by reading reviews and using the "Search Inside" feature.

- **a.** Use the information to develop a list of subquestions to help you narrow your focus.
- **b.** Write down the names of three books you might purchase to further aid your research.
- **c.** Summarize how this website can assist you with your research efforts, and identify any risks of using this technique.

11.5 **Finding Secondary Information** Using online, database, or printed sources, find the following information. Be sure to properly cite your source, using the formats discussed in Appendix B (*Hint:* Start with Table 11.3, Important Resources for Business Research.)

- **a.** Contact information for the American Management Association
- **b.** Median weekly earnings of men and women by occupation
- **c.** Current market share for Perrier water
- **d.** Performance ratios for office supply retailers
- **e.** Annual stock performance for Hewlett-Packard
- **f.** Number of franchise outlets in the United States
- **g.** Composition of the U.S. workforce by profession

11.6 **Finding Information: Company Information** Select any public company and find the following information.

- **a.** Names of the company's current officers
- **b.** List of the company's products or services (if the company has a large number of products, list the product lines instead)
- **c.** Current issues in the company's industry
- **d.** Outlook for the company's industry as a whole

11.7 **Finding Information: Secondary Information** You'd like to know if it's a good idea to buy banner ads on other websites to drive more traffic to your company's website. You're worried about the expense and difficulty of running an experiment to test banner effectiveness, so you decide to look for some secondary data. Using databases available through your library, identify three secondary sources that might offer helpful data on this issue.

11.8 **Finding Information: Search Techniques** Analyze any recent school or work assignment that required you to conduct research. How did you approach your investigation? Did you rely mostly on sources of primary information or mostly on sources of secondary information? Now that you have studied this chapter, can you identify two ways to improve the research techniques you used during that assignment? Briefly explain.

11.9 Finding Information: Surveys You work for a movie studio that is producing a young director's first motion picture—the story of a group of unknown musicians finding work and making a reputation in a competitive industry. Unfortunately, some of your friends say that the 182-minute movie is simply too long. Others say they couldn't imagine any sequences to cut out. Your boss wants to test the movie on a regular audience and ask viewers to complete a questionnaire that will help the director decide whether edits are needed and, if so, where. Design a questionnaire that you can use to solicit valid answers for a report to the director about how to handle the audience's reaction to the movie.

11.10 Finding Information: Interviews You're conducting an information interview with a manager in another division of your company. Partway through the interview, the manager shows clear signs of impatience. How should you respond? What might you do differently to prevent this from happening in the future? Explain your answers.

11.11 Teamwork: Evaluating Sources Break into small groups and surf the Internet to find websites that provide business information such as company or industry news, trends, analysis, facts, or performance data. Using the criteria discussed under "Evaluating Your Sources," evaluate the credibility of the information presented at these websites.

11.12 Processing Information: Reading and Taking Notes Select an article from a business magazine such as *BusinessWeek*, *Fortune*, *Forbes*, *Fast Company*, or *Business 2.0*. Read the article and highlight the article's key points. Summarize the article in fewer than 100 words, paraphrasing the key points.

11.13 Analyzing Data: Calculating the Mean Your boss has asked you to analyze and report on your division's sales for the first nine months of this year. Using the following data from company invoices, calculate the mean for each quarter and all averages for the year to date. Then identify and discuss the quarterly sales trends.

January	$24,600	April	$21,200	July	$29,900
February	25,900	May	24,600	August	30,500
March	23,000	June	26,800	September	26,600

11.14 Teamwork: Unsolicited Proposal Break into small groups and identify an operational problem occurring at your campus that involves either registration, university housing, food services, parking, or library services. Then develop a workable solution to that problem. Finally, develop a list of pertinent facts that your team will need to gather to convince the reader that the problem exists and that your solution will work.

11.15 Analyzing the Situation: Statement of Purpose Sales at The Style Shop, a clothing store for men, have declined for the third month in a row. Your boss is not sure if this decline is due to a weak economy or if it's due to another unknown reason. She has asked you to investigate the situation and to submit a report to her highlighting some possible reasons for the decline. Develop a statement of purpose for your report.

11.16 Organizing Reports: Structuring Analytical Reports Three years ago, your company (a carpet manufacturer) modernized its Georgia plant in anticipation of increasing demand for carpets. Because of the depressed housing market, the increase in demand for new carpets has been slow to materialize. As a result, the company has excess capacity at its Georgia and California plants. On the basis of your research, you have recommended that the company close the California plant. The company president, J. P. Lawrence, has asked you to prepare a justification report to support your recommendation. Here are the facts you gathered by interviewing the respective plant managers:

Operational Statistics

- *Georgia plant:* This plant has newer equipment, productivity is higher, it employs 100 nonunion production workers, and it ships $12 million in carpets a year. The hourly base wage is $16.
- *California plant:* California plant employs 80 union production workers and ships $8 million in carpets a year. The hourly base wage is $20.

Financial Implications

- *Savings by closing California plant:* (1) Increase productivity by 17%; (2) reduce labor costs by 20% (total labor savings would be $1 million per year; see assumptions); (3) annual local tax savings of $120,000 (Georgia has a more favorable tax climate).
- *Sale of Pomona, California, land:* Purchased in 1952 for $200,000. Current market value $2.5 million. Net profit (after capital gains tax) over $1 million.
- *Sale of plant and equipment:* Fully depreciated. Any proceeds a windfall.
- *Costs of closing California plant:* One-time deductible charge of $250,000 (relocation costs of $100,000 and severance payments totaling $150,000).

Assumptions

- Transfer 5 workers from California to Georgia.
- Hire 45 new workers in Georgia.
- Lay off 75 workers in California.
- Georgia plant would require a total of 150 workers to produce the combined volume of both plants.
  - **a.** Which approach (focus on conclusions, recommendations, or logical arguments) will you use to structure your report to the president? Why?
  - **b.** Suppose this report were to be circulated to plant managers and supervisors instead. What changes, if any, might you make in your approach?
  - **c.** List some conclusions that you might draw from the above information to use in your report.
  - **d.** Using the structure you selected for your report to the president, draft a final report outline with first- and second-level informative headings.

Expand Your Knowledge

Learning More on the Web

Check Out This 24-Hour Library

www.ipl.org

Start your business research by visiting the Internet Public Library, at www.ipl.org. Visit the reference center and explore the many online references available. These cover topics such as business, economics, law, government, science, technology, computers, education, and more. You can even submit questions for the IPL staff.

1. Click on "Ready Reference" (left side of the page) and follow some of the reference links. How might these links help you when performing business research?
2. Click on "Business" under "Subject Collections" and locate the "Consumer Issues & Services" subheading. Find three sites that help consumers make better-informed decisions.
3. Click on "Business," find "Business Directories," and use one of the sites listed to select five companies. Find contact information (address, phone, website, officers' names, and so on) for each company. What kinds of contact information did you find at the company websites?

Sharpening Your Career Skills Online

Bovée and Thill's Business Communication Web Search, at http://businesscommunicationblog.com/websearch, is a unique research tool designed specifically for business communication research. Use the Web Search function to find a website, video, PDF document, podcast, or PowerPoint presentation that offers advice on conducting research for business reports. Write a brief e-mail message to your instructor, describing the item that you found and summarizing the career skills information you learned from it.

Improve Your Grammar, Mechanics, and Usage

The following exercises help you improve your knowledge of and power over English grammar, mechanics, and usage. Turn to the Handbook of Grammar, Mechanics, and Usage at the end of this book and review all of Sections 2.1 (Periods), 2.2 (Question Marks), and 2.3 (Exclamation Points). Then look at the following 10 items. Circle the letter of the preferred choice in the following groups of sentences. (Answers to these exercises appear on page AK-3.)

1. a. Dr. Eleanor H Hutton has requested information on TaskMasters, Inc.?
   b. Dr. Eleanor H. Hutton has requested information on TaskMasters, Inc.
2. a. That qualifies us as a rapidly growing new company, don't you think?
   b. That qualifies us as a rapidly growing new company, don't you think.
3. a. Our president is a C.P.A. On your behalf, I asked him why he started the firm.
   b. Our president is a CPA. On your behalf, I asked him why he started the firm.
4. a. Contact me at 1358 N. Parsons Ave., Tulsa, OK 74204.
   b. Contact me at 1358 N. Parsons Ave, Tulsa, OK. 74204.
5. a. Jeb asked, "Why does he want to know! Maybe he plans to become a competitor."
   b. Jeb asked, "Why does he want to know? Maybe he plans to become a competitor!"
6. a. The debt load fluctuates with the movement of the U.S. prime rate.
   b. The debt load fluctuates with the movement of the US prime rate.
7. a. Is consumer loyalty extinct? Yes and no!
   b. Is consumer loyalty extinct? Yes and no.
8. a. Will you please send us a check today so that we can settle your account.
   b. Will you please send us a check today so that we can settle your account?
9. a. Will you be able to speak at the conference, or should we find someone else.
   b. Will you be able to speak at the conference, or should we find someone else?
10. a. So I ask you, "When will we admit defeat?" Never!
    b. So I ask you, "When will we admit defeat"? Never!

For additional exercises focusing on periods, question marks, and exclamation points, visit mybcommlab. Click on Chapter 11, click on "Additional Exercises to Improve Your Grammar, Mechanics, and Usage," and click on "17. Punctuation B."

Writing Reports and Proposals

12

Learning Objectives

After studying this chapter, you will be able to

1 Explain how to adapt to your audiences when writing reports and` proposals, and provide an overview of the process of drafting report content

2 Provide an overview of the process of drafting proposal content, and list six strategies to strengthen your proposal argument

3 Identify five characteristics of effective writing in online reports, and explain how to adapt your writing approach for wikis

4 Discuss six principles of graphic design, and explain how to choose which points in your message to illustrate

5 Identify the most common types of visuals used to present data, information, concepts, and ideas

6 Explain how to integrate visuals with text effectively and how to verify the quality of your visuals

On the Job: Communicating at Tellabs

The annual reports written by Tellabs's George Stenitzer go beyond regulatory compliance to helping investors understand the business and its financial performance.

Redefining the Annual Report with Audience-Focused Writing

Few reports get as much scrutiny as corporate annual reports, and the feedback from many readers is not particularly positive.

These compliance reports are required of every company listed on U.S. stock exchanges, and investors pore over them, looking for clues about a company's financial health and prospects. However, investor surveys suggest that many readers don't believe they are getting the information they need in order to make intelligent decisions about investing in a company's stock. Some companies have even been sued in recent years over their annual reports, with investors accusing them of withholding or obscuring vital information.

In this environment of uncertainty and outright mistrust, writers who communicate clearly and openly tend to stand out from the crowd. One such writer is George Stenitzer, vice president of corporate communication for Tellabs, a major producer of equipment for Internet service providers based in Naperville,

Illinois. According to one widely respected consultant who assesses the quality of annual reports, Stenitzer's work practically demands to be read, thanks to its brevity, forthright style, full disclosure of important financial information, numerous features that enhance readability, and attractive design.

While annual report writers must comply with a complex array of legal compliance requirements, Stenitzer's view is that accuracy and compliance—while vital—are not enough. He recognizes that many companies still lean in the direction of minimal disclosure, saying just enough to satisfy government regulations, but Stenitzer's goal is to help investors truly understand the nature of Tellabs's business and its financial performance. As he puts it, "The test for investor communications is shifting from technical accuracy and legal compliance to clear communication and investor understanding."

The proof of his approach seems to bear out in investor surveys. In an environment in which many investors are extremely skeptical of, or even confused by, what they read in annual reports, one of Tellabs's recent annual reports was rated "good" or "very good" by an overwhelming 83 percent of readers.[1]
www.tellabs.com

CRAFTING REPORTS AND PROPOSALS

George Stenitzer (profiled in the chapter-opening "On the Job" vignette) can tell you how important the writing stage is in the development of successful reports and proposals. This chapter builds on the writing techniques and ideas you learned in Chapter 5, focusing on issues that are particularly important when preparing longer message formats. In addition, you'll get an introduction to creating effective visuals, which are a vital aspect of many reports and proposals.

As with shorter messages, take a few moments before you start writing to make sure you're ready to adapt your approach to your audience.

ADAPTING TO YOUR AUDIENCE

1 LEARNING OBJECTIVE

Explain how to adapt to your audiences when writing reports and proposals, and provide an overview of the process of drafting report content.

Successful report writers adapt to their intended audiences by being sensitive to audience needs, building strong relationships with the audience, and controlling style and tone.

Long or complex reports demand a lot from readers, making the "you" attitude especially important.

Chapter 5 introduces four aspects of audience sensitivity, and all four apply to reports and proposals: adopting the "you" attitude, maintaining a strong sense of etiquette, emphasizing the positive, and using bias-free language. Reports and proposals that are highly technical, complex, or lengthy can put heavy demands on your readers, so the "you" attitude is especially important with these long messages.

Many companies have specific guidelines for reports, particularly those intended for external audiences.

Be sure to plan how you will adapt your style and your language to reflect the image of your organization. Many companies have specific guidelines for communicating with public audiences, so make sure you're aware of these preferences before you start writing.

If you know your readers reasonably well and your report is likely to meet with their approval, you can adopt a fairly informal tone (as long as this is appropriate in your organization, of course). A more formal tone is appropriate for longer reports, especially those that deal with controversial or complex information. You also need a more formal tone when your report will be sent to other parts of the organization or to outsiders, such as customers, suppliers, or members of the community (see Figure 12.1).

Reports destined for audiences outside the United States often require a more formal tone to match the expectations of audiences in many other countries.

Communicating with people in other cultures often calls for more formality—for two reasons. First, the business environment outside the United States tends to be more formal in general, and that formality must be reflected in your communication. Second, the things you do to make a document informal (such as using humor and idiomatic language) tend to translate poorly or not at all from one culture to another, so you risk offending or confusing your readers.

COMPOSING REPORTS AND PROPOSALS

When you compose reports and proposals, follow the writing advice offered in Chapter 5: Select the best words, create the most effective sentences, and develop coherent paragraphs. As with other written business communications, the text of reports and proposals has three main sections: an introduction, a body, and a close.

FIGURE 12.1 Choosing the Right Tone for Business Reports
Yahoo! is known for using a playful, informal tone in its advertising and in most communication with customers, but the company's tone is more formal when communicating with the public on more serious matters.

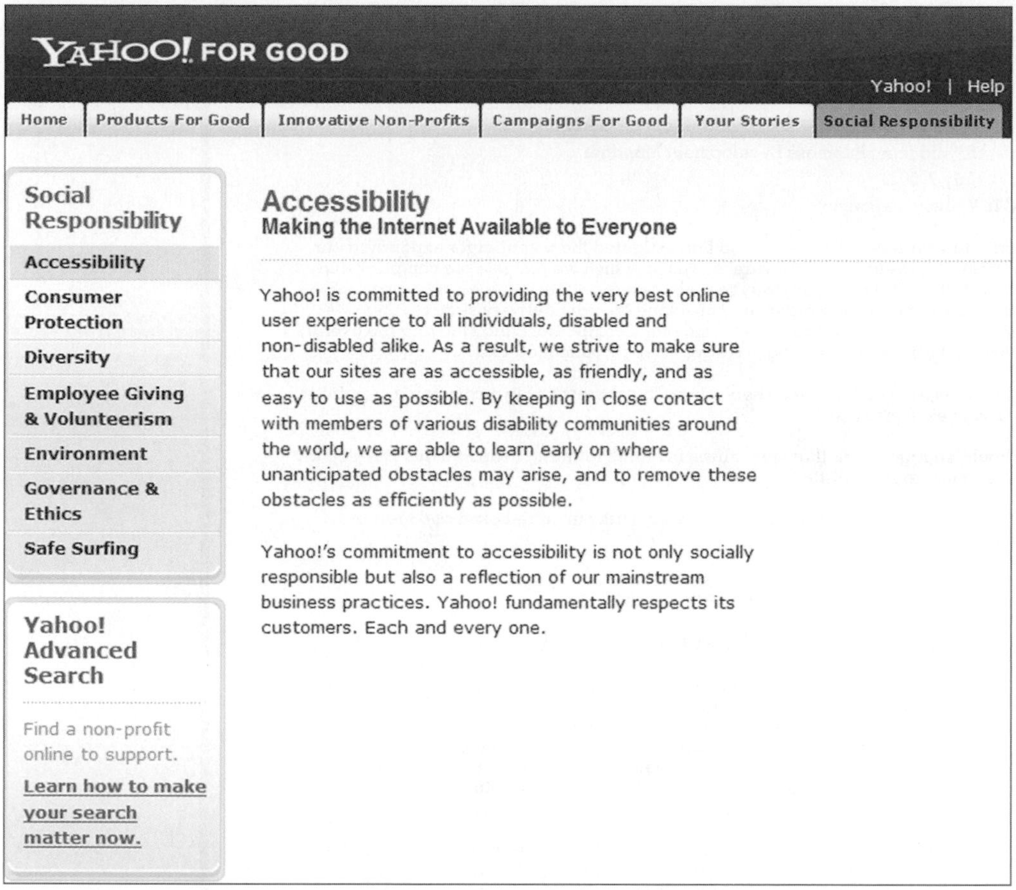

The *introduction* (or *opening*) is the first section in the text of any report or proposal. An effective introduction accomplishes at least four things:

Your introduction needs to put the report in context for the reader, introduce the subject, preview main ideas, and establish the tone of the document.

- Puts the report or proposal in a broader context by tying it to a problem or an assignment
- Introduces the subject or purpose of the report or proposal and indicates why the subject is important
- Previews the main ideas and the order in which they'll be covered
- Establishes the tone of the document and the writer's relationship with the audience

The *body* presents, analyzes, and interprets the information gathered during your investigation and supports the recommendations or conclusions discussed in your document (see Figure 12.2 on the next page).

The body of your report presents, analyzes, and interprets the information you gathered during your investigation.

The *close* has three important functions:

- Emphasizes the main points of the message
- Summarizes the benefits to the reader if the document suggests a change or some other course of action
- Brings all the action items together in one place and gives the details about who should do what, when, where, and how

The close might be the only part of your report some readers have time for, so make sure it conveys the full weight of your message.

Research shows that the final section of a report or proposal leaves a lasting impression. The close gives you one last chance to make sure your report says what you intended.[2]

FIGURE 12.2 Effective Problem-Solving Report Focusing on Recommendations
In this report recommending that her firm expand its website to full e-commerce capability, Alycia Jenn uses the body of her report to provide enough information to support her argument, without burdening her high-level readership with a lot of tactical details.

MEMO

TO: Board of Directors, Executive Committee members
FROM: Alycia Jenn, Business Development Manager
DATE: July 7, 2010
SUBJECT: Website expansion

Reminds readers of the origin and purpose of the report

In response to your request, my staff and I investigated the potential for expanding our website from its current "brochureware" status (in which we promote our company and its products but don't provide any way to place orders online) to full e-commerce capability (including placing orders and checking on order delivery status). After analyzing the behavior of our customers and major competitors and studying the overall development of electronic retailing, we have three recommendations:

1. We should expand our online presence from "brochureware" to e-commerce capability within the next 6 months.
2. We should engage a firm that specializes in online retailing to design and develop the new e-commerce capabilities.
3. We must take care to integrate online retailing with our store-based and mail-order operations.

Clarifies the recommendation by listing the necessary actions in clear, direct language

1. WE SHOULD EXPAND THE WEBSITE TO FULL E-COMMERCE CAPABILITY

Presents logical reasons for recommending that the firm expand its website to include e-commerce

First, does e-commerce capability make sense today for a small company that sells luxury housewares? Even though books and many other products are now commonly sold online, in most cases, this enterprise involves simple, low-cost products that don't require a lot of hands-on inspection before purchasing. As we've observed in our stores, shoppers like to interact with our products before purchasing them. However, a small but growing number of websites do sell specialty products, using such tactics as "virtual product tours" (in which shoppers can interactively view a product in three dimensions, rather than simply looking at a static photograph) and generous return policies (to reduce the perceived risk of buying products online).

Second, do we need to establish a presence now in order to remain competitive in the future? The answer is an overwhelming "yes." The initial steps taken by our competitors are already placing us at a disadvantage among those shoppers who are already comfortable buying online, and every trend indicates our minor competitive weakness today will turn into a major weakness in the next few years:

- Several of our top competitors are beginning to implement full e-commerce, including virtual product tours. Our research suggests that these companies aren't yet generating significant financial returns from these online investments, but their online sales are growing.
- Younger consumers who grew up with the World Wide Web will soon be reaching their peak earning years (ages 35–54). This demographic segment expects e-commerce in nearly every product category, and we'll lose them to the competition if we don't offer it.
- The web is erasing geographical shopping limits, presenting both a threat and an opportunity. Even though our customers can now shop websites anywhere in the world (so that we have thousands of competitors instead of a dozen), we can now target customers anywhere in the world.

Supports the reasoning with evidence

(continued)

Drafting Report Content

Your credibility and career advancement are on the line with every business report you write, so make sure your content is

- **Accurate.** Be sure to double-check your facts and references and to check for typos. If an audience ever gets an inkling that your information is shaky, they'll start to view all your work with skepticism.
- **Complete.** Tell your readers what they need to know—no more, no less—and present the information in a way that is geared to their needs. In a recent Tellabs annual

FIGURE 12.2 *(Continued)*

2

2. WE SHOULD ENGAGE A CONSULTANT TO IMPLEMENT THE SITE

Implementing a competitive retailing site can take anywhere from 1,000 to 1,500 hours of design and programming time. We have some of the expertise needed in-house, but the marketing and information systems departments have only 300 person-hours available in the next 6 months. I recommend that we engage a web design firm to help us with the design and to do all the programming.

Goes beyond the basic recommendation of what to do by suggesting how to do it

3. WE MUST INTEGRATE THE WEB INTO EXISTING OPERATIONS

The studies we reviewed showed that the most successful web retailers are careful to integrate their online retailing with their store- and mail-based retailing. Companies that don't integrate carefully find themselves with higher costs, confused customers, and websites that don't generate much business. Before we begin designing our website, we should develop a plan for integrating the web into our existing marketing, accounting, and production systems. The online site could affect every department in the company, so it's vital that everyone has a chance to review the plans before we proceed.

Addresses some important concerns that must be dealt with if the recommended action is taken

SUMMARY

Concludes with a concise summary of the recommended action

1. Begin working immediately to expand our website to include full e-commerce capability. Even though the financial returns might be minimal in the near term, every sign indicates they will grow in the future. Moreover, we will start to lose customers to other e-commerce sites if we don't expand.

2. Use the services of a web designer because we don't have enough person-hours available in-house.

3. Integrate the website with existing operations, particularly in marketing, accounting, and production.

report, for example, George Stenitzer and his team provided a concise and easily understandable overview of the company's complex and technical product line. The subject matter is presented in a way that any investor interested in the company's stock can comprehend.[3]

- **Balanced.** Present all sides of the issue fairly and equitably and include all the essential information, even if some of the information doesn't support your line of reasoning. Omitting relevant information or facts can bias your report.
- **Clear and logical.** Save your readers time by making sure your writing is uncluttered and proceed logically from point to point.
- **Documented properly.** If you use primary and secondary sources for your report or proposal, be sure to properly document and give credit to your sources.

Keeping these points in mind will help you draft the most effective introduction, body, and close for your report (see Figure 12.3 on the next page).

Report Introduction

The specific elements you should include in an introduction depend on the nature and length of the report, the circumstances under which you're writing the report, and your relationship with the audience. An introduction could contain any or all of the following:

Carefully select the elements to include in your introduction; strive for a balance between necessary, expected information and brevity.

- **Authorization.** When, how, and by whom the report was authorized; who wrote it; and when it was submitted. This material is especially important when you don't accompany the report with a *letter of transmittal* (see Chapter 13).
- **Problem/opportunity/purpose.** The reason the report was written and what is to be accomplished as a result of your having written it.
- **Scope.** What is and what isn't covered in the report. The scope also helps with the critical job of setting the audience's expectations.

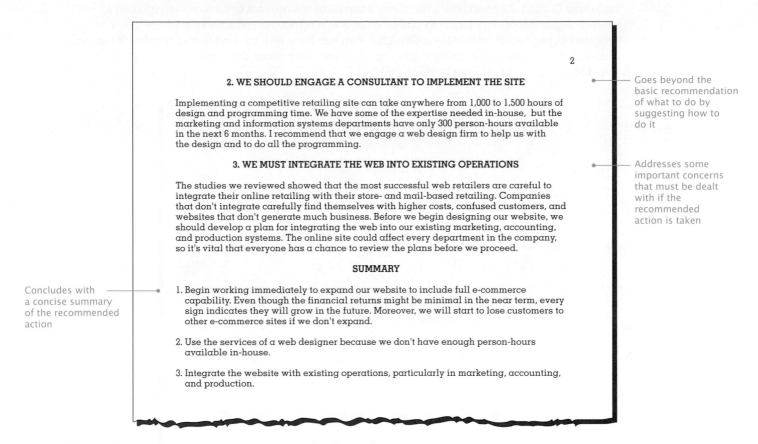

FIGURE 12.3 Effective Progress Report Offering Complete Content (Excerpt)
Note how Carlyce Johnson offers her client a complete but efficient update of her company's landscaping services. In addition to providing routine information, she also informs the client of progress in two problem areas—one that her firm has been able to resolve and one that it has just discovered. Johnson does the right thing by telling the client about the problems as early as possible, giving the client time to react and plan.

Johnson Landscaping

1500 Dakota, Seattle, WA 98105 • (206) 745-8636 / Fax: (206)0745-6361
E-mail: info@johnscape.com

May 30, 2010

Mr. Steve Gamvrellis, Facilities Manager
United Food Processing
9000 235th St., SW
Everett, WA 98204

Dear Mr. Gamvrellis:

This report will bring you up to date on the work done for your company by Johnson Landscaping during the month of May 2010.

GROUND PREPARATION AND SPRINKLER INSTALLATION

Initial ground preparation and sprinkler system installation is complete. We cleared, tilled, leveled, and raked 8,000 square meters for lawn and beds. Installation of the sprinkler system for 4,500 square meters of lawn and beds was completed on May 19.

BED PLANTING

From May 22 to May 30, shrubs and ornamental perennials were planted in 2,100 square meters of beds. Beds were prepared for 1,000 square meters of annuals.

SPECIAL ISSUES AND SOLUTIONS

We've resolved the flooding discovered last month near the south end of the shipping and receiving dock. It appears that an old plumbing repair had failed under the employee cafeteria, causing water to flow under the building and occasionally flood a small portion of the new lawn area.

In several of the perennial borders we've created along the east side of the main building, a series of soil samples indicates an extremely high level of acidity, much higher than would occur under natural conditions. We suspect that the problem may have been caused by a small chemical spill at some point in the past. We'll try to resolve this issue next month with soil amendments. I'll contact you if this solution is likely to affect your budget planning.

PLANS FOR JUNE

1. Distribute beauty bark and plant remaining annuals.
2. Resolve the soil quality issue in the perennial bed and make soil amendments as needed.
3. Monitor and adjust the automated sprinkling system to ensure adequate watering.

Uses letter format, which is appropriate for a simple interim progress report

Introduces the purpose of the report

Uses clear subheadings to help the reader find items of interest

Doesn't hesitate to bring up problems that need to be solved but offers possible solutions for further investigation

Outlines plans for the next reporting period (the month of June)

- **Background.** Any relevant historical conditions or factors that can help readers grasp the report's message.
- **Sources and methods.** The primary and secondary sources of information used. As appropriate, this section can also explain how the information was collected.
- **Definitions.** Definitions of important terms used in the report. Define any terms that might be unfamiliar to the audience or any terms you use in an unfamiliar way.
- **Limitations.** Factors beyond your control that affect the quality of the report, such as budgets, schedule constraints, or limited access to information or people. However, don't apologize or try to explain away personal shortcomings, such as your own poor planning.
- **Report organization.** The organization of the report. This "road map" helps readers understand what's coming in the report and why.

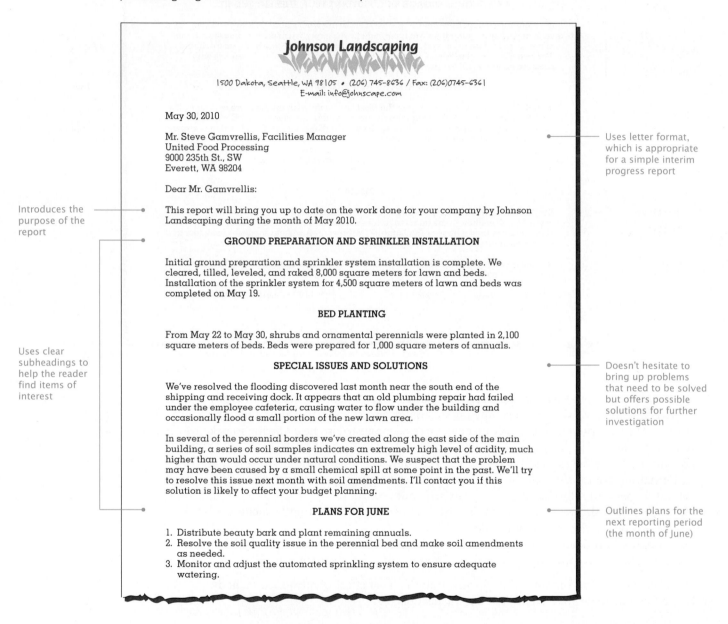

In a brief report, these topics may be discussed in only a paragraph or two. In a longer formal report, the discussion of these topics may span several pages and constitute a significant section within the report.

Report Body

As with the introduction, the body of your report can require some tough decisions about which elements to include and how much detail to offer. Here again, your decisions depend on many variables, including the needs of your audience. Provide only enough detail in the body to support your conclusions and recommendations.

The topics commonly covered in a report body include

- Explanations of a problem or opportunity
- Facts, statistical evidence, and trends
- Results of studies or investigations
- Discussion and analyses of potential courses of action
- Advantages, disadvantages, costs, and benefits of a particular course of action
- Procedures or steps in a process
- Methods and approaches
- Criteria for evaluating alternatives and options
- Conclusions and recommendations
- Supporting reasons for conclusions or recommendations

The report body should contain only enough information to convey your message in a convincing fashion; don't overload readers with interesting but unnecessary material.

For analytical reports that use the direct approach, you generally state your conclusions or recommendations in the introduction and use the body to provide your evidence and support (as illustrated in Figures 12.2 and 12.3). If you're using the indirect approach, you're likely to use the body to discuss your logic and reserve your conclusions or recommendations until the very end.

Report Close

The content and length of your report close depend on your choice of direct or indirect order, among other variables. If you're using the direct approach, you can end with a summary of key points, listed in the order in which they appear in the report body. If you're using the indirect approach, you can use the close to present your conclusions or recommendations if you didn't end the body with them. Just remember that a conclusion or recommendation isn't the place to introduce new facts; your readers should have all the information they need by the time they reach this point in your report.

The nature of your close depends on the type of report (informational or analytical) and the approach (direct or indirect).

If your report is intended to prompt others to action, use the ending to spell out exactly what should happen next and who is responsible for each task. If you'll be taking all the actions yourself, make sure your readers understand this fact so that they know what to expect from you (see Figure 12.4 on the next page).

In a short report, the close may be only a paragraph or two. However, the close of a long report may have separate sections for conclusions, recommendations, and actions. Using separate sections helps your reader locate this material and focus on each element. Such an arrangement also gives you a final opportunity to emphasize this important content. If you have multiple conclusions, recommendations, or actions, you may want to number and list them as well for easier reference.

For long reports, you may need to divide your close into separate sections for conclusions, recommendations, and actions.

2 LEARNING OBJECTIVE

Provide an overview of the process of drafting proposal content, and list six strategies to strengthen your proposal argument.

Drafting Proposal Content

With proposals, the content for each section is governed by many variables—the most important of which is the source of your proposal. If your proposal is unsolicited, you have some latitude in the scope and organization of content. However, if you are responding to a request for proposals (RFP), you need to follow the instructions in the RFP in every detail. Most RFPs spell out precisely what a proposal must cover and in what order so that all bids will be similar in form and therefore easier to compare.

FIGURE 12.4 Effective Report Expressing Action Plan in the Close
Roger Watson's personal activity report for July is a good example of efficiently conveying key information points, including a clear plan of action in the close. Note the use of hyperlinks to maps, photos, and a related report, all of which are stored on the same secure intranet site.

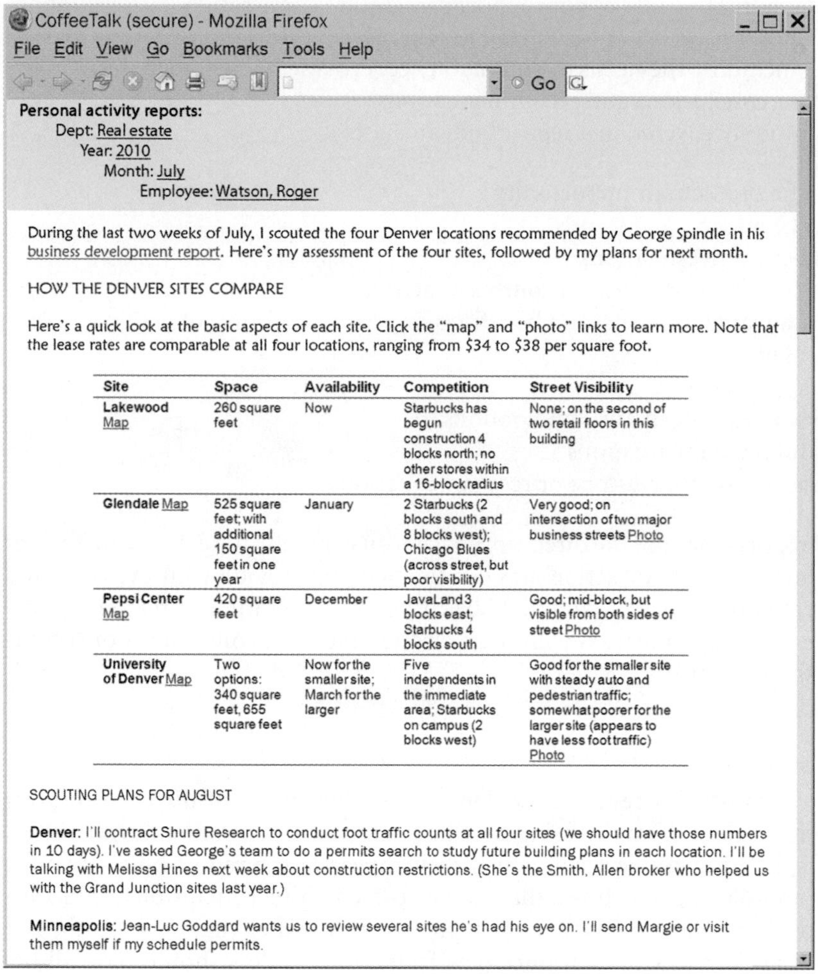

Personal activity reports:
Dept: Real estate
Year: 2010
Month: July
Employee: Watson, Roger

During the last two weeks of July, I scouted the four Denver locations recommended by George Spindle in his business development report. Here's my assessment of the four sites, followed by my plans for next month.

HOW THE DENVER SITES COMPARE

Here's a quick look at the basic aspects of each site. Click the "map" and "photo" links to learn more. Note that the lease rates are comparable at all four locations, ranging from $34 to $38 per square foot.

Site	Space	Availability	Competition	Street Visibility
Lakewood Map	260 square feet	Now	Starbucks has begun construction 4 blocks north; no other stores within a 16-block radius	None; on the second of two retail floors in this building
Glendale Map	525 square feet; with additional 150 square feet in one year	January	2 Starbucks (2 blocks south and 8 blocks west); Chicago Blues (across street, but poor visibility)	Very good; on intersection of two major business streets Photo
Pepsi Center Map	420 square feet	December	JavaLand 3 blocks east; Starbucks 4 blocks south	Good; mid-block, but visible from both sides of street Photo
University of Denver Map	Two options: 340 square feet, 655 square feet	Now for the smaller site; March for the larger	Five independents in the immediate area; Starbucks on campus (2 blocks west)	Good for the smaller site with steady auto and pedestrian traffic; somewhat poorer for the larger site (appears to have less foot traffic) Photo

SCOUTING PLANS FOR AUGUST

Denver: I'll contract Shure Research to conduct foot traffic counts at all four sites (we should have those numbers in 10 days). I've asked George's team to do a permits search to study future building plans in each location. I'll be talking with Melissa Hines next week about construction restrictions. (She's the Smith, Allen broker who helped us with the Grand Junction sites last year.)

Minneapolis: Jean-Luc Goddard wants us to review several sites he's had his eye on. I'll send Margie or visit them myself if my schedule permits.

Approach proposals the same way you approach persuasive messages.

The general purpose of any proposal is to persuade readers to do something, such as purchase goods or services, fund a project, or implement a program. Thus, your writing approach for a proposal is similar to that used for persuasive messages (see Chapter 10). As with other persuasive messages, the AIDA model of gaining attention, building interest, creating desire, and motivating action is an effective structure. Here are key strategies to strengthen your argument:[4]

- Demonstrate your knowledge in terms that are meaningful to the audience.
- Provide concrete information and examples.
- Research the competition so you know what other proposals your audience is likely to read.
- Prove that your proposal is appropriate and feasible for your audience.
- Relate your product, service, or personnel to the reader's exact needs.
- Package your proposal attractively.

In addition, make sure your proposal is letter perfect, inviting, and readable. Readers will prejudge the quality of your products, services, and capabilities by the quality of the proposal you submit.

Proposal Introduction

The introduction of a proposal presents and summarizes the problem or opportunity you want to address, along with your proposed solution. If your proposal is solicited, follow the RFP's instructions about indicating which RFP you're responding to. If your proposal is unsolicited, your introduction should mention any factors that led you to submit your proposal, such as previous conversations you've had with readers. The following topics are commonly covered in a proposal introduction:

- **Background or statement of the problem or opportunity.** Briefly review the reader's situation and establish the need for action. Remember that readers may not perceive a problem or an opportunity the same way you do. In unsolicited proposals, you need to convince them that a problem or an opportunity exists before you can convince them to accept your solution.
- **Solution.** Briefly describe the change you propose and highlight your key selling points and their benefits, showing how your proposal will help readers meet their business objectives.
- **Scope.** States the boundaries of the proposal—what you will and will not do. Sometimes called "Delimitations."
- **Organization.** Orients the reader to the remainder of the proposal and calls attention to the major divisions of information.

In an unsolicited proposal, your introduction needs to convince readers that a problem or an opportunity exists.

In short proposals, your discussion of these topics will be brief—perhaps only a sentence or two for each. For long, formal proposals, each topic may warrant separate subheadings and several paragraphs of discussion.

Proposal Body

The proposal's body gives complete details on the proposed solution and specifies what the anticipated results will be. Because a proposal is by definition a persuasive message, your audience expects you to promote your offering in a confident but professional manner.

Readers understand that a proposal is a persuasive message, so they're willing to accommodate a degree of promotional emphasis—as long as it is focused on their needs.

In addition to providing facts and evidence to support your conclusions, an effective body covers this information:

- **Proposed solution.** Describe what you have to offer: your concept, product, or service. Stress the benefits of your product, service, or investment opportunity that are relevant to your readers' needs and point out any advantages that you have over your competitors.
- **Work plan.** Explain the steps you'll take, the methods or resources you'll use, and the person(s) responsible. For solicited proposals, make sure your dates match those specified in the RFP. Keep in mind that if your proposal is accepted, the work plan is contractually binding, so don't promise more than you can deliver.
- **Statement of qualifications.** Describe your organization's experience, personnel, and facilities—all in relation to reader needs. You can supplement your qualifications by including a list of client references, but get permission ahead of time to use those references.
- **Costs.** Cover pricing, reimbursable expenses, discounts, and other financial concerns.

The work plan indicates exactly how you will accomplish the solution presented in the proposal.

In an informal proposal, discussion of some or all of these elements may be grouped together and presented in a letter format, as the proposal in Figure 12.5 (on the next page) does. In a formal proposal, the discussion of these elements can be quite long and thorough. The format may resemble long reports with multiple parts, as Chapter 13 discusses.

Proposal Close

The final section of a proposal generally summarizes your key points, emphasizes the benefits readers will get from your solution, and asks for a decision from the reader. The close is your last opportunity to persuade readers to accept your proposal. In both formal and informal proposals, make this section relatively brief, assertive (but not brash or abrupt), and confident.

The close is your last chance to convince the reader of the merits of your proposal, so make especially sure it's clear, compelling, and audience oriented.

FIGURE 12.5 Effective Solicited Proposal in Letter Format
This informal solicited proposal provides the information the customer needs to make a purchase. Note that by signing the proposal and returning it, the customer enters into a legal contract to pay for the services described.

JWS Remodeling Solutions
1701 Lake Street • Traverse City, Michigan 49685
(231) 946-8845 • Fax: (231) 946-8846 • E-mail: jws@worldnet.att.net

October 29, 2010

Mr. Daniel Yurgren
Data Dimensions
15 Honeysuckle Lane
Traverse City, Michigan 49686

Dear Mr.Yurgren:

Subject: Proposal for Home Office Construction

JWS Remodeling Solutions would be happy to convert your existing living room area into a home office according to the specifications discussed during our October 14 meeting. We can schedule the project for the week beginning November 12, 2010 (two weeks from today). The project will take roughly three weeks to complete.

Our construction approach is unique. We provide a full staff of licensed tradespeople and schedule our projects so that when one trade finishes, the next trade is ready to begin. To expedite this project, as you requested, we have agreed to overlap several trades whose work can be done concurrently.

JWS Remodeling Solutions will provide the following work:

- Remove baseboard, door casing, fluted casing, and sheetrock to prepare for construction of new partition wall at north end of living room.
- Partition and finish walls to create two separate storage closets at north end of living room with access through two 36" six-panel door units. Replace all disturbed sheetrock.
- Hang and trim new door units and replace all disturbed baseboards and door casings.
- Install 60" double French door unit in location of current cased opening at the SW entrance to living room adjacent to foyer. Trim appropriately.
- Provide all rough and finished electrical, using recessed lighting in the ceiling and appropriate single pole switches and duplex outlets.
- Move cold air return from west wall to east wall of living room.
- Paint or finish all surfaces/trim to match specs used throughout house.

The work does *not* include custom office cabinetry, carpeting, or phone or cable wiring. We would be happy to bid on these projects in the future.

Acknowledges the scope of project

Uses the introduction to grab the reader's attention with expedited completion date—a key selling point

Itemizes the specific tasks to be performed

Uses the body to explain how the company will expedite the schedule, outline the approach, provide a work plan, and (on the next page) list qualifications and state costs

Avoids confusion by identifying work that is outside the scope of the proposal

(continued)

3 LEARNING OBJECTIVE

Identify five characteristics of effective writing in online reports, and explain how to adapt your writing approach for wikis.

Drafting Online Content

The basic principles of report writing apply to online content, but keep these five additional points in mind as well:

- Take special care to build trust with your intended audiences because careful readers can be skeptical of online content. Make sure your content is accurate, current, complete, and authoritative.
- As much as possible, adapt your content for a global audience. Translating content is expensive, so some companies compromise by *localizing* the homepage while keeping the deeper, more detailed content in its original language.

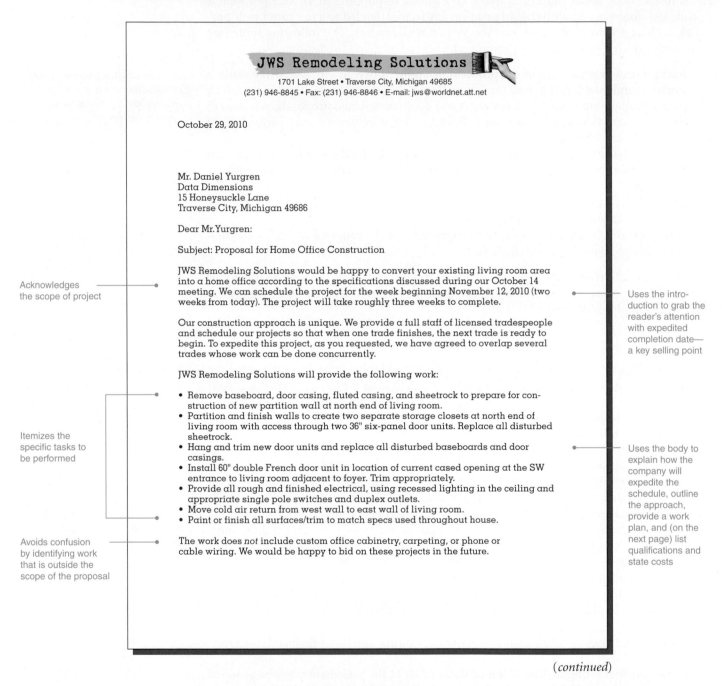

FIGURE 12.5 Effective Solicited Proposal in Letter Format *(Continued)*

Mr. Daniel Yurgren | Page 2 | October 29, 2010

JWS Remodeling Solutions has been in business in the Michigan area for over 17 years. We have a strong reputation for being a quality builder. We take great pride in our work and we treat all projects with the same high-level attention, regardless of their size or scope. Our tradespeople are all licensed, insured professionals with years of experience in their respective crafts. Enclosed is a copy of our company brochure discussing our qualifications in greater detail, along with a current client list. Please contact any of the names on this list for references.

Increases desire by highlighting qualifications

Helps reader accept the cost total by breaking it down into specific categories

The total cost for this project is $6,800, broken down as follows:

Materials and supplies	$3,800
Labor	2,700
Disposal fees	300
Total	$6,800

An initial payment of $3,800 is due upon acceptance of this proposal. The remaining $3,000 is due upon completion of the work.

If you would like to have JWS Remodeling Solutions complete this work, please sign one copy of this letter and return it to us with your deposit in the enclosed envelope. We currently anticipate no construction delays, since the materials needed for your job are in stock and our staff of qualified workers is available during the period mentioned. If you have any questions regarding the terms of this proposal, please call me.

Sincerely,

Jordan W. Spurrier
President

Enclosures (3)

Accepted by:

Makes letter a binding contract, if signed

Daniel Yurgren ______________________ Date ______________

- In an environment that presents many reading challenges, compelling, reader-oriented content is key to success.[5] Wherever you can, use the *inverted pyramid* style, in which you cover the most important information briefly at first and then gradually reveal successive layers of detail—letting readers choose to see those additional layers if they want to.
- Present your information in a concise, skimmable format. Effective websites use a variety of means to help readers skim pages quickly, including lists, careful use of color and boldface, informative headings, and helpful summaries that give readers a choice of learning more if they want to.
- Write effective links that serve for both site navigation and content skimming. Above all else, clearly identify where a link will take readers; don't force them to click through and try to figure out where they're going.

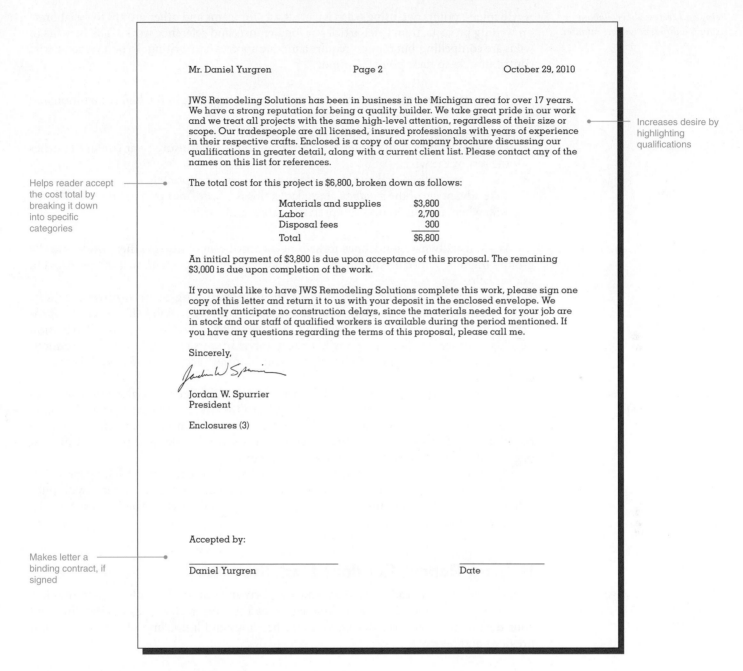

Collaborating on Wikis

Being an effective wiki collaborator requires a different writing mindset.

As Chapter 2 points out, using wikis is a great way for teams and other groups to collaborate on writing projects, from brief articles to long reports and reference works. The benefits of wikis are compelling, but they do require a unique approach to writing. To be a valuable wiki contributor, keep these points in mind:[6]

- Let go of traditional expectations of authorship, including individual recognition and control.
- Encourage all team members to improve each other's work.
- Use page templates and other formatting options to make sure your content matches the rest of the wiki.
- Use the separate editing and discussion capabilities appropriately.
- Take advantage of the *sandbox*, if available; this is a "safe," nonpublished section of the wiki where team members can practice editing and writing.

Wikis usually have guidelines to help new contributors integrate their work into the group's ongoing effort. Be sure to read and understand these guidelines; don't be afraid to ask for help.

If you are creating a new wiki, think through your long-term purpose carefully, just as you would with a new blog or podcast channel. Doing so will help you craft appropriate guidelines, editorial oversight, and security policies. For instance, the PlayStation development team at Sony uses a wiki to keep top managers up to date on new products, and because this information is highly confidential, access to the wiki is tightly controlled.[7]

Make sure you understand how a new wiki page will fit in with the existing content.

If you are adding a page or an article to an existing wiki, figure out how this new material fits in with the existing organization. Also, learn the wiki's preferred style for handling incomplete articles. For example, on the wiki that contains the user documentation for the popular WordPress blogging software, contributors are discouraged from adding new pages until the content is "fairly complete and accurate."[8]

If you are revising or updating an existing wiki article, use the checklist on page 155 in Chapter 6 to evaluate the content before you make changes. If you don't agree with published content and plan to revise it, you can use the wiki's discussion facility to share your concerns with other contributors.

Helping Report Readers Find Their Way

Help your audiences navigate through your reports by providing clear directions to key pieces of content.

Today's time-pressed readers want to browse reports and quickly find information of interest. To help them find what they're looking for and stay on track as they navigate through your documents, learn to make good use of headings and links, smooth transitions, and previews and reviews:

- **Headings and links.** Readers should be able to follow the structure of your document and pick up the key points of your message from the headings and subheadings. (See Chapter 6 for a review of what makes an effective heading.) Follow a simple, consistent arrangement that clearly distinguishes levels.
- **Transitions.** Chapter 5 defines transitions as words or phrases that tie ideas together and show how one thought is related to another. In a long report, an entire paragraph might be used to highlight transitions from one section to the next.
- **Previews and reviews.** *Preview sections* introduce important or complex topics by helping readers get ready for new information. *Review sections* come after a body of material and summarize key points to help readers absorb the information just read.

Previews help readers prepare for upcoming information, and reviews help them verify and clarify what they've just read.

To review the tasks discussed in this section, see "Checklist: Composing Business Reports and Proposals."

CHECKLIST: Composing Business Reports and Proposals

A. Review and fine-tune your outline.
- Match your parallel headings to the tone of your report or proposal.
- Understand how the introduction, body, and close work together to convey your message.

B. Draft report content.
- Use the introduction to establish the purpose, scope, and organization of your report or proposal.
- Use the body to present and interpret the information you gathered.
- Use the close to summarize major points, discuss conclusions, or make recommendations.

C. Draft proposal content.
- Use the introduction to discuss the background or problem, your solution, the scope, and organization.
- Use the body to persuasively explain the benefits of your proposed approach.
- Use the close to emphasize reader benefits and summarize the merits of your approach.

D. Help readers find their way.
- Provide headings to improve readability and clarify the framework of your ideas.
- Use hyperlinks online to allow readers to jump from section to section.
- Create transitions that tie together ideas and show how one thought relates to another.
- Preview important topics to help readers get ready for new information.
- Review key information to help readers absorb details and keep the big picture in mind.

USING TECHNOLOGY TO CRAFT REPORTS AND PROPOSALS

Creating lengthy reports and proposals can be a huge task, so take advantage of technological tools that can help you throughout the process. You've read about some of these tools in earlier chapters; here are some of the most important ones for developing reports and proposals:

Look for ways to use technology to reduce the mechanical work involved in writing long reports.

- **Templates.** Beyond simply formatting documents, report templates can identify the specific sections required for each type of report and even automatically insert headings for each section.
- **Linked and embedded documents.** In many reports and proposals, you need to include graphics, spreadsheets, databases, and other elements produced in other software programs. Make sure you know how the software handles the files. For instance, in Microsoft Office, *linking* to a second file ensures that the first file will be updated whenever the second one is changed. However, *embedding* the second file breaks the connection, so to speak, and changes to the second file will not show up in the first file.
- **Electronic forms.** For recurring forms such as sales reports and compliance reports, consider creating a word processing file that combines boilerplate text for material that doesn't change from report to report.
- **Electronic documents.** Portable document format (PDF) files have become a universal replacement for printed reports and proposals. With a copy of Adobe Acrobat (a separate product from the free Acrobat Reader), you can quickly convert reports and proposals to PDF files that are easy and safe to share electronically.
- **Multimedia documents.** When the written word isn't enough, combine your report with video clips, animation, presentation software slides, and other elements.
- **Proposal-writing software.** Basic features of proposal-writing software include automatically personalizing proposals, ensuring proper structure, and organizing storage of all your boilerplate text. Products such as Sant's RFPMaster can also scan RFPs to identify questions and requirements and fill in potential answers from a centralized knowledge base that contains input from all the relevant experts in your company.[9]

4 LEARNING OBJECTIVE

Discuss six principles of graphic design, and explain how to choose which points in your message to illustrate.

ILLUSTRATING YOUR REPORTS WITH EFFECTIVE VISUALS

Well-designed visual elements can enhance the communication power of textual messages and, in some instances, even replace textual messages. Visuals can often convey some message points (such as spatial relationships, correlations, procedures, and emotions) more

FIGURE 12.6 Visual Symbolism
A red cross (with equal-length arms) on a white background is the well-known symbol of the Red Cross relief organization. It is also used to indicate the medical branches of many nations' military services. The red cross symbol is based on the flag of Switzerland (where the first Red Cross organization was formed), which over the course of hundreds of years developed from battle flags that originally used the Christian cross symbol. Although the Red Cross emblem is not based directly on the Christian symbol, the organization uses a red crescent in countries where Islam is the dominant religion and is known as the Red Crescent. To avoid association with religious symbols, the International Federation of Red Cross and Red Crescent Societies (the global umbrella organization for all national Red Cross and Red Crescent organizations) recently adopted the Red Crystal as its new symbol.

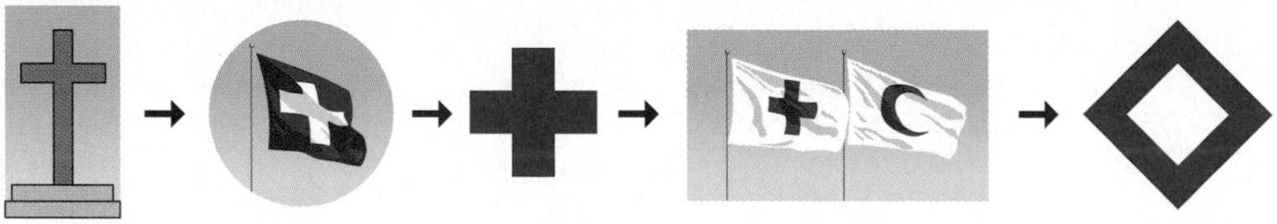

effectively and more efficiently than words. Generally speaking, in a given amount of time, well-designed images can convey much more information than text.[10] Visuals attract and hold people's attention, helping your audience understand and remember your message. Busy readers often jump to visuals to try to get the gist of a message, and attractive visuals can draw readers more deeply into your reports and presentations. Using pictures is also an effective way to communicate with the diverse audiences that are common in today's business environment.

Like words, visuals often carry connotative or symbolic meanings.

As you read in Chapter 5, many words and phrases carry connotative meanings, which are all the mental images, emotions, and other impressions that the word or phrase evokes in audience members. A significant part of the power—and risk—of visual elements derives from their connotative meanings as well. Even something as simple as a watermark symbol embedded in letterhead stationery can boost reader confidence in the message printed on the paper.[11] Many colors, shapes, and other design elements have **visual symbolism**, and their symbolic, connotative meanings can evolve over time and mean different things in different cultures (see Figure 12.6).

Understanding Visual Design Principles

Visual literacy is the ability to create and interpret visual messages.

Given the importance of visuals in today's business environment, **visual literacy**—the ability (as a sender) to create effective images and (as a receiver) to correctly interpret visual messages—has become a key business skill.[12] Just as creating effective sentences, paragraphs, and documents requires working knowledge of the principles of good writing, creating effective visuals requires some knowledge of the principles of good design. Even without any formal training in design, being aware of the following six principles will help you be a more effective visual communicator (see Figure 12.7):

- **Consistency.** Think of continuity as *visual parallelism*, in the same way that textual parallelism helps audiences understand and compare a series of ideas.[13] You can achieve visual parallelism in a variety of ways, through the consistent use of color, shape, size, texture, position, scale, or typeface.
- **Contrast.** Use visual choices such as size and color to emphasize contrasting quantities or ideas. To emphasize similarities, on the other hand, make the visual differences more subtle.

PDF — REAL-TIME UPDATES
Learn More

See why visual design is a lot more than just "eye candy"

The visual design of a website is more than mere decoration—it is an essential, functional part of the website and a key factor in the communication process. Go to **http://real-timeupdates.com/ebc** and click on "Learn More." If you are using mybcommlab, you can access Real-Time Updates within each chapter or under Student Study Tools.

FIGURE 12.7 Ineffective and Effective Visual Designs
The slide in Figure 12.7a violates numerous principles of effective design, as you can see in the annotations. Figure 12.7b will never win any awards for exciting or innovative design, but it does its job efficiently and effectively.

(a) Ineffective Design

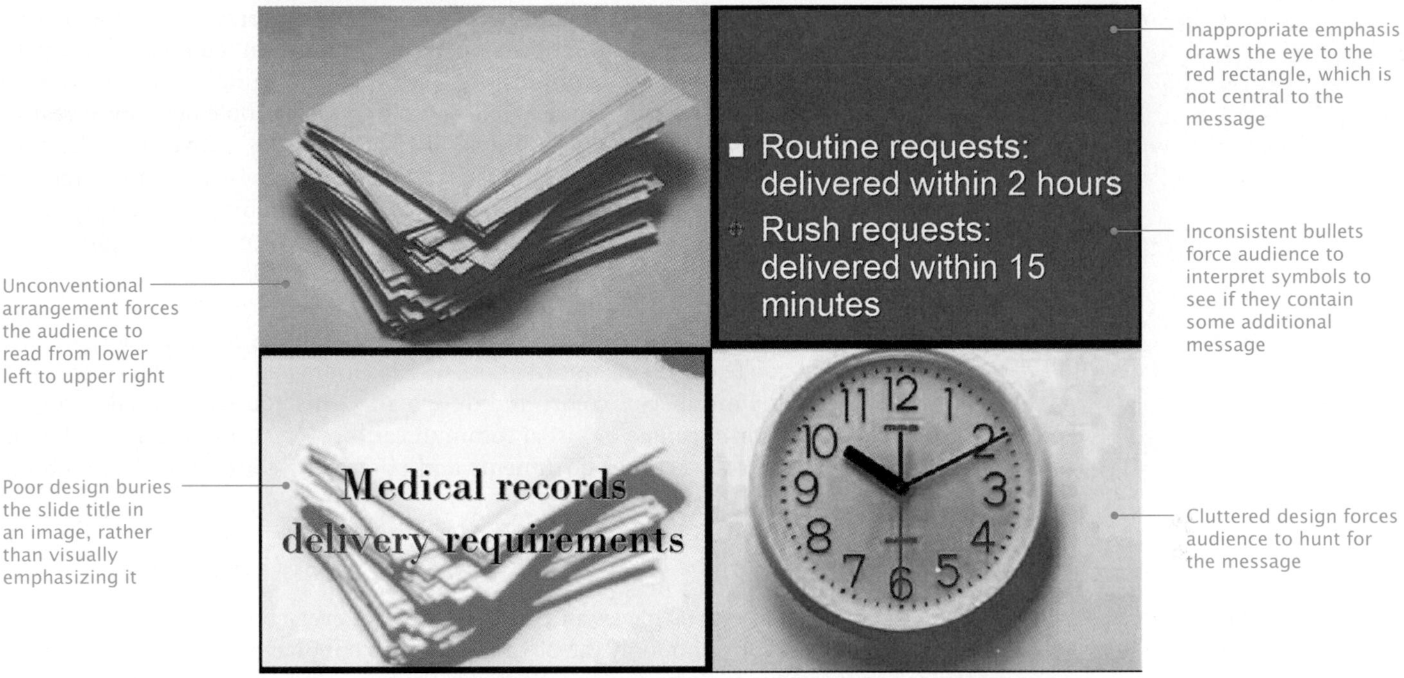

(b) Effective Design

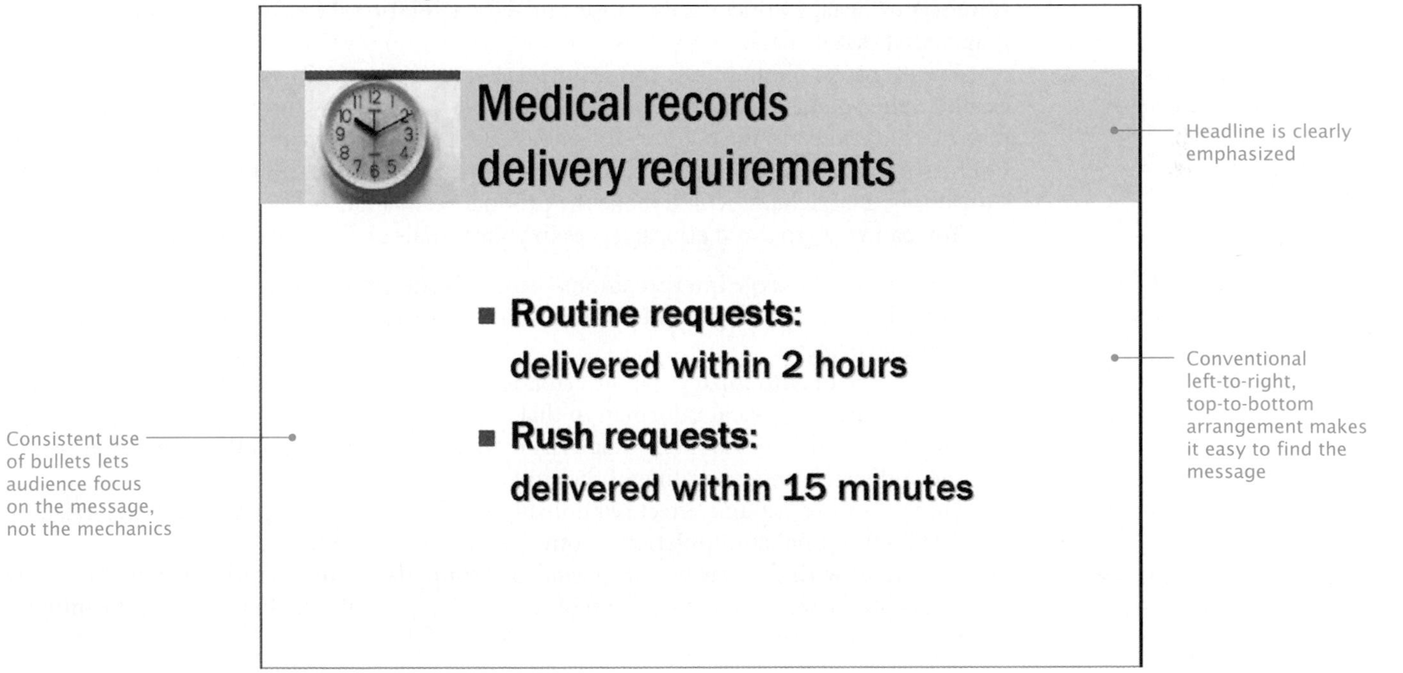

- **Balance.** Images that appear to be out of balance can be as unsettling as a building that looks like it's about to tip over. Balance can be either *formal*, in which the elements in the images are arranged symmetrically around a central point or axis, or *informal*, in which elements are not distributed evenly but stronger and weaker elements are arranged in a way that achieves an overall effect of balance. Generally speaking, formal balance is calming and serious, whereas informal balance tends to feel dynamic and engaging (which is why most advertising uses this approach, for example).

- **Emphasis.** Audiences usually assume that the dominant element in a design is the most important, so make sure that the visually dominant element really does represent the most important information. You can do this through color, position, size, or placement, for instance.
- **Convention.** Just as written communication is guided by an array of spelling, grammar, punctuation, and usage conventions, visual communication is guided by a variety of generally accepted rules or conventions that dictate virtually every aspect of design.[14] Moreover, many conventions are so ingrained that people don't even realize they are following conventions. For example, if English is your native language, you assume that ideas progress across the page from left to right because that's the direction in which English text is written. However, if you are a native Arabic or Hebrew speaker, you might automatically assume that flow on a page or screen is from right to left because that is the direction in which those languages are written.
- **Simplicity.** As Figure 12.7 indicates, simpler is usually better when it comes to visuals for business communication. When you're designing graphics for your documents, remember that you're conveying information, not decorating an apartment or creating artwork. Limit the number of colors and design elements you use and take care to avoid *chartjunk*, a term coined by visual communication specialist Edward R. Tufte for decorative elements that clutter documents and potentially confuse readers without adding any relevant information.[15]

Understanding the Ethics of Visual Communication

When you communicate with visuals, you must do so ethically.

The potential power of visuals places an ethical burden on every business communicator. This responsibility involves not only the obvious requirement of avoiding intentional ethical lapses but the more complicated and often more subtle requirement of avoiding unintentional lapses as well. Ethical problems can include photos that play on racial or gender stereotypes, images that imply cause-and-effect relationships that may not exist, and graphs that distort data.

You can take many steps to emphasize or de-emphasize specific elements in your visuals, but make sure you don't inadvertently commit an ethical lapse while doing so.

For example, photographs can influence perceptions of physical size (and perhaps of quality, value, danger, or other associated variables), depending on the way the various elements are arranged in the picture. To increase the perceived size of a product, an advertiser might show a close-up of it being held by someone with smaller-than-average hands. Conversely, a large hand would make the product seem smaller.

You can work to avoid ethical lapses in your visuals by following these guidelines:[16]

Visuals can't always speak for themselves; make sure your audience has enough context to interpret your visuals correctly.

- Consider all possible interpretations—and misinterpretations.
- Provide enough background information to help audiences interpret the visual information correctly.
- Don't hide or minimize visual information that runs counter to your argument—and don't exaggerate visual information that supports your argument.
- Don't oversimplify complex situations by hiding complications that are important to the audience's understanding of the situation.
- Don't imply cause-and-effect relationships without providing proof that they exist.
- Avoid emotional manipulation or other forms of coercion.
- Be careful with the way you *aggregate*, or group, data. For example, aggregating daily sales data by weeks or months can obscure daily fluctuations that could be meaningful to your audience.

Identifying Points to Illustrate

To help identify which parts of your message can benefit from visuals, step back and consider the flow of the entire message from the audience's point of view. Which parts might seem complex, open to misinterpretation, or even just a little bit dull? Are there any connections between ideas or data sets that might not be obvious if they are addressed only in text? Is there a lot of numeric data or other discrete factual content that would be difficult to read if presented in paragraph form? Is there a chance the main idea won't jump off the page if it's covered only in text? Will readers greet the message with skepticism and therefore look for plenty of supporting evidence?

If you answer yes to any of these questions, you probably need one or more visuals. When you're deciding which points to present visually, think of the five Cs:

- **Clear.** If you're having difficultly conveying an idea in words, take a minute to brainstorm some visual possibilities.
- **Complete.** Visuals, particularly tables, can complement your text to provide readers all the information they need.
- **Concise.** If a particular section of your message seems to require extensive description or explanation, see whether there's a way to convey that information visually in order to reduce your word count.
- **Connected.** A key purpose of many business messages is to show connections of some sort—similarities or differences, correlations, cause-and-effect relationships, and so on.
- **Compelling.** Will one or more illustrations make your message more persuasive, more interesting, or more likely to get read?

5 LEARNING OBJECTIVE

Identify the most common types of visuals used to present data, information, concepts, and ideas.

As you identify which points in your document would benefit from visuals, make sure that each visual you decide on has a clear purpose (see Table 12.1).

You have many types of visuals to choose from, and each is best suited to particular communication tasks.

Selecting the Right Type of Visual

After you've identified which points would benefit most from visual presentation, your next decision is choosing what type of visual to use for each message point (see Figure 12.8). For certain types of information, the decision is usually obvious. To present a large set of numeric values or detailed textual information, a table is the obvious choice in most cases. However, if you're presenting data broken down geographically, a color-coded map might be more effective. Also, certain visuals are commonly used for certain applications, such as line charts for showing trends over time.

REAL-TIME UPDATES
Learn More

Quickly peruse dozens of data and information display techniques

This "periodic table of visualization methods" shows dozens of ways to display data, information, concepts, strategies, and more. Go to **http://real-timeupdates.com/ebc** and click on "Learn More." If you are using mybcommlab, you can access Real-Time Updates within each chapter or under Student Study Tools.

Visuals for Presenting Data

Business professionals have a tremendous number of choices for presenting data, from general-purpose line, bar, and pie charts to specialized charts for product portfolios, financial analysis, and other professional functions. The visuals most

TABLE 12.1 When to Use Visuals

PURPOSE	EXAMPLES OF APPLICATIONS
To clarify	Support text descriptions of quantitative or numeric information, trends, spatial relationships, and physical constructions.
To simplify	Break complicated descriptions into components that can be depicted with conceptual models, flowcharts, organization charts, or diagrams.
To emphasize	Call attention to particularly important points by illustrating them with line, bar, and pie and other types of charts.
To summarize	Review major points in the narrative by providing a chart or table that summarizes key items.
To reinforce	Present information in both visual and written forms to increase readers' retention.
To attract	Engage readers visually and emotionally; provide visual relief from long blocks of text.
To impress	Build credibility by putting ideas into visual form to convey the impression of authenticity and precision.
To unify	Depict the relationship among points, such as visually connecting the steps in a process by presenting them in a flowchart.

FIGURE 12.8 Selecting the Best Visual
For each point you want to illustrate, make sure to choose the most effective type of visual.

Communication Challenge	Effective Visual Choice	
Presenting Data		
To present individual, exact values	Table	(see table below)
To show trends in one or more variables, or the relationship between those variables, over time	Line chart, bar chart	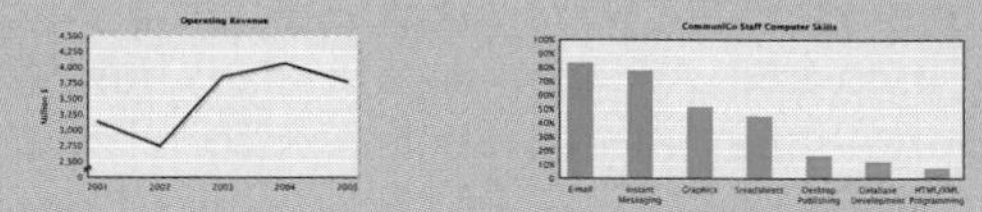
To compare two or more sets of data	Bar chart, line chart	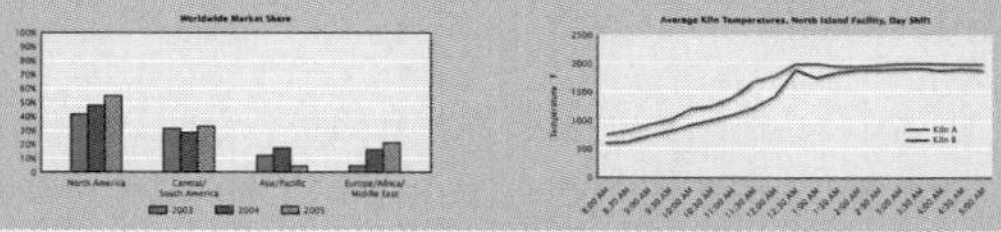
To show frequency or distribution of parts in a whole	Pie chart	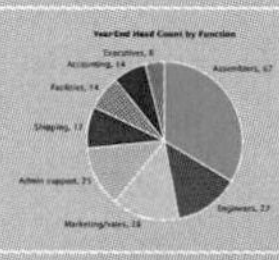
To show massive data sets, complex quantities, or dynamic data	Data visualization	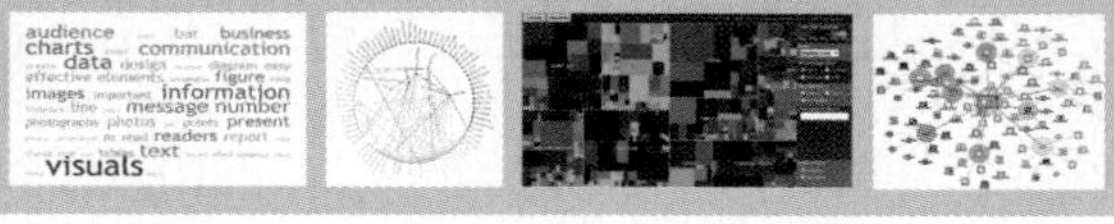
Presenting Information, Concepts, and Ideas		
To show geographic relationships or comparisons	Map	
To illustrate processes or procedures	Flowchart, diagram	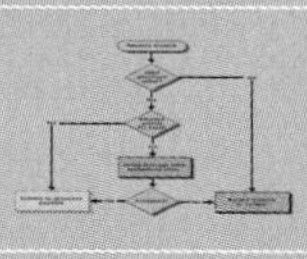
To show conceptual or spatial relationships (simplified)	Drawing	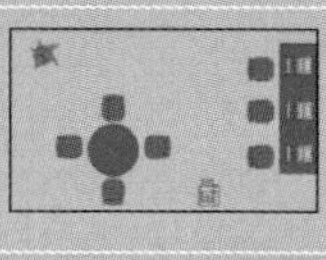
To show spatial relationships (realistic)	Photograph	
To show processes, transformations, and other activities	Animation, video	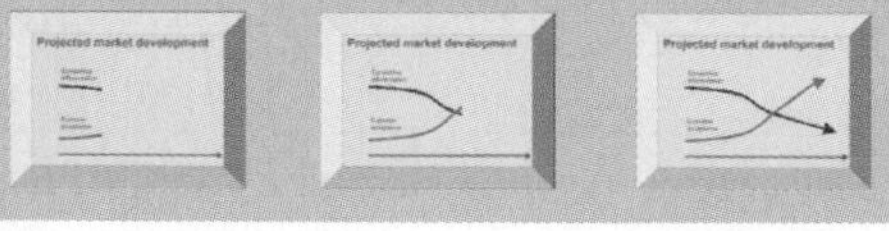

Station	Pretest	Posttest	Change
Bark peeler	0.08	0.07	+13%
Slab saw	1.12	1.18	-5%
Edger	0.45	0.30	+33%
Trim saw	2.27	2.07	+9%
Chop saw	3.62	3.68	-2%

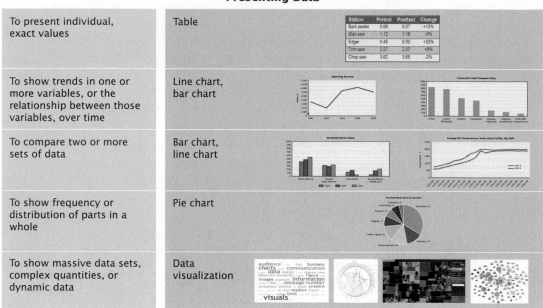

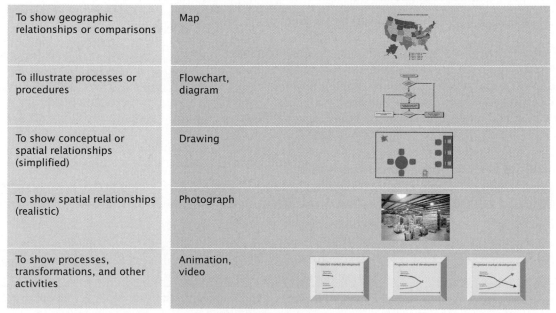

commonly used to present data include tables, line and surface charts, bar charts, and pie charts.

Printed tables can display extensive amounts of data, but tables for online display and electronic presentations need to be simpler.

Tables

When you need to present detailed, specific information, choose a **table**, a systematic arrangement of data in columns and rows. Most tables contain the standard parts illustrated in Figure 12.9. For printed documents, you can adjust font size and column/row

FIGURE 12.9 **Parts of a Table**
Here are the standard parts of a table. No matter which design you choose, make sure the layout is clear and that individual rows and columns are easy to follow.

	Multicolumn Heading			
Subheading	**Subheading**	**Subheading**	**Subheading**	**Single-Column Heading**
Row heading	x x x	x x x	x x x	x x x
Row heading	x x x	x x x	x x x	x x x
Subheading	x x x	x x x	x x x	x x x
Subheading	x x x	x x x	x x x	x x x
Total	x x x	x x x	x x x	x x x

Source: (In the same format as a text footnote; see Appendix B)

*Footnote (For an explanation of elements in the table, a superscript number or small letter may be used instead of an asterisk or other symbol.)

spacing to fit a considerable amount of information on the page and still maintain readability. For online documents, you often need to reduce the number of columns and rows to make sure your tables are easily readable online. Tables for oral presentations usually need to be the simplest of all because you can't expect audiences to read detailed information from the screen.

Although complex information may require formal tables that are set apart from the text, you can present some data more simply within the text. Such text tables are usually introduced with a sentence that leads directly into the tabular information. Here's an example:[17]

Here is how the five leading full-service restaurant chains compare in terms of number of locations and annual revenue:

	OSI RESTAURANT PARTNERS	APPLEBEE'S	CARLSON	BRINKER	DARDEN
Major Chain(s)	Outback Steakhouse, Carrabba's	Applebee's	Friday's, Pick Up Stix	Chili's, On the Border, Romano's	Red Lobster, Olive Garden
Locations	1,400	1,970	1,000	1,800	1,700
Revenue ($ Million)	$4,150	$1,338	$2,400 (est. from 2004)	$4,235	$6,627

Source: Hoover's Online [accessed 3 December 2008] www.hoovers.com

When you prepare tables, follow these guidelines to make your tables easy to read:

- Use common, understandable units and clearly identify the units you're using.
- Express all items in a column in the same unit and round off for simplicity.
- Label column headings clearly and use a subhead, if necessary.
- Separate columns or rows with lines or extra space to make the table easy to follow; in complex tables, consider highlighting every other row or column in a pale contrasting color.
- Provide totals or averages of columns or rows when relevant.
- Document the source of the data, using the same format as for a text footnote (see Appendix B).

FIGURE 12.10 Line Chart
This two-line line chart compares the temperatures measured inside two cement kilns from 8:00 A.M. to 5:00 P.M.

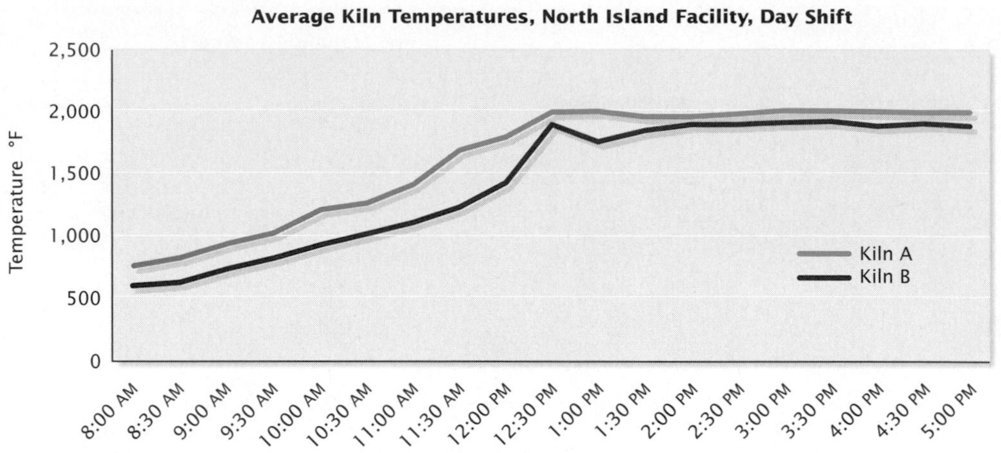

FIGURE 12.11 Surface Chart
Surface, or area, charts can show a combination of trends over time and the individual contributions of the components of a whole.

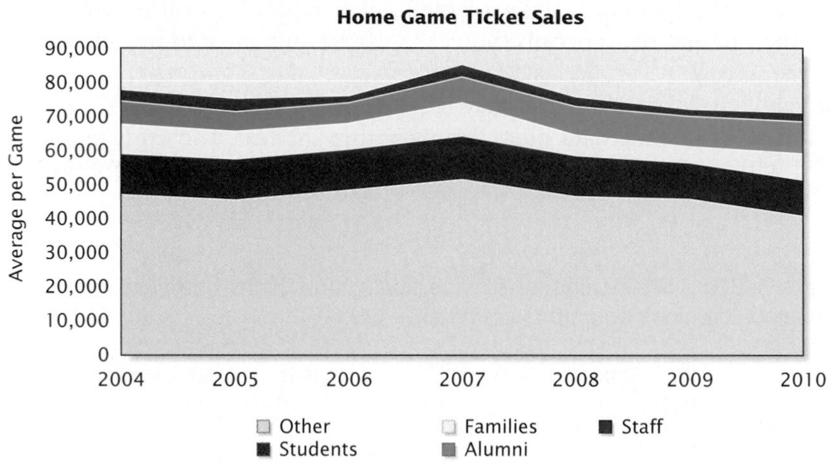

Line Charts and Surface Charts

Line charts are commonly used to show trends over time or the relationship between two variables.

A **line chart**, or *line graph*, illustrates trends over time or plots the relationship of two variables. In line charts that show trends, the vertical, or *y*, axis shows the amount, and the horizontal, or *x*, axis shows the time or other quantity against which the amount is being measured. Moreover, you can plot just a single line or overlay multiple lines to compare different entities (see Figure 12.10).

A **surface chart**, also called an **area chart**, is a form of line chart that shows a cumulative effect; all the lines add up to the top line, which represents the total (see Figure 12.11). This form of chart helps you illustrate changes in the composition of something over time. When preparing a surface chart, put the most important segment against the baseline and restrict the number of strata to four or five.

Bar Charts and Pie Charts

A **bar chart**, or *bar graph*, portrays numbers with the height or length of its rectangular bars, making one or more series of numbers easy to read or understand. Bar charts are particularly valuable when you want to show or compare quantities over time. As the charts in Figure 12.12 suggest, bar charts can appear in various forms. Specialized bar charts such as *timelines* and *Gantt charts* are used often in project management, for example.

FIGURE 12.12 The Versatile Bar Chart
Here are six of the dozens of variations possible with bar charts: singular (12.12a), grouped (12.12b), deviation (12.12c), segmented (12.12d), combination (12.12e), and paired (12.12f).

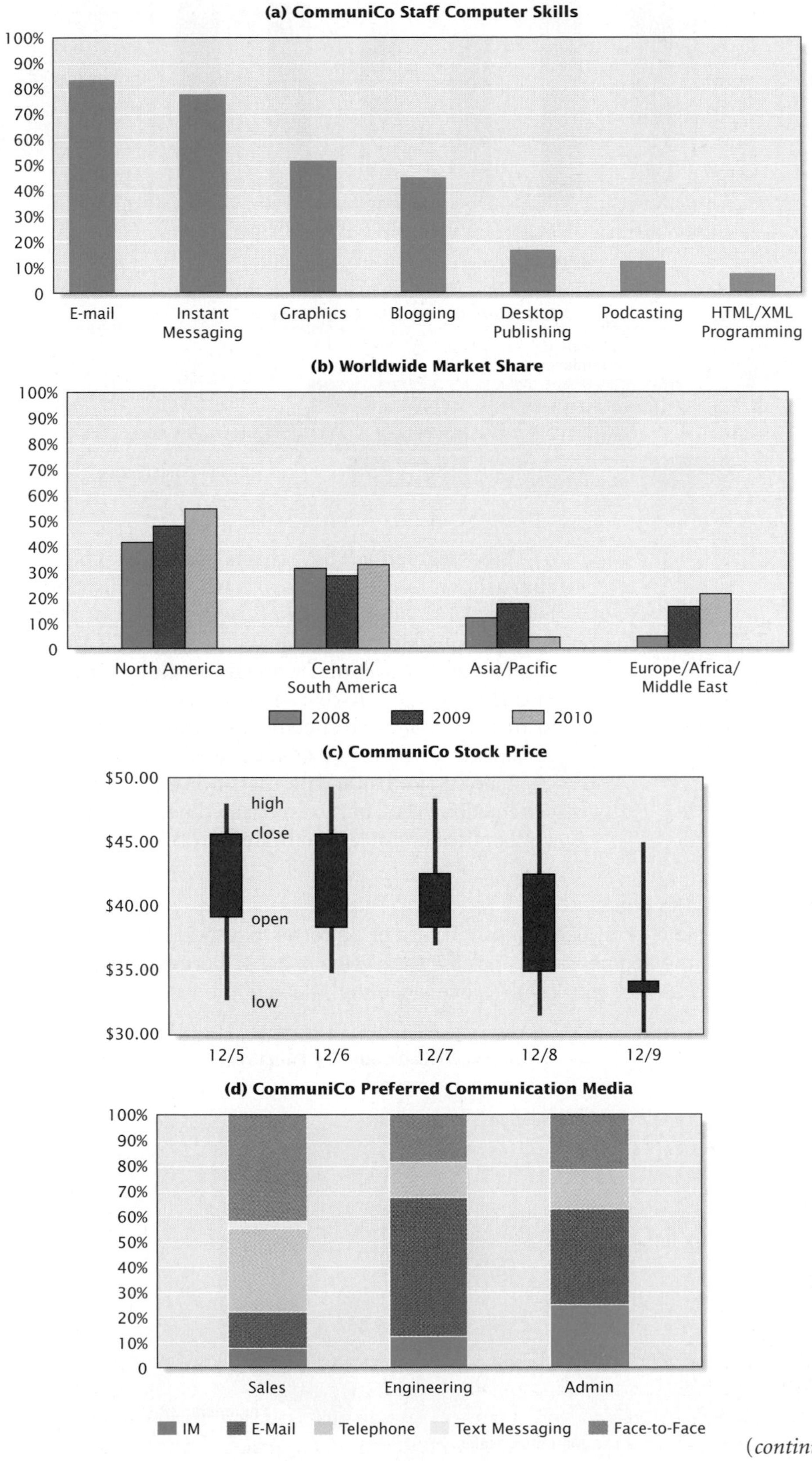

(continued)

FIGURE 12.12 The Versatile Bar Chart *(continued)*

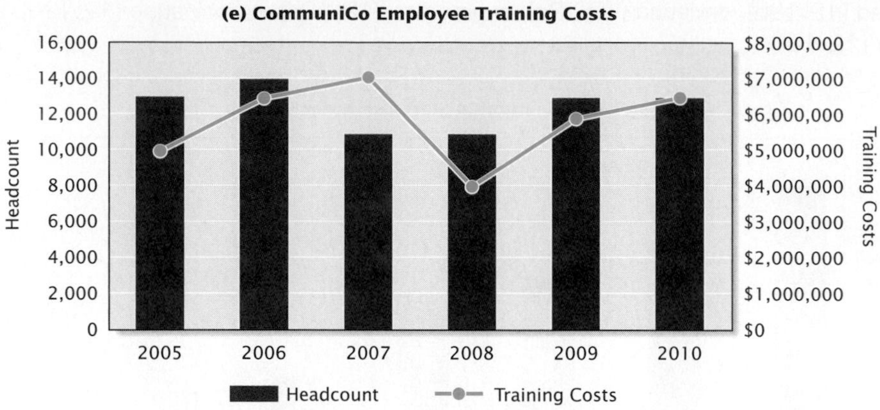

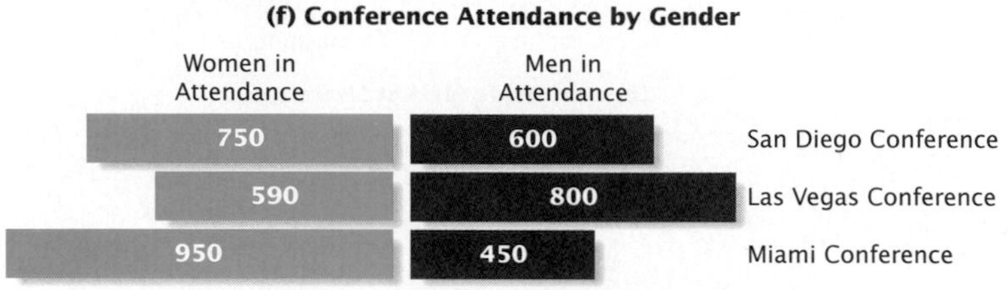

REAL-TIME UPDATES
Learn More

Data visualization gateway: A comprehensive collection for business communicators

This unique web resource offers links to a vast array of data visualization techniques and examples. Go to **http://real-timeupdates.com/ebc**, click on "Learn More," and then select Chapter 12.

Like segmented bar charts and area charts, a **pie chart** shows how the parts of a whole are distributed (see Figure 12.13). Pie charts can be useful to show relative percentages quickly and dramatically, such as if you want to emphasize that part of a whole is much larger than all the rest. However, pie charts can be difficult when readers need to find and compare specific amounts. In such instances, consider a bar chart or a table instead.

Line, surface, bar, and pie charts will meet most of your data presentation needs, but for specialized needs, explore the other chart options available in software such as Microsoft Excel.

Pie charts are effective if you want to show dramatic differences in proportions; to convey specific details, however, a bar chart or table might be more effective.

FIGURE 12.13 Pie Chart
When creating pie charts, use different colors or patterns to distinguish the various pieces. Label all the segments and indicate their value in either percentages or units of measure so that your readers can judge the values of the wedges.

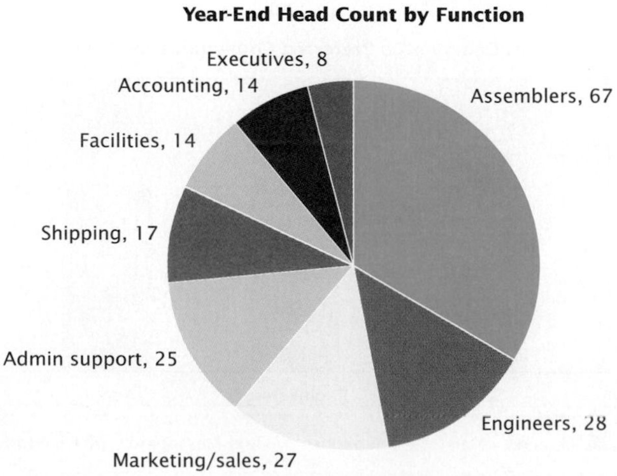

Data Visualization

Data visualization tools let you display vast data sets, dynamic data, and textual information graphically.

Conventional charts and graphs are limited in two ways: They can represent only numeric data, and most types show only a limited number of data points before the display becomes too cluttered to interpret. A diverse class of display capabilities known as **data visualization** overcomes both of these drawbacks (see Figure 12.14). First, some types of data visualization displays can show hundreds, thousands, or even millions of data points, using a variety of graphical presentations. For instance, regional sales data can be displayed in three-dimensional "topography" maps to quickly show strong and weak areas. Second, other kinds of visualization

FIGURE 12.14 Data Visualization

The range of data visualization displays is virtually endless; here are a few of the many different ways to display complex sets of data.

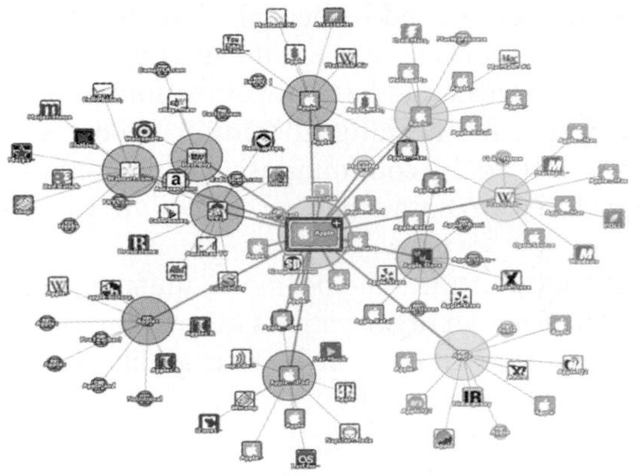

(a) Website Linkage Map Showing the Most Active Links to and from Apple's Homepage (**www.apple.com**)

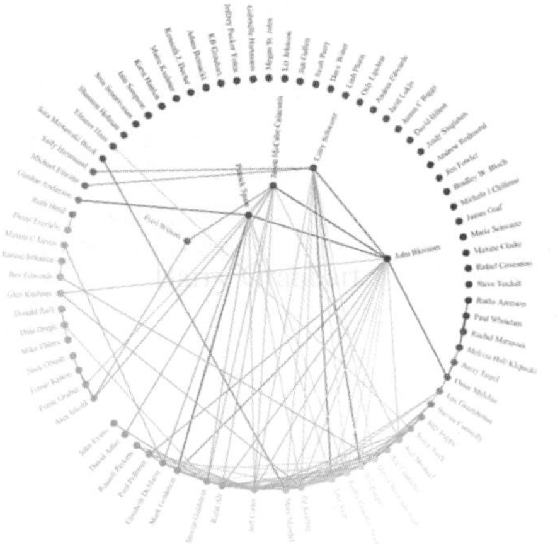

(b) Facebook "Friend Wheel" Showing How the Connections of One Facebook User Are Connected with One Another

(c) A Tag Cloud Showing the Relative Frequency of the 50 Most-Used Words in This Chapter (other than common words such as *and*, *or*, and *the*)

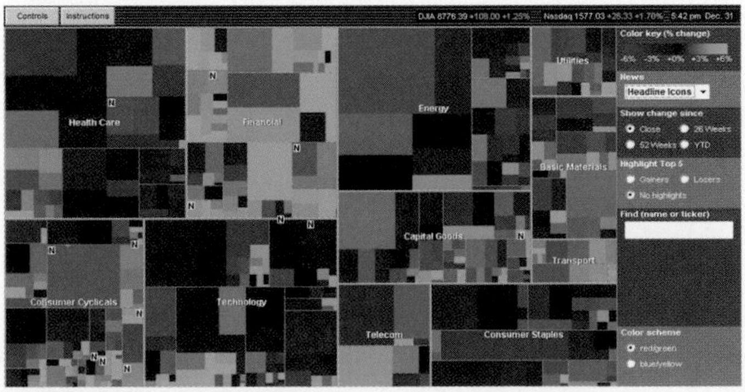

(d) A Real-Time "HeatMap" Showing Price Increases (green) and Decreases (red) for Stocks in Various Industry Sectors

tools combine data with textual information to communicate complex or dynamic data much faster than conventional presentations. A common example of this type of display is a *tag cloud*, which shows the relative frequency of terms, or *tags* (user-applied content labels) in an article, a blog, a website, survey data, or another collection of text.[18] Data visualization is an exciting, dynamic field, and you can expect to see many innovations in the coming years.

Visuals for Presenting Information, Concepts, and Ideas

In addition to facts and figures, you may need to present other types of information, from spatial relationships (such as the floor plan for a new office building) to abstract ideas (such as progress or competition). The most common types of visuals for these applications include flowcharts, organization charts, maps, drawings, diagrams, photographs, animation, and video.

Flowcharts and Organization Charts

A **flowchart** (see Figure 12.15) illustrates a sequence of events from start to finish; it is an indispensable tool for illustrating processes, procedures, and sequential relationships. For general business purposes, you don't need to be too concerned about the specific shapes in a flowchart, but use them consistently. However, you should be aware of the formal flowchart "language," in which each shape has a specific meaning (diamonds are decision points, rectangles are process steps, and so on). If you're communicating with computer programmers and others who are accustomed to formal flowcharting, make sure you use the correct symbols to avoid confusion.

As the name implies, an **organization chart** illustrates the positions, units, or functions of an organization and the way they interrelate. An organization's normal communication channels are almost impossible to describe without the benefit of a chart like the one in Figure 1.2 on page 6. These charts aren't limited to organization structures, of course; as you saw Chapter 4, they can also be used to outline messages.

FIGURE 12.15 **Flowchart**
Flowcharts show sequences of events and are most valuable when the process or procedure has a number of decision points and variable paths.

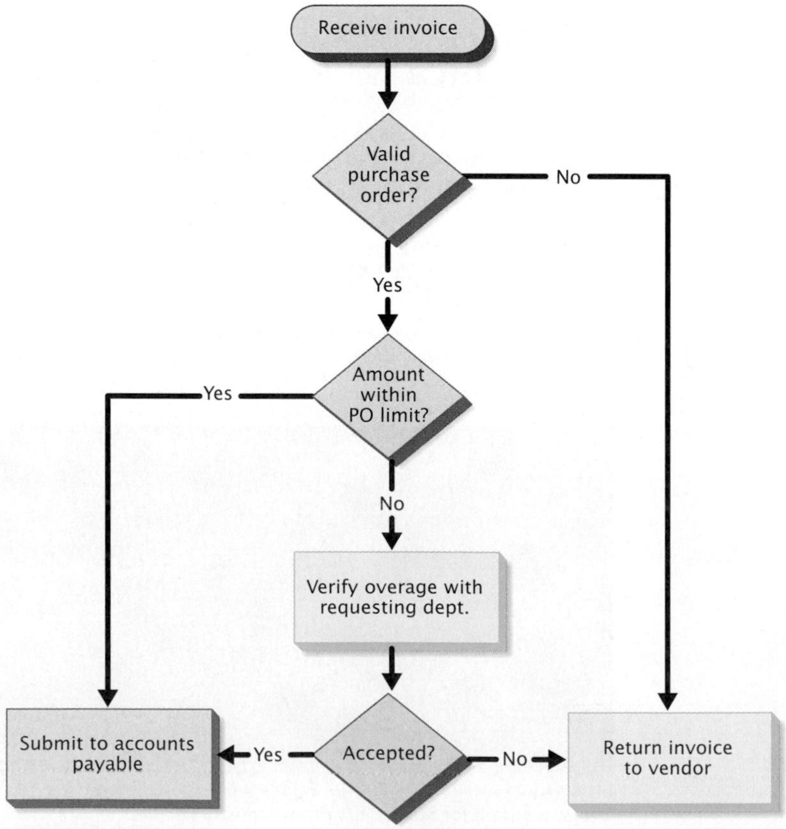

Maps, Drawings, Diagrams, and Photographs

Maps are useful for showing market territories, distribution routes, facility locations, and other geographically significant data (see Figure 12.16). Simple maps are available via clip art libraries for word processing and presentation software, but more powerful uses

Use maps to represent statistics by geographic area and to show spatial relationships.

FIGURE 12.16 Map

Maps offer many opportunities for displaying data and information. The map in Figure 12.16a shows population projections for each state in the United States. When combined with databases in geographic information systems (GIS), maps become extremely powerful visual reporting tools. The map in Figure 12.16b is a simple example of a GIS; more sophisticated systems can show overlays of population profiles, optimized transportation routes, and other information.

(a) Map Showing Statistical Data

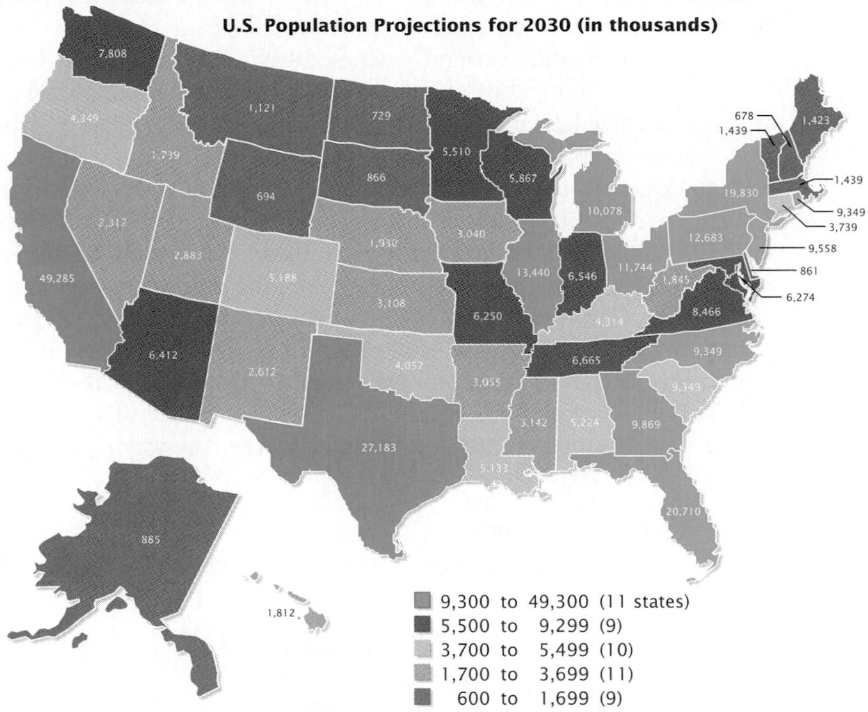

(b) Simple Geographic Information System

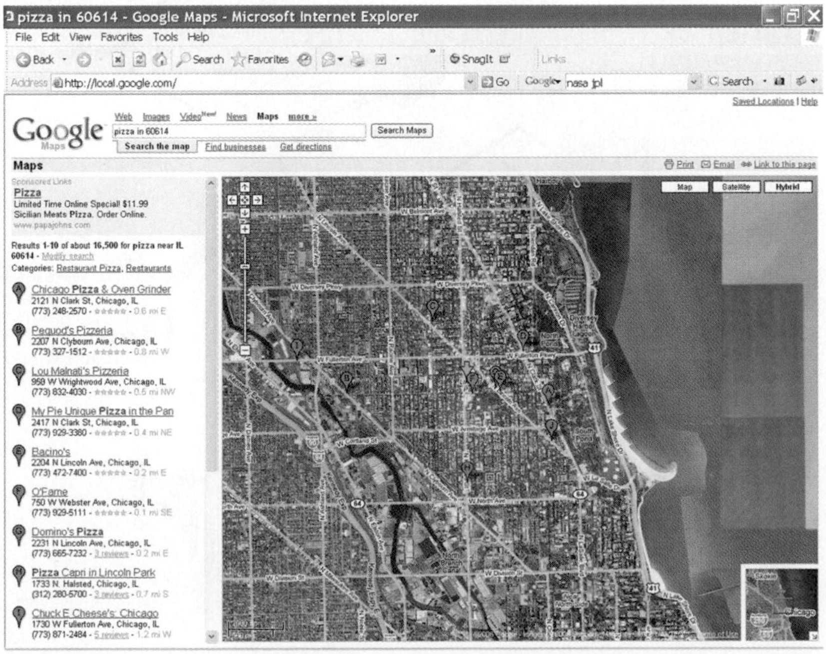

(such as automatically generating color-coded maps based on data inputs) usually require the specialized capabilities of *geographic information systems.* You may also want to explore online resources such as Google Earth (http://earth.google.com) and Bing maps (www.bing.com/map), which offer a variety of mapping and aerial photography features.

Although drawings, diagrams, and photographs are often created by people working in communication specialties such as web design or technical writing, all managers encounter situations in which such images can help get their messages across (see Figure 12.17). Simple drawings can show the network of suppliers in an industry, the flow of funds through a company, or the process for completing the payroll each week. More complex diagrams can convey technical topics such as the operation of a machine or repair procedures.

Word processing programs and presentation software provide basic drawing capabilities, but for more precise drawings or complex illustrations, you need a specialized package such as Microsoft Visio, Adobe Illustrator, or Google SketchUp (which is free). Moving a level beyond those programs, computer-aided design (CAD) systems such as Autodesk's AutoCAD can produce extremely detailed architectural and engineering drawings.

Use photographs for visual appeal and to show exact appearances.

Photographs offer both functional and decorative value. In the past, their use was limited to specialized documents such as annual reports and product brochures; however, with low-cost digital photography now widely available, virtually all writers have the ability to add photographs to printed documents, presentations, and webpages. In addition, photo libraries such as Getty Images (www.gettyimages.com) and various search engines make it easy to find digital photographs. Some of these photos are available for free, but the professional collections, such as Getty Images, require either a one-time payment for unlimited use (often called *royalty free*) or an annual payment or other limited-use purchase (often called *rights managed*). You can also find photos and other images through Creative Commons (http://creativecommons.org), with various levels of licensing terms.

Nothing else can demonstrate the exact appearance of a new facility, a piece of property, a new product, or even a retiring co-worker the way a photograph can. However, in

FIGURE 12.17 Diagram
Clearly drawn diagrams can help audiences grasp technical information quickly.

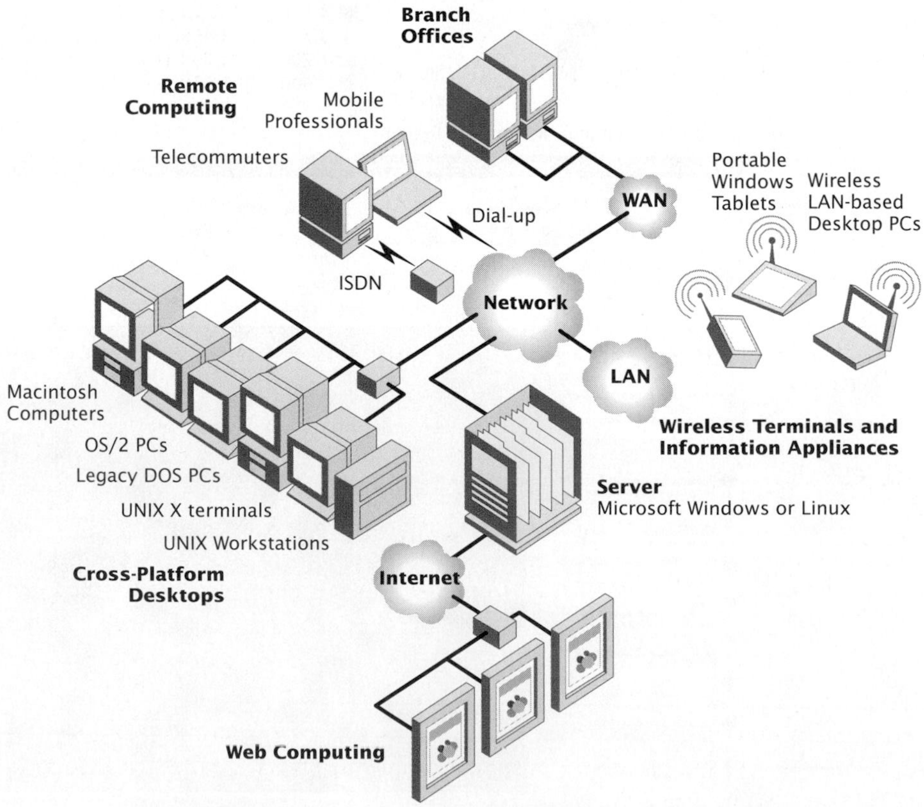

some situations, a photograph may show too much detail, which is one reason assembly and repair manuals frequently use drawings instead of photos, for instance. With a drawing, you can select how much detail to show, and you can focus the reader's attention on particular parts or places. The disadvantage of such technical illustrations is the time, skill, and special tools often required to create them.

Technology makes it easy to use photographs in reports and presentations, but it also presents an important ethical concern. Software tools such as Photoshop allow you to easily make dramatic changes to photos—without leaving a clue that they've been altered. You can remove people from photographs, put Person A's head on Person B's body, and make products look more attractive than they really are. Most people would agree that it's acceptable to make cosmetic improvements, such as brightening an underexposed photo to make it easier to view. But to avoid ethical lapses, don't make any alterations that mislead the viewer or substantially change the message conveyed by the photo—at least not without informing your audience of the changes.[19]

To show investors what a new building would look like in its environment, an artist combined a photograph of a scale model of the building with a photograph of the actual street scene. Because the target audience clearly understands that the building doesn't exist, this sort of image manipulation is not unethical.

Animation and Video

Computer animation and video are among the most specialized forms of business visuals; when they are appropriate and done well, they offer unparalleled visual impact. At a simple level, you can animate shapes and text within electronic presentations (see Chapter 14). At a more sophisticated level, software such as Adobe Flash enables the creation of multimedia files that include computer animation, digital video, and other elements.

The combination of low-cost digital video cameras and video-sharing websites such as YouTube has spurred a revolution in business video applications in recent years. Product demonstrations, company overviews, promotional presentations, and training seminars are among the most popular applications of business video. With a little creativity, you can use video in everything from recruiting to contests that get customers or employees involved in the promotional process. For example, before moving into his career in the insurance industry, Hamline University graduate Eric Binfet used his creative and technical skills to write and produce the winning video in a Dairy Queen employee contest. The video did such a great job of showcasing some important new branding elements that the store owner pitched it to corporate as a potential commercial.[20]

PRODUCING AND INTEGRATING VISUALS

6 LEARNING OBJECTIVE

Explain how to integrate visuals with text effectively and how to verify the quality of your visuals.

Now that you understand the communication power of visuals and have chosen the best visuals to illustrate key points in your report, website, or presentation, it's time to get creative. This section offers advice on creating visuals, integrating them with your text, and verifying the quality of your visual elements.

Creating Visuals

Computer software offers a variety of tools but doesn't automatically give you the design sensibility that is needed for effective visuals.

Computers make it easy to create visuals, but they also make it easy to create ineffective, distracting, and even downright ugly visuals. However, by following the basic design principles discussed on pages 368–370, you can create all the basic visuals you need—visuals

REAL-TIME UPDATES
Learn More

Jumpstart your visual creativity

The notion that visual creativity is a skill that only artists have—or should care about—is simply not true. Every professional can develop visual thinking and design skills that will improve problem solving and communication. Go to **http://real-timeupdates.com/ebc** and click on "Learn More." If you are using mybcommlab, you can access Real-Time Updates within each chapter or under Student Study Tools.

that are attractive and effective. If possible, have a professional designer set up a *template* for the various types of visuals you and your colleagues need to create. In addition to helping ensure an effective design, using templates saves you the time of making numerous design decisions every time you create a chart or graphic.

Remember that the style and quality of your visuals communicate a subtle message about your relationship with the audience. A simple sketch might be fine for a working meeting but inappropriate for a formal presentation or report. On the other hand, elaborate, full-color visuals may be viewed as extravagant for an informal report but may be entirely appropriate for a message to top management or influential outsiders.

Integrating Visuals with Text

For maximum effectiveness and minimum disruption for the reader, visual elements need to be carefully integrated with the text of your message so that readers can move back and forth between text and visuals with as little disruption as possible. Successful integration involves four decisions: maintaining a balance between visuals and text, referring to visuals in the text, placing the visuals in the document, and writing titles and other descriptions.

Balancing Illustrations and Words

Maintain a balance between text and visuals and pace your visuals in a way that emphasizes your key points.

Strong visuals enhance the descriptive and persuasive power of your writing, but putting too many visuals into a report can distract your readers. Constantly referring to visuals makes it difficult for readers to maintain focus on the thread of your message. The space occupied by visuals can also disrupt the flow of text on the page or screen. The pacing of visuals throughout the text is also an important consideration. Although it isn't always possible to have perfect distribution throughout the report, try to have a fairly even flow of text and visuals from page to page or screen to screen.

As always, take into account your readers' specific needs. If you're addressing an audience with multiple language backgrounds or widely varying reading skills, you can shift the balance toward more visual elements to help get around any language barriers. The professional experience, education, and training of your audience should influence your approach as well. For instance, detailed statistical plots and mathematical formulas are everyday reading material for quality-control engineers but not for most salespeople or top executives.

Referencing Visuals

To tie visuals to the text, introduce them in the text and place them near the points they illustrate.

Unless a visual element clearly stands on its own, as in the *sidebars* you often see in magazines, visuals should be clearly referred to by number in the text of your report. Some report writers refer to all visuals as "exhibits" and number them consecutively throughout the report; many others number tables and figures separately (everything that isn't a table is regarded as a figure). In a long report with numbered sections, illustrations may have a double number (separated by a period or a hyphen) representing the section number and the individual illustration number within that section. Whatever scheme you use, make sure it's clear and consistent.

Help your readers understand the significance of visuals by referring to them before readers encounter them in the document or onscreen. The following examples show how you can make this connection in the text:

> Figure 12.1 summarizes the financial history of the motorcycle division over the past five years, with sales broken into four categories.
>
> Total sales were steady over this period, but the mix of sales by category changed dramatically (see Figure 12.2).

> The underlying reason for the remarkable growth in our sales of youth golf apparel is suggested by Table 4, which shows the growing interest in junior golf around the world.

When describing the data shown in your visuals, be sure to emphasize the main point you are trying to make. Don't make the mistake of simply repeating the data to be shown.

Placing Visuals

Try to position your visuals so that your audience doesn't have to flip back and forth (in printed documents) or scroll (onscreen) between the visuals and the text. Ideally, it's best to place each visual within, beside, or immediately after the paragraph it illustrates so that readers can consult the explanation and the visual at the same time. If possible, try to avoid bunching several visuals in one section of the document. (Bunching is unavoidable in some cases, such as when multiple visuals accompany a single section of text—as in this chapter, for instance.)

Writing Titles, Captions, and Legends

Titles, captions, and legends provide more opportunities to connect your visual and textual messages. A **title** is similar to a subheading, providing a short description that identifies the content and purpose of the visual, along with whatever label and number you're using to refer to the visual. A **caption** usually offers additional discussion of the visual's content and can be several sentences long, if appropriate. Captions can also alert readers that additional discussion is available in the accompanying text. Titles usually appear above visuals, and captions appear below, but effective designs can place these two elements in other positions. Sometimes titles and captions are combined in a single block of text as well. As with all other design decisions, be consistent throughout your report or website. A **legend** helps readers "decode" the visual by explaining what various colors, symbols, or other design choices mean.

A descriptive title simply identifies the topic of an illustration; an information title helps the reader understand the conclusion to be drawn from the illustration.

REAL-TIME UPDATES
Learn More

Understand why some visuals work and some don't

Learn from the insightful analysis of more than a dozen commonly used displays for data and information, along with redesigned visuals that addresses the identified problems. Go to **http://real-timeupdates.com/ebc** and click on "Learn More." If you are using mybcommlab, you can access Real-Time Updates within each chapter or under Student Study Tools.

Readers should be able to grasp the point of a visual without digging into the surrounding text. For instance, a title that says simply "Refineries" doesn't say much at all. A **descriptive title** that identifies the topic of the illustration, such as "Relationship Between Petroleum Demand and Refinery Capacity in the United States" provides a better idea of what the chart is all about. An **informative title** tells even more by calling attention to the conclusion that ought to be drawn from the data, such as "Refinery Capacity Declines as Petroleum Demand Continues to Grow."

Verifying the Quality of Your Visuals

Visuals have a particularly strong impact on your readers and on their perceptions of you and your work, so verifying their quality is vital. Take a few extra minutes to make sure your visuals are absolutely accurate, properly documented, and honest:

Review each visual to make sure it doesn't intentionally or unintentionally distort the meaning of the underlying information.

- **Is the visual accurate?** Be sure to check visuals for mistakes such as typographical errors, inconsistent color treatment, confusing or undocumented symbols, and misaligned elements. Does each visual deliver your message accurately?
- **Is the visual properly documented?** As with the textual elements in your reports and presentations, visuals based on other people's research, information, and ideas require full citation. (Note that in many books, including this one, source notes for visuals are collected in one place at the end of the book.)
- **Is the visual honest?** As a final precaution, step back and make sure your visuals communicate truthful messages (see "Practicing Ethical Communication: Distorting the Data").

Practicing Ethical Communication

Distorting the Data

Take a quick look at these three line charts, all of which display the level of impurities found in a particular source of drinking water. Chart A suggests that the source has a consistently high level of impurities throughout the year, Chart B indicates that the level of impurities jumps up and down throughout the year, and Chart C shows an impurity level that is fairly consistent throughout the year—and fairly low.

Here's the catch: All three charts are displaying *exactly the same data.*

Look again at Chart A. The vertical scale is set from 0 to 120, sufficient to cover the range of variations in the data. However, what if you wanted to persuade an audience that the variations from month to month were quite severe? In Chart B, the scale is "zoomed in" on 60 to 110, making the variations look much more dramatic. The result could be a stronger emotional impact on the reader, creating the impression that these impurities are out of control.

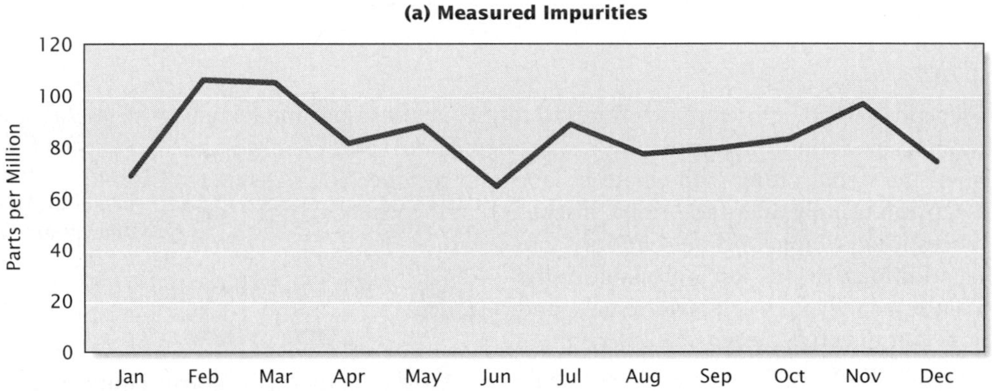

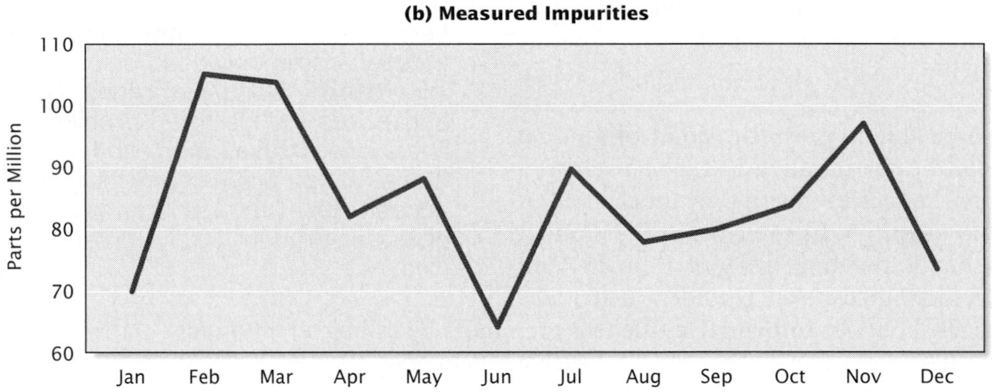

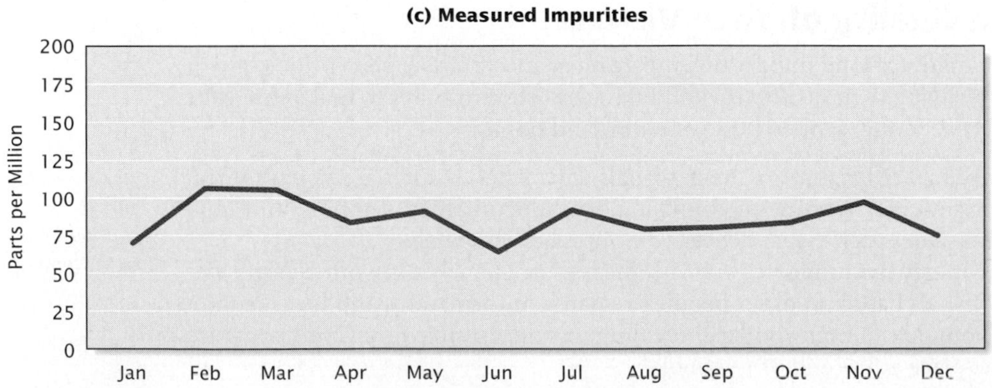

On the other hand, what if you wanted to create the impression that things were humming along just fine, with low levels of impurities and no wild swings from month to month? You would follow the example in Chart C, where the scale is expanded from 0 to 200, which appears to minimize the variations in the data. This graph is visually "calmer," potentially creating the impression that there's really nothing to worry about.

If all three graphs show the same data, is any one of them more honest than the others? The answer to this question depends on your intent and your audience's information needs. For instance, if dramatic swings in the measurement from month to month suggest a problem with the quality of your product or the safety of a process that affects the public, then visually minimizing the swings might well be considered dishonest.

CAREER APPLICATIONS

1. What sort of quick visual impression would such a chart give if the vertical scale is set to 0 to 500? Why?
2. If the acceptable range of impurities in this case is from 60 to 120 parts per million, which of these three charts is the fairest way to present the data? Why?

Make sure they don't hide information the audience needs, imply conclusions that your information doesn't support, or play on audience emotions in manipulative or coercive ways.

For the latest information on report writing and visuals, visit **http://real-timeupdates.com/ebc** and click on "Chapter 12."

For a review of the important points to remember when creating visuals, see "Checklist: Creating Effective Visuals."

Document Makeover

Improve This Policy Report

To practice correcting drafts of actual documents, visit the "Document Makeovers" section in mybcommlab. Refer to the User Guide for specific instructions on how to access the content for this chapter. You will find a policy report that contains problems and errors related to what you've learned in this chapter about writing business reports and proposals. Use the Final Draft decision tool to create an improved version of this report. Check the message for an effective opening; consistent levels of formality or informality; and the use of headings, lists, transitions, and previews and reviews to help orient readers.

CHECKLIST: Creating Effective Visuals

- Emphasize visual consistency to connect parts of a whole and minimize audience confusion.
- Avoid arbitrary changes of color, texture, typeface, position, or scale.
- Highlight contrasting points through color, position, and other design choices.
- Decide whether you want to achieve formal or informal balance.
- Emphasize dominant elements and de-emphasize less important pieces in a design.
- Understand and follow (at least most of the time) the visual conventions your audience expects.
- Strive for simplicity and clarity; don't clutter your visuals with meaningless decoration.
- Follow the guidelines for avoiding ethical lapses.
- Carefully consider your message, the nature of your information, and your audience to choose which points to illustrate.
- Select the proper types of graphics for the information at hand and for the objective of the message.
- Be sure the visual contributes to overall understanding of the subject.
- Understand how to use your software tools to maximize effectiveness and efficiency.
- Integrate visuals and text by maintaining a balance between illustrations and words, clearly referring to visuals within the text, and placing visuals carefully.
- Use titles, captions, and legends to help readers understand the meaning and importance of your visuals.
- Verify the quality of your visuals by checking for accuracy, proper documentation, and honesty.

On the Job: Solving Communication Dilemmas at Tellabs

You wanted to start your career in corporate communications with an opportunity to learn from one of the best, so you're excited to be on George Stenitzer's team at Tellabs. Using the skills you've been practicing in this course, respond to these challenges.

1. The "CEO's letter" in a corporate annual report serves as an introduction to the rest of the report. In Tellabs's 2006 report, CEO Krish Prabhu opened his letter with the following:

> More. I can't think of a better word to describe what's happening in communications today. All across the world, people want to see more. Do more. Interact more. Learn more. And everywhere we look, the world's communications providers are rushing to respond.
>
> This transition to tomorrow's networks represents a unique growth opportunity for Tellabs. That's because making more possible is what this company is all about. We do it by supplying the solutions that providers need to make their networks smarter, faster and better-suited to the kinds of high-bandwidth applications that will define the future of communications.
>
> In fact, that future is already with us. As I write this, YouTube, the immensely popular videosharing Web site, is already one of the top 15 Web sites in the world, even though it has yet to celebrate its second birthday. YouTube originates an average of 100 million video streams each day. And thanks to a partnership with Verizon, those videos are now accessible even when we're away from our computers.
>
> The YouTube success story is merely one illustration of the remarkable changes that are taking place in the way we communicate and entertain ourselves.

After reviewing a draft, Stenitzer suggested that a heading would help intrigue and prepare readers for the information in this section. Which of the following headings does the best job of introducing this section of Prabhu's letter? (The purpose of discussing these changes in online communication and networking is to convince investors that the market opportunities for Tellabs's products will continue to grow.)

a. There's No Stopping Us Now!
b. Exciting Opportunities in the Exciting New World of High-Bandwidth Communication
c. Growth Opportunities in a Growing Market
d. Growth Opportunities: Market Drivers

2. Like many other companies associated with the Internet, Tellabs's business declined when the dot-com boom of the late 1990s began to fizzle out by early 2001. The following excerpt from the company's 2005 annual report describes the effect this had on the company's operations. (The *carriers* and *service providers* referred to are the companies that buy Tellabs's products; *material charges* are expenses that are significant enough to affect the company's stock price.) As you review these two paragraphs (don't worry about all the technical and financial details), you can see that the first discusses the period from 2001 to 2003, when the company's financial results suffered. The second discusses the upturn that began in 2003 and continued through 2005.

> The markets for our products have undergone dynamic change over the last few years. Beginning in 2001, carrier overcapacity, a softening economy and other factors caused our customers to reduce their capital spending significantly. The impact on Tellabs was a dramatic decline in revenue for each of the years 2001 through 2003. In addition, we had manufacturing overcapacity, excess inventories and a cost structure that could not be supported by our smaller revenue base. We responded by closing manufacturing facilities, reducing global head count, consolidating office space, exiting certain product lines and instituting cost controls across the organization. We also reviewed our product portfolio and cut back or stopped development efforts on some products. In addition, at the end of 2003, we moved to outsource the majority of our remaining manufacturing operations to third-party electronics manufacturing services providers to take advantage of their greater purchasing power and other efficiencies. These actions caused us to record material charges in 2001 through 2005 for excess and obsolete inventory and excess purchase commitments, severance costs, facilities shutdown costs, including accelerated depreciation on certain manufacturing and office buildings and equipment due to shortened useful lives, and various contractual obligations. We also recorded charges for other impaired and surplus assets.
>
> Market stability began in 2003 and continued in 2004 and 2005 as service providers invested in their networks at levels

at or above 2003. This stability enabled us to post year-over-year revenue growth in 2004 for the first time since fiscal 2000. Growing demand for wireless services, including third-generation (3G) services, drove capital investments by both wireless and wireline service providers and helped drive sales of our transport and managed access products.

Which of the following transition sentences would be the best choice to add at the beginning of the second paragraph, signaling to readers that the story is about to change from the negative news of 2001 to 2003 to the more positive results that began in 2003?

a. Were we glad to see the dark days of 2001 to 2003 behind us!
b. Fortunately, those bad times didn't last forever.
c. These aggressive measures helped the company survive the extended downturn and prepared us to grow again when the market recovered.
d. Transitioning forward, the situation began to improve beginning in 2003.

3. You've just helped a team from the marketing and engineering departments draft a report on the prospects for the electronic communication market over the next five years. Thanks to the team's diligent research, you're confident that the information is as about as current as it could possibly be. However, so many things associated with the Internet can change so quickly that you can't guarantee the information will be accurate several months from now, much less several years from now. Which of the following statements would be the best way to express this limitation of the report?

a. It must be pointed out that the information in this report may become obsolete as market conditions change. This is a function of the dynamic nature of the market and is not an issue with the quality of our research.
b. The information contained herein was current as of the time of publication. We cannot guarantee its accuracy in the future.
c. The dynamic nature of the electronic communication industry means that information is likely to change over time. Please accept our apologies for this limitation.
d. The dynamic nature of the electronic communication industry means that information is likely to change over time. Please check with us for the latest news and insights before making any major strategic or financial decisions based on the content of this report.

4. To help readers quickly assess the relative contributions of Tellabs's various product lines to the company's overall revenues, year by year over a 10-year period, which type of visual would be most effective?

a. Ten pie charts, one per year, showing the breakdown of sales by product line
b. A table, with the years in columns and the product lines in rows
c. An area chart
d. A bar chart

LEARNING OBJECTIVES CHECKUP

Assess your understanding of the principles in this chapter by reading each learning objective and studying the accompanying exercises. For fill-in-the-blank items, write the missing text in the blank provided; for multiple-choice items, circle the letter of the correct answer. You can check your responses against the answer key on page AK-2.

Objective 12.1: Explain how to adapt to your audiences when writing reports and proposals, and provide an overview of the process of drafting report content.

1. Why is the "you" attitude particularly important with long or complex reports and proposals?
    a. The "you" attitude takes less time to write, so you'll save considerable time with long documents.
    b. Professionals are accustomed to reading long reports, so they don't require a lot of "hand holding."
    c. People simply don't read reports that don't demonstrate good business etiquette.
    d. The length and complexity of these reports put a heavy demand on readers, making it particularly important to be sensitive to their needs.
2. Which of these sentences has the most formal tone?
    a. We discuss herein the possibility of synergistic development strategies between our firm and U.S. Medical.
    b. This report explores the potential for a strategic partnership with U.S. Medical.
    c. My report is the result of a formal investigation into the possibility of a strategic partnership with U.S. Medical.
    d. In this report, I address the potential for a strategic partnership with U.S. Medical.
3. Which of these does not belong in the body of an informational or analytical report?
    a. An explanation of weaknesses in the report
    b. Facts, statistical evidence, and trends
    c. Conclusions and recommendations
    d. Criteria for evaluating alternatives and options

4. Where would you list action items in a report?
 a. In the opening
 b. In the body
 c. In the close
 d. Action items are never listed in reports.

5. Which of the following is *not* a characteristic of effective report content?
 a. Balanced
 b. Logical
 c. Entertaining
 d. Accurate

6. How are audiences likely to react if they spot several errors in your reports?
 a. They'll become skeptical about the quality of all your work.
 b. They'll forgive you and move on without thinking any more about it; everybody makes mistakes.
 c. They'll stop reading your reports.
 d. They'll respect the fact that you don't waste time proofreading.

Objective 12.2: Provide an overview of the process of drafting proposal content, and list six strategies to strengthen your proposal argument.

7. Which of the following is not a recommended strategy for strengthening your proposal argument?
 a. Provide concrete examples of the value of your proposal.
 b. Demonstrate your knowledge.
 c. Identify the amount of time you've invested in the proposal.
 d. Adopt a "you" attitude.

8. If packaging and presentation are only superficial, why are they so important in proposal writing?
 a. Readers tend to prejudge the quality of your products and services based on the quality of your proposal.
 b. They show that you're more than just a "numbers" person—that you can think creatively.
 c. They show the audience that you're willing to invest time and money in getting your proposal accepted.
 d. Attractive documents almost always have high-quality information in them.

9. Which of the following elements is usually *not* part of a proposal's introduction?
 a. Background or statement of the problem
 b. Detailed cost analysis
 c. Organization of the proposal
 d. Scope of the proposal

10. The primary purpose of the body of a proposal is to
 a. List your firm's qualifications for the project in question
 b. Explain why the recipient needs to address a particular problem or opportunity
 c. Communicate your passion for solving the problem or addressing the opportunity
 d. Give complete details on the proposed solution and its anticipated benefits

11. If a proposal is being sent in response to an RFP, how should the body of the proposal address the issue of costs?
 a. It should avoid any mention of costs.
 b. It should provide a total cost figure without wasting the reader's time with a lot of details.
 c. It should follow whatever your company's policy is regarding cost estimates.
 d. It should follow the instructions in the RFP exactly.

Objective 12.3: Identify five characteristics of effective writing in online reports, and explain how to adapt your writing approach for wikis.

12. _________ goes a step beyond translating, making sure web content reflects not only the native language of your readers but also their cultural norms, weights, measures, currency, and other specific elements.

13. Which of the following is the most effectively worded link to a webpage that describes a company's products and services?
 a. <u>Click here</u> to learn more about what we do.
 b. Learn more about <u>our products and services</u>.
 c. <u>Next page</u>
 d. You have problems? We have <u>solutions</u>.

14. Which of the following best summarizes some key advice for wiki collaboration?
 a. Because so many writers can be involved in a wiki, managerial control of content and process is essential.
 b. Personal responsibility is paramount with wikis, so all contributors must safeguard their contributions against unwelcome editing.
 c. Conventional web security measures such as access control should never be used on wikis because they inhibit free collaboration.
 d. Wikis writers need to let go of traditional expectations of authorship, including individual recognition and control.

Objective 12.4: Discuss six principles of graphic design, and explain how to choose which points in your message to illustrate.

15. Why is consistency important in visual design?
 a. It shows the audience that you're not wasting precious time doing artistic designs.
 b. It reduces confusion by eliminating arbitrary changes that force people to relearn your design scheme every time they encounter another visual.
 c. It saves on ink and toner when reports are printed.
 d. It shows the audience that you're serious and businesslike.

16. Which of the following steps could you take to call attention to the most important elements in a visual?
 a. Use a dominant color for the important elements.
 b. Call attention to the important elements in the caption or in the text of your report.
 c. Make the important elements larger.
 d. Do all of the above.

17. Which of the following is a good candidate for illustrating in a report?
 a. Comparison of customer satisfaction ratings of 12 stores across a 12-month period
 b. Percentage of employees who have attended 10 different training courses

c. Ranking of webpages on a website, from most visited to least visited
d. All of the above

18. Which of the following is *not* a good reason to use a visual in a report?
a. To communicate more effectively with multilingual audiences
b. To help unify the separate parts of a process, an organization, or another entity, such as by using a flowchart to depict the various steps in a process
c. To simplify access to specific data points, such as by listing them in a quick-reference table
d. To demonstrate your creative side

Objective 12.5: Identify the most common types of visuals used to present data, information, concepts, and ideas.

19. _________ overcomes two shortcomings of conventional charts and graphs—the ability to represent only numeric data and the ability to show only a limited number of data points before the display becomes too cluttered to interpret.

20. Which of these is a good reason to use a diagram instead of a photograph?
a. Diagrams are more colorful and aren't limited to colors found in real life.
b. Diagrams are more realistic than photographs.
c. Diagrams allow you to control the amount of detail shown to focus reader attention on particular parts of the image.
d. All of the above are true.

Objective 12.6: Explain how to integrate visuals with text effectively and how to verify the quality of your visuals.

21. Which of the following steps should you take to verify the accuracy of the visuals in your reports?
a. Make sure that data presentations such as line charts and bar charts accurately portray the data that you intended to show.
b. Make sure flowcharts and other computer-generated artwork are correct and clear.
c. Make sure that you've inserted the correct visuals at each place in your report.
d. Do all of the above.

22. Assume that you have a line chart with a vertical axis scaled from 0 to 100 and data points that vary within a range of roughly 10 to 90. How would you influence audience perceptions if you increased the vertical scale so that it stretched from 0 to 200 instead of 0 to 100?
a. The scaling change would have no affect on audience perceptions.
b. The scaling change would maximize the perceived variations in the data.
c. The scaling change would minimize the perceived variations in the data.
d. You have no way of predicting in advance how the scaling change would affect perceptions.

PEARSON **mybcommlab**™

Log on to www.mybcommlab.com to access the following study and assessment aids associated with this chapter:

- Video applications
- Real-Time Updates
- Peer review activity
- Quick Learning Guides
- Pre/post test
- Personalized study plan
- Model documents
- Sample presentations

If you are not using mybcommlab, you can access Real-Time Updates and Quick Learning Guides through http://real-timeupdates.com/ebc. The Quick Learning Guide (located under "Learn More" on the website) hits all the high points of this chapter in just two pages. This guide, especially prepared by the authors, will help you study for exams or review important concepts whenever you need a quick refresher.

Apply Your Knowledge

1. Should a report always explain the writer's method of gathering evidence or solving a problem? Why or why not?
2. What similarities do you see between visuals and nonverbal communication? Explain your answer.
3. When you read a graph, how can you be sure that the visual impression you are receiving is an accurate reflection of reality? Please explain.
4. If you want your audience to agree to a specific course of action, should you exclude any references to alternatives that you don't want the audience to consider? Why or why not?
5. **Ethical Choices** After studying the designs of corporate websites, Penn State University professor S. Shyam Sundar discovered quite an interesting phenomenon: The more interactive and engaging a website is, the more likely visitors are to "buy into whatever is being advocated" on the site. In other words, if two websites have identical content, the site with greater interactivity and more "bells and whistles"

would be more persuasive.[21] Is it ethical to increase the persuasive power of a website simply by making it more interactive? Why or why not?

Practice Your Knowledge

Messages for Analysis

Message 12.A: Revising Web Content with a "You" Attitude

To access this wiki exercise, visit http://real-timeupdates.com/ebc, click on "Student Assignments," and select Chapter 12, page 390, Message 12.A. Follow the instructions for evaluating the existing content and revising it to make it more reader oriented.

Message 12.B: Improving the Effectiveness of a Wiki Article

To access this wiki exercise, go to http://real-timeupdates.com/ebc, click on "Student Assignments," and select Chapter 12, Page 390, Message 12.B. Follow the instructions for evaluating the existing content and revising it to make it clear and concise.

Message 12.C: Improving a Solicited Proposal

Read Figure 12.18, a solicited proposal, and then (1) analyze the strengths and weaknesses of this document and (2) revise the document so that it follows this chapter's guidelines.

FIGURE 12.18 Solicited Proposal

Morning Star Travel Service Ltd.
Room 201, Bank Centre,
35 Nathan Road, Kowloon, Hong Kong.

April 15, 2009

PROJECT: Incentive Travel Scheme 89UX2 Contract No. 9194

Dear Mr. Wong:

Morning Star Travel Service Ltd. proposes to be the sole organizer for the Incentive Travel Scheme 89UX2 for 90 staff of your company. The itinerary and the price are shown in the following table:

Incentive Travel Scheme Details

Destination	Length of Stay	Tour Group Size	Price/head*	Total
Beijing	4 days 3 nights	30	HK$3,200.00	HK$96,000.00
Tokyo	5 days 4 nights	30	HK$7,000.00	HK$210,000.00
Seoul	5 days 4 nights	30	HK$4,000.00	HK$120,000.00

*Price/head refers to the total price covering the whole length of stay for each tour member. It includes all taxes but excludes high-season surcharge.

The following items clarify and qualify the scope of our services:

1. Morning Star Travel Service Ltd. will send one tour guide and one escort for each tour group.
2. Accommodation will be four-star hotels or equivalent. All meals are included.
3. One air-conditioned coach will be provided to each tour group.
4. Every member joining the above-mentioned tour groups is responsible for obtaining the entry visa for the respective countries.
5. Travel Service shall not be liable for the travel insurance of individual travelers.
6. The itinerary may be altered in case of adverse weather conditions.
7. The minimum and maximum number per tour group is 20 and 35. Morning Star Travel Service Ltd. shall be paid strictly based on the actual number of travelers in each group.
8. Morning Star Travel Service Ltd. may withdraw this bid if we do not receive a written confirmation from your company within 10 days of your receipt of this proposal.
9. Morning Star Travel Service Ltd. shall not provide a refund for travelers who withdraw from the tour group five working days before the tour commencement.
10. A deposit of $129 is required of each traveler.

If you have any questions, feel free to contact me at the phone number listed below.

Sincerely,

William Fung
Marketing Manager
Morning Star Travel Service Ltd.
Office: (852) 2771 2208
Fax: (852) 2771 8800
E-mail: William_Fung@morningstar.com.hk

Adapted from: Morning Star Travel Service Ltd. website (http:www.morning-star.com.hk) Accessed on 15 April 2009.

Exercises

Active links for all websites in this chapter can be found on mybcommlab; see your User Guide for instructions on accessing the content for this chapter.

12.1 Adapting Reports to the Audience Review the reports shown in Figures 12.3 and 12.4. Give specific examples of how each of these reports establishes a good relationship with the audience. Consider such things as using the "you" attitude, emphasizing the positive, establishing credibility, being polite, using bias-free language, and projecting a good company image.

12.2 Composing Reports: Report Content You are writing an analytical report on the U.S. sales of your newest product. Of the following topics, identify those that should be covered in the report's introduction, body, and close. Briefly explain your decisions.

- **a.** Regional breakdowns of sales across the country
- **b.** Date the product was released in the marketplace
- **c.** Sales figures from competitors selling similar products worldwide
- **d.** Predictions of how the struggling U.S. economy will affect sales over the next six months
- **e.** Method used for obtaining the above predictions
- **f.** The impact of similar products being sold in the United States by Japanese competitors
- **g.** Your recommendation as to whether the company should sell this product internationally
- **h.** Actions that must be completed by year end if the company decides to sell this product internationally

12.3 Composing Business Reports Your boss, Len Chow (vice president of corporate planning), has asked you to research opportunities in the cosmetics industry and to prepare a report that presents your findings and your recommendation for where you think the company should focus its marketing efforts. Here's a copy of your note cards (data were created for this exercise):

Sub: Demand Industrywide sales have grown consistently for several decades, fueled by both a growing population and increased per capita consumption	ref: 1.1
Sub: Competition 700 companies currently in cosmetics industry	ref: 1.2
Sub: Niches Focusing on special niches avoids head-on competition with industry leaders	ref: 1.3
Sub: Competition Industry dominated by market leaders: Revlon, Procter & Gamble, Avon, Gillette	ref: 1.4
Sub: Demand Industry no longer recession-proof: Past year, sales sluggish; consumer spending is down; most affected were mid- to high-priced brands; consumers traded down to less expensive lines	ref: 1.5
Sub: Competition Smaller companies (Neutrogena, Mary Kay, Softsoap, and Noxell) survive by: specializing in niches, differentiating product line, focusing on market segment	ref: 1.6
Sub: Demand Consumption of cosmetics relatively flat for past five years	ref: 1.7
Sub: Competition Prices are constant while promotion budgets are increasing	ref: 1.8
Sub: Niches Men: 50 percent of adult population; account for one-fifth of cosmetic sales; market leaders have attempted this market but failed	ref: 1.9
Sub: Demand Cosmetic industry is near maturity, but some segments may vary. Total market currently produces annual retail sales of $14.5 billion: Cosmetics/lotions/fragrances—$5.635 billion; Personal hygiene products—$4.375 billion; Hair-care products—$3.435 billion; Shaving products—$1.055 billion	ref: 1.10
Sub: Niches Ethnic groups: Some firms specialize in products for African Americans; few firms oriented toward Hispanic, Asian, or Native Americans, which tend to be concentrated geographically	ref: 1.11
Sub: Demand Average annual expenditure per person for cosmetics is $58	ref: 1.12
Sub: Competition Competition is intensifying and dominant companies are putting pressure on smaller ones	ref: 1.13
Sub: Demand First quarter of current year, demand is beginning to revive; trend expected to continue well into next year	ref: 1.14
Sub: Niches Senior citizens: large growing segment of population; account for 6% of cosmetic sales; specialized needs for hair and skin not being met; interested in appearance	ref: 1.15
Sub: Demand Demographic trends: (1) Gradual maturing of baby-boomer generation will fuel growth by consuming greater quantities of shaving cream, hair-coloring agents, and skin creams; (2) population is increasing in the South and Southwest, where some brands have strong distribution	ref: 1.16

List the main idea of your message (your recommendation), the major points (your conclusions), and supporting evidence. Then construct a final report outline with first- and second-level informative headings focusing on your conclusions. Because Chow requested this report, you can feel free to use the direct approach. Finish by writing a draft of your memo report to Chow.

12.4 Composing Reports Find an article in a business newspaper or journal (in print or online) that recommends a solution to a problem. Identify the problem, the recommended solution(s), and the supporting evidence provided by the author to justify his or her recommendation(s). Did the author cite any formal or informal studies as evidence? What facts or statistics did the author include? Did the author cite any criteria for evaluating possible options? If so, what were they?

12.5 Composing Reports: Navigational Clues Review a long business article in a journal or newspaper. Highlight examples of how the article uses headings, transitions, and previews and reviews to help the readers find their way.

12.6 Ethical Choices Your boss has asked you to prepare a feasibility report to determine whether the company should advertise its custom-crafted cabinetry in the weekly neighborhood newspaper. Based on your primary research, you think they should. As you draft the introduction to your report, however, you discover that the survey administered to the neighborhood newspaper subscribers was flawed. Several of the questions were poorly written and misleading. You used the survey results, among other findings, to justify your recommendation. The report is due in three days. What actions might you want to take, if any, before you complete your report?

12.7 Improving Visual Design Find a communication example that you believe could be improved by applying the visual design principles you learned in this chapter. It can be from any medium—a webpage, a magazine ad, a promotional e-mail message, an illustration from a report—anything that you can either copy or scan into a word processing file. With the image in your word processing program, annotate it with notes that identify visual weaknesses and describe ways to fix those weaknesses. (In Microsoft Word, for example, you can use the "AutoShapes Callouts" feature to place notes wherever you'd like on the page.) In a paragraph of accompanying text, explain why you believe the message isn't as effective as it could be and how your suggestions would make it more effective.

12.8 Preparing Line Charts The pet food manufacturer you work for is interested in the results of a recent poll of U.S. pet-owning households. Look at the statistics that follow and decide on the most appropriate scale for a chart; then create a line chart of the trends in cat ownership. What conclusions do you draw from the trend you've charted? Draft a paragraph or two discussing the results of this poll and the potential consequences for the pet food business. Support your conclusions by referring readers to your chart.

> In 1990, 22 million U.S. households owned a cat. In 1995, 24 million households owned a cat. In 2000, 28 million households owned a cat. In 2005, 32 million households owned a cat.

12.9 Selecting the Right Visual You're preparing the annual report for FretCo Guitar Corporation. For each of the following types of information, select an appropriate chart or visual to illustrate the text. Explain your choices.

a. Data on annual sales for the past 20 years
b. Comparison of FretCo sales, product by product (electric guitars, bass guitars, amplifiers, acoustic guitars), for this year and last year
c. Explanation of how a FretCo acoustic guitar is manufactured
d. Explanation of how the FretCo Guitar Corporation markets its guitars
e. Data on sales of FretCo products in each of 12 countries
f. Comparison of FretCo sales figures with sales figures for three competing guitar makers over the past 10 years

12.10 Selecting the Right Chart Here are last year's sales figures for the appliance and electronics megastore where you work. Construct charts based on these figures to help explain to the store's general manager seasonal variations in each department.

STORE SALES IN 2009 (IN $ THOUSANDS)

MONTH	HOME ELECTRONICS	COMPUTERS	APPLIANCES
January	$68	$39	$36
February	72	34	34
March	75	41	30
April	54	41	28
May	56	42	44
June	49	33	48
July	54	31	43
August	66	58	39
September	62	58	36
October	66	44	33
November	83	48	29
December	91	62	24

12.11 Creating Maps You work for C & S Holdings, a company that operates coin-activated, self-service car washes. Research shows that the farther customers live from a car wash, the less likely they are to visit. You know that 50 percent of customers at each of your car washes live within a 4-mile radius of the location, 65 percent live within 6 miles, 80 percent live within 8 miles, and 90 percent live within 10 miles. C & S's owner wants to open two new car washes in your city and has asked you to prepare a report recommending locations. Using a map of your city (print or online), choose two possible locations for car washes and create a visual depicting the customer base surrounding each location. (Make up whatever population data you need.)

12.12 Internet One of the best places to see how data can be presented visually is in government statistical publications, which are often available on the Internet. For example, the International Trade Administration (ITA), a branch of the U.S. Department of Commerce, publishes monthly reports about U.S. trade with other countries. Visit the report page of its website, at **http://trade.gov**, and follow the link to the latest monthly International Trade Update (you should find the link on the right side of the homepage). Download the complete issue as a PDF file. Using what you learned in this chapter, evaluate the charts in the report. Do they present the data clearly? Are they missing any elements? What would you do to improve the charts? Print a copy of the report to turn in with your answers and indicate which charts you are evaluating.

12.13 Creating Photographs As directed by your instructor, team up with other students, making sure that at least one of you has a digital camera or camera phone capable of downloading images to your word-processing software. Find a busy location on campus or in the surrounding neighborhood, someplace with lots of signs, storefronts, pedestrians, and traffic. Scout out two different photo opportunities, one that maximizes the visual impression of crowding and clutter, and one that minimizes this impression. For the first, assume that you are someone who advocates reducing the crowding and clutter, so you want to show how bad it is. For the second, assume that you are a real estate agent or someone else who is motivated to show people that even though the location offers lots of shopping, entertainment, and other attractions, it's actually a rather calm and quiet neighborhood. Insert the two images in a word-processing document and write a caption for each that emphasizes the two opposite messages just described. Finally, write a brief paragraph, discussing the ethical implications of what you've just done. Have you distorted reality or just presented it in ways that work to your advantage? Have you prevented audiences from gaining the information they would need to make informed decisions?

Expand Your Knowledge

Learning More on the Web

Brush Up on Your Computer-Graphics Skills

http://graphicssoft.about.com

Need some help using graphics software? Get started at the About.com Graphics Software website. Take the tutorials and learn how to manage fonts and images and to perform a variety of graphics-related tasks. View the illustrated demonstrations. Read the instructional articles. Learn how to use the most common file formats for graphics. Expand your knowledge of the basic principles of graphic design, and master some advanced color tips and theory. Don't leave without following the links to recommended books and magazines. Explore About.com's Graphics Software section and answer these questions:

1. What are the most common file formats for online visuals?
2. What does color depth mean in computer visuals?
3. What is dithering, and how can it affect your visuals?

Sharpening Your Career Skills Online

Bovée and Thill's Business Communication Web Search, at http://businesscommunicationblog.com/websearch, is a unique research tool designed specifically for business communication research. Use the Web Search function to find a website, video, PDF document, podcast, or PowerPoint presentation that offers advice on writing business reports or on creating effective visuals for documents and presentations. Write a brief e-mail message to your instructor, describing the item that you found and summarizing the career skills information you learned from it.

Improve Your Grammar, Mechanics, and Usage

The following exercises help you improve your knowledge of and power over English grammar, mechanics, and usage. Turn to the Handbook of Grammar, Mechanics, and Usage at the end of this book and review all of Sections 2.7 (Dashes) and 2.8 (Hyphens). Then look at the following 10 items. Circle the letter of the preferred choice in the following groups of sentences. (Answers to these exercises appear on page AK-3.)

1. a. Three qualities—speed, accuracy, and reliability are desirable in any applicant.
   b. Three qualities—speed, accuracy, and reliability—are desirable in any applicant.
2. a. A highly placed source explained the top-secret negotiations.
   b. A highly-placed source explained the top-secret negotiations.
   c. A highly placed source explained the top secret negotiations.
3. a. The file on Mary Gaily—yes—we finally found it reveals a history of tardiness.
   b. The file on Mary Gaily, yes—we finally found it—reveals a history of tardiness.
   c. The file on Mary Gaily—yes, we finally found it—reveals a history of tardiness.
4. a. They're selling a well designed machine.
   b. They're selling a well-designed machine.
5. a. Argentina, Brazil, Mexico—these are the countries we hope to concentrate on.
   b. Argentina, Brazil, Mexico—these are the countries—we hope to concentrate on.
6. a. Only two sites maybe three—offer the things we need.
   b. Only two sites—maybe three—offer the things we need.
7. a. How many owner operators are in the industry?
   b. How many owner—operators are in the industry?
   c. How many owner-operators are in the industry?
8. a. Your ever-faithful assistant deserves—without a doubt—a substantial raise.
   b. Your ever faithful assistant deserves—without a doubt—a substantial raise.
9. a. The charts are well placed—on each page—unlike the running heads and footers.
   b. The charts are well-placed on each page—unlike the running heads and footers.
   c. The charts are well placed on each page—unlike the running heads and footers.
10. a. Your devil-may-care attitude affects everyone in the decision-making process.
    b. Your devil may care attitude affects everyone in the decision-making process.
    c. Your devil-may-care attitude affects everyone in the decision making process.

For additional exercises focusing on dashes and hyphens, visit mybcommlab. Click on Chapter 12, click on "Additional Exercises to Improve Your Grammar, Mechanics, and Usage," and click on "18. Punctuation C."

CASES

Applying the Three-Step Writing Process to Cases

Apply each step to the following cases, as assigned by your instructor.

INFORMATIONAL REPORTS

1. My progress to date: Interim progress report on your academic career. As you know, the bureaucratic process involved in getting a degree or certificate is nearly as challenging as any course you could take.

Your task: Prepare an interim progress report detailing the steps you've taken toward completing your graduation or certification requirements. After examining the requirements listed in your college catalog, indicate a realistic schedule for completing those that remain. In addition to course requirements, include steps such as completing the residency requirement, filing necessary papers, and paying necessary fees. Use memo format for your report, and address it to anyone who is helping or encouraging you through school.

2. Time well spent: Personal activity report of your current school term. Success in any endeavor doesn't happen all at once. For example, success in college is built one quarter or semester at a time, and the way to succeed in the long term is to make sure you succeed in the short term. After all, even a single quarter or semester of college involves a significant investment of time, money, and energy.

Your task: Imagine you work for a company that has agreed to send you to college full time, paying all your educational expenses. You are given complete freedom in choosing your courses, as long as you graduate by an agreed-upon date. All your employer asks in return is that you develop your business skills and insights as much as possible so that you can make a significant contribution to the company when you return to full-time work after graduation. To make sure that you are using your time—and your company's money—wisely, the company requires a brief personal activity report at the end of every quarter or semester (whichever your school uses). Write a brief informational report that you can e-mail to your instructor, summarizing how you spent your quarter or semester. Itemize the classes you took, how much time you spent studying and working on class projects, whether you got involved in campus activities and organizations that help you develop leadership or communication skills, and what you learned that you can apply in a business career. (For the purposes of this assignment, your time estimates don't have to be precise.)

3. Check that price tag: Informational report on trends in college costs. Your college's administration has asked you to compare your college's tuition costs with those of a nearby college and determine which has risen more quickly. Research the trend by checking your college's annual tuition costs for each of the most recent four years. Then research the four-year tuition trends for a neighboring college. For both colleges, calculate the percentage change in tuition costs from year to year and between the first and fourth years.

Your task: Prepare an informal report (using letter format) that presents your findings and conclusions to the president of your college. Include graphics that explain and support your conclusions.

BLOGGING SKILLS TEAM SKILLS

4. With experience comes wisdom: Sharing your wisdom with future college students. If you're like many other college students, your first year was more than you expected: more difficult, more fun, more frustrating, more expensive, more exhausting, more rewarding—more of everything, positive and negative. Oh, the things you know now that you didn't know then!

Your task: With several other students, identify five or six things you wish you would've realized or understood better before you started your first year of college. These can relate to your school life (such as "I didn't realize how much work I would have for my classes" or "I should've asked for help as soon as I got stuck") and your personal and social life ("I wish I would've been more open to meeting people"). Use these items as the foundation of a brief informational report that you could post on a blog that is read by high school students and their families. Your goal with this report is to help the next generation of students make a successful and rewarding transition to college.

ANALYTICAL REPORTS

5. Learning opportunity: Analyzing a significant mistake or failure in your life. Mistakes can be wonderful learning opportunities if we're honest with ourselves and receptive to learning from the mistake.

Your task: Identify a mistake you've made—something significant enough to have cost you a lot of money, wasted a lot of time, harmed your health, damaged a relationship, created serious problems at work, prevented you from pursuing what could've been a rewarding opportunity, or otherwise had serious consequences. Now figure out why you made that mistake. Did you let emotions get in the way of clear thinking? Did you make a serious financial blunder because you didn't take the time to understand the consequences of a decision? Were you too cautious? Not cautious enough? Perhaps several factors led to a poor decision.

Write a brief analytical report to your instructor that describes the situation and outlines your analysis of why the failure occurred and how you can avoid making a similar mistake in the future. If you can't think of a significant mistake or failure that you're comfortable sharing with your instructor, write about a mistake that a friend or family member made (without revealing the person's identify or potentially causing him or her any embarrassment).

E-MAIL SKILLS

6. Staying the course: Unsolicited proposal using the 2 + 2 = 4 approach. Think of a course you would love to see added to the core curriculum at your school. Conversely, if you would like to see a course offered as an elective rather than being required, write your e-mail report accordingly.

Your task: Write a short e-mail proposal using the 2 + 2 = 4 approach (refresh your memory in Chapter 11, if necessary). Prepare your proposal to be submitted to the academic dean by e-mail. Be sure to include all the reasons that support your idea.

7. Planning my program: Problem-solving report using the yardstick approach. Assume that you will have time for only one course next term.

Your task: List the pros and cons of each of four or five courses that interest you and use the yardstick approach to settle on the course that is best for you to take at this time. Write your report in memo format and address it to your academic adviser.

LETTER WRITING SKILLS

8. Restaurant review: Troubleshooting report on a restaurant's food and operations. Visit any restaurant, possibly your school cafeteria. The workers and fellow customers will assume that you are an ordinary customer, but you are really a spy for the owner.

Your task: After your visit, write a short letter to the owner, explaining (a) what you did and what you observed, (b) any violations of policy that you observed, and (c) your recommendations for improvement. The first part of your report (what you did and what you observed) will be the longest. Include a description of the premises, inside and out. Tell how long it took for each step of ordering and receiving your meal. Describe the service and food thoroughly. You are interested in both the good and bad aspects of the establishment's décor, service, and food. For the second section (violations of policy), use some common sense. If all the servers but one have their hair covered, you may assume that policy requires hair to be covered; a dirty window or restroom obviously violates policy. The last section (recommendations for improvement) involves professional judgment. What management actions will improve the restaurant?

9. On the books: Troubleshooting report on improving the campus bookstore. Imagine that you are a consultant hired to improve the profits of your campus bookstore.

Your task: Visit the bookstore and look critically at its operations. Then draft a letter to the bookstore manager, offering recommendations that would make the store more profitable, perhaps suggesting products it should carry, hours it should remain open, or added services that it should make available to students. Be sure to support your recommendations.

10. Day and night: Problem-solving report on stocking a 24-hour convenience store. When a store is open all day, every day, when's the best time to restock the shelves? That's the challenge at Store 24, a retail chain that never closes. Imagine you're the assistant manager of a Store 24 branch that just opened near your campus. You want to set up a restocking schedule that won't conflict with prime shopping hours. Think about the number of customers you're likely to serve in the morning, afternoon, evening, and overnight hours. Consider, too, how many employees you might have during these four periods.

Your task: Write a problem-solving report in letter form to the store manager (Isabel Chu) and the regional manager (Eric Angstrom), who must agree on a solution to this problem. Discuss the pros and cons of each of the four periods, and include your recommendation for restocking the shelves.

PROPOSALS

11. "Would you carry it?" Unsolicited sales proposal recommending a product to a retail outlet. Select a product you are familiar with and imagine that you are the manufacturer trying to get a local retail outlet to carry it. Use the Internet and other resources to gather information about the product.

Your task: Write an unsolicited sales proposal in letter format to the owner (or manager) of the store, proposing that the item be stocked. Use the information you gathered to describe some of the product's features and benefits to the store. Then make up some reasonable figures, highlighting what the item costs, what it can be sold for, and what services your company provides (return of unsold items, free replacement of unsatisfactory items, necessary repairs, and so on).

PORTFOLIO BUILDER

12. Where is everybody? Proposal to sell GPS fleet tracking system. As a sales manager for Air-Trak, one of your responsibilities is writing sales proposals for potential buyers of your company's Air-Trak tracking system. The system uses global positioning system (GPS) technology to track the location of vehicles and other assets. For example, the dispatcher for a trucking company can simply click a map display on a computer screen to find out where all the company's trucks are at that instant. Air-Trak lists the following as benefits of the system:

- Making sure vehicles follow prescribed routes with minimal loitering time
- "Geofencing," in which dispatchers are alerted if vehicles leave
- Route optimization, in which fleet managers can analyze routes and destinations to find the most time- and fuel-efficient path for each vehicle
- Comparisons between scheduled and actual travel
- Enhanced security to protect both drivers and cargos

Your task: Write a brief proposal to Doneta Zachs, fleet manager for Midwest Express, 338 S.W. 6th, Des Moines, Iowa, 50321. Introduce your company, explain the benefits of the Air-Trak system, and propose a trial deployment in which you would equip five Midwest Express trucks. For the purposes of this assignment, you don't need to worry about the technical details of the system; focus on promoting the benefits and asking for a decision regarding the test project. (You can learn more about Air-Trak at **www.air-trak.com**.)[22]

13 Completing Reports and Proposals

Learning Objectives

After studying this chapter, you will be able to

1. Characterize the four tasks involved in completing business reports and proposals
2. Explain how computers have both simplified and complicated the report-production process
3. Identify the circumstances in which you should include letters of authorization and letters of acceptance in your reports
4. Explain the difference between a synopsis and an executive summary
5. Describe the three supplementary parts of a formal report
6. Explain how prefatory parts of a proposal differ, depending on whether the proposal is solicited or unsolicited

On the Job: Communicating at the Bill & Melinda Gates Foundation

In his role as CEO of the Bill & Melinda Gates Foundation, Jeff Raikes (left) relies on numerous reports and proposals to guide the foundation's long-term strategy, monitor results, and build partnerships.

Creating Effective Partnerships to Tackle Some of the World's Most Challenging Problems

Microsoft co-founder Bill Gates is accustomed to creating change on a global scale, and he now applies that same energy and strategic thinking to charitable causes. Backed by billions of dollars in endowments, the Bill & Melinda Gates Foundation acts as a catalyst, bringing resources together in a way that "increases the momentum, scale, and sustainability of change." The strategy is applied to such important social challenges as containing the AIDS epidemic, eradicating malaria, improving high schools, and making sure people everywhere have access to the digital revolution made possible by the Internet.

Meeting challenges of such staggering complexity and coordinating the resources of organizations all over the world is no small task, and communication plays a vital role in this effort. In particular, reports and proposals link the various groups involved in the foundation's activities and inform the public about ongoing challenges and progress. As just one measure of the foundation's enormous scope, it receives several thousand formal grant requests each month.

The foundation is staffed with people who have demonstrated effective leadership and communication skills. Jeff Raikes, a former Microsoft executive who took over as chief executive officer in 2008, is deeply involved in reports and proposals—as a writer and as a reader. Raikes examines proposals from various angles, listening to his colleagues' perspectives and asking probing questions: Does this proposal align with our core values and goals? Is this really the best approach? What's going to make the biggest difference? How do we define *success* in this effort? Could this proposal be a catalyst that attracts other organizations to participate? Raikes and other staffers have learned to read between the lines, too. As his predecessor Patty Stonesifer put it, "It's amazing what people won't tell you when you have billions of dollars to give away."

Raikes and his colleagues recognize that they are tackling problems of almost unimaginable complexity, but with systematic thinking, unstoppable optimism, unmatched financial resources, and effective communication skills, they remain committed to improving life for people the world over.[1]

www.gatesfoundation.org

PUTTING THE FINAL TOUCHES ON REPORTS AND PROPOSALS

1 LEARNING OBJECTIVE

Characterize the four tasks involved in completing business reports and proposals.

Experienced business communicators such as Jeff Raikes (profiled in the chapter-opening "On the Job" vignette) recognize that the process of writing a report or proposal doesn't end with a first draft. This chapter addresses all four tasks involved in completing longer messages: revising, producing, proofreading, and distributing. Although the tasks covered in this chapter are similar in concept to those you studied for short messages in Chapter 6, the completion stage for reports and proposals can require considerably more work. And as you've probably experienced with school reports already, computers, copiers, and other resources have an uncanny knack for going haywire when you're frantic to finish and have no time to spare. When completing an important report on the job, try to leave yourself double or even triple the amount of time you think you'll need so that last-minute glitches don't compromise the quality of all your hard work.

Formal reports have a higher degree of polish and production quality, and they often contain elements not found in informal reports.

Most of the discussion in this chapter applies to *formal* reports and proposals—documents that require an extra measure of polish and professionalism. Few reports and proposals require every component described in this chapter, but be sure to carefully select the elements you want to include in each of your documents.

REVISING REPORTS AND PROPOSALS

The revision process is essentially the same for reports as for any other business message, although it may take considerably more time, depending on the length of your document. Evaluate your organization, style, and tone to make sure you've said what you want to say in a logical, audience-focused way. Then work to improve the report's readability by varying sentence length, keeping paragraphs short, using lists and bullets, and adding headings and subheadings. Keep revising the content until it is clear, concise, and compelling.

Revising for clarity and conciseness is especially important for online reports because reading online can be difficult.

Tight, efficient writing that is easy to skim is always a plus, but it's especially important for impatient online audiences.[2] Review online report content carefully; strip out all information that doesn't meet audience needs and condense everything else as much as possible. Audiences will gladly return to sites that deliver quality information quickly—and they'll avoid sites that don't.

The virtually unlimited graphical and technical possibilities of web design have had the unfortunate side effect of producing too many websites that are difficult to read. You've no doubt visited some of these hard-to-read sites yourself—webpages with backgrounds so busy that you can't make out the words, tiny type that has you reaching for a magnifying glass, quirky fonts that are difficult to read at any size, lines of text that are stretched and wrapped around images, unlabeled graphical hyperlinks that force you to click on them to see what each page is about, and so on. Even when these sites are visually attractive, which isn't often, they fail to meet the primary objective of providing information to the reader. Web-design expert Dean Allen put it perfectly when he wrote that "the primary goal of communication design is to make vital, engaging work intended above all to be read."[3]

2 LEARNING OBJECTIVE

Explain how computers have both simplified and complicated the report-production process.

PRODUCING REPORTS AND PROPOSALS

When you are satisfied with your text, you're ready to produce your report by incorporating the design elements discussed in Chapter 6. At this point, you should also start to add charts, graphs, and other visuals, as well as any missing textual elements, such as previews and reviews.

In some organizations, you'll be able to rely on the help of specialists in design and production, particularly when you are working on important, high-visibility reports or proposals. You may also have clerical help available to assist with mechanical assembly and distribution. However, for most reports in many of today's lean-staffed companies, you should count on doing most or all of the production work yourself.

The good news is that computer tools are now generally easy enough for the average businessperson to use productively. A software suite such as Microsoft Office or Word Perfect Office lets you produce reports that incorporate graphics, spreadsheet data, and database records. Even features such as photography are relatively simple to include these days, thanks to low-cost digital cameras, color desktop scanners, and photo-quality printers.

The bad news is that these continually improving computer tools increase your audience's expectations. People are influenced by packaging, so a handsomely bound report with full-color graphics will impress your audience more than a plain report, even though the two documents may contain the same information. In other words, you may find yourself spending more time on production just to keep up with the competition.

Components of a Formal Report

Length, audience expectations, and organizational traditions all dictate what you should include in a formal report.

The parts you include in a report depend on the type of report you are writing, how long it is, what your audience expects and requires, and what your organization dictates. The components listed in Figure 13.1 fall into three categories, depending on where they are found

(Text continued on page 414)

FIGURE 13.1 Parts of a Formal Report
Depending on the level of formality you need to achieve, you can select from these elements to complete your formal report.

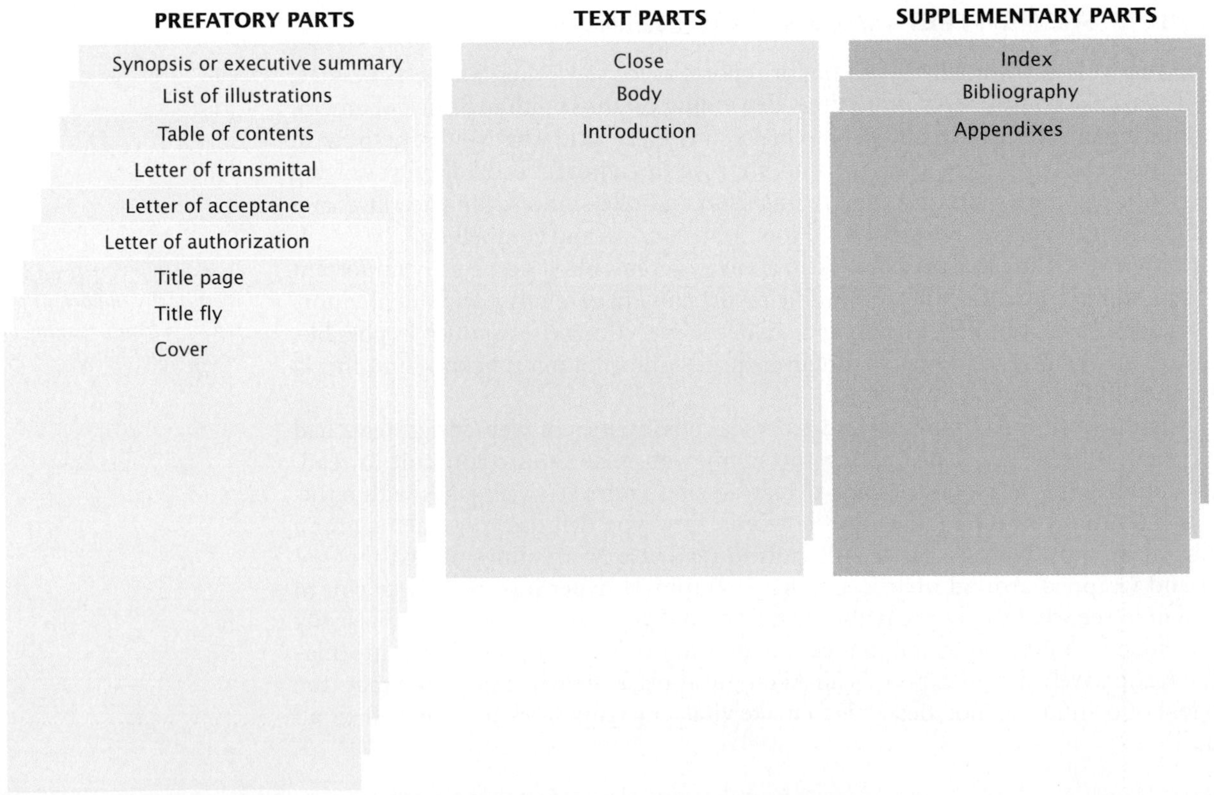

Report Writer's Notebook: Analyzing a Formal Report

The report presented in the following pages was prepared by Linda Moreno, manager of the cost accounting department at Electrovision, a high-tech company based in Los Gatos, California. Electrovision's main product is optical character recognition equipment, which is used by the U.S. Postal Service for sorting mail. Moreno's job is to help analyze the company's costs. She has this to say about the background of the report:

> For the past three or four years, Electrovision has been on a roll. Our A-12 optical character reader was a real breakthrough, and the post office grabbed up as many as we could make. Our sales and profits kept climbing, and morale was fantastic. Everybody seemed to think that the good times would last forever. Unfortunately, everybody was wrong. When the Postal Service announced that it was postponing all new equipment purchases because of cuts in its budget,we woke up to the fact that we are essentially a one-product company with one customer. At that point, management started scrambling around looking for ways to cut costs until we could diversify our business a bit.
>
> The vice president of operations, Dennis McWilliams, asked me to help identify cost-cutting opportunities in travel and entertainment. On the basis of his personal observations, he felt that Electrovision was overly generous in its travel policies and that we might be able to save a significant amount by controlling these costs more carefully. My investigation confirmed his suspicion.
>
> I was reasonably confident that my report would be well received. I've worked with Dennis for several years and know what he likes: plenty of facts, clearly stated conclusions, and specific recommendations for what should be done next. I also knew that my report would be passed on to other Electrovision executives, so I wanted to create a good impression. I wanted the report to be accurate and thorough, visually appealing, readable, and appropriate in tone.

When writing the analytical report that follows, Moreno based the organization on conclusions and recommendations presented in direct order. The first two sections of the report correspond to Moreno's two main conclusions: that Electrovision's travel and entertainment costs are too high and that cuts are essential. The third section presents recommendations for achieving better control over travel and entertainment expenses. As you review the report, analyze both the mechanical aspects and the way Moreno presents her ideas. Be prepared to discuss the way the various components convey and reinforce the main message.

Puts the title all in capital letters

REDUCING ELECTROVISION'S
TRAVEL AND ENTERTAINMENT COSTS

Centers lines horizontally (if this report were left-bound, you would allow an extra half-inch margin on the left side)

Prepared for
Dennis McWilliams,
Vice President of Operations
Electrovision, Inc.

Follows the title with the name, title, and organization of the recipient

Balances the white space between the items on the page

Puts all lines other than title in uppercase and lowercase letters

Prepared by
Linda Moreno, Manager
Cost Accounting Services
Electrovision, Inc.

February 16, 2010

Includes the report's publication date for future reference

The "how-to" tone of Moreno's title is appropriate for an action-oriented report that emphasizes recommendations. A more neutral title, such as "An Analysis of Electrovision's Travel and Entertainment Costs," would be more suitable for an informational report.

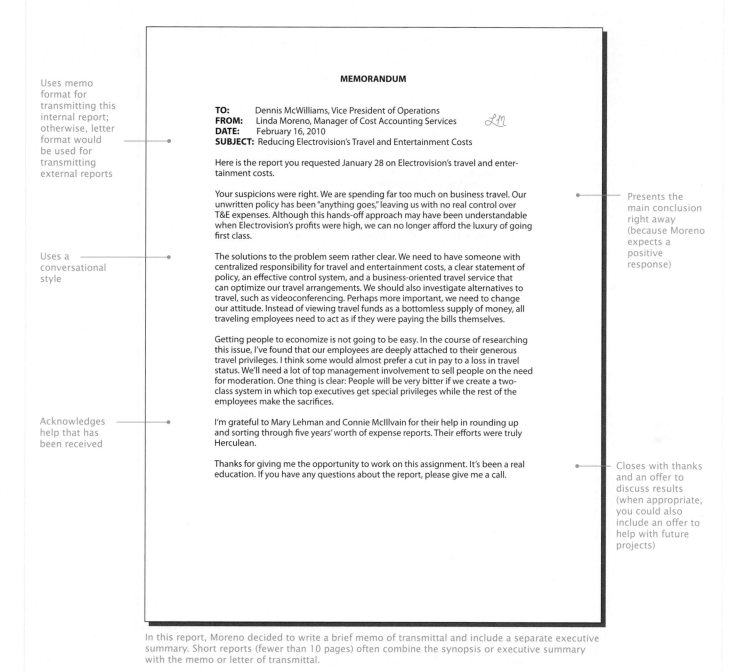

Uses memo format for transmitting this internal report; otherwise, letter format would be used for transmitting external reports

Uses a conversational style

Acknowledges help that has been received

Presents the main conclusion right away (because Moreno expects a positive response)

Closes with thanks and an offer to discuss results (when appropriate, you could also include an offer to help with future projects)

MEMORANDUM

TO: Dennis McWilliams, Vice President of Operations
FROM: Linda Moreno, Manager of Cost Accounting Services *LM*
DATE: February 16, 2010
SUBJECT: Reducing Electrovision's Travel and Entertainment Costs

Here is the report you requested January 28 on Electrovision's travel and entertainment costs.

Your suspicions were right. We are spending far too much on business travel. Our unwritten policy has been "anything goes," leaving us with no real control over T&E expenses. Although this hands-off approach may have been understandable when Electrovision's profits were high, we can no longer afford the luxury of going first class.

The solutions to the problem seem rather clear. We need to have someone with centralized responsibility for travel and entertainment costs, a clear statement of policy, an effective control system, and a business-oriented travel service that can optimize our travel arrangements. We should also investigate alternatives to travel, such as videoconferencing. Perhaps more important, we need to change our attitude. Instead of viewing travel funds as a bottomless supply of money, all traveling employees need to act as if they were paying the bills themselves.

Getting people to economize is not going to be easy. In the course of researching this issue, I've found that our employees are deeply attached to their generous travel privileges. I think some would almost prefer a cut in pay to a loss in travel status. We'll need a lot of top management involvement to sell people on the need for moderation. One thing is clear: People will be very bitter if we create a two-class system in which top executives get special privileges while the rest of the employees make the sacrifices.

I'm grateful to Mary Lehman and Connie McIllvain for their help in rounding up and sorting through five years' worth of expense reports. Their efforts were truly Herculean.

Thanks for giving me the opportunity to work on this assignment. It's been a real education. If you have any questions about the report, please give me a call.

In this report, Moreno decided to write a brief memo of transmittal and include a separate executive summary. Short reports (fewer than 10 pages) often combine the synopsis or executive summary with the memo or letter of transmittal.

Doesn't include any elements that appear before the "Contents" page

Words the headings exactly as they appear in the text

Numbers figures consecutively throughout the report

Numbers the contents page with lowercase Roman numerals centered at the bottom margin

Includes only the page numbers where sections begin

CONTENTS

LIST OF ILLUSTRATIONS

iii

Moreno included only first- and second-level headings in her table of contents, even though the report contains third-level headings. She prefers a shorter table of contents that focuses attention on the main divisions of thought. She used informative titles, which are appropriate for a report to a receptive audience.

Begins by stating the purpose of the report

Presents the points in the executive summary in the same order as they appear in the report, using subheadings that summarize the content of the main sections of the report

EXECUTIVE SUMMARY

This report analyzes Electrovision's travel and entertainment (T&E) costs and presents recommendations for reducing those costs.

Travel and Entertainment Costs Are Too High

Travel and entertainment is a large and growing expense category for Electrovision. The company spends over $16 million per year on business travel, and these costs have been increasing by 12 percent annually. Company employees make roughly 3,390 trips each year at an average cost per trip of $4,720. Airfares are the biggest expense, followed by hotels, meals, and rental cars.

The nature of Electrovision's business does require extensive travel, but the company's costs are excessive: Our employees spend more than twice the national average on travel and entertainment. Although the location of the company's facilities may partly explain this discrepancy, the main reason for our high costs is a management style that gives employees little incentive to economize.

Cuts Are Essential

Electrovision management now recognizes the need to gain more control over this element of costs. The company is currently entering a period of declining profits, prompting management to look for every opportunity to reduce spending. At the same time, rising airfares and hotel rates are making T&E expenses more significant.

Electrovision Can Save $6 Million per Year

Fortunately, Electrovision has a number of excellent opportunities for reducing T&E costs. Savings of up to $6 million per year should be achievable, judging by the experience of other companies. A sensible travel-management program can save companies as much as 35 percent a year (Gilligan 39–40), and we should be able to save even more, since we purchase many more business-class tickets than the average. Four steps will help us cut costs:

1. Hire a director of travel and entertainment to assume overall responsibility for T&E spending, policies, and technologies, including the hiring and management of a national travel agency.
2. Educate employees on the need for cost containment, both in avoiding unnecessary travel and reducing costs when travel is necessary.
3. Negotiate preferential rates with travel providers.
4. Implement technological alternatives to travel, such as virtual meetings.

As necessary as these changes are, they will likely hurt morale, at least in the short term. Management will need to make a determined effort to explain the rationale for reduced spending. By exercising moderation in their own travel arrangements, Electrovision executives can set a good example and help other employees accept the changes. On the plus side, using travel alternatives such as web conferencing will reduce the travel burden on many employees and help them balance their business and personal lives.

iv

Targets a receptive audience with a hard-hitting tone in the executive summary (a more neutral approach would be better for hostile or skeptical readers)

Executive summary uses the same font and paragraph treatment as the text of the report

Continues numbering the executive summary pages with lowercase Roman numerals

Moreno decided to include an executive summary because her report is aimed at a mixed audience, some of whom are interested in the details of her report and others who just want the "big picture." The executive summary is aimed at the second group, giving them enough information to make a decision without burdening them with the task of reading the entire report.

Her writing style matches the serious nature of the content without sounding distant or stiff. Moreno chose the formal approach because several members of her audience are considerably higher up in the organization, and she did not want to sound too familiar. In addition, her company prefers the impersonal style for formal reports.

Centers the title of the report on the first page of the text, 2 inches from the top of the page

REDUCING ELECTROVISION'S TRAVEL AND ENTERTAINMENT COSTS

INTRODUCTION

Electrovision has always encouraged a significant amount of business travel. To compensate employees for the stress and inconvenience of frequent trips, management has authorized generous travel and entertainment (T&E) allowances. This philosophy has been good for morale, but last year Electrovision spent $16 million on travel and entertainment—$7 million more than it spent on research and development.

Opens by establishing the need for action

This year's T&E costs will affect profits even more, due to increases in airline fares and hotel rates. Also, the company anticipates that profits will be relatively weak for a variety of other reasons. Therefore, Dennis McWilliams, Vice President of Operations, has asked the accounting department to explore ways to reduce the T&E budget.

The purpose of this report is to analyze T&E expenses, evaluate the effect of recent hotel and airfare increases, and suggest ways to tighten control over T&E costs. The report outlines several steps that could reduce Electrovision's expenses, but the precise financial impact of these measures is difficult to project. The estimates presented here provide a "best guess" view of what Electrovision can expect to save.

In preparing this report, the accounting department analyzed internal expense reports for the past five years to determine how much Electrovision spends on travel and entertainment. These figures were then compared with average statistics compiled by Dow Jones (publisher of the *Wall Street Journal*) and presented as the Dow Jones Travel Index. We also analyzed trends and suggestions published in a variety of business journal articles to see how other companies are coping with the high cost of business travel.

Mentions sources and methods to increase credibility and to give readers a complete picture of the study's background

THE HIGH COST OF TRAVEL AND ENTERTAINMENT

Although many companies view travel and entertainment as an incidental cost of doing business, the dollars add up. At Electrovision the bill for airfares, hotels, rental cars, meals, and entertainment totaled $16 million last year. Our T&E budget has increased by 12 percent per year for the past five years. Compared to the average U.S. business traveler, Electrovision's expenditures are high, largely because of management's generous policy on travel benefits.

1

Uses the arabic numeral 1 for the first page, centering the number about 1 inch from the bottom of the page

In her brief introduction, Moreno counts on topic sentences and transitions to indicate that she is discussing the purpose, scope, and limitations of the study.

2

Uses arabic numerals to number the second and succeeding pages of the text in the upper right-hand corner where the top and right-hand margins meet

$16 Million per Year Spent on Travel and Entertainment

Electrovision's annual budget for travel and entertainment is only 8 percent of sales. Because this is a relatively small expense category compared with such things as salaries and commissions, it is tempting to dismiss T&E costs as insignificant. However, T&E is Electrovision's third-largest controllable expense, directly behind salaries and information systems.

Last year Electrovision personnel made about 3,390 trips at an average cost per trip of $4,720. The typical trip involved a round-trip flight of 3,000 kilometers, meals, and hotel accommodations for two or three days, and a rental car. Roughly 80 percent of trips were made by 20 percent of the staff—top management and sales personnel traveled most, averaging 18 trips per year.

Figure 1 illustrates how the T&E budget is spent. The largest categories are airfares and lodging, which together account for $7 out of $10 that employees spend on travel and entertainment. This spending breakdown has been relatively steady for the past five years and is consistent with the distribution of expenses experienced by other companies.

Places the visual as close as possible to the point it illustrates

Figure 1
Airfares and Lodging Account for Over Two-Thirds of Electrovision's T&E Budget

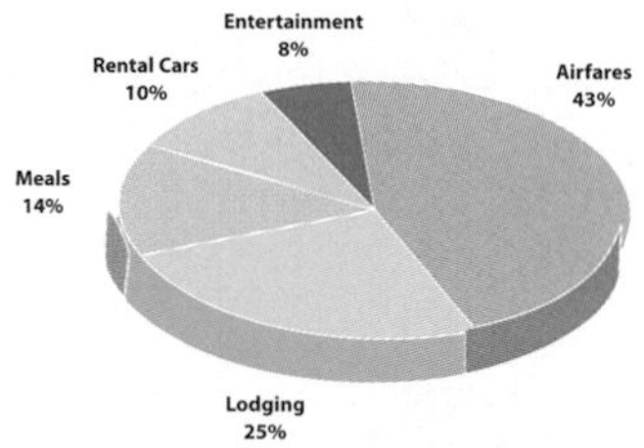

Although the composition of the T&E budget has been consistent, its size has not. As mentioned earlier, these expenditures have increased by about 12 percent per year for the past five years, roughly twice the rate of the company's sales growth (see Figure 2). This rate of growth makes T&E Electrovision's fastest-growing expense item.

Gives each visual a title that clearly indicates what it's about; titles are consistently placed to the left of each visual

Figure 2
T&E Expenses Continue to Increase as a Percentage of Sales

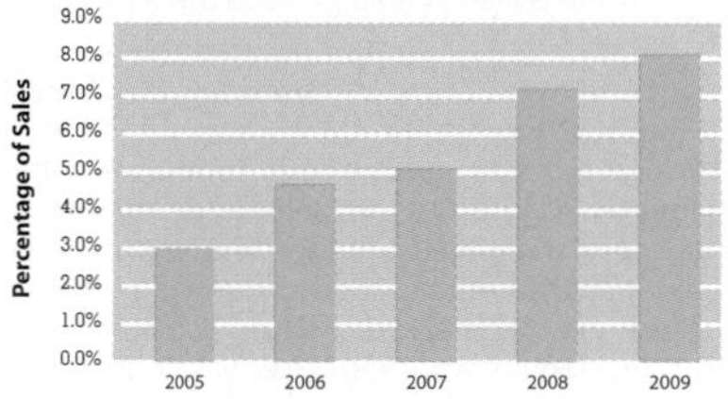

Moreno opens the first main section of the body with a topic sentence that introduces an important fact about the subject of the section. Then she orients the reader to the three major points developed in the section.

3

Electrovision's Travel Expenses Exceed National Averages

Much of our travel budget is justified. Two major factors contribute to Electrovision's high T&E budget:

- With our headquarters on the West Coast and our major customer on the East Coast, we naturally spend a lot of money on cross-country flights.
- A great deal of travel takes place between our headquarters here on the West Coast and the manufacturing operations in Detroit, Boston, and Dallas. Corporate managers and division personnel make frequent trips to coordinate these disparate operations.

However, even though a good portion of Electrovision's travel budget is justifiable, the company spends considerably more on T&E than the average business traveler (see Figure 3).

Introduces visuals before they appear and indicates what readers should notice about the data

Numbers the visuals consecutively and refers to them in the text by their numbers

Figure 3
Electrovision Employees Spend Over Twice as Much as the Average Business Traveler

Source: *Wall Street Journal* and company records

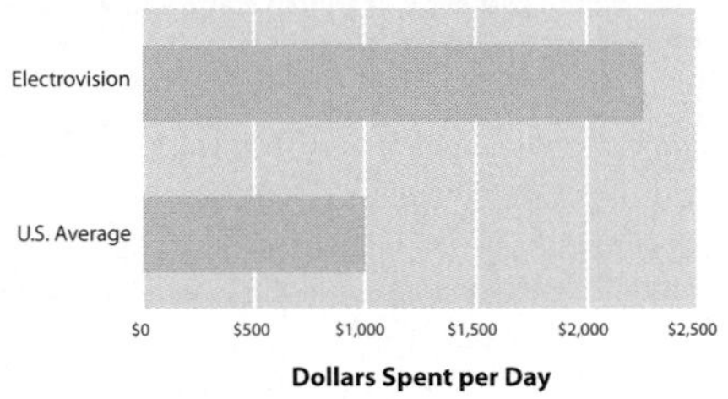

The Dow Jones Travel Index calculates the average cost per day of business travel in the United States, based on average airfare, hotel rates, and rental car rates. The average fluctuates weekly as travel companies change their rates, but it has been running at about $1,000 per day for the last year or so. In contrast, Electrovision's average daily expense over the past year has been $2,250—a hefty 125 percent higher than average. This figure is based on the average trip cost of $4,720 listed earlier and an average trip length of 2.1 days.

Spending Has Been Encouraged

Although a variety of factors may contribute to this differential, Electrovision's relatively high T&E costs are at least partially attributable to the company's philosophy and management style. Since many employees do not enjoy business travel, management has tried to make the trips more pleasant by authorizing business-class airfare, luxury hotel accommodations, and full-size rental cars. The sales staff is encouraged to entertain clients at top restaurants and to invite them to cultural and sporting events.

The chart in Figure 3 is simple but effective; Moreno includes just enough data to make her point. Notice how she is as careful about the appearance of her report as she is about the quality of its content.

Uses a bulleted list to make it easy for readers to identify and distinguish related points

Leaves an extra line of white space above headings to help readers associate each heading with the text it describes

Uses informative headings to focus reader attention on the main points (such headings are appropriate when a report uses direct order and is intended for a receptive audience; however, descriptive headings are more effective when a report is in indirect order and readers are less receptive)

4

The cost of these privileges is easy to overlook, given the weakness of Electrovision's system for keeping track of T&E expenses:

- The monthly financial records do not contain a separate category for travel and entertainment; the information is buried under Cost of Goods Sold and under Selling, General, and Administrative Expenses.
- Each department head is given authority to approve any expense report, regardless of how large it may be.
- Receipts are not required for expenditures of less than $100.
- Individuals are allowed to make their own travel arrangements.
- No one is charged with the responsibility for controlling the company's total spending on travel and entertainment.

GROWING IMPACT ON THE BOTTOM LINE

During the past three years, the company's healthy profits have resulted in relatively little pressure to push for tighter controls over all aspects of the business. However, as we all know, the situation is changing. We're projecting flat to declining profits for the next two years, a situation that has prompted all of us to search for ways to cut costs. At the same time, rising airfares and hotel rates have increased the impact of T&E expenses on the company's financial results.

Lower Profits Underscore the Need for Change

The next two years promise to be difficult for Electrovision. After several years of steady increases in spending, the Postal Service is tightening procurement policies for automated mail-handling equipment. Funding for the A-12 optical character reader has been canceled. As a consequence, the marketing department expects sales to drop by 15 percent. Although Electrovision is negotiating several other promising R&D contracts, the marketing department does not foresee any major procurements for the next two to three years.

At the same time, Electrovision is facing cost increases on several fronts. As we have known for several months, the new production facility now under construction in Salt Lake City, Utah, is behind schedule and over budget. Labor contracts in Boston and Dallas will expire within the next six months, and plant managers there anticipate that significant salary and benefits concessions may be necessary to avoid strikes.

Moreover, marketing and advertising costs are expected to increase as we attempt to strengthen these activities to better cope with competitive pressures. Given the expected decline in revenues and increase in costs, the Executive Committee's prediction that profits will fall by 12 percent in the coming fiscal year does not seem overly pessimistic.

Moreno designed her report to include plenty of white space so even those pages that lack visuals are still attractive and easy to read.

Airfares and Hotel Rates Are Rising

Business travelers have grown accustomed to frequent fare wars and discounting in the travel industry in recent years. Excess capacity and aggressive price competition, particularly in the airline business, made travel a relative bargain.

Documents the facts to add weight to Moreno's argument

However, that situation has changed as weaker competitors have been forced out and the remaining players have grown stronger and smarter. Airlines and hotels are better at managing inventory and keeping occupancy rates high, which translates into higher costs for Electrovision. Last year saw some of the steepest rate hikes in years. Business airfares (tickets most likely to be purchased by business travelers) jumped more than 40 percent in many markets. The trend is expected to continue, with rates increasing another 5 to 10 percent overall (Phillips 331; "Travel Costs Under Pressure" 30; Dahl B6).

Given the fact that air and hotel costs account for almost 70 percent of our T&E budget, the trend toward higher prices in these two categories will have serious consequences, unless management takes action to control these costs.

METHODS FOR REDUCING T&E COSTS

Gives recommendations an objective flavor by pointing out both the benefits and the risks of taking action

By implementing a number of reforms, management can expect to reduce Electrovision's T&E budget by as much as 40 percent. This estimate is based on the general assessment made by American Express (Gilligan 39) and on the fact that we have an opportunity to significantly reduce air travel costs by eliminating business-class travel. However, these measures are likely to be unpopular with employees. To gain acceptance for such changes, management will need to sell employees on the need for moderation in T&E allowances.

Four Ways to Trim Expenses

By researching what other companies are doing to curb T&E expenses, the accounting department has identified four prominent opportunities that should enable Electrovision to save about $6 million annually in travel-related costs.

Institute Tighter Spending Controls

A single individual should be appointed director of travel and entertainment to spearhead the effort to gain control of the T&E budget. More than a third of all U.S. companies now employ travel managers ("Businesses Use Savvy Managers" 4). The director should be familiar with the travel industry and should be well versed in both accounting and information technology. The director should also report to the vice president of operations. The director's first priorities should be to establish a written T&E policy and a cost-control system.

Electrovision currently has no written policy on travel and entertainment, a step that is widely recommended by air travel experts (Smith D4). Creating a policy would clarify management's position and serve as a vehicle for communicating the need for moderation.

Moreno creates a forceful tone by using action verbs in the third-level subheadings of this section. This approach is appropriate to the nature of the study and the attitude of the audience. However, in a status-conscious organization, the imperative verbs might sound a bit too presumptuous coming from a junior member of the staff.

6

At a minimum, the policy should include the following:

- All travel and entertainment should be strictly related to business and should be approved in advance.
- Except under special circumstances to be approved on a case-by-case basis, employees should travel by coach and stay in mid-range business hotels.
- The T&E policy should apply equally to employees at all levels.

Breaks up text with bulleted lists, which not only call attention to important points but also add visual interest

To implement the new policy, Electrovision will need to create a system for controlling T&E expenses. Each department should prepare an annual T&E budget as part of its operating plan. These budgets should be presented in detail so that management can evaluate how T&E dollars will be spent and can recommend appropriate cuts. To help management monitor performance relative to these budgets, the director of travel should prepare monthly financial statements showing actual T&E expenditures by department.

The director of travel should also be responsible for retaining a business-oriented travel service that will schedule all employee business trips and look for the best travel deals, particularly in airfares. In addition to centralizing Electrovision's reservation and ticketing activities, the agency will negotiate reduced group rates with hotels and rental car firms. The agency selected should have offices nationwide so that all Electrovision facilities can channel their reservations through the same company. This is particularly important in light of the dizzying array of often wildly different airfares available between some cities. It's not uncommon to find dozens of fares along commonly traveled routes (Rowe 30). In addition, the director can help coordinate travel across the company to secure group discounts whenever possible (Barker 31; Miller B6).

Specifies the steps required to implement recommendations

Reduce Unnecessary Travel and Entertainment

One of the easiest ways to reduce expenses is to reduce the amount of traveling and entertaining that occurs. An analysis of last year's expenditures suggests that as much as 30 percent of Electrovision's travel and entertainment is discretionary. The professional staff spent $2.8 million attending seminars and conferences last year. Although these gatherings are undoubtedly beneficial, the company could save money by sending fewer representatives to each function and perhaps by eliminating some of the less valuable seminars.

Similarly, Electrovision could economize on trips between headquarters and divisions by reducing the frequency of such visits and by sending fewer people on each trip. Although there is often no substitute for face-to-face meetings, management could try to resolve more internal issues through telephone, electronic, and written communication.

Electrovision can also reduce spending by urging employees to economize. Instead of flying business class, employees can fly coach class or take advantage of discount fares. Rather than ordering a $50 bottle of wine, employees can select a less expensive bottle or dispense with

Moreno takes care not to overstep the boundaries of her analysis. For instance, she doesn't analyze the value of the seminars that employees attend every year, so she avoids any absolute statements about reducing travel to seminars.

7

alcohol entirely. People can book rooms at moderately priced hotels and drive smaller rental cars.

Obtain Lowest Rates from Travel Providers

Apart from urging employees to economize, Electrovision can also save money by searching for the lowest available airfares, hotel rates, and rental car fees. Currently, few employees have the time or knowledge to seek out travel bargains. When they need to travel, they make the most convenient and comfortable arrangements. A professional travel service will be able to obtain lower rates from travel providers.

Judging by the experience of other companies, Electrovision may be able to trim as much as 30 to 40 percent from the travel budget simply by looking for bargains in airfares and negotiating group rates with hotels and rental car companies. Electrovision should be able to achieve these economies by analyzing its travel patterns, identifying frequently visited locations, and selecting a few hotels that are willing to reduce rates in exchange for guaranteed business. At the same time, the company should be able to save up to 40 percent on rental car charges by negotiating a corporate rate.

Points out possible difficulties to show that all angles have been considered and to build confidence in her judgment

The possibilities for economizing are promising; however, making the best travel arrangements often requires trade-offs such as the following:

- The best fares might not always be the lowest. Indirect flights are usually cheaper, but they take longer and may end up costing more in lost work time.
- The cheapest tickets often require booking 14 or even 30 days in advance, which is often impossible for us.
- Discount tickets are usually nonrefundable, which is a serious drawback when a trip needs to be canceled at the last minute.

Replace Travel with Technological Alternatives

Less-expensive travel options promise significant savings, but the biggest cost reductions over the long term might come from replacing travel with virtual meeting technology. Both analysts and corporate users say that the early kinks that hampered online meetings have largely been worked out, and the latest systems are fast, easy to learn, and easy to use (Solheim 26). For example, Webex (a leading provider of webconferencing services) offers everything from simple, impromptu team meetings to major online events with up to 3,000 participants ("Online Meeting Solutions").

One of the first responsibilities of the new travel director should be an evaluation of these technologies and a recommendation for integrating them throughout Electrovision's operations.

Note how Moreno makes the transition from section to section. The first sentence under the second heading on this page refers to the subject of the previous paragraph and signals a shift in thought.

8

The Impact of Reforms

By implementing tighter controls, reducing unnecessary expenses, negotiating more favorable rates, and exploring alternatives to travel, Electrovision should be able to reduce its T&E budget significantly. As Table 1 illustrates, the combined savings should be in the neighborhood of $6 million, although the precise figures are somewhat difficult to project.

Uses complete sentence to help readers focus immediately on the point of the table

Table 1
Electrovision Can Trim Travel and Entertainment Costs
by an Estimated $6 Million per Year

Uses informative title in the table, which is consistent with the way headings are handled in this report and is appropriate for a report to a receptive audience

SOURCE OF SAVINGS	ESTIMATED SAVINGS
Switching from business-class to coach airfare	$2,300,000
Negotiating preferred hotel rates	940,000
Negotiating preferred rental car rates	460,000
Systematically searching for lower airfares	375,000
Reducing interdivisional travel	675,000
Reducing seminar and conference attendance	1,250,000
TOTAL POTENTIAL SAVINGS	**$6,000,000**

Includes financial estimates to help management envision the impact of the suggestions, even though estimated savings are difficult to project

To achieve the economies outlined in the table, Electrovision will incur expenses for hiring a director of travel and for implementing a T&E cost-control system. These costs are projected at $115,000: $105,000 per year in salary and benefits for the new employee and a one-time expense of $10,000 for the cost-control system. The cost of retaining a full-service travel agency is negligible, even with the service fees that many are now passing along from airlines and other service providers.

The measures required to achieve these savings are likely to be unpopular with employees. Electrovision personnel are accustomed to generous T&E allowances, and they are likely to resent having these privileges curtailed. To alleviate their disappointment

- Management should make a determined effort to explain why the changes are necessary.
- The director of corporate communication should be asked to develop a multifaceted campaign that will communicate the importance of curtailing T&E costs.
- Management should set a positive example by adhering strictly to the new policies.
- The limitations should apply equally to employees at all levels in the organization.

Note how Moreno calls attention in the first paragraph to items in the following table, without repeating the information in the table.

Uses a descriptive heading for the last section of the text (in informational reports, this section is often called "Summary"; in analytical reports, it is called "Conclusions" or "Conclusions and Recommendations")

Summarizes conclusions in the first two paragraphs—a good approach because Moreno organized her report around conclusions and recommendations, so readers have already been introduced to them

Emphasizes the recommendations by presenting them in list format

9

CONCLUSIONS AND RECOMMENDATIONS

Electrovision is currently spending $16 million per year on travel and entertainment. Although much of this spending is justified, the company's costs are high relative to competitors' costs, mainly because Electrovision has been generous with its travel benefits.

Electrovision's liberal approach to travel and entertainment was understandable during years of high profitability; however, the company is facing the prospect of declining profits for the next several years. Management is therefore motivated to cut costs in all areas of the business. Reducing T&E spending is particularly important because the bottom-line impact of these costs will increase as airline fares increase.

Electrovision should be able to reduce T&E costs by as much as 40 percent by taking four important steps:

1. *Institute tighter spending controls.* Management should hire a director of travel and entertainment who will assume overall responsibility for T&E activities. Within the next six months, this director should develop a written travel policy, institute a T&E budget and a cost-control system, and retain a professional, business-oriented travel agency that will optimize arrangements with travel providers.

2. *Reduce unnecessary travel and entertainment.* Electrovision should encourage employees to economize on T&E spending. Management can accomplish this by authorizing fewer trips and by urging employees to be more conservative in their spending.

3. *Obtain lowest rates from travel providers.* Electrovision should also focus on obtaining the best rates on airline tickets, hotel rooms, and rental cars. By channeling all arrangements through a professional travel agency, the company can optimize its choices and gain clout in negotiating preferred rates.

4. *Replace travel with technological alternatives.* With the number of computers already installed in our facilities, it seems likely that we could take advantage of desktop videoconferencing and other distance-meeting tools. Technological alternatives won't be quite as feasible with customer sites, since these systems require compatible equipment at both ends of a connection, but such systems are certainly a possibility for communication with Electrovision's own sites.

Because these measures may be unpopular with employees, management should make a concerted effort to explain the importance of reducing travel costs. The director of corporate communication should be given responsibility for developing a plan to communicate the need for employee cooperation.

Moreno doesn't introduce any new facts in this section. In a longer report she might have divided this section into subsections, labeled "Conclusions" and "Recommendations," to distinguish between the two.

Lists references alphabetically by the author's last name, and when the author is unknown, by the title of the reference (see Appendix B for additional details on preparing reference lists)

10

WORKS CITED

Barker, Julie. "How to Rein in Group Travel Costs." *Successful Meetings* Feb. 2008: 31.

"Businesses Use Savvy Managers to Keep Travel Costs Down." *Christian Science Monitor* 17 July 2008: 4.

Dahl, Jonathan. "2000: The Year Travel Costs Took Off." *Wall Street Journal* 29 Dec. 2007: B6.

Gilligan, Edward P. "Trimming Your T&E Is Easier Than You Think." *Managing Office Technology* Nov. 2008: 39–40.

"Meet With Anyone, Anywhere, Anytime," *Webex.com*. 2009. WebEx, 2 February 2009, <http://www.webex.com/solutions/online-meeting-suc.html>.

Miller, Lisa. "Attention, Airline Ticket Shoppers." *Wall Street Journal* 7 July 2007: B6.

Phillips, Edward H. "Airlines Post Record Traffic." *Aviation Week & Space Technology* 8 Jan. 2007: 331.

Rowe, Irene Vlitos. "Global Solution for Cutting Travel Costs." *European* 12 Oct. 2008: 30.

Smith, Carol. "Rising, Erratic Airfares Make Company Policy Vital." *Los Angeles Times* 2 Nov. 2007: D4.

Solheim, Shelley. "Web Conferencing Made Easy." *eWeek* 22 Aug. 2008: 26.

"Travel Costs Under Pressure." *Purchasing* 15 Feb. 2007: 30.

Moreno's list of references follows the style recommended in The MLA Style Manual. The box below shows how these sources would be cited following APA style.

10

REFERENCES

Barker, J. (2008, February). How to rein in group travel costs. *Successful Meetings,* 31.

Businesses use savvy managers to keep travel costs down. (2008, July 17). *Christian Science Monitor,* 4.

Dahl, J. (2007, December 29). 2000: The year travel costs took off. *Wall Street Journal,* B6.

Gilligan, E. (2008, November). Trimming your T&E is easier than you think. *Managing Office Technology,* 39–40.

Miller, L. (2007, July 7). Attention, airline ticket shoppers. *Wall Street Journal,* B6.

Phillips, E. (2007, January 8). Airlines post record traffic. *Aviation Week & Space Technology,* 331.

Rowe, I. (2008, October 12). Global solution for cutting travel costs. *European,* 30.

Smith, C. (2007, November 2). Rising, erratic airfares make company policy vital. *Los Angeles Times,* D4.

Solheim, S. (2008, August 22). Web conferencing made easy. *eWeek,* 26.

Travel costs under pressure. (2007, February 15). *Purchasing,* 30.

Webex.com. (2009). *Meet With Anyone, Anywhere, Anytime.* Retrieved 2 February 2009, from http://www.webex.com/solutions/online-meeting-suc.html.

in a report: prefatory parts, text of the report, and supplementary parts. For an illustration of how the various parts fit together, see Linda Moreno's Electrovision report in "Report Writer's Notebook: Analyzing a Formal Report."

Many of the components in a formal report start on a new page, but not always. Inserting page breaks consumes extra paper and adds to the bulk of your report. On the other hand, starting a section on a new page helps your readers navigate the report and recognize transitions between major sections or features.

If you want a section to stand out, start it on a new page.

When you want a particular section to stand apart, start it on a new page (in the same way that each chapter in this book starts on a new page). Most prefatory parts, such as the table of contents, should also be placed on their own pages. However, the various parts in the report text are often run together. If your introduction is only a paragraph long, don't bother with a page break before moving into the body of your report. If the introduction runs longer than a page, however, a page break can signal the reader that a major shift is occurring in the flow of the report.

Prefatory Parts

Formal reports can contain a variety of prefatory parts, from a cover page to a synopsis or an executive summary.

Prefatory parts are front-end materials that provide key preliminary information so that readers can decide whether and how to read the report.[4] Note that many of these parts—such as the table of contents, list of illustrations, and executive summary—are easiest to prepare after the text has been completed because they directly reflect the contents. When your text is complete, you can use your word processor to automatically compile the table of contents and the list of illustrations. You can prepare other parts at almost any time.

Cover

Many companies have standard covers for reports, made of heavy paper and imprinted with the company's name and logo. If your company doesn't have such covers, you can usually find something suitable in a good stationery store. Look for a cover that is attractive, convenient, and appropriate to the subject matter. Also, make sure it can be labeled with the report title, the writer's name (optional), and the submission date (also optional).

Think carefully about the title you put on the cover. A business report is not a mystery novel, so give your readers all the information they need: the who, what, when, where, why, and how of the subject. At the same time, try to be concise. You can reduce the length of your title by eliminating phrases such as *A Report of*, *A Study of*, or *A Survey of.*

Title Fly and Title Page

The **title fly** is a single sheet of paper with only the title of the report on it. You don't really need one, but it adds a touch of formality. The **title page** includes four blocks of information: (1) the title of the report; (2) the name, title, and address of the person(s), group, or organization that authorized the report (if anyone); (3) the name, title, and address of the person(s), group, or organization that prepared the report; and (4) the date on which the report was submitted. On some title pages, the second block of information is preceded by the words *Prepared for* or *Submitted to*, and the third block of information is preceded by *Prepared by* or *Submitted by*. In some cases, the title page serves as the cover of the report, especially if the report is relatively short and is intended solely for internal use.

3 LEARNING OBJECTIVE

Identify the circumstances in which you should include letters of authorization and letters of acceptance in your reports.

Letter of Authorization and Letter of Acceptance

A letter of authorization is the document that instructed you to produce a report; a letter of acceptance is your written agreement to produce the report.

If you received written authorization to prepare a report, you may want to include that letter or memo in your report. This **letter of authorization** (or *memo of authorization*) is a document you received, asking or directing you to prepare the report. If you wrote a **letter of acceptance** (or *memo of acceptance*) in response to that communication, accepting the assignment and clarifying any conditions or limitations, you might also include that letter in the report's prefatory parts. If there is any chance that your report might not meet your audience's expectations, the letter of acceptance can remind your readers what you agreed to do and why.

In general, letters of authorization and acceptance are included in only the most formal reports. However, in any case in which a significant amount of time has passed since you received the letter of authorization or you do not have a close working relationship with the audience, consider including both letters to make sure everyone is clear about the report's intent and the approach you took to create it. You don't want your weeks or months of work to be diminished by any misunderstandings.

Letter of Transmittal

The **letter of transmittal** (or *memo of transmittal*), a specialized form of a cover letter, introduces your report to your audience. The letter of transmittal says what you'd say if you were handing the report directly to the person who authorized it, so its style is often less formal than that of the rest of the report. If your audience is likely to be skeptical of or even hostile to something in your report, the transmittal letter is a good opportunity to acknowledge their concerns and explain how the report addresses the issues they care about.

A letter or memo of transmittal introduces your report to your audience.

Depending on the nature of your report, your letter of transmittal can follow either the direct approach for routine and positive messages described in Chapter 8 or the indirect approach for negative messages described in Chapter 9. Open by officially conveying the report to your readers and summarizing its purpose. Such a letter typically begins with a statement such as "Here is the report you asked me to prepare on . . ." The rest of the introduction includes information about the scope of the report, the methods used to complete the study, limitations, and any special messages you need to convey.

In the body of the transmittal letter, you may also highlight important points or sections of the report, give suggestions for follow-up studies, and offer any details that will help readers understand and use the report. You may also want to acknowledge help given by others. The conclusion of the transmittal letter often includes a note of thanks for having been given the report assignment, an expression of willingness to discuss the report, and an offer to assist with future projects.

If the report does not have a synopsis, the letter of transmittal may summarize the major findings, conclusions, and recommendations. This material would be placed after the opening of the letter.

If you don't include a synopsis, you can summarize the report's content in your letter of transmittal.

Table of Contents

The table of contents (usually titled simply *Contents*) indicates in outline form the coverage, sequence, and relative importance of the information in the report. The headings used in the text of the report are the basis for the table of contents. Depending on the length and complexity of the report, you may need to decide how many levels of headings to show in the contents; you want to strike a balance between simplicity and completeness. If a detailed table of contents could have dozens or even hundreds of entries, consider including two tables: a high-level table that shows only major headings, followed by a detailed table that includes everything (as this and many other textbooks do). No matter how many levels you include, make sure readers can easily distinguish between them.

Also, take extra care to verify that your table of contents is accurate, consistent, and complete. To ensure accuracy, construct the table of contents after your report is complete, thoroughly edited, and proofed. This way, the headings and subheadings aren't likely to change or move from page to page. And if at all possible, use the automatic features in your word processing software to generate the table of contents. Doing so helps improve accuracy by eliminating typing mistakes, and it keeps your table current in the event that you do have to repaginate or revise headings late in the process.

To save time and reduce errors, use the table of contents generator in your word processor.

List of Illustrations

If you have more than a handful of illustrations in your report, or if you want to call attention to your illustrations, include a list of illustrations after the table of contents. For simplicity's sake, some reports refer to all visuals as *illustrations* or *exhibits*. In other reports, as in Moreno's Electrovision report, tables are labeled separately from other types of visuals, which are called *figures*. Regardless of the system you use, be sure to include titles and page numbers.

If you have enough space on a single page, include the list of illustrations directly beneath the table of contents. Otherwise, put the list on the page after the contents page. When tables and figures are numbered separately, they should also be listed separately.

4 LEARNING OBJECTIVE

Explain the difference between a synopsis and an executive summary.

A synopsis is a brief preview of the most important points in your report.

Synopsis or Executive Summary

A **synopsis** is a brief overview (one page or less) of a report's most important points, designed to give readers a quick preview of the contents (see Figure 13.2). A synopsis is often included in long informational reports dealing with technical, professional, or academic subjects and can also be called an **abstract**. The phrasing of a synopsis can be either informative or descriptive. An informative synopsis presents the main points of the report in the order in which they appear in the text. A descriptive synopsis, on the other hand, simply tells what the report is about, using only moderately greater detail than the table of contents; the actual findings of the report are omitted.

The way you handle a synopsis reflects the approach you use in the text. If you're using an indirect approach in your report, you're better off with a descriptive synopsis because an informative synopsis "gives away the ending" of your report. No matter which type of synopsis you use, be sure to present an accurate picture of the report's contents.[5]

An executive summary is a "mini" version of your report.

Many business report writers prefer to include an **executive summary** instead of a synopsis or an abstract. Whereas a synopsis is a "prose table of contents" that outlines the main points of the report, an executive summary is a fully developed "mini" version of the report itself. An executive summary is more comprehensive than a synopsis; many contain headings, well-developed transitions, and even visual elements. They are usually organized in the same way as the report, using a direct or an indirect approach, depending on the audience's receptivity.

Executive summaries are intended for readers who lack the time or motivation to study the complete text. As a general rule, keep the length of an executive summary proportionate to the length of the report. A brief business report may have only a one-page or shorter executive summary. A longer business report may have a two- or three-page summary. Anything longer, however, might cease to be a summary.[6]

FIGURE 13.2 Report Synopsis
The introductory page of this online brochure serves as a synopsis, giving readers a brief overview of the main points covered. Those who want more information can click on the "Details" link to the left to get additional information.

Many reports require neither a synopsis nor an executive summary. Length is usually the determining factor. Most reports of fewer than 10 pages either omit such a preview or combine it with the letter of transmittal. However, if your report is over 20 or 30 pages long, you'll probably want to include either a synopsis or an executive summary as a convenience for readers.

Text of the Report

No matter how many separate elements are in a formal report, the heart of the report is still the introduction, body, and close.

Although reports may contain a variety of components, the heart of a report is always composed of three main parts: an introduction, a body, and a close (which may consist of a summary, conclusions, or recommendations or some combination of the three). As Chapter 11 points out, the length and content of each of these parts vary with the length and type of report, the organizational structure, and the reader's familiarity with the topic. Following is a brief review of the three major parts of the report text.

Introduction

A good introduction invites audience members to continue reading by telling them what the report is about, why the audience should be concerned, and how the report is organized. If your report has a synopsis or an executive summary, minimize redundancy by balancing the introduction with the material in your summary—as Linda Moreno does in her Electrovision report. For example, Moreno's executive summary is fairly detailed, so she keeps her introduction brief. If you believe that your introduction needs to repeat information that has already been covered in one of the prefatory parts, try to vary the wording to minimize the feeling of repetition.

Body

The body of a report contains the information that supports your conclusions and recommendations as well as your analysis, logic, and interpretation of the information. See the body of Linda Moreno's Electrovision report for an example of the types of supporting detail commonly included in this section. Pay close attention to her effective use of visuals. Most inexperienced writers have a tendency to include too much data in their reports or place too much data in paragraph format instead of using tables and charts. Such treatment increases the chance of boring or losing an audience. If you find yourself with too much information, include only the essential supporting data in the body, use visuals, and place any additional information in an appendix.

Close

The close of your report should summarize your main ideas, highlight your conclusions or recommendations (if any), and list any courses of action that you expect readers to take or that you will be taking yourself. In a long report, this section may be labeled "Summary" or "Conclusions and Recommendations." If you have organized your report in a direct pattern, your close should be relatively brief, like Linda Moreno's. With an indirect organization, you may use this section to present your conclusions and recommendations for the first time, in which case this section might be fairly extensive.

Supplementary Parts

5 LEARNING OBJECTIVE

Describe the three supplementary parts of a formal report.

Supplementary parts follow the text of the report and provide information for readers who seek more detailed discussion. For online reports, you can put supplements on separate webpages and allow readers to link to them from the main report pages. Supplements are more common in long reports than in short ones, and they typically include appendixes, a bibliography, and an index.

Appendixes

Use an appendix for materials that are too lengthy for the body or not directly relevant to all audience members.

An **appendix** contains materials related to the report but not included in the text because they are lengthy, bulky, or perhaps not relevant to everyone in the audience. If your company has an intranet, shared workspaces, or other means of storing and accessing information online, consider putting your detailed supporting evidence there and referring readers to those sources for more detail.

The content of report appendixes varies widely; an appendix can include sample questionnaires and cover letters, sample forms, computer printouts, statistical formulas, financial statements and spreadsheets, copies of important documents, and multipage illustrations that would break up the flow of text. You might also include a glossary as an appendix or as a separate supplementary part.

If you have multiple categories of supporting material, give each type a separate appendix. Appendixes are usually identified with a letter and a short, descriptive title—for example, "Appendix A: Questionnaire," "Appendix B: Computer Printout of Raw Data," and so on. All appendixes should be mentioned in the text and listed in the table of contents.

Bibliography

A bibliography fulfills your ethical obligation to credit your sources, and it allows readers to consult those sources for more information.

To fulfill your ethical and legal obligation to credit other people for their work and to assist readers who want to research your topic further, include a **bibliography**, a list of the secondary sources you consulted when preparing your report. You can label this "Works Cited" if it contains only the works that were mentioned in the report or "References" if it includes works consulted but not mentioned in the report. Alternative formats include the *author-date system* (see page A-21) or numbered footnotes or endnotes. For more information on citing sources, see Appendix B, "Documentation of Report Sources."

In addition to providing a bibliography, some authors prefer to cite references in the report text. Acknowledging your sources in the body of your report demonstrates that you have thoroughly researched your topic. Furthermore, mentioning the names of well-known or important authorities on the subject helps build credibility for your message. Such source references should be handled as smoothly as possible. One approach, especially for internal reports, is simply to mention a source in the text:

> According to Dr. Lewis Morgan of Northwestern Hospital, hip replacement operations account for 7 percent of all surgeries performed on women age 65 and over.

However, if your report will be distributed to outsiders, include additional information on where you obtained the data. Most college students are familiar with citation methods suggested by the Modern Language Association (MLA) or the American Psychological Association (APA). *The Chicago Manual of Style* is a reference often used by typesetters and publishers. All these sources encourage the use of in-text citations (inserting the author's last name and a year of publication or a page number directly in the text).

Index

If your report is lengthy, an index can help readers locate specific topics quickly.

An **index** is an alphabetical list of names, places, and subjects mentioned in a report, along with the pages on which they occur. (See the indexes in this book for examples.) If you think your readers will need to access specific points of information in a lengthy report, consider including an index that lists all key topics, product names, markets, important persons—whatever is relevant to your subject matter. As with your table of contents, accuracy is critical. The good news is that you can also use your word processor to compile the index. Just be sure to update the index (and any automatically generated elements, for that matter) right before you produce and distribute the format.

—REAL-TIME UPDATES
Learn More

Get practical advice on developing research reports

The Online Writing Lab offers advice on developing all the sections of a typical research report. Go to **http://real-timeupdates.com/ebc** and click on "Learn More." If you are using mybcommlab, you can access Real-Time Updates within each chapter or under Student Study Tools.

Components of a Formal Proposal

The goal of a proposal is to impress readers with your professionalism and to make your offering and your company stand out from the competition. Consequently, proposals addressed to external audiences, including potential customers and investors, are nearly always formal. For smaller projects and situations in which you already have a working relationship with the audience, the proposal can be less formal and skip some of the components described in this section.

FIGURE 13.3 Parts of a Formal Proposal
As with formal reports, you can select from a variety of components to complete a formal proposal.

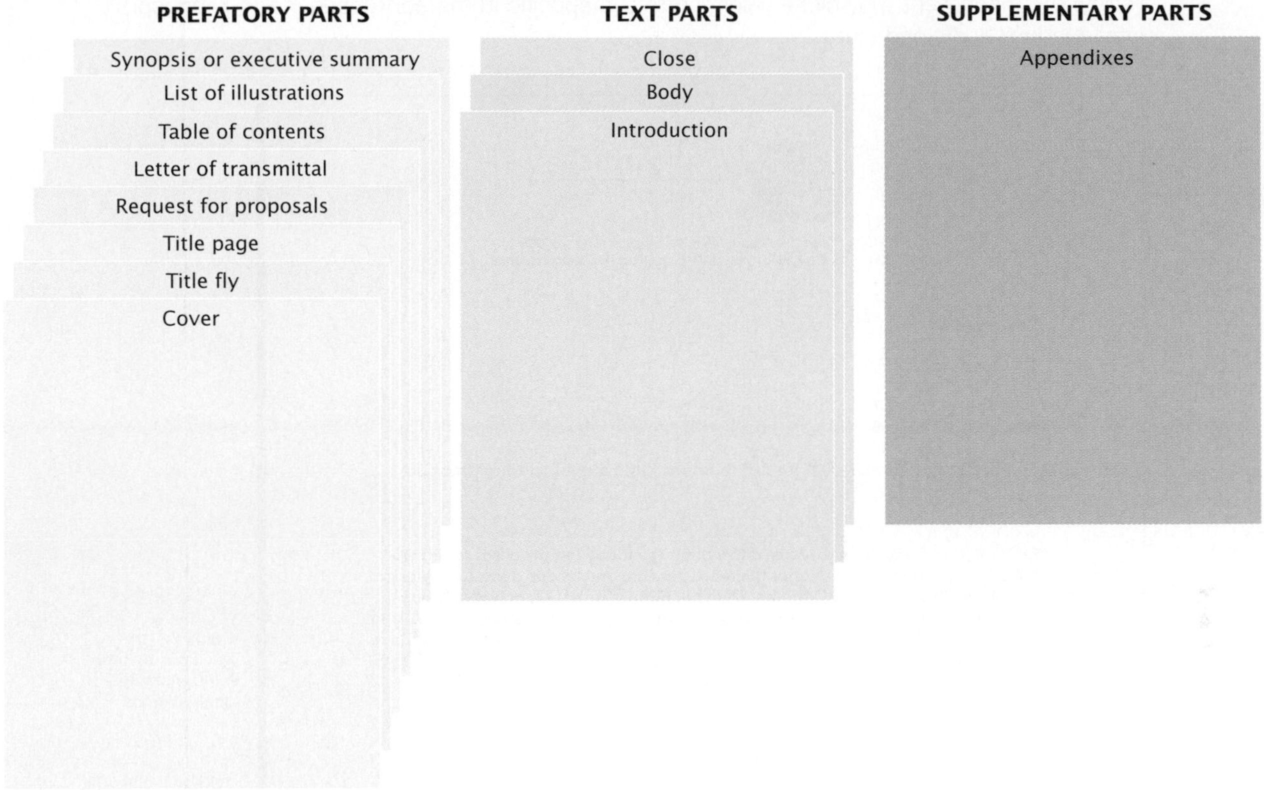

Formal proposals contain many of the same components as other formal reports (see Figure 13.3). The difference lies mostly in the text, although a few of the prefatory parts are also different. With the exception of an occasional appendix, most proposals have few supplementary parts. As always, if you're responding to a request for proposals (RFP), follow its specifications to the letter, being sure to include everything it asks for and nothing it doesn't ask for.

Prefatory Parts

6 LEARNING OBJECTIVE

Explain how prefatory parts of a proposal differ, depending on whether the proposal is solicited or unsolicited.

The cover, title fly, title page, table of contents, and list of illustrations are handled in formal proposals the same as in other formal reports. However, you'll want to handle other prefatory parts a bit differently, such as the copy of the RFP, the synopsis or executive summary, and the letter of transmittal.

Copy of the RFP

An RFP may require you to include a copy of the RFP in your prefatory section; just be sure to follow instructions carefully.

RFPs usually have specific instructions for referring to the RFP itself in the proposal because the organizations that issue RFPs need a methodical way to track all their active RFPs and the incoming responses. Some organizations require that you include a copy of the entire RFP in your proposal; others simply want you to refer to the RFP by name or number or perhaps include just the introductory section of the RFP. Make sure you follow the instructions in every detail. If there are no specific instructions, use your best judgment, based on the length of the RFP and whether you received a printed copy or accessed it online. In any event, make sure your proposal refers to the RFP in some way so that the audience can associate your proposal with the correct RFP.

Synopsis or Executive Summary

Although you may include a synopsis or an executive summary for your reader's convenience when your proposal is quite long, these components are often less useful in a formal proposal than they are in a formal report. If your proposal is unsolicited, your transmittal

FIGURE 13.4 Dixon O'Donnell's Informal Solicited Proposal
This proposal was submitted by Dixon O'Donnell, vice president of O'Donnell & Associates, a geotechnical engineering firm that conducts a variety of environmental testing services. As you review this document, pay close attention to the specific items addressed in the proposal's introduction, body, and close.

O'Donnell & Associates, Inc.

1793 East Westerfield Road, Arlington Heights, Illinois 60005
(847) 398-1148 Fax: (847) 398-1149 E-mail: dod@ix.netcom.com

July 28, 2010

Ms. Joyce Colton, P.E.
AGI Builders, Inc.
1280 Spring Lake Drive
Belvidere, Illinois, 61008

Subject: Proposal No. F-0087 for AGI Builders, Elgin Manufacturing Campus

Dear Ms. Colton:

Uses opening paragraph in place of an introduction

O'Donnell & Associates is pleased to submit the following proposal to provide construction testing services for the mass grading operations and utility work at the Elgin Manufacturing Campus, 126th St., Elgin, Illinois. Our company has been providing construction-testing services in the Chicago area since 1972 and has performed numerous large-scale geotechnical investigations across Illinois, including more than 100 at O'Hare International Airport, Midway Airport, Meig's Field, and other airports.

Grabs reader's attention by highlighting company qualifications

Uses headings to divide proposal into logical segments for easy reading

Background

It is our understanding that the work consists of two projects: (1) the mass grading operations will require approximately six months, and (2) the utility work will require approximately three months. The two operations are scheduled as follows:

Acknowledges the two projects and their required timeline

Mass Grading Operation	September 2010–February 2011
Utility Work	March 2011–May 2011

Proposed Approach and Work Plan

Describes scope of project and outlines specific tests the company will perform

O'Donnell & Associates will perform observation and testing services during both the mass grading operations and the excavation and backfilling of the underground utilities. Specifically, we will perform field density tests on the compacted material as required by the job specifications using a nuclear moisture/density gauge. We will also conduct appropriate laboratory tests such as ASTM D-1557 Modified Proctors. We will prepare detailed reports summarizing the results of our field and laboratory testing. Fill materials to be placed at the site may consist of natural granular materials (sand), processed materials (crushed stone, crushed concrete, slag), or clay soils. O'Donnell & Associates will provide qualified personnel to perform the necessary testing.

(*continued*)

letter will already have caught the reader's interest, making a synopsis or an executive summary redundant. It may also be less important if your proposal is solicited because the reader is already committed to studying your proposal to find out how you intend to satisfy the terms of a contract. The introduction of a solicited proposal would provide an adequate preview of the contents.

Letter of Transmittal

The way you handle the letter of transmittal depends on whether the proposal is solicited or unsolicited. If the proposal is solicited, approach the transmittal letter as a positive message, highlighting the aspects of your proposal that may give you a competitive advantage. If the proposal is unsolicited, approach the transmittal letter as a persuasive message. The

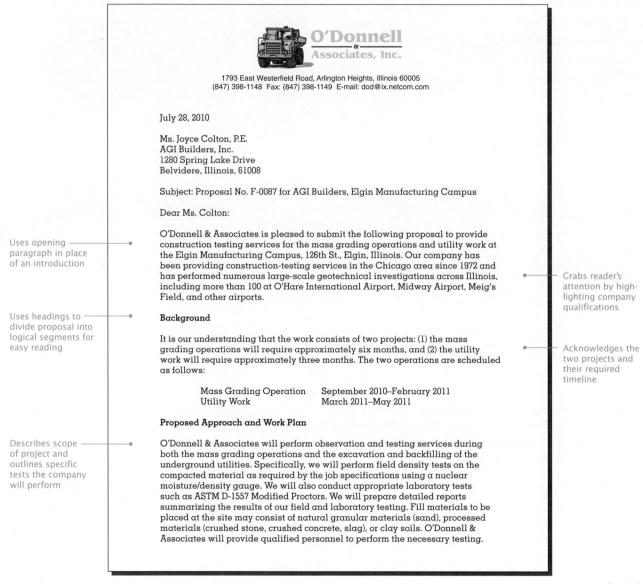

FIGURE 13.4 (Continued)

O'Donnell & Associates, Inc. Page 2 July 28, 2010

Explains who will be responsible for the various tasks

Kevin Patel will be the lead field technician responsible for the project. A copy of Mr. Patel's résumé is included with this proposal for your review. Kevin will coordinate field activities with your job site superintendent and make sure that appropriate personnel are assigned to the job site. Overall project management will be the responsibility of Joseph Proesel. Project engineering services will be performed under the direction of Dixon O'Donnell, P.E. All field personnel assigned to the site will be familiar with and abide by the Project Site Health and Safety Plan prepared by Carlson Environmental, Inc., dated April 2010.

Encloses résumé rather than listing qualifications in the document

Qualifications

O'Donnell & Associates has been providing quality professional services since 1972 in the areas of

Grabs attention by mentioning compelling qualifications

- Geotechnical engineering
- Materials testing and inspection
- Pavement evaluation
- Environmental services
- Engineering and technical support (CADD) services

The company provides Phase I and Phase II environmental site assessments, preparation of LUST site closure reports, installation of groundwater monitoring wells, and testing of soil/groundwater samples for environmental contaminants. Geotechnical services include all phases of soil mechanics and foundation engineering, including foundation and lateral load analysis, slope stability analysis, site preparation recommendations, seepage analysis, pavement design, and settlement analysis.

O'Donnell & Associates materials testing laboratory is certified by AASHTO Accreditation Program for the testing of Soils, Aggregate, Hot Mix Asphalt and Portland Cement Concrete. A copy of our laboratory certification is included with this proposal. In addition to in-house training, field and laboratory technicians participate in a variety of certification programs, including those sponsored by the American Concrete Institute (ACI) and Illinois Department of Transportation (IDOT).

Gains credibility by describing certifications (approvals by recognized industry associations or government agencies)

Costs

On the basis of our understanding of the scope of the work, we estimate the total cost of the two projects to be $100,260.00, as follows:

(continued)

letter must persuade the reader that you have something worthwhile to offer, something that justifies the time required to read the entire proposal.

Text of the Proposal

Just as with reports, the text of a proposal is composed of three main parts: an introduction, a body, and a close. The content and depth of each part depend on whether the proposal is solicited or unsolicited, formal or informal. Here's a brief overview:[7]

- **Introduction.** This section presents and summarizes the problem you intend to solve and your solution to that problem, including any benefits the reader will receive from your solution.
- **Body.** This section explains the complete details of the solution: how the job will be done, how it will be broken into tasks, what method will be used to do it (including the required equipment, material, and personnel), when the work will begin and end, how

FIGURE 13.4 *(Continued)*

O'Donnell & Associates, Inc. Page 3 July 28, 2010

Cost Estimates

Cost Estimate: Mass Grading	**Units**	**Rate ($)**	**Total Cost ($)**
Field Inspection			
Labor	1,320 hours	$38.50	$ 50,820.00
Nuclear Moisture Density Meter	132 days	35.00	4,620.00
Vehicle Expense	132 days	45.00	5,940.00
Laboratory Testing			
Proctor Density Tests (ASTM D-1557)	4 tests	130.00	520.00
Engineering/Project Management			
Principal Engineer	16 hours	110.00	1,760.00
Project Manager	20 hours	80.00	1,600.00
Administrative Assistant	12 hours	50.00	600.00
Subtotal			**$ 65,860.00**

Itemizes costs by project and gives supporting details

Cost Estimate: Utility Work	**Units**	**Rate ($)**	**Total Cost ($)**
Field Inspection			
Labor	660 hours	$ 38.50	$ 25,410.00
Nuclear Moisture Density Meter	66 days	5.00	2,310.00
Vehicle Expense	66 days	45.00	2,970.00
Laboratory Testing			
Proctor Density Tests (ASTM D-1557)	2 tests	130.00	260.00
Engineering/Project Management			
Principal Engineer	10 hours	110.00	1,100.00
Project Manager	20 hours	80.00	1,600.00
Administrative Assistant	15 hours	50.00	750.00
Subtotal			**$ 34,400.00**
Total Project Costs			**$100,260.00**

This estimate assumes full-time inspection services. However, our services may also be performed on an as-requested basis, and actual charges will reflect time associated with the project. We have attached our standard fee schedule for your review. Overtime rates are for hours in excess of 8.0 hours per day, before 7:00 a.m., after 5:00 p.m., and on holidays and weekends.

Provides alternative option in case full-time service costs exceed client's budget

(continued)

much the entire job will cost (including a detailed breakdown, if required or requested), and why your company is qualified.

- **Close.** This section emphasizes the benefits that readers will realize from your solution, and it urges readers to act.

Figure 13.4, starting on page 420, provides an example of an informal proposal.

PROOFREADING REPORTS AND PROPOSALS

After you have assembled all the components of a report or proposal, revised the document for clarity and conciseness, and designed the document to ensure readability and a positive impression on your readers, you have essentially produced your document in its final form.

FIGURE 13.4 (*Continued*)

O'Donnell & Associates, Inc. Page 4 July 28, 2010

Authorization

With a staff of over 30 personnel, including registered professional engineers, resident engineers, geologists, construction inspectors, laboratory technicians, and drillers, we are convinced that O'Donnell & Associates is capable of providing the services required for a project of this magnitude.

Uses brief close to emphasize qualifications and ask for client decision

If you would like our firm to provide the services as outlined in this proposal, please sign this letter and return it to us along with a certified check in the amount of $10,000 (our retainer) by August 13, 2010. Please call me if you have any questions regarding the terms of this proposal or our approach.

Provides deadline and makes response easy

Sincerely,

Dixon O'Donnell

Dixon O'Donnell
Vice President

Enclosures

Accepted for AGI BUILDERS, INC.

By________________________ Date ________________________

Makes letter a binding contract, if signed

Now you need to review it thoroughly one last time, looking for inconsistencies, errors, and missing components. Proofing can catch minor flaws that might diminish your credibility—and major flaws that might damage your career. If you need specific tips on proofreading documents, refer to Chapter 6 for some reminders on what to look for when proofreading text and how to proofread like a pro.

Whenever possible, arrange for someone with "fresh eyes" to proofread the report, somebody who hasn't been involved with the text so far. At this point in the process, you are so familiar with the content that your mind is likely to fill in missing words, fix misspelled words, and subconsciously compensate for other flaws without your even being aware of it. Someone with fresh eyes might see mistakes that you've passed over a dozen times without noticing. An ideal approach is to have two people review it—one who is an expert in the subject matter and one who isn't. The first person can ensure its technical accuracy, and the second can ensure that a wide range of readers will understand it.[8]

Ask for proofreading assistance from someone who hasn't been involved in the development of your proposal; he or she might see errors that you've been overlooking.

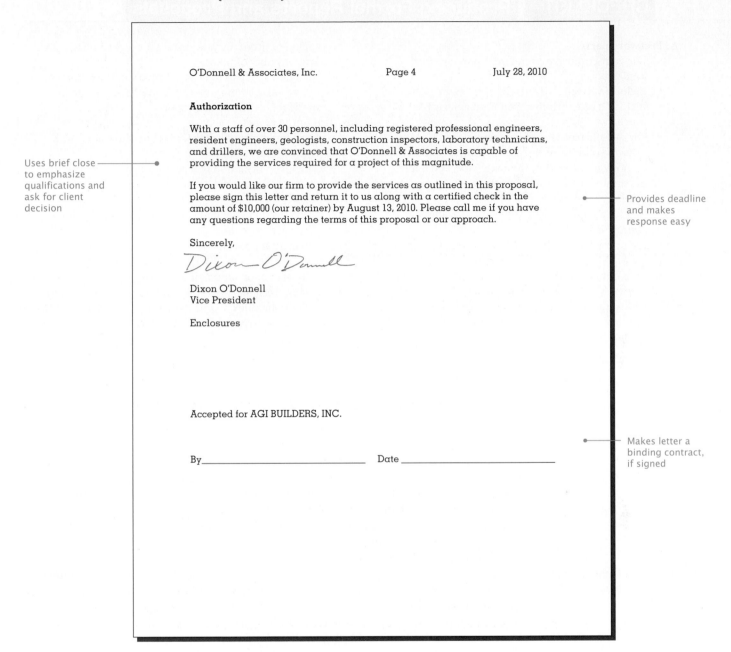

CHECKLIST: Producing Formal Reports and Proposals

A. Prefatory parts
- Use your company's standard report covers, if available.
- Include a concise, descriptive title on the cover.
- Include a title fly only if you want an extra-formal touch.
- On the title page, list the (1) report title; (2) name, title, and address of the group or person(s) who authorized the report; (3) name, title, and address of the group or person(s) who prepared the report; and (4) date of submission.
- Include a copy of the letter of authorization, if appropriate.
- Include a copy of the RFP (or its introduction only if the document is long), if appropriate.
- Include a letter of transmittal that introduces the report.
- Provide a table of contents in outline form, with headings worded exactly as they appear in the body of the report.
- Include a list of illustrations if the report contains a large number of them.
- Include a synopsis (a brief summary of the report) or an executive summary (a condensed, "mini" version of the report) for longer reports.

B. Text of the report
- Draft an introduction that prepares the reader for the content that follows.
- Provide information that supports your conclusions, recommendations, or proposals in the body of the report.
- Don't overload the body with unnecessary detail.
- Close with a summary of your main idea.

C. Supplementary parts
- Use appendixes to provide supplementary information or supporting evidence.
- List any secondary sources you used in a bibliography.
- Provide an index if your report contains a large number of terms or ideas and is likely to be consulted over time.

DISTRIBUTING REPORTS AND PROPOSALS

All the distribution issues you explored in Chapter 6 apply to reports and proposals, as long as you take into account the length and complexity of your documents. For physical distribution, consider spending the few extra dollars for a professional courier or package delivery service, if doing so will help your document stand apart from the crowd. The online tracking offered by FedEx, UPS, and other services can verify that your document arrived safely. On the other hand, if you've prepared the document for a single person or small group, delivering it in person can be a nice touch. Not only can you answer any immediate questions about it, you can promote the results in person—reminding the recipient of the benefits contained in your report or proposal.

Adobe's PDF is a safe and common way to distribute reports electronically.

For electronic distribution, unless your audience specifically requests a word-processor file, provide documents as portable document format (PDF) files. If your company or client expects you to distribute your reports via a web-based content management system, intranet, or extranet, be sure to upload the correct file(s) to the correct online location. Verify the onscreen display of your report after you've posted it, too; make sure graphics, charts, links, and other elements are in place and operational.

When you've completed your formal report or proposal and sent it off to your audience, your next task is to wait for a response. If you don't hear from your readers within a week or two, you might want to ask politely whether the report arrived. (Some RFPs specify a response time frame. In such a case, *don't* pester the recipient ahead of schedule, or you'll hurt your chances.) In hope of stimulating a response, you might ask a question about the report, such as "How do you think accounting will react to the proposed budget increase?" You might also offer to answer any questions or provide additional information. To review the ideas presented in this chapter, see "Checklist: Producing Formal Reports and Proposals." For the latest information on completing reports and proposals, visit http://real-timeupdates.com/ebc and click on Chapter 13.

Document Makeover

Improve This Executive Summary

To practice correcting drafts of actual documents, visit the "Document Makeovers" section in mybcommlab. Refer to the User Guide for specific instructions on how to access the content for this chapter. You will find an excerpt from an executive summary that contains problems and errors related to what you've learned in this chapter about completing formal reports and proposals. Use the "Final Draft" decision tool to create an improved version of this document. Check the executive summary for an appropriate degree of formality, parallel structures, the skillful inclusion or exclusion of detail, and a consistent time perspective.

On the Job: Solving Communication Dilemmas at the Bill & Melinda Gates Foundation

A decade into your business career, you've decided to put your communication skills to use in an effort to improve global health. You recently joined the Gates Foundation as a program officer in global health strategies.

Malaria is one of the foundation's primary health concerns. This mosquito-borne disease has been largely eradicated in many parts of the world, but it remains an active and growing menace in other areas (particularly sub-Saharan Africa). Worldwide, malaria kills more than a million people every year, most of whom are children. You are writing an informational report that will be made available on the foundation's website, summarizing the current crisis and progress being made toward the eventual control and eradication of malaria. How will you handle the following challenges?[9]

1. A wide variety of people visit the foundation's website, from researchers who are interested in applying for grants to reporters writing about health and education issues to members of the general public. Consequently, you can't pin down a specific audience for your report. In addition, because people will simply download a PDF file of the report from the website, you don't have the opportunity to write a traditional letter or memo of transmittal. How should you introduce your report to website visitors?

a. Write a brief description of the report, explaining its purpose and content; post this information on the website, above the link to the PDF file so that people can read it before they decide whether to download the file.
b. Provide an e-mail link that people can use to send you an e-mail message if they'd like to know more about the report before reading it.
c. Write a news release describing the report and post this document on the website's "Newsroom" section.
d. Count on the title of the report to introduce its purpose and content; don't bother writing an introduction.

2. Which of the following report titles would do the best job of catching readers' attention with an emotional "hook" that balances the urgency of the crisis with the reasons for hope?

a. Children Who Don't Need to Die: The Urgent Global Malaria Crisis
b. Preventing a Million Malaria Deaths Every Year: The Urgent Global Challenge—And Reasons for Hope
c. Malaria: It Killed Two Thousand More Children Today
d. Malaria: Progress Toward Eradicating This Global Disease

3. The Gates Foundation is known around the world for the quality of its work, and that includes the quality of its communication efforts. Which of the following proofreading strategies should you use to make sure your report is free of errors?

a. Take advantage of technology. Double-check the settings in your word processor to make sure every checking tool is activated as you type, including the spell checker, grammar checker, and style checker. When you're finished with the first draft, run each of these tools again, just to make sure the computer didn't miss anything.
b. Recognize that no report, particularly a complex 48-page document with multiple visuals and more than 60 sources, is going to be free of errors. Include a statement on the title page apologizing for any errors that may still exist in the report. Provide your e-mail address and invite people to send you a message when they find errors.
c. As soon as you finish typing the first draft, immediately review it for accuracy while the content is still fresh in your mind. After you have done this, you can be reasonably sure that the document is free from errors. If you wait a day or two, you'll start to forget what you've written, thereby lowering your chances of catching errors.
d. Put the report aside for at least a day and then proofread it carefully. Also, recruit two colleagues to review it for you—one who can review the technical accuracy of the material and one who has a good eye for language and clarity.

4. One of the sources used in your report is an article titled "Making Antimalarial Agents Available in Africa," by Kenneth J. Arrow, Hellen Gelband, and Dean T. Jamison. The article appeared in the July 28, 2005, edition (volume 353, issue 4) of the *New England Journal of Medicine,* on pages 333 to 335. Which of the following is the correct way to cite this source using APA guidelines?

a. Arrow, K. J., Gelband H., & Jamison, D. T. (2005). Making antimalarial agents available in Africa. *New England Journal of Medicine, 353* (4), 333–335.
b. Kenneth J. Arrow, Hellen Gelband, and Dean T. Jamison, "Making Antimalarial Agents Available in

Africa," *New England Journal of Medicine*, 28 July 2005, 333 (3 pgs).

c. "Making Antimalarial Agents Available in Africa," *New England Journal of Medicine:* Vol. 353, Iss. 4, Pgs. 333–335.

d. Arrow, Kenneth J., Gelband, Hellen, and Jamison, Dean T. "Making Antimalarial Agents Available in Africa." *New England Journal of Medicine* 353.4 (2005):333–335.

LEARNING OBJECTIVES CHECKUP

Assess your understanding of the principles in this chapter by reading each learning objective and studying the accompanying exercises. For fill-in-the-blank items, write the missing text in the blank provided; for multiple-choice items, circle the letter of the correct answer. You can check your responses against the answer key on page AK-2.

Objective 13.1: Characterize the four tasks involved in completing business reports and proposals.

1. Which of the following is *not* one of the four major tasks involved in completing business reports and proposals?
   a. Revising the report's organization, style, tone, and readability
   b. Formatting the report
   c. Deciding which visuals to create for the report
   d. Proofreading the report

2. The following sentence appears in your first draft of a report that analyzes perceived shortcomings in your company's employee health benefits: "Among the many criticisms and concerns expressed by the workforce, at least among the 376 who responded to our online survey (out of 655 active employees), the issues of elder care, health insurance during retirement, and the increased amount that employees are being forced to pay every month as the company's contribution to health insurance coverage has declined over the past two years were identified as the most important." You realize that this 69-word sentence could be shorter, more direct, and more powerful. Which of these revisions is the most effective?
   a. The employees who responded to our online survey (376 out of 655 active employees) identified these three issues as the most important: elder care, insurance coverage after they retire, and rising monthly payments.
   b. Elder care, insurance coverage after they retire, and rising monthly payments were the three most important issues identified in our survey of employees regarding their complaints and criticisms of health care benefits. Out of a current active workforce of 655 people, 376 employees completed the online survey. They complained about quite a range of issues, but these three were the most important to them overall.
   c. The top three employee concerns: elder care, insurance coverage after they retire, and increases in the amounts that employees pay every month for health insurance.
   d. Based on responses from 376 employees (out of 655) who responded to an online survey, the top three concerns our employees have regarding their health benefits are elder care, insurance coverage after they retire, and increases in the monthly cost of insurance.

Objective 13.2: Explain how computers have both simplified and complicated the report-production process.

3. How have computers and related technology (such as low-cost color printers) made it easier in recent years for all businesspeople to produce top-quality reports and proposals?
   a. Tasks that once required expensive equipment and specialized skills can now be accomplished on most desktop computers by regular businesspeople with minimal training.
   b. Most companies now have dedicated desktop publishing departments, so business professionals are no longer expected to create their own charts, graphs, and other report elements.
   c. The support personnel who will do all your typing for you can now produce all your visuals and other report elements, so you no longer need to work with a variety of different people.
   d. The Internet has improved everyone's design sensibilities.

4. How has the widespread availability of computer publishing tools made life more difficult for report writers?
   a. The Internet is slower than ever before.
   b. Since prices have fallen so low, most companies expect employees to purchase their own computers.
   c. More and more readers are growing tired of the slick, overproduced reports available these days; they want to see more simple, black-and-white, "typewriter-style" reports.
   d. In terms of production quality, audience expectations are higher, and the competition is tougher than ever before.

Objective 13.3: Identify the circumstances in which you should include letters of authorization and letters of acceptance in your reports.

5. In what situation should you consider including a letter or memo of authorization in a formal report?
   a. If you're getting paid to write the report
   b. If you received written authorization to write the report
   c. If the audience outranks you
   d. If you outrank the audience

6. What is the purpose of including a letter of acceptance in a formal report?
   a. It reminds your audience what you previously agreed to address in the report and why you were assigned to write it.
   b. It makes your report feel more formal and official.
   c. It prevents others from taking credit for your work.
   d. It summarizes the key points of your report for people who are too busy to read the report itself.

Objective 13.4: Explain the difference between a synopsis and an executive summary.

7. A/an ________ is a brief overview (usually one page or less) of a report's most important points.

8. A/an ________ is a fully developed "mini" version of the report itself.

9. Which of the following may contain headings, visual aids, and enough information to help busy executives make quick decisions?
   a. An executive summary
   b. A synopsis
   c. Both
   d. Neither

Objective 13.5: Describe the three supplementary parts of a formal report.

10. Which of the following is *not* a typical supplementary part of a formal report?
    a. Appendixes
    b. Bibliography
    c. Letter of authorization
    d. Index

Objective 13.6: Explain how prefatory parts of a proposal differ, depending on whether the proposal is solicited or unsolicited.

11. If you've submitted a proposal that is in response to an RFP, and the RFP doesn't include specific instructions for referring to the RFP, what steps can you take to make sure the recipient understands which RFP you're responding to?
    a. Include the formal title of the RFP (and its reference number, if it has one) as a footnote in the first appendix of your report.
    b. If the RFP is short, include it with the other prefatory parts of your proposal; if the RFP is lengthy, include just the introductory page(s) from it.
    c. Include the entire RFP in the body of your proposal, no matter how long it is.
    d. The RFP was written by someone else, so you can ignore it in your report.

12. How should you handle the letter of transmittal for an unsolicited proposal?
    a. Treat the letter as a routine message; businesspeople get proposals all the time, so they don't expect anything more than a simple announcement that identifies you and your proposal.
    b. Treat the letter as a positive message, highlighting the good news that you have to offer in the proposal.
    c. Treat the letter as a persuasive message, persuading the reader that your report offers information of value.
    d. Don't waste the reader's time with a letter of transmittal; get right to the point with the body of your proposal.

PEARSON mybcommlab™

Log on to www.mybcommlab.com to access the following study and assessment aids associated with this chapter:

- Video applications
- Real-Time Updates
- Peer review activity
- Quick Learning Guides
- Pre/post test
- Personalized study plan
- Model documents
- Sample presentations

If you are not using mybcommlab, you can access Real-Time Updates and Quick Learning Guides through http://real-timeupdates.com/ebc. The Quick Learning Guide (located under "Learn More" on the website) hits all the high points of this chapter in just two pages. This guide, especially prepared by the authors, will help you study for exams or review important concepts whenever you need a quick refresher.

Apply Your Knowledge

1. Is an executive summary a persuasive message? Explain your answer.
2. Under what circumstances would you include more than one index in a lengthy report?
3. If you were submitting a solicited proposal to build a small shopping center, would you include as references the names and addresses of other clients for whom you recently built similar facilities? Where in the proposal would you include these references? Why?
4. If you included a bibliography in your report, would you also need to include in-text citations? Please explain.
5. **Ethical Choices** How would you report on a confidential survey in which employees rated their managers' capabilities? Both employees and managers expect to see the results. Would you give the same report to employees and managers? What components would you include or exclude for each audience? Explain your choices.

Practice Your Knowledge

Message for Analysis

Visit the website of the U.S. Citizenship and Immigration Services at www.uscis.gov. Click on "About USCIS," followed by "Reports and Studies," and then find the report titled "The Triennial Comprehensive Report on Immigration." Download this PDF file and read the executive summary. Using the information in this chapter, analyze the executive summary and offer specific suggestions for revising it.

Exercises

Active links for all websites in this chapter can be found on mybcommlab; see your User Guide for instructions on accessing the content for this chapter.

13.1 Revising for Clarity and Conciseness The following sentence appears in your first draft of a report that analyzes perceived shortcomings in your company's employee health benefits:

> Among the many criticisms and concerns expressed by the workforce, at least among the 376 who responded to our online survey (out of 655 active employees), the issues of elder care, health insurance during retirement, and the increased amount that employees are being forced to pay every month as the company's contribution to health insurance coverage has declined over the past two years were identified as the most important.

Revise this 69-word sentence to make it shorter, more direct, and more powerful.

13.2 Teamwork You and a classmate are helping Linda Moreno prepare her report on Electrovision's travel and entertainment costs (see "Report Writer's Notebook"). This time, however, the report is to be informational rather than analytical, so it will not include recommendations. Review the existing report and determine what changes would be needed to make it an informational report. Be as specific as possible. For example, if your team decides the report needs a new title, what title would you use? Draft a transmittal memo for Moreno to use in conveying this informational report to Dennis McWilliams, Electrovision's vice president of operations.

13.3 Producing Reports: Letter of Transmittal You are president of the Friends of the Library, a nonprofit group that raises funds and provides volunteers to support your local library. Every February, you send a report of the previous year's activities and accomplishments to the County Arts Council, which provides an annual grant of $1,000 toward your group's summer reading festival. Now it's February 6, and you've completed your formal report. Here are the highlights:

- Back-to-school book sale raised $2,000.
- Holiday craft fair raised $1,100.
- Promotion and prizes for summer reading festival cost $1,450.
- Materials for children's program featuring local author cost $125.
- New reference databases for library's career center cost $850.
- Bookmarks promoting library's website cost $200.

Write a letter of transmittal to Erica Maki, the council's director. Because she is expecting this report, you can use the direct approach. Be sure to express gratitude for the council's ongoing financial support.

13.4 Internet Government reports vary in purpose and structure. Read through the U.S. Department of Education's report "Helping Your Child Become a Reader," available at www.ed.gov. What is the purpose of this document? Does the title communicate this purpose? What type of report is this, and what is the report's structure? Which prefatory and supplementary parts are included? Analyze the visuals. What types of visuals are included in this report? Are they all necessary? Are the titles and legends sufficiently informative? How does this report take advantage of the online medium to enhance readability?

13.5 Ethical Choices: Team Challenge You submitted what you thought was a masterful report to your boss over three weeks ago. The report analyzes current department productivity and recommends several steps that you think will improve employee output without increasing individual workloads. Brilliant, you thought. But you haven't heard a word from your boss. Did you overstep your boundaries by making recommendations that might imply that she has not been doing a good job? Did you overwhelm her with your ideas? You'd like some feedback. In your last e-mail to her, you asked if she had read your report. So far, you've received no reply. Yesterday, you overheard the company vice president talk about some productivity changes in your department. The changes were ones that you recommended in your report. Now you're worried that your boss submitted your report to senior management and will take full credit for your terrific ideas. What, if anything, should you do? Should you confront your boss about this? Should you ask to meet with the company vice president? Discuss this situation with your teammates and develop a solution to this sticky situation. Present your solution to the class, explaining the rationale behind your decision.

Expand Your Knowledge

Learning More on the Web

Preview Before You Produce

www.dogpile.com

A good way to get ideas for the best style, organization, and format of a report is by looking at copies of professional business reports. To find samples of various types of reports, you can use a metasearch engine such as Dogpile. Choose a metasearch engine (refer to Table 11.4 on page 327). Try several search terms—such as *status report, progress report, sales report, business plan,* or *marketing plan*—until you uncover an interesting-looking report. Review the report and then answer the following questions:

1. What is the purpose of the report you read? Who is its target audience? Explain why the structure and style of the report make it easy or difficult to follow the main idea.
2. What type of report did you read? Briefly describe the main message. Is the information well organized? If you answer yes, explain how you can use the report as a guide for a report you might write. If you answer no, explain why the report is not helpful.
3. Drawing on what you know about the qualities of a good business report, review a report and describe the features that contribute to its readability.

Sharpening Your Career Skills Online

Bovée and Thill's Business Communication Web Search, at **http://businesscommunicationblog.com/websearch**, is a unique research tool designed specifically for business communication research. Use the Web Search function to find a website, video, PDF document, or PowerPoint presentation that offers advice on producing formal reports and proposals. Write a brief e-mail message to your instructor, describing the item that you found and summarizing the career skills information you learned from it.

Improve Your Grammar, Mechanics, and Usage

The following exercises help you improve your knowledge of and power over English grammar, mechanics, and usage. Turn to the Handbook of Grammar, Mechanics, and Usage at the end of this book and review all of Sections 2.10 (Quotation Marks), 2.11 (Parentheses), and 2.12 (Ellipses). Then look at the following 10 items. Circle the letter of the preferred choice in the following groups of sentences. (Answers to these exercises appear on page AK-3.)

1. a. Be sure to read (How to Sell by Listening) in this month's issue of *Fortune.*
   b. Be sure to read "How to Sell by Listening" in this month's issue of *Fortune.*
   c. Be sure to read "How to Sell by Listening . . ." in this month's issue of *Fortune.*

2. a. Her response . . . see the attached memo . . .is disturbing.
   b. Her response (see the attached memo) is disturbing.
   c. Her response "see the attached memo" is disturbing.

3. a. We operate with a skeleton staff during the holidays (December 21 through January 2).
   b. We operate with a skeleton staff during the holidays "December 21 through January 2".
   c. We operate with a skeleton staff during the holidays (December 21 through January 2.)

4. a. "The SBP's next conference . . ." the bulletin noted, ". . . will be held in Minneapolis."
   b. "The SBP's next conference," the bulletin noted, "will be held in Minneapolis."
   c. "The SBP's next conference," the bulletin noted, "will be held in Minneapolis".

5. a. The term "up in the air" means "undecided."
   b. The term "up in the air" means *undecided.*
   c. The term *up in the air* means "undecided."

6. a. Her assistant (the one who just had the baby) won't be back for four weeks.
   b. Her assistant (the one who just had the baby), won't be back for four weeks.
   c. Her assistant . . . the one who just had the baby . . . won't be back for four weeks.

7. a. "Ask not what your country can do for you," begins a famous John Kennedy quotation.
   b. ". . . Ask not what your country can do for you" begins a famous John Kennedy quotation.
   c. "Ask not what your country can do for you . . ." begins a famous John Kennedy quotation.

8. a. Do you remember who said, "And away we go?"
   b. Do you remember who said, "And away we go"?

9. a. Refinements may prove profitable. (More detail about this technology appears in Appendix A).
   b. Refinements may prove profitable. (More detail about this technology appears in Appendix A.)

10. a. The resignation letter begins, "Since I'll never regain your respect . . .," and goes on to explain why that's true.
   b. The resignation letter begins, "Since I'll never regain your respect, . . ." and goes on to explain why that's true.
   c. The resignation letter begins, "Since I'll never regain your respect . . ." and goes on to explain why that's true.

For additional exercises focusing on quotation marks, parentheses, and ellipses, visit mybcommlab. Click on Chapter 13, click on "Additional Exercises to Improve Your Grammar, Mechanics, and Usage," and then click on "19. Punctuation D."

CASES

Applying the Three-Step Writing Process to Cases

Apply each step to the following cases, as assigned by your instructor.

SHORT FORMAL REPORTS REQUIRING NO ADDITIONAL RESEARCH

PORTFOLIO BUILDER

1. Giving it the online try: Report analyzing the advantages and disadvantages of corporate online learning. As the newest member of the corporate training division of Paper Products, Inc., you have been asked to investigate and analyze the merits of creating online courses for the company's employees. The president of your company thinks e-learning might be a good employee benefit as well as a terrific way for employees to learn new skills that they can use on the job. You've already done your research, and here's a copy of your notes:

Online courses open up new horizons for working adults, who often find it difficult to juggle conventional classes with jobs and families.
Adults over 25 now represent nearly half of higher-ed students; most are employed and want more education to advance their careers.
Some experts believe that online learning will never be as good as face-to-face instruction.
Online learning requires no commute and is appealing for employees who travel regularly.
Enrollment in courses offered online by postsecondary institutions is expected to increase from 4 million students in 2009 to 7 million students in 2014.
E-learning is a cost-effective way to get better-educated employees.
More than one-third of the $50 billion spent on employee training every year is spent on e-learning.
At IBM, some 200,000 employees received education or training online last year, and 75 percent of the company's Basic Blue course for new managers is online. E-learning cut IBM's training bill by $350 million last year—mostly because online courses don't require travel.
There are no national statistics, but a recent report from the *Chronicle of Higher Education* found that institutions are seeing dropout rates that range from 20 to 50 percent for online learners. The research does not adequately explain why the dropout rates for e-learners are higher.
A recent study of corporate online learners reported that employees want the following things from their online courses: college credit or a certificate; active correspondence with an online facilitator who has frequent virtual office hours; access to 24-hour, seven-day-a-week technical support; and the ability to start a course anytime.
Corporate e-learners said that their top reason for dropping a course was lack of time. Many had trouble completing courses from their desktops because of frequent distractions caused by co-workers. Some said they could only access courses through the company's intranet, so they couldn't finish their assignments from home.
Besides lack of time, corporate e-learners cited the following as e-learning disadvantages: lack of management oversight, lack of motivation, problems with technology, lack of student support, individual learning preferences, poorly designed courses, substandard/inexperienced instructors.
A recent study by GE Capital found that finishing a corporate online course was dependent on whether managers gave reinforcement on attendance, how important employees were made to feel, and whether employee progress in the course was tracked.
Sun Microsystems found that interactivity can be a critical success factor for online courses. Company studies showed that only 25 percent of employees finish classes that are strictly self-paced. But 75 percent finish when given similar assignments and access to tutors through e-mail, phone, or online discussion groups.
Company managers must supervise e-learning just as they would any other important initiative.
For online learning to work, companies must develop a culture that takes online learning just as seriously as classroom training.
For many e-learners, studying at home is optimal. Whenever possible, companies should offer courses through the Internet or provide intranet access at home. Having employees studying on their own time will more than cover any added costs.
Corporate e-learning has flared into a $2.3 billion market, making it one of the fastest-growing segments of the education industry.
Rather than fly trainers to 7,000 dealerships, General Motors University now uses interactive satellite broadcasts to teach salespeople the best way to highlight features of the new Buick.
Fast and cheap, e-training can shave companies' training costs while it saves employees' travel time.
Pharmaceutical companies such as Merck are conducting live, interactive classes over the web, allowing sales reps to learn about the latest product information at home rather than fly to a conference center.
McDonald's trainers can log into Hamburger University to learn such skills as how to assemble a made-to-order burger or properly place a drink on a tray.

One obstacle to the spread of online corporate training is the mismatch between what employees really need—customized courses that are tailored to a firm's products and its unique corporate culture—and what employers can afford.
Eighty percent of companies prefer developing their own online training courses in-house. But creating even one customized e-course can take months, involve armies of experts, and cost anywhere from $25,000 to $50,000. Thus, most companies either stick with classroom training or buy generic courses on such topics as how to give performance appraisals, understanding basic business ethics, and so on. Employers can choose from a wide selection of noncustomized electronic courses.
For online learning to be effective, content must be broken into short "chunks" with lots of pop quizzes, online discussion groups, and other interactive features that let students demonstrate what they've learned. For instance, Circuit City's tutorial on digital camcorders consists of three 20-minute segments. Each contains audio demonstrations of how to handle customer product queries, tests on terminology, and "try-its" that propel trainees back onto the floor to practice what they've learned.
Dell expects 90 percent of its learning solutions to be totally or partially technology enabled.
The Home Depot has used e-training to cut a full day from the time required to train new cashiers.
Online training has freed up an average of 17 days every year for Black & Decker's sales representatives.

Your task: Write a short (three to five pages) memo report to the director of human resources, Kerry Simmons, presenting the advantages and disadvantages of e-learning and making a recommendation about whether Paper Products, Inc., should invest time and money in training its employees this way. Be sure to organize your information so that it is clear, concise, and logically presented. Simmons likes to read the "bottom line" first, so be direct: Present your recommendation up-front and support your recommendation with your findings.[10]

PORTFOLIO BUILDER

2. Grumbling in the ranks: When departments can't agree on the value of work. You've been in your new job as human resources director for only a week, and already you have a major personnel crisis on your hands. Some employees in the marketing department got their hands on a confidential salary report, only to learn that, on average, marketing employees earn less than engineering employees. In addition, several top performers in the engineering group make significantly more money than anybody in marketing. The report was passed around the company instantly by e-mail, and now everyone is discussing the situation. You'll deal with the data security issue later; for now, you need to address the dissatisfaction in the marketing group.

Table 1 lists the salary and employment data you were able to pull from the employee database. You also had the opportunity to interview the engineering and marketing directors to get their opinions on the pay situation; their answers are listed in Table 2 on page 432.

Your task: The CEO has asked for a short report, summarizing the data and information you have on engineering and marketing salaries. Feel free to offer your own interpretation of the situation as well (make up any information you need), but keep in mind that as a new manager with almost no experience in the company, your opinion might not have a lot of influence.

PORTFOLIO BUILDER

3. Building a new magazine: Finding opportunity in the remodeling craze. Spurred on in part by the success of numerous television shows and even entire cable networks devoted to remodeling, homeowners across the country are redecorating and rebuilding like never before. Many people are content with superficial changes, such as new paint or new accessories, but some are more ambitious. These homeowners want to move walls, add rooms, redesign kitchens, convert garages to home theaters—the big stuff.

With many consumer trends, publishers try to create magazines that appeal to carefully identified groups of potential readers and the advertisers who'd like to reach them. The do-it-yourself (DIY) market is already served by numerous magazines, but you see an opportunity in those homeowners who tackle the heavy-duty projects. Tables 3 through 5 on page 432 summarize the results of some preliminary research you asked your company's research staff to conduct.

Your task: You think the data show a real opportunity for a "big projects" DIY magazine, although you'll need more extensive research to confirm the size of the market and refine the editorial direction of the magazine. Prepare a brief analytical report that presents the data you have, identifies the opportunity or opportunities you've found (suggest your own ideas based on the tables), and requests funding from the editorial board to pursue further research.

TABLE 1 Selected Employment Data for Engineers and Marketing Staff

EMPLOYMENT STATISTIC	ENGINEERING DEPARTMENT	MARKETING DEPARTMENT
Average number of years of work experience	18.2	16.3
Average number of years of experience in current profession	17.8	8.6
Average number of years with company	12.4	7.9
Average number of years of college education	6.9	4.8
Average number of years between promotions	6.7	4.3
Salary range	$58–165k	$45–85k
Median salary	$77k	$62k

TABLE 2 Summary Statements from Department Director Interviews

QUESTION	ENGINEERING DIRECTOR	MARKETING DIRECTOR
1. Should engineering and marketing professionals receive roughly similar pay?	In general, yes, but we need to make allowances for the special nature of the engineering profession. In some cases, it's entirely appropriate for an engineer to earn more than a marketing person.	Yes.
2. Why or why not?	Several reasons: (1) Top engineers are extremely hard to find, and we need to offer competitive salaries; (2) the structure of the engineering department doesn't provide as many promotional opportunities, so we can't use promotions as a motivator the way marketing can; (3) many of our engineers have advanced degrees, and nearly all pursue continuous education to stay on top of the technology.	Without marketing, the products the engineers create wouldn't reach customers, and the company wouldn't have any revenue. The two teams make equal contributions to the company's success.
3. If we decide to balance pay between the two departments, how should we do it?	If we do anything to cap or reduce engineering salaries, we'll lose key people to the competition.	If we can't increase payroll immediately to raise marketing salaries, the only fair thing to do is freeze raises in engineering and gradually raise marketing salaries over the next few years.

TABLE 3 Rooms Most Frequently Remodeled by DIYers

ROOM	PERCENTAGE OF HOMEOWNERS SURVEYED WHO HAVE TACKLED OR PLAN TO TACKLE AT LEAST A PARTIAL REMODEL
Kitchen	60
Bathroom	48
Home office/study	44
Bedroom	38
Media room/home theater	31
Den/recreation room	28
Living room	27
Dining room	12
Sun room/solarium	8

TABLE 4 Average Amount Spent on Remodeling Projects

ESTIMATED AMOUNT	PERCENTAGE OF SURVEYED HOMEOWNERS
Under $5k	5
$5–10k	21
$10–20k	39
$20–50k	22
More than $50k	13

TABLE 5 Tasks Performed by Homeowner on a Typical Remodeling Project

TASK	PERCENTAGE OF SURVEYED HOMEOWNERS WHO PERFORM OR PLAN TO PERFORM MOST OR ALL OF THIS TASK THEMSELVES
Conceptual design	90
Technical design/ architecture	34
Demolition	98
Foundation work	62
Framing	88
Plumbing	91
Electrical	55
Heating/cooling	22
Finish carpentry	85
Tile work	90
Painting	100
Interior design	52

SHORT FORMAL REPORTS REQUIRING ADDITIONAL RESEARCH

PORTFOLIO BUILDER

4. Reconciling the experts: Resolving the advice on writing business plans. Like any other endeavor that combines hard-nosed factual analysis and creative freethinking, the task of writing business plans generates a range of opinions.

Your task: Find at least six sources of advice on writing successful business plans (focus on start-up businesses that are likely to seek outside investors). Use at least two books, two magazine or journal articles, and two websites or blogs. Analyze the advice you find and identify points where most or all the experts agree and points where they don't agree. Wherever you find points of significant disagreement, identify which opinion you find most convincing and explain why. Summarize your findings in a brief formal report.

TEAM SKILLS PORTFOLIO BUILDER

5. Averse to verse? Report suggesting ways to increase sales of poetry. Anyone looking at the fragmented 21st-century landscape of media and entertainment options might be surprised to learn that poetry was once a dominant medium for not only creative literary expression but also philosophical, political, and even scientific discourse. Alas, such is no longer the case.

Your task: With a team of fellow students, your challenge is to identify opportunities to increase sales of poetry—any kind of poetry, in any medium. The following suggestions may help you get started:

- Research recent bestsellers in the poetry field and try to identify why they have been popular.
- Interview literature professors, professional poets, librarians, publishers, and bookstore personnel.
- Conduct surveys and interviews to find out why consumers don't buy more poetry.
- Review professional journals that cover the field of poetry, including *Publishers Weekly* and *Poets & Writers*, from both business and creative standpoints.

Summarize your findings in a brief formal report; assume that your target readers are executives in the publishing industry.

PORTFOLIO BUILDER

6. A ready-made business: Finding the right franchise opportunity. After 15 years in the corporate world, you're ready to strike out on your own. Rather than building a business from the ground up, however, you think that buying a franchise is a better idea. Unfortunately, some of the most lucrative franchise opportunities, such as the major fast-food chains, require significant start-up costs—some more than a half-million dollars. Fortunately, you've met several potential investors who seem willing to help you get started in exchange for a share of ownership. Between your own savings and money from these investors, you estimate that you can raise from $350,000 to $600,000, depending on how much ownership share you want to concede to the investors.

You've worked in several functional areas already, including sales and manufacturing, so you have a fairly well-rounded business résumé. You're open to just about any type of business, too, as long as it provides the opportunity to grow; you don't want to be so tied down to the first operation that you can't turn it over to a hired manager and expand into another market.

Your task: To convene a formal meeting with the investor group, you need to first draft a report that outlines the types of franchise opportunities you'd like to pursue. Write a brief report, identifying five franchises that you would like to explore further. (Choose five based on your own personal interests and the criteria already identified.) For each possibility, identify the nature of the business, the financial requirements, the level of support the company provides, and a brief statement of why you could run such a business successfully (make up any details you need). Be sure to carefully review the information you find about each franchise company to make sure you can qualify for it. For instance, McDonald's doesn't allow investment partnerships to buy franchises, so you won't be able to start up a McDonald's outlet until you have enough money to do it on your own.

For a quick introduction to franchising, see How Stuff Works (http://money.howstuffworks.com/franchising.htm). You can learn more about the business of franchising at Franchising.com (www.franchising.com) and search for specific franchise opportunities at Francorp Connect (www.francorpconnect.com). In addition, many companies that sell franchises, such as Subway, offer additional information on their websites.

LONG FORMAL REPORTS REQUIRING NO ADDITIONAL RESEARCH

PORTFOLIO BUILDER

7. You can get anything online these days: Shopping for automobiles on the Internet. As a researcher in your state's consumer protection agency, you're frequently called on to investigate consumer topics and write reports for the agency's website. Thousands of consumers have arranged the purchase of cars online, and millions more do at least some of their research online before heading to a dealership. Some want to save time and money, some want to be armed with as much information as possible before talking to a dealer, while others want to completely avoid the often-uncomfortable experience of negotiating prices with car salespeople. In response, a variety of online services have emerged to meet these consumer needs. Some let you compare information on various car models, some connect you to local dealers to complete the transaction, and some complete nearly all of the transaction details for you, including negotiating the price. Some search the inventory of thousands of dealers, whereas others search only a single dealership or a network of affiliated dealers. In other words, a slew of new tools are available for car buyers, but it's not always easy to figure out where to go and what to expect. That's where your report will help.

By visiting a variety of car-related websites and reading magazine and newspaper articles on the car-buying process, you've compiled a variety of notes related to the subject:

- **Process overview.** The process is relatively straightforward and fairly similar to other online shopping experiences, with two key differences. In general, a consumer identifies the make and model of car he or she wants, and then the online car-buying service searches the inventories of car dealers nationwide and presents the available choices. The consumer chooses a particular car from that list, and the service handles the communication and purchase details with the dealer. When the paperwork is finished, the consumer then visits the dealership and picks up the car. The two biggest differences with online auto buying are that (1) you can't actually complete the purchase over the Internet (in most cases, you must visit a local dealer to pick up the car and sign the papers, although in some cities, a dealer or a local car-buying service will deliver it to your home), and (2) in most states, it's illegal to purchase a new car from anyone other than a franchise dealer (i.e., you can't buy directly from the manufacturer, the way you can buy a Dell computer directly from Dell, for instance).

- **Information you can find online (not all information is available at all sites).** The information you can find online includes makes, models, colors, options, option packages (often, specific options are available only as part of a package; you need to know these constraints before you select your options), photos, specifications (everything from engine size to interior space), fuel efficiency estimates, performance data, safety information, predicted resale value, reviews, comparable models, insurance costs, consumer ratings, repair and reliability histories, available buyer incentives and rebates, true ownership costs (including fuel, maintenance, repairs, etc.), warranty information, loan and lease payments, and maintenance requirements.
- **Advantages of shopping online.** Advantages of shopping online include shopping from the comfort and convenience of home, none of the dreaded negotiating at the dealership (in many cases), the ability to search far and wide for a specific car (even nationwide, on many sites), rapid access to considerable amounts of data and information, and reviews from both professional automotive journalists and other consumers. In general, online auto shopping reduces a key advantage that auto dealers used to have: control of most of the information in the purchase transaction. Now consumers can find out how reliable each model is, how quickly it will depreciate, how often it is likely to need repairs, what other drivers think of it, how much the dealer paid the manufacturer for it, and so on.
- **Changing nature of the business.** The relationship between dealers and third-party websites (such as CarsDirect.com and Vehix.com) continues to evolve. At first, the relationship was antagonistic, as some third-party sites and dealers frequently competed for the same customers, and each side made bold proclamations about driving the other out of business. However, the relationship is more collaborative in many cases now, with dealers realizing that some third-party sites already have wide brand awareness and nationwide audiences. As the percentage of new car sales that originate via the Internet continues to increase, dealers are more receptive to working with third-party sites.
- **Comparing information from multiple sources.** Consumers shouldn't rely solely on the information from a single website. Each site has its own way of organizing information, and many have their own ways of evaluating car models and connecting buyers with sellers.
- **Understanding what each site is doing.** For instance, some search thousands of dealers, regardless of ownership connections. Others, such as AutoNation, search only affiliated dealers. A search for a specific model might yield only a half-dozen cars on one site but dozens of cars on another site. Find out who owns the site and what their business objectives are, if you can; this will help you assess the information you receive.
- **Leading websites.** Consumers can check out a wide variety of websites, some of which are full-service operations, offering everything from research to negotiation; others provide more specific and limited services. For instance, CarsDirect (www.carsdirect.com) provides a full range of services, whereas Carfax (www.carfax.com) specializes in uncovering the repair histories of individual used cars. Table 6 lists some of the leading car-related websites.

TABLE 6 Leading Automotive Websites

SITE	URL
AutoAdvice	www.autoadvice.com
Autobytel	www.autobytel.com
Autos.com	www.autos.com
AutoVantage	www.autovantage.com
Autoweb	www.autoweb.com
CarBargains	www.carbargains.com
Carfax	www.carfax.com
CarPrices.com	www.carprices.com
Cars.com	www.cars.com
CarsDirect	www.carsdirect.com
CarSmart	www.carsmart.com
Consumer Reports	www.consumerreports.org
eBay Motors	www.motors.ebay.com
Edmunds	www.edmunds.com
iMotors	www.imotors.com
IntelliChoice	www.intellichoice.com
InvoiceDealers	www.invoicedealers.com
JDPower	www.jdpower.com
Kelly Blue Book	www.kbb.com
MSN Autos	http://autos.msn.com
PickupTrucks.com	www.pickuptrucks.com
The Car Connection	www.thecarconnection.com
Vehix.com	www.vehix.com
Yahoo! Autos	http//autos.yahoo.com

Your task: Write an informational report, based on your research notes. The purpose of the report is to introduce consumers to the basic concepts of integrating the Internet into their car-buying activities and to educate them about important issues.[11]

PORTFOLIO BUILDER

8. Moving the workforce: Understanding commute patterns. Your company is the largest private employer in your metropolitan area, and the 43,500 employees in your workforce have a tremendous impact on local traffic. A group of city and county transportation officials recently approached your CEO with a request to explore ways to reduce this impact. The CEO has assigned you the task of analyzing the workforce's transportation habits and attitudes as a first step toward identifying potential solutions. He's willing to consider anything from subsidized bus passes to company-owned shuttle buses to telecommuting, but the decision requires a thorough understanding of employee transportation needs. Tables 7 through 11 summarize data you collected in an employee survey.

TABLE 7 Employee Carpool Habits

FREQUENCY OF USE: CARPOOLING	PORTION OF WORKFORCE
Every day, every week	10,138 (23%)
Certain days, every week	4,361 (10%)
Randomly	983 (2%)
Never	28,018 (64%)

TABLE 8 Use of Public Transportation

FREQUENCY OF USE: PUBLIC TRANSPORTATION	PORTION OF WORKFORCE
Every day, every week	23,556 (54%)
Certain days, every week	2,029 (5%)
Randomly	5,862 (13%)
Never	12,053 (28%)

TABLE 9 Effect of Potential Improvements to Public Transportation

WHICH OF THE FOLLOWING WOULD ENCOURAGE YOU TO USE PUBLIC TRANSPORTATION MORE FREQUENTLY (CHECK ALL THAT APPLY)	PORTION OF RESPONDENTS
Increased perceptions of safety	4,932 (28%)
Improved cleanliness	852 (5%)
Reduced commute times	7,285 (41%)
Greater convenience: fewer transfers	3,278 (18%)
Greater convenience: more stops	1,155 (6%)
Lower (or subsidized) fares	5,634 (31%)
Nothing could encourage me to take public transportation	8,294 (46%)

Note: This question was asked of respondents who use public transportation randomly or never, a subgroup that represents 17,915 employees, or 41 percent of the workforce.

TABLE 10 Distance Traveled to/from Work

DISTANCE YOU TRAVEL TO WORK (ONE WAY)	PORTION OF WORKFORCE
Less than 1 mile	531 (1%)
1–3 miles	6,874 (16%)
4–10 miles	22,951 (53%)
11–20 miles	10,605 (24%)
More than 20 miles	2,539 (6%)

TABLE 11 Is Telecommuting an Option?

DOES THE NATURE OF YOUR WORK MAKE TELECOMMUTING A REALISTIC OPTION?	PORTION OF WORKFORCE
Yes, every day	3,460 (8%)
Yes, several days a week	8,521 (20%)
Yes, random days	12,918 (30%)
No	18,601 (43%)

Your task: Present the results of your survey in an informational report, using the data provided in Tables 7 through 11.

LONG FORMAL REPORTS REQUIRING ADDITIONAL RESEARCH

PORTFOLIO BUILDER

9. Face-off: Informational report comparing two companies in the same industry. The partners in your accounting firm have agreed to invest some of the company's profits in the stock market. A previous team effort identified two leading companies in each of five different industries:

- Boeing; Airbus (aerospace)
- Hewlett-Packard; Dell (computers and software)
- Applebee's; OSI Restaurant Partners (casual dining)
- Barnes & Noble; Amazon.com (retailing)
- UPS; FedEx (delivery and logistics)

The partners have already done an in-depth financial analysis of all 10 firms, and they have asked you to look for more qualitative information, such as

- Fundamental philosophical differences in management styles, launch and handling of products and services, marketing of products and services, and approach to e-commerce that sets one rival company apart from the other
- Future challenges that each competitor faces
- Important decisions made by the two competitors and how those decisions affected their company
- Fundamental differences in each company's vision of its industry's future (for instance, do they both agree on what consumers want, what products to deliver, and so on?)
- Specific competitive advantages of each rival
- Past challenges each competitor has faced and how each met those challenges
- Strategic moves made by one rival that might affect the other
- Company success stories
- Brief company background information
- Brief comparative statistics, such as annual sales, market share, number of employees, number of stores, types of equipment, number of customers, sources of revenue, and so on

Your task: Select two competitors from the preceding list (or another list provided by your instructor) and write a long formal informational report comparing how the two companies are addressing the topics outlined by the partners. Of course, not every topic will apply to each company, and some will be more important than others—depending on the companies you select. The partners will invest in only one of the two companies in your report. (*Note:* Because these topics require considerable research, your instructor may choose to make this a team project.)

10. Is there any justice? Report critiquing legislation. Plenty of people complain about their state legislators, but few are specific about their complaints. Here's your chance.

Your task: Write a long formal report about a law that you believe should not have been enacted or that should be enacted. Be objective. Write the report using specific facts to support your beliefs. Reach conclusions and offer a recommendation at the end of the report. As a final step, send a copy of the report to an appropriate state official or legislator.

11. Travel opportunities: Report comparing two destinations. You are planning to take a two-week trip abroad sometime within the next year. Because there are a couple of destinations that appeal to you, you are going to have to do some research before you can make a decision.

Your task: Prepare a lengthy comparative study of two countries that you would like to visit. Begin by making a list of important questions you will need to answer. Do you want a relaxing vacation or an educational experience? What types of services will you require? What will your transportation needs be? Where will you have the least difficulty with the language? Using resources in your library, the Internet, and perhaps travel agencies, analyze the suitability of these two destinations with respect to your own travel criteria. At the end of the report, recommend the better country to visit this year.

PORTFOLIO BUILDER

12. Secondary sources: Report based on library and online research. As a college student and an active consumer, you may have considered one or more of the following questions at some point in the past few years:

- **a.** What criteria distinguish the top-rated MBA programs in the country? How well do these criteria correspond to the needs and expectations of business? Are the criteria fair for students, employers, and business schools?
- **b.** Which of three companies you might like to work for has the strongest corporate ethics policies?
- **c.** What will the music industry look like in the future? What's next after online stores such as Apple iTunes and digital players such as the iPod?
- **d.** Which industries and job categories are forecast to experience the greatest growth—and therefore the greatest demands for workers—in the next 10 years?
- **e.** What has been the impact of Starbucks's aggressive growth on small, independent coffee shops? On mid-sized chains or franchises? In the United States or in another country?
- **f.** How large is the "industry" of major college sports? How much do the major football or basketball programs contribute—directly or indirectly—to other parts of a typical university?
- **g.** How much have minor league sports—baseball, hockey, arena football—grown in small- and medium-market cities? What is the local economic impact when these municipalities build stadiums and arenas?

Your task: Answer one of these questions, using secondary research sources for information. Be sure to document your sources in the correct form. Make conclusions and offer recommendations where appropriate.

PORTFOLIO BUILDER

13. Doing business abroad: Report summarizing the social and business customs of a foreign country. Your company would like to sell its products overseas. Before they begin negotiating on the international horizon, however, the management team members must have a clear understanding of the social and business customs of the countries where they intend to do business.

Your task: Choose a non-English-speaking country and write a long formal report, summarizing the country's social and business customs. Review Chapter 3 and use Table 3.1 as a guide for the types of information you should include in your report.

FORMAL PROPOSALS

PORTFOLIO BUILDER

14. Polishing the presenters: Offering your services as a presentation trainer. Presentations can make or break both careers and businesses. A good presentation can bring in millions of dollars in new sales or fresh investment capital. A bad presentation might cause a number of troubles, from turning away potential customers to upsetting fellow employees to derailing key projects. To help business professionals plan, create, and deliver more effective presentations, you offer a three-day workshop that covers the essentials of good presentations:

- Understanding your audience's needs and expectations
- Formulating your presentation objectives
- Choosing an organizational approach
- Writing openings that catch your audience members' attention
- Creating effective graphics and slides
- Practicing and delivering your presentation
- Leaving a positive impression on your audience
- Avoiding common mistakes with Microsoft PowerPoint
- Making presentations online using webcasting tools
- Handling questions and arguments from the audience
- Overcoming the top 10 worries of public speaking (including "How can I overcome stage fright?" and "I'm not the performing type; can I still give an effective presentation?")

Here is some additional information about the workshop:

- **Workshop benefits:** Students will learn how to prepare better presentations in less time and deliver them more effectively.
- **Who should attend:** Top executives, project managers, employment recruiters, sales professionals, and anyone else who gives important presentations to internal or external audiences.
- **Your qualifications:** 18 years of business experience, including 14 years in sales and 12 years in public speaking. Experience speaking to audiences as large as 5,000 people. More than a dozen speech-related articles published in professional journals. Have conducted successful workshops for nearly 100 companies.

- **Workshop details:** Three-day workshop (9 A.M. to 3:30 P.M.) that combines lectures, practice presentations, and both individual and group feedback. Minimum number of students: 6. Maximum number of students per workshop: 12.
- **Pricing:** The cost is $3,500, plus $100 per student. 10 percent discount for additional workshops.
- **Other information:** Each attendee will have the opportunity to give three practice presentations that will last from three to five minutes. Everyone is encouraged to bring PowerPoint files containing slides from actual business presentations. Each attendee will also receive a workbook and a digital video recording of his or her final class presentation. You'll also be available for phone or e-mail coaching for six months after the workshop.

Your task: Identify a company in your local area that might be a good candidate for your services. Learn more about the company by visiting its website so you can personalize your proposal. Using the information listed earlier in this exercise, prepare a sales proposal that explains the benefits of your training and what students can expect during the workshop.

PORTFOLIO BUILDER

15. Healthy alternatives: Proposal to sell snacks and beverages at local schools. For years, a controversy has been brewing over the amount of junk food and soft drinks being sold through vending machines in local schools. Schools benefit from revenue-sharing arrangements, but many parents and health experts are concerned about the negative effects of these snacks and beverages. You and your brother have almost a decade of experience running espresso and juice stands in malls and on street corners, and you'd love to find some way to expand your business into schools. After a quick brainstorming session, the two of you craft a plan that makes good business sense while meeting the financial concerns of school administrators and the nutritional concerns of parents and dietitians. Here are the notes from your brainstorming session:

- Set up portable juice bars on school campuses, offering healthy fruit and vegetable drinks along with simple healthy snacks.
- Offer schools 30 percent of profits in exchange for free space and long-term contracts.
- Provide job training opportunities for students (during athletic events, etc.).
- Provide detailed dietary analysis of all products sold.
- Establish a nutritional advisory board composed of parents, students, and at least one certified health professional.
- Assure schools and parents that all products are safe (e.g., no stimulant drinks, no dietary supplements, and so on).
- Support local farmers and specialty food preparers by buying locally and giving these vendors the opportunity to test-market new products at your stands.

Your task: Based on the ideas listed, draft a formal proposal to the local school board, outlining your plan to offer healthier alternatives to soft drinks and prepackaged snack foods. Invent any details you need to complete your proposal.

PORTFOLIO BUILDER

16. Career connections: Helping employees get the advice they need to move ahead. Seems like everybody in the firm is frustrated. On the one hand, top executives complain about the number of lower-level employees who want promotions but just don't seem to "get it" when it comes to dealing with customers and the public, recognizing when to speak out and when to be quiet, knowing how to push new ideas through the appropriate channels, and performing other essential but difficult-to-teach tasks. On the other hand, ambitious employees who'd like to learn more feel that they have nowhere to turn for career advice from people who've been there. In between, a variety of managers and midlevel executives are overwhelmed by the growing number of mentoring requests they're getting, sometimes from employees they don't even know.

You've been assigned the challenge of proposing a formal mentoring program—and a considerable challenge it is:

- The number of employees who want mentoring relationships far exceeds the number of managers and executives willing and able to be mentors. How will you select people for the program?
- The people most in demand for mentoring also tend to be some of the busiest people in the organization.
- After several years of belt tightening and staff reductions, the entire company feels overworked; few people can imagine adding another recurring task to their seemingly endless to-do lists.
- What's in it for the mentors? Why would they be motivated to help lower-level employees?
- How will you measure success or failure of the mentoring effort?

Your task: Identify potential solutions to the issues (make up any information you need) and draft a proposal to the executive committee for a formal, companywide mentoring program that would match selected employees with successful managers and executives.

14 Designing and Delivering Oral and Online Presentations

Learning Objectives

After studying this chapter, you will be able to

1. Describe the tasks involved in planning an oral presentation
2. Explain how to adapt to your audience, compose your presentation, and craft an effective introduction
3. Explain how to connect ideas and hold the audience's attention during the body of a presentation and how to close effectively
4. Outline the key steps in creating powerful presentation visuals
5. Identify the tasks needed to complete your presentation materials
6. Explain how to excel at presentation delivery by overcoming anxiety, handling questions responsively, and giving presentations online

On the Job: Communicating at Hewlett-Packard

Dan Talbott (far right) led a team whose presentation skills helped land a multibillion-dollar contract for Hewlett-Packard.

Making a Compelling Presentation with $3 Billion on the Line

Making presentations with millions or billions of dollars on the line? That's business as usual for Dan Talbott of HP Managed Services, a unit of Hewlett-Packard that manages computer operations for other companies.

A great example was the pursuit of a huge contract with Procter & Gamble (P&G), the consumer-products giant that markets more than 300 brands, including Charmin, Crest, and Tide. P&G was looking to lower its costs by hiring an outside organization to take over its global information system—a network of more than 80,000 computers. HP faced two tough competitors for the contract, Electronic Data Systems (EDS) and IBM, and was considered a distant third-place contender because it had never landed a contract the size of the P&G deal. And as if that weren't enough, P&G had published a 10,000-page request for proposals (RFP) and limited the response time to just 56 days—when 9 to 12 months is typical on projects of this magnitude.

As a seasoned industry veteran but a rookie at HP, Talbott was eager to show that he could bring his new employer this mammoth piece of business. He moved his team into an HP office near P&G's Cincinnati headquarters, tapped the brainpower of 80 colleagues from around the world, and began developing the series of presentations that were specified in the RFP. Talbott told the group, "Our job is to ensure that every conversation is a win." However, HP's initial presentation was shaky, so he asked the presenters to print their PowerPoint slides—more than 200 in all—and post them on the walls of a conference room. He conducted a slide-by-slide critique, questioning every slide that lacked a clear message. The team revised and kept revising until the presentation was audience centered and crystal clear from beginning to end.

That rigorous review produced a string of successful presentations that ultimately helped Talbott and his team win a 10-year contract worth $3 billion—a stunning success that announced HP's arrival as a serious contender in computer services.[1]
www.hp.com

BUILDING YOUR CAREER WITH PRESENTATIONS

Dan Talbott's experience (profiled in the chapter-opening "On the Job" vignette) is solid proof that presentation skills are vital in today's business environment. Oral presentations offer important opportunities to put all your communication skills on display—not just in research, planning, writing, and visual design but also in interpersonal and nonverbal communication. Presentations can also let you demonstrate your ability to think on your feet, grasp complex issues, and handle challenging situations—all attributes that executives look for when searching for talented employees to promote. Although you *develop* presentations more than *write* them word for word, the three-step writing process works quite well for oral presentations, with some modifications (see Figure 14.1).

Presentations involve all your communication skills, from conducting research to using nonverbal communication.

PLANNING YOUR PRESENTATION

1 LEARNING OBJECTIVE

Describe the tasks involved in planning an oral presentation.

Planning oral presentations is much like planning any other business message: You (1) analyze the situation, (2) gather information, (3) select the right medium, and (4) organize the information. Gathering information for oral presentations is essentially the same as it is for

FIGURE 14.1 The Three-Step Process for Presentations
Although you rarely "write" a presentation or speech in the sense of composing every word ahead of time, the tasks in the three-step writing process adapt quite well to the challenge of planning, creating, and delivering oral and online presentations.

1 Plan →

Analyze the Situation
Define your purpose and develop a profile of your audience, including their likely emotional states and language preferences.

Gather Information
Determine audience needs and obtain the information necessary to satisfy those needs.

Select the Right Medium
Choose the best medium or combination of media for delivering your presentation, including handouts and other support materials.

Organize the Information
Define your main idea, limit your scope and verify timing, select the direct or indirect approach, and outline your content.

2 Write →

Adapt to Your Audience
Adapt your content, presentation style, and room setup to the audience and the specific situation. Be sensitive to audience needs and expectations with a "you" attitude, politeness, positive emphasis, and bias-free language. Plan to establish your credibility as required.

Compose Your Presentation
Outline an attention-getting introduction, body, and close. Prepare supporting visuals and speaking notes.

3 Complete

Revise the Message
Evaluate your content and speaking notes.

Master Your Delivery
Choose your delivery mode and practice your presentation.

Prepare to Speak
Verify facilities and equipment, including online connections and software setups. Hire an interpreter if necessary.

Overcome Anxiety
Take steps to feel more confident and appear more confident on stage.

REAL-TIME UPDATES
Learn More

Practical advice for making presentations that stick

Presentation expert Andy Bounds describes his simple RAP method for great presentations: start with the desired results in mind, understand audience motivations, and only then can you prepare effectively. Go to **http://real-timeupdates.com/ebc** and click on "Learn More." If you are using mybcommlab, you can access Real-Time Updates within each chapter or under Student Study Tools.

written communication projects. The other three planning tasks have some special applications when it comes to oral presentations; they are covered in the following sections.

Analyzing the Situation

As with written communications, in oral communications, analyzing the situation involves defining your purpose and developing an audience profile. The purpose of most of your presentations will be to inform or to persuade, although you may occasionally need to make a collaborative presentation, such as when you're leading a problem-solving or brainstorming session. The guidelines in Chapter 4 will help you identify and refine your purpose.

Knowing your audience's state of mind will help you adjust your message and your delivery.

When you develop your audience profile, start with the advice in Chapter 4 and then consider two other issues that are particularly important for oral presentations. First, try to anticipate what sort of emotional state your audience members are likely to be in. Consider what you know about the audience, the topic of your presentation, and your relationship with the audience. Will your listeners be supportive, hostile, or somewhere in between? Figure 14.2 offers some tips on preparing for audiences in various mindsets.

After considering your audience's emotional state, determine whether they are comfortable listening to the language you speak. Listening to an unfamiliar language is much more difficult than reading that language, so an audience that might be able to read a written report might not be able to understand an oral presentation covering the same material (see "Communicating Across Cultures: Five Tips for Making Presentations Around the World").

As you analyze the situation, also consider the specific circumstances in which you'll be making your presentation. Will you speak in a conference room, where you can control everything from light to sound to temperature? Or will you be demonstrating a product

FIGURE 14.2 Planning for Various Audience Mindsets
Try to learn the emotional state of your audience ahead of time so you can plan your presentation approach accordingly.

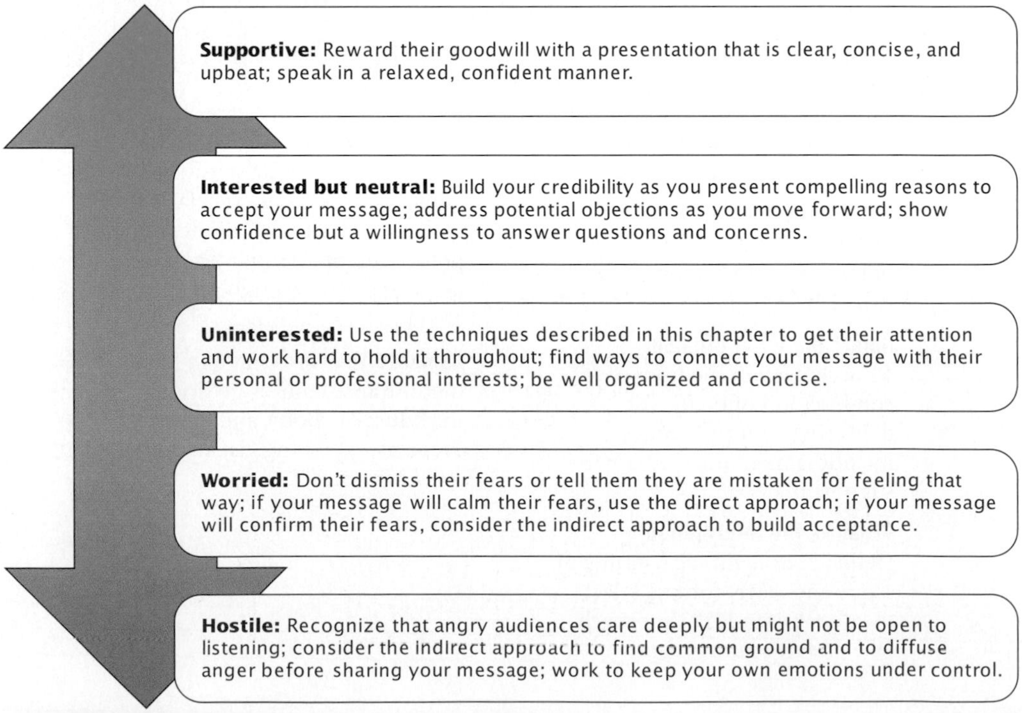
Supportive: Reward their goodwill with a presentation that is clear, concise, and upbeat; speak in a relaxed, confident manner.
Interested but neutral: Build your credibility as you present compelling reasons to accept your message; address potential objections as you move forward; show confidence but a willingness to answer questions and concerns.
Uninterested: Use the techniques described in this chapter to get their attention and work hard to hold it throughout; find ways to connect your message with their personal or professional interests; be well organized and concise.
Worried: Don't dismiss their fears or tell them they are mistaken for feeling that way; if your message will calm their fears, use the direct approach; if your message will confirm their fears, consider the indirect approach to build acceptance.
Hostile: Recognize that angry audiences care deeply but might not be open to listening; consider the indirect approach to find common ground and to diffuse anger before sharing your message; work to keep your own emotions under control.

on the floor of a trade show and have little control over the environment? Will everyone be in the same room, or will your audience participate from remote locations via the Internet? What equipment will you use? All these variables can influence not only the style of your presentation but even the content. Table 14.1 offers a summary of the key steps in analyzing an audience for oral presentations.

Be sure to research the setting and circumstances of your presentation, from the size of the audience to potential interruptions.

Selecting the Right Medium

The task of selecting the right medium might seem obvious—after all, you are speaking, so it's an oral medium. However, technology offers an array of choices these days, ranging from live, in-person presentations to *webcasts* that people view on your website whenever doing so fits their individual schedules. Explore these options early on so that you can take full advantage of the ones at your disposal.

Organizing Your Presentation

Organizing a presentation involves the same tasks as organizing a written message: Define your main idea, limit your scope, select the direct or indirect approach, and outline your content. Remember that when people read written reports, they can skip back and forth if they're confused or don't need certain information. However, in an oral presentation, audiences are more or less trapped in your time frame and sequence. For some presentations, you should plan to be flexible and respond to audience feedback, such as skipping over sections the audience doesn't need to hear and going into more detail in other sections.

REAL-TIME UPDATES
Learn More

Apply cognitive learning theory for better presentations

Build your presentation around the way audience members learn. Go to **http://real-timeupdates.com/ebc** and click on "Learn More." If you are using mybcommlab, you can access Real-Time Updates within each chapter or under Student Study Tools.

Communicating Across Cultures

Five Tips for Making Presentations Around the World

When making presentations to international audiences, language fluency might vary widely, so take special care to ensure clear communication:

- **Speak slowly and distinctly.** The most common complaint of international audiences is that English speakers talk too fast. Articulate every word carefully, emphasize consonants for clarity, and pause frequently.
- **Repeat key words and phrases.** When audiences are not terribly familiar with your language, they need to hear important information more than once. Also, they may not be familiar with various synonyms, so word key points in the same way throughout your presentation.
- **Aim for clarity.** Keep your message simple. Eliminate complex sentence structure, abbreviations, and acronyms. Replace two-word verbs with one-word alternatives (such as *review* instead of *look over*). Two-word verbs are confusing because the definition of each separate word differs from the meaning of the two words combined. Avoid cultural idioms, such as *once in a blue moon*, which may be unfamiliar to an international audience.
- **Communicate with body language.** Emphasize and clarify verbal information with gestures and facial expressions. For instance, smile to emphasize positive points and use gestures to illustrate the meaning of words such as *up*, *down*, or *under*.
- **Support your oral message with visuals.** For most audiences, visual messages support and clarify spoken words. To eliminate problems with rapid speech, unclear pronunciations, or strange accents, prepare captions both in English and in your audience's native language.

CAREER APPLICATIONS

1. One of the most important changes speakers need to make when addressing audiences in other cultures is to avoid colloquial figures of speech. Replace each of these phrases with wording that is more likely to be understood by non-native English speakers or audiences in other countries: "hit one out of the park," "go for broke," and "get your ducks in a row."
2. Make a list of 10 two-word verbs. How does the meaning of each separate word differ from the definition of the combined words? Replace each two-word verb with a single, specific word that will be clearer to an international audience.

TABLE 14.1 Analyzing an Audience for an Oral Presentation

TASK	ACTIONS
To determine audience size and composition	• Estimate how many people will attend and whether they will all attend in person, online, or a mix of both. • Find out if the audience members share professional interests or other affiliations that can help you establish common ground with them. • Analyze demographic and psychographic variables to see whether any significant differences or similarities should influence the content and style of your presentation.
To predict the audience's probable reaction	• Analyze why audience members are attending the presentation. • Predict the mood that people will be in when you speak to them: supportive, interested but neutral, uninterested, apprehensive, or hostile. • Find out what kind of backup information will impress and influence the audience: technical data, historical information, financial data, demonstrations, samples, and so on. • Consider whether the audience has any biases that might work against you. • Anticipate possible objections or questions.
To gauge the audience's level of understanding	• Analyze whether everybody has the same background and experience. • Determine what the audience already knows about the subject. • Decide what background information the audience will need to better understand the subject. • Consider whether the audience is familiar with your vocabulary. • Analyze what the audience expects from you. • Think about the mix of general concepts and specific details you will need to present.

Defining Your Main Idea

If your can't express your main idea in a single sentence, you probably haven't defined it clearly enough.

If you've ever heard a speaker struggle to get his or her main point across ("What I really mean to say is . . ."), you know how frustrating such an experience can be for an audience. To avoid that struggle, figure out the one key message you want audience members to walk away with. Then compose a one-sentence summary that links your subject and purpose to your audience's frame of reference. Here are some examples:

- Convince management that reorganizing the technical support department will improve customer service and reduce employee turnover.
- Convince the board of directors that we should build a new plant in Texas to eliminate manufacturing bottlenecks and improve production quality.
- Address employee concerns regarding a new health-care plan by showing how the plan will reduce costs and improve the quality of their care.

Each of these statements puts a particular slant on the subject, one that directly relates to the audience's interests. By focusing on your audience's needs and using the "you" attitude, you help keep their attention and convince them that your points are relevant.

Limiting Your Scope

Limiting your scope is important for two reasons: to fit your allotted time and to make sure your content meets audience needs and expectations.

Limiting your scope is important with any message, but it's particularly vital with presentations, for two reasons. First, for many presentations, you must work within strict time limits. For example, at DEMO and TechCrunch, two influential conferences in which entrepreneurs present their business plans to potential investors, presentations are limited to six and eight minutes, respectively.[2] Second, you can count on having audience attention for only a finite amount of time, and you'll lose the audience if you try to cover too much material. For example, studies show that audience attention levels and retention rates drop sharply after 20 minutes.[3]

If you're using conventional structured slides, allow 3 or 4 minutes per slide as a rough guideline.

When you've decided on the right amount of information to cover, do your best to estimate the time required to present that material or to estimate the amount of material you can cover within a fixed amount of time. The only sure way to do this is to practice. As an alternative, if you're using conventional structured slides (see page 449) you can figure on 3 or 4 minutes per slide as a rough guide.[4] For instance, if you have 20 minutes, plan on being able to cover roughly six or seven slides.

Of course, be sure to factor in time for introductions, coffee breaks, demonstrations, question-and-answer sessions, and anything else that takes away from your speaking time.

FIGURE 14.3 Effective Outline for a 10-Minute Progress Report
Here is an outline of a short presentation that updates management on the status of a key project; the presenter has some bad news to deliver, so she opted for an indirect approach to lay out the reasons for the delay before sharing the news of the schedule slip.

Progress Report: August 2010

Purpose: To update the Executive Committee on our product development schedule.

I. Review goals and progress.
   A. Mechanical design:
      1. Goal: 100%
      2. Actual: 80%
      3. Reason for delay: Unanticipated problems with case durability
   B. Software development:
      1. Goal: 50%
      2. Actual: 60%
   C. Material sourcing:
      1. Goal: 100%
      2. Actual: 45% (and materials identified are at 140% of anticipated costs)
      3. Reason for delay: Purchasing is understaffed and hasn't been able to research sources adequately.
II. Discuss schedule options.
   A. Option 1: Reschedule product launch date.
   B. Option 2: Launch on schedule with more expensive materials.
III. Suggest goals for next month.
IV. Q&A

Choosing Your Approach

Organize short presentations the same way you would a letter or brief memo.

With a well-defined main idea to guide you and a clear idea about the scope of your presentation, you can begin to arrange your message. If you have 10 minutes or less to deliver your message, organize your presentation much as you would a letter or a brief memo: Use the direct approach if the subject involves routine information or good news, and use the indirect approach if the subject involves bad news or persuasion. Figure 14.3 presents an outline of a short presentation that updates management on the status of a key project; the presenter has some bad news to deliver, so she opted for an indirect approach to lay out the reasons for the delay before sharing the news of the schedule slip.

Longer presentations are organized like reports. If the purpose is to motivate or inform, use a direct approach and a structure imposed naturally by the subject: importance, sequence, chronology, spatial orientation, geography, or category (as discussed in Chapter 11). If your purpose is to analyze, persuade, or collaborate, organize your material around conclusions and recommendations or around a logical argument. Use a direct approach if the audience is receptive and an indirect approach if you expect resistance.

Preparing Your Outline

A presentation outline helps you plan your speaking notes as well as your presentation.

A presentation outline performs the same function as an outline for a written report: It helps you organize your message in a way that maximizes its impact on your audience. To ensure effective organization, prepare your outline in several stages:[5]

- State your purpose and main idea and then use these to guide the rest of your planning.
- Organize your major points and subpoints in logical order, expressing each major point as a single, complete sentence.

- Identify major points in the body first and then outline the introduction and close.
- Identify transitions between major points or sections and then write these transitions in full-sentence form.
- Prepare your bibliography or source notes; highlight the sources you want to identify by name during your talk.
- Choose a compelling title; even if the title won't be published, it will help you focus your thoughts around your main idea.

The outline in Figure 14.4 is for a 30-minute analytical presentation. It is organized around conclusions and presented in direct order. This outline is based on Chapter 13's Electrovision report, written by Linda Moreno.

FIGURE 14.4 Effective Outline for a 30-Minute Presentation
This outline clearly identifies the purpose and the distinct points to be made in the introduction, body, and close. Notice also how the speaker wrote her major transitions in full-sentence form to be sure she can clearly phrase these critical passages when it's time to speak.

OUR TRAVEL AND ENTERTAINMENT COSTS ARE OUT OF CONTROL

Includes the statement of purpose

Purpose: To explain why Electrovision's travel and entertainment (T&E) costs are so high and to propose a series of changes to bring them under control.

INTRODUCTION

I. Our T&E costs are way above average, and they pose a threat to the company's financial health; fortunately, we can fix the problem in four straightforward steps that could save as much as $6 million a year.

Highlights the purpose in the introduction

II. How we approached the investigation
   A. We analyzed internal expense reports.
   B. We compared our cost data with nationwide averages.
   C. We analyzed published information on trends and cost-control suggestions.

Explains the investigation process

(Transition: This presentation reviews Electrovision's spending patterns, analyzes the impact on company profits, and recommends four steps for reducing the budget.)

BODY

I. Analysis of spending patterns
   A. The amount we've been spending on T&E:
      1. Airfares, hotels, rental cars, restaurants, and entertainment totaled $16 million last year.
      2. T&E budget increased by 12 percent per year for the past five years.
   B. Where the money goes:
      1. We took 3,390 trips last year at an average cost per trip of $4,725.
      2. Airfares and lodging represent 70 percent of T&E expenses.
   C. How our spending compares with national averages:
      1. Facilities and customers spread from coast to coast force us to spend a lot on travel.
      2. However, we spend 125 percent more than the national average for every day of travel. (Source: Dow Jones)
   D. Why do we spend so much?
      1. First-class travel has been viewed as compensation for the demands of extensive travel.
      2. The sales staff is encouraged to entertain clients.
      3. T&E costs are hard for managers to view and study.
      4. No one has central responsibility for controlling costs.

Uses a logical and simple organization

Explains why the problem exists

(Transition: We need to control spending for two reasons: (1) profits are projected to be flat or declining over the next two years, and (2) hotel rates and airfares continue to rise sharply.)

(continued)

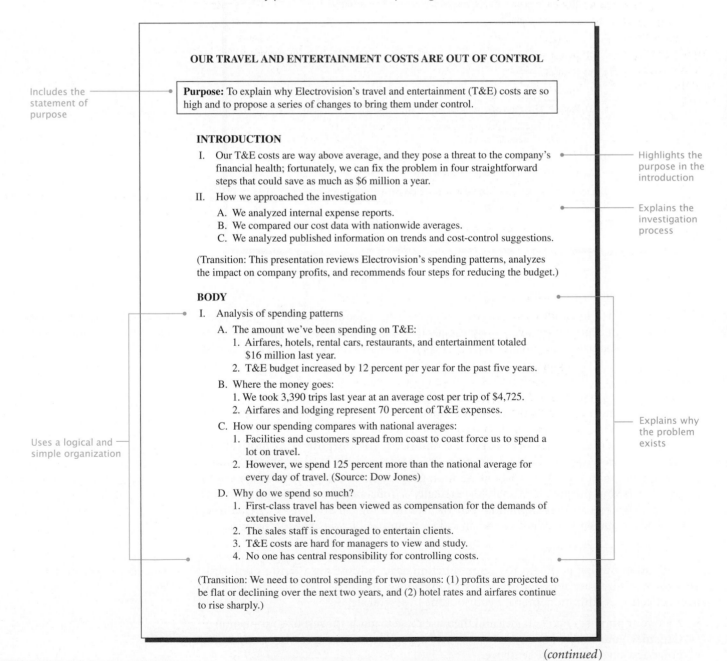

FIGURE 14.4 *(Continued)*

II. Impact on profits
  A. T&E costs continue to rise, as do other company costs.
  B. Revenue is projected to decline in coming years.
  C. Bottom line: We're headed for trouble.

(Transition: By implementing a number of reforms, management can expect to reduce Electrovision's T&E budget by as much as 40 percent. We can cut expenses in four ways.)

III. Solution
  A. We should institute tighter spending controls:
    1. Hire a travel manager to control costs and negotiate group discounts.
    2. Develop a formal, written policy to contain costs.
    3. Give departmental managers the data they need to make smarter decisions.
  B. We can reduce unnecessary travel and entertainment costs:
    1. Cut down on discretionary trips (seminars, etc.).
    2. Reduce the number of intracompany trips and employees sent on each trip.
    3. Encourage employees to economize.
  C. We can find lower travel rates:
    1. Negotiate corporate discounts.
    2. Plan trips more carefully to take advantage of lower fares.
  D. We can replace some travel with technological alternatives:
    1. Conference calls
    2. Videoconferences
    3. Other possibilities
  E. Potential impact of all these changes: As much as $6 million in reduced costs (Source: American Express)

(Transition: This presentation reviews Electrovision's spending patterns, analyzes the impact on company profits, and recommends four steps for reducing the budget.)

CLOSE

I. We spend more on T&E than we should
II. Four fairly obvious steps will yield significant cost savings
  A. Establish tighter controls
  B. Rein in unnecessary T&E costs
  C. Find lower travel rates
  D. Reduce travel by using technological alternatives

Explains why T&E costs are a problem

Maintains the logical organization throughout

Provides the four-step solution mentioned in the introduction, then makes a recommendation for implementing the steps

Restates the four recommended steps

Many speakers like to prepare both a detailed *planning outline* and a simpler *speaking outline* that provides all the cues and reminders they need to present their material.[6] To prepare an effective speaking outline, follow these steps:[7]

You might find it helpful to create a simpler speaking outline from your planning outline.

- Start with the planning outline and condense points and transitions to key words or phrases that will jog your memory.
- Add delivery cues, such as places in your outline where you plan to pause for emphasis or use a visual.
- Arrange your notes on numbered cards or use the "notes" field in your presentation software.

DEVELOPING YOUR PRESENTATION

2 LEARNING OBJECTIVE

Explain how to adapt to your audience, compose your presentation, and craft an effective introduction.

Although you may never actually write out a presentation word for word, you still engage in the writing process—developing your ideas, structuring support points, phrasing your transitions, and so on. Before you get to the actual writing phase, consider how you should adapt your style to your audience.

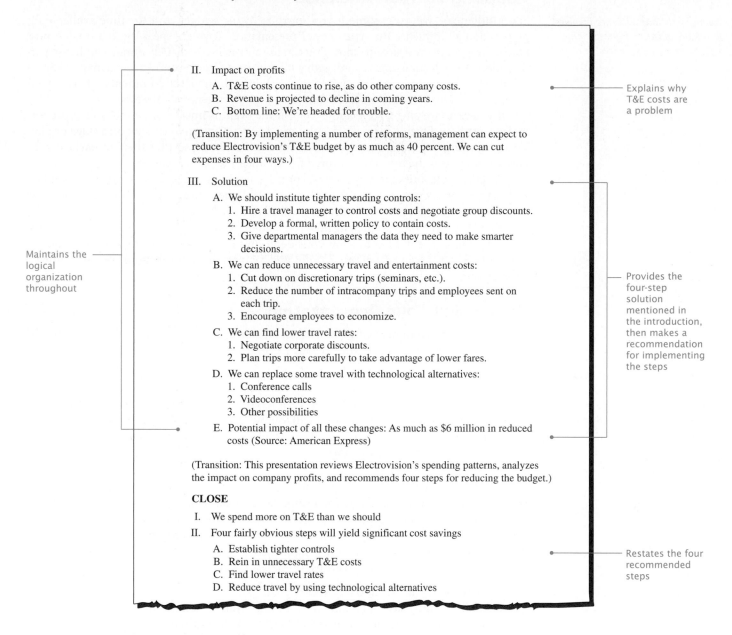

Adapting to Your Audience

Adapting to your audience involves a number of issues, from speaking style to technology choices.

Your audience's size, your subject, your purpose, your budget, and the time available for preparation all influence the style of your presentation. If you're speaking to a small group, particularly people you already know, you can use a casual style that encourages audience participation. A small conference room, with your audience seated around a table, may be appropriate. Use simple visuals and invite your audience to interject comments. Deliver your remarks in a conversational tone, using notes to jog your memory, if necessary.

If you're addressing a large audience or if the event is important, establish a more formal atmosphere. During formal presentations, speakers are often located on a stage or platform, standing behind a podium and using a microphone so that their remarks can be heard throughout the room or captured for broadcasting or webcasting.

Whether your presentation is formal or informal, strive for simple, familiar vocabulary and define any special terms you need to use. And keep things simple. If you repeatedly stumble over a word as you rehearse, use a different one.[8]

Finally, when you're pondering how you'll adapt to your audience, take public speaking etiquette into account. Plan to show consideration for your audience by making good use of their time, addressing them respectfully, and maintaining a professional presence during your speech.

Composing Your Presentation

Presentations are composed of three distinct elements: the introduction, the body, and the close, and each plays a specific role in your communication effort.

Introduction

An effective introduction arouses interest in your topic, establishes your credibility, and prepares the audience for the body of your presentation.

A good introduction arouses the audience's interest in your topic, establishes your credibility, and prepares the audience for what will follow. That's a lot to accomplish in the first few minutes, so give yourself plenty of time to develop the words and visuals you'll use to get your presentation off to a great start.

Getting Your Audience's Attention

Some subjects are naturally more interesting to some audiences than others. If you will be discussing a matter of profound significance that will personally affect the members of your audience, chances are they'll listen, regardless of how you begin. All you really have to do is announce your topic, and you'll have their attention. Other subjects call for more imagination. Here are six ways to arouse audience interest:[9]

- Unite the audience around a common goal.
- Tell an intriguing story that illustrates an important and relevant point.
- Pass around an example or otherwise appeal to listeners' senses.
- Ask a question that will get your audience thinking about your message.
- Share an intriguing, unexpected, or shocking detail.
- Open with an amusing observation about yourself, the subject matter of the presentation, or the circumstances surrounding the presentation—but make sure any humorous remarks are relevant, appropriate, and not offensive to anyone in the audience.

Regardless of which technique you choose, make sure you can give audience members a reason to care and to believe that the time they're about to spend listening to you will be worth their while.[10]

Building Your Credibility

In addition to grabbing the audience's attention, your introduction has to establish your credibility. If you're a well-known expert in the subject matter or have earned your audience's trust in other situations, you're ahead of the game. However, if you have no working relationship with your audience or if you're speaking in an area outside your presumed expertise, you need to establish your credibility and do so quickly; people tend to decide within a few minutes whether you're worth listening to.[11]

Techniques for building credibility vary, depending on whether you will be introducing yourself or having someone else introduce you. If a master of ceremonies, conference chair, or other person will introduce you, he or she can present your credentials so that you won't appear boastful. If you will be introducing yourself, keep your comments simple but don't be afraid to mention your accomplishments. Your listeners will be curious about your qualifications, so tell them briefly who you are and why you're there. Generally, you need to mention only a few aspects of your background, including your position in an organization, your profession, and the name of your company. You might say something like this:

If someone else will be introducing you to the audience, you can ask this person to present your credentials as well.

> I'm Karen Whitney, a market research analyst with Information Resources Corporation. For the past five years, I've specialized in studying high-technology markets. Your director of engineering, John LaBarre, has asked me to talk to you about recent trends in computer-aided design so that you'll have a better idea of how to direct your research efforts.

This speaker establishes credibility by tying her credentials to the purpose of her presentation. By mentioning her company's name, her specialization and position, and the name of the audience's boss, she lets her listeners know immediately that she is qualified to tell them something they need to know. She connects her background to their concerns.

Previewing Your Message

In addition to getting the audience's attention and building your credibility, a good introduction gives your audience a preview of what's ahead. Your preview should summarize the main idea of your presentation, identify major supporting points, and indicate the order in which you'll develop those points. Of course, if you're using the indirect approach, you'll have to decide how much information to review in your introduction.

Use the introduction as a preview of the importance, the structure, and the content of your message.

Body

The bulk of your speech or presentation is devoted to a discussion of the main points in your outline. As you convey your information, make sure that the organization of your presentation is clear and your presentation holds the audience's attention.

3 LEARNING OBJECTIVE

Explain how to connect ideas and hold the audience's attention during the body of a presentation and how to close effectively.

Connecting Your Ideas

In written documents, you can show how ideas are related on the page or screen by using a variety of design clues: headings, paragraph indentions, white space, and lists. However, with oral communication—particularly when you aren't using visuals for support—you have to rely primarily on words to link various parts and ideas.

For the small links between sentences and paragraphs, use one or two transitional words: *therefore, because, in addition, in contrast, moreover, for example, consequently, nevertheless,* or *finally.* To link major sections of a presentation, use complete sentences or paragraphs, such as "Now that we've reviewed the problem, let's take a look at some solutions." Every time you shift topics, be sure to stress the connection between ideas. Summarize what's been said and then preview what's to come.

The longer your presentation, the more important your transitions. If you will be presenting many ideas, audience members may have trouble absorbing them and seeing the relationships among them. Your listeners need clear transitions to guide them to the most important points. Furthermore, they'll appreciate brief, interim summaries to pick up any ideas they may have missed. By repeating key ideas in your transitions, you can compensate for lapses in your audience's attention. When you actually give your presentation, you might also want to call attention to the transitions by using gestures, changing your tone of voice, or introducing a new visual.

Use transitions to repeat key ideas, particularly in longer presentations.

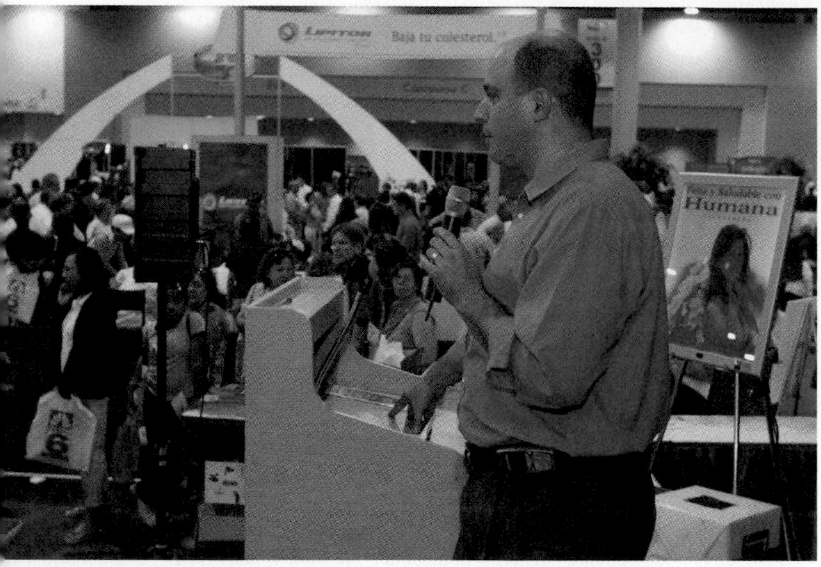

When attempting to hold an audience's attention, public speakers sometimes encounter distractions in the background. It takes a focused speaker to overcome such physical interruptions and get his or her message across.

Holding Your Audience's Attention

After you've successfully captured your audience's attention in your introduction, you need to work to keep it throughout the body of your presentation. Here are a few helpful tips for keeping the audience tuned into your message:

- **Relate your subject to your audience's needs.** People are interested in things that affect them personally. As much as possible, present every point in light of your audience's needs and interests.
- **Anticipate your audience's questions.** Try to anticipate as many questions as you can and address these questions in the body of your presentation or during the question-and-answer period.
- **Use clear, vivid language.** People become bored quickly when they don't understand the speaker. If your presentation will involve abstract ideas, show how those abstractions connect with everyday life. Use familiar words, short sentences, and concrete examples. Avoid repeating the same words and phrases, too.
- **Explain the relationship between your subject and familiar ideas.** Show how your subject is related to ideas that audience members already understand and give people a way to categorize and remember your points.[12]
- **Ask for opinions or pause occasionally for questions or comments.** Audience feedback helps you determine whether your listeners understand a key point before you launch into another section. Feedback also gives your audience members a chance to switch for a time from listening to participating, which helps them engage with your message and develop a sense of shared ownership.
- **Illustrate your ideas with visuals.** Visuals enliven your message, help you connect with audience members, and help them remember your message more effectively (see "Enhancing Your Presentations with Effective Visuals," page 449).

The most important way to hold an audience's attention is to show how your message relates to their individual needs and concerns.

Close

Plan your close carefully so that your audience leaves with your main idea fresh in their minds.

The close of a speech or presentation is critical for two reasons: Audiences tend to focus more carefully as they wait for you to wrap up, and they leave with your final words ringing in their ears. Before closing your presentation, tell listeners that you're about to finish so they'll make one final effort to listen intently. Don't be afraid to sound obvious. Consider saying something such as "In conclusion" or "To sum it all up." You want people to know this is the final segment of your presentation.

Restating Your Main Points

After you announce your close, repeat your main idea and reinforce it with your key support points. Emphasize what you want your audience to do or to think and stress the key motivating factor that will encourage them to respond that way. For instance, to conclude a presentation on your company's executive compensation program, you can repeat your specific recommendations and finish with a memorable statement to motivate your audience to take action:

> We can all be proud of the way our company has grown. However, if we want to continue that growth, we need to adjust our executive compensation program to reflect competitive practices. If we don't, our best people will look for opportunities elsewhere.
>
> In summary, our survey has shown that we need to take four steps to improve executive compensation:
>
> - Increase the overall level of compensation
> - Install a cash bonus program
> - Offer a variety of stock-based incentives
> - Improve health insurance and pension benefits
>
> By making these improvements, we can help our company remain competitive with the industry's largest competitors.

Such repetition of key ideas greatly improves the chance that your audience will hear your message in the way you intended.

Ending with Clarity and Confidence

If you've been successful with the introduction and body of your presentation, your listeners now have the information they need, and they're in the right frame of mind to put that information to good use. Now you're ready to end on a strong note that confirms expectations about any actions or decisions that will follow the presentation—and to bolster the audience's confidence in you and your message one final time.

Some presentations require the audience to reach a decision or agree to take specific action, in which case the close provides a clear wrap-up. If the audience agrees on an issue covered in the presentation, briefly review the consensus. If they don't agree, make the lack of consensus clear by saying something like, "We seem to have some fundamental disagreement on this question." Then be ready to suggest a method of resolving the differences.

If you need to have the audience make a decision or agree to take action, make sure the responsibilities for doing so are clear.

If you expect any action to occur as a result of your speech, be sure to explain who is responsible for doing what. One effective technique is to list the action items, with an estimated completion date and the name of the person or team responsible. You can present this list in a visual and ask each person on the list to agree to accomplish his or her assigned task by the target date. This public commitment to action is good insurance that something will happen.

Make sure your final remarks are upbeat and memorable. After summarizing your key points, conclude with a quote, a call to action, or some encouraging words. For instance, you might stress the benefits of action or express confidence in the listeners' ability to accomplish the work ahead. An alternative is to end with a question or a statement that will leave your audience thinking.

Plan your final statement carefully so you can end on a strong, positive note.

At the completion of your presentation, your audience should feel satisfied. The close is not the place to introduce new ideas or to alter the mood of the presentation. Even if parts of your presentation are downbeat, try to close on a positive note. Compose your closing remarks carefully. You don't want to wind up on stage with nothing to say but "Well, I guess that's it."

Enhancing Your Presentations with Effective Visuals

4 LEARNING OBJECTIVE

Outline the key steps in creating powerful presentation visuals.

Visuals can improve the quality and impact of your oral presentation by creating interest, illustrating points that are difficult to explain in words alone, adding variety, and increasing the audience's ability to absorb and remember information. Behavioral research has shown that visuals can improve learning by up to 400 percent because humans can process visuals 60,000 times faster than text.[13]

You can select from a variety of visuals to enhance oral presentations, including old-school technologies such as overhead transparencies, chalkboards, whiteboards, and flipcharts—all of which have value in the right circumstances. However, the medium of choice for most business presentations is an electronic presentation using Microsoft PowerPoint, Apple Keynote, or similar software. Electronic presentations are easy to edit and update; you can add sound, photos, video, and animation; they can be incorporated into online meetings, webcasts, and *webinars* (a common term for web-based seminars); and you can record self-running presentations for trade shows, websites, and other uses.

Thoughtfully designed visuals create interest, illustrate complex points in your message, add variety, and help the audience absorb and remember information.

When designing presentation slides, let accuracy and simplicity guide you. Doing so has several advantages. First, simple materials take less time to create than complex materials. Second, simple visuals reduce the chances of distraction and misinterpretation. Third, the more "bells and whistles" you have in your presentation, the more likely something will go wrong. In addition, make sure your visual style is appropriate for the subject and the setting (see Figure 14.5 on the next page)

Accuracy and simplicity are keys to effective visuals.

Choosing Structured or Free-Form Slides

Perhaps the most important design choice you face when creating slides is whether to use conventional *structured slides* or the looser, *free-form slides* that many presentation specialists now advocate. Compare the two rows of slides in Figure 14.6 on page 451. The structured

Structured slides are usually based on templates that give all the slides in a presentation the same general look; free-form slides typically don't follow any set design plan.

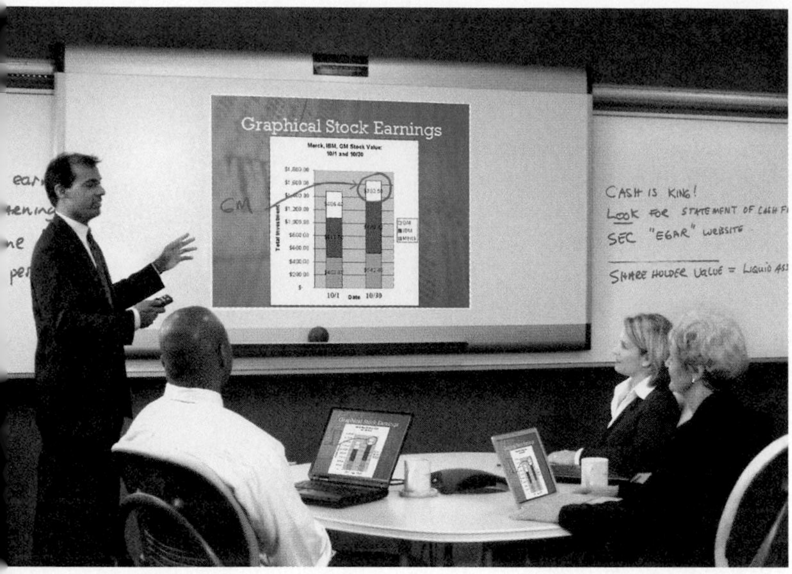

Electronic whiteboards let you capture notes and feedback during presentations and then print them out or e-mail them to audience members.

slides in the top row follow the same basic format throughout the presentation; in fact, they're based directly on the templates built into PowerPoint. The free-form slides in the bottom row don't follow a rigid structure—and most definitely not a PowerPoint template. However, this doesn't mean free-form designs are just random from one slide to the next. Effectively designed slides should still be unified by design elements such as color and font selections, for example, as Figures 14.6c and 14.6d are. Also, note how Figure 14.6d combines visual and textual messages to convey the point about listening without criticizing. This complementary approach of pictures and words is a highlight of free-form design.

Because the amount of content varies so dramatically between the two design approaches, the number of slides in a presentation also varies dramatically. For instance, someone using structured slides might have six or seven slides for a 20-minute presentation, but someone using free-form slides for the same presentation might have 60 or 80 slides or more and spend only 15 or 20 seconds on each one. In the extreme, a 20-minute free-form presentation could have *hundreds* of slides, with some slides sometimes displayed for less than a second.[14] Both design strategies have advantages and disadvantages, and one or the other can be a better choice for specific situations.

Free-form slides often have far less content per slide than structured designs, which requires many more slides to cover a presentation of equal length.

Structured slides are usually the best choice for project updates and other routine information presentations, particularly if the slides are intended to be used only once.

Well-designed free-form slides help viewers understand, process, and remember the speaker's message.

Structured slides have the advantage of being easy to create; you simply choose an overall design scheme for the presentation, select a template for a new slide, and start typing. If you're in a schedule crunch, going the structured route might save the day because at least you'll have *something* ready to show. Given the speed and ease of creating them, structured slides can be a more practical choice for routine presentations such as project status updates. Also, because more information can usually be packed on each slide, structured slides can be more effective at conveying complex ideas or sets of interrelated data to the right audiences.

The goal of free-form slide design is to overcome the drawbacks of text-heavy structured design by fulfilling three criteria that researchers have identified as important for successful presentations: (1) providing complementary information through both textual and visual means; (2) limiting the amount of information delivered at any one time to prevent cognitive overload; and (3) helping viewers process information by identifying priorities and connections, such as by highlighting the most important data points in a graph.[15] With appropriate imagery, free-form designs can also create a more dynamic and engaging experience for the audience. Given their ability to excite and engage, free-form designs are

FIGURE 14.5 Presentation Style
Presentation software makes it easy to create an endless variety of visual styles. Compare the staid, "quiet" style on the left with the more dynamic style on the right.

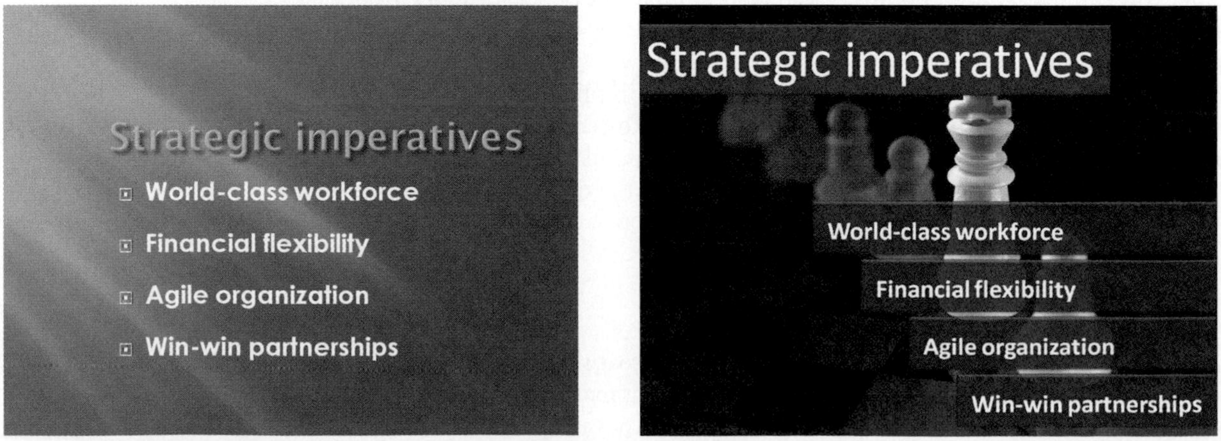

FIGURE 14.6 Structured Versus Free-Form Slide Design
Compare the rigid, predictable design of the two slides in the top row with the free-form designs in the bottom row. Although the two free-form slides don't follow the same design structure, they are visually linked by color and font choices.

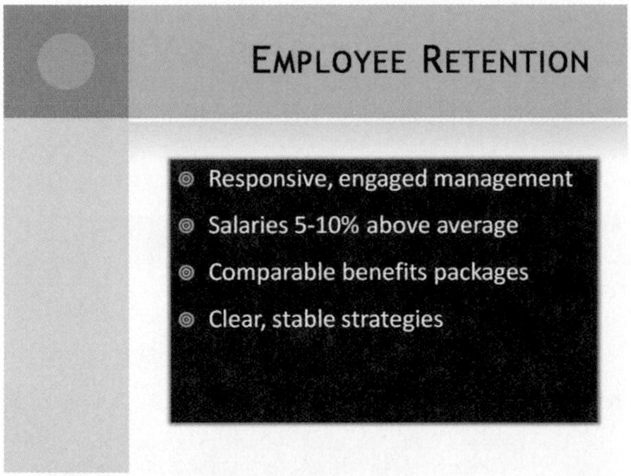

Figure 14.6a

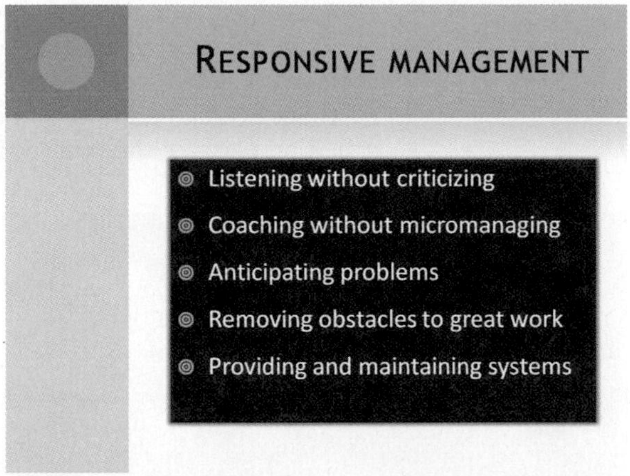

Figure 14.6b

Figure 14.6c

Figure 14.6d

particularly good for motivational, educational, and persuasive presentations—particularly when the slides will be used multiple times and therefore compensate for the extra time and effort required to create them.

Writing Readable Content

One of the most common mistakes beginners make—and one of the chief criticisms leveled at structured slide designs in general—is stuffing slides with too much text. Doing so creates several problems: It overloads the audience with too much information too fast; it takes attention away from the speaker by forcing people to read more; and it requires the presenter to use smaller type, which in turns makes the slides even harder to read.

Effective text slides supplement your words and help the audience follow the flow of ideas (see Figure 14.7 on the next page). Use them to highlight key points, summarize and preview your message, signal major shifts in thought, illustrate concepts, or help create interest in your spoken message.

Use slide text to emphasize key points, not to convey your entire message.

REAL-TIME UPDATES
Learn More

Way beyond bullet points: A stunning example of free-form slide design

Online identity specialist Dick Hardt wowed his audience with this high-speed slide presentation. See how a creative mind can transform electronic slides into something far more compelling than conventional bullet points. Go to **http://real-timeupdates.com/ebc** and click on "Learn More." If you are using mybcommlab, you can access Real-Time Updates within each chapter or under Student Study Tools.

FIGURE 14.7 Writing Readable Content
Effective text slides are clear, simple guides that help the audience understand and remember the speaker's message. Notice the progression toward simplicity in these slides: Figure 14.7a is a paragraph that would distract the audience for an extended period of time. Figure 14.7b simplifies the message somewhat, but these bullet points are too long, and the slide is too crowded. Figure 14.7c offers concise, readable bullets, although too many slides in a row in this structured design would become tedious. Figure 14.7d distills the message down to a single compelling thought, without even a headline. It is easy to read, but the speaker will need to fill in the missing parts of the message.

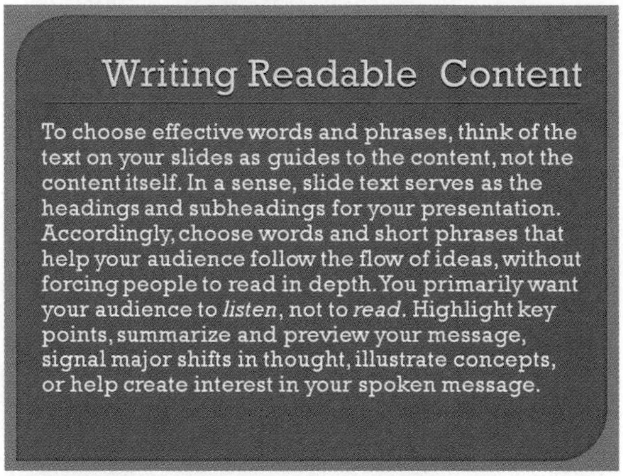

Writing Readable Content
To choose effective words and phrases, think of the text on your slides as guides to the content, not the content itself. In a sense, slide text serves as the headings and subheadings for your presentation. Accordingly, choose words and short phrases that help your audience follow the flow of ideas, without forcing people to read in depth. You primarily want your audience to *listen*, not to *read*. Highlight key points, summarize and preview your message, signal major shifts in thought, illustrate concepts, or help create interest in your spoken message.

Figure 14.7a

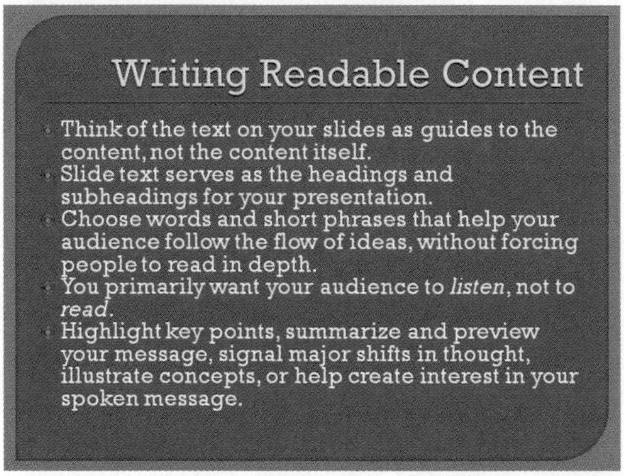

Writing Readable Content
Think of the text on your slides as guides to the content, not the content itself.
Slide text serves as the headings and subheadings for your presentation.
Choose words and short phrases that help your audience follow the flow of ideas, without forcing people to read in depth.
You primarily want your audience to *listen*, not to *read*.
Highlight key points, summarize and preview your message, signal major shifts in thought, illustrate concepts, or help create interest in your spoken message.

Figure 14.7b

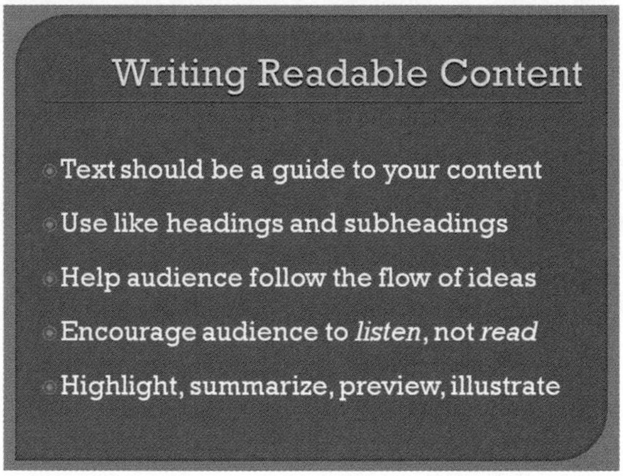

Writing Readable Content
Text should be a guide to your content
Use like headings and subheadings
Help audience follow the flow of ideas
Encourage audience to *listen*, not *read*
Highlight, summarize, preview, illustrate

Figure 14.7c

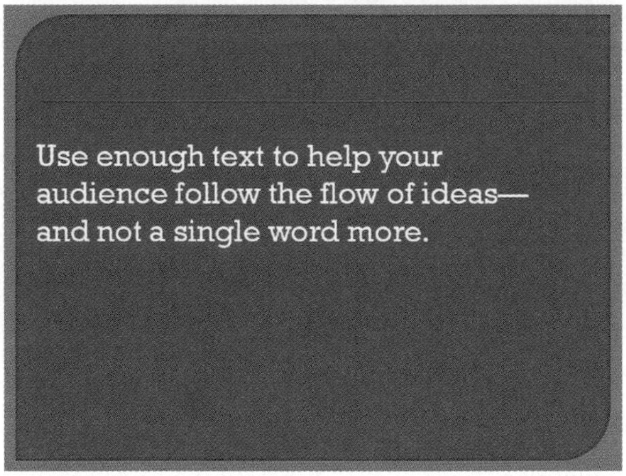

Use enough text to help your audience follow the flow of ideas—and not a single word more.

Figure 14.7d

Modifying Graphics for Slides

Visuals created for printed documents may need to be simplified for use in presentations.

The visual design principles you learned in Chapter 12 apply to presentation visuals as well, with one important caution: Visuals for presentations need to be simpler than visuals for printed documents. Detailed images that look fine on the printed page can be too dense and complicated for presentations.

If you're adapting visuals originally created for a written report, start by reducing the level of detail, eliminating anything that is not absolutely essential to the message. If necessary, break information into more than one illustration. Whenever you can do so without confusing the audience, look for shorter variations of numeric values. For instance, round off a number such as $12,500.72 to $12 or $12.5, and then label the axis to indicate thousands.

With the basic design in place, use graphical elements to highlight key points. Leave plenty of white space, use colors that stand out from the slide's background, and choose a

TABLE 14.2 Color and Emotion

COLOR	SELECTED EMOTIONAL ASSOCIATIONS (CAN VARY BY CULTURE)	BEST USES
Blue	Peaceful, soothing, tranquil, cool, trusting	Background for presentation slides (usually dark blue); safe and conservative
White	Neutral, innocent, pure, wise	Font color of choice for most presentation slides that have a dark background
Yellow	Warm, bright, cheerful, enthusiastic	Text bullets and subheadings on a dark background
Red	Passionate, dangerous, active, painful	To promote action or stimulate the audience; seldom used as background ("In the red" specifically refers to financial losses.)
Green	Assertive, prosperous, envious, relaxed	Highlight and accent color (Green symbolizes money in the United States but not in other countries.)

font that's clear and easy to read. Use arrows, boldface type, and color to direct your audience's eyes to the main point of a visual.

Selecting Design Elements

As you create slides, pay close attention to the interaction of color, background and foreground designs, artwork, fonts, and type styles.

Choose design elements carefully to create slides that help audiences grasp each slide's message.

- **Color.** Color is a critical design element that can grab attention, emphasize important ideas, create contrast, and stimulate various emotions (see Table 14.2). Research shows that color visuals can account for 60 percent of an audience's acceptance or rejection of an idea. Color can increase willingness to read by up to 80 percent, and it can enhance learning and improve retention by more than 75 percent.[16] Color is powerful, though, so use it carefully.
- **Background designs and artwork.** The *background* is the equivalent of paper in a printed report. Keep the background simple; cluttered or flashy backgrounds distract from your message.
- **Foreground designs and artwork.** The *foreground* contains the unique text and graphic elements that make up each individual slide. In the foreground, artwork can be either functional or decorative. *Functional artwork* includes photos, technical drawings, charts, and other visual elements containing information that's part of your message. In contrast, *decorative artwork* simply enhances the look of your slides, and it should be using sparingly.
- **Fonts and type styles.** Type is harder to read onscreen than on the printed page because projectors have lower *resolution* (the ability to display fine details) than most printed pages. Sans serif fonts are usually easier to read than serif fonts (see Figure 14.8 on the next page). In general, avoid script or decorative fonts, italicized type, and all capitals. Use plenty of white space between lines of text, and limit the number of fonts to two or three. Choose font sizes that are easy to read from anywhere in the room. Venture capitalist Guy Kawasaki, who has sat through hundreds and hundreds of PowerPoint presentations, suggests using no type smaller than 30 points. Doing so not only ensures readable slides but forces you to distill every idea down to its essential core, simply because you won't have room to be wordy.[17]

Color is more than just decoration; colors have meanings themselves, based on both cultural experience and the relationships you establish between the colors in your designs.

Artwork in the foreground of your slides can be either decorative or functional; use decorative artwork sparingly.

Many of the fonts available on your computer are difficult to read onscreen, so they aren't good choices for presentation slides.

Maintaining design consistency is critical because audiences start to assign meaning to visual elements beginning with the first slide. For instance, if yellow is used to call attention to the first major point in your presentation, viewers will expect the next occurrence of yellow to also signal an important point. The *slide master* feature makes consistency easy to achieve because it applies design choices to every slide in a presentation.

Design inconsistencies confuse and annoy audiences; don't change colors and other design elements randomly throughout your presentation.

Adding Animation and Multimedia

Today's presentation software offers many options for livening up your slides, including sound, animation, video clips, transition effects, and hyperlinks. Think about the impact that all these effects will have on your audience and use only those special effects that support your message.[18]

You can animate just about everything in an electronic presentation; resist the temptation to do so—make sure an animation has a purpose.

FIGURE 14.8 Selecting Fonts for Projection
Times New Roman is a standard font for many print documents; however, as Figure 14.8a demonstrates, the serifs at the end of each letter make it difficult to read on-screen. Sans serif fonts such as the Calibri font shown in Figure 14.8b are a better choice for slides; they are cleaner and easier to read from a distance.

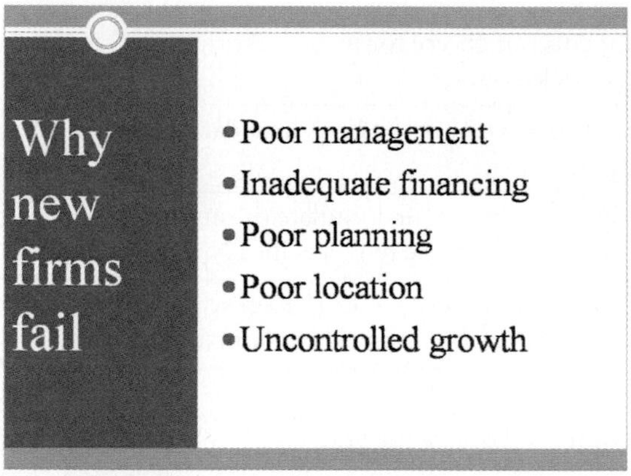

Figure 14.8a Times New Roman (serif) font

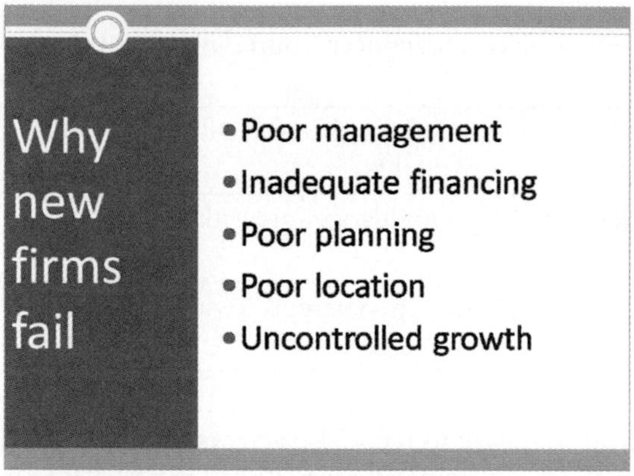

Figure 14.8b Calibri (sans serif) font

REAL-TIME UPDATES
Learn More

Effective presentation slides: Learn from one of the best

Respected presentation expert Garr Reynolds offers 10 great tips to improve the quality of your presentation slides. Go to **http://real-timeupdates.com/ebc** and click on "Learn More." If you are using mybcommlab, you can access Real-Time Updates within each chapter or under Student Study Tools.

Functional animation involves motion that is directly related to your message, such as a highlight arrow that moves around the screen to emphasize specific points in a technical diagram. Such animation is also a great way to demonstrate sequences and procedures. In contrast, *decorative animation*, such as having a block of text cartwheel in from offscreen, needs to be used with great care. These effects don't add any functional value, and they easily distract audiences.

Some of the slide transitions available in presentation software are distracting and amateurish.

Transitions control how one slide replaces another, such as having the current slide gently fade out before the next slide fades in. Subtle transitions like this can ease your viewers' gaze from one slide to the next, but many of the transition effects now available are little more than distractions, so choose carefully. **Builds** control the release of text, graphics, and other elements on individual slides. With builds, you can make key points appear one at a time rather than having all of them appear on a slide at once, thereby making it easier for you and the audience to focus on each new message point.

Hyperlinks let you jump to different slides, websites, or other displays.

A **hyperlink** instructs your computer to jump to another slide in your presentation, to a website, or to another program entirely. Using hyperlinks is also a great way to build flexibility into your presentations so that you can instantly change the flow of your presentation in response to audience feedback.

Make sure multimedia elements are relevant, interesting, and brief.

Multimedia elements offer the ultimate in active presentations. Using audio and video clips can be a great way to complement your textual message. You can incorporate various media elements with PowerPoint by using tools such as the Microsoft Producer add-in. In addition, dozens of software programs are now available to assist with video editing, from basic tools sometimes included with digital cameras or camcorders to professional packages such as Adobe Premiere Pro.

5 LEARNING OBJECTIVE

Identify the tasks needed to complete your presentation materials.

COMPLETING YOUR PRESENTATION

The completion state for presentations involves a wider range of tasks than printed documents require. Make sure you allow enough time to test your presentation slides, verify equipment operation, practice your speech, and create handout materials. With a first draft of your presentation in hand, revise your slides to make sure they are readable, concise,

FIGURE 14.9 Slide Sorter View
Examining thumbnails of slides on one screen is the best way to check the overall design of your final product. The slide sorter also makes it easy to ponder the order and organization of your presentation; you can change the position of any slide simply by clicking and dragging it to a new position.

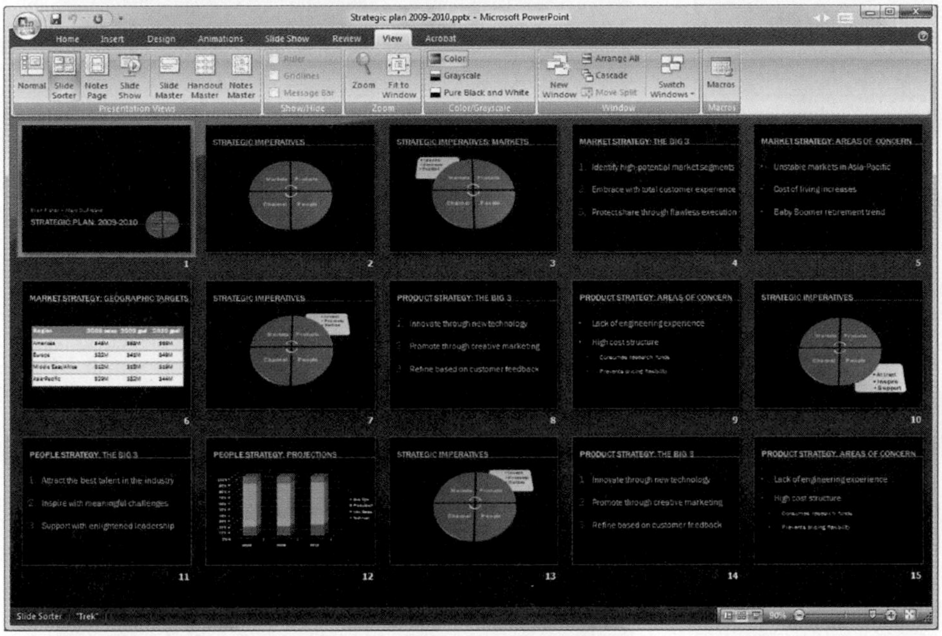

consistent, and fully operational (including transitions, builds, animation, and multimedia). Then complete your presentation by finalizing your slides and support materials.

Finalizing Slides and Support Materials

Electronic presentation software can help you throughout the editing and revision process. As Figure 14.9 shows, the *slide sorter view* lets you see some or all of the slides in your presentation on a single screen. Use this view to add and delete slides, reposition slides, and check slides for design consistency.

Use the slide sorter view to verify and modify the organization of your slides.

In addition to the content slides that you've already created, you can help your audience follow the flow of your presentation by creating slides for your title, agenda and program details, and navigation flow:

Navigational slides help your audience keep track of what you've covered already and what you plan to cover next.

- **Title slide(s).** Make a good first impression on your audience with one or two title slides, the equivalent of a report's cover and title page (see Figures 14.10a and 14.10b on the next page). A title slide should contain the title of your presentation (and subtitle, if appropriate), your name, your department affiliation (for internal audiences), and your company affiliation (for external audiences).
- **Agenda and program details.** These slides communicate both the agenda for your presentation and any additional information your audience might need, such as lunch plans (see Figures 14.10c and 14.10d).
- **Navigation slides.** To tell your audience where you're going and where you've been, you can use a series of **navigation slides** based on your outline or agenda. This technique is most useful in longer presentations with several major sections. As you complete each section, repeat the slide but indicate which material has been covered and which section you are about to begin (see Figure 14.11 on the next page).

With your slides working properly and in clear, logical order, consider whether some additional material will help your audience either during or after your presentations. *Handouts* are a great way to offer your audience additional material without overloading your slides with information.

Use handout materials to support the points made in your presentation and to offer the audience additional information on your topic.

FIGURE 14.10 Navigation and Support Slides
You can use a variety of navigation and support slides to introduce yourself and your presentation, to let the audience know what your presentation will cover, and to provide essential details.

Figure 14.10a Title slide

Figure 14.10b Title slide 2

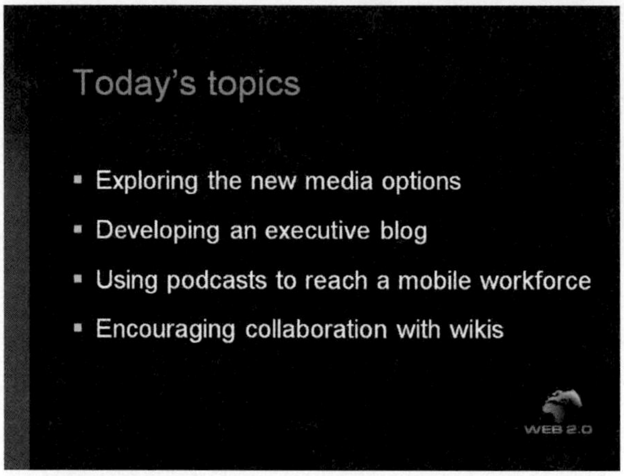

Figure 14.10c Agenda

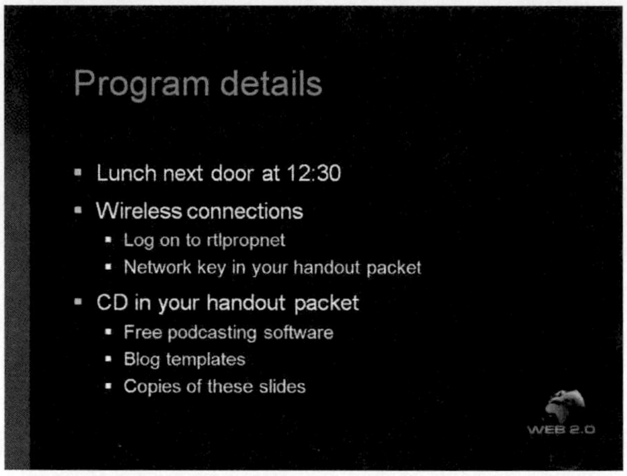

Figure 14.10d Program details

FIGURE 14.11 Moving Blueprint Slides
Here are two of the ways you can use a *blueprint slide* as a navigational aid to help your audience stay on track with the presentation. Figure 14.11a visually "mutes" and checks off the sections of the presentation that have already been covered. In contrast, Figure 14.11b uses a sliding highlight box to indicate the next section to be covered.

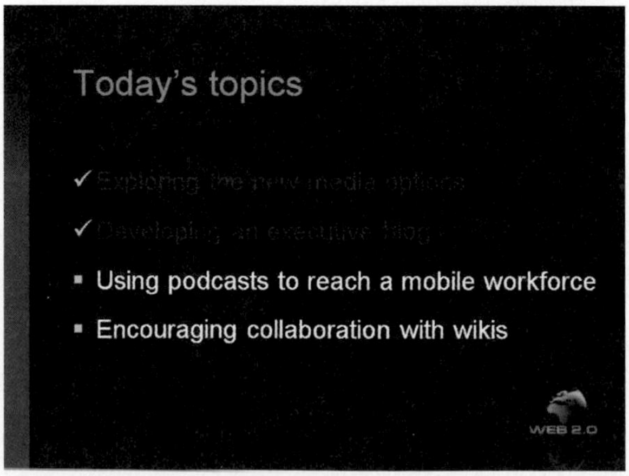

Figure 14.11a "Muting" topics already covered

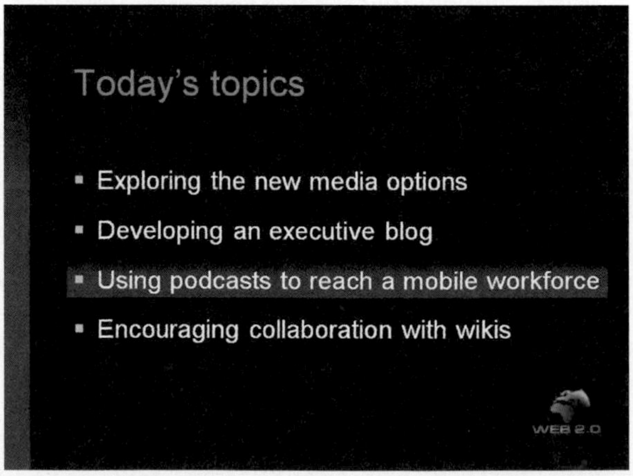

Figure 14.11b Highlighting the next topic

Preparing to Speak

With all your materials ready, your next step is to decide which method of speaking you want to use. You have three options: memorizing your material word for word, reading a printout of your material, or speaking from notes. Memorizing is usually not a good choice. In the best of circumstances, you'll probably sound stilted; in the worst, you might forget your lines. Reading your speech is sometimes necessary, such as when delivering legal information, policy statements, or other messages that must be conveyed in an exact manner. However, for most business presentations, reading is a poor choice because it limits your interaction with the audience and lacks the fresh, dynamic feel of natural talking.

Speaking from notes, with the help of an outline, note cards, or visuals, is usually the most effective and easiest delivery mode. This approach gives you something to refer to and still allows for plenty of eye contact, interaction with the audience, and improvisation in response to audience feedback.

Speaking from carefully prepared notes is the easiest and most effective delivery mode for most speakers.

From time to time, you may have to give an *impromptu*, or unrehearsed, speech when you have virtually no time at all to prepare. Take a moment to think through what you'll say and then focus on your key points. If you absolutely cannot say something intelligent and effective on the subject at hand, it's usually better to explain that you can't and ask for an opportunity to prepare some remarks for a later time or date.

Learning to focus on the audience and interact with them while using electronic slides or other visuals takes practice.

Practicing Your Delivery

Many things can go wrong in a major presentation, including equipment glitches, timing problems, and that sinking feeling that you don't know what to say next. That's why experienced speakers always practice important presentations. A day or two before you're ready to step on stage for an important talk, make sure you can give a positive response to the following questions:

- Can you present your material naturally, without reading your slides word-for-word?
- Is the equipment working—and do you know how to work it?
- Is your timing on track?
- Can you easily pronounce all the words you plan to use?
- Have you decided how you're going to introduce your slides?
- Have you anticipated likely questions and objections?

With experience, you'll get a feel for how much practice is enough in any given situation. For an important presentation, four or five practice runs is not excessive. Your credibility is dramatically enhanced when you move seamlessly through your presentation, matching effective words with each slide. Practicing helps keep you on track, helps you maintain a conversational tone with your audience, and boosts your confidence and composure.

You'll know you've practiced enough when you can present the material at a comfortable pace and in a conversational tone, without the need to read your slides or constantly refer to your notes.

6 LEARNING OBJECTIVE

Explain how to excel at presentation delivery by overcoming anxiety, handling questions responsively, and giving presentations online.

DELIVERING YOUR PRESENTATION

It's show time. This section offers practical advice for two important aspects of delivery: overcoming anxiety and responding to questions.

Overcoming Anxiety

Even speakers with years of experience feel some anxiety about getting up in front of an audience. Think of nervousness as an indication that you care about your audience, your topic, and the occasion. Such stimulation can give you the extra energy you need to make

Preparation is the best antidote for anxiety.

your presentation sparkle. Here are some ways to harness your nervous energy to become a more confident speaker:[19]

- **Prepare more material than necessary.** Combined with having a genuine interest in your topic, having extra knowledge will reduce your anxiety.
- **Practice.** The more familiar you are with your material, the less panic you'll feel.
- **Think positively.** See yourself as polished and professional, and your audience will, too.
- **Visualize your success.** Visualize mental images of yourself in front of the audience, feeling confident, prepared, and able to handle any situation that might arise.[20]
- **Take a few deep breaths.** Before you begin to speak, remember that your audience wants you to succeed, too.
- **Be ready.** Have your first sentence memorized and on the tip of your tongue.
- **Be comfortable.** Dress appropriately for the situation but as comfortably as possible. Drink plenty of water before your scheduled presentation time to ensure that your voice is well hydrated (bring a bottle of water with you, too).
- **Don't panic.** If you sense that you're starting to race—a natural response when you're nervous—stop for a second and arrange your notes or perform some other small task while taking several deep breaths. Then start again at your normal pace.
- **Concentrate on your message and your audience, not on yourself.** When you're busy thinking about your subject and observing your audience's response, you tend to forget your fears.
- **Maintain eye contact with friendly audience members.** When your presentation is under way, be particularly careful to maintain eye contact with your audience, shifting your gaze periodically around the room.
- **Keep going.** Things usually get better as you move along, with each successful minute giving you more and more confidence.

Handling Questions Responsively

Don't leave the question-and-answer period to chance: Anticipate likely questions and think through your answers.

The question-and-answer (Q&A) period is one of the most important parts of an oral presentation. It gives you a chance to obtain important information, to emphasize your main idea and supporting points, and to build enthusiasm for your point of view. When you're speaking to high-ranking executives in your company, the Q&A period will often consume most of the time allotted for you presentation.[21]

Whether or not you can establish ground rules for Q&A depends on the audience and the situation. If you're presenting to a small group of upper managers or potential investors, for example, you will probably have no say in the matter: Audience members will ask as many questions as they want to get the information they need. On the other hand, if you are presenting to your peers or a large public audience, establish some guidelines, such as the number of questions allowed per person and the overall time limit for questions.

If you ever face hostile questions, don't duck; respond honestly and directly while keeping your cool.

Don't assume that you can handle whatever comes up without some preparation.[22] Learn enough about your audience members to get an idea of their concerns and think through answers to potential questions.

When people ask questions, pay attention to nonverbal signals to help determine what each person really means. Repeat the question to confirm your understanding and to ensure that the entire audience has heard it. If the question is vague or confusing, ask for clarification; then give a simple, direct answer.

If you are asked a difficult or complex question, avoid the temptation to sidestep it or try to laugh it off without answering. Offer to meet with the questioner afterward if giving an adequate answer would take too long. If you don't know the answer, don't pretend that you do. Instead, offer to get a complete answer as soon as possible.

Be on guard for audience members who use questions to make impromptu speeches or to take control of your presentation. Without offending anyone, find a way to stay in control. You might admit that you and the questioner

REAL-TIME UPDATES
Learn More

Get a quick reminder of the elements of a successful presentation

The Memphis Public Library offers succinct reminders of the planning and design choices that lead to successful presentations. Go to **http://real-timeupdates.com/ebc** and click on "Learn More." If you are using mybcommlab, you can access Real-Time Updates within each chapter or under Student Study Tools.

have differing opinions and, before calling on someone else, offer to get back to the questioner after you've done more research.[23]

If a question ever puts you on the hot seat, respond honestly but keep your cool. Look the person in the eye, answer the question as well as you can, and keep your emotions under control. Defuse hostility by paraphrasing the question and asking the questioner to confirm that you've understood it correctly. Maintain a businesslike tone of voice and a pleasant expression.[24]

When the time allotted for your presentation is almost up, prepare the audience for the end by saying something like, "Our time is almost up. Let's have one more question." After you reply to that last question, summarize the main idea of the presentation and thank people for their attention. Conclude the way you opened: by looking around the room and making eye contact. Then leave the podium with the same confident demeanor you've had from the beginning. For a reminder of the steps to take in developing an oral presentation, refer to "Checklist: Developing Oral Presentations."

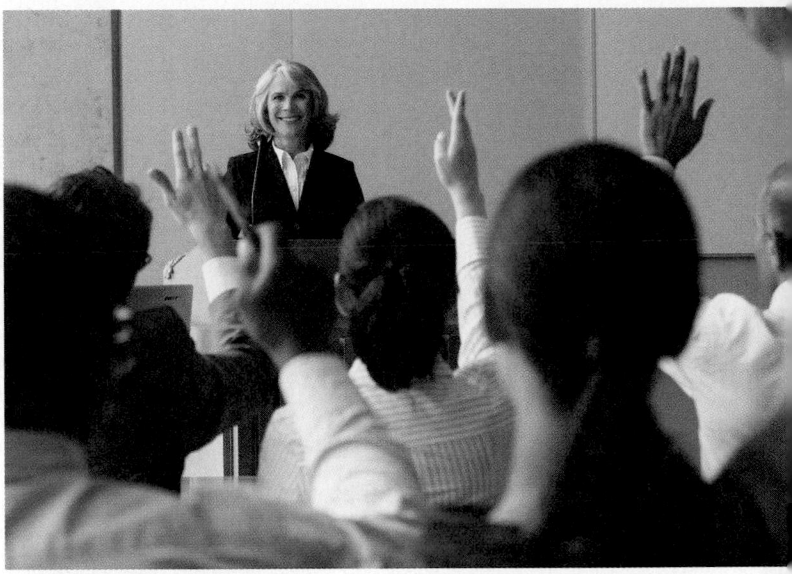

The question-and-answer session is often the most valuable part of a presentation, so prepare for it by researching answers to likely questions.

Giving Presentations Online

In some companies, online presentations have already become a routine matter, conducted via internal groupware, virtual meeting systems, or webcast systems designed specifically for online presentations. In most cases, you'll communicate through some combination of audio, video, data presentations (for instance, PowerPoint slides), and perhaps *screencasts* ("movies" made by recording screen activity). Your audience members will view your presentation either on their individual computer screens or via a projector in a conference room.

Online presentations give you a way to reach many people in a short time, but they require special preparation and skills.

The benefits of online presentations are considerable, including the opportunity to communicate with a geographically dispersed audience at a fraction of the cost of travel and the ability for a project team or an entire organization to meet at a moment's notice. However, the challenges for a presenter can be significant, thanks to that layer of technology between you and your audience. Many of those "human moments" that guide and encourage you through an in-person presentation won't travel across the digital divide. For instance, it's often difficult to tell whether audience members are bored or confused because your view of them is usually confined to small video images (and sometimes not even that).

CHECKLIST: Developing Oral Presentations

A. Plan your oral presentation.
- Analyze the situation by defining your purpose and developing an audience profile.
- Select the right medium.
- Organize your presentation by defining the main idea, limiting the scope, choosing your approach, and preparing your outline.

B. Write your oral presentation.
- Adapt to your audience by tailoring your style and language.
- Compose your presentation by preparing an introduction, a body, and a close.
- Use your introduction to arouse audience interest, build your credibility, and preview your message.
- Use the body to connect your ideas and hold your audience's attention.
- Use the close to restate your main points and describe the next steps.

C. Complete your oral presentation.
- Master the art of delivery by choosing a delivery method, knowing your material, and practicing your delivery.
- Check the location and equipment in advance.
- Determine whether you should use an interpreter.
- Overcome anxiety by preparing thoroughly.
- Handle questions responsively.

To ensure successful online presentations, keep the following advice in mind:

- **Consider sending preview study materials ahead of time.** Doing so allows audience members to familiarize themselves with any important background information. Also, by using a free service such as SlideShare (**www.slideshare.net**), you can distribute your presentation slides to either public or private audiences, and you can record audio narrative to make your presentations function on their own.[25]
- **Keep your presentation as simple as possible.** Break complicated slides down into multiple slides if necessary and keep the direction of your discussion clear so that no one gets lost.
- **Ask for feedback frequently.** You won't have as much of the visual feedback that alerts you when audience members are confused, and many online viewers will be reluctant to call attention to themselves by interrupting you to ask for clarification.
- **Consider the viewing experience from the audience members' point of view.** Will they be able to see what you think they can see? For instance, webcast video is typically displayed in a small window on-screen, so viewers may miss important details.
- **Make sure your audience can receive the sort of content you intend to use.** For instance, some corporate *firewalls* (network security devices) don't allow streaming media, so your webcast video might not survive the trip.[26]
- **Allow plenty of time for everyone to get connected and familiar with the screen they're viewing.** Build extra time into your schedule to ensure that everyone is connected and ready to start.

Document Makeover

Improve This Presentation

To practice correcting drafts of actual documents, visit the "Document Makeovers" section in mybcommlab. Refer to the User Guide for specific instructions on how to access the content for this chapter. You will find a presentation draft that contains problems and errors related to what you've learned in this chapter about preparing effective oral presentations. Use the "Final Draft" decision tool to create an improved version of this presentation. Check the message for effective choices in scope, style, opening, use of transitions, and close.

When you master the technology, you can spend less time thinking about it and more time thinking about the most important elements of the presentation: your message and your audience.

Last but not least, don't get lost in the technology. Use these tools whenever they'll help but remember that the most important aspect of any presentation is getting the audience to receive, understand, and embrace your message. For the latest information on online presentations, visit **http://real-timeupdates.com/ebc** and click on Chapter 14.

On the Job: Solving Communication Dilemmas at Hewlett-Packard

After leading the successful effort to land the huge Procter & Gamble computer services contract, Dan Talbott is now HP's senior client relationship director for the P&G program. You work for him as an assistant manager on the program, and one of your key responsibilities is coordinating communication efforts across the far-flung team of people who now operate P&G's computer network. When HP landed the contract to take over P&G's information systems, it not only acquired several P&G facilities but also hired a large number of P&G employees who had previously worked on those systems. Although both companies have highly respected—and widely emulated—corporate cultures, you appreciate that the transition is difficult for some of the P&G staff. Many of these people joined P&G right out of college, and some have worked there for 20 years or more. They might be doing the same jobs as before and even working in the same facilities, but they have a new employer with different policies, different leadership, and so on. They also need to adjust to working for a high-technology firm instead of a consumer-goods firm. How will you address these challenges?[27]

1. You've been preparing a series of presentations on what it's like to work at HP, and the presentation you're developing now is on the concept of the "agile organization." Here's how HP's website describes the concept:

> By working together, we become a smart organization that thinks imaginatively, acts decisively and delivers quickly. Time-to-market, time-to-customer, time-to-revenue and time-to-profit are our critical drivers, as we take calculated risks to outpace competitors and anticipate market changes.

Which of the following main idea statements does the best job of encapsulating this rather complicated thought?

a. Talk about how speed is critical to HP's success—creating new products quickly, acquiring new customers quickly, generating new revenue quickly, and realizing profits quickly.

b. Explain how teamwork plays a vital role in HP's ability to outpace competitors and anticipate market changes.
c. Make sure the ex-P&G people understand that business moves quickly at HP and that everyone is responsible for making HP an agile organization.
d. By working together, we become a smart organization that thinks imaginatively, acts decisively, and delivers quickly.

2. Eventually, some of the people who've recently joined from P&G may be transferred to other positions within HP, including working on HP's own internal information systems or working on programs for other HP clients. However, the vast majority are still focused on the P&G program, so HP's overall mission and competitive concerns are probably not of immediate interest to many of them. What approach should you take in your presentation to encourage them to care about the concept of the "agile organization" and their individual roles in it?
a. Begin your presentation by immediately asking them what they've heard about the "agile organization" so far. Encourage them to ask any questions before you begin your presentation. This way you can squash any rumors before explaining what the "agile organization" means.
b. Start your introduction with a few recent news items about layoffs in other high-technology companies and then emphasize that in order to avoid that fate, everyone who works for HP needs to embrace the idea of agility. This will scare them into paying attention.
c. Share with them an insider's view of the sales process that Dan Talbott's team used to land the P&G contract, focusing on how the team responded so quickly to the opportunity. It's a great example of agility in action, and this situation affected all of them personally (and many of them probably wonder why HP was able to win the contract when EDS and IBM seemed to most people in the industry as more obvious choices for such a huge project). As HP employees now, they will care about how HP will continue to win big contracts and thereby avoid layoffs, keep providing good benefits, and create opportunities for career advancement.
d. Start your presentation with several short video clips that communicate the idea of speed, such as race cars, rockets, foot races at the Olympics, and a microwave oven cooking a meal in a matter of minutes. From these scenes, they'll get the idea that speed is vital in today's fast-paced world.

3. In the body of your presentation, you plan to show a PowerPoint slide that explains the various aspects of the company's description of what it means to be an agile organization. You'll present a text slide, talk the audience through the description, and then open the floor to questions. Which of the following is the best way to arrange the text for this slide?

a.

The Agile Organization

By working together, we become a smart organization that thinks imaginatively, acts decisively and delivers quickly. Time-to-market, time-to-customer, time-to-revenue, and time-to-profit are our critical drivers, as we take calculated risks to outpace competitors and anticipate market changes.

b.

What Does It Mean to Be Agile?

By working together, we become a smart organization that thinks imaginatively, acts decisively, and delivers quickly. Time-to-market, time-to-customer, time-to-revenue, and time-to-profit are our critical drivers, as we take calculated risks to outpace competitors and anticipate market changes.

c.

What Does It Mean to Be Agile?

- Teamwork creates a smart organization:
  - Imaginative thinking
  - Decisive action
  - Quick delivery
- Time is our primary motivating force:
  - Time-to-market
  - Time-to-customer
  - Time-to-revenue
  - Time-to-profit
- A strategy of taking calculated risks yields major benefits:
  - Outpace competitors
  - Anticipate market changes

d.

What Does It Mean to Be Agile?

- Teamwork creates a smart organization
- Time is our primary motivating force
- A strategy of taking calculated risks yields major benefits

4. You've completed your slide show on the agile organization, and you've been looking forward to giving the presentation for the first time. The presentation is going along nicely until you notice one employee in the back of the room snickering from time to time and whispering to people next to him. You've never met this person, and you're not even sure what his position is, but he's starting to distract you. After a few more minutes of this annoying behavior, the employee begins openly laughing at some of your remarks about corporate agility. Unfortunately, your emotions get the best of you, and you lose your cool, stop the presentation, and demand to know what the employee finds so funny. You realize immediately that you've made a mistake, particularly when the employee responds, "If HP is so freakin' agile, why have you been forced to lay off thousands of employees in the past couple of years? How soon until we lose our jobs, too?" You're not prepared to respond to such a complex question (the layoffs were the result of both the merger with Compaq and the general downturn in the technology market a few years ago), nor are you authorized to speak for the company on such a sensitive subject. On the other hand, you don't want to appear weak or ill prepared. After you take a deep breath and calm down a bit, how should you respond?

a. Use humor to defuse the situation. Tell the questioner, "HP laid off other employees to make room for charming new additions like you."
b. Recognize that this is not a question you should try to handle under these circumstances, particularly since you don't know how many other people might share the questioner's anxiety; you might lose control of the situation entirely. Respond by saying, "This is not an appropriate time or place to discuss such matters, and I'd like to return to the focus of our discussion today so that those employees who would like to learn more can get the information they came for."
c. Express empathy with the questioner's anxiety and explain that the best way to avoid layoffs in the future is for everyone to contribute to the company's efforts of becoming more agile: "As a fellow employee, I certainly share your concern about job security. However, I also know that the only part I can control is my contribution to the company's efforts to become more agile. Rather than digressing into past difficulties, why don't we focus on what each of us can do to ensure profitable growth into the future?"
d. Ignore the question entirely. Count to 10 silently, look back around the room at the friendly faces you were making eye contact with earlier, and resume your presentation.

LEARNING OBJECTIVES CHECKUP

Assess your understanding of the principles in this chapter by reading each learning objective and studying the accompanying exercises. For fill-in-the-blank items, write the missing text in the blank provided; for multiple-choice items, circle the letter of the correct answer. You can check your responses against the answer key on page AK-2.

Objective 14.1: Describe the tasks involved in planning an oral presentation.

1. If you are facing an audience that is apprehensive about what you might have to say in a presentation, which of the following approaches is best?
   a. Even if your presentation will confirm their worst fears, use the direct approach to confront the negative emotions head-on.
   b. If your message will calm their fears, use the direct approach; if your message will confirm their fears, consider the indirect approach to build acceptance.
   c. Ignore the emotional undercurrents and focus on the practical content of your message.
   d. Diffuse the situation with a humorous story that dismisses the audience members' fears.

2. If you are using conventional structured slide design, roughly how many slides should you plan to use in a 30-minute presentation?
   a. 100–150
   b. 30–40
   c. 60–65
   d. 8–10

3. A/an _____ outline is similar to an outline for a written memo or report, whereas a/an _____ outline is a simplified version designed to help you during the delivery of your presentation.

Objective 14.2: Explain how to adapt to your audience, compose your presentation, and craft an effective introduction.

4. Which of the following is true about "writing" a presentation?
   a. You should always write every word of every presentation, leaving nothing to chance.
   b. You should never write presentations in the sense of writing a memo or a report.
   c. In most cases, you don't write out every word of a presentation; instead, you think through key phrases and perhaps draft your opening and closing statements.
   d. The three-step writing process does not apply to presentations.

5. Which of the following is the best way to arouse interest in a presentation to a group of fellow employees on the importance of taking ownership of the problem whenever a customer calls in with a complaint?
   a. "If customers leave, so do our jobs."
   b. "Everything we want as employees of this company—from stable jobs to pay raises to promotional opportunities—depends on one thing: satisfied customers."

c. "How are customers supposed to get their problems solved if we keep passing the buck from one person to the next without ever doing anything?"
d. "The company's profit margins depend on satisfied customers, and it's up to us to make sure those customers are satisfied."

6. If you suspect that your audience doesn't really care about the topic you plan to discuss, how can you generate interest in your presentation?
a. Look for ways to help them relate to the information on a personal level, such as helping the company ensure better job security.
b. Speak louder and, if possible, use lots of sound effects and visual special effects in your presentation.
c. Show your passion for the material by speaking faster than normal and pacing the room in an excited fashion.
d. Show that you care about their feelings by saying up front that you don't really care about the topic either, but you've been assigned to talk about it.

7. If you're giving a presentation in a subject area that you've researched thoroughly but in which you don't have any hands-on experience (suppose your topic is coordinating a major facility relocation or hiring a tax attorney, for instance), which of these steps should you take to build credibility?
a. During your introduction, explain that your presentation is the result of research that you've done and briefly explain the extent of the research.
b. Explain that you don't have any experience in the subject area, but you've done some research.
c. Emphasize that you know a great deal about the subject matter.
d. Sidestep the issue of credibility entirely in the introduction and let your knowledge shine through during the body of your presentation.

Objective 14.3: Explain how to connect ideas and hold the audience's attention during the body of a presentation and how to close effectively.

8. Which of the following would do the best job of holding an audience's attention during a presentation on the growing importance of blogs in corporate communication? In this particular case, the audience members are all managers of the same company, but they represent a half dozen countries and speak four different native languages (although they all have basic English skills).
a. "Blogs are now an important feature in the corporate communication landscape."
b. "Successful managers around the world now view blogging as an essential tool in their communication efforts."
c. "Millions of customers and employees are now hip to the latest wave to blow through corporate communication, the clumsily named but nevertheless vital blog."
d. "I personally read more than a dozen blogs every day, which is solid evidence of how important blogs have become."

9. Your company recently relocated from another state, and the owners are eager to begin building a positive relationship with the local community. You've been asked to speak to employees about volunteering in various community organizations. Which of the following statements does the best job of communicating the owners' wishes while appealing to employees' personal interests?
a. "Becoming involved in community organizations is a great way for you and your families to meet new people and feel more at home in your new city."
b. "Becoming involved in community organizations shows our new neighbors that we're an organization of positive, caring people—and it's a great way for you and your families to meet new people and feel more at home in your new city."
c. "We really owe it to our new community to give back by volunteering."
d. "The owners feel it is vital for us to become more involved in the community."

10. Which of these techniques is mentioned in the chapter as a way to hold an audience's attention during a presentation?
a. Speak louder than average
b. Tell people that management expects them to pay attention
c. Use clear and vivid language
d. None of the above

Objective 14.4: Outline the key steps in creating powerful presentation visuals.

11. Which of the following is true about visuals?
a. They can add interest to your presentations.
b. They can help you illustrate and clarify important points.
c. They can help your audience absorb and understand information.
d. They can do all of the above.

12. Which of these is an advantage of electronic presentations?
a. You can edit and update your slides right up to the beginning of your presentation.
b. Electronic presentations are less expensive.
c. Electronic presentations require you to talk less.
d. None of the above.

13. Why is consistent use of colors, fonts, size, and other design elements important in presentations?
a. Consistency is not important; in fact, it's a sign of a dull presentation.
b. Consistency shows that you're a smart businessperson who doesn't waste time on trivial details.
c. Consistency simplifies the viewing and listening process for your audience and enables them to pay closer attention to your message rather than spending time trying to figure out your visuals.
d. Consistency shows that you're a team player who can follow instructions.

Objective 14.5: Identify the tasks needed to complete your presentation materials.

14. How does the completion stage of the three-step writing process differ between reports and presentations?
    a. Completion is exactly the same for reports and presentations.
    b. Presentations are never proofread or tested ahead of time; doing so would destroy the spontaneity of your delivery.
    c. You never revise presentation slides because they're locked in place once you create them.
    d. The completion state for presentations involves a wider range of tasks, including testing your presentation slides, verifying equipment operation, practicing your speech, and creating handout materials.

15. What advice would you give to a novice presenter regarding practicing before a big presentation?
    a. Don't practice—it destroys the spontaneity you need to give an upbeat presentation.
    b. Make multiple practice runs, a half dozen if needed, to make sure you can deliver the material smoothly and confidently.
    c. Write out a script and memorize it word for word; you can't risk forgetting any key points.
    d. One practice session is adequate; use the extra time to polish your presentation slides instead.

Objective 14.6: Explain how to excel at presentation delivery by overcoming anxiety, handling questions responsively, and giving presentations online.

16. Which of the following is an effective way to respond if you feel nervous right before giving a presentation?
    a. Think up a short joke to begin your presentation; the audience's laughter will help you relax.
    b. Begin your presentation by telling people that you're nervous and asking them to be sympathetic if you make any mistakes.
    c. Begin your presentation by telling the audience how much you dislike speaking in public; most of them dislike public speaking, too, so they'll be more sympathetic toward you.
    d. Remind yourself that everybody gets nervous and that being nervous simply means you care about doing well; use the nervousness to be more energetic when you begin speaking.

17. Which of the following is a disadvantage of conducting presentations online?
    a. The lack of audio communication
    b. The inability of most people to participate, since most businesses don't have Internet access
    c. The inability to use PowerPoint slides online
    d. The shortage (or sometimes complete lack) of nonverbal signals such as posture, which can provide vital feedback during a presentation

18. Which of the following is an advantage of online presentations?
    a. Lower travel costs
    b. More opportunities for employees to meet customers in person
    c. The ability to multitask during meetings
    d. All of the above

19. Which of these actions should you take when an audience member asks you a question?
    a. Observe the questioner's body language and facial expression to help determine what the person really means.
    b. Nod your head or show some other sign that you acknowledge the question.
    c. Repeat the question to confirm your understanding and to ensure that the entire audience has heard it.
    d. Do all of the above.

20. If you receive a question that is important and relevant to the topic you're presenting but you lack the information needed to answer it, which of the following would be the best response?
    a. "I'm sorry; I don't know the answer."
    b. "You've asked an important question, but I don't have the information needed to answer it properly. I'll research the issue after we're finished here today and then send everyone an e-mail message with the answer."
    c. "Let me get back to you on that."
    d. "I'd really like to stay focused on the material that I prepared for this presentation."

PEARSON mybcommlab™

Log on to www.mybcommlab.com to access the following study and assessment aids associated with this chapter:

- Video applications
- Real-Time Updates
- Peer review activity
- Quick Learning Guides
- Pre/post test
- Personalized study plan
- Model documents
- Sample presentations

If you are not using mybcommlab, you can access Real-Time Updates and Quick Learning Guides through http://real-timeupdates.com/ebc. The Quick Learning Guide (located under "Learn More" on the website) hits all the high points of this chapter in just two pages. This guide, especially prepared by the authors, will help you study for exams or review important concepts whenever you need a quick refresher.

Apply Your Knowledge

1. Would you rather (a) deliver an oral presentation to an outside audience, (b) be interviewed for a news story, or (c) make a presentation at a departmental meeting? Why? How do the communication skills differ among those situations? Explain.
2. How might the audience's attitude affect the amount of audience interaction during or after a presentation? Explain your answer.
3. If you were giving an oral presentation on the performance of a company product, what three attention-getters might you use to enliven your speech?
4. For a high-energy sales presentation, would you choose structured slide designs or free-form designs? Why?
5. **Ethical Choices** Is it ethical to use design elements and special effects to persuade an audience? Why or why not?

Practice Your Knowledge

Messages for Analysis

Message 14.A: Improving a Slide

Examine the slide in Figure Figure 14.12 and point out any problems you notice. How would you correct these problems?

Message 14.B: Simplifying a Graph

Examine the graph in Figure 14.13 on page 466 and explain how to modify it for an electronic presentation using the guidelines discussed in this chapter.

Message 14.C: Analyzing Animation

To access this PowerPoint presentation, visit http://real-timeupdates.com/ebc, click on "Student Assignments," and select Chapter 14, page 465, Message 14.C. Download and watch the presentation in slide show mode. (After you select Slide Show from the View menu, simply click your mouse to advance through the slides.) After you've watched the presentation, identify at least three ways in which various animations, builds, and transitions either enhanced or impeded your understanding of the subject matter.

Exercises

Active links for all websites in this chapter can be found on mybcommlab; see your User Guide for instructions on accessing the content for this chapter.

14.1 **Mastering Delivery: Analysis** Attend a presentation at your school or in your town or watch a speech on television. Categorize the presentation or speech as one that motivates or entertains, one that informs or analyzes, or one that persuades or urges collaboration. Then compare the speaker's delivery with this chapter's "Checklist: Developing Oral Presentations." Write a two-page report analyzing the speaker's performance and suggesting improvements.

14.2 **Mastering Delivery: Nonverbal Signals** Observe and analyze the delivery of a speaker in a school, at work, or in another setting. What type of delivery did the speaker use? Was this delivery appropriate for the occasion? What nonverbal signals did the speaker use to emphasize key points? Were these signals effective? Which nonverbal

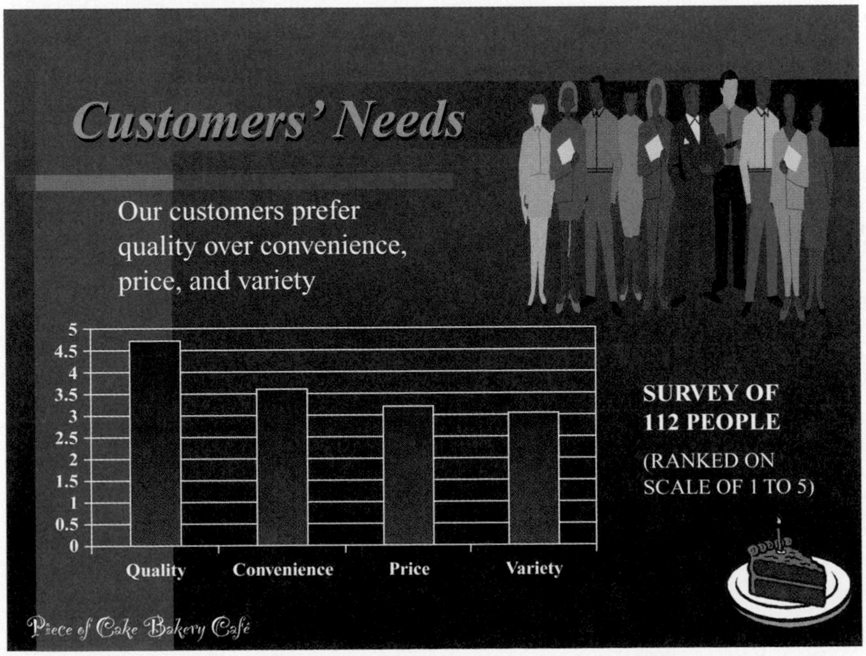

FIGURE 14.12 Piece of Cake Bakery Customer Survey

FIGURE 14.13 CommuniCo Employee Training Costs

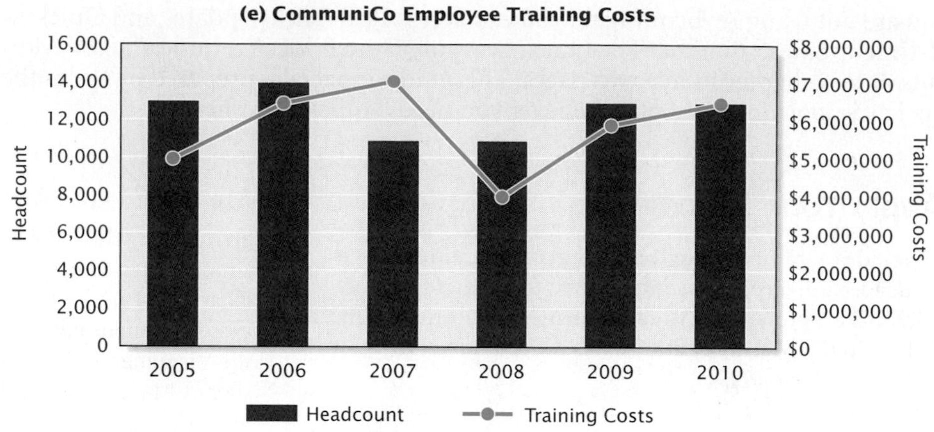

signals would you suggest to further enhance the delivery of this oral presentation—and why?

14.3 **Ethical Choices** Think again about the oral presentation you observed and analyzed in Exercise 14.2. How could the speaker have used nonverbal signals to unethically manipulate the audience's attitudes or actions?

14.4 **Teamwork** You've been asked to give an informative 10-minute presentation on vacation opportunities in your home state. Draft your introduction, which should last no more than two minutes. Then pair off with a classmate and analyze each other's introductions. How well do these two introductions arouse the audience's interest, build credibility, and preview the presentation? Suggest how these introductions might be improved.

14.5 **Completing Oral Presentations: Self-Assessment** How good are you at planning, writing, and delivering oral presentations? Rate yourself using the self-assessment at the bottom of the page. Then examine your ratings to identify where you are strongest and where you can improve, using the tips in this chapter.

14.6 **Creating Effective Slides: Content** Look through recent issues (print or online) of *BusinessWeek*, *Fortune*, or other business publications for articles that discuss challenges that a specific company or industry is facing. Based on the articles and the guidelines discussed in this chapter, create three to five slides that summarize these issues.

14.7 **Creating Effective Slides: Content and Design** You've been asked to give an informative 10-minute talk to a group of convention attendees on great things to see and do while visiting your hometown. Choose a structured or free-form design and create enough slides to fill your 10-minute time slot.

14.8 **Completing Electronic Presentations: Slide Sorter View** Download any business-oriented PowerPoint presentation from the Internet and use the *slide sorter view* to critique the content, layout, and design elements of this presentation. Edit and revise the slides to improve their overall effectiveness.

14.9 **Creating Effective Slides: Structured Versus Free-Form Design** Find a business-related slide presentation on SlideShare (**www.slideshare.net**) and analyze the design. Do you consider it structured or free form? Does the design help the audience understand and remember the

ELEMENT OF PRESENTATION PROCESS	ALWAYS	FREQUENTLY	OCCASIONALLY	NEVER
1. I start by defining my purpose.	____	____	____	____
2. I analyze my audience before writing an oral presentation.	____	____	____	____
3. I match my presentation length to the allotted time.	____	____	____	____
4. I begin my oral presentations with an attention-getting introduction.	____	____	____	____
5. I look for ways to build credibility as a speaker.	____	____	____	____
6. I cover only a few main points in the body of my presentation.	____	____	____	____
7. I use transitions to help listeners follow my ideas.	____	____	____	____
8. I review main points and describe next steps in the close.	____	____	____	____
9. I practice my presentation beforehand.	____	____	____	____
10. I prepare in advance for questions and objections.	____	____	____	____
11. I conclude oral presentations by summarizing my main idea.	____	____	____	____

message? Why or why not? What improvements would you suggest to the design?

14.10 Internet Creating hyperlinks to live websites can perk up an electronic presentation, but it requires being prepared for the unexpected. What are some of the obstacles you might encounter when creating live Internet links? How can you prepare in advance to overcome such obstacles?

Expand Your Knowledge

Learning More on the Web

Learn from the Presentation Pros

www.presentations.com

The online home of *Presentations* magazine offers a wealth of articles that offer practical advice on creating and delivering business presentations. Under the "Presentations" tab, browse the "Creation," "Delivery," "Venue," "Technology," and "Products" sections to find resources that will help you complete the following tasks.

1. Find several articles that discuss the unique challenges of making presentations at trade shows. Identify three to five tips that will help you succeed in these environments.
2. Find a recent article that discusses tips, techniques, or traps of using PowerPoint for business presentations. Summarize the article's advice in a brief message that could be posted on your company's internal blog.
3. Find one or more articles that discuss techniques for improving vocal delivery. Identify three points that speakers can use to make more effective use of their voice during presentations.

Sharpening Your Career Skills Online

Bovée and Thill's Business Communication Web Search, at **http://businesscommunicationblog.com/websearch**, is a unique research tool designed specifically for business communication research. Use the Web Search function to find a website, video, PDF document, podcast, or PowerPoint presentation that offers advice on developing and delivering business presentations. Write a brief e-mail message to your instructor, describing the item that you found and summarizing the career skills information you learned from it.

Improve Your Grammar, Mechanics, And Usage

The following exercises help you improve your knowledge of and power over English grammar, mechanics, and usage. Turn to the Handbook of Grammar, Mechanics, and Usage at the end of this book and review all of Sections 3.1 (Capitalization), 3.2 (Underscores and Italics), and 3.3 (Abbreviations). Then look at the following 10 items. Circle the letter of the preferred choice in the following groups of sentences. (Answers to these exercises appear on pages AK-3 and AK-4.)

1. a. Send this report to Mister H. K. Danforth, RR 1, Albany, NY 12885.
b. Send this report to Mister H. K. Danforth, Rural Route 1, Albany, New York 12885.
c. Send this report to Mr. H. K. Danforth, RR 1, Albany, NY 12885.

2. a. She received her MBA degree from the University of Michigan.
b. She received her Master of Business Administration degree from the university of Michigan.

3. a. Sara O'Rourke (a reporter from The <u>Wall Street Journal</u>) will be here Thursday.
b. Sara O'Rourke (a reporter from <u>The Wall Street Journal</u>) will be here Thursday.
c. Sara O'Rourke (a reporter from *The Wall Street Journal*) will be here Thursday.

4. a. The building is located on the corner of Madison and Center streets.
b. The building is located on the corner of Madison and Center Streets.

5. a. Call me at 8 a.m. tomorrow morning, PST, and I'll have the information you need.
b. Call me at 8 tomorrow morning, PST, and I'll have the information you need.
c. Call me tomorrow at 8 a.m. PST, and I'll have the information you need.

6. a. Whom do you think *Time* magazine will select as its Person of the Year?
b. Whom do you think *Time magazine* will select as its *Person of the Year*?
c. Whom do you think *Time magazine* will select as its Person of the Year?

7. a. The art department will begin work on Feb. 2, just one wk. from today.
b. The art department will begin work on February 2, just one week from today.
c. The art department will begin work on Feb. 2, just one week from today.

8. a. You are to meet him on friday at the UN building in NYC.
b. You are to meet him on Friday at the UN building in NYC.
c. You are to meet him on Friday at the un building in New York city.

9. a. You must help her distinguish between *i.e.* (which means "that is") and *e.g.* (which means "for example").
b. You must help her distinguish between <u>i.e.</u> (which means "that is") and *e.g.* (which means "for example").
c. You must help her distinguish between *i.e.* (which means <u>that is</u>) and *e.g.* (which means <u>for example</u>).

10. a. We plan to establish a sales office on the West coast.
b. We plan to establish a sales office on the west coast.
c. We plan to establish a sales office on the West Coast.

For additional exercises focusing on mechanics, visit mybcommlab. Click on Chapter 14, click on "Additional Exercises to Improve Your Grammar, Mechanics, and Usage," and then click on "20. Capitals" or "21. Word division."

CASES

Applying the Three-Step Writing Process to Cases

Apply each step to the following cases, as assigned by your instructor (refer to Figure 14.1).

PRESENTATION SKILLS PORTFOLIO BUILDER

1. Is anybody out there? Explaining Loopt's social mapping service.

How many times have you been out shopping or clubbing and wondered if any of your friends were in the neighborhood? A new *social mapping* service from Loopt can provide the answer. It lets you put yourself on a map that your friends can see on their mobile phones, and you can see their locations as well. You can even get automatic alerts whenever friends are near.

Your task: Create a brief presentation explaining the Loopt concept to someone who is comfortable using text messaging and other mobile phone features. Be sure to explain what type of phone is required and include one slide that discusses safety issues. You can learn more about it at www.loopt.com.[28]

PRESENTATION SKILLS PORTFOLIO BUILDER

2. I'll find my space somewhere else, thanks: Promoting alternatives to MySpace.

With a user base well on its way toward 200 million people, MySpace is the king of social networking sites. However, it doesn't appeal to everyone. Some people want to be able to customize their online presence more than MySpace allows, while others want more control over who sees what aspects of their online profiles.

Your task: Choose one of the lesser-known alternatives to MySpace, such as the customizable social networking site Ning (www.ning.com), the blogging site Vox (www.vox.com), the content sharing site eSnips (www.esnips.com), or any other site that offers some degree of social networking. Compare its features and functions to those of MySpace and prepare a brief presentation that highlights the similarities and differences of the two sites. In your presentation, identify the sort of people most likely to prefer the site you've chosen over MySpace.[29]

PRESENTATION SKILLS

3. Face to face: Updating management on your monthly progress.

Imagine that you've just completed the impressive-looking online progress report shown in Figure 12.4 (page 362), when your boss decides he'd like to hear a presentation from you instead.

Your task: Adapt the information in Figure 12.4 to a brief electronic slide show. Your boss might want to see maps of the four locations listed, so have slides with maps ready. (Because you don't have the specific addresses, just capture an online map for each general area. Lakewood and Glendale are suburbs of Denver, the University of Denver is south of downtown, and Pepsi Center is downtown.)

PRESENTATION SKILLS PORTFOLIO BUILDER

4. Hot topics: Identifying key elements in an important business issue.

In your job as a business development researcher for a major corporation, you're asked to gather and process information on a wide variety of subjects. Management has gained confidence in your research and analysis skills and would now like you to begin making regular presentations at management retreats and other functions. Topics are likely to include the following:

- Offshoring of U.S. jobs
- Foreign ownership of U.S. firms
- Employment issues involving immigrants
- Tax breaks offered by local and state governments to attract new businesses
- Economic impact of environmental regulations
- Government bailouts of troubled industries

Your task: Choose one of the topics from this list and conduct enough research to familiarize yourself with the topic. Identify at least three important issues that anyone involved with this topic should know about. Prepare a 10-minute presentation that introduces the topic, comments on its importance to the U.S. economy, and discusses the issues you've identified. Assume that your audience is a cross-section of business managers who don't have any particular experience in the topic you've chosen.

PRESENTATION SKILLS PORTFOLIO BUILDER

5. Check out my skill set: Describing five skills you've learned or developed in this class.

Depending on the sequence your instructor chose for this course, you've probably covered at least a dozen chapters at this point and learned or improved many valuable skills. Think through your progress and identify five business communication skills that you've either learned for the first time or developed during this course.

Your task: Create a six-slide presentation (using PowerPoint or another software or online solution, as directed by your instructor), with a title slide and five slides that describe each of the five skills you've identified. Be sure to explain how each skill could help you in your career. Use any visual style that you feel is appropriate for the assignment.

PRESENTATION SKILLS

6. Verizon on the horizon: Promoting the benefits of joining this communications giant.

In its competitive battles with AT&T, Sprint, T-Mobile, and other carriers, Verizon competes to attract and keep not just customers but top employees. Engineers and technicians obviously play a vital role in a technology company such as Verizon, but the firm also needs specialists in everything from accounting to public relations to real estate.

Your task: Prepare a brief presentation that Verizon recruiters could use at job fairs and other venues to entice both new graduates and experienced professionals to consider joining the company. Choose a structured or free-form design and then create an appropriate number of slides for a presentation that is at least 10 minutes but no longer than 15 (not including a question-and-answer period). Assume that the audience members have heard of Verizon but don't have any in-depth knowledge about the company. You can learn more about the company and the benefits of working there by visiting www22.verizon.com/jobs.

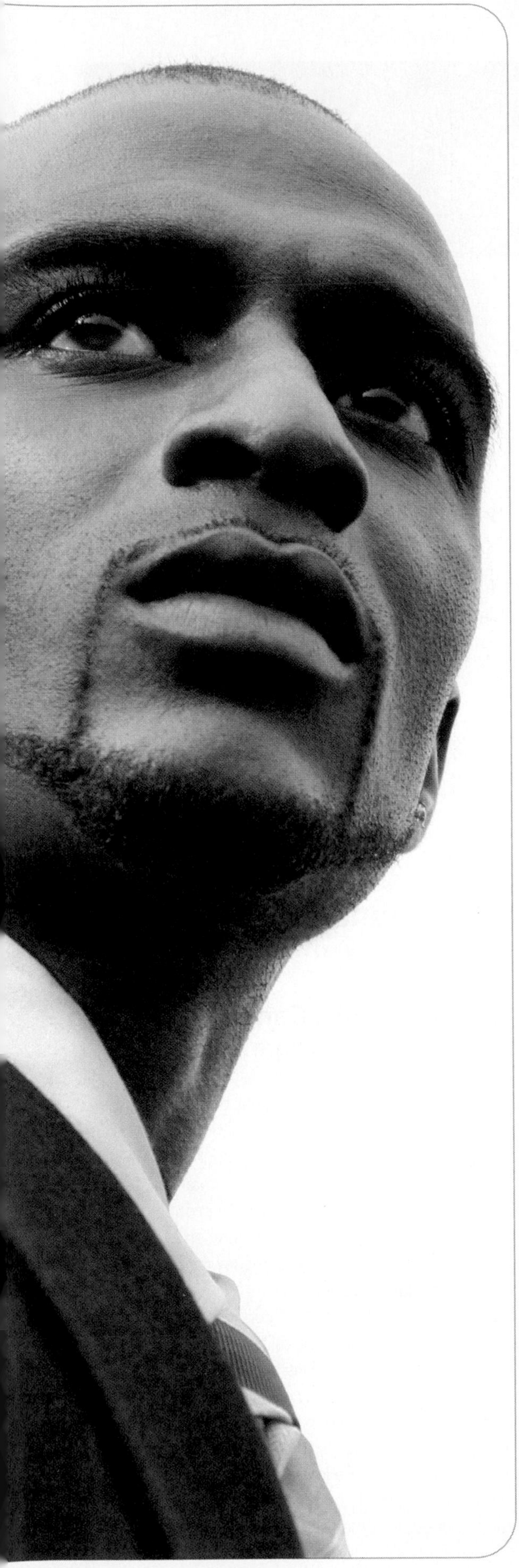

Part 5

Writing Employment Messages and Interviewing for Jobs

The same techniques you use to succeed in your career can also help you launch and manage that career. Understand the employer's perspective on the hiring process so that you can adapt your approach and find the best job in the shortest possible time. Learn the best ways to craft a résumé and the other elements in your job search portfolio. Understand the interviewing process to make sure you're prepared for every stage and every type of interview.

15 Building Careers and Writing Résumés

Learning Objectives

After studying this chapter, you will be able to

1. Describe the approach most employers take to finding potential new employees
2. Explain the importance of networking in your career search
3. Discuss how to choose the appropriate résumé organization, and list the advantages and disadvantages of the three common options
4. List the major sections of a traditional résumé
5. Identify six different formats in which you can produce a résumé
6. Describe what you should do to adapt your résumé to a scannable format

On the Job: Communicating at Hersha Hospitality Management

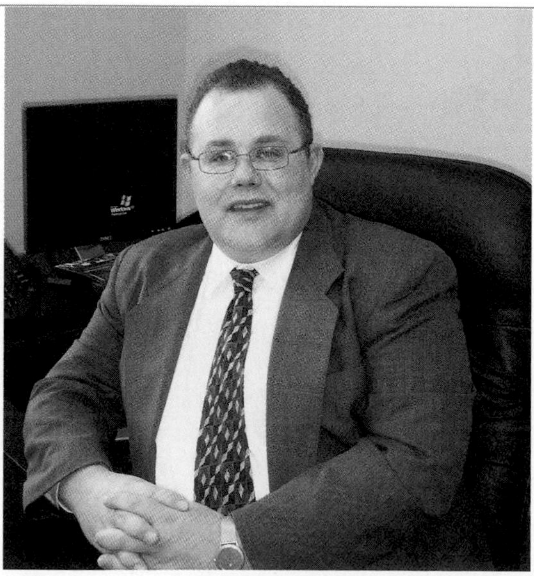

An applicant tracking system has helped Jeffrey Wade and his team at Hersha Hospitality Management efficiently recruit the customer service–driven employees on which Hersha relies.

Serving Up the Right Candidates for a Service-Driven Organization

For applicants, the job search process might be long and grueling, but at least it has a definite beginning, middle, and end. But for managers in charge of recruiting, such as Hersha Hospitality Management's vice president of human resources, Jeffrey Wade, the process never ends. Hersha provides operational management services to a growing number of hotels in the eastern United States, and as the company grows, its need to add top-quality employees continues.

Expansion is not the only force that puts demands on Wade and his team. "Recruiting in the hospitality industry is always a challenge because many of the positions are lower-wage jobs, and front-office positions are often filled by college students who want to move on with their careers," he explains. In other words, even as the company expands and needs to bring in more new employees, many existing employees are looking to move up and out. The result is relentless pressure to select new people to join the Hersha family. Moreover, Wade isn't interested in hiring just anybody; the company has extremely high customer service standards for everyone from entry-level hotel workers to top management.

Many managers in Wade's position, particularly in small to midsize companies, *outsource* the recruiting function, paying an outside company to find and filter candidates. However, Wade believes that recruiting is too essential to Hersha's success to be left in the hands of an outsider.

His answer to the challenge of endless hiring is to use an *applicant tracking system*, a computer-based solution that integrates the entire recruiting and employee records management effort—from job seekers' submission of online résumés and applications through interviewing, hiring, orientation, promotions, and eventual departure from the company. Although it is highly computerized, the process is far from impersonal. In fact, by managing all the details, the system frees up Wade and his staff to spend time with applicants, assessing their personalities and potential fit with Hersha's service-oriented culture.[1]

www.hershahotels.com

SECURING EMPLOYMENT IN TODAY'S JOB MARKET

Hersha's approach to managing the employee application process (profiled in the chapter-opening "On the Job" vignette) highlights the ever-evolving nature of the job market. To keep up with the demand for good employees—and the flood of résumés coming in from all over the Internet—many companies now use some form of automation to find the best candidates and shepherd them through the selection process.

Understanding how employers approach the hiring process is just one of many insights and skills you need in order to conduct a successful job search. Figure 15.1 shows the six most important tasks in the job search process. This chapter discusses the first two, and Chapter 16 explores the final four.

1 LEARNING OBJECTIVE

Describe the approach most employers take to finding potential new employees.

Understanding Employers' Approach to the Employment Process

You can save considerable time and effort in your job search by understanding how employers approach the recruiting process. Look at Figure 15.2 on the next page, and you'll notice that the easiest way for you to find out about new opportunities—through the employer's outside advertising—is the employer's *least-preferred* way of finding new employees. Some top employers find as many as 40 percent of new hires through employee referrals.[2] In fact, according to some estimates, up to 80 percent of all job openings are never advertised, a phenomenon known as the *hidden job market.*[3] In other words, employers have looked in quite a few other places before they come looking for you. To find the best opportunities, it's up to you to take action to get yourself noticed.

It's important to understand that the easiest way for you to find jobs (that is, through companies' help-wanted advertising) is the least-preferred channel for many companies to find new employees.

FIGURE 15.1 The Employment Search
Finding the ideal job opportunity is a six-step process that you might repeat a number of times during your career.

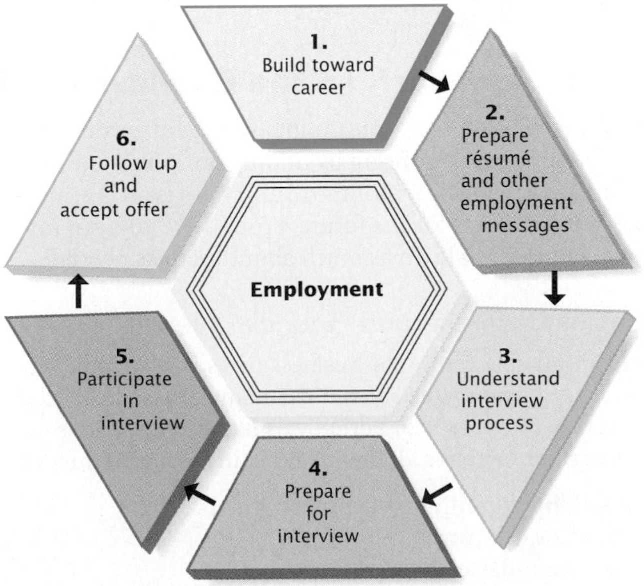

FIGURE 15.2 How Organizations Prefer to Find New Employees
Employers often prefer to look at their existing workforce to find candidates for new jobs and promotions. If no suitable candidates can be found, they begin to look outside the firm, starting with people whom company insiders already know.

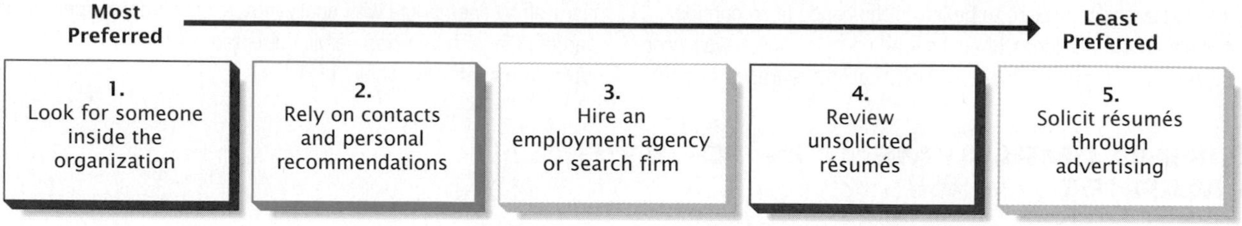
Most Preferred
Least Preferred
1. Look for someone inside the organization
2. Rely on contacts and personal recommendations
3. Hire an employment agency or search firm
4. Review unsolicited résumés
5. Solicit résumés through advertising

Beyond personal referrals, employers use a variety of methods to identify potential employees. According to one recent survey of large employers, companies' own websites are the number-one source of external hires.[4] Employers recruit candidates through on-campus visits, employment agencies, state employment services, temporary staffing services, the employment bureaus operated by some trade associations, and *headhunters* (recruiters who specialize in finding experienced executives and professionals for specific job openings). A growing number of employers now use social networking sites to develop relationships with potential employees.[5] Employers advertise job openings in a variety of news media, through search-engine advertising, and on *job boards* such as Monster and CareerBuilder.

REAL-TIME UPDATES
Learn More

Innovative job searches using social networking

Entrepreneur Willy Franzen describes a fascinating experiment he conducted in which job seekers used advertising on Facebook to target specific employers. Go to **http://real-timeupdates.com/ebc** and click on "Learn More." If you are using mybcommlab, you can access Real-Time Updates within each chapter or under Student Study Tools.

Many specialized websites are also now springing up to focus on narrow parts of the job market or offer technology that promises to do a better job of matching employers and job searchers. For example, Jobfox (**www.jobfox.com**) uses in-depth questionnaires to match employers and employees,[6] while Jobster (**www.jobster.com**) uses the latest social networking technologies to create a vast referral network that its corporate clients use to find potential employees.[7]

To keep tabs on all the applicants in various stages of the recruiting process, companies such as Hersha now use computerized **applicant tracking systems** to capture and store the hundreds or thousands of résumés they receive each year. These systems use a variety of filtering techniques to help recruiters find good prospects for current openings, so having the right terminology on your résumé is essential (see the information on keyword summaries on pages 488–490).[8]

Organizing Your Approach to the Employment Process

The employment process can be time-consuming, so organize your efforts carefully to be efficient and maximize your chances. Begin by finding out where the job opportunities are, which industries are strong, which parts of the country are growing, and which specific job categories offer the best prospects for the future. From there you can investigate individual organizations, doing your best to learn as much about them as possible.

Staying Abreast of Business and Financial News

With so many print and electronic resources available today, it's easy to stay in touch with what's happening in the business world.

Thanks to the Internet, staying on top of business news is easy today. In fact, your biggest challenge will be selecting new material from the many available sources. To help you get started, here is a selection of websites of periodicals that offer business news (in some cases, you need to be a subscriber to access all the material, including archives):

- *Wall Street Journal*: **http://online.wsj.com/public/us**
- *New York Times*: **www.nyt.com**
- *USA Today*: **www.usatoday.com**

- *BusinessWeek*: www.businessweek.com
- *Business 2.0*: www.business2.com
- *Fast Company*: www.fastcompany.com
- *Fortune*: www.fortune.com
- *Forbes*: www.forbes.com

In addition, thousands of bloggers and podcasters offer news and commentary on the business world. To identify some that you might find helpful, start with directories such as Technorati (www.technorati.com/blogs/tag/business) for blogs or Podcast Alley (www.podcastalley.com; select the "Business" genre) for podcasts. AllTop (http://alltop.com) is another good resource for finding people who write about topics that interest you. For all these online resources, use a newsfeed aggregator to select the type of stories you're interested in and have them delivered to your screen automatically.

Twitter has also become a great resource for business news, job leads, and other employment-related information. Using services such as TweepSearch (http://tweepsearch.com) or Just Tweet It (http://justtweetit.com) you can find Twitter users who specialize in your industry or profession.

— REAL-TIME UPDATES
Learn More

Use these checklists to organize your job search

A job search can be a long, exhausting process, but getting organized with these handy checklists will help you make the best use of your time. Go to **http://real-timeupdates.com/ebc** and click on "Learn More." If you are using mybcommlab, you can access Real-Time Updates within each chapter or under Student Study Tools.

Researching Specific Companies

Chapter 11 discusses how to find information on individual industries and companies, and it provides a list of helpful research resources. Review those sources, as well as professional journals and websites in the fields that interest you. When you've identified a promising industry and career field, consult directories of employers at your college library, at your career center, or on the web and compile a list of specific organizations that appeal to you.

Most companies, even small firms, offer at least basic information about themselves on their websites. Look for the "About Us" or "Company" part of the site to find a company profile, executive biographies, press releases, financial information, and information on employment opportunities. Any company's website is going to present the firm in the most positive light possible, of course, so look for outside sources as well, including the business sections of local newspapers and trade publications that cover the company's industries and markets.

Don't limit your research to easily available sources, however. Companies are likely to be impressed by creative research, such as interviewing their customers to learn more about how the firm does business. "Detailed research, including talking to our customers, is so rare it will almost guarantee you get hired," explains the recruiting manager at Alcon Laboratories.[9]

Go beyond every company's own communication materials; find out what others in their industries and communities think about them.

Table 15.1 lists some of the many websites where you can learn more about companies and find job openings. Start with The Riley Guide, www.rileyguide.com, which offers links to hundreds of specialized websites that post openings in specific industries and professions. Your college's career center placement office probably maintains an up-to-date list as well.

2 LEARNING OBJECTIVE

Explain the importance of networking in your career search.

Networking

Networking is the process of making informal connections with mutually beneficial business contacts. Networking takes place wherever and whenever people talk: at industry functions, at social gatherings, at sports events and recreational activities, at alumni reunions, and so on. Social networks, including Facebook, www.facebook.com, and business-oriented websites such as www.linkedin.com, www.ryze.com, and www.spoke.com, have become powerful networking resources. Read news sites, blogs, and other online sources. Follow industry leaders on Twitter or on *lifestreaming* sites, which integrate a person's text, audio, and video content from multiple social networking tools. Participate in

— REAL-TIME UPDATES
Learn More

Tweet your way to a sweet job

This simple introduction to Twitter focuses on using the microblogging service for career networking. Go to **http://real-timeupdates.com/ebc** and click on "Learn More." If you are using mybcommlab, you can access Real-Time Updates within each chapter or under Student Study Tools.

JOBS ON WEB LOOKING

TABLE 15.1 Netting a Job on the Web

WEBSITE*	URL	HIGHLIGHTS
Riley Guide	www.rileyguide.com	Vast collection of links to both general and specialized job sites for every career imaginable; don't miss this one—it'll save you hours and hours of searching
CollegeRecruiter.com	www.collegerecruiter.com	Focused on opportunities for graduates with less than three years of work experience
Monster	www.monster.com	One of the most popular job sites, with hundreds of thousands of openings, many from hard-to-find small companies; extensive collection of advice on the job search process
MonsterTrak	www.monstertrak.com	Focused on job searches for new college grads; your school's career center site probably links here
Yahoo! Hotjobs	http://hotjobs.yahoo.com	Another leading job board; like Monster and CareerBuilder, offers extensive advice for job seekers
CareerBuilder	www.careerbuilder.com	One of the largest job boards; affiliated with more than 150 newspapers around the country
Jobster	www.jobster.com	Uses social networking to link employers with job seekers
USAJOBS	www.usajobs.opm.gov	The official job search site for the U.S. government, featuring everything from jobs for economists to astronauts to border patrol agents
IMDiversity	www.imdiversity.com	Good resource on diversity in the workplace, with job postings from companies that have made a special commitment to promoting diversity in their workforces
Dice.com	www.dice.com	One of the best sites for high-technology jobs
Net-Temps	www.nettemps.com	Popular site for contractors and freelancers looking for short-term assignments
WetFeet	www.wetfeet.com	Posts listings from companies looking for interns in a wide variety of professions
Simply Hired Indeed	www.simplyhired.com www.indeed.com	Specialized search engines that look for job postings on hundreds of websites worldwide; they find many postings that aren't listed on job board sites such as Monster

Note: This list represents only a small fraction of the hundreds of job-posting sites and other resources available online; be sure to check with your college's career center for the latest information.

Remember that you need to contribute to the networking process, too.

student business organizations, especially those with ties to professional organizations. Visit *trade shows* to learn about various industries and rub shoulders with people who work in those industries.[10] Don't overlook volunteering; you not only meet people but also demonstrate your ability to solve problems, plan projects, and so on. You can do some good while creating a network for yourself.

Remember that networking is about people helping each other, not just about other people helping you. Pay close attention to networking etiquette: Try to learn something about the people you want to connect with, don't overwhelm others with too many messages or requests, be succinct in all your communication efforts, don't give out other people's names and contact information without their permission to do so, never e-mail your résumé to complete strangers, and remember to say thank you every time someone helps you.[11]

To become a valued network member, you need to be able to help others in some way. You may not have any influential

— REAL-TIME UPDATES
Learn More

Follow these people to a new career

Alison Doyle maintains a great list of career experts to follow on Twitter. Go to **http://real-timeupdates.com/ebc** and click on "Learn More." If you are using mybcommlab, you can access Real-Time Updates within each chapter or under Student Study Tools.

contacts yet, but because you're actively researching a number of industries and trends in your own job search, you probably have valuable information you can share. Or you might simply be able to connect one person with another who can help. The more you network, the more valuable you become in your network—and the more valuable your network becomes to you.

Seeking Career Counseling

Your college's career center probably offers a wide variety of services, including individual counseling, job fairs, on-campus interviews, and job listings. Counselors can give you advice on résumé-writing software and provide workshops in job search techniques, résumé preparation, job readiness training, interview techniques, self-marketing, and more.[12] You can also find career planning advice online. Many of the websites listed in Table 15.1 offer articles and online tests to help you choose a career path, identify essential skills, and prepare to enter the job market.

Don't overlook the many resources available through your college's placement office.

PREPARING RÉSUMÉS

The job search process involves many forms of communication, but the centerpiece of this effort is a well-written résumé. Some job seekers are intimidated by the prospect of writing a résumé, but it is really just another specialized business message. Follow the three-step writing process, and it'll be easier than you think (see Figure 15.3).

FIGURE 15.3 Three-Step Writing Process for Résumés
Following the three-step writing process will help you create a successful résumé in a short time. Remember to pay particular attention to the "you" attitude and presentation quality; your résumé will probably get tossed aside if it doesn't speak to audience needs or if it contains mistakes.

1 Plan →

Analyze the Situation
Recognize that the purpose of your résumé is to get an interview, not to get a job.

Gather Information
Research target industries and companies so that you know what they're looking for in new hires; learn about various jobs and what to expect; learn about the hiring manager, if possible.

Select the Right Medium
Start with a traditional paper résumé and develop scannable, electronic plain-text, HTML, or PDF versions, as needed. Consider using PowerPoint and video for your e-portfolio.

Organize the Information
Choose an organizational model that highlights your strengths and downplays your shortcomings; use the chronological approach unless you have a strong reason not to.

2 Write →

Adapt to Your Audience
Plan your wording carefully so that you can catch a recruiter's eye within seconds; translate your education and experience into attributes that target employers find valuable.

Compose the Message
Write clearly and succinctly, using active, powerful language that is appropriate to the industries and companies you're targeting; use a professional tone in all communications, even when using e-mail.

3 Complete

Revise the Message
Evaluate content and review readability and then edit and rewrite for conciseness and clarity.

Produce the Message
Use effective design elements and suitable layout for a clean, professional appearance; seamlessly combine text and graphical elements.

Proofread the Message
Review for errors in layout, spelling, and mechanics; mistakes can cost you interview opportunities.

Distribute the Message
Deliver your résumé following the specific instructions of each employer or job board website.

Planning Your Résumé

As with other business messages, planning a résumé means analyzing your purpose and your audience, gathering information, choosing the best medium, and organizing your content.

Analyzing Your Purpose and Audience

When you view your résumé as a persuasive business message, it's easier to decide what should and shouldn't be in it.

A **résumé** is a structured, written summary of a person's education, employment background, and job qualifications. Before you begin writing a résumé, make sure you understand its true function: It is a persuasive business message intended to stimulate an employer's interest in meeting you and learning more about you (see Table 15.2). A successful résumé inspires a prospective employer to invite you to interview with the company. In other words, your purpose in writing your résumé is to create interest—*not* to tell readers every little detail.[13]

Because you've already completed a good deal of research on specific companies, you should know quite a bit about the organizations you'll be applying to. But take some time now to learn what you can about the individuals who may be reading your résumé. For example, if you learned of an opportunity through your networking efforts, chances are you'll have both a contact name and some personalized advice to help fine-tune your writing. Search online using the person's name; you might find him or her mentioned in a news release, magazine article, or blog. Any bit of information can help you craft a more effective message. Even if you can't identify a specific hiring manager, try to put yourself in his or her shoes so that you can tailor your résumé to satisfy your audience's needs. Why would that person be interested in learning more about you?

By the way, if employers ask to see your "CV," they're referring to your *curriculum vitae*, the term used instead of *résumé* in some professions and in many countries outside the United States. Résumés and CVs are essentially the same, although CVs can be more detailed. If you need to adapt a U.S.-style résumé to CV format, or vice versa, see Monster.com, which offers helpful guidelines on the subject.

Gathering Pertinent Information

If you haven't been building an employment portfolio thus far, you may need to do some research on yourself at this point. Gather all the pertinent personal history you can think of, including all the specific dates, duties, and accomplishments from any previous jobs you've held. Collect every piece of relevant educational experience that adds to your qualifications—formal degrees, skills certificates, academic awards, or scholarships. Also, gather any relevant information about personal endeavors: dates of your membership in associations, offices you have held in any club or professional organization, any presentations you

TABLE 15.2 Fallacies and Facts About Résumés

FALLACY	FACT
The purpose of a résumé is to list all your skills and abilities.	The purpose of a résumé is to kindle employer interest and generate an interview.
A good résumé will get you the job you want.	All a résumé can do is get you in the door.
Your résumé will always be read carefully and thoroughly.	In most cases, your résumé needs to make a positive impression within 30 or 45 seconds; only then will someone read it in detail. Moreover, it may be screened by a computer looking for keywords first—and if it doesn't contain the right keywords, a human being may never see it.
The more good information you present about yourself in your résumé, the better, so stuff your résumé with every positive detail you can think of.	Recruiters don't need that much information about you at the initial screening stage, and they probably won't read it.
If you want a really good résumé, have it prepared by a résumé service.	You have the skills needed to prepare an effective résumé, so prepare it yourself—unless the position is especially high level or specialized. Even then, you should check carefully before using a service.

have given to community groups. You probably won't use every piece of information you come up with, but you'll want to have it at your fingertips before you begin composing your résumé.

Selecting the Best Medium

You should expect to produce your résumé in several media; "Producing Your Résumé" on page 486 explores the various options. No matter how many different media you eventually use, however, it's always a good idea to prepare a traditional paper résumé and keep copies on hand. You never know when someone might ask for it, and not all employers want to bother with electronic media when all they want to know is your basic profile. In addition, starting with a paper résumé is a great way to organize your background information and identify your unique strengths.

Organizing Your Résumé Around Your Strengths

3 LEARNING OBJECTIVE

Discuss how to choose the appropriate résumé organization, and list the advantages and disadvantages of the three common options.

Organize your résumé to highlight several qualities employers seek: that you (1) think in terms of results, (2) know how to get things done, (3) are well rounded, (4) show signs of career progress and professional development, (5) have personal standards of excellence, (6) are flexible and willing to try new things, and (7) communicate effectively.

In each category, align your career objectives with the needs of your target employers, without distorting or misrepresenting the facts.[14] If you have any significant weaknesses in your history, here are some common problems and quick suggestions for overcoming them:[15]

The key to organizing a résumé is aligning your personal strengths with both the general and specific qualities that your target employers are looking for.

Frequent job changes and gaps in your work history are two of the most common issues that employers may perceive as weaknesses, so plan to address these if they pertain to you.

- **Frequent job changes or contracting assignments.** Group similar jobs and contracts under a single heading. If past job positions were eliminated as a result of layoffs or mergers, find a subtle way to convey that information (if not in your résumé, then in your cover letter).
- **Gaps in work history.** Mention relevant experience and education you gained during employment gaps, such as volunteer or community work. If gaps are due to personal circumstances such as injuries, illness, or caring for a relative, you can use a cover letter to offer honest but general explanations about your absences ("I had serious health concerns and had to take time off to fully recover").
- **Inexperience.** Mention related volunteer work. List relevant course work and internships. If appropriate, offer hiring incentives such as "willing to work nights and weekends."
- **Overqualification.** Tone down your résumé, focusing exclusively on the experience and skills that relate to the position.
- **Long-term employment with one company.** Itemize each position held at the firm to show career progress with increasing responsibilities.
- **Job termination for cause.** Be honest with interviewers. Show that you're a hard-working employee and counter their concerns with proof, such as recommendations and examples of completed projects.
- **Criminal record.** You don't necessarily need to disclose on your résumé a criminal record or time spent incarcerated, but you may be asked about it on a job application form. Laws regarding what employers may ask (and whether they can conduct a criminal background check) vary by state and profession, but if you are asked and the question applies to you, you must answer truthfully, or you risk being terminated later if the employer finds out. Use the interview process to explain any mitigating circumstances and to emphasize your rehabilitation and commitment to being a law-abiding, trustworthy employee.[16]

To focus attention on your strongest points, adopt the appropriate organizational approach for your résumé, based on your background and your goals.

The Chronological Résumé

In a **chronological résumé**, the work experience section dominates and is placed in the most prominent slot, immediately after your name and address and optional objective. List your jobs sequentially in reverse order, beginning with the most recent position. Under each listing, describe your responsibilities and accomplishments, giving the most space to the most recent and most relevant positions. If you're just graduating from college and have limited professional experience, you can vary this chronological approach by putting your educational qualifications before your experience.

The chronological résumé is the most common résumé approach, but it might not be right for you at a particular stage in your career.

The chronological approach is the most common way to organize a résumé, and many employers prefer it. This approach has three key advantages: (1) Employers are familiar with it and can easily find information, (2) it highlights growth and career progression, and (3) it highlights employment continuity and stability.[17] As vice president with Korn/Ferry International, Robert Nesbit speaks for many hiring managers and recruiters when he says, "Unless you have a really compelling reason, don't use any but the standard chronological format. I want to be able to grasp quickly where a candidate has worked, how long, and in what capacities."[18]

The chronological approach is especially appropriate if you have a strong employment history and are aiming for a job that builds on your current career path (see Figures 15.4 and 15.5).

FIGURE 15.4 Ineffective Chronological Résumé
This chronological résumé exhibits a wide range of problems. The language is self-centered and unprofessional, and the organization forces the reader to dig out essential details—and today's recruiters don't have the time or the patience for that. Compare this with the improved version in Figure 15.5.

Roberto Cortez

5687 Crosswoods Drive, Falls Church, Virginia 22046
Home: (703) 987-0086 Office: (703) 549-6624
Email: rcortez@silvernet.com

Fails to provide an introductory statement of any kind, forcing the reader to piece together what this applicant is all about

I have been staff accountant/financial analyst at Inter-American Imports in Alexandria, Virginia, from March 2005 to present.

Organizes information chronologically but hides that fact with awkward format

- I have negotiated with major suppliers.
- I speak both Spanish and German fluently, and I was recently encouraged to implement an electronic funds transfer for vendor disbursements.
- In my current position, I am responsible for preparing accounting reports.
- I have audited financial transactions.
- I have also been involved in the design of a computerized model to adjust accounts for fluctuations in currency exchange rates.
- I am skilled in the use of Excel, Access, Microsoft Dynamics, and SAP Business One.
- I am deeply knowledgeable regarding Sarbox reporting.

Uses bulleted lists ineffectively: items are poorly organized, lack parallelism, use "I" too often, use too many words, and fail to highlight most important skills

Fails to highlight skills and attributes that will be valuable to a future employer

Was staff accountant with Monsanto Agricultural Chemicals in Mexico City, Mexico (October 2001 to March 2005).

- While with Monsanto in Mexico City, I was responsible for budgeting and billing.
- I am responsible for credit-processing functions.
- I was also responsible for auditing the travel and entertainment expenses for the sales department.
- I launched an online computer system to automate all accounting functions.
- Also during this time, I was able to travel extensively in Latin America.

Fails to use headings, making it difficult to find key information

Uses too many words to describe education and lacks parallelism

I have my Master of Business Administration with emphasis on international business, which I earned while attending George Mason University in Fairfax, Virginia, from 1999 to 2001.

Bachelor of Business Administration, Accounting (1996–1999), earned while attending University of Texas in Austin, Texas.

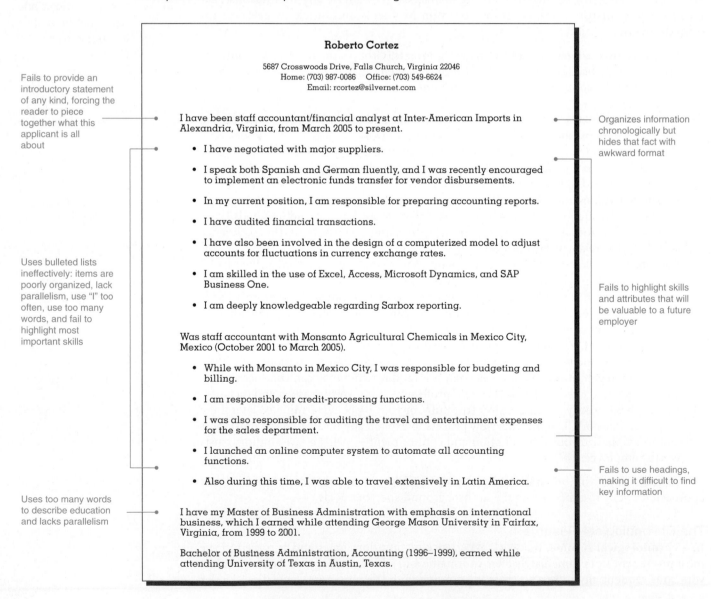

FIGURE 15.5 Effective Chronological Résumé
This version does a much better job of presenting the candidate's ability to contribute to a new employer. Notice in particular how easy it is to scan through this résumé to find sections of interest.

ROBERTO CORTEZ
5687 Crosswoods Drive
Falls Church, Virginia 22046
Home: (703) 987-0086 Office: (703) 549-6624
E-mail: RCortez@silvernet.com

International Accounting Management — Experienced international accountant and financial analyst with proven leadership, planning, negotiating, and intercultural communication skills. Demonstrated ability to improve process efficiency and reduce operating costs.

Experience

3/2005 to present — **Staff Accountant/Financial Analyst**
Inter-American Imports: Alexandria, Virginia

- Prepare accounting reports for wholesale giftware importer ($15 million annual sales)
- Audit financial transactions with suppliers in 12 Latin American countries
- Verify Sarbanes-Oxley process and reporting standards
- Serve as project and team leader
- Created a computerized model to adjust accounts for fluctuations in currency exchange rates
- Negotiated joint-venture agreements with major suppliers in Mexico and Colombia
- Implemented electronic funds transfer for vendor disbursements, improving cash flow and eliminating payables clerk position

10/2001 to 3/2005 — **Staff Accountant**
Monsanto Agricultural Chemicals: Mexico City, Mexico

- Handled budgeting, billing, and credit-processing functions for the Mexico City branch
- Audited travel & entertainment expenses for Monsanto's 30-member Latin American sales force
- Helped launch an online system to automate all accounting functions, improving reporting accuracy by 65%

Education

6/2001 — **Master of Business Administration with emphasis in international business**
George Mason University, Fairfax, Virginia

5/1999 — **Master of Business Administration Accounting**
University of Texas, Austin, Texas

Special Skills

Cultural
- Fluent in Spanish and German
- Extensive business contacts in Latin America

Technical
- Proficient with a wide range of financial software and systems, including Excel, Access, Microsoft Dynamics, and SAP Business One

"Brands" himself as a management candidate with this title for his qualifications summary—and also subtly expresses his career objective

Succinctly summarizes his qualifications for an international accounting management job; an employer can "get" who he is in a matter of seconds

Presents specific skills and accomplishments in easy-to-skim bullet format

Uses side heads to make major sections easy to find

Doesn't go into detail about education because he has been out of college for almost a decade

Highlights a few special skills, focusing on talents that employers value in this position

1 Plan →

Analyze the Situation
Decide on the best way to combine finance and international experience.

Gather Information
Research target positions to identify key employer needs.

Select the Right Medium
Start with a traditional paper résumé and develop scannable or plain-text versions as needed.

Organize the Information
Open with a qualifications summary that also signals the career objective; choose the chronological format since it fits this strong employment history perfectly.

2 Write →

Adapt to Your Audience
Translate specific experience into general qualifications that all multinational companies will find valuable.

Compose the Message
Write clearly and succinctly, using active, powerful language that is appropriate to the accounting management profession.

3 Complete

Revise the Message
Evaluate content and review readability, clarity, and accuracy.

Produce the Message
Use effective design elements and suitable layout for a clean, professional appearance.

Proofread the Message
Review for errors in layout, spelling, and mechanics.

Distribute the Message
Deliver the résumé and other employment messages following the specific instructions of each employer or job board website.

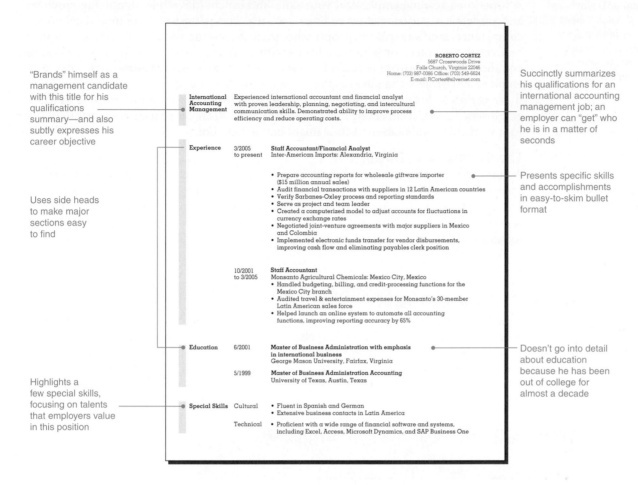

The Functional Résumé

The functional résumé is often used by people with little employment history or with gaps in their work history, but some employers suspect that people who use this approach are trying to hide weaknesses in their backgrounds.

A **functional résumé** emphasizes your skills and capabilities while identifying employers and academic experience in subordinate sections. This pattern stresses individual areas of competence, so it's useful for people who are just entering the job market, who want to redirect their careers, or who have little continuous career-related experience. However, you should be aware that because a functional résumé can obscure your work history, many employment professionals are suspicious of it—and some assume that candidates who use it are trying to hide something. In fact, Monster lists the functional résumé as one of employers' "Top 10 Pet Peeves."[19] If you don't have a strong, uninterrupted history of relevant work, the combination résumé might be a better choice.

The Combination Résumé

If you don't have a lot of work history, consider a combination résumé to highlight your skills while still providing a chronological history of your employment.

A **combination résumé** includes the best features of the chronological and functional approaches (see Figure 15.6). Nevertheless, it is not commonly used, and it has two major disadvantages: (1) It tends to be longer than a chronological résumé, and (2) it can be repetitious if you have to list your accomplishments and skills in both the functional section and the chronological job descriptions.[20]

FIGURE 15.6 Combination Résumé

With her limited work experience in her field of interest, Erica Vorkamp opted for a combination résumé to highlight her skills. Her employment history is complete and easy to find, but it isn't featured to the same degree as the other elements. Note that even though this is a webpage, she mimicked a conventional résumé design to make her information easy to find. Having an HTML version as part of her e-portfolio also lets her provide instant links to other information, such as samples of her work and testimonials from people who have worked with her in the past.

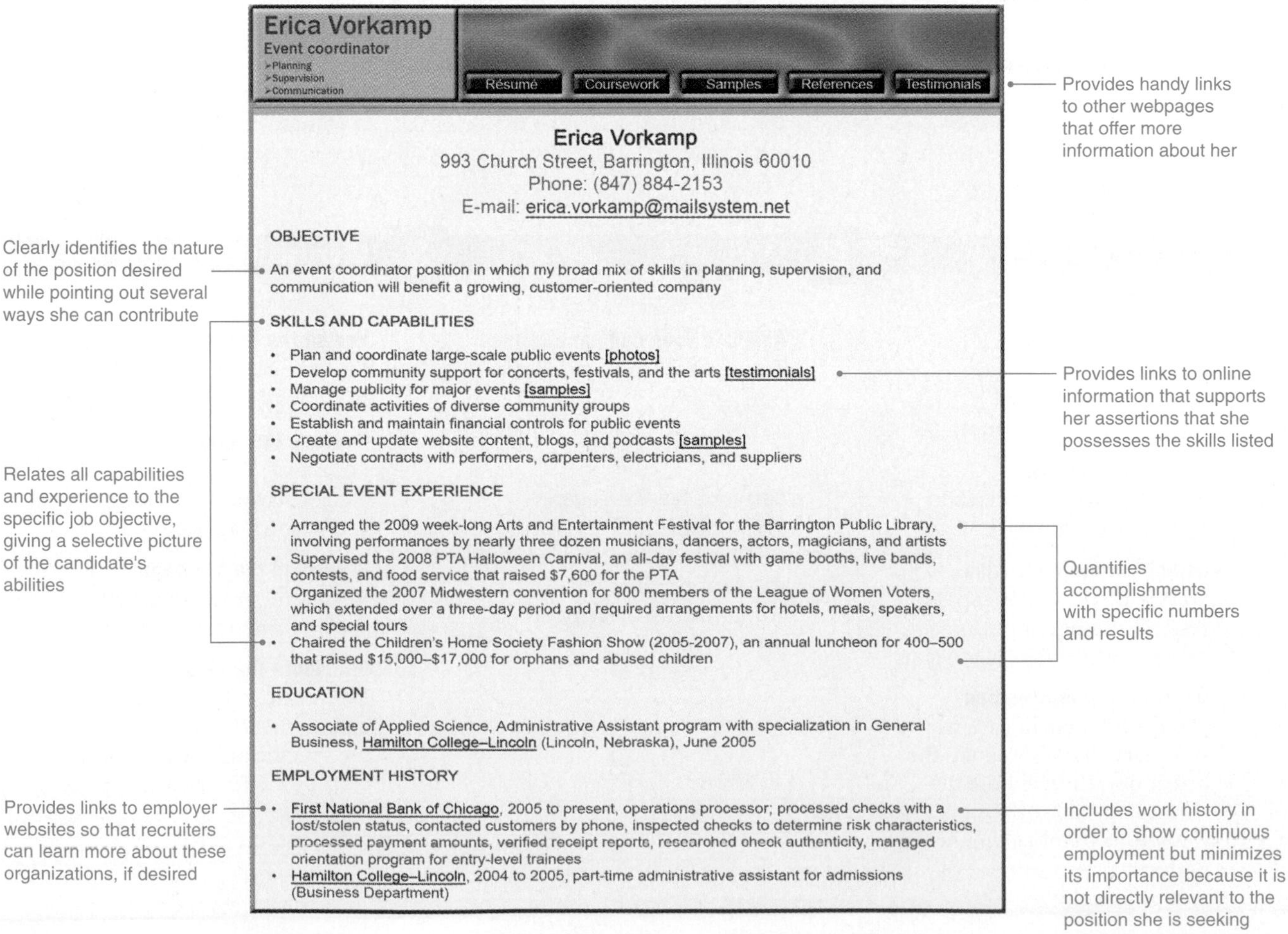

Erica Vorkamp
Event coordinator
>Planning
>Supervision
>Communication

Résumé | Coursework | Samples | References | Testimonials

Erica Vorkamp
993 Church Street, Barrington, Illinois 60010
Phone: (847) 884-2153
E-mail: erica.vorkamp@mailsystem.net

OBJECTIVE

An event coordinator position in which my broad mix of skills in planning, supervision, and communication will benefit a growing, customer-oriented company

SKILLS AND CAPABILITIES

- Plan and coordinate large-scale public events [photos]
- Develop community support for concerts, festivals, and the arts [testimonials]
- Manage publicity for major events [samples]
- Coordinate activities of diverse community groups
- Establish and maintain financial controls for public events
- Create and update website content, blogs, and podcasts [samples]
- Negotiate contracts with performers, carpenters, electricians, and suppliers

SPECIAL EVENT EXPERIENCE

- Arranged the 2009 week-long Arts and Entertainment Festival for the Barrington Public Library, involving performances by nearly three dozen musicians, dancers, actors, magicians, and artists
- Supervised the 2008 PTA Halloween Carnival, an all-day festival with game booths, live bands, contests, and food service that raised $7,600 for the PTA
- Organized the 2007 Midwestern convention for 800 members of the League of Women Voters, which extended over a three-day period and required arrangements for hotels, meals, speakers, and special tours
- Chaired the Children's Home Society Fashion Show (2005-2007), an annual luncheon for 400–500 that raised $15,000–$17,000 for orphans and abused children

EDUCATION

- Associate of Applied Science, Administrative Assistant program with specialization in General Business, Hamilton College–Lincoln (Lincoln, Nebraska), June 2005

EMPLOYMENT HISTORY

- First National Bank of Chicago, 2005 to present, operations processor; processed checks with a lost/stolen status, contacted customers by phone, inspected checks to determine risk characteristics, processed payment amounts, verified receipt reports, researched check authenticity, managed orientation program for entry-level trainees
- Hamilton College–Lincoln, 2004 to 2005, part-time administrative assistant for admissions (Business Department)

Provides handy links to other webpages that offer more information about her
Clearly identifies the nature of the position desired while pointing out several ways she can contribute
Provides links to online information that supports her assertions that she possesses the skills listed
Relates all capabilities and experience to the specific job objective, giving a selective picture of the candidate's abilities
Quantifies accomplishments with specific numbers and results
Provides links to employer websites so that recruiters can learn more about these organizations, if desired
Includes work history in order to show continuous employment but minimizes its importance because it is not directly relevant to the position she is seeking

As you look at a number of sample résumés, you'll probably notice variations on the three basic formats presented here. Study these other options in light of effective communication principles; if you find one that seems like a good fit for your unique situation, by all means use it.

Writing Your Résumé

Early in the evaluation process, your résumé might be the only information employers have about you, so make sure that information is clear and compelling.

As you follow the three-step process to develop your résumé, keep four points in mind. First, treat your résumé with the respect it deserves. A single mistake or oversight can cost you interview opportunities. Second, give yourself plenty of time. Don't put off preparing your résumé until the last second and then try to write it in one sitting. Third, learn from good models. You can find sample résumés online at college websites and job sites such as Monster.com. Fourth, don't get frustrated by the conflicting advice you'll read about résumés. Résumés are more art than science, and there is more than one way to be successful with them. Consider the alternatives and choose the approach that makes the most sense to you, given everything you know about successful business communication.

If you feel uncomfortable writing about yourself, you're not alone. Many people, even accomplished writers, find it difficult to write their own résumés. If you get stuck, find a classmate or friend who is also writing a résumé and swap projects for a while. By working on each other's résumés, you might be able to speed up the process for both of you.

Keeping Your Résumé Honest

Somehow, the idea that "everybody lies on their résumés" has crept into popular consciousness, and dishonesty in the job search process has reached epidemic proportions. Estimates vary, but one comprehensive study uncovered lies about work history in more than 40 percent of the résumés tested.[21] And it's not just the simple fudging of facts here and there. Dishonest applicants are getting bolder all the time—going so far as to buy fake diplomas online, pay a computer hacker to insert their names into prestigious universities' graduation records, and sign up for services that offer phony employment verification.[22]

Applicants with integrity know they don't need to lie on their résumés to catch the attention of potential employers.

Applicants with integrity know they don't need to stoop to lying to compete in the job market. If you are tempted to stretch the truth, bear in mind that professional recruiters have seen every trick in the book, and employers who are fed up with the dishonesty are getting more aggressive at uncovering the truth. Nearly all employers do some form of background checking, from contacting references to verifying employment to checking for criminal records. In addition to using their own resources, U.S. companies now spend more than $2 billion each year on outside services that specialize in verifying résumés and application information.[23] Employers are also beginning to craft certain interview questions specifically to uncover dishonest résumé entries.[24]

More than 90 percent of companies that find lies on résumés refuse to hire the offending applicants, even if that means withdrawing formal job offers.[25] And even if you do sneak past these filters and get hired, you'll probably be exposed on the job when you can't live up to your own résumé. Résumé fabrications have been known to catch up to people many years into their careers, with embarrassing consequences. Given the networked nature of today's job market, lying on a résumé could haunt you for years—and you could be forced to keep lying throughout your career to hide the original misrepresentations on your résumé.[26]

If you're not sure whether to include or exclude a particular point, ask yourself this: Would you be willing to say the same thing to an interviewer in person? If not, don't say it in your résumé. Keep your résumé honest so that it represents who you really are and leads you toward jobs that are truly right for you.

Adapting Your Résumé to Your Audience

One of the biggest challenges in writing a résumé is to make your unique qualities quickly apparent to readers; they won't search through details if you don't look like an appealing candidate.

Your résumé needs to make a positive impression in a matter of seconds, so be sure to adopt a "you" attitude and think about your résumé from the employer's perspective. The single most important concept to keep in mind as you write your résumé is to translate your past accomplishments into perceived future potential. In other words, employers are certainly interested in what you've done for other organizations in the past, but they're more interested in what you can do for them in the future. If necessary, customize your résumé for individual companies, too.

You may also need to translate your skills and experiences into the terminology of the hiring organization. For instance, military experience can help a person develop a number of skills that are valuable in business, but military terminology can sound like a foreign language to people who aren't familiar with it. Isolate the important general concepts and present them in common business language. Similarly, educational achievements in other countries might not align with U.S. definitions of high schools, community colleges, technical and trade schools, and colleges and universities. If necessary, include a brief statement explaining how your degree or certificate relates to U.S. expectations—or how your U.S. degree relates to expectations in other countries, if you're applying for work abroad.

Although your résumé is a highly factual document, it should still tell the "story of you," giving readers a clear picture of the sort of employee you are.

Regardless of your background, it's up to you to combine your experiences into a straightforward message that communicates what you can do for your potential employer.[27] Think in terms of an image or a theme you'd like to project. Are you academically gifted? A strong leader? A well-rounded person? A creative genius? A technical wizard? By knowing yourself and your audience, you'll be able to focus on the strengths that potential employers want.

Composing Your Résumé

Draft your résumé using short, crisp phrases built around strong verbs and nouns.

Write your résumé using a simple and direct style. Use short, crisp phrases instead of whole sentences and focus on what your reader needs to know. Avoid using the word *I*, which can sound both self-involved and repetitious by the time you outline all your skills and accomplishments. Instead, start your phrases with strong action verbs such as these:[28]

accomplished	coordinated	initiated	participated	set up
achieved	created	installed	performed	simplified
administered	demonstrated	introduced	planned	sparked
approved	developed	investigated	presented	streamlined
arranged	directed	joined	proposed	strengthened
assisted	established	launched	raised	succeeded
assumed	explored	maintained	recommended	supervised
budgeted	forecasted	managed	reduced	systematized
chaired	generated	motivated	reorganized	targeted
changed	identified	operated	resolved	trained
compiled	implemented	organized	saved	transformed
completed	improved	oversaw	served	upgraded

For instance, you might say, "Created a campus organization for students interested in entrepreneurship" or "Managed a fast-food restaurant and four employees." Whenever you can, quantify the results so that your claims don't come across as empty puffery. Don't just say you're a team player or detail oriented—show you are by offering concrete proof.[29] Here are some examples of phrasing accomplishments using active statements that show results:

AVOID WEAK STATEMENTS	USE ACTIVE STATEMENTS THAT SHOW RESULTS
Responsible for developing a new filing system	Developed a new filing system that reduced paperwork by 50 percent
I was in charge of customer complaints and all ordering problems	Handled all customer complaints and resolved all product order discrepancies
I won a trip to Europe for opening the most new customer accounts in my department	Generated the highest number of new customer accounts in my department
Member of special campus task force to resolve student problems with existing cafeteria assignments	Assisted in implementing new campus dining program that balances student wishes with cafeteria capacity

Providing specific supporting evidence is vital but make sure you don't go overboard with small details.[30]

Name and Contact Information

4 LEARNING OBJECTIVE

List the major sections of a traditional résumé.

Be sure to provide complete and accurate contact information; mistakes in this section of the résumé are surprisingly common.

Your name and contact information constitute the heading of your résumé; include the following:

- Name
- Physical address (both permanent and temporary, if you're likely to move during the job search process; however, if you're posting a résumé in an unsecured location online, leave off your physical address for security purposes)
- E-mail address
- Phone number(s)
- The URL of your personal webpage or e-portfolio (if you have one)

Be sure that everything in your résumé heading is well organized and clearly laid out on the page.

If you don't already have one, get a professional-sounding e-mail address for business correspondence (such as firstname.lastname @something.com), if you don't already have one.

If the only e-mail address you have is through your current employer, get a free personal e-mail address from one of the many services that offer them. It's not fair to your current employer to use company resources for a job search; moreover, it sends a bad signal to potential employers. Also, if your personal e-mail address is anything like precious .princess@something.com or PsychoDawg@something.com, get a new e-mail address for your business correspondence.

Introductory Statement

Of all the parts of a résumé, the brief introductory statement that follows your name and contact information probably generates the most disagreement. You can put one of three things here:[31]

If you choose to open with a career objective, make sure it is phrased in terms of meeting an employer's needs, not your needs.

- **Career objective.** A career objective identifies either a specific job you want to land or a general career track you would like to pursue. Some experts advise against including a career objective because it can categorize you so narrowly that you miss out on interesting opportunities, and it is essentially about fulfilling your desires, not about meeting the employer's needs. In the past, most résumés included a career objective, but in recent years, more job seekers are using a qualifications summary or a career summary. However, if you have little or no work experience in your target profession, a career objective might be your best option. If you do opt for an objective, word it in a way that relates your qualifications to employer needs (see Figure 15.6 on page 480). Avoid such self-absorbed (but all too common) statements as "A fulfilling position that provides ample opportunity for career growth and personal satisfaction."
- **Qualifications summary.** A qualifications summary offers a brief view of your key qualifications. The goal is to let a reader know within a few seconds what you can deliver. You can title this section generically as "Qualifications Summary" or "Summary of Qualifications," or if you have one dominant qualification, you can use that as the title (see the career summary in Figure 15.5 on page 479 for an example). Consider using a qualifications summary if you have one or more important qualifications but don't yet have a long career history. Also, if you haven't been working long but your college education has given you a dominant professional "theme," such as multimedia design or taxation, you can craft a qualifications summary that highlights your educational preparedness.

A qualifications summary gives a quick overview of the value you can offer an employer.

- **Career summary.** A career summary offers a brief recap of your career, with the goal of presenting increasing levels of responsibility and performance. A career summary can be particularly useful for executives who have demonstrated the ability to manage increasingly larger and more complicated business operations—a key consideration when companies look to hire upper-level managers.

Education

Your education is likely to be one of your strongest selling points, so think carefully about how to present it.

If you're still in school, education is probably your strongest selling point. Present your educational background in depth, choosing facts that support your "theme." Give this section a heading such as "Education," "Technical Training," or "Academic Preparation," as appropriate. Then, starting with the most recent, list the name and location of each school you have attended, the month and year of your graduation (say "anticipated graduation in ____" if you haven't graduated yet), your major and minor fields of study, significant skills and abilities you've developed in your course work, and the degrees or certificates you've earned. If you're still working toward a degree, include in parentheses the expected date of completion. Showcase your qualifications by listing courses that have directly equipped you for the job you are seeking and indicate any scholarships, awards, or academic honors you've received.

The education section should also include relevant training sponsored by business or government organizations. Mention high school or military training only if the associated achievements are pertinent to your career goals.

Whether you list your grade point average (GPA) depends on the job you want and the quality of your grades. If you don't show your GPA on your résumé—and there's no rule saying you have to—be prepared to answer questions about it during the interview process because many employers will assume that your GPA is not spectacular if you didn't show it on your résumé. If you choose to show a GPA, be sure to mention the scale, especially if it isn't a four-point scale. If your grades are better within your major than in other courses, you can also list your GPA as "Major GPA" and include only those courses within your major.

Work Experience, Skills, and Accomplishments

When you describe past job responsibilities, be sure to relate them to the needs of potential employers; identify the skills and knowledge from these previous jobs that you can apply to a future job.

Like the education section, the work experience section should focus on your overall theme. Align your past with the employer's future. Call attention to the skills you've developed on the job and to your ability to handle increasing responsibility.

List your jobs in reverse chronological order (starting with the most recent). Include military service and any internships and part-time or temporary jobs related to your career objective. Include the name and location of the employer, and if readers are unlikely to recognize the organization, briefly describe what it does. When you want to keep the name of your current employer confidential, you can identify the firm by industry only ("a large video game developer"). If an organization's name or location has changed since you worked there, state the current name and location and include the old information preceded by "formerly . . . " Before or after each job listing, state your job title and list the years you worked in the job; use the phrase "to present" to denote current employment. Indicate whether a job was part time.

Whenever you can, quantify your accomplishments in numeric terms: sales increases, customer satisfaction scores, measured productivity, and so on.

Devote the most space to the jobs that are related to your target position. If you were personally responsible for something significant, be sure to mention it ("Devised a new collection system that accelerated payment of overdue receivables"). Facts about your skills and accomplishments are the most important information you can give a prospective employer, so quantify them whenever possible:

> Created an online ad campaign that increased sales by 9 percent
> Raised $2,500 in 15 days for cancer research

One helpful exercise is to write a 30-second "commercial" for each major skill you want to highlight. The commercial should offer proof that you really do possess the skill. For your résumé, distill the commercials down to brief phrases; you can use the more detailed proof statements in cover letters and as answers to interview questions.[32]

If you've held a number of part-time, temporary, or entry-level jobs that don't relate to your career objective, you have to use your best judgment when it comes to including or excluding them. On the one hand, employers will be impressed by the fact that you can land and keep jobs while you're progressing toward your career goals. On the other hand, too many minor and irrelevant work details can clutter your résumé, particularly if you've been in the professional workforce for a few years. Generally speaking, if you don't have a long employment history, use these jobs to show your ability and willingness to work.

You can also include information describing other aspects of your background that pertain to your career objective, such as fluency in multiple languages. If samples of your work might increase your chances of getting a job, insert a line at the end of your résumé, offering to supply them on request or indicating that they're available in your e-portfolio.

Activities and Achievements

Don't overlook personal accomplishments that indicate special skills or qualities, but make sure they are relevant to the jobs you're seeking.

Include activities and achievements outside of a work context only if they make you a more attractive job candidate. For example, membership in the Toastmasters public-speaking organization shows an interest in becoming a better communicator, which is something every smart employer values. Similarly, artistic awards could weigh in your favor if you are applying for work at a web design company or an advertising agency. However, unless you are applying to a running-shoe company such as Nike or New Balance, the fact that you are a long-distance runner is irrelevant. Also consider mentioning publications and other accomplishments that required relevant business skills.

Because many employers are involved in their local communities, they tend to look positively on applicants who are active and concerned members of their communities as well. Consider including community service activities that suggest leadership, teamwork, communication skills, technical aptitude, or other valuable attributes.

You should generally avoid indicating membership or significant activity in religious or political organizations (unless, of course, you're applying to such an organization) because doing so might raise concerns for people with differing beliefs or affiliations. However, if you want to highlight skills you developed while involved with such a group, you can refer to it generically as a "not-for-profit organization."

Finally, if you have little or no job experience and not much to discuss outside your education, indicating involvement in athletics or other organized student activities lets employers know that you don't spend all your free time hanging around your apartment, playing video games. However, this information becomes increasingly irrelevant the longer you have been out of school.

Personal Data

Do not include any personal data unless there is a specific reason to do so (there rarely is).

In nearly all instances, your résumé should not include any personal data beyond the information described in the previous sections. When applying to U.S. companies, never include any of the following: physical characteristics, age, gender, marital status, sexual orientation, religious or political affiliations, race, national origin, salary history, reasons for leaving jobs, names of previous supervisors, names of references, Social Security number, or student ID number. Also, never include a photo on or with your résumé—some employers won't even look at résumés with photos for fear of being accused of discrimination based on personal characteristics.[33]

Note that standards can vary in other countries. For example, you might be expected to include your citizenship, nationality, or marital status.[34] However, verify such requirements before including any personal data.

Prepare a list of references, using the same design and layout as your résumé.

The availability of references is usually assumed, so you don't need to put "References available upon request" at the end of your résumé. However, be sure to have a list of several references ready when you begin applying for jobs; you will probably be asked for it at some point in the selection process. Prepare your reference sheet with your name and contact information at the top. For a finished look, use the same design and layout you use for your résumé. Then list three or four people who have agreed to serve as references. (Don't list anyone who hasn't agreed to be listed.) Include each person's name, job title, organization, address, telephone number, and e-mail address (if the reference prefers to be contacted by e-mail).

Completing Your Résumé

As with any other business message, completing your résumé involves revising it for quality, producing it in an appropriate form, and proofreading it for any errors before distributing it to your target employers.

Sharpening Your Career Skills

Don't. Just Don't.

Even though employment recruiters might think they've seen it all by now, innovative job applicants will keep finding new ways to get their résumés tossed into the recycling bin. Here are a few examples for your amusement—and warning, if you're inclined to share a little too much information:

- The passing of a beloved pet is never easy, but should grief over a departed cat keep someone out of the workforce for three months? That's how one job applicant explained a three-month gap in his employment history.
- One applicant's résumé arrived in an envelope that had a picture of a car on it, along with an explanation saying this would be a gift for the hiring manager.
- A person's family medical history is obviously important to him or her, but it's not something to put on a résumé, as one job seeker did, for reasons unknown.
- In a valiant effort to cram as many mistakes as possible onto a single page, one creative candidate included a full body photo of herself—in thigh-high boots, no less—and used oversized, fluorescent pink paper. This résumé probably did look pretty as it fluttered off a recruiter's desk into the trash can.
- Expressing strong interest in a job is good, but not if that interest is expressed like this: "to keep my parole officer from putting me back in jail."
- One applicant's mother was proud of her, to be sure, but including a letter from her with a résumé made the applicant look like, well, a child.

These cringe-inducing blunders are worth more than a quick chuckle: They're a great reminder of why it is crucial to understand the purpose of a résumé and the effect a résumé has on hiring managers.

CAREER APPLICATIONS

1. Is it a good idea to "show some personality" in your résumé? Explain your answer.
2. How should you handle the employment section of your résumé if you really did take three months off work to grieve the loss of a pet?

The ideal length of your résumé depends on the depth of your experience and the level of the positions for which you are applying. As a general guideline, if you have fewer than 10 years of professional experience, try to keep your résumé to one page. If you have more experience and are applying for a higher-level position, you may need to prepare a somewhat longer résumé.[35] For highly technical positions, longer résumés are often the norm as well because the qualifications for such jobs can require more description.

Revising Your Résumé

Avoid common errors that will get your résumé excluded from consideration.

Ask professional recruiters to list the most common mistakes they see on résumés, and you'll hear the same things over and over again. Keep your résumé out of the recycling bin by avoiding these flaws:

- Too long or too wordy
- Too short or sketchy
- Difficult to read
- Poorly written
- Displaying weak understanding of the business world or of a particular industry
- Poor-quality printing or cheap paper
- Full of spelling and grammar errors
- Boastful
- Gimmicky design

Producing Your Résumé

Effective résumé designs are simple, clean, and professional—not gaudy, clever, or cute.

Good design is a must, and it's not difficult to achieve. As you can see in Figures 15.5 and 15.6, good designs are simple, are clearly organized, have plenty of white space, and use straightforward typefaces such as Times Roman or Arial. Make your subheadings easy to find and easy to read, placing them either above each section or in the left margin. Use lists to itemize important points. Color is not necessary by any means, but if you add color, make it subtle and sophisticated, such as using a thin horizontal line under your name and address. The most common way to get into trouble with résumé design is going overboard (see Figure 15.7). An amateurish design could end your chances of getting an interview.

FIGURE 15.7 Ineffective Résumé Design
This résumé tries too hard to be creative and eye-catching, resulting in a document that is difficult to read—and that probably won't get read. Recruiters have seen every conceivable design gimmick, so don't try to stand out from the crowd with unusual design. Instead, provide compelling, employer-focused information that is easy to find.

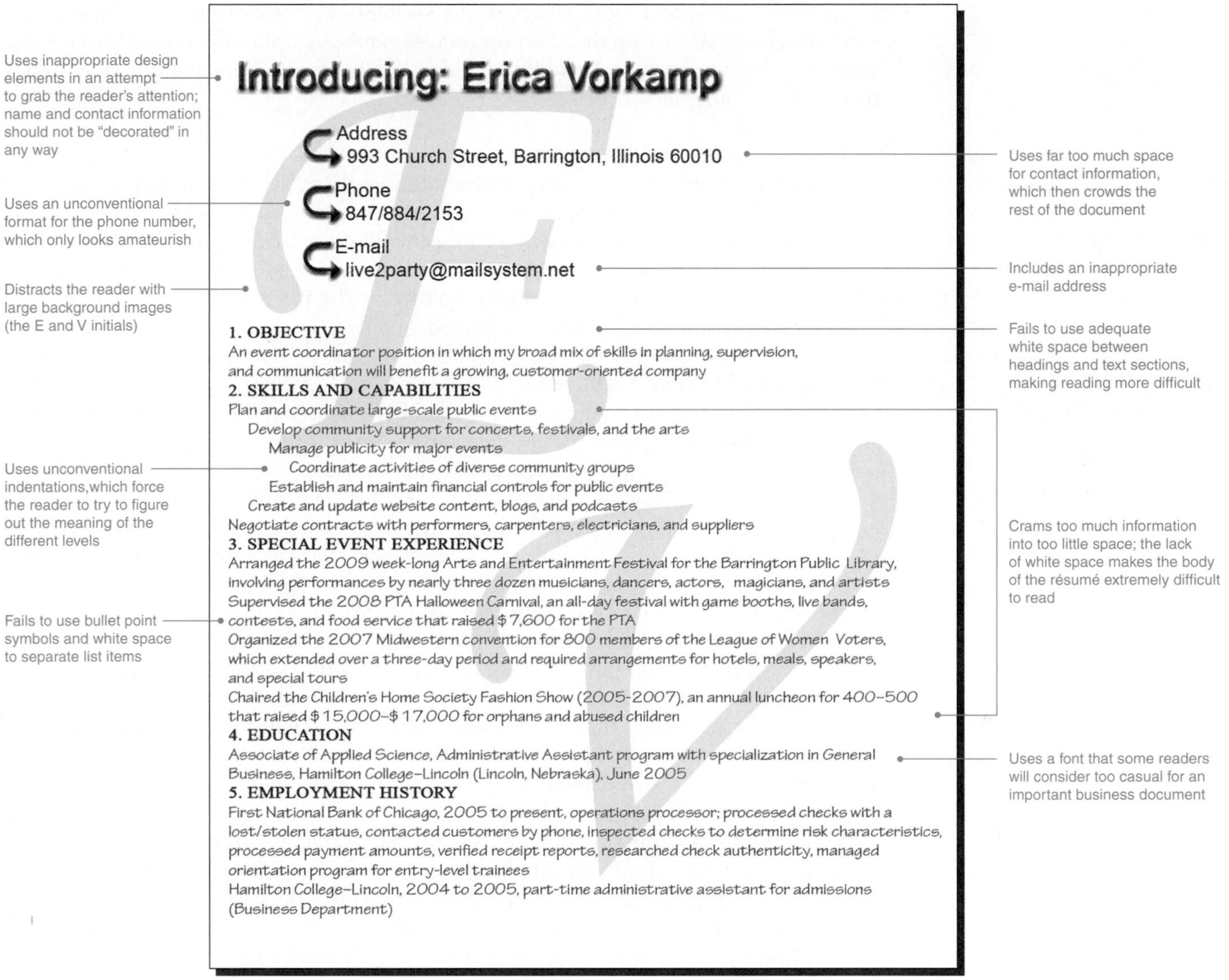
Introducing: Erica Vorkamp

Address
993 Church Street, Barrington, Illinois 60010

Phone
847/884/2153

E-mail
live2party@mailsystem.net

1. OBJECTIVE
An event coordinator position in which my broad mix of skills in planning, supervision, and communication will benefit a growing, customer-oriented company

2. SKILLS AND CAPABILITIES
Plan and coordinate large-scale public events
Develop community support for concerts, festivals, and the arts
Manage publicity for major events
Coordinate activities of diverse community groups
Establish and maintain financial controls for public events
Create and update website content, blogs, and podcasts
Negotiate contracts with performers, carpenters, electricians, and suppliers

3. SPECIAL EVENT EXPERIENCE
Arranged the 2009 week-long Arts and Entertainment Festival for the Barrington Public Library, involving performances by nearly three dozen musicians, dancers, actors, magicians, and artists
Supervised the 2008 PTA Halloween Carnival, an all-day festival with game booths, live bands, contests, and food service that raised $7,600 for the PTA
Organized the 2007 Midwestern convention for 800 members of the League of Women Voters, which extended over a three-day period and required arrangements for hotels, meals, speakers, and special tours
Chaired the Children's Home Society Fashion Show (2005-2007), an annual luncheon for 400-500 that raised $15,000-$17,000 for orphans and abused children

4. EDUCATION
Associate of Applied Science, Administrative Assistant program with specialization in General Business, Hamilton College-Lincoln (Lincoln, Nebraska), June 2005

5. EMPLOYMENT HISTORY
First National Bank of Chicago, 2005 to present, operations processor; processed checks with a lost/stolen status, contacted customers by phone, inspected checks to determine risk characteristics, processed payment amounts, verified receipt reports, researched check authenticity, managed orientation program for entry-level trainees
Hamilton College-Lincoln, 2004 to 2005, part-time administrative assistant for admissions (Business Department)

As one experienced recruiter put it, "At our office, these résumés are rejected without even being read."[36] Of course, if you are applying for a graphic design position or some other opportunity in which visual creativity is expected, you can certainly use your résumé as a way to demonstrate your design skills.[37]

Depending on the companies you apply to, you might want to produce your résumé in as many as six forms (all are explained in the following sections):

- Printed traditional résumé
- Printed scannable résumé
- Electronic plain-text file
- Microsoft Word file
- HTML format
- PDF file

Some applicants also create PowerPoint presentations or videos to supplement a conventional résumé. Two key advantages of a PowerPoint supplement are flexibility and

5 LEARNING OBJECTIVE

Identify six different formats in which you can produce a résumé.

Start with a traditional printed résumé but realize that you may need to create several other versions during your job search.

Using a PowerPoint presentation or a video can be a great way to supplement your résumé, but not all employers will view them.

multimedia capabilities. For instance, you can present a menu of choices on the opening screen and allow viewers to click through to such items as a brief biography or photos that document important accomplishments (such as screen shots of websites you designed).

A video résumé can be a compelling supplement as well, but videos are not without controversy. Some employment law experts advise employers not to view videos, at least not until after candidates have been evaluated solely on their credentials. The reason for this caution is the same as with photographs: Seeing visual cues of the age, ethnicity, and gender of candidates early in the selection process exposes employers to complaints of discriminatory hiring practices. In addition, videos are more cumbersome to evaluate than paper or electronic résumés.[38]

Printing a Traditional Résumé

Strive for a clean, classy look in your printed résumé, using professional-grade paper and a clean, high-quality printer.

The traditional paper résumé still has a place in this world of electronic job searches, if only to have a few copies ready whenever one of your networking contacts asks for one. Avoid basic, low-cost white bond paper intended for general office use and gimmicky papers with borders and backgrounds. Choose a heavier, higher-quality paper designed specifically for résumés and other important documents. White or slightly off-white is the best color choice. Finally, be sure to use a well-maintained, quality printer.

6 LEARNING OBJECTIVE

Describe what you should do to adapt your résumé to a scannable format.

Printing a Scannable Résumé

To cope with the flood of unsolicited paper résumés in recent years, many companies now optically scan incoming paper résumés into applicant tracking systems that hiring managers can search for attractive candidates. Whether they use simpler keyword matching or sophisticated linguistic analysis, these systems display lists of possible candidates, each with a percentage score indicating how closely the résumé reflects a given position's requirements.[39] Nearly all large companies now use these systems, as do many midsized companies and even some small firms.[40]

The use of scanning has important implications for your résumé. First, computers are interested only in matching information to search parameters, not in artistic attempts at résumé design. In fact, complex designs can cause errors in the scanning process. Second, *optical character recognition* (*OCR*) software doesn't technically "read" anything; it merely looks for shapes that match stored profiles of characters. If OCR software can't make sense of your fancy fonts or creative page layout, it will enter gibberish into the database. Third, even the most sophisticated databases cannot conduct a search with the nuance and intuition of an experienced human recruiter.

For job searchers, this situation creates two requirements for a successful scannable résumé: (1) Use a plain font and simplified design and (2) compile a **keyword summary** that lists all the terms that could help match your résumé to the right openings. Other than the keyword summary, a scannable résumé contains the same information as your traditional résumé but is formatted to be OCR friendly (see Figure 15.8):[41]

- Use a clean sans serif font such as Verdana or Arial and size it between 10 and 14 points.
- Make sure characters do not touch one another, including the slash (/).
- Don't use side-by-side columns.
- Don't use ampersands (&), percent signs (%), accented characters (such as é and ö), or bullet symbols (use a hyphen, not a lowercase *o*, in place of a bullet symbol).
- Put each phone number and e-mail address on its own line.
- Print on plain white paper.

Your scannable résumé will probably be longer than your traditional résumé; if it runs more than one page, make sure your name appears on each subsequent page. Before sending a scannable résumé, check the company's website or call the human resources department to see whether it has any specific requirements other than those discussed here.

Think carefully about the keywords you include in your scannable résumé; they need to appeal to recruiters and reflect your qualities accurately.

When adding a keyword summary (see Figure 15.8) to your résumé, keep your audience in mind. Employers generally search for nouns (because verbs tend to be generic rather than specific to a particular position or skill), so make your keywords nouns as well. Use abbreviations sparingly and only when they are well known and unambiguous, such as

FIGURE 15.8 Scannable Résumé
This version of the chronological résumé from Figure 15.5 shows the changes necessary to ensure successful scanning. Notice that the résumé doesn't have any special characters, formatting, or design elements that are likely to confuse the scanning software.

ROBERTO CORTEZ
5687 Crosswoods Drive
Falls Church, Virginia 22046
Home: (703) 987-0086
Office: (703) 549-6624
E-mail: RCortez@silvernet.com

Puts each contact element on its own line

KEYWORDS

Adds a summary of keywords taken from job descriptions and industry publications

Financial executive, accounting management, international finance, financial analyst, accounting reports, financial audit, exchange rates, Sarbanes-Oxley, joint-venture agreements, budgets, billing, credit processing, MBA, fluent Spanish, fluent German, Microsoft Dynamics, SAP Business One, leadership, planning, negotiating, Latin America

Uses enough white space to ensure successful scanning, without worrying about a pleasing visual design

INTERNATIONAL ACCOUNTING MANAGEMENT

Experienced international accountant and financial analyst with proven leadership, planning, negotiating, and intercultural communication skills. Demonstrated ability to improve process efficiency and reduce operating costs.

EXPERIENCE

Staff Accountant Financial Analyst, Inter-American Imports, Alexandria, Virginia, March 2005 to present
- Prepare accounting reports for wholesale giftware importer ($15 million annual sales)
- Audit financial transactions with suppliers in 12 Latin American countries
- Verify Sarbanes-Oxley process and reporting standards
- Serve as project and team leader
- Created a computerized model to adjust accounts for fluctuations in currency exchange rates
- Negotiated joint-venture agreements with major suppliers in Mexico and Colombia
- Implemented electronic funds transfer for vendor disbursements, improving cash flow and eliminating payables clerk position

Uses a clean, scanner-friendly font

Removes slashes, bullet points, ampersands (&), and other characters that might confuse the OCR software

Staff Accountant, Monsanto Agricultural Chemicals, Mexico City, Mexico, October 2001 to March 2005
- Handled budgeting, billing, and credit-processing functions for the Mexico City branch
- Audited travel and entertainment expenses for Monsanto's 30-member Latin American sales force
- Helped launch an online system to automate all accounting functions, improving reporting accuracy by 65 percent

EDUCATION

Master of Business Administration with emphasis in international business, George Mason University, Fairfax, Virginia, June 2001
Bachelor of Business Administration, Accounting, University of Texas, Austin, Texas, May 1999

Simplifies layout by removing multiple-column format

CULTURAL SKILLS

- Fluent in Spanish and German
- Extensive business contacts in Latin America

TECHNICAL SKILLS

Proficient with a wide range of financial software and systems, including Excel, Access, Microsoft Dynamics, and SAP Business One

MBA. List 20 to 30 words and phrases that define your skills, experience, education, and professional affiliations as they relate to your target position. Place this list right after your name and address. Note that you can also use your keywords as tags on your blog, social networking profile, or other elements of your online presence.[42]

One good way to identify which keywords to include in your summary is to find all the skills listed in ads for the types of jobs you're interested in. Another advantage of staying up to date with industry news and networking widely is that you'll develop a good ear for current terminology.

REAL-TIME UPDATES
Learn More

Practical advice on preparing a scannable résumé

Take advantage of these great tips on successfully transforming your résumé for optical scanning. Go to **http://real-timeupdates.com/ebc** and click on "Learn More." If you are using mybcommlab, you can access Real-Time Updates within each chapter or under Student Study Tools.

If you're tempted to toss in impressive keywords that don't really apply to you, don't. Increasingly sophisticated résumé analysis systems can now detect whether your keywords truly relate to the job descriptions and other information on your résumé. If a system suspects that you've padded your keyword list, it could move you to the bottom of the ranking or delete your résumé entirely.[43]

Creating a Plain-Text File of Your Résumé

A plain-text version of your résumé is simply a computer file without any of the formatting that you typically apply using a word-processing program.

Make sure you verify the plain-text file that you create with a word-processing program and adjust it as needed.

Many employers now prefer to enter résumé information directly into their tracking systems through the use of electronic **plain-text versions** (sometimes referred to as *ASCII text versions*). If you have the option of mailing a scannable résumé or submitting plain text online, go with plain text because it is less prone to errors. Note that a plain-text version should include a keyword summary (see the previous section).

Plain text is just what it sounds like: no font formatting, no bullet symbols, no colors, no lines or boxes, and so on. A plain-text version is easy to create with your word processor. Start with the file you used to create your scannable résumé, use the "Save As" choice to save it as "plain text" or whichever similarly labeled option your software has, and verify the result by using a basic text editor (such as Microsoft Notepad). If necessary, reformat the page manually, moving text and inserting space as needed. For simplicity's sake, left-justify all your headings rather than try to center them manually.

Creating a Word File of Your Résumé

In some cases, an employer or a job-posting website will let you upload a Microsoft Word file directly. (Although there are certainly other word-processing programs on the market, Microsoft Word is the de facto standard in business these days.) Read the instructions on each site carefully. For instance, you can upload a Word résumé to Monster, but the site asks you to follow some specific formatting instructions to make sure your file doesn't become garbled.[44]

Before you submit a Word file to anyone, make sure your computer system is virus free. Infecting a potential employer's network is not a way to make a good first impression.

Creating an HTML Version of Your Résumé

You have many options for posting your résumé online. Remember that you could be displaying your personal information for all the world to see, so think carefully about privacy and security.

You can probably find several uses for an HTML (webpage) version of your résumé, including sending it as a fully formatted e-mail message and including it in your e-portfolio. A key advantage of an HTML version is that you can provide links to supporting details and other materials from within your résumé. Even if you don't have HTML experience, you can save your résumé as a webpage from within Word. This method won't necessarily create the most spectacularly beautiful webpage, but it should at least be functional.

As you design your HTML résumé, think of important keywords to use as hyperlinks—words that will grab an employer's attention and make the recruiter want to click on that hyperlink to learn more about you. You can link to papers you've written, recommendations you've received, and sound or video clips that directly support your résumé. However, be sure to have permission to publish or link to material created for a previous employer.

Creating a PDF Version of Your Résumé

Creating a PDF version of your résumé is a simple procedure, but you need the right software. Adobe Acrobat (not the free Adobe Reader) is the best-known program, but many others are available, including some free versions. You can also use Adobe's online service at **http://createpdf.adobe.com** to create PDFs without buying software.

Proofreading Your Résumé

Your résumé can't be "pretty good" or "almost perfect"—it needs to be perfect, so proofread it thoroughly and ask several other people to verify it, too.

Employers view your résumé as a concrete example of your attention to quality and detail. Your résumé doesn't need to be good or pretty good—it needs to be *perfect.* In a recent survey, an overwhelming majority of executives said that just one or two errors in the job application package are enough to doom a candidate's chances.[45] Job seekers have committed every conceivable error, from forgetting to put their own names on their résumés to misspelling "Education.[46] Your résumé is one of the most important documents you'll ever write, so don't cut corners when it comes to proofreading. Check all headings and lists for clarity and parallelism and be sure that your grammar, spelling, and punctuation are correct. Ask at least three other people to read it, too. As the creator of the material, you could stare at a mistake for weeks and not see it.

You also need to make sure your résumé works in every format you create, so double- and triple-check your scannable, plain-text, and HTML versions closely. Many personal computer users now have low-cost scanners with OCR software, so you can even test the scannability of your résumé. These OCR tools aren't as accurate as commercial systems, but you'll get a rough idea of what your résumé will look like on the other end of the scanning process. Test your plain-text version by copying it into an e-mail message and sending it to yourself and several friends on different e-mail systems.

Distributing Your Résumé

How you distribute your résumé depends on the number of employers you target and their preferences for receiving résumés. Employers usually list their preferences on their websites, so verify this information to make sure your résumé ends up in the right format and in the right channel. Beyond that, here are some general distribution tips:

When distributing your résumé, pay close attention to the specific wishes of each employer.

- **Mailing your traditional and scannable résumés.** Take some care with the packaging. Spend a few extra cents to mail these documents in a flat 9 × 12 envelope, or better yet, use a Priority Mail flat-rate envelope, which gives you a sturdy cardboard mailer and faster delivery for just a few more dollars. Consider sending both standard and scannable versions to each employer. In your cover letter, explain that for the employer's convenience, you're sending both formats. However, if an employer provides the means to submit a résumé electronically, go with that option, as it increases the chances that your information will get into the applicant tracking system quickly and correctly.
- **Faxing your traditional and scannable résumés.** If you know that an employer prefers résumés via fax, be sure to send a standard fax cover sheet, along with your cover letter, followed by your résumé. Set the fax machine to "fine" mode to help ensure a high-quality printout on the receiving end. Note that a faxed résumé is probably the least desired format for many employers, so choose this route only if the employer requests faxes.
- **E-mailing your résumé.** Unless someone specifically asks for a Word document as an e-mail attachment, chances are a Word file won't get opened (because of virus concerns). Instead, insert plain text into the body of the e-mail message, attach a PDF file, or include a hyperlink in the e-mail that links to a résumé on your website or in your e-portfolio. If you have a reference number or a job ad number, include it in your e-mail subject line.
- **Posting your résumé online.** The range of options for posting résumés online seems to grow every year, particularly with the emergence of social networks and specialized job search websites. Consider all the following in your job search: (1) create an e-portfolio (see the Prologue for an example); (2) create a personal website, which can include your e-portfolio; (3) create a profile on one or more social networking sites; (4) post your résumé on "general-purpose" job websites, such as Monster and CareerBuilder; (5) post your résumé on specialized websites, such as Jobster and Jobfox (note that some specialized sites focus on higher-level positions, so they might not be available to you early in your career); (6) post your résumé with a staffing service, such as Volt (**http://jobs.volt.com**); and (7) keep an eye out for any new channels that emerge in the coming years. In every case, pay close attention to the instructions. For instance, some sites let you upload a Word file, whereas others want you to copy and paste individual sections of a résumé into an online application form.

Spend some time exploring the many options for posting your résumé (or sections of information from it) online.

Before you upload your résumé to any site, learn about its confidentiality protection. Some sites allow you to specify levels of confidentiality, such as letting employers search your qualifications without seeing your personal contact information or preventing your current employer from seeing your résumé. In any case, carefully limit the amount of personal information you provide online. Never put your Social Security number, student ID number, or driver's license number online, and don't post your résumé to any

CHECKLIST: Writing an Effective Résumé

A. Plan your résumé.
- Analyze your purpose and audience carefully to make sure your message meets employers' needs.
- Gather pertinent information about your target companies.
- Select the best medium by researching the preferences of each employer.
- Organize your résumé around your strengths, choosing the chronological, functional, or combination structure. (Be careful about using the functional structure.)

B. Write your résumé.
- Keep your résumé honest.
- Adapt your résumé to your audience to highlight the qualifications each employer is looking for.
- Use powerful language to convey your name and contact information, career objective or summary of qualifications, education, work experience, skills, work or school accomplishments, and personal activities and achievements.

C. Complete your résumé.
- Revise your résumé until it is clear, concise, and compelling.
- Produce your résumé in all the formats you might need: traditional printed résumé, scannable, plain-text file, Microsoft Word file, HTML format, or PDF.
- Proofread your résumé to make sure it is absolutely perfect.
- Distribute your résumé using the means that each employer prefers.

Document Makeover

Improve This Résumé

To practice correcting drafts of actual documents, visit the "Document Makeovers" section in mybcommlab. Refer to the User Guide for specific instructions on how to access the content for this chapter. You will find a résumé that contains problems and errors related to what you've learned in this chapter about writing effective résumés and application letters. Use the "Final Draft" decision tool to create an improved version of this document. Check the résumé for spelling and grammatical errors, effective use of verbs and pronouns, inclusion of unnecessary information, and omission of important facts.

website that doesn't give you the option of restricting the display of your contact information. (Only employers that are registered clients of the service should be able to see your contact information.)[47]

For a quick summary of the steps to take when planning, writing, and completing your résumé, refer to "Checklist: Writing an Effective Résumé." For the latest information on résumé writing and distribution, visit **http://real-timeupdates.com/ebc** and click on Chapter 15.

On the Job: Solving Communication Dilemmas at Hersha Hospitality Management

You recently joined Jeffrey Wade's recruiting team at Hersha, and your responsibilities include analyzing résumés and applications to help the company identify the most promising candidates to be interviewed. Your current task is finding candidates to fill a staff accountant position in the corporate finance group.

1. You've learned to pay close attention to the career objectives on résumés to make sure you match applicants' interests with appropriate job openings. You've selected four résumés for the accountant position; from them, which of the following is the most compelling statement of objectives for this position?
   a. An entry-level financial position in a large company
   b. To invest my accounting and financial talent and business savvy in shepherding Hersha toward explosive growth
   c. A position in which my degree in business administration and my experience in cash management will make a valuable contribution
   d. To learn all I can about accounting in an exciting environment with a company whose reputation is as outstanding as Hersha's

2. Of the education sections included in the résumés, which of the following is the most effective?

a. Morehouse College, Atlanta, GA, 2001–2004. Received BA degree with a major in Business Administration and a minor in Finance. Graduated with a 3.65 grade point average. Played varsity football and basketball. Worked 15 hours per week in the library. Coordinated the local student chapter of the American Management Association. Member of Alpha Phi Alpha social fraternity.

b. I attended Wayne State University in Detroit, Michigan, for two years and then transferred to the University of Michigan at Ann Arbor, where I completed my studies. My major was economics, but I also took many business management courses, including employee motivation, small business administration, history of business start-ups, and organizational behavior. I selected courses based on the professors' reputation for excellence, and I received mostly A's and B's. Unlike many college students, I viewed the acquisition of knowledge—rather than career preparation—as my primary goal. I believe I have received a well-rounded education that has prepared me to approach management situations as problem-solving exercises.

c. University of Connecticut, Storrs, Connecticut. Graduated with a BA degree in 2004. Majored in Physical Education. Minored in Business Administration. Graduated with a 2.85 average.

d. North Texas State University and University of Texas at Tyler. Received BA and MBA degrees. I majored in business as an undergraduate and concentrated in financial management during my MBA program. Received a special $2,500 scholarship offered by Rotary international recognizing academic achievement in business courses. I also won the MEGA award in 2003. Dean's List.

3. Which of the résumés does the best job of portraying each candidate's work experience?

a. **McDonald's, Peoria, IL, 2000–2001. Part-time cook**. Worked 15 hours per week while attending high school. Prepared all menu items. Received employee-of-the-month award for outstanding work habits.
University Grill, Ames, IA, 2001–2004. Part-time cook. Worked 20 hours per week while attending college. Prepared hot and cold sandwiches. Helped manager purchase ingredients. Trained new kitchen workers. Prepared work schedules for kitchen staff.

b. Although I have never held a full-time job, I have worked part-time and during summer vacations throughout my high school and college years. During my freshman and sophomore years in high school, I bagged groceries at the A&P store three afternoons a week, where I was generally acknowledged as one of the hardest-working employees. During my junior and senior years, I worked at the YMCA as an after-school counselor for elementary school children. I know I made a positive difference in their lives because I still get letters from some of them. During summer vacations while I was in college, I did construction work for a local homebuilder. The job paid well, and I also learned a lot about carpentry. I also worked part-time in college in the student cafeteria.

c. **Macy's Department Store, Sherman Oaks, CA, Summers, 2002–2005. Sales Consultant, Furniture Department**. Interacted with a diverse group of customers while endeavoring to satisfy their individual needs and make their shopping experience efficient and enjoyable. Under the direction of the sales manager, prepared employee schedules and completed departmental reports. Demonstrated computer skills and attention to detail while assisting with inventory management, working the cash register, and handling a variety of special orders and customer requests. Received the CEO Award (for best monthly sales performance) three times.

d. **Athens, GA, Civilian Member of Public Safety Committee, January-December 2004.**
• Organized and promoted a lecture series on vacation safety and home security for the residents of Athens, GA; recruited and trained seven committee members to help plan and produce the lectures; persuaded local businesses to finance the program; designed, printed, and distributed flyers; wrote and distributed press releases; attracted an average of 120 people to each of three lectures
• Developed a questionnaire to determine local residents' home security needs; directed the efforts of 10 volunteers working on the survey; prepared written report for city council and delivered oral summary of findings at town meeting; helped persuade city to fund new home security program
• Initiated the Business Security Forum as an annual meeting at which local business leaders could meet to discuss safety and security issues; created promotional flyers for the first forum; convinced 19 business owners to fund a business security survey; arranged press coverage of the first forum

4. While you are analyzing four résumés suggested by your applicant tracking system, a fellow employee hands you the following résumé and says this person would be great for the opening in accounting. What action will you take?
   a. Definitely recommend that Hersha take a look at this outstanding candidate.
   b. Reject the application. He doesn't give enough information about when he attended college, what he majored in, or where he has worked.
   c. Review the candidate's web-based e-portfolio, in which he has posted many of his school projects. If the assessment contains the missing information and the candidate sounds promising, recommend him for a closer look. If vital information is still missing, send the candidate an e-mail requesting additional information. Make the decision once you receive all necessary information.
   d. Consider the candidate's qualifications relative to those of other applicants. Recommend him if you cannot find three or four other applicants with more directly relevant qualifications.

Darius Jaidee
809 N. Perkins Rd, Stillwater, OK 74075
Phone: (405) 369-0098
E-mail: dariusj@okstate.edu

Career Objective: To build a successful career in financial management

Summary of Qualifications: As a student at the University of Oklahoma, Stillwater, completed a wide variety of assignments that demonstrate skills related to accounting and management. For example:

Planning skills: As president of the university's foreign affairs forum, organized six lectures and workshops featuring 36 speakers from 16 foreign countries within a nine-month period. Identified and recruited the speakers, handled their travel arrangements, and scheduled the facilities.

Communication skills: Wrote more than 25 essays and term papers on various academic topics, including at least 10 dealing with business and finance. As a senior, wrote a 20-page analysis of financial trends in the petroleum industry, interviewing five high-ranking executives in accounting and finance positions at ConocoPhillip's refinery in Ponca City, Oklahoma, and company headquarters in Houston, Texas.

Accounting and computer skills: Competent in all areas of Microsoft Office, including Excel spreadsheets and Access databases. Assisted with bookkeeping activities in parents' small business, including the conversion from paper-based to computer-based accounting (Peachtree software). Have taken courses in accounting, financial planning, database design, web design, and computer networking.

For more information, including employment history, please access my e-portfolio at **http://dariusjaidee.tripod.com**.

LEARNING OBJECTIVES CHECKUP

Assess your understanding of the principles in this chapter by reading each learning objective and studying the accompanying exercises. For fill-in-the-blank items, write the missing text in the blank provided; for multiple-choice items, circle the letter of the correct answer. You can check your responses against the answer key on page AK-2.

Objective 15.1: Describe the approach most employers take to finding potential new employees.

1. What is the first step that employers usually take when they need to find candidates to interview for a job opening?
   a. They search online for personal websites and e-portfolios that might contain information about potential candidates.
   b. They look inside the company for likely candidates.
   c. They post job openings on job boards such as Monster.com and CareerBuilder.com.
   d. They run ads in the local newspaper.
2. Which of these most accurately characterizes the respective approaches that employers use to find new employees and employees use to find new opportunities?
   a. Employers and employees look in the same places, in the same general sequence.
   b. The respective approaches of employers and employees is essentially opposite, with employers starting inside the firm and gradually moving toward help wanted ads as a last resort and employees starting with help wanted ads and moving in the other direction.
   c. Because websites are the only places that employers now communicate news of job openings, the web is the only place employees should look.
   d. The approaches of employees and employers have nothing in common.
3. According to the chapter, what percentage of job openings are never advertised (a phenomenon known as the *hidden job market*)?
   a. 15 percent
   b. 5 percent
   c. 28 percent
   d. 80 percent

Objective 15.2: Explain the importance of networking in your career search.

4. Which of the following best describes the process of networking as it applies to your career?

a. Making sure you are plugged into the online scene so that you don't miss out on any new Internet developments
b. Making informal connections with a broad sphere of mutually beneficial business contacts
c. Asking as many people as possible to alert you to interesting job opportunities
d. Making sure you get to know everyone in your company shortly after accepting a new position

5. If you don't yet have significant work experience but still want to become a valued network member, which of the following tactics should you consider?
a. Limit your networking to people whose work experience is similar to yours so that you can share similar information.
b. Create a convenient, foldable, business-card-size version of your résumé that you can give to everyone you meet so they don't have to carry a full-size copy of your résumé.
c. Avoid networking until you have enough work experience to be able to offer insider tips on the job market in your industry.
d. Research recent trends in the business world in order to have interesting and useful information at your fingertips whenever you encounter people in your network.

Objective 15.3: Discuss how to choose the appropriate résumé organization, and list the advantages or disadvantages of the three common options.

6. A/an ____ résumé highlights employment experience, listing jobs in reverse order from most recent to earliest.

7. A/an ____ résumé focuses on a person's particular skills and competencies, without itemizing his or her job history.

8. A/an ____ résumé uses elements of both the chronological and functional formats.

9. Which of the following is an advantage of the chronological résumé?
a. It helps employers easily locate necessary information.
b. It highlights your professional growth and career progress.
c. It emphasizes continuity and stability in your employment background.
d. It performs all of these communication functions.

10. Why are many employers suspicious of the functional résumé?
a. It allows applicants to hide or downplay lengthy periods of unemployment or a lack of career progress.
b. It doesn't scan into computer databases as effectively as other résumé formats.
c. It doesn't provide any information about education.
d. It encourages applicants to include accomplishments that were the result of teamwork rather than individual efforts.

11. Which of the following is a disadvantage of the combination résumé?
a. It is impossible to convert to scannable format.
b. It tends to be longer than other formats and can be repetitious.
c. It doesn't work for people who have extensive job experience.
d. The combination résumé has no disadvantages.

Objective 15.4: List the major sections of a traditional résumé.

12. Which of the following sections should be included in any résumé, regardless of the format you've chosen?
a. Contact information, education, and work experience
b. Contact information, education, and personal references
c. Personal data, contact information, and education
d. Education, personal references, and career objectives

13. Why do some experts recommend not including a career objective on your résumé?
a. It can limit your possibilities as a candidate, particularly if you want to be considered for a variety of positions.
b. It shows that you're selfish and only thinking about your own success.
c. It shows that you're unrealistic, since no one can plan a career that might last for 40 or 50 years.
d. It helps focus you as a candidate in the minds of potential employers.

14. Should a summary of qualifications focus on the past or the future?
a. It should focus on the past, covering things that you've already accomplished.
b. It should focus on the future, identifying valuable traits that you can offer a new employer.
c. It should combine elements of both the past and the future, offering solid evidence of what you've accomplished while being phrased in a way that relates to a future employer's needs.
d. It should focus on the future, explaining what you'd like to accomplish in your career in the coming years.

Objective 15.5: Identify six different formats in which you can produce a résumé.

15. A/an ____ version of your résumé has the same content as a traditional résumé but has had all the formatting removed so that it can be easily e-mailed or copied into online forms.

16. Which of these is a significant advantage of an HTML format résumé?
a. You can save money on printing paper résumés.
b. You can provide links to additional information, such as samples of your work.
c. You can use lots of color.
d. You can use the flexibility of the web to provide extensive details on your life history.

Objective 15.6: Describe what you should do to adapt your résumé to a scannable format.

17. Which of the following formatting steps is necessary to convert a traditional résumé to a scannable format?
a. Remove all font formatting, such as boldface and italics.
b. Replace bullet point characters with hyphens.
c. Convert all multiple columns to a single column.
d. Do all of the above.

18. What is the primary purpose of the list of keywords in a scannable résumé?
   a. It shows employers that you've done your research.
   b. It increases the probability that a computer database will select your résumé for the types of opportunities in which you're interested.
   c. It fills up space when you don't have enough work experience.
   d. Keywords should never be included in a scannable résumé.

PEARSON mybcommlab™

Log on to www.mybcommlab.com to access the following study and assessment aids associated with this chapter:

- Video applications
- Real-Time Updates
- Peer review activity
- Quick Learning Guides
- Pre/post test
- Personalized study plan
- Model documents
- Sample presentations

If you are not using mybcommlab, you can access Real-Time Updates and Quick Learning Guides through http://real-timeupdates.com/ebc. The Quick Learning Guide (located under "Learn More" on the website) hits all the high points of this chapter in just two pages. This guide, especially prepared by the authors, will help you study for exams or review important concepts whenever you need a quick refresher.

Apply Your Knowledge

1. How should you present a past job that is unrelated to your current career plans?
2. One of the disadvantages of computerized résumé scanning is that some qualified applicants will be missed because the technology isn't perfect. However, more and more companies are using this approach to deal with the flood of résumés they receive. Do you think that scanning is a good idea? Explain.
3. Can you use a qualifications summary if you don't yet have extensive professional experience in your desired career? Why or why not?
4. Some people don't have a clear career path when they enter the job market. If you're in this situation, how would your uncertainty affect the way you write your résumé?
5. **Ethical Choices** Between your sophomore and junior years, you quit school for a year to earn the money to finish college. You worked as a loan-processing assistant in a finance company, checking references on loan applications, typing, and filing. Your manager made a lot of the fact that he had never attended college. He seemed to resent you for pursuing your education, but he never criticized your work, so you thought you were doing okay. After you'd been working there for six months, he fired you, saying that you'd failed to be thorough enough in your credit checks. You were actually glad to leave, and you found another job right away at a bank, doing similar duties. Now that you've graduated from college, you're writing your résumé. Will you include the finance company job in your work history? Explain.

Practice Your Knowledge

Message for Analysis

Read the following résumé information and then (1) analyze the strengths or weaknesses of the information and (2) revise the résumé so that it follows the guidelines presented in this chapter.

Message 15.A: Writing a Résumé

Sylvia Manchester
765 Belle Fleur Blvd.
New Orleans, LA 70113
(504) 312-9504
smanchester@rcnmail.com

PERSONAL: Single, excellent health, 5'8", 116 lbs.; hobbies include cooking, dancing, and reading.

JOB OBJECTIVE: To obtain a responsible position in marketing or sales with a good company.

EDUCATION: BA degree in biology, University of Louisiana, 1998. Graduated with a 3.0 average. Member of the varsity cheerleading squad. President of Panhellenic League. Homecoming queen.

WORK EXPERIENCE

Fisher Scientific Instruments, 2004 to now, field sales representative. Responsible for calling on customers and explaining the features of Fisher's line of laboratory instruments. Also responsible for writing sales letters, attending trade shows, and preparing weekly sales reports.

Fisher Scientific Instruments, 2001–2003, customer service representative. Was responsible for handling incoming phone calls from customers who had questions about delivery, quality, or operation of

Fisher's line of laboratory instruments. Also handled miscellaneous correspondence with customers.

Medical Electronics, Inc., 1998–2001, administrative assistant to the vice president of marketing. In addition to handling typical secretarial chores for the vice president of marketing, I was in charge of compiling the monthly sales reports, using figures provided by members of the field sales force. I also was given responsibility for doing various market research activities.

New Orleans Convention and Visitors Bureau, 1995–1998, summers, tour guide. During the summers of my college years, I led tours of New Orleans for tourists visiting the city. My duties included greeting conventioneers and their spouses at hotels, explaining the history and features of the city during an all-day sightseeing tour, and answering questions about New Orleans and its attractions. During my fourth summer with the bureau, I was asked to help train the new tour guides. I prepared a handbook that provided interesting facts about the various tourist attractions, as well as answers to the most commonly asked tourist questions. The Bureau was so impressed with the handbook they had it printed up so that it could be given as a gift to visitors.

University of Louisiana, 1995–1998, part-time clerk in admissions office. While I was a student in college, I worked 15 hours a week in the admissions office. My duties included filing, processing applications, and handling correspondence with high school students and administrators.

Exercises

Active links for all websites in this chapter can be found on mybcommlab; see your User Guide for instructions on accessing the content for this chapter.

15.1 Internet Based on the preferences you identified in your career self-assessment (see page xxxiii) and the academic, professional, and personal qualities you have to offer, perform an online search for a career that matches your interests (starting with the websites listed in Table 15.1). Draft a brief report for your instructor, indicating how the career you select and the job openings you find match your strengths and preferences.

15.2 Teamwork Working with another student, change the following statements to make them more effective for a résumé by using action verbs.

a. Have some experience with database design.
b. Assigned to a project to analyze the cost accounting methods for a large manufacturer.
c. I was part of a team that developed a new inventory control system.
d. Am responsible for preparing the quarterly department budget.
e. Was a manager of a department with seven employees working for me.
f. Was responsible for developing a spreadsheet to analyze monthly sales by department.
g. Put in place a new program for ordering supplies.

15.3 Résumé Preparation: Work Accomplishments Using your team's answers to exercise 15.2, make the statements stronger by quantifying them. (Make up any numbers you need.)

15.4 Ethical Choices Assume that you achieved all the tasks shown in exercise 15.2 not as an individual employee but as part of a work team. In your résumé, must you mention other team members? Explain your answer.

15.5 Résumé Preparation: Electronic Plain-Text Version Using your revised version of Message for Analysis 15.A, prepare a fully formatted print résumé. What formatting changes would Sylvia Manchester need to make if she were uploading her résumé to a website as a plain-text file? Develop a keyword summary and make all the changes needed to complete this plain-text résumé.

15.6 Résumé Preparation: HTML Version Using your revised version of the résumé in Message for Analysis 15.A, prepare a webpage version. Your instructor may direct you to a particular HTML editing tool, or you can use the "Save as Web Page" function in Microsoft Word. Word also lets you insert hyperlinks, so somewhere in the Work Experience section, create a hyperlink that takes the reader to a secondary page in order to show a work sample. For this new page, you can either use one of your own assignments from this course or simply create a blank page titled "Work Sample for Sylvia Manchester." On this page, create a hyperlink that takes the reader back to the main résumé page.

Be sure to test your finished files using a web browser. Adjust your formatting as necessary to ensure a clean, professional design. When your files are complete, submit as your instructor indicates.

15.7 It's Show Time: Creating a Vidcast to Supplement Your Application Imagine that you are applying for work in a field that involves speaking in front of an audience, such as sales, consulting, management, or training. Using material you created for any of the exercises or cases in Chapter 14, plan a two- to three-minute video demonstration of your speaking and presentation skills. Using a digital camcorder, a digital camera with video capability, or a webcam, record yourself speaking to an imaginary audience. If possible, use PowerPoint slides or other visuals. As your instructor directs, either submit this movie clip or use it to create a video podcast. For a good tutorial on creating vidcasts on Apple computers running Mac OS X, visit www.apple.com/quicktime/tutorials/videopodcasts.html; for Windows computers, visit www.apple.com/quicktime/tutorials/videopodcasts_win.html.

Expand Your Knowledge

Exploring the Best of the Web

Post a Résumé Online

www.careerbuilder.com

At CareerBuilder, you'll find sample résumés, tips on preparing different types of résumés (including scannable ones), links to additional articles, and expert advice on creating résumés that bring positive results. After you've polished your résumé-writing skills, you can search for jobs online, using the site's numerous links to national and international industry-specific websites. You can access the information at CareerBuilder to develop your résumé and then post it with prospective employers—all free of charge. Use the site's advice to complete these tasks:

1. Before writing a new résumé, make a list of action verbs that describe your skills and experience.

2. Describe the advantages and disadvantages of chronological and functional résumé formats. Do you think a combination résumé would be an appropriate format for your new résumé? Explain why or why not.
3. List some of the tips you learned for preparing a résumé for online posting.

Sharpening Your Career Skills Online

Bovée and Thill's Business Communication Web Search, at **http://businesscommunicationblog.com/websearch**, is a unique research tool designed specifically for business communication research. Use the Web Search function to find a website, video, PDF document, podcast, or PowerPoint presentation that offers advice on creating an effective résumé. Write a brief e-mail message to your instructor, describing the item that you found and summarizing the career skills information you learned from it.

Improve Your Grammar, Mechanics, and Usage

The following exercises help you improve your knowledge of and power over English grammar, mechanics, and usage. Turn to the Handbook of Grammar, Mechanics, and Usage at the end of this book and review all of Sections 4.1 (Frequently Confused Words), 4.2 (Frequently Misused Words), and 4.3 (Frequently Misspelled Words). Then look at the following 10 items. Underline the preferred choice within each set of parentheses. (Answers to these exercises appear on page AK-4.)

1. Everyone (*accept, except*) Barbara King has registered for the company competition.
2. We need to find a new security (*device, devise*).
3. The Jennings are (*loath, loathe*) to admit that they are wrong.
4. That decision lies with the director, (*who's whose*) in charge of this department.
5. In this department, we see (*a lot, alot*) of mistakes like that.
6. In my (*judgement, judgment*), you'll need to redo the cover.
7. He decided to reveal the information, (*irregardless, regardless*) of the consequences.
8. Why not go along when it is so easy to (*accomodate, accommodate*) his demands?
9. When you say that, do you mean to (*infer, imply*) that I'm being unfair?
10. All we have to do is try (*and, to*) get along with him for a few more days.

For additional exercises focusing on frequently confused, misused, or misspelled words, visit mybcommlab. Click on Chapter 15, click on "Additional Exercises to Improve Your Grammar, Mechanics, and Usage," and then click on "21. Frequently confused words," "22. Frequently misused words," or "23. Frequently misspelled words."

CASES

Applying the Three-Step Writing Process to Cases

Apply each step to the following cases, as assigned by your instructor.

1. The right job, right now: Imagining your ideal résumé. Think about yourself. What are some things that come easily to you? What do you enjoy doing? In what part of the country would you like to live? Do you like to work indoors? Outdoors? A combination of the two? How much do you like to travel? Would you like to spend considerable time on the road? Do you like to work closely with others or more independently? What conditions make a job unpleasant? Do you delegate responsibility easily, or do you like to do things yourself? Are you better with words or numbers? Better at speaking or writing? Do you like to work under fixed deadlines? How important is job security to you? Do you want your supervisor to state clearly what is expected of you, or do you like the freedom to make many of your own decisions?

Your task: After answering these questions, gather information about possible jobs that suit your current qualifications by consulting reference materials (from your college library or placement center) and by searching online. Next, choose a location, a company, and a job that interests you. Write a résumé that matches your qualifications and the job description; use whatever format your instructor specifies.

E-MAIL SKILLS

2. The dream job in the future: What will it take to get there? Chances are you won't be able to land your dream job right out of college, but that doesn't mean you shouldn't start planning right now to make that dream come true.

Your task: Using online job search tools, find a job that sounds just about perfect for you, even if you're not yet qualified for it. It might even be something that would take 10 or 20 years to reach. Don't settle for something that's not quite right—find a job that is so "you" and so exciting that you would jump out of bed every morning, eager to go to work (such jobs really do exist!). Start with the job description you found online and then supplement it with additional research so that you get a good picture of what this job and career path are all about. Compile a list of all the qualifications you would need in order to have a reasonable chance of landing such a job. Now compare this list with your current résumé. Write a brief e-mail to your instructor that identifies all the areas in which you would need to improve your skills, work experience, education, and other qualifications in order to land your dream job.

PRESENTATION SKILLS

3. The multimedia me: Creating a PowerPoint presentation for your e-portfolio. Using PowerPoint presentations and other multimedia supplements can be a great way to expand on the brief overview that a résumé provides.

Your task: Starting with any version of a résumé that you've created for yourself, create a PowerPoint presentation that expands on your résumé information to give potential employers a more complete picture of what you can contribute. Include samples of your work, testimonials from current or past employers and colleagues, videos of speeches you've made, and anything else that tells the story of the professional "you." If you have a specific job or type of job in mind, focus your presentation on that. Otherwise, present a more general picture that shows why you would be a great employee for any company to consider. Be sure to review the information from Chapter 14 about creating professional-quality presentations.

16 Applying and Interviewing for Employment

Learning Objectives

After studying this chapter, you will be able to

1. Define the purpose of application letters and explain how to apply the AIDA model to them
2. Describe the typical sequence of job interviews
3. Describe briefly what employers look for during an employment interview and preemployment testing
4. List six tasks you need to complete to prepare for a successful job interview
5. Explain the three stages of a successful employment interview
6. Identify the most common employment messages that follow an interview, and explain when you would use each one

On the Job: Communicating at Google

Arnnon Geshuri heads Google's recruiting effort as the company looks to hire thousands of the most innovative online business and technical specialists in the world.

The Search Engine Leader's Search for the Best Talent on the Web

When you prepare for your job interviews, knowing just the basic facts and figures about a company isn't always enough to impress top recruiters. For instance, most web surfers know Google as the leading online search engine, but the company is also helping to revolutionize advertising, publishing, geographic information systems, shopping—if it involves digital information, chances are that Google has looked into opportunities to build a business out of it.

As Google continues its rapid growth, recruiting manager Arnnon Geshuri and his staff dedicate considerable time, energy, and resources to employee recruiting. However, finding the right people is so important to the company that contributing to the recruiting effort is considered the responsibility of virtually every manager and employee. In fact, John Sullivan of San Francisco State University, who has studied the company's recruiting efforts closely, says that recruiting permeates the company so thoroughly that Google has created what he terms the world's first "recruiting culture." Acting on the belief that hiring choices are the most important decisions a company can make, Google has been known to wait several years to find the right people to fill some posts—even though it receives more than a million résumés a year.

Moreover, as befits a company focused on innovation, Google pursues people who don't fit the traditional corporate mold. Most are either risk takers with adventurous outside interests or experienced superstars from top research labs or respected technology firms. Googlers, as employees are informally known, hail from every corner of the business world—and beyond. As the company puts it, "Googlers have been Olympic athletes and Jeopardy champions; professional chefs and independent filmmakers."

You may never apply to Google, but gaining similar insights about the companies you are interested in will give you a competitive edge. Google provides quite a bit of information on its website about work life at the company, but you can't always hop on a company website to find these insights. Doing some extra digging through magazines, reading employment-related blogs, networking with others in your chosen field, and taking other opportunities to learn will help you prepare for every stage of the employment search process.[1]

www.google.com

WRITING APPLICATION LETTERS AND OTHER EMPLOYMENT MESSAGES

Whether you plan to apply to Google (profiled in the chapter-opening "On the Job" vignette) or any other company, your résumé will usually be the centerpiece of your job search package. However, it needs support from several other employment messages, including application letters, job-inquiry letters, application forms, and follow-up notes.

Application Letters

1 LEARNING OBJECTIVE

Define the purpose of application letters, and explain how to apply the AIDA model to them.

Whenever you submit your résumé, accompany it with an **application letter** to let readers know what you're sending, why you're sending it, and how they can benefit from reading it. (Application letters are sometimes called *cover letters*, and they can be either printed or e-mailed.) Start by researching the organization and then focus on your audience so that you can show you've done your homework. During your research, try to find out the name, title, and department of the person you're writing to. If you can't find a specific name, use something like "Dear Hiring Manager."[2]

Use the three-step process to create attention-getting application letters.

Remember that your reader's in-box is probably overflowing with résumés and application letters, and respect his or her time. Avoid gimmicks and don't repeat information that already appears in your résumé. Keep your letter straightforward, fact based, short, upbeat, and professional. Here are some quick tips to help you write effective application letters:[3]

Impress your reader with knowledge and professionalism—not gimmicks.

- Be as clear as possible about the kind of opportunity you seek.
- Show that you understand the company and the position.
- Never volunteer salary information unless an employer asks for it.
- Keep it short; in just two or three paragraphs, convey how your strengths and character would fit the position.
- Show some personality; doing so will help balance the choppy, shorthand style of your résumé.
- Meticulously check your spelling, mechanics, and grammar; errors will send your message directly to the recycling bin. And be aware that potential employers will treat your e-mail messages every bit as seriously as formal, printed letters.[4]

If you're sending a **solicited application letter** in response to an announced job opening, you'll usually know what qualifications the organization is seeking (see Figure 16.1 on the next page). In contrast, if you're sending an **unsolicited application letter** to an organization that has not announced an opening, you'll need to do some research to identify the requirements the position is likely to have (see Figure 16.2 on page 503).

Getting Attention

Like your résumé, your application letter is a form of advertising, so organize it as you would a marketing or sales message: Use the AIDA model, focus on your audience, and emphasize reader benefits (as discussed in Chapter 10). Make sure your style projects confidence without being arrogant.

FIGURE 16.1 Effective Solicited Application Message
In this response to an online job posting, Dalton Smith highlights his qualifications while mirroring the requirements specified in the posting. Following the AIDA model, he grabs attention immediately by letting the reader know that he is familiar with the company and the global transportation business.

Position			Supply Chain Pricing Analyst		Apply
Position code	T23-6678	Location	Tacoma, WA	Status	Full-time

Sea-Air Global Transport has an immediate opening for a supply chain pricing analyst in our Tacoma, WA, headquarters. This challenging position requires excellent communication skills in a variety of media, a polished customer service presence both in person and over the phone, and proven aptitude in statistical analysis and business mathematics.

The minimum educational requirement for this position is a bachelors degree or equivalent, preferably in business, statistical methods, or applied mathematics. Experience in customer service is highly desirable, and experience in transportation or logistics is a major plus.

Click here to learn more about Sea-Air or click here to explore the attractive compensation and benefits packages we offer all employees.

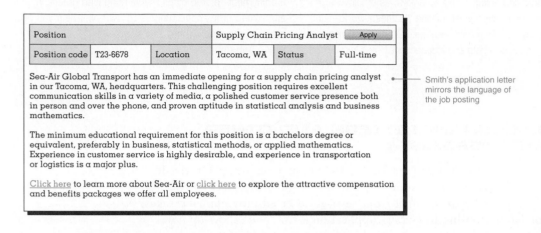

Smith's application letter mirrors the language of the job posting

27225 Eucalyptus Avenue
Long Beach, CA 90806
March 12, 2010

Sea-Air Global Transport
5467 Port of Tacoma Rd., Suite 230
Tacoma, WA 98421

Dear Hiring Manager:

Immediately grabs attention by indicating knowledge of the company and its industry

Sea-Air Global Transport consistently appeared as a top transportation firm in the research I did for my senior project in global supply chain management, so imagine my delight when I discovered the opening for an export pricing analyst in your Tacoma headquarters (Position Code: T23-6678). With a major in business and a minor in statistical methods, my education has been ideal preparation for the challenges of this position.

Identifies the specific job to which he is applying

In fact, my senior project demonstrates most of the skills listed in your job description, including written communication skills, analytical abilities, and math aptitude. I enjoyed the opportunity to put my math skills to the test as part of the statistical comparison of various freight modes.

Echoes qualifications stated in the job posting

Emphasizes his customer service orientation and also shows he has done his homework by researching the company

As you can see from my résumé, I also have more than three years of part-time experience working with customers in both retail and commercial settings. This experience taught me the importance of customer service, and I want to start my professional career with a company that truly values the customer. In reviewing your website and reading several articles on Lloyd's List and other trade websites, I am impressed by Sea-Air's constant attention to customer service in this highly competitive industry.

My verbal communication skills would be best demonstrated in an interview, of course. I would be happy to meet with a representative of your company at the earliest convenience. I can be reached at dalton.k.smith@gmail.com or by phone at (562) 555-3737.

Politely asks for an interview in a way that emphasizes yet another job-related skill

Sincerely,

Doesn't include a handwritten signature because the letter was uploaded to a website along with his résumé

Dalton Smith

The opening paragraph of your application letter needs to clearly convey the reason you're writing and give the recipient a compelling reason to keep reading.

The opening paragraph of your application letter has two important tasks to accomplish: (1) clearly stating your reason for writing and (2) giving the recipient a reason to keep reading. Why would a recruiter want to keep reading your letter instead of the hundred others piling up on his or her desk? Because you show some immediate potential for meeting the company's needs. You've researched the company and the position, and you know something about the industry and its current challenges. Consider this opening:

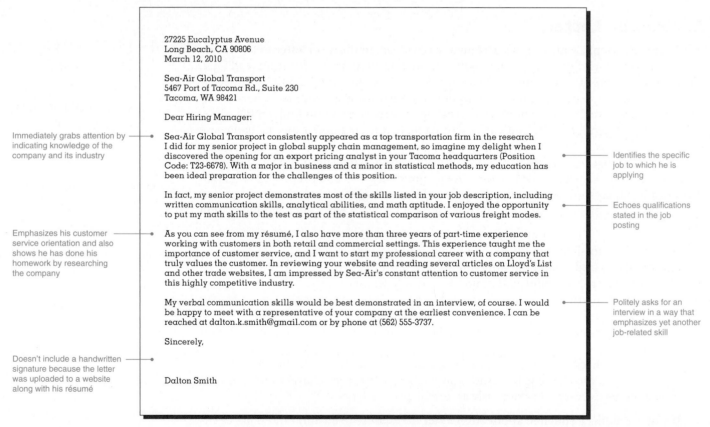

FIGURE 16.2 Effective Unsolicited Application Letter
Glenda Johns's experience as a clerk and an assistant manager gives her a good idea of the qualities that Walmart is likely to be looking for in future managers. She uses these insights to craft the opening of her letter. Also, because this is an unsolicited letter, she also uses the opening to explain her purpose in writing.

457 Mountain View Rd.
Clear Lake, IA 50428
June 16, 2010

Ms. Patricia Downings, Store Manager
Walmart
840 South Oak
Iowa Falls, IA 50126

Dear Ms. Downing:

You want retail clerks and managers who are accurate, enthusiastic, and experienced. You want someone who cares about customer service, who understands merchandising, and who can work with others to get the job done. When you're ready to hire a manager trainee or a clerk who is willing to work toward promotion, please consider me for the job.

Gains attention in the first paragraph by speaking directly to the reader's needs

Working as a clerk and then as an assistant manager in a large department store has taught me how to anticipate customer problems and deliver the type of service that keeps customers coming back. Moreover, my recent BA degree in retailing, which encompassed such courses as retailing, marketing, management, and business information systems, will provide your store with a well-rounded associate. (Please refer to my enclosed résumé for more information.) You'll find that I'm interested in every facet of retailing, eager to take on responsibility, and willing to continue learning throughout my career.

Points out personal qualities that aren't specifically stated in her résumé

I understand that Walmart prefers to promote its managers from within the company, and I would be pleased to start out with an entry-level position until I gain the necessary experience. Do you have any associate positions opening up soon? Could we discuss my qualifications? I will phone you early next Wednesday to arrange a meeting at your convenience.

Builds the reader's interest by demonstrating knowledge of the company's policy regarding promotion

Focuses on the reader and displays the "you" attitude, even though the last paragraph uses the word "I"

Sincerely,

Glenda Johns

Glenda Johns

Enclosure

> With the recent slowdown in corporate purchasing, I can certainly appreciate the challenge of new fleet sales in this business environment. With my high energy level and 16 months of new-car sales experience, I believe I can produce the results you listed as vital in your September 23 advertisement in the *Baltimore Sun*.

This applicant does a smooth job of mirroring the company's stated needs while highlighting his personal qualifications, along with evidence that he understands the broader market.

Table 16.1 on the next page highlights some ways you can spark interest and grab attention in your opening paragraph. All these openings demonstrate the "you" attitude, and many indicate how the applicant can serve the employer.

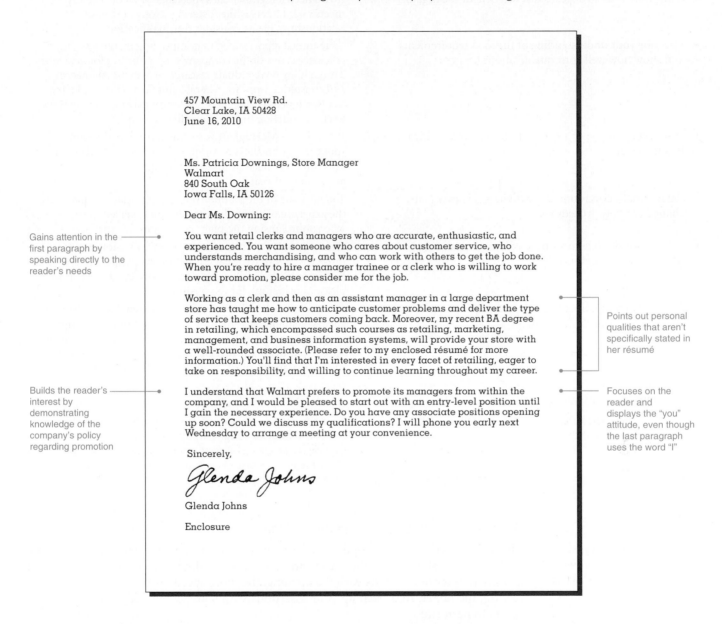

TABLE 16.1 Tips for Getting Attention in Application Letters

TIP	EXAMPLE
UNSOLICITED APPLICATION LETTERS	
• Show how your strongest skills will benefit the organization.	If you need a regional sales specialist who consistently meets sales targets while fostering strong customer relationships, please consider my qualifications.
• Describe your understanding of the job's requirements and show how well your qualifications fit them.	Your annual report stated that improving manufacturing efficiency is one of the company's top priorities for next year. Through my postgraduate research in systems engineering and consulting work for several companies in the industry, I've developed reliable methods for quickly identifying ways to cut production time while reducing resource use.
• Mention the name of a person known to and highly regarded by the reader.	When Janice McHugh of your franchise sales division spoke to our business communication class last week, she said you often need promising new marketing graduates at this time of year.
• Refer to publicized company activities, achievements, changes, or new procedures.	Today's issue of the *Detroit News* reports that you may need the expertise of computer programmers versed in robotics when your Lansing tire plant automates this spring.
• Use a question to demonstrate your understanding of the organization's needs.	Can your fast-growing market research division use an interviewer with two years of field survey experience, a B.A. in public relations, and a real desire to succeed? If so, please consider me for the position.
• Use a catchphrase opening if the job requires ingenuity and imagination.	*Haut monde*—whether referring to French, Italian, or Arab clients, it still means "high society." As an interior designer for your Beverly Hills showroom, not only could I serve and sell to your distinguished clientele, but I could do it in all these languages. I speak, read, and write them fluently.
SOLICITED APPLICATION LETTERS	
• Identify where you discovered the job opening; describe what you have to offer.	Your ad in the April issue of *Travel & Leisure* for a cruise-line social director caught my eye. My eight years of experience as a social director in the travel industry would allow me to serve your new Caribbean cruise division well.

Building Interest and Increasing Desire

Use the middle section of your letter to expand on your opening, presenting a more complete picture of your strengths.

The middle section of your application letter presents your strongest selling points in terms of their potential benefit to the organization, thereby building interest in you and creating a desire to interview you. As with the opening, the more specific you can be in the middle section, the better. And back up your assertions with some convincing evidence of your ability to perform:

> **Poor:** I completed three college courses in business communication, earning an A in each course, and have worked for the past year at Imperial Construction.
>
> **Improved:** Using the skills gained from three semesters of college training in business communication, I developed a collection system for Imperial Construction that reduced annual bad-debt losses by 25 percent. Emphasizing a win-win scenario for the company and its clients with incentives for on-time payment, the system was also credited with improving customer satisfaction.

When writing a solicited letter, be sure to discuss each requirement specified in the advertisement. If you are deficient in any of these requirements, stress other solid selling points to help strengthen your overall presentation.

Don't restrict your message to just core job duties. Also highlight personal characteristics that apply to the targeted position, such as your diligence or your ability to work hard, learn quickly, handle responsibility, or get along with people:

> While attending college full-time, I trained three hours a day with the varsity track team. In addition, I worked part-time during the school year and up to 60 hours a week each summer in order to be totally self-supporting while in college. I can offer your organization the same level of effort and perseverance.

Another matter you might bring up in this section is your salary requirements—but *only* if the organization has asked you to state them. If you don't know the salary that's appropriate for the position and someone with your qualifications, you can find salary ranges for hundreds of jobs at the Bureau of Labor Statistics website (**www.bls.gov**) or a number of commercial sites, including Monster.com. If you do state a target salary, tie it to the benefits you would bring to the organization:

Don't bring up salary in your application letter unless the recipient has previously asked you to include your salary requirements.

> For the past two years, I have been helping a company similar to yours organize its database marketing efforts. I would therefore like to receive a salary in the same range (the mid-60s) for helping your company set up a more efficient customer database.

Toward the end of this section, refer the reader to your résumé by citing a specific fact or general point covered there:

> As you can see in the enclosed résumé, I've been working part-time with a local publisher since my sophomore year. During that time, I've used client interactions as an opportunity to build strong customer service skills.

Motivating Action

The final paragraph of your application letter has two important functions: to ask the reader for a specific action and to facilitate a reply. Don't demand an interview, however; try to sound natural and appreciative. Offer to come to the employer's office at a convenient time or, if the firm is some distance away, to meet with its nearest representative or arrange a telephone interview. Make the request easy to fulfill by stating your phone number and the best time to reach you—or, if you want to be in control, by mentioning that you will follow up with a phone call in a few days. Refer again to your strongest selling point and, if desired, your date of availability:

In the final paragraph of your application letter, respectfully ask for specific action and make it easy for the reader to respond.

> After you have reviewed my qualifications, could we discuss the possibility of putting my marketing skills to work for your company? Because I will be on spring break the week of March 8, I would like to arrange a time to talk then. I will call in late February to schedule a convenient time when we could discuss employment opportunities at your company.

After you have edited and proofread your application letter, give it a final quality check by referring to "Checklist: Writing Application Letters." Then send it along with your résumé promptly, especially if you are responding to an advertisement or online job posting.

Application Follow-Ups

If your application letter and résumé fail to bring a response within a month or so, follow up with a second letter to keep your file active. This follow-up letter also gives you a chance to update your original application with any recent job-related information:

CHECKLIST: Writing Application Letters

- Open the letter by capturing the reader's attention in a businesslike way.
- Use specific language to clearly state your interests and objectives.
- Build interest and desire in your potential contribution by presenting your key qualifications for the job.
- Link your education, experience, and personal qualities to the job requirements.
- Outline salary requirements only if the organization has requested that you provide them.
- Request an interview at a time and place that is convenient for the reader.
- Make it easy to comply with your request by providing your complete contact information and good times to reach you.
- Adapt your style for cultural variations, if required.

> Since applying to you on May 3 for a position in your management training program, I have completed three courses in business and management at South River Community College and received straight A's.
>
> Please keep my application in your active file; I would welcome another opportunity to apply for the program.

Even if you've received a letter acknowledging your application and saying that it will be kept on file, don't hesitate to send a follow-up letter three months later to show that you are still interested:

Think creatively about a follow-up message; show that you've continued to add to your skills or that you've learned more about the company or the industry.

> Three months have elapsed since I applied to you for an underwriting position, but I want to let you know that I am still very interested in joining your company.
>
> I recently completed a four-week temporary work assignment at a large local insurance agency. I learned several new verification techniques and gained experience in using the online computer system. This experience could increase my value to your underwriting department.
>
> Please keep my application in your active file and let me know when a position opens for a capable underwriter.

Understand the interview process so you can prepare for the different types of interviews you will encounter.

You can write this sort of follow-up message even if you have no new accomplishments to share. Do some quick research on the company and its industry to find something that you can feature in your message ("I've been reading about the new technical challenges facing your industry . . ."). Your initiative and knowledge will impress recruiters. Without a follow-up communication from you, the human resources office is likely to assume that you've already found a job and are no longer interested in the organization. Moreover, a company's requirements change. A follow-up letter can demonstrate that you're sincerely interested in working for the organization, persistent in pursuing your goals, and committed to upgrading your skills. And it might just get you an interview.

UNDERSTANDING THE INTERVIEWING PROCESS

All recruiters, including Google's Arnnon Geshuri, have lists of qualities and accomplishments they are looking for in job candidates. An **employment interview** is a formal meeting during which you and a prospective employer ask questions and exchange information. These meetings have a dual purpose: (1) The organization's main objective is to find the best person available for the job by determining whether you and the organization are a good match, and (2) your main objective is to find the job best suited to your goals and capabilities. While recruiters are trying to decide whether you are right for them, you must decide whether a company is right for you.

Large organizations that hire hundreds of new employees every year typically take a more systematic approach to the recruiting and interviewing process than small local businesses that hire only a few new people each year. In many cases, the easiest way to connect with a big company is through your campus career center, while the most efficient way to reach a smaller business is often by contacting the company directly.

Be aware that interviewing takes time, so begin the process well in advance of the date you want to start work. During downturns in the economy, early planning is especially crucial. Whatever shape the economy is in, try to secure as many interviews as you can, both to improve your chances of receiving a job offer and to give yourself more options when you do get offers.

REAL-TIME UPDATES
Learn More

Looking for an international adventure?

Finding a job in another country is a long and complex process, but these tips can help you reach your goal as quickly as possible. Go to **http://real-timeupdates.com/ebc** and click on "Learn More." If you are using mybcommlab, you can access Real-Time Updates within each chapter or under Student Study Tools.

The Typical Sequence of Interviews

2 LEARNING OBJECTIVE

Describe the typical sequence of job interviews.

Most employers interview an applicant multiple times before deciding to make a job offer. At the most selective companies, you might have a dozen or more individual interviews across several stages.[5] Depending on the company and the position, the process may stretch out over many weeks, or it may be completed in a matter of days.[6]

Most organizations interview an applicant several times before extending a job offer.

The interviewing process starts with a *screening stage*, in which an employer filters out applicants who are unqualified or otherwise not a good fit for the position. Screening can take place on campus, at company offices, or via telephone or computer. If your screening interview will take place by phone, try to schedule it for a time when you can be focused and free from interruptions.[7]

During the screening stage, try to differentiate yourself from other candidates.

Your best approach to an interview at the screening stage is to follow the interviewer's lead. Keep your responses short and to the point. Time is limited, so taking too long to answer any single question can be a mistake. To differentiate yourself and demonstrate your strengths and qualifications, try to emphasize the "theme" you used in developing your résumé.

During the selection stage, you may interview with several people, perhaps at the same time.

The next stage of interviews helps the organization narrow the field a little further. During this *selection stage*, show interest in the job, relate your skills and experience to the organization's needs, listen attentively, ask insightful questions that show you've done your research, and display enthusiasm. Typically, if you're invited to visit a company, you will talk with several people in succession, such as a member of the human resources department, one or two potential colleagues, and one or more managers, including your potential supervisor. At Google, for example, recruits talk with at least four interviewers, both managers and potential colleagues.[8]

During the final stage, the interviewer may try to sell you on working for the firm.

If the interviewers agree that you're a good candidate, you may receive a job offer, either on the spot or a few days later by phone, mail, or e-mail. In other cases, you may be invited back for a final evaluation, often by a higher-ranking executive. The objective of this *final stage* is often to sell you on the advantages of joining the organization.

Common Types of Interviews

Employers can use a number of interviewing methods, so you need to recognize the various types and be prepared for each one. These methods can be distinguished by the way they are structured, the number of people involved, and the purpose of the interview.

Structured Versus Unstructured Interviews

A structured interview follows a set sequence of questions, allowing the interview team to compare answers from all candidates.

In a **structured interview**, the interviewer (or a computer) asks a series of prepared questions in a set order. Structured interviews help employers identify candidates who don't meet basic job criteria, and they allow the interview team to compare answers from multiple candidates.[9]

In an open-ended interview, the interviewer adapts the line of questioning based on your responses and questions.

In contrast, in an **open-ended interview**, the interviewer adapts his or her line of questioning based on the answers you give and any questions you ask. Even though it may feel like a conversation, remember that it's still an interview, so keep your answers focused and professional.

Panel and Group Interviews

In a panel interview, you meet with several interviewers at once; in a group interview, several candidates meet with one or more interviewers at once.

Many of your interviews will be conventional one-on-one interviews, with just you and a single interviewer. However, in a **panel interview**, you will meet with several interviewers at once (some companies have up to 50 employees on the panel, but that is unusual).[10] Try to make a connection with each person on the panel and remember that each one has a different perspective, so tailor your responses accordingly.[11] For example, an upper-level manager is likely to be interested in your overall business sense and strategic perspective, whereas a potential colleague might be more interested in your technical skills and ability to work as part of a team.

Some organizations perform **group interviews**, in which one or more interviewers meet with several candidates simultaneously. A key purpose of the group interview is to observe how the candidates interact.[12]

Behavioral, Situational, Working, and Stress Interviews

Behavioral interviews, in which you are asked to describe how you handled situations from your past, are commonly used.

Perhaps the most common type of interview these days is the **behavioral interview**, in which you are asked to relate specific incidents and experiences from your past.[13] Whereas traditional, generic interview questions can often be answered with "canned" responses, behavioral questions require candidates to use their own experiences and attributes to craft answers. Employers use these questions to assess such areas as your job-related technical skills and your ability to work under pressure, coordinate with others, and resolve conflict.[14]

Interviewers also look to see if the ways you handled challenges in the past reflect the organization's core values. To prepare for a behavioral interview, start by researching these values, which you can usually find discussed in the "About Us" section of the company's website. For example, one firm might emphasize innovation and technical excellence, while another might emphasize teamwork and commitment to customers. Next, review your work history and experience on school projects to recall several instances in which you demonstrated an important job-related skill or attribute that can be expressed in terms of those values. By discussing your experiences and accomplishments in the context of the company's values, you demonstrate that you understand what is important to the company and that you can be counted on to uphold those values.

In situational interviews, you're asked to explain how you would handle various hypothetical situations.

A **situational interview** is similar to a behavioral interview except that the questions focus on how you would handle various hypothetical situations on the job. The situations will likely relate to the job you're applying for, so the more you know about the position, the better prepared you'll be.

In a working interview, you perform real or simulated work-related tasks.

A **working interview** is the most realistic of all: You actually perform a job-related activity during the interview. You may be asked to lead a brainstorming session (sometimes with other job candidates), solve a business problem, engage in role playing, or even make a presentation.[15]

Stress interviews help recruiters see how you handle yourself under pressure.

The most unnerving type of interview is the **stress interview**, during which you might be asked questions designed to unsettle you or even subject you to long periods of silence, criticism, interruptions, and or hostile reactions by the interviewer. The theory behind this approach is that you'll reveal how well you handle stressful situations, although some experts find the technique of dubious value.[16] If you find yourself in a stress interview, recognize what is happening and collect your thoughts for a few seconds before you respond.

Interview Media

Expect to use a variety of media when you interview, from in-person conversations to virtual meetings.

Expect to be interviewed through a variety of media. Employers trying to cut travel costs and the demands on staff time now interview candidates via telephone, e-mail, instant messaging, virtual online systems, and videoconferencing, in addition to traditional face-to-face meetings.

Treat a telephone interview as seriously as you would an in-person interview.

To succeed at a telephone interview, make sure you treat it as seriously as an in-person interview. Be ready with a copy of all the materials you have sent the employer, and prepare some note cards with key message points you'd like to make and your supporting evidence (such as an impressive success story from your current job). If possible, arrange to speak on a landline so you don't have to worry about mobile phone reception problems. And remember that you won't be able to use a pleasant smile, a firm handshake, and other nonverbal signals to create a good impression. A positive, alert tone of voice is therefore vital.[17]

E-mail and IM are sometimes used in the screening stage. While you have even less opportunity to send and receive nonverbal signals with these formats, you do have the major advantage of being able to review and edit each response before you send it. Maintain a professional style in your responses and be sure to ask questions that demonstrate your knowledge of the company and the position.[18]

When interviewing via e-mail or IM, be sure to take a moment to review your responses before sending them.

Many employers use video technology for both live and recorded interviews. Live video interviews can involve a videoconferencing facility or simply a webcam attached to your personal computer. (Some companies will arrange to send you a webcam if you don't have one.) With recorded video interviews, an online system asks a set of questions and records each respondent's answers. Some systems also include online questionnaires in which you type your answers.[19] Prepare for a video interview as you would for an in-person interview and take the extra steps needed to become familiar with the equipment and the process. If you're interviewing from home, arrange the space so that the webcam doesn't pick up anything distracting or embarrassing in the background. During any video interview, remember to sit up straight and focus on the camera.

In a video interview, speak to the camera as though you are addressing the interviewer in person.

Virtual online interviews can range from simple structured interviews to sophisticated job simulations that are similar to working interviews. People applying for teller positions at SunTrust, a regional bank based in Atlanta, interact with video-game-like characters while performing job-related tasks. These job simulations not only identify good candidates but also reduce the risk of employment discrimination lawsuits because they closely mimic actual job skills.[20] And as one might expect from an innovator in search technology, Google is testing an extensive online interview system that measures attitudes, behaviors, personality, and personal history in an attempt to find candidates who match the profiles of successful Google employees.[21] Virtual worlds such as Second Life are also likely to see increased use in the interviewing process in years to come (see Figure 16.3).[22]

Computer-based virtual interviews range from simple structured interviews to realistic job simulations to meetings in virtual worlds.

What Employers Look for in an Interview

3 LEARNING OBJECTIVE

Describe briefly what employers look for during an employment interview and preemployment testing.

Interviews give employers the chance to go beyond the basic data of your résumé to get to know you and to answer two essential questions. The first is whether you can handle the responsibilities of the position. You'll probably be asked to describe your education, previous job experiences, and skill set. You may also be asked how you would apply those skills to

FIGURE 16.3 Finding Real Jobs in a Virtual World
Virtual job fairs, such as the Working Worlds event hosted by Luxembourg's GAX Technologies, allow candidates and recruiters to interact without the time and expense of travel.

Suitability for a specific job is judged on the basis of
- *Academic preparation*
- *Work experience*
- *Job-related personality traits*

Compatibility with an organization and a position is judged on the basis of personal background, attitudes, and style.

hypothetical situations on the job. By learning as much as you can about the company, the industry, and the specific job, you have a great opportunity to stand apart from the competition.

The second essential question is whether you will be a good fit with the organization and the target position. This line of inquiry includes both a general aspect and a specific aspect. The general aspect concerns your overall personality and approach to work. All good employers want people who are confident, dedicated, positive, curious, courteous, ethical, and willing to commit to something larger than their own individual goals. You could have superstar qualifications, but if an employer suspects that you might be a negative presence in the workplace, you probably won't get a job offer.

The specific aspect involves the fit with a particular company and position. Just like people, companies have different "personalities." Some are more intense; others are more laid back. Some emphasize teamwork; others expect employees to forge their own way and even to compete with one another. Expectations also vary from job to job within a company and from industry to industry. An outgoing personality is essential for sales but less so for research, for instance. Numerous candidates might have the technical qualifications for a particular job, but not all will have the right mix of personal attributes.

Preemployment Testing and Background Checks

Preemployment tests attempt to provide objective, quantitative information about a candidate's skills, attitudes, and habits.

In an effort to improve the predictability of the selection process and reduce the reliance on the brief interaction that an interview allows, many employers now conduct a variety of preemployment tests.[23] Here is an overview of the most common types of tests:

- **Integrity tests.** You might not think that a test could identify job candidates who are likely to steal from their employers or commit other ethical or legal infractions, but employers have had some success in using integrity tests.[24]
- **Personality tests.** Some employers use personality tests to profile overall intellectual ability, attitudes toward work, interests, managerial potential, dependability, commitment, honesty, and motivation.[25] The use of personality tests in hiring is controversial, however; recent research suggests that current tests are not a reliable predictor of job success.[26]
- **Job skills tests.** The most common type of preemployment tests are those designed to assess the competency or specific abilities needed to perform a job.[27] Some larger employers, including Google and Capital One, have created custom evaluation systems that test applicants and continue to track employees after they're hired.[28]
- **Substance tests.** Drug and alcohol testing is one of the most controversial issues in business today. Some employers believe such testing is absolutely necessary to maintain workplace safety and protect companies from lawsuits, whereas others view it as an invasion of employee privacy and a sign of disrespect. In recent years, as many as 80 percent of U.S. employers have conducted drug testing, but that percentage appears to be declining.[29]
- **Background checks.** In addition to testing, most companies conduct some sort of *background check* on job candidates.[30] Such checks can include reviewing your credit record, checking to see whether you have a criminal history, and verifying your education. To help prevent a background check from tripping you up, make sure your college transcript and credit record are correct and up to date.[31] And if you have anything posted online at MySpace, Facebook, or anywhere else that might be potentially embarrassing, take it down now. Recruiters routinely search for information about candidates online.[32] Employers can also find "unscripted references" from online social networks—that is, people who know you in some capacity but whom you haven't listed as references.[33]

If you're concerned about any preemployment test, ask the employer for more information or ask your college placement office for advice. You can also get more information from the Equal Employment Opportunity Commission (EEOC), at www.eeoc.gov.

4 LEARNING OBJECTIVE

List six tasks you need to complete to prepare for a successful job interview.

PREPARING FOR A JOB INTERVIEW

Preparation will help you feel more confident and perform better under pressure, and preparation starts with learning about the organization.

Learning About the Organization

A potential employer expects serious candidates to demonstrate an understanding of the company's operations, its markets, and its strategic and tactical challenges.[34] You've already done some initial research to identify companies of interest, but when you're invited to interview, it's time to dig a little deeper (see Table 16.2). Making this effort demonstrates your interest in the company, and it identifies you as a business professional who knows the importance of investigation and analysis.

Interviewers expect serious candidates to know some basic information about the company and its industry.

Thinking Ahead About Questions

Planning ahead for the interviewer's questions will help you handle them more confidently and successfully. As you consider answers to questions you might encounter, think in terms of how you can relate your qualifications to the organization's needs. In addition, you will want to prepare insightful questions of your own.

As you plan your responses to potential interview questions, be prepared to relate your qualifications to the organization's needs.

TABLE 16.2 Investigating an Organization and a Job Opportunity

WHERE TO LOOK AND WHAT YOU CAN LEARN

- *Company website:* Overall information about the company, including key executives, products and services, locations and divisions, employee benefits, and job descriptions
- *Competitors' websites:* Similar information from competitors, including the strengths those companies claim to have
- *Industry-related websites:* Objective analysis and criticism of the company, its products, its reputation, and its management
- *Marketing materials* (*brochures, catalogs, etc.*): The company's marketing strategy and customer communication style
- *Company publications* (*both print and electronic*): Key events, stories about employees, and new products
- *Blogs:* Analysis and criticism (not always fair or unbiased) of the company, its products and services, its reputation, and its management
- *Social networks:* Names and job titles of potential contacts in a company
- *Periodicals* (*newspapers and trade journals, both print and online*): In-depth stories about the company and its strategies, products, successes, and failures; you may find profiles of top executives
- *Career center at your college:* A wide array of information about companies that hire graduates
- *Current and former employees:* Insights into the work environment

POINTS TO LEARN ABOUT THE ORGANIZATION

- Full name
- Location (headquarters and divisions, branches, subsidiaries, or other units)
- Ownership (public or private; whether it is owned by another company)
- Age and brief history
- Products and services
- Industry position (whether the company is a leader or a minor player; whether it is an innovator or more of a follower)
- Key financial points (such as stock price and trend, if a public company)
- Growth prospects (whether the company is investing in its future through research and development; whether it is in a thriving industry)

POINTS TO LEARN ABOUT THE POSITION

- Title
- Functions and responsibilities
- Qualifications and expectations
- Possible career paths
- Salary range
- Travel expectations and opportunities
- Relocation expectations and opportunities

Communicating Across Cultures

Successfully Interviewing Across Borders

Interviewing for a job in another country can be one of the most exciting steps in your career. To succeed, you need to pay especially close attention to the important elements of the interviewing process, including personal appearance, an awareness of what interviewers are really trying to learn about you, and what you should learn about the organization you're hoping to join.

Some countries and cultures place a much higher importance on dress and personal grooming than many employees in the United States are accustomed to; moreover, expectations of personal appearance can vary dramatically from country to country. Ask people who've been to the country before and observe local businesspeople when you arrive. Many people interpret inappropriate dress as more than a simple fashion mistake; they view it as an inability or unwillingness to understand another culture.

Whether or not these things should matter isn't the question; they do matter, and successful job candidates learn how to respond to different expectations. For instance, business image consultant Ashley Rothschild points out that you could get away with wearing a boldly colored suit in Italy but probably not in Japan. Business professionals do tend to dress formally in Italy, but as a worldwide fashion leader, the country has a broad definition of what is appropriate business attire.

Smart U.S. recruiters always analyze both nonverbal signals and verbal messages to judge whether an applicant truly has the qualities necessary for a job. In international employment situations, you'll probably be under even closer scrutiny. Recruiters abroad will want to know if you really have what it takes to succeed in unfamiliar social settings, how your family will handle the transition, and whether you can adapt your personal work style and habits enough to blend in with the hiring organization.

Remember to ask plenty of questions and do your research, both before and after the interview. Some employees view overseas postings as grand adventures, only to collide headfirst with the reality of what it's like to live and work in a completely different culture. For instance, if you've grown accustomed to the independent work style you enjoy in your current job or in school, could you handle a more structured work environment with a hierarchical chain of command? Make sure to get a sense of the culture both within the company and within its social community before you commit to a job in another country.

CAREER APPLICATIONS

1. Explain how you could find out what is appropriate dress for a job interview in South Africa.
2. Would it be appropriate to ask an interviewer to describe the culture in his or her country? Explain your answer.

Planning for the Employer's Questions

In addition to questions about specific jobs and organizational needs, you can expect to be asked a variety of questions about your skills, achievements, goals, attitudes toward work and school, relationships with others, and occasionally your hobbies and interests. You'll also need to anticipate and give a little extra thought to a few particularly tough questions, such as these:

- **What is the hardest decision you've ever had to make?** Be prepared with a good example, explaining why the decision was difficult and how you finally made it.
- **What are your greatest weaknesses?** This question seems to be a stock favorite of some interviewers, although it probably rarely yields useful information. One recommended way to answer this question is to mention a relatively minor shortcoming and explain how you're working to improve in that area.
- **What didn't you like about previous jobs you've held?** Answer this one carefully: The interviewer is trying to predict whether you'll be an unhappy or difficult employee.[35] Describe something that you didn't like in a way that puts you in a positive light, such as having limited opportunities to apply your skills or education. Avoid making negative comments about former employers or colleagues.
- **Where do you want to be five years from now?** This questions tests (1) whether you're merely using this job as a stopover until something better comes along and (2) whether you've given thought to your long-term goals. Whatever you plan to say, your answer should reflect your desire to contribute to the employer's long-term goals. Whether this question yields useful information is a matter of debate but be prepared to answer it.[36]
- **Tell me something about yourself.** Ask if the interviewer would like to know about your specific skills or attributes. If this point is clarified, respond accordingly. If it isn't, explain how your skills can contribute to the job and the organization. This is a great chance to sell yourself.

Continue your preparation by jotting down a brief answer to each question in Table 16.3 You can also find typical interview questions at websites such as InterviewUp (www.interviewup.com), where candidates share actual questions they have faced in recent interviews.[37]

— REAL-TIME UPDATES
Learn More

Study the classics to ace your next interview

No, not Homer and Ovid—classic interview questions. Prepare answers to these old standbys so you can respond with clarity and confidence. Go to **http://real-timeupdates.com/ebc** and click on "Learn More." If you are using mybcommlab, you can access Real-Time Updates within each chapter or under Student Study Tools.

Planning Questions of Your Own

Remember that an interview is a two-way street: The questions you ask are just as important as the answers you provide. By asking insightful questions, you can demonstrate your understanding of the organization, you can steer the discussion into areas that allow you to present your qualifications to best advantage, and you can verify for yourself whether this is a good opportunity. Plus, interviewers expect you to ask questions, so you must be prepared for that. Here's a list of some things you might want to find out:

Plan questions that will help you decide whether the work and the organization are compatible with your goals and values.

- **Are these my kind of people?** Observe the interviewers, and if you can, arrange to talk with other employees.

TABLE 16.3 Twenty-Five Common Interview Questions

QUESTIONS ABOUT COLLEGE

1. What courses in college did you like most? Least? Why?
2. Do you think your extracurricular activities in college were worth the time you spent on them? Why or why not?
3. When did you choose your college major? Did you ever change your major? If so, why?
4. Do you feel you did the best scholastic work you are capable of?
5. How has your college education prepared you for this position?

QUESTIONS ABOUT EMPLOYERS AND JOBS

6. What jobs have you held? Why did you leave?
7. What percentage of your college expenses did you earn? How?
8. Why did you choose your particular field of work?
9. What are the disadvantages of your chosen field?
10. Have you served in the military? What rank did you achieve? What jobs did you perform?
11. What do you think about how this industry operates today?
12. Why do you think you would like this particular type of job?

QUESTIONS ABOUT PERSONAL ATTITUDES AND PREFERENCES

13. Do you prefer to work in any specific geographic location? If so, why?
14. How much money do you hope to be earning in 5 years? In 10 years?
15. What do you think determines a person's progress in a good organization?
16. What personal characteristics do you feel are necessary for success in your chosen field?
17. Tell me a story.
18. Do you like to travel?
19. Why should I hire you?

QUESTIONS ABOUT WORK HABITS

20. Do you prefer working with others or by yourself?
21. What type of boss do you prefer?
22. Have you ever had any difficulty getting along with colleagues or supervisors? With instructors? With other students?
23. What would you do if you were given an unrealistic deadline for a task or project?
24. How do you feel about overtime work?
25. What have you done that shows initiative and willingness to work?

TABLE 16.4 Ten Questions to Ask an Interviewer

QUESTION	REASON FOR ASKING
1. What are the job's major responsibilities?	A vague answer could mean that the responsibilities have not been clearly defined, which is almost guaranteed to cause frustration if you take the job.
2. What qualities do you want in the person who fills this position?	This will help you go beyond the job description to understand what the company really wants.
3. How do you measure success for someone in this position?	A vague or incomplete answer could mean that the expectations you will face are unrealistic or ill defined.
4. What is the first problem that needs the attention of the person you hire?	Not only will this help you prepare, but it can signal whether you're about to jump into a problematic situation.
5. Would relocation be required now or in the future?	If you're not willing to move often or at all, you need to know those expectations now.
6. Why is this job now vacant?	If the previous employee got promoted, that's a good sign. If the person quit, that might not be such a good sign.
7. What makes your organization different from others in the industry?	The answer will help you assess whether the company has a clear strategy to succeed in its industry and whether top managers communicate it to lower-level employees.
8. How would you define your organization's managerial philosophy?	You want to know whether the managerial philosophy is consistent with your own working values.
9. What is a typical workday like for you?	The interviewer's response can give you clues about daily life at the company.
10. What systems and policies are in place to help employees stay up to date in their professions and continue to expand their skills?	If the company doesn't have a strong commitment to employee development, chances are it isn't going to stay competitive very long.

- **Can I do this work?** Compare your qualifications with the requirements described by the interviewer.
- **Will I enjoy the work?** Will the work give you real feelings of accomplishment and satisfaction?
- **Is the job what I want?** Will it make use of your best capabilities? Does it offer a career path to the long-term goals you've set?
- **Does the job pay what I'm worth?** By comparing jobs and salaries before you're interviewed, you'll know what's reasonable for someone with your skills in your industry.
- **What kind of person would I be working for?** Keep in mind that you will likely work for more than one boss during your tenure at a company, so don't focus too much on one individual.
- **What sort of future can I expect with this organization?** Is this organization in healthy financial shape? Will it grow enough to offer you opportunities to advance?

For a list of good questions that you might use as a starting point, see Table 16.4.

Think ahead about ways to relate your skills and accomplishments through brief, memorable stories.

As you prepare answers, look for ways to frame your responses as brief stories (30 to 90 seconds) rather than simple declarative statements.[38] Instead of just saying you are good at finding ways to reduce costs, tell a story of a time you did just that. Cohesive stories tend to stick in the listener's mind more effectively than disconnected facts and statements.

Bolstering Your Confidence

The best way to build your confidence is to prepare thoroughly and address shortcomings as best you can—in other words, to take action.

Interviewing is stressful for everyone, so some nervousness is natural. However, you can take steps to feel more confident. Start by reminding yourself that you have value to offer the employer, and the employer already thinks highly enough of you to invite you to an interview.

If some aspect of your appearance or background makes you uneasy, correct it if possible or offset it by emphasizing positive traits such as warmth, wit, intelligence, or charm. Instead of dwelling on your weaknesses, focus on your strengths. Instead of worrying about how you will perform in the interview, focus on how you can help the organization succeed. As with public speaking, the more prepared you are, the more confident you'll be.

Polishing Your Interview Style

Competence and confidence are the foundation of your interviewing style, and you can enhance them by giving the interviewer an impression of poise, good manners, and good judgment. You can develop an adept style by staging mock interviews with a friend or using an interview simulator. Record these mock interviews so you can evaluate yourself. Your career center may have computer-based systems for practicing interviews as well (see Figure 16.4).

After each practice session, look for opportunities to improve. Have your mock interview partner critique your performance, or critique yourself if you're able to record your practice interviews, using the list of warning signs shown in Table 16.5 on the next page. Pay close attention to the length of your planned answers as well. Interviewers want you to give complete answers, but they don't want you to take up valuable time or test their patience by chatting about minor or irrelevant details.[39]

Staging mock interviews with a friend is a good way to hone your style.

Evaluate your nonverbal behavior as well. In the United States and most other Western cultures, you are more likely to have a successful interview if you maintain eye contact, smile frequently, sit in an attentive position, and use frequent hand gestures. These nonverbal signals convince the interviewer that you're alert, assertive, dependable, confident, responsible, and energetic.[40]

Nonverbal behavior has a significant effect on the interviewer's opinion of you.

The sound of your voice can also have a major impact on your success in a job interview.[41] Recording your voice can help you overcome voice problems. If you tend to speak too rapidly, practice speaking more slowly. If your voice sounds too loud or too soft, practice adjusting it. Work on eliminating speech mannerisms such as *you know*, *like*, and *um*, which make you sound hesitant or inarticulate.

The way you speak is almost as important as what you say.

FIGURE 16.4 Interview Simulators

Experts recommend practicing your interview skills as much as possible. You can use a friend or classmate as a practice partner, or you might be able to use one of the interview simulators now available, such as this system from Perfect Interview. Ask at your career center for more information.

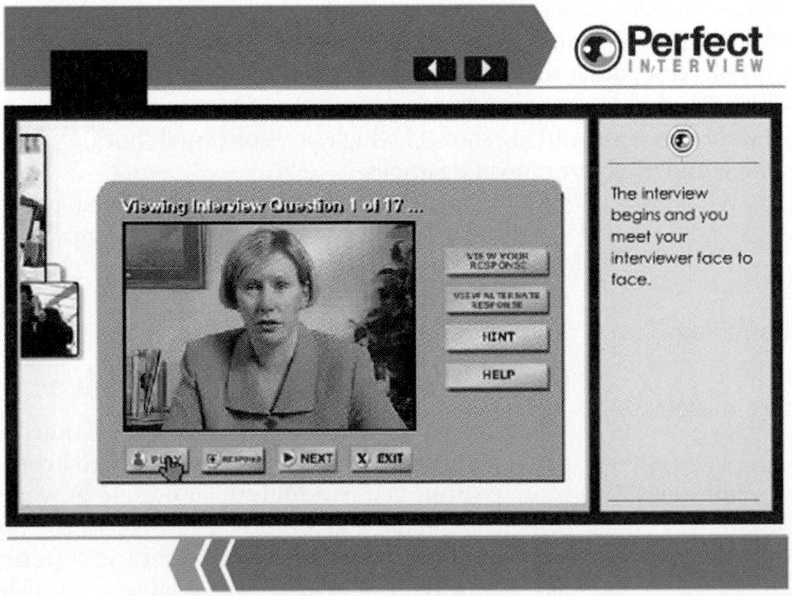

TABLE 16.5 Warning Signs: 25 Attributes That Interviewers Don't Like to See

1. Poor personal appearance
2. Overbearing, overaggressive, or conceited demeanor; a "superiority complex"; a know-it-all attitude
3. Inability to express ideas clearly; poor voice, diction, or grammar
4. Lack of knowledge or experience
5. Poor preparation for the interview
6. Lack of interest in the job
7. Lack of planning for career; lack of purpose or goals
8. Lack of enthusiasm; passive and indifferent demeanor
9. Lack of confidence and poise; appearance of being nervous and ill at ease
10. Insufficient evidence of achievement
11. Failure to participate in extracurricular activities
12. Overemphasis on money; interested only in the best dollar offer
13. Poor scholastic record; just got by
14. Unwillingness to start at the bottom; expecting too much too soon
15. Tendency to make excuses
16. Evasive answers; hedging on unfavorable factors in record
17. Lack of tact
18. Lack of maturity
19. Lack of courtesy; being ill mannered
20. Condemnation of past employers
21. Lack of social skills
22. Marked dislike for schoolwork
23. Lack of vitality
24. Failure to look interviewer in the eye
25. Limp, weak handshake

Presenting a Professional Image

Dress conservatively and be well groomed for every interview; you will be judged on how well you can sense what is appropriate in the work environment.

Clothing and grooming are important elements of preparation because they reveal something about a candidate's personality, professionalism, and ability to sense the unspoken "rules" of a situation. Your research into various industries and professions should give you insight into expectations for business attire. If you're not sure what to wear, refer to Table 2.4 on page 53 for tips on selecting appropriate business attire or ask someone who works in the same industry. And don't be afraid to call the company for advice.

If you want to be taken seriously, dress and act seriously.

Send a clear signal that you understand the business world and know how to adapt to it. You won't be taken seriously otherwise. You don't need to spend a fortune on interview clothes, but your clothes must be clean, pressed, and appropriate. The following conservative look will serve you well in just about any interview situation:[42]

- Neat, "adult" hairstyle
- Conservative business suit (for women, that means no exposed midriffs, no short skirts, and no plunging necklines), in a dark solid color or a subtle pattern such as pinstripes
- White shirt for men; coordinated blouse for women
- Conservative tie (classic stripes or subtle patterns) for men
- Limited jewelry (men should wear very little jewelry)
- No visible piercings other than one or two earrings (for women only)
- No visible tattoos
- Stylish but professional-looking shoes (no high heels or casual shoes)
- Clean hands and nicely trimmed fingernails
- Little or no perfume or cologne (some people are allergic, and many people are put off by strong smells)
- Subtle makeup (for women)
- Exemplary personal hygiene

REAL-TIME UPDATES
Learn More

Do you know the difference between business casual and business formal?

Go shopping with a business style expert to select the appropriate wear for any interview. Go to **http://real-timeupdates.com/ebc** and click on "Learn More." If you are using mybcommlab, you can access Real-Time Updates within each chapter or under Student Study Tools.

Being Ready When You Arrive

When you go to your interview, take a small notebook, a pen, a list of the questions you want to ask, several copies of your résumé (protected in a folder), an outline of what you have learned about the organization, and any past correspondence about the position. You may also want to take a small calendar, a transcript of your college grades, a list of references, and a portfolio containing samples of your work, performance reviews, and certificates of achievement.[43] Carry all these items in a good-quality briefcase.

Be sure you know when and where the interview will be held. The worst way to start any interview is to be late. Verify the route and time required to get there, even if that means traveling there ahead of time. Plan to arrive early.

When you arrive, you may have to wait for a while. Use this time to review the key messages about yourself you want to get across in the interview. Conduct yourself professionally while waiting, and show respect for everyone you encounter. Avoid chewing gum, eating, or drinking. Anything you do or say at this stage may get back to the interviewer, so make sure your best qualities show from the moment you enter the premises. To review the steps for planning a successful interview, see "Checklist: Planning for a Successful Job Interview."

Make a positive first impression with careful grooming and attire. You don't need to spend a fortune on new clothes, but you do need to look clean, prepared, and professional.

INTERVIEWING FOR SUCCESS

At this point, you have a good sense of the overall process and know how to prepare for your interviews. The next step is to get familiar with the three stages of every interview: the warm-up, the question-and-answer session, and the close.

5 LEARNING OBJECTIVE

Explain the three stages of a successful employment interview.

The Warm-Up

Of the three stages, the warm-up is the most important, even though it may account for only a small fraction of the time you spend in the interview. Studies suggest that many interviewers, particularly those who are poorly trained in interviewing techniques, make up their minds within the first 20 seconds of contact with a candidate.[45] Don't let your guard down if the interviewer wants to engage in what feels like small talk; these exchanges are every bit as important as structured questions.

The first minute of an interview is crucial, so be ready and stay on your toes.

Body language is crucial. Stand up or sit up straight, maintain regular but natural eye contact, and don't fidget. When the interviewer extends a hand, respond with a firm but not overpowering handshake. Repeat the interviewer's name when you're introduced ("It's a pleasure to meet you, Ms. Litton"). Wait until you're asked to be seated or the interviewer has taken a seat. Let the interviewer start the discussion and be ready to answer one or two substantial questions right away. Common openers include[46]

- Why do you want to work here?
- What do you know about us?
- Tell me a little about yourself.

CHECKLIST: Planning for a Successful Job Interview

- Learn about the organization, including its operations, markets, and challenges.
- Plan for the employer's questions, including questions about tough decisions you've made, your perceived shortcomings, what you didn't like about previous jobs, and your career plans.
- Plan questions of your own to find out whether this is really the job and the organization for you and to show that you've done your research.
- Bolster your confidence by removing as many sources of apprehension as you can.
- Polish your interview style by staging mock interviews.
- Present a professional appearance with appropriate dress and grooming.
- Be ready when you arrive and bring along a pen, paper, a list of questions, copies of your résumé, an outline of your research on the company, and any correspondence you've had regarding the position.
- Double-check the location and time of the interview and map out the route beforehand.
- Relax and be flexible; the schedule and interview arrangements may change when you arrive.

Sharpening Your Career Skills

Make Sure You Don't Talk Yourself Out of a Job

Even well-qualified applicants sometimes talk themselves right out of an opportunity by making avoidable blunders during a job interview. Take care to avoid these all-too-common mistakes:

Being defensive. An interview isn't an interrogation, and the interviewer isn't out to get you. Treat interviews as business conversations, an exchange of information in which both sides have something of value to share. You'll give (and get) better information that way.

Failing to ask questions. Interviewers expect you to ask questions, both during the interview and at its conclusion, when they ask if you have any questions. If you have nothing to ask, you come across as someone who isn't really interested in the job or the company. Prepare a list of questions before every interview.

Failing to answer questions—or trying to bluff your way through difficult questions. If you can't answer a question, don't try to talk your way around it or fake your way through it. Remember that sometimes interviewers ask strange questions just to see how you'll respond. What kind of fish would you like to be? How would you go about nailing jelly to the ceiling? Why are manhole covers round? Some of these questions are designed to test your grace under pressure, whereas others are used to get you to think through a logical answer. (Manhole covers are round because a circle is the only shape that can't fall through an open hole of slightly smaller size, by the way.) Don't act like the question is stupid or refuse to answer it. As Lynne Sarikas, director of the MBA Career Center at Northeastern University, explains, these questions offer an opportunity to "demonstrate quick thinking, poise, creativity, and even a sense of humor."[44]

Freezing up. The human brain seems to have the capacity to just freeze up in stressful situations. An interviewer might have asked you a simple question, or perhaps you are halfway through an intelligent answer, and poof!—all your thoughts disappear and you can't organize words in any logical order. Try to quickly replay the last few seconds of the conversation in your mind to see if you can recapture the conversational thread. If that fails, you're probably better off explaining to the interviewer that your mind has gone blank and asking him or her to repeat the question. Doing so is embarrassing but not as embarrassing as chattering on and on with no idea of what you're saying, hoping you'll stumble back onto the topic.

Failing to understand your potential to contribute to the organization. Interviewers care less about your history than about how you can help their organization in the future. Be sure to understand ahead of time how your skills can help the company meet its challenges.

CAREER APPLICATIONS

1. What should you do if you suddenly realize that something you said earlier in the interview is incorrect or incomplete? Explain your answer.
2. How would you answer the following question: "How do you respond to colleagues who make you angry?" Explain your answer.

The Question-and-Answer Stage

You could face substantial questions as soon as the interview starts, so make sure you are prepared and ready to go.

Questions and answers will consume the greatest part of the interview. The interviewer will ask you about your qualifications and discuss many of the points mentioned in your résumé. You'll also be asking questions of your own.

Dealing with Questions

Let the interviewer lead the conversation and never answer a question before he or she has finished asking it. As much as possible, avoid one-word, yes-or-no answers. Use the opportunity to expand on a positive response or explain a negative response. If you're asked a difficult question, pause before responding. Think through the implications of the question; for instance, the recruiter may know that you can't answer a question and only want to see how you'll handle the situation.

Whenever you're asked if you have any questions, or whenever doing so naturally fits the flow of the conversation, ask a question from the list you've prepared. Probe for what the company is looking for in its new employees so that you can show how you meet the firm's needs. Also try to zero in on any reservations the interviewer might have about you so that you can dispel them.

TABLE 16.6 Interview Questions That Employers Are and Are Not Allowed to Ask

INTERVIEWERS MAY ASK THIS . . .	BUT NOT THIS
What is your name?	What was your maiden name?
Are you over 18?	When were you born?
Did you graduate from high school?	When did you graduate from high school?
[No questions about race are allowed.]	What is your race?
Can you perform [specific tasks]?	Do you have physical or mental disabilities?
	Do you have a drug or alcohol problem?
	Are you taking any prescription drugs?
Would you be able to meet the job's requirement to frequently work weekends?	Would working on weekends conflict with your religion?
Do you have the legal right to work in the United States?	What country are you a citizen of?
Have you ever been convicted of a felony?	Have you ever been arrested?
This job requires that you speak Spanish. Do you?	What language did you speak in your home when you were growing up?

Listening to the Interviewer

Paying attention when an interviewer speaks can be as important as giving good answers or asking good questions. Review the tips on listening offered in Chapter 2. The interviewer's facial expressions, eye movements, gestures, and posture may tell you the real meaning of what is being said. Be especially aware of how your comments are received. Does the interviewer nod in agreement or smile to show approval? If so, you're making progress. If not, you might want to introduce another topic or modify your approach.

Paying attention to both verbal and nonverbal messages can help you turn the question-and-answer stage to your advantage.

Handling Discriminatory Questions

Employers cannot legally discriminate against a job candidate on the basis of race, color, gender, age (if the candidate is 40 or older), marital status, religion, national origin, or disability. Accordingly, regulations are in place to prevent interviewers from asking questions in ways that would allow them to discriminate according to any of these factors (see Table 16.6).

Well-trained interviewers are aware of questions they shouldn't ask.

If an interviewer asks an unlawful question, consider your options carefully before you respond. You can answer the question as it was asked, you can ask tactfully whether the question might be prohibited, you can simply refuse to answer it, or you can try to answer "the question behind the question."[47] For example, if an interviewer inappropriately asks whether you are married or have strong family ties in the area, he or she might be trying to figure out if you're willing to travel or relocate—both of which are acceptable questions. Only you can decide which is the right choice based on the situation.

Think about how you might respond if you are asked a potentially unlawful question.

Even if you do answer the question as it was asked, think hard before accepting a job offer from this company if you have alternatives. Was the off-limits question possibly accidental (it happens) and therefore not really a major concern? If you think it was intentional, would you want to work for an organization that condones illegal or discriminatory questions or that doesn't train its employees to avoid them?

If you believe an interviewer's questions are unreasonable, unrelated to the job, or an attempt to discriminate, you have the option of filing a complaint with the EEOC (www.eeoc.gov) or with the agency in your state that regulates fair employment practices.

The Close

Like the warm-up, the end of the interview is more important than its brief duration would indicate. These last few minutes are your last opportunity to emphasize your value to the organization and to correct any misconceptions the interviewer might have. Be aware that many interviews will ask if you have any more questions at this point, so save one or two from your list.

REAL-TIME UPDATES
Learn More

Evaluating a job offer

Explore the many steps needed to determine whether a job offer is right for you, your family, and your future. Go to **http://real-timeupdates.com/ebc** and click on "Learn More." If you are using mybcommlab, you can access Real-Time Updates within each chapter or under Student Study Tools.

Concluding Gracefully

You can usually tell when the interviewer is trying to conclude the session. He or she may ask whether you have any more questions, check the time, sum up the discussion, or simply tell you that the allotted time for the interview is up. When you get the signal, be sure to thank the interviewer for the opportunity and express your interest in the organization. If you can do so comfortably, try to pin down what will happen next, but don't press for an immediate decision.

Conclude an interview with courtesy and enthusiasm.

If this is your second or third visit to the organization, the interview may end with an offer of employment. If you have other offers or need time to think about this offer, it's perfectly acceptable to thank the interviewer for the offer and ask for some time to consider it. If no job offer is made, the interview team may not have reached a decision yet, but you may tactfully ask when you can expect to know the decision.

Discussing Salary

Research salary ranges in your job, industry, and geographic region before you try to negotiate salary.

If you receive an offer during an interview, you'll naturally want to discuss salary. However, let the interviewer raise the subject. If you are asked your salary requirements during the interview or on a job application, you can say that your salary requirements are open or negotiable or that you would expect a competitive compensation package.[48] If you have added qualifications, point them out: "With my 18 months of experience in the field, I would expect to start in the middle of the normal salary range."

How far you can negotiate depends on several factors, including market demand for your skills, the strength of the job market, the company's compensation policies, the company's financial health, and whether you have other job offers. Remember that you're negotiating a business deal, not asking for personal favors, so focus on the unique value you can bring to the job. The more information you have, the stronger your position will be.

Negotiating benefits may be one way to get more value from an employment package.

Salary will probably be the most important component of your compensation and benefits package, but it's not the only factor by any means. And even if salary isn't negotiable, you may find flexibility in a signing bonus, profit sharing, pension and other retirement benefits, health coverage, vacation time, stock options, and other valuable elements in the overall compensation and benefits package.[49]

To review the important tips for successful interviews, see "Checklist: Making a Positive Impression in Job Interviews."

Interview Notes

Keep a written record of your job interviews, and keep your notes organized so that you can compare companies and opportunities.

Maintain a notebook or simple database with information about each company, interviewers' answers to your questions, contact information for each interviewer, the status of thank-you notes and other follow-up communication, and future interview appointments. Carefully organized notes will help you decide which company is the right fit for you when it comes time to choose from the job offers you've received.

For the latest information on interviewing strategies, visit http://real-timeupdates.com/ebc and click on Chapter 16.

REAL-TIME UPDATES
Learn More

Follow these negotiating tips to get the best job offer

Make sure you get the best compensation package when you get a job offer. Go to **http://real-timeupdates.com/ebc** and click on "Learn More." If you are using mybcommlab, you can access Real-Time Updates within each chapter or under Student Study Tools.

FOLLOWING UP AFTER THE INTERVIEW

Staying in contact with a prospective employer after an interview shows that you really want the job and are determined to get it. Doing so also gives you another chance to demonstrate your communication skills and sense of business

CHECKLIST: Making a Positive Impression in Job Interviews

A. Be ready for the warm-up stage.
- Stay on your toes; even initial small talk is part of the interviewing process.
- Greet the interviewer by name, with a smile and direct eye contact.
- Offer a firm (not crushing) handshake if the interviewer extends a hand.
- Take a seat only after the interviewer invites you to sit or has taken his or her own seat.
- Listen for clues about what the interviewer is trying to get you to reveal about you and your qualifications.

B. Understand the question-and-answer stage.
- Let the interviewer lead the conversation.
- Never answer a question before the interviewer finishes asking it.
- Listen carefully to the interviewer and watch for nonverbal signals.
- Don't limit yourself to simple yes-or-no answers; expand on the answer to show your knowledge of the company (but don't ramble on).
- If you encounter a potentially discriminatory question, decide how you want to respond before you say anything.
- When you have the opportunity, ask questions from the list you've prepared; remember that interviewers expect you to ask questions.

C. Close on a strong note.
- Watch and listen for signs that the interview is about to end.
- Quickly evaluate how well you've done and correct any misperceptions the interviewer might have.
- If you receive an offer and aren't ready to decide, it's entirely appropriate to ask for time to think about it.
- Don't bring up salary but be prepared to discuss it if the interviewer raises the subject.
- End with a warm smile and a handshake and thank the interviewer for meeting with you.

etiquette. You have several opportunities to communicate after an interview, starting with a thank-you message.

6 LEARNING OBJECTIVE

Identify the most common employment messages that follow an interview, and explain when you would use each one.

Thank-You Message

Write a thank-you letter or e-mail within two days of the interview, even if you feel you have little chance of being offered the job. Not only is this good etiquette, but it can be an essential step in promoting yourself to the employer. The thank-you message gives you the opportunity to reinforce the reasons that you are a good choice for the position, and it lets you respond to any negatives that might've arisen in the interview.[50] Acknowledge the interviewer's time and courtesy, convey your continued interest, reinforce the reasons that you are a good fit for the position, and then ask politely for a decision (see Figure 16.5 on the next page). Keep your message brief, demonstrate the "you" attitude, and sound positive without sounding overconfident.

Six types of follow-up messages:
- *Thank-you message*
- *Message of inquiry*
- *Request for a time extension*
- *Letter of acceptance*
- *Letter declining a job offer*
- *Letter of resignation*

Message of Inquiry

If you're not advised of the interviewer's decision by the promised date or within two weeks, you can inquire about the status of the decision—particularly if you've received a job offer from a second firm and don't want to accept it before you have an answer from the first. Use the following message as a model:

When we talked on April 7 about the fashion coordinator position in your Park Avenue showroom, you indicated that a decision would be made by May 1. I am still enthusiastic about the position and eager to know what conclusion you've reached.

Identifies the position and introduces the main idea

To complicate matters, another firm has now offered me a position and has asked that I reply within the next two weeks.

Places the reason for the request second

Because your company seems to offer a greater challenge, I would appreciate knowing about your decision by Thursday, May 12. If you need more information before then, please let me know.

Makes a courteous request for specific action last, while clearly stating a preference for this organization

FIGURE 16.5 Thank-You Message
In three brief paragraphs, Michael Espinosa acknowledges the interviewer's time and consideration, expresses his continued interest in the position, explains a crucial discussion point that he has reconsidered, and asks for a decision.

Thank you for yesterday's interview (HTML)

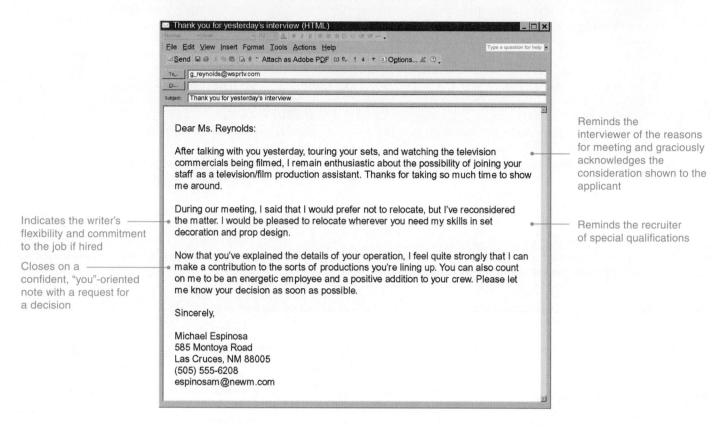

To... g_reynolds@wsprtv.com

Cc...

Subject: Thank you for yesterday's interview

Dear Ms. Reynolds:

After talking with you yesterday, touring your sets, and watching the television commercials being filmed, I remain enthusiastic about the possibility of joining your staff as a television/film production assistant. Thanks for taking so much time to show me around.

During our meeting, I said that I would prefer not to relocate, but I've reconsidered the matter. I would be pleased to relocate wherever you need my skills in set decoration and prop design.

Now that you've explained the details of your operation, I feel quite strongly that I can make a contribution to the sorts of productions you're lining up. You can also count on me to be an energetic employee and a positive addition to your crew. Please let me know your decision as soon as possible.

Sincerely,

Michael Espinosa
585 Montoya Road
Las Cruces, NM 88005
(505) 555-6208
espinosam@newm.com

Reminds the interviewer of the reasons for meeting and graciously acknowledges the consideration shown to the applicant

Indicates the writer's flexibility and commitment to the job if hired

Reminds the recruiter of special qualifications

Closes on a confident, "you"-oriented note with a request for a decision

Request for a Time Extension

If you receive a job offer while other interviews are still pending, you can ask the employer for a time extension. Open with a strong statement of your continued interest in the job, ask for more time to consider the offer, provide specific reasons for the request, and assure the reader that you will respond by a specific date (see Figure 16.6).

Letter of Acceptance

Use the model for positive messages when you write a letter of acceptance.

When you receive a job offer that you want to accept, reply within five days. Begin by accepting the position and expressing thanks. Identify the job that you're accepting. In the next paragraph, cover any necessary details. Conclude by saying that you look forward to reporting for work. As always, a positive message such as this should convey your enthusiasm and eagerness to contribute:

Confirms the specific terms of the offer with a good-news statement at the beginning

> I'm delighted to accept the graphic design position in your advertising department at the salary of $2,975 a month.

Covers miscellaneous details in the middle

> Enclosed are the health insurance forms you asked me to complete and sign. I've already given notice to my current employer and will be able to start work on Monday, January 18.

Closes with another reference to the good news and a look toward the future

> The prospect of joining your firm is exciting. Thank you for giving me this opportunity to contribute to [the company's] long-term success.

Be aware that a job offer and a written acceptance of that offer can constitute a legally binding contract—for you and the employer. Before you write an acceptance letter, be sure you want the job.

FIGURE 16.6 Request for a Time Extension
If you need to request more time to make a decision about a job offer, be sure to explain why you need the extension and reaffirm that you are still interested in the job.

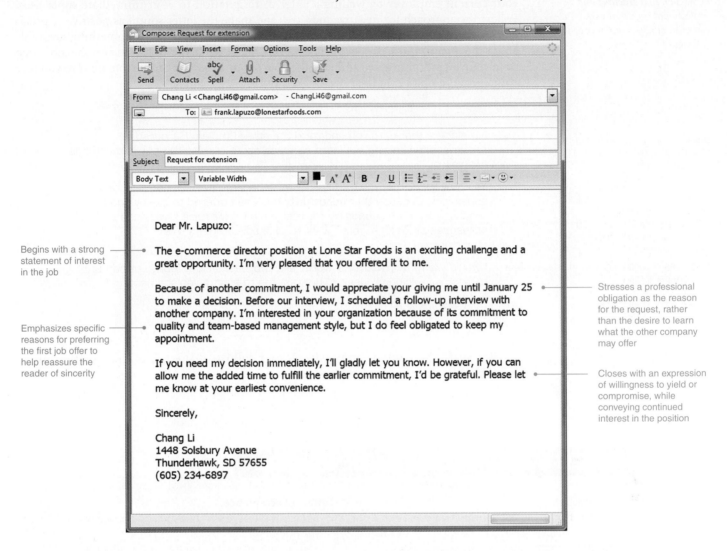

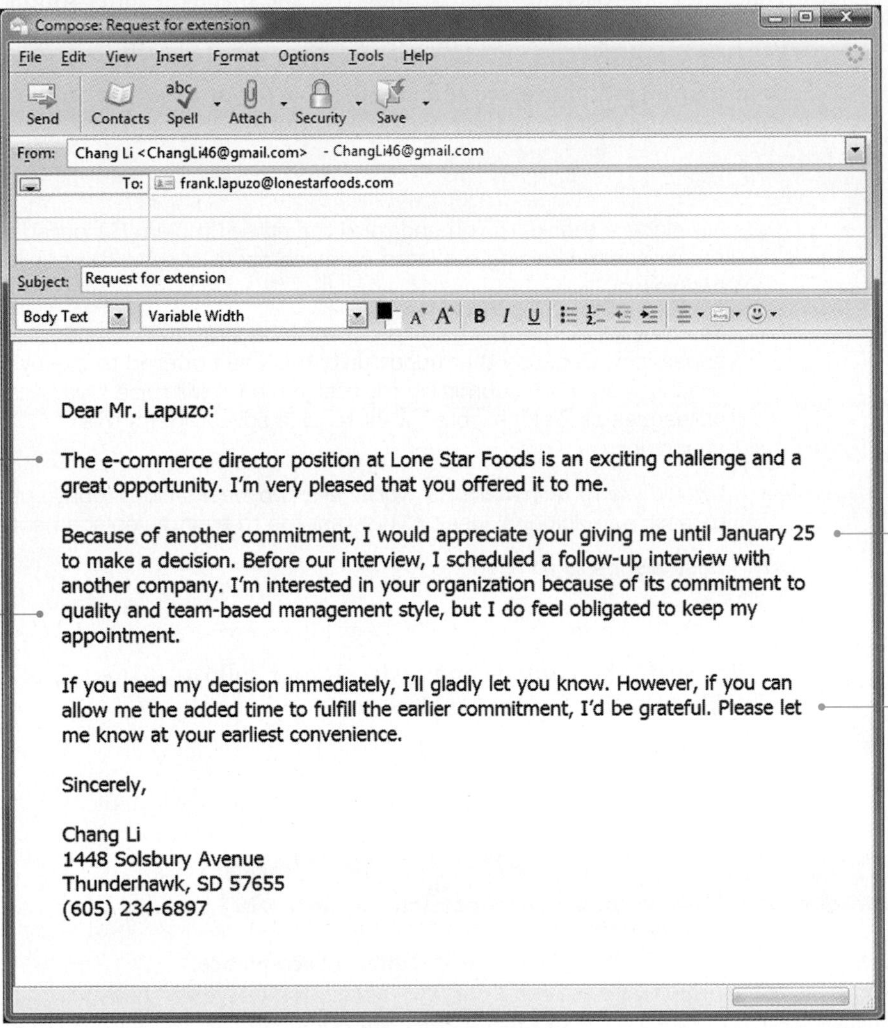

Dear Mr. Lapuzo:

The e-commerce director position at Lone Star Foods is an exciting challenge and a great opportunity. I'm very pleased that you offered it to me.

Because of another commitment, I would appreciate your giving me until January 25 to make a decision. Before our interview, I scheduled a follow-up interview with another company. I'm interested in your organization because of its commitment to quality and team-based management style, but I do feel obligated to keep my appointment.

If you need my decision immediately, I'll gladly let you know. However, if you can allow me the added time to fulfill the earlier commitment, I'd be grateful. Please let me know at your earliest convenience.

Sincerely,

Chang Li
1448 Solsbury Avenue
Thunderhawk, SD 57655
(605) 234-6897

Begins with a strong statement of interest in the job

Emphasizes specific reasons for preferring the first job offer to help reassure the reader of sincerity

Stresses a professional obligation as the reason for the request, rather than the desire to learn what the other company may offer

Closes with an expression of willingness to yield or compromise, while conveying continued interest in the position

Letter Declining a Job Offer

After all your interviews, you may find that you need to write a letter declining a job offer. Use the techniques for negative messages (see Chapter 9): Open warmly, state the reasons for refusing the offer, decline the offer explicitly, and close on a pleasant note, expressing gratitude. By taking the time to write a sincere, tactful letter, you leave the door open for future contact:

A letter declining a job offer should follow the model for negative messages.

Thank you for your hospitality during my interview at your Durham facility last month. I'm flattered that you would offer me the computer analyst position that we talked about.

I was fortunate to receive two job offers during my search. Because my desire to work abroad can more readily be satisfied by another company, I have accepted that job offer.

I deeply appreciate the time you spent talking with me. Thank you again for your consideration and kindness.

Uses a buffer in the opening paragraph

Precedes the bad news with tactfully phrased reasons for the applicant's unfavorable decision and leaves the door open

Lets the reader down gently with a sincere and cordial ending

Letter of Resignation

Letters of resignation should always be written in a gracious and professional style that avoids criticism of your employer or your colleagues.

If you get a job offer and are currently employed, you can maintain good relations with your current employer by writing a letter of resignation to your immediate supervisor. Follow the approach for negative messages and make the letter sound as positive as possible. Don't use this letter to vent any frustrations you may have. Say something favorable about the organization, the people you work with, or what you've learned on the job. Then state your intention to leave and give the date of your last day on the job. Be sure you give your current employer at least two weeks' notice:

Uses an appreciative opening to serve as a buffer

My sincere thanks to you and to all the other Emblem Corporation employees for helping me learn so much about serving the public these past two years.

States reasons before the bad news itself, using tactful phrasing to help keep the relationship friendly, should the writer later want letters of recommendation

You may recall that my goal has been to become a customer relations supervisor. Because that opportunity has been offered to me by another organization, I am submitting my resignation. I will miss my friends and colleagues at Emblem, but I want to take advantage of this opportunity.

Discusses necessary details in an extra paragraph

I would like to terminate my work here two weeks from today but can arrange to work an additional week if you want me to train a replacement.

Tempers any disappointment with a cordial close

Best wishes to all of you.

To verify the content and style of your follow-up messages, consult the tips in "Checklist: Writing Follow-Up Messages."

CHECKLIST: Writing Follow-Up Messages

A. Thank-you messages.
- Write a brief thank-you letter within two days of the interview.
- Acknowledge the interviewer's time and courtesy.
- Restate the specific job you're applying for.
- Express your enthusiasm about the organization and the job.
- Add any new facts that may help your chances.
- Politely ask for a decision.

B. Messages of inquiry.
- If you haven't heard from the interviewer by the promised date, write a brief message of inquiry.
- Use the direct approach: main idea, necessary details, specific request.

C. Requests for a time extension.
- Request an extension if you have pending interviews and need time to decide about an offer.
- Open on a friendly note.
- Explain why you need more time and express continued interest in the company.
- In the close, promise a quick decision if your request is denied and ask for a confirmation if your request is granted.

D. Letters of acceptance.
- Send this message within five days of receiving the offer.
- State clearly that you accept the offer, identify the job you're accepting, and confirm vital details such as salary and start date.
- Make sure you want the job; an acceptance letter can be treated as a legally binding contract.

E. Letters declining a job offer.
- Use the model for negative messages.
- Open on a warm and appreciative note and then explain why you are refusing the offer.
- End on a sincere, positive note.

F. Letters of resignation.
- Send a letter of resignation to your current employer as soon as possible.
- Begin with an appreciative buffer.
- In the middle section, state your reasons for leaving and actually state that you are resigning.
- Close cordially.

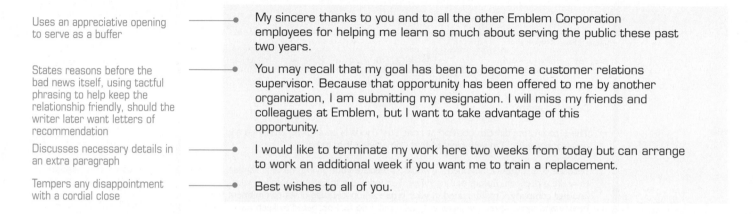

Document Makeover

Improve This Letter

To practice correcting drafts of actual documents, visit the "Document Makeovers" section in mybcommlab. Refer to the User Guide for specific instructions on how to access the content for this chapter. You will find a letter that contains problems and errors related to what you've learned in this chapter about applying and interviewing for employment. Use the "Final Draft" decision tool to create an improved version of this request for a time extension. Check the letter for all the elements necessary to reassure the potential employer, ask for the extension, explain the reasons for the request, offer to compromise, and facilitate a quick reply.

On the Job: Solving Communication Dilemmas at Google

Much of Google's recruiting effort focuses on the software engineers and other technical specialists who create and refine the company's search technologies. However, as those technologies get put to use in a wider array of commercial applications, business specialists will play an increasingly important role in the company's future. You're on the interview team assigned to fill one such position, that of corporate development analyst/associate in Google's Mountain View, California, offices. Here is how Google's website describes the position ("M&A" is an abbreviation for mergers and acquisitions):

> This is a great opportunity to join the team at Google focusing on enhancing our corporate mission through M&A transactions. We are looking for an associate to join our corporate development team where you will be mentored by some of the best deal people in the business. In this role, you will screen external inquiries for potential acquisition deals, research domestic and international market segments, and participate in deal activities working closely with corporate development managers, principals and the director.
>
> Our ideal candidate is a top performer who brings high levels of energy and enthusiasm; works well with large and diverse teams and has a demonstrated ability to think creatively.
>
> **Requirements:**
>
> - Bachelor's degree required.
> - 1–3 years of experience in strategic consulting, investment banking or relevant corporate experience preferred.
> - Strong quantitative and qualitative analytical ability required.
> - Excellent oral and written communication skills.
> - Demonstrated ability to manage multiple projects simultaneously.
> - Must be a team player with a sense of humor.

With these job requirements in mind, how would you respond to these recruiting situations?

1. Because written communication skills are such an important part of the job, you pay close attention to application letters. Based on the following opening paragraphs, which of these four candidates has done the best job of capturing your attention and interest?

a. I LOVE GOOGLE! I relied on your awesome search engine to get me through a zillion research papers in college, and I continue to use it in my new job as a legislative analyst in the mayor's office (that would be the Honorable Jack R. Spiker, mayor of Cheyenne, Wyoming, in whose employ I currently serve).

b. Guess what I found when I Googled myself? A five-page listing of all the awards I've received, speeches I've given, articles I've written, and projects I've managed. Try it yourself and see what you can see about my work.

c. Given Google's reputation for hiring only the best and brightest, the big question is why the heck don't I work there yet? I'm driven, way smarter than the average bear, and not afraid to tell my mom I work at some place called "Google"!

d. It's amazing how many times Google's name keeps popping up around the espresso machine here at Ignito Strategic Consulting, whenever my colleagues and I discuss smart acquisitions. Your firm continues to execute strategic moves that are creatively imagined, carefully researched, and cleverly implemented—exactly the kind of business deals I've been training for my entire career. And although that career is only one year old at the moment, my first annual performance review just said that I already have the deal-making acumen of a five-year veteran.

2. You like to put applicants at ease right away, so you usually start interviews by asking a humorous question to break the tension while also revealing something about the candidate's personality and knowledge. For this round of interviews, which of these questions would you choose to start each interview?
   a. What's the dumbest business deal you've ever heard of?
   b. If we wanted to lose $10 million on a business deal, what would you suggest we do?
   c. Ever have one of those days when life seems like one endless job interview?
   d. So . . . buying that weekly lottery ticket still hasn't worked out, eh?

3. Google places a great deal of emphasis on creative thinking, so you and your colleagues spend much of your time probing candidates' abilities to think through challenges and propose clever solutions. Which of these questions would you use to judge a candidate's ability to grasp a problem and begin developing a solution?
   a. You're a scientist with the Environmental Protection Agency, specializing in toxic waste from electronic products. You're testifying before a congressional committee, and a senator wants to know how many mobile phone batteries will be thrown away in the next 10 years. Without access to any additional information, how would you start to construct an estimate of this number?
   b. Guess how old I am.
   c. Why do telephone numbers in movies and TV shows always start with 555?
   d. How would you explain the concept of a human family to a creature from another planet?

4. At the end of each interview, you make a point to ask candidates if they have any questions for you. Which of the following responses impresses you the most?
   a. No, thanks. I think I'm all set.
   b. Hey, if I have any questions, I'll just Google away when I get back to my computer, right?
   c. Yes, one of my top priorities in searching for a new job is finding a greater sense of intellectual and professional freedom. Is Google the kind of place where top performers can really pursue their own dreams?
   d. Yes, a couple of questions, actually. First, Google's stated mission of organizing the world's information and making it universally accessible leaves the door open to a lot of different possibilities. For instance, do you see the company ever moving into traditional publishing, with books or magazines?

LEARNING OBJECTIVES CHECKUP

Assess your understanding of the principles in this chapter by reading each learning objective and studying the accompanying exercises. For fill-in-the-blank items, write the missing text in the blank provided; for multiple-choice items, circle the letter of the correct answer. You can check your responses against the answer key on page AK-2.

Objective 16.1: Define the purpose of application letters, and explain how to apply the AIDA model to them.

1. What is the primary reason for sending an application letter?
   a. To encourage the reader to look at your résumé
   b. To ask for a job
   c. To itemize your qualifications
   d. To ask for an application form

2. Which of the following is a good technique to gain attention in the opening paragraph of an application letter?
   a. Explain how your work skills could benefit the organization.
   b. Explain how your qualifications fit the job.
   c. Show that you understand the organization's needs.
   d. Do all of the above.

Objective 16.2: Describe the typical sequence of job interviews.

3. Which of these interview stages happens first?
   a. The selection stage
   b. The screening stage
   c. The filtering stage
   d. The sorting stage

4. A/an ______ interview, often used in the screening stage, features a series of prepared questions in a set order.

5. A/an ______ interview is a relatively informal and unstructured format, in which the interviewer poses broad questions that require more than simple yes or no answers.

6. A/an ______ interview tries to uncover how the candidate would behave when faced with various challenges on the job.

Objective 16.3: Describe briefly what employers look for during an employment interview and preemployment testing.

7. What are the two most important factors that employers look for during interviews?
   a. Fit with the organization and motivation
   b. Motivation and ability to perform the job

c. Motivation and years of experience
d. Fit with the organization and ability to perform the job

8. Which of the following preemployment tests might you encounter while applying for jobs?
a. Integrity tests
b. Substance tests
c. Personality tests
d. All of the above

9. Approximately what percentage of U.S. companies requires applicants to undergo preemployment drug testing?
a. 3 percent
b. 12 percent
c. 50 percent
d. 80 percent

Objective 16.4: List six tasks you need to complete to prepare for a successful job interview.

10. If an interviewer asks you to describe your biggest weakness, which of the following is the best strategy for your response?
a. Explain the weakness in depth; doing so will convince the interviewer of your honesty.
b. Describe a weakness so that it sounds like a strength, such as saying that you drive yourself too hard.
c. Respectfully explain to the interviewer that the question is illegal.
d. Explain that you don't have any major weaknesses.

11. What is the best strategy for asking questions of your own during an interview?
a. Try to ask all of them at the beginning of the interview so that you don't run out of time.
b. Wait until after the interview and then e-mail your questions to the interviewer.
c. Try to work your questions in naturally throughout the course of the interview.
d. Wait until the interviewer asks if you have any questions.

12. If you believe that you have a particular disadvantage related to some aspect of your appearance, interviewing skills, job skills, or work experience, how should you handle the situation when preparing for an interview?
a. Plan to make a joke about your weakness early in the interview; this will break the tension and allow you to focus on the interviewer's questions.
b. Compensate by focusing on your strengths, both while you're preparing and during the interview.
c. Correct the perceived shortcoming if possible; if not, focus on your positive attributes.
d. Ignore the situation; there's nothing you can do about a weakness at this point.

13. If you're not sure what style of clothing to wear to a particular interview and you're not able to ask someone at the company for advice, what should you do?
a. Dress in a fairly conservative style; it's better to be a little too dressy than too casual.
b. Dress as you would like to dress on the job.
c. Dress in an eye-catching style that will make a lasting impression on the interviewer.
d. Arrive early with several different changes of clothes; try to see what people there are wearing, then find a place to change into whichever outfit you have that most closely matches.

Objective 16.5: Explain the three stages of a successful employment interview.

14. Studies show that many interviewers, particularly those with poor training, make up their minds about candidates
a. In the first 20 seconds of the interview
b. In the final 20 seconds of the interview
c. On the basis of the résumé
d. On the basis of the cover letter

15. Which of the following is an advisable response to an interviewer who asks you about your marital status, how many children you have, and what their ages are?
a. Answer the questions; it is perfectly within the interviewer's right to ask you such personal questions, even if they are not directly related to the job you are applying for.
b. Tell the interviewer that such questions are illegal and threaten to sue for invasion of privacy.
c. Sidestep the questions—which are illegal—by asking if the interviewer has some specific concerns about your commitment to the job, your willingness to travel, or some other factor.
d. If you want the job, refuse to answer the questions but promise that you won't report the illegal questioning to the EEOC.

16. What should you do if the interviewer tells you the salary for the job being offered?
a. Always take whatever the company offers.
b. Respond with a figure higher than what is offered.
c. Respond with a figure lower than what is offered.
d. Ask if there is any room to negotiate on salary.

Objective 16.6: Identify the most common employment messages that follow an interview, and explain when you would use each one.

17. Following a job interview, you should send a thank-you message
a. Within two days after the interview
b. Only if you think you got the job
c. That follows the AIDA organizational model
d. That does all of the above

18. A letter declining a job offer should follow
a. The direct approach
b. The AIDA model
c. A negative news approach
d. The polite plan

PEARSON mybcommlab

Log on to www.mybcommlab.com to access the following study and assessment aids associated with this chapter:

- Video applications
- Real-Time Updates
- Peer review activity
- Quick Learning Guides
- Pre/post test
- Personalized study plan
- Model documents
- Sample presentations

If you are not using mybcommlab, you can access Real-Time Updates and Quick Learning Guides through http://real-timeupdates.com/ebc. The Quick Learning Guide (located under "Learn More" on the website) hits all the high points of this chapter in just two pages. This guide, especially prepared by the authors, will help you study for exams or review important concepts whenever you need a quick refresher.

Apply Your Knowledge

1. How can you distinguish yourself from other candidates in a screening interview and still keep your responses short and to the point? Explain.
2. How can you prepare for a situational or behavioral interview if you have no experience with the job for which you are interviewing?
3. If you want a new job because you can't work with your current supervisor, how can you explain this situation to a prospective employer? Give an example.
4. If you lack one important qualification for a job but have made it past the initial screening stage, how should you prepare to handle this issue during the next round of interviews? Explain your answer.
5. **Ethical Choices** Why is it important to distinguish unethical or illegal interview questions from acceptable questions? Explain.

Practice Your Knowledge

Messages for Analysis

Read the following documents and then (1) analyze the strengths or weaknesses of each document and (2) revise each document so that it follows this chapter's guidelines.

Message 16.A: Writing an Application Letter

I'm writing to let you know about my availability for the brand manager job you advertised. As you can see from my enclosed résumé, my background is perfect for the position. Even though I don't have any real job experience, my grades have been outstanding, considering that I went to a top-ranked business school.

I did many things during my undergraduate years to prepare me for this job:

- Earned a 3.4 out of a 4.0, with a 3.8 in my business courses
- Elected representative to the student governing association
- Selected to receive the Lamar Franklin Award
- Worked to earn a portion of my tuition

I am sending my résumé to all the top firms, but I like yours better than any of the rest. Your reputation is tops in the industry, and I want to be associated with a business that can pridefully say it's the best.

If you wish for me to come in for an interview, I can come on a Friday afternoon or anytime on weekends when I don't have classes. Again, thanks for considering me for your brand manager position.

Message 16.B: Writing Application Follow-Up Messages

Did you receive my résumé? I sent it to you at least two months ago and haven't heard anything. I know you keep résumés on file, but I just want to be sure that you keep me in mind. I heard you are hiring health-care managers and certainly would like to be considered for one of those positions.

Since I last wrote you, I've worked in a variety of positions that have helped prepare me for management. To wit, I've become lunch manager at the restaurant where I work, which involved a raise in pay. I now manage a waitstaff of 12 girls and take the lunch receipts to the bank every day.

Of course, I'd much rather be working at a real job, and that's why I'm writing again. Is there anything else you would like to know about me or my background? I would really like to know more about your company. Is there any literature you could send me? If so, I would really appreciate it.

I think one reason I haven't been hired yet is that I don't want to leave Atlanta. So I hope when you think of me, it's for a position that wouldn't require moving. Thanks again for considering my application.

Message 16.C: Thank-You Message

Thank you for the really marvelous opportunity to meet you and your colleagues at Starret Engine Company. I really enjoyed touring your facilities and talking with all the people there. You have quite a crew! Some of the other companies I have visited have been so rigid and uptight that I can't imagine how I would fit in. It's a relief to run into a group of people who seem to enjoy their work as much as all of you do.

I know that you must be looking at many other candidates for this job, and I know that some of them will probably be more experienced than I am. But I do want to emphasize that my two-year hitch in the Navy involved a good deal of engineering work. I don't think I mentioned all my shipboard responsibilities during the interview.

Please give me a call within the next week to let me know your decision. You can usually find me at my dormitory in the evening after dinner (phone: 877-9080).

Message 16.D: Letter of Inquiry

I have recently received a very attractive job offer from the Warrington Company. But before I let them know one way or another, I would like to consider any offer that your firm may extend. I was quite impressed with your company during my recent interview, and I am still very interested in a career there.

I don't mean to pressure you, but Warrington has asked for my decision within 10 days. Could you let me know by Tuesday whether you plan to offer me a position? That would give me enough time to compare the two offers.

Message 16.E: Letter Declining a Job Offer

I'm writing to say that I must decline your job offer. Another company has made me a more generous offer, and I have decided to accept. However, if things don't work out for me there, I will let you know. I sincerely appreciate your interest in me.

Exercises

Active links for all websites in this chapter can be found on mybcommlab; see your User Guide for instructions on accessing the content for this chapter.

16.1 **Internet** Select a large company (one that you can easily find information on) where you might like to work. Use Internet sources to gather some preliminary research on the company; don't limit your search to the company's own website.

1. What did you learn about this organization that would help you during an interview there?
2. What Internet sources did you use to obtain this information?
3. Armed with this information, what aspects of your background do you think might appeal to this company's recruiters?
4. Based on what you've learned about this company's culture, what aspects of your personality should you try to highlight during an interview?

16.2 **Teamwork** Divide the class into two groups. Half the class will be recruiters for a large chain of national department stores, looking to fill manager trainee positions (there are 16 openings). The other half of the class will be candidates for the job. The company is specifically looking for candidates who demonstrate these three qualities: initiative, dependability, and willingness to assume responsibility.

1. Have each recruiter select and interview an applicant for 10 minutes.
2. Have all the recruiters discuss how they assessed the applicant in each of the three desired qualities. What questions did they ask, or what did they use as an indicator to determine whether the candidate possessed the quality?
3. Have all the applicants discuss what they said to convince the recruiters that they possessed each of these qualities.

16.3 **Interviews: Understanding Qualifications** Write a short e-mail to your instructor, discussing what you believe are your greatest strengths and weaknesses from an employment perspective. Next, explain how these strengths and weaknesses would be viewed by interviewers evaluating your qualifications.

16.4 **Interviews: Being Prepared** Prepare written answers to 10 of the questions listed in Table 16.3.

16.5 **Ethical Choices** You have decided to accept a new position with a competitor of your company. Write a letter of resignation to your supervisor, announcing your decision.

1. Will you notify your employer that you are joining a competing firm? Explain.
2. Will you use the direct or the indirect approach? Explain.
3. Will you send your letter by e-mail, send it by regular mail, or place it on your supervisor's desk?

Expand Your Knowledge

Learning More on the Web

Prepare and Practice Before That First Interview

www.job-interview.net

How can you practice for a job interview? What are some questions you might be asked? How should you respond? What questions are you not obligated to answer? Job-interview.net provides mock interviews based on actual job openings. It provides job descriptions, questions and answers for specific careers and jobs, and links to company guides and annual reports. You'll find a step-by-step plan that outlines key job requirements, lists practice interview questions, and helps you put together practice interviews. The site offers tips on the keywords to look for in a job description, which will help you narrow your search and anticipate the questions you might be asked on your first or next job interview. Explore the site and then answer these questions:

1. What are some problem questions you might be asked during a job interview? How would you handle these questions?
2. Choose a job title from the list and read more about it. What did you learn that could help during an actual interview for the job you selected?
3. Developing an "interview game plan" ahead of time helps you make a strong, positive impression during an interview. What are some of the things you can practice to help make everything you do during an interview seem to come naturally?

Sharpening Your Career Skills Online

Bovée and Thill's Business Communication Web Search, at **http://businesscommunicationblog.com/websearch**, is a unique research tool designed specifically for business communication research. Use the Web Search function to find a website, video, PDF document, or PowerPoint presentation that offers advice on interviewing. Write a brief e-mail message to your instructor, describing the item that you found and summarizing the career skills information you learned from it.

Improve Your Grammar, Mechanics, and Usage

The following exercises help you improve your knowledge of and power over English grammar, mechanics, and usage. Turn to the Handbook of Grammar, Mechanics, and Usage at the end of this book and review all of Section 3.4 (Numbers). Then look at the following 10 items. Circle the letter of the preferred choice in the following groups of sentences. (Answers to these exercises appear on page AK-4.)

1. **a.** We need to hire one office manager, four bookkeepers, and 12 clerk-typists.
b. We need to hire one office manager, four bookkeepers, and twelve clerk-typists.
c. We need to hire 1 office manager, 4 bookkeepers, and 12 clerk-typists.

2. **a.** The market for this product is nearly 6 million people in our region alone.
b. The market for this product is nearly six million people in our region alone.
c. The market for this product is nearly 6,000,000 million people in our region alone.

3. **a.** Make sure that all 1,835 pages are on my desk no later than 9:00 a.m.
b. Make sure that all 1835 pages are on my desk no later than nine o'clock in the morning.
c. Make sure that all 1,835 pages are on my desk no later than nine o'clock a.m.

4. **a.** Our deadline is 4/7, but we won't be ready before 4/11.
b. Our deadline is April 7, but we won't be ready before April 11.
c. Our deadline is 4/7, but we won't be ready before April 11.

5. **a.** 95 percent of our customers are men.
b. Ninety-five percent of our customers are men.
c. Of our customers, ninety-five percent are men.

6. **a.** More than half the U.S. population is female.
b. More than 1/2 the U.S. population is female.
c. More than one-half the U.S. population is female.

7. **a.** Last year, I wrote 20 15-page reports, and Michelle wrote 24 three-page reports.
b. Last year, I wrote 20 fifteen-page reports, and Michelle wrote 24 three-page reports.
c. Last year, I wrote twenty 15-page reports, and Michelle wrote 24 three-page reports.

8. **a.** Our blinds should measure 38 inches wide by 64 and one-half inches long by 7/16 inches deep.
b. Our blinds should measure 38 inches wide by 64-1/2 inches long by 7/16 inches deep.
c. Our blinds should measure 38 inches wide by 64-8/16 inches long by 7/16 inches deep.

9. **a.** Deliver the couch to 783 Fountain Rd., Suite 3, Procter Valley, CA 92074.
b. Deliver the couch to 783 Fountain Rd., Suite three, Procter Valley, CA 92074.
c. Deliver the couch to seven eighty-three Fountain Rd., Suite three, Procter Valley, CA 92074.

10. **a.** Here are the corrected figures: 42.7% agree, 23.25% disagree, 34% are undecided, and the error is 0.05%.
b. Here are the corrected figures: 42.7% agree, 23.25% disagree, 34.0% are undecided, and the error is .05%.
c. Here are the corrected figures: 42.70% agree, 23.25% disagree, 34.00% are undecided, and the error is 0.05%.

For an overall review of your grammar, mechanics, and usage skills, visit mybcommlab. Click on Chapter 16, click on "Additional Exercises to Improve Your Grammar, Mechanics, and Usage," and then click on "25. Grammar and usage."

CASES

Applying the Three-Step Writing Process to Cases

Apply each step to the following cases, as assigned by your instructor.

PREPARING OTHER TYPES OF EMPLOYMENT MESSAGES

E-MAIL SKILLS

1. Online application: Electronic application letter introducing a résumé. While researching a digital camera purchase, you stumble on the webzine *Megapixel* (www.megapixel.net), which offers product reviews on a wide array of camera models. The quality of the reviews and the stunning examples of photography on the site inspire a new part-time business idea: You'd like to write a regular column for *Megapixel.* The webzine does a great job addressing the information needs of experienced camera users, but you see an opportunity to write for "newbies," people who are new to digital photography and need a more basic level of information.

Your task: Write an e-mail message that will serve as your application letter and address your message to Denys Bouton, who edits the English edition of *Megapixel.* (It is also published in French.) Try to limit your message to one screen (generally 20–25 lines). You'll need a creative "hook" and a reassuring approach that identifies you as the right person to launch this new feature in the webzine. (Make up any details about your background that you may need to complete the letter.)

PORTFOLIO BUILDER

2. All over the map: Application letter to Google Earth. You've applied yourself with vigor and resolve for four years, and you're just about to graduate with your business degree. While cruising the web to relax one night, you stumble on something called Google Earth. You're hooked instantly by the ability to zoom all around the globe and look at detailed satellite photos of places you've been to or dreamed of visiting. You can even type in the address of your apartment and get an aerial view of your neighborhood. You're amazed at the three-dimensional renderings of major U.S. cities. Plus, the photographs and maps are linked to Google's other search technologies, allowing you to locate everything from ATMs to coffees shops in your neighborhood.

You've loved maps since you were a kid, and discovering Google Earth is making you wish you'd majored in geography. Knowing how important it is to follow your heart, you decide to apply to Google anyway, even though you don't have a strong background in geographic information systems. You do have a ton of passion for maps and a good head for business.

Your task: Visit http://earth.google.com and explore the system's capabilities. (You can download a free copy of the software.) In particular, look at the business and government applications of the technology, such as customized aerial photos and maps for real estate sales, land use and environmental impact analysis, and emergency planning for homeland security agencies. Be sure to visit the Community pages as well, where you can learn more about the many interesting applications of this technology. Draft an application e-mail to Google (address it to jobs@google.com), asking to be considered for the Google Earth team. Think about how you could help the company develop the commercial potential of this product line and make sure your enthusiasm shines through in the message.

INTERVIEWING WITH POTENTIAL EMPLOYERS

TEAM SKILLS

3. Digging for insights: Compiling a list of questions to ask in an interview. Research is a critical element of the job search process. With information in hand, you increase the chance of finding the right opportunity (and avoiding bad choices), and you impress interviewers in multiple ways by demonstrating initiative, curiosity, research and analysis skills, an appreciation for the complex challenges of running a business, and willingness to work to achieve results.

Your task: With a small team of classmates, use online job listings to identify an intriguing job opening that at least one member of the team would seriously consider pursuing as graduation approaches. (You'll find it helpful if the career is related to at least one team member's college major or on-the-job experience so that the team can benefit from some knowledge of the profession in question.) Next, research the company, its competitors, its markets, and this specific position to identify five questions that would (1) help the team member decide if this is a good opportunity and (2) show an interviewer that you've really done your homework. Go beyond the basic and obvious questions to identify current, specific, and complex issues that only deep research can uncover. For example, is the company facing significant technical, financial, legal, or regulatory challenges that threaten its ability to grow or perhaps even survive in the long term? Or is the market evolving in a way that positions this particular company for dramatic growth? In a brief report, list your five questions, identify how you uncovered the issue, and explain why each is significant.

4. Interviewers and interviewees: Classroom exercise in interviewing. Interviewing is clearly an interactive process that involves at least two people. The best way to practice for interviews is to work with others.

Your task: You and all other members of your class are to write letters of application for an entry-level or management-trainee position that requires a pleasant personality and intelligence but a minimum of specialized education or experience. Sign your letter with a fictitious name that conceals your identity. Next, polish (or create) a résumé that accurately identifies you and your educational and professional accomplishments.

Now, three members of the class who volunteer as interviewers divide up all the anonymously written application letters. Then each interviewer selects a candidate who seems the most pleasant and convincing in his or her letter. At this time, the selected candidates identify themselves and give the interviewers their résumés.

Each interviewer then interviews his or her chosen candidate in front of the class, seeking to understand how the items on the résumé qualify the candidate for the job. At the end of the interviews, the class may decide who gets the job and discuss why this candidate was successful. Afterward, retrieve your letter, sign it with your name, and submit it to the instructor for credit.

5. Internet interview: Exercise in interviewing. Locate the website of a company in an industry in which you might like to work and then identify an interesting position within the company. Study the company, using any of the online business resources discussed in Chapter 11, and prepare for an interview with that company.

Your task: Working with a classmate, take turns interviewing each other for your chosen positions. Interviewers should take notes during the interview. When the interview is complete, critique each other's performance. (Interviewers should critique how well candidates prepared for the interview and answered the questions; interviewees should critique the quality of the questions asked.) Write a follow-up letter, thanking your interviewer, and submit the letter to your instructor.

FOLLOWING UP AFTER AN INTERVIEW

LETTER WRITING SKILLS

6. A slight error in timing: Letter asking for delay of an employment decision. Thanks to a mix-up in your job application scheduling, you accidentally applied for your third-choice job before going after what you really wanted. What you want to do is work in retail marketing with the upscale department store Neiman Marcus in Dallas; what you have been offered is a similar job with Longhorn Leather and Lumber, 55 dry and dusty miles away in Commerce, just south of the Oklahoma panhandle.

You review your notes. Your Longhorn interview was three weeks ago with the human resources manager, R. P. Bronson, a congenial person who has just written to offer you the position. The store's address is 27 Sam Rayburn Drive, Commerce, TX 75428. Mr. Bronson notes that he can hold the position open for 10 days. You have an interview scheduled with Neiman Marcus next week, but it is unlikely that you will know the store's decision within this 10-day period.

Your task: Write to R. P. Bronson, requesting a reasonable delay in your consideration of his job offer.

LETTER WRITING SKILLS

7. Job hunt: Set of employment-related letters to a single company. Where would you like to work? Choose one of your favorite products, and find out what company either manufactures it or sells it in the United States (if it's manufactured in another country). Assume that a month ago, you sent your résumé and application letter. Not long afterward, you were invited to come for an interview, which seemed to go very well.

Your task: Use your imagination to write the following: (1) a thank-you letter for the interview, (2) a note of inquiry, (3) a request for more time to decide, (4) a letter of acceptance, and (5) a letter declining the job offer.

LETTER WRITING SKILLS

8. Breaking up is hard to do: Resignation letter to a valued mentor. Leaving a job is rarely stress free, but it's particularly difficult when you are parting ways with a mentor who played an important role in advancing your career. A half-dozen years into your career, you have benefited greatly from the advice, encouragement, and professional connections offered by your mentor, who also happens to be your current boss. She seemed to believe in your potential from the very beginning and went out of her way on numerous occasions to help you. You returned the favor by becoming a stellar employee who has made important contributions to the success of the department your boss leads.

Unfortunately, you find yourself at a career impasse. You believe you are ready to move into a management position, but your company is not growing enough to create many opportunities. Worse yet, you joined the firm during a period of rapid expansion, so there are many eager and qualified internal candidates at your career level interested in the few managerial jobs that do become available. You fear it may be years before you get the chance to move up in the company. Through your online networking activities, you found an opportunity with a firm in another industry and have decided to pursue it.

Your task: You have a close relationship with your boss, so you will announce your intention to leave the company in a private, one-on-one conversation. However, you also recognize the need to write a formal letter of resignation, which you will hand to your boss during this meeting. This letter is addressed to your boss, but as formal business correspondence that will become part of your personnel file, it should not be a "personal" letter. Making up whatever details you need, write a brief letter of resignation.

Appendix A
Format and Layout of Business Documents

The format and layout of business documents vary from country to country; they even vary within regions of the United States. In addition, many organizations develop their own variations of standard styles, adapting documents to the types of messages they send and the kinds of audiences they communicate with. The formats described here are more common than others.

FIRST IMPRESSIONS

Your documents tell readers a lot about you and about your company's professionalism. So all your documents must look neat, present a professional image, and be easy to read. Your audience's first impression of a document comes from the quality of its paper, the way it is customized, and its general appearance.

Paper

To give a quality impression, businesspeople consider carefully the paper they use. Several aspects of paper contribute to the overall impression:

- **Weight.** Paper quality is judged by the weight of four reams (each a 500-sheet package) of letter-size paper. The weight most commonly used by U.S. business organizations is 20-pound paper, but 16- and 24-pound versions are also used.
- **Cotton content.** Paper quality is also judged by the percentage of cotton in the paper. Cotton doesn't yellow over time the way wood pulp does, plus it's both strong and soft. For letters and outside reports, use paper with a 25 percent cotton content. For memos and other internal documents, you can use a lighter-weight paper with lower cotton content. Airmail-weight paper may save money for international correspondence, but make sure it isn't too flimsy.[1]
- **Size.** In the United States, the standard paper size for business documents is 8½ by 11 inches. Standard legal documents are 8½ by 14 inches. Executives sometimes have heavier 7-by-10-inch paper on hand (with matching envelopes) for personal messages such as congratulations.[2] They may also have a box of note cards imprinted with their initials and a box of plain folded notes for condolences or for acknowledging formal invitations.
- **Color.** White is the standard color for business purposes, although neutral colors such as gray and ivory are sometimes used. Memos can be produced on pastel-colored paper to distinguish them from external correspondence. In addition, memos are sometimes produced on various colors of paper for routing to separate departments. Light-colored papers are appropriate, but bright or dark colors make reading difficult and may appear too frivolous.

Customization

For letters to outsiders, U.S. businesses commonly use letterhead stationery, which may be either professionally printed or designed in-house using word processing templates and graphics. The letterhead includes the company's name and address, usually at the top of the page but sometimes along the left side or even at the bottom. Other information may be included in the letterhead as well: the company's telephone number, fax number, cable address, website address, product lines, date of establishment, officers and directors, slogan, and symbol (logo). Well-designed letterhead gives readers[3]

- Pertinent reference data
- A favorable image of the company
- A good idea of what the company does

For as much as it's meant to accomplish, the letterhead should be as simple as possible. Too much information makes the page look cluttered, occupies space needed for the message, and might become outdated before all the stationery can be used. If you correspond frequently with people abroad, your letterhead must be intelligible to foreigners. It must include the name of your country in addition to your cable, telex, e-mail, or fax information.

In the United States, businesses always use letterhead for the first page of a letter. Successive pages are usually plain sheets of paper that match the letterhead in color and quality. Some companies use a specially printed second-page letterhead that bears only the company's name. Other countries have other conventions.

Many companies also design and print standardized forms for memos and frequently written reports that always require the same sort of information (such as sales reports and expense reports). These forms may be printed in sets for use with carbon paper or in carbonless-copy sets that produce multiple copies automatically. More and more organizations use computers to generate their standardized forms, which can save them both money and time.[4]

Appearance

Nearly all business documents are produced using an inkjet or laser printer; make sure to use a clean, high-quality printer. Certain documents, however, should be handwritten (such as a short informal memo or a note of condolence). Be sure to handwrite, print, or type the envelope to match the document. However, even a letter on the best-quality paper with the best-designed letterhead may look unprofessional if it's poorly produced. So pay close attention to all the factors affecting appearance, including the following:

- **Margins.** Companies in the United States make sure that documents (especially external ones) are centered on the page, with margins of at least 1 inch all around. Using word processing software, you can achieve this balance simply by defining the format parameters.
- **Line length.** Lines are rarely justified, because the resulting text looks too much like a form letter and can be hard to read (even with proportional spacing). Varying line length makes the document look more personal and interesting.
- **Line spacing.** You can adjust the number of blank lines between elements (such as between the date and the inside address) to ensure that a short document fills the page vertically or that a longer document extends at least two lines of the body onto the last page.
- **Character spacing.** Use proper spacing between characters and after punctuation. For example, U.S. conventions include leaving one space after commas, semicolons, colons, and sentence-ending periods. Each letter in a person's initials is followed by a period and a single space. However, abbreviations such as U.S.A. or MBA may or may not have periods, but they never have internal spaces.
- **Special symbols.** Take advantage of the many special symbols available with your computer's selection of fonts. (In Microsoft Word, click on the Insert menu, then select Symbol.) Table A.1 shows some of the more common symbols used in business documents. In addition, see if your company has a style guide for documents, which may include other symbols you are expected to use.
- **Corrections.** Messy corrections are unacceptable in business documents. If you notice an error after printing a document with your word processor, correct the mistake and reprint. (With informal memos to members of your own team or department, the occasional small correction in pen or pencil is acceptable, but never in formal documents.)

TABLE A.1 Special Symbols on a Computer

	COMPUTER SYMBOL
Case fractions	½
Copyright	©
Registered trademark	®
Cents	¢
British pound	£
Paragraph	¶
Bullets	●, ♦, ■, □, ✓, ☑, ⊗
Em dash	—
En dash	–

LETTERS

All business letters have certain elements in common. Several of these elements appear in every letter; others appear only when desirable or appropriate. In addition, these letter parts are usually arranged in one of three basic formats.

Standard Letter Parts

The letter in Figure A.1 shows the placement of standard letter parts. The writer of this business letter had no letterhead available but correctly included a heading. All business letters typically include these seven elements.

Heading

Most companies have preprinted *letterhead* sheets that show the company name, address, telephone number, website URL, and a general e-mail address. Executive letterhead also bears the name of an individual within the organization. Computers allow you to design your own letterhead (either one to use for all correspondence or a new one for each piece of correspondence). If letterhead stationery is not available, the heading includes a return address (but no name) and starts 13 lines from the top of the page, which leaves a 2-inch top margin.

Date

If you're using letterhead, place the date at least one blank line beneath the lowest part of the letterhead. Without letterhead, place the date immediately below the return address. The standard method of writing the date in the United States uses the full name of the month (no abbreviations), followed by the day (in numerals, without *st*, *nd*, *rd*, or *th*), a comma, and then the year: July 14, 2010 (7/14/2010). Some organizations follow other conventions (see Table A.2). To maintain the utmost clarity in international correspondence, always spell out the name of the month in dates.[5]

When communicating internationally, you may also experience some confusion over time. Some companies in the United States refer to morning (A.M.) and afternoon (P.M.), dividing a 24-hour day into 12-hour blocks so that they refer to four o'clock in the morning (4:00 A.M.) or four o'clock in the afternoon (4:00 P.M.). The U.S. military and European companies refer to one 24-hour period so that 0400 hours (4:00 A.M.) is always in the morning and 1600 hours (4:00 P.M.) is always in the afternoon.[6] Make sure your references to time are as clear as possible, and be sure you clearly understand your audience's time references.

FIGURE A.1 Standard Letter Parts

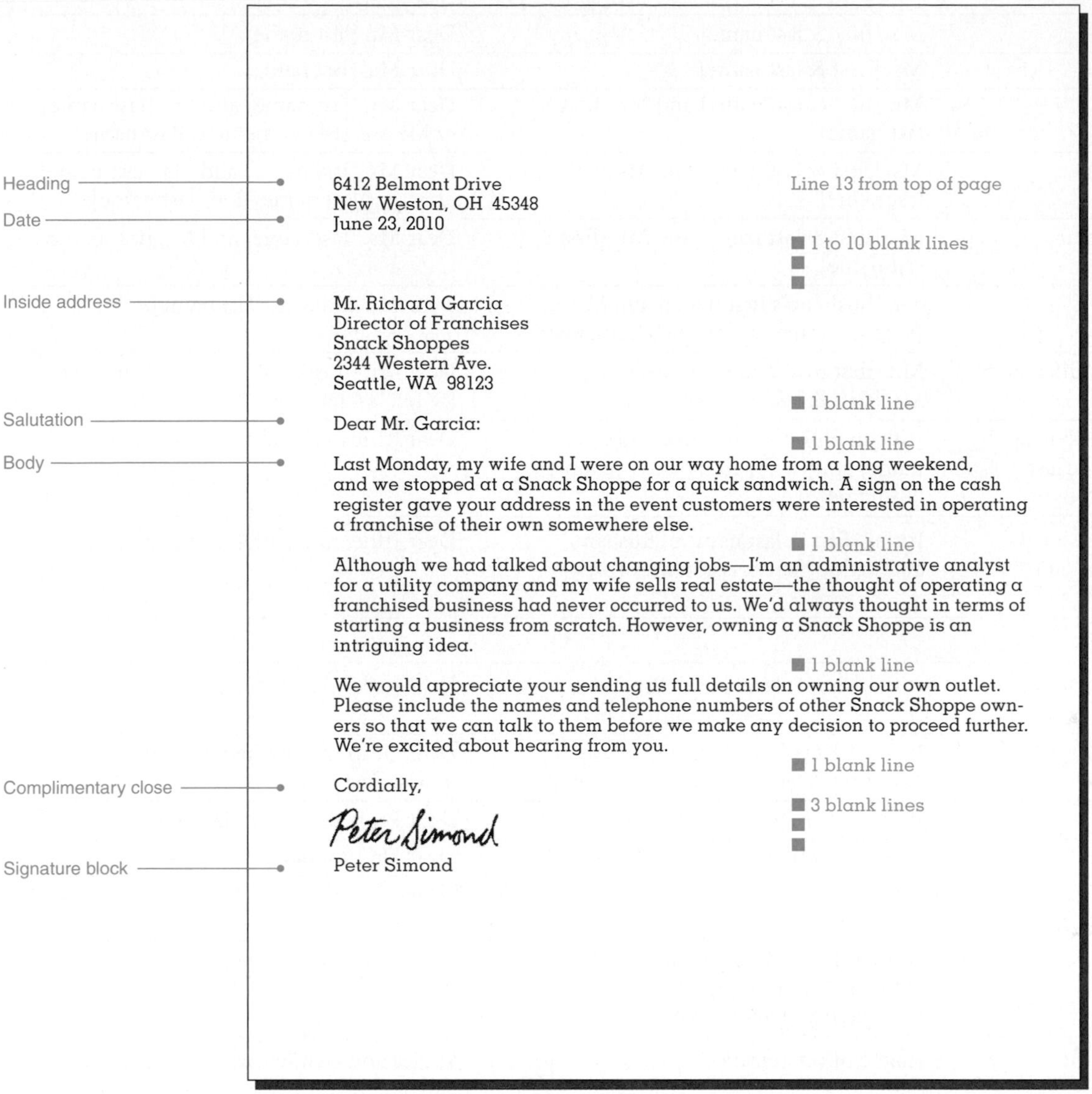

Heading ———————• 6412 Belmont Drive Line 13 from top of page
Date ———————————• New Weston, OH 45348
 June 23, 2010
 ■ 1 to 10 blank lines
 ■
 ■
Inside address ———————• Mr. Richard Garcia
 Director of Franchises
 Snack Shoppes
 2344 Western Ave.
 Seattle, WA 98123
 ■ 1 blank line
Salutation ———————• Dear Mr. Garcia:
 ■ 1 blank line
Body ———————————• Last Monday, my wife and I were on our way home from a long weekend,
 and we stopped at a Snack Shoppe for a quick sandwich. A sign on the cash
 register gave your address in the event customers were interested in operating
 a franchise of their own somewhere else.
 ■ 1 blank line
 Although we had talked about changing jobs—I'm an administrative analyst
 for a utility company and my wife sells real estate—the thought of operating a
 franchised business had never occurred to us. We'd always thought in terms of
 starting a business from scratch. However, owning a Snack Shoppe is an
 intriguing idea.
 ■ 1 blank line
 We would appreciate your sending us full details on owning our own outlet.
 Please include the names and telephone numbers of other Snack Shoppe owners so that we can talk to them before we make any decision to proceed further.
 We're excited about hearing from you.
 ■ 1 blank line
Complimentary close ———• Cordially,
 ■ 3 blank lines
 ■
 Peter Simond ■

Signature block ———————• Peter Simond

Inside Address

The inside address identifies the recipient of the letter. For U.S. correspondence, begin the inside address at least one line below the date. Precede the addressee's name with a courtesy title, such as *Dr., Mr.,* or *Ms.* The accepted courtesy title for women in business is *Ms.,* although a woman known to prefer the title *Miss* or *Mrs.* is always accommodated.

If you don't know whether a person is a man or a woman (and you have no way of finding out), omit the courtesy title. For example, *Terry Smith* could be either a man or a woman. The first line of the inside address would be just *Terry Smith*, and the salutation would be *Dear Terry Smith.* The same is true if you know only a person's initials, as in *S. J. Adams.*

TABLE A.2 Common Date Forms

CONVENTION	DESCRIPTION	DATE—MIXED	DATE—ALL NUMERALS
U.S. standard	Month (spelled out) day, year	July 14, 2010	7/14/10
U.S. government and some U.S. industries	Day (in numerals) month (spelled out) year	14 July 2010	14/7/10
European	Replace U.S. solidus (diagonal line) with periods	14 July 2010	14.7.2010
International standard	Year month day	2010 July 14	2010,7,14

TABLE A.3 Forms of Address

PERSON	IN ADDRESS	IN SALUTATION
Personal Titles		
Man	Mr. [first & last name]	Dear Mr. [last name]:
Woman*	Ms. [first & last name]	Dear Ms. [last name]:
Two men (or more)	Mr. [first & last name] and Mr. [first & last name]	Dear Mr. [last name] and Mr. [last name] *or* Messrs. [last name] and [last name]:
Two women (or more)	Ms. [first & last name] and Ms. [first & last name]	Dear Ms. [last name] and Ms. [last name] *or* Mses. [last name] and [last name]:
One woman and one man	Ms. [first & last name] and Mr. [first & last name]	Dear Ms. [last name] and Mr. [last name]:
Couple (married)	Mr. [husband's first name] and Mrs. [wife's first name] [couple's last name]	Dear Mr. and Mrs. [last name]:
Couple (married with different last names)	Mr. [first & last name of husband] Ms. [first & last name of wife]	Dear Mr. [husband's last name] and Ms. [wife's last name]:
Couple (married professionals with same title and same last name)	[title in plural form] [husband's first name] and [wife's first name] [couple's last name]	Dear [title in plural form] [last name]:
Couple (married professionals with different titles and same last name)	[title] [first & last name of husband] and [title] [first & last name of wife]	Dear [title] and [title] [last name]:
Professional Titles		
President of a college or university	[title] [first & last name], President	Dear [title] [last name]:
Dean of a school of college	Dean [first & last name] *or* Dr., Mr., *or* Ms. [first & last name], Dean of [title]	Dear Dean [last name]: *or* Dear Dr., Mr., *or* Ms. [last name]:
Professor	Professor *or* Dr. [first & last name]	Dear Professor *or* Dr. [last name]:
Physician	[first & last name], M.D.	Dear Dr. [last name]:
Lawyer	Mr. *or* Ms. [first & last name] Attorney at Law	Dear Mr. *or* Ms. [last name]:
Military personnel	[full rank, first & last name, abbreviation of service designation] (add *Retired* if applicable)	Dear [rank][last name]:
Company or corporation	[name of organization]	Ladies and Gentlemen: *or* Gentlemen and Ladies:
Governmental Titles		
President of the United States	The president	Dear Mr. *or* Madam President:
Senator of the United States	Honorable [first & last name]	Dear Senator [last name]:
Cabinet member	Honorable [first & last name]	Dear Mr. *or* Madam Secretary:
Postmaster General		Dear Mr. *or* Madam Postmaster General:
Attorney General		Dear Mr. *or* Madam Attorney General:
Mayor	Honorable [first & last name], Mayor of [name of city]	Dear Mayor [last name]:
Judge	The Honorable [first & last name]	Dear Judge [last name]:

*Use *Mrs.* or *Miss* only if the recipient has specifically requested that you use one of these titles; otherwise *always* use *Ms.* in business correspondence. Also, never refer to a married woman by her husband's name (e.g., Mrs. Robert Washington) unless she specifically requests that you do so.

Spell out and capitalize titles that precede a person's name, such as *Professor* or *General* (see Table A.3 for the proper forms of address). The person's organizational title, such as *Director*, may be included on this first line (if it is short) or on the line below; the name of a department may follow. In addresses and signature lines, don't forget to capitalize any professional title that follows a person's name:

Mr. Ray Johnson, Dean

Ms. Patricia T. Higgins
Assistant Vice President

However, professional titles not appearing in an address or signature line are capitalized only when they directly precede the name:

President Kenneth Johanson will deliver the speech.

Maria Morales, president of ABC Enterprises, will deliver the speech.

The Honorable Helen Masters, senator from Arizona, will deliver the speech.

If the name of a specific person is unavailable, you may address the letter to the department or to a specific position within the department. Also, be sure to spell out company names in full, unless the company itself uses abbreviations in its official name.

Other address information includes the treatment of buildings, house numbers, and compass directions (see Table A.4). The following example shows all the information that may be included in the inside address and its proper order for U.S. correspondence:

Ms. Linda Coolidge, Vice President
Corporate Planning Department
Midwest Airlines
Kowalski Building, Suite 21-A
7279 Bristol Ave.
Toledo, OH 43617

Canadian addresses are similar, except that the name of the province is usually spelled out:

Dr. H. C. Armstrong
Research and Development
Commonwealth Mining Consortium
The Chelton Building, Suite 301
585 Second St. SW
Calgary, Alberta T2P 2P5

The order and layout of address information vary from country to country. So when addressing correspondence for other countries, carefully follow the format and information that appear in the company's letterhead. However, when you're sending mail from the United States, be sure that the name of the destination country appears on the last line of the address in capital letters. Use the English version of the country name so that your mail is routed from the United States to the right country. Then, to be sure your mail is routed correctly within the destination country, use the foreign spelling of the city name (using the characters and diacritical marks that would be commonly used in the region). For example, the following address uses *Köln* instead of *Cologne*:

H. R. Veith, Director	Addressee
Eisfieren Glaswerk	Company name
Blaubachstrasse 13	Street address
Postfach 10 80 07	Post office road
D-5000 Köln I	District, city
GERMANY	Country

For additional examples of international addresses, see Table A.5.

Be sure to use organizational titles correctly when addressing international correspondence. Job designations vary around the world. In England, for example, a managing director is often what a U.S. company would call its chief executive officer or president, and a British deputy is the equivalent of a vice president. In France, responsibilities are assigned to individuals without regard to title or organizational structure, and in China the title *project manager* has meaning, but the title *sales manager* may not.

To make matters worse, businesspeople in some countries sign correspondence without their names typed below. In Germany, for example, the belief is that employees represent the company, so it's inappropriate to emphasize personal names.[7] Use the examples in Table A.5 as guidelines when addressing correspondence to countries outside the United States.

Salutation

In the salutation of your letter, follow the style of the first line of the inside address. If the first line is a person's name, the salutation is *Dear Mr.* or *Ms. Name.* The formality of the salutation depends on your relationship with the addressee. If in conversation you would say "Mary," your letter's salutation should be *Dear Mary,* followed by a colon. Otherwise, include the courtesy title and last name, followed by a colon. Presuming to write *Dear Lewis* instead of *Dear Professor Chang* demonstrates a disrespectful familiarity that the recipient will probably resent.

If the first line of the inside address is a position title such as *Director of Personnel,* then use *Dear Director.* If the addressee is unknown, use a polite description, such as *Dear Alumnus, Dear SPCA Supporter,* or *Dear Voter.* If the first line is plural (a department or company), then use *Ladies and*

TABLE A.4 Inside Address Information

DESCRIPTION	EXAMPLE
Capitalize building names.	Empire State Building
Capitalize locations within buildings (apartments, suites, rooms).	Suite 1073
Use numerals for all house or building numbers, except the number *one.*	One Trinity Lane; 637 Adams Ave., Apt. 7
Spell out compass directions that fall within a street address	1074 West Connover St.
Abbreviate compass directions that follow the street address	783 Main St., N.E., Apt. 27

TABLE A.5 International Addresses and Salutations

COUNTRY	POSTAL ADDRESS	ADDRESS ELEMENTS	SALUTATIONS
Argentina	Sr. Juan Pérez Editorial Internacional S.A. Av. Sarmiento 1337, 8° P. C. C1035AAB BUENOS AIRES–CF ARGENTINA	S.A. = Sociedad Anónima (corporation) Av. Sarmiento (name of street) 1337 (building number) 8° – 8th. P = Piso (floor) C (room or suite) C1035AAB (postcode + city) CF = Capital Federal (federal capital)	Sr. = Señor (Mr.) Sra. = Señora (Mrs.) Srta. = Señorita (Miss) Don't use given names except with people you know well.
Australia	Mr. Roger Lewis International Publishing Pty. Ltd. 166 Kent Street, Level 9 GPO Box 3542 SYDNEY NSW 2001 AUSTRALIA	Pty. Ltd. – Proprietory Limited (corp.) 166 (building number) Kent Street (name of street) Level (floor) GPO Box (P.O. box) City + state (abbrev.) + postcode	Mr. and Mrs. used on first contact. Ms. not common (avoid use). Business is informal—use given name freely.
Austria	Herrn Dipl.-Ing.J.Gerdenitsch International Verlag Ges.m.b.H. Glockengasse 159 1010 WIEN AUSTRIA	Herrn – To Mr. (separate line) Dipl.-Ing. (engineering degree) Ges.m.b.H. (a corporation) Glockengasse (street name) 159 (building number) 1010 (postcode + city) WIEN (Vienna)	Herr (Mr.) Frau (Mrs.) Fräulein (Miss) obsolete in business, so do not use. Given names are almost never used in business.
Brazil	Ilmo. Sr. Gilberto Rabello Ribeiro Editores Internacionais S.A. Rua da Ajuda, 228–6° Andar Caixa Postal 2574 20040–000 RIO DE JANEIRO–RJ BRAZIL	Ilmo. = Ilustrissimo (honorific) Ilma. = Ilustrissima (hon. female) S.A. – Sociedade Anônima (corporation) Rua = street, da Ajuda (street name) 228 (building number) 6° = 6th. Andar (floor) Caixa Postal (P.O. box) 20040–000 (postcode + city)–RJ (state abbrev.)	Sr. = Senhor (Mr.) Sra. = Senhora (Mrs.) Srta. = Senhorita (Miss) Family name at end, e.g., Senhor Ribeiro (Rabello is mother's family name) Given names readily used in business.
China	Xia Zhiyi International Publishing Ltd. 14 Jianguolu Chaoyangqu BEIJING 100025 CHINA	Ltd. (limited liability corporation) 14 (building number) Jianguolu (street name), lu (street) Chaoyangqu (district name) (city + postcode)	Family name (single syllable) first. Given name (2 syllables) second, sometimes reversed. Use Mr. or Ms. at all times (Mr. Xia).
France	Monsieur LEFÈVRE Alain Éditions Internationales S.A. Siège Social Immeuble Le Bonaparte 64–68, av. Galliéni B.P. 154 75942 PARIS CEDEX 19 FRANCE	S.A. = Société Anonyme (corporation) Siège Social (head office) Immeuble (building + name) 64–68 (building occupies 64, 66, 68) av. = avenue (no initial capital) B.P. = Boîte Postale (P.O. box) 75942 (postcode + city) CEDEX (postcode for P.O. box)	Monsieur (Mr.) Madame (Mrs.) Mademoiselle (Miss) Best not to abbreviate. Family name is sometimes in all caps with given name following.
Germany	Herrn Gerhardt Schneider International Verlag GmbH Schillerstraße 159 44147 DORTMUND GERMANY	Herrn = To Mr. (on a separate line) GmbH (inc.—incorporated) –straße (street—'ß' often written 'ss') 159 (building number) 44147 (postcode – city)	Herr (Mr.) Frau (Mrs.) Fräulein (Miss) obsolete in business. Business is formal: (1) do not use given names unless invited, and (2) use academic titles precisely.

COUNTRY	POSTAL ADDRESS	ADDRESS ELEMENTS	SALUTATIONS
India	Sr. Shyam Lal Gupta International Publishing (Pvt.) Ltd. 1820 Rehaja Centre 214, Darussalam Road Andheri East BOMBAY–400049 INDIA	(Pvt.) (privately owned) Ltd. (limited liability corporation) 1820 (possibly office #20 on 18th floor) Rehaja Centre (building name) 214 (building number) Andheri East (suburb name) (city + hyphen + postcode)	Shri (Mr.), Shrimati (Mrs.) but English is common business language, so use Mr., Mrs., Miss. Given names are used only by family and close friends.
Italy	Egr. Sig. Giacomo Mariotti Edizioni Internazionali S.p.A. Via Terenzio, 21 20138 MILANO ITALY	Egr. = Egregio (honorific) Sig. = Signor (not nec. a separate line) S.p.A. = Società per Azioni (corp.) Via (street) 21 (building number) 20138 (postcode + city)	Sig. = Signore (Mr.) Sig.ra = Signora (Mrs.) Sig.a (Ms.) Women in business are addressed as Signora. Use given name only when invited.
Japan	Mr. Taro Tanaka Kokusai Shuppan K.K. 10–23, 5-chome, Minamiazabu Minato-ku TOKYO 106 JAPAN	K.K. = Kabushiki Kaisha (corporation) 10 (lot number) 23 (building number) 5-chome (area #5) Minamiazabu (neighborhood name) Minato-ku (city district) (city + postcode)	Given names not used in business. Use family name + job title. Or use family name + "-san" (Tanaka-san) or more respectfully, add "-sama" or "-dono."
Korea	Mr. Kim Chang-ik International Publishers Ltd. Room 206, Korea Building 33–4 Nonhyon-dong Kangnam-ku SEOUL 135–010 KOREA	English company names common Ltd. (a corporation) 206 (office number inside the building) 33–4 (area 4 of subdivision 33) -dong (city neighborhood name) -ku (subdivision of city) (city + postcode)	Family name is normally first but sometimes placed after given name. A two-part name is the given name. Use Mr. or Mrs. in letters, but use job title in speech.
Mexico	Sr. Francisco Pérez Martínez Editores Internacionales S.A. Independencia No. 322 Col. Juárez 06050 MEXICO D.F.	S.A. – Sociedad Anónima (corporation) Independencia (street name) No. = Número (number) 322 (building number) Col. = Colonia (city district) Juárez (locality name) 06050 (postcode + city) D.F. = Distrito Federal (federal capital)	Sr. = Señor (Mr.) Sra. = Señora (Mrs.) Srta. = Señorita (Miss) Family name in middle: e.g., Sr. Pérez (Martínez is mother's family). Given names are used in business.
South Africa	Mr. Mandla Ntuli International Publishing (Pty.) Ltd. Private Bag X2581 JOHANNESBURG 2000 SOUTH AFRICA	Pty. = Proprietory (privately owned) Ltd. (a corporation) Private Bag (P.O. Box) (city + postcode) or (postcode + city)	Mnr. = Meneer (Mr.) Mev. = Mevrou (Mrs.) Mejuffrou (Miss) is not used in business. Business is becoming less formal, so the use of given names is possible.
United Kingdom	Mr. N. J. Lancaster International Publishing Ltd. Kingsbury House 12 Kingsbury Road EDGEWARE Middlesex HA8 9XG ENGLAND	N. J. (initials of given names) Ltd. (limited liability corporation) Kingsbury House(building name) 12 (building number) Kingsbury Road (name of street/road) EDGEWARE (city—all caps) Middlesex (county—not all caps) HA8 9XG	Mr. and Ms. used mostly. Mrs. and Miss sometimes used in North and by older women. Given names—called Christian names—are used in business after some time. Wait to be invited.

Gentlemen (look again at Table A.3). When you do not know whether you're writing to an individual or a group (for example, when writing a reference or a letter of recommendation), use *To whom it may concern.*

In the United States some letter writers use a "salutopening" on the salutation line. A salutopening omits *Dear* but includes the first few words of the opening paragraph along with the recipient's name. After this line, the sentence continues a double space below as part of the body of the letter, as in these examples:

Thank you, Mr. Brown, for your prompt payment of your bill.	Salutopening Body
Congratulations, Ms. Lake! Your promotion is well deserved.	Salutopening Body

Whether your salutation is informal or formal, be especially careful that names are spelled correctly. A misspelled name is glaring evidence of carelessness, and it belies the personal interest you're trying to express.

Body

The body of the letter is your message. Almost all letters are single-spaced, with one blank line before and after the salutation or salutopening, between paragraphs, and before the complimentary close. The body may include indented lists, entire paragraphs indented for emphasis, and even subheadings. If it does, all similar elements should be treated in the same way. Your department or company may select a format to use for all letters.

Complimentary Close

The complimentary close begins on the second line below the body of the letter. Alternatives for wording are available, but currently the trend seems to be toward using one-word closes, such as *Sincerely* and *Cordially.* In any case, the complimentary close reflects the relationship between you and the person you're writing to. Avoid cute closes, such as *Yours for bigger profits.* If your audience doesn't know you well, your sense of humor may be misunderstood.

Signature Block

Leave three blank lines for a written signature below the complimentary close, and then include the sender's name (unless it appears in the letterhead). The person's title may appear on the same line as the name or on the line below:

Cordially,

Raymond Dunnigan
Director of Personnel

Your letterhead indicates that you're representing your company. However, if your letter is on plain paper or runs to a second page, you may want to emphasize that you're speaking legally for the company. The accepted way of doing that is to place the company's name in capital letters a double space below the complimentary close and then include the sender's name and title four lines below that:

Sincerely,
WENTWORTH INDUSTRIES

(Ms.) Helen B. Taylor
President

If your name could be taken for either a man's or a woman's, a courtesy title indicating gender should be included, with or without parentheses. Also, women who prefer a particular courtesy title should include it:

Mrs. Nancy Winters
(Ms.) Juana Flores
Ms. Pat Li
(Mr.) Jamie Saunders

Additional Letter Parts

Letters vary greatly in subject matter and thus in the identifying information they need and the format they adopt. The letter in Figure A.2 shows how these additional parts should be arranged. The following elements may be used in any combination, depending on the requirements of the particular letter:

- **Addressee notation.** Letters that have a restricted readership or that must be handled in a special way should include such addressee notations as *Personal, Confidential,* or *Please Forward.* This sort of notation appears a double space above the inside address, in all-capital letters.
- **Attention line.** Although not commonly used today, an attention line can be used if you know only the last name of the person you're writing to. It can also direct a letter to a position title or department. Place the attention line on the first line of the inside address and put the company name on the second.[8] Match the address on the envelope with the style of the inside address. An attention line may take any of the following forms or variants of them:

  Attention Dr. McHenry
  Attention Director of Marketing
  Attention Marketing Department

- **Subject line.** The subject line tells recipients at a glance what the letter is about (and indicates where to file the letter for future reference). It usually appears below the salutation, either against the left margin, indented (as a paragraph in the body), or centered. It can be placed above the salutation or at the very top of the page, and it can be underscored. Some businesses omit the word *Subject,* and some organizations replace it with *Re:* or *In re:* (meaning "concerning" or "in the matter of"). The

FIGURE A.2 Additional Letter Parts

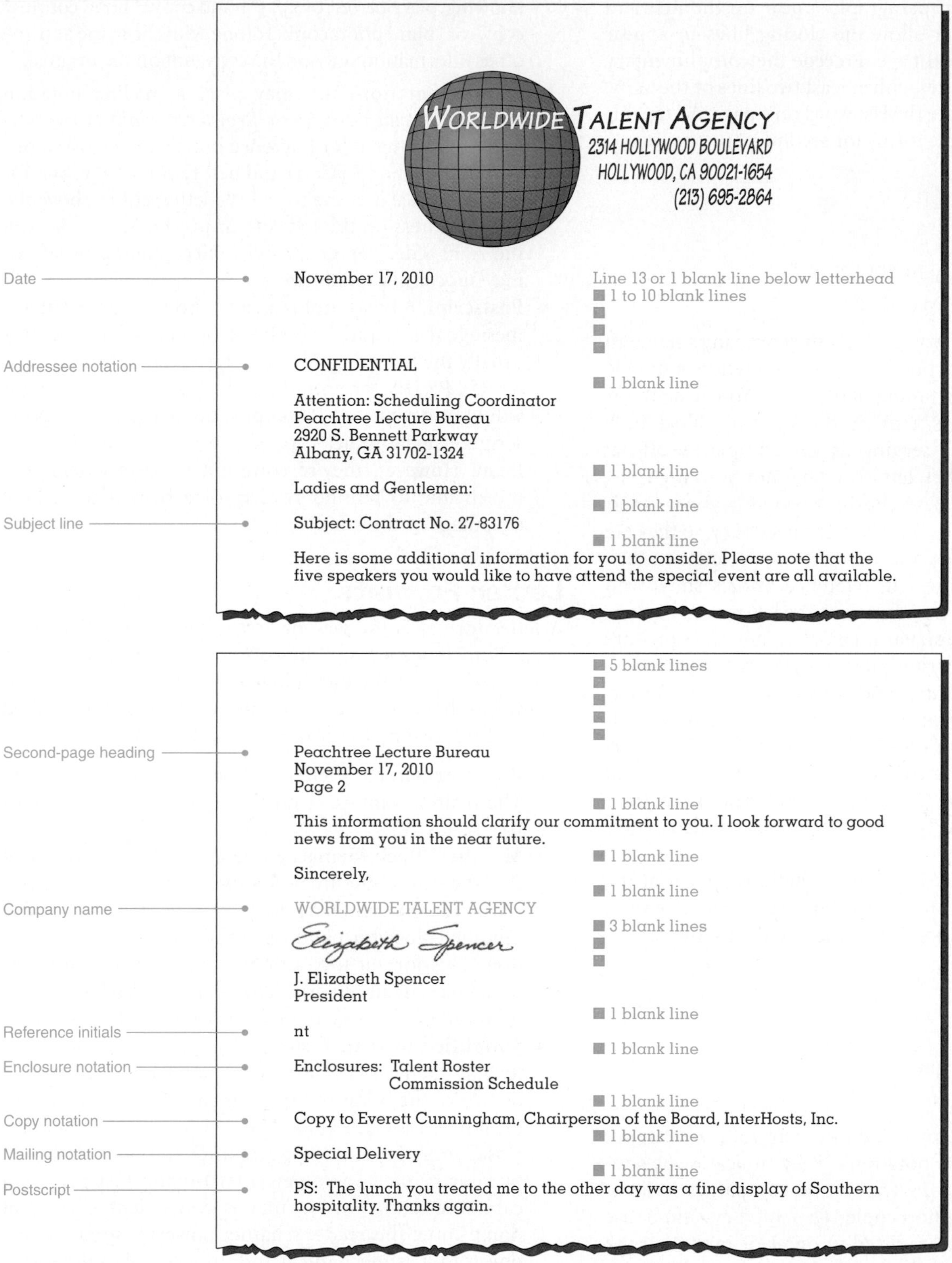

subject line may take a variety of forms, including the following:

Subject: RainMaster Sprinklers

About your February 2, 2010, order

FALL 2010 SALES MEETING

Reference Order No. 27920

- **Second-page heading.** Use a second-page heading whenever an additional page is required. Some companies have second-page letterhead (with the company name and address on one line and in a smaller typeface). The heading bears the name (person or organization) from the first line of the inside address, the page number, the date, and perhaps a reference number. Leave two blank lines before the body. Make sure that at least two lines of a continued paragraph appear on the first and second pages. Never allow the closing lines to appear alone on a continued page. Precede the complimentary close or signature lines with at least two lines of the body. Also, don't hyphenate the last word on a page. All the following are acceptable forms for second-page headings:

Ms. Melissa Baker
May 10, 2010
Page 2

Ms. Melissa Baker, May 10, 2010, Page 2

Ms. Melissa Baker -2- May 10, 2010

- **Company name.** If you include the company's name in the signature block, put it all in capital letters a double space below the complimentary close. You usually include the company's name in the signature block only when the writer is serving as the company's official spokesperson or when letterhead has not been used.
- **Reference initials.** When businesspeople keyboard their own letters, reference initials are unnecessary, so they are becoming rare. When one person dictates a letter and another person produces it, reference initials show who helped prepare it. Place initials at the left margin, a double space below the signature block. When the signature block includes the writer's name, use only the preparer's initials. If the signature block includes only the department, use both sets of initials, usually in one of the following forms: *RSR/sm, RSR:sm,* or *RSR:SM* (writer/preparer). When the writer and the signer are different people, at least the file copy should bear both their initials as well as the typist's: *JFS/RSR/sm* (signer/writer/preparer).
- **Enclosure notation.** Enclosure notations appear at the bottom of a letter, one or two lines below the reference initials. Some common forms include the following:

Enclosure

Enclosures (2)

Enclosures: Résumé
Photograph
Attachment

- **Copy notation.** Copy notations may follow reference initials or enclosure notations. They indicate who's receiving a *courtesy copy* (*cc*). Some companies indicate copies made on a photocopier (*pc*), or they simply use *copy* (*c*). Recipients are listed in order of rank or (rank being equal) in alphabetical order. Among the forms used are the following:

cc: David Wentworth, Vice President

pc: Dr. Martha Littlefield

Copy to Hans Vogel
748 Chesterton Road
Snohomish, WA 98290

c: Joseph Martinez with brochure and technical sheet

When sending copies to readers without other recipients knowing, place *bc, bcc,* or *bpc* ("blind copy," "blind courtesy copy," or "blind photocopy") along with the name and any other information only on the copy, not on the original.

- **Mailing notation.** You may place a mailing notation (such as *Special Delivery* or *Registered Mail*) at the bottom of the letter, after reference initials or enclosure notations (whichever is last) and before copy notations. Or you may place it at the top of the letter, either above the inside address on the left side or just below the date on the right side. For greater visibility, mailing notations may appear in capital letters.
- **Postscript.** A postscript is an afterthought to the letter, a message that requires emphasis, or a personal note. It is usually the last thing on any letter and may be preceded by *P.S., PS., PS:,* or nothing at all. A second afterthought would be designated *P.P.S.* (post postscript). Since postscripts usually indicate poor planning, generally avoid them. However, they're common in sales letters as a punch line to remind readers of a benefit for taking advantage of the offer.

Letter Formats

A letter format is the way of arranging all the basic letter parts. Sometimes a company adopts a certain format as its policy; sometimes the individual letter writer or preparer is allowed to choose the most appropriate format. In the United States, three major letter formats are commonly used:

- **Block format.** Each letter part begins at the left margin. The main advantage is quick and efficient preparation (see Figure A.3).
- **Modified block format.** Same as block format, except that the date, complimentary close, and signature block start near the center of the page (see Figure A.4). The modified block format does permit indentions as an option. This format mixes preparation speed with traditional placement of some letter parts. It also looks more balanced on the page than the block format does.
- **Simplified format.** Instead of using a salutation, this format often weaves the reader's name into the first line or two of the body and often includes a subject line in capital letters (see Figure A.5). With no complimentary close, your signature appears after the body, followed by your printed (or typewritten) name (usually in all capital letters). This format is convenient when you don't know the reader's name; however, some people object to it as mechanical and impersonal (a drawback you can overcome with a warm writing style). Because certain letter parts are eliminated, some line spacing is changed.

These three formats differ in the way paragraphs are indented, in the way letter parts are placed, and in some punctuation. However, the elements are always separated by at least one blank line, and the printed (or typewritten) name is always separated from the line above by at least three blank

FIGURE A.3 Block Letter Format

Delauny Music
56 Commerce Circle • Davenport, IA 52806
(563) 555-4001 • delaunymusic.net

June 21, 2010 — Line 13 or one line below letterhead

■ 1 to 10 blank lines
■

Ms. Claudia Banks
122 River Heights Drive
Bettendorf, IA 52722

■ 1 blank line

Dear Ms. Banks:

■ 1 blank line

Thank you for your recent purchase. We wish you many years of satisfaction with your new Yamaha CG1 grand piano. The CG1 carries more than a century of Yamaha's heritage in design and production of world-class musical instruments and will give you many years of playing and listening pleasure.

■ 1 blank line

Our commitment to your satisfaction doesn't stop with your purchase, however. As a vital first step, please remember to call us sometime within three to eight months after your piano was delivered to take advantage of the Yamaha Servicebond^{SM} Assurance Program. This free service program includes a thorough evaluation and adjustment of the instrument after you've had some time to play your piano and your piano has had time to adapt to its environment.

■ 1 blank line

In addition to this important service appointment, a regular program of tuning is essential to ensure your piano's impeccable performance. Our piano specialists commend four tunings during the first year and two tunings every year thereafter. As your local Yamaha dealer, we are ideally positioned to provide you with optimum service for both regular tuning and any maintenance or repair needs you may have.

■ 1 blank line

Sincerely,

■ 3 blank lines
■
■

Madeline Delauny
Owner

■ 1 blank line

tjr

■ 1 blank line

lines to allow space for a signature. If paragraphs are indented, the indention is normally five spaces. The most common formats for intercultural business letters are the block style and the modified block style.

In addition to these three letter formats, letters may also be classified according to their style of punctuation. *Standard*, or *mixed, punctuation* uses a colon after the salutation (a comma if the letter is social or personal) and a comma after the complimentary close. *Open punctuation* uses no colon or comma after the salutation or the complimentary close. Although the most popular style in business communication is mixed punctuation, either style of punctuation may be used with block or modified block letter formats. Because the simplified letter format has no salutation or complimentary close, the style of punctuation is irrelevant.

ENVELOPES

For a first impression, the quality of the envelope is just as important as the quality of the stationery. Letterhead and envelopes should be of the same paper stock, have the same color ink, and be imprinted with the same address and logo. Most envelopes used by U.S. businesses are No. 10 envelopes (9½ inches long), which are sized for an 8½-by-11-inch piece of paper folded in thirds. Some occasions call for a smaller, No. 6¾, envelope or for envelopes proportioned to fit special stationery. Figure A.6 shows the two most common sizes.

Addressing the Envelope

No matter what size the envelope, the address is always single-spaced with all lines aligned on the left. The address on the envelope is in the same style as the inside address and

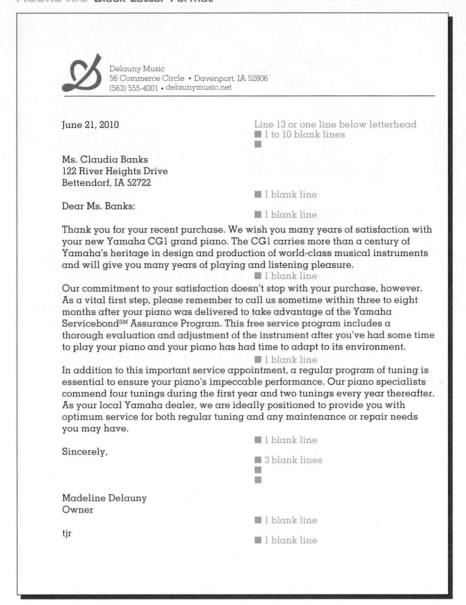

FIGURE A.4 Modified Block Letter Format

GREYHOUND

Ronald Struthers
Regional Sales Director

■ line 13 from top of page November 2, 2010
■ 1 to 10 blank lines
■

Ms. Eugenia Preston, President
Garden Valley High School PTA
P.O. Box 335
Garden Valley, ID 83622
■ 1 blank line
Dear Ms. Preston:
■ 1 blank line

350 N. St. Paul Street
Dallas, TX 75201
Phone: 972-789-7380
Fax: 214-849-8410

Thank you for inviting us to participate in your "Day of Government" program. So that your honors students can experience state government firsthand, we will be delighted to provide one of our motor coaches next May at a 15% discount to transport up to 40 students and 7 advisers from Garden Valley to Boise and back.
■ 1 blank line
Our buses seat 47 passengers, are fully equipped with restrooms and reclining seats, and are climate controlled for year-round comfort. You can rely on us for your charter transportation needs:
■ 1 blank line
- Our intensive, ongoing driver-training program ensures your safety and satisfaction.
- Our competitive pricing allows us to compete both locally and nationwide.
- Our state-of-the-art maintenance facilities are located in all major U.S. cities to ensure quality, reliability, and excellent service.

■ 1 blank line
Please give me a call at (208) 997-4646 to discuss the specific date of your event, departure times, and the discounted price for your trip. Together, we'll make sure your students have a day that's not only fun and educational but safe and secure. I look forward to hearing from you.
■ 1 blank line
Sincerely,
■ 3 blank lines
■
■

Ronald Struthers
Regional Sales Director
■ 1 blank line
pf
■ 1 blank line
Enclosure

presents the same information. The order to follow is from the smallest division to the largest:

1. Name and title of recipient
2. Name of department or subgroup
3. Name of organization
4. Name of building
5. Street address and suite number, or post office box number
6. City, state, or province, and zip code or postal code
7. Name of country (if the letter is being sent abroad)

Because the U.S. Postal Service uses optical scanners to sort mail, envelopes for quantity mailings, in particular, should be addressed in the prescribed format. Everything is in capital letters, no punctuation is included, and all mailing instructions of interest to the post office are placed above the address area (see Figure A.6). Canada Post requires a similar format, except that only the city is all in capitals, and the postal code is placed on the line below the name of the city. The post office scanners read addresses from the bottom up, so if a letter is to be sent to a post office box rather than to a street address, the street address should appear on the line above the box number. Figure A.6 also shows the proper spacing for addresses and return addresses.

The U.S. Postal Service and the Canada Post Corporation have published lists of two-letter mailing abbreviations for states, provinces, and territories (see Table A.6). Postal authorities prefer no punctuation with these abbreviations, but some executives prefer to have state and province names spelled out in full and set off from city names by a comma. The issue is unresolved, although the comma is most often included. Quantity mailings follow post office requirements. For other letters, a reasonable compromise is to use traditional punctuation,

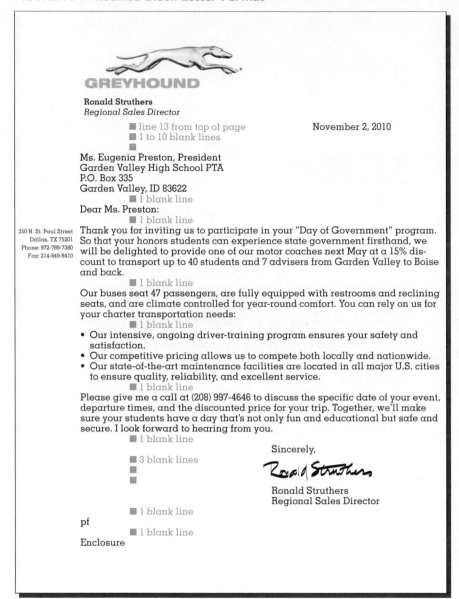

FIGURE A.5 Simplified Letter Format

LJT
Workplace Solutions

May 5, 2010 — Line 13 from top of page

1 to 10 blank lines

Ms. Gillian Wiles, President
Scientific and Technical Contracts, Inc.
6348 Morehouse Dr.
San Diego, CA 92121

2 blank lines

NEW SERVICES

2 blank lines

Thank you, Ms. Wiles, for your recent inquiry about our services. Our complete line of staffing services offers high-level professionals with the skills you require. From the office to the factory, from the tech site to the trade show, from the law firm to the lab—we can provide you with the people and the expertise you need.

1 blank line

I have enclosed a package of information for your review, including specific information on our engineers, designers/drafters, and engineering support personnel. The package also contains reprints of customer reviews and a comparison sheet showing how our services measure up against those of competing companies. We identify qualified candidates and recruit through a network of professional channels to reach candidates whose skills match the specific engineering disciplines you require.

1 blank line

Please call me with any questions you may have. Whether you need a temporary employee for a day or an entire department staffed indefinitely, our staffing solutions give you the freedom you need to focus and the support you need to succeed. I will be glad to help you fill your staffing needs with Kelly professionals.

3 blank lines

Rudy Cohen

RUDY COHEN
CUSTOMER SERVICE SPECIALIST

1 blank line

jn

1 blank line

Enclosures

999 WEST BIG BEAVER ROAD • TROY, MICHIGAN 48084-4782
TELEPHONE (248) 362-4444

uppercase and lowercase letters for names and street addresses, but two-letter state or province abbreviations, as shown here:

Mr. Kevin Kennedy
2107 E. Packer Dr.
Amarillo, TX 79108

For all out-of-office correspondence, use zip and postal codes that have been assigned to speed mail delivery. The U.S. Postal Service has divided the United States and its territories into 10 zones (0 to 9); this digit comes first in the zip code. The second and third digits represent smaller geographical areas within a state, and the last two digits identify a "local delivery area." Canadian postal codes are alphanumeric, with a three-character "area code" and a three-character "local code" separated by a single space (K2P 5A5). Zip and postal codes should be separated from state and province names by one space. Canadian postal codes may be treated the same or may be put in the bottom line of the address all by itself.

The U.S. Postal Service has added zip 4 codes, which add a hyphen and four more numbers to the standard zip codes. The first two of the new numbers may identify an area as small as a single large building, and the last two digits may identify one floor in a large building or even a specific department of an organization. The zip 4 codes are especially useful for business correspondence. The Canada Post Corporation achieves the same result with special postal codes assigned to buildings and organizations that receive a large volume of mail.

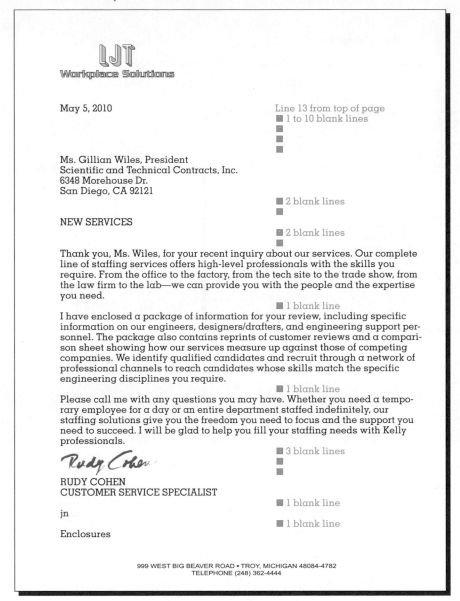

FIGURE A.6 Prescribed Envelope Format

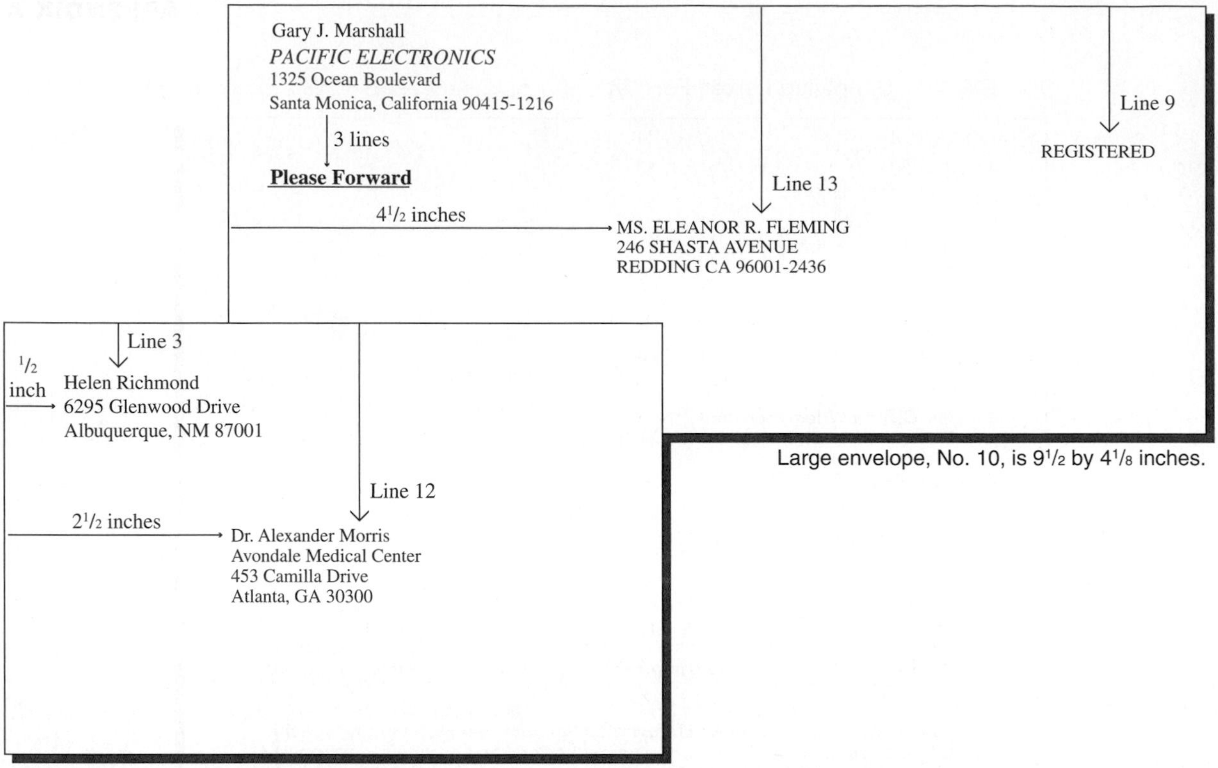

Large envelope, No. 10, is $9^1/_2$ by $4^1/_8$ inches.

Small envelope, No. $6^3/_4$, is $6^1/_2$ by $3^5/_8$ inches.

TABLE A.6 Two-Letter Mailing Abbreviations for the United States and Canada

STATE/ TERRITORY/ PROVINCE	ABBREVIATION	STATE/ TERRITORY/ PROVINCE	ABBREVIATION	STATE/ TERRITORY/ PROVINCE	ABBREVIATION
United States		Massachusetts	MA	Texas	TX
Alabama	AL	Michigan	MI	Utah	UT
Alaska	AK	Minnesota	MN	Vermont	VT
American Samoa	AS	Mississippi	MS	Virginia	VA
Arizona	AZ	Missouri	MO	Virgin Islands	VI
Arkansas	AR	Montana	MT	Washington	WA
California	CA	Nebraska	NE	West Virginia	WV
Canal Zone	CZ	Nevada	NV	Wisconsin	WI
Colorado	CO	New Hampshire	NH	Wyoming	WY
Connecticut	CT	New Jersey	NJ	**Canada**	
Delaware	DE	New Mexico	NM	Alberta	AB
District of Columbia	DC	New York	NY	British Columbia	BC
Florida	FL	North Carolina	NC	Labrador	NL
Georgia	GA	North Dakota	ND	Manitoba	MB
Guam	GU	Northern Mariana	MP	New Brunswick	NB
Hawaii	HI	Ohio	OH	Newfoundland	NL
Idaho	ID	Oklahoma	OK	Northwest Territories	NT
Illinois	IL	Oregon	OR	Nova Scotia	NS
Indiana	IN	Pennsylvania	PA	Nunavur	NU
Iowa	IA	Puerto Rico	PR	Ontario	ON
Kansas	KS	Rhode Island	RI	Prince Edward Island	PE
Kentucky	KY	South Carolina	SC	Quebec	PQ
Louisiana	LA	South Dakota	SD	Saskatchewan	SK
Maine	ME	Tennessee	TN	Yukon Territory	YT
Maryland	MD	Trust Territories	TT		

Folding to Fit

The way a letter is folded also contributes to the recipient's overall impression of your organization's professionalism. When sending a standard-size piece of paper in a No. 10 envelope, fold it in thirds, with the bottom folded up first and the top folded down over it (see Figure A.7); the open end should be at the top of the envelope and facing out. Fit smaller stationery neatly into the appropriate envelope simply by folding it in half or in thirds. When sending a standard-size letterhead in a No. 6¾ envelope, fold it in half from top to bottom and then in thirds from side to side.

International Mail

Postal service differs from country to country, so it's always a good idea to investigate the quality and availability of various services before sending messages and packages internationally. Also, compare the services offered by delivery companies such as UPS and FedEx to find the best rates and options for each destination and type of shipment. No matter which service you choose, be aware that international mail requires more planning than domestic mail. For example, for anything beyond simple letters, you generally need to prepare *customs forms* and possibly other documents, depending on the country of destination and the type of shipment. You are responsible for following the laws of the United States and any countries to which you send mail and packages.

The U.S. Postal Service currently offers four classes of international delivery, listed here from the fastest (and most expensive) to the slowest (and least expensive):

- **Global Express Guaranteed** is the fastest option. This service, offered in conjunction with FedEx, provides delivery in one to three business days to more than 190 countries and territories.
- **Express Mail International** guarantees delivery in three to five business days to a limited number of countries, including Australia, China, Hong Kong, Japan, and South Korea.
- **Priority Mail International** offers delivery guarantees of 6 to 10 business days to more than 190 countries and territories.
- **First Class Mail International** is an economical way to send correspondence and packages weighing up to four pounds to virtually any destination worldwide.

To prepare your mail for international delivery, follow the instructions provided at www.usps.com/international. There you'll find complete information on the international services available through the U.S. Postal Service, along with advice on addressing and packaging mail, completing customs forms, and calculating postage rates and fees. The *International Mail Manual*, also available on this website, offers the latest information and regulations for both outbound and inbound international mail. For instance, you can click on individual country names to see current information about restricted or prohibited items and materials, required customs forms, and rates for various classes of service.[9] Various countries have specific and often extensive lists of items that may not be sent by mail at all or that must be sent using particular postal service options.

MEMOS

Many organizations have memo forms preprinted, with labeled spaces for the recipient's name (or sometimes a checklist of all departments in an organization or all persons in a

FIGURE A.7 *Folding Standard-Size Letterhead*

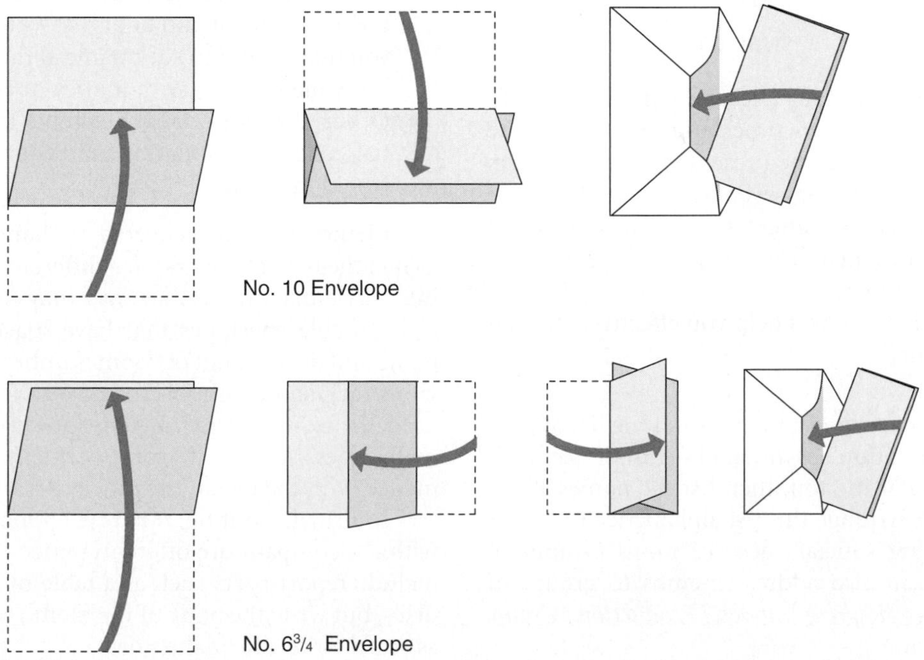

FIGURE A.8 Preprinted Memo Form

MEMO

TO: ____________

DEPT: ____________ FROM: ____________

DATE: ____________ TELEPHONE: ____________

SUBJECT: ____________ For your ☐ APPROVAL ☐ INFORMATION ☐ COMMENT

department), the sender's name, the date, and the subject (see Figure A.8). If such forms don't exist, you can use a memo template (which comes with word processing software and provides margin settings, headings, and special formats), or you can use plain paper.

On your document, include a title such as MEMO or INTEROFFICE CORRESPONDENCE (all in capitals) centered at the top of the page or aligned with the left margin. Also at the top, include the words *To, From, Date,* and *Subject*—followed by the appropriate information—with a blank line between as shown here:

MEMO

TO:

FROM:

DATE:

SUBJECT:

Sometimes the heading is organized like this:

MEMO

TO:	DATE:
FROM:	SUBJECT:

You can arrange these four pieces of information in almost any order. The date sometimes appears without the heading *Date.* The subject may be presented with the letters *Re:* (in place of *SUBJECT:*) or may even be presented without any heading (but in capital letters so that it stands out clearly). You may want to include a file or reference number, introduced by the word *File.*

The following guidelines will help you effectively format specific memo elements:

- **Addressees.** When sending a memo to a long list of people, include the notation *See distribution list* or *See below* in the *To* position at the top; then list the names at the end of the memo. Arrange this list alphabetically, except when high-ranking officials deserve more prominent placement. You can also address memos to groups of people—*All Sales Representatives, Production Group, New Product Team.*
- **Courtesy titles.** You need not use courtesy titles anywhere in a memo; first initials and last names, first names, or even initials alone are often sufficient. However, use a courtesy title if you would use one in a face-to-face encounter with the person.
- **Subject line.** The subject line of a memo helps busy colleagues quickly find out what your memo is about. Although the subject "line" may overflow onto a second line, it's most helpful when it's short (but still informative).
- **Body.** Start the body of the memo on the second or third line below the heading. Like the body of a letter, it's usually single-spaced with blank lines between paragraphs. Indenting paragraphs is optional. Handle lists, important passages, and subheadings as you do in letters. If the memo is very short, you may double-space it.
- **Second page.** If the memo carries over to a second page, head the second page just as you head the second page of a letter.
- **Writer's initials.** Unlike a letter, a memo doesn't require a complimentary close or a signature, because your name is already prominent at the top. However, you may initial the memo—either beside the name appearing at the top of the memo or at the bottom of the memo—or you may even sign your name at the bottom, particularly if the memo deals with money or confidential matters.
- **Other elements.** Treat elements such as reference initials, enclosure notations, and copy notations just as you would in a letter.

Memos may be delivered by hand, by the post office (when the recipient works at a different location), or through interoffice mail. Interoffice mail may require the use of special reusable envelopes that have spaces for the recipient's name and department or room number; the name of the previous recipient is simply crossed out. If a regular envelope is used, the words *Interoffice Mail* appear where the stamp normally goes, so that it won't accidentally be stamped and mailed with the rest of the office correspondence.

Informal, routine, or brief reports for distribution within a company are often presented in memo form. Don't include report parts such as a table of contents and appendixes, but write the body of the memo report just as carefully as you'd write a formal report.

E-MAIL

Because e-mail messages can act both as memos (carrying information within your company) and as letters (carrying information outside your company and around the world), their format depends on your audience and purpose. You may choose to have your e-mail resemble a formal letter or a detailed report, or you may decide to keep things as simple as an interoffice memo. A modified memo format is appropriate for most e-mail messages.[10] All e-mail programs include two major elements: the header and the body (see Figure A.9).

Header

The e-mail header depends on the particular program you use. Some programs even allow you to choose between a shorter and a longer version. However, most headers contain similar information:

- **To:** Contains the audience's e-mail address (see Figure A.10). Most e-mail programs also allow you to send mail to an entire group of people all at once. First, you create a distribution list. Then you type the name of the list in the *To:* line instead of typing the addresses of every person in the group.[11] The most common e-mail addresses are addresses such as

  nmaa.betsy@c.si.edu (Smithsonian Institute's National Museum of American Art)

  webwsj@dowjones.com (*Wall Street Journal*)

  relpubli@mairie-toulouse.mipnet.fr (Municipal Services, Toulouse, France)

- **From:** Contains your e-mail address.
- **Date:** Contains the day of the week, date (day, month, year), time, and time zone.

FIGURE A.9 A Typical E-Mail Message

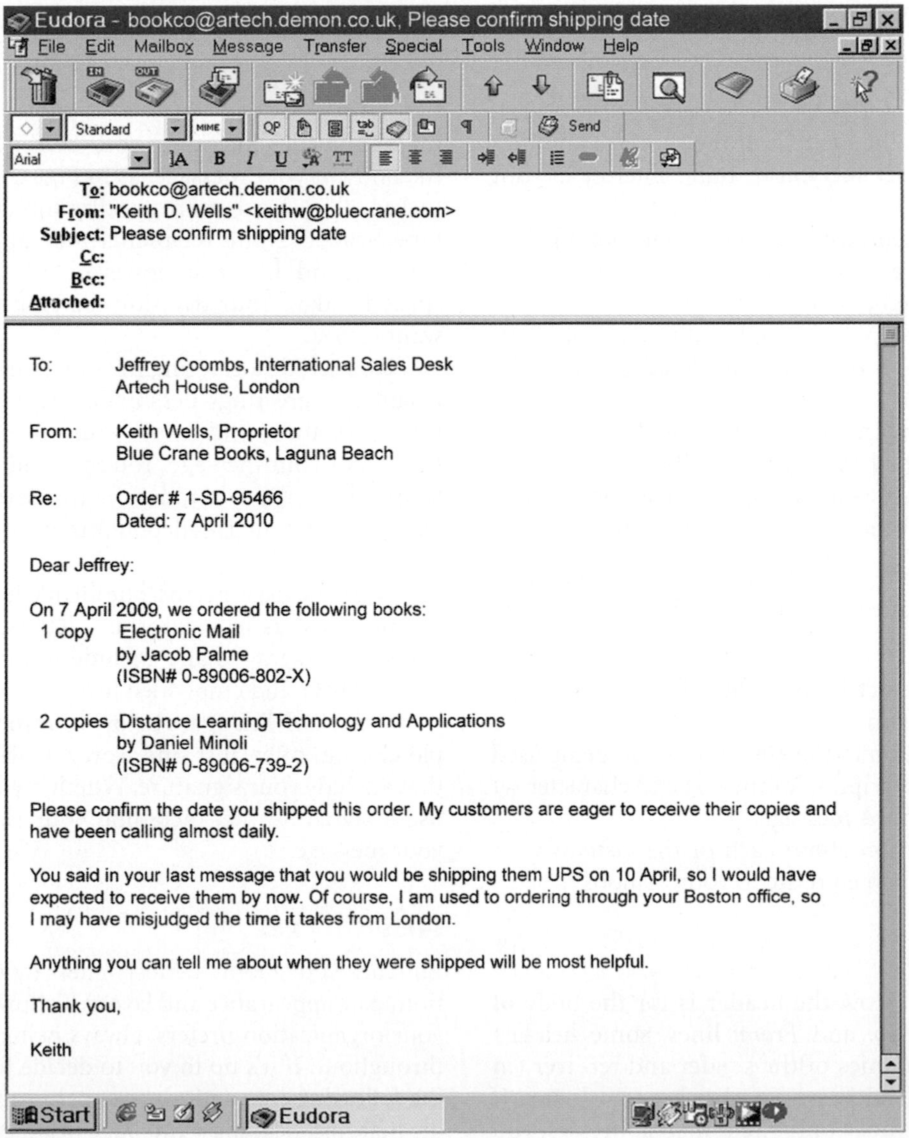

To: Jeffrey Coombs, International Sales Desk
Artech House, London

From: Keith Wells, Proprietor
Blue Crane Books, Laguna Beach

Re: Order # 1-SD-95466
Dated: 7 April 2010

Dear Jeffrey:

On 7 April 2009, we ordered the following books:
1 copy Electronic Mail
by Jacob Palme
(ISBN# 0-89006-802-X)

2 copies Distance Learning Technology and Applications
by Daniel Minoli
(ISBN# 0-89006-739-2)

Please confirm the date you shipped this order. My customers are eager to receive their copies and have been calling almost daily.

You said in your last message that you would be shipping them UPS on 10 April, so I would have expected to receive them by now. Of course, I am used to ordering through your Boston office, so I may have misjudged the time it takes from London.

Anything you can tell me about when they were shipped will be most helpful.

Thank you,

Keith

FIGURE A.10 Anatomy of an E-Mail Address

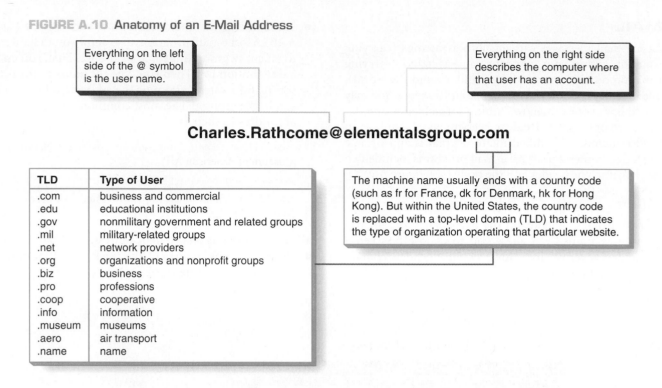

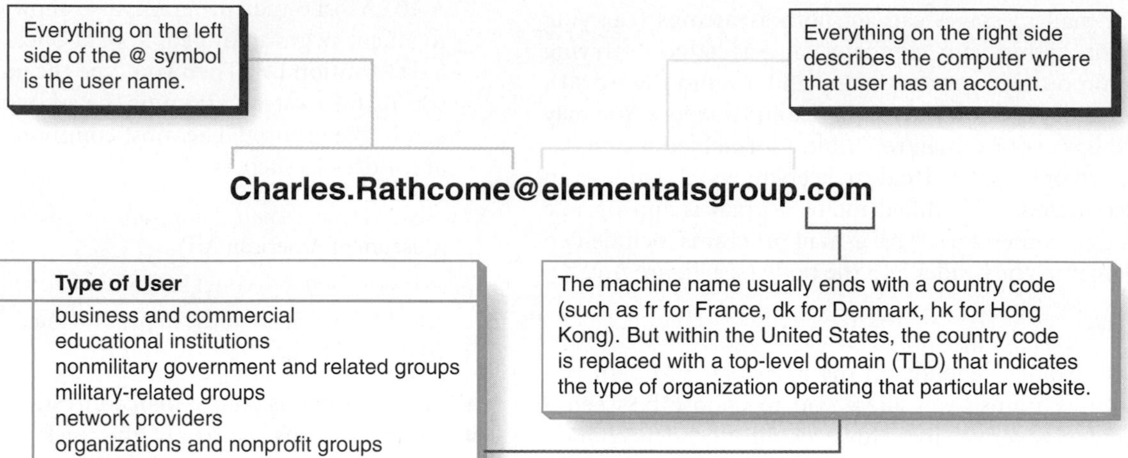
Everything on the left side of the @ symbol is the user name.
Everything on the right side describes the computer where that user has an account.
Charles.Rathcome@elementalsgroup.com
The machine name usually ends with a country code (such as fr for France, dk for Denmark, hk for Hong Kong). But within the United States, the country code is replaced with a top-level domain (TLD) that indicates the type of organization operating that particular website.

TLD	Type of User
.com	business and commercial
.edu	educational institutions
.gov	nonmilitary government and related groups
.mil	military-related groups
.net	network providers
.org	organizations and nonprofit groups
.biz	business
.pro	professions
.coop	cooperative
.info	information
.museum	museums
.aero	air transport
.name	name

- **Subject:** Describes the content of the message and presents an opportunity for you to build interest in your message.
- **Cc:** Allows you to send copies of a message to more than one person at a time. It also allows everyone on the list to see who else received the same message.
- **Bcc:** Lets you send copies to people without the other recipients knowing—a practice considered unethical by some.[12]
- **Attachments:** Contains the name(s) of the file(s) you attach to your e-mail message. The file can be a word processing document, a digital image, an audio or video message, a spreadsheet, or a software program.[13]

Most e-mail programs now allow you the choice of hiding or revealing other lines that contain more detailed information, including

- **Message-Id:** The exact location of this e-mail message on the sender's system
- **X-mailer:** The version of the e-mail program being used
- **Content type:** A description of the text and character set that is contained in the message
- **Received:** Information about each of the systems your e-mail passed through en route to your mailbox[14]

Body

The rest of the space below the header is for the body of your message. In the *To:* and *From:* lines, some headers actually print out the names of the sender and receiver (in addition to their e-mail addresses). Other headers do not. If your mail program includes only the e-mail addresses, you might consider including your own memo-type header in the body of your message, as in Figure A.9. The writer even included a second, more specific subject line in his memo-type header. Some recipients may applaud the clarity of such second headers; however, others will criticize the space it takes. Your decision depends on how formal you want to be.

Do include a greeting in your e-mail. As pointed out in Chapter 7, greetings personalize your message. Leave one line space above and below your greeting to set it off from the rest of your message. You may end your greeting with a colon (formal), a comma (conversational), or even two hyphens (informal)—depending on the level of formality you want.

Your message begins one blank line space below your greeting. Just as in memos and letters, skip one line space between paragraphs and include headings, numbered lists, bulleted lists, and embedded lists when appropriate.

One blank line space below your message, include a simple closing, often just one word. A blank line space below that, include your signature. Whether you type your name or use a signature file, including your signature personalizes your message.

REPORTS

Enhance your report's effectiveness by paying careful attention to its appearance and layout. Follow whatever guidelines your organization prefers, always being neat and consistent throughout. If it's up to you to decide formatting questions, the following conventions may help you decide how to handle margins, headings, and page numbers.

FIGURE A.11 Margins for Formal Reports

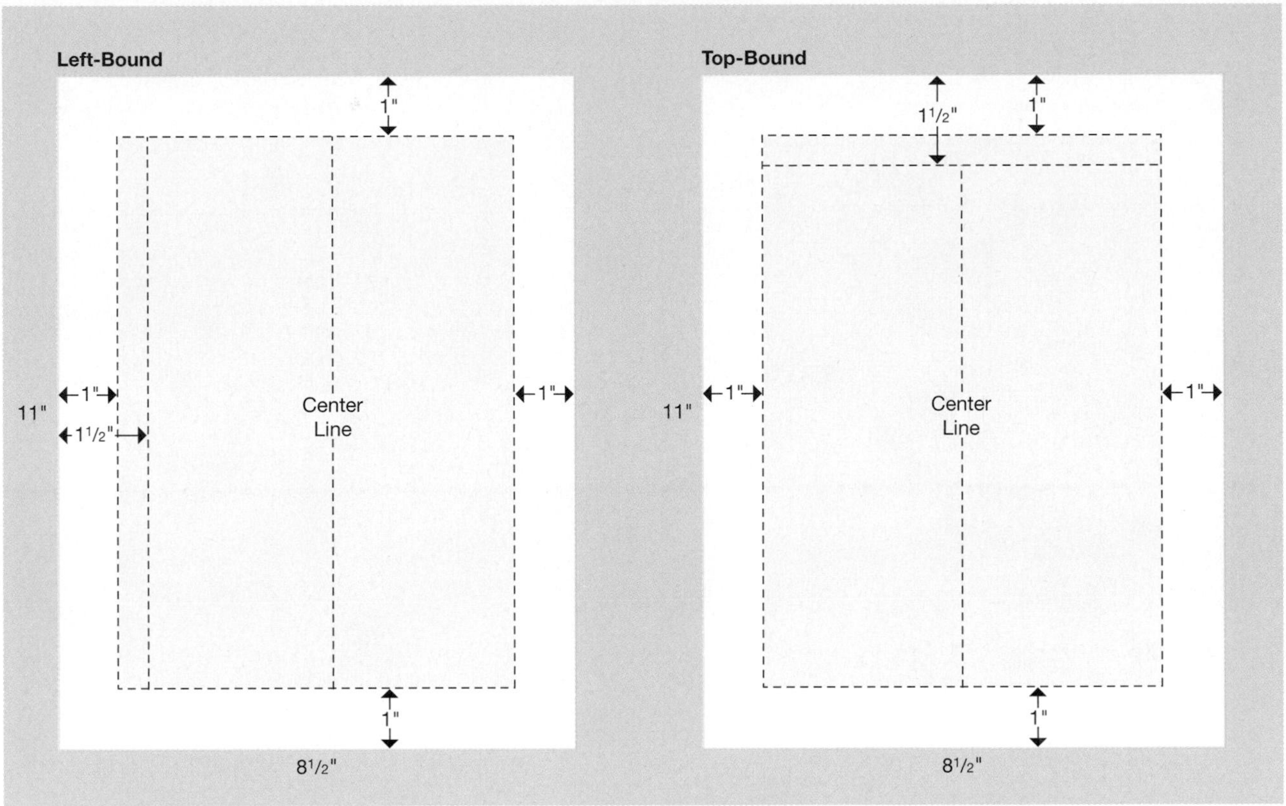

Margins

All margins on a report page are at least 1 inch wide. For double-spaced pages, use 1-inch margins; for single-spaced pages, set margins between 1¼ and 1½ inches. The top, left, and right margins are usually the same, but the bottom margins can be 1½ times deeper. Some special pages also have deeper top margins. Set top margins as deep as 2 inches for pages that contain major titles: prefatory parts (such as the table of contents or the executive summary), supplementary parts (such as the reference notes or bibliography), and textual parts (such as the first page of the text or the first page of each chapter).

If you're going to bind your report at the left or at the top, add half an inch to the margin on the bound edge (see Figure A.11): The space taken by the binding on left-bound reports makes the center point of the text a quarter inch to the right of the center of the paper. Be sure to center headings between the margins, not between the edges of the paper. The "center" paragraph format setting in your word processor does this automatically.

Headings

Headings of various levels provide visual clues to a report's organization. Figure 12.2, on page 358, illustrates one good system for showing these levels, but many variations exist. No matter which system you use, be sure to be consistent.

Page Numbers

Remember that every page in the report is counted; however, not all pages show numbers. The first page of the report, normally the title page, is unnumbered. All other pages in the prefatory section are numbered with a lowercase roman numeral, beginning with *ii* and continuing with *iii, iv, v,* and so on. The unadorned (no dashes, no period) page number is centered at the bottom margin.

Number the first page of the text of the report with the unadorned arabic numeral 1, centered at the bottom margin (double- or triple-spaced below the text). In left-bound reports, number the following pages (including the supplementary parts) consecutively with unadorned arabic numerals (2, 3, and so on), placed at the top right-hand margin (double- or triple-spaced above the text). For top-bound reports and for special pages having 2-inch top margins, center the page numbers at the bottom margin.

Appendix B
Documentation of Report Sources

By providing information about your sources, you improve your own credibility as well as the credibility of the facts and opinions you present. Documentation gives readers the means for checking your findings and pursuing the subject further. Also, documenting your report is the accepted way to give credit to the people whose work you have drawn from.

What style should you use to document your report? Experts recommend various forms, depending on your field or discipline. Moreover, your employer or client may use a form different from those the experts suggest. Don't let this discrepancy confuse you. If your employer specifies a form, use it; the standardized form is easier for colleagues to understand. However, if the choice of form is left to you, adopt one of the styles described here. Whatever style you choose, be consistent within any given report, using the same order, punctuation, and format from one reference citation or bibliography entry to the next.

A wide variety of style manuals provide detailed information on documentation. These publications explain the three most commonly used styles:

- American Psychological Association, *Publication Manual of the American Psychological Association*, 5th ed. (Washington, D.C.: American Psychological Association, 2001). Details the author–date system, which is preferred in the social sciences and often in the natural sciences as well.
- *The Chicago Manual of Style*, 15th ed. (Chicago: University of Chicago Press, 2003). Often referred to only as "*Chicago*" and widely used in the publishing industry; provides detailed treatment of source documentation and many other aspects of document preparation.
- Joseph Gibaldi, *MLA Style Manual and Guide to Scholarly Publishing*, 3rd ed. (New York: Modern Language Association, 2008). Serves as the basis for the note and bibliography style used in much academic writing and is recommended in many college textbooks on writing term papers; provides a lot of examples in the humanities.

For more information on these three guides, visit http://real-timeupdates.com/ebc and click on Appendix B. Although many schemes have been proposed for organizing the information in source notes, all of them break the information into parts: (1) information about the author (name), (2) information about the work (title, edition, volume number), (3) information about the publication (place, publisher), (4) information about the date, and (5) information on relevant page ranges.

In the following sections, we summarize the major conventions for documenting sources in three styles: *The Chicago Manual of Style* (Chicago), the *Publication Manual of the American Psychological Association* (APA), and the *MLA Style Manual* (MLA).

CHICAGO HUMANITIES STYLE

The Chicago Manual of Style recommends two types of documentation systems. The *documentary-note*, or *humanities*, style gives bibliographic citations in notes—either footnotes (when printed at the bottom of a page) or endnotes (when printed at the end of the report). The humanities system is often used in literature, history, and the arts. The other system strongly recommended by *Chicago* is the *author-date* system, which cites the author's last name and the date of publication in the text, usually in parentheses, reserving full documentation for the reference list (or bibliography). For the purpose of comparing styles, we will concentrate on the humanities system, which is described in detail in *Chicago*.

In-Text Citation—*Chicago* Humanities Style

To document report sources in text, the humanities system relies on superscripts—arabic numerals placed just above the line of type at the end of the reference:

> Toward the end of his speech, Myers sounded a note of caution, saying that even though the economy is expected to grow, it could easily slow a bit.[10]

The superscript lets the reader know how to look for source information in either a footnote or an endnote (see Figure B-1). Some readers prefer footnotes so that they can simply glance at the bottom of the page for information. Others prefer endnotes so that they can read the text without a clutter of notes on the page. Also, endnotes relieve the writer from worrying about how long each note will be and how much space it will take away from the page. Both footnotes and endnotes are handled automatically by today's word processing software.

For the reader's convenience, you can use footnotes for **content notes** (which may supplement your main text with asides about a particular issue or event, provide a cross-reference to another section of your report, or direct the reader to a related source). Then you can use endnotes for **source notes** (which document direct quotations, paraphrased passages, and visual aids). Consider which type of note is most common in your report, and then choose whether to present these notes all as endnotes or all as footnotes. Regardless of the method you choose for referencing textual information in your report, notes for visual aids (both content notes and source notes) are placed on the same page as the visual.

FIGURE B-1 Sample Endnotes—*Chicago* Humanities Style

NOTES

Journal article with volume and issue numbers	1. Jonathan Clifton, "Beyond Taxonomies of Influence," *Journal of Business Communication* 46, no. 1 (2009): 57–79.
Brochure	2. BestTemp Staffing Services, *An Employer's Guide to Staffing Services,* 2d ed. (Denver: BestTemp Information Center, 2008), 31.
Newspaper article, no author	3. "Might Be Harder Than It Looks," *Los Angeles Times,* 30 January 2009, sec. A, p. 22.
Annual report	4. The Walt Disney Company, *2007 Annual Report* (Burbank, Calif.: The Walt Disney Company, 2008), 48.
Magazine article	5. Kerry A. Dolan, "A Whole New Crop" *Forbes*, 2 June 2008, 72–75.
Television broadcast	6. Daniel Han, "Trade Wars Heating Up Around the Globe," *CNN Headline News* (Atlanta: CNN, 5 March 2002).
Internet, World Wide Web	7. "Intel—Company Capsule," Hoover's Online [cited 19 June 2008], 3 screens; available from www.hoovers.com/intel/-ID_13787-/free-co-factsheet.xhtml.
Book, component parts	8. Sonja Kuntz, "Moving Beyond Benefits," in *Our Changing Workforce,* ed. Randolf Jacobson (New York: Citadel Press, 2001), 213–27.
Unpublished dissertation or thesis	9. George H. Morales, "The Economic Pressures on Industrialized Nations in a Global Economy" (Ph.D. diss., University of San Diego, 2001), 32–47.
Paper presented at a meeting	10. Charles Myers, "HMOs in Today's Environment" (paper presented at the Conference on Medical Insurance Solutions, Chicago, Ill., August 2001), 16–17.
Online magazine article	11. Leo Babauta, "17 Tips to Be Productive with Instant Messaging," in *Web Worker Daily* [online] (San Francisco, 2007 [updated 14 November 2007; cited 14 February 2008]); available from http://webworkerdaily.com.
CD-ROM encyclopedia article, one author	12. Robert Parkings, "George Eastman," *The Concise Columbia Encyclopedia* (New York: Columbia University Press, 1998) [CD-ROM].
Interview	13. Georgia Stainer, general manager, Day Cable and Communications, interview by author, Topeka, Kan., 2 March 2000.
Newspaper article, one author	14. Evelyn Standish, "Global Market Crushes OPEC's Delicate Balance of Interests," *Wall Street Journal,* 19 January 2002, sec. A, p. 1.
Book, two authors	15. Miriam Toller and Jay Fielding, *Global Business for Smaller Companies* (Rocklin, Calif.: Prima Publishing, 2001), 102–3.
Government publication	16. U.S. Department of Defense, *Stretching Research Dollars: Survival Advice for Universities and Government Labs* (Washington, D.C.: GPO, 2002), 126.

Bibliography—*Chicago* Humanities Style

The humanities system may or may not be accompanied by a bibliography (because the notes give all the necessary bibliographic information). However, endnotes are arranged in order of appearance in the text, so an alphabetical bibliography can be valuable to your readers. The bibliography may be titled *Bibliography, Reference List, Sources, Works Cited* (if you include only those sources you actually cited in your report), or *Works Consulted* (if you include uncited sources as well). This list of sources may also serve as a reading list for those who want to pursue the subject of your report further, so you may want to annotate each entry—that is, comment on the subject matter and viewpoint of the source, as well as on its usefulness to readers. Annotations may be written in either complete or incomplete sentences. (See the annotated list of style manuals early in this appendix.) A bibliography may also be more manageable if you subdivide it into categories (a classified bibliography), either by type of reference (such as books, articles, and unpublished material) or by subject matter (such as government regulation, market forces, and so on). Following are the major conventions for developing a bibliography according to *Chicago* style (see Figure B-2):

- Exclude any page numbers that may be cited in source notes, except for journals, periodicals, and newspapers.
- Alphabetize entries by the last name of the lead author (listing last name first). The names of second and succeeding authors are listed in normal order. Entries without an

FIGURE B-2 Sample Bibliography—*Chicago* Humanities Style

BIBLIOGRAPHY

Journal article with volume and issue numbers	Clifton, Jonathan. "Beyond Taxonomies of Influence." *Journal of Business Communication* 46, no. 1 (2009): 57–79.
Online magazine article	Babauta, Leo. "17 Tips to Be Productive with Instant Messaging," In *Web Worker Daily* [online], San Francisco, 2007 [updated 14 November 2007, cited 14 February 2008]. Available from http://webworkerdaily.com.
Brochure	BestTemp Staffing Services. *An Employer's Guide to Staffing Services.* 2d ed. Denver: BestTemp Information Center, 2008.
Newspaper article, no author	"Might Be Harder Than It Looks." *Los Angeles Times,* 30 January 2009, sec. A, p. 22.
Magazine article	Dolan, Kerry A. "A Whole New Crop," *Forbes*, 2 June 2008, 72–75.
Television broadcast	Han, Daniel. "Trade Wars Heating Up Around the Globe." *CNN Headline News.* Atlanta: CNN, 5 March 2002.
Internet, World Wide Web	"Intel—Company Capsule." *Hoover's Online* [cited 19 June 2008]. 3 screens; Available from www.hoovers.com/intel/-ID_13787-/free-co-factsheet.xhtml.
Book, component parts	Kuntz, Sonja. "Moving Beyond Benefits." In *Our Changing Workforce*, edited by Randolf Jacobson. New York: Citadel Press, 2001.
Unpublished dissertation or thesis	Morales, George H. "The Economic Pressures on Industrialized Nations in a Global Economy." Ph.D. diss., University of San Diego, 2001.
Paper presented at a meeting	Myers, Charles. "HMOs in Today's Environment." Paper presented at the Conference on Medical Insurance Solutions, Chicago, Ill., August 2001.
CD-ROM encyclopedia article, one author	Parkings, Robert. "George Eastman." *The Concise Columbia Encyclopedia.* New York: Columbia University Press, 1998. [CD-ROM].
Interview	Stainer, Georgia, general manager, Day Cable and Communications. Interview by author. Topeka, Kan., 2 March 2000.
Newspaper article, one author	Standish, Evelyn. "Global Market Crushes OPEC's Delicate Balance of Interests." *Wall Street Journal,* 19 January 2002, sec. A, p. 1.
Book, two authors	Toller, Miriam, and Jay Fielding. *Global Business for Smaller Companies.* Rocklin, Calif.: Prima Publishing, 2001.
Government publication	U.S. Department of Defense. *Stretching Research Dollars: Survival Advice for Universities and Government Labs.* Washington, D.C.: GPO, 2002.
Annual report	The Walt Disney Company, *2007 Annual Report,* Burbank, Calif.: The Walt Disney Company, 2008.

author name are alphabetized by the first important word in the title.

- Format entries as hanging indents (indent second and succeeding lines three to five spaces).
- Arrange entries in the following general order: (1) author name, (2) title information, (3) publication information, (4) date, (5) periodical page range.
- Use quotation marks around the titles of articles from magazines, newspapers, and journals. Capitalize the first and last words, as well as all other important words (except prepositions, articles, and coordinating conjunctions).
- Use italics to set off the names of books, newspapers, journals, and other complete publications. Capitalize the first and last words, as well as all other important words.
- For journal articles, include the volume number and the issue number (if necessary). Include the year of publication inside parentheses and follow with a colon and the page range of the article: *Journal of Business Communication* 46, no. 1 (2009): 57–79. (In this source, the volume is 46, the number is 1, and the page range is 57–79.)
- Use brackets to identify all electronic references: [Online database] or [CD-ROM].
- Explain how electronic references can be reached: Available from www.spaceless.com/WWWVL.
- Give the citation date for online references: Cited 23 August 2010.

APA STYLE

The American Psychological Association (APA) recommends the author–date system of documentation, which is popular in the physical, natural, and social sciences. When using this system, you simply insert the author's last name and the year of publication within parentheses following the text discussion of the material cited. Include a page number if you use a direct quote. This approach briefly identifies the source so that readers can locate complete information in the alphabetical reference list at the end of the report. The author–date system is both brief and clear, saving readers time and effort.

In-Text Citation—APA Style

To document report sources in text using APA style, insert the author's surname and the date of publication at the end of a statement. Enclose this information in parentheses. If the author's name is referred to in the text itself, then the name can be omitted from parenthetical material.

> Some experts recommend both translation and back-translation when dealing with any non-English-speaking culture (Clifton, 2009).
>
> Toller and Fielding (2001) make a strong case for small companies succeeding in global business.

Personal communications and interviews conducted by the author would not be listed in the reference list at all. Such citations would appear in the text only.

> Increasing the role of cable companies is high on the list of Georgia Stainer, general manager at Day Cable and Communications (personal communication, March 2, 2009).

List of References—APA Style

For APA style, list only those works actually cited in the text (so you would not include works for background or for further reading). Report writers must choose their references judiciously. Following are the major conventions for developing a reference list according to APA style (see Figure B-3):

- Format entries as hanging indents.
- List all author names in reversed order (last name first), and use only initials for the first and middle names.
- Arrange entries in the following general order: (1) author name, (2) date, (3) title information, (4) publication information, (5) periodical page range.
- Follow the author name with the date of publication in parentheses.
- List titles of articles from magazines, newspapers, and journals without underlines or quotation marks. Capitalize only the first word of the title, any proper nouns, and the first word to follow an internal colon.
- Italicize titles of books, capitalizing only the first word, any proper nouns, and the first word to follow a colon.
- Italicize names of magazines, newspapers, journals, and other complete publications. Capitalize all the important words.
- For journal articles, include the volume number (in italics) and, if necessary, the issue number (in parentheses). Finally, include the page range of the article: *Journal of Business Communication, 46*(1), 57–79. (In this example, the volume is 46, the number is 1, and the page range is 57–79.)
- Include personal communications (such as letters, memos, e-mail, and conversations) only in text, not in reference lists.
- Electronic references include author, date of publication, title of article, name of publication (if one), volume, date of retrieval (month, day, year), and the source.
- For electronic references, indicate the actual year of publication and the exact date of retrieval.
- For electronic references, specify the URL; leave periods off the ends of URLs.

MLA STYLE

The style recommended by the Modern Language Association of America is used widely in the humanities, especially in the study of language and literature. Like APA style, MLA style uses brief parenthetical citations in the text. However, instead of including author name and year, MLA citations include author name and page reference.

In-Text Citation—MLA Style

To document report sources in text using MLA style, insert the author's last name and a page reference inside parentheses following the cited material: (Matthews 63). If the author's name is mentioned in the text reference, the name can be omitted from the parenthetical citation: (63). The citation indicates that the reference came from page 63 of a work by Matthews. With the author's name, readers can find complete publication information in the alphabetically arranged list of works cited that comes at the end of the report.

> Some experts recommend both translation and back-translation when dealing with any non-English-speaking culture (Clifton 57).
>
> Toller and Fielding make a strong case for small companies succeeding in global business (102–03).

List of Works Cited—MLA Style

The *MLA Style Manual* recommends preparing the list of works cited first so that you will know what information to give in the parenthetical citation (for example, whether to add a short title if you're citing more than one work by the same author, or whether to give an initial or first name if you're citing two authors who have the same last name). The list of works cited appears at the end of your report, contains all the works that you cite in your text, and lists them in alphabetical order. Following are the major conventions

FIGURE B-3 Sample References—APA Style

REFERENCES

Journal article with volume and issue numbers	Clifton, J. (2009). Beyond Taxonomies of Influence. *Journal of Business Communication 46* (1), 57.
Online magazine article	Babauta, L. (2007, November 14), 17 tips to be productive with instant messaging. *Web Worker Daily*. Retrieved February 14, 2008, from http://webworkerdaily.com.
Brochure	BestTemp Staffing Services. (2008). *An employer's guide to staffing services* (2d ed.) [Brochure]. Denver: BestTemp Information Center.
Newspaper article, no author	Might be harder than it looks. (2009, January 30). *Los Angeles Times,* p. A22.
Magazine article	Dolan, K. A. (2008, June 2). A whole new crop. *Forbes*, 72–75.
Television broadcast	Han, D. (2002, March 5). Trade wars heating up around the globe. *CNN Headline News*. [Television broadcast]. Atlanta, GA: CNN.
Internet, World Wide Web	Hoover's Online. (2003). *Intel—Company Capsule*. Retrieved June 19, 2008, from http://www.hoovers.com/intel/-ID_13787-/free-co-factsheet.xhtml.
Book, component parts	Kuntz, S. (2001). Moving beyond benefits. In Randolph Jacobson (Ed.), *Our changing workforce* (pp. 213–227). New York: Citadel Press.
Unpublished dissertation or thesis	Morales, G. H. (2001). *The economic pressures on industrialized nations in a global economy*. Unpublished doctoral dissertation, University of San Diego.
Paper presented at a meeting	Myers, C. (2001, August). *HMOs in today's environment*. Paper presented at the Conference on Medical Insurance Solutions, Chicago, IL.
CD-ROM encyclopedia article, one author	Parkings, R. (1998). George Eastman. On *The concise Columbia encyclopedia.* [CD-ROM]. New York: Columbia University Press.
Interview	*Cited in text only, not in the list of references.*
Newspaper article, one author	Standish, E. (2002, January 19). Global market crushes OPEC's delicate balance of interests. *Wall Street Journal*, p. A1.
Book, two authors	Toller, M., & Fielding, J. (2001). *Global business for smaller companies*. Rocklin, CA: Prima Publishing.
Government publication	U.S. Department of Defense. (2002). *Stretching research dollars: Survival advice for universities and government labs*. Washington, DC: U.S. Government Printing Office.
Annual report	The Walt Disney Company. (2008). *2007 Annual Report.* Burbank, Calif.: The Walt Disney Company.

for developing a reference list according to MLA style (see Figure B-4):

- Format entries as hanging indents.
- Arrange entries in the following general order: (1) author name, (2) title information, (3) publication information, (4) date, (5) periodical page range.
- List the lead author's name in reverse order (last name first), using either full first names or initials. List second and succeeding author names in normal order.
- Use quotation marks around the titles of articles from magazines, newspapers, and journals. Capitalize all important words.
- Italicize the names of books, newspapers, journals, and other complete publications, capitalizing all main words in the title.
- For journal articles, include the volume number and the issue number (if necessary). Include the year of publication inside parentheses and follow with a colon and the page range of the article: *Journal of Business Communication* 46, 1 (2009): 57. (In this source, the volume is 46, the number is 1, and the page is 57.)
- Electronic sources are less fixed than print sources, and they may not be readily accessible to readers. So citations for electronic sources must provide more information.

FIGURE B-4 Sample Works Cited—MLA Style

WORKS CITED

Journal article with volume and issue numbers	Clifton, Jonathan. "Beyond Taxonomies of Influence." *Journal of Business Communication* 46, 1 (2009): 57–79.
Online magazine article	Babauta, Leo. "17 Tips to Be Productive with Instant Messaging," *Web Worker Daily* 14 Nov. 2007. 14 Feb. 2008. <http://webworkerdaily.com>.
Brochure	BestTemp Staffing Services. *An Employer's Guide to Staffing Services*. 2d ed. Denver: BestTemp Information Center, 2008.
Newspaper article, no author	"Might Be Harder Than It Looks." *Los Angeles Times,* 30 Jan. 2009: A22.
Magazine article	Dolan, Kerry A. "A Whole New Crop" *Forbes*, 2 June 2008: 72–75.
Television broadcast	Han, Daniel. "Trade Wars Heating Up Around the Globe." *CNN Headline News*. CNN, Atlanta. 5 Mar. 2002.
Internet, World Wide Web	"Intel—Company Capsule." *Hoover's Online*. 2008. Hoover's Company Information. 19 June 2008 <http://www.hoovers.com/intel/-ID_13787/free-co-factsheet.xhtml.
Book, component parts	Kuntz, Sonja. "Moving Beyond Benefits." *Our Changing Workforce*. Ed. Randolf Jacobson. New York: Citadel Press, 2001. 213–27.
Unpublished dissertation or thesis	Morales, George H. "The Economic Pressures on Industrialized Nations in a Global Economy." Diss. U of San Diego, 2001.
Paper presented at a meeting	Myers, Charles. "HMOs in Today's Environment." Conference on Medical Insurance Solutions. Chicago. 13 Aug. 2001.
CD-ROM encyclopedia article, one author	Parkings, Robert. "George Eastman." *The Concise Columbia Encyclopedia*. CD-ROM. New York: Columbia UP, 1998.
Interview	Stainer, Georgia, general manager, Day Cable and Communications. Telephone interview. 2 Mar. 2000.
Newspaper article, one author	Standish, Evelyn. "Global Market Crushes OPEC's Delicate Balance of Interests." *Wall Street Journal,* 19 Jan. 2002: A1.
Book, two authors	Toller, Miriam, and Jay Fielding. *Global Business for Smaller Companies*. Rocklin, CA: Prima Publishing, 2001.
Government publication	United States. Department of Defense. *Stretching Research Dollars: Survival Advice for Universities and Government Labs*. Washington: GPO, 2002.
Annual report	The Walt Disney Company, *2007 Annual Report*. Calif.: The Walt Disney Company, 2008.

Always try to be as comprehensive as possible, citing whatever information is available (however, see the note below about extremely long URLs).

- The date for electronic sources should contain both the date assigned in the source and the date accessed by the researcher.
- The URL for electronic sources must be as accurate and complete as possible, from access-mode identifier (such as http or ftp) to all relevant directory and file names. If the URL is extremely long, use the URL of the website's home page or the URL of the site's search page if you used the site's search function to find the article. Be sure to enclose this path inside angle brackets: http://www.hoovers.com/capsules/13787.html.

Appendix C
Correction Symbols

Instructors often use these short, easy-to-remember correction symbols and abbreviations when evaluating students' writing. You can use them too, to understand your instructor's suggestions and to revise and proofread your own letters, memos, and reports. Refer to the Handbook of Grammar, Mechanics, and Usage (pages H-1–H-26) for further information.

CONTENT AND STYLE

Acc	Accuracy. Check to be sure information is correct.
ACE	Avoid copying examples.
ACP	Avoid copying problems.
Adp	Adapt. Tailor message to reader.
App	Follow proper organization approach. (Refer to Chapter 4.)
Assign	Assignment. Review instructions for assignment.
AV	Active verb. Substitute active for passive.
Awk	Awkward phrasing. Rewrite.
BC	Be consistent.
BMS	Be more sincere.
Chop	Choppy sentences. Use longer sentences and more transitional phrases.
Con	Condense. Use fewer words.
CT	Conversational tone. Avoid using overly formal language.
Depers	Depersonalize. Avoid attributing credit or blame to any individual or group.
Dev	Develop. Provide greater detail.
Dir	Direct. Use direct approach; get to the point.
Emph	Emphasize. Develop this point more fully.
EW	Explanation weak. Check logic; provide more proof.
Fl	Flattery. Avoid compliments that are insincere.
FS	Figure of speech. Find a more accurate expression.
GNF	Good news first. Use direct order.
GRF	Give reasons first. Use indirect order.
GW	Goodwill. Put more emphasis on expressions of goodwill.
H/E	Honesty/ethics. Revise statement to reflect good business practices.
Imp	Imply. Avoid being direct.
Inc	Incomplete. Develop further.
Jar	Jargon. Use less specialized language.
Log	Logic. Check development of argument.
Neg	Negative. Use more positive approach or expression.
Obv	Obvious. Do not state point in such detail.
Oc	Overconfident. Adopt humbler language.
Om	Omission.
Org	Organization. Strengthen outline.
OS	Off the subject. Close with point on main subject.
Par	Parallel. Use same structure.
Pom	Pompous. Rephrase in down-to-earth terms.
PV	Point of view. Make statement from reader's perspective rather than your own.
RB	Reader benefit. Explain what reader stands to gain.
Red	Redundant. Reduce number of times this point is made.
Ref	Reference. Cite source of information.
Rep	Repetitive. Provide different expression.
Rs	Resale. Reassure reader that he or she has made a good choice.
SA	Service attitude. Put more emphasis on helping reader.
Sin	Sincerity. Avoid sounding glib or uncaring.
SL	Stereotyped language. Focus on individual's characteristics instead of on false generalizations.
Spec	Specific. Provide more specific statement.
SPM	Sales promotion material. Tell reader about related goods or services.
Stet	Let stand in original form.
Sub	Subordinate. Make this point less important.
Sx	Sexist. Avoid language that contributes to gender stereotypes.
Tone	Tone needs improvement.
Trans	Transition. Show connection between points.
UAE	Use action ending. Close by stating what reader should do next.
UAS	Use appropriate salutation.
UAV	Use active voice.
Unc	Unclear. Rewrite to clarify meaning.
UPV	Use passive voice.
USS	Use shorter sentences.
V	Variety. Use different expression or sentence pattern.
W	Wordy. Eliminate unnecessary words.
WC	Word choice. Find a more appropriate word.
YA	"You" attitude. Rewrite to emphasize reader's needs.

GRAMMAR, MECHANICS, AND USAGE

Ab	Abbreviation. Avoid abbreviations in most cases; use correct abbreviation.
Adj	Adjective. Use adjective instead.
Adv	Adverb. Use adverb instead.
Agr	Agreement. Make subject and verb or noun and pronoun agree.
Ap	Appearance. Improve appearance.
Apos	Apostrophe. Check use of apostrophe.
Art	Article. Use correct article.
BC	Be consistent.
Cap	Capitalize.
Case	Use cases correctly.
CoAdj	Coordinate adjective. Insert comma between coordinate adjectives; delete comma between adjective and compound noun.
CS	Comma splice. Use period or semicolon to separate clauses.
DM	Dangling modifier. Rewrite so that modifier clearly relates to subject of sentence.
Exp	Expletive. Avoid expletive beginnings, such as it is, there are, there is, this is, and these are.
F	Format. Improve layout of document.
Frag	Fragment. Rewrite as complete sentence.
Gram	Grammar. Correct grammatical error.
HCA	Hyphenate compound adjective.
lc	Lowercase. Do not use capital letter.
M	Margins. Improve frame around document.
MM	Misplaced modifier. Place modifier close to word it modifies.
NRC	Nonrestrictive clause (or phrase). Separate from rest of sentence with commas.
P	Punctuation. Use correct punctuation.
Par	Parallel. Use same structure.
PH	Place higher. Move document up on page.
PL	Place lower. Move document down on page.
Prep	Preposition. Use correct preposition.
RC	Restrictive clause (or phrase). Remove commas that separate clause from rest of sentence.
RO	Run-on sentence. Separate two sentences with comma and coordinating conjunction or with semicolon.
SC	Series comma. Add comma before *and.*
SI	Split infinitive. Do not separate *to* from rest of verb.
Sp	Spelling error. Consult dictionary.
S-V	Subject–verb pair. Do not separate with comma.
Syl	Syllabification. Divide word between syllables.
WD	Word division. Check dictionary for proper end-of-line hyphenation.
WW	Wrong word. Replace with another word.

PROOFREADING MARKS

Symbol	Meaning	Symbol Used in Context	Corrected Copy
═	Align horizontally	meaningful result	meaningful result
‖	Align vertically	1. Power cable 2. Keyboard	1. Power cable 2. Keyboard
(bf)	Boldface	Recommendations (bf)	**Recommendations**
≡	Capitalize	Pepsico, Inc.	PepsiCo, Inc.
][	Center	]Awards Banquet[	Awards Banquet
⁀‿	Close up space	self- confidence	self-confidence
ℓ	Delete	harrassment ~~and abuse~~	harassment
(ds)	Double-space	text in first line text in second line (ds)	text in first line text in second line
∧	Insert	tirquoise shirts (u; and white)	turquoise and white shirts
’	Insert apostrophe	our teams goals	our team’s goals
,	Insert comma	a, b and c	a, b, and c
=	Insert hyphen	third quarter sales	third-quarter sales
⊙	Insert period	Harrigan et al	Harrigan et al.
“ ”	Insert quotation marks	This team isn’t cooperating.	This “team” isn’t cooperating.
#	Insert space	realestate testcase	real estate test case
(ital)	Italics	Quarterly Report (ital)	*Quarterly Report*
/	Lowercase	TULSA, South of here	Tulsa, south of here
⊔	Move down	Sincerely,	Sincerely,
[	Move left	Attention: [Security	Attention: Security
]	Move right	February 2, 2010]	February 2, 2010
⊓	Move up	THIRD-QUARTER SALES	THIRD-QUARTER SALES
(STET)	Restore	staff talked ~~openly and frankly~~ (STET)	staff talked openly
⊂	Run lines together	Manager, Distribution	Manager, Distribution
(ss)	Single space	text in first line text in second line (ss)	text in first line text in second line
◯	Spell out	COD	cash on delivery
(sp)	Spell out	(sp) Assn. of Biochem. Engrs.	Association of Biochemical Engineers
⌐	Start new line	Marla Fenton, Manager, Distri-bution	Marla Fenton, Manager, Distribution
¶	Start new paragraph	¶ The solution is easy to determine but difficult to implement in a competitive environment like the one we now face.	The solution is easy to determine but difficult to implement in a competitive environment like the one we now face.
∼	Transpose	airy, light, casaul tone	light, airy, casual tone

Video Guide

Your instructor may elect to show you one or more of the videos described on the following pages. These programs supplement course concepts with real-life examples of businesspeople meeting important communication challenges. This video guide includes several review and analysis questions as well as exercises for each video. Be sure to review the appropriate page ahead of time so that you'll know what to look for when you watch the video. (To access backup copies of the online articles mentioned in the follow-up assignments and research projects, visit and click on "Student Assignments.")

EFFECTIVE COMMUNICATION

Learning Objectives

After viewing this video, you will be able to

1. Recognize the importance of communication in the business environment
2. Recognize the elements that distinguish effective from ineffective communication
3. Understand why brevity is an important part of effective communication

Background Information

Effective communication delivers a number of business benefits, including stronger decision making and faster problem solving, earlier warning of potential problems, increased productivity and steadier workflow, stronger business relationships, clearer and more persuasive marketing messages, enhanced professional images for both employers and companies, lower employee turnover and higher employee satisfaction, better financial results, and higher return for investors. To be considered effective, communication efforts need to provide practical information, give facts rather than vague impressions, present information concisely, clarify expectations and responsibilities, and offer persuasive arguments and recommendations.

The Video

This video portrays a new employee at an advertising agency as he learns the importance of effective communication—and learns how to improve his communication efforts. As he goes through a typical day accompanied by a "message mentor," he observes the results of both effective and ineffective communication.

Discussion Questions

1. Why might new hires fresh out of college face challenges in learning how to communicate in the workplace?
2. How should you handle situations in which you are asked to provide solid information but the only information available to you is imprecise and potentially unreliable?
3. How can effective communication improve employee morale?
4. How can you judge how much information to provide your audience in any given situation?
5. Can communication efforts be both effective and unethical? For example, what about a marketing campaign that uses compelling information to persuade people to buy an inferior product when a better product is available from the competition?

Follow-Up Assignment

Most companies make an effort to define external communication strategies, but many don't have a formal strategy for internal communication—which is every bit as essential to their success. Read the article, "Internal Communication Strategies—The Neglected Strategic Element," at http://workhelp.org/content/view/171/46/ and then answer the following questions:

1. What are the advantages of effective internal communication?
2. How does communication help align the efforts of everyone in the organization toward common goals?
3. Why is it important to have a companywide strategy for internal communication?

For Further Research

The *HR Magazine* article "Great Communicators, Great Communication" emphasizes the role communication plays in creating great workplaces. Visit www.shrm.org, use the search function to find the article, and then summarize the steps companies have taken to be included among the magazine's list of the 50 best small and medium companies to work for in the United States.

ETHICAL COMMUNICATION

Learning Objectives

After viewing this video, you will be able to

1. Describe a process for deciding what is ethical or unethical
2. Explain the importance of meeting your personal and professional responsibilities in an ethical manner
3. Discuss the possible consequences of ethical and unethical choices and talk about the impact of these choices on direct and related audiences

Background Information

Communication is ethical when it includes all relevant information, when it's true in every sense, and when it isn't deceptive in any way. In contrast, communication is unethical when it includes false information, fails to include important information, or otherwise misleads an audience. To avoid unethical choices in your communication efforts, you must consider not only legal issues but also the needs of your audience and the expectations of society and your employer. In turn, companies that demonstrate high standards of ethics maintain credibility with employees, customers, and other stakeholders.

The Video

This video identifies two important tools in a communicator's toolbox: honesty and objectivity. These tools help businesspeople resolve ethical dilemmas and avoid ethical lapses, both within the company and during interactions with outside audiences. Poor ethical choices can damage a company's credibility and put employees, customers, and the surrounding community at risk. Unfortunately, some ethical choices are neither clear nor simple, and you may face situations in which the needs of one group or individual must be weighed against the needs of another.

Discussion Questions

1. Would you ever consider compromising your ethics for self-gain? If so, under what circumstance? If not, why?
2. The video mentions the role of misrepresentations in the collapse of Enron. If you were the head of communications at Enron and had some knowledge of the true nature of the company's financial condition, what would you have done?
3. Identify risks involved when you choose to act in an unethical manner.
4. How can you be an effective business communicator without credibility?
5. Is it ethical to call in sick to work, even though you are not ill? What happens to your credibility if someone finds out you were not sick?

Follow-Up Assignment

Many businesses, from small companies to large corporations, formulate codes of ethics that outline ethical standards for employees. Download IBM's Business Conduct Guidelines from www.ibm.com/investor/pdf/BCG2009.pdf and answer the following questions:

1. What does IBM want employees to do if they are aware of unethical situations within the organization?
2. How does IBM view misleading statements or innuendoes about competitors?
3. What advice does IBM give employees on the subject of receiving gifts from people outside the company?

For Further Research

Advertising communications, particularly advertising aimed at children, can present a variety of ethical concerns. Visit the American Psychological Association's website, at www.apa.org, and search for the article "Advertising to children: Is it ethical?" After reading this article, do you believe it is unethical for psychologists to advise companies on how to target children more effectively through advertising? Why or why not?

BUSINESS ETIQUETTE

Learning Objectives

After viewing this video, you will be able to

1. Recognize the negative impact that poor etiquette can have in the workplace
2. Identify the five goals that every bad-news message should seek to achieve
3. Identify situations in which the indirect approach is likely to be more effective than the direct approach

Background Information

Etiquette strikes some people as a fine idea for tea parties but something that has little relevance in the contemporary workplace. However, the stresses and strains of today's business environment make etiquette more important than ever. Poor etiquette harms relationships, hinders communication, lowers morale and productivity, and limits career potential. Successful professionals know that taking the time and effort to treat others with respect—through their words and their actions—pays off for everyone in the long run.

The Video

This video shows a young employee learning firsthand the value of business etiquette. A business associate whom he has offended through clumsy communication turns the tables and helps him understand the negative effect that poor etiquette has on people in the workplace. She then helps him grasp the steps needed to present himself respectably and to communicate in ways that get his point across without unnecessarily stirring up negative emotions.

Discussion Questions

1. Is paying attention to standards of etiquette likely to save time or cost time in the workplace? Why?
2. If you need to deliver bad news to a person with whom you will probably never interact again, how can you justify taking extra time and effort to communicate carefully and respectfully? Are you wasting your company's money by spending time on such efforts?
3. How does a well-written buffer in an indirect negative message help the receiver accept the bad news?
4. Can a buffer also make the task of delivering negative messages less stressful? Why or why not?

5. Is the indirect approach to negative messages deceptive? Shouldn't communication always be straightforward and direct? Be prepared to explain your answer.

Follow-Up Assignment

Visit www.executiveplanet.com and click on any country that interests you. Explore the Public Behaviour section(s) for that country and identify three tips that would help anyone from the United States who is preparing to do business there.

For Further Research

Take the brief business etiquette quiz at http://www.gradview.com/articles/careers/etiquette.html. Were you able to figure out answers to these situations? Do you agree with the responses that the website identifies as being correct?

LEARNING TO LISTEN: SECOND CITY COMMUNICATIONS

CREATIVITY: SECOND CITY COMMUNICATIONS

Learning Objectives

After viewing this video, you will be able to

1. Understand the functions of interpersonal communication in the workplace
2. Identify the ways to overcome barriers to effective communication
3. Discuss the importance of active listening both socially and professionally

Background Information

Chicago's Second City Improv is more than the world's best-known comedy theater. Second City now brings its famous brand of humor to corporate giants such as Coca-Cola, Motorola, and Microsoft. With over 40 years of experience in corporate services, Second City's teachers help business professionals develop communication skills through lessons in improvisational theater. Business communications training is Second City's fastest-growing practice, fueled by the demands of more than 200 Fortune 500 companies. Workshops are tailored to clients' needs in such areas as listening and giving presentations, collaborative leadership and team skills, interviewing, breaking down barriers to successful communication, and using humor to convey important messages. The next time you watch improvisational sketch comedy, ask yourself how a lesson in the art of "improv" might give your career a boost.

The Video

In these two video segments, you'll see Second City's training techniques in action. The first segment addresses the need to listen actively, and the second explores techniques for encouraging innovation. The second clip is less focused on communication, but you can see how the techniques for stimulating innovation work equally well for fostering meaningful, two-way conversation that encourages people to open up rather than shut down.

Discussion Questions

1. How do the exercises featured in this video address the contrasting needs of the trial lawyer, the divorce lawyer, and the media buyer?
2. Would ABC's talkative guest Kay Jarman, the 47-year-old award-winning salesperson, be a good candidate for Second City's training workshop?
3. What other workshops might Tom Yorton want to offer companies in response to the current economic and political climate?
4. How might the "Yes and" rule of improvisation be used to train customer service representatives at an L.L. Bean or a Dell call center? Without physical cues, such as facial expression and body language, is the "Yes and" rule still effective?
5. As president and managing director of Second City Communications, Tom Yorton says the following: "You have to be willing to fail to be able to get the results you want . . . to connect with an audience." Do you agree that this statement is as true in business as it is in comedy? Support your chosen position.

Follow-Up Assignment

Enjoy Second City Communications's website, at www.secondcity.com. If you are a loyal fan, you might want to check out the book titles offered and read more about the group's history. Now explore Second City's Corporate Services: Scan the client roster, read the testimonials, and select a case study that you find compelling. If you are currently employed, which workshop would be most beneficial to you and to your work team? Explain your choice. If you are not currently employed, how might you and your fellow business students benefit from a Second City workshop? Which workshop would you most like to participate in? Explain how you think it might help you in terms of your social life, your career planning, and your interviewing skills.

For Further Research

The importance of active listening is at the core of *consultative selling*, an approach that emphasizes posing questions to the potential buyer in order to identify needs and expectations—rather than rattling off a prepared sales speech. PublicSpeakingSkills.com (www.publicspeakingskills.com) is one of many companies that offer training in consultative selling. Review the description of the company's Consultative Selling and Negotiating Skills course. Do the principles espoused match the concept of the "you" attitude and the elements of ethical communication that you've learned so far?

COMMUNICATING IN THE GLOBAL WORKPLACE

Learning Objectives

After viewing this video, you will be able to

1. Discuss the challenges of communicating in the global workplace
2. Identify barriers to effective communication across borders
3. Explain the critical role of time in global communication efforts

Background Information

Many businesses are crossing national boundaries to engage in international business. However, operating in a global environment presents a variety of challenges related to culture and communication. Understanding and respecting these challenges can mean the difference between success and failure, so executives must make sure that employees are educated on cultural issues before attempting to do business in other countries.

The Video

This video identifies the challenges to effective communication in the global marketplace, including the barriers posed by language, culture, time, and technology. You will see that a significant amount of research needs to be conducted before a company can engage in successful global business ventures. For instance, if communicators are unaware of differences in gestures, expressions, and dialect, they can inadvertently offend or confuse their audiences. In addition, time zone differences require organizations to plan carefully in advance so that they can develop, translate, and deliver information in a timely manner.

Discussion Questions

1. Language can be a barrier to effective communication. What steps can a company take to minimize language barriers across borders?
2. What characteristics of a country's culture need to be researched to ensure business success across borders?
3. How does a company ensure that a message is properly translated into the local language and dialect of the people it conducts business with?
4. What challenges does a company face when trying to hold a conference call or video meeting with affiliates and employees around the world?
5. The video mentions that some companies have trusted contacts in a country they wish to do business with, while other companies rely on a significant amount of research to learn more about culture and other local characteristics. What method do you feel is most effective for gathering useful, accurate, and up-to-date information regarding cultural issues?

Follow-Up Assignment

The Coca-Cola Company has local operations in more than 200 countries throughout the world. Visit www.coca-cola.com and click on "Change Country" at the top of the page to learn more about the company's business activities in a variety of countries. What steps does Coke take to communicate through its website with customers around the world? Does the company strive to develop products that meet local tastes and needs? If so, how and why?

For Further Research

Choose a country other than the United States and research your selection, using both online and library resources to identify important cultural characteristics specific to that country. For example, you might want to gather information about gestures and other nonverbal communication that would be considered offensive, about work habits, or about laws related to conducting business in that country. The characteristics you identify should be useful and accurate.

Based on what you've learned about this country and your personal beliefs, values, and life experiences, is there any risk that you might have a prejudiced or ethnocentric viewpoint regarding people from this country? Why or why not?

IMPACT OF CULTURE ON BUSINESS: SPOTLIGHT ON LATIN AMERICA

Learning Objectives

After viewing this video, you will be able to

1. List key aspects of Latin American cultures and indicate the influences on their development
2. Identify factors that might lead to cultural change in Latin America
3. Explain some of the major cultural contrasts within Latin America and their impact on international business operations

Background Information

To a large degree, culture defines the way all human beings interpret and respond to life's changing circumstances. When you interact with people from your own culture, your shared experiences and expectations usually enhance the communication process by providing a common language and frame of reference. However, when you communicate across cultural boundaries, a lack of awareness of your audience's culture—and the subconscious ways that your own culture shapes your perceptions—can result in partial or even total failure of the communication process. Moreover, culture is rarely static, so impressions you may have gathered at one point in your life may need to be revisited and revised over time.

The Video

This video takes a broad look at Latin America's various countries and cultures and explores the business implications of cultural similarities and differences. You'll learn how cultural groups that may appear identical on the surface can in fact have subtle but profound differences. Although communication is just one of many topics discussed in the video, you will get a sense of just how important—and challenging—communication can be when conducting business across cultural boundaries.

Discussion Questions

1. Explain what the video means when it says that your own culture can "sneak up on you."
2. How is business influencing the economic gulf between urban and rural populations in Latin America?
3. How have imperial conquests and slavery affected the populations and cultures of Latin America?
4. How do many outsiders view the issue of business and government corruption in Latin America?
5. Is business etiquette in most of Latin America considered relatively formal or relatively informal?

Follow-Up Assignment

The World Bank plays an important role in today's fast-changing, closely meshed global economy. Visit the bank's website, at www.worldbank.org, and explore the programs and initiatives under way in the Latin American region. How is the bank using this website to foster better communication between Latin America and the rest of the world?

For Further Research

In today's global marketplace, knowing as much as possible about your international customers' business practices and customs could give you a strategic advantage. To help you successfully conduct business around the globe, visit www.buyusainfo.net and select any country from the drop-down menu. How can resources such as this website help U.S. businesses communicate more successfully with customers, employees, and other groups in Latin America?

EFFECTIVE ORAL PRESENTATIONS

Learning Objectives

After viewing this video, you will be able to

1. Reiterate the importance of knowing your audience before creating and delivering oral presentations
2. Discuss the role of teamwork in preparing and delivering complex presentations
3. Explain the importance of anticipating objections likely to be raised during a presentation

Background Information

Oral presentations are a vital communication medium in most companies. In particular, important decisions often involve one or more presentations, either in person or online, in which people advocating a specific choice present their case to the people responsible for making the decision. Such presentations usually combine informational and analytical reporting, along with the persuasive aspects of a proposal. Beyond the mere delivery of information, however, presentations also involve an element of performance. Audiences search for both verbal and nonverbal clues to help them assess presenters' knowledge, confidence, and credibility.

The Video

This video follows three colleagues as they create and deliver a presentation that seeks to convince the audience to approve the purchase of a particular software system that will be used to manage the company's sales force. The presenters explain the importance of understanding the expectations of their audience, from the types of visuals they prefer to the objections they are likely to raise. The team also explains how they took advantage of each member's individual strengths to create a more effective presentation.

Discussion Questions

1. How did the presenters demonstrate their knowledge of the audience?
2. Why did one presenter use a $100 bill as a prop?
3. What are the risks of using props such as the $100 bill?
4. How did the presenters prepare for objections raised by the audience?
5. How would the team need to modify its presentation for an online webcast instead of an in-person oral presentation?

Follow-Up Assignment

Podcasts (audio only) and vidcasts (podcasts with video) are quickly catching on as a medium for business presentations. Visit www.technorati.com and click on the Business channel. Select any three podcasts. Listen to them, taking careful notes so that you can compare the three selections in terms of grabbing your attention, keeping your attention, and effectively communicating the podcast's information. Which of the three podcasts is the most effective? Why?

For Further Research

Musicians, actors, jugglers—virtually everyone who performs in public experiences *performance anxiety*, or *stage fright*, as it is commonly known. This anxiety is simply the natural outcome of caring about how well you do. After all, if you didn't care, you wouldn't feel anxious. Seasoned performers not only recognize that anxiety is natural but they also have learned how to use this emotion to their advantage by giving them extra energy. Visit www.petethomas.co.uk/performance-nerves.html and www.jugglingdb.com (search for "stage fright" and then click on "Collective wisdom on stage fright") and read how these accomplished performers handle the anxiety of performing in public. How can you adapt their techniques to business presentations?

INTERVIEWING SKILLS

Learning Objectives

After viewing this video, you will be able to

1. Explain how the AIDA approach helps create effective application letters
2. Identify mistakes that can cause an otherwise qualified candidate to lose out on a job opportunity
3. Explain why planning for tough questions is such an important part of your interviewing strategy

Background Information

Most companies would admit that an employment interview is an imperfect test of a candidate's skills and personality fit with the organization. In response, some are beginning to add testing, job simulations, and other evaluation tools to the selection process. However, the classic face-to-face interview remains the dominant decision-making tool in the hiring process, so developing your interviewing skills will be vital to your success at every stage in your career.

The Video

This video follows the progress of two candidates applying and interviewing for a technical writing position. One candidate has more experience in this area, but his approach to the interview process ends up costing him the job opportunity. In contrast, a candidate with less experience takes a confident and creative approach that nets her the job.

Discussion Questions

1. Why are multiple StayCom managers involved in this interviewing process? Couldn't one manager handle it?
2. Why does one of the managers compare an application letter to a news story?
3. What steps did Cheryl Yung take to overcome a potential shortcoming in her qualifications?
4. What mistakes did candidate Buddy McCoy make in his interview?
5. Why would the interviewers care about the interpersonal skills of someone who will be writing for a living?

Follow-Up Assignment

Nonverbal cues are important in every communication scenario, but they are perhaps never more important than in job interviews. Not only are interviewers looking for any clues they can find that will guide their decisions but they tend to make up their minds quickly—perhaps even before the candidate has said anything at all. Use the Web Search feature at http://businesscommunicationblog.com/ websearch to find advice on nonverbal communication in interviews. Distill this information down to a half dozen or so key points that you can write on a note card to study before you step into your next job interview.

For Further Research

You look great in your new interview outfit, your hair is perfect but not too perfect, your smile radiates positive energy, and you're ready to dazzle the interviewer. Then, oops—you discover that your first interview will be held over the telephone, so none of your visual cues will help you at this stage. Don't fret; read the telephone interviewing advice at www.collegegrad.com/jobsearch/phone-Interviewing-Success/, and you'll be ready to dazzle the interviewer long distance.

Handbook of Grammar, Mechanics, and Usage

The rules of grammar, mechanics, and usage provide the guidance every professional needs in order to communicate successfully with colleagues, customers, and other audiences. Understanding and following these rules helps you in two important ways. First, the rules determine how meaning is encoded and decoded in the communication process. If you don't encode your messages using the same rules your readers or listeners use to decode them, chances are your audiences will not extract your intended meaning from your messages. Without a firm grasp of the basics of grammar, mechanics, and usage, you risk being misunderstood, damaging your company's image, losing money for your company, and possibly even losing your job. In other words, if you want to get your point across, you need to follow the rules of grammar, mechanics, and usage. Second, apart from transferring meaning successfully, following the rules tells your audience that you respect the conventions and expectations of the business community.

You can think of *grammar* as the agreed-upon structure of a language, the way that individual words are formed and the manner in which those words are then combined to form meaningful sentences. *Mechanics* are style and formatting issues such as capitalization, spelling, and the use of numbers and symbols. *Usage* involves the accepted and expected way in which specific words are used by a particular community of people—in this case, the community of businesspeople who use English. This handbook can help you improve your knowledge and awareness in all three areas. It is divided into the following sections:

- **Diagnostic Test of English Skills.** Testing your current knowledge of grammar, mechanics, and usage helps you find out where your strengths and weaknesses lie. This test offers 50 items taken from the topics included in this handbook.
- **Assessment of English Skills.** After completing the diagnostic test, use the assessment form to highlight the areas you most need to review.
- **Essentials of Grammar, Mechanics, and Usage.** This section helps you quickly review the basics. You can study the things you've probably already learned but may have forgotten about grammar, punctuation, mechanics (including capitalization, abbreviation, number style, and word division), and vocabulary (including frequently confused words, frequently misused words, frequently misspelled words, and transitional words and phrases). Practice sessions throughout this section help you test yourself and reinforce what you learn. Use this essential review not only to study and improve your English skills but also as a reference for any questions you may have during this course.

DIAGNOSTIC TEST OF ENGLISH SKILLS

Use this test to determine whether you need more practice with grammar, punctuation, mechanics, or vocabulary. When you've answered all the questions, ask your instructor for an answer sheet so that you can score the test. On the Assessment of English Skills form (page H-3), record the number of questions you answered incorrectly in each section.

The following choices apply to items 1–5. Write in each blank the letter of the choice that best describes the part of speech that is underlined.

A. noun
B. pronoun
C. verb
D. adjective
E. adverb
F. preposition
G. conjunction
H. article

____ **1.** The new branch location will be decided by next week.
____ **2.** We must hire only qualified, ambitious graduates.
____ **3.** After their presentation, I was still undecided.
____ **4.** See me after the meeting.
____ **5.** Margaret, pressed for time, turned in unusually sloppy work.

In the blanks for items 6–15, write the letter of the word or phrase that best completes each sentence.

____ **6.** (A. Russ's, B. Russ') laptop was stolen last week.
____ **7.** Speaking only for (A. me, B. myself), I think the new policy is discriminatory.
____ **8.** Of the five candidates we interviewed yesterday, (A. who, B. whom) do you believe is the best choice?
____ **9.** India has increased (A. it's, B. its) imports of corn and rice.
____ **10.** Anyone who wants to be (A. their, B. his or her) own boss should think about owning a franchise.
____ **11.** If the IT department can't (A. lie, B. lay) the fiber-optic cable by March 1, the plant will not open on schedule.
____ **12.** Starbucks (A. is, B. are) opening five new stores in San Diego in the next year.
____ **13.** The number of women-owned small businesses (A. has, B. have) increased sharply in the past two decades.
____ **14.** Greg and Bernyce worked (A. good, B. well) together.
____ **15.** They distributed the supplies (A. among, B. between) the six staff members.

The following choices apply to items 16–20. Write in each blank the letter of the choice that best describes the sentence structure problem with each item.

A. sentence fragment
B. comma splice
C. misplaced modifier
D. fused sentence
E. lack of parallelism
F. unclear antecedent

_____ **16.** The number of employees who took the buyout offer was much higher than expected, now the entire company is understaffed.
_____ **17.** The leader in Internet-only banking.
_____ **18.** Diamond doesn't actually sell financial products rather it acts as an intermediary.
_____ **19.** Helen's proposal is for not only the present but also for the future.
_____ **20.** When purchasing luxury products, quality is more important than price for consumers.

For items 21–30, circle the letter of the preferred choice in each of the following groups of sentences.

21. A. What do you think of the ad slogan "Have it your way?"
B. What do you think of the ad slogan "Have it your way"?

22. A. Send copies to Jackie Cross, Uniline, Brad Nardi, Peale & Associates, and Tom Griesbaum, MatchMakers.
B. Send copies to Jackie Cross, Uniline; Brad Nardi, Peale & Associates; and Tom Griesbaum, MatchMakers.

23. A. They've recorded 22 complaints since yesterday, all of them from long-time employees.
B. They've recorded 22 complaints since yesterday; all of them from long-time employees.

24. A. We are looking for two qualities in applicants: experience with computers and an interest in people.
B. We are looking for two qualities in applicants; experience with computers and an interest in people.

25. A. At the Center for the Blind the clients we serve have lost vision, due to a wide variety of causes.
B. At the Center for the Blind, the clients we serve have lost vision due to a wide variety of causes.

26. A. Replace your standard light bulbs with new, compact fluorescent bulbs.
B. Replace your standard light bulbs with new, compact, fluorescent bulbs.
C. Replace your standard light bulbs with new compact fluorescent bulbs.

27. A. Blue Cross of California may have changed its name to Anthem Blue Cross but the company still has the same commitment to California.
B. Blue Cross of California may have changed its name to Anthem Blue Cross, but the company still has the same commitment to California.

28. A. Only eight banks in this country—maybe nine can handle transactions of this magnitude.
B. Only eight banks in this country—maybe nine—can handle transactions of this magnitude.

29. A. Instead of focusing on high-growth companies, we targeted mature businesses with only one or two people handling the decision making.
B. Instead of focusing on high growth companies, we targeted mature businesses with only one or two people handling the decision-making.

30. A. According to board president Damian Cabaza "having a crisis communication plan is a high priority."
B. According to board president Damian Cabaza, "Having a crisis communication plan is a high priority."

For items 31–40, select the best choice from among those provided.

31. A. At her previous employer, Mary-Anne worked in Marketing Communications and Human Resources.
B. At her previous employer, Mary-Anne worked in marketing communications and human resources.

32. A. By fall, we'll have a dozen locations between the Mississippi and Missouri rivers.
B. By Fall, we'll have a dozen locations between the Mississippi and Missouri Rivers.

33. A. The Board applauded President Donlan upon her reelection for a fifth term.
B. The board applauded president Donlan upon her reelection for a fifth term.
C. The board applauded President Donlan upon her reelection for a fifth term.

34. A. If you want to travel to France, you need to be au courant with the business practices.
B. If you want to travel to France, you need to be "au courant" with the business practices.

35. A. As the company's CEO, Thomas Spurgeon handles all dealings with the FDA.
B. As the company's C.E.O., Thomas Spurgeon handles all dealings with the F.D.A.

36. A. The maximum speed limit in most states is 65 mph.
B. The maximum speed limit in most states is 65 m.p.h.

37. A. Sales of graphic novels increased nine percent between 2008 and 2009.
B. Sales of graphic novels increased 9 percent between 2008 and 2009.

38. A. Our store is open daily from nine a.m. to seven P. M.
B. Our store is open daily from 9:00 A.M. to 7:00 P.M.

39. A. The organizing meeting is scheduled for July 27, and the event will be held in January 2010.
B. The organizing meeting is scheduled for July 27th, and the event will be held in January, 2010.

40. A. We need six desks, eight file cabinets, and 12 trashcans.
B. We need 6 desks, 8 file cabinets, and 12 trashcans.

For items 41–50, write in each blank the letter of the word that best completes each sentence.

____ **41.** Will having a degree (A. affect, B. effect) my chances for promotion?
____ **42.** Try not to (A. loose, B. lose) this key; we will charge you a fee to replace it.
____ **43.** I don't want to discuss my (A. personal, B. personnel) problems in front of anyone.
____ **44.** Let us help you choose the right tie to (A. complement, B. compliment) your look.
____ **45.** The repairman's whistling (A. aggravated, B. irritated) all of us in accounting.
____ **46.** The bank agreed to (A. loan, B. lend) the Smiths $20,000 for their start-up.
____ **47.** The credit card company is (A. liable, B. likely) to increase your interest rate if you miss a payment.
____ **48.** The airline tries to (A. accommodate, B. accomodate) disabled passengers.
____ **49.** Every company needs a policy regarding sexual (A. harrassment, B. harassment).
____ **50.** Use your best (A. judgment, B. judgement) in selecting a service provider.

ASSESSMENT OF ENGLISH SKILLS

In the space provided, record the number of questions you answered incorrectly.

QUESTIONS	SKILLS AREA	NUMBER OF INCORRECT ANSWERS
1–5	Parts of speech	________
6–15	Usage	________
16–20	Sentence structure	________
21–30	Punctuation	________
31–40	Mechanics	________
41–50	Vocabulary	________

If you had more than two incorrect answers in any of the skills areas, focus on those areas in the appropriate sections of this handbook.

ESSENTIALS OF GRAMMAR, MECHANICS, AND USAGE

The following sentence looks innocent, but is it really?

> We sell tuxedos as well as rent.

You sell tuxedos, but it's highly unlikely that you sell rent—which is what this sentence says. Whatever you're selling, some people will ignore your message because of a blunder like this. The following sentence has a similar problem:

> Vice President Eldon Neale told his chief engineer that he would no longer be with Avix, Inc., as of June 30.

Is Eldon or the engineer leaving? No matter which side the facts are on, the sentence can be read the other way. Now look at this sentence:

> The year before we budgeted more for advertising sales were up.

Confused? Perhaps this is what the writer meant:

> The year before, we budgeted more for advertising. Sales were up.

Or maybe the writer meant this:

> The year before we budgeted more for advertising, sales were up.

These examples show that even short, simple sentences can be misunderstood because of errors on the part of the writer. As you've learned in numerous courses over your schooling, an English sentence consists of the parts of speech being combined with punctuation, mechanics, and vocabulary to convey meaning. Making a point of brushing up on your grammar, punctuation, mechanics, and vocabulary skills will help ensure that you create clear, effective business messages.

1.0 GRAMMAR

Grammar is the study of how words come together to form sentences. Categorized by meaning, form, and function, English words fall into various parts of speech: nouns, pronouns, verbs, adjectives, adverbs, prepositions, conjunctions, articles, and interjections. You will communicate more clearly if you understand how each of these parts of speech operates in a sentence.

1.1 Nouns

A **noun** names a person, a place, a thing, or an idea. Anything you can see or detect with one of your senses has a noun to name it. Some things you can't see or sense are also nouns—ions, for example, or space. So are things that exist as ideas, such as accuracy and height. (You can see that something is accurate or that a building is tall, but you can't see the idea of accuracy or the idea of height.) These names for ideas are known as **abstract nouns**. The simplest nouns are the names of things you can see or touch: *car, building, cloud, brick*; these are termed **concrete nouns**. A few nouns, such as *algorithm, software*, and *code*, are difficult to categorize as either abstract or concrete but can reasonably be considered concrete even though they don't have a physical presence.

1.1.1 Proper Nouns and Common Nouns

So far, all the examples of nouns have been **common nouns**, referring to general classes of things. The word *building* refers to a whole class of structures. Common nouns such as *building* are not capitalized.

If you want to talk about one particular building, however, you might refer to the Glazier Building. The name is capitalized, indicating that *Glazier Building* is a **proper noun**.

Here are three sets of common and proper nouns for comparison:

Common	**Proper**
city	Kansas City
company	Blaisden Company
store	Books Galore

1.1.2 Nouns as Subject and Object

Nouns may be used in sentences as subjects or objects. That is, the person, place, thing, or idea that is being or doing (subject) is represented by a noun. So is the person, place, idea, or thing that is being acted on (object). In the following sentence, the nouns are underlined:

The <u>web designer</u> created the <u>homepage</u>.

The web designer (subject) is acting in a way that affects the home page (object). The following sentence is more complicated:

The <u>installer</u> delivered the <u>carpet</u> to the <u>customer</u>.

Installer is the subject. *Carpet* is the object of the main part of the sentence (acted on by the installer), and *customer* is the object of the phrase *to the customer*. Nevertheless, both *carpet* and *customer* are objects.

1.1.3 Plural Nouns

Nouns can be either singular or plural. The usual way to make a plural noun is to add *s* or *es* to the singular form of the word:

Singular	**Plural**
file	files
tax	taxes
cargo	cargoes

Many nouns have other ways of forming the plural. Some plurals involve a change in a vowel (*mouse/mice, goose/geese, woman/women*), the addition of *en* or *ren* (*ox/oxen, child/children*), the change from *y* to *ies* (*city/cities, specialty/specialties*), or the change from *f* to *v* (*knife/knives, half/halves;* some exceptions: *fifes, roofs*). Some words of Latin origin offer a choice of plurals (*phenomena/phenomenons, indexes/indices, appendixes/appendices*). It's always a good idea to consult a dictionary if you are unsure of the correct or preferred plural spelling of a word.

The plurals of compound nouns are usually formed by adding *s* or *es* to the main word of the compound (*fathers-in-law, editors-in-chief, attorneys-at-law*).

Some nouns are the same whether singular or plural (*sleep, deer, moose*). Some nouns are plural in form but singular in use (*ethics, measles*). Some nouns are used in the plural only (*scissors, trousers*).

Letters, numbers, and words used as words are sometimes made plural by adding an apostrophe and an *s* (*A's, Ph.D.'s, I's*). However, if no confusion would be created by leaving off the apostrophe, it is common practice to just add the *s* (*1990s, RFPs, DVDs*).

1.1.4 Possessive Nouns

A noun becomes possessive when it's used to show the ownership of something. Then you add *'s* to the word:

the man's car	the woman's apartment

However, ownership does not need to be legal:

the secretary's desk	the company's assets

Also, ownership may be nothing more than an automatic association:

a day's work	the job's prestige

An exception to the rule about adding *'s* to make a noun possessive occurs when the word is singular and already has two "s" sounds at the end. In cases like the following, an apostrophe is all that's needed:

crisis' dimensions	Mr. Moses' application

When the noun has only one "s" sound at the end, however, retain the *'s:*

Chris's book	Carolyn Nuss's office

With compound (hyphenated) nouns, add *'s* to the last word:

Compound Noun	**Possessive Noun**
mother-in-law	mother-in-law's
mayor-elect	mayor-elect's

To form the possessive of plural nouns, just begin by following the same rule as with singular nouns: add *'s*. However, if the plural noun already ends in an *s* (as most do), drop the one you've added, leaving only the apostrophe:

the clients' complaints	employees' benefits

To denote joint possession by two or more proper nouns, add the *'s* to the last name only (*Moody, Nation,* and *Smith's* ad agency). To denote individual possession by two or more persons, add an *'s* to each proper noun (*Moody's, Nation's,* and *Smith's* ad agencies).

1.1.5 Collective Nouns

Collective nouns encompass a group of people or objects: *crowd, jury, committee, team, audience, family, couple, herd, class.* They are often treated as singular nouns. (For more on collective nouns, see Section 1.3.4, Subject–Verb Agreement.)

1.2 Pronouns

A **pronoun** is a word that stands for a noun; it saves repeating the noun:

> Employees have some choice of weeks for vacation, but *they* must notify the HR office of *their* preference by March 1.

The pronouns *they* and *their* stand in for the noun *employees.* The noun that a pronoun stands for is called the **antecedent** of the pronoun; *employees* is the antecedent of *they* and *their.*

When the antecedent is plural, the pronoun that stands in for it has to be plural; *they* and *their* are plural pronouns because *employees* is plural. Likewise, when the antecedent is singular, the pronoun has to be singular:

> We thought the contract had expired, but we soon learned that *it* had not.

1.2.1 Multiple Antecedents

Sometimes a pronoun has a double (or even a triple) antecedent:

> Kathryn Boettcher and Luis Gutierrez went beyond *their* sales quotas for January.

If taken alone, *Kathryn Boettcher* is a singular antecedent. So is *Luis Gutierrez.* However, when together they are the plural antecedent of a pronoun, so the pronoun has to be plural. Thus the pronoun is *their* instead of *her* or *his.*

1.2.2 Unclear Antecedents

In some sentences the pronoun's antecedent is unclear:

> Sandy Wright sent Jane Brougham *her* production figures for the previous year. *She* thought they were too low.

To which person does the pronoun *her* refer? Someone who knew Sandy and Jane and knew their business relationship might be able to figure out the antecedent for *her.* Even with such an advantage, however, a reader might receive the wrong meaning. Also, it would be nearly impossible for any reader to know which name is the antecedent of *she.*

The best way to clarify an ambiguous pronoun is usually to rewrite the sentence, repeating nouns when needed for clarity:

> Sandy Wright sent her production figures for the previous year to Jane Brougham. Jane thought they were too low.

The noun needs to be repeated only when the antecedent is unclear.

1.2.3 Pronoun Classes

Personal pronouns consist of *I, you, we/us, he/him, she/her, it,* and *they/them.*

Compound personal pronouns are created by adding *self* or *selves* to simple personal pronouns: *myself, ourselves, yourself, yourselves, himself, herself, itself, themselves.* Compound personal pronouns are used either *intensively,* to emphasize the identity of the noun or pronoun (I *myself* have seen the demonstration), or *reflexively,* to indicate that the subject is the receiver of his or her own action (I promised *myself* I'd finish by noon). Compound personal pronouns are used incorrectly if they appear in a sentence without their antecedent:

> Walter, Virginia, and *I* (not *myself*) are the top salespeople.
>
> You need to tell *her* (not *herself*) about the mixup.

Relative pronouns refer to nouns (or groups of words used as nouns) in the main clause and are used to introduce clauses:

> Purina is the brand *that* most dog owners purchase.

The relative pronouns are *which, who, whom, whose,* and *what.* Other words used as relative pronouns include *that, whoever, whomever, whatever,* and *whichever.*

Interrogative pronouns are those used for asking questions: *who, whom, whose, which,* and *what.*

Demonstrative pronouns point out particular persons, places, or things:

> *That* is my desk.   *This* can't be correct.

The demonstrative pronouns are *this, these, that,* and *those.*

Indefinite pronouns refer to persons or things not specifically identified. They include *anyone, someone, everyone, everybody, somebody, either, neither, one, none, all, both, each, another, any, many,* and similar words.

1.2.4 Case of Pronouns

The case of a pronoun tells whether it's acting or acted upon:

> *She* sells an average of five packages each week.

In this sentence, *she* is doing the selling. Because *she* is acting, *she* is said to be in the **nominative case.** Now consider what happens when the pronoun is acted upon:

> After six months, Ms. Browning promoted *her.*

In this sentence, the pronoun *her* is acted upon and is thus said to be in the **objective case.**

Contrast the nominative and objective pronouns in this list:

Nominative	Objective
I	me
we	us
he	him
she	her
they	them
who	whom
whoever	whomever

Objective pronouns may be used as either the object of a verb (such as *promoted*) or the object of a preposition (such as *with*):

> Rob worked with *them* until the order was filled.

In this example, *them* is the object of the preposition *with* because Rob acted upon—worked with—them. Here's a sentence with three pronouns, the first one nominative, the second the object of a verb, and the third the object of a preposition:

> *He* paid *us* as soon as the check came from *them.*

He is nominative; *us* is objective because it's the object of the verb *paid; them* is objective because it's the object of the preposition *from.*

Every writer sometimes wonders whether to use *who* or *whom:*

> (*Who, Whom*) will you hire?

Because this sentence is a question, it's difficult to see that *whom* is the object of the verb *hire.* You can figure out which pronoun to use if you rearrange the question and temporarily try *she* and *her* in place of *who* and *whom:* "Will you hire *she?*" or "Will you hire *her?*" *Her* and *whom* are both objective, so the correct choice is "Whom will you hire?" Here's a different example:

> (*Who, Whom*) logged so much travel time?

Turning the question into a statement, you get:

> He logged so much travel time.

Therefore, the correct statement is:

> Who logged so much travel time?

1.2.5 Possessive Pronouns

Possessive pronouns work like possessive nouns—they show ownership or automatic association:

her job	their preferences
his account	its equipment

However, possessive pronouns are different from possessive nouns in the way they are written. Possessive pronouns never have an apostrophe:

Possessive Noun	**Possessive Pronoun**
the woman's estate	her estate
Roger Franklin's plans	his plans
the shareholders' feelings	their feelings
the vacuum cleaner's attachments	its attachments

The word *its* is the possessive of *it.* Like all other possessive pronouns, *its* has no apostrophe. Some people confuse *its* with *it's,* the contraction of *it is.* (Contractions are discussed in Section 2.9, Apostrophes.)

1.2.6 Pronoun–Antecedent Agreement

Like nouns, pronouns can be singular or plural. Pronouns must agree in number with their antecedents—a singular antecedent requires a singular pronoun:

> The president of the board tendered *his* resignation.

Multiple antecedents require a plural pronoun:

> The members of the board tendered *their* resignations.

A pronoun referring to singular antecedents connected by *or* or *nor* should be singular:

> Neither Sean nor Terry made his quota.

But a pronoun referring to a plural and a singular antecedent connected by *or* or *nor* should be plural:

> Neither Sean nor the twins made *their* quotas.

Formal English prefers the nominative case after the linking verb *to be:*

> It is *I.*　　　That is *he.*

However, for general usage it's perfectly acceptable to use the more natural "It's me" and "That's him."

1.3 Verbs

A **verb** describes an action or acts as a link between a subject and words that define or describe that subject:

> They all *quit* in disgust.
> Working conditions *were* substandard.

The English language is full of **action verbs**. Here are a few you'll often run across in the business world:

verify	perform	fulfill
hire	succeed	send
leave	improve	receive
accept	develop	pay

You could undoubtedly list many more.

The most common linking verbs are all the forms of *to be:* I *am, was,* or *will be;* you *are, were,* or *will be.* Other words that can serve as linking verbs include *seem, become, appear, prove, look, remain, feel, taste, smell, sound, resemble, turn,* and *grow:*

> It *seemed* a good plan at the time.
>
> She *sounds* impressive at a meeting.
>
> The time *grows* near for us to make a decision.

These verbs link what comes before them in the sentence with what comes after; no action is involved. (See Section 1.7.5 for a fuller discussion of linking verbs.)

An **auxiliary verb** is one that helps another verb and is used for showing tense, voice, and so on. A verb with its helpers is called a **verb phrase.** Verbs used as auxiliaries include *do, did, have, may, can, must, shall, might, could, would,* and *should.*

1.3.1 Verb Tenses

English has three simple verb tenses: present, past, and future.

Present:	Our branches in Hawaii *stock* other items.
Past:	We *stocked* Purquil pens for a short time.
Future:	Rotex Tire Stores *will stock* your line of tires when you begin a program of effective national advertising.

With most verbs (the regular ones), the past tense ends in *ed*, and the future tense always has *will* or *shall* in front of it. But the present tense is more complex, depending on the subject:

	First Person	Second Person	Third Person
Singular	I stock	you stock	he/she/it stocks
Plural	we stock	you stock	they stock

The basic form, *stock*, takes an additional *s* when *he*, *she*, or *it* precedes it. (See Section 1.3.4 for more on subject–verb agreement.)

In addition to the three simple tenses, the three **perfect tenses** are created by adding forms of the auxiliary verb *have*. The present perfect tense uses the past participle (regularly the past tense) of the main verb, *stocked*, and adds the present-tense *have* or *has* to the front of it:

(I, we, you, they) *have stocked.*

(He, she, it) *has stocked.*

The past perfect tense uses the past participle of the main verb, *stocked*, and adds the past-tense *had* to the front of it:

(I, you, he, she, it, we, they) *had stocked.*

The future perfect tense also uses the past participle of the main verb, *stocked*, but adds the future-tense *will have:*

(I, you, he, she, it, we, they) *will have stocked.*

Verbs should be kept in the same tense when the actions occur at the same time:

When the payroll checks *came in*, everyone *showed up* for work.

We *have found* that everyone *has pitched* in to help.

When the actions occur at different times, you may change tense accordingly:

The shipment *came* last Wednesday, so if another one *comes* in today, please return it.

The new employee *had been* ill at ease, but now she *has become* a full-fledged member of the team.

1.3.2 Irregular Verbs

Many verbs don't follow some of the standard p:atterns for verb tenses. The most irregular of these verbs is *to be*:

Tense	Singular	Plural
Present:	I *am*	we *are*
	you *are*	you *are*
	he, she, it *is*	they *are*
Past:	I *was*	we *were*
	you *were*	you *were*
	he, she, it *was*	they *were*

The future tense of *to be* is formed in the same way that the future tense of a regular verb is formed.

The perfect tenses of *to be* are also formed as they would be for a regular verb, except that the past participle is a special form, *been*, instead of just the past tense:

Present perfect:	you have been
Past perfect:	you had been
Future perfect:	you will have been

Here's a sampling of other irregular verbs:

Present	Past	Past Participle
begin	began	begun
shrink	shrank	shrunk
know	knew	known
rise	rose	risen
become	became	become
go	went	gone
do	did	done

Dictionaries list the various forms of other irregular verbs.

1.3.3 Transitive and Intransitive Verbs

Many people are confused by three particular sets of verbs:

lie/lay sit/set rise/raise

Using these verbs correctly is much easier when you learn the difference between transitive and intransitive verbs.

Transitive verbs require a receiver; they "transfer" their action to an object. Intransitive verbs do not have a receiver for their action. Some intransitive verbs are complete in themselves and need no help from other words (prices *dropped*; we *won*). Other intransitive words must be "completed" by a noun or adjective called a **complement**. Complements occur with linking verbs.

Here are some sample uses of transitive and intransitive verbs:

Intransitive	Transitive
We should include in our new offices a place to *lie* down for a nap.	The workers will be here on Monday to *lay* new carpeting.
Even the way an interviewee *sits* is important.	That crate is full of stemware, so *set* it down carefully.
Salaries at Compu-Link, Inc., *rise* swiftly.	They *raise* their level of production every year.

The workers *lay* carpeting, you *set down* the crate, they *raise* production; each action is transferred to something. In the intransitive sentences, a person *lies down*, an interviewee *sits*, and salaries *rise* without affecting anything else. Intransitive sentences are complete with only a subject and a verb; transitive sentences are not complete unless they also include an object; or something to transfer the action to.

Tenses are a confusing element of the lie/lay problem:

Present	Past	Past Participle
I *lie*	I *lay*	I *have lain*
I *lay* (something down)	I *laid* (something down)	I *have laid* (something down)

The past tense of *lie* and the present tense of *lay* look and sound alike, even though they're different verbs.

1.3.4 Subject–Verb Agreement

Whether regular or irregular, every verb must agree with its subject, both in person (first, second, or third) and in number (single or plural).

	First Person	Second Person	Third Person
Singular	I *am*	you *are*	he/she/it *is*
	I *write*	you *write*	he/she/it *writes*
Plural	we *are*	you *are*	they *are*
	we *write*	you *write*	they *write*

In a simple sentence, making a verb agree with its subject is a straightforward task:

Hector Ruiz *is* a strong competitor. (third-person singular)

We *write* to you every month. (first-person plural)

Confusion sometimes arises when sentences are a bit more complicated. For example, be sure to avoid agreement problems when words come between the subject and verb. In the following examples, the verb appears in italics, and its subject is underlined:

The analysis of existing documents *takes* a full week.

Even though *documents* is a plural, the verb is in the singular form. That's because the subject of the sentence is *analysis*, a singular noun. The phrase *of existing documents* can be disregarded. Here is another example:

The answers for this exercise *are* in the study guide.

Take away the phrase *for this exercise* and you are left with the plural subject *answers*. Therefore, the verb takes the plural form.

Verb agreement is also complicated when the subject is a collective noun or pronoun or when the subject may be considered either singular or plural. In such cases, you often have to analyze the surrounding sentence to determine which verb form to use:

The staff *is* quartered in the warehouse.

The staff *are* at their desks in the warehouse.

The computers and the staff *are* in the warehouse.

Neither the staff nor the computers *are* in the warehouse.

Every computer *is* in the warehouse.

Many a computer *is* in the warehouse.

Did you notice that words such as *every* use the singular verb form? In addition, when an *either/or* or a *neither/nor* phrase combines singular and plural nouns, the verb takes the form that matches the noun closest to it.

In the business world, some subjects require extra attention. Company names, for example, are considered singular and therefore take a singular verb in most cases—even if they contain plural words:

Stater Brothers *offers* convenient grocery shopping.

In addition, quantities are sometimes considered singular and sometimes plural. If a quantity refers to a total amount, it takes a singular verb; if a quantity refers to individual, countable units, it takes a plural verb:

Three hours *is* a long time.

The eight dollars we collected for the fund *are* tacked on the bulletin board.

Fractions may also be singular or plural, depending on the noun that accompanies them:

One-third of the warehouse *is* devoted to this product line.

One-third of the products *are* defective.

To decide whether to use a singular or plural verb with subjects such as *number* and *variety*, follow this simple rule: If the subject is preceded by *a*, use a plural verb:

A number of products *are* being displayed at the trade show.

If the subject is preceded by *the*, use a singular verb:

The variety of products on display *is* mind-boggling.

For a related discussion, see Section 1.7.1, Longer Sentences.

1.3.5 Voice of Verbs

Verbs have two voices, active and passive. When the subject comes first, the verb is in **active voice**; when the object comes first, the verb is in **passive voice**:

Active:	The buyer *paid* a large amount.
Passive:	A large amount *was paid* by the buyer.

The passive voice uses a form of the verb *to be*, which adds words to a sentence. In the example, the passive-voice sentence uses eight words, whereas the active-voice sentence uses only six to say the same thing. The words *was* and *by* are unnecessary to convey the meaning of the sentence. In fact, extra words usually clog meaning. So be sure to opt for the active voice when you have a choice.

At times, however, you have no choice:

> Several items *have been taken*, but so far we don't know who took them.

The passive voice becomes necessary when you don't know (or don't want to say) who performed the action; the active voice is bolder and more direct.

1.3.6 Mood of Verbs

Verbs can express one of three moods: indicative, imperative, or subjunctive. The **indicative mood** is used to make a statement or to ask a question:

> The secretary mailed a letter to each supplier.
>
> Did the secretary mail a letter to each supplier?

Use the **imperative mood** when you wish to command or request:

> Please mail a letter to each supplier.

With the imperative mood, the subject is the understood *you*.

The **subjunctive mood** is used to express doubt or a wish or a condition contrary to fact:

> If I *were* you, I wouldn't send that e-mail.

The subjunctive is also used to express a suggestion or a request:

> I asked that Rosario *be* [not *is*] present at the meeting.

1.3.7 Verbals

Verbals are verbs that are modified to function as other parts of speech. They include infinitives, gerunds, and participles.

Infinitives are formed by placing a *to* in front of the verb (*to go, to purchase, to work*). They function as nouns. Although many of us were taught that it is "incorrect" to split an infinitive—that is, to place an adverb between the *to* and the verb—that rule is not a hard and fast one. In some cases, the adverb is best placed in the middle of the infinitive to avoid awkward constructions or ambiguous meaning:

> Production of steel is expected to *moderately exceed* domestic use.

Gerunds are verbals formed by adding *ing* to a verb (*going, having, working*). Like infinitives, they function as nouns. Gerunds and gerund phrases take a singular verb:

> *Borrowing* from banks *is* preferable to getting venture capital.

Participles are verb forms used as adjectives. The present participle ends in *ing* and generally describes action going on at the same time as other action:

> *Checking* the schedule, the contractor was pleased with progress on the project.

The past participle is usually the same form as the past tense and generally indicates completed action:

> When *completed*, the project will occupy six city blocks.

The **perfect participle** is formed by adding *having* to the past participle:

> *Having completed* the project, the contractor submitted his last invoice.

1.4 Adjectives

An **adjective** modifies (tells something about) a noun or pronoun. Each of the following phrases says more about the noun or pronoun than the noun or pronoun would say alone:

an *efficient* staff	a *heavy* price
brisk trade	*light* web traffic

Adjectives modify nouns more often than they modify pronouns. When adjectives do modify pronouns, however, the sentence usually has a linking verb:

They were *attentive.*	It looked *appropriate.*
He seems *interested.*	You are *skillful.*

1.4.1 Types of Adjectives

Adjectives serve a variety of purposes. **Descriptive adjectives** express some quality belonging to the modified item (*tall, successful, green*). **Limiting or definitive adjectives**, on the other hand, point out the modified item or limit its meaning without expressing a quality. Types include:

- Numeral adjectives (one, fifty, second)
- Articles (a, an, the)
- Pronominal adjectives: pronouns used as adjectives (his desk, each employee)
- Demonstrative adjectives: this, these, that, those (these tires, that invoice)

Proper adjectives are derived from proper nouns:

Chinese customs	*Orwellian* overtones

Predicate adjectives complete the meaning of the predicate and are introduced by linking verbs:

The location is *perfect.*	Prices are *high.*

1.4.2 Comparative Degree

Most adjectives can take three forms: simple, comparative, and superlative. The simple form modifies a single noun or pronoun. Use the comparative form when comparing two items. When comparing three or more items, use the superlative form:

Simple	Comparative	Superlative
hard	harder	hardest
safe	safer	safest
dry	drier	driest

The comparative form adds *er* to the simple form, and the superlative form adds *est*. (The *y* at the end of a word changes to *i* before the *er* or *est* is added.)

A small number of adjectives are irregular, including these:

Simple	Comparative	Superlative
good	better	best
bad	worse	worst
little	less	least

When the simple form of an adjective has two or more syllables, you usually add *more* to form the comparative and *most* to form the superlative:

Simple	Comparative	Superlative
useful	more useful	most useful
exhausting	more exhausting	most exhausting
expensive	more expensive	most expensive

The most common exceptions are two-syllable adjectives that end in *y*:

Simple	Comparative	Superlative
happy	happier	happiest
costly	costlier	costliest

If you choose this option, change the *y* to *i* and tack *er* or *est* onto the end.

Some adjectives cannot be used to make comparisons because they themselves indicate the extreme. For example, if something is perfect, nothing can be more perfect. If something is unique or ultimate, nothing can be more unique or more ultimate.

1.4.3 Hyphenated Adjectives

Many adjectives used in the business world are actually combinations of words: *up-to-date* report, *last-minute* effort, *fifth-floor* suite, *well-built* engine. As you can see, they are hyphenated when they come before the noun they modify. However, when such word combinations come after the noun they modify, they are not hyphenated. In the following example, the adjectives appear in italics and the nouns they modify are underlined:

> The <u>report</u> is *up to date* because of our team's *last-minute* <u>efforts</u>.

Hyphens are not used when part of the combination is a word ending in *ly* (because that word is usually not an adjective). Hyphens are also omitted from word combinations that are used so frequently that readers are used to seeing the words together:

> We live in a *rapidly shrinking* world.
>
> Our *highly motivated* employees will be well paid.
>
> Please consider renewing your *credit card* account.
>
> Send those figures to our *data processing* department.
>
> Our new intern is a *high school* student.

1.5 Adverbs

An **adverb** modifies a verb, an adjective, or another adverb:

Modifying a verb:	Our marketing department works *efficiently*.
Modifying an adjective:	She was not dependable, although she was *highly* intelligent.
Modifying another adverb:	When signing new clients, he moved *extremely* cautiously.

An adverb can be a single word (*clearly*), a phrase (*very clearly*), or a clause (*because it was clear*).

1.5.1 Types of Adverbs

Simple adverbs are simple modifiers:

> The door opened *automatically*.
>
> The order arrived *yesterday*.
>
> Top companies were *there*.

Interrogative adverbs ask a question:

> *Where* have you been?

Conjunctive adverbs connect clauses:

> We can't start *until* Maria gets here.
>
> Jorge tried to explain *how* the new software works.

Words frequently used as conjunctive adverbs include *where, wherever, when, whenever, while, as, how, why, before, after, until*, and *since*.

Negative adverbs include *not, never, seldom, rarely, scarcely, hardly*, and similar words. Negative adverbs are powerful words and therefore do not need any help in conveying a negative thought. Avoid using double negatives like these:

> I don't want no mistakes.
> (Correct: "I don't want any mistakes," or "I want no mistakes.")
>
> They couldn't hardly read the report.
> (Correct: "They could hardly read the report," or "They couldn't read the report.")
>
> They scarcely noticed neither one.
> (Correct: "They scarcely noticed either one," or "They noticed neither one.")

1.5.2 Adverb–Adjective Confusion

Many adverbs are adjectives turned into adverbs by adding *ly*: *highly, extremely, officially, closely, really*. In addition, many words can be adjectives or adverbs, depending on their usage in a particular sentence:

The *early* bird gets the worm. [adjective]	We arrived *early*. [adverb]
It was a *hard* decision. [adjective]	He hit the wall *hard*. [adverb]

Because of this situation, some adverbs are difficult to distinguish from adjectives. For example, in the following sentences, is the underlined word an adverb or an adjective?

They worked well.

The baby is well.

In the first sentence, *well* is an adverb modifying the verb *worked*. In the second sentence, *well* is an adjective modifying the noun *baby*. To choose correctly between adverbs and adjectives, remember that linking verbs are used to connect an adjective to describe a noun. In contrast, you would use an adverb to describe an action verb:

Adjective	Adverb
He is *good* worker. (What kind of worker is he?)	He works *well*. (How does he work?)
It is a *real* computer. (What kind of computer is it?)	It *really* is a computer. (To what extent is it a computer?)
The traffic is *slow*. (What quality does the traffic have?)	The traffic moves *slowly*. (How does the traffic move?)
This food tastes *bad* without salt. (What quality does the food have?)	This food *badly* needs salt. (How much is it needed?)

1.5.3 Comparative Degree

Like adjectives, adverbs can be used to compare items. Generally, the basic adverb is combined with *more* or *most*, just as long adjectives are. However, some adverbs have one-word comparative forms:

One Item	Two Items	Three Items
quickly	more quickly	most quickly
sincerely	less sincerely	least sincerely
fast	faster	fastest
well	better	best

1.6 Other Parts of Speech

Nouns, pronouns, verbs, adjectives, and adverbs carry most of the meaning in a sentence. Four other parts of speech link them together in sentences: prepositions, conjunctions, articles, and interjections.

1.6.1 Prepositions

A preposition is a word or group of words that describes a relationship between other words in a sentence. A simple preposition is made up of one word: *of, in, by, above, below*. A *compound preposition* is made up of two prepositions: *out of, from among, except for, because of*.

A **prepositional phrase** is a group of words introduced by a preposition that functions as an adjective (an adjectival phrase) or as an adverb (adverbial phrase) by telling more about a pronoun, noun, or verb:

The shipment will be here *by next Friday*.

Put the mail *in the out-bin*.

Prepositional phrases should be placed as close as possible to the element they are modifying:

Shopping *on the Internet* can be confusing for the uninitiated. (*not* Shopping can be confusing for the uninitiated *on the Internet*.)

Some prepositions are closely linked with a verb. When using phrases such as *look up* and *wipe out*, keep them intact and do not insert anything between the verb and the preposition.

You may have been told that it is unacceptable to put a preposition at the end of a sentence. However, that is not a hard-and-fast rule, and trying to follow it can sometimes be a challenge. You can end a sentence with a preposition as long as the sentence sounds natural and as long as rewording the sentence would create awkward wording:

I couldn't tell what they were interested in.

What did she attribute it to?

What are you looking for?

Avoid using unnecessary prepositions. In the following examples, the prepositions in parentheses should be omitted:

All (of) the staff members were present.

I almost fell off (of) my chair with surprise.

Where was Mr. Steuben going (to)?

They couldn't help (from) wondering.

The opposite problem is failing to include a preposition when you should. Consider these two sentences:

Sales were over $100,000 for Linda and Bill.

Sales were over $100,000 for Linda and for Bill.

The first sentence indicates that Linda and Bill had combined sales over $100,000; the second, that Linda and Bill each had sales over $100,000, for a combined total in excess of $200,000. The preposition *for* is critical here.

When the same preposition can be used for two or more words in a sentence without affecting the meaning, only the last preposition is required:

We are familiar (with) and satisfied with your company's products.

But when different prepositions are normally used with the words, all the prepositions must be included:

> We are familiar with and interested in your company's products.

Some prepositions have come to be used in a particular way with certain other parts of speech. Here is a partial list of some prepositions that have come to be used with certain words:

according to	independent of
agree to (a proposal)	inferior to
agree with (a person)	plan to
buy from	prefer to
capable of	prior to
comply with	reason with
conform to	responsible for
differ from (things)	similar to
differ with (person)	talk to (without interaction)
different from	talk with (with interaction)
get from (receive)	wait for (person or thing)
get off (dismount)	wait on (like a waiter)

If you are unsure of the correct idiomatic expression, check a dictionary.

Some verb–preposition idioms vary depending on the situation: You agree *to* a proposal but *with* a person, *on* a price, or *in* principle. You argue *about* something, *with* a person, and *for* or *against* a proposition. You compare one item *to* another to show their similarities; you compare one item *with* another to show differences.

Here are some other examples of preposition usage that have given writers trouble:

> **among/between:** *Among* is used to refer to three or more (Circulate the memo *among* the staff); *between* is used to refer to two (Put the copy machine *between* Judy and Dan)
>
> **as if/like:** *As if* is used before a clause (It seems *as if* we should be doing something); *like* is used before a noun or pronoun (He seems *like* a nice guy).
>
> **have/of:** *Have* is a verb used in verb phrases (They should *have* checked first); *of* is a preposition and is never used in such cases.
>
> **in/into:** *In* is used to refer to a static position (The file is *in* the cabinet); *into* is used to refer to movement toward a position (Put the file *into* the cabinet).

1.6.2 Conjunctions

Conjunctions connect the parts of a sentence: words, phrases, and clauses. A coordinating conjunction connects two words, phrases, or clauses of equal rank. The simple coordinating conjunctions include *and, but, or, nor, for, yet,* and *so.* Correlative conjunctions are coordinating conjunctions used in pairs: *both/and, either/or, neither/nor, not only/but also.* Constructions with correlative conjunctions should be parallel, with the same part of speech following each element of the conjunction:

> The purchase was *not only* expensive *but also* unnecessary.
>
> The purchase *not only was* expensive *but also was* unnecessary.

Conjunctive adverbs are adverbs used to connect or show relationships between clauses. They include *however, nevertheless, consequently, moreover,* and *as a result.*

A **subordinate conjunction** connects two clauses of unequal rank; it joins a dependent (subordinate) clause to the independent clause on which it depends (for more on dependent and independent clauses, see Section 1.7.1). Subordinate conjunctions include *as, if, because, although, while, before, since, that, until, unless, when, where,* and *whether.*

1.6.3 Articles and Interjections

Only three articles exist in English: *the, a,* and *an.* These words are used, like adjectives, to specify which item you are talking about. *The* is called the *definite article* because it indicates a specific noun; *a* and *an* are called the *indefinite articles* because they are less specific about what they are referring to.

If a word begins with a vowel (soft) sound, use *an;* otherwise, use *a.* It's *a history,* not *an history, a hypothesis,* not *an hypothesis.* Use *an* with an "h" word only if it is a soft "h," as in *honor* and *hour.* Use *an* with words that are pronounced with a soft vowel sound even if they are spelled beginning with a consonant (usually in the case of abbreviations): *an SEC application, an MP3 file.* Use *a* with words that begin with vowels if they are pronounced with a hard sound: *a university, a Usenet account.*

Repeat an article if adjectives modify different nouns: *The red house and the white house are mine.* Do not repeat an article if all adjectives modify the same noun: *The red and white house is mine.*

Interjections are words that express no solid information, only emotion:

Wow!	Well, well!
Oh, no!	Good!

Such purely emotional language has its place in private life and advertising copy, but it only weakens the effect of most business writing.

1.7 Sentences

Sentences are constructed with the major building blocks, the parts of speech. Take, for example, this simple two-word sentence:

> Money talks.

It consists of a noun (*money*) and a verb (*talks*). When used in this way, the noun works as the first requirement for a sentence, the **subject**, and the verb works as the second requirement, the **predicate**. Without a subject (who or what does something) and a predicate (the doing of it), you have merely a collection of words, not a sentence.

1.7.1 Longer Sentences

More complicated sentences have more complicated subjects and predicates, but they still have a simple subject and a predicate verb. In the following examples, the subject is underlined once, the predicate verb twice:

> Marex and Contron enjoy higher earnings each quarter.

Marex [and] *Contron* do something; *enjoy* is what they do.

> My interview, coming minutes after my freeway accident, did not impress or move anyone.

Interview is what did something. What did it do? It *did* [not] *impress* [or] *move.*

> In terms of usable space, a steel warehouse, with its extremely long span of roof unsupported by pillars, makes more sense.

Warehouse is what *makes.*

These three sentences demonstrate several things. First, in all three sentences, the simple subject and predicate verb are the "bare bones" of the sentence, the parts that carry the core idea of the sentence. When trying to find the subject and predicate verb, disregard all prepositional phrases, modifiers, conjunctions, and articles.

Second, in the third sentence, the verb is singular (*makes*) because the subject is singular (*warehouse*). Even though the plural noun *pillars* is closer to the verb, *warehouse* is the subject. So *warehouse* determines whether the verb is singular or plural. Subject and predicate must agree.

Third, the subject in the first sentence is compound (*Marex* [and] *Contron*). A compound subject, when connected by *and*, requires a plural verb (*enjoy*). Also, the second sentence shows how compound predicates can occur (*did* [not] *impress* [or] *move*).

Fourth, the second sentence incorporates a group of words—*coming minutes after my freeway accident*—containing a form of a verb (*coming*) and a noun (*accident*). Yet, this group of words is not a complete sentence for two reasons:

- Not all nouns are subjects: *Accident* is not the subject of *coming.*
- Not all verbs are predicates: A verb that ends in *ing* can never be the predicate of a sentence (unless preceded by a form of *to be*, as in *was coming*).

Because they don't contain a subject and a predicate, the words *coming minutes after my freeway accident* (called a **phrase**) can't be written as a sentence. That is, the phrase cannot stand alone; it cannot begin with a capital letter and end with a period. So a phrase must always be just one part of a sentence.

Sometimes a sentence incorporates two or more groups of words that do contain a subject and a predicate; these word groups are called **clauses**:

> My interview, because it came minutes after my freeway accident, did not impress or move anyone.

The **independent clause** is the portion of the sentence that could stand alone without revision:

> My *interview* did not impress or move anyone.

The other part of the sentence could stand alone only by removing *because.*

> (because) It came minutes after my freeway accident.

This part of the sentence is known as a **dependent clause**; although it has a subject and a predicate (just as an independent clause does), it's linked to the main part of the sentence by a word (*because*) showing its dependence.

In summary, the two types of clauses—dependent and independent—both have a subject and a predicate. Dependent clauses, however, do not bear the main meaning of the sentence and are therefore linked to an independent clause. Nor can phrases stand alone, because they lack both a subject and a predicate. Only independent clauses can be written as sentences without revision.

1.7.2 Types of Sentences

Sentences come in four main types, depending on the extent to which they contain clauses. A simple sentence has one subject and one predicate; in short, it has one main independent clause:

> Boeing is the world's largest aerospace company.

A **compound sentence** consists of two independent clauses connected by a coordinating conjunction (*and, or, but,* etc.) or a semicolon:

> Airbus outsold Boeing for several years, but Boeing has recently regained the lead.

A **complex sentence** consists of an independent clause and one or more dependent clauses:

> Boeing is betting [independent clause] that airlines will begin using moderately smaller planes to fly passengers between smaller cities [dependent clause introduced by *that*].

A **compound-complex sentence** has two main clauses, at least one of which contains a subordinate (dependent clause):

> Boeing is betting [independent clause] that airlines will begin using moderately smaller planes to fly passengers between smaller cities [dependent clause], and it anticipates that new airports will be developed to meet passenger needs [independent clause].

1.7.3 Sentence Fragments

An incomplete sentence (a phrase or a dependent clause) that is written as though it were a complete sentence is called a **fragment**. Consider the following sentence fragments:

> Marilyn Sanders, having had pilferage problems in her store for the past year. Refuses to accept the results of our investigation.

This serious error can easily be corrected by putting the two fragments together:

> Marilyn Sanders, having had pilferage problems in her store for the past year, refuses to accept the results of our investigation.

The actual details of a situation will determine the best way for you to remedy a fragment problem.

The ban on fragments has one exception. Some advertising copy contains sentence fragments, written knowingly to convey a certain rhythm. However, advertising is the only area of business in which fragments are acceptable.

1.7.4 Fused Sentences and Comma Splices

Just as there can be too little in a group of words to make it a sentence, there can also be too much:

> All our mail is run through a postage meter every afternoon someone picks it up.

This example contains two sentences, not one, but the two have been blended so that it's hard to tell where one ends and the next begins. Is the mail run through a meter every afternoon? If so, the sentences should read:

> All our mail is run through a postage meter every afternoon. Someone picks it up.

Perhaps the mail is run through a meter at some other time (morning, for example) and is picked up every afternoon;

> All our mail is run through a postage meter. Every afternoon someone picks it up.

The order of words is the same in all three cases; sentence division makes all the difference. Either of the last two cases is grammatically correct. The choice depends on the facts of the situation.

Sometimes these so-called **fused sentences** have a more obvious point of separation:

> Several large orders arrived within a few days of one another, too many came in for us to process by the end of the month.

Here, the comma has been put between two independent clauses in an attempt to link them. When a lowly comma separates two complete sentences, the result is called a **comma splice**. A comma splice can be remedied in one of three ways:

- Replace the comma with a period and capitalize the next word: ". . . one another. Too many ". . ."
- Replace the comma with a semicolon and do not capitalize the next word: " . . . one another; too many. . ." This remedy works only when the two sentences have closely related meanings.
- Change one of the sentences so that it becomes a phrase or a dependent clause. This remedy often produces the best writing, but it takes more work.

The third alternative can be carried out in several ways. One is to begin the sentence with a subordinating conjunction:

> Whenever several large orders arrived within a few days of one another, too many came in for us to process by the end of the month.

Another way is to remove part of the subject or the predicate verb from one of the independent clauses, thereby creating a phrase:

> Several large orders arrived within a few days of one another, too many for us to process by the end of the month.

Finally, you can change one of the predicate verbs to its *ing* form:

> Several large orders arrived within a few days of one another, too many coming in for us to process by the end of the month.

In many cases, simply adding a coordinating conjunction can separate fused sentences or remedy a comma splice:

> You can fire them, or you can make better use of their abilities.
>
> Margaret drew up the designs, and Matt carried them out.
>
> We will have three strong months, but after that sales will taper off.

Be careful with coordinating conjunctions: Use them only to join simple sentences that express similar ideas.

Also, because they say relatively little about the relationship between the two clauses they join, avoid using coordinating conjunctions too often: *and* is merely an addition sign; *but* is just a turn signal; *or* only points to an alternative. Subordinating conjunctions such as *because* and *whenever* tell the reader a lot more.

1.7.5 Sentences with Linking Verbs

Linking verbs were discussed briefly in the section on verbs (Section 1.3). Here, you can see more fully the way they function in a sentence. The following is a model of any sentence with a linking verb:

> A *(verb)* B.

Although words such as *seems* and *feels* can also be linking verbs, let's assume that the verb is a form of *to be:*

> A *is* B.

In such a sentence, A and B are always nouns, pronouns, or adjectives. When one is a noun and the other is a pronoun, or when both are nouns, the sentence says that one is the same as the other:

> She is president.
>
> Rachel is president.
>
> She is forceful.

Recall from Section 1.3.3 that the noun or adjective that follows the linking verb is called a *complement.* When it is a noun or noun phrase, the complement is called a *predicate nominative*, when the complement is an adjective, it is referred to as a *predicate adjective.*

1.7.6 Misplaced Modifiers

The position of a modifier in a sentence is important. The movement of *only* changes the meaning in the following sentences:

> Only we are obliged to supply those items specified in your contract.
>
> We are obliged only to supply those items specified in your contract.
>
> We are obliged to supply only those items specified in your contract.
>
> We are obliged to supply those items specified only in your contract.

In any particular set of circumstances, only one of those sentences would be accurate. The others would very likely cause problems. To prevent misunderstanding, place such modifiers as close as possible to the noun or verb they modify.

For similar reasons, whole phrases that are modifiers must be placed near the right noun or verb. Mistakes in placement create ludicrous meanings:

> Antia Information Systems bought new computer chairs for the programmers with more comfortable seats.

The anatomy of programmers is not normally a concern of business writers. Obviously, the comfort of the chairs was the issue:

> Antia Information Systems bought programmers the new computer chairs with more comfortable seats.

Here is another example:

> I asked him to file all the letters in the cabinet that had been answered.

In this ridiculous sentence, the cabinet has been answered, even though no cabinet in history is known to have asked a question. *That had been answered* is too far from *letters* and too close to *cabinet.* Here's an improvement:

> I asked him to file in the cabinet all the letters that had been answered.

The term **dangling modifier** is often used to refer to a clause or phrase that because of its position in the sentence seems to modify a word that it is not meant to modify. For instance:

> Lying motionless, co-workers rushed to Barry's aid.

Readers expect an introductory phrase to modify the subject of the main clause. But in this case it wasn't the *co-workers* who were lying motionless but rather *Barry* who was in this situation. Like this example, most instances of dangling modifiers occur at the beginning of sentences. The source of some danglers is a passive construction:

> To find the needed information, the whole book had to be read.

In such cases, switching to the active voice can usually remedy the problem:

> To find the needed information, you will need to read the whole book.

1.7.7 Parallelism

Two or more sentence elements that have the same relation to another element should be in the same form. Otherwise, the reader is forced to work harder to understand the meaning of the sentence. When a series consists of phrases or clauses, the same part of speech (preposition, gerund, etc.) should introduce them. Do not mix infinitives with participles or adjectives with nouns. Here are some examples of nonparallel elements:

> Andersen is hiring managers, programmers, and people who work in accounting. [nouns not parallel]
>
> Andersen earns income by auditing, consulting, and by bookkeeping. [prepositional phrases not parallel]
>
> Andersen's goals are to win new clients, keeping old clients happy, and finding new enterprises. [infinitive mixed with gerunds]

2.0 PUNCTUATION

On the highway, signs tell you when to slow down or stop, where to turn, and when to merge. In similar fashion, punctuation helps readers negotiate your prose. The proper use of punctuation keeps readers from losing track of your meaning.

2.1 Periods

Use a period (1) to end any sentence that is not a question, (2) with certain abbreviations, and (3) between dollars and cents in an amount of money.

2.2 Question Marks

Use a question mark after any direct question that requests an answer:

> Are you planning to enclose a check, or shall we bill you?

Don't use a question mark with commands phrased as questions for the sake of politeness:

> Will you send us a check today.

A question mark should precede quotation marks, parentheses, and brackets if it is part of the quoted or parenthetical material; otherwise, it should follow:

> This issue of *Inc.* has an article titled "What's Your Entrepreneurial IQ?"
>
> Have you read the article "Five Principles of Guerrilla Marketing"?

Do not use the question mark with indirect questions or with requests:

> Mr. Antonelli asked whether anyone had seen Nathalia lately.

Do not use a comma or a period with a question mark; the question mark takes the place of these punctuation marks.

2.3 Exclamation Points

Use exclamation points after highly emotional language. Because business writing almost never calls for emotional language, you will seldom use exclamation points.

2.4 Semicolons

Semicolons have three main uses. One is to separate two closely related independent clauses:

> The outline for the report is due within a week; the report itself is due at the end of the month.

A semicolon should also be used instead of a comma when the items in a series have commas within them:

> Our previous meetings were on November 11, 2004; February 20, 2005; and April 28, 2006.

Finally, a semicolon should be used to separate independent clauses when the second one begins with a conjunctive adverb such as *however*, *therefore*, or *nevertheless* or a phrase such as *for example* or *in that case:*

> Our supplier has been out of part D712 for 10 weeks; however, we have found another source that can ship the part right away.
>
> His test scores were quite low; on the other hand, he has a lot of relevant experience.

Section 4.4 provides more information on using transitional words and phrases.

Semicolons should always be placed outside parentheses.

> Events Northwest has the contract for this year's convention (August 23–28); we haven't awarded the contract for next year yet.

2.5 Colons

Use a colon after the salutation in a business letter. You should also use a colon at the end of a sentence or phrase introducing a list or (sometimes) a quotation:

> Our study included the three most critical problems: insufficient capital, incompetent management, and inappropriate location.

A colon should not be used when the list, quotation, or idea is a direct object of the verb or preposition. This rule applies whether the list is set off or run in:

> We are able to supply
>
> staples
>
> wood screws
>
> nails
>
> toggle bolts
>
> This shipment includes 9 DVDs, 12 CDs, and 4 USB flash drives.

Another way you can use a colon is to separate the main clause and another sentence element when the second explains, illustrates, or amplifies the first:

> Management was unprepared for the union representatives' demands: this fact alone accounts for their arguing well into the night.

However, in contemporary usage, such clauses are frequently separated by a semicolon.

Like semicolons, colons should always be placed outside parentheses.

> He has an expensive list of new demands (none of which is covered in the purchase agreement): new carpeting, network cabling, and a new security system.

2.6 Commas

Commas have many uses; the most common is to separate items in a series:

> He took the job, learned it well, worked hard, and succeeded.
>
> Put paper, pencils, and paper clips on the requisition list.

Company style may dictate omitting the final comma in a series. However, if you have a choice, use the final comma; it's often necessary to prevent misunderstanding.

A second place to use a comma is between independent clauses that are joined by a coordinating conjunction (*and*, *but*, or *or*).

> She spoke to the sales staff, and he spoke to the production staff.
>
> I was advised to proceed, and I did.

A third use for the comma is to separate a dependent clause at the beginning of a sentence from an independent clause:

> Because of our lead in the market, we may be able to risk introducing a new product.

However, a dependent clause at the end of a sentence is separated from the independent clause by a comma only when the dependent clause is unnecessary to the main meaning of the sentence:

> We may be able to introduce a new product, although it may involve some risk.

A fourth use for the comma is after an introductory phrase or word:

> Starting with this amount of capital, we can survive in the red for one year.
>
> Through more careful planning, we may be able to serve more people.
>
> Yes, you may proceed as originally planned.

However, with short introductory prepositional phrases and some one-syllable words (such as *hence* and *thus*), the comma is often omitted:

> Before January 1 we must complete the inventory.
>
> Thus we may not need to hire anyone.
>
> In July we will complete the move to Tulsa.

Fifth, paired commas are used to set off nonrestrictive clauses and phrases. A **restrictive clause** is one that cannot be omitted without altering the meaning of the main clause, whereas a **nonrestrictive clause** can be:

> The *Time Magazine* website, which is produced by Steve Conley, has won several design awards. [nonrestrictive: the material set off by commas could be omitted]
>
> The website that is produced by Steve Conley has won several design awards. [restrictive: no commas are used before and after *that is produced by Steve Conley* because this information is necessary to the meaning of the sentence—it specifies which website]

A sixth use for commas is to set off appositive words and phrases. (An **appositive** has the same meaning as the word it is in apposition to.) Like nonrestrictive clauses, appositives can be dropped without changing or obscuring the meaning of the sentence:

> Conley, a freelance designer, also produces the websites for several nonprofit corporations.

Seventh, commas are used between adjectives modifying the same noun (coordinate adjectives):

> She left Monday for a long, difficult recruiting trip.

To test the appropriateness of such a comma, try reversing the order of the adjectives: *a difficult, long recruiting trip.* If the order cannot be reversed, leave out the comma (a *good old friend* isn't the same as an *old good friend*). A comma should not be used when one of the adjectives is part of the noun. Compare these two phrases:

> a distinguished, well-known figure
>
> a distinguished public figure

The adjective–noun combination of *public* and *figure* has been used together so often that it has come to be considered a single thing: *public figure.* So no comma is required.

Eighth, commas are used both before and after the year in sentences that include month, day, and year:

> It will be sent by December 15, 2007, from our Cincinnati plant.

Some companies write dates in another form: 15 December 2007. No commas should be used in that case. Nor is a comma needed when only the month and year are present (December 2007).

Ninth, commas are used to set off a variety of parenthetical words and phrases within sentences, including state names, dates, abbreviations, transitional expressions, and contrasted elements:

> They were, in fact, prepared to submit a bid.
>
> Habermacher, Inc., went public in 1999.
>
> Our goal was increased profits, not increased market share.
>
> Service, then, is our main concern.
>
> The factory was completed in Chattanooga, Tennessee, just three weeks ago.
>
> Joanne Dubiik, M.D., has applied for a loan from First Savings.
>
> I started work here on March 1, 2003, and soon received my first promotion.

Tenth, a comma is used to separate a quotation from the rest of the sentence:

> Your warranty reads, "These conditions remain in effect for one year from date of purchase."

However, the comma is left out when the quotation as a whole is built into the structure of the sentence:

> He hurried off with an angry "Look where you're going."

Finally, a comma should be used whenever it's needed to avoid confusion or an unintended meaning. Compare the following:

> Ever since they have planned new ventures more carefully.
>
> Ever since, they have planned new ventures more carefully.

2.7 Dashes

Use dashes to surround a comment that is a sudden turn in thought:

> Membership in the IBSA—it's expensive but worth it—may be obtained by applying to our New York office.

A dash can also be used to emphasize a parenthetical word or phrase:

> Third-quarter profits—in excess of $2 million—are up sharply.

Finally, use dashes to set off a phrase that contains commas:

> All our offices—Milwaukee, New Orleans, and Phoenix—have sent representatives.

Don't confuse a dash with a hyphen. A dash separates and emphasizes words, phrases, and clauses more strongly than commas or parentheses can; a hyphen ties two words so tightly that they almost become one word.

When using a computer, use the em dash symbol. When typing a dash in e-mail, type two hyphens with no space before, between, or after.

A second type of dash, the en dash, can be produced with computer word processing and page-layout programs. This kind of dash is shorter than the regular dash and longer than a hyphen. It is reserved almost exclusively for indicating "to" or "through" with numbers such as dates and pages: *2001–2002, pages 30–44.*

2.8 Hyphens

Hyphens are mainly used in three ways. The first is to separate the parts of compound words beginning with such prefixes as *self-*, *ex-*, *quasi-*, and *all-*:

self-assured	quasi-official
ex-wife	all-important

However, do not use hyphens in words that have prefixes such as *pro, anti, non, re, pre, un, inter,* and *extra*:

prolabor	nonunion
antifascist	interdepartmental

Exceptions occur when (1) the prefix occurs before a proper noun or (2) the vowel at the end of the prefix is the same as the first letter of the root word:

pro-Republican	anti-American
anti-inflammatory	extra-atmospheric

When in doubt, consult your dictionary.

Hyphens are used in some types of spelled-out numbers. For instance, they are used to separate the parts of a spelled-out number from *twenty-one* to *ninety-nine* and for spelled-out fractions: *two-thirds, one-sixth* (although some style guides say not to hyphenate fractions used as nouns).

Certain compound nouns are formed by using hyphens: *secretary-treasurer, city-state.* Check your dictionary for compounds you're unsure about.

Hyphens are also used in some compound adjectives, which are adjectives made up of two or more words. Specifically, you should use hyphens in compound adjectives that come before the noun:

an interest-bearing account	well-informed executives

However, you need not hyphenate when the adjective follows a linking verb:

> This account is interest bearing.
>
> Their executives are well informed.

You can shorten sentences that list similar hyphenated words by dropping the common part from all but the last word:

> Check the costs of first-, second-, and third-class postage.

Finally, hyphens may be used to divide words at the end of a typed line. Such hyphenation is best avoided, but when you have to divide words at the end of a line, do so correctly (see Section 3.5). Dictionaries show how words are divided into syllables.

2.9 Apostrophes

Use an apostrophe in the possessive form of noun (but not in a pronoun):

> On his desk was a reply to Bette *Ainsley's* application for the *manager's* position.

Apostrophes are also used in place of the missing letter(s) of a contraction:

Whole Words	Contraction
we will	we'll
do not	don't
they are	they're

2.10 Quotation Marks

Use quotation marks to surround words that are repeated exactly as they were said or written:

> The collection letter ended by saying, "This is your third and final notice."

Remember: (1) When the quoted material is a complete sentence, the first word is capitalized. (2) The final comma or period goes inside the closing quotation marks.

Quotation marks are also used to set off the title of a newspaper story, magazine article, or book chapter:

> You should read "Legal Aspects of the Collection Letter" in *Today's Credit.*

Quotation marks may also be used to indicate special treatment for words or phrases, such as terms that you're using in an unusual or ironic way:

> Our management "team" spends more time squabbling than working to solve company problems.

When you are defining a word, put the definition in quotation marks:

> The abbreviation *etc.* means "and so forth."

When using quotation marks, take care to insert the closing marks as well as the opening ones.

Although periods and commas go inside any quotation marks, colons and semicolons generally go outside them. A question mark goes inside the quotation marks only if the quotation is a question:

> All that day we wondered, "Is he with us?"

If the quotation is not a question but the entire sentence is, the question mark goes outside:

> What did she mean by "You will hear from me"?

For quotes within quotes, use single quotation marks within double:

> As David Pottruck, former co-CEO of Charles Schwab, told it, "I assembled about 100 managers at the base of the Golden Gate Bridge and gave them jackets emblazoned with the phrase 'Crossing the Chasm' and then led them across the bridge."

Otherwise, do not use single quotation marks for anything, including titles of works—that's British style.

2.11 Parentheses and Brackets

Use parentheses to surround comments that are entirely incidental or to supply additional information:

> Our figures do not match yours, although (if my calculations are correct) they are closer than we thought.
>
> These kinds of supplements do not require FDA (Food and Drug Administration) approval.

Parentheses are used in legal documents to surround figures in arabic numerals that follow the same amount in words:

> Remittance will be One Thousand Two Hundred Dollars ($1,200).

Be careful to put punctuation marks (period, comma, and so on) outside the parentheses unless they are part of the statement in parentheses. And keep in mind that parentheses have both an opening and a closing mark; both should always be used, even when setting off listed items within text: *(1)*, not *1)*.

Brackets are used for notation, comment, explanation, or correction within quoted material:

> In the interview, multimillionaire Bob Buford said, "One of my major influences was Peter [Drucker], who encourages people and helps them believe in themselves."

Brackets are also used for parenthetical material that falls within parentheses:

> Drucker's magnum opus *(Management: Tasks, Responsibilities, Practices* [Harper & Row, 1979]) has influenced generations of entrepreneurs.

2.12 Ellipses

Use ellipsis points, or three evenly spaced periods, to indicate that material has been left out of a direct quotation. Use them only in direct quotations and only at the point where material was left out. In the following example, the first sentence is quoted in the second:

> The Dow Jones Industrial Average fell 276.39 points, or 2.6%, during the week to 10292.31.
>
> According to the *Wall Street Journal*, "The Dow Jones Industrial Average fell 276.39 points . . . to 10,292.31."

The number of dots in ellipses is not optional; always use three. Occasionally, the points of an ellipsis come at the end of a sentence, where they seem to grow a fourth dot. Don't be fooled: One of the dots is a period. Ellipsis points should always be preceded and followed by a space.

Avoid using ellipses to represent a pause in your writing; use a dash for that purpose:

> At first we had planned to leave for the conference on Wednesday—but then we changed our minds. [not *on Wednesday . . . but then*]

3.0 MECHANICS

The most obvious and least tolerable mistakes that a business writer makes are probably those related to grammar and punctuation. However, a number of small details, known as writing mechanics, demonstrate the writer's polish and reflect on the company's professionalism.

When it comes to mechanics, also called *style*, many of the "rules" are not hard and fast. Publications and organizations vary in their preferred styles for capitalization, abbreviations, numbers, italics, and so on. Here, we'll try to differentiate between practices that are generally accepted and those that can vary. When you are writing materials for a specific company or organization, find out the preferred style (such as *The Chicago Manual of Style* or Webster's *Style Manual*). Otherwise, choose a respected style guide. The key to style is consistency: If you spell out the word *percent* in one part of a document, don't use the percent sign in a similar context elsewhere in the same document.

3.1 Capitalization

With capitalization, you can follow either an "up" style (when in doubt, capitalize: *Federal Government, Board of Directors*) or a "down" style (when in doubt, use lowercase: *federal government, board of directors*). The trend over the last few decades has been toward the down style. Your best bet is to get a good style manual and consult it when you have a capitalization question. Following are some rules that most style guides agree on.

Capital letters are used at the beginning of certain word groups:

- **Complete sentence:** Before hanging up, he said, "We'll meet here on Wednesday at noon."
- **Formal statement following a colon:** She has a favorite motto: Where there's a will, there's a way.
- **Phrase used as sentence:** Absolutely not!
- **Quoted sentence embedded in another sentence:** Scott said, "Nobody was here during lunch hour except me."
- **List of items set off from text:** Three preliminary steps are involved:

  Design review

  Budgeting

  Scheduling

Capitalize proper adjectives and proper nouns (the names of particular persons, places, and things):

> Darrell Greene lived in a Victorian mansion.
>
> We sent Ms. Larson an application form, informing her that not all applicants are interviewed.
>
> Let's consider opening a branch in the West, perhaps at the west end of Tucson, Arizona.
>
> As office buildings go, the Kinney Building is a pleasant setting for TDG Office Equipment.
>
> We are going to have to cancel our plans for hiring French and German sales reps.

Larson's name is capitalized because she is a particular applicant, whereas the general term *applicant* is left uncapitalized. Likewise, *West* is capitalized when it refers to a particular place but not when it means a direction. In the same way, *office* and *building* are not capitalized when they are general terms (common nouns), but they are capitalized when they are part of the title of a particular office or building (proper nouns). Some proper adjectives are lowercased when they are part of terms that have come into common use, such as *french fries* and *roman numerals.*

Titles within families or companies as well as professional titles may also be capitalized:

> I turned down Uncle David when he offered me a job. I wouldn't be comfortable working for one of my relatives.
>
> We've never had a president quite like President Sweeney.

People's titles are capitalized when they are used in addressing a person, especially in a formal context. They are not usually capitalized, however, when they are used merely to identify the person:

> Address the letter to Chairperson Anna Palmer.
>
> I wish to thank Chairperson Anna Palmer for her assistance.
>
> Anna Palmer, chairperson of the board, took the podium.

Also capitalize titles if they are used by themselves in addressing a person:

> Thank you, Doctor, for your donation.

Always capitalize the first word of the salutation and complimentary close of a letter:

> *Dear* Mr. Andrews: *Yours* very truly,

The names of organizations are capitalized, of course; so are the official names of their departments and divisions. However, do not use capitals when referring in general terms to a department or division, especially one in another organization:

> Route this memo to Personnel.
>
> Larry Tien was transferred to the Microchip Division.
>
> Will you be enrolled in the Psychology Department?
>
> Someone from the personnel department at EnerTech stopped by the booth.

Capitalization is unnecessary when using a word like *company, corporation*, or *university* alone:

> The corporation plans to issue 50,000 shares of common stock.

Likewise, the names of specific products are capitalized, although the names of general product types are not:

> Apple Inc. Xerox machine
> Tide laundry detergent

When it comes to government terminology, here are some guides to capitalization: (1) Lowercase *federal* unless it is part of an agency name; (2) capitalize names of courts, departments, bureaus, offices, and agencies but lowercase such references as *the bureau* and *the department* when the full name is not used; (3) lowercase the titles of government officers unless they precede a specific person's name: *the secretary of state, the senator, the ambassador, the governor, and the mayor* but *Mayor Gonzalez* (Note: style guides vary on whether to capitalize *president* when referring to the president of the United States without including the person's name); capitalize the names of laws and acts: *the Sherman Antitrust Act, the Civil Rights Act*; (5) capitalize the names of political parties but lowercase the word *party: Democratic party, Libertarian party.*

One problem that often arises in writing about places is the treatment of two or more proper nouns of the same type. When the common word comes before the specific names, it is capitalized; when it comes after the specific names, it is not:

> Lakes Ontario and Huron
>
> Allegheny and Monongahela rivers

The names of languages, races, and ethnic groups are capitalized: Japanese, Caucasian, Hispanic. But racial terms that denote only skin color are not capitalized: black, white.

When referring to the titles of books, articles, magazines, newspapers, reports, movies, and so on, you should capitalize the first and last words and all nouns, pronouns, adjectives, verbs, and adverbs, and capitalize prepositions and conjunctions with five letters or more. Except for the first and last words, do not capitalize articles:

> *Economics During the Great War*
>
> "An Investigation into the Market for Long-Distance Services"
>
> "What Successes Are Made Of"

When *the* is part of the official name of a newspaper or magazine, it should be treated this way too:

> *The Wall Street Journal*

Style guides vary in their recommendations regarding capitalization of hyphenated words in titles. A general guide is to capitalize the second word in a temporary compound (a compound that is hyphenated for grammatical reasons and not spelling reasons), such as *Law-Abiding Citizen*, but to lowercase the word if the term is always hyphenated, such as *Son-in-law*).

References to specific pages, paragraphs, lines, and the like are not capitalized: *page 73, line 3.* However, in most other numbered or lettered references, the identifying term is capitalized:

> *Chapter 4* *Serial No. 382-2203* *Item B-11*

Finally, the names of academic degrees are capitalized when they follow a person's name but are not capitalized when used in a general sense:

> I received a bachelor of science degree.
>
> Thomas Whitelaw, Doctor of Philosophy, will attend.

Similarly, general courses of study are not capitalized, but the names of specific classes are:

> She studied accounting as an undergraduate.
>
> She is enrolled in Accounting 201.

3.2 Underscores and Italics

Usually a line typed underneath a word or phrase either provides emphasis or indicates the title of a book, magazine, or newspaper. If possible, use italics instead of an underscore. Italics (or underlining) should also be used for defining terms and for discussing words as words:

> In this report, *net sales* refers to after-tax sales dollars.
>
> The word *building* is a common noun and should not be capitalized.

Also use italics to set off foreign words, unless the words have become a common part of English:

> Top Shelf is considered the *sine qua non* of comic book publishers.
>
> Chris uses a laissez-faire [no italic] management style.

3.3 Abbreviations

Abbreviations are used heavily in tables, charts, lists, and forms. They're used sparingly in prose. Here are some abbreviation situations to watch for:

- In most cases do not use periods with acronyms (words formed from the initial letter or letters of parts of a term): *CEO, CD-ROM, DOS, YWCA, FDA*; but *Ph.D., M.A., M.D.*
- Use periods with abbreviations such as *Mr., Ms., Sr., Jr., a.m., p.m., B.C.,* and *A.D.*
- The trend is away from using periods with such units of measure as *mph, mm,* and *lb.*
- Use periods with such Latin abbreviations as *e.g., i.e., et al.,* and *etc.* However, style guides recommend that you avoid using these Latin forms and instead use their English equivalents *(for example, that is, and others,* and *and so on,* respectively). If you must use these abbreviations, such as in parenthetical expressions or footnotes, do not put them in italics.
- Some companies have abbreviations as part of their names *(&, Co., Inc., Ltd.)*. When you refer to such firms by name, be sure to double-check the preferred spelling, including spacing: *AT&T; Barnes & Noble; Carson Pirie Scott & Company; PepsiCo; Kate Spade, Inc.; National Data Corporation; Siemens Corp.; Glaxo Wellcome PLC; US Airways; U.S. Business Reporter.*
- Most style guides recommend that you spell out *United States* as a noun and reserve *U.S.* as an adjective preceding the noun modified.

One way to handle an abbreviation that you want to use throughout a document is to spell it out the first time you use it, follow it with the abbreviation in parentheses, and then use the abbreviation in the remainder of the document.

3.4 Numbers

Numbers may be correctly handled many ways in business writing, so follow company style. In the absence of a set style, however, generally spell out all numbers from one to nine and use arabic numerals for the rest.

There are some exceptions to this general rule. For example, never begin a sentence with a numeral:

> Twenty of us produced 641 units per week in the first 12 weeks of the year.

Use numerals for the numbers one through nine if they're in the same list as larger numbers:

> Our weekly quota rose from 9 to 15 to 27.

Use numerals for percentages, time of day (except with o'clock), dates, and (in general) dollar amounts:

> Our division is responsible for 7 percent of total sales.
>
> The meeting is scheduled for 8:30 a.m. on August 2.
>
> Add $3 for postage and handling.

When using numerals for time, be consistent: It should be *between 10:00 a.m. and 4:30 p.m.,* not *between 10 a.m. and 4:30 p.m.* Expressions such as *4:00 o'clock* and *7 a.m. in the morning* are redundant.

Use a comma in numbers expressing thousands (1,257), unless your company specifies another style. When dealing with numbers in the millions and billions, combine words and figures: 7.3 million, 2 billion.

When writing dollar amounts, use a decimal point only if cents are included. In lists of two or more dollar amounts, use the decimal point either for all or for none:

> He sent two checks, one for $67.92 and one for $90.00.

When two numbers fall next to each other in a sentence, use figures for the number that is largest, most difficult to spell, or part of a physical measurement; use words for the other:

> I have learned to manage a classroom of 30 twelve-year-olds.
>
> She won a bonus for selling 24 thirty-volume sets.
>
> You'll need twenty 3-inch bolts.

In addresses, all street numbers except One are in numerals. So are suite and room numbers and zip codes. For street names that are numbered, practice varies so widely that you should use the form specified on an organization's letterhead or in a reliable directory. All the following examples are correct:

One Fifth Avenue	297 Ninth Street
1839 44th Street	11026 West 78 Place

Telephone numbers are always expressed in numerals. Parentheses may separate the area code from the rest of the number, but a slash or a hyphen may be used instead, especially if the entire phone number is enclosed in parentheses:

> 382-8329 (602/382-8329) 602-382-8329

Percentages are always expressed in numerals. The word *percent* is used in most cases, but % may be used in tables, forms, and statistical writing.

Ages are usually expressed in words—except when a parenthetical reference to age follows someone's name:

> Mrs. Margaret Sanderson is seventy-two.
>
> Mrs. Margaret Sanderson, 72, swims daily.

Also, ages expressed in years and months are treated like physical measurements that combine two units of measure: *5 years 6 months.*

Physical measurements such as distance, weight, and volume are also often expressed in numerals: *9 kilometers, 5 feet 3 inches, 7 pounds 10 ounces.*

Decimal numbers are always written in numerals. In most cases, add a zero to the left of the decimal point if the number is less than one and does not already start with a zero:

1.38 .07 0.2

In a series of related decimal numbers with at least one number greater than one, make sure that all numbers smaller than one have a zero to the left of the decimal point: 1.20, 0.21, 0.09.

Simple fractions are written in words, but more complicated fractions are expressed in figures or, if easier to read, in figures and words:

two-thirds 9/32 2 hundredths

Most style guides recommend that you use a comma with numbers consisting of four digits: *2,345*, not *2345*.

When typing ordinal numbers, such as *3rd edition* or *21st century*, your word processing program may automatically make the letters *rd* (or *st*, *th*, or *nd*) into a superscript. Do yourself a favor and turn that formatting function off in your "Preferences," as superscripts should not be used in regular prose or even in bibliographies.

3.5 Word Division

In general, avoid dividing words at the end of lines. When you must do so, follow these rules:

- Don't divide one-syllable words (such as *since, walked*, and *thought*), abbreviations (*mgr.*), contractions (*isn't*), or numbers expressed in numerals (*117,500*).
- Divide words between syllables, as specified in a dictionary or word-division manual.
- Make sure that at least three letters of the divided words are moved to the second line: *sin-cerely* instead of *sincere-ly*.
- Do not end a page or more than three consecutive lines with hyphens.
- Leave syllables consisting of a single vowel at the end of the first line (*impedi-ment* instead of *imped-iment*), except when the single vowel is part of a suffix such as *-able, -ible, -ical,* or *-ity* (*re-spons-ible* instead of *re-sponsi-ble*).
- Divide between double letters (*tomor-row*), except when the root word ends in double letters (*call-ing* instead of *cal-ling*).
- Wherever possible, divide hyphenated words at the hyphen only: instead of *anti-inde-pendence*, use *anti-independence*.
- Whenever possible, do not break URLs or e-mail addresses. If you have to break a long URL or e-mail address, do not insert a hyphen at the end of the first line.

4.0 VOCABULARY

Using the right word in the right place is a crucial skill in business communication. However, many pitfalls await the unwary.

4.1 Frequently Confused Words

Because the following sets of words sound similar, be careful not to use one when you mean to use the other:

Word	Meaning
accede	to comply with
exceed	to go beyond
accept	to take
except	to exclude
access	admittance
excess	too much
advice	suggestion
advise	to suggest
affect	to influence
effect	the result
allot	to distribute
a lot	much or many
all ready	completely prepared
already	completed earlier
born	given birth to
borne	carried
capital	money; chief city
capitol	a government building
cite	to quote
sight	a view
site	a location
complement	complete amount; to go well with
compliment	expression of esteem; to flatter
corespondent	party in a divorce suit
correspondent	letter writer
council	a panel of people
counsel	advice; a lawyer
defer	to put off until later
differ	to be different
device	a mechanism
devise	to plan
die	to stop living; a tool
dye	to color
discreet	careful
discrete	separate
envelop	to surround
envelope	a covering for a letter
forth	forward
fourth	number four
holey	full of holes
holy	sacred
wholly	completely
human	of people
humane	kindly
incidence	frequency
incidents	events

Word	Meaning
instance	example
instants	moments
interstate	between states
intrastate	within a state
later	afterward
latter	the second of two
lead	a metal; to guide
led	guided
lean	to rest at an angle
lien	a claim
levee	embankment
levy	tax
loath	reluctant
loathe	to hate
loose	free; not tight
lose	to mislay
material	substance
materiel	equipment
miner	mineworker
minor	underage person
moral	virtuous; a lesson
morale	sense of well-being
ordinance	law
ordnance	weapons
overdo	to do in excess
overdue	past due
peace	lack of conflict
piece	a fragment
pedal	a foot lever
peddle	to sell
persecute	to torment
prosecute	to sue
personal	private
personnel	employees
precedence	priority
precedents	previous events
principal	sum of money; chief; main
principle	general rule
rap	to knock
wrap	to cover
residence	home
residents	inhabitants
right	correct
rite	ceremony
write	to form words on a surface
role	a part to play
roll	to tumble; a list

Word	Meaning
root	part of a plant
rout	to defeat
route	a traveler's way
shear	to cut
sheer	thin, steep
stationary	immovable
stationery	paper
than	as compared with
then	at that time
their	belonging to them
there	in that place
they're	they are
to	a preposition
too	excessively; also
two	the number
waive	to set aside
wave	a swell of water; a gesture
weather	atmospheric conditions
whether	if
who's	contraction of "who is" or "who has"
whose	possessive form of who

In the preceding list, only enough of each word's meaning is given to help you distinguish between the words in each group. For more complete definitions, consult a dictionary.

4.2 Frequently Misused Words

The following words tend to be misused for reasons other than their sound. Reference books (including the *Random House College Dictionary*, revised edition; Follett's *Modern American Usage*; and Fowler's *Modern English Usage*) can help you with similar questions of usage:

a lot: When the writer means "many," *a lot* is always two separate words, never one.

aggravate/irritate: *Aggravate* means "to make things worse." Sitting in the smoke-filled room *aggravated* his sinus condition. *Irritate* means "to annoy." Her constant questions *irritated* [not *aggravated*] me.

anticipate/expect: *Anticipate* means "to prepare for": Macy's *anticipated* increased demand for athletic shoes in spring by ordering in November. In formal usage, it is incorrect to use *anticipate* for *expect*: I *expected* (not *anticipated*) a better response to our presentation than we actually got.

compose/comprise: The whole comprises the parts:

The company's distribution division *comprises* four departments.

It would be incorrect usage to say

The company's distribution division *is comprised of* four departments.

In that construction, *is composed of* or *consists of* would be preferable. It might be helpful to think of *comprise* as meaning "encompasses" or "contains."

continual/continuous: *Continual* refers to ongoing actions that have breaks:

> Her *continual* complaining will accomplish little in the long run.

Continuous refers to ongoing actions without interruptions or breaks:

> A *continuous* stream of paper came out of the fax machine.

convince/persuade: One is *convinced* of a fact or that something is true; one is *persuaded* by someone else to do something. The use of *to* with *convince* is unidiomatic—you don't convince someone to do something, you persuade them to do it.

correspond with: Use this phrase when you are talking about exchanging letters. Use *correspond to* when you mean "similar to." Use either *correspond with* or *correspond to* when you mean "relate to."

dilemma/problem: Technically, a *dilemma* is a situation in which one must choose between two undesirable alternatives. It shouldn't be used when no choice is actually involved.

disinterested: This word means "fair, unbiased, having no favorites, impartial." If you mean "bored" or "not interested," use *uninterested*.

etc.: This abbreviated form of the Latin phrase *et cetera* means "and so on" or "and so forth," so it is never correct to write *and etc.* The current tendency among business writers is to use English rather than Latin.

example/sample: An *example* is a model to be followed or one item that represents a group. A *sample* is a preview of a product or another entity, intended to demonstrate the product's qualities. In statistics, a sample is selected to represent the characteristics of a larger population.

flaunt/flout: To *flaunt* is to be ostentatious or boastful; to *flout* is to mock or scoff at.

impact: Avoid using *impact* as a verb when *influence* or *affect* is meant.

imply/infer: Both refer to hints. Their great difference lies in who is acting. The writer *implies*, the reader *infers*, sees between the lines.

lay: This word is a transitive verb. Never use it for the intransitive *lie*. (See Section 1.3.3.)

lend/loan: *Lend* is a verb; *loan* is a noun. Usage such as "Can you *loan* me $5?" is therefore incorrect.

less/fewer: Use *less* for uncountable quantities (such as amounts of water, air, sugar, and oil). Use *fewer* for countable quantities (such as numbers of jars, saws, words, pages, and humans). The same distinction applies to *much* and *little* (uncountable) versus *many* and *few* (countable).

liable/likely: *Liable* means "responsible for": I will hold you *liable* if this deal doesn't go through. It is incorrect to use *liable* for "possible": Anything is *likely* (not *liable*) to happen.

literally: *Literally* means "actually" or "precisely"; it is often misused to mean "almost" or "virtually." It is usually best left out entirely or replaced with *figuratively*.

many/much: See *less/fewer*.

regardless: The *less* suffix is the negative part. No word needs two negative parts, so don't add *ir* (a negative prefix) to the beginning. There is no such word as *irregardless*.

try: Always follow with *to*, never *and*.

verbal: People in the business community who are careful with language frown on those who use *verbal* to mean "spoken" or "oral." Many others do say "verbal agreement." Strictly speaking, *verbal* means "of words" and therefore includes both spoken and written words. Follow company usage in this matter.

4.3 Frequently Misspelled Words

All of us, even the world's best spellers, sometimes have to check a dictionary for the spelling of some words. People who have never memorized the spelling of commonly used words must look up so many that they grow exasperated and give up on spelling words correctly.

Don't expect perfection and don't surrender. If you can memorize the spelling of just the words listed here, you'll need the dictionary far less often and you'll write with more confidence:

absence
absorption
accessible
accommodate
accumulate
achieve
advantageous
affiliated
aggressive
alignment
aluminum
ambience
analyze
apparent
appropriate
argument
asphalt
assistant
asterisk
auditor

bankruptcy
believable
brilliant
bulletin

calendar
campaign
category
ceiling

changeable
clientele
collateral
committee
comparative
competitor
concede
congratulations
connoisseur
consensus
convenient
convertible
corroborate
criticism

definitely
description
desirable
dilemma
disappear
disappoint
disbursement
discrepancy
dissatisfied
dissipate

eligible
embarrassing
endorsement
exaggerate

exceed
exhaust
existence
extraordinary

fallacy
familiar
flexible
fluctuation
forty

gesture
grievous

haphazard
harassment
holiday

illegible
immigrant
incidentally
indelible
independent
indispensable
insistent
intermediary
irresistible

jewelry
judgment
judicial

labeling
legitimate
leisure
license
litigation

maintenance
mathematics
mediocre
minimum

necessary
negligence
negotiable
newsstand
noticeable

occurrence
omission

parallel
pastime
peaceable
permanent
perseverance
persistent
personnel
persuade
possesses
precede
predictable
preferred
privilege
procedure
proceed
pronunciation
psychology
pursue

questionnaire

receive
recommend
repetition
rescind
rhythmical
ridiculous

salable
secretary
seize
separate
sincerely
succeed
suddenness
superintendent
supersede
surprise

tangible
tariff
technique
tenant
truly

unanimous
until

vacillate
vacuum
vicious

4.4 Transitional Words and Phrases

The following sentences don't communicate as well as they could because they lack a transitional word or phrase:

> Production delays are inevitable. Our current lag time in filling orders is one month.

A semicolon between the two sentences would signal a close relationship between their meanings, but it wouldn't even hint at what that relationship is. Here are the sentences again, now linked by means of a semicolon, with a space for a transitional word or phrase:

> Production delays are inevitable; _______________, our current lag time in filling orders is one month.

Now read the sentence with *nevertheless* in the blank space. Then try *therefore, incidentally, in fact,* and *at any rate* in the blank. Each substitution changes the meaning of the sentence.

Here are some transitional words (conjunctive adverbs) that will help you write more clearly:

accordingly	furthermore	moreover
anyway	however	otherwise
besides	incidentally	still
consequently	likewise	therefore
finally	meanwhile	

The following transitional phrases are used in the same way:

as a result	in other words
at any rate	in the second place
for example	on the other hand
in fact	to the contrary

When one of these words or phrases joins two independent clauses, it should be preceded by a semicolon and followed by a comma:

> The consultant recommended a complete reorganization; moreover, she suggested that we drop several products.

Answer Keys

ANSWER KEY FOR "LEARNING OBJECTIVES CHECKUP"

Chapter 1

1. a
2. c
3. b
4. c
5. b
6. improvement
7. a
8. sense, select, perceive
9. d
10. information, people
11. a
12. c
13. d
14. dilemma, lapse

Chapter 2

1. d
2. d
3. d
4. a
5. b
6. a
7. decode
8. c
9. d
10. a
11. d
12. d
13. c
14. a
15. a

Chapter 3

1. d
2. d
3. b
4. b
5. c
6. d
7. ethnocentrism
8. stereotyping
9. d
10. a
11. c
12. b
13. a
14. nonverbal
15. d
16. a
17. b
18. b

Chapter 4

1. b
2. c
3. d
4. a
5. general purpose
6. b
7. a
8. c
9. c
10. d
11. d
12. richness
13. d
14. a
15. b
16. direct
17. indirect
18. a

Chapter 5

1. a
2. d
3. d
4. b
5. c
6. c
7. passive
8. active
9. a
10. b
11. c
12. a
13. a
14. c
15. c
16. examples
17. similarities, differences
18. a

Chapter 6

1. d
2. a
3. c
4. a
5. b
6. d
7. d
8. b
9. b
10. a
11. c
12. b
13. white space
14. c
15. a
16. c
17. d
18. a
19. b

Chapter 7

1. b
2. a
3. c
4. b
5. a
6. c
7. b
8. a
9. c
10. d
11. b
12. a
13. b
14. viral marketing
15. c
16. c
17. d
18. podcast channel
19. syndication
20. a

Chapter 8

1. b
2. a

3. d
4. c
5. b
6. d
7. b
8. the good news
9. d
10. d
11. b
12. a
13. d
14. d

Chapter 9

1. h
2. d
3. c
4. a
5. a
6. c
7. c
8. buffer
9. b
10. d
11. b
12. c
13. b
14. a
15. a

Chapter 10

1. c
2. d
3. d
4. b
5. b
6. c
7. d
8. c
9. emotional
10. logical
11. b
12. a
13. b
14. d
15. c
16. b
17. a
18. d

Chapter 11

1. a
2. a
3. informational
4. analytical
5. proposals
6. d
7. d
8. primary
9. secondary
10. a
11. c
12. a
13. c
14. c
15. a
16. summary
17. conclusion
18. recommendation
19. b
20. information architecture
21. a
22. a

Chapter 12

1. d
2. b
3. a
4. c
5. c
6. a
7. c
8. a
9. b
10. d
11. d
12. localizing
13. b
14. d
15. b
16. d
17. b
18. d
19. data visualization
20. c
21. d
22. c

Chapter 13

1. c
2. d
3. a
4. d
5. b
6. a
7. synopsis
8. executive summary
9. a
10. c
11. b
12. c

Chapter 14

1. b
2. d
3. planning, speaking
4. c
5. b
6. a
7. a
8. b
9. b
10. c
11. d
12. a
13. c
14. d
15. b
16. d
17. d
18. a
19. d
20. b

Chapter 15

1. b
2. b
3. d
4. b
5. d
6. chronological
7. functional
8. combination
9. d
10. a
11. b
12. a
13. a
14. c
15. plain-text
16. b
17. d
18. b

Chapter 16

1. a
2. d
3. b
4. structured
5. open-ended
6. situational
7. d
8. d
9. d
10. b
11. c
12. c
13. a
14. a
15. c
16. d
17. a
18. c

ANSWER KEY FOR "IMPROVE YOUR GRAMMAR, MECHANICS, AND USAGE" EXERCISES

Chapter 1

1. boss's (1.1.4)
2. sheep (1.1.3)
3. 1990s (1.1.3)
4. Joneses, stopwatches (1.1.3)
5. attorneys (1.1.3)
6. copies (1.1.3)
7. employees' (1.1.4)
8. sons-in-law, businesses (1.1.3, 1.1.4)
9. parentheses (1.1.3)
10. Ness's, week's (1.1.4)

Chapter 2

1. its (1.2.5)
2. their (1.2.5)
3. its (1.2.5)
4. their (1.2.1)
5. his or her (1.2.3)
6. his or her (1.2.3)
7. a, them (1.2.3, 1.2.4)
8. who (1.2.4)
9. whom (1.2.4)
10. its (1.2.5)

Chapter 3

1. b (1.3.1)
2. b (1.3.1)
3. a (1.3.1)
4. b (1.3.5)
5. a (1.3.5)
6. a (1.3.4)
7. b (1.3.4)
8. b (1.3.4)
9. a (1.3.4)
10. b (1.3.4)

Chapter 4

1. greater (1.4.1)
2. perfect (1.4.1)
3. most interesting (1.4.1)
4. hardest (1.4.1)
5. highly placed, last-ditch (1.4.2)
6. top-secret (1.4.2)
7. 30-year-old (1.4.2)
8. all-out, no-holds-barred struggle (1.4)
9. tiny metal (1.4)
10. usual cheerful, prompt (1.4)

Chapter 5

1. good (1.5)
2. surely (1.5)
3. sick (1.5)
4. well (1.5)
5. good (1.5)
6. faster (1.5.2)
7. better (1.5.2)
8. any (1.5.1)
9. ever (1.5.1)
10. can, any (1.5.1)

Chapter 6

1. leading (1.6.1)
2. off (1.6.1)
3. aware of (1.6.1)
4. to (1.6.1)
5. among (1.6.1)
6. for (1.6.1)
7. to (1.6.1)
8. from (1.6.1)
9. not only in (1.6.1, 1.7.7)
10. into (1.6.2)

Chapter 7

1. b (1.6.2)
2. b (1.6.1)
3. a (1.6.1)
4. b (1.6.1)
5. b (1.6.1)
6. a (1.6.1)
7. a (1.6.3)
8. b (1.6.2)
9. b (1.6.3)
10. b (1.6.3)

Chapter 8

1. b (1.7.3)
2. a (1.7.2)
3. b (1.7.6)
4. a (1.7.4)
5. b (1.7.4)
6. b (1.7.6)
7. a (1.7.6)
8. b (1.7.4)
9. a (1.7.3)
10. b (1.7.2)

Chapter 9

1. c (2.6)
2. a (2.6)
3. b (2.6)
4. a (2.6)
5. b (2.6)
6. c (2.6)
7. b (2.6)
8. a (2.6)
9. c (2.6)
10. b (2.6)

Chapter 10

1. a (2.4)
2. a (2.5)
3. c (2.4)
4. a (2.5)
5. b (2.5)
6. b (2.4)
7. a (2.4)
8. c (2.4)
9. b (2.4)
10. c (2.5)

Chapter 11

1. b (2.1)
2. a (2.2)
3. b (2.1)
4. a (2.1)
5. b (2.2, 2.3)
6. b (2.1)
7. b (2.2, 2.1)
8. a (2.2)
9. b (2.2)
10. a (2.2, 2.3)

Chapter 12

1. b (2.7)
2. a (2.8)
3. c (2.7)
4. b (2.8)
5. a (2.7)
6. b (2.7)
7. c (2.8)
8. a (2.8, 2.7)
9. c (2.8, 2.7)
10. a (2.8)

Chapter 13

1. b (2.10)
2. b (2.11)
3. a (2.11)
4. b (2.10)
5. c (2.10)
6. a (2.11)
7. c (2.10, 2.12)
8. b (2.10)
9. b (2.11)
10. c (2.10, 2.12)

Chapter 14

1. c (3.1, 3.3)
2. a (3.1, 3.3)
3. c (3.1, 3.2)
4. a (3.1)
5. c (3.3)

6. a (3.1, 3.2)
7. b (3.1, 3.3)
8. b (3.1, 3.3)
9. a (3.2)
10. c (3.1)

Chapter 15

1. except (4.1)
2. device (4.1)
3. loath (4.1)
4. who's (4.1)
5. a lot (4.2)
6. judgment (4.3)
7. regardless (4.2)
8. accommodate (4.3)
9. imply (4.2)
10. to (4.2)

Chapter 16

1. c (3.4)
2. a (3.4)
3. a (3.4)
4. b (3.4)
5. b (3.4)
6. a (3.4)
7. b (3.4)
8. c (3.4)
9. a (3.4)
10. c (3.4)

References

PROLOGUE

1. "The Small Business Economy, 2009," U.S. Small Business Administration website [accessed 8 August 2009] www.sba.gov; "Advocacy Small Business Statistics and Research," U.S. Small Business Administration website [accessed 3 July 2007] www.sba.gov; Malik Singleton, "Same Markets, New Marketplaces," *Black Enterprise*, September 2004, 34; Edmund L. Andrews, "Where Do the Jobs Come From?" *New York Times*, 21 September 2004, E1, E11; Maureen Jenkins, "Yours for the Taking," *Boeing Frontiers Online*, June 2004 [accessed 25 September 2005] www.boeing.com; "Firm Predicts Top 10 Workforce/Workplace Trends for 2004," *Enterprise*, 8–14 December 2003, 1–2; Scott Hudson, "Keeping Employees Happy," *Community Banker*, September 2003, 34+; Marvin J. Cetron and Owen Davies, "Trends Now Changing the World: Technology, the Workplace, Management, and Institutions," *Futurist* 35, no. 2 (March/April 2001): 27–42.
2. "Career Planning: Do it Directionally," Leadership Now blog, 27 June 2007 [accessed 7 July 2008] www.leadershipnow.com
3. Alina Tugend, "Putting Yourself Out There on a Shelf to Buy," *New York Times*, 27 March 2009 [accessed 9 August 2009] www.nytimes.com.
4. Vivian Yeo, "India Still Top Choice for Offshoring," *BusinessWeek*, 27 June 2008 [accessed 7 July 2008] www.businessweek.com; Jim Puzzanghera, "Coalition of High-Tech Firms to Urge Officials to Help Keep U.S. Competitive," *San Jose Mercury News*, 8 January 2004 [accessed 14 February 2004] www.ebscohost.com.
5. Amanda Bennett, "GE Redesigns Rungs of Career Ladder," *Wall Street Journal*, 15 March 1993, B1, B3.
6. Robin White Goode, "International and Foreign Language Skills Have an Edge," *Black Enterprise*, May 1995, 53.
7. Nancy M. Somerick, "Managing a Communication Internship Program," *Bulletin of the Association for Business Communication* 56, no. 3 (1993): 10–20.
8. Fellowforce website [accessed 8 August 2009] www.fellowforce.com.
9. Joan Lloyd, "Changing Workplace Requires You to Alter Your Career Outlook," *Milwaukee Journal Sentinel*, 4 July 1999, 1; Camille DeBell, "Ninety Years in the World of Work in America," *Career Development Quarterly* 50, no. 1 (September 2001): 77–88.
10. Jeffrey R. Young, "'E-Portfolios' Could Give Students a New Sense of Their Accomplishments," *The Chronicle of Higher Education*, 8 March 2002, A31.
11. Brian Carcione, e-portfolio [accessed 20 December 2006] http://eportfolio.psu.edu.

CHAPTER 1

1. Six Apart website [accessed 19 June 2009] www.sixapart.com; David Kirkpatrick and Daniel Roth, "Why There's No Escaping the Blog," *Fortune*, 10 January 2005, 44–50; "People of the Year," *PC Magazine*, 12 December 2004 [accessed 21 June 2005] www.pcmag.com; Thomas Mucha, "A Motor City Marketing Lesson," *Business 2.0*, 10 March 2005 [accessed 13 March 2005] www.business2.com; Lee Gomes, "How the Next Big Thing in Technology Morphed into a Really Big Thing," *Wall Street Journal*, 4 October 2004, B1; David Kirkpatrick, "It's Hard to Manage if You Don't Blog," *Fortune*, 4 October 2004, 46.
2. Caroline Kealey, "Web 2.0: The Medium Is the Message, but What's the Result?" *CW Bulletin*, October 2007 [accessed 24 July 2008] www.iabc.com.
3. Julie Connelly, "Youthful Attitudes, Sobering Realities," *New York Times*, 28 October 2003, E1, E6; Nigel Andrews and Laura D'Andrea Tyson, "The Upwardly Global MBA," *Strategy + Business* 36: 60–69; Jim McKay, "Communication Skills Found Lacking," *Pittsburgh Post-Gazette*, 28 February 2005 [accessed 28 February 2005] www.delawareonline.com.
4. Richard L. Daft, *Management*, 6th ed. (Cincinnati: Thomson South-Western, 2003), 580.
5. "Majority of Global Companies Face an Engagement Gap," Internal Comms Hub website, 23 October 2007 [accessed 5 July 2008] www.internalcommshub.com; Gary L. Neilson, Karla L. Martin, and Elizabeth Powers, "The Secrets to Successful Strategy Execution," *Harvard Business Review*, June 2008, 61–70; Nicholas Carr, "Lessons in Corporate Blogging," *BusinessWeek*, 18 July 2006, 9; Susan Meisinger, "To Keep Employees, Talk—and Listen—to Them!" *HR Magazine*, August 2006, 10.
6. Charlotte Huff, "Why Business Can't Write—and What to Do About It," *Workforce Management*, October 2008 [accessed 14 October 2008] www.workforce.com.
7. Daft, *Management*, 147.
8. Gareth R. Jones and Jennifer M. George, *Contemporary Management*, 3rd ed. (New York: McGraw-Hill Irwin, 2003), 512, 517.
9. Philip C. Kolin, *Successful Writing at Work*, 6th ed. (Boston: Houghton Mifflin, 2001), 17–23.
10. Tim Laseter and Rob Cross, "The Craft of Connection," *Strategy + Business*, Autumn 2006, 26–32.
11. "CEOs to Communicators: 'Stick to Common Sense'," Internal Comms Hub website, 23 October 2007 [accessed 11 July 2008] www.internalcommshub.com; "A Writing Competency Model for Business," BizCom101.com, 14 December 2007 [accessed 11 July 2008] www.businesswriting-courses.com; Sue Dewhurst and Liam FitzPatrick, "What Should Be the Competency of Your IC Team?" white paper, 2007 [accessed 11 July 2008] http://competentcommunicators.com.
12. Don Hellriegel, Susan E. Jackson, and John W. Slocum, Jr., *Management: A Competency-Based Approach* (Cincinnati: Thomson South-Western, 2002), 447.
13. Paul Martin Lester, *Visual Communication: Images with Messages* (Belmont, Calif.: Thomson South-Western, 2006), 6–8.
14. Michael R. Solomon, *Consumer Behavior: Buying, Having, and Being*, 6th ed. (Upper Saddle River, N.J.: Pearson Prentice Hall, 2004), 65.
15. Anne Field, "What You Say, What They Hear," *Harvard Management Communication Letter*, Winter 2005, 3–5.
16. Chuck Williams, *Management*, 2nd ed. (Cincinnati: Thomson South-Western, 2002), 690.
17. Charles G. Morris and Albert A. Maisto, *Psychology: An Introduction*, 12th ed. (Upper Saddle River, N.J.: Pearson Prentice Hall, 2005), 226–239; Saundra K. Ciccarelli and Glenn E. Meyer, *Psychology* (Upper Saddle River, N.J.: Prentice Hall, 2006), 210–229; Mark H. Ashcraft, *Cognition*, 4th ed. (Upper Saddle River, N.J.: Prentice Hall, 2006), 44–54.
18. Stephanie Armour, "Music Hath Charms for Some Workers—Others It Really Annoys," *USA Today*, 24 March 2006, B1–B2.
19. Hellriegel et al., *Management: A Competency-Based Approach*, 451.
20. Laura L. Myers and Mary L. Tucker, "Increasing Awareness of Emotional Intelligence in a Business Curriculum," *Business Communication Quarterly*, March 2005, 44–51.

21. John Owens, "Good Communication in Workplace Is Basic to Getting Any Job Done," *Knight Ridder/Tribune Business News*, 9 July 2003, 1.
22. Williams, *Management*, 706–707.
23. Tara Craig, "How to Avoid Information Overload," *Personnel Today*, 10 June 2008, 31; Jeff Davidson, "Fighting Information Overload," *Canadian Manager*, Spring 2005, 16+.
24. Information Overload Research Group website [accessed 19 July 2008] www.iorgforum.org.
25. Sushil K. Sharma and Jatinder N. D. Gupta, "Improving Workers' Productivity and Reducing Internet Abuse," *Journal of Computer Information Systems*, Winter 2003–2004, 74–78.
26. Eric J. Sinrod, "Perspective: It's My Internet—I Can Do What I Want," News.com, 29 March 2006 [accessed 12 August 2006] www.news.com.
27. Eric J. Sinrod, "Time to Crack Down on Tech at Work?" News.com, 14 June 2006 [accessed 12 August 2006] www.news.com.
28. Jack Trout, "Beware of 'Infomania,'" *Forbes*, 11 August 2006 [accessed 5 October 2006] www.forbes.com.
29. Steve Lohr, "As Travel Costs Rise, More Meetings Go Virtual," *New York Times*, 22 July 2008 [accessed 23 July 2008] www.nytimes.com.
30. A. Thomas Young, "Ethics in Business: Business of Ethics," *Vital Speeches*, 15 September 1992, 725–730.
31. Kolin, *Successful Writing at Work*, 24–30.
32. Nancy K. Kubasek, Bartley A. Brennan, and M. Neil Browne, *The Legal Environment of Business*, 3rd ed. (Upper Saddle River, N.J.: Prentice Hall, 2003), 172.
33. Rich Phillips and John Zarrella, "Live Bombs Haunt Orlando Neighborhood," CNN.com, 1 July 2008 [accessed 24 July 2008] www.cnn.com.
34. Daft, *Management*, 155.
35. "Less Than Half of Companies Encourage Discussion of Ethical Issues at the Workplace," press release, International Association of Business Communicators Research Foundation website, 23 May 2006 [accessed 12 August 2006] www.iabc.com.
36. Kent Hoover, "Most Employees See Ethical Misconduct at Work," *Washington Business Journal*, 10 December 2007 [accessed 24 July 2008] www.bizjournals.com.
37. Gap, Inc., "Code of Business Conduct," updated 4 January 2005 [accessed 24 July 2008] www.gapinc.com.
38. Based in part on Robert Kreitner, *Management*, 9th ed. (Boston: Houghton Mifflin, 2004), 163.
39. Henry R. Cheeseman, *Contemporary Business and E-Commerce Law*, 4th ed. (Upper Saddle River, N.J.: Prentice Hall, 2003), 841–843.
40. Cheeseman, *Contemporary Business and E-Commerce Law*, 201.
41. John Jude Moran, *Employment Law: New Challenges in the Business Environment*, 2nd ed. (Upper Saddle River, N.J.: Prentice Hall, 2002), 186–187; Kubasek et al., *The Legal Environment of Business*, 562.
42. Cheeseman, *Contemporary Business and E-Commerce Law*, 325.
43. Kubasek et al., *The Legal Environment of Business*, 306.

CHAPTER 2

1. Evelyn Nussenbaum, "Boosting Teamwork with Wikis," *Fortune Small Business*, 12 February 2008 [accessed 15 August 2008] http://money.cnn.com; Doug Cornelius, "Wikis at the Rosen Law Firm," KM Space blog, 28 February 2008 [accessed 15 August 2008] http://kmspace.blogspot.com; Rosen Law Firm website [accessed 15 August 2008] www.rosen.com.
2. Courtland L. Bovée and John V. Thill, *Business in Action*, 3rd ed. (Upper Saddle River, N.J.: Pearson Prentice Hall, 2005), 175.
3. "Five Case Studies on Successful Teams," *HR Focus*, April 2002, 18+.
4. Stephen R. Robbins, *Essentials of Organizational Behavior*, 6th ed. (Upper Saddle River, N.J.: Prentice Hall, 2000), 98.
5. Max Landsberg and Madeline Pfau, "Developing Diversity: Lessons from Top Teams," *Strategy + Business*, Winter 2005, 10–12.
6. "Groups Best at Complex Problems," *Industrial Engineer*, June 2006, 14.
7. Lynda McDermott, Bill Waite, and Nolan Brawley, "Executive Teamwork," *Executive Excellence*, May 1999, 15.
8. Nicola A. Nelson, "Leading Teams," *Defense AT&L*, July-August 2006, 26–29; Larry Cole and Michael Cole, "Why Is the Teamwork Buzz Word Not Working?" *Communication World*, February-March 1999, 29; Patricia Buhler, "Managing in the 90s: Creating Flexibility in Today's Workplace," *Supervision*, January 1997, 241; Allison W. Amason, Allen C. Hochwarter, Wayne A. Thompson, and Kenneth R. Harrison, "Conflict: An Important Dimension in Successful Management Teams," *Organizational Dynamics*, Autumn 1995, 201.
9. Richard L. Daft, *Management*, 6th ed. (Cincinnati: Thomson South-Western, 2003), 614.
10. Geoffrey Colvin, "Why Dream Teams Fail," *Fortune*, 12 June 2006, 87–92.
11. Vijay Govindarajan and Anil K. Gupta, "Building an Effective Global Business Team," *MIT Sloan Management Review*, Summer 2001, 631.
12. Louise Rehling, "Improving Teamwork Through Awareness of Conversational Styles," *Business Communication Quarterly*, December 2004, 475–482.
13. Jon Hanke, "Presenting as a Team," *Presentations*, January 1998, 74–82.
14. William P. Galle, Jr., Beverly H. Nelson, Donna W. Luse, and Maurice F. Villere, *Business Communication: A Technology-Based Approach* (Chicago: Irwin, 1996), 260.
15. Mary Beth Debs, "Recent Research on Collaborative Writing in Industry," *Technical Communication*, November 1991, 476–484.
16. "TWiki Success Stories," TWiki website [accessed 18 August 2006] www.twiki.org.
17. Mark Choate, "What Makes an Enterprise Wiki?" CMS Watch website, 28 April 2006 [accessed 18 August 2006] www.cmswatch.com.
18. Choate, "What Makes an Enterprise Wiki?"
19. Tony Kontzer, "Learning to Share," *InformationWeek*, 5 May 2003, 28; Jon Udell, "Uniting Under Groove," *InfoWorld*, 17 February 2003 [accessed 9 September 2003] www.elibrary.com; Alison Overholt, "Virtually There?" *Fast Company*, 14 February 2002, 108.
20. Colvin, "Why Dream Teams Fail," 87–92.
21. Tiziana Casciaro and Miguel Sousa Lobo, "Competent Jerks, Lovable Fools, and the Formation of Social Networks," *Harvard Business Review*, June 2005, 92–99.
22. Stephen P. Robbins and David A. DeCenzo, *Fundamentals of Management*, 4th ed. (Upper Saddle River, N.J.: Prentice Hall, 2004), 266–267; Jerald Greenberg and Robert A. Baron, *Behavior in Organizations*, 8th ed. (Upper Saddle River, N.J.: Prentice Hall, 2003), 279–280.
23. "Team Building: Managing the Norms of Informal Groups in the Workplace," Accel-Team website [accessed 16 August 2006] www.accel-team.com.
24. B. Aubrey Fisher, *Small Group Decision Making: Communication and the Group Process*, 2nd ed. (New York: McGraw-Hill, 1980), 145–149; Robbins and De Cenzo, *Fundamentals of Management*, 334–335; Daft, *Management*, 602–603.
25. Michael Laff, "Effective Team Building: More Than Just Fun at Work," *Training + Development*, August 2006, 24–35.
26. Claire Sookman, "Building Your Virtual Team," *Network World*, 21 June 2004, 91.
27. Jared Sandberg, "Brainstorming Works Best if People Scramble for Ideas on Their Own," *Wall Street Journal*, 13 June 2006, B1.
28. Mark K. Smith, "Bruce W. Tuckman—Forming, Storming, Norming, and Performing in Groups," Infed.org [accessed 5 July 2005] www.infed.org.
29. Robbins and DeCenzo, *Fundamentals of Management*, 258–259.
30. Daft, *Management*, 609–612.
31. Andy Boynton and Bill Fischer, *Virtuoso Teams: Lessons from Teams That Changed Their Worlds* (Harrow, UK: FT Prentice Hall, 2005), 10.

32. Thomas K. Capozzoli, "Conflict Resolution—A Key Ingredient in Successful Teams," *Supervision*, November 1999, 14–16.
33. Jesse S. Nirenberg, *Getting Through to People* (Paramus, N.J.: Prentice Hall, 1973), 134–142.
34. Nirenberg, *Getting Through to People*, 134–142.
35. Nirenberg, *Getting Through to People*, 134–142.
36. Christopher Carfi and Leif Chastaine, "Social Networking for Businesses & Organizations," white paper, Cerado website [accessed 13 August 2008] www.cerado.com.
37. David Pescovitz, "Technology of the Year: Social Network Applications," *Business 2.0*, November 2003, 113–114.
38. "Better Meetings Benefit Everyone: How to Make Yours More Productive," *Working Communicator Bonus Report*, July 1998, 1.
39. Ken Blanchard, "Meetings Can Be Effective," *Supervisory Management*, October 1992, 5.
40. Cyrus Farivar, "How to Run an Effective Meeting," BNET website [accessed 12 August 2008] www.bnet.com.
41. "Better Meetings Benefit Everyone," 1.
42. Steve Lohr, "As Travel Costs Rise, More Meetings Go Virtual," *New York Times*, 22 July 2008 [accessed 23 July 2008] www.nytimes.com.
43. IBM Jam program website [accessed 15 August 2006] www.collaborationjam.com; "Big Blue Brainstorm," *BusinessWeek*, 7 August 2006 [accessed 15 August 2006] www.businessweek.com; Roger O. Crockett, "The 21st Century Meeting," *BusinessWeek*, 26 February 2007, 72–79.
44. Augusta M. Simon, "Effective Listening: Barriers to Listening in a Diverse Business Environment," *Bulletin of the Association for Business Communication* 54, no. 3 (September 1991): 73–74.
45. Judi Brownell, *Listening*, 2nd ed. (Boston: Allyn & Bacon, 2002), 9, 10.
46. Anne Fisher, "The Trouble with MBAs," *Fortune International*, 30 April 2007, 33–34.
47. Robyn D. Clarke, "Do You Hear What I Hear?" *Black Enterprise*, May 1998, 129.
48. Dennis M. Kratz and Abby Robinson Kratz, *Effective Listening Skills* (New York: McGraw-Hill, 1995), 45–53; J. Michael Sproule, *Communication Today* (Glenview, Ill.: Scott Foresman, 1981), 69.
49. Brownell, *Listening*, 230–231.
50. Kratz and Kratz, *Effective Listening Skills*, 78–79.
51. Bill Brooks, "The Power of Active Listening," *American Salesman*, June 2003, 12; "Active Listening," Study Guides and Strategies website [accessed 5 February 2005] www.studygs.net.
52. Bob Lamons, "Good Listeners Are Better Communicators," *Marketing News*, 11 September 1995, 13+; Phillip Morgan and H. Kent Baker, "Building a Professional Image: Improving Listening Behavior," *Supervisory Management*, November 1985, 35–36.
53. Clarke, "Do You Hear What I Hear?"; Dot Yandle, "Listening to Understand," *Pryor Report Management Newsletter Supplement* 15, no. 8 (August 1998): 13.
54. Brownell, *Listening*, 14; Kratz and Kratz, *Effective Listening Skills*, 8–9; Sherwyn P. Morreale and Courtland L. Bovée, *Excellence in Public Speaking* (Orlando, Fla.: Harcourt Brace, 1998), 72–76; Lyman K. Steil, Larry L. Barker, and Kittie W. Watson, *Effective Listening: Key to Your Success* (Reading, Mass.: Addison Wesley, 1983), 21–22.
55. Patrick J. Collins, *Say It with Power and Confidence* (Upper Saddle River, N.J.: Prentice Hall, 1997), 40–45.
56. Morreale and Bovée, *Excellence in Public Speaking*, 296.
57. Judee K. Burgoon, David B. Butler, and W. Gill Woodall, *Nonverbal Communication: The Unspoken Dialog* (New York: McGraw-Hill, 1996), 137.
58. Dale G. Leathers, *Successful Nonverbal Communication: Principles and Applications* (New York: Macmillan, 1986), 19.
59. Gerald H. Graham, Jeanne Unrue, and Paul Jennings, "The Impact of Nonverbal Communication in Organizations: A Survey of Perceptions," *Journal of Business Communication* 28, no. 1 (Winter 1991): 45–62.
60. Virginia P. Richmond and James C. McCroskey, *Nonverbal Behavior in Interpersonal Relations* (Boston: Allyn & Bacon, 2000), 153–157.
61. Richmond and McCroskey, *Nonverbal Behavior in Interpersonal Relations*, 2–3.
62. John Hollon, "No Tolerance for Jerks," *Workforce Management*, 12 February 2007, 34.
63. Marilyn Pincus, *Everyday Business Etiquette* (Bloomington, Ind.: Authorhouse, 2003), 136.
64. Dana May Casperson, *Power Etiquette: What You Don't Know Can Kill Your Career* (New York: Amacom, 1999), 23.
65. Maggie Jackson, "Turn Off That Cellphone. It's Meeting Time," *New York Times*, 2 March 2003, sec. 3, 12.
66. Casperson, *Power Etiquette*, 10–14; Ellyn Spragins, "Introducing Politeness," *Fortune Small Business*, November 2001, 30.
67. Tanya Mohn, "The Social Graces as a Business Tool," *New York Times*, 10 November 2002, sec. 3, 12.
68. Casperson, *Power Etiquette*, 44–46.
69. Casperson, *Power Etiquette*, 109–110.
70. Pete Babb, "The Ten Commandments of Blog and Wiki Etiquette," *InfoWorld*, 28 May 2007 [accessed 3 August 2008] www.infoworld.com; Judith Kallos, "Instant Messaging Etiquette," NetM@anners blog [accessed 3 August 2008] www.netmanners.com; Michael S. Hyatt, "E-Mail Etiquette 101," From Where I Sit blog, 1 July 2007 [accessed 3 August 2008] www.michaelhyatt.com.

CHAPTER 3

1. "IBM Innovation Embraces All Races, Cultures and Genders," Diversity Careers website [accessed 16 August 2008] www.diversitycareers.com; Regina Tosca and Rima Matsumoto, "Diversity and Inclusion: A Driving Force for Growth and Innovation at IBM," 2 February 2007, Hispanic Association on Corporate Responsibility website [accessed 12 February 2007] www.hacr.org; IBM website [accessed 16 August 2008] www.ibm.com; "Executive Corner: Letter from IBM's Vice President, Global Workforce Diversity," IBM website [accessed 12 February 2007] www.ibm.com; "IBM—Diversity as a Strategic Imperative," TWI website [accessed 6 July 2005] www.diversityatwork.com; Cliff Edwards, "The Rewards of Tolerance," *BusinessWeek*, 15 December 2003 [accessed 6 July 2005] www.businessweek.com; David A. Thomas, "IBM Finds Profit in Diversity," *HBS Working Knowledge*, 27 September 2004 [accessed 5 July 2005] http://hbswk.hbs.edu; "IBM Diversity Executive to Speak at the University of Virginia," *University of Virginia News*, 7 November 2003 [accessed 5 July 2005] www.virginia.edu.
2. Michael R. Carrell, Everett E. Mann, and Tracey Honeycutt Sigler, "Defining Workforce Diversity Programs and Practices in Organizations: A Longitudinal Study," *Labor Law Journal*, Spring 2006, 5–12.
3. "Top Trading Partners—Total Trade, Exports, Imports June 2008," U.S. Census Bureau website [accessed 16 August 2008] www.census.gov.
4. Nancy R. Lockwood, "Workplace Diversity: Leveraging the Power of Difference for Competitive Advantage," *HR Magazine*, June 2005, special section 1–10.
5. Podcast interview with Ron Glover, IBM website [accessed 17 August 2008] www.ibm.com.
6. "More Than 300 Counties Now 'Majority-Minority,'" press release, U.S. Census Bureau website, 9 August 2007 [accessed 16 August 2008] www.census.gov; Robert Kreitner, *Management*, 9th ed. (Boston: Houghton Mifflin, 2004), 84.
7. Linda Beamer and Iris Varner, *Intercultural Communication in the Workplace*, 2nd ed. (New York: McGraw-Hill Irwin, 2001), xiii.
8. Tracy Novinger, *Intercultural Communication, A Practical Guide* (Austin, Tex.: University of Texas Press, 2001), 15.
9. Larry A. Samovar and Richard E. Porter, "Basic Principles of Intercultural Communication," in *Intercultural Communication: A Reader*, 6th ed., edited by Larry A. Samovar and Richard E. Porter (Belmont, Calif.: Wadsworth, 1991), 12.

10. Beamer and Varner, *Intercultural Communication in the Workplace*, 3.
11. "Languages of the USA," Ethnologue website [accessed 22 August 2006] www.ethnologue.com.
12. Philip R. Harris and Robert T. Moran, *Managing Cultural Differences*, 3rd ed. (Houston: Gulf, 1991), 394–397, 429–430.
13. Lillian H. Chaney and Jeanette S. Martin, *Intercultural Business Communication*, 2nd ed. (Upper Saddle River, N.J.: Prentice Hall, 2000), 6.
14. Beamer and Varner, *Intercultural Communication in the Workplace*, 4.
15. Chaney and Martin, *Intercultural Business Communication*, 2nd ed., 9.
16. Richard L. Daft, *Management*, 6th ed. (Cincinnati: Thomson South-Western, 2003), 455.
17. Lillian H. Chaney and Jeanette S. Martin, *Intercultural Business Communication*, 4th ed. (Upper Saddle River, N.J.: Pearson Prentice Hall, 2007), 53.
18. Project Implicit website [accessed 17 August 2008] http://implicit.harvard.edu/implicit.
19. Linda Beamer, "Teaching English Business Writing to Chinese-Speaking Business Students," *Business Communication Quarterly*, 57, no. 1, (March 1994): 12–18.
20. Edward T. Hall, "Context and Meaning," in *Intercultural Communication*, 6th ed., edited by Larry A. Samovar and Richard E. Porter (Belmont, Calif.: Wadsworth, 1991), 46–55.
21. Daft, *Management*, 459.
22. Charley H. Dodd, *Dynamics of Intercultural Communication*, 3rd ed. (Dubuque, Ia.: Brown, 1991), 69–70.
23. Daft, *Management*, 459.
24. Beamer and Varner, *Intercultural Communication in the Workplace*, 230–233.
25. James Wilfong and Toni Seger, *Taking Your Business Global* (Franklin Lakes, N.J.: Career Press, 1997), 277–278.
26. Guo-Ming Chen and William J. Starosta, *Foundations of Intercultural Communication* (Boston: Allyn & Bacon, 1998), 288–289.
27. Mark Landler and Michael Barbaro, "Wal-Mart Finds That Its Formula Doesn't Fit Every Culture," *New York Times*, 2 August 2006 [accessed 23 August 2006] www.nytimes.com.
28. Mary A. DeVries, *Internationally Yours* (New York: Houghton Mifflin, 1994), 194.
29. Robert O. Joy, "Cultural and Procedural Differences That Influence Business Strategies and Operations in the People's Republic of China," *SAM Advanced Management Journal*, Summer 1989, 29–33.
30. Chaney and Martin, *Intercultural Business Communication*, 2nd ed., 122–123.
31. Mansour Javidan, "Forward-Thinking Cultures," *Harvard Business Review*, July-August 2007, 20.
32. IBM website [accessed 17 August 2008] www.ibm.com; Wendy Harris, "Out of the Corporate Closet," *Black Enterprise*, May 2007, 64–66; David A. Thomas, "Diversity as Strategy," *Harvard Business Review*, September 2004, 98–108; Joe Mullich, "Hiring Without Limits," *Workforce Management*, June 2004, 53–58; Mike France and William G. Symonds, "Diversity Is About to Get More Elusive, Not Less," *BusinessWeek*, 7 July 2003 [accessed 24 January 2005] www.businessweek.com.
33. Novinger, *Intercultural Communication: A Practical Guide*, 54.
34. Peter Coy, "Old. Smart. Productive." *BusinessWeek*, 27 June 2005 [accessed 24 August 2006] www.businessweek.com; Beamer and Varner, *Intercultural Communication in the Workplace*, 107–108.
35. Beamer and Varner, *Intercultural Communication in the Workplace*, 107–108.
36. Nancy Sutton Bell and Marvin Narz, "Meeting the Challenges of Age Diversity in the Workplace," *The CPA Journal*, February 2007 [accessed 17 August 2008] www.nysscpa.org.
37. Tonya Vinas, "A Place at the Table," *IndustryWeek*, 1 July 2003, 22.
38. Daft, *Management*, 445.
39. John Gray, *Mars and Venus in the Workplace* (New York: HarperCollins, 2002), 10, 25–27, 61–63.
40. Chaney and Martin, *Intercultural Business Communication*, 4th ed., 62.
41. Todd Henneman, "A New Approach to Faith at Work," *Workforce Management*, October 2004, 76–77.
42. Mark D. Downey, "Keeping the Faith," *HR Magazine*, January 2008, 85–88.
43. Vadim Liberman, "What Happens When an Employee's Freedom of Religion Crosses Paths with a Company's Interests?" *Conference Board Review*, September/October 2007, 42–48.
44. IBM Accessibility Center [accessed 24 August 2006] www-03.ibm.com/able ; AssistiveTech.net [accessed 24 August 2006] www.assistivetech.net; Business Leadership Network website [accessed 24 August 2006] www.usbln.org; National Institute on Disability and Rehabilitation Research website [accessed 24 August 2006] www.ed.gov/about/offices/list/osers/nidrr; Rehabilitation Engineering & Assistive Technology Society of North America website [accessed 24 August 2006] www.resna.org.
45. Daphne A. Jameson, "Reconceptualizing Cultural Identity and Its Role in Intercultural Business Communication," *Journal of Business Communication*, July 2007, 199–235.
46. Leslie Knudson, "Diversity on a Global Scale," *HR Management* [accessed 17 August 2008] www.hrmreport.com.
47. Craig S. Smith, "Beware of Green Hats in China and Other Cross-Cultural Faux Pas," *The New York Times*, 30 April 2002, C11.
48. Sana Reynolds and Deborah Valentine, *Guide for Internationals: Culture, Communication, and ESL* (Upper Saddle River, N.J.: Pearson Prentice Hall, 2006), 3–11, 14–19, 25.
49. P. Christopher Earley and Elaine Mosakowsi, "Cultural Intelligence," *Harvard Business Review*, October 2004, 139–146.
50. Wendy A. Conklin, "An Inside Look at Two Diversity Intranet Sites: IBM and Merck," *The Diversity Factor*, Summer 2005.
51. Paul Johnson, "Must the Whole World Speak English?" *Forbes*, 29 November 2004, 39; Randolph E. Schmid, "Study Says English Language Is Losing Cultural Dominance," *Desert Sun*, 29 February 2004, A25.
52. Mary Beth Sheridan, "Learning the New Language of Labor," *Washington Post*, 20 August 2002, A1.
53. Phillip M. Perry, "Found in Translation," *Kitchen & Bath Business*, September 2006, 44–46.
54. Bob Nelson, "Motivating Workers Worldwide," *Global Workforce*, November 1998, 25–27.
55. Mona Casady and Lynn Wasson, "Written Communication Skills of International Business Persons," *Business Communication Quarterly*, 57, no. 4, (December 1994): 36–40.
56. Lynn Gaertner-Johnston, "Found in Translation," Business Writing blog, 25 November 2005 [accessed 18 August 2008] www.businesswritingblog.com.
57. "From Plain English to Global English," Quality Web Content website [accessed 24 August 2006] www.webpagecontent.com.
58. Myron W. Lustig and Jolene Koester, *Intercultural Competence*, 4th ed. (Boston: Allyn & Bacon, 2003), 196.
59. Wilfong and Seger, *Taking Your Business Global*, 232.
60. Mark Lasswell, "Lost in Translation," *Business 2.0*, August 2004, 68–70.
61. Sheridan Prasso, ed., "It's All Greek to These Sites," *BusinessWeek*, 22 July 2002, 18.

CHAPTER 4

1. Shel Israel, "Twitterville Notebook: HR Block's Paula Drum," Global Neighbourhoods blog, 22 December 2008 [accessed 25 January 2009] http://redcouch.typepad.com/weblog; "H&R Block's Paula Drum Talks Up Value of Online 'Presence,'" The Deal website, video interview, 6 June 2008 [accessed 28 August 2008] www.thedeal.com; Shel Israel, "SAP Global Survey: H&R Block's Paula Drum," Global Neighbourhoods blog, 4 April 2008 [accessed 28 August 2008] http://redcouch.typepad.com/weblog;

"Tango in Plain English," video [accessed 27 August 2008] www.youtube.com; "H&R Block, Inc.," Hoovers [accessed 27 August 2008] www.hoovers.com; Linda Zimmer, "H&R Blocks Tangoes into Second Life," Business Communicators of Second Life blog, 17 March 2007 [accessed 27 August 2008] http://freshtakes.typepad.com/sl_communicators; H&R Block website [accessed 25 January 2009] www.hrblock.com; "H&R Block Launches First Virtual Tax Experience in Second Life," press release [accessed 27 August 2008] www.hrblock.com.

2. Laurey Berk and Phillip G. Clampitt, "Finding the Right Path in the Communication Maze," *IABC Communication World*, October 1991, 28–32.
3. Linda Duyle, "Get Out of Your Office," *HR Magazine*, July 2006, 99–101.
4. Caroline McCarthy, "The Future of Web Apps Will See the Death of E-Mail," Webware blog, 29 February 2008 [accessed 25 August 2008] http://news.cnet.com; Kris Maher, "The Jungle," *Wall Street Journal*, 5 October 2004, B10; Kevin Maney, "Surge in Text Messaging Makes Cell Operators :-)," *USA Today*, 28 July 2005, B1–B2.
5. David Kirkpatrick, "It's Hard to Manage if You Don't Blog," *Fortune*, 4 October 2004, 46; Lee Gomes, "How the Next Big Thing in Technology Morphed into a Really Big Thing," *Wall Street Journal*, 4 October 2004, B1; Jeff Meisner, "Cutting Through the Blah, Blah, Blah," *Puget Sound Business Journal*, 19–25 November 2004, 27–28; Lauren Gard, "The Business of Blogging," *BusinessWeek*, 13 December 2004, 117–119; Heather Green, "Online Video: The Sequel," *BusinessWeek*, 10 January 2005, 40; Michelle Conlin and Andrew Park, "Blogging with the Boss's Blessing," *BusinessWeek*, 28 June 2004, 100–102.
6. Berk and Clampitt, "Finding the Right Path in the Communication Maze."
7. Samantha R. Murray and Joseph Peyrefitte, "Knowledge Type and Communication Media Choice in the Knowledge Transfer Process," *Journal of Managerial Issues*, Spring 2007, 111–133.
8. Raymond M. Olderman, *10 Minute Guide to Business Communication* (New York: Alpha Books, 1997), 19–20.
9. Mohan R. Limaye and David A. Victor, "Cross-Cultural Business Communication Research: State of the Art and Hypotheses for the 1990s," *Journal of Business Communication* 28, no. 3 (Summer 1991): 277–299.
10. Mind Mapping Software Weblog [accessed 1 February 2008] http://mindmapping.typepad.com; bubbl.us website [accessed 1 February 2008] http://bubbl.us.
11. Holly Weeks, "The Best Memo You'll Ever Write," *Harvard Management Communication Letter*, Spring 2005, 3–5.

CHAPTER 5

1. "An Interview with Joi Ito, CEO of Creative Commons," audio interview [accessed 6 September 2008] www.businessweek.com; Kenji Hall, "Online Sharing with Creative Commons," *BusinessWeek*, 15 August 2008 [accessed 6 September 2008] www.businessweek.com; Creative Commons website [accessed 6 September 2008] www.creativecommons.org; Ariana Eunjung Cha, "Creative Commons Is Rewriting Rules of Copyright," *The Washington Post*, 15 March 2005 [accessed 3 August 2005] www.washingtonpost.com; Steven Levy, "Lawrence Lessig's Supreme Showdown," *Wired*, October 2002 [accessed 3 August 2005] www.wired.com; "Happy Birthday: We'll Sue," Snopes.com [accessed 3 August 2005] www.snopes.com.
2. Annette N. Shelby and N. Lamar Reinsch, Jr., "Positive Emphasis and You Attitude: An Empirical Study," *Journal of Business Communication* 32, no. 4 (1995): 303–322.
3. Sherryl Kleinman, "Why Sexist Language Matters," *Qualitative Sociology* 25, no. 2 (Summer 2002): 299–304.
4. Judy E. Pickens, "Terms of Equality: A Guide to Bias-Free Language," *Personnel Journal*, August 1985, 24.
5. Lisa Taylor, "Communicating About People with Disabilities: Does the Language We Use Make a Difference?" *Bulletin of the Association for Business Communication* 53, no. 3 (September 1990): 65–67.
6. Susan Benjamin, *Words at Work* (Reading, Mass.: Addison-Wesley, 1997), 136–137.
7. Stuart Crainer and Des Dearlove, "Making Yourself Understood," *Across the Board*, May/June 2004, 23–27.
8. Plain English Campaign website [accessed 3 October 2003] www.plainenglish.co.uk.
9. Plain Language website [accessed 3 September 2008] www.plainlanguage.gov.
10. Creative Commons website [accessed 2 September 2008] www.creativecommons.org.
11. Susan Jaderstrom and Joanne Miller, "Active Writing," *Office Pro*, November/December 2003, 29.
12. Portions of this section are adapted from Courtland L. Bovée, *Techniques of Writing Business Letters, Memos, and Reports* (Sherman Oaks, Calif.: Banner Books International, 1978), 13–90.
13. Catherine Quinn, "Lose the Office Jargon; It May Sunset Your Career," *The Age* (Australia), 1 September 2007 [accessed 5 February 2008] www.theage.com.au.
14. Visuwords website [accessed 5 February 2008] www.visuwords.com.
15. David A. Fryxell, "Lost in Transition?" *Writers Digest*, January 2005, 24–26.
16. Food Allergy Initiative website [accessed 5 September 2008] www.foodallergyinitiative.org; Diana Keough, "Snacks That Can Kill; Schools Take Steps to Protect Kids Who Have Severe Allergies to Nuts," *Plain Dealer*, 15 July 2003, E1; "Dawdling over Food Labels," *The New York Times*, 2 June 2003, A16; Sheila McNulty, "A Matter of Life and Death," *Financial Times*, 10 September 2003, 14.
17. Apple iTunes website [accessed 23 September 2006] www.apple.com/itunes.

CHAPTER 6

1. Mercedes-AMG website [accessed 7 September 2008] www.mercedes-amg.com; Razorfish website [accessed 25 September 2006] www.razorfish.com; "Mercedes-AMG Website Wins Webby Award," 12 June 2006, eMercedesBenz website [accessed 25 September 2006] www.emercedesbenz.com.
2. Deborah Gunn, "Looking Good on Paper," *Office Pro*, March 2004, 10–11.
3. Jacci Howard Bear, "Desktop Publishing Rules of Page Layout," About.com [accessed 22 August 2005] www.about.com.
4. Jacci Howard Bear, "Desktop Publishing Rules for How Many Fonts to Use," About.com [accessed 22 August 2005] www.about.com.
5. The writing samples in this exercise were adapted from material on the Mercedes-AMG website [accessed 2 October 2006 and 9 September 2008] www.mercedes-amg.com.
6. The writing sample in this exercise was adapted from material on the Marsh Risk Consulting website [accessed 2 October 2006] www.marshriskconsulting.com.

CHAPTER 7

1. "Welcome to the 'New and Improved' Nuts About Southwest—A User's Guide," Nuts About Southwest blog [accessed 19 July 2009] www.blogsouthwest.com; Bill Owens, "Why Can't I Make Reservations Further in Advance?" Nuts About Southwest blog, 24 January 2007 [accessed 15 May 2007] www.blogsouthwest.com; Bill Owens, "I Blogged. You Flamed. We Changed." Nuts About Southwest blog, 18 April 2007 [accessed 10 May 2007] www.blogsouthwest.com; "Southwest Airlines Is Nuts About Blogging," Southwest Airlines press release, 27 April 2007 [accessed 15 May 2007] www.prnewswire.com.
2. Specialized Bicycle Components website [accessed 14 September 2008] www.specialized.com; Specialized Riders Club website [accessed 14 September 2008] www.specializedriders.com; Steven Outing, "Enabling the Social Company," white paper, September 2007 [accessed 14 September 2008] www.enthusiastgroup.com.
3. Kate Maddox, "Warrillow Finds 39% of Small-Business Owners Use Text Messaging," BtoB, 1 August 2008 [accessed 15 September 2008]

www.btobonline.com; Dave Carpenter, "Companies Discover Marketing Power of Text Messaging," *Seattle Times*, 25 September 2006 [accessed 25 September 2006] www.seattletimes.com.

4. Catherine Toole, "My 7 Deadly Sins of Writing for Social Media—Am I Right?" Econsultancy blog, 19 June 2007 [accessed 16 September 2008] www.econsultancy.com; Muhammad Saleem, "How to Write a Social Media Press Release," Copyblogger [accessed 16 September 2008] www.copyblogger.com; Melanie McBride, "5 Tips for (Better) Social Media Writing," Melanie McBride Online, 11 June 2008 [accessed 16 September 2008] http://melaniemcbride.net.
5. Hilary Potkewitz and Rachel Brown, "Spread of E-Mail Has Altered Communication Habits at Work," *Los Angeles Business Journal*, 18 April 2005 [accessed 30 April 2006] www.findarticles.com; Nancy Flynn, *Instant Messaging Rules* (New York: AMACOM, 2004), 47–54.
6. Dana Mattioli, "Leaks Grow in World of Blogs," *Wall Street Journal*, 20 July 2009 [accessed 20 July 2009] http://online.wsj.com.
7. "Employee Communication Is Cause for Concern," Duane Morris LLP website, 23 August 2006 [accessed 4 October 2006] www.duanemorris.com.
8. Greg Burns, "For Some, Benefits of E-Mail Not Worth Risk," *San Diego Union-Tribune*, 16 August 2005, A1, A8; Pui-Wing Tam, Erin White, Nick Wingfield, and Kris Maher, "Snooping E-Mail by Software Is Now a Workplace Norm," *Wall Street Journal*, 9 March 2005, B1+.
9. Matt Cain, "Managing E-Mail Hygiene," ZD Net Tech Update, 5 February 2004 [accessed 19 March 2004] www.techupdate.zdnet.com.
10. Lizette Alvarez, "Got 2 Extra Hours for Your E-Mail?" *New York Times*, 10 November 2005 [accessed 10 November 2005] www.nytimes.com.
11. Jack Trout, "Beware of 'Infomania,'" *Forbes*, 11 August 2006 [accessed 5 October 2006] www.forbes.com.
12. Reid Goldsborough, "'Creeping Informality' Can Be Big Mistake in Business E-Mails," *New Orleans City Business*, 14 March 2005, 18; Jack E. Appleman, "Bad Writing Can Cost Insurers Time & Money," *National Underwriter*, 27 September 2004, 34; Adina Genn, "RE: This Is an Important Message, Really," *Long Island Business News*, 5–11 December 2003, 21A; Lynn Lofton, "Regardless of What You Thought, Grammar Rules *Do* Apply to E-Mail," *Mississippi Business Journal*, 23–29 May 2005, 1.
13. Mary Munter, Priscilla S. Rogers, and Jone Rymer, "Business E-Mail: Guidelines for Users," *Business Communication Quarterly*, March 2003, 26+; Renee B. Horowitz and Marian G. Barchilon, "Stylistic Guidelines for E-Mail," *IEEE Transactions on Professional Communication* 37, no. 4 (December 1994): 207–212.
14. Reid Goldborough, "More Trends for 2009: What to Expect with Personal Technology," *Public Relations Tactics*, February 2009, 9.
15. Douglas MacMillan, "The End of Instant Messaging (As We Know It)," *BusinessWeek*, 16 November 2008 [accessed 16 December 2008] www.businessweek.com.
16. Vayusphere website [accessed 22 January 2006] www.vayusphere.com; Christa C. Ayer, "Presence Awareness: Instant Messaging's Killer App," *Mobile Business Advisor*, 1 July 2004 [accessed 22 January 2006] www.highbeam.com; Jefferson Graham, "Instant Messaging Programs Are No Longer Just for Messages," *USA Today*, 20 October 2003, 5D; Todd R. Weiss, "Microsoft Targets Corporate Instant Messaging Customers," *Computerworld*, 18 November 2002, 12; "Banks Adopt Instant Messaging to Create a Global Business Network," *Computer Weekly*, 25 April 2002, 40; Michael D. Osterman, "Instant Messaging in the Enterprise," *Business Communications Review*, January 2003, 59–62; John Pallato, "Instant Messaging Unites Work Groups and Inspires Collaboration," *Internet World*, December 2002, 14+.
17. Paul Mah, "Using Text Messaging in Business," Mobile Enterprise blog, 4 February 2008 [accessed 16 September 2008] http://blogs.techrepublic.com.com/wireless; Paul Kedrosky, "Why We Don't Get the (Text) Message," *Business 2.0*, 2 October 2006 [accessed 4 October 2006] www.business2.com; Carpenter, "Companies Discover Marketing Power of Text Messaging."
18. Mark Gibbs, "Racing to Instant Messaging," *NetworkWorld*, 17 February 2003, 74.
19. "E-Mail Is So Five Minutes Ago," *BusinessWeek*, 28 November 2005 [accessed 31 July 2009] www.businessweek.com.
20. "SANS Top-20 2007 Security Risks," SANS Institute [accessed 16 September 2008] www.sans.org; Tom Espiner, "Spim, Splog on the Rise," CNET News, 6 July 2006 [accessed 16 September 2008] http://news.cnet.com; Anita Hamilton, "You've Got Spim!" *Time*, 2 February 2004 [accessed 1 March 2004] www.time.com; Elizabeth Millard, "Instant Messaging Threats Still Rising," Newsfactor.com, 6 July 2005 [accessed 5 October 2006] www.newsfactor.com.
21. Clint Boulton, "IDC: IM Use Is Booming in Business," InstantMessagingPlanet.com, 5 October 2005 [accessed 22 January 2006] www.instantmessagingplanet.com; Jenny Goodbody, "Critical Success Factors for Global Virtual Teams," *Strategic Communication Management*, February/March 2005, 18–21; Ann Majchrzak, Arvind Malhotra, Jeffrey Stamps, and Jessica Lipnack, "Can Absence Make a Team Grow Stronger?" *Harvard Business Review*, May 2004, 131–137; Christine Y. Chen, "The IM Invasion," *Fortune*, 26 May 2003, 135–138; Yudhijit Bhattacharjee, "A Swarm of Little Notes," *Time*, September 2002, A3–A8; Mark Bruno, "Taming the Wild Frontiers of Instant Messaging," *Bank Technology News*, December 2002, 30–31; Richard Grigonis, "Enterprise-Strength Instant Messaging," Convergence.com, 10–15 [accessed March 2003] www.convergence.com.
22. Pallato, "Instant Messaging Unites Work Groups and Inspires Collaboration," 14+.
23. Dr. Laundry blog [accessed 15 September 2008] www.drlaundryblog.com.
24. GM FastLane blog [accessed 15 September 2008] http://fastlane.gmblogs.com.
25. Fredrik Wackå, "Six Types of Blogs—A Classification," CorporateBlogging, 10 August 10 2004 [accessed 5 October 2006] www.corporateblogging.info; Stephen Baker, "The Inside Story on Company Blogs," *BusinessWeek*, 14 February 2006 [accessed 15 February 2006] www.businessweek.com; Jeremy Wright, *Blog Marketing* (New York: McGraw-Hill, 2006), 45–56; Paul Chaney, "Blogs: Beyond the Hype!" 26 May 2005 [accessed 4 May 2006] http://radiantmarketinggroup.com.
26. Evolve24 website [accessed 18 July 2009] www.evolve24.com.
27. Ann Smarty, "16 Examples of Huge Brands Using Twitter for Business," *Search Engine Journal*, 7 October 2008 [accessed 16 October 2008] www.searchenginejournal.com; Heather Green, "Creative Business Uses of Twitter," *BusinessWeek*, 30 April 2006 [accessed 15 September 2008] www.businessweek.com.
28. Adam C. Haver, personal communication, 25 November 2008.
29. Stephen Baker and Heather Green, "Blogs Will Change Your Business," *BusinessWeek*, 2 May 2005, 57–67.
30. Julie Moran Alterio, "Podcasts a Hit Inside and Outside IBM," *The Journal News* (White Plains, NY), 9 January 2006 [accessed 5 May 2006] www.thejournalnews.com.
31. "Turn Your Feed into a Podcast," Lifehacker blog, 12 January 2006 [accessed 6 May 2006] www.lifehacker.com.
32. "Set Up Your Podcast for Success," FeedForAll website [accessed 4 October 2006] www.feedforall.com.
33. Shel Holtz, "Ten Guidelines for B2B Podcasts," WebProNews, 12 October 2005 [accessed 9 March 2006] www.webpronews.com.
34. Todd Cochrane, *Podcasting: The Do-It-Yourself Guide* (Indianapolis, Ind.: Wiley, 2005), 107–109.
35. Michael W. Goeghegan and Dan Klass, *Podcast Solutions: The Complete Guide to Podcasting* (Berkeley, Calif.: Friends of Ed, 2005), 57–86; Cochrane, *Podcasting: The Do-It-Yourself Guide*, 87–136.
36. "Syndication Format," Answers.com [accessed 5 October 2006] www.answers.com.
37. FeedBurner website [accessed 15 September 2008] www.feedburner.com.
38. Adapted from Comic-Con website [accessed 16 January 2007] www.comic-con.org; Tom Spurgeon, "Welcome to Nerd Vegas: A

Guide to Visiting and Enjoying Comic-Con International in San Diego, 2006!" The Comics Reporter, 11 July 2006 [accessed 16 January 2007] www.comicsreporter.com; Rebecca Winters Keegan, "Boys Who Like Toys," *Time*, 19 April 2007 [accessed 15 May 2007] www.time.com.

39. Adapted from Tom Lowry, "ESPN.COM: Guys and Dollars," *BusinessWeek*, 17 October 2005 [accessed 16 January 2007] www.businessweek.com.
40. Adapted from Lisa Marsh, "Why Fashion Loves Skinny," MSN Lifestyle [accessed 17 September 2008] http://lifestyle.msn.com.
41. Adapted from Seymour Powell website [accessed 16 January 2007] www.seymourpowell.com; Sam Roberts, "51% of Women Now Living Without a Spouse," *New York Times*, 16 January 2007 [accessed 16 January 2007] www.nytimes.com.
42. Adapted from Bruce Einhorn and Ben Elgin, "Helping Big Brother Go High Tech," *BusinessWeek*, 18 September 2006, 47–52.
43. Adapted from Crutchfield website [accessed 17 January 2007] www.crutchfield.com.
44. Adapted from *Logan* website [accessed 18 July 2009] www.loganmagazine.com.
45. Adapted from "Major New Study Shatters Stereotypes About Teens and Video Games," MacArthur Foundation, 16 September 2008 [accessed 18 September 2008] www.macfound.org.
46. Adapted from "Side Impact Protection Explained," Britax website [accessed 18 September 2008] www.britaxusa.com.
47. JetBlue Twitter website [accessed 18 September 2008] http://twitter.com/JetBlue; "JetBlue Lands on eBay," JetBlue website [accessed 18 September 2008] http://jetblue.com/ebay.

CHAPTER 8

1. Get Satisfaction website [accessed 20 July 2009] http://getsatisfaction.com; Matt Marshall, "Get Satisfaction Gets New CEO and Funding Amid Growth," VentureBeat, 17 February 2009 [accessed 20 July 2009], http://venturebeat.com; Dan Fost, "On the Internet, Everyone Can Hear You Complain," *New York Times*, 25 February 2008 [accessed 2 October 2008] www.nytimes.com.
2. Fraser P. Seitel, *The Practice of Public Relations*, 9th ed. (Upper Saddle River, N.J.: Prentice Hall, 2004), 402–411; *Techniques for Communicators* (Chicago: Lawrence Ragan Communication, 1995), 34, 36.
3. David Meerman Scott, *The New Rules of Marketing and PR* (Hoboken, N.J.: Wiley, 2007), 62.
4. Mary Mitchell, "The Circle of Life—Condolence Letters," LiveandLearn.com [accessed 18 July 2005] www.liveandlearn.com; Donna Larcen, "Authors Share the Words of Condolence," *Los Angeles Times*, 20 December 1991, E11.
5. See Note 1; some exercise questions adapted from content on the Get Satisfaction website.
6. Adapted from Tom Abate, "Need to Preserve Cash Generates Wave of Layoffs in Biotech Industry," *San Francisco Chronicle*, 10 February 2003 [accessed 18 July 2005] www.sfgate.com.
7. Adapted from Lisa DiCarlo, "IBM Gets the Message—Instantly," *Forbes*, 7 July 2002 [accessed 22 July 2003] www.forbes.com; "IBM Introduces Breakthrough Messaging Technology for Customers and Business Partners," *M2 Presswire*, 19 February 2003 [accessed 24 July 2003] www.proquest.com; "IBM and America Online Team for Instant Messaging Pilot," *M2 Presswire*, 4 February 2003 [accessed 24 July 2003] www.proquest.com.
8. Adapted from CES website [accessed 18 July 2005] www.cesweb.org.
9. Adapted from Floorgraphics website [accessed 25 October 2006] www.floorgraphics.com; John Grossman, "It's an Ad, Ad, Ad, Ad World," *Inc.*, March 2000, 23–26; David Wellman, "Floor 'Toons," *Supermarket Business*, 15 November 1999, 47; "Floorshow," *Dallas Morning News*, 4 September 1998, 11D.
10. Adapted from Jamba Juice website [accessed 26 October 2006] http://www.jambajuice.com/#/jobs_careers/; Brenda Paik Sunoo, "Blending a Successful Workforce," *Workforce*, March 2000, 44–48; Michael Adams, "Kirk Perron: Jamba Juice," *Restaurant Business*, 15 March 1999, 38; "Live in a Blender," *Restaurant Business*, 1 December 2000, 48–50; David Goll, "Jamba Juices Up 24-Hour Fitness Clubs," *East Bay Business Times*, 30 June 2000, 6.
11. Adapted from Burt Helm, "Wal-Mart, Please Don't Leave Me," *BusinessWeek*, 9 October 2006, 84–89.
12. "Entrepreneurs Across America," *Entrepreneur Magazine* [accessed 12 June 1997] www.entrepreneur.com.
13. Adapted from SitePoint website [accessed 12 May 2006] www.sitepoint.com; Dylan Tweney, "The Defogger: Slim Down That Homepage," *Business 2.0*, 13 July 2001 [accessed 1 August 2001] www.business2.com.
14. Adapted from SolarCity website [accessed 2 October 2008] www.solarcity.com.
15. Adapted from Public Relations Society of America website [accessed 18 June 2005] www.prsa.org.
16. Adapted from Keith H. Hammonds, "Difference Is Power," *Fast Company*, 36, 258 [accessed 11 July 2000] www.fastcompany.com.
17. Adapted from Jeff Nachtigal, "It's Easy and Cheap Being Green," *Fortune*, 16 October 2006, 53; Adobe Wins Platinum Certification Awarded by U.S. Green Building Council," press release, 3 July 2006 [accessed 15 October 2006] www.adobe.com.

CHAPTER 9

1. Jessica Marquez, "Breaking the Bad News on 401(k)s," *Workforce Management*, 22 June 2009, 30–32; Leviton website [accessed 21 July 2009] www.leviton.com; Jessica Marquez, "A Bad Economy Doesn't Dampen Auto Increase in 401(k) Plans," *Workforce Management*, February 2009 [accessed 21 July 2009] www.workforce.com; "Leviton Recognized for Caliber of Employee Wellness by Leading Healthcare Services Company," Lighting Controls Association website [accessed 21 July 2009] www.aboutlightingcontrols.org.
2. Katie Grasso, "Deliver Bad News to Workers Face-to-Face, with Empathy," *Courier-Post* (Camden, N.J.), 8 February 2006 [accessed 14 May 2006] www.courierpostonline.com.
3. Letter from Sheila Zuckerman, Countrywide Office of the President, 6 September 2008.
4. Carol David and Margaret Ann Baker, "Rereading Bad News: Compliance-Gaining Features in Management Memos," *Journal of Business Communication*, October 1994 [accessed 1 December 2003] www.elibrary.com.
5. Ian McDonald, "Marsh Can Do $600 Million, but Apologize?" *Wall Street Journal*, 14 January 2005, C1, C3; Adrienne Carter and Amy Borrus, "What if Companies Fessed Up?" *BusinessWeek*, 24 January 2005, 59–60; Patrick J. Kiger, "The Art of the Apology," *Workforce Management*, October 2004, 57–62.
6. Golnar Motevalli, "Reputational Risk: Is It time for Bankers to Risk an Apology?" *Insurance Journal*, 20 October 2008 [accessed 30 January 2009] www.insurancejournal.com; Del Jones, "Why 'Sorry' Isn't in Many CEOs' Vocabularies Anymore," *USA Today*, 21 October 2008 [accessed 29 October 2008] www.usatoday.com.
7. Ameeta Patel and Lamar Reinsch, "Companies Can Apologize: Corporate Apologies and Legal Liability," *Business Communication Quarterly*, March 2003 [accessed 1 December 2003] www.elibrary.com.
8. John Guiniven, "Sorry! An Apology as a Strategic PR Tool," *Public Relations Tactics*, December 2007, 6.
9. Iris I. Varner, "A Comparison of American and French Business Correspondence," *Journal of Business Communication* 24, no. 4 (Fall 1988): 55–65.
10. Susan Jenkins and John Hinds, "Business Letter Writing: English, French, and Japanese," *TESOL Quarterly* 21, no. 2 (June 1987): 327–349; Saburo Haneda and Hiosuke Shima, "Japanese Communication Behavior as Reflected in Letter Writing," *Journal of Business Communication* 19, no. 1 (1982): 19–32.
11. James Calvert Scott and Diana J. Green, "British Perspectives on Organizing Bad-News Letters: Organizational Patterns Used by Major U.K. Companies," *Bulletin of the Association for Business Communication* 55, no. 1 (March 1992): 17–19.
12. Dana Mattioli, "Leaks Grow in World of Blogs," *Wall Street Journal*, 20 July 2009 [accessed 20 July 2009] http://online.wsj.com.

13. "Advice from the Pros on the Best Way to Deliver Bad News," *Report on Customer Relationship Management*, 1 February 2003 [accessed 1 December 2003] www.elibrary.com.
14. Ben Levisohn, "Getting More Workers to Whistle," *BusinessWeek*, 28 January 2008, 18.
15. "Less Than Half of Privately Held Businesses Support Whistleblowing," Grant Thornton website [accessed 13 October 2008] www.internationalbusinessreport.com.
16. Courtland L. Bovée, John V. Thill, George P. Dovel, and Marian Burk Wood, *Advertising Excellence* (New York: McGraw-Hill, 1995), 508–509; John Holusha, "Exxon's Public-Relations Problem," *New York Times*, 12 April 1989, D1.
17. "Throw Out the Old Handbook in Favor of Today's Crisis Drills," *PR News*, 27 January 2003, 1.
18. Thomas S. Brice and Marie Waung, "Applicant Rejection Letters: Are Businesses Sending the Wrong Message?" *Business Horizons*, March-April 1995, 59–62.
19. Gwendolyn N. Smith, Rebecca F. Nolan, and Yong Dai, "Job-Refusal Letters: Readers' Affective Responses to Direct and Indirect Organizational Plans," *Business Communication Quarterly* 59, no. 1 (1996): 67–73; Brice and Waung, "Applicant Rejection Letters."
20. Judi Brownell, "The Performance Appraisal Interviews: A Multipurpose Communication Assignment," *Bulletin of the Association for Business Communication* 57, no. 2 (1994): 11–21.
21. Gary Dessler, *A Framework for Human Resource Management*, 3rd ed. (Upper Saddle River, N.J.: Pearson Prentice Hall, 2004), 198.
22. Patricia A. McLagan, "Advice for Bad-News Bearers: How to Tell Employees They're Not Hacking It and Get Results," *IndustryWeek*, 15 February 1993, 42; Michael Lee Smith, "Give Feedback, Not Criticism," *Supervisory Management*, 1993, 4; "A Checklist for Conducting Problem Performer Appraisals," *Supervisory Management*, December 1993, 7–9.
23. Carrie Brodzinski, "Avoiding Wrongful Termination Suits," *National Underwriter Property & Casualty—Risk & Benefits Management*, 13 October 2003 [accessed 2 December 2003] www.elibrary.com.
24. "Writing Effective Employee Evaluations," *Healthcare Executive*, September/October 2008, 82.
25. Jane R. Goodson, Gail W. McGee, and Anson Seers, "Giving Appropriate Performance Feedback to Managers: An Empirical Test of Content and Outcomes," *Journal of Business Communication* 29, no. 4 (1992): 329–342.
26. "A Legal Termination," *Supervision*, September 2008, 22–25; Craig Cox, "On the Firing Line," *Business Ethics*, May-June 1992, 33–34.
27. Cox, "On the Firing Line."
28. Adapted from "FDA Notifies Public That Vail Products, Inc., Issues Nationwide Recall of Enclosed Bed Systems," FDA press release, 30 June 2005 [accessed 18 August 2005] www.fda.gov.
29. Adapted from "Bathtub Curve," *Engineering Statistics Handbook*, National Institute of Standards and Technology website [accessed 16 April 2005] www.nist.gov; Robert Berner, "The Warranty Windfall," *BusinessWeek*, 20 December 2004, 84–86; Larry Armstrong, "When Service Contracts Make Sense," *BusinessWeek*, 20 December 2004, 86.
30. Adapted from Twitter/JetBlue website [accessed 29 October 2008] http://twitter.com/JetBlue.
31. "Viral Effect of Email Promotion," Alka Dwivedi blog [accessed 19 October 2006] www.alkadwivedi.net; Teresa Valdez Klein, "Starbucks Makes a Viral Marketing Misstep," Blog Business Summit website [accessed 19 October 2006] www.blogbusinesssummit.com.
32. Adapted from Lee Valley website [accessed 29 October 2008] www.leevalley.com.
33. Adapted from Fookes Software website [accessed 28 October 2008] www.fookes.com.
34. Adapted from Environmental Quality Company press releases [accessed 27 October 2006] www.eqonline.com; "N.C. Residents to Return After Fire," *Science Daily*, 6 October 2006 [accessed 27 October 2006] www.sciencedaily.com; "Hazardous Waste Plant Fire in N.C. Forces 17,000 to Evacuate," FOXNews.com, 6 October 2006 [accessed 27 October 2006] www.foxnews.com.
35. Adapted from Rodney Manley, "Milledgeville Plan to Close; 150 to Lose Jobs," Macon.com, 28 January 2009 [accessed 1 February 2009] www.macon.com; Jamie Jones, "Shaw Plant Closing in Milledgeville," *The Daily Citizen* (Dalton, Georgia), 29 January 2009 [accessed 1 February 2009] www.northwestgeorgia.com.
36. Adapted from "Recall Safety Notice," Bombardier Recreational Products website, 10 September 2008 [accessed 30 October 2008] www.brp.com; Bombardier Recreational Products website [accessed 30 October 2008] www.brp.com.
37. Adapted from Pui-Wing Tam, Erin White, Nick Wingfield, and Kris Maher, "Snooping E-Mail by Software Is Now a Workplace Norm," *Wall Street Journal*, 9 March 2005, B1+.
38. Adapted from Stanton website [accessed 18 August 2005] www.stantondj.com.
39. Adapted from "Feds Warn Carter's Baby Clothes May Cause Rash," CNN.com, 25 October 2008 [accessed 30 October 2008] www.cnn.com; "A Message from Carter's on 'Tag-Less' Labels," Carter's website [accessed 30 October 2008] www.carters.com.
40. Adapted from Alion website [accessed 19 August 2005] www.alionscience.com.

CHAPTER 10

1. CafeMom website [accessed 21 July 2009] www.cafemom.com; Claire Cain Miller, "The New Back Fence," *Forbes*, 7 April 2008 [accessed 21 July 2009] www.forbes.com; "ClubMom Introduces the MomNetwork—The Web's First Social Network for Moms," press release, 8 May 2006 [accessed 22 October 2006] www.hcp.com; "Laura Fortner Named Senior Vice President, Business Development at ClubMom," press release, 20 September 2006 [accessed 22 October 2006] http://newyork.dbusinessnews.com.
2. Jay A. Conger, "The Necessary Art of Persuasion," *Harvard Business Review*, May-June 1998, 84–95; Jeanette W. Gilsdorf, "Write Me Your Best Case for...," *Bulletin of the Association for Business Communication* 54, no. 1 (March 1991): 7–12.
3. "Vital Skill for Today's Managers: Persuading, Not Ordering Others," *Soundview Executive Book Summaries*, September 1998, 1.
4. Mary Cross, "Aristotle and Business Writing: Why We Need to Teach Persuasion," *Bulletin of the Association for Business Communication* 54, no. 1 (March 1991): 3–6.
5. IKEA website [accessed 3 March 2008] www.ikea.com; Liz C. Wang, Julie Baker, Judy A. Wagner, and Kirk Wakefield, "Can a Retail Web Site Be Social?" *Journal of Marketing* 71, no. 3 (July 2007), 143–157.
6. Robert T. Moran, "Tips on Making Speeches to International Audiences," *International Management*, April 1980, 58–59.
7. Conger, "The Necessary Art of Persuasion."
8. Wesley Clark, "The Potency of Persuasion," *Fortune*, 12 November 2007, 48; W. H. Weiss, "Using Persuasion Successfully," *Supervision*, October 2006, 13–16.
9. Tom Chandler, "The Copywriter's Best Friend," The Copywriter Underground blog, 20 December 2006 [accessed 4 March 2008] http://copywriterunderground.com.
10. Raymond M. Olderman, *10-Minute Guide to Business Communication* (New York: Macmillan Spectrum/Alpha Books, 1997), 57–61.
11. John D. Ramage and John C. Bean, *Writing Arguments: A Rhetoric with Readings*, 3rd ed. (Boston: Allyn & Bacon, 1995), 430–442.
12. Philip Vassallo, "Persuading Powerfully: Tips for Writing Persuasive Documents," *Et Cetera*, Spring 2002, 65–71.
13. Dianna Booher, *Communicate with Confidence* (New York: McGraw-Hill, 1994), 102.
14. *Overview of the Web Accessibility Initiative*, W3C website [accessed 20 October 2006] www.w3.org.
15. iPod nano main product page, Apple website [accessed 4 March 2008] www.apple.com/ipodnano.

16. "HealthGrades Reveals America's Best Hospitals," Ivanhoe, 27 February 2008 [accessed 4 March 2008] www.ivanhoe.com.
17. Saturn VUE product page, Saturn website [accessed 8 December 2003] www.saturn.com.
18. Lancôme website [accessed 4 March 2008] www.lancome-usa.com.
19. *Living in France* product page, Insider Paris Guides website [accessed 4 March 2008] www.insiderparisguides.com.
20. U.S. Department of Energy, Energy Efficiency and Renewable Energy website [accessed 4 March 2008] www.eere.energy.gov.
21. Microsoft Office website [accessed 4 March 2008] http://office.microsoft.com.
22. Fast Break Backpack product page, Lands' End website [accessed 8 December 2003] www.landsend.com.
23. iPod nano main product page, Apple website [accessed 4 March 2008] www.apple.com/ipodnano.
24. "Technical Specifications," iPod nano, Apple website [accessed 4 March 2008] www.apple.com/ipodnano.
25. Larry Weber, *Marketing to the Social Web* (Hoboken, N.J.: Wiley, 2007), 12–14; David Meerman Scott, *The New Rules of Marketing and PR* (Hoboken, N.J.: Wiley, 2007), 62; Paul Gillin, *The New Influencers* (Sanger, Calif.: Quill Driver Books, 2007), 34–35; Jeremy Wright, *Blog Marketing: The Revolutionary Way to Increase Sales, Build Your Brand, and Get Exceptional Results* (New York: McGraw-Hill, 2006), 263–365.
26. Gilsdorf, "Write Me Your Best Case for..."
27. "Undercover Marketing Uncovered," CBSnews.com, 25 July 2004 [accessed 11 April 2005] www.cbsnews.com; Stephanie Dunnewind, "Teen Recruits Create Word-of-Mouth 'Buzz' to Hook Peers on Products," *Seattle Times*, 20 November 2004 [accessed 11 April 2005] www.seattletimes.com.
28. *Frequently Asked Advertising Questions: A Guide for Small Business*, U.S. Federal Trade Commission website [accessed 9 December 2003] www.ftc.gov.
29. Adapted from Samsung website [accessed 22 October 2006] www.samsung.com.
30. Adapted from GM Fastlane Blog [accessed 6 November 2008] http://fastlane.gmblogs.com.
31. Adapted from Starbucks website [accessed 23 August 2005] www.starbucks.com.
32. Adapted from IBM website [accessed 15 January 2004] www.ibm.com; "DAS Faces an Assured Future with IBM," IBM website [accessed 16 January 2004] www.ibm.com; "Sametime," IBM website [accessed 16 January 2004] www.ibm.com.
33. Adapted from CNET Shopper.com [accessed 1 October 2001] http://shopper.cnet.com.
34. Adapted from Courtland L. Bovée and John V. Thill, *Business in Action*, 3rd ed. (Upper Saddle River, N.J.: Prentice Hall, 2005), 236–237; International Telework Coalition website [accessed 24 August 2005] www.telcoa.org; Jason Roberson, "Rush-Hour Rebellion," *Dallas Business Journal*, 22 June 2001, 31; Carole Hawkins, "Ready, Set, Go Home," *Black Enterprise*, August 2001, 118–124; Wayne Tompkins, "Telecommuting in Transition," *Courier-Journal* (Louisville, Ky.), 9 July 2001, 1C.
35. Adapted from Give Life website [accessed 23 August 2005] www.givelife.org; American Red Cross website [accessed 3 October 2001] www.redcross.org; American Red Cross San Diego Chapter website [accessed 3 October 2001] www.sdarc.org.
36. Adapted from Web Accessibility Initiative, World Wide Web Consortium website [accessed 7 November 2008] www.w3.org.
37. Adapted from American Beefalo International website [accessed 31 October 2006] www.ababeefalo.org.
38. Adapted from The Podcast Bunker website [accessed 25 August 2005] www.podcastbunker.com.
39. Adapted from Time Inc. website [accessed 25 August 2005] www.timewarner.com.
40. Adapted from Insure.com website [accessed 24 August 2005] www.insure.com.
41. Adapted from Kelly Services website [accessed 9 January 2004] www.kellyservices.com.
42. Adapted from Hangers Cleaners (Kansas City) website [accessed 7 November 2008] www.hangerskc.com; Charles Fishman, "The Greener Cleaners," Fast Company website [accessed 11 July 2000] http://fastcompany.com; Micell Technologies website [accessed 1 September 2000] www.micell.com; Cool Clean Technologies, Inc., website [accessed 9 January 2004] www.coolclean.com.

CHAPTER 11

1. Fresh & Easy website [accessed 22 July 2009] www.freshandeasy.com; Tesco website [accessed 22 July 2009] www.tesco.com; "Competition and Profit," Food Marketing Institute website [accessed 5 November 2006] www.fmi.org; John E. Forsyth, Nicolo Galante, and Todd Guild, "Capitalizing on Customer Insights," *McKinsey Quarterly*, 2006 Issue 3, 42–53; "Company Spotlight: Tesco PLC," *MarketWatch: Global Round-Up*, July 2006, 76–81; James Quilter, "Tesco Hands Senior Role to Brand Planning Chief," *Marketing*, 2 August 2006, 4; Don Longo, "The British Are Coming," *Progressive Grocer*, 15 April 2006, 66–75.
2. Legal-Definitions.com [accessed 17 December 2003] www.legal-definitions.com.
3. Information for this section was obtained from "Finding Industry Information" [accessed 3 November 1998] www.pitt.edu/~buslibry/industries.htm; Thomas P. Bergman, Stephen M. Garrison, and Gregory M. Scott, *The Business Student Writer's Manual and Guide to the Internet* (Upper Saddle River, N.J.: Prentice Hall, 1998), 67–80; Ernest L. Maier, Anthony J. Faria, Peter Kaatrude, and Elizabeth Wood, *The Business Library and How to Use It* (Detroit: Omnigraphics, 1996), 53–76; Sherwyn P. Morreale and Courtland L. Bovée, *Excellence in Public Speaking* (Fort Worth: Harcourt Brace College Publishers, 1998), 166–171.
4. AllTheWeb.com advanced search page [accessed 27 August 2005] www.alltheweb.com; Google advanced search page [accessed 27 August 2005] www.google.com; Yahoo! advanced search page [accessed 27 August 2005] www.yahoo.com.
5. "Copyright Office Basics," U.S. Copyright Office website [accessed 2 November 2006] www.copyright.gov.
6. A. B. Blankenship and George Edward Breen, *State of the Art Marketing Research* (Chicago: NTC Business Books, 1993), 136.
7. Naresh K. Malhotra, *Basic Marketing Research* (Upper Saddle River, N.J.: Prentice-Hall, 2002), 314–317; "How to Design and Conduct a Study," *Credit Union Magazine*, October 1983, 36–46.
8. Product features page, SurveyMonkey.com [accessed 29 October 2006] www.surveymonkey.com.
9. American Marketing Association website [accessed 14 December 2003] www.marketingpower.com.
10. Karen J. Bannan, "Companies Save Time, Money with Online Surveys," *B to B*, 9 June 2003, 1+; Allen Hogg, "Online Research Overview," American Marketing Association website [accessed 15 December 2003] www.marketingpower.com.
11. Tesco website [accessed 5 November 2006] www.tesco.com.
12. Morreale and Bovée, *Excellence in Public Speaking*, 177.
13. Morreale and Bovée, *Excellence in Public Speaking*, 182.
14. A. B. Blankenship and George Edward Breen, *State of the Art Marketing Research* (Lincolnwood, Ill.: NTC Business Books, 1992), 225.
15. Lynn Quitman Troyka, *Simon & Schuster Handbook for Writers*, 6th ed. (Upper Saddle River, N.J.: Simon & Schuster, 2002), 481.
16. "How to Paraphrase Effectively: 6 Steps to Follow," ResearchPaper.com [accessed 26 October 1998] www.researchpaper.com/writing_center/30.html.
17. Jakob Nielsen, "How Users Read on the Web" [accessed 11 November 2004] www.useit.com/alertbox/9710a.html.
18. Reid Goldsborough, "Words for the Wise," *Link-Up*, September-October 1999, 25–26.
19. Julie Rohovit, "Computer Eye Strain: The Dilbert Syndrome," Virtual Hospital website [accessed 9 November 2004] www.vh.org.

CHAPTER 12

1. Adapted from Tellabs website [accessed 24 July 2009] www.tellabs.com; Sid Cato, "World's Best 2005 Reports," Sid Cato's Office Annual Report Website [accessed 11 November 2006] www.sidcato.com; George Stenitzer, "New Challenges for Annual Reports," Presentation to National Investor Relations Institute, November 2005 [accessed 11 November 2006] www.niri-chicago.org; Tellabs 2006 Annual Report [accessed 24 July 2009] www.tellabs.com.
2. A. S. C. Ehrenberg, "Report Writing—Six Simple Rules for Better Business Documents," *Admap*, June 1992, 39–42.
3. "Tellabs Solutions and Applications," Tellabs 2005 Annual Report [accessed 11 November 2006] www.tellabs.com.
4. Philip C. Kolin, *Successful Writing at Work*, 6th ed. (Boston: Houghton Mifflin, 2001), 552–555.
5. "Web Writing: How to Avoid Pitfalls," *Investor Relations Business*, 1 November 1999, 15.
6. "Codex: Guidelines," WordPress website [accessed 16 February 2008] http://wordpress.org; Michael Shanks, "Wiki Guidelines," Traumwerk website [accessed 18 August 2006] http://metamedia.stanford.edu/projects/traumwerk/home; Joe Moxley, MC Morgan, Matt Barton, and Donna Hanak, "For Teachers New to Wikis," Writing Wiki [accessed 18 August 2006] http://writingwiki.org; "Wiki Guidelines," Psi [accessed 18 August 2006] http://psi-im.org.
7. Rachael King, "No Rest for the Wiki," *BusinessWeek*, 12 March 2007 [accessed 14 February 2008] www.businessweek.com.
8. "Codex: Guidelines," WordPress website [accessed 14 February 2008] http://wordpress.org.
9. Dan MacDougall, "Orchestrating Your Proposal," *Canadian Consulting Engineer*, March-April 2003, 51–56; Sant Corporation website [accessed 7 December 2008] www.santcorp.com.
10. Alexis Gerard and Bob Goldstein, *Going Visual* (Hoboken, N.J.: Wiley, 2005), 18.
11. Charles Kostelnick and Michael Hassett, *Shaping Information: The Rhetoric of Visual Conventions* (Carbondale, Ill.: Southern Illinois University Press, 2003), 177.
12. Gerard and Goldstein, *Going Visual*, 103–106.
13. Edward R. Tufte, *Visual Explanations: Images and Quantities, Evidence and Narrative* (Cheshire, Conn.: Graphics Press, 1997), 82.
14. Kostelnick and Hassett, *Shaping Information: The Rhetoric of Visual Conventions*, 17.
15. Edward R. Tufte, *The Visual Display of Quantitative Information* (Cheshire, Conn.: Graphic Press, 1983), 113.
16. Based in part on Tufte, *Visual Explanations: Images and Quantities, Evidence and Narrative*, 29–37, 53; Paul Martin Lester, *Visual Communication: Images with Messages*, 4th ed. (Belmont, Calif.: Thomson Wadsworth, 2006), 95–105, 194–196.
17. Hoover's Online [accessed 3 December 2008] www.hoovers.com.
18. "Data Visualization: Modern Approaches," *Smashing Magazine*, 2 August 2007 [accessed 15 March 2008] www.smashingmagazine.com; "7 Things You Should Know About Data Visualization," EDUCAUSE Learning Initiative website [accessed 15 March 2008] www.educause.edu; TagCrowd website [accessed 15 March 2008] www.tagcrowd.com.
19. Sheri Rosen, "What Is Truth?" *IABC Communication World*, March 1995, 40.
20. Eric Binfet, personal communication, 26 November 2008.
21. "Interactive Web Sites Draw Minds, Shape Public Perception," *ScienceDaily*, 27 May 2008 [accessed 3 December 2008] www.sciencedaily.com.
22. Adapted from Air-Trak website [accessed 24 July 2009] www.air-trak.com.

CHAPTER 13

1. "CEO's Letter: A Message from Patty Stonesifer," Bill & Melinda Gates Foundation 2007 Annual Report [accessed 13 December 2008] www.gatesfoundation.org; Bill & Melinda Gates Foundation website [accessed 13 December 2008] www.gatesfoundation.org; Richard Klausner and Pedro Alonso, "An Attack on All Fronts," *Nature*, 19 August 2004, 930–931; "Richard Klausner Spends to Save Lives," *Fast Company*, November 2002, 128; Kent Allen, "The Gatekeeper," *U.S. News & World Report*, 8 December 2003, 64–66.
2. John Morkes and Jakob Nielsen, "Concise, Scannable, and Objective: How to Write for the Web," UseIt.com [accessed 13 November 2006] www.useit.com.
3. Dean Allen, "Reading Design," *A List Apart*, 23 November 2001 [accessed 9 November 2004] www.alistapart.com.
4. Michael Netzley and Craig Snow, *Guide to Report Writing* (Upper Saddle River, N.J.: Prentice Hall, 2001), 57.
5. Oswald M. T. Ratteray, "Hit the Mark with Better Summaries," *Supervisory Management*, September 1989, 43–45.
6. Netzley and Snow, *Guide to Report Writing*, 43.
7. Alice Reid, "A Practical Guide for Writing Proposals" [accessed 31 May 2001] http://members.dca.net/areid/proposal.htm.
8. Toby B. Gooley, "Ocean Shipping: RFPs That Get Results," *Logistics Management*, July 2003, 47–52.
9. See Note 1.
10. Adapted from "Home Depot Says E-Learning Is Paying for Itself," *Workforce Management*, 25 February 2004 [accessed 28 February 2004] www.workforce.com; Robert Celaschi, "The Insider: Training," *Workforce Management*, August 2004, 67–69; Joe Mullich, "A Second Act for E-Learning," *Workforce Management*, February 2004, 51–55; Gail Johnson, "Brewing the Perfect Blend," *Training*, December 2003, 30+; Tammy Galvin, "2003 Industry Report," *Training*, October 2003, 21+; William C. Symonds, "Giving It the Old Online Try," *BusinessWeek*, 3 December 2001, 76–80; Karen Frankola, "Why Online Learners Drop Out," *Workforce*, October 2001, 52–60; Mary Lord, "They're Online and on the Job; Managers and Hamburger Flippers Are Being E-Trained at Work," *U.S. News & World Report*, 15 October 2001, 72–77.
11. Adapted from Ieva M. Augstumes, "Buyers Take the Driver's Seat," *Dallas Morning News*, 20 February 2004 [accessed 30 June 2004] www.highbeam.com; Jill Amadio, "A Click Away: Automotive Web Sites Are Revved Up and Ready to Help You Buy," *Entrepreneur*, 1 August 2003 [accessed 30 June 2004] www.highbeam.com; Dawn C. Chmielewski, "Car Sites Lend Feel-Good Info for Haggling," *San Jose Mercury News*, 1 August 2003 [accessed 30 June 2004] www.highbeam.com; Cromwell Schubarth, "Autoheroes Handle Hassle of Haggling," *Boston Herald*, 24 July 2003 [accessed 30 June 2004] www.highbeam.com; Rick Popely, "Internet Doesn't Change Basic Shopping Rules," *Chicago Tribune*, 28 February 2004 [accessed 30 June 2004] www.highbeam.com; Matt Nauman, "Walnut Creek, Calif., Firm Prospers as Online Car Buying Becomes More Popular," *San Jose Mercury News*, 21 June 2004 [accessed 30 June 2004] www.highbeam.com; Cliff Banks, "e-Dealer 100," Ward's Dealer Business, 1 April 2004 [accessed 30 June 2004] www.highbeam.com; Cars.com website [accessed 30 June 2004] www.cars.com; CarsDirect website [accessed 30 June 2004] www.carsdirect.com.

CHAPTER 14

1. James Rogers, "The Tech Investor's Guide to 2009," 26 December 2008, TheStreet.com [accessed 27 December 2008] www.thestreet.com; "Culture and Philosophy" and "Procter & Gamble Case Study," HP website [accessed 20 September 2005] www.hp.com; Paul McDougall, "Procter & Gamble's Deal with HP Grows," *InformationWeek*, 16 August 2004 [accessed 20 September 2005] www.outsourcingpipeline.com; Bill Breen, "The Big Score," *Fast Company*, September 2003, 64; "HP Finalizes $3 Billion Outsourcing Agreement to Manage Procter & Gamble's IT Infrastructure," press release, HP website, 6 May 2003 [accessed 10 October 2003] www.hp.com; "HP Selected by P&G for $3 Billion, 10-Year Services Contract," press release, HP website, 11 April 2003 [accessed 10 October 2003] www.hp.com.
2. Carmine Gallo, "Loaded for Bore," *BusinessWeek* online, 5 August 2005 [accessed 19 September 2005] www.businessweek.com.

3. Carmine Gallo, "How to Deliver a Presentation Under Pressure," *BusinessWeek* online, 18 September 2008 [accessed 15 August 2009] www.businessweek.com.
4. Sarah Lary and Karen Pruente, "Powerless Point: Common PowerPoint Mistakes to Avoid," *Public Relations Tactics*, February 2004, 28.
5. Sherwyn P. Morreale and Courtland L. Bovée, *Excellence in Public Speaking* (Fort Worth, Tex.: Harcourt Brace College Publishers, 1998), 234–237.
6. Morreale and Bovée, *Excellence in Public Speaking*, 230.
7. Morreale and Bovée, *Excellence in Public Speaking*, 241–243.
8. "Choose and Use Your Words Deliberately," *Soundview Executive Book Summaries*, 20, no. 6, pt. 2 (June 1998): 3.
9. Adapted from Eric J. Adams, "Management Focus: User-Friendly Presentation Software," *World Trade*, March 1995, 92.
10. Carmine Gallo, "Grab Your Audience Fast," *BusinessWeek*, 13 September 2006, 19.
11. Walter Kiechel III, "How to Give a Speech," *Fortune*, 8 June 1987, 180.
12. *Communication and Leadership Program* (Santa Ana, Calif.: Toastmasters International, 1980), 44, 45.
13. "Polishing Your Presentation," 3M Meeting Network [accessed 25 May 2007] www.3m.com/meetingnetwork/readingroom/meetingguide_pres.html.
14. An example of such a presentation is Dick Hardt's keynote presentation at OSCON 2005; the presentation can be viewed at www.identity20.com/media/OSCON2005.
15. Cliff Atkinson, "The Cognitive Load of PowerPoint: Q&A with Richard E. Mayer," Sociable Media [accessed 15 August 2009] http://www.sociablemedia.com/articles_mayer.htm.
16. "The Power of Color in Presentations," 3M Meeting Network [accessed 25 May 2007] www.3m.com/meetingnetwork/readingroom/meetingguide_power_color.html.
17. Guy Kawasaki, "Rule of Thumb," *Entrepreneur*, May 2008, 44.
18. Sarah Lary and Karen Pruente, "Powerless Point: Common PowerPoint Mistakes to Avoid," *Public Relations Tactics*, February 2004, 28.
19. Morreale and Bovée, *Excellence in Public Speaking*, 24–25.
20. Jennifer Rotondo and Mike Rotondo, Jr., *Presentation Skills for Managers* (New York: McGraw-Hill, 2002), 9.
21. Rick Gilbert, "Presentation Advice for Boardroom Success," *Financial Executive*, September 2005, 12.
22. Rotondo and Rotondo, *Presentation Skills for Managers*, 151.
23. Teresa Brady, "Fielding Abrasive Questions During Presentations," *Supervisory Management*, February 1993, 6.
24. Robert L. Montgomery, "Listening on Your Feet," *The Toastmaster*, July 1987, 14–15.
25. SlideShare website [accessed 24 December 2008] www.slideshare.net.
26. TechWeb website [accessed 20 March 2008] www.techweb.com; "Webcasting Tips & Advice," Spider Eye Studios [accessed 13 February 2004] www.spidereye.com.
27. See Note 1.
28. Adapted from Loopt website [accessed 25 July 2009] www.loopt.com; Boost Mobile website [accessed 9 December 2006] www.boostmobile.com.
29. Adapted from Vox website [accessed 27 December 2008] www.vox.com; eSnips website [accessed 27 December 2008] www.esnips.com; Robert D. Hof, "There's Not Enough 'Me' in MySpace," *BusinessWeek*, 4 December 2006, 40.

CHAPTER 15

1. Hersha Hospitality Management website [accessed 30 December 2008] www.hershahotels.com; Charles Handler, "What You Need to Know About What's Happening in the Pre-Employment Assessment Market," Ere.net, 20 July 2006 [accessed 12 December 2006] www.ere.net; Fay Hansen, "Growing into Applicant Tracking Systems, *Workforce Management*, 10 October 2006 [accessed 12 December 2006] www.workforce.com; Connie Winkler, "Job Tryouts Go Virtual," *HR Magazine*, September 2006, 131–134; "Hersha Hospitality Management Selects ERC's Selectech Workforce Management Recruiting Solution," 7 December 2006, ERC Dataplus website [accessed 12 December 2006] www.ercdataplus.com.
2. Anne Fisher, "How to Get Hired by a 'Best' Company," *Fortune*, 4 February 2008, 96.
3. Caroline A. Drakeley, "Viral Networking: Tactics in Today's Job Market," *Intercom*, September-October 2003, 4–7.
4. "CareerXroads 6th Annual Sources of Hire Study, 2006," CareerXroads website [accessed 30 March 2008] www.careerxroads.com.
5. Caroline Kealey, "Web 2.0: The Medium Is the Message, but What's the Result?" IABC website [accessed 29 December 2008] www.iabc.com; Alina Tugend, "Job Hunting Is, and Isn't, What It Used to Be," *New York Times*, 26 September 2008 [accessed 29 December 2008] www.nytimes.com.
6. Jobfox website [accessed 29 December 2008] www.jobfox.com; Olga Kharif, "The Job of Challenging Monster," *BusinessWeek* online, 6 September 2005 [accessed 25 September 2005] www.businessweek.com; "Job Sites: The 'Second Generation,'" *BusinessWeek* online, 7 September 2005 [accessed 25 September 2005] www.businessweek.com.
7. Jobster website [accessed 29 December 2008] www.jobster.com; Jeanette Borzo, "Taking on the Recruiting Monster," *FSB*, May 2007, 89–90.
8. Douglas MacMillan, "The Art of the Online Résumé," *BusinessWeek*, 7 May 2007, 86.
9. Fisher, "How to Get Hired by a 'Best' Company."
10. Anne Fisher, "Greener Pastures in a New Field," *Fortune*, 26 January 2004, 48.
11. Liz Ryan, "Etiquette for Online Outreach," Yahoo! Hotjobs website [accessed 26 March 2008] http://hotjobs.yahoo.com.
12. Career and Employment Services, Danville Area Community College website [accessed 23 March 2008] www.dacc.edu/career; Career Counseling, Sarah Lawrence College website [accessed 23 March 2008] www.slc.edu/occ/index.php; Cheryl L. Noll, "Collaborating with the Career Planning and Placement Center in the Job-Search Project," *Business Communication Quarterly* 58, no. 3 (1995): 53–55.
13. Rockport Institute, "How to Write a Masterpiece of a Résumé" [accessed 24 March 2008] www.rockportinstitute.com.
14. Pam Stanley-Weigand, "Organizing the Writing of Your Resume," *Bulletin of the Association for Business Communication* 54, no. 3 (September 1991): 11–12.
15. Susan Vaughn, "Answer the Hard Questions Before Asked," *Los Angeles Times*, 29 July 2001, W1-W2.
16. John Steven Niznik, "Landing a Job with a Criminal Record," About.com [accessed 12 December 2006] http://jobsearchtech.about.com.
17. Richard H. Beatty and Nicholas C. Burkholder, *The Executive Career Guide for MBAs* (New York: Wiley, 1996), 133.
18. Adapted from Burdette E. Bostwick, *How to Find the Job You've Always Wanted* (New York: Wiley, 1982), 69–70.
19. Norma Mushkat Gaffin, "Recruiters' Top 10 Resume Pet Peeves," Monster.com [accessed 19 February 2004] www.monster.com; Beatty and Burkholder, *The Executive Career Guide for MBAs*, 151.
20. Rockport Institute, "How to Write a Masterpiece of a Résumé."
21. "How to Ferret Out Instances of Résumé Padding and Fraud," *Compensation & Benefits for Law Offices*, June 2006, 1+.
22. "Resume Fraud Gets Slicker and Easier," CNN.com [accessed 11 March 2004] www.cnn.com.
23. Lisa Takeuchi Cullen, "Getting Wise to Lies," *Time*, 1 May 2006, 59; "Resume Fraud Gets Slicker and Easier"; Employment Research Services website [accessed 18 March 2004] www.erscheck.com.
24. "How to Ferret Out Instances of Résumé Padding and Fraud."
25. Jacqueline Durett, "Redoing Your Résumé? Leave Off the Lies," *Training*, December 2006, 9; "Employers Turn Their Fire on Untruthful CVs," *Supply Management*, 23 June 2005, 13.

26. Cynthia E. Conn, "Integrating Writing Skills and Ethics Training in Business Communication Pedagogy: A Résumé Case Study Exemplar," *Business Communication Quarterly*, June 2008, 138–151; Marilyn Moats Kennedy, "Don't Get Burned by Résumé Inflation," *Marketing News*, 15 April 2007, 37–38.
27. Sal Divita, "If You're Thinking Résumé, Think Creatively," *Marketing News*, 14 September 1992, 29.
28. Rockport Institute, "How to Write a Masterpiece of a Résumé."
29. Lora Morsch, "25 Words That Hurt Your Resume," CNN.com, 20 January 2006 [accessed 20 January 2006] www.cnn.com.
30. Liz Ryan, "The Reengineered Résumé," *BusinessWeek*, 3 December 2007, SC12.
31. Anthony Balderrama, "Resume Blunders That Will Keep You from Getting Hired," CNN.com, 19 March 2008 [accessed 26 March 2008] www.cnn.com; Michelle Dumas, "5 Resume Writing Myths," Distinctive Documents blog, 17 July 2007 [accessed 26 March 2008] http://blog.distinctiveweb.com; Kim Isaacs, "Resume Dilemma: Recent Graduate," Monster.com [accessed 26 March 2008] http://career-advice.monster.com.
32. Karl L. Smart, "Articulating Skills in the Job Search," *Business Communication Quarterly* 67, no. 2 (June 2004): 198–205.
33. "25 Things You Should Never Include on a Resume," HR World website 18 December 2007 [accessed 25 March 2008] www.hrworld.com.
34. "When to Include Personal Data," ResumeEdge.com [accessed 25 March 2008] www.resumeedge.com.
35. "Résumé Length: What It Should Be and Why It Matters to Recruiters," *HR Focus*, June 2007, 9.
36. Ed Tazzia, "Wanted: A Résumé That Really Works," *Brandweek*, 15 May 2006, 26.
37. Rachel Zupek, "Seven Exceptions to Job Search Rules," CNN.com, 3 September 2008 [accessed 29 December 2008] www.cnn.com.
38. John Sullivan, "Résumés: Paper, Please," *Workforce Management*, 22 October 2007, 50; "Video Résumés Offer Both Pros and Cons During Recruiting," *HR Focus*, July 2007, 8.
39. Ellen Joe Pollock, "Sir: Your Application for a Job Is Rejected; Sincerely, Hal 9000," *Wall Street Journal*, 30 July 1998, A1, A12.
40. "Scannable Resume Design," ResumeEdge.com [accessed 19 February 2004] www.resumeedge.com.
41. Kim Isaacs, "Tips for Creating a Scannable Resume," Monster.com [accessed 19 February 2004] www.monster.com.
42. Christian Anderson, "New Year's Resolutions—Jobster Style," Jobster blog, 21 December 2007 [accessed 28 March 2008] www.jobster.blogs.com.
43. Sarah E. Needleman, "Why Sneaky Tactics May Not Help Resume; Recruiters Use New Search Technologies to Ferret Out Bogus Keywords," *Wall Street Journal*, 6 March 2007, B8.
44. Kim Isaacs, "Enhance Your Resume for Monster Upload," Monster.com [accessed 19 February 2004] www.monster.com.
45. "10 Reasons Why You Are Not Getting Any Interviews," *Miami Times*, 7–13 November 2007, 6D.
46. "The Rogue's Gallery of 25 Awful Résumé Mistakes," CareerExplorer.net [accessed 19 February 2004] www.careerexplorer.net.
47. "Protect Yourself From Identity Theft When Hunting for a Job Online," *Office Pro*, May 2007, 6.

CHAPTER 16

1. Guy Logan, "Hiring Policy Makes Google Best Place to Work in the UK," Personnel Today, 3 June 2008, 3; John Sullivan, "A Case Study of Google Recruiting," 5 December 2005, *Electronic Recruiting Exchange* [accessed 16 December 2006] www.ere.net; "What's It Like to Work at Google?" Google website [accessed 26 September 2005] www.google.com; Fred Vogelstein, "Can Google Grow Up?" *Fortune*, 8 December 2003, 102; Quentin Hardy, "All Eyes on Google," *Forbes*, 26 May 2003, 100; Keith H. Hammonds, "Growth Search," *Fast Company*, April 2003, 74–81; Stanley Bing, "How Not to Success (*sic*) in Business," *Fortune*, 30 December 2002, 210; Pierre Mornell, "Zero Defect Hiring," *Inc.*, March 1998, 74.
2. "The Writer Approach," *Los Angeles Times*, 17 November 2002, W1.
3. Toni Logan, "The Perfect Cover Story," *Kinko's Impress* 2 (2000): 32, 34.
4. James Gonyea, "Money Talks: Salary History Versus Salary Requirements," Monster.com [accessed 19 October 2004] www.monster.com; Marguerite Higgins, "Tech-Savvy Job Hunters Not So Suave in Writing; E-Mail Résumés Appall Employers," *Washington Times*, 17 December 2002 [accessed 22 February 2004] www.highbeam.com; "Keep Goal in Mind When Crafting a Résumé," *Register-Guard* (Eugene, Ore.), 3 August 2003 [accessed 22 February 2004] www.highbeam.com; Anis F. McClin, "Effects of Spelling Errors on the Perception of Writers," *Journal of General Psychology*, January 2002 [accessed 22 February 2004] www.highbeam.com.
5. Anne Fisher, "How to Get Hired by a 'Best' Company," *Fortune*, 4 February 2008, 96.
6. Sarah E. Needleman, "Speed Interviewing Grows as Skills Shortage Looms; Strategy May Help Lock in Top Picks; Some Drawbacks," *Wall Street Journal*, 6 November 2007, B15.
7. Scott Beagrie, "How to Handle a Telephone Job Interview," *Personnel Today*, 26 June 2007, 29.
8. "Hiring Process," Google website [accessed 2 January 2009] www.google.com.
9. John Olmstead, "Predict Future Success with Structured Interviews," *Nursing Management*, March 2007, 52–53.
10. Fisher, "How to Get Hired by a 'Best' Company."
11. Erinn R. Johnson, "Pressure Sessions," *Black Enterprise*, October 2007, 72.
12. "What's a Group Interview," About.com Tech Careers [accessed 5 April 2008] http://jobsearchtech.about.com.
13. Fisher, "How to Get Hired by a 'Best' Company."
14. "FAQs About Behavioral Based Interviewing," University of Wisconsin-Eau Clair website [accessed 5 April 2008] www.uwec.edu; "Advice on Mastering the 'Behavioral' Interview," *Financial Executive*, November 2007, 11.
15. Chris Pentilla, "Testing the Waters," *Entrepreneur*, January 2004 [accessed 27 May 2006] www.entrepreneur.com; Terry McKenna, "Behavior-Based Interviewing," *National Petroleum News*, January 2004, 16; Nancy K. Austin, "Goodbye Gimmicks," *Incentive*, May 1996, 241.
16. William Poundstone, "Beware the Interview Inquisition," *Harvard Business Review*, May 2003, 18+.
17. Peter Vogt, "Mastering the Phone Interview," Monster.com [accessed 13 December 2006] www.monster.com; Nina Segal, "The Global Interview: Tips for Successful, Unconventional Interview Techniques," Monster.com [accessed 13 December 2006] www.monster.com.
18. Segal, "The Global Interview: Tips for Successful, Unconventional Interview Techniques."
19. HireVue website [accessed 4 April 2008] www.hirevue.com; in2View website [accessed 4 April 2008] www.in2view.biz; Victoria Reitz, "Interview Without Leaving Home," *Machine Design*, 1 April 2004, 66.
20. Connie Winkler, "Job Tryouts Go Virtual," *HR Magazine*, September 2006, 131–134.
21. Saul Hansell, "Google Answer to Filling Jobs Is an Algorithm," *New York Times*, 3 January 2007 [accessed 3 January 2007] www.nytimes.com.
22. Gina Ruiz, "Job Candidate Assessment Tests Go Virtual," *Workforce Management*, January 2008 [accessed 1 January 2009] www.workforce.com.
23. Dino di Mattia, "Testing Methods and Effectiveness of Tests," *Supervision*, August 2005, 4–5.
24. David W. Arnold and John W. Jones, "Who the Devil's Applying Now?" *Security Management*, March 2002, 85–88.
25. Arnold and Jones, "Who the Devil's Applying Now?" 86.
26. Frederick P. Morgeson, Michael A. Campion, Robert L. Dipboye, John R. Hollenbeck, Kevin Murphy, and Neil Schmitt, "Are We

Getting Fooled Again? Coming to Terms with Limitations in the Use of Personality Tests in Personnel Selection," *Personnel Psychology* 60, no. 4 (Winter 2007): 1029–1049.
27. Adam Agard, "Preemployment Skills Testing: An Important Step in the Hiring Process," *Supervision*, June 2003, 7+.
28. Ashlea Ebeling, "Corporate Moneyball," *Forbes*, 23 April 2007, 102+.
29. "Drug Test Company Official Disputes Report Pre-employment Tests Falling," *Drug Detection Report*, 23 March 2006, 43.
30. Matthew J. Heller, "Digging Deeper," *Workforce Management*, 3 March 2008, 35–39.
31. "Check Yourself Before Employer Does," *CA Magazine*, June/July 2005, 12.
32. Scott Medintz, "Talkin' 'Bout MySpace Generation," *Money*, February 2006, 27.
33. Michael Kaplan, "Job Interview Brainteasers," *Business 2.0*, September 2007, 35–37.
34. Nancy K. Austin, "Goodbye Gimmicks," *Incentive*, May 1996, 241.
35. Katherine Spencer Lee, "Tackling Tough Interview Questions," *Certification Magazine*, May 2005, 35.
36. Nick Corcodilos, "How to Answer a Misguided Interview Question," *Seattle Times*, 30 March 2008 [accessed 5 April 2008] www.seattletimes.com.
37. InterviewUp website [accessed 5 April 2008] www.interviewup.com.
38. Joe Turner, "An Interview Strategy: Telling Stories," Yahoo! HotJobs [accessed 5 April 2008] http://hotjobs.yahoo.com.
39. "A Word of Caution for Chatty Job Candidates," *Public Relations Tactics*, January 2008, 4.
40. Robert Gifford, Cheuk Fan Ng, and Margaret Wilkinson, "Nonverbal Cues in the Employment Interview: Links Between Applicant Qualities and Interviewer Judgments," *Journal of Applied Psychology* 70, no. 4 (1985): 729.
41. Dale G. Leathers, *Successful Nonverbal Communication* (New York: Macmillan, 1986), 225.
42. Randall S. Hansen, "When Job-Hunting: Dress for Success," QuintCareers.com [accessed 5 April 2008] www.quintcareers.com; Alison Doyle, "Dressing for Success," About.com [accessed 5 April 2008] http://jobsearch.about.com.
43. William S. Frank, "Job Interview: Pre-Flight Checklist," *The Career Advisor* [accessed 28 September 2005] http://careerplanning.about.com.
44. "Because You Asked: Interviews Get a Little Strange," ManageSmarter, 25 September 2008 [accessed 2 January 2009] www.managesmarter.com.
45. T. Shawn Taylor, "Most Managers Have No Idea How to Hire the Right Person for the Job," *Chicago Tribune*, 23 July 2002 [accessed 29 September 2005] www.ebsco.com.
46. "10 Minutes to Impress," *Journal of Accountancy*, July 2007, 13.
47. Todd Anten, "How to Handle Illegal Interview Questions," Yahoo! HotJobs [accessed 7 August 2009] http://hotjobs.yahoo.com.
48. "Negotiating Salary: An Introduction," *InformationWeek* online [accessed 22 February 2004] www.infoweek.com.
49. "Negotiating Salary: An Introduction."
50. Joan S. Lublin, "Notes to Interviewers Should Go Beyond a Simple Thank You," *Wall Street Journal*, 5 February 2008, B1.

Acknowledgments

TEXT

224 (Practicing Ethical Communication: What's Right to Write in a Recommendation Letter?) Adapted from Diane Cadrain, "HR Professionals Stymied by Vanishing Job References," *HR Magazine*, November 2004, 31–40; "Five (or More) Ways You Can Be Sued for Writing (or Not Writing) Recommendation Letters," *Fair Employment Practice Guidelines*, July 2006, 1, 3–4; Rochelle Kaplan, "Writing a Recommendation Letter," National Association of Colleges and Employers website [accessed 12 October 2006] www.naceweb.org; Maura Dolan and Stuart Silverstein, "Court Broadens Liability for Job References," *Los Angeles Times*, 28 January 1997, A1, A11; David A. Price, "Good References Pave Road to Court," *USA Today*, 13 February 1997, 11A; Frances A. McMorris, "Ex-Bosses Face Less Peril Giving Honest Job References," *Wall Street Journal*, 8 July 1996, B1, B8; Dawn Gunsch, "Gray Matters: Centralize Control of Giving References," *Personnel Journal*, September 1992, 114, 116–117; Betty Southard Murphy, Wayne E. Barlow, and D. Diane Hatch, "Manager's Newsfront: Job Reference Liability of Employees," *Personnel Journal*, September 1991, 22, 26; Ross H. Fishman, "When Silence Is Golden," *Nation's Business*, July 1991, 48–49. **260 (Business Communication 2.0: Controlling Rumors in a Social Media Environment)** Augie Ray, "Combating Rumors in Social Media: Sarah Palin and Babygate," Experience: The Blog, 1 September 2008 [accessed 18 October 2008] www.experiencetheblog.com; Michelle Conlin, "Web Attack," *BusinessWeek*, 16 April 2007 [accessed 27 February 2008] www.businessweek.com; Melissa Allison, "Corporations Seek to Clean Up Online Rumors," *Seattle Times*, 4 March 2007 [accessed 4 March 2007] www.seattletimes.com; Charles Wolrich, "Top Corporate Hate Web Sites," *Forbes*, 8 March 2005 [accessed 16 August 2005] www.forbes.com; PlanetFeedback.com [accessed 27 February 2008] www.planetfeedback.com; "Health Related Hoaxes and Rumors," Centers for Disease Control and Prevention website [accessed 16 August 2005] www.cdc.gov; Snopes.com [accessed 16 August 2005] www.snopes.com; "Pranksters, Activists and Rogues: Know Your Adversaries and Where They Surf," *PR News*, 26 June 2000 [accessed 3 December 2003] www.elibrary.com. **290 (Business Communication 2.0: Building an Audience Through Search Engine Optimization)** Adapted from P.J. Fusco, "How Web 2.0 Affects SEO Strategy," ClickZ, 23 May 2007 [accessed 6 November 2008] www.clickz.com; "Law Firm Marketing Now Dependent on Search Engine Optimization," *Law Office Management & Administration Report*, June 2006, 1, 10–12; "Pandia Search Engine Marketing 101," Pandia website [accessed 25 March 2007] www.pandia.com; Mike Grehan, "Does Textbook SEO Really Work Anymore?" 17 April 2006, ClickZ [accessed 25 March 2007] www.clickz.com; Shari Thurow, "Web Positioning Metrics and SEO," 24 October 2005, ClickZ [accessed 25 March 2007] www.clickz.com. **336 (Sharpening Your Career Skills: Creating an Effective Business Plan)** Adapted from Michael Gerber, "The Business Plan That Always Works," *Her Business*, May/June 2004, 23–25; J. Tol Broome, Jr., "How to Write a Business Plan," *Nation's Business*, February 1993, 29–30; Albert Richards, "The Ernst & Young Business Plan Guide," *R & D Management*, April 1995, 253; David Lanchner, "How Chitchat Became a Valuable Business Plan," *Global Finance*, February 1995, 54–56; Marguerita Ashby-Berger, "My Business Plan—And What Really Happened," *Small Business Forum*, Winter 1994–1995, 24–35; Stanley R. Rich and David E. Gumpert, *Business Plans That Win $$$* (New York: Harper Row, 1985). **441 (Communicating Across Cultures: Five Tips for Making Presentations Around the World)** Adapted from Patricia L. Kurtz, *The Global Speaker* (New York: AMACOM, 1995), 35–47, 56–68, 75–82, 87–100; David A. Victor, *International Business Communication* (New York: HarperCollins, 1992), 39–45; Lalita Khosla, "You Say Tomato," *Forbes*, 21 May 2001, 36; Stephen Dolainski, "Are Expats Getting Lost in the Translation?" *Workforce*, February 1997, 32–39. **486 (Sharpening Your Career Skills: Communication Miscues: Don't. Just Don't.)** Adapted from Rosemary Haefner, "Biggest Resume Mistakes," CNN.com, 21 May 2007 [accessed 30 December 2008] www.cnn.com; Sue Campbell, "Eight Worst Resume Mistakes," 1st-Writer.com [accessed 30 December 2008] www.1st-writer.com; "150 Funniest Resume Mistakes, Bloopers, and Blunders Ever," The Best Article Every Day blog, 2 June 2008 [accessed 30 December 2008] www.bspcn.com; "Hiring Managers Share Top 12 Wackiest Resume Blunders in New CareerBuilder.com Survey," CareerBuilder.com, 25 April 2007 [accessed 30 December 2008] www.careerbuilder.com. **518 (Sharpening Your Career Skills: Make Sure You Don't Talk Yourself Out of a Job)** Adapted from Thomas Pack, "Good Answers to Job Interview Questions," *Information Today*, January 2004, 35+; John Lees, "Make Them Believe You Are the Best," *The Times* (London), 21 January 2004, 3; "Six Interview Mistakes," Monster.com [accessed 23 February 2004] www.monster.com.

FIGURES AND TABLES

37 (Figure 2.1: Using a Wiki for Collaborative Communication) Used with permission of Wikia, Inc. **42 (Table 2.2: Business Uses of Social Networking Technology)** Source: Adapted from Christopher Carfi and Leif Chastaine, "Social Networking for Businesses & Organizations," white paper, Cerado website [accessed 13 August 2008] www.cerado.com; Anusorn Kansap, "Social Networking," PowerPoint presentation, Silpakorn University [accessed 14 August 2008] http://real-timeupdates.com; "Social Network Websites: Best Practices from Leading Services," white paper, 28 November 2007, FaberNovel Consulting [accessed 14 August 2008] www.fabernovel.com. **47 (Figure 2.6: Web-Based Meetings)** Courtesy of InstantPresenter. **48 (Figure 2.7: Virtual Meetings in a Virtual World)** Courtesy of Cranial Tap. **50 (Table 2.3: What Makes an Effective Listener?)** Source: Madelyn Burley-Allen, *Listening: The Forgotten Skill* (New York: Wiley, 1995), 70–71, 119–120; Judi Brownell, *Listening: Attitudes, Principles, and Skills* (Boston: Allyn and Bacon, 2002); 3, 9, 83, 89, 125; Larry Barker and Kittie Watson, *Listen Up* (New York: St. Martin's, 2000), 8, 9, 64. **54 (Table 2.5: Quick Tips for Improving Your Phone Skills)** Source: Alf Nucifora, "Voice Mail Demands Good Etiquette from Both Sides," *Puget Sound Business Journal*, 5–11 September 2003, 24; Ruth Davidhizar and Ruth Shearer, "The Effective Voice Mail Message," *Hospital Materiel Management Quarterly*, November 2000, 45–49; "How to Get the Most Out of Voice Mail," *The CPA Journal*, February 2000, 11; Jo Ind, "Hanging on the Telephone," *Birmingham Post*, 28 July 1999, PS10; Larry Barker and Kittie Watson, *Listen Up* (New York: St. Martin's Press, 2000), 64–65; Lin Walker, *Telephone Techniques* (New York: Amacom, 1998), 46–47; Dorothy Neal, *Telephone Techniques*, 2d ed. (New York: Glencoe McGraw-Hill, 1998), 31; Jeannie Davis, *Beyond "Hello"* (Aurora, Col.: Now Hear This, Inc., 2000), 2–3; "Ten Steps to Caller-Friendly Voice Mail," *Managing Office Technology*, January 1995, 25; Rhonda Finniss, "Voice Mail: Tips for a Positive Impression," *Administrative Assistant's Update*, August 2001, 5. **65 (Figure 3.1: Languages of the World)** Copyright (c) 2005, SIL International, from the database of Ethnologue: Languages of the World, 15th ed., www.ethnologue.com. **69 (Figure 3.2: How Cultural Context Affects Business)** Source: Mary O'Hara-Devereaux and Robert Johansen, *Global Work: Bridging Distance, Culture, and Time*

(San Francisco: Jossey-Bass, 1994), 55, 59. **71 (Figure 3.3: Future Orientation and National Competitiveness)** Source: Mansour Javidan, "Forward-Thinking Cultures," *Harvard Business Review*, July–August 2007, 20. **71 (Figure 3.4: Avoiding Nonverbal Mishaps)** Source: Adapted from Roger Axtell, *Gestures: The Do's and Taboos of Body Language Around the World* (New York: Wiley, 1991), 117–119. **91 (Figure 4.1: The Three-Step Writing Process)** Source: Adapted from Kevin J. Harty and John Keenan, *Writing for Business and Industry: Process and Product* (New York: Macmillan Publishing Company, 1987), 3–4; Richard Hatch, *Business Writing* (Chicago: Science Research Associates, 1983), 88–89; Richard Hatch, *Business Communication Theory and Technique* (Chicago: Science Research Associates, 1983), 74–75; Center for Humanities, *Writing as a Process: A Step-by-Step Guide, Four Filmstrips and Cassettes* (Mount Kisko, NY: Center for Humanities, 1987); Michael L. Keene, *Effective Professional Writing* (New York: D.C. Heath, 1987), 28–34. **97 (Figure 4.4: An Audience-Focused Report (Selected Pages))** Used by permission of Alderwood Water & Wastewater. **99 (Figure 4.6: Electronic Oral Media)** Used by permission of World Voyager Vacations. **148 (Figure 6.1: Improving a Message Through Careful Revision)** Letterhead provided by Yamaha Corporation of America; text written by the authors. **149 (Figure 6.2: Revised Customer Letter)** Letterhead provided by Yamaha Corporation of America; text written by the authors. **162 (Figure 6.6: Multimedia Tools)** Photo by Ryan Lackey. Adobe product screen shot(s) reprinted with permission from Adobe Systems Incorporated. **164 (Figure 6.7: A Typical Business Memo)** Used with permission of Carnival Corporation. **186 (Figure 7.3: Video Blogging)** Used with permission of Joe Foley. **187 (Table 7.2: Tips for Effective Business Blogging)** Robert Scoble and Shel Israel, *Naked Conversations* (Hoboken, N.J.: John Wiley & Sons, 2006), 78–81, 190–194; Paul McFedries, *The Complete Idiot's Guide to Creating a Web Page & Blog*, 6th ed. (New York: Alpha, 2004), 206–208, 272–276; Shel Holtz and Ted Demopoulos, *Blogging for Business* (Chicago: Kaplan, 2006), 54–59, 113–114; Denise Wakeman, "Top 10 Blog Writing Tips," Blogarooni.com [accessed 1 February 2006] www.blogarooni.com; Dennis A. Mahoney, "How to Write a Better Weblog," 22 February 2002, A List Apart [accessed 1 February 2006] www.alistapart.com. **194 (Figure 7.7: Viewing Blog Updates in Web Browsers)** Used with permission of David Meerman Scott. **210 (Figure 8.1: Routine Messages)** Google blog screenshot © Google Inc. and is used with permission. **220 (Figure 8.6: Personalized Reply to a Request for Information)** Courtesy of Herman Miller. **225 (Figure 8.8: Effective Recommendation Letter)** Letterhead provided by Airbus Americas, Inc.; text written by the authors. **246 (Figure 9.2: Negative Message Using the Direct Approach)** Used with permission of Spherion Corporation. **290 (Figure 10.3: Marketing Messages)** Used with permission of Maine Coast Properties. **292 (Figure 10.4: Explaining the Benefits of Product Features)** Blackberry®, RIM®, Research in Motion®, Sure Type®, SurePress™ and related trademarks, names and logos are the property of Research in Motion Limited and are registered and/or used in the U.S. and countries around the world. **294 (Figure 10.5b: Emotional and Logical Appeals in Marketing and Sales Messages)** Gladiator GarageWorks website photograph used with permission of Whirlpool Corporation. **295 (Figure 10.7: The Call to Action in a Sales Message)** Reprinted with permission from the American Council on Exercise. **279 (Table 10.1: Human Needs That Influence Motivation)** Adapted from Saundra K. Ciccarelli and Glenn E. Meyer, *Psychology* (Upper Saddle River, N.J.: Prentice Hall, 2006), 336–346; Courtland L. Bovée, John V. Thill, and Michael H. Mescon, *Excellence in Business*, 3rd ed. (Upper Saddle River, N.J.: Prentice Hall, 2006), 327–333; Abraham H. Maslow, "A Theory of Human Motivation," *Psychological Review* 50 (1943): 370–396. **291 (Table 10.2: Features Versus Benefits)** Adapted from "What Is the HYBRID HEAT Dual Fuel System by Carrier?" Carrier website [accessed 5 November 2008] www.residential.carrier.com. **326 (Figure 11.6: Searching Printed Sources Online)** © Google, Inc. **329 (Figure 11.7: Desktop Search Engines)** Used with permission of Copernic. **323 (Table 11.3: Important Resources for Business Research)** Source: Adapted from H.W. Wilson website [accessed 20 November 2008] www.hwwilson.com; Bowker website [accessed 20 November 2008] www.bowker.com; University of Washington Libraries online card catalog [accessed 20 November 2008] http://uwashington.worldcat.org; D&B website [accessed 20 November 2008] www.dnb.com; "Industry Information," Thomas J. Long Business and Economics Library website, University of California, Berkeley [accessed 6 November 2006] www.lib.berkeley.edu; Hoovers website [accessed 20 November 2008] www.hoovers.com; MarketResearch.com [accessed 6 November 2006] www.marketresearch.com; Risk Management Association website [accessed 6 November 2006] www.rmahq.org; "Subscribed Sites," Sno-Isle Regional Library System [accessed 18 December 2003] www.sno-isle.org; "Business Directories: A Research Guide," University of Delaware Library website [accessed 6 November 2006] www.lib.udel.edu; Thomas P. Bergman, Stephen M. Garrison, and Gregory M. Scott, *The Business Student Writer's Manual and Guide to the Internet* (Paramus, N.J.: Prentice Hall, 1998), 67–80; Ernest L. Maier, Anthony J. Faria, Peter Kaatrude, and Elizabeth Wood, *The Business Library and How to Use It* (Detroit: Omnigraphics, 1996), 53–76. **377 (Figure 12.14: Data Visualization)** **(a)** Used with permission of TouchGraph. **(b)** Used with permission of Barry Graubart. **(d)** Copyright 2009 SmartMoney.All rights reserved. **416 (Figure 13.2: Report Synopsis)** Reprinted by permission of Sprint Nextel. **453 (Table 14.2: Color and Emotion)** Adapted from Claudyne Wilder and David Fine, *Point, Click & Wow* (San Francisco: Jossey-Bass Pfeiffer, 1996), 63, 527. **472 (Figure 15.2: How Organizations Prefer to Find New Employees)** Adapted from Richard Nelson Bolles, *What Color Is Your Parachute?* (Berkeley, Calif.: Ten Speed Press, 1997), 67. **474 (Table 15.1: Netting a Job on the Web)** Source: The Riley Guide [accessed 5 August 2009] www.rileyguide.com; SimplyHired website [accessed 5 August 2009] www.simplyhired.com; Indeed website [accessed 5 August 2009] www.indeed.com; College Recruiter.com [accessed 5 August 2009] www.collegerecruiter.com; Jobster website [accessed 30 March 2008] www.jobster.com; InternshipPrograms.com [accessed 30 March 2008] http://internshipprograms.com. **509 (Figure 16.3: Finding Real Jobs in a Virtual World)** Used with permission of Working Worlds. **513 (Table 16.3: Twenty-Five Common Interview Questions)** Adapted from InterviewUp website [accessed 6 April 2008] www.interviewup.com; *The Northwestern Endicott Report* (Evanston, Ill.: Northwestern University Placement Center). **514 (Table 16.4: Ten Questions to Ask an Interviewer)** Adapted from Joe Conklin, "Turning the Tables: Six Questions to Ask Your Interviewer," *Quality Progress*, November 2007, 55; Andrea N. Browne, "Keeping the Momentum at the Interview; Ask Questions, Do Your Research, and Be a Team Player," *Washington Post*, 29 July 2007, K1; Marilyn Sherman, "Questions R Us: What to Ask at a Job Interview," *Career World*, January 2004, 20; H. Lee Rust, *Job Search: The Complete Manual for Jobseekers* (New York: American Management Association, 1979), 56. **516 (Table 16.5: Warning Signs: 25 Attributes That Interviewers Don't Like to See)** Adapted from *The Northwestern Endicott Report* (Evanston, Ill.: Northwestern University Placement Center). **519 (Table 16.6: Interview Questions That Employers Are and Are Not Allowed to Ask)** Adapted from Deanna G. Kucler, "Interview Questions: Legal or Illegal?" *Workforce Management* [accessed 28 September 2005] www.workforce.com; "Illegal Interview Questions," *USA Today*, 29 January 2001 [accessed 28 September 2005] www.usatoday.com"; "Dangerous Questions," *Nation's Business*, May 1999, 22.

PHOTOS

Cover iStockphoto.com. **1.** Getty Images–BLOOMimages. **2 and 28** Mena & Ben Trott, Co-founders of Six Apart, Ltd. **9** Walter Hodges, Getty Images Inc.—Stone Allstock. **13** Ellen Isaacs/age Fotostock, Art Life Images. **18, left top** Belkin International, Inc. **18, right top** Getty Images–Digital Vision. **18, left bottom** Lance Davies Photography, Polyvision, a Steelcase Company. **18, right bottom** Ethan Hill Photography. **19, left bottom** Studio M, Stock Connection. **19, right top** Instant-Presenter. **19, right bottom** Ethan Hill Photography. **20, right middle** United Parcel Service. **20, right bottom** Peter Christopher, Masterfile Corporation. **21, right top** Photolibrary.com. **21, right bottom** Staples, Inc. **21, left middle** Marcio Jose Sanchez, AP Wide World Photo. **34 and 56** Rosen Law Firm. **45** Peter Wynn Thompson/The

New York Times, Redux Pictures. **63 and 82** IBM Corporation. **66** Mark Richards, PhotoEdit, Inc. **72** Steve Cole, Getty Images–Photodisc. **81** Diego Azubel/epa, CORBIS-NY. **89** Getty Images, Inc. **90 and 111** H&R Block World Headquarters. **118 and 138** Mizuka Ito, Creative Commons. **146 and 167** Daimler Chrysler AG. **175** Getty Images, Inc.–PhotoDisc **176 and 195** Southwest Airlines Co. **177** Chris Strangemore. **188** Ric Feld, AP Wide World Photos. **192** Promethius Consulting, LLC. **208 and 230** Thor Muller. **242 and 264** Jupiter Unlimited. **247** Tom Hindman, AP Wide World Photos. Caption based on Ken Ward, Jr., "Bayer Admits 'We Fell Short' in Fire Response," redOrbit, 9 October 2008 [accessed 11 October 2008] www.redorbit.com; "Plant Manager Apologizes for Lack of Communication," *Charleston Daily Mail*, 11 October 2008 [accessed 11 October 2008] www.dailymail.com. **289** ImageState, Alamy Images. **313** Getty Images, Inc. **314 and 349** Getty Images–Editorial. **341 and 368** Robert Seale, Tellabs. **381** Alan Gough, Alan Gough Photography. **396 and 425** Paul Sakuma, AP Wide World Photos. **438 and 460** Hewlett Packard. **448** Jeff Greenberg, PhotoEdit, Inc. **450** Lance Davies Photography, Polyvision, a Steelcase Company. **457** Dennis MacDonald, PhotoEdit, Inc. **459** Noel Hendrickson, Getty Images, Inc.—Image Bank. **469** Getty Images, Inc.–DK Stock. **470 and 492** Hersha Hospitality Management. **500 and 525** Google, Inc. **506** AGE Fotostock America, Inc.—Royalty-free. **517** Jon Feingersh/Zefa.

Brand, Organization, Name, and Website Index

P

Q

R

S

T

U

V

W

X

Y

Z

Subject Index

A

D

F

M

N

O

Q

R

S

XYZ